Ernest Hemingway
A LIFE STORY

Ernest Hemingway

A LIFE STORY

By

CARLOS BAKER

"To live, to err, to fall, to triumph,
to recreate life out of life . . ."

—JAMES JOYCE, *A Portrait of the Artist as a Young Man*

Collier Books
Macmillan Publishing Company
New York

Collier Books
Macmillan Publishing Company
866 Third Avenue, New York, N.Y. 10022
Collier Macmillan Canada, Inc.

Library of Congress Cataloging-in-Publication Data
Baker, Carlos, 1909–1987.
Ernest Hemingway: a life story / by Carlos Baker—1st Collier Books ed.
p.   cm.
Originally published: New York: Scribner, 1969.
Bibliography: p.
Includes index.
1. Hemingway, Ernest, 1899–1961—Biography. 2. Authors,
American—20th century—Biography. I. Title.
PS3515.E37Z575 1988
813'.52—dc 19   87-29955
[B]   CIP

ISBN 0-02-001690-5

ILLUSTRATION ACKNOWLEDGMENTS
The following illustrations are used with the kind permission
of the owners indicated below:

Lloyd Arnold: 72–76; Estate of Lawrence T. Barnett: 15, 16, 21, 23; Mrs. Raymond O. Barton: 84; Mrs. H. W. Blakely: 82; Cano: 96, 97; Robert Cromie: 83; John Dos Passos: 47; Mrs. John Gardner: 12; Carl Hayden: 98, 99; Mary Hemingway (Family Collection): 1–11, 13, 17–20, 22, 25, 37, 42, 43, 45, 55, 65–68; Mrs. Barklie M. Henry: 64; Mrs. Guy Hickok: 28; Imperial War Museum (London): 80; Clinton King: 39; Ramon Lavalle: 77; Colonel Charles T. Lanham, USA Ret.: 86, 89; *Life*: 85, 88, 95; *Look*: 93, 94; Herbert Matthews: 69, 71; Mrs. E. J. Miller: 90; Mrs. Paul S. Mowrer: 24, 26, 27, 44, 49; Mrs. Olive Nordquist: 57; Waldo Pierce: 46; PIP Photos, Inc. by Interfoto Features: 91; Princeton University (Silvia Beach Collection): 29–31, 33, 36; Collection of Man Ray: 40; Royal Air Force: 79; Mrs. Gustav Regler: 70; Scribner Art Files: 41; Henry Strater: 32, 48, Copyright by Henry Strater; Allen Tanner annd Yale University Collection of American Literature: 35; United Press International Photos: 78, 92; William Walton: 81; Wide World Photos: 34.

Macmillan books are available at special discounts for bulk purchases for sales promotions, premiums, fund-raising, or educational use. For details, contact:

Special Sales Director
Macmillan Publishing Company
866 Third Avenue
New York, N.Y. 10022

First Collier Books Edition 1988

10 9 8 7 6 5 4 3 2 1

Printed in the United States of America

To my friend
BUCK LANHAM
and my wife
DOROTHY BAKER
who fought it out by my side during
the seven-year siege

FOREWORD

HE used to say that he wanted no biography written while he was alive, and preferably for a hundred years after he was dead. In another mood, he remarked that if he were ever to be mounted, he would prefer to have the job done by Jonas Brothers of Yonkers, New York, the finest taxidermists in the land. Of these three wishes, he got only the first, which is probably just as well. Had it been possible to write his biography during his lifetime, it would have been impossible to tell what has here been told about his life and work. If the preparation of a biography had been put off for a century, much valuable evidence would inevitably have been lost or destroyed. Even the best of taxidermists could not have preserved that complex and many-sided man and artist whose adventures are recorded in the following life story.

No biography can portray a man as he actually was. The best that can be hoped for is an approximation, from which all that is false has been expunged and in which most of what is true has been set forth, whether by statement or by implication. If Ernest Hemingway is to be made to live again, it must be by virtue of a thousand pictures, both still and moving, a thousand scenes in which he was involved, a thousand instances when he wrote or spoke both publicly and privately of those matters that most concerned him. The small boy who shouted "Fraid o'nothing" became the man who discovered that there was plenty to fear, including that vast cosmic nothingness which Goya named *Nada*. The adolescent, wounded in Italy, learned that no man was exempt from mortality. The romantic activist, the center and in many ways the originator of his own universe, became the pragmatic moralist whose leading aim was to find out how to live in life, how to last and (having lasted) how to convert a carefully cultivated stoical fortitude into the stuff of which his fictional heroes were made. The ethical hedonist sought and found a million pleasures while learning, over and over, that human life, his own included, is forever punctuated with pain. *Il faut (d'abord) durer* became his watchword as well as the rule by which he lived until the concept of lasting gave way to an overriding conviction that it was time for him to die.

If all the pictures are not here, there may still be enough of them for the reader to work with as he attempts to comprehend the phenomenon of Ernest Hemingway. There is, first, the immensely ambitious young man, unfailingly competitive, driven by an urge to excel in whatever he undertook, to be admired and looked up to, to assert his superiority by repeated example, to display for the benefit of others his strength and his endurance; his hatred of politicians, poseurs, intellectuals, cowards, and apron strings; his rulership over fear and pain; his proud defiance of death. There is next the man of many contradictions: the shy and diffident man and the incredible braggart; the sentimentalist quick to tears and the bully who used his anger like a club; the warm and generous friend and the ruthless and overbearing enemy; the man who stayed loyal to some of his oldest friends while picking quarrels with others because he feared that they were beginning to assume a proprietary interest over him; the non-hero longing for heroic status and sometimes achieving it; the man of action harnessed to the same chariot as the man of words; the author who constantly impugned all cheap and easy writing, yet boiled as many pots as the next man before he was through. There is the perpetual student, the omnivorous reader, the brilliant naturalist, the curious questioner, the skilled and retentive observer, the careful expositor, the temperamental teacher, the assiduous cultivator of the atavistic and the elemental. He was superstitious in the presence of the mysteries, rubbing his lucky stones between his calloused palms, turning to and then away from the Church, arriving finally at a kind of nonintellectualized humanism while protesting that he missed the ghostly comforts of institutionalized religion as a man who is cold and wet misses the consolations of good whiskey. There is the romantic liar for whom the line between fact and fiction was thinner than a hair, who invented stories for a living and saw no reason to turn off the mechanism when writing letters or conversing with friends and acquaintances. There is also the man who once admitted that he would have liked to be a king. He could be lordly with underlings, but also fiercely democratic; surly with sycophants, though ready enough to surround himself with them; gracious with those he felt to be his equals; warmly affectionate with close friends; shy in large companies; and deferential among those whose offices or abilities he respected. He divided all the world into good guys and jerks. With some notable exceptions, he preferred the lower and middle to the upper classes, although his taste in people (again with exceptions) was usually excellent.

There is the man driven by pride, which he often defined as a deadly sin yet embraced as his personal and well-loved daemon. He was proud of his manhood, his literary and athletic skills, his staying and recuperative powers, his reputation, his capacity for drink, his prowess as fisherman and wing shot, his earnings, his self-reliance, his wit, his poetry, his medical and military knowledge, his skill in map reading, navigation, and the sizing up of terrain. There is the temperamental manic-depressive, the inveterate hypochondriac and valetudinarian who spoke seriously of suicide at intervals throughout his life, yet possessed enormous powers of resilience and recuperation that could bring him back from the brink to the peak within days and sometimes within hours. He was a persistent worrier who wryly cautioned others against this pernicious habit. He was plagued all his adult life by insomnia and in sleep by nightmares, both the result of a highly developed imagination. He could be thrown into a slump by weather that was cold and damp or hot and sticky. He could be lifted from the depths by early morning, the time of sunset, breezy sunlight, crisp cold, hills and mountains, and the sea.

There was the fierce individualist who resisted fad and fashion like the plague, who held that a writer must be an "outlyer" like a gypsy, who believed that that government is best which governs least, who hated tyranny, bureaucracy, taxation, propaganda, and oratory; who thought that human greed and rapaciousness were everywhere destroying the parts of the world he loved best; who resented the incursions of modern civilization upon the shrinking wilderness, and the intrusions of the machine into the garden.

There was the physical presence, powerful enough to electrify any room into which he stepped, ingratiating enough to overcome any antipathy he had aroused. One's first impression of him was of size and strength. He was six feet tall and usually weighed about 210 pounds. He had a tendency to put on weight and was once up to 260. He wore a size eleven shoe. His eyes were brown, his complexion ruddy, and there were dimples in both his cheeks which his beard later concealed. His hair at first was brownish black and straight. In his forties, it began to grow thin on top and in his late fifties he became bald, a condition which he concealed by combing his hair forward over the crown of his head in a hyacinthine bang. His beard at first was raven black, in middle life beaver-colored, then pepper-and-salt, and at last white. He could not stand confinement around the throat and customarily wore open-necked shirts. He believed that a leather hunting vest protected his kidneys and made a great point of wearing one. His gait was rolling and purposeful. He had a habit of standing poised on the balls of his feet, and there was often a noticeable side-to-side motion of his head when he talked or listened. Acute listeners could detect a slight speech impediment in which ls and rs tended to take on a semblance of the w sound. He is said by those who know to have been a perfectly satisfactory lover without being a Don Juan. According to his closest friends, he was indubitably a man's man. He formed many friendships with women, at first older and later younger than he, as if he were aiming at some middle ground. He boasted on occasion, somewhat ambiguously, that he had had every woman he ever wanted. He enjoyed telling yarns about his conquests to his cronies, especially in his youth and in his fifties; in the interval between, he said little. He had three sons and longed to have a daughter. He was likely to address pretty women with the title of "Daughter." Among women he often assumed the role of big brother, like a man accustomed to having sisters, as he in fact was. The women he preferred were not invariably beautiful or even pretty, but he admired those who were doers as against those who were spoiled, petulant, overdependent, overassertive, overintellectual. He was especially conscious of women's hair, its length, its texture, its arrangement, its care and treatment. He disliked the use of cold cream, unguents, salves, most perfumes, excessive makeup, girdles, and false bosom-builders.

He admired courage and stoical endurance in women as in men, disliked hard backtalk, fishwifely screaming, false accusations, true accusations. He liked to show off his skill in verbal fencing and witty phrasing in the presence of women. In his treatment of those he liked or loved there was often something of the chivalric; once he had turned against them he could be excessively cruel and abusive. When drunk or sufficiently provoked he sometimes slapped or cuffed them. He was unchivalrously outspoken to friends and even to relatively new acquaintances about his internal domestic affairs, particularly after the age of thirty-five and increasingly as he grew older. When things were going well, he spoke of his wives in a standard phrase: they were happy, healthy, hard as a rock, and well-tanned.

He was one of the foremost writers that America has produced, an epoch-making stylist with a highly original talent who spawned imitators by the score and dealt, almost single-handed, a permanent blow against the affected, the namby-pamby, the pretentious, and the false. The writing of fiction was hard for him. The intensity of his application was so great that a few hours of it literally exhausted him, and a day's work for him normally did not exceed five or six hundred words. "Truly," he wrote in 1951, "it is a tough métier; no matter how much you love it. I love it more than anything. But it is quite difficult if a man really works at it." Although most of his adventures made their way sooner or later into his work, it is his writing, rather than his career as a man of action, which justifies a biography.

The narrative that follows is not a "definitive" biography, nor was it meant to be. Although it seeks to tell in considerable detail the story of his life from birth to death, it will be after the year 2000 before anything like a definitive work can be undertaken. Many lines of investigation remain to be followed out, as they will be, by generations of scholars. Again, although the present work offers a substantial amount of information about the origin, development, and reception of his writings, it is not what is commonly called a "critical biography," in which the biographer seeks to explore, analyze, and evaluate the full range of his subject's literary output simultaneously with the record of his life. This idea was early considered and rejected because the present biographer had already made an intensive examination of Hemingway's fiction in a volume still in print. Finally, this is not a "thesis" biography. Even though certain patterns of attitude and behavior emerge clearly from the mosaic of Hemingway's life, no one of them in itself exclusively dominates his psychological outlook or fully explains the nature and direction of his career as man and artist.

Most of the story is drawn directly or indirectly from manuscript sources, including many pages of his unpublished work, approximately 2500 of his letters, and at least an equal number of letters to him from friends, members of his family, and chance associates. These materials have been supplemented with numerous interviews, much correspondence with those who knew him best, and by visits to many, though not to all, of the regions that Hemingway frequented, both early and late. The documentation is extensive and will be found at the back of the book, so arranged that readers can easily locate the sources of all statements made in the text. An enormous fund of misinformation about him is already in print. Apart from stating the facts about his life and work, no attempt has been made to refute errors that have hitherto passed as truths.

This biography was undertaken at the invitation of Charles Scribner, Jr., president of the publishing company which brought out all of Hemingway's major works from 1926 onwards. The work was carried on with the full knowledge and cooperation of Mary Welsh Hemingway, the author's widow and literary executor, who generously permitted the biographer to examine whatever documents he wished to see without attempting to influence his judgments or his interpretations.

No work of this magnitude could have been brought to completion without the willing assistance of many people. The list of those who magnanimously contributed their information, time, energy, and encouragement will be found elsewhere in this volume under the heading of Debts and Credits. Except for considerations of space, the biographer would have wished to place all their names on the title page. Further debts have been systematically acknowledged in the sources and notes to each of the seventy-six sections. The biographer thanks his collaborators one and all from a very full heart.

Carlos Baker

Princeton, New Jersey
1961–1968

CONTENTS

VIII. EAST AND WEST

IX. ANOTHER WAR

X. RETURNINGS

XI. A MATTER OF LIFE AND DEATH

Ernest Hemingway

A LIFE STORY

CHAPTER 1

Midwestern Boyhood

1. THE COUNTRY AND THE TOWN

As soon as it was safe for the boy to travel, they bore him away to the northern woods. It was a long and complicated journey for a child only seven weeks old. From the suburban town of Oak Park, Illinois, they took the train to Chicago, a horse cab to the pier on Lake Michigan, the steamer *Manitou* to Harbor Springs on Little Traverse Bay, the curving tracks of the small railroad to the depot in Petoskey, an even smaller branch line to the foot of Bear Lake, and at last a rowboat to the shore-front property that Dr. Ed Hemingway had bought from Henry Bacon the summer before. They were going to build a summer cottage and they had come to complete the arrangements.

It was the closing year of the old century. The early September weather was already sharp, and the leaves on the aspens across the milk-blue lake were beginning to turn gold. Bacon's four-square white farmhouse stood well back from the shore among pastures and orchards, pens and barns and chicken coops. In the patch of woods between his farm and the sandy road that led over the hills to Petoskey stood the shacks of a settlement of Ottawa Indians. Some of the women did washing and wove baskets of sweet grass to sell to the summer people. The most aggressive of the group was a half-breed sawyer named Nick Boulton. He worked for a lumbering outfit that ran logs across the lake to the sawmill. When the wind was right, the distant scream of the saw could be heard all the way to Bacon's farm. The lumber for the Hemingway cottage was already piled in a corner of the newly cleared lot. Grace Hemingway took some snapshots of her infant son, howling lustily in his father's arms on a beech log by the sandy shore. Then it was time to go back to Illinois and take up the work of the winter.

The child's father was Clarence Edmonds Hemingway, commonly known as Ed. A graduate of Oberlin, he had earned his M.D. at Rush Medical College in Chicago, satisfied his wanderlust with a European tour in 1895, and then settled down as a general practitioner. He was the eldest son of Anson T. Hemingway, a straight-backed, gray-bearded Civil War veteran who maintained a prosperous real-estate business in Chicago. Anson and his wife Adelaide had chosen to raise their children in a large white frame house in Oak Park. At twenty-eight, Ed Hemingway stood six feet tall, with powerful arms and shoulders and a barrel chest. He wore a black beard to increase the maturity of his appearance. His Roman nose was rather hawklike and his brown eyes were phenomenally farsighted. He was an avid collector of coins and stamps, as well as a great store of Pottawatomi Indian arrowheads, gathered in his boyhood. He practiced amateur taxidermy with small animals and birds, and also collected snakes, which he preserved in alcohol in sealed glass jars. Apart from collecting, his chief avocations were fishing, hunting, and cooking. He greatly relished all kinds of fish and game. On a trip to the Great Smoky Mountains of North Carolina following his graduation from Oberlin, he had astonished his companions with a fresh blackberry pie, sweetened with wild honey from a bee tree and baked to a turn beside the campfire where some squirrels were stewing. He had rolled out the pie crust on a peeled log with an empty beer bottle.

He had first met Grace Hall while they were students at Oak Park High School. She had a good contralto voice, and her mother as well as her teachers had encouraged her to follow a career in grand opera. For five years after her graduation from high school she taught music at home, working at languages and voice training, though constantly troubled with defective eyesight. As a child of seven, after scarlet fever, she had been totally blind for several months. Her eyes were still so acutely sensitive to light that she suffered recurrent headaches. Apart from these problems, she had at least the look of a potential opera star. At the time of her mother's death she had just turned twenty-three, a girl of Junoesque proportions, with prominent features, china-blue eyes, light-brown hair, and high English coloring. That winter she went to work at the Art Students League in New York and made her professional debut in the spring at Madison Square Garden. But the glare of the footlights was more than her eyes could bear. She went abroad with her father that summer and returned to marry young Dr. Hemingway on October 1, 1896.

After the wedding, they moved in with Grace's widowed father, Ernest Hall, who lived at 439 North Oak Park Avenue, across the street from Anson and Adelaide. Dr. Hemingway resumed his practice, Grace gave music lessons, and the management of the household was given over to a hardworking German girl named Sophie Stelzel. Money was not a problem. Mr. Hall commuted daily to his wholesale cutlery business in Chicago. He was a gentle, godly man who worshipped on Sundays at Grace Episcopal Church, knelt on the Brussels carpet in the parlor to lead evening prayer, and softly asked the blessing at the dinner table. Like Anson he was a Civil War veteran, having been a corporal with Troop L, First Iowa Volunteer Cavalry. He still carried a Confederate minié ball in one thigh, but never allowed the war to be discussed in his presence. His only vice was tobacco, which he consumed after dinner in the small library behind closed doors, often in the company of his brother-in-law, Tyley Hancock. Tyley at forty-eight was still a traveling salesman with the firm of Miller Hall and Sons, which made brass and iron bedsteads. He was a frequent visitor to the house, a merry tyke of a man with a pipe aslant in his mouth and a tweed hat cocked rakishly over one eye.

Ernest Hall's first grandson was born at eight o'clock in the morning of July 21, 1899, in the south front bedroom of the house. He weighed nine and a half pounds and measured twenty-three inches tall. His hair was black and thick, though it would later turn yellow, and his eyes were dark blue, though they would later become brown. His complexion was mahogany, there were dimples in both his cheeks, and his voice from the first sounded remarkably masculine. His older sister Marcelline had arrived in the dead of winter, in January, 1898, but the summer sun shone hot in a clear sky the day the boy was born. "The robins," wrote his mother, "sang their sweetest songs to welcome the little stranger into this beautiful world." They waited for the christening until after the flying trip to Bear Lake. Shortly before noon on the first of October, Grace's third wedding anniversary, the child was baptized Ernest Miller Hemingway at the First Congregational Church. Both his given names were from Grace's side of the family—Ernest for his grandfather Hall, and Miller for his great-uncle, the bedstead manufacturer. After the ceremony Grace wrote piously that the child had been carried "as an offering unto the Lord, to receive his name and hence forth be counted as one of God's little lambs."

All through his first winter, the child was placid, well-behaved, and above all well-fed, since he slept with his mother and lunched frequently, as she put it, whenever he awoke in the night. His first doll was a rubber papoose from Sophie Stelzel and his second a white Eskimo from his father. In January he cut his first tooth. During the spring Grace indulged her fancy for dressing Ernest and Marcelline alike. At the age of nine months he had his picture taken in a pink gingham dress and a wide hat ornamented with flowers.

But he began to assert his boyhood during the summer of 1900 when the family occupied their cottage at Bear Lake for the first time. It smelt pleasantly of new lumber and fresh varnish. Grace wished to call it Windermere after the famous lake in her ancestral England, but subsequent longhand spellings fixed the name as Windemere. The cottage faced southwest, with a panorama of low green hills, blue water, and pastel sunsets. The living room was finished in white pine and dominated by a huge brick fireplace with cushioned window seats on either side. There were two small bedrooms, a narrow dining room, and a kitchen with a wood-burning range and an iron pump for the well water. Lighting was by oil lamp. In a clump of evergreens up the slope stood the small outhouse. The lake itself was the only bathtub. The beach at the foot of the slope was clean and sandy, sheltered from the north wind by a wooded promontory called Murphy's Point.

It was an environment ideally suited to manly endeavors. The child played, ate, and slept with a kind of passionate enjoyment. On July 13th, shortly before his first birthday, he took the occasion of a barn-raising party at Bacon's farm to walk alone for the first time. He relished scraped apple and discovered a great liking for fish, which he pronounced "hish" and soon began to use as a generic term for all meats. His father brought home a splendid rowboat, with *Marcelline of Windemere* painted on its bows. All that summer Ernest and Marce were in and out of it like frogs. They gamboled naked in the wet sand, using the family washtub as an auxiliary skiff. He was a notably happy child, dancing and jigging, roaring in a lion's voice, and riding a cane for a hobbyhorse. Wearing a blue grass-length smock, he drove Bacon's sheep with a stick, crying "hig, hig." According to his mother his "sturdy little body" was all muscle, and his hands were already larger and stronger than Marcelline's. When thwarted in his wishes, he was known to storm, kick, and dance with rage. Yet at play he proudly took any amount of rough usage without losing his temper. On being put to bed, he never protested, placing the pillow over his face to keep out the light. He knelt at his mother's knee while she began to say his prayers. But after a sentence or two he always leaped up, roaring "Amen" with great finality.

Picture books enthralled him, especially some large bound volumes of a monthly serial called *Birds of Nature*. He also liked to have animals drawn for him in caricature, laughing with pleasure when he recognized them. He would listen to any and all stories, though his favorite was the one about Prince, a black horse that drew his father's buggy in Oak Park. According to Dr. Hemingway, Prince's neck was so short and his legs so long that he had to kneel down in order to crop the grass. Hanging on each word, Ernest always shouted "kneel" or "knee" just before his father said it, and would then kneel laughing on the floor to illustrate Prince's youthful eating habits. Back in town that September he developed a liking for stories about owls, having seen one in a tree across the street. He described a black bruise on one of his toes as an "owl's eye."

Nothing pleased him more than the naming of names. His early version of his own was Nurnie, the first of many nicknames. Ernest Hall became Abba Bear, his grandmother Adelaide Amma Bear, and his current nurse Lillie Bear. His rocking horse, two cut-out horse figures joined by a seat, was called Prince and Charlie. Vaccinated against smallpox in January, he described the scab as a "wose bud." His name for his mother was Fweetee. He astonished her in February by correctly identifying seventy-three birds in the *Birds of Nature* volume. He was already showing other signs of verbal aptitude. His first recorded joke was a pun on dandelions. "Dandy lions," he cried. "Dandy hosses."

He had learned the art of kissing with a loud and genuine smack. "He comes and slaps you if you don't suit him," wrote his mother, "and kisses you when he is sorry." He had long since graduated from diapers and bedwetting, an achievement justly praised in the household. His first complete sentence, uttered on St. Patrick's Day of 1901, was, "I don't know Buffalo Bill." On being taken to see Pawnee Bill's Wild West Show, he promptly became a cowboy and was photographed astride the patient Prince. In April he was taken to Ringling Brothers Circus, coming home to show his grandfather how the elephants had walked, and emulating the acrobats by turning somersaults with grave concentration. His equivalent of a circus cart was a three-by-two wooden box on red wheels, widely distributed at this time by hardware stores as an advertisement for Berry Brothers Varnishes and Architectural Finishes.

His mother described him at two as "round and fat and strong as a five-year-old. His hair is yellow worn in bangs and curly ends around his head, a healthy brown complexion, light brown eyes, strong black eyebrows, perfect mouth and dimples." When she called him a Dutch dolly, he stamped his foot, saying, "I not a Dutch dolly, I Pawnee Bill. Bang, I shoot Fweetee." His other family nicknames were Punch, Chipmunk, and Bobby. He sang, slightly off-key, such favorites as "Three Blind Mice" and "I Went to the Animal Fair." Bear Lake had lately been renamed Walloon, and Grace composed a waltz called "Lovely Walloona." Ernest adapted it to the song about the Animal Fair. Instead of "an old baboon by the light of the moon," he sang, "Oh, Walloon, light a da moon." It struck his parents as a brilliant interpolation.

"When asked what he is afraid of," wrote Grace, "he shouts out *fraid a nothing* with great gusto." His aspiration was to be taken for a man. He stomped about with half an old musket on his shoulder. He memorized some stanzas from Tennyson's "Charge of the Light Brigade" and became forthwith a soldier, gathering various pieces of wood which he called his blunderbuss, his shotgun, his rifle, his Winchester, and his pistol. His parents were much impressed by his courage and endurance. He took to dramatizing passages from Longfellow's *Hiawatha,* with Marcelline as the dark-eyed daughter of the old Arrow-maker in the Land of the Dacotahs.

His domestic side was evinced in Grace's sewing room in Oak Park. "He loves to sew," she wrote, "his idea always being to sew something for Papa to wear. He delights in mending Daddy's pants, an old pair which Mama keeps for him to sew on." He was also very tender-hearted, "crying bitterly over the death of a fly he had tried to revive on sugar and water." He loved all animals, especially wild ones. He talked to his playthings and personified each one. He longed to have a baby brother, and was greatly disappointed by the arrival of his sister Ursula in April, 1902. There was a tear in his eye when he learned the news. "I think maybe Jesus will send my baby brother tomorrow," said he.

Back at the lake for his third birthday he went fishing with his father for the first time. "He caught the biggest fish of the crowd," wrote Grace. "He knows when he gets a bite and lands them all himself. . . . He is a natural scientist, loving everything in the way of bugs, stones, shells, birds, animals, insects, and blossoms." A year later he was equally enthusiastic about nature. His birthday present the day he was four was an all-day fishing trip with his father. Rain fell steadily, but he was not disconcerted, babbling constantly about all he saw, perfectly content with the lake and the forest, excited by glimpses of chip-

munks and squirrels, and eager to help with the rowing on the long pull back
to Windemere.

His best friend in that summer of 1903 was a blue-eyed, tow-headed boy of
eleven named Wesley Dilworth. He came from Horton Bay on Lake Charlevoix, two miles beyond the low hills that closed the Hemingways' western
horizon. His father, Jim, ran a blacksmith shop across from the township
school. His mother, Liz, whom the Hemingway children called Aunty Beth,
conducted a chicken-dinner establishment called Pinehurst Cottage on the hill
overlooking the lake. Horton Bay was only a cluster of houses, with a general
store and post office and a small Methodist church. But in the years of Ernest's
childhood, it was almost as familiar to him as Windemere and Walloon Lake.
The bay was blue and often whitecapped with the breeze that blew from Lake
Michigan; enormous ore barges moved majestically between Boyne City and
Charlevoix; the hillside was cool and shady, smelling pleasantly of sandy loam,
sun-warmed pine needles, and Liz Dilworth's fried chicken.

Ernest was enrolled that fall in Miss Annie L. Howe's Ingleside Kinder-
garten. He also joined the local branch of the Agassiz Club, a nature-study
group organized by his father. Each Saturday morning through the spring he
strode manfully along with the older boys, gathering specimens in Thatcher's
Woods and identifying birds in the thickets along the banks of the Des Plaines
River. His grandfather Hall gave him a microscope for his fifth birthday. "He
is delighted," wrote his mother, "to look at specimens of rocks and insects
by the hour." Six months later she summarized her son's attainments.

Ernest Miller at 5½ years old is a little man—no longer lazy—dresses himself
completely and is a good helper for his father. He wears suspenders just like
Papa. Is very proud to be a member of Agassiz. He counts up to 100, can spell
by ear very well. His ear in singing is improving, though far from correct. He
likes to build cannons and forts with building blocks. Collects cartoons of the
Russo-Japanese War. He loves stories about Great Americans—can give you good
sketches of all the great men of American History.

He had just begun to accept his two-year-old sister Ursula, whom he called
Mrs. Gigs, when he learned from his mother that another child was imminent.
"My darling boy was *so* delighted," she wrote, "when he came into my bed one
morning . . . and I told him the happy secret that God was going to give us
another little baby." He was still hoping for a brother. But when the child
appeared on November 28th, 1904, it was another girl. They named her
Madelaine for a cousin of Grace's, but her nickname was the one that stuck.
She was not a month old when they all began to call her Sunny Jim, after the
good-humored baby whose likeness advertised a breakfast cereal.

Grandfather Hall spent the winter in California with his son Leicester. He
returned in the spring gravely ill with Bright's disease. Although the children
were kept away from the sickroom as much as possible, young Ernest burst in
one day with the news that he had stopped a runaway horse single-handed. His

grandfather was much amused. "Mark my words, Chumpy dear," he told his daughter, "this boy is going to be heard from some day. If he uses his imagination for good purposes, he'll be famous, but if he starts the wrong way, with all his energy, he'll end in jail." But Ernest Hall heard no more of his grandson's tall stories. He died on May 10, 1905, and was buried on the 12th with a funeral service held at the house.

The long summer in Michigan was crammed with more events than Ernest was prepared for. A second rowboat, the *Ursula of Windemere,* was added to the fleet and christened with a bottle of water. A forty-acre farmstead across the lake was on the point of being sold for taxes. The Hemingways bought it, renaming it Longfield Farm. Dr. Hemingway planted hundreds of fruit trees and hardwoods. Ernest ran gleefully up and down the new acreage, wearing an Indian suit with fringed leggings. It was his sixth vacation in Michigan and the final summer of his Dutch-boy haircut. In the fall, entering first grade, he was going to abandon long hair forever.

But these changes were as nothing to the one that lay ahead. Grace Hemingway was determined to sell her father's Victorian house, where the family had lived for the past nine years and where all four of her children had been born. She was ambitious for a place of grander proportions and more modern appointments, and was already dreaming of a lofty room where she could play and sing, returning to her former career as a music teacher after all the years of childbearing. In October the cash sale was completed and the family moved into a rented house next door to Oak Park's public library. "I remember," wrote Ernest a long time later, "after my grandfather died we moved away from that house . . . Many things that were not to be moved were burned in the back-yard and I remember those jars from the attic being thrown in the fire, and how they popped in the heat and the fire flamed up from the alcohol. I remember the snakes burning in the fire in the back-yard."

The new location was a corner lot at 600 North Kenilworth Avenue and Iowa Street. Grace's plans called for a three-story stucco house with eight bedrooms, a music room, and a medical office for the doctor. The space was necessary. Besides the six Hemingways, there were two servants who lived in, and one of the bedrooms was allotted to Uncle Tyley Hancock, who had grown accustomed to staying with the family whenever he was in town. They all gathered inside the shell of the house one day in April, 1906, for a ceremony of dedication. Anson and Adelaide were there. Dr. Hemingway had brought a tin box of family relics to be cemented into the hearth. A mason covered it over, the architect inscribed the date, the Congregational minister said a prayer, and Grace led them all in the singing of "Blest Be the Tie That Binds."

That summer's vacation in Michigan was a good deal shorter than usual. Ernest was allowed to invite a neighbor boy named Harold Sampson to serve as a playmate. The boys spent as much time as possible at Longfield Farm across the lake. There was a track with wooden cross-ties and rails that teamsters used to haul lumber in large open wagons. Ernest and Sam hitched rides to Horton Bay behind the slow-moving teams. Wesley Dilworth took them fishing at Horton Creek, west of Fox's store on the road to Charlevoix. They ate fried trout and chicken dinners at Pinehurst Cottage and roasted marshmallows to cinders over a campfire on the beach at Windemere. Then, all at once, the summer was over, in fact if not in date. Bag and baggage in the midst of August, the Hemingways returned to occupy their new house in Oak Park. Ernest took it all in stride. At the age of two, he had stated with gusto that he was afraid of nothing. At seven he still felt the same way.

2. ARTS AND SCIENCES

ART and science contended for mastery in the new house on Kenilworth Avenue. The center of Grace's artistic interest was the music room, thirty feet square and fifteen high, with a small balcony. This rather grandiose retreat gave off the north side of the living room through double oaken doors. Grace had gone to great pains to make it acoustically perfect. Her proudest possession was the shining new Steinway grand piano. Beside it was a small carpeted dais for her pupils' solo recitals. She kept a battered upright piano in the dining room for the practice sessions of the younger children and the drumming of infant hands. When Dr. Hemingway found time to play his cornet, usually a shade off-key, it was his custom to retire to the basement.

The pursuit of science took place at the other end of the house, where the doctor had his office and waiting room. Patients sat in the family library, finished in golden oak, with bound classics in serried rows. Here also were kept the birds and animals he had mounted—a moth-eaten squirrel with bright glass eyes, a brace of chipmunks, an owl, and a small raccoon he had shot on a hunting trip in southern Illinois with his brother-in-law, Frank Hines. Out of sight in the untidy little room that he used as a laboratory were covered jars containing a pickled appendix and a monkeylike human fetus. There was also a skeleton in the closet which he called, with humor that was rather rare with him, "Susie Bone-a-part."

Two such positive personalities as Grace and Ed were bound to clash. The domestic quarrels, when they came, centered mainly on questions of money and the raising of the children. The construction and furnishing of the new house had greatly diminished Grace's patrimony. She was by nature somewhat extravagant, and much given to dressing up in *grande-dame* clothes and hats with ostrich plumes, as befitted a woman who had once planned a career in opera. She felt that in marrying and bearing children she had made a considerable personal sacrifice. Her lack of interest in housekeeping, like her determination to be cultured and creative, made servants a necessity rather than a luxury. Their wages, though small enough by modern standards, caused a steady drain on the family income, which was not in any case abundant. A whole succession of cooks and nursemaids came and went. In the intervals, Dr. Hemingway was obliged to do most of the cooking. One of his patients remembered that, during a house visit, the doctor used the telephone to call home, telling whoever answered that it was time to take that pie out of the oven. The family was lucky in that he counted cooking, as well as the canning of fruits and vegetables, among his hobbies. He also did the marketing, kept chickens and rabbits in the back yard, and served as medical examiner for a dairy. Ernest afterwards remembered that twelve quarts of milk were delivered daily at the back door.

In the regulation of the children the doctor was by far the stricter of the two. He was always so nervously busy that any signs of idleness or procrastination among his brood roused him to sharp words and sudden scoldings. He forbade all recreational activity on the Lord's Day—no play with friends, no games, no concerts. Except in times of illness, attendance at church and Sunday school was compulsory. Major infractions of the rules were swiftly punished with a razor strop (Grace employed a hairbrush), followed by injunctions to kneel and ask God's forgiveness. Grace was on the whole a good deal more permissive. She said repeatedly that she wanted her children to enjoy life. To her this meant above all an awareness of the arts. She saw from the first that they all had music lessons. As soon as they were old enough, she bought them tickets for symphony concerts, operatic performances, and the better plays that came to Chicago, and they were encouraged quite early to acquaint themselves with the paintings and drawings at the Chicago Art Institute. Her own deep-dyed belief in creativity made her long to develop the talents of her children to the highest possible level.

The great gift of the doctor to his children was a knowledge and love of nature. He taught Ernest how to build fires and cook in the open, how to use an ax to make a woodland shelter of hemlock boughs, how to tie wet and dry flies, how to make bullets in a mold that Anson had brought back from the Civil War, how to prepare birds and small animals for mounting, how to dress fish and fowl for the frying pan or the oven. He insisted on the proper handling and careful preservation of guns, rods, and tackle, and taught his son the rudiments of physical courage and endurance. The boy's later memories of his father were nearly always in outdoor settings—flushing jacksnipe on the prairies; walking through dead grass or harvest fields where corn stood in shocks; passing by grist or cider mills or trickling lumber dams. He thought of his father whenever he saw a lake or an open fire or a horse and buggy or a flight of wild geese, or whenever there was wood to be split or water to be hauled. He remembered that his father "had frost in his beard in cold weather" while "in hot weather he sweated very much," as in fact Ernest did, too. "He liked to work in the sun on the farm because he did not have to," and loved all forms of manual labor, as Ernest in his maturity did not.

Along with his compassion for wounded animals went a belief that God had provided wild game for the nurture and enjoyment of mankind. He shot all kinds of edible animals for the cooking pot, and taught Ernest from the beginning to like venison, squirrel, possum, and raccoon, as well as pheasant, duck, quail, partridge, doves, and all kinds of fish. He was merciless with all predators, which he referred to as "vermin." One of his letters from Oak Park to Ernest at Walloon Lake said "Don't tell but I saw a great grey cat in our chicken coop the other evening while Uncle Tyley had the chickens out in the yard. So I ran and got Mama's .22-long-smokeless Winchester and went out in the yard and out came Mr. Tom Cat who had the nerve to look me in the eye as I raised the rifle. In an instant a squibb-like report and Mr. Tom Cat turned a summersault in the air and will never steal eggs or baby chickens again."

While Ernest slowly ascended the rungs of the grammar-school ladder from second grade in 1906–1907 through eighth grade in 1912–1913, he spent much of every winter dreaming of the summer that lay ahead. His bare feet became so accustomed to the route from Windemere to Bacon's farm, where he went daily for the milk, that he could have followed it in the dark. He long remembered the pine-needle loam in the hemlock woods, the black muck of the swamp, the sunbaked earth across the pasture, the fresh warm manure behind Bacon's barn, the quaking bog of the creek bottom where killdeer plover fed. On one of these "milk runs," galloping downhill with a stick in his mouth, he stumbled and fell, driving the sharp end of the stick into the back of his throat. It was luckily one of the times when his father was on hand, and he quickly stanched the bleeding and cauterized the wound.

Although he was obliged to carry on his practice in Oak Park while the rest of the family was at Windemere, Ed spent as much time as possible in Michigan, wearing old clothes and a wide straw hat, larding the soil of Longfield Farm, rowing and fishing on the lake, and teaching the lore of nature to his growing brood. Ernest later said that the domestic quarrels between his father and mother led them to plan separate vacations, and that he customarily took sides with one or the other in order to preserve what he called "an armed neutrality." Except for fishing trips with Uncle Tyley to Brevoort Lake in the northern peninsula of Michigan or the hunting trips in the fall to his sister Nettie Hines's place in southern Illinois, the doctor spent most of every year with his wife. His most protracted absence came in 1908, when he took a four months' post-graduate course in obstetrics at the New York Lying-In Hospital. According to his daughter Marcelline, Grace paid his expenses with money she had earned from giving music lessons. On the way back, he followed a circuitous route, taking passage on the SS *Comus* from New York to New Orleans, coming up the Mississippi on a river steamer, and reaching home at last in November. On his arrival in New Orleans he found a message from Ernest, dated October 19th, 1908. It said, with some boyish misspellings, that a clam which Ernest had brought from the Des Plaines River had shut down on the tail of a Japanese goldfish in the school aquarium. This communication was enclosed in a letter from Grace. She said that she hoped Dr. Hemingway was getting a good rest in that "pleasant southern town" and that God would bless and keep him safe. If Ernest's parents sometimes quarreled at home, it was the bond of Christian faith that most united them.

Apart from the annual pilgrimages to Michigan, Ernest himself did little traveling. But he made up for it by poring over a series, edited by Marian George and published in Chicago, comprising *Little Journeys to France and Switzerland,* as well as Germany, Holland, Belgium, and Denmark. His birthday book in the summer of 1909 was G. A. Henty's *True to the Old Flag,* while at Christmas he was given *Ivanhoe* and *Robinson Crusoe,* along with Dickens's *Christmas Stories for Children,* which came from his Uncle Leicester in far-off California. His first extended journey came in September, 1910, when he accompanied his mother to Nantucket. Leaving Windemere on August 29th, they went by boat and train to Woods Hole, where they boarded the steamer for the island. They stayed in a century-old house at 45 Pearl Street, boarding with a spinster named Annie Ayers. It was Ernest's first sight of any ocean. He went swimming daily, as he later said, "among the kelp and horse-shoe crabs." His mother, who sunburned easily, contented herself with partial immersion in the salt-water baths. On Sundays she sang in the choir loft at the First Congregational Church on Centre Street, proud of the fact that the building dated from 1711 and that her father and mother had been choristers there in the 1880s. Ernest went fishing for mackerel and sea bass and shipped home a swordfish sword as a marine specimen for the Agassiz Club collection. On the way home, as Grace had done with Marcelline the year before, they made a sightseeing tour of historical sights in Boston and Cambridge, Lexington and Concord.

Several weeks late for his sixth-grade classes, Ernest went reluctantly back to work, still sunburned from his month beside the sea. There was now a good deal of intrafamily talk about his becoming a doctor, like his father and his uncle Will. Dr. Hemingway took notice of these aspirations on a picture postcard of St. Mary's Hospital at the Mayo Brothers Clinic in Rochester, Minnesota, where he had gone for a quick course in the latest surgical techniques, particularly in obstetrics:

October 12, 1910

My dear Ernest: Here is a picture of the world's surgical headquarters. Your dad is having an excellent trip, it will be only a few years before you and Papa will be visiting clinics together. Much love to all, Lovingly your father, C. E. Hemingway, M.D.

On Easter Sunday, 1911, Ernest and Marcelline were confirmed in a ceremony at the Third Congregational Church, where Grace was choir director and soloist. She was large with her fifth child and her heart was filled with motherly solicitude and religious sentiment. Ernest spoke much later of "the feeling you expected to have and did not have when you made your first communion."

Whatever his emotions may have been, he was activated next day to write the earliest of his short stories as an exercise for his sixth-grade English class at the Holmes Grammar School. Although he mentioned the island of Martha's Vineyard, which he had seen on the way to Nantucket the previous summer, he owed the rest of the yarn to his Great-uncle Tyley Hancock. Like the boy in the story, Tyley had lost his mother when he was four, and had afterwards accompanied his father, Captain Alexander Hancock, on a voyage round Cape Horn to Australia aboard the three-masted bark *Elizabeth*.

Mon April 17 1911   Ernest H

MY FIRST SEA VOUGE

I was born in a little white house on the Island of Marthas Vineyard in the State of Massachuset. My mother died when I was four years old and my father, the catain of the three masted schooner "Elizabeth" took me and my little brother around the "Horn" with him to Australia.

Going we had fine weather and we would see the porpoises playing around the ship and the big white albatross winging its way across the ocean or following the brig for scraps of food; the sailors caught one on a huge hook baited with a biscuit but they let him go as soon as they had caught him for they are very superstitious about these big birds.

One time the sailors went out on a barrel fastened on the bow sprit and speared a porpoise (or sea pig as they call them) and hauled him up on deck and cut out the liver and we had it fried for supper it tasted like pork only it was greesier.

We arrived in Sydney Australia after a fine vouge and had just as good a vouge going back.

This was not the last time in his career as a writer that Ernest would pass off another's story as his own. He had altered Uncle Tyley's account only by having the narrator embark from Martha's Vineyard instead of Liverpool, and by the substitution of "my little brother" for Tyley's older sisters, Caroline and Annie. If any reflection of his inmost yearnings was to be found in the story, it was the allusion to "my little brother." He had wanted one for the past nine years.

That summer at Windemere he was disappointed yet again when his fourth sister, Carol, arrived in the southwest bedroom at Windemere, the first and last of the Hemingway children to be born in Michigan. She was born only two days before Ernest's twelfth birthday, which was quietly celebrated with a small party on the screened porch. In the snapshots taken that day, Ernest looked rather morose. In fact, however, he was inwardly bubbling with joy. His grandfather Anson had made him a gift of a single-barrel 20-gauge shotgun.

The baby was a month old when relatives began to arrive. Dr. Willoughby Hemingway, with his wife Mary and two small daughters, was home from China on furlough, the first since his marriage in 1903. Grace referred to it as "that beautiful time when Uncle Will's family lived with us at Windemere."

When Tyler and George Hemingway came over from George's place in Ironton with their wives and children and Ernest's grandmother Adelaide, the family group numbered two dozen people. From time to time, Grace retired from the hubbub with sick headaches.

Willoughby was something of a hero in the eyes of his older brother Ed. Despite the loss of his right index finger in a boyhood accident with a cornsheller, he had managed, in eight years' time, to become a highly successful and much loved missionary surgeon in Shansi province. Dr. Hemingway yearned to emulate him. According to his son, "he was offered chances to go to Guam or to Greenland," while "at another point he was determined to settle in Nevada, where he could at least escape city life." But Grace, the "cultural arbiter, dealt firmly with this wanderlust." Uncle Will entertained the assembled family with a modest account of his recent meeting with the Dalai Lama. Although the borders of Tibet were still closed to foreign interlopers, Willoughby had managed to catch up with the Lama when he made a royal progress through Mongolia in 1910. To a boy of twelve, like Ernest, this vision of Oriental exoticism was like a sudden translation to another planet.

Although Ernest worshipped no heroes among the Indians who lived in the woods near Bacon's farm, he was constantly aware of their presence, like atavistic shadows moving along the edges of his consciousness, coming and going without a sound. They picked berries along the sandy road that led over the hills to Petoskey and brought them down to sell to the cottagers—"wild, red raspberries crushing with their own weight, covered with basswood leaves to keep them cool" and later in the season brimming pails of blackberries, "firm and fresh-shining." He never heard their footfalls until they were suddenly there, standing beside the kitchen door. But sometimes, reading in the hammock, he thought that he could actually smell them "coming through the gate past the woodpile and around the house." They all smelled alike to him, a curious sweetish odor which he had first detected "when Grandpa Bacon rented the shack by the point to Indians and after they had left he went inside the shack and it all smelt that way." One occupant of the shack was a very tall Indian who had given Ernest a canoe paddle made from ashwood. He "lived alone in the shack and drank pain-killer and walked through the woods alone at night." The manner of his death was memorable. One Fourth of July he went to Petoskey to celebrate by getting drunk. On the way home he fell asleep on the Pere Marquette railway tracks and was run over by the midnight train.

The Indians that Ernest saw most often were the sawyers, Nick Boulton and Billy Tabeshaw. Nick was a muscular man, "very lazy but a great worker once he was started." Some of the farmers in the area "believed he was really a white man." Billy Tabeshaw was short and plump "with only a few hairs of mustache like a Chinaman." One day that summer, Dr. Hemingway summoned them to cut up some beech logs for use in the stove and fireplace. The logs had broken away from the boom up the lake and drifted ashore in front of the cottage. The day the Indians arrived, carrying cant hooks, axes, wedges, and a long cross-cut saw, Dr. Hemingway found his camera and followed them down to the beach to photograph them while they worked. The pictures were good and clear, and he mounted them in his "Bear Lake Book" as a memento of the occasion. Ernest hung about watching, taking in every word that was said. A long time later he would write a short story about it, fictionizing the incident, and of course making a far better job of it than his "Sea Vouge" story of the preceding April.

Apart from Nick Boulton and his daughter Prudence, who sometimes worked for Grace Hemingway, the Indian that Ernest knew best was old Simon Green. He owned a good-sized farm on Horton's Creek and could often be seen, as Ernest wrote, "sitting in a chair in front of [Jim Dilworth's] blacksmith shop at Horton Bay, perspiring in the sun while his horses were being shod inside." He was "an old fat Indian" and a great admirer of Dr. Hemingway's prowess with rifle and shotgun. Ernest was out with his father and Simon Green the day he saw his first covey of partridges. They were "dusting and feeding in the sun beside the grist mill on Horton's Creek" and looked to the boy's eyes as big as turkeys. When they flew, he was so much excited by the clack and whir of their wings that he could not hit any of them. But Dr. Hemingway, "shooting an old lever action Winchester pump," brought down five birds in quick succession. "I can remember the Indian picking them up and laughing," wrote Ernest. "My father . . . was a beautiful shot, the fastest I have ever seen."

Later that fall, he watched his father shooting again when they went to southern Illinois to see Ernest's cousins. Dr. Hemingway's older sister, Nettie, christened Anginette, had been married in 1898 to a widower named Frank Bristow Hines. Hines began as a Congregationalist minister, then became president of the Southern Collegiate Institute in Albion, and at last turned to farming, growing fruit and breeding stock on several large homesteads in the western part of the state. A friendly and jolly man, Hines lived with his wife and seven children in a handsome brick house in Albion. The house was dark and cool even in the heat of summer, with tall narrow windows and shade maples in the yard. The Hines children owned three ponies, Sorghum, Kitty, and Kitty's colt, Princess. The atmosphere of the region, which lay close to the banks of the Wabash, was as southern as Indiana and Kentucky, the bordering states to the east. The fields stood high with corn and wheat, loud with the summer chorus of a million fiddling insects, and the Hines table groaned beneath an abundance of southern dishes. As often as his practice would permit, Dr. Hemingway made the 300-mile trip from Chicago to Albion. Nettie's lively children called him "Uncle Doctor," and in the fall of the year there was always the prospect of a three-day, two-night hunting expedition for quail, coon, and possum on one of Frank Hines's farms in Union County south of Carbondale.

This time the boy and his father were borne away from the station in the

Hines family buggy to the brick house where the younger children waited—
Margarette, Anginette, Adelaide, Anson, and the eldest son, Frank, Junior.
Though Ernest was twelve and Frank only eight, they became good companions almost at once. The pony called Sorghum had just been sold, and the
boys set off to deliver it to its new owner. Ernest was in the saddle and Frank
followed in the pony buggy, driving Kitty. They had gone no more than a mile
or two when Sorghum's belly-band broke, pitching Ernest into the dust. "A
cool Ernest and a cool Sorghum kept everything under control," wrote Margarette. "Neither boy nor pony got excited." When they reached home, the
rest of the family had gone to prayer meeting. The boys began playing football
with a sofa cushion in the parlor, and managed to shatter a large green vase,
ornamented with gold, that had been Nettie's wedding present from Dr. and
Mrs. Hemingway.

There was, in fact, so much breakage that Ernest remembered it afterwards
as "an unlucky trip." When they reached the farm in Union County, Dr. Hemingway wanted to show off his son's skill with the new birthday shotgun by
letting him shoot pigeons. The birds made ghostly moving targets high up
among the rafters in the shadowy gable of the dairy barn, and Ernest soon
killed enough to make a large pigeon pie of the breast meat. When his father
judged that he had proved his marksmanship and refused him further shells,
the boy began to practice swinging on the pigeons, snapping the hammer of
his gun against the empty chamber. It did not take much of this before the
hammer spring broke. Disconsolately picking up the pigeons to carry them to
the kitchen, he had just emerged from the barn when two older boys came
along the road. One asked him about the pigeons. Ernest said he had just shot
them. The boy said he had not. Ernest called him a liar, and the smaller of
the two then "whipped hell" out of Ernest.

It was known in the family that Ernest loved to dramatize everything, continuing his boyhood habit of making up stories in which he was invariably the
swashbuckling hero. His first actual experience on the stage came in March
of 1912, when he appeared in the seventh-grade play, *Robin Hood,* wearing
high buckled boots, a wig, a velvet cap, and a long soutane, and carrying a
homemade longbow through the simulated glades of Sherwood Forest. He was
now singing regularly in the vested choir at the Third Congregational Church,
and had even tried his hand at some verses about the Chicago Cubs:

April 12, 1912   Ernest H.

The Opening Game

1st Inning

    With Chance on first and Evers on Third,
    Great things from the Cubs will soon be heard.
    Then up comes Shulte to the bat,
    On the plate his bat does rap,
    Takes a slug at that old ball,
    Makes it clear the right field wall. . . .

Two summers and a winter remained before Ernest could enter high school. The first of the summers went by like the wind. The family initiated a ceremony called "bringing home the birthday tree," a small hemlock cut in the woods and brought home in a wheelbarrow to be hung with gifts for the joint birthday party of Ernest and the baby. They also bought a second motor launch and named it for Carol. In September, at Harbor Springs on the way home, Ernest saw his first seaplane—a frail-looking craft manned by a pilot in grease-stained pants and a baseball cap with the visor turned backwards. The fall was replete with parties. Nineteen Hemingways gathered to help Dr. Hemingway celebrate his forty-first birthday and the whole family dressed up and sat for a formal picture on Grace and Ed's sixteenth wedding anniversary. In February, Marcelline and Ernest gave a Valentine's Day party for their classmates in the eighth grade. On successive Saturdays in May, they performed in a Japanese pageant play at the Chicago Coliseum. A contrite note from Ernest to his father refers to one of these visits. "My conduct at the Coloseum yesterday was bad and my conduct at Church this morning was bad. My conduct tomorrow will be good." He signed it formally and gave the date—May 11, 1913. Within a month he and Marcelline had been graduated from the Holmes Grammar School, with diplomas listing their achievements, and were setting off once more for Windemere.

It was Ernest's fourteenth season in Michigan. He pitched a tent just inside the rail fence behind the cottage and slept there all summer. Harold Sampson came up again for the final weeks of August, and a girl named Ruth McCollum arrived to visit Marcelline. One night they all read Bram Stoker's *Dracula* aloud before the cottage fireplace. Ernest's imagination was so much inflamed that soon after midnight he awakened the household with a yelling nightmare. Another day, the Bacons' dog attacked a porcupine in the woods. They brought it moaning to Dr. Hemingway for surgical attention. He talked to the dog quietly and cut out the barbed quills one by one. After the ordeal, Ernest and Harold went hunting for the porcupine. They found and killed it in a lumber clearing behind the Bacon farm, returning in triumph side by side, carrying their trophy by the hind legs. If they had expected praise, they were disappointed. Dr. Hemingway read them a lecture on the needless destruction of harmless animals. Having shot it, said he, they were now obliged to eat it. "We cooked the haunches for hours," wrote Harold, "but they were still about as tender and tasty as a piece of shoe leather."

To a remarkable degree, the child was father to the man: many traits of Ernest's boyish character held on with only slight modifications well into his adult life. "Afraid of nothing"—the maxim he had first uttered at the age of two—was an ideal of behavior in the face of adversity long after he had discovered that many things and events might legitimately arouse fear. All his life he sought scrupulously to uphold the code of physical courage and endurance which his father, and sometimes his mother, had early impressed upon him. The love of nature, of hunting and fishing, of the freedom to be found in the woods or on the water, stayed solidly with him to the end of his life. He shared his father's pleasure in good eating, especially of fish and game. Even his liking for onions dated back to the time when his father had pointed out that wild onions, stripped clean of clinging loam, made an excellent filling for sandwiches. Because he lacked his father's phenomenal eyesight, he could never match his skill with shotgun or rifle, though in time and with the aid of spectacles, he became a superb wingshot. Like his father he was never able to carry a tune quite on key, nor was he ever to be so fully at home in the realms of music as his mother would have wished. But he soon moved far past her in the judgment and appreciation of the graphic arts, particularly oil painting, while the impulse to creativity, which he clearly owed to her both by inheritance and youthful training, took directions in his own life that she could neither understand nor approve.

After adolescence, he quickly abandoned the manual labor in which his father took so much pleasure, though he was always willing to expend equal energy in sundry forms of sport. He loved swimming, walking, and hiking throughout his life. Nothing pleased him more than working up a good swingeing sweat: he and his father both believed that it cleared the brain and cleansed the body. He shared his father's determination to do things "properly" (a favorite adverb in both their vocabularies), whether building a fire, rigging a rod, baiting a hook, casting a fly, handling a gun, or roasting a duck or a haunch of venison. Neither he nor his father before him was much good in the diagnosis and repair of faulty engines. The ills and accidents of his boyhood and manhood confirmed Ernest's respect for the profession of medicine, though he entertained some remarkably naive physiological beliefs. In later life he shared the tendency of both his parents to take on weight, and it may even be that the luxuriant beards he grew in adulthood were motivated partly by the fact that he had never known his father to be without one.

Within these limits, and with the exceptions noted, he owed his knowledge of the arts and the sciences to both his parents and to the manner of his upbringing in suburban Oak Park and rural Michigan. Because he was a kind of genius, he would surpass both his immediate forebears in ways not yet fully visible in the fourteenth year of his life. The nature of his gifts would eventually oblige him to rebel from certain mores and moral and religious standards which they held dear. But that time was not yet upon him as he packed his suitcase for the return to Oak Park in September, 1913.

3. JUVENILIA

Now it was time for high school, the great adventure of Ernest's adolescence. The Oak Park and River Forest Township High School was as big as a palace: a new and imposing structure of yellow brick, with four floors, two wings, an assembly hall, a lunchroom, and a massive front door reached by a curving stairway of stone. On opening day, he walked over to get his class schedule for Algebra, Latin, English, and General Science. The English did not scare him, but the other subjects did. He found first-year Latin so difficult that his mother, who had hated it in her girlhood, hired a tutor to start him off right. The English classes were almost a pleasure. They were conducted by Frank J. Platt, head of the department, in the elegant English Club room, with leather armchairs and a Tudor-style beamed ceiling.

As a freshman, Ernest was much ashamed of his height. He was a whole head shorter than Marcelline, who looked in her sixteenth year like the young woman she already was, and he longed vainly for comparable stature. At five feet four inches he was still too small and light for football. He tried to make up for his physical shortcomings by working on his marksmanship, in which he was consistently able to score 112 out of a possible 150 at a range of twenty yards. He blamed the mistakes on the sight of his left eye, which had been deficient from the time of his birth, and believed that this was a heritage from his mother, whose difficulty with her eyes was constantly evident. All through the busy spring of his freshman year, he stayed restively at five feet five. It was not until he reached Walloon Lake that summer of his fifteenth birthday that the long-awaited miracle took place. As if a weight had fallen from a hidden spring, he suddenly began to grow at the rate of an inch or more a month.

When Harold Sampson came up to join him for a working vacation, they pitched a tent on a rise of ground at Longfield Farm, gathering hay, attending to the truck garden, and milking a cow named Topsy. Ernest and Sam used the motor launch *Carol* to establish a water-borne vegetable route, peddling new potatoes, beans, carrots, peas, and rutabagas to the small hotels and cottages around the lake. They ended their "vegetarian" summer—the hardest-working season of their lives—by harvesting fifty bushels of potatoes in rough and blowing weather.

Having now outgrown all his clothes, Ernest was allowed his first pair of long pants in the middle of October. He wore them to a reception given at home by his parents for the Sons and Daughters of the American Revolution. He was out for lightweight football, though the coach took little notice of him. He was also sawing away at his cello in the school orchestra, and working part time in the school lunchroom. On October 17th, with no great enthusiasm, he took Marcelline to their first lesson at Miss Belle Ingram's dancing class at the Colonial Club, a huge old structure on Forest Avenue. Both in football and in dancing, his large feet and indifferent coordination were a hazard to himself and others. But in biology class he made a minor triumph with a six-page paper on the anatomy of grasshoppers, without once mentioning that he had been using them for years as trout bait. The paper was graded 90 and marked "very good."

Grace was now pregnant for the sixth time. The baby was due in April, and all the children still hoped for a brother. It was plainly now or never, for Grace was in her forties, and further children were unlikely. Just before Christmas vacation, Ernest began walking home with a freshman named Dorothy Davies. "It is the very first notice he has ever taken of any girl," wrote his mother, "and we notice the increased interest in personal appearance." Besides the long pants, he was now wearing a stiff collar and a necktie. In January, 1915, he took Dorothy to a basketball game. It was his first date. "All his bachelor friends," said Grace, "were nearly in a state of apoplexy over it."

These bachelor classmates included Lewis Clarahan, Ray Ohlsen, Lloyd Golder, Paul Haase, Proctor Gilbert (called Bunny), Tom Cusack, Lyman Worthington, Hale Printup, Morris Musselman, and George Madill, who was called Pickles. Ernest disdained such nicknames as Bunny and Pickles and was pleased when Lew Clarahan addressed him as Porthos, after the largest of the Three Musketeers. He also liked the name Butch, and at home urged Marcelline to call him "The Old Brute." But the name he preferred to all others, and in fact kept all his life, was Hemingstein. It originated at a period before anti-Semitic jokes had become unfashionable and when, indeed, a few were even permitted in the high-school publications. Ernest had a locker on the ground floor of the school beside those of Lloyd Golder and Ray Ohlsen. He drew three circles in yellow chalk on the locker doors and said that they represented a pawnshop. Golder became Goldberg and Ohlsen Cohen. "We deal in funds," said the sophomoric Hemingstein. "We don't lend. You lend to us. We promise to use any money anyone wants to contribute and we promise never to return it."

The whole gang passed the usual hectic spring of high-school sophomores. Ernest spent long hours of orchestra rehearsal for the ambitious production of Balfe's three-act operetta, *The Bohemian Girl.* After Grace's years as choir director at the Third Congregational Church, the family had now returned to the First Church, where Ernest became a stalwart pillar of the Plymouth League for young people. He supplemented his weekly allowance of fifteen cents (one penny for each year of his age) by shoveling snow and delivering *Oak Leaves,* the local weekly. On Washington's Birthday, he joined the boys' Hiking Club in a jaunt of thirty-two miles, and on the following Saturday made another which covered twenty-five. He was still as much concerned with distance and endurance as he had been at the age of four. In the ninth annual cross-country run, forty-six candidates turned out at Phipps Field and did the course in heavy rain. Although Ernest came in forty-third, he finished the race. During the spring recess, he and Lew Clarahan hiked to Lake Zurich, some thirty-five miles northwest of Oak Park, returning home on April 3rd. While they were away, Grace had her sixth child. It was a boy, born on April Fool's Day, and much given to raucous bellowing. But he had come too late to be the companion that Ernest had long desired. They called him Leicester Clarence in honor of Grace's brother and her husband. Ernest nicknamed him Leicester De Pester after a comic-strip character. This was presently shortened to "The Pest," in allusion to his crying, though "The Last of the Flock" might have been a happier designation.

When the school year ended on June 19th, Ernest and Lew Clarahan packed up and set out for Walloon Lake. Ray Ohlsen went along for the boat-ride aboard the *Missouri* as far as Frankfort, Michigan. The boys shared a stateroom and got into trouble with the purser because of loud roughhousing. At Frankfort they left Ray to return home and began the long hike to Windemere by way of Traverse City and Charlevoix. Ernest talked, sang, and shouted most of the way, "his imagination going full steam." Sometimes they rode a few miles in passing country wagons, but mainly they walked. Their chief entertainment was fishing. Once a bobcat leaped across the road in front of them. They tried swimming in Traverse Bay, but it was icy cold and they had to settle for wading. After four or five days on a diet of fresh-caught trout and canned beans, they plodded into Horton Bay for a dinner with the Dilworths. Wesley Dilworth was now twenty-five and about to marry a twenty-year-old schoolteacher named Kathryn Kennedy. But the high school sophomores were only mildly interested. They spent the final days of June at Windemere, removing shutters and otherwise preparing the cottage for summer occupancy. The rest of the time they camped in their tent at Longfield Farm. Whenever they grew tired of their own cooking, Pinehurst Cottage was just over the ridge.

Wesley married Kathryn on July 12th. A week later, Dr. Hemingway sent Ernest a birthday message from Oak Park. "I am so pleased and proud," he wrote, "you have grown to be such a fine big manly fellow and will trust your development will continue symmetrical and in harmony with our highest Christian ideals. . . . When I get back, you shall have a good trout fish." On the 23rd, he wrote again, enclosing his own prints of the pictures Ernest and Lew had taken on their hiking trip. The launch *Carol* was leaking and needed a new bilge pump. Ernest was instructed to get it repaired. He was also to take good care of the garden and the stock at Longfield, and to dress chickens for his mother whenever she needed them.

At sixteen, he looked older than he was. Inside he was still a boy, striving to live in harmony with "Christian ideals" and much given to worry whenever he ran into difficulties with the Establishment. Shortly after his birthday he got into a minor scrape which he afterwards remembered, and characteristically exaggerated, as the worst of his boyhood. It began with an innocent picnic. His only companion was his eleven-year-old sister, Sunny, the leading tomboy among the Hemingway daughters. In the launch *Carol,* with the rowboat *Ursula* in tow, they headed for a spot called the "Cracken" on the shore of Mud Lake. This was a region of tall reeds, turtles, frogs, and sedimentary mud at the far extremity of the West Arm of Walloon. They had just reached their destination when they scared up a large blue heron. Ernest impulsively shot it.

He wrapped it in a newspaper and left it in the launch while they went ashore to eat. When they came back, the bird was gone. The son of the local game warden had discovered and impounded the bird. He approached in a skiff and asked who the culprit was. Ernest lied smoothly. A man had given it to him, said he, and he was going to take it home and stuff it. The boy went off to report to his father. Ernest hurried home, blurted out the story, and set off at once for Longfield to lie low until the storm was over.

An oafish man named Smith who said that he was the game warden presently appeared at the Hemingway cottage. He was full of "beastly, insinuating, sneering questions." He was looking for a young man of about eighteen who owned a shotgun and a red sweater. That was her son, said Grace. He was sixteen years old and was working on the farm across the lake. When Smith asked to borrow a rowboat, Grace gave him a dressing down in her most imperious manner, sent Sunny for the shotgun, and ordered him off the property. "Lady," said Smith, as he edged out of range, "I've learned a lesson."

Ernest fled over the ridge to Dilworth's. Wesley promised to intercede with the warden, whom he knew, and the fugitive went on to his Uncle George Hemingway's summer place at Ironton, beyond Lake Charlevoix. On the night of the 30th, under cover of darkness, he made a dramatic trip back to Longfield, where he picked some string beans, dug some potatoes, and killed a chicken so that his mother would not lack for food in his absence. Then he retreated to Ironton until it was safe to come home again. His father wrote from Oak Park, advising him to insist on a jury trial and to plead guilty of shooting the heron but innocent of a legal offense. Ernest told his story to the judge at Boyne City, paid a fine of fifteen dollars, and returned in a chastened mood to help with the haying. The story greatly amused Lew Clarahan. "I wish I had been there," he wrote. "What was your time from the farm to Dilworth's?" But Ernest took a far more serious view. He had tangled with the law. He had been a bad boy. All the rest of his life he regarded game wardens with the utmost suspicion. The older he grew, the larger the episode bulked in his memory. In his fifties, he solemnly assured a professor of English that two game wardens had once chased him all over Michigan and that he was lucky not to have been sent to reform school. He also set down a puerile story based on the incident. The fictional game wardens stayed overnight at Windemere, getting drunk on whiskey, while Ernest and Sunny fled ever deeper into the wilderness.

He spent the fall of 1915 as substitute tackle on the lightweight football team. Phipps Field, where they practiced, was three miles from home, and the Spartan effort often left him too tired to study. He was also dieting—"eating a negative quantity of nothing" he called it—in an attempt to maintain his weight at 135 pounds. He was now finding Latin easier than football. "Cicero is a pipe," he wrote. "I could write better stuff with both hands tied behind me." He had lately earned a grade of 100 on an ancient-history test. But he still preferred hiking and shooting to team sports or studying. One of his favorite Saturday morning haunts was a game farm on the prairie beyond the Des Plaines River, about two miles west of the Hemingway house. It was run by Wallace Evans for the cultivation of wild game, especially pheasants.

Ernest was poaching on these preserves the day he shot his first pheasant. Long afterwards he recalled what a miracle it had seemed when the cock came roaring up from under his feet "to top a sweet briar thicket" and plummet down with its wings still pounding. He waited until nightfall before he dared to carry his prize home. "You can feel the bulk of him still," he wrote, "inside your shirt with his long tail up under your armpit, walking in to town in the dark along the dirt road [North Avenue] where the gypsy wagons used to camp."

Early in 1916, Ernest discovered an enthusiasm for boxing. He was large for his age and husky from his work on the farm in the summer, and there was a streak of the bully in his nature which began to emerge when he learned of the power in his fists. For a time he used the music room for a ring, taking on a whole succession of his schoolmates, many of them smaller than he. Grace drove them out when the boxing began to "degenerate into fighting," and the locale was shifted to the small gymnasium in Tom Cusack's basement. They also fought outdoors. "I remember boxing Ernie on the prairie back of 822 North Euclid," wrote his diminutive friend, Lew Clarahan, "and getting knocked out by EMH." Ernest often spoke in later years of having learned to box before he was sixteen from professional fighters in Chicago. His sparring partners and instructors included (so he said) Sam Langford, Jack Blackburn, Eddie McGoorty, Tommy Gibbons, Jack Dillon, and Harry Greb. These sessions allegedly took place in gyms like those of Kid Howard or Forbes and Ferretti. Ernest allowed his listeners to infer that the faulty vision of his left eye had been caused by the dirty tactics of his opponents (resin on the heel of the glove, loose drawstrings deftly flicked against an eyeball), and told his stories with such wholehearted conviction that his auditors swallowed them whole. On the show-off side of his character, which was as real as his shy and modest side, he secretly enjoyed the open-mouthed belief that his yarns engendered. It helped to enhance his reputation as the tough kid he wanted them to think he had been, and also paid silent tribute to his considerable powers as actor-narrator. There is no surviving evidence to prove that he boxed professionals in Chicago, either then or later. This, after all, was the same boy who had sought, aged five, to convince his grandfather that he had stopped a runaway horse in mid-career. The best evidence is that he learned the rough rudiments boxing in his mother's music room, Tom Cusack's basement gymnasium, and out on the prairie back of Tom's house at 822 North Euclid.

On the other hand, his interest in boxing may well have prompted him to make a few Saturday morning visits to Forbes and Ferretti's or Kid Howard's just to see how it was done. If he kept his eyes and ears open and listened to yarns by some of the old guard, there was always a chance of fresh material for short stories. In April, just when his boxing enthusiasm was at its height, the *Tabula* printed one of his earliest short stories. "A Matter of Colour" was a humorous tale told by an old fight manager to a youthful listener.

Even the opening sentence sounded like something Ernest might have picked up on a Saturday morning visit to a Chicago gym. " 'What, you never heard the story about Joe Gans's first fight?' said old Bob Armstrong, as he tugged at one of his gloves. 'Well, son, that kid I was just giving the lesson to reminded me of the Big Swede that gummed the best frame-up we ever almost pulled off.' " Old Bob went on to tell how he had matched an up-and-coming lightweight named Montana Dan Morgan against Joe Gans, "a pusson of color." Having bet heavily on Dan, he had hired the Big Swede to stand behind the curtain at one side of the ring, and knock Joe out with a baseball bat when Dan had maneuvered him into position. But the Swede knocked out the wrong man. Old Bob gave him hell after the fight. "Why in the name of the Prophet did you hit the white man instead of the black one?" he cried. "Mister Armstrong," said the Swede, "I bane color blind."

"A Matter of Colour" was the second of his short stories to appear in the school's elaborate literary magazine. The first had appeared in February. It was a bloody tale of mayhem and suicide with a setting in the northern woods. A Cree Indian named Pierre, believing that his white partner had stolen his wallet, set a trap for him along the trail they customarily followed. When he found that a red squirrel was the actual thief, Pierre ran off to rescue his friend. It was too late. Tracks of timber wolves were "all over the bloody snow" while a pair of ravens, like the "Twa Corbies" of the medieval ballad, were picking "at the shapeless something that had once been Dick Haywood." Pierre was so shocked that he stepped into a bear trap. This, as he knew, was "The Judgment of Manitou" for having mistrusted his partner. As the story closed he was reaching for his rifle to save the wolves the trouble of killing him.

Along with his work in fiction, Ernest was also acting as a reporter for *The Trapeze,* the school's weekly newspaper. His first by-line appeared in January over an account of a concert by the Chicago Symphony. Through February and March he did a series on the Hanna Club, a school organization which imported speakers from Chicago and its suburbs, many of them with inspirational messages. But the life of action attracted him most. His best reporting in the spring of 1916 was a three-inch story on an attempted suicide in the old pond down by the waterworks one evening in May. The hero of the story was Lyman Worthington, one of Ernest's boxing partners, who dived in and pulled the victim ashore. "Worthington was highly complimented by the police and Public Service company for his bravery and prompt action," wrote Ernest. "He said when interviewed that the only bad effect . . . was the loss from his coat pocket of a fine lot of jokes for the *Tabula.*"

From boxing and reporting he now turned to canoeing, making moonlight trips along the Des Plaines River in a Storm class canoe. His companions were mostly his male classmates, but once or twice he took Frances Coates, who had now succeeded Dorothy Davies in his affections. His interest dated from a performance of the three-act opera, *Martha,* in which Frances had appeared during April. Playing his cello in the orchestra pit, Ernest could hardly keep his eyes on the score. His friend Al Dungan, a gifted cartoonist, made a caricature of a boy with desperate eyes and labeled it: "Erney sees a girl named Frances." He was too shy to ask her to the Junior-Senior Prom on May 19th. "Ernest and Marcelline went together," wrote his mother, "altho Marcelline had other invitations." But at the end of the month Frances and Marcelline, Ernest and Harold Sampson took what Grace described as "a beautiful canoe trip up the Des Plaines River, with supper on the banks near the University Camp."

The hiking trip of the year before had turned out so well that Ernest now persuaded Lew Clarahan to try it again. They set forth as soon as school was out, at four o'clock on the afternoon of Saturday, June 10th. Both of them were well loaded down with tent and blankets, ax and cooking kit, fishing equipment, can opener, toilet paper, safety pins, matches, pink pills, salt and pepper, a compass, a watch, a pedometer, a packet of postcards, adhesive tape, two maps, malted milk, German sweet chocolate, two spoons, two combination knife-forks, extra socks, a can of worms, and, not least important, a supply of bacon and cornmeal for cooking the trout they hoped to catch. Ernest had drawn seven dollars from the bank to finance the trip.

The steamer hooted its way deliberately across the foggy lake. This time they headed south from Frankfort and hiked from Onekama along the Manistee River to Bear Creek, a clear stream fifty feet wide. "Camped in dandy spot on bank of stream," wrote Ernest in his diary. "Many trout. . . . Killed water moccasin on R.R. track." Next morning they were out at seven. "Many trout jumping," wrote Ernest. "Great fighters." Between them that day they caught four. Ernest's were 14 and 18 inches long. On Tuesday they broke camp and went to Walton Junction for midday dinner. It was a dirty hamlet dominated by railroad tracks—the place, as Ernest wrote, "that put the junk in junction." In the afternoon they went on to Mayfield and hiked from there to the Boardman, a narrow, deep river "with a devilish current." The fish were not biting and they made a "spruce house bed," turning in early under lowering skies. About two in the morning they were awakened by a deluge. Rain was still falling steadily as they worked downstream to an old lumber dam, where Lew caught a pair of two-foot suckers. "They gave us some sensation," wrote Ernest, "while we thot they were trout." In Mayfield next morning they traded the suckers to an old couple in exchange for a quart of milk. "The old woman smoked a pipe," wrote Ernest. "The old man is 78 years old and the woman 85. They were delighted with the suckers."

They took the train to Kalkaska and hiked to Rapid River, the fastest fishing stream in Ernest's limited experience. "There is a small water electric power plant out here in the wilderness run by a fellow from Chicago," wrote Ernest. "He had a rainbow 20 inches long." The boys' blankets were still so wet that they stayed up all night fishing in "a nifty pool below the power house." It was great romantic fun, Ernest thought, "fighting them in the dark in the deep swift river." Towards dawn, Lew fell asleep inside the power plant, but Ernest kept on fishing through the open window, adding more trout to the pile in the basket. "A lot of people," said Ernest, "were sorry to see us go. . . . The whole town [of Rug, Michigan] came down to see us off." It was a typical instance of his lifelong pleasure in being popular. They ate a midday dinner in a "lumberjack joint" at Kalkaska. Lew Clarahan said good-bye and caught the southbound train for home.

Ernest went on alone to the "rough burg" of Mancelona and waited seven hours for the train to Petoskey. He whiled away some of the time by watching an Indian girl about his own age, and talking with a friendly lumberjack from Alba. He was already thinking of how much "good stuff" he had gathered in the past week "for stories and essays." He made a little list in the back pages of his diary: "(1) Old people at Boardman. (2) Mancelona Indian girl. (3) Bear Creek. (4) Rapid River." One story was already forming in his head: "Mancelona. Rainy night. Tough looking lumberjack. Young Indian girl. Kills self and girl." It was the kind of plot his adolescent imagination found easiest to hatch.

That Saturday night in Petoskey he paid seventy-five cents for a bed at the Hotel Perry, and next morning hiked to Horton Bay. The Dilworths gave him dinner at noon and he had supper with Wesley and Kathryn. The rain was easing off at last and the weather was turning cold. He shot a crow for the Dilworths to use as a scarecrow and on Tuesday split some wood and plucked a chicken. Afterwards he caught eight rainbows in Horton's Creek and brought them back for dinner at the Dilworths'. The family would soon be reaching Windemere for the summer, but in the meantime he was taking pleasure in being on his own, doing as he liked, and dreaming about tough lumberjacks and Indian girls in the tough burg of Mancelona.

As if he had decided to enforce his newfound independence, Ernest spent more time than ever at Horton Bay. Apart from the Dilworth family, his chief associates were Bill and Katy Smith. They lived with their aunt, Mrs. Joseph William Charles, the wife of a doctor in St. Louis. She had raised them since their mother's death of tuberculosis in 1899, and had bought and fixed over the Horton Bay farmhouse to provide healthy summers for her foster children. Ernest had known them vaguely for several years. Now he found them so gay and witty and so ready to share in his own love of the woods and the lake that it was easy to forget the discrepancy in their ages. Katy was nearly twenty-five and Bill was a college student going on twenty-one. He was a slender, good-looking boy with light hair slicked down close to his head. He spoke with a slow Missouri drawl and a droll sense of humor that ran lightly to puns and polysyllabics. Katy was neither quite pretty nor quite plain, an outspoken girl with flyaway hair like Jo March in *Little Women*. She was always brushing it out of her eyes with the back of her slender hand. Her most arresting feature was her eyes, which were green as a cat's and almost made you think that she could see in the dark. Bill pleased Ernest by accepting him as a coeval; Katy treated him with a kind of condescending affection, like a slightly older sister who was not averse to pointing out that his fingernails were dirty, as in fact they usually were.

Ernest maintained his distance from domestic entanglements by sleeping in a tent in the yard behind Windemere cottage and setting up a camp of his own at Murphy's Point, half a mile away. If he sometimes felt the normal rebelliousness of a seventeen-year-old towards the family circle, or if he lost his virginity in some forest glade to Nick Boulton's nubile daughter Prudy—as he often boasted in subsequent fiction and letters—he naturally took pains to conceal his emotions from his parents and his sisters. Outwardly, at least, he remained the dutiful son, "leading a life in harmony with our highest Christian ideals." If his fictional account of his father can be trusted, he did not find their discussions of sex highly illuminating. When he read in the paper that Enrico Caruso had been arrested for mashing, he asked his father what the word meant. "It is one of the most heinous crimes," said Dr. Hemingway, and Ernest was left to picture "the great tenor doing something strange, bizarre, and heinous with a potato masher to a beautiful lady who looked like the pictures of Anna Held on the inside of cigar boxes." Dr. Hemingway "summed up the whole matter by stating that masturbation produced blindness, insanity, and death, while a man who went with prostitutes would contract hideous venereal diseases and that the thing to do was to keep your hands off people." As with his stories of learning to box from the professionals in Chicago, Ernest's fictional accounts of sexual initiation with Prudy Boulton were more likely the product of wishful thinking than of fact.

When he returned to Oak Park for his senior year, Ernest stood nearly six feet tall and weighed 150 pounds. Further lightweight football was out of the question and he went out for the first team. He was still so awkward that the best he could hope for was a position as second- or third-string guard. His big feet were as troublesome in football as in dancing, and they were soon a legend among his teammates. None of the mud-caked football shoes in the bin at school would fit him. Gordon Shepherd, the team captain, suggested that a cobbler might nail cleats to an old pair of Ernest's own high-laced shoes. This did not end the difficulties. Coach Thistlewaite had instructed his guards to lock ankles with Shepherd, who played defensive center. Whenever Ernest was sent in as a substitute, Shepherd began to worry. "He was so slow in moving," said he, "that I was always in difficulty in getting my foot worked loose from his so that I could play the game as it should be played." The season went well enough, including a 35–19 victory over Waite High of Toledo. On this trip, Dr. Hemingway accompanied the team. He was touchingly eager to make sure that Ernest won his varsity letter, and tried to persuade both Shepherd and Thistlewaite that his strapping son was the best linesman in the league. Both were politely noncommittal until the end of the season, when Ernest was awarded a large OP to wear on his sweater. It was a kind of triumph. So was his membership on the swimming team that winter, and his election as captain of the new water-basketball squad.

But writing came easier than team sports. "His themes were almost always read aloud in class," wrote Susan Lowrey, "as examples of what we should all strive for." His favorite English teachers were Fannie Biggs and Margaret Dixon. "They were both very nice," said Ernest, "and especially nice to me because I had to try to be an athlete as well as try to learn to write English." Miss Biggs was a small, wiry spinster whose greatest interest lay in imaginative writing. Miss Dixon was "frank, straightforward, honest, [and] down-to-earth." Whatever else may be said of Ernest's fiction at this period, most of it was tough-minded, firmly plotted, original, and astonishingly free of those ineptitudes common to high-school writing. Shortly after the end of football season, the *Tabula* brought out the third of his stories. It drew on his acquaintance with the Indians in Michigan and was called "Sepi Jingan." Sepi Jingan was the name of a large dog belonging to Billy Tabeshaw. "A long, lean, copper-colored, ham-faced" Ojibway, the fictional Billy had nothing in common with his real-life namesake. It was a story of vengeance. A bad Indian named Paul Black Bird had killed Billy's cousin. For two years, Billy trailed the murderer without success. He was walking along the Pere Marquette tracks one Fourth of July when someone knocked him out. It was Paul Black Bird. He boasted that he was going to kill Billy and his dog, destroying the evidence by tying them to the tracks. But the villain had reckoned without the power of the dog. Even as Paul Black Bird spoke, Sepi Jingan, with bared fangs, was stalking him from behind.

The greater part of Ernest's writing in his senior year was journalism for the *Trapeze*. Between November, 1916, and May, 1917, he averaged better than a story a week. Many dealt with sports, some seriously, some humorously. His chief model for the humorous pieces was Ring Lardner, whose column in the Chicago *Tribune* was widely acclaimed. One of Ernest's stories printed in December carried the headline: OUR RING LARDNER, JR. BREAKS INTO PRINT WITH ALL-COOK COUNTY ELEVEN. He had not yet mastered Lardner's pseudo-illiterate style, and much of his work was loose and silly, beaten out on a second-hand typewriter in the relative privacy of his third-floor bedroom at home, and submitted without revision to John Gehlmann, the faculty adviser. Ernest was not a supremely capable speller. He never learned, for example, that verbs like *have* drop the final e in forming the present participle, or that *nor* does not properly follow a previous negative. All his life he confused *already* with *all ready* and believed that there was such a word as *alright*. Yet the pieces he wrote in high school showed enough dash and energy to make up for such minor deficiencies. Later, as he was fond of saying, you could always hire people to correct your mistakes.

His enthusiasm for canoeing renewed itself when the ice melted. During spring vacation, on April 2–6, 1917, he left with Ray Ohlsen for a canoe trip on the Illinois River to Starved Rock State Park in La Salle County, near Ottawa, Illinois. They were still calling each other Cohen and Stein, making motions with their hands which they took to be appropriate to pawnbrokers. They were three days out when Dr. Hemingway sent a letter to his wife and oldest daughter, who had gone to Ohio to enter Marcelline in Oberlin College. "Dear Gracie and Marcelline: The children are all OK up stairs, three have had their swims and Ursula is in the tub now. It has just started to rain, harder now every minute. Ernest has had three good days and now comes the rain. Ray Ohlsen's father got a letter from 'Ole' today saying they had a rather hard day their second day, only made 15 miles as they had to portage several times and had been held up by the Soldiers guarding the [Illinois] Canal and searched—but passed OK. A good thing they had no arms or ammunition or dynamite."

The soldiers doing guard duty on the Canal were the first visible sign of the entry of the United States into the war in Europe. In common with many of his classmates, Ernest talked of wanting to go. When required to set down the college of his choice for publication in the commencement *Tabula,* he teamed with Ohlsen and Wilcoxen in naming the University of Illinois. But it was only a half-hearted gesture. There is no evidence that he actually applied. His Uncle Tyler was in the lumber business in Kansas City, and Dr. Hemingway wrote to see if Ernest could be taken on as a cub reporter on the *Star.* But the word came back that there would be no openings until September or October. It was no great blow. Ernest was already dreaming of another summer in northern Michigan.

The second scrape of his boyhood came near the close of his senior year. He was out on a camping trip with Jack Pentecost and Morrie Musselman on the banks of the Des Plaines River. The Chicago papers had lately told of a "squad of prowlers which had been terrorizing the Oak Park and Proviso Districts." About two in the morning, the sleeping campers were attacked by a howling gang who slashed their tent ropes and began to carry their equipment into the woods. Jack Pentecost caught one with a hard right to the nose, and Ernest threw an ax at the head of another, missing by inches. When three of the gang started dragging him away, Ernest fought back so wildly that they pitched him into the muddy river. Only as he crawled out did he discover that the whole affair was a practical joke. The attackers were all seniors from Oak Park High. They were having a stag party at Tom Cusack's house when the idea suddenly struck them. Ten boys drove out in cars to North Avenue and sneaked through the woods to the camp. "Peace was made," said the account in the weekly *Trapeze.* "Not even the victims of the hoax claimed that it was a failure." But Ernest could not forget his hurling of the ax. What if the blade had split open Clarence Kohler's skull? A Chicago reporter called George Shaffer had named both the axman and his intended victim. Ernest went to some trouble to make sure that no reference to the ax throwing was included in the version of the story that appeared in the *Trapeze.* Once again, as in the episode of the blue heron, he was frightened of "the law." Again, too, the incident grew in his imagination out of all proportion to its importance. As a man of fifty, eager to have it supposed that he had led a dangerous life in his boyhood, he muttered darkly about having thrown an ax at another man's head with intent to kill. But it was only another of his exaggerations.

Commencement week began on the eighth of June. The motif was patriotic. Baskets of red, white, and blue flowers festooned the auditorium on Class Day. In recognition of his literary attainments, Ernest was Class Prophet. His narrative, strongly military in flavor, was judged to be the climax of the program and was delivered with "quite some pep." The commencement exercises on Thursday evening ran through a program of prayers, hymns, school songs, cheers, five student speakers (including Marcelline Hemingway and Edward Wagenknecht), and the presentation of diplomas to a graduating class of one hundred and fifty. Ernest received all this with the high seriousness befitting his station. He was still enough of a Latinist and an idealist to appreciate the implications of the class motto—*Qui Pro Viribus Agit Bene Agit*—although he had not yet determined precisely what form of action he was going to follow.

His first postgraduate opportunity came in the form of a letter from Lloyd Harter of the Boys' Department at the First Congregational Church:

My dear Ernest:
I want you to take three or four minutes to talk to the younger boys of the Department who are to go on with the game where you leave off. Tell them in an intimate personal way some of the deeper things about your high school experience and especially what the Church and our [Sunday school] Class has meant to you and finally what you are planning to do next year. Won't you take as much time as necessary to prepare your thoughts for this little talk and make it count for yourself and the younger boys? Put your soul into it and bring them a message that they will never forget. This is your day and your graduating address. Here, old fellow, is a chance to get in some of your serious world. Give the chaps the best you've got right from the shoulder.

Yours faithfully,
Lloyd E. Harter

Four other boys had also been asked to speak. The generic title for all their little talks was "Hail and Farewell." That Sunday noon, along with Bob Cole, Clarence Kohler, Gordon Shepherd, and Lyman Worthington, Ernest gave the chaps the best he had straight from the shoulder. At least presumably. The text of his remarks has not survived. This is a pity, since it was the final act of his years of formal education.

4. THE ENORMOUS ROOM

COLLEGE, war, and work were the choices that confronted him after his graduation from high school. He rejected college, though his father had wanted him to go to Oberlin with Marcelline, while he would have been welcomed at Illinois by Lewis Clarahan, who was doing well as a member of the class of 1920. Dr. Hemingway was against his going to war because of his age, and Ernest was not in any hurry. The job on the Kansas City *Star* would not be available until October. Meantime there was plenty to be done on the farm in Michigan. The great world, such as it was, could wait for a few months more.

Dr. Hemingway was eager to drive north in his Model T Ford touring car, taking Grace and his two sons, and camping along the way. They left one morning in the third week of June. The roads were primitive. Punctures assailed them. They dug out of mudholes and traps of loose sand. It took them five days to reach Uncle George's summer place at Ironton. Next day they completed the journey, bumping down past Bacon's farm and pulling up triumphantly behind Windemere Cottage. They were as proud, said Marcelline, as if they had discovered a new continent.

They got to work at once on Longfield Farm across the lake. Dr. Hemingway hired a thin, mustached farmer in galluses and a sweat-stained hat. His name was Warren Sumner and he owned a team of mules and a homemade stoneboat. They jacked up the old tenant farmhouse and moved it off the property, built a shed and stocked it with sawdust to hold the coming winter's crop of ice, cut and cured twenty acres of hay, and planted the usual large vegetable garden. Ernest took respite from these labors on long weekends at Horton Bay, fishing in Horton's Creek and Lake Charlevoix, seeing the Dilworths of both generations, and renewing his friendship with Bill and Katy Smith. A young bachelor named Carl Edgar made a constant fourth in their comings and goings. Carl was in love with Katy. She would not hear of marriage, though her suitor had a good job and a small apartment in Kansas City. If Ernest came out to work for the *Star,* said Carl, he would be welcome to move into the apartment and share expenses.

Ernest was inclined to go as soon as the *Star* would have him. He was beginning to yearn for experience outside the provincial domains of his upbringing, as well as freedom from family ties and pressures. His high-school work in fiction and journalism had taught him only the barest rudiments of writing. He still had much to learn about accuracy, immediacy, and economy of utterance. He counted on the *Star* to polish his prose and on Kansas City to educate him in the seamier sides of human experience. How else but by an enlargement of his scope could he improve on such yarns as he had published in the Oak Park *Tabula?* One day that summer he put this question to Trumbull White, manager of the Chautauqua program at Bay View, the cottage colony on Little Traverse Bay near Petoskey, where Marcelline was spending July as a guest of the White family. Trumbull White was a journalist of some renown who had recently retired from the editorship of *Everybody's Magazine.* He received Ernest kindly and told him that any neophyte must learn to write by writing. As for subjects, the best were those drawn directly from personal experience. For a boy of Ernest's years and inclinations, the advice could hardly have been better.

There were some signs now of a normal rebelliousness against the edicts of his father. Ursula and Sunny had saved up to buy a canoe from Oldtown, Maine. When Ernest took Sunny to pick it up at the freight office in Walloon Village, the place was closed for the day. Ernest wrote a note to the baggage-master, pried open the door of a freight car on the siding, lifted out the canoe, and towed it home. Somewhat to their astonishment, neither the baggage-master nor Dr. Hemingway had anything to say. In view of Ernest's illegal action, his father's silence was unusual. The doctor's ideas of right and wrong were firm and fixed. Any offenses were likely to rouse him to instantaneous indignation. His children remembered many occasions when his "dimpled cheeks and charming smile" gave sudden place to the glinting eyes and tautly drawn mouth of one whose moral sensibilities have been mortally exasperated. Grace, on the other hand, habitually maintained an air of ladylike serenity, saving up her complaints and spending them all at once in outbursts of ag-grieved rectitude. Sometimes like his mother, Ernest would harbor wounded feelings until they festered, and continued all his life to hold grudges against those who had unwittingly offended him. At other times, especially in the throes of what he regarded as unjust punishment, he met his father's anger with a black rage of his own. One arresting instance of the way his mind worked was revealed to Bill Smith that fall. Bill had stopped over in Oak Park on his way home to St. Louis. Ernest mentioned the small shed for garden tools in the back yard at Windemere. It commanded a view of the path into which Dr. Hemingway sometimes stepped while working among his tomato vines. Ernest reported that when his father had punished him and he was angry, he had sometimes sat in the open door of the shed with his shotgun, drawing a bead on his father's head.

Such brooding rages were forgotten in mid-October when Ernest took the train for Kansas City. Marcelline had left in September to study music at Oberlin, and Ernest was permanently disgusted with tearful farewells. Dr. Hemingway accompanied him to the station and stood with him beside the train until the moment of departure. Ernest remembered the occasion for many years and gave it fictional form in *For Whom the Bell Tolls:* "He had been afraid to go and he did not want anyone to know it and, at the station, just before the conductor picked up the box he would step up on to reach the steps of the day coach, his father had kissed him good-by and said, 'May the Lord watch between me and thee while we are absent the one from the other.' His father had been a very religious man and he had said it simply and sincerely. But his moustache had been moist and his eyes were damp with emotion." All of it so much embarrassed the boy—"the damp religious sound of the prayer . . . his father kissing him good-by"—that he "felt suddenly so much older than his father and sorry for him that he could hardly bear it."

Ernest's departure coincided with the final day of the World Series. Chicago was leading three games to two, and Ernest, as a White Sox fan, was hoping that they would win the final game in New York. Late that afternoon the train drew up on a siding just east of the Mississippi River; when it started again, a news butcher came swaying down the aisle. Ernest asked how the game had come out. "White Sox," the man said, "four and two." Ernest was elated. He bought a *Saturday Evening Post* and settled back to read. But they were near the river now, and he kept glancing out of the window. It was his first sight of the Mississippi, and he had expected tall bluffs on the eastern bank. Instead he saw flat fields and "an endless seeming bayou." At last the locomotive came into view up ahead, pulling the train in a slow curve onto a long bridge. The muddy river "seemed to move solidly down stream, not to flow but to move like a solid shifting lake, swirling a little where the abutments of the bridge jutted out." Visions of Mark Twain, Huck Finn, Tom Sawyer, the explorer La Salle, and Happy Felsch, the White Sox center fielder, crowded one another in his mind. "Anyway," he thought happily, "I've seen the Mississippi."

Uncle Tyler Hemingway met him at Union Station and drove him home to the tall Victorian house in the 3600 block of Warwick Boulevard. It was a polite neighborhood of neat green lawns, with well-kept shrubs and shade trees. Men were raking the leaves along the sidewalks. The house was made of rosy brick, with rather small rooms and high ceilings. Ernest's Aunt Arabella was the daughter of J. B. White, who had made a fortune in lumber and was grooming his son-in-law to succeed him in the business. Arabella was short, sturdily built like her father, intelligent, and attractive. Ernest thought her rather beautiful. Tyler was nervous in manner and slight of build. He walked quickly and impatiently, snapping out orders. Of all his uncles, Ernest liked Tyler least. He gave the boy a night to recover from his train trip and then took him downtown to meet Henry J. Haskell of the *Star*.

The *Star* building stood at 1729 Grand Avenue between 17th and 18th Streets. Three stories high and made of brick, it occupied most of a city block. But its most impressive aspect met Ernest's eyes when he stepped off the elevator onto the second floor. It was an enormous room, filled with the clatter of typewriters and thronged with reporters, copy editors, sportswriters, columnists, and critics. Battered desks were ranged row on row. There were neither cubicles nor partitions of any kind, and the October sun, shining through the dusty windows, gilded them all alike. Harry Haskell was the chief editorial writer, a graduate of Harvard, studious and aloof. He passed the young man along to George Longan, the city editor, who offered him a reporter's job at fifteen dollars a week. At the next desk sat C. G. Wellington, called Pete, the assistant city editor. Pete was a pale undersized man of thirty with a poker face and a calm demeanor. He had served his apprenticeship on the Topeka *Capitol* in Kansas. Lately the army had turned him down because of a heart disorder. His smile was quiet and his manner was dry. He handled young reporters with a faint undertone of sarcasm.

The boy at Wellington's desk that morning looked big and gangling, healthy and tan. His brown eyes were lively and there were dimples in both his red cheeks. The summer of work on the farm had so greatly enlarged his muscles that he seemed on the point of bursting out of his clothes. In manner he was gay and likable, talkative, deferential, anxious to please, a little awkward. There was a shade of w-sound in the way he pronounced his l's. Wellington explained that enlistments and the draft were raising hell with their reportorial staff. He showed Ernest to one of the empty desks in the huge room. The boy sat down on the desktop and grinned broadly. For the first time in his life, he was a bona-fide reporter on a big-city newspaper. He looked as if nothing could have pleased him more.

Through most of October he stayed on with his aunt and uncle, and even consented to make a date with a pretty young girl named Sally Carrighar who lived next door. They walked five blocks to a neighborhood movie house and watched Douglas Fairbanks in a light comedy. The star was faultlessly dressed in ice-cream pants and a straw hat with a bright ribbon. For Sally, at least, his dapper and romantic image redeemed an otherwise dreary evening. Ernest had rung her front doorbell looking so unkempt that when they reached the crowded lobby of the theater she walked briskly ahead, hoping that no one would recognize this rough-looking character as her escort. After the show they had ice-cream sodas at a nearby drugstore. Ernest seemed morose and said very little. They parted in amity and that was that.

After what he regarded as a decent interval, Ernest moved in with Carl Edgar, his friend from Horton Bay, who was renting a small apartment in Agnes Street. It was farther away from the *Star* building than Uncle Tyler's house and could be reached only by an interminable ride on the Prospect Avenue trolley cars. But Ernest was untroubled. Life in the rather dingy apartment represented a new access of freedom. Only on the hikes with Lew Clarahan had he known anything like it. The trips to Nantucket and Albion hardly counted. He had never in his life been out of the sight of parents and relatives for more than a few days at a time. He got on well with Carl Edgar, whom he usually addressed as Odgar. Carl's only complaint was that Ernest kept wanting to talk about "the romance of newspaper work" when it would have been better for them both to get some sleep. Sometimes that fall, working late on an assignment or too lazy to make the long trolley ride, Ernest stayed overnight in the pressroom at the Hotel Muehlbach at Baltimore and 12th Street, sleeping in the bathtub with towels for a mattress, reveling in the rare experience of being on his own.

He was beginning to affect a worldly air beyond his years and knowledge, but also getting to know something of the rougher side of the city. "I covered the short-stop run," he said in retrospect, "which included the 15th Street police station, the Union Station, and the General Hospital [at 24th and Cherry]. At the 15th Street station you covered crime, usually small, but you never knew when you might hit something larger. Union Station was everybody going in and out of town . . . some shady characters I got to know, and interviews with celebrities going through. The General Hospital was up a long hill from Union Station and there you got accidents and a double check on crimes of violence." In the dark foggy days of November, the lighted hospital windows stood out like beacons from the jumble of buildings on the hillside. Even from a distance he sometimes thought that he could smell "its antiseptic concord of odors."

He was "constantly talking to older writers on the staff about how they got their stories and how they wrote them." The *Star* maintained a literary department, which "clipped magazines, quoted from books new and old, and ransacked American and foreign newspapers for material that would both interest and elevate subscribers." To work on the paper was to learn how "to write declarative sentences," how "to avoid hackneyed adjectives," and how "to tell an interesting narrative." There was also a stylebook which the young reporters were supposed to study. It said that the key to fine reporting was to "use short sentences. Use short first paragraphs. Use vigorous English, not forgetting to strive for smoothness. Be positive, not negative." The stylebook, the literary department, the example of his elders, and the constant supervision of Pete Wellington gave Ernest his first real education in journalism.

But he was by no means averse to legwork. He enraged his boss by failing to keep in touch with the newsroom. "When we would put in a call for him at the hospital," said Wellington, "we would learn that he had gone out on an ambulance call. He seemed always to want to be wherever the action was." One day he was hurrying through Union Station when a man fell unconscious on the floor with an attack of smallpox. Ernest, who had long since been vaccinated, carried the man to a hack and took him to the hospital, afterwards advising the hackman to fumigate his vehicle. The municipal doctor who handled the case soon became a fast friend of Ernest's, regaling him with shocking anecdotes about the rougher districts of the city and about the prevalence of dope-taking among the local prostitutes. Although Ernest had yet to attain the distinction of a by-line, he sweated over an account of the smallpox epidemic, as well as another, "very sad," about a whore who stood weeping outside an elegant dancehall while the soldier she loved whirled gaily around inside "with his smartly dressed partners."

He was finding plenty to see and hear. Kansas City was a metropolis of 300,000, only two decades removed from the brawling frontier town of the late nineteenth century. Ernest thought the city both "wonderful and unsavory," especially the region that ran from Union Station down through the stockyards to the Missouri River. It was also growing fast. In 1911, when the *Star* moved uptown from its former headquarters at 8th and Main Streets, wiser heads held that the new building on Grand Avenue was much too far from the center of activity. Yet it had taken only six years to crowd all the space between. Crime was rife and justice crude. Dale Wilson, a young copy reader on the *Star,* remembered an occasion when a dozen Negroes were arraigned in court for running a crap game. The judge grinned, lined them up, gave the tall ones five days in jail, and dismissed charges against the short ones. Prostitutes plying their trade were so common on Twelfth Street that one wit nicknamed it "Woodrow Wilson Avenue, a piece at any price." Though forbidden to solicit customers at the tables of cheap hotels, the girls were allowed to join any who came to their tables with a specific request, and the hotel stood ready to provide a room.

The man on the *Star* who most dramatically embodied the city's rougher side was an egotistical, hard-drinking, hard-fighting reporter and rewrite man named Lionel Calhoun Moise (pronounced Mo-ees). Although Ernest knew him "only slightly," he was impressed by his facility with words, his prodigious vitality, and his undisciplined talent. Whenever he drank, his native energy "overflowed into violence." His writing style was forceful and flamboyant. Ernest admired him as a picturesque throwback to the older school of yellow journalism, though he could not help deploring his prodigal waste of his endowments. "Lionel Moise," he once wrote in a sketch, "was a great rewrite man. He could carry four stories in his head and go to the telephone and take a fifth and then write all five at full speed to catch an edition. There would be something alive about each one. He was always the highest paid man on every paper he worked on. If any other man was getting more money he quit or had his pay raised. He never spoke to the other reporters unless he had been drinking. He was tall and thick and had long arms and big hands. He was the fastest man on a typewriter I ever knew. He drove a motor car and it was understood in the office that a woman had given it to him. One night she stabbed him in it out on the Lincoln Highway halfway to Jefferson City. He took the knife away from her and [broke her jaw: *crossed out*] threw it out of the car. Then he did something awful to her. She was lying in the back of the car when they found them. Moise drove the car all the way into Kansas City with her fixed that way."

But Moise was a crass and distant demigod enthroned between his typewriter and his telephone in a far corner of the enormous room. Ernest's regular associates were closer to his own age and temperament. One was Dale Wilson, a Missourian from Corder, aged twenty-three, who was waiting to be called up for service with the Navy. Others included George (Punk) Wallace, Harry Kohr the telegraph editor, John Collins, Bill Moorehead the police-court reporter, Tod Armiston, and Wilson Hicks. Ernest was still too close to high school to have given up his boyish sport with nicknames. He spoke of himself as Hemingstein and Ernest De La Mancha Hemingway, and quickly invented titles for his associates. "Smith the Beamer" was a grinning backslapper named H. Merle Smith. A young Australian became "The Tasmanian Woodsman."

Charlie Hopkins, the afternoon assignment editor, a swarthy Oklahoman who had liked Ernest on sight, was called Hoopkins or sometimes the Hooper. A myopic copyreader named Harry Godfrey, who wore thick glasses and liked to give advice, was nicknamed "the pensive Hebrew." Leo Fitzpatrick, a stocky little Irishman who was something of a dude and a girl charmer, was known to Ernest as "Lovely Leo." Ernest's only accident of the winter happened one evening when he tried to defend Leo from a bully. They were eating Saturday night supper in a lunchroom at Grand Avenue and 17th Street when an aggressive teamster began to bait Leo about his resplendent necktie. Ernest threw a chivalric haymaker and his fist on the follow-through broke a glass showcase containing cigars. His hand was cut enough to need a bandage. For some days he enjoyed a hero's status. Yet for all his bumptiousness and occasional bragging, he struck Dale Wilson as basically shy. When he teased his fellow reporters, it was usually with a twisted smile and a twinkle in his eyes.

From his brief stay in Kansas City he salvaged material for three later sketches. One was a rough vignette in which an Irish policeman shot down two Hungarians who had robbed a cigar store. The city supported two burlesque houses where the girls cavorted in flesh-colored tights on a runway before the usual appreciative audience. Ernest later wrote a sketch about an advance man for a burlesque company who had succumbed to drink and dope and lay in bed all day with the sheet drawn over his face. The best of the three was "God Rest You Merry, Gentlemen," a sardonic Christmas tale in which two City Hospital internes argued over the case of a neurotic youth who had emasculated himself from motives of mistaken piety.

Apart from his determination to learn how to write, the chief subject of Ernest's conversations was the war and how he could get into it. His father still opposed his enlistment, and the defective vision in his left eye seemed to make the whole question academic. "We all have that bad eye like Mother's," he wrote his sister Marcelline. "But I'll make it to Europe some way in spite of this optic. I can't let a show like this go on without getting into it." He soon found out how it could be done from a Kansas City boy named Theodore Brumback who had begun work at the *Star* a month after Ernest's arrival. Ted was a dark-haired boy of twenty-two whose most striking feature was a glass eye. He had entered Cornell University in 1913. In the spring of 1915 a golf ball had hit a tree and bounced back into his face. After the loss of his eye he was too restive to finish college. In the summer of 1917 he enlisted in the American Field Service and spent four months driving ambulances in France. His tales of life in Europe were romantic, but he advised crossing over in the spring rather than the winter, when rain fell continuously and all the roads were quagmires. By Christmas, Ted and Ernest had made a pact with Wilson Hicks: as soon as possible after New Year's, they would apply to the Red Cross as ambulance drivers. Dr. Hemingway reluctantly withdrew his objections. Ernest was the youngest of the trio, and could scarcely contain his boyish exuberance at the prospect of crossing the Atlantic.

He had now moved out of Carl Edgar's apartment to a "tiny dismal room in the attic of an old-fashioned frame house" not far away. Late one evening he asked Ted Brumback over for the night. They rode the owl car through the snowy streets and climbed the stairs to Ernest's attic. It was after one in the morning and Brumback was deadly sleepy. But Ernest brought out a jug of red wine and a volume of Browning's poems and began to read aloud in a "clear penetrating voice." When Brumback awoke at four, Ernest was still at it, looking fresh as a daisy. Next day he "got through his work as if nothing had happened." His energy was boundless and it seemed to Brumback the one certain sign of his incipient genius. "When the rest of us mortals have finished our work," wrote Ted, "we're ready for play or bed. But your genius has only started." It was true. His six-month job with the *Star* "only started" Ernest on the path to whatever eminence he was going to attain. But it was at least a useful beginning.

CHAPTER 2

Veteran Out of the Wars

5. THE SCHIO COUNTRY CLUB

"I was an awful dope when I went to the last war," said Hemingway in 1942. "I can remember just thinking that we were the home team and the Austrians were the visiting team." It still seemed like the greatest game in the world on the last day of April, 1918, when Ernest and Ted Brumback drew their final paychecks from the *Star* and climbed aboard the Chicago-bound train at Union Station. Wilson Hicks had been obliged to withdraw from the pact. Charlie Hopkins and Carl Edgar, who were waiting to be called up by the Army and the Navy, went along with Ernest and Ted for a final fishing trip to Horton Bay. They stopped overnight with the Hemingways in Oak Park and then left for Michigan. Dr. Hemingway agreed to notify them when orders arrived from the Red Cross headquarters in St. Louis. The Dilworths greeted (and fed) them, and they began an intensive period of fishing. They had scarcely got their feet wet when the telegram came through. Hemingway and Brumback were to report for physical examinations in New York no later than May 8th.

They rushed back to Chicago, said their good-byes, and caught the east-bound train. In New York, the Red Cross boarded them at the Hotel Earle in Waverly Place, along with seventy other volunteers who came drifting in from all corners of the country. Most were either too young for the armed services or had already been rejected for various disabilities, mainly eyesight. Fred Spiegel and Larry Barnett had been classmates at New Trier High School in Winnetka, Illinois. Bus Scudder and Dick Hawes came from St. Louis. Bill Horne of Yonkers, New York, teamed with his college roommate, Percy Norton, from the state of Washington; they were both Princeton graduates in the class of 1913. The group lined up for physicals at the Life Extension Institute offices on West 45th Street. Ernest passed with a B rating and a blood-pressure reading of 128 over 75, although his vision was so defective that Dr. Dunn, the examining physician, recommended the attention of an oculist and the purchase of a pair of glasses.

38

Ernest ignored the recommendation and entered enthusiastically upon the two-week indoctrination period. His father had made him a parting gift of $150, and he had another hundred left over from his earnings in Kansas City. He invested thirty dollars in a handsome pair of cordovan leather boots to lend distinction to his uniform—a high-collared, choke-necked blouse, baggy pants, and an overseas cap. Small crosses of red enamel ornamented the collar and the cap. Ernest and Ted dressed up and strolled down Broadway in the Maytime twilight, wearing the bars of honorary second lieutenants. Their first inoculation against typhoid made them ache in every joint. But the "Croix Rouge," as Ernest reported, took "very good care" of them, and they "lacked for nothing."

His boyish exuberance seemed boundless. It was his first visit to New York. He had been there ten days when he wrote Dale Wilson in Kansas City: "Ha Ha Ha Ha Ha Ha! Tis none other than the greatest of the Hemingsteins that indicts this epistle. Woodrow me lad, comma, how are you?" He told Wilson a cock-and-bull story about his current love affair with Mae Marsh, the actress he had seen in *The Birth of a Nation.* He had "sunk" the "150 plunks" that his "Pop" had given him in an engagement ring. Mae had promised to await his return from the wars. He had also got a "fine look" at President Woodrow Wilson, who had come to New York to launch the city's Red Cross War Fund Drive. Ernest was one of the 75,000 men and women who paraded down Fifth Avenue from 82nd to 8th Street to salute the occasion. His view of the President was all the better, he said, because "by virtue of his manly form and perfect complexion," the great Hemingstein had been chosen as right guide to the first platoon.

On the morning of the 23rd they went aboard a venerable French Line ship happily named the *Chicago.* Early that afternoon she slipped quietly out of the harbor bound for Bordeaux. The boys agreed that she was "the rottenest old tub afloat." But the food was good, the rules were lax, and for two days they cruised through placid seas in weather so warm and bright that Ernest was reminded of Walloon Lake. On the third day they ran into a storm. The *Chicago* pitched, rolled, and swung in "wide lugubrious circles." The dining salons emptied rapidly and the rails were lined with retching men. Ernest's boast was that he had "heaved but four times" during the two days of storm.

Afterwards he took to standing on the deck at night, watching the phosphorescence in the wake of the ship. When the wind was up, the blowing crests of the billows reminded him of brands from a campfire. By day he saw nothing but a few flying fish and an occasional school of porpoise. The *Chicago's* course took her well to the south of the usual sea lanes and they met no other ships until the 27th, when a westbound American cruiser appeared off the port beam and heliograph and flag signals were exchanged. German U-boats were said to be lurking in these waters and the portholes were blacked out at night. Ernest was hoping for action, but none came. The only other vexation was the second of his typhoid shots. It left him "sick as a dog."

Besides Brumback, his chief crony was a "cocky little rooster of a boy" named Howell Jenkins, who stood about five feet four, sported a small reddish mustache, and spoke sardonically from the corner of his mouth. He was variously known as Jenks, Howie, The Carper, Carpative, Little Fever, or Fever, the last in allusion to his fondness for crap games. Ernest also befriended a pair of Polish lieutenants from Buffalo, New York. They were going to France to join a Troupe Polonaise. Their names were Leon Chocianowicz and Anton Galinski. Ernest called them "dandy fellows," and said that they proved the breadth of the gap between Poles and Polacks. The only woman aboard was a blond French girl named Gaby, who was said to be spending most of her time in lifeboats with a succession of swains. Ernest and Leon discussed Gaby, and the values of drink and sex, while the *Chicago* made her slow way to Bordeaux.

There they gorged themselves with red wine and French cooking until the night train left for Paris. At the station next morning, they were treated with unusual deference: Belleau Wood had just fallen to the American Marines. High-ranking French combat officers saluted their wrinkled, ill-fitting uniforms. They were quartered in a small hotel near the Madeleine. German artillery was trying to destroy French morale with a huge long-range gun, known among the Allies as Big Bertha. High explosive shells were falling in the streets of Paris. Ernest was as excited, wrote Ted Brumback, "as if he'd been sent on special assignment to cover the biggest story of the year." He and Brumback hired a decrepit taxi in the hope of seeing a fresh crater or two. It was a tantalizing chase. "When we heard a shell explode," wrote Ted, "we would drive towards the sound as fast as our two-lunger could make it. . . . But we'd arrive there to hear another explosion in some far distant part of the city." They had just given up and were going back to the hotel when one of the shells "hit the façade of the Madeleine, chipping off a foot or two of stone." This was close enough, even for Ernest. For a split second the projectile had sounded as if it might land in their laps.

Ernest soon became bored with sightseeing, which was anyway never his strong point. "I wish they'd hurry up," said he, "and ship us off to the front." They were obliged to wait only until another contingent of volunteers came in from London, swelling the group to 150. Within two days they were aboard the train for Italy. At Modane, they transferred to boxcars for the trip through the Mount Cenis tunnel. Crossing the frontier, singing and laughing, they dangled their legs through the open doorways and enjoyed what Bill Horne called "the loveliest train ride through the beautifulest scenery of my life."

Even the Alps could not compare with their welcome to Milan. "Having a wonderful time!!" said Ernest's postcard to the *Star*. "Had my first baptism of fire my first day here when an entire munition factory exploded. We carried them in like at the General Hospital, Kansas City." But it was far more gory than anything he had seen in the Midwest, or anywhere else. "One becomes so accustomed to all the dead being men," he wrote afterwards, "that the sight of a dead woman is quite shocking. I first saw inversion of the usual sex of the dead after the explosion of a munition factory which had been situated in the countryside near Milan. . . . We drove to the scene of the disaster in trucks along poplar-shaded roads. . . . Arriving where the munition plant had been, some of us were put to patrolling about those large stocks of munitions which for some reason had not exploded, while others were put at extinguishing a fire which had gotten into the grass of an adjacent field; which task being concluded, we were ordered to search the immediate vicinity and surrounding fields for bodies. We found and carried to an improvised mortuary a good number of these and I must admit, frankly, the shock it was to find that those dead were women rather than men." The final task was to gather human fragments from what was left of the heavy barbed wire fence around the factory. This also was a considerable shock to one whose contact with the dead had hitherto been limited to the shooting of birds and small animals.

Milan itself was busy and crowded with men in uniform. La Scala was open and there were daily races at the San Siro track. The boys strolled through the Galleria and into the vast dim cathedral. But there was little time for sightseeing. A Red Cross captain named Meade Detweiler divided them into groups of twenty-five. Along with Larry Barnett, Dick Baum, Walter Feder, Jerome Flaherty, Bill Horne, Howie Jenkins, Fred Spiegel, Zalmon Simmons, and some fifteen others, Hemingway and Brumback were assigned to ARC Section Four. Two days after the munitions explosion, they got aboard the train for Vicenza. Ambulances were waiting to drive them to Schio, 24 kilometers to the northwest in the foothills of the Dolomites.

The road to Schio passed through neat farming country. From far off the boys could see the mocha-colored town, its roofs and campaniles nestled under the scarred brows of several large mountains. The biggest was Monte Pasubio. Over its right shoulder was where the fighting was. The ambulances jounced over the cobblestones through ancient narrow streets. In one of the squares was a bust of Garibaldi, and in another a small cathedral that resembled a Greek temple. The driver jerked his thumb at the crossed swords on the hanging sign of the Albergo Due Spadi, the best of the eating places. A *torrente* called the Leogra flowed through the midst of the town, which specialized in peacetime in the manufacture of wool. The headquarters for Section Four was an abandoned factory building. It had a paved courtyard with open sheds for the ambulances, seventeen large Fiats and half a dozen smaller Fords. The barracks on the second floor had been used for the storage of wool. It was a single room, fifty by a hundred feet, lined with rows of army cots. The one assigned to Ernest was halfway down the right-hand side. Downstairs in the messhall were long refectory tables. Italian waiters served spaghetti, rabbit stews, and a dark bread reputed to contain burlap. Once a week the boys were given fried eggs. There were large pots of apricot jam, a product of the region. For the first time in his life, Ernest had all the wine he wanted. He made up for the dry years as well as he could.

They called their quarters the Schio Country Club. The section published a newspaper of sorts called *Ciao,* which was printed in Vicenza whenever enough copy had accumulated. Ernest borrowed a typewriter and beat out a contribution. Like some of his Ring Lardner imitations in high school, it was cast in the form of a letter. "Well Al we are here in this old Italy," he wrote, "and now that I am here I am not going to leave it. And that is not no New Years revolution Al but the truth. Well Al I am now an officer and if you would meet me you would have to salute me. What I am is a provisional acting second lieutenant without a commission but the trouble is that all the other fellows are too. There ain't no privates in our army Al and the Captain is called a chef. But he don't look to me as tho he could cook a dam bit."

During his three weeks of driving for Section Four, Ernest took turns at the wheel of a lumbering Fiat. It was a clumsy vehicle, painted battleship gray with a large red cross on top. The road up Pasubio was a wilderness of hairpin turns, closely flanked with barbed wire which scraped and screeched against the sides of the cars. Two thirds of the work was done in daylight, and the three ambulances on call each made one run a day, evacuating wounded to the *smistamenti,* or distributing stations. Sometimes they stopped at a soup kitchen on Mount Pasubio, run by a volunteer from Philadelphia named Gifford Corcoran. Americans alone or in pairs were always appearing in unlikely places. One day in Dolo, Ernest met a tall, brown-eyed young man who introduced himself as John Dos Passos, a fellow Chicagoan. He was three years older than Ernest, and had been graduated from Harvard in 1916, afterwards serving in France with the Norton-Harjes Ambulance Corps. He was now detached for service in Italy, where he had spent the winter in the region behind Mount Grappa and the valley around Bassano. He was on the point of leaving for Paris to join the Ambulance and Medical Corps of the U.S. Army. The two boys talked for a while and went their ways. Afterwards Dos Passos remembered that he had not even caught the name of the hefty, dark-haired youngster in whose company he had spent a couple of pleasant hours.

The Austrians had now turned their attention to the Piave River valley north of Venice. The chef of Section Four, Lieutenant Charles B. Griffin, took a unit of six cars with American drivers and Italian mechanics to evacuate wounded at the apex of the drive. Ernest resented the fact that he was not among them. "I'm fed up," he told Brumback one day late in June. "There's nothing here but scenery and too damn much of that. I'm going to get out of this ambulance section and see if I can't find out where the war is." For a while the Schio Country Club had been fun, with vinous dinners at the Due Spadi Hotel and occasional evenings of beer drinking in a gardenlike *trattoria* under a spreading wistaria bush in one of the back streets of Schio. Yet none of that consoled him. Fred Spiegel saw that he was becoming "increasingly itchy." As Pete Wellington had discovered in Kansas City, Ernest "wanted always to go where the action was."

The opportunity he wanted soon came. The Red Cross maintained a number of canteens, mostly situated on well-traveled roads where troops were likely to pass. Others were established a few kilometers back of the lines. One ARC *tenente* was in charge of each, living in a hut adjoining a larger building which served as a rest billet. These held tables, writing materials, phonographs and records, and long counters where coffee, soup, candy, jam, and cigarettes were handed out. After hours, the *tenente* sometimes carried cigarettes, candy, and postcards to the men in the lines.

Because the pressure of work had lessened in the mountains and mightily increased in the valley of the Piave, men could be spared from Section Four to help activate a series of emergency canteens in the small towns bordering the river. Along the west bank the Italians were dug in for miles in a system of trenches, earthworks, and forward listening posts. When Lieutenant Griffin called for volunteers to man these canteens, Ernest was among the first to step forward. Others were Bill Horne, Fever Jenkins, Dick Baum, and Warren Pease. They were taken by ambulance to Mestre and placed under the command of Captain Jim Gamble, a wealthy young man whose family ran the soap-manufacturing firm of Procter and Gamble. Gamble's official title was Inspector of Rolling Canteens, but his chief concern at the moment was distribution of cigarettes to the thousands of Italian troops upriver. He gave the volunteers a short leave in Mestre, though Venice itself was off limits. Some of them went to inspect the Italian officers' brothel, generically known as the Villa Rosa. According to Fever Jenkins, Ernest was extremely shy, and blushed furiously when accosted by one of the whores.

From the railhead at Mestre, they were distributed along the Piave front. Ernest dropped off at Fossalta, a low-lying, heavily damaged village behind grassy dikes at a point where the river made an L-shaped bend. Horne and Pease went on to San Pedro Norello, a neighboring village, and set up their cots on the second floor of a ramshackle building which was used for the nurture of silkworms. "For a week, nothing happened," said Bill. "No canteen. No supplies for a canteen. No instructions. No action. Nothing but silkworms gnawing and mosquitoes stinging." Ernest came over on his bicycle and spent a night with Pease and Horne. "That night," he wrote afterwards, "we lay on the floor in the room and I listened to the silk-worms eating. The silk-worms fed in racks of mulberry leaves and all night you could hear them eating and a dropping sound in the leaves. . . . You can hear silk-worms eating very clearly in the night and I lay with my eyes open and listened to them." The volunteers were experiencing the familiar military phenomenon of "hurry up and wait." Ernest was still as restive as ever. Yet at least and at last he was within earshot of the guns and in daily contact with the soldiers who were doing the fighting.

As provisional lieutenants, the Americans were eligible to mess with the

Italian officers of the Brigata Ancona, comprising the 69th and 70th Infantry. One of the chaplains was a young priest called Don Giuseppe Bianchi, a native of Florence. He wore a cross in dark red velvet above the left-hand pocket of his tunic and quickly befriended Ernest who treated him with sympathy and respect. Among the actual warriors, Ernest's behavior was both modest and bellicose. His position as director of the still nonexistent emergency canteen made him, as he later said, "a very minor sort of camp follower." But he gloried in his proximity to the field of battle.

The combination of inaction, mosquitoes, and gnawing silkworms soon drove Bill Horne back to Schio. There at least he could do some good by driving ambulances, while the mud and wreckage of the Basso Piave was no substitute for the lovely view of the Dolomites from the north windows of the Schio Country Club. But Ernest was in his element now. He elected to stay on in Fossalta, where canteen supplies were starting to filter in. Bill had been back with Section Four for about a week when the news came through. Around midnight on July 8th, in a forward listening post on the west bank of the river near Fossalta, Ernest had been severely wounded.

In bits and pieces the story of Ernest's remarkable exploit came drifting back to his friends. The night in the valley had been hot and moonless. At sunset the sluggish river shone like brass. After dark it was invisible except when the star shells climbed and broke in flowerings of white light. At intervals all day the opposing forces had been exchanging desultory small-arms and mortar fire. Near midnight the duel intensified. Ernest had left off his underwear because of the heat and was sweating heavily through his tunic as he leaned his bicycle against the back wall of a forward command post and ducked into the trenches, wearing a helmet and keeping low. He was carrying a supply of cigarettes, chocolate, and postcards for the soldiers. Some of them he had met before and for a while they talked in pidgin Italian. His pronunciation amused them. He said that he had come down from the mountains to be among them here on the plain. They said that they would prefer to be in the mountains. It would be quieter in the mountains. The stuff from the Austrian side was coming too close.

Soon after midnight, one of the Austrian Minenwerfer crews sent another of their projectiles hurtling across the river. It was about the size of a five-gallon tin and was probably of 420 caliber. The canister was filled with steel rod fragments and miscellaneous metal junk. It was designed to explode on contact, scattering its contents at ground level. They all heard it coming—the far cough as it left the muzzle, and the strange "chuh-chuh-chuh" sound as it arched and descended. "Then there was a flash, as when a blast-furnace door is swung open, and a roar that started white and went red." It was like a hurricane of such force that it tore the eardrums and snatched away the breath. "I tried to breathe," wrote Ernest afterwards, "but my breath would not come. . . . The ground was torn up and in front of my head there was a splintered beam of wood. In the jolt of my head I heard somebody crying. . . .

I tried to move but I could not move. I heard the machine guns and rifles firing across the river."

His legs felt as if he were wearing rubber boots filled with warm water. Beside him was a man who made no sound. Just beyond him was another, badly hurt and crying piteously. Ernest groped for his neck and legs, heaved him up in a fireman's carry, and began to stagger back towards the command post. He had covered fifty yards when a round from a heavy machine gun tore into his right leg at the knee. It felt like an icy snowball. He stumbled and fell with the man on his shoulder. He never afterwards remembered how he had covered the final hundred yards. But he made it, delivered his man, and lost consciousness.

His tunic and breeches were so thickly soaked with Italian blood that they thought at first he had been shot through the chest. They got him onto a stretcher and the two bearers began the long trip to the nearest dressing station. But the place had come under artillery fire and been evacuated. Nothing remained for shelter but a roofless shed. They lowered him to the ground and sat down to wait for an ambulance. Much later he said that he was surrounded by so many dead and dying that to die seemed more natural and normal than to go on living: for a time he even thought seriously of shooting himself with his officer's pistol. The night sky was lighted hideously by the star shells and faintly by the stars.

He lay there two hours, waiting and praying: "Now I lay me." Near dawn an ambulance took him to a *smistamento,* a converted schoolhouse near Fornaci. His legs felt as if he had been stung by a thousand hornets. The doctor-in-charge gave him morphine and antitetanus. There was a white-haired man in a dirty gray-green uniform, sitting with his back to the wall and looking at the blood-soaked emergency dressing which covered the shattered stump of his wrist. Ernest spoke to him. He came from the Abruzzi, and he said that he would be fifty-five years old in August. "You're too old, Dad, for this war," said Ernest. The soldier looked at him. *"Corpo di Bacco,"* he said. "I can die as well as any man." The little Florentine priest came along the line of wounded men, murmuring the holy words, anointing each as he passed. He recognized Ernest and did the same for him. When his turn came at the bloody table, they probed and removed twenty-eight *scaggia* fragments from his feet and legs. There were hundreds more, too deep to be reached. A long time later, an ambulance picked up the wounded that could be moved. Ernest was taken to a field hospital near Treviso. He spent five days in a long ward, swathed in bandages from heel to thigh, a badly injured hero of the home team. On the morning of the 15th, a slow hospital train pulled away for Milano.

Outside Mestre the cars stood for hours on a siding in the thick heat of mid-July. From where they lay they could not see the magical city of Venice stretching out into the Adriatic. The boy in the berth did not care. Flies coursed through the open windows to settle on his bandages and rode along undisturbed as the train gathered speed. There were further long waits at Vicenza and

Verona. He did not see the Lago di Garda nor did he know when they reached Brescia. They had been two full days in transit by the time the train pulled into the freight yards of Milano. It was Wednesday, July 17th, 1918, at six o'clock in the morning. In four more days, Ernest would be nineteen years old.

6. MILANO

THE sound of the words ran in his ears like music: Ospedale Croce Rossa Americana, 10 Via Alessandro Manzoni, Milano, Italia. He was back where he had begun his tour of duty only six weeks before, but this time on a stretcher. The Italian orderlies got him into the lift and up to the top floor. There were eighteen Red Cross nurses for only four patients. One of them hovered busily over the wounded youngster. She was a short and motherly woman named Elsie Macdonald, who spoke with the hint of a burr. She kept smiling and patting Ernest while they lowered him into the bed, and told him, laughing, that he was her "broken doll, who had come all the way from the Piave to be glued together again."

He could hardly have had a more fashionable address. The large mansion, built in the old heroic style of stone and stucco, stood only two short blocks from the Piazza La Scala, which in turn gave upon the Galleria, the Piazza del Duomo, and the Cova. Ernest's room was dim and cool, with a window that looked out onto the tops of old trees and the shuttered windows of adjacent buildings. Even his surgeon was the best that could be found—a dark, spare, mustached man named Captain Sammarelli, who had the bandages cut away and examined the wounds with a critical eye. There was no evidence of infection and everything was healing nicely. When Ted Brumback hurried over from Schio to pay a call, he was told (wrongly) that Ernest was "fast on the road to recovery" and would be out, "a whole man once again," in a couple of weeks. Ted wrote a cheerful letter to the elder Hemingways, describing the accident and Ernest's heroic conduct. The hero himself added a postscript: "I am all O.K. and include much love to ye parents. I'm not near so much of a hell roarer as Brummy makes me out. Don't worry, Pop! Lots of love. Ernie."

His first real letter home, written on his nineteenth birthday, was meant to be equally reassuring. Accompanied by Elsie Macdonald, he had taken an ambulance to the Misericordia Hospital to have X-ray pictures made. They revealed a machine-gun slug in his right foot and another which had lodged just behind his right kneecap. The one in the knee had entered transversely without smashing the patella. The surgeon planned to remove both bullets before the end of July. It was a peach of a hospital, said Ernest. In addition to the excellent treatment, he stood to gain one of Italy's highest honors: he had been recommended for the silver medal of valor.

Miss Macdonald and the rest of the nurses occupied the floor below. Ernest soon got to know them all. He and Elsie were constantly joking and quarreling.

She called him Ernesto and Broken Doll. His nickname for her was The
Spanish Mackerel or Spanish Mac. The nurse in charge was Katharine C.
de Long, who had been Superintendent at Bellevue Hospital in New York and
was universally known as Gumshoe Casey. Three much younger Bellevue
graduates of the Class of 1917 were also on the staff: Ruth Brooks, Loretta
Cavanaugh (Sis Cavie), and Agnes Hannah von Kurowsky, whom everyone
called Von. Ruth was something of a flirt; she and Ernest did not hit it off. He
liked Sis Cavie and adored Elsie Macdonald. But the one who chiefly caught
his eye was Agnes.

She was a tall and dark-haired girl who had been reared in Washington,
D.C. After her father's death in 1910, she had worked as an assistant in the
Washington Public Library, and had then gone on to nursing school at Bellevue, hoping eventually to be sent abroad. In January, 1918, she applied for
admission to the Red Cross Nursing Service and late in June sailed for Europe
on her first foreign assignment. She was kind, generous, and bright, fond of
people, and full of bubbling energy. Since she "rather liked night duty" and
often volunteered to take the place of other nurses, she was in charge on the
evening of August first when they brought in young Henry Villard with a bad
case of jaundice and a touch of malaria. He had been driving ambulances for
Section One at Bassano. After the filthy train trip, during which he was continuously assailed by the dry nausea characteristic of his disease, he came into
the hospital as into "a bit of heaven." There was even an angel to receive him
"in the form of a beautiful night nurse named Agnes." She gave him a hot
bath, a dose of castor oil, a cocktail, and an eggnog. In the comfortable bed,
with real sheets and pillowcases, he drifted away into his first sound sleep in
months. Agnes was "doubly attractive so far from home, cheerful, quick,
sympathetic, with an almost mischievous sense of humor—an ideal personality
for a nurse."

All the other young men shared these sentiments, Ernest included. There
was a universal determination among them to get well quickly so that they
could have a date with Agnes. It was not an easy goal. The Red Cross nursing
rules conformed to Italian custom, which forbade unchaperoned dates, especially in the evenings. Agnes was not by nature a breaker of rules. She made
one exception on August 10th in response to a dinner invitation from Captain
Enrico Serena, a blond North Italian with vehement manners and a patch over
one of his eyes. He had formed the habit of dropping in at the hospital, and
had already befriended Ernest, whom he addressed as "Baby"—never imagining that he would one day serve as the prototype of Captain Rinaldi, the
surgeon in *A Farewell to Arms*. Serena had engaged a private dining room,
which included a piano and a seductive-looking couch. Agnes chattered
nervously, looking askance at the couch, and managing to get away unscathed
on the plea that she had to report for night duty at the hospital.

It was the evening after the morning of Ernest's second operation. Captain
Sammarelli had successfully removed the machine-gun slugs from Ernest's

knee and foot. Elsie Macdonald had accompanied him to the operating room, where Ernest told the doctor that if for any reason he failed to pull through, Spanish Mac was to receive all his back pay, his insurance claims, and "the trophy of the bloody boot." "Gee, Kid," wrote Elsie afterwards, "the tears came to my eyes that morning, and next morning I could not get to the Red Cross office quick enough to cable your Dad and let him know that you were all right."

Many others besides Agnes and Elsie were concerned about his welfare. He was the first American to be wounded in Italy, and all the newspapers in the Chicago area gave prominence to his story. He was pleased at all the acclaim. "I have begun to think," he wrote his parents, "that maybe you didn't appreciate me when I used to reside in the bosom. It's the next best thing to getting killed and reading your own obituary." He gave a graphic account of his rescue of the Italian soldier. "The Italian I had with me had bled all over my coat, and my pants looked like somebody had made currant jelly in them and then punched holes to let the pulp out. . . . I told them in Italian that I wanted to see my legs, though I was afraid to look. . . . So we took off my trousers and the old limbs were still there but gee they were a mess. They couldn't figure out how I had walked 150 yards with a load with both knees shot through and my right shoe punctured [in] two big places also over 200 flesh wounds." But Dr. Sammarelli's operation had been "a peach of a job." He had closed the incisions in the knee and the foot with twenty-eight stitches, and immobilized the leg in a plaster splint. "I wouldn't be really comfortable now unless I had some pain," said Ernest. He wanted all his friends at home to know the full details of his wounding, his behavior, and his rank. Someone had sent a letter addressed to Private Ernest Hemingway. "What I am," he wrote firmly, "is . . . Soto Tenente Ernest Hemingway. That is my rank and it means 2nd Lieut. I hope to be a Tenente or 1st Lieut. soon."

He enjoyed the brotherly admiration of his comrades-in-arms, and gloried in his consciousness of having behaved well throughout his ordeal by fire and the long recuperation. Day after hot day in August, he sat or lay in his bed like a king on a throne, holding court and greeting all comers. Red Cross captains came to sit at his feet and listen to his monologues: Meade Detweiler, the Milan representative; Bob Bates, the Inspector of Ambulances; and Jim Gamble, the Inspector of Rolling Canteens. Captain Serena appeared bearing gifts, treating him with fraternal solicitude. For three weeks in August, Bill Horne was his constant companion, having been hospitalized with gastroenteritis, the most persistent foe of foreigners in Italy.

"We [all] took turns conversing with him," said Henry Villard, "and encouraging him to forget his wounds." For a time there had been some loose talk about possible amputation, but Ernest insisted on piece-by-piece extraction of the *scaggia,* "no matter how long it took or how great the pain." He even pried out some of the smaller fragments as they worked their way to the surface, using the point of a penknife, and bolstering his courage with nips from a bottle of cognac which he kept hidden under his pillow. They all noticed his "everlasting good nature," though at times he could assert himself "with obstinacy and no little authority when things were not exactly right or the discipline became irksome." He did not appear to be cowed by Miss de Long's anger when she found his closet full of empty cognac bottles. Mistakes by underlings or even good friends could make him imperious as a ruling monarch. Elsie Macdonald felt the weight of his displeasure after she had carelessly left some Victrola records on the terrace, where they soon melted like toffee in the sun.

"You know how he was," said Agnes, long afterwards. "Men loved him. You know what I mean." What she meant was that there were elements in his personality that elicited a kind of hero worship. Bill Smith and Carl Edgar had discovered his special qualities in the summers at Walloon Lake and Horton Bay: the youth, the pride in strength, the animal charm, the boyish ebullience and good humor, the love of yarn-spinning. Now that he was older, with more experience, he communicated a new sense of fortitude, tenacity of purpose, stamina, and independence: perhaps above all the willed determination to be a free soul, untrapped by tradition, living his life in accordance with pragmatic principles. He gave the impression of having discovered them for himself, without apparent indebtedness to models or examples. From childhood he had enjoyed the company of men who could do things; in high school he had surrounded himself with a coterie of like-minded contemporaries. Now that he was nineteen, men several years older than he were ready to accept him as a coeval to be looked up to. Good companions like Bill Horne, Ted Brumback, or Fever Jenkins neither noticed, nor would have minded if they had, his habit of measuring himself against them, his competitive spirit, his determination to excel them all. They were not only content but even eager to tan themselves like sunbathers in the rays he generated. One great part of his power over others was that he knew he had it, yet somehow managed not to be spoiled by it.

For the first time in his life he was also discovering that he was attractive to and attracted by women. Villard noticed how the nurses "liked to exhibit him to visitors as their prize specimen of a wounded hero." His experience in being blown up, in rescuing a wounded companion, in courageously enduring the pain of his wounds, had enlarged his confidence. Without loss of his endearing boyish qualities, he had suddenly taken on some of the qualities of manhood. Most of the adolescent awkwardness was gone: he had become quite handsome in a distinctively masculine fashion, with a good jaw, strong white teeth, a clear ruddy complexion, and a more becoming way of wearing his hair. Older women like Elsie Macdonald adopted, mothered, worshipped, and bickered with him while he grinned and scolded. Younger women like Agnes von Kurowsky were soon aware of a newly aggressive sexuality, hitherto sublimated but now brought forth by the long confinement in bed, the kindly attention of pretty nurses, and the romantic setting of a hospital in wartime Milano.

By the middle of August, Ernest was "wildly" in love with Agnes von Kurowsky. She was beginning to reciprocate, though not to the degree that he would have liked. It was his first adult love affair—there is no trustworthy indication of any before it—and he hurled himself into it with uncommon devotion. She was the night nurse most of the time through August and early September. Although she was far too careful a nurse to neglect her other charges, her duties brought her frequently into his room, and she often returned to see him after the other boys had settled down. Elsie Macdonald was one of Agnes's closest friends. Whenever she was troubled with insomnia, she had a habit of coming upstairs in felt slippers and gossiping with Agnes late into the night. This enraged Ernesto. "You had a great case on her," Elsie recalled later on. "Remember how I could not sleep and would come up to visit her on night duty when out you would come on your crutches and lay me out, call me all manner of Spanish names. Hee Hee! That was great fun." It was far more fun for Elsie than it was for Ernest.

Agnes refused to permit the affair to progress beyond the kissing stage. She took her duties too seriously to think of getting married and settling down, as Ernest wanted to do. On the other hand, though hardly a flirt, she recognized the need of some variety. The boys on the top floor all adored her. Sometimes she let them take her to dinner, as she had done with Captain Serena, and as she did with Henry Villard after his jaundice was cured. She called Ernest Kid and herself Mrs. Kid, and let him address her as Ag or Aggie, a privilege she granted to few others. She also missed him when they were apart, though, as she said, "maybe not quite as wildly." She carried his picture in the pocket of her uniform, and wrote to him nearly every night. Yet she probably suspected, as he evidently did not, that this wartime romance was unlikely to last.

By September 11th, Ernest could get around the streets with a cane or crutches, though still unable to wear a shoe on his right foot. He made daily trips to the Ospedale Maggiore for therapy and exercise. His left leg was now fully functional, but he told his father that it resembled the hide of some old horse that had been branded and rebranded by at least fifty owners. One thing was certain, said he: he could never appear in kilts. Dr. Sammarelli's operation had left him with an eight-inch scar like a centipede on the sole of his right foot, and a neat little puncture on the instep where the copper-jacketed bullet had entered. He said proudly that his promotion to First Lieutenant had now come through. This meant that he could wear a Sam Browne belt and two gold stripes on each of his sleeves. His silver medal of valor was reputedly on the way, and there was a rumor that he would also be given a Croce di Guerra. The doctor had told him that he could not drive an ambulance for another six months. Meantime, he said carelessly, he would probably take command of a front-line post in the mountains, since his new commission entitled him to serve in the regular Italian Army. This last was one of his daydreams, though the rest of his news was real enough.

When he had recovered sufficiently to go to the races at San Siro track, he refused to budge from his room until his wound stripes had been sewn to his uniform. He had a mortal fear of being mistaken for a loafer or malingerer. Agnes and Elsie Macdonald wore the capes and high-crowned sailor hats that were the official street uniform for the nurses. Two young lieutenants of aviation, George Pay and George Lewis, also came along. They rode out in open carriages through the park and past the villas of the suburbs. It was a clear fall afternoon and the mountains showed blue in the distance. The turf in the paddock was fresh and green, the grandstand worn and weathered after four years of war. They had a drink at the bar under the stands and bet a few lire on the horses. None of them made any money, but the change in routine made it seem like a vacation. Ernest romanticized the afternoon. Some day he might use it in a short story or even a novel.

Late in September he went further afield for a holiday at the Gran Hotel Stresa on Lago Maggiore. His companion was a Minnesota boy named Johnny Miller, who had been driving ambulances all summer for Sections Two and Three. They were adopted by a small, elderly Italian, the Conte Giuseppe Greppi, an "uomo politico" with lengthy diplomatic experience who seemed eager to discuss American politics. It was Ernest's later boast that the Count had "brought him up politically." They played at billiards in the game room of the hotel, and the Count provided successive bottles of well-iced champagne. Ernest reveled in being adopted by Italian nobility. He was full of gay talk and literary opinions. He had brought along a copy of the *Saturday Evening Post* and discoursed to Johnny Miller on the excellence of Ring Lardner, whom he then placed as high "as Jupiter on tiptoes."

Agnes remembered afterwards the way he looked on his return from Stresa, stepping from the lift on the *quatro piano,* and holding out his arms to her in the hospital corridor. He was wearing a new British-style tunic of olive-drab whipcord, the work of Spagnolini, the eminent Milanese military tailor, and he cut a romantic figure. But she had news that plunged him into the deepest gloom he had known since July. She had volunteered for service at the Territorial Hospital in Florence to help with an outbreak of influenza. They spent a final evening of talk in the hospital library and he saw her off on the night train to the south. It was the middle of October, a time of clear bright weather. Her hospital was in the Via di Camerata on a hilltop with a splendid view of Florence and the soup-green Arno. "I'm all alone with my patient and another —a British Tommy—with the Floo," she wrote Ernest, "so I expect you'll get more letters than you know how to answer. I'll send some to the [Anglo-American Officers'] Club because I don't want any suspicions cast on you. Dear old thing, you are so far away. . . . All my love—and double. As ever, *your* Agnes."

He wrote to her daily, sometimes twice a day. She answered as often as her duties would allow. She called him "The Light of My Existence, My Dearest and Best, Most Ernest of Ernies, More Precious Than Gold, and My Hero," and complained that her evenings were lonely. "Gosh," she wrote, "if you were only here, I'd dash in and make you up about now, and you'd smile at me and hold out your brawny arms— What's the use of wishing?" On the 24th, five of his letters came in a batch, and there was another from Sis Cavie which said that Ernest was "very sad." He had made up his mind to go back to the front. Even if he could not drive an ambulance, he could at least see friends like Brummy and Bill and Howie Jenkins. "I knew you'd have to go sometime," wrote Agnes. But she longed for the war to be over and done with.

Other letters than hers diversified his days. One was from the Polish lieutenant, Leon Chocianowicz, who was now somewhere in France with the Troupe Polonaise. There was another from the Reverend William E. Barton in Oak Park, who said that the bell on the First Congregational Church was rung every day at noon for the boys who were at war. Marcelline sent the astonishing news that she had seen him in a newsreel, sitting in a wheelchair on the hospital porch, accompanied by a pretty nurse, with a lap robe of knitted wool squares. The whole family went next day for their first sight of Ernest since May.

There was also a month-old letter from his father, asking when Ernest would be coming home. He replied that he felt duty-bound to stay until the war was over. No army in the world would take him with his "bum leg and foot," but he was determined to serve in Italy as long as there was a war to hobble to. "It does give you an awfully satisfactory feeling to be wounded," said Ernest. "There are no heroes in this war. . . . All the heroes are dead. . . . Dying is a very simple thing. I've looked at death and really I know. If I should have died, it would have been . . . quite the easiest thing I ever did. . . . And how much better to die in all the happy period of undisillusioned youth, to go out in a blaze of light, than to have your body worn out and old and illusions shattered." Like so many of his letters now and later, this one was a mixture of truth and disingenuousness. He wished to stay abroad for patriotic reasons. But he could not tell his parents that his mode of life in Italy had turned him permanently away from the life he had been raised to. Nor did he mention his newly acquired taste for cognac and cigarettes, or the fact that he had fallen in love with his night nurse.

He was nevertheless quite sincere in stating that he would hobble away to the war so long as it was there to hobble to. He proved it a week later by returning for what he hoped would be another period of association with his comrades of Section Four. But he found only a skeleton force at the Schio Country Club. A group of their ambulances had been assigned to Section One, which was extremely active around Bassano in the vicinity of Mount Grappa. The huge Vittorio-Veneto offensive against the Austrians was about to be launched, and Ernest was eager to be present. Still limping on his cane, he rode an ambulance to a village near Bassano where Bill Horne and Emmett Shaw were standing by with Ambulance Number 8. A regiment of Arditi was stationed nearby, tough shock troops who swaggered past in distinctive gray uniforms and immediately entered Ernest's gallery of heroes. He arrived in time to witness the tremendous artillery barrage from the Italian guns. It continued through the whole night and lighted up the mountains around them like a perpetual thunderstorm. The boys sat up all night watching it and waiting for orders to pick up the casualties.

Next day, October 25th, Shaw and Horne drove to the top of Mount Grappa for what turned out to be a week of steady labor carrying the wounded. But Ernest was not with them. He had hardly finished watching the artillery barrage of the 24th when he was overtaken by a severe attack of jaundice. He knew the symptoms from his talks in August with Henry Villard. The closest comparable sensation, as he often said afterwards, was that of being kicked in the scrotum with a large army brogan. He hurried back to Milan and crawled miserably into bed. The whites of his eyes were the color of mustard and his skin, as he complained to Agnes, took on a "mongolian cast." The worst of it was that he was forbidden to drink. Agnes was sympathetic. "To think," she wrote, "you had to go and be sick when I wasn't there to take care of you."

But he was basically in fairly good health and quickly threw off his affliction. He had recovered sufficiently to be out and around the town by November 3rd. Towards noon that day he limped into the lounge of the Officers' Club and sat down to read the papers. A young British infantry officer was sitting nearby, drinking a glass of German export ale. Neither of them spoke until a girl named Maria, who looked after the Club, came rushing over with the news that an armistice had been signed between Italy and Austria. This was more than enough to bring the two strangers together. The acting major, an Irishman by birth, was Eric Dorman-Smith, who had been commanding troops on the Asiago Plateau behind Mount Pasubio until he came down with gastroenteritis. He was now officer-in-charge of British troops in Milano. In some fashion—possibly from Ernest's lively imagination—he got the impression that "this harmless-looking Red Cross youngster had been badly wounded leading Arditi troops on Monte Grappa." But Dorman-Smith had no reason to doubt the story, and the friendship ripened rapidly. He was amused and touched when Ernest began to quiz him relentlessly about the background of his wound stripes and the shape of his previous career.

He was the eldest son of an Irish major with an ancestral estate in Bellamont Forest, Cootehill, County Cavan. Although he was only twenty-three, he had been fighting since 1914 with the Northumberland Fusiliers. He had been wounded three times and mentioned three times in despatches, and held the Military Cross for extraordinary heroism. He was well-read, witty, sardonic, and charming, speaking in the clipped British fashion which Ernest admired and sought to imitate. They got on famously, lunching at the Club, drinking at the Cova, dining at Biffi's in the Galleria, and dropping in at the

Teatro Scala. The Irishman's nickname was Chink, and he called Ernest Hem, or sometimes Popplethwaite. Hem appointed himself as Chink's ADC, and repeatedly led the conversations into the subjects of war and death, the behavior of men under fire, and the enthralling topic of personal courage. Chink was full of anecdotes, some of them relating to the war in Belgium. Once they had lain in a garden at Mons, potting Boche infantry as they came climbing over the garden wall. Another time they had made a "priceless" barricade from a wrought-iron gate. There was a more recent story about a British Tommy in a village in the Dolomites. He had swaggered into a bar, pointed to a bottle, and asked, "What's that bloody stuff?" When they said it was Strega, he bought a bottle, drank its contents down like beer—and promptly died.

Apropos of a discussion of death on the field of battle, Chink came out one day with a quotation from Shakespeare that Ernest had never heard of. He liked it so well that he got Chink to write it out on a slip of paper and afterwards committed it to memory. It came from *The Second Part of Henry the Fourth:* "By my troth, I care not; a man can die but once; we owe God a death . . . and let it go which way it will, he that dies this year is quit for the next." It precisely echoed the view of death that he had recently espoused in the letter to his parents. "Dying is a very simple thing," he had written. For those times in the night when he did not fully believe in such bravado, Chink Smith's Shakespearean passage could serve as a literary talisman.

Agnes returned from Florence in mid-November, bringing with her an ARC nurse named Elsie Jessup, who had been granted a period of sick leave. Miss Jessup was blond, somewhat English in manner, and carried a swagger stick. Ernest listened and watched with his customary care. Like the little priest from the Abruzzi, to say nothing of Elsie Macdonald, Captain Serena, and Count Greppi, Miss Jessup might some day serve as a character in one of his stories. He squired the two girls around the city, though Elsie's presence made it hard to see Agnes alone. Captain Jim Gamble had now offered him a full year in Italy, with all expenses paid. When Agnes saw that he was half-inclined to accept, she summoned her courage and began to argue against it, fearing that it might make "the Kid" into a "sponger, a floater, and a bum." She herself was convinced, and had told Ernest, that it was "wonderful to be alive in these stirring times," but only if one could do some good. The devastated house of Europe needed rebuilding and she wanted to make whatever contribution she could.

She had been "home" hardly a week when she was again sent away—this time to Treviso, near Padua, where another epidemic was raging among the American troops. The forty-eight beds in her ward were almost constantly filled. Some of the boys died of pneumonia. She worked long hours under adverse conditions while managing, by some miracle of loyalty, to keep on writing Ernest every other day. He soon hinted that he might come over to pay her a visit. "I keep looking out of the windows," said Agnes in reply, "and every now and then I jump because I think I see a familiar stalwart figure in a good-looking English uniform and overseas cap with a cane. It's a mighty queer thing, and I've been sadly disappointed several times." When he suddenly appeared on Monday, December 9th, he was disappointed in his turn. He looked exactly as she had imagined, limping through the ward. The recuperating soldiers were sprawled smoking in their beds and a portable Victrola was blaring. Something in Ernest's appearance and manner made them laugh at him. It is not clear whether or not he noticed it. If he did, it may explain why he was so loud and self-assertive when Agnes introduced him to some of the other nurses.

She scolded him afterwards for having been "so brutally outspoken." It was a newly emergent trait, visible in times of nervous stress. Yet she reflected that if he were faultless, she would like him less. "Perfect people are not nearly so lovable," she wrote, "and of course you have some very fine qualities also." One result of their reunion in Treviso was that he had promised to go home right away. "It's strange," said Agnes, "how circumstances can affect one. When I was with Jessup I wanted to do all sorts of wild things—anything but go home—and when you [were] with Captain Gamble you felt the same way. But I think maybe we have both changed our minds—and the old États-Unis are going to look très, très bien to our world-weary eyes."

In such ways as this, gently and obliquely, she continued to urge him to keep his promise to go home. She even hinted that in due course, perhaps a year or two, they might be married. Yet she was well aware that her twenty-seventh birthday was less than a month away, while his twentieth would not come until July. Her affection for Ernest was genuine, but she was also eager to continue her work as a nurse. In December she told him quietly that she would not be in Milano to celebrate their first Christmas. But she hoped that he would "be cheerful and contented anyhow."

He did his best, joining Chink Smith in a round of pre-Christmas parties, including one to celebrate his emergence from the Red Cross Hospital. There was no further talk of dying, but only of how to live. On Christmas Day he went to a dance at the Cova. A number of officers from the 332nd A.E.F. were on hand. Ernest befriended some of them, including a young First Lieutenant named Carl Hugo Trik, who came from Philadelphia and had fallen in love with an Italian girl named Pia. After the dance they went to a party. Ernest's date was a pretty dark-haired girl who stood on a chair and made an impassioned speech about cabbages and kings. They played charades in Italian and Carl Trik envied Ernest his seeming mastery of the language.

The time in Italy was now growing short. Ernest was booked to sail from Genoa early in January aboard the SS *Giuseppe Verdi*. Captain Gamble was still persistent. He had rented a house in Taormina, and asked his young friend down for a visit. Between Christmas and New Year's Ernest took the night train from Naples, his first excursion through southern Italy. But according to the story he told on his return, he never reached Taormina. He assured

Dorman-Smith that he had "seen nothing of Sicily except from a bedroom window because his hostess in the first small hotel he stopped in had hidden his clothes and kept him to herself for a week. The food she brought him was excellent and she was affectionate; Hem had no complaints except that he saw very little of the country." In the light of his love of yarning, this story should probably be taken with skepticism. Since the age of four he had delighted in tall tales, usually with himself as hero. Now that he was nineteen, the content had merely become a little more worldly. Yet in other respects, his wounding, his five months' convalescence, and the unconsummated love affair with Agnes had matured him faster than anything else he had done. Like the *scaggia* that remained in his legs, the memory of the north of Italy in 1918 would stay with him all the rest of his life.

7. *SOLDIER'S HOME*

THE minute he limped down the gangplank of the *Giuseppe Verdi* on January 21st, he found that he was a celebrity—the one man among all the uniformed passengers to be singled out by a reporter from the *New York Sun*. Hyperbole dominated the interview. The reporter believed that the 227 scars on Ernest's legs proved that he had taken more punishment than "any other man, in or out of uniform," who had "defied the shrapnel of the Central Powers." He also got the impression that Ernest had spent much of October and early November fighting in the vicinity of Monte Grappa, an impression that Ernest did not deny.

Bill Horne was on hand to greet him, accompanied by a pretty girl named Ann Sage. Bill had spent a hard week carrying wounded on Monte Grappa during the October offensive, returned to Schio just as Section Four was breaking up, and reached New York in time for Christmas with his parents. In his new civilian clothes he was hardly a match for the tall, brown-haired young officer in the cordovan leather boots and the long black broadcloth Italian officer's cape, held at the throat with a silver clasp. Ann Sage could hardly take her eyes off the homecoming hero when they went to the Plaza for tea. That night the boys stayed up late reminiscing at Bill's house in Yonkers. They were still talking when Ernest got aboard the day train at Grand Central.

In Chicago he stepped stiffly down into the cavernous cold gloom of the La Salle Street train shed. His father and Marcelline were there to meet him, shedding tears of thanksgiving for his safe return. He leaned on his cane and limped slowly, taking the stairs one by one. They dropped Marcelline at the Congregational Training School and drove home through snow-covered streets. All the lights were shining in the house on Kenilworth. Ursula was away at college, but Grace, Sunny, Carol, and Leicester were waiting. Sunny was fourteen and still in high school. Carol, aged seven, and Leicester, aged four, were awake but very sleepy. On the front-hall table were several letters from Italy.

As soon as he could, Ernest clumped upstairs to his third-floor bedroom to read his mail in privacy.

Two of the letters were from Agnes. One told of her attendance at a reception for President and Mrs. Woodrow Wilson, who had stopped over in Milan during their Italian tour. The other had been scribbled by lantern light in the ward of her hospital at Padua. "Well, good night, dear Kid," she concluded, "and how I wish I knew how you are at this moment, but I know you're O.K. . . . A rivederla, carissimo tenente, suo cattivo ragazza [your naughty girl], Agnes."

Ernest was already homesick for Italy. Each morning he lay late in his green-painted bed with the knitted lap robe he had brought from Milan spread over him as a counterpane. After lunch with the family he usually went for a walk, wearing his uniform and the cordovan boots, and leaning heavily on his cane. A girl reporter named Roselle Dean "beguiled him into *The Oak Parker* office" for an interview. She found him little "disposed to talk about himself," and most reluctant to be called a hero. "I went because I wanted to go," said he. "I was big and strong, my country needed me, and I went and did whatever I was told—and anything I did outside of that was simply my duty." He was ready to admit that war was "great sport" and that he would go again if the occasion arose.

Two little eleven-year-olds named Dorothy Reynolds and Katherine De Voe had begun to worship him from a suitable distance. They made him a huge lacy Valentine and delivered it to his house, ringing the doorbell and running away, though "not very fast or very far." By way of reward, he took them out into the back yard and shot off an Italian star shell. Later, in Grace's music room, he spent hours talking to them about his war souvenirs, which he had shipped home in a trunk and arranged on the small carpeted dais beside the Steinway. They marveled at his ring, set with a piece of the metal that had been taken from his legs. He told the little girls "wonderful stories" of the war. They reciprocated with "corny jokes." Afterwards it occurred to Dorothy that perhaps he was lonely.

He was lonely indeed. When Marcelline came home on weekends, she thought he resembled someone "put in a box with the cover nailed down." Most of his former friends were away or at work. He wrote to Agnes, telling her about shooting off the star shells, and sympathizing with her because she must be lonely, too. She answered that she was far too busy to be unhappy. She had moved from Treviso to Torre di Mosta, where she was "having the time of [her] young life." A captain of Arditi had come to sleep at the hospital until he could find suitable quarters elsewhere. All the Arditi were wild men. "You'd certainly adore them," thought Agnes. There was an Alpini major there, too. One of his arms was paralyzed, but he was "full of pep." He had spent five years in the war, including forty months in various hospitals. He was about thirty, very small in stature, but already a great friend to everyone in the hospital. Sis Cavanaugh had been "very cruel" to Agnes lately, accusing her of being a flirt, and putting her in the same class with Ruth Brooks. "You know I don't do anything like that, don't you?" wrote Agnes.

None of this helped Ernest much in getting out of his box. He had brought home some liqueurs, including a bear-shaped bottle of Kümmel. He gave some to Al Dungan and some more to Marcelline. She took a small mouthful but was afraid to swallow it. "Don't be afraid," said Ernest. "There's great comfort in that small bottle. . . . Taste everything, Sis. . . . Sometimes I think we only half live over here. The Italians live all the way." He was a little consoled when some of the Italian-Americans from Chicago and the suburbs gave a party in his honor. On two different Sundays they came to the house in chattering cavalcades, bringing hampers of food, jugs of red wine, and musical instruments. They hung a large Italian flag from the balcony in the music room and staged an impromptu concert. Some of them were attached to the Chicago Opera Company. They stood on Grace's little dais and bellowed famous arias. Ernest sang the song about General Cadorna, only slightly off-key:

> *Il generale Cadorna*
> *Scrive alla Regina*
> *Se vuole vedere Trieste*
> *Compra la cartolina!*

The company raised their glasses and joined in the chorus: *"Boum, Boum, Boum, Rumor di cannonado!"* Afterwards they ate spaghetti, fish salad, and large frosted cakes. Dr. Hemingway, the Sabbatarian teetotaler, joined in as well as he could. But the second such party was too much. All this loud singing and shouting was a nuisance to the neighbors, he muttered, stomping angrily off to bed.

Roselle Dean's piece in *The Oak Parker* brought Ernest a number of invitations to talk about his war experiences in public. The most successful of these was the Friday assembly of March 14th at the high school. Ernest took along some of his trophies for exhibition: an Austrian helmet, a revolver, the star-shell pistol, and even the breeches he had worn on the night of his wounding. His classmate Caroline Bagley introduced him as the well-known Hemingstein. He opened his speech by saying that no one could spit when sufficiently scared. Then he launched into an account of the mortar explosion that had scared him so badly in July. He told of carrying the wounded soldier back to the command post, and held up for inspection his incredibly torn and bloodstained uniform breeches. After that he began to tell them stories about the Arditi whom he had seen at Bassano. Those men were really tough, said Ernest. They rode to battle in camions, singing the song about General Cadorna's letter to the Queen. Ernest sang it to the audience and then translated it. He told of having met an Arditi captain who plugged the bulletholes in his chest with cigarette stubs and went on fighting. The speech was an immense success. None of the children had heard anything like it. Afterwards

Ernest went over to the YMCA swimming pool with Al Dungan and some of the boys. They all shuddered with horror and admiration when they saw the terrible network of scars on his legs.

Late in March there was a crisis. He had continued to write to Agnes every day—"wonderful long letters bulging with news." One of hers, sent from Torre di Mosta on March first, told of the arrival of a whole bushel from him, so many that she had not even had time to read them. She said that he must not write so often. With all she had to do at the hospital, she couldn't keep to such a pace. "I'm not all the perfect being you think I am. But, as I am, I always was, only it's just beginning to creep out. I'm feeling very *cattivo* tonight, so good-night, Kid, and don't do anything rash but have a good time. Afft., Aggie." Anyone less in love than Ernest might have read the signs of approaching disaster between the lines of Agnes's letter. She had in fact fallen in love with a handsome young Neapolitan, Tenente Domenico Caracciolo, and the blow was not long deferred. Sometime in March, not unkindly, she told him the truth of the matter. "She was sorry," as he later recorded it, "and she knew he would probably not be able to understand, but might some day forgive her, and be grateful to her. She hoped he would have a great career, and believed in him absolutely."

He was beside himself with horror and dismay. He began to run a temperature and was obliged to go to bed. When he got up again, he was in a black rage over her perfidious conduct. He sent off a crackling letter to Elsie Macdonald, telling her the news and adding that when Agnes disembarked in New York on her way home, he hoped that she would stumble on the dock and knock out all her front teeth. He presently began to assure his friends that he had "cauterized" the memory of Agnes with a course of "booze and other women." As usual he was exaggerating. In the mild weather of April and May, he made a few dates with a pretty girl named Kathryn Longwell, resuming his prewar habit of canoeing on the Des Plaines River. "We'd paddle for miles," she wrote, "and other times we would come to my home and read stories he had written, while eating little Italian cakes that he brought from the city." On one occasion he presented Kathryn with his Italian officer's cloak, which made Grace Hemingway so angry that she demanded its return.

Y. K. Smith, the older brother of Bill and Katy, was now living in an apartment on North Oak Park Avenue. He had recently recovered from tuberculosis at the famous Trudeau Sanatorium in the Adirondacks. He was tall and slender, clever and bright, much interested in literature and the other arts. His wife, Doodles, played the piano, a short and rather plump girl with gray eyes and long brown hair. Bill stopped in to see them on his way to Horton Bay and spent a night or two with Ernest. It was their first meeting since the summer of 1917 and they stayed up half the night while Ernest told gaudy yarns. He had still not got the Arditi out of his system. He said he had been talking to one of them up in the Dolomites. The soldier had showed Ernest how to use the short sword like a dagger, hitting the heart through the hollow under the left shoulder blade. To illustrate, said Ernest, the soldier had called over an Austrian prisoner—and killed him with a single stroke.

Next evening they went to Chicago for dinner at an Italian restaurant. Their companion was a short and swarthy friend of Ernest's named Nick Neroni. They drank several pitchers of red wine, and Ernest spoke Italian with Neroni, proud of his mastery of the language. As they were riding the El back to Oak Park, they happened to meet Kathryn Longwell. The conversation turned, as usual, to the war. Kathryn asked Ernest many questions about the girls in Paris. She was unaware that his two-day sojourn in the City of Light had been spent chasing shells instead of women. But the red wine at dinner had lubricated his imagination, and he was still talking about the French girls when he and Bill got back to Oak Park and went to bed.

He was doing more short stories like those he had shown to Kathryn Longwell. One was called "The Passing of Pickles McCarty, or The Woppian Way." The lead paragraph was breezy.

Back in the days when we were eating of the fruit of the tree of watchful waiting, when people still cared where the Giants finished, before the draft had even begun to form in the cave of the winds . . . there was a ringsman by the name of Pickles McCarty.

His name was really Neroni, the story said, but he had needed an Irish monicker to get anywhere in the fight game. Under his ring name he came along fast. Just as he was emerging into the big time, he suddenly disappeared. When he turned up again, it was as a member of a battalion of Arditi at Bassano in the Dolomites, proudly wearing the resplendent gray uniform, with black roll puttees and a tasseled black fez. All through June he had fought the Austrians along the lower Piave. Now he was back in the mountains, ready to attack a mountainside village still in Austrian hands. Ernest's story reached a stirring climax in which Pickles McCarty, a knife in each hand, cut his way through fierce opposition to the spot where his commanding officer had fallen. After such victories, there was no point in returning to anything as tame as prizefighting.

"The Passing of Pickles McCarty" was an attempt to bridge the gap between Ernest's high-school fiction and more ambitious stories in which he could use the knowledge he had picked up during seven months in wartime Italy. He was still trying to follow the advice of Trumbull White from the summer of 1917: to write of subjects that he knew from personal experience. He had in fact known many "a June twilight in the Dolomites," walked through Vicenza "under a bombing moon," and drunk beer in the little *trattoria* in Schio under the purple blossoms of wistaria. Perhaps he had sampled Strega at Cittadella between Bassano and Padua. He had seen a detachment of Arditi riding camions to attack the Austrians above Bassano. But he had not yet learned to discipline his prose, economize his dialogue, curb his powers of invention, or understand that scenes of carnage were not in themselves the ideal climax for the stories he had to tell.

Nevertheless, he was trying to write again, and he took his little store of manuscripts along when he went up to Horton Bay early in June. At first he stayed with Bill Smith at Mrs. Charles's farm, assisting as well as he could with the spraying of the apple trees and the planting of the garden. After work they often went roaring around the countryside in Bill's Buick. On several occasions, emergent bits of *scaggia* bothered him so much that he was obliged to climb the narrow dark stairway to Dr. Guy Conkle's office in Boyne City to have his legs bandaged. But his infirmities did not deter him from fishing. By the middle of the month, they had taken six rainbows that averaged three pounds apiece, and Ernest was bubbling with his usual enthusiasm. "Gosh," he said, "those fish sure could put up a fight." He had renamed them "the Arditi of the lakes."

Now that he was free of the restrictions of his family, he had resumed drinking and cigarette smoking. His taste in cigarettes was somewhat exotic —a Russian brand, with dark brown paper, "very slimy looking," and procurable only at a tobacco shop just off Wabash Avenue in Chicago. They cost plenty—thirty cents for a packet of ten—but he assured his friends that they were far and away the "best weeds" (he also called them "pills") that he had ever smoked. He gaily predicted that Chicago would never go dry, and urged Fever Jenkins to bring along "a couple of quarts" when he came north in August.

One day in June he received a letter with an Italian postmark and familiar handwriting. It was from Agnes, who had been transferred yet again, this time to Rome, where she was working with Sis Cavanaugh. Her love affair with Tenente Domenico Caracciolo was now finished. He had taken her to Naples to meet his family. Only then had she discovered that Domenico stood to inherit a dukedom upon the death of his father. The proud old family forbade their son to marry her, supposing (quite falsely) that Agnes was an American adventuress seeking the distinction of an Italian title. So, Agnes reported, it was all over, and she was thinking of coming home in July. Ernest wrote to Jenkins that she had probably got exactly what was coming to her. But he was not vengeful. All he could feel was pity. "Poor damned kid," said he. "I'm sorry as hell for her." He had loved her once; she had "gypped" him; there was nothing further to be done. All of it there in Milano, he said, seemed "long ago and far away," and there were "no busses running from the Bank to Mandalay." So, with successive bows to W. H. Hudson and Rudyard Kipling, he closed the most romantic chapter in the first twenty years of his life, and turned, almost with relief, to his first postwar summer in the northern woods.

By early July his legs were strong enough to carry him on his first fishing trip in almost two years. They drove in Bill's Buick to Vanderbilt, twenty miles southeast of Horton Bay. Beyond Vanderbilt in the same direction was a region called the Pine Barrens. It was dotted with ponds and intersected by three excellent trout streams, the Sturgeon, the Pigeon, and the Black. They went five days without seeing a house or even a clearing—"wild as the devil," said Ernest. On the banks of the Pigeon River they startled a bear. There were occasional deer and they flushed many partridges. Fishing the Black and camping at a new spot almost every night, they took more trout than they could eat. With a wet fly on one hook and a grasshopper on the other, Bill twice landed two fish at once. On the last day they caught sixty-four trout between them. They drove home triumphantly along the dusty roads, smelling of fish, citronella, and woodsmoke, and sporting seven-day beards.

The rest of the Hemingway family was now back at Windemere. The great project of their summer was Grace's plan to build herself a small summer cottage at Longfield Farm. The site was the high knoll in the middle of the property that she and Ed had once named Red Top Mountain. "This was to be Grace's own studio, where she could escape into privacy from her large, noisy family." She was now forty-seven and looking forward to the change. One day that summer, she took Marce into her confidence. Even though she loved her husband deeply, they "frequently got on each other's nerves." He could not comprehend her need to be alone. Ernest, on the other hand, took after his mother rather than his father. As soon as he had learned to stop "fighting himself and everybody else," said Grace, he would turn into a "fine man."

Having now accumulated a small cache of short stories in the style of "The Woppian Way," Ernest was casting about for a suitable fiction market. A kindly man of thirty-five named Edwin Balmer was summering at Walloon Lake. He was a native of Chicago, a graduate of Northwestern and Harvard, and a former reporter for the *Chicago Tribune.* In collaboration with his brother-in-law, William McHarg, he had already written some novels. When Ernest came to see him, they spent several hours sitting in the shade of Balmer's boathouse, talking about the art of fiction and listening to the gentle lapping of the water under the dock. Balmer was encouraging—or at least not discouraging. He scribbled down the names of several magazine editors for Ernest to try: George Horace Lorimer of the *Saturday Evening Post,* Virginia Roderick of *Everybody's Magazine,* Charles Agnew MacLean of *Popular Magazine,* and Karl Harriman of *Red Book* and *Blue Book.* The conference produced little more than friendship and hope, but hope was a quality on which Ernest was more than ever dependent as he struggled awkwardly through his first experiments with adult writing.

He was now enthusiastically planning another trip to the Pine Barrens. Fever Jenkins was coming up in August with Larry Barnett, another former member of the Schio Country Club. Larry had been promised the loan of his father's Chalmers Master Six, a touring car with the top down, the last word in current fashion. Ernest urged Jenks to bring his Austrian carbine and a good supply of shells: it would be a darned good weapon to have around in case they saw another bear. He and Bill Smith had assembled a camping outfit for four men. They would have a peach of a time, especially if Jenks could scare up "heavy supplies of the grog." Ernest painted a happy picture of the four of them sitting around a campfire before their tent on the banks of the Black, with a full moon on the horizon and a good meal of trout in their bellies, smoking "pills," passing around a bottle of "the grog," and singing all the rousing songs they knew.

The trip went off as planned. The weather was good and they spent a week wading the Black and "catching and eating many beautiful trout." Ernest rolled them in cornmeal, fried them in Crisco, and basted them slowly with bacon slices. "We went unshaven for a week or so," wrote Larry, "and started back one evening loaded down with tents and camping equipment. Passing through Boyne City, Smith and Hemingway in the back thought it would be good clean fun to shoot out the overhead street lights as we passed under them. This was done for perhaps five or six when we all decided it was not just prankish and we might get in trouble, so the shooting ceased and we sped homeward. A few miles later a motorcycle with siren came from behind and stopped us. The cop looked over the four unshaven, roughly dressed characters and timidly asked if we had seen a large touring car with four men, top down, loaded with equipment. This we denied and acted horrified to hear that such a car had recently passed through Boyne City with guns a-blazin'. . . . We assured him we would report any such car should we see it, and he returned eastward. Of course we fitted the description completely, but apparently the officer was a bit unnerved seeing such a rough crowd on that dark road—and alone." Ernest remembered this occasion, like the heron shooting episode, as one of his youthful tangles with the law. In his fifties, he was still boasting about having "shot up" the towns of Boyne Falls and Boyne City for no other reason than high spirits. He did not bother to explain that the shooting-up was nothing more daring than plugging half a dozen street lights from a passing car.

His final camping trip of the summer went farther afield, this time to a ghost town called Seney in the Upper Peninsula of Michigan, only fifteen miles from the chilly shores of Lake Superior. The trip gave him the background for "Big Two-Hearted River," the story of Nick Adams on a lone hiking-and-fishing expedition to recuperate from the effects of his wounding in the war. He later recalled that he was still badly hurt in body, mind, spirit, and morals at this time. When he got off the train at Seney, said he, the brakeman told the engineer to pause longer than usual so that Ernest could get down. "Hold her up," the brakeman said. "There's a cripple and he needs time to get his stuff down." The remark shocked Ernest, who had never thought of himself as a cripple. After that, said he, he stopped being one in his mind. The anecdote may or may not be true. But Ernest was not alone on the trip to Seney. His companions were a boy named Al Walker and Jack Pentecost, his high-school classmate. Their purpose was to fish the Fox River, which teemed with rainbows and brook trout. During the week that they spent on the Fox they caught nearly two hundred.

Except for the adventure of camping in the wilderness, they need not have left home. They had been back only a few days when hundreds of enormous rainbows began to appear in the cove at Horton Bay. "You can see 'em jumping from Dilstein's porch," said Ernest. He meant the porch of Liz Dilworth's Pinehurst Cottage, where he had taken to sitting out after supper, watching the sunsets, smoking Russian cigarettes, and waiting for Marjorie Bump to get off from work. Marjorie and her friend Connie Curtis had come from Petoskey to wait on tables at Mrs. Dilworth's. She was seventeen, with red hair and freckles, dimpled cheeks, and a sunny disposition. Wesley's wife Kathryn thought that Marjorie was "much enamored of Ernest," and used to watch her at the breadboard in Liz Dilworth's kitchen, making sandwiches to take along when she and Ernest went out to the Point for long evenings beside a driftwood campfire. Opinions differ as to the seriousness of their association. But Ernest subsequently used her first name and characteristically romanticized their friendship in a pair of related stories, "The End of Something" and "The Three-Day Blow."

After Marjorie and Connie had gone back to high school in Petoskey, Ernest stayed on through September and the first week of October, helping with the seed-potato harvest. The potatoes were stored in bags in a large shed called the Potato House. This and another building called the Bean House flanked the large dock at the foot of the sandy lane that led past Dilworth's down to the Bay. The dock was the scene of an event which Ernest later converted into a short story. One of the Pinehurst Cottage waitresses, a pretty and forward girl somewhat older than Marjorie and Connie, had stayed past Labor Day to help Liz Dilworth restore order to her house after the heavy traffic of July and August. She and Ernest took to strolling out together in the evenings after her work was done. One night their stroll ended in a mutual seduction on the chilly planking of the dock in the shadows behind the Potato House. Ernest had boasted in June of having cauterized the wound of Agnes's rejection with a course of women and booze. The surviving evidence makes it seem far more likely that his encounter with the waitress at Horton Bay was the first of its kind. It evidently impressed him. Two years later, he wrote a fictional account of the episode in a story called "Up in Michigan." It dealt so frankly and graphically with sexual intercourse that he had difficulty in getting it published in the United States.

8. NORTH COUNTRY

THE revels ended, such as they were, and Ernest rode home with Bill Smith at the end of the first week in October. But Oak Park was only a way station. He told his family that he wanted to do some serious writing and hurried back to the easy atmosphere of the Dilworths'. By the end of the month he had decided to move to Petoskey, where he rented a large front bedroom on the second floor of a gabled frame house at 602 State Street. It was run as a rooming and boarding house by a widow named Evva Potter and her daughter Hazel. Hazel worked in Mancelona, coming home on weekends to help her mother. Every morning the house resounded with the clack of young Hemingway's typewriter.

When high school let out in the afternoon, he was often on hand to meet Marjorie Bump and walk her home. He wore a cloth cap with a visor and a black leather jacket lined with sheepskin. Soon he was a familiar figure around Petoskey. One of his admirers was Grace Quinlan, a pretty little fourteen-year-old with dark eyes and Indian-black hair. He nicknamed her Sister Luke and took to sitting in the Quinlans' kitchen, popping corn and telling yarns about his life in Italy. His best friends among the boys were Dutch Pailthorp, whose father was a lawyer, and Luman Ramsdell, the doctor's son. Dutch was a thin, red-haired boy who had just withdrawn from the University of Michigan because of illness. He and Ernest put down a keg of cider, which they fortified with cracked corn and raisins and set to fermenting over the hot-air register in Ernest's room.

Around Thanksgiving, the cider had turned hard enough to drink. They decided to have a party at the Ramsdells' summer cottage in Bay View, the Methodist cultural colony. They asked Irene Goldstein, Bernice Babbitt, and a boy called Homer Zipp. Irene was Ernest's date, a handsome girl exactly his age who was home on vacation from a college of physical education in Chicago. They all piled into Luman's Whippet with the cider and some sandwiches. The Ramsdell house had been closed for the season and the iron cold was everywhere. They built a fire in the fireplace and spent a raucous evening sampling the cider and talking. Ernest hiked up his pants leg to show Irene his scars and discoursed at length on the wines of Italy and the guinea red he said he had drunk at the Venice Café on Wabash Avenue in Chicago.

Among the stories he was beating out in the rented room at Mrs. Potter's was one called "Wolves and Doughnuts." The locale was an Italian restaurant in Chicago.

If you are . . . curious, [he wrote] about pearl fishing conditions in the Marquesas, the possibility of employment on the projected trans-Gobi railway, or the potentialities of any of the hot tamale republics, go to the Café Cambrinus on Wabash Avenue, Chicago. There at the rear of the dining room where the neo-bohemians struggle nightly with their spaghetti and ravioli is a small, always smoke-filled room that is a clearing house for the camp-followers of fortune. When you enter the room, and you have no more chance than the zoological entrant in the famous camel-needle's eye gymkana of entering the room unless you are approved by Cambrinus, there will be a sudden silence. Then a varying number of eyes will look you over with that detached intensity that comes of a periodic contemplation of death. This inspection is not merely boorishness. If you are recognized favourably, all right. If you are unknown, it is all right, Cambrinus has passed on you. After a time the talk picks up again. But one time the door was pushed open, men looked up, glances of recognition shot across the room, a man half rose from one of the card tables, his hand behind him, there was a roar from the doorway and what had had its Genesis in the Malay Archipelago finished in the back room of the Café Cambrinus. But that's not this.

I came out of the wind-scoured midnight nakedness of Wabash Avenue in January into the cosy bar of the Cambrinus and armed with a smile from Cambrinus himself passed through the dining-room where the waiters were clearing away the debris of the table d'hotes into the . . . [End of fragment.]

For every story he wrote down he poured a dozen others into the avid ears of Luman Ramsdell and Dutch Pailthorp. The most horrifying centered on the Arditi. He told how they got rid of Austrian prisoners, tying them wrist to wrist in hollow squares and then tossing in a hand grenade. He said they had taught him the art of throwing knives and even offered him an Austrian to practice on. There was also an elaborate yarn about a gorgeous number who had picked him up on a train. They spent several happy days at her villa on the Riviera. Then the girl's husband appeared. Ernest recognized him as a famous Italian ace. A duel was arranged with pistols, to be fired at point-blank range. But the girl intervened at the last moment and Ernest departed in a cab. His last sight of the lady was her long and loving wink.

He was asked to give a talk on his wartime adventures at the December meeting of the Ladies' Aid Society in the Petoskey Public Library on Mitchell Street. He wore the sweeping cloak with the silver clasp and his well-polished cordovan boots. The speech was roughly a duplicate of the one he had given at Oak Park High School in March. Out of deference to the ladies, he omitted the racy anecdotes he had told to Dutch and Luman. But he spoke admiringly of the Arditi and exhibited his well-riddled khaki breeches. The audience sighed in sympathy when he spoke of lying wounded in the roofless stable. It had seemed, he told them, "more reasonable to die than to live."

One of his auditors was a handsome white-haired lady named Harriet Gridley Connable, who had come from Toronto to visit her mother. Her husband, Ralph, was a tall, dynamic man, head of the Canadian branch of the F. W. Woolworth five-and-ten-cent stores. The Connables were planning to spend a few months in Palm Beach that winter, accompanied by their daughter, Dorothy, a gentle girl of twenty-six. Their son Ralph was a year younger than Ernest and had been lame from birth. Mr. Connable asked Ernest to serve as a companion to Ralph, Jr., during their absence. The boys could attend hockey and boxing matches, plays and concerts, and there were plenty of servants to look after them at home. Dutch Pailthorp would also be there, working for the Woolworth stores. Ernest grabbed at the chance. He had not sold any stories and his bank account was nearly empty. "I'm going to

Toronto," he wrote Howie Jenkins. "This Toronto thing looks like the original Peruvian doughnuts."

He checked in at Oak Park for the holidays, determined to make up for the small-town life in Petoskey and the polite life he expected to lead in Toronto. On New Year's Eve, he went to a dance at the Country Club and next day drank afternoon tea with a pretty neighbor named Isabelle Simmons, a senior at Oak Park High. He and Jack Pentecost went to Chicago with Howie Jenkins for a Chianti lunch at the Venice Café. That night he joined fifteen veterans of the Schio Country Club at a reunion dinner. He was on hand to hear Titta Ruffo in *Pagliacci* at the Chicago Opera House and to "lamp" the latest edition of the Ziegfeld Follies the next night. On the sixth of January, he and Jenkins made a double date with Irene Goldstein and her college roommate, Marian Holbrook, taking the girls to a basement speakeasy on Wabash Avenue.

On the eighth he caught the train for Toronto and moved into the Connable family mansion at 153 Lyndhurst Avenue. It was a large and comfortable house on the edge of a wooded ravine just south of St. Clair Avenue. The music room held a pipe organ and enough instruments to supply a small orchestra. The billiard room reminded Ernest of the one in Stresa where he had played with Count Greppi. The tennis court behind the house was flooded to serve as a skating rink. Beside it was a roofless cabin with a fireplace and benches, where the skaters could rest and drink hot chocolate from thermos jugs. A large box in the loggia held extra skates for visitors. It was altogether a more stately mansion than Ernest had ever known before.

In spite of his painful legs, he was ready to join in the impromptu games of hockey, the first he had played since his return from Italy. The regulars included the chauffeur's son, who was just learning to skate, a lady goalkeeper, and a Scot from Nova Scotia named Ernest Smith, who had served overseas with both the Canadian Army and the British Navy. Smith handicapped himself by using a broom and wearing shoes, since he had played collegiate hockey at the University of Toronto. Dorothy and Ernest, along with Dutch Pailthorp (who was living at the YMCA and often came over on Sundays) rounded out the group. The Connable skates were invariably unsharpened, and there was much falling down. Ernest was more persistent than skillful. "They had snow piled about waist-high on every side," said Smith. "When Ernest would start out for you, all you had to do was sidestep and he couldn't stop—he'd take a header into the snowbank. Then he would get up, take another bearing, and start off again."

He struck all the Connables as a "modest, sensitive, and wonderfully considerate guest." Dorothy had done work with the YMCA in France and Germany after the Armistice. Ernest pleased her by saying that they were both "very young old soldiers." But he was too eager for action to hang around the house. He had not been there a week before he asked Mr. Connable about working on Ontario's leading newspaper, *The Toronto Star,* which published both a daily and a weekly edition. Connable presented him to Arthur Donaldson, chief of advertising layout for both papers, and Donaldson took him on a tour of the shoddy old four-story building at 20 King Street West. The interior smelt pleasantly of dust, disinfectant, tobacco smoke, and printer's ink. Donaldson concluded the tour by introducing Ernest to a pair of young staff members who shared a tiny smoke-filled room on the second floor back.

Their names were Greg Clark and Jimmy Frise. Greg was a bumptious, tweedy little man, five feet tall, who was features editor for the weekly. Jimmy Frise was dark, slender, and sardonic, and served as chief cartoonist. They looked up from their work to see a tall ruddy-faced youth in a red shirt and a black leather jacket. Although he seemed very shy and curiously inarticulate, they were impressed when he sat down on the radiator, unbuttoned his jacket, and said that he had once been a reporter on the Kansas City *Star.* "So I looked at him," said Gregory Clark, "and I thought to myself, 'Hell, this kid worked for them, did he?' It was like saying he'd been on the *Manchester Guardian:* the Kansas City *Star* was the beau ideal of newspaper men all over the continent."

Ernest took to dropping in almost every day. He and Jimmy Frise were soon good friends and went skiing once or twice, initiating Hemingway into a sport in which he would later become an enthusiast. Gregory Clark was at first distrustful. "Look, Jimmy," said he, "don't encourage this kid hanging around. He'll borrow ten bucks off ya and that's the last you'll see of him." But Ernest continued to haunt the place, eager for the newspaper atmosphere, leaning forward on the balls of his feet, swaying slightly, and asking interminable questions. At last Clark capitulated. "For God's sake, Hemingway," he cried one morning, "do you want a job?" When Hemingway said yes, Clark took him in to see "dear old Cranston, who gave him space rates in the weekly bulldog section."

Cranston was a mild-mannered editor, serious and pious, dedicated to the encouragement of young Canadian writers, and anxious to make the *Star Weekly* into a people's paper, filled with human-interest stories and humorous slants on life around Toronto. He soon discovered that "Hemingway could write in good, plain Anglo-Saxon, and had a certain much prized gift of humor." Ernest's first piece, printed in the Valentine's Day issue, was a thousand-word account of a scheme in which socially prominent women of Toronto rented original oil paintings from local artists. Between the middle of February and the middle of May, 1920, he did ten other articles. Cranston liked them well enough to give him a by-line and raise his pay to a penny a word.

He was still trying vainly to market the stories he had written in Petoskey. He sent several along to Edwin Balmer in Evanston, Illinois. Balmer replied helpfully on February 1, saying that one or two of the pieces seemed clearly salable, though not necessarily immediately. "The funny feature of the writing business," said he, "is that you simply can not tell what will go; I've seen things in print that I wouldn't believe anyone could possibly buy; and I've seen things turned down that I couldn't see how anyone could pass up. But those do not remain forever turned down." This observation exactly defined Ernest's problem in breaking into the fiction market. He could always sell feature articles to a friendly newspaper. But his conception of what constituted a salable short story was not in line with prevailing editorial opinion. To a considerable extent he would have to create the taste by which his stories would eventually be judged.

His family took pride in his newspaper work. Dr. Hemingway wrote in praise of his war record and his writing for the *Star*. His Croce di Guerra had just come and been forwarded to Toronto, clear evidence of the esteem in which Italy held him. Ernest's grandmother and mother were both unwell. Adelaide in her seventies was growing feeble, and Grace at forty-eight was suffering from emotional difficulties, which she was trying to overcome with a course in manual training. Dr. Hemingway believed that she might soon get back to normal. But he felt that Ernest ought to make a special point of coming home to Oak Park before he went to spend the summer in Michigan. "You will never regret," said his father, "all the love you can express to your Grand Parents and Parents and brother and sisters."

While the Connables were in Florida, Ernest and Dutch escorted young Ralph to hockey and boxing matches at the Mutual Street Arena Gardens and the pseudo-medieval pile of Massey Hall. Ralph was sickened by the blood at one gory fight between Rocky Kansas and Fern Bull, which Ernest watched with obvious enjoyment. Dutch was not deceived by Ernest's carefully culti-vated toughness in public places. "Inside," thought Dutch, "Hemmy was soft as a meringue pie." His softer side appeared in the course of a few dates with Bonnie Bonnell, a striking six-foot brunette who was related to the wealthy family of Massey, who had endowed Massey Hall. They rode horse-back through the western suburbs and called themselves the Bathurst Street Hunt Club. Ernest borrowed a tailcoat from Ernest Smith and took Bonnie dancing at the Grange, incongruously shod in Indian moccasins.

When the Connables returned in March, he resumed his endless conversa-tions with both Dorothy and her mother. He showed great affection for Har-riet Connable, stopping at her desk for a visit every morning, and offering advice about the secretary's report which she was preparing for the spring meeting of the Women's Patriotic League. He could not understand, he said, why her sentences were so long when his own were so short and terse. When he discovered that Dorothy had not read O. Henry, he went downtown and bought her a copy of *Cabbages and Kings,* which he inscribed "To the Negative from the Affirmative." Another gift book was D'Annunzio's *The Flame* with an inscription absolving her from any responsibility in owning it.

Ernest's escape valve from the genteel Connable household was the news-paper office on King Street West. Most of his fellow workers had now succumbed to his boyish charm. He told endless lies with a straight face, convincing Cranston that he had been a vagabond from the day he left high school, living in hobo jungles and riding the rods from place to place. He said also that he "had eaten all kinds of . . . slugs, earthworms, lizards, all the delicacies that the savage tribes of the world fancy, just to get their taste." They laughed among themselves at his red shirt and black leather jacket, now much worn around the buttonholes; at the trouble he had in pronouncing his *l*'s; at the way his upper lip and chin were always heavily bedewed with perspiration; at his habit of standing poised on the balls of his feet; at the faint habitual weaving of his head from side to side, like a boxer feinting or a king cobra about to strike. He surprised Greg Clark with his skill at fishing when they went after trout in the Credit River. He was also a great fomenter of literary arguments. His opinions were always extreme: a book was either "great stuff" or it was "putrid," without intermediate shading. He had a flair for the invention of ingenious news pegs on which to drape his always lively though often rather sophomoric prose, and he seemed to be skilled in turning almost any subject into a salable human-interest story. John Bone, the tough-minded managing editor of the daily *Star,* was beginning to hint that he might have a future with the paper.

But Ernest was not yet ready to be tied down. When his term with the Connables expired in May, he said that he would have to leave for another summer in Michigan. In parting from Toronto, he earned eleven dollars with a report on Georges Carpentier, the light-heavyweight champion of Europe, who fought a listless exhibition bout with the Belgian Jules Lanaers at the Arena Gardens on May 8th. He earned his train fare back to Oak Park with a piece on Canadian rum-running, gathering his materials on the way through Detroit and Ann Arbor by the simple expedient of talking with his fellow travelers about Scotch whiskey and summarizing what they said.

His stay in Oak Park was again as brief as decency would allow. Bill Smith was coming from St. Louis on his annual jaunt to Horton Bay, and Ernest chafed impatiently all through the last week of May. When Bill clanked in on the 31st, he had burnt out a bearing in his Buick, and the boys did not get away until June 3rd. On the trip north, Ernest was full of his plans for the fall. He and Ted Brumback would ship out of San Francisco bound for Japan, China, and India. Brummy would hire on as an able seaman at seventy "seeds" a week. Ernest was thinking of using his mighty thews as a stoker. It was a better-paid job than that of common sailor. Not only would it provide him with more capital for the exploration of Yokohama, Hong Kong, and Madras, but it would also keep his record clean: since his days on the Kansas City *Star* he had always earned more than Brumback, and he did not intend to fall behind.

His competitive spirit was constantly in evidence. He got on well with the easygoing Bill Smith, who readily accepted his rage for leadership. Except for some rather one-sided boxing bouts, they never had any physical fights.

But once while they were crossing the ridge from the western shore of Walloon to Horton Bay, stumbling through the rough and sandy soil, Ernest sharply accused Bill of holding something in reserve for a sprint finish. A simple hike through the woods had suddenly become in his mind a serious athletic contest. He also felt obliged to demonstrate his imperviousness to pain. Swimming off Wesley Dilworth's dock one day, he pointed to the remnants of a smashed milk bottle. He would walk over the shards of broken glass to show them all how tough the soles of his feet were. "He cut his foot in a couple of places," said Bill, "but he made it." It was the same all over again when he went to Petoskey to play tennis with Irene Goldstein. He always made a special point of winning, and when her aunt and uncle, the Rosenthals, asked him to dinner, he insisted on lugging over an enormous fish which he had bought at the market while managing to leave the impression that he had caught it himself. For all his six-foot stature, his battle scars, his love affair with Agnes, and his mild success at newspaper work, Ernest was still a boy.

Grace's current emotional disorders made her particularly sensitive to Ernest's boyish behavior. It seemed to her that he was refusing to capitalize on his innate abilities, and she was much upset by his failure to cooperate in such domestic problems as plucking chickens and getting out the family boat dock. He had begun to use what his father called "vitriolistic words" and always seemed to be fishing in the Pine Barrens when he was needed at home. He appeared with Ted Brumback and Bill Smith for his twenty-first birthday supper, and afterwards stayed around for a few days, washing the dishes, digging holes for garbage disposal, and painting the outside of the cottage. But he made no attempt to disguise his view that this was the work of a hired man.

I surely will expect you to be a greater comfort to your parents and sisters [wrote his father]. "Try and not be a sponger. . . . It is best for you [and Ted] to change camps and go to new fields to conquer, it is all together too hard on your mother to entertain you and your friends, when she is not having help and you are so hard to please and are so insulting to your dear mother. So please pack up and try elsewhere until you are again invited . . . to Windemere. . . . Try and look this matter right square in the face as an honest boy and be as kind and considerate to your mother and sisters as you are to Madam Charles and Bill Smith.

Shortly after Ernest turned twenty-one, he was involved in a trivial incident which raised his mother's emotions to the boiling point. The Hemingway girls and their neighbors, the Loomises, secretly planned a midnight picnic at Ryan's Point, a sandbar with trees in the West Arm of the lake. Ursula and Sunny, Bob Loomis and Beverly Hugle, took the launch to the foot of the lake that afternoon and laid in a supply of food. Elizabeth Loomis and Jean Reynolds invited Ernest and Ted to make it a party of eight. Both households went to bed at the usual time. At midnight the conspirators sneaked out, took a rowboat and a canoe, and spent a couple of hours around a bonfire at the Point, singing songs to Brummy's mandolin, eating and chattering, taking dips off the sandy shore, and no doubt kissing the girls beyond the edge of the firelight. It was nearly three when they doused the fire and paddled home. From the lake they could see the bobbing light of a lantern on the shore. Grace Hemingway and Mrs. Loomis had found the empty beds, and Ruth Arnold, the housekeeper, had tearfully revealed the secret. Mrs. Loomis blamed Ernest and Ted, who were older than the others. She refused to see Ernest when he volunteered to apologize. All the girls were forbidden dates for the rest of the summer. Ted and Ernest were banished from Windemere.

The crucial postscript to the Ryan's Point picnic was a letter which Grace wrote Ernest next day.

For years [she wrote], since you decided at the age of 18 years that you did not need any further advice or guidance from your parents, I have tried to keep silence and let you work out your own salvation. By that, I mean your own philosophy of life, your code of ethics in dealing with men, women, and children. Now at the age of 21, and being (according to some of your best friends and wellwishers) so sadly in need of good guidance, I shall brave your anger and speak this once more to you.

Here Grace developed at length an elaborate simile about the resemblance between a mother's love and a bank account. When the child is born, the mother deposits great stores of love and patience, on which the child subsequently draws for sustenance. Ernest, she felt, had overdrawn his account many times over.

Unless you, my son Ernest, come to yourself; cease your lazy loafing and pleasure seeking; borrowing with no thought of returning; stop trying to graft a living off anybody and everybody; spending all your earnings lavishly and wastefully on luxuries for yourself; stop trading on your hansome [sic] face to fool little gullable [sic] girls, and neglecting your duties to God and your Savior, Jesus Christ; unless, in other words, you come into your manhood, there is nothing before you but bankruptcy—you have overdrawn. . . . When you have changed your ideas and aims in life, you will find your mother waiting to welcome you, whether it be this world or the next—loving you and longing for your love. The Good Lord watch between me and thee, while we are absent one from the other.

And signed the letter, "Your still hoping and praying mother, Grace Hall Hemingway."

Ernest took it hard. A week later he complained to Grace Quinlan that he was now literally homeless—kicked out permanently for no good reason. Brummy had been thrown out at the same time. Even if a man didn't use his home, it made him feel "kind of rotten" to know that he hadn't any. But he consoled himself by taking a fishing trip to the Black River with Brummy, Jack Pentecost, Howell Jenkins, and Dick Smale. They were gone for six days in a rented car with a trailer. In the evenings, Brummy played his mandolin and Ernest read aloud from the tales of Lord Dunsany. Afterwards, he courted sleep by lying wrapped in his blankets, gazing at the moon, and thinking what he described as "long, long thoughts." There was a superstition that a man would become moonstruck if he slept with moonlight on his face. "Maybe," said Ernest, "that's what ails me." He renewed his dreams of shipping out for the Far East. After all, as he explained to Grace Quinlan, his mother had been glad of the excuse to throw him out. She had "more or less hated" him ever since he had opposed her using up two or three thousand "seeds" to build her studio, Grace Cottage, at Longfield Farm. The "jack" should have been used to send the younger kids to college. All families, he said airily, have skeletons in their closets, but the Hemingsteins have heaps. He did not pause to reflect on the wisdom of making such remarks to a fifteen-year-old girl.

I shall continue to pray for Ernest [wrote his father], that he will develop a sense of greater responsibility, for if he does not the Great Creator will cause him to suffer a whole lot more than he ever has so far. . . . Ernest's last letter to me . . . was written in anger and filled with expressions that were untrue to a gentleman and a son who has had everything done for him. . . . He must get busy and make his own way, and suffering alone will be the means of softening his Iron Heart of selfishness.

But this was written in ignorance of Grace's letter to Ernest. She waited six weeks before sending her husband a copy. When he read it on September 2nd, he told her that it was a masterpiece. He would always prize it as embodying the "Mother's part of the game of Family life." "Keep up your courage, my darling," the doctor wrote. "It is a long session of the family's existence, and we must be brave. There are relatively few storms in our sea of life as compared to many you and I know, if you only stop and count your blessings."

Grace prepared "a nice lunch" for Ernest on her last day in Michigan, but he was staying at a boardinghouse in Boyne City and did not appear. Sailing on Lake Charlevoix with Katy Smith and Carl Edgar, he caught his belly on a boat cleat and complained to his mother of severe internal hemorrhaging. It was not very severe and looked like a bid for sympathy. "I hope your internal injury is giving you no more trouble," his mother wrote. "I could not sleep the night after you told me about it (sympathetic nervous pain). So sorry you should have to suffer so much torture." But the torture was short-lived. The doctor lanced his navel and the difficulty subsided. He earned a little money by helping to plant nine acres of seed clover and picking apples in Mrs. Charles's orchard. One day in the Catholic Church at Charlevoix, he and Katy burnt a votive candle while Ernest prayed, as he said, for all the things he wanted and never expected to get.

His expectations remained indefinite. He spoke no more of romantic voyages to the Far East, and seemed to be weighing the idea of going back to Kansas City to work for the *Star,* perhaps continuing to do feature articles for the other *Star* in Toronto. He told Fever Jenkins that the Kansas City job was crying for a Hemingstein to fill it. They had asked him to name his own price.

It was a lie, of course. But the mere telling of it gave him the confidence he needed in a jobless situation. When his father came up in October to close Windemere Cottage, he went over to call at Horton Bay. Ernest was picking apples in Mrs. Charles's orchard. Bill Smith was laid up with a sprained ankle. As soon as he recovered the boys were planning to drive south. The extravagant summer of 1920 was now in the past. There was little to be gained in trying to extend it. The leaves had fallen and the nights were cold. Bill's brother Kenley had now moved into an apartment at 100 East Chicago Avenue on the Near North Side of Chicago. Ernest could stay there while he looked for a job. By the time Bill's ankle was strong enough to walk on, Ernest was ready, too. He gathered up his equipment and his dog-eared typescripts and rode down with Bill and Katy and Mrs. Charles. He did not know what the future held, but he knew it would hold something.

CHAPTER 3

Emergence

9. HADLEY

ALL that summer of 1920, while Ernest was disporting himself in Michigan, a girl in St. Louis had been attending to her dying mother. Elizabeth Hadley Richardson was twenty-eight, a tall girl with auburn hair. She had lost her father by suicide in 1903, and lived with her mother and her married sister at 5739 Cates Avenue in the western section of the city. The sister, Mrs. Roland Usher, occupied the apartment downstairs with her husband and two small children. In the sickroom upstairs, Hadley was awake much of every night from June to September, "rubbing, pleading, cajoling, and pitying" the slowly sinking patient.

When Florence Richardson died, Hadley was fatigued and distraught. Even her piano playing had fallen away to silence. None of her beaux greatly interested her, and she seemed to herself to be poised on the verge of spinsterhood. She had been graduated in 1910 from Mary Institute, a private school for girls in St. Louis, and afterwards had spent a single year at Bryn Mawr. Since then she had lived at home. She thought of her life as sheltered and uneventful, and of herself as naive and inexperienced. She was both touched and heartened when she heard from Katy Smith, her close friend and classmate from the days at Mary Institute. Katy was going to be living and working in Chicago in the fall. She asked Hadley to come up for a good long visit. She could stay with Kenley and Doodles in their new apartment. Late in October Hadley packed up and took the train to Chicago.

She was almost overcome by the crowd of young men who came surging into Kenley's apartment. Y.K. himself was thirty-one, a tall aquiline man with strong intellectual interests and a dry, sardonic wit. Among his bachelor boarders were Don Wright, Bobby Rouse, and a slim, blue-eyed boy in glasses who came from Yonkers, New York, and worked for a firm called Standard Parts. His name was Bill Horne and he had driven ambulances in Italy during the war. But the most impressive member of Kenley's crew was another veteran of the war in Italy—a "hulky, bulky something masculine" who had just driven down from Horton Bay with Bill and Katy. His name was Ernest Hemingway, but they called him Ernie, Oinbones, Nesto, Hemmy, Hemingstein, Stein, and Wemedge. They all talked a curious lingo, in which food was eatage, death was mortage, and risibility was laughage. Ernest's name had become Weminghay, then Wemage, and at last Wemedge through a kind of pig Latin that they all threw around like crazy Jesuits. Bill and Ernie called each other Bird or Boid, referring to Katy as Stut or Butstein. It was all very confusing. Bill Horne was Horney Bill, Edith Foley was Fedith, and a funny little man whose real name Hadley never caught was indiscriminately addressed as Carper and Little Fever. Dollars were seeds and cigarettes were pills. Hadley contributed a nickname of her own. Her intimates in St. Louis called her Hash.

She stayed for three exciting weeks. Afterwards she summed up her first impression of Ernest as "a pair of very red cheeks and very brown eyes straddling the piano bench while Bill wrote down statistics (all wrong) that Katy and I gave as to population in China." She was a little tongue-tied in his presence, but she thought to herself that he liked her for three reasons: her hair was red, her skirt was a good length, and she played nicely on Doodles's piano. When she went home to St. Louis, they began to exchange letters every week. She wanted him to come down for a visit but he could not afford the train fare. His supply of seeds was as low, he said, as if he had been a navel orange.

He was having trouble getting a job. An Oak Parker named Tubby Williams hired him on a piecework basis to write advertising copy for Firestone Tires, and he collaborated halfheartedly with his high-school classmate, Morrie Musselman, who was trying to write a comedy for the stage. Bill Horne came to his rescue in November by inviting him to share a third-floor room on North State Street. Horne paid the rent and they ate around the corner at a Greek lunchroom called Kitsos, which employed a colored cook and offered steak and potatoes for sixty cents. On Sundays they often went out to Oak Park to stoke up on Dr. Hemingway's homemade chicken pies. Ernest boasted to his friends that he was "grinding out stuff" each day for the Toronto *Star Weekly*. In fact, however, Cranston printed only a handful of his articles between the end of October and the turn of the year.

In December he answered a want ad in the *Chicago Tribune*. An editor named Richard Loper needed a man to write for *The Cooperative Commonwealth*, a slick-paper monthly magazine put out by the Cooperative Society of America. The starting salary was forty dollars a week and Ernest grabbed at the chance. The December number contained twenty pages of advertising and eighty of reading matter, much of it dashed off by Ernest himself. He wrote his mother that he was going to use his first salary check to buy some clothes, both over and under, and that he was trying to follow her instructions by being "very busy, very good, and very tired." Christmas had sneaked up on him, with no time left for shopping. His presents for his sisters would have to be "paper seeds in small denominations." He wished all the family a Merry Christmas, but not a Happy New Year. Any new year, said he, morosely, was just one more lurch nearer the grave.

When Bill Horne went home to Yonkers, Ernest moved in once more with Y.K. Smith, who had now leased a seven-room apartment in an elegant establishment called "The Belleville," with a marble entrance hall and a curving staircase. Y.K.'s wife Doodles had gone to study music in New York and would be there until May. Y.K. had hired a priceless cook named Della and invited Ernest and several others to share his bachelor quarters. Since Ernest was supposed to do much of his editorial planning at home, the arrangement suited him exactly. He got to the office about 9:30 each morning, stayed until noon or one, took his "usual siesta" until 4:30, and returned for an hour or two in the late afternoon. The bad time came at the end of the month when they worked all hours putting the magazine to bed. Ernest caught a sore throat and lolled around the apartment reading Havelock Ellis's *The Dance of Life.*

His letters to Hadley had what she called a "clutched-in-the-hand, stuffed-in-the-pocket look to them," but they were always full of news. He spoke of a strange young man named Krebs Friend who worked beside him at the Cooperative Commonwealth, and of boxing with Y.K. Smith and Nick Neroni on the roof of the apartment. He was photographed in long underwear, a scarlet sash, and a false mustache, pretending to be John L. Sullivan. He took Katy Smith out dancing and went to see Ann Pennington in *George White's Scandals.* He told Hadley about an invitation from Jim Gamble, the Red Cross captain he had known in 1918. Gamble had gone back to Italy and wanted Ernest to come along. He was half inclined to accept. Italian sunshine would be a great improvement over the gray slush of Chicago.

Hadley wrote to say that he was hers, her own. "I can't think of anything unsympathetic in you," she said, "and I do love you very much. And I want to love you more. I mean to find more ways to show a thing so sweet and rare." She was calling him "Dearest Nesto" and had coined the adjective "Ernestoic." He told her rather gloomily that he hoped to go on loving her for "a little while at least." Was this the skittishness of a confirmed bachelor or the philosophic reflection of one who had already loved and lost? She wasn't sure. He had already told her about Agnes von Kurowsky, the girl who had "given him so much" and then had "gone away." Didn't he have the capacity to stand the long strain of things and circumstances? She hoped so. If he didn't, now was the time to speak. Unless it would greatly help his work, she did not want him to follow Jim Gamble to Rome. Perhaps instead he would come to St. Louis to see her. He was "always invited—always hoped for."

On the weekend of March 11th, he went down to see her, wearing a brand-new Brooks Brothers suit. He carried the Italian officer's cape and a scrapbook containing the articles he had done for the Toronto *Star.* Howie Jenkins called him aside before he left and strongly advised him against getting married. But the courtship continued. Two weeks later, Hadley returned the visit, accompanied by her friends Ruth Bradfield and Helen and George Breaker. She arrived in a fit of doubt, mainly about Ernest's marital intentions and the eight-year discrepancy in their ages. But when she saw and touched him again in the front hall of Kenley Smith's domicile, all things became as "sweetly normal" as before. Ruth Bradfield thought Ernest

a beautiful youth. He was slender and moved well. His face had the symmetry of fine bony structure and he had a small elastic mouth that stretched from ear to ear when he laughed. He laughed aloud a lot from quick humor. . . . His focussed attention to the person he was talking with was immensely flattering. . . . He generated excitement because he was so intense about everything, about writing and boxing, about good food and drink. Everything we did took on new importance when he was with us.

The group at the "Domicile" in Division Street were all mad about writing. "They had jobs and pounded typewriters all night and boxed on the roof. They refused to make friends with anybody who lived more than fifty cents away by taxi. Everybody was a little crazy with the joy of being alive." The girls from St. Louis blossomed in this heady atmosphere. Hadley and Ernest went on a double date with Katy Smith and Bill Horne, eating spaghetti and drinking red wine at the Victor House on Grand Avenue. Ernest bubbled over with his usual enthusiastic charm, and Hadley bloomed like a rose in her black satin dress with Bulgarian embroidery. "Allah be praised," she wrote him afterwards, "that we are living at the same time and know each other."

The night before she went home, they had a long talk about her "filthy lucre." She had a small trust fund that could be counted on to bring in two or three thousand a year. With "its aid and abetment" they might be able to "go Woplandwards in November." Twice in the next two months she sent him substantial sums to be invested in Italian lire. Ernest said that he was trying to live on two pennies a day, eating scrappily to save money, and boxing as a sparring partner to make some more. In that tone of mild self-pity which he tended to adopt from time to time, he remarked that he might now be an undergraduate at Princeton if his mother had not used the money to build Grace Cottage. "You don't need a university," said Hadley, admiringly. She was already dreaming of the Italian tour, a visit to San Miniato, perhaps a prayer at Ernest's side in the *duomo* of Milan.

But Sherwood Anderson said that they ought to go to Paris instead. He was a friend of Y.K. Smith's, and lived nearby with his second wife, Tennessee, a teacher of music. He was a confirmed romantic with warm brown eyes, ruffled hair, and a love of conversation. At forty-five he was already famous as the author of *Winesburg, Ohio* and *Poor White*. He dropped in often at the Domicile, telling endless stories about his rebellion from the straitlaced

1. Clarence E. Hemingway on vacation in the Great Smoky Mountains, N.C., 1891.

2. Grace Hall on vacation at Lake Geneva, Wis., shortly before her marriage.

3. Grace with Ernest, aged 7 weeks, Bear (later Walloon) Lake, Sept. 6, 1899.

4. Ernest's birthplace, 439 N. Oak Park Ave., Oak Park, Ill.

5. Ernest's grandfather Ernest Hall

6. Anson and Adelaide Hemingway with 5 of their 6 children: Nettie, Alfred, Clarence, George, Grace.

7. Ursula, Ernest, and Marcelline with parents, Oct., 1903.

8. Ernest trout fishing at age 5, Horton Creek, July, 1904.

9. Dr. Hemingway's new house, 600 N. Kenilworth Ave., Oak Park, 1906.

10. Ernest feeding a stuffed squirrel, Feb., 1910.

11. Ernest and Grace off for Nantucket, Aug. 29, 1910.

12. Grace with her six offspring: Leicester, Carol, Sunny, Ursula, Ernest, Marcelline, Windemere Cottage, 1916.

13. LEFT. Ernest as a 17-year-old, Walloon Lake, summer, 1916.

14. Lightweight football player (at center), Oak Park High, Nov., 191

15. TOP. Woolen-mill barracks, nicknamed the Schio Country Club, June, 1918.

16 CENTER. Section 4 Fiat and Ford ambulances, Schio, June, 1918.

17. BELOW. Italian Lancers on the road to Fossalta, Basso Piave, June, 1918.

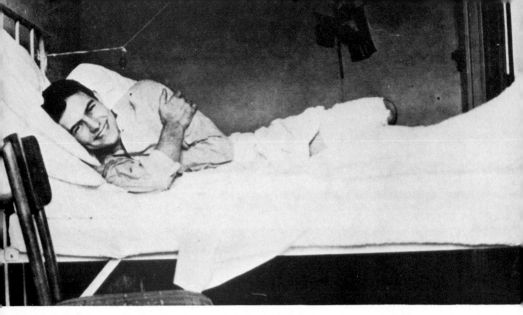

18. The youngest patient in the Red Cross Hospital, Via Manzoni, Milan, late July, 1918.

19. On the mend in September.

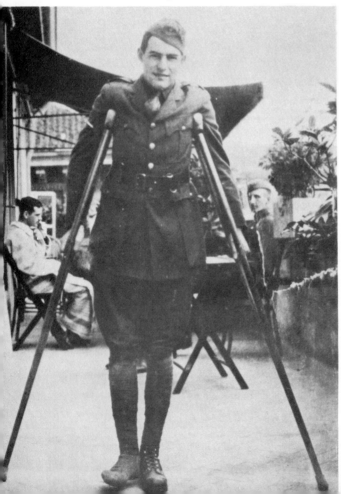

20. Agnes von Kurowsky, Aug., 1918.

21. Back home in Oak Park, April, 1919.

22. Ernest mimicking John L. Sullivan, Y. K. Smith's apartment, Chicago, ca. Jan., 1921.

23. Larry Barnett, Ernest, and Jack Pentecost, Oak Park, April, 1919.

24. Hadley Richardson, 1918.

25. Ernest in his Spagnolini uniform, 1918.

26. The wedding day: Ursula, Hadley, Ernest, Grace, and Leicester, Horton Bay, Sept. 3, 1921.

small-town society of Ohio. He took Ernest out to see his little suburban house in Palos Park. In May, he said, he and Tennessee were going to Paris with a friend named Paul Rosenfeld, who was paying all the bills. They would live among the famous expatriates on the Left Bank. Sherwood could hardly wait to get away from the oppressions of midland America.

One Saturday night after his departure, Ernest went with Katy, Y.K., and Krebs Friend on a tour of German family resorts, where dinners cost fifty cents and beer came to forty cents a stein. Y.K. watched with bemusement the slow dissipation of Krebs's frozen loneliness under the combined effects of beer and wiener schnitzel. Krebs, too, it appeared, wanted to go to Paris. That was where they really knew how to live. He even contrived to look like a Frenchman when he clapped a tall hat on his head and stood up to lead the German band at Wurz 'n' Zepp's, a renowned beer hall on North Avenue.

The fact of the wedding, if not the date, was already settled when Ernest and Bill Horne went to St. Louis for the Memorial Day weekend. Hadley had recently received "a peach of a letter" from Grace Hall Hemingway, offering them Windemere Cottage for their honeymoon. Bill Horne immediately took to Ruth Bradfield, whom he christened B.L.G.—for Beautiful Little Girl—and the two couples went for a Sunday canoe trip on the Meramec, stopping for a picnic and a long talk on the riverbank. Hadley was impressed by the way Ernest made cigarette smoke pour from his nostrils, as well as by his skills in "boxing, fishing, writing, . . . leaving folks fall in fits of admiration around about you, intriguing Kenley, teaching Horney you can't expect 'em to be attractive and good simultaneous, getting war medals, playing bridge, swirling about in the black cape . . . swimming, paddling, tennis, charm, good looks, knowledge of clothes, love of women, domesticity." She took a girlish pleasure in showing Ernest off at George and Helen Breaker's Memorial Day party. For her he meant the end of a long period of monotony. "The world's a jail," she said, "and we're going to break it together."

Ernest knew that marriage would destroy the kind of life he had been leading. During the spring, he "damned near went cuckoo" dreaming of camping trips to the Sturgeon and the Black. All his life, he wrote Bill Smith, a man loved two or three streams better than anything else in the world. Then he fell in love with a girl and the "goddam streams [could] dry up" for all he cared. Except, of course, that he continued to long for the Michigan wilderness. With the arrival of warm weather, he took to sleeping on the apartment roof, laboriously carrying up several loads of clean gravel to serve as a foundation for his blankets.

Ernest and Bill Horne went along when Y. K. Smith returned to his former apartment at 100 East Chicago Avenue. There was a large four-poster bed in one of the rooms and Ernest told Hadley that it might be assigned to them when they returned from their honeymoon. "I think our little room at 100 will be terribly adorable," said Hadley. In one momentary mood she told Ernest that she sometimes wondered whether she wouldn't perhaps prefer to have him for her papa. But when her friend Georgia Riddle asked if she didn't think the time of being engaged was better than the time of marriage, Hadley said no. "Seems to me everything lovely and wonderful is to come," she wrote Ernest. "Sort of like the difference between studying the sun through astronomical methods and simply and joyously living in a country saturated with sunlight."

Grace Hemingway had to prod Hadley to set the wedding date and buy a dress. Ernest came down with an attack of low spirits. "What's this?" asked Hadley. "Not truly so low as to crave mortage, are you?" The mood had disappeared when she came to Chicago for the weekend of July 12. She praised the way he walked, "so big, and paddy, and rhythmic," and gave him a Corona typewriter for his twenty-second birthday in the mistaken belief that he was twenty-three. Ernest tapped out something that he said was a poem: "Desire, and all the sweet pulsing aches and gentle hurtings that were you . . ." He was working on some other verses which he thought of submitting to the *Dial* or Harriet Monroe's *Poetry*. He had also done a satirical story called "A Divine Gesture." Hadley read it straight through, breathless and eager. It seemed to her of far greater importance than the fact that the wedding-invitation list had reached four hundred and fifty.

The time and place of the wedding had now been fixed for September 3rd in the country church at Horton Bay. Hadley was going to spend August in a cabin near State Line, Wisconsin, reaching Horton Bay three days before the ceremony. On the way north she stopped over in Chicago to spend a week with Ernest. She said afterwards that she was "selfishly, deliciously engulfed" in his companionship. On the scorching Friday when she had to entrain for Wisconsin, they spent most of the afternoon in the dark, cool back room at Wurz 'n' Zepp's. "We did love each other so," she wrote him next day. But she had been in such a dither that she had left her umbrella at Y. K. Smith's, her jewelry in the safe at the Virginia Hotel, and one of the bridesmaid's hats in Helen Breaker's stateroom on the train.

A few points remained to be settled. The organist at Horton Bay knew only one piece, "Throw Out the Lifeline." Hadley asked Ernest to find a more talented musician and a minister in Petoskey. Ernest sent Grace Quinlan a desperate note. "Pick me a prelate," said he. The only provisos were that he must not wear a celluloid collar or chew tobacco. Hadley's sister was going to be matron of honor. Her other attendants would be Helen Breaker, Ruth Bradfield, and Katy Smith. Bill Smith was best man. Jenkins, Bill Horne, Carl Edgar, Jack Pentecost, and Art Meyer were the ushers. The girls would stay with Mrs. Charles and the boys with the Dilworths. "In two weeks from today," wrote Hadley, "we'll be playing together at Walloon Lake with a day and a night behind us and many days and nights ahead of us to love each other in."

Ernest reached Horton Bay the Sunday before his wedding, pale and hollow-eyed from lack of sleep. Next day he set off for the Sturgeon River with

Howie Jenkins and Charlie Hopkins to use up the last three days of the fishing season in a final bachelor's splurge. The day he returned, Hadley arrived from Wisconsin with the Breakers and Ruth Bradfield. Ruth and Katy decorated the church altar with bittersweet, swamp lilies, and clumps of pollinating goldenrod. Windemere Cottage was ready for the honeymooners with a new porch roof and freshly varnished floors.

The day of the wedding was clear and warm. Dutch Pailthorp and Luman Ramsdell drove over from Petoskey in Luman's Whippet, and went into Ernest's room at Dilworth's while he dressed. He had been swimming and was washing the dirt off his feet after the walk up the hill. Later he would type off a page about the scene, telling how "the room was hot and Dutch and Luman were both standing around looking nervous." He got out "a clean suit of underwear, clean silk socks, new garters, [and] a white shirt and collar, and put them on." He tied his striped tie before the mirror. "Dutch and Luman reminded him of dressing rooms before fights and football games. He enjoyed their nervousness. He wondered if it would be this way if he were going to be hanged. Probably. He could never realize anything until it happened."

Hadley was a little late in reaching the church because she had also been swimming and her thick hair did not dry easily. Harriet Connable and her son Ralph came over from Walloon and sat in one of the pews at the back. Dr. Hemingway was perspiring in a gray suit and vest with a starched wing collar. Grace looked motherly and overheated in a long flowered dress with a tasseled cord at the waist. Carol kept turning around to see if Hadley had come yet and Ursula had to whisper to her to face the front. The seven-year-old Leicester was restive and miserable. Then Hadley came down the aisle on George Breaker's arm. She wore a wreath around her slightly damp auburn hair. A veil hung down her back and she carried a bouquet of baby's breath. The organist from Petoskey roared out the usual wedding march. Ernest had trouble kneeling because of his wounded legs. The minister read the service and Hadley marched out with Ernest into the warm September evening. For an hour they posed for group pictures outside Pinehurst Cottage. Then Liz Dilworth called them in for one of her famous chicken dinners.

Night had fallen when Ernest and Hadley threw their bags into the back of John Kotesky's Ford and made their getaway. John drove them over the ridge to Longfield Farm and from there they rowed across the lake to Windemere. The honeymoon lasted two weeks. They both came down with bad colds and made a brew of mulled wine to cure their hacking coughs. Hadley was enraged when Ernest took her to Petoskey to meet some of his former girls, including Marjorie Bump, the hardware dealer's daughter. He explained rather lamely that he had supposed she would think more highly of him when she saw the girls he had rejected in her favor.

During the summer, Y.K.'s wife Doodles had spilled her private thoughts to Ernest, who had maliciously blabbed them to Don Wright. Y.K. was so angry at this perfidious gossip that he withdrew his offer to let Ernest and

Hadley live in the room with the four-poster bed. They took instead a small, top-floor apartment in the 1300 block of North Clark Street. It was grubby and depressing. Grace came to see Hadley for a little talk about the value of sentiment. She and the doctor had been married for twenty-five years. They were celebrating with a reception on the first of October and wanted Hadley and Ernest to be guests of honor. On hearing that his mother had also invited Kenley and Doodles, Ernest sent Kenley a note, flatly rescinding his mother's invitation and adding that he would soon drop in at the Domicile to collect his clothes and his "probably well-thumbed correspondence." Y.K. answered immediately, listing the items Ernest had left in storage and closing out the friendship. It was not the last time in Ernest's life that he would pick a quarrel with an erstwhile benefactor.

He and Hadley were now living exclusively on the income from her trust fund. He had given up his job with the *Cooperative Commonwealth* in the face of persistent rumors that the parent organization was crooked and would soon collapse into bankruptcy. He kept his hand in with the *Toronto Star* by submitting occasional articles to Cranston. One was a satire on wedding gifts, which appeared with a special cartoon by Jimmy Frise:

> Three traveling clocks
> Tick
> On the mantelpiece
> Comma
> But the young man is starving.

The reference to starvation was a typical overstatement, though they were living as simply as possible in order to save up for the long-anticipated trip to Europe. They went round to dinner with Sherwood and Tennessee Anderson, who had recently returned from Paris. Sherwood said that it was all very well to talk about fishing and playing tennis in Italy, but Paris was the place for a serious writer. The rate of exchange made living cheap and the Left Bank abounded with important people. Until they found an apartment, they could stay where the Andersons had stayed, the little Hôtel Jacob et d'Angleterre at 44 rue Jacob, right in the middle of everything. Ernest could doubtless earn enough to live on by sending back a series of European letters to John Bone at the *Toronto Star*.

By the Monday after Thanksgiving, it was all arranged. They booked passage on the *Leopoldina,* a cumbersome old ship belonging to the French Line. Sherwood volunteered to write letters of introduction to some of the famous expatriates he had met in Paris. One was Gertrude Stein, who lived with a companion named Alice B. Toklas in the rue de Fleurus. She collected Picasso and other modern painters, looked like an *Erdmutter,* and talked like an angel. Another was Sylvia Beach, a little sharp-eyed woman from Princeton, New Jersey. Sylvia ran a bookshop called Shakespeare and Company in the rue de l'Odéon, and knew everybody worth knowing, including the incomparable

Irishman, James Joyce. Ernest would certainly like Lewis Galantière, who worked for the International Chamber of Commerce and occupied a handsome flat in the rue Jean Goujon. He spoke French like a native and was helping Madame Marguerite Gay with the translation of Anderson's books. Finally there was Ezra Pound, a tall poet from Idaho who had lived in England before the war and was now a power in the literary worlds of London, Paris, and New York.

Anderson's letter to Galantière called Ernest a "quite wonderful newspaper man" whose "extraordinary talent" would take him far beyond journalism. The other letters were all alike: Mr. Hemingway was "a writer instinctively in touch with everything worthwhile" in the United States; he and his wife were "delightful people to know." Anderson was a generous spirit, much given to superlatives. He did not say that the young man he was recommending was only twenty-two, unpublished and unknown. Just before they got aboard the train for New York, Ernest tried to reciprocate by carrying over all the unused canned goods from the apartment in North Clark Street. "That was a nice idea," thought Anderson, "bringing thus to a fellow-scribbler the food he had to abandon." For a long time he would remember the picture Ernest made when he brought the loaded haversack—"a magnificent broad-shouldered man" climbing the dark stairs and shouting as he came.

10. ONE TRUE SENTENCE

NOTHING could exceed Ernest's exuberance as he set forth on his second voyage to Europe. He danced and sang, shadow-boxed and shouted. Even seasickness did not keep him down for long. There was a French girl with a squalling infant traveling steerage. She had been deserted by her American husband, a veteran of the A.E.F., and her money had dwindled to ten francs. Ernest arranged a three-round exhibition boxing match as a benefit for the girl. His opponent was Henry Cuddy, an Italian fighter from Salt Lake City. They pushed back the tables in the dining salon and Hadley acted as her husband's second. Ernest outweighed his opponent and brought him to the verge of a knockout in the final minute. Or so he boasted afterwards, adding that Cuddy had urged him to fight professionally in Paris.

The jubilation continued when the *Leopoldina* made a four-hour stop at Vigo in the third week of December. It was his second glimpse of Spain. The *Giuseppe Verdi* had touched briefly at Algeciras on the homeward voyage in 1919. The harbor at Vigo reminded him of Little Traverse Bay in Michigan, though the town was far more exotic than Petoskey. Small boats with lateen sails skimmed before the wind. The waters teemed with mackerel, sea bass, and six-foot tuna which leaped clear of the water and fell again with a noise like horses jumping off a dock. The brown mountains along the coast looked to his eyes like tired old dinosaurs. He and Hadley walked up the cobblestoned street to the fish market. Some of the tuna lay gutted on the marble slabs. Anyone strong enough to boat one of these, thought Ernest, ought to be able to "enter unabashed into the presence of the very elder gods."

This Kiplingesque mood prevailed when they arrived in Paris. The city was cold, damp, crowded, jolly, and beautiful. As Anderson had promised, the Hôtel Jacob was clean and cheap, and they ate at the Pré aux Clercs in the rue Bonaparte. Dinner for two came to only twelve francs and good Pinard wine cost sixty centimes a bottle. There was a note from Anderson's friend Lewis Galantière, who asked them to dinner at the Restaurant Michaud. Lewis was a small, dynamic man of twenty-six, an excellent mimic. Hadley almost dissolved with laughter. Afterwards Ernest proposed a little friendly sparring in his room at the Hôtel Jacob. Lewis agreed reluctantly. He had boxed before, but Ernest was twice his size. They put on the gloves and squared off. Ernest bored in with a flurry of blows. After one round Lewis had had enough. He pulled off his gloves and put on his rimless glasses. But Ernest was still bobbing and weaving. His left hand darted out and broke Lewis's glasses. He mumbled an apology and helped pick up the pieces. Even his bully's behavior could not destroy his personal charm.

After the holidays, Lewis helped them find a place to live. It was a fourth-floor apartment at 74, rue du Cardinal Lemoine, a plebeian street that wound up from the Seine near Pont Sully and ended in a cobblestoned square called the Place de la Contrescarpe. Beside the front entrance at 74 was an angular building which housed a workmen's dance hall, or Bal Musette. Around the corner was the Café des Amateurs, "the cesspool of the rue Mouffetard," as Ernest called it, crowded with drunks and thick with smells. The stairway to the Hemingways' flat was dark and narrow, with a toilet niche on each landing. Their living-bedroom was nearly filled with a heavily gilded mahogany bed. Hadley rather liked the black mantelpiece over the fireplace. But the chairs and table in the dining room struck her as hideous, while the bathroom was a bowl and a pitcher inside a small closet and the kitchen was medieval. When they moved in on January 9, 1922, Ernest wrote his friends that they were living in "the best part of the Latin Quarter."

For the first time since the winter in Petoskey, he was free to write as he chose. He was determined to begin afresh with brand-new standards of truth and simplicity. "All you have to do is write one true sentence," he told himself. "Write the truest sentence that you know." It must be above all a "true simple declarative sentence" without scrollwork or ornamental language of any sort. It must deal with something he knew from personal experience. Stories like "The Passing of Pickles McCarty" or "Wolves and Doughnuts" had been largely invented. They grazed his own experience in Italy and Illinois without keeping the central facts in focus. Now he wanted to place his faith in the direct transcription of what he saw. That and no more. Somehow the emotion that he wanted to convey would filter through the reported facts.

They were hardly settled on the Montagne Sainte Geneviève when they

left for a two-week holiday in a pension at Chamby in the mountains above
Montreux. The family who owned it were German Swiss named Gangwisch.
The place and the people reminded Ernest of the Dilworths' at Horton Bay.
Room and board cost less than five dollars a day. They both liked the Swiss
cleanliness and comfort, with books and good food and a window open at
night on the bright, near-looking stars. Ernest called it an ideal blend of wilderness and civilization. He saw deer tracks beside a sweep of dark forest. The
valleys looked as wild as any he had seen at home. Then, just around a bend
in the road, one came suddenly on four large hotels, filled with ruddy English
families on holiday, pale men with tuberculosis, and slick-haired young men
who lived off the wealthy old widows.

The only flaw was the absence of his male cronies. He longed to introduce
Bill Smith, Howie Jenkins, and Jack Pentecost to the arts of skiing and bobsledding. He wrote to urge Chink Dorman-Smith, his Irish soldier friend of
the days in Milan, to come and join them among the Alps. But Chink answered
that he was working nine hours a day for trifling pay as Adjutant to the Fifth
Northumberland Fusiliers in the barracks at Carlow, Ireland. He had had
only five nights' leave since 1920 and could not get away. Ernest swallowed
his disappointment. With "the men" along, said he, Switzerland would be the
greatest show on earth.

When they got back to Paris, the December rains were gone and the weather
was clear and cold. After the vast reaches of Switzerland, the apartment
seemed small and crowded. Ernest rented a bedroom nearby on the top floor
of the tall old hotel where Paul Verlaine had died exactly twenty-five years
before. Here he could be quiet and alone, taking contemplative turns around
his chilly citadel, keeping warm with the bundles of twigs he bought in the
streets, and gazing out between sentences on all the roofs and chimney pots of
Paris. Sometimes in the afternoons he went to walk the graveled paths of the
Luxembourg, stopping in at the Musée for a look at the Cézannes and the
Monets, thinking inside himself that they had done with paint and canvas what
he had been striving to do with words all morning in his room at the old hotel.

He left Hadley much alone while he sat for hours poring over the small,
recalcitrant sentences and slowly developing paragraphs. Now and then he
spoke bravely of the novel he had begun the previous winter in Chicago. But
his chief interest centered in short, impressionistic pieces, where every word
must count both for itself and for its effect on all the others. It was hard going.
His blue notebooks were filled with false starts, deletions, and interlinear afterthoughts. His goals were concentration and clarity. As in Chicago, but more
fiercely now, he deplored all pretentiousness. "Artist, art, artistic!" he had
cried to his friends at Y. K. Smith's. "Can't we ever hear the last of that stuff?"
He had nothing but scorn for the loafing expatriates who crowded the Dôme
and the Rotonde, warming their hands at the charcoal braziers. The real
artists of Paris seldom went to such places. For all his eccentricity, said
Ernest, Baudelaire had rejected the notion that good poetry could be written

in cafés. When he carved and sweated out *Les Fleurs du Mal,* he must have worked alone.

Ernest was shy and slow about seeking out the famous Americans to whom Anderson had written in his behalf. He was still inwardly rebellious when he took Hadley to tea at Ezra Pound's gloomy studio in the rue Notre Dame des Champs. Hadley thought that even "low-voiced words seemed a little presumptuous" in such a setting. Dorothy Pound served tea, a pretty woman with the studied reserve of a British matron. Ezra drank cup after cup, slouching in his chair, talking pontifically, running his fingers through his sandy hair. Ernest sat at his feet, listening and saying little. His true opinion came out some days later when he handed Lewis Galantière a satire which attacked Pound's pretentious Bohemianism, his wild hair, his unclipped goatee, his open Byronic collar. Lewis asked him what he proposed to do with it. Ernest said that he had just been talking with Margaret Anderson and Jane Heap, the editors of *The Little Review.* They had said they were eager to print something he had written. Lewis patiently explained that this would never do. They would have to reject so outrageous an attack on a man who had served for years, undoubtedly without pay, as their foreign editor. Ernest wisely tore up his little satire.

He did not regret it. Pound presently told him that he liked some of his poetry, and surprised him by saying that he would like to learn boxing. He was not a boxer by nature and was usually winded before Ernest had even worked up a sweat. Still, thought Ernest, it was sporting of him to risk his dignity by allowing large gloves to be stuck into his face. He pleased Ernest further by taking six of his poems to send to Scofield Thayer at the *Dial,* and tentatively accepting a story for *The Little Review.* Although Miss Anderson rejected the story and Thayer the poems, Ernest was convinced of Pound's editorial wisdom. He reported his discovery to Lewis Galantière. Ezra was a great guy and a wonderful editor. "He's teaching me to write," stuttered Ernest, enthusiastically, "and I'm teaching him to box."

It was March before he summoned up courage to call on Gertrude Stein. He walked with Hadley through the Luxembourg Gardens, found 27 rue de Fleurus, and was admitted to a handsome apartment so filled with paintings that it might have been a museum. "There was a big fireplace," he wrote in retrospect, "and it was warm and comfortable and they gave you good things to eat and tea and natural distilled liqueurs made from purple plums, yellow plums, or wild raspberries." Gertrude at forty-eight was old enough to be his mother. She reminded him of a peasant woman from the region near Milan— short, solidly built, with beautiful dark eyes and thick immigrant hair. The tiny Alice Toklas, whom Ernest for months kept calling Miss Tocraz, was also dark, with a hooked nose, a Joan of Arc haircut, and a lapful of needlepoint, on which she worked steadily while the talk flowed around her.

Gertrude thought Ernest very handsome and "rather foreign-looking." The expression in his eyes indicated that he was "passionately interested" in what she was saying. Presently she and Alice went to call on the Hemingways in the rue du Cardinal Lemoine. Gertrude hoisted herself up the steep and narrow stairs and took up her station on the gilded mahogany bed. Ernest brought out some poems and the fragment of his novel. She rather liked the poems, which were "direct and Kiplingesque," but she did not care for the novel. "There is a great deal of description in this," she said, "and not particularly good description. Begin over again and concentrate." Ernest pricked up his ears. This was exactly the position he had independently arrived at during his repeated attempts to write one true sentence in his private office atop the old hotel. He took his courage in his hands and showed her "Up in Michigan," one of the stories he had written since coming to Paris. Gertrude read it quickly. She did not much care for Jim Gilmore's seduction of Liz Coates on the dock at Horton Bay. "It's good," she said. "That's not the question at all. But it is *inaccrochable*. That means it is like a picture that a painter paints and then he cannot hang it."

He was amused by Gertrude's literary prejudices. She seemed to ignore Sherwood Anderson's writing, but was full of praise for his "great, beautiful, warm, Italian eyes." She could not forgive James Joyce for having written *Ulysses,* a work as *inaccrochable* as "Up in Michigan." If you brought up Joyce's name more than once in her presence, said Ernest, "you would not be invited back." He himself thought *Ulysses* a "most god-damn wonderful book," though he could not credit the popular report that the Joyce family was starving. "The whole celtic crew of them" dined every night at Michaud's, where Ernest and Hadley could afford to eat no more than once a week. Joyce's lady-publisher, Sylvia Beach, ran the lending library and bookstore called Shakespeare and Company at 12, rue de l'Odéon. Like Gertrude's apartment, it was warm and cheerful. The shelves were crammed with books and the walls were crowded with photographs of the famous, both dead and alive. Sylvia herself had a sharply sculptured face, brown eyes "as gay as a young girl's," and brown hair which she wore "brushed back from her fine forehead." She was usually dressed in a brown velvet jacket. "She had pretty legs," thought Ernest, "and she was kind, cheerful, and interested, and loved to make jokes and gossip." He would often say later what he had first felt in that spring of 1922: "No one that I ever knew was nicer to me."

Along with his new literary friends, Ernest was enlarging his acquaintance among the foreign correspondents of Paris. He attended the weekly meetings of the Anglo-American Press Club and soon struck up a gay friendship with Guy Hickok of the *Brooklyn Daily Eagle.* Guy was a genial and seasoned reporter and an enthusiastic gourmet. He wore a handsome black mustache and shared Ernest's interest in boxing, horse racing, human interest stories, and tall tales. Ernest never crossed the Seine without dropping in at the sign of the *Eagle* in the Boulevard de la Madeleine. Laughter was always skyrocketing through the smoke-filled rooms. Hadley took at once to Guy's wife Mary, and Ernest fell in love with Guy's mother, Clara, an indefatigable little woman who paid regular visits to the prisons of Paris, carrying small gifts for the prisoners.

Ernest had been slow in beginning work for the *Toronto Star*. The first of his mailed pieces reached Bone's desk on February 2, almost two months after his departure from New York. After that, however, his articles began to appear at the rate of two a week. The subjects were various: Swiss tourism, the depreciation of the German mark, tuna fishing at Vigo, the election of Pope Pius XI, and the place of Tiger Clemenceau in the political life of France. There was even a book review, the first he had ever tried, of a novel about Africa by René Maran, who had won a Goncourt Prize for his harsh indictment of French imperialism. Bone was almost invariably pleased with what Ernest sent —some thirty articles up to the end of March. "My impression," Bone wrote, "is that we have used or will use most of them. Personally I find them exceedingly interesting." In April he asked Ernest to cover the Conferenza Internazionale Economica di Genova, where statesmen from thirty-four nations were going to convene in the great hall of the Palazzo San Giorgio.

As Ernest made new friends, he shed some older ones. The quarrel with Kenley Smith which had embittered the last days in Chicago led to an estrangement between his brother Bill and Ernest, the closest of cronies since 1916. Ernest sent Bill an insulting letter about Y.K. but Bill sided with Kenley on the grounds that blood is thicker than water. He did not care, he said, for the 1922 edition of Ernest Miller Hemingway. It was as different from what he had been as vinegar was from champagne, and he could only hope that time would reverse the trend. Ernest concluded that Mrs. Charles had been poisoning Bill's mind against him. He composed and sent an ugly poem which threw all the blame where it did not belong:

> "Blood is thicker than water,"
> The young man said
> As he knifed his friend
> For a drooling old bitch
> And a house full of lies.

After he had sent it off he began to worry about $800 in drafts of Italian lire that he had left with Katy to be kept in her safety-deposit box and forwarded at his request. She had not written to him all winter. He was going to Genoa for the *Star* and would need the money to pay his train fare. He asked Jenkins to intercede.

The southbound train was filled with foreign correspondents. Ernest teamed up with George Slocombe, a red-bearded man in a wide black hat who worked for the London *Daily Herald,* and a slender ascetic-looking American named Bill Bird, who ran the Continental branch of the Consolidated Press from an office in the rue d'Antin. Like Hickok, Bird was a college graduate, with a bachelor's degree from Trinity College in Hartford, Connecticut. His humor was dry, his wits were sharp, and he had a rather handsome, hollow-cheeked Renaissance face. Bird soon saw the color of Hemingway's blood. They had just reached Genoa and signed into the hotel when a hot-water heater exploded while Ernest was taking a bath, wounding his chest and arms with bits of flying metal. The cuts were superficial but the effect was gory. The bath towels, said Bill, looked like those in the loser's locker room after a championship fight.

When the conference opened on April 9th, the streets of Genoa resembled an armed camp. The seating of the eighty-member Soviet delegation under Georgi Chicherin had touched off demonstrations among the North Italian Communists. They clashed frequently in back streets with ardent young Fascists who were intent on protecting their country from the Red menace. Neither group greatly impressed Ernest, though he sensed at once the implicit threat from the "brood of dragon's teeth" which had sprung up in 1920 to crush an incipient Bolshevik uprising in Italy. His account of the famous statesmen was heavy with youthful cynicism; Chicherin, with his ragged beard, looked like a country storekeeper; Maxim Litvinov had a face like a ham; the German chancellor, Dr. Karl Joseph Wirth, resembled a tuba player in a beer-hall band. To Ernest's mind the most distinctive man at the conference was Alexander Stambouliski of Bulgaria, a sturdy character whose weatherbeaten red face stood out from all the rest "like a ripe blackberry in a bunch of daisies." But Ernest stayed away from the Palazzo whenever possible. One day he went with Slocombe, Bird, and George Seldes to inspect the unutterable slums of Genoa, the chief spawning ground, according to Slocombe, of the whole Communist movement in northern Italy.

Ernest got on well with Max Eastman, who looked "like a big, jolly, middle-western college professor" but was in fact an editor of a Communist journal called *The Masses*. Eastman thought Ernest "a modest and princely mannered boy," who pleased him with his frank confession that "he had been scared to death in the war." He agreed to read through a sheaf of Ernest's experimental sketches, which he liked well enough to send along to Claude McKay and Mike Gold for possible publication. Lincoln Steffens, the wrinkled old muckraker, asked Ernest to join a group which met frequently at a small *trattoria* around a two-gallon flask of Chianti. The group included George Seldes, Sam Spewack, and the bearded sculptor Jo Davidson, who had come to make some portrait heads of the leading foreign statesmen. Ernest described in detail his wounding at Fossalta and his recuperation in Milan, and taught them all to sing the rousing song about General Cadorna's letter to the Queen. In the closing days of the conference he drove out to Rapallo with Eastman and Slocombe. They paid a call on Max Beerbohm, the English caricaturist, who handed round small glasses of Marsala and discussed the revolt of creative artists against the evils of commercial journalism.

It was a topic of great interest to Ernest. He had sent the *Star* no fewer than fifteen articles on the Genoa Conference, and accordingly felt justified in returning once more to his experimental work in prose and poetry. He was encouraged in May when *The Double Dealer* of New Orleans published his fable, "A Divine Gesture," along with a program note which said that he was now living in Paris, enjoying the favor of Ezra Pound, and that he would shortly bring out a book of verse. It was true that he had some poems, though not enough for a book. He gathered up half a dozen and sent them off to Harriet Monroe in Chicago, asking her to consider them for *Poetry: A Magazine of Verse.* One of them compared his typewriter to a machine gun:

> The mills of the gods grind slowly;
> But this mill
> Chatters in mechanical staccato,
> Ugly short infantry of the mind,
> Advancing over difficult terrain,
> Make this Corona
> Their mitrailleuse.

Another looked back to his boyhood in Michigan:

> A porcupine skin,
> Stiff with bad tanning,
> It must have ended somewhere.
> Stuffed horned owl
> Pompous
> Yellow-eyed;
> Chuck-wills-widow on a biased twig
> Sooted with dust.
> Piles of old magazines,
> Drawers of boys' letters
> And the line of love
> They must have ended somewhere.
> Yesterday's *Tribune* is gone
> Along with youth
> And the canoe that went to pieces on the beach
> The year of the big storm
> When the hotel burned down
> At Seney, Michigan.

These were true sentences cast loosely in the forms of verse. But Ernest's true forte was displayed in a series of carefully pruned statements which he worked out in his blue notebooks and then copied down in longhand on three telegraph blanks. He headed them *Paris 1922* as if they had been despatches to the *Star*. But they were not journalism. They were the most concentrated distillation that he could make of what he had seen in Paris during five months' residence in the Latin Quarter.

I have seen the favourite crash into the Bulfinch and come down in a heap kicking, while the rest of the field swooped over the jump . . . and the crowd raced across the pelouze to see the horses come into the stretch. . . . I have seen Peggy Joyce at 2 A.M. in a Dancing in the Rue Camartin quarreling with the shellac haired young Chilean who had manicured finger nails, blew a puff of cigarette smoke into her face, wrote something in a notebook, and shot himself at 3:30 the same morning. . . . I have watched the police charge the crowd with swords as they milled back into Paris through the Porte Maillot on the first of May and seen the frightened proud look on the white beaten-up face of the sixteen year old kid who looked like a prep school quarter back and had just shot two policemen. . . . I have stood on the crowded back platform of a seven o'clock Batignolles bus as it lurched along the wet lamp lit street while men who were going home to supper never looked up from their newspapers as we passed Notre Dame grey and dripping in the rain. . . . I have seen the one legged street walker who works the Boulevard Madelaine between the Rue Cambon and Bernheim Jeune's limping along the pavement through the crowd on a rainy night with a beefy red-faced Episcopal clergyman holding an umbrella over her. . . . I have watched two Senegalese soldiers in the dim light of the snake house of the Jardin des Plantes teasing the King Cobra who swayed and tightened in tense erect rage as one of the little brown men crouched and feinted at him with his red fez.

He had set out in January to write one true sentence. By the end of May he had managed to write six—declarative, straightforward, and forceful as a right to the jaw. After all the false starts in Petoskey and Chicago, he was on his way at last.

11. GOING BACK

Despite his talk of Italy while he was courting Hadley, Ernest had still not taken her back to the scenes of his former triumphs. During the spring they had temporarily assuaged their love of travel with a few short trips—to Enghien to see the steeplechasing; to Meaux with Gertrude and Alice in Gertrude's Ford runabout for a picnic lunch with Mildred Aldrich, the "fine old femme" who had written *A Hilltop on the Marne;* and to the neighborhood of Compiègne on a long hike with knapsacks, stopping at inns along the way to eat pasties made of wild boar meat, cooked with onions and mushrooms, and well laced with country wine. But Ernest was eager for Italy, and for once there was enough money to go. Bone had paid him well for his Genoa despatches, and Hadley's trust fund had yielded several checks. In the middle of May, they set out on a month-long trip. This time Chink Dorman-Smith arranged a furlough and joined them at the Gangwisch pension at Chamby.

Chink had not changed. Even in his British sporting kit and hobnailed mountain boots, he carried himself like a professional soldier. His black hair was neatly cut and he still wore the military mustache. He grinned his sidelong grin at Hadley, named her Mrs. Popplethwaite, and at once settled down with Ernest into the old argumentative camaraderie. They slid on the Maytime snow-crust and climbed the Cap au Moine, a 7000-foot peak. Across from the

station at Aigle stood a café with a galloping golden horse on the roof and a
"great wistaria vine, as thick through as a small tree," where bees hummed in
the purple blossoms. They sat at green tables under the arbor, drinking strong
dark beer in quart-sized mugs. One evening Ernest and Chink entered a beer-
drinking contest in a nearby mountain village and came home drunkenly
singing through fields of narcissus silver in the moonlight. They had a great
argument on whether chestnut blossoms could be spoken of as waxen cande-
labra. Hadley and Chink settled down to reading at the inn in Aigle while
Ernest went out alone to fish the Stockalper, still swollen and gray with snow
water, and the fast-flowing Rhône Canal, barely a yard wide. Afterwards he
sat down under a pine tree, reading the *Daily Mail* he had wrapped his trout in,
eating cherries out of a paper sack, and gazing at a far-off waterfall that
plunged silently over the brown face of a cliff.

On the last day of May they rode the train to Bourg St. Pierre, getting down
at the tiny station to begin their hike into Italy. All next day they climbed
through knee-deep snow up the Pass of St. Bernard. Chink and Ernest wore
stout boots, but Hadley had brought nothing better than "a rather neat pair of
tan American Oxfords" which were soaked through and beginning to split
open before they had covered two kilometers. She barely made it to the gaunt
Hospice of St. Bernard, which looked to Chink like a barracks in a moonscape.
He had to fend off a hostile St. Bernard dog before he could ring the almoner's
bell. The monks took them in and gave them quarters for the night. Waiting
for supper in dry clothes and bedroom slippers, Hadley tiptoed curiously down
a long stone corridor. All the doors opened silently as she passed. Behind each
was a tonsured brother in a long black robe. Ernest assured her that she had
committed the greatest sin in ten centuries: no other woman had ever invaded
these ascetic premises. She did penance next day on the route to Aosta. When
they came into town she had turned into a "human blister," with Ernest and
Chink like crutches on either side. She slept all the way on the train to Milan,
where Chink left them to return to his military station on the Rhine.

For Ernest, at least, Milan was a homecoming of sorts. He showed his wife
the tall old building in the Via Manzoni which had served as the Red Cross
hospital; they went into the Duomo and afterwards stopped off at Biffi's in
the Galleria, holding hands under the table and drinking Capri with fresh
peaches and strawberries from a tall pitcher that tinkled with ice. The newspapers were black with headlines about the Fascist attack on Bologna, where
15,000 arrogant young nationalists had seized the city and held it for a day in
a "counter-campaign of terrorism" against the Communist working classes.
When Ernest heard that Mussolini, the emergent leader of the Black Shirts,
was actually in Milan, he used his press card to arrange an interview.

Mussolini received him in the editor's office of the *Popolo d'Italia*. He spoke
slowly in simple Italian. Beside his chair, playing with wadded newspapers,
was a wolfhound puppy whose ears he sometimes fondled as he talked. At
thirty-nine he stood on the verge of power. Ernest did not find him the mon-

ster of popular legend, but rather a "big, brown-faced man with a high forehead, a slow-smiling mouth, and large expressive hands." He talked more like
a quick-thinking intellectual than a rabble-rouser, and described the organization of his Black Shirts, 250,000 strong, who served as shock troops for the
newly formed Fascist Party. "Garibaldi had red shirts," he said, smiling and
spreading his hands. "We are not out to oppose any Italian government. We
are not against the law. But we have force enough to overthrow any government that might try to oppose or destroy us." Ernest thanked him and went
back to the hotel to write up his notes. Italian Fascism had entered its third
phase. First it had been an organization of anti-Communists, then a political
party. Now it was a military and political movement bent upon dominating
Italy from Rome to the Alps. Mussolini sat at the fuse of a powder keg. The
question in Ernest's mind was what he would do with his matches.

Ernest still thought of Schio as "one of the finest places on earth" and
wanted to spend a night with Hadley at the Two Swords Hotel. They could
see the mill that had housed the Schio Country Club, the stream where the
boys had swum in the heat of the day, and the small *trattoria,* festooned with
wistaria, where they had drunk beer under a bombing moon. But when they
took the bus from Milan on June 13th the sky had gone gray with a hint of
rain, and his nostalgic dream was soon dissipated. Schio had shrunk in the
years between. Even the mountains looked "rain-furrowed and dull." The Due
Spadi was only "a small mean inn" where the bed squeaked and the only light
came from a fly-specked bulb suspended from the middle of the ceiling. The
wool factory was back in operation, the old entrance had been bricked up,
and a flow of black muck from the washing of the wool had polluted the
swimming hole. Ernest strolled in the rain down the long, winding main street,
looking at the shirts and postcards and cheap china dishes in the shop windows.
On a stool behind the bar in the principal wineshop sat a girl who was knitting
a sweater.

"The town is changed," said Ernest.

The girl nodded without missing a stitch.

"I was here during the war," he said.

"So were many others," said the girl.

Ernest drank his drink and left the place. He knew enough now not to try
to find the garden with the plane tree and the wistaria vine. Perhaps it had
never existed. Back at the Two Swords the dinner was poor and he could not
see to read by the light of the single bulb. Early next morning, after a sleepless
night, he and Hadley left in a hired car for Rovereto. It was still raining.

They made the circuit of Lago di Garda, spent a quiet evening on the point
of land at Sirmione, turned in the car at Verona, and took the train for Mestre,
"traveling first class with an assorted carriageful of evil-smelling Italian
profiteers going to Venice for vacations." With the last of their time and
money Ernest wanted to show Hadley the riverbank where he had been
wounded almost four years before. At Mestre they hired another car with an

Italian driver. Ernest sat in the back seat studying a map and gazing out at the "poisonous green Adriatic marshes." The long straight road ran like a causeway through the flat wasteland. Near Porto Grande the car broke down and the driver began poking under the hood, getting a splinter of steel in one of his fingers. Hadley dug it out with a needle from her rucksack. The mist blew away and the sun shone hot. Far away beyond the swamp and the blue lagoon they could see the magical skyline of Venice, "standing gray and yellow like a fairy city."

At last the driver wiped his hands on his hair and they drove on to Fossalta. When Ernest had seen it last, it had been a heap of rubble. Now he could not recognize a single landmark. "All the shattered, tragic dignity of the wrecked town was gone," he wrote. "In its place was a new, smug, hideous collection of plaster houses." They were all painted in garish colors. The shell scars on the trees had grown over and healed. When they drove out to the bank of the river, all the old trenches and dugouts had vanished without a trace. Ernest climbed the grassy slope above the sunken road. The Piave was clean and blue and he watched a cement barge moving slowly upstream, towed by horses with long hawsers attached to singletrees. The bargemen were working just where the listening post had been. But now there was only a smooth green slope stretching down to the river. In one of the hedgerows he found a rusty shell fragment, the only surviving sign of the front where he had once bled and thousands had died.

"There was nothing more to say," wrote Ernest. "A shattered village in the war always had a dignity, as though it had died for something. . . . It was all part of the great sacrifice." Now everything was back to normal—"except a little worse." He had tried and failed to re-create a former actuality for his wife's benefit and perhaps for his own. But the past, he concluded, was as dead as a smashed Victrola record. "Chasing yesterdays," said he, "is a bum show, and if you have to prove it, go back to your old front." In half a dozen years he would discover how to catch and hold the past in the forms of fiction. Now he could only stand ruefully among the rebuilt houses of Fossalta-di-Piave on that hot afternoon in the middle of June, 1922.

12. BLACK FOREST, BLACK SEA

AFTER Italia they settled back for two months in the noisy neighborhood of the Place de la Contrescarpe. No major news stories broke that summer. The best Ernest could do for the *Star* was a few make-work essays on the mendacity of Armenian rug vendors, the scarcity of apartments in Paris, and the equestrian ineptitudes of Sinclair Lewis, the famous novelist, who had been rebuked by his Cockney groom while cantering down a bridle path in London. The June number of the New Orleans *Double Dealer* contained a poem of Ernest's side by side with some prose by an obscure young Mississippian named William Faulkner. The poem did not amount to much—a couple of lines about a man who struggled to spit out the truth—but it had one distinction: it was the first of his adult poems to be published in the United States.

People from home were always dropping in. One was Pinard Baum, a veteran of the Schio Country Club, who was much dejected because he had been forbidden to drink the very wine that had given him his nickname. Another was John Dos Passos, the Harvard man Ernest had met at Dolo in 1918. He stayed long enough for a convivial lunch at Lipp's Brasserie. He had crammed half a lifetime of travel into the past four years, exploring Spain, Portugal, and most of the Middle East. Two of his books had already appeared —*One Man's Initiation, 1917* and a novel called *Three Soldiers*. He still had half a mind to become a painter or to indulge his "faint hankering after the theatre." Dos blew in and out of Paris like a brown-eyed whirlwind.

Ernest had now taken to working in the early mornings. The rest of the day there was too much noise in the streets, and every night the clamor was compounded by accordion music from the Bal Musette downstairs. Sometimes the Hemingways went down to take a whirl. The place was dark and narrow, with wooden tables and benches along the walls, and a small bare space for dancing. The atmosphere, Hadley thought, was "real old workmen's France." There was a scattering of sailors and *poules* among the customers. Patrons bought coins for each dance and anyone could dance with anyone else. Hadley's wealthy cousin, Bates Wyman, was shocked at the roughness of the neighborhood and the rudeness of the clientele, and Hadley was occasionally frightened by the ruffians who asked her to dance. But Ernest seemed to revel in the smoky atmosphere. Spinning around the floor, wearing a striped Breton fisherman's shirt, he might have been mistaken for a native of the place. During the Bastille Day celebration, the accordionist moved out into the street, joining two drummers, a bagpiper, and a cornetist. For four nights they played from dark to dawn, sitting in a wagonbox supported by winecasks, while dozens of couples danced to the music and no one in the neighborhood even attempted to sleep.

In the midst of August they escaped the heat and din of Paris with a fishing trip to Germany. They asked Bill and Sally Bird and Lewis Galantière and his fiancée, Dorothy Butler. The plan was to hike through the Black Forest, catching trout all day and spending the nights in country inns. Bill Nash of the *Chicago Daily News* advised a flight to Strasbourg: the same trip that took ten hours by train could be made by plane in two and a half. Ernest bought two press-rate tickets from a sinister-sounding outfit called the Franco-Rumanian Aero Company. The others agreed to follow by train.

Next morning the Hemingways rose at four, roused the taxi driver, who doubled as accordion player at the Bal Musette, and rattled out to Le Bourget through the dark streets. A small biplane was waiting. They slid their haversacks under the seats, stuffed their ears with cotton, and took off into the summer dawn. The pilot was a broad-nosed man in goggles, with a stained sheepskin jacket and a visored cap worn backwards. The engine smelt strongly of castor oil. Ernest peered down at the green velvet forests, the red rooftops of Bar le Duc and Nancy, and the wartime trenches outside St. Mihiel. They hedgehopped along a weedy canal, then climbed through misty rain over the Vosges mountains. The pilot tapped Ernest's shoulder and pointed off to the right at a mud-colored ribbon. It was the Rhine. Hadley awoke as they came down onto the sunburnt grass of the Strasbourg airfield. For the first flight of their lives it had all been very casual.

Strasbourg looked to Ernest like an illustration in a Grimm Brothers fairy tale. They stayed in a *Gasthaus* on the cobblestoned square beside the Lutheran Church, and dined on brook trout in the fifteenth-century *Kammerzell*, drinking Rhine wine in tall dark bottles and a plum liqueur called quetsch. According to Ernest, it tasted exactly as plums look as if they ought to taste but never do. It was all very inexpensive. Occupied Germany was gripped by severe inflation. At full pension with tips included, the four days in Freiburg cost them the equivalent of eighty cents apiece.

But the Black Forest was not the Michigan-like wilderness that Ernest had longed for in the baking streets of Paris. It was a region of low wooded mountains, diversified with railroads, potato fields, fenced-in pastures, and enormous hotels. It was also densely populated. The five-hour trip to Triberg was accomplished in a train crammed with large, rude Germans in *Lederhosen*. Their heads were shaved and they all carried rucksacks hung with aluminum cooking pots that clanked like cowbells. Even the fishing licenses were a problem. All through the Kingdom of Baden Ernest's cry was "Ve wishen der fishencarten." In the end they rented a stretch of trout stream that ran through a birch grove. Sally and Dorothy did not like fishing, but Hadley caught three good ones the first time she tried. Ernest took five others from the River Elz with one of his old McGintys. The natives were often unfriendly. Farmers armed with wooden pitchforks chased them off a stream near Uberprechtal, and once or twice they were denounced as "alien profiteers" in the *Gasthaus* dining rooms. One afternoon in the forest, Ernest tripped over a log and landed heavily on his back. He did not try to laugh it off, but took to his bed, refusing to eat and staying incommunicado all the rest of the day. Next morning, still in bed, he told them that he would probably die while they were off enjoying themselves in the woods. But he was only playing Ajax. That night he rejoined the company with a hearty appetite.

Early in September Ernest and Hadley saw the others off to Paris and went to pay a call on Chink Dorman-Smith at the British Occupation Garrison in Cologne. Chink showed them an equestrian statue of Wilhelm II which an angry mob had lately defaced, hacking off the spurs and pulling down the enormous sword blade. The rioters had also murdered a German policeman. It was a macabre story and Ernest sent it off to John Bone as an example of the present state of unrest in Germany.

During the attack on the statue [he wrote], a policeman appeared and tried to quiet the mob. The mob threw the policeman into the river. In the cold swift swell of the Rhine against the base of the bridge the policeman hung onto one of the abutments and shouted up that he knew who was in the mob and would see that they were all punished. So the mob swarmed down and tried to push the policeman loose into the current. It meant drowning for the policeman to let go—and he hung on. Then the mob chopped his fingers loose from the stone with the hatchet with which they had been attacking the statue.

Another form of violence had erupted in the Middle East. Ernest had not been back in Paris more than a week when a cable from the *Star* ordered him to Constantinople to cover the war between Greece and Turkey. Late in August, the Turks had launched an offensive to drive the Greeks from Anatolia. The action had just culminated in the Turkish occupation and burning of the port of Smyrna. The Turks also threatened to take over the neutral zone which the Allies had established to guard the Straits from the Black Sea on the north to the Dardanelles in the south. Units of Turkish cavalry advanced to the British barbed wire at Chanak on the Dardanelles, and it was generally supposed that Kemal Pasha would soon occupy Constantinople.

Hadley was determined that Ernest should not go. They quarreled "dreadfully" and she refused to speak to him for three days before he left. "He suffered," she said, "but finally went without a word from me." The taxi to the Gare de Lyon on the night of September 25th was driven by a drunken chauffeur who hurled Ernest's suitcase out of the cab with such exuberance that the Corona typewriter inside was useless to him all through the long trip south. At Sofia he mailed a batch of scribbled postcards and sent off a handwritten piece to the *Star*. He was worried about his relations with John Bone. Before leaving Paris he had reached a secret agreement with Frank Mason of Hearst's International News Service to cable spot news stories to INS even though he was supposed to be under exclusive contract to the *Star*.

On the morning of the 29th the long brown train rolled through the flatlands and plunged at noon among the ramshackle tenements of the city. Ernest took a cab to the Hôtel de Londres, got his typewriter repaired, and tapped out the lead sentence of his first despatch: "Constantinople is noisy, hot, hilly, dirty, and beautiful . . . packed with uniforms and rumors." British troops had arrived to head off the expected Turkish invasion, but all the foreigners were scared. They remembered the tales of Turkish atrocities at the sacking of Smyrna and had booked all outgoing train space for weeks ahead. The Greek Christian who owned the hotel told Ernest that he would rather fight than lose his property to the puritanical Turks. Kemal Pasha had sworn to rid the city of all liquor, gambling, dancing, nightclubs, and bordellos.

Ernest got a glimpse of Galata, the sinkhole of venery halfway up the hill from the port. Despite his later boasting, it was enough to turn his tired stomach. The storied "magic of the East" appeared briefly in the mornings, with minarets slim in the rising sun and the muezzins calling the faithful to prayer in voices that soared and dipped like arias from Russian opera. But in the small dark hours one stepped cautiously along sidewalks where lean mongrels nosed the heaps of garbage, rats lay rotting in the gutters, and the all-night drunken roar of the metropolis seemed to invite the housecleaning that Kemal had promised.

He made a few acquaintances among the military personnel, pumping them for authoritative pronouncements on the probable course of events. One of the most talkative was a brusk, red-faced soldier of fortune named Colonel Charles Sweeny, who spoke like a man of the world and amazed Ernest with his grasp of military science and tactics. But Ernest was fighting a battle of his own against the inroads of malaria. Glancing into the mirror in his room at the Hôtel de Londres, he saw that his face was speckled with bug bites. He moved to the Hôtel Montreal to avoid further traffic with insect life. It did no good. He was too ill to join the other correspondents aboard a British destroyer on a briefing trip to Mytilene. On October 6th, John Bone cabled that his spot news stories were duplicating those of the wire services, as in fact they were, owing to Ernest's secret duplicity with INS. There were other difficulties, including the stupidity of the censors and the refusal of the military to allow newsmen at the Conference of Mudania, which ceded eastern Thrace to the Turks and gave the Greek army three days to evacuate the territory. The day the document was signed, Ernest was shivering with malaria and paying a doctor ten piasters for a supply of quinine pills.

The Mudania agreement now shifted attention from Constantinople to Thrace. On the 14th Ernest bought some lice-free blankets and headed for Muradli, eighty miles to the west. All day he passed columns of "dirty, tired, unshaven, windbitten" Greek infantrymen in ill-fitting American uniforms. They shambled across the barren countryside, preceded by cavalry patrols and followed by heavy-wheeled baggage carts drawn by buffaloes. The telegraph wires they had cut dangled from the poles "like Maypole ribbons." These dogged troops, said Ernest, were "the last of the glory that was Greece."

He borrowed a shotgun and shot some quail, but his malaria made him too miserable to do much more. On the 17th he packed his typewriter and caught the westbound train for Adrianople, a hundred and thirty miles along the homeward route to Paris. At eleven that night he got down in the rain with his new blankets over his shoulder. The station at Adrianople was a cheerless mudhole, lighted by kerosene flares and crowded with soldiers, civilians, bundles, bedsprings, sewing machines, squawling babies, and broken carts. One of the soldiers guided him to the only hotel, run by a Croatian named Madame Marie. A barefoot Frenchman told him at the door that all rooms were booked solid. If he wished, he could spread his blankets on the floor in the hotel office. But a car came in just then from Rodosto, bearing two American cameramen who had been filming the evacuation. The taller man, whose name was Shorty Wornall, offered Ernest a folding cot and they all turned in. Twice in the night he awoke with severe chills, which he dosed heavily with aspirin and quinine. In the morning light they saw that every surface in the room was swarming with lice. Madame Marie, a large and slovenly woman, served them coffee and black bread in the hotel office. When Ernest complained of the lice, she only shrugged. "It is better than sleeping in the road?" she said. "Eh, monsieur? It is better than that?"

The cameramen were driving back to Rodosto and Ernest accompanied them a few miles down the road. In the gray drizzle of the October morning he saw a sight that he never forgot. Almost the entire Christian population of Thrace jammed the long stone road which led westward through Adrianople and on towards Karagatch. There were twenty miles of refugee carts, drawn by bullocks, cows, and water buffaloes. Thousands of exhausted men, women, and children walked blindly through the rain with blankets over their heads. Mud-splashed Greek cavalrymen herded them along. No one spoke or even grunted. It was all they could do to keep moving. In one of the carts was a woman in labor, her groans the only sound. Her husband had spread a blanket to keep off the driving rain. The small daughter watched with horror and began to cry. The slow procession moved on.

Ernest went back across the bridge to Adrianople. The Maritza River was in flood, with brick-red water a quarter-mile wide. At Madame Marie's he stopped to dry out and write a despatch. An Italian colonel agreed to file it for him at the telegraph office next day, sending it collect to Frank Mason of INS with instructions to relay it to the London office of the Toronto *Star*. Ernest's fever was up again, and Madame Marie brought him a bottle of sweet Thracian wine to wash down his quinine and aspirin. That night he got thankfully aboard the Orient Express for the four-day ride back to Paris.

When the train chuffed into the Gare de Lyon at half past six on the morning of October 21, he had been away for more than three weeks. He was covered with bug bites and his hair was so lousy that he had to have his head shaved. But he came bearing other gifts to Hadley than his fever-and-lice-ridden person: a necklace of ivory and one of amber, and a bottle of attar of roses. The amber necklace was a genuine antique, he explained, bought from a member of the Russian nobility who was waiting on tables in Constantinople. Hadley accepted the peace offerings. She was glad enough to have him back.

13. LAUSANNE

FOR a week after his return from Adrianople, Ernest did nothing but sleep. But his labors in the Middle East had brought him the princely reward of $400 in back salary from John Bone, and when he had recovered his strength he used the money and the leisure to get back to what he called "serious writing." Ezra Pound was his chief catalyst, having conceived, during the summer, the notion of conducting "an inquest into the state of contemporary English prose." The program was more modest than Ezra's grandiloquent description of it. It would consist of half a dozen little books, handsomely printed, bound in boards, and issued under his personal editorship. The publisher would be William Bird, who had just bought a printshop at 29 Quai d'Anjou on the Île St.-Louis and announced the establishment of the Three Mountains Press. When Pound asked Ernest to contribute to the series, he was highly flattered. He sent off a jubilant letter to Harriet Monroe, explaining that Bill Bird would shortly bring out some of his "stuff" under Ezra's aegis, and asking permission to use the six poems that Miss Monroe had accepted for *Poetry*.

At this time also he had his first portrait painted. It was done by Henry Strater, a graduate of Princeton whose nickname was Mike. Ernest met him at Pound's studio, where they drank whiskey out of Dorothy's fragile teacups and discovered a common interest in boxing. They presently agreed to a friendly match. Strater lived with his wife Maggie and a small child in the Hameau Béranger not far from the race track at Auteuil. He was a six-footer, weighing close to 200 pounds. On the streetcar going out, Ernest had some fear of being bested. But a few stiff rounds proved that they were evenly matched. He took a bath in the large tin tub and stayed for lunch. Strater urged him to sit for a portrait, full-face, downward-gazing, and wearing a gray sweatshirt. Mike immediately named it the "boxer portrait." It was the first likeness of Ernest to show the new mustache which he had begun to cultivate that summer in the Black Forest.

Ernest's spirits ran high all through early November. After several home-comings to the flat in the rue du Cardinal Lemoine, he was beginning to feel like a veteran expatriate. Sylvia Beach even asked his advice about publishing Frank Harris's sex-ridden autobiography. Ernest told her to go right ahead: it would be "the finest fiction ever written." Gertrude Stein, taking the sun in Provence, sent the Hemingways a candied casaba melon as big as a Thanksgiving pumpkin. They began visiting cafés, playing checkers and drinking hot rum punch. Ernest became so sanguine about his future that he even sent a friendly letter to Agnes von Kurowsky, telling her of his residence in Paris, his marriage to Hadley, and the expected appearance of his first book.

He was still uncertain of the contents, except that it would include both poetry and prose. He had in hand the seduction story, "Up in Michigan," and had embarked on another called "My Old Man," the longest he had tried since "Pickles McCarty." It was an invented story about a boy who learned with sick dismay that his adored jockey father was a crook. Ernest drew on his memories of the San Siro race track in Milan and his more recent observations at Enghien and Auteuil, where he and Hadley had been betting on the horses whenever they had enough money. The narrative manner showed traces of the influence of Sherwood Anderson, though Ernest was never willing to admit it. "The only writing that was any good was what you made up, what you imagined," he wrote two years later. "Like when [you] wrote 'My Old Man' [you'd] never seen a jockey killed and the next week Georges Parfrement was killed at that very jump and that was the way it looked."

Between sessions with fiction, he kept in practice by composing satirical sketches about people he did not like. Literary poseurs always brought out the latent streak of cruelty in his nature. One of these was Ernest Walsh, whom he first met in Pound's studio. Walsh was a tubercular young man with a pale face and burning eyes who liked to pose as a man marked for early death, cultivating a social manner both dark and intense. Another was the British novelist, Ford Madox Hueffer, known since the war as Ford Madox Ford, who came to Paris in November and was pointed out to Ernest in one of the cafés. Was this arrogant fat man with the walrus mustache and pale blue eyes the famous friend and collaborator of Joseph Conrad? Ernest, who had admired Conrad's work for several years, found it hard to believe that he should ever have taken up with Ford.

He tapped out a sketch on an American businessman-turned-poet who had known Hadley in St. Louis and had now come abroad with two sons and a daughter for an indefinite stay. At forty-eight, Dave O'Neil had retired from a prosperous lumber business to follow the arts. Ernest liked Dave's wife Barbara far better.

Dave gets his political opinions from the *Daily Mail* [wrote Ernest], and then reads the *Daily Mail* to get facts to support them. He talks about his intuitions. He is sentimentally Irish. When he meets another, he says, 'You're Irish. Well, God bless you.' He would like to be the Irish poet laureate. All his poems are the same. A poem to Dave is a combination of words about something he doesn't understand. It is therefore poetic. He has written, quickly, several hundred poems. He called his book of poems *A Cabinet of Jade* on the suggestion of Zoe Akins. Now that several people have told him Zoe isn't so much he would like to have given it another title.

Ernest had been writing about the decline of Georges Clemenceau without ever having met the fierce old man. Clemenceau was spending the fall in his seaside retreat at St. Vincent du Jard near Les Sables d'Olonne in the Vendée. When Ernest heard that Bill Bird was going down for an interview, he asked to come along. Clemenceau was eighty-one. He wore gray gloves and stained mustaches and spoke with loquacious bitterness. He told them about his forthcoming lecture tour in the United States. Ernest suggested a side trip to Toronto. *"Jamais,"* cried Clemenceau. "Never will I set foot in Canada." He explained gruffly that Canada had not done her part in the war. In the taxi afterwards, Ernest wanted to stop at Les Sables to send off a cable to Bone. Bird advised him to think it over. Instead he sent a crackling feature story by mail. Bone refused to print it. "He can say these things," said Bone, "but he cannot say them in our paper."

The *Star* was eager for Ernest to cover the Lausanne Peace Conference, which was convened on November 20th to settle the territorial dispute between Greece and Turkey. The meeting place this time was the Château Ouchy, a stone building so ugly, said Ernest, that it made the Odd Fellows Hall in Petoskey look like the Parthenon by comparison. He arrived on the 22nd, having taken the assignment of running a twenty-four-hour wire coverage for the two Hearst agencies of INS and Universal Service. It kept him so busy for the next three weeks that nothing from his typewriter relating to Lausanne appeared in the *Star* until late January.

Hadley's plans to join him were delayed by a severe cold which kept her in bed in Paris. Ernest wired her twice, using their intramural baby talk in which she was Wickey or Feather Cat and he was Poo or Wax Puppy. Not to be outdone by her illness, he gave a graphic account of his own. He was coughing up "green stuff with black specks" and using "millions of handkerchiefs" for his stuffed-up nose. He had to keep the wire open from nine in the morning until midnight, and was heartily sick of tramping up and down hill to keep abreast of developments at the Château Ouchy. After all, said he, "I'm only a tiny wax puppy."

Many of the correspondents Ernest had met in Genoa and Paris were on hand at Lausanne. He showed the horse-race story, "My Old Man," to Lincoln Steffens, who liked it so well that he insisted on sending it with his personal imprimatur to Ray Long at *Cosmopolitan*. Ernest also brought out his despatch about the Thracian refugees on the bridge at Adrianople. Steffens was immensely impressed by the vividness and vigor of Ernest's prose. But Ernest was embarrassed by the praise. "No," he said, "just read the cablese, only the cablese. Isn't it a great language?" Steffens was more than ever convinced that Hemingway had the surest future of any youngster on the European literary scene.

One of his new acquaintances was a brilliant and sardonic young South African named William Bolitho Ryall, who had been gravely wounded as an infantry officer in France in 1917. He was now serving as European correspondent for the *Manchester Guardian,* a strange-looking man with "a white lantern-jawed face"—the kind, said Ernest, "that is supposed to haunt you if seen suddenly in a London fog." It was Ryall's counsel in Lausanne that marked the real beginning of Ernest's education in international politics. They met nearly every evening for dinner. Over the brandy, Ryall held forth repeatedly on "the malady of power." It was a complex disease, starting with suspicion of one's associates and quickly evolving into a conviction of one's own indispensability.

These lectures immediately began to color Ernest's political opinions. Ryall's forte lay in the debunking of the great. The small dark Ismet Pasha looked to him, and so to Ernest, more like an Armenian lace salesman than a Turkish general. In the Palace bar one night, Ernest was chosen to present

Ismet's bodyguard with an exploding cigar. "He took it very graciously," wrote Ernest, "and offered me a cigarette in exchange." When the cigar went off, the bodyguard pulled all four pistols at once. Under Ryall's tutelage, Ernest quickly revised his former opinion of Benito Mussolini, whom he now called "the biggest bluff in Europe." Every adolescent Italian Fascist aped his scowl. In Lausanne he appeared wearing a black shirt and white spats, a deplorable combination even in one who persistently strove for histrionic effect. Ernest watched with scorn while Mussolini rolled his "big-whited African eyes" at a pretty girl reporter named Claire Sheridan. At one of his press conferences he sat scowling behind a large desk with an open book in his hands. "I tiptoed over behind him to see what the book was," wrote Ernest. "It was a French-English dictionary held upside down."

He had been urging Hadley to fly down whenever she felt "travelly." The prospect of dodging among the snowy mountains was not very tempting and she took the train instead. But the journey was made under conditions so harrowing for her and so horrible for Ernest that neither of them was ever able to forget it. She decided to take all his manuscripts in a separate small valise so that he could get on with his writing during the Christmas season. Except for "Up in Michigan," which was gathering dust in a drawer, and "My Old Man," which Steffens had sent off to *Cosmopolitan*, she gathered up all the fiction and poetry she could find. Then she took a taxi to the Gare de Lyon and got a porter to carry her luggage to the compartment. During the very brief time when the bags were out of her sight, the valise with the manuscripts was stolen.

She made the trip in frozen horror.

I had never seen anyone hurt by a thing other than death or unbearable suffering [wrote Ernest later], except Hadley when she told me about the things being gone. She . . . cried and cried and could not tell me. I told her that no matter what the dreadful thing was that had happened, nothing could be that bad. . . . Finally she told me. I was sure that she could not have brought the carbons too and I hired someone to cover for me on my newspaper job . . . and took the train for Paris. It was true all right and I remember what I did in the night after I let myself into the flat and found it was true.

Whatever it was he did that December night remained his secret for the rest of his life. Next day he went over to see Gertrude and Alice. They were suitably sympathetic and gave him "a very fine lunch." He stayed there until train time, talking and reading "a lot of [Gertrude's] new stuff." On the train he went into the *wagon-restaurant* and ordered a large dinner with a bottle of Beaune, which he drank all by himself while the train roared south through the Jura. He was facing the double prospect of meeting his tearful wife and reopening the Hearst wire services. In a mood of Byronic defiance he set down a new poem on the Lausanne Conference—a very Ryallesque free-for-all in free verse in which he attacked all the statesmen from Lord Curzon, the alleged lover of young boys, to Mussolini with his "nigger eyes" and the pink-cheeked ambassador, Richard Washburn Child, who had come with his wife as American representative for President Warren G. Harding. "Mrs. Child has flat breasts," wrote Ernest, maliciously, "and Mr. Child is an idealist and wrote Harding's campaign speeches. . . . Lincoln Steffens is with Child. The big C makes the joke easy."

His raffish mood continued into the Christmas season. On Saturday, December 16th, he concluded his work for the wire services, collected his salary, took Hadley up the funicular to the Gangwisch pension, drank hot rum punch with Chink Dorman-Smith, and tried to forget the loss of his manuscripts by skiing down innumerable slopes across the smooth new snow. Not least among his holiday pleasures was a long letter from Agnes von Kurowsky:

After I recovered from the surprise [of getting your letter], I never was more pleased over anything in my life. You know there has always been a little bitterness over the way our comradeship ended, especially since I got back and [Elsie Macdonald] read me the very biting letter you wrote to her about me. . . . Anyhow I always knew that it would turn out right in the end, and that you would realize it was the best way, as I'm positive you must believe, now that you have Hadley. . . . How proud I will be some day . . . to say, 'Oh, yes. Ernest Hemingway. Used to know him well during the war.' I've always known you would stand out some day from the background, and it is always a pleasure to have one's judgment confirmed.

He was ready to luxuriate in the new access of freedom: the old brown chalet, the fields of crisp snow, the clear cold days, and evenings by the fire with Chink and Hadley. He went bobsledding on the Col de Sonloup *piste* in the Canton of Vaud, accompanied by Dave O'Neil's seventeen-year-old son George, wearing his shapeless felt hat and holding down the tail end of the sled. Chink's leave soon ended, but his place was taken by Isabelle Simmons, Ernest's next-door neighbor from Oak Park, who arrived on New Year's Day for a fortnight of skiing. They were out every day while the snow lasted, sweeping down the saddle of the Dent de Jaman and coming home at dusk along a road so icy that they fell every twenty yards. One day George lost a ski into the gulf below. Next morning Ernest went to retrieve it in a blinding snowstorm. By ten o'clock the snow had turned to warm and steady rain. Ernest half slid, half floundered down to a clump of willows, found the ski, and struggled up the slope through snow that sometimes reached his armpits. Whenever he stopped to rest, he glanced up at the acres of loosening snow poised on the peaks above. It was like climbing towards the snout of a machine gun with an epileptic at the trigger. Hadley and Isabelle were waiting beside the road. They took shelter in a small barn built into the mountainside, eating a picnic lunch and watching the rain through the open door. In the next two hours Ernest counted fourteen avalanches roaring from the heights into the valley below. Whether it was for this reason or some other, the wind and rain of a season of thaw were always afterwards associated in his mind with the prospect of imminent disaster.

14. RAPALLO AND CORTINA

AFTER Isabelle had left for Paris, Ernest and Hadley began to talk of going to Rapallo. It was the town that Ezra had adopted in exchange for the damps of Paris. He was down there working on his Malatesta Cantos. Mike Strater was also there with his wife and baby, painting seascapes of the Mediterranean. Ernest remembered the place from the time of the Genoa Conference: the glint of light on the water, the small boats in the bay, and the stucco villas among the green trees on the slopes above the esplanade. He could box with Mike and play mixed doubles with the Pounds and the Straters. Living would be cheap and easy at the Hotel Splendide down by the waterfront. Perhaps he could write some short stories to replace those he had lost.

Ezra kept urging the Hemingways to come. He wanted them as company on a walking tour of the Romagna with Dorothy, visiting the places that were associated with the career of Sigismondo Malatesta. "As I was very vague as to who Sigismondo was," wrote Ernest, "and had no wish to eat bad food and sleep in poor inns in Italy in February following the trail of a historic personage, . . . I put off going as long as possible."

He temporized until the snows of Chamby melted to slush, the clear cold weather gave way to bone-chilling dampness, and the whole Swiss prospect became gray and uninviting. The real turning point came when Hadley announced that she was going to have a baby. She thought that her first pregnancy would succeed far better in the warm sun by the Mediterranean. In the end, they "cashed a check and went down the mountains to Montreux," taking the train through the Simplon Tunnel, and following the shores of Lago Maggiore through Stresa and Gallarate to Milan, where they celebrated with a splendid dinner at Campari's before going on to Rapallo.

At first he was disappointed with Ezra's famous hideout. After the bracing heights above Montreux, it was hard to breathe in the humid atmosphere of sea level. The Mediterranean seemed "weak and dull," with a one-inch tide and paltry waves that broke on the shingle of the shore with a sound like a bucket of ashes being dumped off the side of a scow. Three days after the Hemingways' arrival, Ezra went off somewhere, promising to come back in a week or two. Mike Strater had sprained an ankle and could neither box nor play tennis. Ernest checked on his progress twice a day. He was so eager to knock Mike out that he said he had even stopped sleeping with Hadley. Mike used the interim to paint both their portraits—Hadley in three-quarter-face with thick auburn hair, and Ernest in profile, with a luxurious mustache and dark brown hair that hung over his ears and reminded Hadley of Balzac.

"Mike spoils many paintings," said Ernest churlishly, "but he has enough money so it does not matter."

What mattered chiefly to Ernest was his own meager productivity. He typed out a lazy fragment which said that he and Hadley were happiest in bed, where there were no problems. "Sheets are over-rated but nice," he wrote. "The big linen ones are damp. Sleeping is good. I used to lie awake all night. That was before. This is after." He sent off a plea to Gertrude Stein. He had been trying, he said, to follow her advice about writing. If she had any more to say, he would be glad to hear it. He needed something to stir up his creativity. "It was a very bad time," he wrote of Rapallo in retrospect, "and I did not think I could write any more."

It was just at this low point that he met Edward O'Brien, who was boarding in a monastery in the hills above the town. O'Brien was nine years older than Ernest, a shy and gentle man from Boston, the author of a volume of poetry called *White Fountains,* and since the war the editor of annual anthologies of the best short stories of the years before. He was "pale, with pale blue eyes, and straight lanky hair he cut himself." He was already gathering material for *The Best Short Stories of 1923,* and asked Ernest if he had any on hand. Ernest pulled the crumpled typescript of "My Old Man" from the depths of his luggage and showed it to O'Brien as a curiosity—"as you might show, stupidly, the binnacle of a ship you had lost . . . or as you might pick up your booted foot and make some joke about it if it had been amputated in a crash." O'Brien took the story up to the monastery. When he brought it back, he said that it was a splendid piece of work. His usual custom was to choose materials that had already appeared in magazines, but he wanted to make an exception with "My Old Man." Ernest could hardly believe his ears. At last he had done something that would appear between hard covers.

Another visitor to Rapallo was Robert Menzies McAlmon, a poet and short-story writer who had been born in Kansas and raised in California. McAlmon was a slender man of twenty-seven with cold blue eyes and a mouth like the lip of a change-purse. Since 1921 he had been married to Annie Winifred Eller-man, a British heiress who wrote under the name of Bryher. Because of his marriage, he was said to have money to burn, and had recently begun a new career as editor and publisher of Contact Editions, with Darantière of Dijon as his printer, and Sylvia Beach's bookshop as his mailing address. He had given out that the manuscripts he wanted must show "individuality, intelligence, talent, a live sense of literature, and . . . the odour and timbre of authenticity." When he met the Hemingways and the Straters in a restaurant at Rapallo, he had yet to discover any such qualities in Ernest. He had heard of him only vaguely as a Canadian journalist, and of Mike as a painter with a degree from Princeton.

He liked Strater at once—"a simple and direct, cleancut young American, unpretending and actually modest." About Hemingway his feelings were mixed. "At times he was deliberately hard-boiled and case-hardened," wrote Mc-

Almon later. "Again he appeared deliberately innocent, sentimental, the hurt, soft, but fairly sensitive boy trying to conceal hurt, wanting to be brave, not bitter or cynical but being somewhat both, and somehow on the defensive, suspicions lurking in his peering analytic glances at a person with whom he was talking. He approached a café with a small-boy, tough-guy swagger, and before strangers of whom he was doubtful, a potential snarl of scorn played on his large-lipped, rather loose mouth." Whatever their future association, it was clear that McAlmon had not succumbed entirely to Ernest's fabled charm.

McAlmon had gone back to Paris by the time the Pounds returned to Rapallo. Ezra lent Ernest a copy of T. S. Eliot's new poem, *The Waste Land,* which had greatly profited by Pound's editorial advice. Ernest was unable to take it seriously, though he echoed it once after watching the antics of a pair of cats on a green table in the hotel garden. "The big cat gets on the small cat," he wrote. "Sweeney gets on Mrs. Porter." He began to make some notes for a short story to be called "Cat in the Rain." It was about himself and Hadley and the manager and chambermaid at the Hotel Splendide. "There were only two Americans stopping at the hotel," it began. "They did not know any of the people they passed on the stairs. . . . Their room was on the second floor facing the sea. It also faced the public garden and the war monument. . . . The American wife stood at the window looking out. . . . Right under their window a cat was crouched under one of the dripping green tables." But he was not yet ready to compose the story, and he put the notes aside until a better day.

Ezra was still determined to take the walking tour. When Ernest finally capitulated, they set off one fair morning with their wives and their rucksacks. It was a fine trip, Hadley thought. Ezra was at his best, and talked learnedly about all the places. Every noonday they lunched al fresco with native cheeses, figs, and wine, spreading the simple fare in the shade of hillside trees in sight of vineyards and olive groves. The route took them southwards through Pisa and Siena. Since Malatesta had been a general as well as a famous patron of artists and writers, they tramped over the fifteenth-century battlegrounds at Piombino and Orbetello where Ernest, as an avid student of military tactics, "tried to explain to [Ezra] how [Malatesta's campaigns] would, more or less, have to have been fought." Pound examined the seaside terrain, his eyes gleaming beneath shaggy eyebrows, and then nodded sagely, striding on with his steady, long-legged lope. After Orbetello, they rode the train to Sirmione on Lago di Garda where they parted—the Pounds for Rapallo and the Hemingways for Cortina d'Ampezzo among the Dolomites north of Venice.

Neither Ernest nor Hadley had seen Cortina before. It reminded them both of Switzerland. The air hung fresh and frosty over broad fields of snow where the valley widened and the enormous rocky peaks seemed to draw back to let in the sunlight from ten until three. The town was small, a haphazard arrangement of Swiss-looking houses and shops along the slanting streets. There were a number of large hotels, filled with winter sportsmen at the season's peak from Christmas through February, but far less crowded now as the spring drew on. They stayed at the Hotel Bellevue in the middle of the village. Hadley met a gifted pianist called Renata Borgatti with whom she discussed both music and babies. They went about together, walking and shopping, wearing blue berets and sturdy mountain boots.

The mountain air soon brought Ernest back to the edge of creativity. He divided his time between the ski slopes and the writing desk. Jane Heap, the mannish coeditor of *The Little Review,* had invited him to contribute to the Exiles number, which would be out in April, and he was already tinkering with a series of short prose sketches. They were based in form and idea on the half-dozen "I have seen" sentences which he had composed the year before under the title of *Paris, 1922.* Now he was trying to enlarge his grasp, stringing sharp sentences into brief paragraphs. Each was the product of a score of crossed-out beginnings. He went over them patiently, pruning extraneous verbiage, carving each sentence as if it had been a cameo, designing miniatures in motion that were supposed to detonate like small grenades inside the reader's head.

In the end he had six, precisely the same magical number as the poems Harriet Monroe had published and the set of six sentences called *Paris, 1922.* All but one were the products of hearsay. Two of them aped the tight-lipped British style that Chink Smith had used in telling him of the fighting around Mons. His source for another was a newspaper clipping about the execution of King Constantine's cabinet ministers (strangely, there were six of them) after they had been convicted of treason the previous November. Ernest concentrated his attention on the one of them who had been half-dead with typhoid, and had been shot sitting down in a puddle with his head on his knees. He tried one account of a bullfight, based on what he had heard from Mike Strater and Gertrude Stein. His only eyewitness report was a version of his cable about the Greek refugees at Adrianople. He had reworked it a good deal since the draft that Lincoln Steffens had admired so extravagantly.

His literary labors were interrupted late in March by a cable from John Bone, who wanted a series of despatches on Franco-German relations in the troubled Ruhr. Ernest packed up his miniatures, left Hadley with Renata Borgatti, and caught the train for Paris. The weather was bad and the flat was dismal. He turned his sketches over to Jane Heap and wrote his father in Oak Park that he was on his way to Germany once more. In the past year he had traveled some ten thousand miles—six times between Paris and Switzerland, three times to Italy, to Constantinople and back, once to the Black Forest, once down the Rhine. He would rejoin Hadley in Cortina when the present assignment was finished, this time with fishing tackle in place of his skis.

The ten articles that Ernest wrote for the *Star* in late March and early April totaled about twenty thousand words. Together they represented his most sustained effort at political analysis and exposition since he had begun work for John Bone. His first three pieces were sent from Paris, where he interviewed politicians and statesmen, discovering a strong undercurrent of opposition to the French occupation of the Ruhr. He knew already that times were bad before he got to Offenburg and Ortenberg. The German working class was still fiercely rebellious; many were Communists; hatred simmered in the grimy streets of Düsseldorf and Essen. Ernest ended his German tour at Cologne with Chink Smith. Conditions were still so parlous there that Chink insisted on giving him a safe-conduct pass for use on the way back to Paris.

When Ernest got back to Cortina in the midst of April, the snow was gone, the skiers had vanished, and bobsleds were rusting in stacks on the porch of the Hotel Concordia. Laborers in stone-dusty jackets were laying the foundations of another new hotel. Once more the heady atmosphere renewed Ernest's urge to write. He had great success with the first full-length short story he had tried since the theft of his manuscripts. It was almost straight autobiography and he called it "Out of Season." The people were a young married couple and a down-at-heel villager named Peduzzi. Ernest later spoke of it as a "very simple story." It was not. Nor was it derivative, like "My Old Man." It was a kind of gateway to the best writing of his career.

With this story, in fact, he discovered for the first time the infinite possibilities of a new narrative technique. This consisted in developing two intrinsically related truths simultaneously, as a good poet does with a metaphor that really works. The "out-of-season" theme applied with equal force to the young man's relations with his wife Tiny, and to the officious insistence by the guide Peduzzi that the young man fish for trout in defiance of the local fishing laws. The real-life Peduzzi was a wine-soaked old reprobate whom all the village scorned. He hanged himself in a stable after Ernest complained to the hotel manager and got him sacked. Ernest did not use the suicide as part of his story. He was evolving "a new theory that you could omit anything if you knew that you omitted, and the omitted part would strengthen the story and make people feel something more than they understood." The theory worked badly in the case of "Out of Season." Peduzzi came through as an oaf but not as a potential suicide. The device that Ernest did not mention—the metaphorical confluence of emotional atmospheres—was what gave the story its considerable distinction. This first successful use of it was the foremost esthetic discovery of Ernest's early career. It was in this, rather than in the flat and uninspired verse of which he seemed so proud, that his true gifts as a poet were to be repeatedly displayed.

15. IBERIA

SPAIN was the only remaining Latin country that Ernest could not boast of knowing from the inside. His brief glimpses of Algeciras in 1919 and Vigo in 1921 hardly counted. One of his miniatures in *The Little Review* had described the goring of a matador, but he had never seen anything of the sort. Now he wanted to know the way it actually was in the bullrings of Spain. He began to promote the idea of a trip with Bill Bird and Bob McAlmon. Bob had plenty of money and was willing to pay the way. They went to lunch with Mike Strater at the Swedish Restaurant to work out an itinerary. Mike annoyed Ernest by pronouncing Seville as Theveeya and Madrid as Madreeth. He drew a map on the back of a menu, with crosses for Burgos and Madrid, Cordoba and Granada, Seville and Ronda.

"What the hell is Ronda?" asked Ernest.

"Oh," said Mike, "it's way down in the south on a sort of a big canyon and it's supposed to be one of the best towns in Spain."

"Where do you stop there?"

"I don't know," Mike said. "I've never been there."

Mike had treated Ernest kindly since their first meeting at Ezra Pound's. But Ernest was already beginning to regard him with a hint of disdain. It was the same pattern he had followed with Bill and Y. K. Smith. Now he looked at Mike across the restaurant table. His neck was too long, thought Ernest, his jaw was unpleasantly twisted, and his nose and mouth were those of a reformer. The worst of it was that he was talking about something he did not know, and using a false Spanish accent to boot.

Bob and Ernest caught the southbound train, leaving Bill to join them in Madrid. Somewhere between Paris and Bayonne, their coach stopped beside a flatcar on which lay the corpse of a dog. Its flesh was alive with maggots and McAlmon looked away in disgust. Ernest took note of the gesture and began to lecture him on the need of facing reality, no matter how ugly it might be. "Hell, Mac," said he, "you write like a realist. Are you going to be a romantic on us?" McAlmon disliked the tone of raillery and Ernest's pose of the veteran insider. Decaying bodies were nothing new to him. He had met them in plenty, both animal and human, while working on a lumber barge in New York harbor. He left Ernest alone and went into the dining car to wash down his rage with a drink.

By the time Bird caught up with his friends at a bullfighters' pension in the Calle San Jerónimo, Ernest was already behaving like a new initiate in a secret society, and laying plans to make a trip through Andalusia with a crew of matadors. When they went to see a *novillada* at one of the lesser bullrings of Madrid, he could talk of nothing but the courage of the bulls and men. He said repeatedly that foreigners were wrong in thinking that bullfights were brutal. Every *corrida* was "a great tragedy." Watching one was like having a ringside seat at a war.

They saw their first major fight during the feast of Corpus Christi in Seville. They had agreed that the goring of the horses might be repellent, and had fortified themselves with brandy. When the first bull dumped a picador and his horse, McAlmon rose in his seat with a yell. Ernest watched him with scorn.

X.Y. [he later wrote], 27 years old; American; male, college education; ridden horses on farm as boy. Took flask of brandy to his first bullfight—took several drinks at ring—when bull charged picador and hit horse, X.Y. gave sudden screeching intake of breath—took drink of brandy—repeated this on each encounter between bull and horse. Seemed to be in search of strong sensations. Doubted genuineness of my enthusiasm for bullfights. Declared it was a pose. He felt no enthusiasm and declared no one else could . . . Does not care for sport of any sort. Does not care for games of chance. Amusements and occupation drinking, night life and gossip. Writes. Travels about.

The night life of Seville was boring to Ernest. They watched a few flamenco dances, where broad-beamed women snapped their fingers to the music of guitars and the dancers rose to stamp and utter long-drawn gypsy howls. "Oh, for Christ's sake," he kept saying, "more flamingos!" He could not rest until Bird and McAlmon agreed to go on to Ronda. It was even better than Mike had predicted—a spectacular village with an ancient bullring high in the mountains above Malaga. The canyon looked like something out of Salvator Rosa. Jackdaws nested among the beetling cliffs, coming out at dusk to dive and circle in the rosy air. Except for Madrid, Ronda seemed to Ernest the finest town in Spain.

By Granada, where they went to see a *novillada* that was rained out, Bill Bird was becoming increasingly aware of the growing coldness between Hemingway and McAlmon. He could not help holding Ernest primarily responsible. Bob's attitude was merely indifferent and at worst contemptuous, but Ernest was often "outrageously insulting." One evening after they had come back from a visit to the gypsy caves, Bill raised the point with Ernest. McAlmon was footing all the bills and buying all the Scotch. Ernest had no right to accept handouts and then bite the hand that was feeding him. But Ernest only laughed sourly. "You know," he told Bird, "I'll take anything from *you*." It did not strike Bill as an adequate response.

McAlmon's skin was evidently a good deal thicker than Bird's. Soon after their return to Paris, he publicly announced his plans to become Ernest's first publisher. He issued a two-page leaflet, listing the forthcoming publications of Contact Editions. These would include volumes of verse by William Carlos Williams, Mina Loy, and Marsden Hartley, a book of McAlmon's own called *Post-Adolescence,* and another of "Short Stories" by Ernest Hemingway. Ernest had only three short stories to his name—"Up in Michigan," "My Old Man," and the new one from Cortina, "Out of Season." But there were always the poems. Ernest obviously fancied himself as a poet, and McAlmon saw no reason why his first book should not include both poetry and prose.

With Ernest's entire output scheduled for publication by McAlmon, there was nothing left over for Bill Bird's Three Mountains Press edition of his work, which was supposed to be the sixth volume in Pound's "inquest" series. Bird issued a little hand-printed broadside announcing it simply as "Blank, by Ernest M. Hemingway." It was up to Ernest to fill in the blank. Bill liked the six experimental miniatures that Jane Heap had printed in *The Little Review,* and length, as such, was happily not a problem. If Ernest could get together a dozen more of the miniatures to add to the first six, the whole would make a respectable little volume, printed on handmade paper and issued in a limited edition of 300 copies.

Ernest now began talking of going back to Spain to get some more firsthand material. Gertrude Stein recommended Pamplona, an upland city on a golden plateau in the Basque country of Navarre. Early in July each year there was a celebration called the Fiesta of San Fermín. It lasted a week and attracted the best matadors and the bravest bulls in all of Spain. Hadley was eager to go. She and Ernest agreed that a session with the bullfights might be a "stalwart" prenatal influence for the baby. They could also escape from the confinement of the flat and the perpetual droning music of the Bal Musette downstairs. All through June Ernest tramped the rainy boulevards, dreaming of Spanish sunlight. He even had a half an idea of bringing back a bull calf "to practice veronicas with."

Neither Hadley nor Ernest knew Spanish or anything about the north of Spain. Nor were they prepared for what they found in Pamplona on the sixth of July. The fiesta began with fireworks and continued through a noisy week of drinking and dancing, with religious processions and special Masses in the churches, and bullfights every afternoon. Each morning at dawn Ernest roused Hadley to watch the bulls come galloping down a mile and a half of cobble-stoned streets to the pens in the Plaza de Toros. Ahead of the bulls ran all the young bucks of Pamplona, flirting with death and showing off to the crowds that were packed six deep along the route. Betweentimes came the riau-riau dancing, with men in blue shirts and red kerchiefs shuffling and singing through the streets and squares to the music of fifes and drums. The celebration reached its daily climax each afternoon at the bullfights. Five of the best matadors in Spain were gored in the first five days.

"By God," wrote Ernest, "they have bullfights in that town!" The Villar bulls were fast and brave, with horns like sword blades. Among the matadors, he singled out two for special attention. One was Nicanor Villalta, a native of Aragon, tall as a telephone pole, brave as a lion, and with a neck so long that he had to develop a special style in order not to look grotesque. The other was Manuel García, called Maera—"dark, thin-hipped, gaunt-eyed . . . arrogant, slouching, and somber." He was also "generous, humorous, proud, bitter, foul-mouthed, and a great drinker. . . . He loved to kill bulls and lived with much passion and enjoyment." Ernest and Hadley agreed that if they had a son they would name him for Nicanor Villalta. But it was to Maera that Ernest paid the highest tribute he could think of: *"Era muy hombre."*

Ernest's chief legacy from Pamplona was his memory of the bullfights. Hadley's was a bad cold. Back in Paris she grew so pale that he began to worry about her. He was also worried about himself. He had made some notes for the sketches he meant to write for the Three Mountains Press book, but that was as far as he got. Each day dribbled away in domestic trivialities. In the morning he bought rolls, made coffee, fed the new puppy, emptied the slop pails, cleaned up the kitchen, and at last, if he was lucky, found an hour to write in before lunchtime. He lay awake nights worrying about his writing. Hadley was agitated by the pregnant woman's desire for exotic foods. One night Ernest tossed until dawn, when he fell into a doze. Hadley awoke him to say that she had a great desire for waffles and muskmelons. Ernest rolled out angrily to make the morning coffee. The words of a new sketch were already forming in his head. But it fell to pieces in his mind while he went through the motions of housework.

Time, he felt, was breathing down his neck. In a month they would be sailing for Canada so that Hadley could have the baby on American soil. He made it clear to his friends that he did not look forward either to Canada or to fatherhood. One day he sat gloomily by the window in Guy Hickok's office while Guy and a visitor were discussing birth control. At last he roused himself. "There is no sure preventative," said he, looking darkly at the others. But all through late July and early August he labored over a series of new miniatures for Bill Bird's little volume. He found material for two in the American Midwest: the hanging of a desperado named Sam Cardinella in Chicago, and the murder of two cigar-store burglars by an Irish policeman in Kansas City. Two others related to the war in Italy. One dealt with a young American named Nick and an Italian named Rinaldi lying wounded at Fossalta-di-Piave. The other summarized Ernest's love affair with Agnes in Milan, concluding with an account of his homecoming and her letter of rejection. Writing it down was a way of getting rid of the dwindling remnants of his spite. There was another sketch about a chance meeting with a young Hungarian Communist in Italy in 1919. Shorty Wornall, the film-maker he had met in Adrianople, had told him about an informal interview with the King of Greece in the garden of the royal palace in Athens. This was good for another laconic anecdote. Like all Greeks, the King had said that he wanted to go to America.

But the other five miniatures were all derived from Ernest's recent observations of the Spanish bullfight. There was an account of a gored horse that broke into a sorry canter with its blue entrails hanging out; an action portrait of a hapless matador in disgrace with the crowd; and another about a Mexican torero so irresponsible that he drunkenly danced in the streets of Pamplona on the very afternoon of a bullfight in which he was supposed to appear. Two of the best among the sketches immortalized Ernest's latest heroes, Villalta and Maera. One showed Villalta making a perfect kill. The other was an imaginary account of Maera's goring and death. This was a curious experiment, since Maera was still very much alive. He continued to fight with his customary brilliance for many months after Ernest's book appeared. When he died at last, it was not from a horn wound but from an advanced case of tuberculosis.

Most of these sketches were done by the hot Sunday afternoon of August 5th when a messenger climbed the stairs to Ernest's flat. The package he brought contained the proof sheets and cover design for the Contact Edition of Ernest's *Three Stories and Ten Poems*. It was a memorable day. Ernest ripped off the paper and read through his book, only slightly dismayed by the slenderness of the contents. It occurred to him that it might be fattened up with blank pages at the beginning and the end. He checked a few of the books on his shelf. Dos Passos's *Three Soldiers* opened with eight blank pages. Max Beerbohm's *Seven Men* and Flaubert's *Madame Bovary* each had four. Ernest took the book to show to Gertrude Stein. She agreed with him that the full table of contents ought to be printed on the front cover in good, bold, black type. Ernest was hoping for bound copies before he sailed for Canada. He typed out a two-page note to McAlmon, filled with marginal notations and postscripts. Then he mailed the epochmaking package back to the printer in Dijon.

Ten days later it was time to go. They packed their bags, gave the new puppy to a neighbor, and went to say good-bye to Gertrude and Alice, the Straters, the Hickoks, and the Pounds. Everybody said they must hurry back to Paris as soon as the baby was ready to travel. Ezra took Hadley aside for a quiet talk about the future. "Never try to change Hem," he said. "Most wives try to change their husbands. With him it would be a terrible mistake. When you come back from Canada with a baby, you won't be the same. Women's minds undergo a softening process when they become mothers." Big with the child she was going to bear, Hadley gazed at Ezra with serious eyes. She had never liked him much. She thought him too imperious, too magisterial. But she would remember his parting admonition all her life.

CHAPTER 4

Sun Ascending

16. THE BEARING OF THE YOUNG

FOR all their talk of a year in limbo, the Hemingways were surrounded by a warm cloud of hospitality the moment they stepped ashore in Quebec from the Cunard liner *Andania*. There was a note from John Bone which made no attempt to conceal his exuberance at Ernest's homecoming, and another from Greg Clark that welcomed "Dear Old Hemmy" to "the land of trouts and deers and spaces." He and his wife Helen were eager to meet Hadley. "The paper needs you bad," said Greg, "and you will be in a position to tear into things and write your name on the skies."

But Greg was mistaken. When Ernest went to work on September 10th, he discovered that his new boss was Harry Hindmarsh, the city editor of the *Daily Star*. Hindmarsh was a large man with heavy shoulders and close-cropped hair, hard-driving and self-assured. He decided at once that Hemingway was too big for his breeches and needed taking down a peg or two. Not only would he get no by-line but he would also be sent to cover assignments out of town. One of his first jobs was the story of an escaped convict in Kingston, Ontario.

Hadley bided her time at a family hotel called the Selby on Sherbourne Avenue. The doctor said that the baby would not arrive until late October or early November. The Connables still lived on Lyndhurst Avenue, where Ernest had stayed in 1920. The Clarks helped the Hemingways to find an apartment in a new brick building called Cedarvale Mansions at 1599 Bathurst Street in the Connables' section of town. They moved in at the end of September. Dr. Hemingway shipped the wedding presents which had been stored in Oak Park. Pictures by the Frenchman Masson and the Japanese Kumae leaned against the walls waiting to be hung when Ernest had time. There was a sunroom looking south towards the ravine behind the Connable estate and a single bedroom with a let-down Murphy bed.

Ernest was looking healthy and handsome, but he missed Paris. Bill Bird was still at work hand-setting the book of sketches. He had lately been toying with the idea of framing each page with a border of newsprint, carefully selected to serve both as decoration and illustration. What could be more fitting for a book by a young journalist? Even the proposed title reflected Ernest's connection with current history: they were going to call it *in our time*. Pound forwarded Bill Bird's letter with a postscript of his own:

> For yr
> ap— or
> disap——proval
> R.S.V.P.—
> romptly.

Hindmarsh sent Ernest to investigate a mining story in the Sudbury Basin north of Georgian Bay, where seams of anthraxolite had lately been discovered. He took along three back numbers of the *Pictorial Review,* which was then serializing Joseph Conrad's novel *The Rover.* Ernest dutifully filed a couple of stories on the mining situation and then settled down to read Conrad in his room at the Nickel Range Hotel in Sudbury. "When morning came," he wrote, "I had used up all my Conrad like a drunkard. I had hoped it would last me the trip, and felt like a young man who has blown his patrimony. But, I thought, he will write more stories. He has lots of time."

The next out-of-town assignment took Ernest to New York to cover the arrival of the British Prime Minister, David Lloyd George, who was accompanied by his daughter Megan. Leaving Hadley in the care of the Connables and the Clarks, Ernest went down by train early in October. He had not seen New York for almost two years and was much impressed by the beauty of the skyscrapers at Broad and Wall. But he would not have lived there for love or money. The city was filled with the "damndest looking people" who never smiled or laughed. One of the strangest was a religious fanatic who was chalking red and yellow signs on the pavement before the Stock Exchange. Ernest stopped to listen along with some messenger boys from the financial district.

"He sent his only begotten Son to die on the tree," the fanatic shouted. "He sent his only begotten Son to hang there and die."

"Pretty tough on de boy," said one of the messengers.

Isabelle Simmons, the girl from Oak Park whom Ernest had taught to ski at Chamby in January, was now enrolled at Barnard College. Ernest collared her one morning just as she was coming from a class. He wanted her help when the British party arrived. She would handle the woman's angle, asking Megan some questions that he would provide. Isabelle reluctantly agreed, boarding the tender with the women reporters, asking the questions, and returning the answers to Ernest. He was convinced that Megan had been brought along to meet a marriageable American millionaire. He had already seen Lloyd George at the Lausanne Peace Conference and his view of the Prime Minister was colored by Ryall's view that he was cantankerous, temperamental, and vicious. He filed half a dozen stories on the great man's arrival but failed to say anything about a speech by Deputy Mayor Hulbert of New York, who had greeted the visitor with a surly lecture on the sins of Great Britain. The New York papers carried the story, but the *Toronto Star* was scooped. The *Star's* publisher, J. E. Atkinson, angrily telephoned the night editor to take Hemingway off the Lloyd George tour immediately. But Ernest was already on his way home aboard the special train.

He was still in transit late in the evening of October 9th when Hadley's labor pains began. Mrs. Connable packed her off to the hospital and the child was born at two o'clock on the morning of the 10th. It was a boy, weighing seven pounds five ounces, with dark-brown hair the color of Ernest's, widely spaced blue eyes, a perfect little torso, and a Hemingway nose. When Ernest hurried in that morning at nine for his first sight of the baby, he told Hadley that the nose made the child resemble the King of Spain. There was even a Spanish flavor in the name they had chosen, John Hadley Nicanor Hemingway, in honor of his mother and the matador Villalta. The only nuisance in the whole affair was Hindmarsh, whom both of them blamed for having sent Ernest to New York at the worst possible time. Hadley sent a note to Isabelle Simmons, complaining that she had been obliged to bear the child "without the heart-warming presence of my Tiny." On reaching the hospital, said Hadley, Ernest had quite broken down "for a while from fatigue and strain," though he was afterwards very "sweet." Yesterday, October 11th, he had been "bawled out by the brute at the office" for having come to the hospital before checking in at the *Star*. "Izz," wrote Hadley, "I think we are going to leave here as soon as I am safely strong again. It is too horrible to describe or linger over and it will kill or scar my Tiny if we stay too long. He is almost crazy and our hearts are heavy, heavy just when we ought to be so happy."

By the middle of October all the trees along the ravine were bright with fall colors and the Hemingway apartment was thick with buzzing flies. The new cat enjoyed hunting them, leaping straight into the air to snap them up with evident relish. The cat's droppings accumulated behind the clawfoot bathtub and Ernest cleaned them up with a copy of the *Daily Star*. He was still angry at Hindmarsh, and the gesture gave him special pleasure. He engaged a practical nurse for Hadley's homecoming, a fine old woman aged eighty-nine who kept the apartment clean and helped with the washing. The child was gaining steadily on four-hour feedings. "Six ten two," wrote Ernest, "six ten two six ten two am and pm." Someone had given them a Canadian mother's book, full of phrases like "Daddy will do it. Won't you, Daddy?" Ernest added one of his own for use at six in the morning: "Daddy will have to push the Canadian mother out of bed, won't you, Daddy?" By the age of one month, the well-fed boy was "beginning to laugh" at his parents. "I am getting very fond of him," wrote his father to Gertrude Stein.

Ernest was now a full-fledged author. In one of the closets he was treasuring a modest pile of copies of *Three Stories and Ten Poems*. The disappointment was that none of the American reviewers had so much as hinted at the book's existence. Then someone sent him a clipping of a column by Burton Rascoe from a Sunday edition of the New York *Tribune*. Rascoe said that he had paid a call on Edmund Wilson, who reviewed books regularly for a powerful monthly magazine called the *Dial*. Wilson had handed Rascoe a copy of the Exiles number of *The Little Review* and called his attention to six prose sketches by a young writer named Hemingway. Rascoe thought them "amusing stuff." He went on to say that Lewis Galantière had lately sent him a copy of *Three Stories and Ten Poems* by the same author. He had not yet got around to reading it.

Rascoe's delay in reading the book struck Ernest as unforgivable. On Armistice Day he sat down in the sun-room and wrote a letter to Edmund Wilson:

Dear Mr. Wilson: In Burton Rascoe's Social and Literary Notes I saw you had drawn his attention to some writing of mine in the *Little Review*. I am sending you *Three Stories and Ten Poems*. As far as I know it has not yet been reviewed in the States. Gertrude Stein writes me she has done a review but I don't know whether she has gotten it published yet. You don't know anything in Canada. I would like to send out some for review but do not know whether to put a dedication, as compulsory in France, or what. Being an unknown name and the books unimposing they would probably be received as [such?] by Mr. Rascoe, who has not yet had time, after three months, to read the copy Galantière sent him. (He could read it all in an hour and a half.) The Contact Publishing Co. is McAlmon. It has published Wm. Carlos Williams, Mina Loy, Marsden Hartley and McAlmon. I hope you like the book. If you are interested could you send me the names of four or five people to send it to to get it reviewed? It would be terribly good of you. This address will be good until January when we go back to Paris. Thanking you very much whether you have the time to do it or not. Yours sincerely, Ernest Hemingway.

Wilson read the book at once and wrote Hemingway that some of it was very good. He did not much care for "Up in Michigan," while "My Old Man" reminded him strongly of Sherwood Anderson's race-track stories. Yet he thought Ernest's prose superior to his poems. He praised the miniatures from *The Little Review* and was amused by the satirical poem on the Lausanne conference which Jane Heap had printed in the same number. He ended by offering to include a notice of *Three Stories and Ten Poems* in the "Briefer Mentions" section of the *Dial*. Ernest replied with suitable modesty. Perhaps it would be better to postpone the "Briefer Mentions" notice until the Three Mountains Press brought out *in our time* in December. Wilson could then review both books at once. Ernest mentioned the forthcoming appearance of "My Old Man" in *The Best Short Stories of 1923*. O'Brien, said he, was planning to dedicate the volume to Hemingway and had even suggested that Ernest might submit a collection of his stories to Boni and Liveright in New

York. Did that mean O'Brien could persuade them to publish such a book? Ernest did not know. Maybe Wilson could advise him.

As for his alleged debt to Anderson, Ernest could not agree. "My Old Man" was about a boy and his father and some race horses. Sherwood had also written about boys and horses, but "very differently." Ernest was sure that he had not been inspired by Anderson, whom he knew pretty well but had not seen in the flesh for several years. Sherwood's recent work seemed "to have gone to hell, perhaps from people in New York telling him too much how good he was." But Ernest was very fond of him. He had written good stories. So had E. E. Cummings, whose *Enormous Room* was the best book Ernest had read in 1922. He was highly critical of another recent war story, Willa Cather's *One of Ours,* which had won a prize and enjoyed big sales. The irony, said Ernest, was that all her war scenes were faked, stolen from the battle sequences in D. W. Griffith's *The Birth of a Nation.* The book was nothing but Griffith Catherized. "Poor woman," said Ernest, "she had to get her war experience somewhere."

Ernest's newspaper work was now confined largely to potboiling feature articles for the *Star Weekly.* He wrote Gertrude Stein that he would probably chuck journalism, as she had often advised him to do, and go all out for serious writing. As soon as the baby was three months old, they would all go back to Paris, sailing from New York on the Cunarder *Antonia,* which Ernest Catherized to *My Antonia.* Working for the *Star* used up all his time and energy. "It is impossible," he wrote Sylvia Beach, "for me to do any writing of my own." He was homesick for Paris. Canada was "a dreadful country." He would "like to swing a *crochet* on the *menton* of Canada." He understood now why men could bring themselves to commit suicide: it was simply because of so great a pile-up of things to be done that they could not see their way clear of the tangle.

It was characteristic of him to overdramatize the demands, difficulties, and complexities of his work for the *Star.* He told Mary Lowrey, the paper's girl reporter, that his three months in Toronto had destroyed ten years of his literary life. His only literary friendship of the fall was formed with Morley Callaghan, a sophomore at the university who worked part time for the *Star.* One day Morley looked up from the table in the library where he was beating out an assigned story. Hemingway was watching him.

He was sitting across from me [wrote Callaghan], leaning close, and there was real sweetness in his smile and a wonderful availability. . . . He made me feel that he was eagerly and deeply involved in everything. We began to talk. . . . He had come to Toronto with good expectations, and now he seemed to feel smothered, though he had good friends here. . . . He gave me a quick rundown on the talents of the better-known reporters. This one was "a good newspaperman." Another one —"There's no one better at the kind of thing he's doing." But with some he was brutal. "Him? He simply has no shame." This one had a homosexual style. Then we began to talk about literature. All his judgments seemed to come out of an intense and fierce conviction, but he offered them to you as if he were letting you in on something. "James Joyce is the greatest writer in the world," he said. *Huckleberry Finn* was a very great book. Had I read Stendhal? Had I read Flaubert? Always appearing to be sharing a secret; yet watching me intently.

He asked Callaghan if he wrote fiction. "A little," said the boy. He would show Ernest one of his stories. When they passed on the stairs some days later, Ernest growled, "You didn't bring that story down." Callaghan said that he had been too busy. "I see," said Ernest, with a sudden snarl. "I just wanted to see if you were another god-damned phoney."

Around the offices of the *Star,* which had meant so much to him in 1920, he could now find little but boredom. He typed out an analysis of some of his fellow workers.

And so they talked. Then they talked some more. Down through the ages. . . . Listen to it. [Bobby] Reade is a Rhodes Scholar with a Cockney wife. . . . Greg [Clark] is an ex-major of infantry and a very good soldier. Neither of them knows a goddam thing about what he is talking about. . . . They don't have to work. . . . Bill Wiggins sneaks in to use a typewriter. . . . Reade and Clark sit around and talk. Talk is cheap. . . . They like to use names. . . . All of the names are a little worn. None of the names comes out clean and hard and sharp. The names come out like old scenery. . . . I am happy because I have the little African fetish from Angola. It is very beautiful and gives me pleasure. It is much better than Leger's drawings. Neither of them would look at it. They only like new ideas when they come out of *Vanity Fair* or some other place like that. They do not like the little fetish. Jimmy [Frise] likes it. He is the only artist on the paper except me. . . . Jimmy understands people and is the best fellow I know. He understands everything. . . . He understood Hadley the first time he met her . . . Bobby Reade is dry inside his head like the vagina of an old whore. Dry and futile. . . . There is really nothing there. . . . I have not done Greg [Clark] justice. Maybe I have hurt him. It would be cruel to hurt him but also difficult because he is not flat but round all around. . . . He loves his wife and his baby. He loves hunting and fishing and fishing tackle. He loves guns and books about guns. . . . He also loves to think. He thinks very well but he never strains himself. He likes it about Canada, too. What I dislike he dislikes too but it does not touch him. . . . Greg is very romantic. But I can never understand all the way inside of him because he is romantic. I am romantic too and that is the trouble. You cannot dismiss him or classify him because he is always acting and you cannot tell how much of it is acting. He also acts inside himself. He is an officer and a gentleman. It is better that way. He does things for people. . . . There is too much India rubber in him. I have never seen him angry. . . . If he has a weakness it is having too much sense. He writes the best of anyone on the paper. I have known him a long time but I do not know much about him. I do not know all about a man until I have seen him cry. Sooner or later you will see every man cry. It is like chemistry. When he cries is when he is separated into his component parts. Greg is my friend and I know less about him than I do about Hindmarsh. Hindmarsh is a son of a bitch and a liar and they are easy to understand. A good man is hard to understand. A son of a bitch always goes by the rules. . . . The only thing I hold against Greg is that he did not know it about horse racing or about boxing. They are the tests on a man. But I don't hold it against him. Besides I have never seen him drunk. . . . I like to see every man drunk. A man does not exist until he is drunk. . . . I love getting drunk. Right from the start it is the best feeling.

Clark's view of Ernest was somewhat more charitable. "He had this dark sort of looking eyes," said Clark, "and this rosy high complexion and a kind of Latin look and this intense [manner]. . . . He was an inarticulate guy. Tried three or four ways to say everything he had to say." Both Clark and Mary Lowrey noticed that he had a slight speech impediment, the inability to pronounce the letter *l*. When he tried to say the name of the matador Villalta, said Clark, "it came out of him as Vewowda." He was "deadly serious" about his writing. When he got the proof sheets of *in our time* from Bill Bird, he brought them round to the office saying, "I've discovered a new form." Morley Callaghan read them admiringly. "What do your friends in Paris say about this work?" he asked. Ernest answered calmly. "Ezra Pound says it is the best prose he has read in forty years." Behind the outward calm Callaghan sensed "that he was willing to be ruthless with himself or with anything or anybody that got in the way of the perfection of his work."

The finished copies of *in our time* arrived for Christmas. It was a handsome little volume with a montage of newspaper headlines on the cover. There was also a woodcut portrait of the artist as a young man, used as a frontispiece and based on Mike Strater's boxer portrait of 1922. But the number to be placed on sale had dwindled from 300, owing to the carelessness of a French printer who had used watermarked paper in reproducing the woodcut. Only 170 perfect copies survived the run. Bird sent fifty of the others for use as gifts and review copies. Ernest lost no time in putting one of them into the mails for Edmund Wilson.

He also paid a flying visit to Oak Park. Hadley did not go because so long a trip might upset the baby and keep them from sailing back to Paris on January 19th. His mother was much impressed with Ernest's new maturity, so like that of his grandfather, Ernest Hall.

As you sat and talked Sunday night [she wrote Ernest afterwards] you expressed the very same views of life which he held. . . . I remember his saying, "Patriotism is the last resort of thugs and scoundrels" so strongly did he feel that only World Patriotism was right. Nothing could have made me happier than to sense the warm heart of you, my boy, in your generous gift to Uncle [Tyley]. The tears just poured down his face, and we cried in each other's arms, off in a corner of the music room. You will never know the joy it is to a mother to find her son is a thoroughbred.

Ernest's opinion of Harry Hindmarsh had not changed; it had only intensified. On his return from Oak Park he typed out a letter of resignation addressed, significantly, to John Bone. He hoped that Bone would not construe his brevity as rudeness. While he was in Europe, he had dealt with Bone;

since then, his boss had been Hindmarsh. Only yesterday, said Ernest, Hindmarsh had proved that he was neither wise, just, nor honest. Under the circumstances there was no use in continuing to work for the *Star* under Mr. Hindmarsh's direction. The effective date of Ernest's resignation was January 1, 1924.

The remaining days in Toronto were spent in preparing for the journey back to Europe. Since they were going to jump their six-month lease at Cedarvale Mansions, they conspired with their friends to carry off their personal possessions to be held for them until they were ready to leave. In this way, one by one, the wedding presents and the pictures disappeared from the premises. By the time Ernest's fellow reporter, Jimmy Cowan, came to be married in the Hemingway flat, nothing remained but the Murphy bed and the rented grand piano. The Connables gave them a farewell party on the evening of the 12th. Mary Lowrey was the only *Star* staffer who came to see them off at the station. The locomotive spat clouds of steam into the frozen air and the train began its long trip to New York. They were both too busy with the baby and the luggage to look back at the receding image of Toronto.

17. CARPENTER'S LOFT

WAITING in New York for the *Antonia's* sailing date, Ernest looked and acted like a man released from prison. Margaret Anderson and Jane Heap were in town and he took them to a prizefight at the Madison Square Garden. His running commentary on the action was a new and baffling science to Miss Anderson. "People sitting near us strained forward to hear what he was saying," she wrote. "Afterward, as we walked through the night streets, he described the fight again, round by round, blow by blow. No one ever talked more excitingly about sports." Isabelle Simmons saw them off at the Cunard pier. So did Ernest's cousin, Walter Johnson, who was much amused by his outfit of tweed golf pants, woolen stockings, beret, and gnarled walking stick. The total effect was as outlandish as Ernest no doubt intended.

The first problem in Paris was to find an apartment. Ezra's *pavillon* in the rue Notre Dame des Champs was too cold and damp for the baby, but there was another available flat on the second floor of a building farther up the hill. It was a pleasant street sloping down from the corner of the Avenue de l'Observatoire and the Boulevard du Montparnasse, an easy stroll from the Luxembourg Gardens, where Hadley could air the baby, a stone's throw from an unspoiled café called La Closerie des Lilas, and much closer to Gertrude Stein's than the former walk-up apartment in the rue du Cardinal Lemoine. The whole neighborhood was a good deal prettier and more polite than that of the Montagne Ste.-Geneviève, though not much quieter. The Hemingways' windows at Number 113 looked down upon a sawmill and lumberyard. It was owned and operated by Pierre Chautard, who lived with his wife and a small dog on the ground floor. The whine of the circular saw, the chuff of the donkey-engine that drove it, the hollow boom of newly sawn planks being laid in piles, and the clatter of the ancient camions that carried the lumber away made such a medley that Ernest was often driven to the haven of the Closerie des Lilas to do his writing.

In the apartment itself, a dark tunnel of a hall led to a kitchen with a stone sink and a two-ring gas burner for cooking. There was a dining room, mostly filled by a large table, and a small bedroom where Ernest sometimes worked. The master bedroom held a stove and double bed, with a small dressing room large enough for the baby's crib. Hadley quickly rehired the *femme de ménage,* Madame Henri Rohrbach, who had worked for her off and on before. Marie was a sturdy peasant from Mur-de-Bretagne. She and her husband, who was called Ton-Ton, lived at 10 bis, Avenue des Gobelins. Her own nickname was Marie Cocotte, from her method of calling the chickens at home on the farm in Brittany. She took at once to the child and often bore him away in a carriage lent by the Straters to see Ton-Ton, who was a retired soldier with time on his hands. Madame Chautard, the wife of the owner of the sawmill, was a plump and childless woman with brassy hair and a voice so harsh that it made the baby cry. She seemed to be envious of Hadley's motherhood. Watching the child drink his daily ration of orange juice she could only say scornfully, *"Il sera un poivrot comme sa mère."* Of the baby's many nicknames—Gallito, Matt, and Joe—the one that stuck was Bumby, which Hadley invented to signify his warm, plump, teddy-bearish, arm-filling solidity which both parents admired and enjoyed.

Ford Madox Ford had now moved to Paris to start a new literary magazine, the *transatlantic review.* His publishing office was a sort of elevated gallery in the rear of Bill Bird's Three Mountains Press on the Quai d'Anjou. While Ernest was in Toronto, Pound had advised him to "come home" to direct the editorial policy of the *transatlantic.* Although Ernest had then supposed that Ezra's invitation was "exaggerated," he now discovered that it was true. The first time they met at Ezra's studio, Pound enthusiastically puffed Ernest to Ford. Ernest was dancing around on his toes shadowboxing, and threatening, as Ford said, "a fat and blinking bonze," one of the relics of Ezra's Chinese period.

"That young man," said Ford, "appears to have Sinophobia." "He's only getting rid of his superfluous energy," said Ezra. "You ought to have had him for your subeditor. He's an experienced journalist. He writes very good verse and he's the finest prose stylist in the world. . . . He's disciplined, too."

Ford professed interest. Hemingway reminded him of an "Eton-Oxford, husky-ish young captain of a midland regiment of His Britannic Majesty." The arrangements were soon consummated. "Ford asked me to read MSS for him," wrote Ernest, "and I used to go down there and take a batch of them out on the Quai and read them. . . . Some of the stories I used to rewrite for fun." He found Ford personally unattractive in the extreme, with colorless eyelashes and eyebrows above the "washed-out blue" of his eyes, a "heavy stained mustache" through which he breathed asthmatically, and a torso which resembled an "ambulatory, well-clothed, up-ended hogshead." He had discovered the Bal Musette in the rue du Cardinal Lemoine and urged Ernest to bring Hadley over for a "little evening" of drinking and dancing. "I lived above it for two years," said Ernest. But Ford was not listening. "It's quite gay," he said. "I stumbled on it quite by chance. I'll draw you a map so you can find it."

Wearing worn tennis shoes and a patched jacket, Ernest appeared when he felt like it at Ford's Thursday literary teas in the Quai d'Anjou. It was there that he first met a well-dressed, dark-haired young man with broad shoulders, a firm chin, and the profile of a classical Greek wrestler. This was Harold Loeb, a Princeton alumnus eleven years out. He had in fact wrestled in college and had recently made a small splash as founder and editor of the little magazine *Broom*. Loeb was eight years older than Ernest and came of two prominent Jewish families in New York: the Loebs and the Guggenheims. He and Kitty Cannell, a beautiful golden-haired girl who had been a professional dancer, occupied adjacent flats in the rue Montessuy near the Eiffel Tower. They presently invited Ernest and Hadley to a lobster dinner at the Nègre de Toulouse. When they called at the apartment above the sawmill, they were much amused at Bumby, whom Ernest had taught "to put up his fists and assume a ferocious expression."

Kitty thought Hadley one of the nicest girls she had ever met. She resented the fact that Ernest was making his wife live an unnecessarily poverty-stricken life in well-worn clothes and a dingy flat. She made a point of taking Hadley out shopping and sometimes made her small gifts of costume jewelry. When she discovered that Ernest resented this, Kitty took a defiant pleasure in setting "a bad example to a submissive wife." But the Hemingways' financial problems were real. Ford paid Ernest nothing for his work as subeditor. There was no longer any income from the *Star*. Worst of all, Hadley's patrimony was rapidly dwindling. She had entrusted the investment of her funds to George Breaker, the husband of her good friend Helen. His bad judgment had quickly cut her available capital almost in half.

In his capacity as manuscript scout for the *transatlantic,* Ernest now conceived the idea of bringing out serially an early book of Gertrude Stein's, *The Making of Americans*. He broached his plan to Gertrude, who was "quite overcome" with excitement. Together they copied out the first fifty pages from the sewn and bound manuscript which had been languishing on her shelves since 1911.

Ford alleges he is delighted with the stuff [wrote Ernest presently], and is going to call on you. . . . He is going to publish the 1st installment in the April No. going to press the 1st part of March. He wondered if you would accept 30 francs a page (his magazine page) and I said I thought I could get you to. (*Be haughty but not too haughty.*) I made it clear it was a remarkable scoop . . . obtained only through my obtaining genius. He is under the impression that you get big prices when you consent to publish. I did not give him this impression but did not discourage it. After all it is [John] Quinn's money and the stuff is worth all of their 35,000 f. Treat him high wide and handsome. . . . It is really a scoop for them you know. They are going to have Joyce in the same number.

The April number of the *transatlantic* made literary history in other respects than the publication of Joyce and Gertrude Stein. It contained the earliest reviews of *Three Stories and Ten Poems* and *in our time*. The three stories were said to show "a sensitive feeling for the emotional possibilities of a situation." Marjorie Reid, Ford's secretary, accurately described the miniatures as seizing upon those "moments when life is condensed and clean-cut and significant," and presenting them "in minute narratives that eliminate every useless word." The April number also contained a short story of Ernest's called "Indian Camp." His own title was omitted in favor of the generic term, *Works in Progress,* which covered also selections from Tristan Tzara, the founder of literary Dadaism, and from Joyce's still-untitled *Finnegans Wake.*

Ernest had written "Indian Camp" since his return from Toronto. It told of a night-time emergency visit to an Indian settlement in northern Michigan. Apart from the Indians, the chief persons were Nick Adams, his father, Dr. Henry Adams, and his Uncle George. Dr. Adams performed a Caesarean section on a young Indian woman, using his jackknife as a scalpel and closing the incision with a nine-foot tapered gut leader from his fishing kit. Only afterwards did he discover that the woman's husband, unable to stand his wife's screams, had committed suicide in the upper bunk by cutting his throat from ear to ear. The story used the Walloon Lake locale and an Indian camp not unlike the settlement near Bacon's farm. The doctor, his brother, and his son were clearly modeled on Dr. Hemingway, his brother George, and Ernest. But the melodramatic circumstances were Ernest's own invention. What he revealed to no one was that he had cut his story rigorously, omitting an entire preliminary episode covering eight longhand pages. This was the story of Nick Adams, a small boy afraid of the dark, firing off a rifle to bring his father and his uncle back from jacklight fishing in the lake. When they returned, he told them a cock-and-bull story about having been scared by some animal "fooling around the tent." It had sounded, he said, "like a cross between a fox and a wolf." Dr. Adams's kindness and sympathy were firmly established as counterpoint to the evident absence of both qualities in Uncle George.

Ernest's reasons for lopping off the original opening of his story remain obscure. He may have shortened it to fit the available space in Ford's review. He may have been trying out his new critical theory that something omitted can still affect the reader as if it were there. He may have decided that the comic aspects of the small-boy story softened unduly the hammerblows of violence in the main story's double climax of birth and death. Finally, he may have made the deletion because it clearly indicated the presence of cowardice in Nick Adams, whom he was planning to develop as a hero of tougher fiber.

When Bumby reached the age of five months, he was taken to be christened at a little ceremony just before vespers in St. Luke's Episcopal Chapel in the rue de la Grande Chaumière. Chink Smith stood up as godfather and Gertrude Stein was godmother. Since Hadley entertained no special denominational loyalties and Ernest was not prepared to raise his son as a Catholic, Gertrude had said that Episcopalianism was as sound a sect as any. She soon began to call Bumby Goddy, as short for godson, and came with Alice Toklas to his six-months' birthday party on April 10th, bringing several rubber animals and a silver christening cup for orange juice. Hadley saluted the occasion with a little supper of oysters and white wine.

At Ford's literary tea that very afternoon Ernest had remarked rather plaintively that it took a man years to get his name known. "Nonsense," said Ford, "you will have a great name in no time at all." Ford had in fact conceived a marked admiration for his twenty-four-year-old subeditor. "I did not read more than six words of his," he wrote in retrospect, "before I decided to publish everything that he sent me." Even in conversation, Ernest behaved like a true artist. He spoke hesitantly. His tendency was to "pause between words and then to speak gently but with great decision." His temperament, thought Ford, "was selecting the instances he should narrate, his mind selecting the words to employ. The impression was one of a person using restraint at the biddings of discipline."

Whatever Ford said, a great name would not come without effort, and Ernest was working fairly hard. He awoke early in the spring mornings, "boiled the rubber nipples and the bottles, made the formula, finished the bottling, gave Mr. Bumby a bottle," and wrote for a time at the dining-room table before Hadley got up. Chautard had not begun his sawing at that hour, the street was quiet, and Ernest's only companions were Mr. Bumby and Mr. Feather Puss, a large cat given them by Kitty Cannell and named with one of Hadley's nicknames. But Ernest was truly domestic only in the early mornings. He took the freedom of Paris as his personal prerogative, roving as widely as he chose. There was a gymnasium in the rue Pontoise where he often went to earn ten francs a round by sparring with professional heavyweights. The job called for a nice blend of skill and forbearance, since hirelings must be polite while fighting back just enough to engage, without enraging, the emotions of the fighters. Ernest had befriended a waiter at the Closerie des Lilas and sometimes helped him weed a small vegetable garden near the Porte d'Orléans. The waiter knew that he was a writer and warned him that the boxing might jar his brains. But Ernest was glad enough to earn the extra money. He had already begun to save up to buy pesetas for another trip to Spain in July.

Although he often said that nothing else could touch bullfighting, Ernest's passion for other sports continued unabated. He boxed for fun with Harold

Loeb, George O'Neil, and a young American architect named Paul Fisher, whose clean-cut profile reminded Loeb of an Arrow collar advertisement. Possibly for that reason Ernest one day unleashed a barrage of heavy blows, explaining to Loeb afterwards that the impulse to blast hell out of Fisher had been too strong to resist. But this was nothing new: he had done the same with Bill Smith in the old days at Horton Bay. An extroverted bank teller named T. H. (Mike) Ward introduced him to six-day bicycle racing in the smoky gloom of the Vélodrome d'Hiver and the outdoor tracks in the Stade Buffalo and the Parc du Prince. When the courts dried out, Ernest and Harold Loeb played tennis on the red-clay courts near the prison and the guillotine in the Boulevard Arago. Dr. William Carlos Williams joined them one day in May and they played until Ernest complained that his knee was giving out. He was also a frequent visitor to the prizefights in the Cirque de Paris, keeping an eye on a colored fighter named Larry Gains, in whom he had taken an interest, and using press tickets supplied by Bird and Hickok.

He was steadily enlarging his circle of acquaintances, partly in the cafés, partly at Sylvia Beach's bookshop, where he often appeared in the afternoon to read or borrow books. He renewed a nascent friendship with Donald Ogden Stewart, whom he had first met in the preceding spring. Stewart was thirty, a Yale graduate of 1916, a wise, witty, and much-traveled writer of humorous fiction. Dos Passos was often in Paris and was once or twice invited to watch the evening ceremony of bathing Bumby. Afterwards, the child left in the care of Madame Rohrbach while they all went out to dinner. On one such evening, during dinner in a Chinese restaurant, Ernest and Dos entertained little Ella Winter, whom Lincoln Steffens was about to marry, with the repeated assurance that anyone could write if he set his mind to it. "*You* can," cried Ernest, feinting at Ella's jaw. "It's hell. It takes it all out of you; it nearly kills you; but you can do it."

He knew about writer's fatigue from personal experience. He had lately begun a very long short story which he was going to call "Big Two-Hearted River." It was about the boy Nick Adams, who had appeared in "Indian Camp." Now he was grown up and making a lone fishing trip to the Fox River near Seney in the northern peninsula of Michigan. He had come back wounded from the war, but the story contained no allusion to his wounds or to the war. Ernest was trying his theory of omission once again. He was also drawing on his personal experience of fishing the Fox in 1919 with Al Walker and Jack Pentecost. They, too, were omitted so that Nick Adams could fight his therapeutic battle alone. As for changing the name of the Fox to the Two-Hearted River, Ernest had done it purposely. He explained later that the change was made "not from ignorance nor carelessness but because Big Two-Hearted River is poetry."

Not all of the stories he was setting down in the blue notebooks looked back to his personal past. He was doing some others about his fellow expatriates, indulging his satirical vein and venting his spite against people he disliked or thought pretentious. The governing spirit in these sketches was like that which had produced his acidulous portrait of Dave O'Neil, George's father, and his disquisition on Greg Clark and Bobby Reade gabbing away the hours at the *Star* offices in Toronto. The major difference was that these were full-fledged short stories. When the strawberry season arrived in Paris, he appropriated the name of his "good cousin," Frank Hines, to serve as narrator of a little story about Ford and his wife Stella Bowen arguing petulantly over the wine at dinner one evening at the Nègre de Toulouse.

Ford's review was now so close to bankrupt that he resolved on a trip to New York, partly to see his American publisher, Thomas Seltzer, but chiefly, he hoped, to secure a further grant-in-aid from John Quinn, who had so far kept the *transatlantic* afloat. The table of contents for the July number was mainly fixed before he left, but he asked Ernest to complete the job with Marjorie Reid, and to add such editorial embellishments as seemed fitting. Ernest at first refused, on the grounds that it would "bitch" his own work for the duration of Ford's absence. But, as Ernest later reported it, Ford replied that unless he were willing to undertake the job, and also to assemble a table of contents for the August number, the *transatlantic* might well blow up and go under. Ernest reluctantly agreed. On the eve of embarking from Plymouth, Ford sent back a public announcement of his decision. "We are journeying Westwards," he wrote, "leaving the helm of the review . . . in the hands of Mr. Ernest Hemingway, whose tastes march more with our own than those of most other men."

While the elephant was away, the young lion chose to play. Ernest seized the occasion of Ford's absence to insert a satirical editorial in the July number. Unsigned, and labeled "And Out of America," it impugned the talents of Tristan Tzara, Jean Cocteau, and Gilbert Seldes, whose book on *The Seven Lively Arts* was more or less favorably reviewed by Lewis Galantière in the same number. Despite Ford's honeyed remarks about having left the review in such capable hands, Ernest seems to have construed their previous conversation on the subject as a sort of quarrel. The tone of his satirical insertion suggested that he was using his newfound editorial powers to "bitch" Ford in return.

Since he was planning to take Hadley to Pamplona early in July, the preparation of the August issue posed a far greater problem—particularly of timing. He solved it in part by hastily assembling material from his friends— a long story by Dos Passos, a short one by Nathan Asch, a nonfiction article by Guy Hickok, and another long excerpt from Gertrude's *The Making of Americans*. His problems were somewhat complicated by the sudden appearance of his cousin, Frank Hines, with whom he had ridden ponies in boyhood in southern Illinois. Frank was now twenty-two and just out of Oberlin College. It amused Ernest that his sole possessions were a gaberdine coat, an extra shirt, a razor, and $85 in cash. Ernest borrowed the razor and shaved as a surprise for Hadley. Frank stayed for two weeks, careful not to obstruct his cousin's mornings, which were devoted to writing and editing in the tiny spare room of the apartment. In the afternoons, they sometimes boxed a little or played tennis with Ezra Pound. Returning from the courts, Ernest pretended that his racquet was a bullfighter's cape. He danced in front of trolley cars, executing correct and incorrect passes, and delightedly enraging the motormen. Twice in the evenings they attended neighborhood prizefights, sitting almost in the ring itself. Ernest seemed to know all the fighters and trainers by name. Afterwards, sitting at a table in the Dôme, he scornfully pointed out the American expatriates. They had come to Paris ostensibly to work, yet now were content merely to be seen in Left Bank gathering places, where they talked about writing and did none.

When Frank left for Italy with some of his Oberlin classmates, the Hemingways began their second (and Ernest's third) trip to Spain. Bumby stayed behind in the care of Madame Rohrbach. From Madrid, Ernest wrote Gertrude with his usual gusto that they were getting a lot of "dope" on bullfighting from the matadors who lived in the pension at 37, Calle San Jerónimo. They saw Gitanillo de Triana in a splendid *corrida* at Aranjuez and watched the long-necked Villalta in action against six bulls from the ranch of Martínez. Boxing looked pale beside this great sport and they could hardly wait for the beginning of the fiesta of San Fermín in Pamplona.

Ernest's enthusiastic reports on the *feria* of 1923 had encouraged a number of others. Chink Smith the soldier "suffered sincerely and deeply at what happened to the horses at his first bullfight," saying that "it was the most hateful thing he had ever seen." But he soon became deeply interested in the technical aspects of the sport. After half-a-dozen *corridas,* he was so sure of his opinions that he sprang to the defense of John Annllo, Nacional II, when another spectator criticized him. Bill and Sally Bird were also present. Sally was moderately horrified by what happened in the ring and did not go again. Dos Passos, Don Stewart, Bob McAlmon, and young George O'Neil completed the party. According to McAlmon, Ernest "had been talking a good deal about courage" and believed that "he must prove himself" at the free-for-all amateur bullfights held each morning. In a boastful letter to the Toronto *Star* he told how he and Don Stewart had handled themselves on the first day. Wearing white pants and waving a red cape, he made the legitimate bull-call—*"Huh, toro, toro!"*—and the animal charged. Ernest manfully grabbed the padded horns and succeeded in bulldogging the animal to the ground. The matadors Maera and Algabeno were standing by to take over if necessary. They "coached" Ernest and Don Stewart, and Ernest immodestly reported that he and Don performed each day before 20,000 fans. It was all very fine because the whole town split into two factions, the humanitarians who wanted them to quit while they were still alive, and the *aficionados* who arrived in a body at six every morning to make certain that the Americanos would appear.

Ernie was so God damned brave [said Stewart] we couldn't let him face the bulls without showing that we too were brave. . . . I was the only one the bull tossed, greatly to the joy of all concerned. Hem was, of course, his usual fearless self. . . . I cracked a couple of ribs when the bull hit me, but the wine of Pamplona had wonderful healing powers, and the fiesta was one of the high and memorable times.

Stewart tried dancing the riau-riau one night in the square before the Hotel de la Perla, doing so well that some of the other dancers lifted him to their shoulders in triumphant tribute to so capable an alien. Hadley was introduced to Maera and Algabeno, but her best news of the week was from Madame Rohrbach: Bumby had cut his first tooth.

Just before the celebration ended, the Birds and Bob McAlmon took the old bus for Burguete, a Basque village in the mountains near the ancient site of Roncevaux. The Hemingways followed them on the 14th, having seen the fiesta week through to the end. Ernest at once proposed a fishing trip to the Irati River a few kilometers away. The innkeeper packed a lunch, including a large slab of Manchego cheese, and they held a *fête champêtre* on the riverbank. Bill was eating a wedge of the cheese when he saw Ernest watching him with horror. "Is all the cheese like that?" he asked. The morsel in Bill's hand was alive with maggots. He hurled it into the river and retired to get rid of what he had already eaten. Hadley caught a half dozen large trout in a pool below a waterfall. Ernest lolled against the trunk of a beech tree, watching his wife in action. Chink Smith presently arrived with Dos Passos and George O'Neil. Along with McAlmon, they were going to hike to Andorra along the Spanish side of the Pyrenees. Ernest walked with them for a few kilometers. He wanted to go the rest of the way, but dutifully decided to return to Hadley.

This was no great hardship, even though he would have liked to be off with the hikers. Nothing could dampen his eager enthusiasm for the region around Burguete. He liked the ice-cold mountain streams, the great beech forests which had never known an ax, and the tall swaying pine-groves higher up towards the crests. He called it the wildest damn country in the Pyrenees. It offered the only trout fishing that had not been ruined by railroads and motorcars. Spain, said he, was the only country left in Europe that had not been shot to pieces. Mussolini's Blackshirts had ruined Italy, which now contained nothing but bad food and hysterics. But the Spaniards were the best people in the world—all of them "good guys" like Jim Dilworth of Horton Bay. Spain, in fact, was the real old stuff.

18. TRANSATLANTIC

PARIS was quiet when they got back to it—except for Bumby, who was cutting teeth and rousing the household at three in the morning. Ernest improved the night watches by cleaning out the trap in the kitchen sink. He felt so virtuous afterwards that he fell asleep in spite of Bumby's wailing.

The mountaineering bachelors returned from the Pyrenees, laden with edelweiss and covered with bedbug bites. Dos Passos, Dorman-Smith, and George O'Neil had walked the full 460 kilometers from Burguete to Andorra in two weeks' time. McAlmon, an enthusiastic starter, had been obliged to drop out with blistered heels. About the same time, Madame Chautard found her small dog dead in the courtyard. She loudly accused the neighbors of having poisoned it until an autopsy revealed that it had been run over. She hired a taxidermist to stuff and mount it as a sentimental trophy, never dreaming that the dog would one day be obliquely immortalized in American literature.

There was a time in August when Ernest would have been glad to see Ford Madox Ford stuffed and mounted. This was when he read the August number of the *transatlantic*. He had laboriously assembled and edited the contents while Ford was away in New York. Ford had returned while Ernest was in Spain. Without Ernest's knowledge, he had inserted a last-minute editorial note. It wryly accused Ernest of having stuffed the issue with an "unusually large sample" of work by his young American friends. Ford ended with a promise that future numbers would resume their normal international aspect. Ernest was enraged by what he took to be an insult. Not only had he published work by many non-Americans, but he had also gone to considerable personal sacrifice to help Ford out of his difficulties.

Ford mollified him somewhat by coming round to see him, mumbling a kind of apology, and pointing out that the magazine's coffers were now so depleted that it would either have to become a quarterly or cease publication. The original angel, John Quinn, had died of cancer, and no wealthy successor had yet appeared. Swallowing his wrath, Ernest said that he knew a man who might take over. This was Krebs Friend, the strange and lonely young war veteran whom he had first befriended in Chicago. Krebs was now in Paris, looking (as Nathan Asch said) like death warmed over, but married to an heiress who was said to be worth millions. Krebs had surprised Ernest by repaying a loan of $15, dating from 1920, and now surprised him even more by agreeing to advance Ford $200 a month for six months. It was like a lifeline to a drowning swimmer. At a directors' meeting on August 15th, Friend was rewarded with the presidency of the *transatlantic review*.

While all this was going on, Ernest had finished "Big Two-Hearted River" in a sudden burst of energy. It was the longest story he had yet written, but he added a coda of some three thousand words. This was mainly an interior monologue by Nick Adams, full of reflections about his old friends in Michigan and his new ones in Europe. There were also some observations on esthetic principles.

The only writing that was any good was what you made up, what you imagined. . . . That was the weakness of Joyce. Daedalus in *Ulysses* was Joyce himself, so he was terrible. Joyce was so damn romantic and intellectual about him. He'd made Bloom up. Bloom was wonderful. He'd made Mrs. Bloom up. She was the greatest in the world. That was the way with Mac [McAlmon]. Mac worked too close to life. You had to digest life and then create your own people. . . . Nick [Adams] in the stories was never himself. He had made him up. Of course he'd never seen an Indian woman having a baby. That was what made it good. . . . He'd seen a woman having a baby on the road to Karagatch and tried to help her. That was the way it was.

[Nick] wanted to be a great writer. He was pretty sure he would be. . . . It was hard to be a great writer if you loved the world and living in it and special people. It was hard when you loved so many places. . . . There were times when you had to write. Not conscience. Just peristaltic action. It was really more fun than anything. . . . It had more bite to it than anything else. . . . He, Nick, wanted to write about country so it would be there like Cézanne had done it in painting. You had to do it from inside yourself. . . . He felt almost holy about it. It was deadly serious. You could do it if you would fight it out. If you'd lived right with your eyes. It was a thing you couldn't talk about. . . . He knew just how Cézanne would paint this stretch of river. God, if he was only here to do it. They died and that was the hell of it. They worked all their lives and then got old and died.

But Ernest was not old: he had just turned twenty-five. Nothing that he said afterwards on the subject of writing had quite the special poignancy of these fumbling attempts to describe his intention, his ambition, his developing esthetic bias, his consuming love both for writing and for the world. Many of the phrases were arresting. Not to work too close to life, but rather to digest and then create from one's imagination. Not conscience, he said, just peristaltic action. Living right with your eyes. More fun than anything, but hell to do. Something deadly serious, almost holy. A job for all his life. Ernest wanted to be a great writer. He was pretty sure he would be. But he still managed a tone of boyish modesty when he wrote to tell Gertrude about having finished "Big Two-Hearted River." He was trying to do the country like Cézanne and having a hell of a time and sometimes getting it a little bit. "It is about 100 pages long," he wrote, "and nothing happens and the country is swell, I made it all up, so I see it all and part of it comes out the way it ought to. . . . But isn't writing a hard job, though? It used to be easy before I met you. I certainly was bad, gosh, I'm awfully bad now but it's a different kind of bad."

These words to Gertrude were, however, only the seeming modesty of a young challenger about to overtake a past master. "Big Two-Hearted River" was the latest in a series of nine remarkable stories that he had written in the seven months since his return from Toronto. His achievement was almost the literary equivalent of a population explosion. Besides "Indian Camp," he had completed "The Doctor and the Doctor's Wife," based on the episode in the summer of 1911 when Nick Boulton and Billy Tabeshaw had come to cut up the beech log on the shore at Windemere Cottage. He had written "Soldier's Home," which showed the town of Oak Park as it had looked to him after his return from the wars in January, 1919. "The End of Something" and "The Three-Day Blow" both grew out of his brief romance with Marjorie Bump at

Horton Bay in the summer of 1919. He had written "Cross-Country Snow" to commemorate his skiing sessions with George O'Neil in January, 1923. "Cat in the Rain" was derived from a rainy day spent with Hadley that February at the Hotel Splendide in Rapallo. He had also written a malicious gossip-story called "Mr. and Mrs. Smith" making fun of the alleged sexual ineptitudes of Mr. and Mrs. Chard Powers Smith.

These nine stories, together with the prose contents of *Three Stories and Ten Poems* and the miniatures from Bill Bird's edition of *in our time,* added up to a very respectable volume, both in length and quality. Stewart and Dos Passos both encouraged him to seek American publication, and offered their personal assistance. Towards the end of September, he sent the typescript off to Don Stewart at the Yale Club in New York. Harold Loeb was also eager to assist. Horace Liveright had just agreed to publish his first novel, *Doodab,* and he was generously convinced that he and Ernest might together take their places as rising stars with the firm of Boni and Liveright.

But Loeb's friend, Kitty Cannell, felt a curious foreboding about Harold's friendship with Ernest. While Hem was personally attractive, with very white teeth, cheeks like rosy apples, and a sudden dimpled smile, there was something about him that struck her as sinister. Outwardly, at least, they got on very well. In his lighter moods, he reminded her of a small boy who had just had his hair cut. They also shared a love of cats. When she had made him a present of Mr. F. Puss, he had thanked her by saying, "The only thing that reconciles me to life now is my kitty." It seemed odd to her that he had not also included his wife and his son. She thought him a good companion, with a wild sense of humor—except about himself. His word portraits of his fellow expatriates were at once very funny and extremely devastating. Beneath that attractive exterior, she thought, ran a streak of vicious cruelty. She warned Harold that Ernest had a way of turning against those who had befriended him.

Leon Fleischman, Liveright's literary scout, now came to Paris with a contract for Loeb's *Doodab.* Harold could not rest until Ernest had met Leon. Kitty was again doubtful, having noticed Hem's occasional anti-Semitic outbursts. But Harold's will prevailed and a meeting was arranged. Leon and his wife Helen had taken a flat just off the Champs Elysées. As usual, Ernest was carelessly dressed. He froze visibly when the genial Fleischman received them in a velvet smoking jacket. He said very little and sat nursing his Scotch and soda with a kind of Indian stolidity. Leon said pleasantly that he would be glad to read Ernest's stories. If he liked them, he would send them along to Liveright with a recommendation. Something in his tone hinted that this would be a great favor. At least, Hemingway took it so, and his demon pride rose darkly. But he said nothing more until the evening ended and they went down the stairs. Then he exploded profanely, calling Fleischman a low-down kike and a string of other epithets. Loeb was taken by surprise. Yet he continued to champion his friend, shrugging off Kitty's prediction that his own turn would come in time.

Ernest had meanwhile discovered an outlet for his work in a German magazine called *Der Querschnitt* (*The Cross-Section*), founded four years earlier at Frankfurt-am-Main by Alfred Flechtheim, an art dealer who owned galleries in Berlin and Dusseldorf. "He was a very able picture-dealer," wrote Ernest. "He was the only Jew who had been an officer in an Uhlan regiment in the . . . war." Flechtheim's Paris representative was one Count Alfred von Wedderkop, sometimes called "Mr. Awfully Nice" in honor of the only two English words he customarily uttered. For mysterious reasons he liked several bawdy poems of Ernest's and bought four of them for publication in *Der Querschnitt*. One was so long that it appeared in two numbers: "The Soul of Spain with McAlmon and Bird the Publishers." Another, in Ernest's worst vein of raillery, was called "The Lady Poets with Foot Notes," possibly as a left-handed satire on Eliot's use of footnotes in *The Waste Land*. Another, somewhat more serious, was "The Age Demanded," which borrowed its title from Pound's "Hugh Selwyn Mauberley." Like the rest of his puppy-doggerel, none of the *Querschnitt* poems seemed likely to enhance his reputation. It was one of the ironies of an undemanding age that Ernest was soon known among the readers of that journal as "Hemingway der Dichter."

Edmund Wilson was speaking of *Three Stories and Ten Poems* when he correctly remarked in the October number of the *Dial* that "Mr. Hemingway's poems are not particularly important." His prose, however, struck Wilson as highly distinctive. Along with Gertrude Stein and Sherwood Anderson, he had developed a special skill in using naive language to convey "profound emotions and complex states of mind." Wilson called his composite review of Ernest's first two books "Mr. Hemingway's Dry-Points" and compared the bullfight scenes from *in our time* to some of Goya's lithographs. He quoted entire the "dry little vignette" about the execution of the Greek Cabinet ministers, and said flatly that *in our time* contained "more artistic dignity than anything else about the period of the war that has as yet been written by an American." He still disliked "Up in Michigan," which "should have been a masterpiece." Instead, the "rude and primitive people" from Horton Bay failed, he felt, to emerge from the shadows into the full light of realization.

Ernest wrote to Wilson to say that he was "awfully glad" his early books had pleased so good a critic. He also alerted Wilson to the fact that he had lately finished and sent off a full-sized book of stories. The vignettes from *in our time* would appear as interchapters among the longer stories. "That is the way they were meant to go," said he, "to give the picture of the whole between examining it in detail." He compared the intended effect to that of watching a coastline from a ship, first with the naked eye and then with binoculars. He closed by praising Wilson's review as cool, clear-minded, decent, impersonal, and sympathetic. Such intelligence as Wilson had displayed was a "damn rare" commodity.

Ernest looked in vain for evidence of decency and intelligence among most of his fellow expatriates in Paris. Few of them escaped his barbs. He bought drinks for a seedy young American poet and race-horse fancier named Evan Shipman, whose society he seemed to enjoy. He also pored with seeming patience over the short stories of Nathan Asch, aged twenty-two, who was seeking to establish himself as a writer in Paris. But behind their backs he took malicious pleasure in gossiping about them. He told McAlmon of a fight between Asch and Shipman from which they both emerged unmarked after half an hour of slugging. Shipman, it seemed, had lent Asch enough money to buy some false teeth. Asch had then hit Shipman out of "kike gratitude." Ernest was nearly as hard on T. S. Eliot, whom he persisted in calling "The Major." He alluded superciliously to the "heavy uncut pages of Eliot's quarterly," the *Criterion*. When Joseph Conrad died and Ford got together a special Conrad supplement for the *transatlantic,* Ernest went out of his way to remark in print that if he could bring Conrad back to life "by grinding Mr. Eliot into a fine dry powder and sprinkling that powder over Conrad's grave in Canterbury," he would "leave for London early tomorrow morning with a sausage-grinder." He continued to admire Pound and was merely quizzical about his eccentricities. But when the Pounds gave up their studio down the street and moved permanently to Rapallo, Ernest gleefully noted that Ezra had contrived a small nervous breakdown in order to evade the work of packing up.

His deep disdain towards any form of meretriciousness or inadequacy was by way of becoming one of his chief motivations to creativity. This was not among the more endearing traits of his character. Yet it was as powerful a force as its opposite—his boyish admiration for Chink Smith fighting at Mons, or Maera killing bulls in the Plaza de Toros at Madrid. Besides his essay on Reade and Clark gabbing away the afternoons in Toronto, and the sketch of Ford and Stella bickering over the wine at the Nègre de Toulouse, and the account of Mr. and Mrs. Smith trying vainly to have a baby, other fragments of the literature of gossip were finding their way into his blue notebooks. There was one about a fat girl who had come to Paris to study piano and if possible to have a love affair. She was still a virgin after a year abroad and Ernest told how she lay listening through the wall of her apartment to the sounds of others making love. It did not matter to him that the fat girl was one of Hadley's good friends. He did another sketch about Bertram Hartman, an American painter. Bertram had met a German girl named Gusta, who was working as assistant to a fashionable photographer in Munich. According to Ernest, Gusta was tiny, dark, and Jewish-looking, and had run away from her family near Bodensee. After their marriage, Gusta made hooked rugs from designs that Bertram painted for her. These remained unsold because Gusta's prices were too high. As Edmund Wilson had shrewdly observed in his review of Ernest's first two books, "Mr. Hemingway" was "not a propagandist even for humanity."

This trait was evident in his treatment of Ford, whom he blamed for the imminent demise of the *transatlantic*. All through the autumn he had simmered with rage over Ford's "megalomaniac blundering" in the conduct of the magazine. He told Gertrude Stein that Ford was also a liar and a crook who concealed his deficiencies behind a mask of the finest synthetic English gentility. These, of course, were exaggerations, as was Ford's own rueful complaint to Miss Stein that his position as editor had made him into "a sort of green baize swing door" that everyone kicked "on entering and leaving" the office on the Quai d'Anjou.

The bad blood between them flared up finally in November when Ford chose to print an apology for Ernest's sausage-grinder assault on Eliot. "Two months ago," wrote Ford, "one of these gentlemen made an attack on Mr. T. S. Eliot. . . . We hesitated a long time over the ethics of the matter, deciding in the end that our standards must prevail. We had invited that writer to write, we had indicated no limits to his bloodthirstiness. . . . We take the opportunity of expressing for the tenth time our admiration for Mr. Eliot's poetry."

All this was mild enough, certainly, and anyone but Ernest might have forgiven Ford his gentlemanly attempt to keep the peace. But Ernest promptly construed it as an arrant insult to his critical integrity and judgment. It came, moreover, only three months after Ford had publicly accused him of overstuffing the August number with Americana. This was the end. He dropped all outward semblance of friendship for Ford, and went out of his way to be as insulting as possible. When Burton Rascoe and his wife came to Paris, Ford took them round to the Bal Musette in the rue du Cardinal Lemoine. He introduced them to Nancy Cunard, E. E. Cummings, Bob McAlmon, and Hadley Hemingway. Ernest was there, but Rascoe noticed that "he and Ford were not speaking." Ernest told Rascoe his name and gratefully shook his hand: this was the journalist who had first brought his work to the attention of Edmund Wilson. But when Ford invited them all to sit at his table near the zinc bar, Ernest flatly refused to join the group. "Pay for your own drinks, do you hear?" he shouted to Hadley above the din. "Don't let [Ford] buy you anything." Although the last two numbers of the dying *transatlantic* printed two more of his stories, he did not relent in his surly grudge against Ford. He even extended it to include the luckless Krebs Friend. Krebs, said he, was out to demonstrate his business acumen by making the magazine GO. But where it was really going was to hell, on or about January 1, 1925. And that, unhappily, was approximately what happened.

19. TO THE EASTERN KINGDOM

WHEN the wet weather of November descended over Paris and the whole family came down with colds, Ernest began dreaming of the Swiss Alps. He had long since vowed never to be absent for longer than he could help from the magical combination of snow and mountains. Once again he was in the mood to move. "We've got only one time to live," he wrote Howell Jenkins, "and so let's have a hell of a good time together." The chief deterrent was the lack of money. Although the Gangwisches still charged less than the Dilworths used to do at Horton Bay, the Hemingways' bank account had dwindled to $1280, with no immediate prospect of additional income.

It was just at this point that they heard from Bertram Hartman about a village called Schruns in the Austrian Vorarlberg. It lay just off the main rail line between Zurich and Innsbruck. The best place to stay was a family hotel called the Taube. Life was simple, the food was good, and the skiing was said to be excellent. The cost to the three Hemingways would be something like two million kronen a week. But the size of the sum was deceptive. Austria was gripped by runaway inflation: an American dollar would buy 70,000 kronen. Ernest did a quick computation in the blue notebook that contained his sketch about the Hartmans. To his astonishment, it came out to $28.50 a week for three. They could sublet the Paris apartment and spend a whole winter among the snowy mountains. The owner of the Taube was Paul Nels. Ernest sent him a letter, reserving two rooms for December 20th.

In the interval before Austria, he made his usual complement of new friends, including Archibald and Ada MacLeish. They were living near the Luxembourg in an apartment on the Boul' Miche. Archie was seven years older than Ernest, a crag-faced Scot who came from Illinois, with an A.B. from Yale and a law degree from Harvard. He had served two years in France during and after the war and had now returned to follow his calling as a poet. He could have taught Ernest much that he needed to know about the art of poetry. But Archie found him unwilling to talk esthetics. Their conversations at the Closerie des Lilas turned chiefly on boxing and baseball. Ernest also met John Herrmann, a native of Michigan who had been studying art history in Munich and was about to marry a pretty girl named Josephine Herbst. Josie was fair, with blue eyes and wheat-colored hair; John was dark, and looked enough like Ernest to be mistaken for his younger brother. Both of them were determined to become serious writers.

So was the tubercular young Ernest Walsh, who had a close friend and patroness named Ethel Moorhead. They were talking of starting a new little magazine to be called *This Quarter*. Ernest had once rejected Walsh as a pretentious poseur. Now he began to say that he was "a pretty nice guy." He frequently appeared in Walsh's rooms at the Vénétia Hôtel, bubbling with talk about writers and artists. The motivation behind these visits must have been clear, even to Walsh. With the *transatlantic review* about to expire, Ernest needed the new outlet for his work that Walsh's magazine could provide.

No such reasoning lay behind his new friendship with Janet Flanner, a handsome and gifted journalist who was just then beginning to write for *The New Yorker* magazine. Ernest often came to her room in the rue Bonaparte, sitting invariably in a low-slung chair that had originally been designed for nursing mothers. Janet had bought it at a flea market and had it re-covered with a print of "galleons and tall sailboats" coursing through maps of the seven seas. This, she thought, appealed to Ernest's love of travel. She called it

"Ernest's chair" mainly because it was the only one in the room large enough to hold him. He sat there talking—always talking—his legs crossed and cocked up in front of him, his white teeth gleaming. Janet liked "his friendly, observant, bright, agate-brown eyes," which had nothing of the molten Latin look. Once he took her to a boxing match at a small old-fashioned ring near the Place de la République. She listened with admiration while Ernest and the French fans yelled advice and insults in the argot of the town. He was, she thought, "a natural quick linguist who learned a language first through his ears because of his constant necessity for understanding people and for communicating."

He was full of shy admiration for a new story called "The Undefeated," which he had begun in September and completed by November 20th. It was a distillation of all he had learned about bullfighting in three visits to Spain. He liked it also for its engagement of a theme he had never tried before—the vain attempt of a superannuated matador named Manuel García to make a comeback in the Plaza de Toros in Madrid during the hot summer of 1918. It was a tragic story, full of color and action. Manuel achieved a Pyrrhic victory against tremendous odds, destroyed but not defeated. Ernest thought that it was the best story he had ever written. But he felt much the same way about "Soldier's Home," which he sold to McAlmon on December 10th for a new anthology called *The Contact Collection of Contemporary Writers*. He was equally excited about the possibilities of "Big Two-Hearted River," except for Nick's long interior monologue at the end. Reading it over, he decided that "all that mental conversation" spoiled the effect he wanted to achieve. Don Stewart had already submitted the typescript of the collected stories to George Doran, his own publisher. Ernest wrote him posthaste to lop off the last nine pages of "Big Two-Hearted River."

Then it was time for Austria. Six days before Christmas, they boarded the train at the Gare de l'Est. Next morning at Buchs, a small lumber town on the border, Ernest walked across the tracks, changed some money, and bought tickets for Bludenz. There they transferred to an electric train which carried them up the Montafon Valley to Schruns. The weather was warm as September. Brown cows still grazed in the meadows and only the higher peaks were covered with snow. Paul Nels's porter met them at the station. The Taube was a substantial five-story building faced with stucco and painted white. The front door gave upon the Kirchplatz, and the musty old church had a dome like an inverted green onion. Their rooms were on the second floor, Ernest on the front corner and Hadley and the baby just behind him on the garden side. The immediate prospect from Ernest's window was a fir-covered valley to the southeast, pleasantly diversified with pastures and small farms, but by leaning out he could see no fewer than ten mountain peaks.

The village was small and homelike. It straddled a fast-flowing stream called Die Litz. Wooden bridges joined the two parts of the town, which consisted of shops and sawmills, a scattering of *Gasthofs,* and a neglected museum. The villagers spoke the Montafoner dialect, a mélange of soft gutturals, and lifted their hats to strangers, saying *"Grüss Gott."* Ernest began to wonder why he could ever have thought of the Austrians as enemies. Theirs was a lovely country, with fine food, thirty-six varieties of beer, commodious rooms, a piano for Hadley to play, and a beautiful *bonne* named Mathilde Braun who lived in the house beside the hotel and at once fell in love with Bumby.

All across Europe the winter was warm and the snow very late in coming. After the feverish productivity of the fall, Ernest's writing entered a state of eclipse. He complained to Harold Loeb that he needed the stimulus of a "big town" like Paris to write in. He took to bowling with Bertram Hartman in the Taube's bowling alley. Don Stewart sent a Christmas letter from New York containing a large check. Ernest's heart leaped. It must be an advance from the publisher Doran. But it was Stewart's personal check, designed to build up his morale. Doran had decided to reject the stories, though he said that he would be glad to see a novel by Hemingway. Stewart had taken the typescript to the great H. L. Mencken for possible transmission to Alfred Knopf. If Mencken did not like the stories, there was always Horace Liveright. Loeb wrote that he could not come to Austria. He was going to New York to check on the progress of his novel *Doodab*. He promised to say a good word to Horace about *In Our Time*.

Snow fell at last, first in the high mountains and then in the valley, blanketing Schruns and the tiny village of Tschagguns a mile and a half to the south. Hadley practiced skiing on the slope behind the hotel and another low hill at Tschagguns where herds of chamois sometimes came to feed. Herr Nels moved the hotel piano into her room, and she played Bach and Haydn in the mornings while Bumby was outdoors cavorting with Mathilde. She also did some knitting with the undyed local wool, gray or black as it came from the sheep, and spun into yarn by the farm wives up the valley. She made Ernest a sweater and ski cap. He put them on and posed for a watercolor sketch by Bertram Hartman.

He was hurling himself into life in the mountains with his customary passion and enjoyment. His appetite was enormous. "Every meal time was a great event," he said afterwards. Frau Nels kept to the kitchen, supervising the preparation of great roasts of beef, with potatoes browned in gravy, jugged hare with wine sauce, venison chops, a special omelette soufflé, and homemade plum pudding. There was an abundance of red wine and an immense variety of beer. Ernest liked the local kirsch and a kind of schnapps distilled from mountain gentians. He was growing a heavy black beard and heard with pleasure that the Montafoners were calling him "The Black Christ" or sometimes "The Black Kirsch-drinking Christ." Gambling was then illegal in Austria but poker games went on each evening in the smoky dining room of the hotel. It was a great joke that one of the players was the captain of the local police. The others included a banker and lawyer, Herr Nels the hotel-keeper, and a tall, thin, sardonic man of fifty named Walther Lent, who had come from Munich to start a ski school. He scorned the practice slopes and spoke of taking his pupils to the Alpine Club huts beyond the Silvretta-Hochalpenstrasse at altitudes above two thousand meters.

One day in January the mails brought a prospectus for Walsh's new magazine, *This Quarter*. Ernest forwarded it to Gertrude Stein, observing that Walsh in the role of a helpmeet to artists struck him as ironic. But he concealed his suspicions from Walsh, to whom he wrote enthusiastically. He enclosed a copy of "Big Two-Hearted River" which he described as far and away his best work to date. He volunteered to name some other possible contributors, applauded Miss Moorhead's decision to pay liberally for contributions to the magazine, and began to advise them, in the fashion of a Dutch uncle, on the details of running a review. They repaid his zeal by accepting his story, sealing the bargain with a check for 1,000 francs. He was at once converted to their cause. He pointed out that in calendar 1924 his total income from serious writing had been 1,100 francs, that neither *Three Stories* nor *in our time* had earned him so much as a sou, and that he and Hadley were trying to subsist on a hundred dollars a month.

In the middle of January, Walther Lent conducted his ski school on a first trip into the high mountains. They went by sleigh up the valley road to Partenen and spent the night at an ancient inn. Next morning they rose before dawn to begin the climb, with sealskins on their skis and rucksacks on their backs. Hired porters carried the heaviest loads—"squat sullen peasants" who "climbed steadily like pack horses," dumped their loads at the top against the stone walls of the Alpine hut, and then "shot down and away on their short skis like gnomes." On the way up the long valley to the frozen Vermunt-Stausee, Ernest saw deer and chamois, many ptarmigan, two martens, and once a fox. The Madlenerhaus was built into the flank of the Kresperspitz at 1,986 meters. All around it lay a vast acreage of virgin snow. They skied all day and bedded down early in bunks like feeding troughs, while the high winds howled at the corners of the building and blew great clouds of snow off the surrounding peaks in the moonlight.

It was the second trip to the Madlenerhaus early in February which marked a change in Ernest's luck. It began with a memorable evening of poker when he drew an ace to fill a royal flush in spades and went to bed the richer by 430,000 kronen. Next day he went out with Lent to ski down the Vermunt-gletscher, starting at an altitude of 3,200 meters and making the five-mile run down the glacier's face in twelve minutes flat. Returning at nightfall, weary and windburned, he found two cables brought up from Schruns. They were from Don Stewart and Harold Loeb. Both of them bore the same ecstatic message: Horace Liveright had agreed to publish *In Our Time*.

At first he could not believe it. But further confirmation awaited him at the Taube in the form of a cable and a letter from Liveright himself. The stories, said Horace, were splendid and generally acceptable. There were only a couple of problems. One was "Mr. and Mrs. Elliot" which contained a passage that Liveright thought obscene. This would of course have to be changed. The major problem was "Up in Michigan," another story involving sex. It was so outspoken that Horace felt it would have to be rejected. Ernest must supply another in its place. He immediately set to work with a borrowed typewriter on a story called "A Great Little Fighting Machine," later shortened to "The Battler." The locale was a hobo jungle near Mancelona, Michigan, and the circumstances were wholly invented. The battler was a punch-drunk prize-fighter named Ad Francis, whose personality was based on two real-life fighters known to Ernest: Ad Wolgast and Bat Nelson. Ad Francis's fictional companion, a polite and patient Negro named Bugs, was modeled on an actual Negro trainer who had looked after Wolgast in the period of his decline. Ernest had begun the story somewhat earlier, perhaps in December shortly after his arrival in Austria. Now he revised and typed it out, working through the night of February 12th and finishing on the morning of Friday the 13th.

For reasons of his own, he postponed his "DELIGHTED ACCEPT" cablegram to Liveright, sending it off at last on March 5th. During the rest of his stay in Austria, he devoted his energies to a pair of projects which gradually coalesced in his mind. One was to find a job in Paris for Bill Smith, who had suddenly written out of the blue to apologize for their three-year-old quarrel. Old Bill, as Ernest wrote to Jenkins, had meantime passed through the toughest possible time, both domestic and financial. He had even spent some months in a sanatorium. Bygones were now gone by. He must be helped to get going again. The other project was Ernest Walsh's plan to make the first number of *This Quarter* into a *Festschrift* for Ezra Pound, with a portrait of the master and a bouquet of tributes. Walsh asked for one from Ernest, who banged away on his sticky Corona from dawn to dusk on March 9th and emerged with a thousand words designed to warm the cockles of Ezra's heart. He said, among other things, that Pound's energy was boundless, that he was like a fine Miura bull, that no one ever shook a cape at him without provoking a charge. He had fought all his fights with "a very gay grimness" and his wounds had healed quickly. Now he had moved to Rapallo where his friends could not wear him out by asking favors, and where his energies could be released for further productivity.

On this generous note the long Austrian vacation came to an end. Except under compulsion, Ernest had written little but letters. Perhaps, as he said, he needed a big town to write in—the stimulus of daily gossip, the mornings alone at the Closerie des Lilas, the trips across the river to see Guy Hickok and Mike Ward. It was not until some months later that he even learned the meaning of the name of the country where he had lived with such good luck through the early weeks of 1925. "You know what Austria (Osterreich) means?" he asked his new friend Fitzgerald the following Christmas. "The Eastern Kingdom. Isn't that swell? Tell Zelda."

20. *THIS QUARTER*

As soon as he heard that the Hemingways were back from Austria Harold Loeb rushed over to pay them a call. He was full of pride and good will because both he and Ernest were going to be published by Boni and Liveright. He asked Hadley and Ernest to come and celebrate by having a drink with him and Kitty Cannell. When they got there, Kitty was entertaining Pauline and Virginia Pfeiffer. They were the daughters of a landowning squire in Piggott, Arkansas. Both were small in stature, with "slender limbs like delicate little birds" and bobbed hair worn in bangs. Pauline, the older of the two, worked for the Paris edition of *Vogue* magazine, though Kitty had the impression that her real purpose in having come to France was to find a suitable husband. Chic, well-dressed, and highly articulate about the current fashions, she glanced sympathetically at Hadley's worn and simple clothes. The sisters were devout Catholics, and had attended the Visitation Convent in St. Louis, not far from Hadley's former home. Pauline was a recent graduate of the University of Missouri. She fell into talk with Harold Loeb while Ernest was telling Jinny about the skiing in Austria. When they got up to go, Pauline put on a handsome coat of chipmunk skins. Ernest told Kitty that he had liked Jinny much the better of the two. "I'd like," said he, "to take her out in her sister's coat."

The sisters shortly came round to see Hadley and Bumby in the flat above the sawmill. It was clear enough that they were accustomed to a higher scale of living. Pauline afterwards remarked to Kitty that she had been shocked by the conditions which Ernest imposed upon his wife and child in the name of art. She had caught a glimpse of the master of the house through the door of the bedroom. He lay in bed reading, unkempt and unshaven. She thought him rather coarse both in manner and appearance. She did not see how Hadley could stand to live in such a place or in the company of such a man.

Almost daily for the first month after his return from Schruns, Ernest haunted the Imprimerie of Herbert Clarke in the rue St. Honoré, attending to arrangements for the ambitious first number of Walsh's *This Quarter* magazine. The contents had inexorably expanded to a substantial volume of 250 pages. Clarke had been the printer for the *transatlantic,* and Ernest was already more than familiar with the problems of putting a magazine to bed. These included late copy, harassing delays, incredible typographical inaccuracies, and now even rats, which had developed an appetite for the rollers on Clarke's printing press. Ernest procured a Man Ray photograph of Pound to be used as a frontispiece and assembled the illustrations. They were mainly photographs of sculptures by Brancusi and of paintings by Miss Moorhead and Bertram Hartman. He also enlisted Hadley's "super-accurate" services as proofreader and devoted several mornings a week to goading the dilatory Clarke.

On the morning of March 27th, in the midst of these labors, "The Undefeated" came back from the *Dial*. The covering letter called it a great story, but too strong for American readers. Ernest's former enthusiasm for the *Dial* cooled rapidly and soon congealed into a grudge that he nurtured all his life. If American editors would not buy his story, he knew perfectly well how to get it published. He merely transferred the dog-eared typescript to another envelope and sent it along to Ernest Walsh. He told Walsh that it had now been turned down by every reputable and disreputable magazine in the United States. This was not true, but it worked. Walsh responded with a laudatory letter, followed by a check from Miss Moorhead. Ernest wrote happily that he was going to use the money to settle the rent with the Chautards, make a down payment on a new suit of clothes, lay in some groceries, and buy tickets to the six-day bike races.

With his two longest stories bought and paid for with Ethel Moorhead's money, and with the first number of the magazine largely in shape, Ernest now concluded that he had served long enough. One Saturday morning early in April, he wrote Walsh that he must stop work on the magazine in order to get on with his own. When he wasn't creating, said he, he was absolutely miserable and ugly. To write as he must, his mind must be free and clear. If Walsh needed an editorial assistant, he ought to consider the merits of Bill Smith, who would be coming to Paris later in April. For 1,000 francs a month, Bill could handle all details of makeup, printing, publicity, and distribution. Walsh met this suggestion with some asperity. He implied that Ernest was interfering where he had no business, and possibly even seeking to extort money from Miss Moorhead on the pretext of securing employment for a close friend. Ernest answered with hurt pride. If this was the effect he had on people, said he, *"tant pis pour moi."* Walsh must be oversuspicious about being cheated. As he had done with Ford and the editors of the *Dial,* he developed a grudge against both Walsh and Miss Moorhead, ignoring the fact that they had cheerfully bought two long stories that he had not been able to sell in the United States.

Still, he had sold a whole book of stories to Boni and Liveright. He signed the contract on March 31st and sent Liveright the new story of "The Battler" as a substitute for the ill-fated "Up in Michigan." He strictly enjoined both Liveright and his chief editor, T. R. Smith, not to alter any of the stories without his approval. As for potential sales, said he, the book had a good 3–1 gambling chance. The classic example of a "really fine book" that did not sell was Cummings's *The Enormous Room,* which Horace had published in 1922. But Cummings's style was difficult. The advantage of *In Our Time,* according to Ernest, was that it would be praised by highbrows and could be read by lowbrows. Nobody with a high-school education would have the slightest trouble with the prose. He also professed to be pleased with "The Battler." It would give the book "additional unity." As he had been saying about some of his other stories, it seemed to him "about the best" he had ever written.

Another editor in New York had recently approached Ernest with a letter of inquiry. This was Maxwell Perkins of Scribners. He had been stirred to action by one of his leading young authors, F. Scott Fitzgerald. Fitzgerald was certain that Hemingway would have a brilliant future. The short pieces Bill Bird had published were remarkable. He was plainly "The real thing." Perkins's first letter to Ernest had miscarried. His second, sent while Ernest was in Austria, had been kept by Sylvia Beach with a pile of other mail. She handed it over to him only five days after he had accepted Horace Liveright's offer. Ernest wrote Perkins about the contract he had lately signed. It gave Boni and Liveright an option on his next three books. Unless they took up the option within sixty days of receipt of a manuscript, the arrangement would lapse. Ernest said that he would have been glad to send *In Our Time* to Scribners. If he were ever in a position to submit another book to Perkins, he would do so. One possibility was a study of the bullfight. It would do for the matadors and the animals what Doughty had done for the nomadic people of the Arabian deserts. It would have to be a large book, filled with wonderful pictures. But such dreams, said Ernest, no doubt made him a poor prospect for an American publisher. Apart from bullfighting, his only other interest was the short story. He thought that the novel was an awfully artificial and worked-out form. Still, some of his stories were lengthening out towards 12,000 words. Maybe in time one might stretch to novel length.

When Bill Smith came to Paris, Ernest hailed him like a long-lost brother and gave him the use of the small study-bedroom. Bill met the Chautards and was both amused and disgusted by Mme. Chautard's stuffed dog. Ernest also introduced him to Pauline Pfeiffer, who seemed to Bill to be working hard to capture Ernest's attention, using such girlish gambits as "I was talking to someone about you." Ernest would then answer, "Oh? And what did he say?" He spent most of every morning writing at a table in the Closerie des Lilas. In the afternoons, he and Bill played tennis with Harold Loeb and Paul Fisher whenever the courts were dry enough.

During these games Loeb's manner was sometimes rather absent. Kitty Cannell was trying to give him the freedom he said he wanted, and he had conceived a passion for a tall and handsome Englishwoman named Lady Duff Twysden. He liked her statuesque figure, gray eyes, and close-cropped blond hair. They had first met casually at a cocktail party. But it was not until some weeks later, dropping in at the Select, that he had heard a murmurous, low-pitched laugh. It seemed to Harold to have the "liquid quality of the lilt of a mockingbird singing to the moon." He could not help thinking of Rima, the mysterious heroine of his favorite romantic novel, W. H. Hudson's *Green Mansions*. In spite of affecting mannish tweed suits and a man's felt hat perched carelessly on the back of her head, Duff had immense natural chic. She wore no makeup and there were some, less ardent than Loeb, who held that she seldom washed. Yet, to the heiress Nancy Cunard, Duff seemed to possess both *beaucoup de cran* and *beaucoup de branche*. Her "well-tailored face," thin and delicate as a cameo, might have been the subject of an eight-eenth-century portrait—perhaps an oil on wood—from the walls of the National Gallery.

Duff was then thirty-two, reputedly a dangerous age. Her recent history had been chequered. She had been christened Mary Duff Stirling Byrom, eldest daughter of B. W. Smurthwaite of Prior House, Richmond, Yorkshire. In January, 1917 (while Ernest was still in high school) she had been married in London to Sir Roger Thomas Twysden, tenth baronet, a recent graduate of the Royal Naval College at Dartmouth. In March, 1918, she had borne him a son named Anthony, who was now being reared by the family of her estranged husband. Her divorce was said to be imminent. Her chief companion in the spring of 1925 was Pat Guthrie, a tall, dissipated Scot with narrow shoulders and a wide-ranging thirst. Loeb thought him a parasite by vocation, but he shared his allowance with Duff, as well as his slick-haired circle of effeminate friends. Pat's behavior in his cups was either silly or sullen, depend-ing on his mood of the moment. Duff carried her liquor so well that she was able to play very decent bridge even after hours of steady toping.

Ernest's view of Duff was tinged with ambiguity. Like Loeb, though a good deal less romantically, he was impressed by her looks, her style, her insouci-ance, her British accent, and her capacity for drink. His habitual scorn for the floaters of Montparnasse lost some of its edge whenever he talked to Duff. Although he does not seem to have been included in the narrow circle of her amours, he felt sufficiently possessive towards her to resent Loeb's steadily developing infatuation.

One day in May he was sitting on a bar stool at the Dingo in the rue Delambre, talking to Duff and Pat, when he heard a voice at his elbow. He looked up to see the man who had recommended him to Maxwell Perkins. Like Ernest, Fitzgerald was a Midwesterner, serious about his writing, im-perious in his critical questioning, young, gay, generous, and enthusiastic. He was better dressed and far more prosperous than Ernest, beside whose manly bulk he looked both boyish and fragile. Fitzgerald introduced himself and the tall young man, a former Princeton athlete, who had entered the Dingo with him. Ernest liked the athlete at once but could not make up his mind about Fitzgerald. "He had very fair wavy hair," he wrote afterwards, "a high fore-head, excited and friendly eyes, and a delicate long-lipped Irish mouth that, on a girl, would have been the mouth of a beauty. His chin was well-built and he had good ears and a handsome, almost beautiful, unmarked nose. . . . The mouth worried you until you knew him and then it worried you even more."

When Duff withdrew, Fitzgerald launched into a laudatory speech about the Nick Adams stories. Ernest found it embarrassingly fulsome. An old high-school rhyme coursed through his head: "Praise to the face is open disgrace." He concentrated on the champagne that Fitzgerald had ordered, responding in monosyllables to the highly personal questions that came out of Fitzgerald like bullets from a machine gun. Suddenly an odd thing happened. Sweatdrops smaller than the pearls on a lady's ring began to form all the way across Fitzgerald's upper lip. His color turned waxen and his eyes went dead as agates. The skin tightened along his cheekbones until the whole face assumed the appearance of a skull. There was nothing to do but get him home. The Princeton athlete told Ernest not to worry. This kind of thing happened all the time.

When they met for the second time some days later at the Closerie des Lilas, Scott said that he wanted Ernest to read *The Great Gatsby*. He talked very intelligently and modestly about the book. Even though he drank a couple of whiskeys, the phenomenon of the Dingo Bar was not repeated. Ernest liked him well enough to accept his invitation to go down to Lyon to pick up his car, and they arranged to meet at the station next day. But he was not at hand when the train pulled out and Ernest went on alone. Fitzgerald appeared at the hotel next morning, full of apologies for having missed the train. When they found the car, Ernest discovered that it had no top. Scott's wife Zelda had ordered it cut away. An hour north of Lyon they were stopped by driving rain. By Chalon-sur-Saône they were both so wet that they checked in at the hotel. Fitzgerald immediately went to bed with what he said was congestion of the lungs. That night at dinner he passed out at the table, very much as he had done at the Dingo. Next morning, driving up through the Côte d'Or, he seemed as healthy and cheerful as ever. He passed the time by providing detailed summaries of the plots in the novels of Michael Arlen.

In the following week, the Hemingways went to lunch at the Fitzgeralds' apartment in the rue de Tilsitt. The place struck Ernest as gloomy and sour, and he took an immediate dislike to Zelda, who happened to be suffering from a hangover. She had the eyes of a predatory hawk and spoke jealously of the trip to Lyon as if it had been a huge success. Ernest gathered that she was jealous of the time Scott gave to writing. When he drank she smiled a secret smile which meant, Ernest believed, that she was glad Scott would not be able to write afterwards. It was not the behavior he cherished in the wife of a writer. But he read *The Great Gatsby* with admiration, and wrote Max Perkins that it was an absolutely first-rate book.

They discussed this and Fitzgerald's earlier novels in the company of Christian Gauss, a professor of French from Princeton. He had come to Paris with his wife Alice for a summer of research and writing. Gauss was a slight, wiry, and sardonic man with a fighter's chin and a pleasantly asymmetrical face. He had known both Fitzgerald and Edmund Wilson during their undergraduate years at Princeton and maintained a quizzical interest in the vagaries of avant-garde literature, both French and American. He asked his companions what they thought of Stevenson's advice to young writers—that each of them should play the sedulous ape to his betters until he had developed a style of his own. Scott said that he had followed this pattern in his Princeton novel, *This Side of Paradise,* which was indebted both to the fiction of Compton Mackenzie and to some pages in Joyce's *Portrait of the Artist as a Young*

Man. Ernest acknowledged a more remote obligation to Sherwood Anderson, to whom he had lately written a warm letter of appreciation for his part in persuading Liveright to accept *In Our Time.* "But both agreed," said Professor Gauss, "that you later had to pay" for such help. It was like weaning oneself from a psychiatrist. Every writer eventually needed freedom from outside influence. Ernest was uncommonly vehement about this matter. Gauss's former student, Edmund Wilson, had said that he belonged to the same school as Anderson and Gertrude Stein. It was a connection that he wanted to live down as rapidly as possible.

Ernest surprised himself one morning in the middle of June by starting to write a novel. Not two months earlier he had condemned the genre as worked-out and artificial. Now he borrowed the title of one of his lyrics and printed it out in capital letters in one of his blue notebooks: "ALONG WITH YOUTH: A NOVEL." Its hero was Nick Adams and its opening locale was the battered troop transport *Chicago,* steaming through the Bay of Biscay one warm night in June, 1918. The story proceeded largely through dialogue between Nick, two Polish officers named Leon Chocianowitz and Anton Galinski, and a drunken youth in the upper berth who was called only The Carper. Nothing much happened. The young men drank and talked on the deck, in one of the cabins, and in a lifeboat on davits overhanging the calm and phosphorescent sea.

But Ernest's intention was clear enough. He was trying to make use of the first big adventure of his youth. He used the actual names of the Polish lieutenants and the nickname of Howell Jenkins, with whom he had recently exchanged letters. His purpose, apparently, was to carry Nick's adventures from Bordeaux to Paris to Milan to Schio to the Basso Piave, and so back to Milan and a love affair with a nurse named Agnes. In "A Very Short Story" he had already summed up the love affair and its aftermath. Perhaps now, almost seven years after the fact, he could at last set it down in the form of a novel. It did not work. *Along with Youth* stopped forever on the twenty-seventh manuscript page one day late in June, 1925. But it was at least a beginning.

21. THE SUN ALSO RISES

ALL through the winter in Schruns and the spring in Paris, Ernest had been dreaming of his third visit to the fiesta of San Fermín in Pamplona. "Gaw," he told Bill Smith, "what a wonderful show!" Bulls were like rattlesnakes. They had been bred for speed and viciousness for 600 years, and reached the summit of their lives when they came tearing into the arena at ninety miles an hour. It was like prehistoric times to watch them chase a picador until they plucked him out of the saddle and gored him to death. Spain was the most Christ-wonderful country in the world.

By the end of the third week in June all plans were in order. Ernest gathered funds from his friends for train fare, bullfight tickets, and hotel reservations.

This year they would stay at Juanito Quintana's Hotel Quintana across the square from the Hotel de la Perla. Juanito was a veteran *aficionado* and matadors often stayed there. Bumby was going to Brittany with the Rohrbachs. Ernest and Hadley were planning a week of trout fishing at Burguete before the fiesta. Bill Smith, Don Stewart, and Harold Loeb would join them. Alfred Flechtheim of *Der Querschnitt* had given Ernest an advance on a book on bull-fighting, the third in a series that had already resulted in books about horses and boxing. It would be illustrated by Picasso, Juan Gris, and other painters, and there would be many photographs.

Harold Loeb told Ernest that he wanted to relax by the sea at St. Jean-de-Luz before joining the others at Burguete. What he did not reveal was that he had persuaded Duff Twysden to spend a week with him in consummation of their romance. Duff called it afterwards "our glorious little dream." She returned alone to Paris and wrote Ernest a note on the back of a bar check. "Please do come at once to Jimmie's Bar—real trouble— Just rung up Parnass and find no word from you. SOS. Duff." Then she wrote a love letter to Harold at St. Jean-de-Luz. "I'm miserable without you," she said. "Things don't seem to improve at all with time. . . . Now for a doubtful glad tidings. I am coming on the Pamplona trip with Hem and your lot. Can you bear it? With Pat [Guthrie] of course. If this appears impossible for you, let me know and I'll try to get out of it. But I'm dying to come and feel that even seeing you and being able to talk to you will be better than nothing."

Harold agreed, even though the scheme would include his rival. He feared that Ernest might be jealous on learning that he had spent a week with Duff at St. Jean-de-Luz. But he was reassured by Ernest's letter of June 21st. It said that Duff had sent to England for money, and added that since she was not going to bring along any of her perverted tribe, Harold should arrange to meet her train with a band of Spanish fairies carrying a daisy chain to make her feel at home. Another letter from Duff further alleviated Harold's worries. "Hem has promised to be good," she wrote, "and we ought to have a marvelous time." She and Harold (and of course Guthrie) could all go to St. Jean-de-Luz to wait until the Pamplona fiesta began. Again Harold complied. Since he did not want to be off in the mountains while Duff was available, he wired Ernest that he would not come to fish at Burguete. They could all meet at Pamplona on the fifth of July.

On Thursday morning, June 25th, Ernest and Hadley were up at dawn to finish their packing. Sylvia Beach had appeared the evening before on an errand for James Joyce. A new section of *Finnegans Wake* was going to appear in the second number of *This Quarter*, and the question was where the typescript should be sent. Ernest paused in the midst of his packing to write a note to Walsh. Joyce's stuff should be sent direct to Herbert Clarke's printshop in the rue St. Honoré. Ernest added the friendly note that Mr. F. Puss, the cat, was upset by the turmoil in the household, and that the first light of dawn was just coming into the sawmill courtyard. He could not conceal his exuberance.

This was his final editorial act for *This Quarter*. In an hour or two he would be leaving for Spain.

Bad luck set in the moment they reached Burguete. The woman at the inn shook her head and looked gloomy. All winter and spring the loggers had been working in the beech and pine forests and it was locally rumored that the fishing had been ruined. Ernest could not believe it. Bill Smith had brought along a box of sure-fire flies, old favorites from the summers at Horton Bay: McGintys, Royal Coachmans, Yellow Sallys. But they soon found that the landlady was right. The dark stream bed of the Irati was filled with loggers' trash. "The irony of it," said Don Stewart. "The pity of it." They put away the flies and used worms and grasshoppers, working along the Río Fábrica and some of the smaller streams. In four days of trying, they did not take a single fish. "Fish killed, pools destroyed, dams broken down," said Ernest. "Made me feel sick."

It was almost as bad at Pamplona. Ernest tried vainly to recapture the glories of his former visits. Nothing was quite the same. Hadley and Don Stewart, who had both been there in 1924, were more than conscious of the change. Both of them knew that it was caused by the new presences, Duff and Pat, Harold Loeb and Bill Smith. They all walked out to the railroad yards to watch the bulls unloaded. Ernest gave them a little lecture on the qualities of the animals, pointing to the "small spot between their shoulder-blades" where the sword must enter at the moment of truth. Next morning they all got up at dawn to watch the running of the bulls through the streets. At the "amateurs" afterwards, Ernest tried his old stunt of bulldogging, wearing a beret, a sweater, and baggy white pants. Don Stewart watched from the sidelines while Bill and Harold followed Ernest into the crowded arena. Bill made the crowd laugh when one of the bulls butted him in the rear. But Harold, resplendent in a Fair Isle sweater, seized the horns of one of the bulls. He held his white sneakers aloft like an acrobat, and was borne rapidly across the field of combat, his horn-rimmed glasses still in place, out-Hemingwaying Hemingway. Ernest's enthusiasm for amateur bullfighting quickly evaporated.

At the afternoon's bullfight, the center of attention was the great new phenomenon, a nineteen-year-old from Ronda named Cayetano Ordóñez, slim and straight as an arrow. It was his first season as a full matador. He had been promoted only that spring after some epochal performances as a *novillero* at Malaga, Seville, and Madrid, and was being hailed everywhere as the "Messiah who had come to save bullfighting." Hadley became at once his most ardent admirer. Ernest shared her views. Ordóñez was "purity of style itself with the cape . . . beautiful with the *muleta*." On several bulls he killed *"recibiendo,"* receiving the animal on the sword in the "old manner" of such eighteenth-century matadors as Pedro Romero.

As he had done in former years, Ernest cocked an observant eye at the reactions of his fellow spectators. Don Stewart seemed genuinely fond of all phases of the bullfight. It was just the opposite with Bill Smith, who was so "shocked and horrified" by the goring of the horses that he was unable to think of anything else. Although Duff did not like the wounding of the horses, she was so much "excited by bullfighters and general strong emotion that she became a partizan of the spectacle," only to drink herself out of all remembrance of it shortly afterwards. Harold Loeb viewed the whole proceeding with distaste. He hated to watch the death agony of the bulls. In some obscure fashion it struck him as shameful.

Apart from the bullfights, Don Stewart was disappointed. He remembered nostalgically the "male revel" of 1924—the "long and eager" lines outside the bordellos, the nonsexual riau-riau dancing in the streets. The atmosphere then had been much like that of a "college reunion," pervaded by a kind of boyish innocence and a sense of release. Now all was changed. "The Garden of Eden wasn't the same." No longer could they even claim to be the only Americans in Pamplona. High society had appeared in limousines from Biarritz. Ambassador Alex Moore and his lady guests were parked in the Plaza near the Hotel de la Perla. Uniformed chauffeurs waited beside the cars. It was like an alien invasion. The "devil sex" was also apparent. Don sensed that something was afoot between Ernest and Duff. Ernest seemed angry that she had spent a week with Loeb at St. Jean-de-Luz. Had Duff fallen for Ernest? Don "was not sure—and did not want to be sure." Then there was the matter of money. Pat Guthrie did not have enough to pay the bills for himself and Duff. Don put up the money, becoming for the moment "good old Don." But he could not help feeling that "something had gone out of Pamplona."

Bill Smith was also aware of the pervasive distemper. Harold Loeb, whom he both liked and pitied, seemed at a very low ebb throughout the fiesta, an object of scorn to both Hemingway and Guthrie. It was clear to Bill that Duff was "wild about Ernest" even though he did not believe they had established an overt sexual connection. Ernest's behavior was that of a dog in the manger. He could not or would not have Duff, yet he made no secret of his resentment over Loeb's temporary success with her during their romance in June.

The abscess broke after dinner on Saturday night. The evening before, Harold and Duff had slipped away from the others for a drink in one of the cafés. Their small carouse had ended in a Spanish clubroom in one of the buildings on the square, where Duff, as the only woman, was like the queen bee in a hive of drones. She refused to leave and Harold was obliged to return to the hotel alone. She appeared for lunch with a black eye and a contusion on her forehead. When Harold asked about it, Ernest cut him short by saying that she had fallen against a railing. "Pat was sour, ugly. Hadley had lost her smile. Don tried a quip that went lame. Bill looked grim." Over the brandy that night, Guthrie suddenly told Harold to get out: he was not wanted. Harold turned to Duff, who said at once that she did not want him to go. Ernest exploded in manly wrath. "You lousy bastard," he shouted at Loeb, "running to a woman." He meant using Duff as a shield and protection against Guthrie's boorishness instead of hitting him, as he no doubt deserved.

Loeb rose unsteadily and asked Hemingway to step outside. Ernest followed silently. They turned into a dark street just off the square, a colonnade of dingy shops. Loeb was frightened: he had boxed with Ernest and knew his black temper. But chiefly he was overcome with sadness. This, he felt, was the pattern of his life: to acquire a friend who suddenly became "a bitter lashing enemy." At last he stopped, took off his jacket, and stowed his horn-rimmed glasses in a side pocket, looking around nearsightedly for a place to lay it down. If his glasses should be broken, said he, there was no one to repair them in Pamplona. Even as he spoke, he saw that Ernest was smiling—the wide, boyish, contagious smile "that made it so hard not to like him." "I don't want to hit you," said Harold. "Me, either," said Ernest, and they walked back the way they had come.

On the morning of July 13th, descending from his room, Loeb was handed a note by the concierge. It was from Ernest, who said that he had been terribly tight and nasty to Harold on the evening of the 12th. He did not want Harold to leave Pamplona with that nasty, insulting business as the last thing of the fiestas. He wished that he could wipe out all the meanness and this note was just to let Harold know that he was thoroughly ashamed of the stinking, unjust, and uncalled-for things he had said.

After it was over, they all dispersed in different directions. Harold and Bill rented a car to drive to Bayonne, carrying Duff and Pat along with them. Don Stewart disappeared in the direction of the French Riviera. Ernest and Hadley, riding third class on a train to Madrid, discovered that they had stepped out of one lark into another. Sharing their compartment was the son of a vintner from Tofalla. He was carrying several large jugs of his father's best wine for sale in the capital of the world. In talking up the qualities of his merchandise he was moved to offer copious samples to his fellow travelers. All members of the group, which included a couple of priests and four members of the Guardia Civil, soon got thoroughly tight. Hadley and the priests conversed happily in Latin while Ernest managed to lose his railway tickets a few stations north of Madrid. This sobered him quickly, but the sympathetic Civil Guards persuaded the conductor that the young Americans should be allowed to proceed. It was all very fine, wrote Ernest to Gertrude Stein, almost the best party he had ever attended.

They took rooms at the old stand in the Calle San Jerónimo. The Pension Aguilar offered bed and board for ten pesetas a day, and their funds were anyway too slender to allow for more fashionable quarters. They divided the week between the newly renovated Prado and the bullfights. Gertrude Stein's old friend Belmonte was gored before their eyes. But shortly before that, the new hero, Cayetano Ordóñez, fresh from his triumphs in Pamplona, had fought a *mano a mano* which in Ernest's opinion made the jut-jawed Belmonte look cheap. Whatever Belmonte did, Ordóñez did better. He dedicated one of his bulls to the bright-haired Hadley, was awarded the ear, and presented it to her. She wrapped it up in a handkerchief of Don Stewart's, and stored it in a bureau drawer at the pension. As it gradually ripened in the heat of July, Ernest argued that she must either throw it away or cut it up to send in letters to her friends in St. Louis. She did neither, having never before owned a bull's ear or the plaudits of a *torero*. On the 15th they attended the great Corrida de la Prensa. Once again Ordóñez singled Hadley out for special honors. Her worries over whether or not Bumby was enjoying himself in Brittany were almost assuaged when he gave her his cape to hold. Both of them thought he was a wonder. None of the others could match his suavity, the smoothness of his capework, or the dignified deliberation with which he moved in for the kill.

Ernest had decided to make him the hero of a novel called *Fiesta*. He had already typed out part of the first chapter. It began by saying that it was half past three in the afternoon in a dark bedroom in the Hotel Montoya in Pamplona. A nineteen-year-old bullfighter named Romero was getting dressed. Two Americans named William Gorton and Jacob Barnes were staying at the same hotel. Montoya himself asked if they wanted to meet Romero. He ushered them into the room and they shook hands. Montoya made a little speech about the Americans' admiration for bullfighting and said that they wanted to wish him luck.

It was a good scene. Ernest fixed the time and place as he had been taught to do by his mentors in Kansas City and Toronto. Romero was the center of interest. Ernest got the shabby room, the company of underlings, the embarrassment of the Americans, and the sense of the bullfighter's aloneness. He was aloof in his native dignity, thinking already of the first of the bulls he must face within that very hour. Then the good beginning was spoiled. Bill Gorton and Jake Barnes crossed the hot square to the Café Iruña. A gray Rolls-Royce was parked there, surrounded by a crowd. It contained the American Ambassador, Ferdinand J. Watson of Ohio, as well as his niece and a flirtatious woman named Mrs. Carelton. Like Zelda Fitzgerald's, her hair was streaked from exposure to the sun; like Duff Twysden, she wore a man's felt hat. Jake and Bill passed the shining car and joined their friends at the café. One was Lady Brett Ashley. Brett said that this was a shabby way to treat an ambassador. She urged Jake to go back and speak to Watson and the ladies. He was angry at himself afterwards for having played up to Mrs. Carelton, and angry at Brett for having "deviled" him into doing it. It gave Brett the upper hand.

After eight days in Madrid, the weather turned so cold that Ernest and Hadley almost froze. Ordóñez's next engagement was in Valencia at the great annual *feria* beginning on the 24th. The Hemingways went down early, both to get warm and to be sure of getting bullfight tickets. They were well settled in by Ernest's twenty-sixth birthday. He was eager to get on with his novel on the events in Pamplona a mere two weeks before. His first attempt had begun well and then disintegrated. He decided to start with Paris and to provide biographical backgrounds for Brett Ashley, Mike Campbell, and Robert Cohn. These were to be based on what he knew of the recent histories of Duff Twysden, Pat Guthrie, and Harold Loeb. He worked at it in bed every morning in Valencia. Each afternoon he and Hadley went down to the beach to swim and then caught the canary-colored streetcar back to the Plaza de Toros to watch another heroic performance by Ordóñez.

His new opening said that this was going to be a novel about a lady. Her name was Lady Ashley and she was living in Paris. Her story was both romantic and highly moral. Her maiden name was Elizabeth Brett Murray. Her title came from her second husband, an officer of the Royal Navy who had become a dipsomaniac. In his drunken moments he even threatened her life, but would not give her a divorce. In the end she ran off to the Continent with Mike Campbell. He was a former soldier who had lost his inheritance in a business venture in Spain and then developed homosexual tendencies. Brett rescued him from his associates. Since then he had been living a party-going life in her vitalizing company.

Jake Barnes met Brett and Mike in Paris. He was an American newspaperman who had been discharged from a British hospital in 1916, worked for a time on the *New York Mail,* and then formed the Continental Press Association, coming to Paris as its European director. He soon found that he could handle his work in four or five hours a day and resolved to write a novel. He was encouraged in this plan by another American named Robert Cohn, whose own first novel had just been accepted by an American publisher. Cohn was a good tennis player and had once been middleweight boxing champion of Princeton. "Do not think," wrote Jake Barnes, "I am very much impressed by that as a boxing title, but it meant a lot to Cohn."

Ernest's original opening had begun well and then fizzled. But he was skilled and practiced enough in the literature of gossip so that the new opening in Paris carried him along with a wondrous momentum. When he and Hadley returned to Madrid for a couple of days early in August, he wrote in "great luxury" in their room at the pension and at a table in a beer joint round the corner in the Pasaje Álvarez. The August heat drove them out of Madrid and they went on to the Hotel Suizo in San Sebastian for two days of swimming in the blue bay behind the sheltering island. From there they moved to the Hotel Grand at Hendaye across the border, where the price was thirty francs a day *tout compris,* including purple mountains and a long white beach embroidered with Atlantic surf. By August 12th, when Hadley took the train for Paris to clean the apartment and prepare for Bumby's return, Ernest had filled two *cahiers* with his boyish longhand.

He stayed on alone at Hendaye for another week. He confided in a letter to Howell Jenkins that he feared to return to Paris because Bill Smith was there. Bill was so depressed that Ernest feared it might be catching. Meantime he was working harder than he had ever worked in his life, often until three or four in the morning. Then he would fall asleep, his head feeling like a frozen cabbage, only to jump awake again a few hours later, with the words already stringing themselves into sentences, clamoring to be set down. By August 19th when he left for Paris his first draft covered more than 250 of the small notebook pages and he thought that the end was almost in sight.

Madame Chautard had written that a lovely surprise awaited the Hemingways. When he got home he found out what it was. One broken window had been repaired and "hideous" new wallpaper had been hung in the dining room. On being thanked, she smiled her witch's smile and said that of course she must now raise the rent. Ernest threatened to move, but did nothing about it. Any such displacement would tear him up by the roots just when he most needed stability. He toyed briefly also with the notion of going to Morocco. Colonel Charlie Sweeny was in town, the soldier of fortune he had first met in Constantinople three years earlier. Sweeny had signed on with a group of officers to go and fight for the French against the Riff rebellion of Abd-el-Krim. But Ernest quickly curbed his wanderlust. It would interrupt his work on the novel.

By the end of August, he was deep in his account of the Pamplona fiesta. Ordóñez, thinly disguised as Pedro Romero, was beginning to dominate the book. In spite of Ernest's preliminary fears, the presence in Paris of Harold Loeb and Bill Smith did nothing to slow him down. Bill and Harold were now as thick as thieves. After Pamplona they had taken a bicycle trip through the Black Forest. For a time they had planned to visit the Loeb family's ancestral seat at Worms, but rains and mud drove them back to Paris by train. They had both booked passage for New York on September 5th.

The night before they left, Kitty Cannell gave them a farewell dinner at the Nègre de Toulouse. She invited Hadley and Ernest and they all walked to the restaurant. Hadley strode on ahead with Bill and Harold while Ernest followed with Kitty. She had been advising him to write stories with real plots in place of the *contes* which she felt were held together only by simple emotions. "Hey, Kitty," said Ernest, "I'm taking your advice. I'm writing a novel full of plot and drama." He gestured ahead towards Harold and Bill. "I'm tearing those bastards apart," he said. "I'm putting everyone in it and that kike Loeb is the villain. But you're a wonderful girl, Kitty, and I wouldn't do anything to annoy you." Kitty said nothing. But she remembered well enough her warnings to Harold that his day would come at last.

At the restaurant they ordered roast duck. Bill was gay and jovial. Hadley and Kitty chattered happily. Ernest drank a good deal of wine. Harold tried not to show his anxiety. He could not forget Ernest's savage outburst in Pamplona. Nothing now must be allowed to go wrong. When the waiter carved the ducks, everyone but Ernest was given breast meat. His share, Harold noticed, was "a helping of the lower anatomy." Ernest glowered, but that was all.

Five days later he filled up the sixth of his little *cahiers* and took up the seventh. He had completed his story of the fiesta and sent Jake Barnes off to recuperate at San Sebastian. There was not much more to say. A telegram from Brett summoned Jake to Madrid. They rode together in a taxi down the Gran Vía. "Oh, Jake," Brett said, "we could have had such a damned good time together." Jake was watching a traffic policeman in a khaki uniform. "It's nice as hell to think so," he said.

Ernest stared for a while at the closing sentence of his first novel. Then he drew a line through it and changed it to a question: "Isn't it nice to think so?" The phrasing was still not quite right but he was too tired to change it. "The End," he wrote. "Paris—Sept. 21—1925."

22. DOUBLE-CROSSINGS

THE drive to finish his novel left Ernest physically and emotionally exhausted. He tried to recuperate by swimming in the icy Seine, but gave it up when he tore a ligament in his right foot. He would have liked to take Hadley on a walking tour in northern Italy, crossing the Pass of St. Bernard, stopping over in Milan, Vicenza, Schio, and Bassano, and then going on to Venice for a little romantic lovemaking. But the plan was impossible because of Bumby, who had come back from Brittany bigger, browner, blonder, and livelier than ever. It was no use going to Italy without a girl, said Ernest, and he did not want to take any of his other girls for fear of such complications as alimony or illegitimate children. There was also the problem of Mussolini's government-by-lead-pipe-and-castor-oil. One sign of its spreading evil was the fact that the murderers of Matteotti had just been let off scot-free. "I've buried Italy," said Ernest, "and why dig it up when there's a chance it still stinks?"

He settled finally for a small trip to Chartres late in September, taking along the manuscript of his novel. He had meant to put it aside until Christmas, when he would "go all over it and cut it and fix it up and type it out." But he found that it could not be dismissed so easily. Part of the problem was the title. So far he had called it *Fiesta,* but he "did not want to use a foreign word." In Chartres he toyed with the idea of calling it *The Lost Generation.* He wrote out a foreword to explain where it came from. That summer Gertrude Stein had stopped at a garage in a village in the Department of Ain. One of the valves in her Ford was stuck and a very young mechanic fixed it quickly and efficiently. Gertrude asked the owner of the garage where he got such good workers. He said that he trained them himself: these young ones learned fast. It was those in the age group twenty-two to thirty who could not be taught. *"C'est une génération perdue,"* the owner said. Ernest listed some alternate titles inside the back cover of one of his *cahiers: River to the Sea, Two Lie Together, The Old Leaven, The Sun Also Rises.* He rejected them all except the last, a quotation from Ecclesiastes. The chief result of his trip to Chartres was the decision to change the name of his first novel to *The Sun Also Rises.*

About this time he had a note from Duff Twysden. It was scribbled on the stationery of the Studio-Apartments Hotel at 9, rue Delambre and left with

Fred, the bartender at the Dingo nearby. Duff was sympathetic about the torn ligament in Ernest's foot, but it was another matter that filled her mind.

Ernest my dear [she wrote], forgive me for this effort but can you possibly lend me some money? I am in a stinking fix but for once only temporary and can pay you back for *sure*. I want 3000 francs—but for Gods sake lend me as much as you can. I hate asking you—but all my friends seem to be in the same boat—broke to the wide. Am living in the country on nothing—but owe the pub a packet and dare not return without it. In the meanwhile—stuck here—and terrified of running it up further. If you can—and will be an angel will you leave me an answer here with Fred—at the bar as soon as you get this? I'm in such a stew so hope you'll really forgive this. I hear you have hurt yourself and do hope it's not serious. Best luck. As ever, Duff Twysden.

Whether or not he complied with Duff's request, there is no doubt that she was much in his mind. He set down in one of his little *cahiers* seven fragments of monologue, obviously remembered from remarks that Duff had made, very likely to himself.

[1] You must make fantastic statements to cover things.
[2] It is like living with fourteen men so no one will know there is someone you love.
[3] We can't do it. You can't hurt people. It's what we believe in in place of God.
[4] I have to have it and I can't have what I want with you so I'm going to take this other thing.
[5] I have never been able to have anything I ever wanted.
[6] And I looked at you and I thought I wouldn't be able to stand it. What a shame he put the top thing down just as we came up.
[7] What are you so merry about. What were you so merry about the other day.

Ernest was doubtless testing out these sentences with a view to putting them into the mouth of Brett Ashley when he revised his novel. Only one of them got in: "It's what we believe in in place of God." All of them were of the sort that might be uttered by a woman involved in a clandestine attachment. She advised the man to lie: "You must make fantastic statements to cover things." She was trying to hide her love for him by going out with other men: "It is like living with fourteen men so no one will know there is someone you love." Others would be hurt if the secret got out: "We can't do it. You can't hurt people. It's what we believe in in place of God." Denied consummation, the woman accepted a lesser substitute: "I have to have it and I can't have what I want with you so I'm going to take this other thing." She complained of her bad luck: "I have never been able to have anything I wanted." She recalled the time when she was nearly overcome with desire, and was hoping to be with the man in the concealment of a fiacre, only to reach the vehicle just as the driver was putting the top down: "And I looked at you and I thought I couldn't stand it. What a shame he put the top thing down just as we came up." Finally, she resented the man's good humor which she was unable to share: "What are you so merry about? What were you so merry about the other day?"

The passage in the notebook pointed up a question about the degree of Ernest's intimacy with Duff. They met often enough in the cafés: indeed, he was talking with her at the Dingo the day he first met Fitzgerald. In times of financial crisis, she turned to him at least twice for loans or assistance, sending the notes in secrecy. Her behavior in Pamplona convinced both Don Stewart and Bill Smith that something was afoot between Duff and Ernest. His explosion against Harold Loeb hinted at something like sexual jealousy. Yet the evidence indicates that if the topic of sexual intercourse arose, as it probably did, Ernest was able to resist temptation. Something of this got into *The Sun Also Rises* in disguised form. Jake Barnes's war wound left him capable of sexual desire but incapable of fulfilling it. The situation between Barnes and Brett Ashley, as Ernest imagined it, could very well be a projection of his own inhibitions about sleeping with Duff.

However it was, Duff and her desires served to underscore the theme of double-crossing, which was much in Ernest's mind that fall on both the conscious and subconscious levels. The only two stories he wrote in these months both turned upon instances of the double-cross. One was "Ten Indians," which he set down in first draft for later revision. It dealt with the presumable betrayal of Nick Adams by his Indian girl, Prudence Mitchell. While Nick was in Petoskey watching a Fourth of July baseball game, Dr. Adams saw Prudy "threshing around" with Frank Washburn in the woods near Walloon Lake. The other story, "Fifty Grand," was based on the welterweight championship bout at the New York Hippodrome on June 26, 1922. In the 13th round of a 15-round contest, Benny Leonard, the world lightweight champion, fouled Jack Britton, the welterweight king, which gave Jack the fight on a foul. Ernest's story doubled the double-cross. Jack Brennan secretly bet $50,000 on his opponent, Jimmy Walcott. When Jimmy fouled him late in the fight, Jack knew that he could not collect his money if he claimed the victory on the foul. With a heroic effort he stayed long enough to foul Walcott in turn. Walcott was awarded the fight and Jack collected his "fifty grand."

Fitzgerald was full of admiration when Ernest showed him the fight story. His only objection was to the opening conversation between Jack Brennan and one of his retainers. They were talking about the opening rounds of another fight.

"How did you handle Benny so easy, Jack?"

"Benny's an awful smart boxer," Jack said. "All the time he's in there he's thinking. All the time he's thinking, I was hitting him."

For years Ernest had been treasuring this remark as "a lovely revelation of the metaphysics of boxing." He was shocked when Scott Fitzgerald said that it was nothing but an old chestnut and would have to be cut out. Although he was humble enough at that time to follow Scott's advice, he came to regret the deletion some months later. Far from being an old chestnut, the anecdote was one that Fitzgerald had heard once, and once only, from a friend.

Both Fitzgerald and Dos Passos were full of talk about a wealthy American couple named Murphy. Gerald was a graduate of Yale—a tall, slender man with a high forehead and neatly combed red hair who was known to his three children by the nickname of Dow-Dow. He had married Sara in 1916 and brought her abroad to live in 1921. They maintained an apartment on the Quai des Grands-Augustins, but spent most of their time at the elegant Villa América at Cap d'Antibes on the Riviera. Gerald had studied architecture and then turned to painting. Everyone loved Sara, who said exactly and forcefully what was on her mind and cared nothing for the pretensions of the high society from which she sprang. The Villa América included a small guest-house called the Bastide or blockhouse, where Dos Passos often paused in his inveterate goings and comings. In spite of his fondness for Sara and his liking for Gerald's conversation, Dos found that four days at a stretch were about all he wanted of the Murphys' largess. He was always relieved to come back to see the Hemingways at the sawmill apartment, and even to assist in the ceremony of giving Bumby his evening bath.

He was on hand the day Ernest bought a large bright canvas called "The Farm" by a small dark Spaniard named Joan Miró. Evan Shipman had been coveting the picture and had persuaded Miró to sell it to him through a dealer. On learning that Ernest wanted to give it to Hadley as a present for her thirty-fourth birthday, Evan magnanimously offered to shoot dice for the right to buy it. Although Ernest won, the price of 5,000 francs was far more than he could afford. They all scurried around borrowing the money and triumphantly brought home the picture in a cab. Miró came to see it where it hung above the bed, content that it had fallen into such good hands. Ernest was ecstatic. Miró, said he, was the only painter who had ever been able to combine in one picture all that you felt about Spain when you were there and all that you felt when you were away and could not go there.

Apart from the acquisition of the picture, the great event of the fall was the publication of *In Our Time* in October. Liveright went to some pains to give the book a proper launching. The jacket flap contained a blurb by Sherwood Anderson, and there were other laudatory comments by Edward J. O'Brien, John Dos Passos, Waldo Frank, and Gilbert Seldes. The edition was small—some 1,300 copies. Nobody but Ernest expected the book to sell. As George Doran had told Don Stewart, novels could usually pay their way. Short stories were a drug on the market. Some of the reviews were nevertheless satisfactory. *The New York Times* spoke of the "lean, pleasing, tough resilience" of the stories and the colloquial freshness of the language. Herbert Gorman said that Hemingway drove "to the crux of the matter with a merciless bareness." The only sour note was sounded by Herschel Brickell. These, he said, could not be called stories in the commonly accepted sense. The exception was "My Old Man"—a beautifully executed race-track story which Sherwood Anderson himself could not have bettered. Ernest was sick of being compared to Anderson. He had said as much to Edmund Wilson as long ago as 1923. Anderson had started well, but his work had lately been going to hell, probably from too much praise by the people in New York. In the dark days of November, Ernest began to meditate a parody-satire. It might help to head off future comparisons between Anderson's work and his own.

Both Hadley and Bumby were down with bad colds when he set to work. He invented a little fable about the effects of the vernal equinox in the lives of two men in Petoskey, Michigan. Turgenev's *The Torrents of Spring* gave him his title, and Fielding's *Tom Jones* provided an epigraph to the effect that the only source of the true ridiculous is affectation. Ernest's method was mainly a parody of the affectations in Anderson's latest novel, *Dark Laughter,* a rather silly book that deserved the lampoon. Ernest's manner was brash. He made no pretense of serious purpose. One of his notes to the reader told how he had written Chapter Twelve straight off on the typewriter in a couple of hours, and then gone off for lunch with Dos Passos. Another mentioned a recent visit from Fitzgerald, who had sat down in the fireplace and refused to let the fire burn anything else but his overcoat. Fitzgerald had in fact appeared sometime after midnight on November 28th. He was so drunk that Ernest had to take him back to his flat in the rue de Tilsitt. On the 30th he sent the Hemingways a note of apology: "It is only fair to say that the deplorable man who entered your apartment Saturday morning was not me but a man named Johnston who has often been mistaken for me."

Fitzgerald left Paris before the book was finished, but Ernest read it aloud to Dos Passos. Dos liked the Michigan Indians—"Hem had a way with Indians," he said—and laughed at a lot of the better tomfoolery. He also agreed that *Dark Laughter* was both silly and sentimental. If someone were going to chastise Sherwood, however, there was no reason why it had to be Hemingway. Why double-cross an aging champion in just this way? Dos tried to argue him out of submitting the book, at least for the time being. It was not "quite good enough to stand on its own feet as a parody" while *In Our Time* was so good that it deserved to be followed by a smash hit. But Ernest hummed while Dos argued. His mind seemed made up. Hadley agreed with Dos. She liked Sherwood personally and "thought the whole idea detestable," though she soon found that "nothing could deter" Ernest from his plan to send the book to Liveright. Gertrude Stein was "very angry." Not only had Ernest called Part Four "The Making and Marring of Americans," but he had also chosen to betray someone whom she regarded as "a part of her apparatus." The only thoroughgoing champion of *The Torrents* was little Pauline Pfeiffer, the *Vogue* fashion editor from Arkansas, who had long since changed her first impression of Ernest as a rough, unshaven loafer and was now becoming one of Hadley's best friends. While the others deplored Ernest's satire, Pauline laughed heartily, told Ernest that it was great, and urged him to submit it to Liveright at once.

He did so, even though some of his friends half suspected a hidden motive. As Anderson's publisher and friend, Liveright could not possibly publish such a book. In turning it down he would automatically release Ernest from the terms of his contractual agreement. Dos could not decide whether Hem was deliberately scheming or merely playing "a heartless boy's prank." Mike Strater had no doubt that the book was a "cold-blooded contract-breaker." If it was, Ernest played his hand out with a poker face. His covering letter, sent with the manuscript on December 7th, was that of a brash young man who felt himself to be in a good bargaining position because of a respectable pile of manuscript called *The Sun Also Rises*. For a long time, Ernest told Horace, he had heard various critics bewailing the lack of good American satirists. When Horace read *The Torrents*, he could tell the critics to stop crying. After all, Fielding's *Joseph Andrews* had parodied Richardson's *Pamela* in the "golden age" of the English novel, and both books were now classics. Here was one more example, which had been read and praised by Scott Fitzgerald, Louis Bromfield, and John Dos Passos—writers already well known in New York. It was about the right length for satire, only five thousand words longer than Don Stewart's *Parody Outline of History*. The only conceivable reason for rejecting the book would be Horace's fear of offending Sherwood. But nobody with any stuff could be hurt by satire. With illustrations by Ralph Barton the cartoonist, sales could easily reach twenty thousand copies. Ernest asked for a $500 advance and an early decision by cable to the Hotel Taube in Schruns. It was a hell of a fine book and could make them both a lot of money.

The news from home was that Ernest's father had bought a copy of *In Our Time* and read the stories "with interest." Grace was gathering up some of the reviews to forward to her son. Around Oak Park, Dr. Hemingway had had "many compliments" about Ernest's latest achievement. But the good doctor could not entirely conceal his belief that the book was somewhat lacking in spiritual uplift. "Trust you will see and describe more of humanity of a different character in future volumes," he wrote. "The brutal you have surely shown the world. Look for the joyous, uplifting, and optimistic and spiritual in character. It is present if found. Remember God holds us each responsible to do our best. My thoughts and prayers are for you dear boy every day."

23. *YEAR OF THE AVALANCHES*

WHEN they got back to Schruns on the 12th of December they found two feet of snow and fine clear mountain weather. Ernest had need of the mountains. He had developed severe laryngitis after first catching a cold and then reading aloud the whole of *The Torrents of Spring* to his new friends, Gerald and Sara Murphy. He thought them "grand people." Their praise was still ringing in his ears when he and Hadley gathered up their child and their luggage and caught the night train from the Gare de l'Est. Bumby chattered steadily all night in the *wagon-lit,* and Hadley was red-eyed from lack of sleep when they changed trains at Bludenz for the final run to Schruns.

Herr Walther Lent had engaged a girl instructor for his *Ski-schule.* She was from Leipzig, a great skier, "small and beautifully built," with a narrow brown face and hair skinned back severely in a tight knot at the back of her head. She was Fräulein Margarete Elisabeth Maria Glaser. Herr Lent remarked that she would be of great use when it was time to ski in the high Silvretta. But that time was not yet, for even now, in December, conditions were ripe for avalanches. The first big loss of life occurred with a party of Germans at Lech in the Arlberg. Herr Lent had wired the Germans not to come and, when they came, refused to take them out. "They said they would ski by themselves" and he took them finally to the safest slope he could think of. "He crossed it himself and then they followed and the whole hillside came down in a rush, rising over them as a tidal wave rises. Thirteen were dug out and nine of them were dead." Herr Lent wisely forbade further skiing parties until the snowfalls had had time to settle and freeze.

Much of the first week Ernest stayed in bed, nursing his throat and chest, eating with gusto, writing letters, and reading Thomas Mann and Turgenev. Books like *Buddenbrooks* and *Fathers and Children* were much better reading, said he, than H. L. Mencken's white-haired boy-writer, Sinclair Lewis, who was making a reputation by exploiting the "much-abused American Scene." This judgment surprised Hadley, who recalled how deeply and carefully Ernest had once studied *Main Street.* Besides Turgenev and Mann, Ernest's book bag contained Maugham's *Of Human Bondage,* Conrad's *Within the Tides,* and Tolstoi's *War and Peace,* which he had carried all over Spain the summer before.

From the fastness of his featherbed, Ernest discoursed at length to Fitzgerald on the importance of subject in fiction. War, said he, was the best subject of all. It offered maximum material combined with maximum action. Everything was speeded up and the writer who had participated in a war gained such a mass of experience as he would normally have to wait a lifetime to get. Dos Passos, for one, had been made by the Kaiser's War, having gone to it twice and grown up in between. This was one reason why his *Three Soldiers* was such a swell book. Other good subjects, according to Ernest, were love, money, avarice, murder, and impotence. *The Sun Also Rises,* which he must now work all winter to revise, engaged none of these except the second and the last, but his hopes for the book were high. As soon as he recovered from his respiratory infection, he would take up the task of revision and typing.

He returned gradually to his former recreations, to which he now added billiards. A fresh storm on the 13th and 14th blanketed the town with three more feet of snow, and he went out twice to try the slopes behind the Taube only to discover that his illness had sapped his strength and weakened his courage. When a sozzle of rain came to melt the snow, he went to bed with Captain Marryat's *Peter Simple,* the satisfying success story of a young fool who makes good. One night he played poker, drinking seven bottles of beer and winning 158,000 kronen. Although at the depressed exchange rate this amounted to only $2.35, it took only half his winnings to buy Bumby a Christmas rocking horse at one of the small shops in the town.

Kitty Cannell was now back in Paris. One day in December she met Pauline Pfeiffer on the street. She was bent nearly double under the weight of a pair of skis and explained with laughter that she was going to Austria to spend Christmas and New Year's with Hadley and Ernest. She had never skied before, but Ernest had promised to teach her. This intelligence surprised Kitty Cannell, who had been unaware of the rapid ripening of Pauline's friendship with the Hemingways and still remembered her former opinion that Ernest was a lazy ne'er-do-well. But Pauline's views had changed. She did not mind at all when the thaw lasted through the holidays and made ski lessons impossible. Just to be near Ernest was enough. She was now, and she knew it, cock-eyed in love with him, and the problem was to keep Hadley from guessing as much.

She had been in Schruns about ten days when Ernest got the news from Horace Liveright about the book she had so much admired. "REJECTING TORRENTS OF SPRING," said the cable, "PATIENTLY AWAITING MANUSCRIPT SUN ALSO RISES WRITING FULLY." To Ernest, who at once sent Fitzgerald a long explanatory letter, the cable was scarcely a surprise. He had known all along that Liveright could not and would not publish something that "made a bum" out of the firm's current ace and bestseller. The contract with Liveright was nothing but a letter; yet it stated very clearly that their option on his first three books would lapse if they rejected Book Number Two. This they had just done. "So," said Ernest, "I'm loose."

He was also in mild demand. Max Perkins at Scribners had written last winter, as of course Fitzgerald knew. Bill Bradley at Knopf had lately sent a letter of inquiry. And Louis Bromfield, whose publisher was Harcourt, Brace, had just sounded out Alfred Harcourt's opinions on Hemingway. Harcourt said that Ernest's first novel might rock the country. He agreed to advance any reasonable sum if Ernest should decide to change publishers. Ernest's immediate inclination was to keep his promise to Max Perkins. The steps were clear enough. First, he would cable Liveright to hand over the manuscript to Don Stewart at the Yale Club. Don could then submit it to Perkins. *The Sun Also Rises* ought, he felt, to help in the bargaining.

Following a worried and sleepless night, Hemingway added a New Year's-morning postscript to his letter to Fitzgerald. He had begun to think ser.ously of a quick trip to New York. It would then be possible to settle matters on the spot, make any required changes in *The Torrents,* and even commandeer the plates of *In Our Time.* He would have to wait until mid-January for a new passport, his old one having lapsed before Christmas. Meantime he would go down to the custom house to claim the small jockey cap, with whip and silks, which the Fitzgeralds had sent Bumby as a Christmas gift to complement the new rocking horse.

Pauline was still in Schruns when Liveright's letter arrived. Horace said frankly that all the people in the office had read the book and unanimously agreed that it was not for them. Quite apart from its being such a bitter and even vicious caricature of the Andersonian manner, it was too cerebral a piece of humor, not at all comparable to the lighthearted work of Don Stewart and Bob Benchley. Far from selling 20,000 copies, as Ernest had predicted, they would be lucky to get rid of seven or eight hundred. To publish it would be in rotten taste and horribly cruel to Anderson. On the other hand, they were all looking forward to *The Sun Also Rises.* If they got it soon enough, they would publish in the fall. Pauline Pfeiffer clenched her small fists and went back to Paris.

Ernest was now well aware of the ongoing process that he later described, in which

an unmarried young woman becomes the temporary best friend of another young woman who is married, goes to live with the husband and wife and then unknowingly, innocently and unrelentingly sets out to marry the husband. When the husband is a writer and doing difficult work so that he is occupied much of the time and is not a good companion or partner to his wife for a big part of the day, the arrangement has advantages until you know how it works out. The husband has two attractive girls around when he has finished work. One is new and strange and if he has bad luck he gets to love them both. Then, instead of the two of them and their child, there are three of them. First it is stimulating and fun and it goes on that way for a while. All things truly wicked start from innocence. So you live day by day and enjoy what you have and do not worry. You lie and hate it and it destroys you and every day is more dangerous, but you live day to day as in a war.

Back in Paris, Pauline labored to keep up the pretense of maidenly friendship with the whole family. She wrote directly to Hadley to ask for the return of a kimono and a hairbrush which she had forgotten, and sent money to get Bumby a present at the toyshop. She praised Hadley's technique at the piano, and Ernest's progress with the novel, which he was then trying, unsuccessfully, to change over from first to third-person narrative. When she learned that Ernest had actually decided to make his business trip to New York, Pauline grew a shade bolder and said that she would like nothing better than to go along with him. Horace Liveright's letter had been a travesty of good taste; what he obviously needed was a *viva voce* lecture on the art of satire. Now that she knew the husky, apple-cheeked Bumby so well, she understood perfectly why Hadley would not leave him behind with Tiddy in order to accompany

Ernest to Paris enroute to his ship. But when Ernest came, she promised to cling to him like a millstone, old moss, or winter ivy.

This was roughly what happened as soon as he reached Paris late in January. Pauline wrote Hadley that there was an immense contrast between seeing Ernest and attending the fashion openings that her job under Mainbocher required. That very afternoon, for example, they were going to look at pictures in the Jeu de Paume. Ernest was being "just splendid," he was "a delight." What form the delight took Pauline did not specify. She had a flat in the rue Picot and Ernest was staying at the Vénétia Hôtel on the Boulevard du Montparnasse. He had already entered that schizophrenic state of being in love with two women at once. He did not want to leave her side to take ship across the Atlantic.

He made the trip alone, not without remorse for his predicament. As soon as the *Mauretania* docked on February 9th, he checked in at the Hotel Brevoort and then made a beeline uptown to Boni and Liveright. The firm occupied an old brownstone front at 61 West 48th Street. He was ushered immediately into Horace's cluttered office on the second floor. They used first names and the meeting was cordial enough. Ernest spoke of his sorrow at having to change publishers. They had a couple of friendly drinks at a nearby speakeasy. That night Ernest got "slightly tight" and slept very little. He was torn by indecision whether to approach Scribners, as Fitzgerald advised, or to try Bromfield's publisher, Alfred Harcourt. By morning he had concluded that his previous promise to Perkins ought to take precedence. He paid the first visit of his life to the Scribner offices on Fifth Avenue. Perkins, an immensely tactful man, at once aloof and warm, was sitting in his paper-strewn office on the fifth floor while the morning traffic flowed by outside. He said that *The Torrents* was a "grand" book, and offered a princely advance of $1500 on both the satire and the still unfinished novel. He also thought that they could work out an unusually munificent flat royalty rate of 15 per cent.

Ernest then went round to see Alfred Harcourt. He mentioned the arrangement with Scribners and explained that he had promised Perkins a first refusal. Harcourt was benign and urbane. Ernest would always be welcome at Harcourt, Brace if the occasion ever arose. They already had such able Midwestern authors as Glenway Wescott. In Paris Ernest had taken a cordial dislike to Wescott, deploring his simulated British accent, which he satirized in a brief scene at the Bal Musette in *The Sun Also Rises*. He told Harcourt rather bearishly that Wescott's stuff was fundamentally unsound. Although slightly embarrassed by his own temerity, he was feeling so "cock-eyed honest" about having kept his promise to Perkins that the condemnation of Wescott popped out almost before he knew it. But Harcourt merely raised his eyebrows and changed the subject.

During the New York visit, which was planned for seven days but stretched to nineteen, Ernest met "any hell's amount of people." He thought that Ernest Boyd was grand; so were Madeleine Boyd and of course Bob Benchley and

Dotty Parker. The literary gossip was that Bromfield and Ford were the most genuinely admired authors among the intelligentsia. Dos Passos's *Manhattan Transfer* had entered its fourth printing and Anderson's *Winesburg, Ohio,* its tenth. Owen Davis had adapted Fitzgerald's *The Great Gatsby* for the stage. Ernest went to see it. He thought that getting one's novels converted to plays was a splendid way of making easy money. He later reported that he had paid to get in, and once or twice would gladly have paid to get out. But on the whole he was pleased by the results, which were "pretty darn close to the book."

Up to the time of his departure, from Hoboken, his social life was joyously hectic. Jack Cowles knew dozens of bootleggers; so did Bobby Rouse, one of the old gang from the Y. K. Smith days in Chicago. Jack had a small house behind a livery stable at 25 Cornelia Street in Greenwich Village. One night they picked up John Herrmann, who had married Josie Herbst and was living in the Village. McAlmon had published John's novel, *What Happens,* an "authentic picture of American youth" which was judged to be so gamy that it was debarred from the United States. They rapped on the window of 50 West Ninth, where the novelist Dawn Powell lived with her husband and baby. Dawn was a tiny woman, pretty and plump, with dark hair cut close to her head like Pauline Pfeiffer's. She went along with them to Jack's house. Ernest sprawled contentedly on the sofa while Cowles made the drinks.

He also looked up Isabelle Simmons, now married to a classical scholar named Godolphin, whom everyone called Frisco. On his last day he went off to Ernest Boyd's, where they finished off three shakers of cocktails before lunch with Cowles and Rouse. After lunch they drank a few bottles of ale and Ernest went woozily to a matinee. When he reached the Hotel Merley for a farewell dinner, everyone else was as "cockeyed" as he was. He fell in love with Elinor Wylie, who pretended to reciprocate. Marc Connelly invited the whole gang to see his show, *The Wisdom Tooth,* but Ernest had to finish packing. On the way to the Brevoort in a cab, he recovered from his love for Elinor. He fell back in again when she accompanied him to the Hoboken pier where the *Roosevelt* sailed at midnight, with Dotty Parker and Bob Benchley among the other passengers.

On reaching Paris, Ernest just had time for lunch and dinner with Scott and Zelda before they left for Nice. Scott urged him to come to the Riviera, and Ernest promised to consider it. The Murphys had asked them to the Villa América in April. But he must have struck the Fitzgeralds as more than usually preoccupied. The novel was not done; Hadley and Bumby awaited his return to Schruns; and in the rue Picot was the "new and strange" girl, small and determined as a terrier, who had chosen Ernest as the man she wanted to marry. "I should have caught the first train from the Gare de l'Est," he wrote long afterwards. "But the girl I was in love with was in Paris then . . . and where we went and what we did, and the unbelievable wrenching, killing happiness, selfishness and treachery of everything we did gave me such a ter-

rible remorse [that] I did not take the first train or the second or the third."
He took the fourth. "When I saw my wife again standing by the tracks as the
train came in by the piled logs at the station, I wished I had died before I
ever loved anyone but her. She was smiling, the sun on her lovely face tanned
by the snow and sun, beautifully built, her hair red gold in the sun, grown out
all winter awkwardly and beautifully, and Mr. Bumby standing with her blonde
and chunky and with winter cheeks looking like a good Voralberg boy."

In March Dos Passos and the Murphys appeared for a visit. Dos was fresh
and tanned from his travels in Morocco and could stay only a week before
leaving for New York. Gerald and Sara looked stylish in their new ski clothes.
They said that they were dying to hear Ernest read his new novel aloud to
them. They were all delighted with the Austrian hideaway: the porcelain
stoves, the *Forellen im blau* for lunch, the hot kirsch in the *Weinstube*. Dos
thought it was "like living in an old-fashioned Christmas card." Both the
Hemingways found the Murphys generous and understanding. They were
somehow able "to give each day the quality of a festival." There was a strain
in Ernest that loved sprawling in luxury: he had once told Hadley that he
would have liked to be a king. Later he would describe himself as a trusting
and stupid bird dog in the Murphys' presence. Gerald and Sara persuaded him
to read aloud a few chapters of *The Sun Also Rises*. They both praised it so
lavishly that he wagged his tail with pleasure, as he put it, and thought that
there was nothing quite so fine as the "fiesta concept of life."

After the charming invaders had gone, he settled at last to his writing. He
had acquired a thick handsome book, like a binder's dummy, with a cover of
black buckram and many blank pages of fine rag paper. Two weeks earlier,
he had signed and dated it "EH, March 6, 1926, Note Book." The first of his
entries said that he must finish *The Sun Also Rises* and then write short stories
for four or five months. He was toying with a title that pleased him: *A New
Slain Knight*. It came from a medieval ballad, "The Twa Corbies." If he did
not use it for a new volume of the short stories, it would do for a novel. Ever
since he had picked out the epigraphs for *The Torrents of Spring* from Fielding's *Tom Jones,* he had been dreaming of doing what he called "a picaresque
novel for America." Its subject went back to one of his first assignments for
the *Star* after his return to Toronto in the fall of 1925. "It will be about Red
Ryan," he wrote in his black book, "and his escape from Kingston Pen. The
flight—the hiding in the woods—the bank robbery in Toronto—the double
crossing by his girl in Minneapolis—the arrest—the double crossing newspaper men in Minneapolis—the trip back to Toronto and Kingston—or it
will be a story of all the tough guys. The jockeys, the bartenders—the Italian
crooks—the pugs—Kid Howards—all the places. It will not be the story of a
weak disappointed youth caught and sucked up by fate. It will be the story of a
tough kid lucky for a long time and finally smashed by fate."

Luck, fate, and the concept of the double-cross were much in his mind these
days. He was more fatigued and distraught than he fully recognized. He used

his black buckram book to set down some of his meditations on suicide. "When I feel low," he wrote, "I like to think about death and the various ways of dying. And I think about probably the best way, unless you could arrange to die some way while asleep, would be to go off a liner at night. That way there could be no doubt about the thing going through and it does not seem a nasty death. There would be only the moment of taking the jump and it is very easy for me to take almost any sort of jump. Also it would never be definitely known what had happened and there would be no post mortems and no expenses left for any one to pay and there would always be the chance that you might be given credit for an accident."

One night in the Löwen, he discussed the matter with Fräulein Glaser, who shared his taste for the macabre. He said that he "wished there were some way of being killed skiing other than an avalanche." She sat there thinking it over, her brown hair skinned back severely from her lean and serious face. She said finally that her idea of a good death would be to have her heart stop while she was on her skis, "running straight down in *pulver Schnee*." This struck Ernest as a "very romantic" way to die. "You might run on for a little after your heart stopped" or else "spill forward instantly." As for avalanches, said Fräulein Glaser, they killed you with varying degrees of nastiness. "One man was found, killed by a powder snow avalanche, standing up, turning, his hand up, waving to his partner, also killed, his face smiling." Ernest doubted the part about smiling unless the partner smiled "after the snow came up and over him." But he remembered for years another of the Fräulein's stories, and eventually convinced himself that he had been present when it happened. This was the case of a man caught in a "heavy wet old snow avalanche" who was not found for two days. "They were digging all the time," said Fräulein Glaser, "and first they found blood in the snow. Then more blood and they dug following the blood . . . and they found him upright and the blood had all come from his neck that he twisted from side to side until it was worn right through to the bone." Of course, she said, he might have been unconscious while he was doing it.

"We became great students of avalanches," wrote Ernest in retrospect, "the different types of avalanches, how to avoid them and how to behave if you were caught in one. Most of the writing that I did that year was in avalanche time." It was still a time of avalanches in the closing weeks of March when he revised the last five chapters of *The Sun Also Rises*, beating them out on the noisy old Corona. Once he had determined to retain the first person narrative method, the work went smoothly. He lavished all his descriptive powers on the climactic bullfights of Pedro Romero, the departure of the revelers, and Jake's farewell to Brett at the Hotel Montana in Madrid. On reaching Paris at the end of the month, he had in hand a completed typescript of ninety thousand words. This was good, and he sent it out for professional typing at a cost of 1,085 francs. The bad part was that the "thing" began once more—just where it had left off some weeks earlier when Ernest kissed his new girl good-bye and caught the train back to Schruns and his *légitime*. No Alpine avalanche, poised for release by the torrents of spring, was potentially more disastrous than Hemingway's situation in Paris at Easter, 1926.

24. THE END OF SOMETHING

THE leaves on the trees in the valley of the Loire were already showing green when Jinny and Pauline Pfeiffer commandeered Hadley for a trip to the château country in Jinny's car. They went down by way of Versailles and Rambouillet to Chartres, taking their time, stopping at good hotels, and dining well each evening. The Loire was running full and fast between its high embankments. The ancient castles with their slate-covered turrets and formal gardens were a special delight to Hadley, who had not seen them before.

They had not been many hours on the journey when Hadley began to notice that Pauline was behaving rather curiously, lapsing into long silences after short bursts of conversation. On being asked a question, she snapped out the answer almost angrily, like a bark. Hadley's feelings were hurt. Jinny, who knew her sister's secret, explained that Pauline had been subject to similar moods since girlhood. But Hadley was skeptical. One day she asked Jinny point-blank whether Ernest was in any way involved. "I think," said Jinny, "that they are very fond of each other." Hadley did not pursue the subject, but her pleasure in the castle country rapidly drained away. On the return trip to Paris, she was the silent one.

The inevitable confrontation was not far off. April and May were dark and wet. Hadley had been coughing with a chest cold ever since Schruns. Bumby was hacking and sometimes vomiting with what sounded like whooping cough. Ernest had trouble sleeping. When Hadley remarked one day that she had reason to think he was in love with Pauline, his face flushed and he drew himself up. Hadley, said he, should not have mentioned the matter. By bringing it out into the open, she had broken the chain that might have held them together. His implication, as Hadley caught it, was that the real fault was hers for having spoken. He stalked downstairs to walk the rainy streets. Hadley wept.

The row at home, as commonly happened, started up the springs of Ernest's urge to write. Early in May he finished a short story called "Alpine Idyll" about a peasant named Olz in the Paznauntal, well to the east of Schruns in the direction of Innsbruck. He may have owed the central anecdote about Frau Olz's condition at the time of her burial to conversations with Fräulein Glaser, whose taste for the macabre had often emerged in her talks with Ernest on death and suicide. Ernest's version of the story turned upon Olz's inhuman lack of feeling for his wife. On the fifth of May he mailed it to Perkins for submission to *Scribner's Magazine*. The editors had found "Fifty Grand" too long to take. "Alpine Idyll" was short and direct.

The quarrel over Pauline, as well as Bumby's whooping cough, changed the Hemingways' plans for another summer in Spain. Ernest was still determined to leave as early as May 12th or 13th. If Bumby were not recovered by then, he would go on to Madrid by himself and Hadley could join him later. He was eager to see the *novilladas* and to write some short stories. He was also feeling bereft and sorry for himself. All his friends were out of town—Fitzgerald at Juan-les-Pins, Archie MacLeish in Persia, Chink Dorman-Smith back in England with the military, and Dos Passos in New York. Ernest closed a letter to Fitzgerald with the announced intention of going out and getting "cock-eyed drunk."

Pauline was on holiday in Italy with her aunt and uncle. A long time later Ernest would complain of her habit of "going away elaborately but only being away at any time long enough so that you would miss her." She had been gone this time less than a week when he packed his bag and caught the night train for Madrid, checking in at the Pension Aguilar. He found the city very dry and dusty and uncommonly cold for May. He arrived too late for the big bullfights on the 13th and the next *corrida,* scheduled for Saturday the 15th, was canceled by the veterinaries because of the inferior condition of the bulls. That Sunday he awoke to find that it had snowed heavily during the night. The San Isidro bullfights had to be called off. He spent the day working in bed to keep warm.

He had brought along the rough drafts of several stories and spent a remarkably productive Sunday completing three of them. Two were chapters in the further education of his young hero, Nick Adams. His first version of "Ten Indians" had concluded with a sentimental midnight meeting between Nick and his Indian girl, Prudy Boulton. He lopped off this episode and ended with Nick's disappointment over Prudy's faithless conduct with Frank Washburn. Another, first called "The Matadors" and afterwards "The Killers," took place in a lunchroom in Petoskey. The hired killers were Chicago gunmen named Al and Max. Their potential victim was an Italian boxer named Neroni, the same who had first appeared in Ernest's early story, "The Passing of Pickles McCarty." That morning in Madrid he renamed his fighter Ole Andreson and changed the locale from Petoskey to Summit, a small town near Chicago. The third item was Ernest's first play, an elementary one-acter about three Roman soldiers drinking in a tavern in Jerusalem the evening after the Crucifixion. It was the least successful of his day's productions. The dialogue read like a locker-room discussion among high-school sophomore football players.

While Ernest was in Madrid, Hadley took Bumby to Cap d'Antibes, staying in the Murphys' guesthouse in the grounds of the Villa América. All went well for a few days. The Fitzgeralds and the MacLeishes were both living nearby. Each morning the company assembled to swim while Bumby, still coughing, played on the shore with the Murphy children. But the child's cough aroused the Murphys' suspicion. Their British doctor quarantined him with whooping cough. The Fitzgeralds had recently moved from the Villa Paquita at Juan-les-

Pins to the much larger Villa St.-Louis, which had a beach of its own and was close to the Casino. Their lease on the smaller house had not expired and they offered it to Hadley, who summoned Madame Rohrbach from Paris and moved in to keep the quarantine.

Still in Madrid, Ernest wrote Sherwood Anderson about *The Torrents of Spring,* which was about to be published by Scribners. He admitted that Sherwood might regard it as a "lousy, snotty letter" about a "lousy, snotty book." But, said he, he felt obliged to explain his seemingly irresistible urge to push Anderson in the face after all his help in getting *In Our Time* published and praised. The whole thing had started the previous November while he and Dos Passos were having lunch and discussing *Dark Laughter.* After lunch, said Ernest, he went back to the flat, "started the *Torrents of Spring* thing" and completed it in a week. It was a joke, not meant to be mean, but absolutely sincere. Writers should not have to pull their punches among themselves. When a man like Sherwood, who was capable of great things, wrote something "rotten," it was Ernest's obligation to "call" him on it. He must not suppose that Ernest was lining up on the side of "smart jews" like Ben Hecht and those other morning glories. Personal feelings excepted, nothing really good could be hurt by satire. Since the book was not intended as a personal attack, the tougher it was, the better.

After three weeks in Spain, Ernest joined Hadley at the Villa Paquita. The Murphys greeted his arrival with a small champagne-and-caviar party on the terrace at the Casino. The early June dusk came tumbling down and the Mediterranean licked softly at the shore. Archie and Ada MacLeish chatted quietly, the Murphys were in the kindest of moods, and Ernest and Hadley both seemed in good form. But when the Fitzgeralds arrived, already tipsy, Scott seemed intent on social sabotage. "To begin with," said Gerald, "he made all sorts of derogatory remarks about the caviar-and-champagne notion . . . evidently because he thought it the height of affectation." Then he stared so long and rudely at a pretty girl at a nearby table that she complained to the head waiter. Next he began tossing ashtrays at another of the tables, laughing with sophomoric glee, until the head waiter had to be called again. Gerald was so disgusted that he left the group and went home.

Hemingway was also disgusted. The Riviera, with close friends close by, was not so good a place to work as the Aguilar in Madrid, and for a simple reason: there was almost no time when he could be alone. But he showed the carbon copy of *The Sun Also Rises* to Scott Fitzgerald, who now, in full sobriety, said that it was an excellent book. But he recommended a number of internal cuts in the opening chapters. His arguments were so persuasive that Ernest resolved almost at once to lop off the first fifteen typed pages of the manuscript—the whole biography of Brett Ashley and Mike Campbell and the autobiography of the narrator Jake Barnes. Most of this emerged, or was somehow explained, later in the novel, and it would anyhow provide a further test of Ernest's leading esthetic theory in these years. It had worked with "Out of Season," "Indian Camp," and "Big Two-Hearted River." It might also work with something as long as a novel. He notified Max Perkins of this momentous decision and sat back to await results.

Max Perkins agreed to the change and wrote that he thought the whole novel "a most extraordinary performance. No one could conceive of a book with more life in it. All the scenes, and particularly those when they cross the Pyrenees and come into Spain, and when they fish in that cold river, and when the bulls are sent in with the steers, and when they are fought in the arena, are of such a quality as to be like actual experience." The bad news was that *Scribner's Magazine* felt obliged to decline "Alpine Idyll." It would be "too hard a blow for the magazine"—or at least so Robert Bridges believed. It was "too terrible, like certain stories by Chekhov and Gorky," and dealt with a stark reality which most people preferred to keep covered up.

Max also sent along some reviews of *The Torrents of Spring*, which had been published May 28th. Harry Hansen in the *New York World* was not much impressed. "Parody," said he, "is a gift of the gods. Few are blessed with it. It missed Hemingway. He is better as a writer of short stories." But Hansen was in the minority. Most of the commentators found the book "great fun," and one called it "the best take-off on Anderson" in existence. Ernest Boyd, with whom Hemingway had drunk three shakers of cocktails in February, said that the old laurels of the Chicago school were now withered. *The Torrents* echoed some of Anderson's seedier mannerisms in the shrewdest possible fashion. But Sherwood himself was considerably upset. Ernest's letter from Madrid had struck him as "possibly the most self-conscious and patronizing" ever written from one literary man to another, while the book itself gave evidence of jealous resentment. It might have been funny, said Anderson, if Max Beerbohm had condensed it to a dozen pages.

Hadley was also hurt that summer, though for a different reason. Pauline Pfeiffer, who said that she was *not* afraid of whooping cough, having had it as a child, came to share the Hemingways' quarantine until it was time to go to Pamplona. The Fitzgeralds' lease on the Villa Paquita had now run out and the Hemingways, with Pauline, rented two rooms at the Hôtel de la Pinède in Juan-les-Pins. It was near the beach and had a small garden where the *ménage à trois* took most of their meals. Each morning they spent on the beach, swimming and taking the sun. After lunch in the garden and a long siesta, they took long bicycle rides along the Golfe de Juan, returning at evening yardarm time for cocktails with the Murphys, the MacLeishes, and the Fitzgeralds. Bumby and Madame Rohrbach lived in a small bungalow nearby, walking among the pines and playing on the rocks. But at the hotel there were three of everything: breakfast trays, bicycles, bathing suits drying on the line —and worst of all two women in love with the same man. Hadley was at some pains to pretend that nothing was amiss.

These arrangements continued until early July, when the Hemingways took Pauline and the Murphys to the fiesta at Pamplona. They stayed at the Hotel

Quintana for the usual noisy week. Each afternoon they occupied *barrera* seats at the bullring, paid for by Gerald. At one of the morning amateurs, Ernest persuaded Gerald into the ring with the yearling bulls—to test his nerve, said Ernest, with that flat look in his brown eyes. Gerald had a raincoat for use as a cape. When one of the bulls charged him at top speed he could not think what to do. But he escaped injury at the last moment by twitching his raincoat to one side, diverting the bull. Ernest congratulated him on having achieved a perfect veronica. But Gerald was apologetic. "Next year," he promised, "I'll do it well, Papa. To want to do a thing well . . . is still one of my complications." Pauline's complication was that she must soon return to Paris, far from the sight and sound of "Papa" Hemingway. As they all sat together in the white wicker chairs outside the Café Iruña, Hadley thought that Pauline looked unhappy and forlorn.

After the fiesta Hadley enjoyed, as well as she could, a welcome respite from Pauline's company at the Hotel Suizo in San Sebastian. The Murphys and Pauline entrained for Bayonne, where they sent back a souvenir postcard from the station buffet. "Well, well, it's all over—three depressed voyagers think of you kindly. À bientôt!" They signed the card in a column of three: *"Sadie . . . Pauline . . . dow-dow."* Yet nothing was really over, even when the Murphys got back to the quiet of the Villa América and Pauline rejoined her sister in Paris. For when the Hemingways went on to the Aguilar in Madrid, it was only to be pursued by Pauline's letters. "I'm going to get a bicycle and ride in the bois," she wrote. "I am going to get a saddle, too. I am going to get everything I want. Please write to me. This means YOU, Hadley." But Hadley was little inclined to comply.

Gerald's letter of thanks said admiringly that the Hemingways graced the earth. "You're so right," said he, "because you're so close to what's elemental. Your values are hitched up to the universe. We're proud to know you. Yours are the things that count." But the Hemingways' universe was coming unhitched. Ernest hinted at the imminence of disaster in a letter to Mike Strater just before the opening of the *feria* in Valencia late in July. He and Hadley had decided to cancel their proposed trip to the United States that fall. Everything, said Ernest, was all shot to hell in every direction. Strater's mother had died that summer and Ernest sent sympathy. He hoped that Mike had been able to discover some way to console his bereaved father: it was such a hopeless business to lose someone you had been in love with and made your life with, even though, as everyone knew, this contingency was one of the "swell things" that are in reserve for "all of us." Ernest's irony was of course intentional. He, too, was about to lose a woman he had loved—and still loved—and with whom he had made his life for the best part of five years. But he was not yet ready to reveal his predicament to Strater, except by such broad hints.

When the Hemingways stopped over at the Villa América early in August, Don Stewart and his bride were spending their honeymoon at Cap d'Antibes. Don was dismayed at the ruin of a marriage which he had thought indestructible. So were the Murphys. On learning that Hadley and Ernest were going to set up separate residences, Gerald offered Ernest the use of a studio he was leasing at 69, rue Froidevaux. Ernest accepted the offer in a kind of daze. He still could not fully believe in the actuality of the coming separation.

The details of their final trip together etched themselves in his memory: the oppressive heat of the southern provinces, the dusty trees and the gray stone hills, the steaming clutter of Marseilles, and the coming at nightfall to Avignon with its ruined bridge. In a field beside the railway a farmhouse was burning. All the rescued furniture stood forlornly on the grass. In the morning on the outskirts of Paris they passed three baggage cars which had been in a wreck. Such images of destruction accorded well with Ernest's state of mind. They took a cab from the Gare de Lyon to the rue Notre Dame des Champs. The apartment was silent and empty; the child was still in Brittany with Marie and Ton-Ton. They found a room for Hadley at the Hôtel Beauvoir, across the Avenue from the Closerie des Lilas. Ernest settled into Gerald's studio and began to read proof on *The Sun Also Rises*. He sent it off to Max Perkins aboard the *Mauretania* on August 27th. His covering letter contained the dedication which he wanted his first novel to carry: THIS BOOK IS FOR HADLEY AND FOR JOHN HADLEY NICANOR. It was, he thought, about the least he could do.

CHAPTER 5

Man of Letters

25. THE HUNDRED DAYS

HADLEY wrote out the agreement on a small slip of paper and signed her name. If Pauline and Ernest would stay apart for a hundred days and were still in love by the end of that time, she would give him a divorce. The only way that the lovers could think of to keep the commitment was to put an ocean between them. Pauline booked passage on the Red Star liner *Pennland,* out of Boulogne for Southampton and New York, sailing September 24th. Next day she cabled from England: AUVOIR ALL MY LOVE. The ship was hardly out of the Channel before she wrote him that separation was no tragedy. There were only three months to be gone through before "Ernest and Pfeiffer" would be together forever.

She stayed at the Waldorf Astoria, recovering from a cold. Dos Passos was also in New York and so were the Murphys. Just before leaving Paris, Gerald had quietly given Ernest $400—over 13,000 francs—by direct deposit to his depleted account at the Guaranty Trust. Having praised the Hemingways' marriage so fulsomely in July, he was now equally certain that Ernest and Hadley had done the wise thing in splitting up. His only fear was that remorse and self-reproach might adversely affect Ernest's writing. He thought it would be a great mistake for Ernest to desert that thing in himself—call it genius—which was of such special value. This was a view that Ernest shared but did not wish to recognize. He never forgave Gerald the writing of that letter.

Her uncle Gus Pfeiffer bought Pauline's train ticket to Arkansas. He was her father's brother, a slender bespectacled man of great wealth who owned a controlling interest in Hudnut perfumes. In the Pullman berth on her westbound train, Pauline considered how to break the news to her parents. Her father, Paul, was president and board chairman of the Piggott Custom Gin Company, which processed cotton for the farmers of Clay County. He was also a land pioneer who had bought up thousands of acres of bottomland both east and west of town. The family lived in a large white frame house on Cherry Street Hill. Pauline's mother Mary was a devout Catholic, mild-mannered, intelligent, simple, and unworldly, given to bridge playing, afternoon naps, regular church attendance, and good works in the community. Pauline waited four days before telling her the news. Mrs. Pfeiffer was profoundly shocked. Her sympathies lay with the wronged wife. "And how does *she* feel?" she kept saying, tears brimming her eyes. Pauline explained the voluntary exile arrangement, and they gradually talked the matter out. All in good time, both parents might come to accept what they could not avoid.

"Oh, you are lovely," wrote Pauline to Ernest. "And a great classic beauty. And smart. And perfect." But he did not feel like such a paragon. He assumed the pose of a sardonic young sufferer when he told Fitzgerald about his separation from Hadley. Their life, said he, had all gone to hell, which was the one thing you could always expect a good life to do. Hadley, of course, had been grand. The fault was his own in every way. Ever since that second Christmas in Austria, when Pauline had come on a skiing visit, he had been living in a personal hell, with plenty of insomnia to light the pathways and assist in the study of the terrain. He had become so used to it that he was even thinking of conducting sightseeing tours around the premises. Still, he was working hard in Gerald's studio in the rue Froidevaux. Jonathan Cape was bringing out an English edition of *In Our Time* and had already asked Scribners for an early look at the proof sheets of *The Sun Also Rises*. Edward O'Brien wanted to print "The Undefeated," which had been translated into both German and French, in *The Best Short Stories of 1926*. *Scribner's Magazine* bought "The Killers" for $200, the first of Ernest's mature stories to be accepted by an American periodical.

After the life of Paris and New York, Pauline found Piggott both rural and restful. Its population was about two thousand and there was little to do. She rode a boy's bicycle along the back roads, and took up a regimen of milk drinking to regain the weight she had lost during the earlier stages of her love affair. She read a good deal, made over some dresses and a coat of her mother's, played bridge, and let her bangs grow out so that she could part her hair on the side. For entertainment she went to a few "picture-shows" with her parents, spent one evening square dancing, and even attended a two-ring circus whose star, aged seventeen, was defiantly billed as "the oldest bucking horse in the world." The daily letters to Ernest were scarcely those of a siren. She had a little postal joke which she enjoyed and repeated: "For two cents I'd come to you in a plain wrapper." But she came no closer than that to a sexual allusion, though she thought his photograph was "very seductive and awfully poignantly beautifully spiritual." Her nightly prayer, as she set it down for Ernest's information, was: "Dear Saint Joseph, send me a good, kind, attractive Catholic husband." She literally counted the days until the time of rustication should be over and she could rejoin him in Paris.

Once in October she was struck by a "madhouse" fit of depression. "I don't know what caused it," she wrote, "except perhaps God." She had suddenly been overcome by the realization that they hadn't given Hadley a chance, had indeed locked her cruelly out of their lives. In a fit of contrition, she sent her a note, offering to extend the period of separation, and promising not even to communicate with Ernest if that would help to keep the bargain.

Ernest was seeing a good deal of the MacLeishes at their apartment in the rue du Bac. Once in October he and Archie made a bachelor trip to a late-season bullfight in Zaragoza. He also sought to persuade Archie to share his own enthusiasm for bicycles, fending off his friend's attempts to talk General Culture by ostentatiously reading a copy of *La Pédale,* the bicyclists' sporting journal. They rode out to Chartres, Ernest pumping furiously to stay ahead and pointing to the peasants plowing the fields far off in the blue distance while Archie, aching in every joint, fought to catch up. Ernest was notably truculent whenever he squired Ada to prizefights or bike races. If anyone even remotely jostled her, he would be invited to stand up and be slugged. Ada was amused to notice that these were nearly all little men, seldom more than five feet tall. Ernest towered and glowered above them like the giant in *Jack and the Beanstalk.* Some friends lent the MacLeishes an apartment on the Avenue du Bois de Boulogne. Archie conceived a violent dislike to the new quarters. Only the frequent presence of "Pappy," as he called Ernest, took "the curse off the blasted place." It was there at an evening party that Ernest insisted on reading aloud a scatalogical poem about Dorothy Parker, whom he had no reason to dislike or attack. Don and Beatrice Stewart were present that night. Don thought the poem vicious and said so. It was the beginning of the end of his friendship with Ernest.

Ernest's aggressive behavior was probably an outward manifestation of continuing remorse. Pauline's letter about her severe depression evoked a long reply in which he said frankly that he was writing it to get rid of the poisonous acids that were circulating through his system. He described it as a lousy, terribly cheap, self-pitying letter, wallowing in bathos and completely contemptible in every way. But Pauline's account of her melancholy seizure had left him absolutely done for and gone to pieces. The time was passing so slowly and so horribly that he felt as if he must scream it out. In his nightmares he seemed to hear Pauline saying that she would not go on with it, that her nerves were destroyed, that both of them were smashed.

He told her that he had even thought seriously of suicide. In perfect calm and without bluffing he had resolved in the fall of 1925 that if the love affair were not settled by Christmas, he would kill himself. It would save Hadley the necessity of divorce and remove the sin from Pauline's life. Later he had promised himself to delay the suicide until Pauline's return. But now everything was getting out of control again. He was not a saint. He would much rather die now while there was still something left of the world instead of going on until everything was hollowed and flat. After death he was perfectly willing to go to Hell. What he could not endure was the hell that lay around him now. If Pauline came back soon enough, he could doubtless survive. They were two against the world. He prayed for her each night for hours and every morning on awakening. He loved her and hoped she would forgive this contemptible letter.

She answered blithely that she had never confused him with sin. She had now regained her composure. Even her mother had begun half-consciously to speak of "when you are married." It would all work out. "Pauline Cézanne Hemingway Pilar Pfeiffer" was "fini mit tragedy." She had sprung back from the brink of her sorrow "like all the king's horses." Thus reassured, Ernest said that he too would probably recover. He was not by nature a "depressed rat," and knew that it was foolish to want to die. What he really longed for was simple oblivion until Pauline's return. The hundred-days arrangement had shot him all to hell inside. It was almost as bad as an abortion. He was thinking of trying to write a play about an "awfully swell" idea. The only hitch was the regular arrival of despair. Every evening around five o'clock it came floating up like fog out of a river bottom.

Even though nothing came of the play project, Ernest managed to siphon off his sorrow in the form of short stories. *Scribner's Magazine* paid him $150 for "A Canary for One," an only slightly fictionalized account of his return journey from Antibes with Hadley that August to establish separate residences in Paris. On November 22nd, he sent them "In Another Country," with the observation that the old days in Milan had now come to seem very real. The story recalled his sessions of physiotherapy at the Ospedale Maggiore. The central figure was an Italian major whose wounded right hand had dwindled to a claw, and whose young wife had just died of pneumonia. While he and the young American worked side by side on the exercise machines, the major discoursed bitterly about his double loss. The finality of his own loss became clear to Ernest when Hadley sent him a list of the items, including furniture, which she wanted him to deliver to her new apartment at 35, rue de Fleurus. He rented a handbarrow and accomplished the move. It required several trips and a separate one for Joan Miró's "The Farm." As he delivered the first of his loads he burst into tears.

Hadley left Bumby in his father's care and went down to Chartres to think her problem through. She wrote back to say that she had really meant her marriage vow in taking him for better or for worse. But since he seemed to want a divorce, he must now begin looking into the legal procedures for getting one. For Bumby's sake, she wanted all the arrangements to be conducted by mail unless something came up that could be settled in a few words without a quarrel. Ernest could see the child whenever he wished. While Hadley was away, Ernest stayed with Bumby in the sixth-floor flat. The child spoke French and had many small jokes, such as calling his father Madame Papa. He liked to pretend that a wolf lived in the flat. *"Il n'est pas gentil, le Monsieur Loup-loup,"* said he. When they rode in a cab to some other part of the city, Ernest always asked him, "Where are we now, Schatz?" and Bumby always replied, *"Ici, papa."* Ernest bought him a harmonica. They sat down at a table in one of the cafés and ordered ice cream. With the ring of vanilla around his mouth, his harmonica clutched in his left hand, and his wide eyes fixed on the passing crowds, Bumby suddenly heaved a great sigh of contentment. *"Ah,"* said he, *"la vie est beau avec papa."*

Ernest waited until Hadley's return before he answered her letter. As always, he told her, she had been brave, unselfish, and generous. He said that he had written to both Scribners and Jonathan Cape asking them to assign to her all royalties from *The Sun Also Rises*. Having done so much to hurt her, he could at least do this to help her. After all, he said, she had supported him with her patrimony while he wrote all his early books, and he could never have done them without her loyal, self-sacrificing, stimulating, loving, and "actual cash-support." As for himself he could always borrow from the "wealthy"—Fitzgerald or MacLeish or Murphy—or accept donations from Pauline's uncle Gus, who was more than eager to help his niece. Finally, in a sweeping and magnanimous gesture, he told Hadley that he was making a new will. The income from all his books, past and future, would be paid into a trust fund for Bumby. The boy's best luck, he said, was to have Hadley for a mother—with all her straight thinking, her good head and heart, and her lovely hands. She was the best, truest, and loveliest person Ernest had ever known.

Next evening Hadley replied straightforwardly: divorce proceedings might now begin. The three-month separation agreement was canceled. She would accept the assignment of the royalties with due thanks. If she decided to return to America during the divorce proceedings, she would take the boy to see his grandparents in Oak Park. Would Ernest please collect his suitcases, which he had left in her dining room? And would he be sure to eat well, sleep well, keep well, and work well? She closed the letter "with Mummy's love."

Among his friends Ernest did not spare himself. He was having a drink with Bill Bird at the Caves Mura when he blurted out the news that he and Hadley were getting a divorce. When Bill asked him why, Ernest answered flatly: "Because I am a son of a bitch." He told Fitzgerald that he had now got past his suicidal phase. He would consider it now only under special circumstances which he did not expect to arise. At any rate, said he, he had not been cowardly enough to turn the gas jet halfway on or slit his wrists superficially with well-sterilized razor blades. He would now go on in his familiar role of *son of a bitch sans peur et sans reproche*. Although he was living on one meal a day in Gerald's unheated studio, he was healthy, his head was in good shape, and he was going well.

The Sun Also Rises was also going well, at least for a first novel. By mid-December, two months after publication, sales stood just short of 7,000 copies. Max Perkins had risked a first printing of six thousand and a second and third of two thousand each; after the holidays he expected a strong performance through the spring season. If not so uniformly eulogistic as Ernest would have liked, the reviewers had extolled the book for some of the right reasons: the vigor of the prose, the vivid dialogue, the sustained tension of the action, the evidence that Hemingway could state and develop a theme at novel length. Hardly anyone seemed to like the people. One reviewer even said that their "extreme moral sordidness" defeated Hemingway's artistic purpose. There was also a widespread tendency to take the book as a prime exhibit of "Lost Generationism." Ernest had helped this along by placing Gertrude Stein's remark, "You are all a lost generation" side by side with the quotation from *Ecclesiastes* about the continuity of the rhythms of the earth. He complained to Perkins that it was the latter, not the former, that he wanted to emphasize. What he had meant to write was "a damn tragedy with the earth abiding forever as the hero."

Around Paris, much of the pleasure in reading the novel lay in identifying those who had served as working models for the cast of characters. Nearly everyone on the Left Bank recognized Brett Ashley, Mike Campbell, and Robert Cohn. A few saw that Braddocks and his wife were based on Ford Madox Ford and Stella Bowen. There was a good deal of ineffectual debate about the identity of Count Mippipopoulos. Harold Stearns, wearing a worn bowler hat and (as Evan Shipman said) "balancing his disreputable life like a comic juggler" was perfectly recognizable as the fictional Harvey Stone. Bill Bird noticed with amusement that Ernest had given Jake Barnes one of Bird's own favorite tricks for getting rid of bothersome friends: you asked them to have a drink at the Caves Mura, and after a suitable interval excused yourself on the plea of having to work. Don Stewart was mildly amused at the caricature of himself in the figure of Bill Gorton. He recognized a few of his own quips in the talk between Bill and Jake, but the whole book struck him as little more than a very clever reportorial *tour de force*.

Hemingway's other victims were generally resentful. The book made Kitty Cannell so angry that she took to her bed for three days. Her deepest indignation was less for herself than for the virtual crucifixion of Harold Loeb. But she was also enraged by the portrait of Frances Cline, Cohn's jealous mistress in the novel. She saw at once that Ernest had listened carefully to her conversational style, which was highly individualized and unmistakable. He had then projected it upon the character and experience of a Jewish secretary who had worked with Loeb in the editing of *Broom*. Loeb himself felt as if he had developed an ulcer. What had he done to evoke such malice? Had he not defended Ernest against the charge of anti-Semitism? Had he not boxed with him, bought him endless oysters and bottles of Pouilly-Fuissé, introduced him to Leon Fleischman, helped him to get published in the United States? Was it for this that he was whispered about at every party as the prototype of Robert Cohn? Duff Twysden came only belatedly to a reading of the novel. Although furious at first, she afterwards relented. When Ernest happened to meet her one night at the Dingo, she said that she had not been at all disturbed. Her only quibble was that she had not in fact slept with the bloody bullfighter.

As might have been expected, Ernest's parents were uncomfortable in the vicarious company of the wastelanders of Pamplona. Dr. Hemingway mailed

Ernest a copy of the *Literary Digest Book Review Magazine*. In red and blue pencil, he had underscored an editorial which said that there was now a strong public reaction against the "sex novel" and the "highbrow realistic novel." But he remained loyal to his son despite his own preference for "healthier" forms of literature, merely expressing the hope that Ernest's future books would deal with a somewhat higher level of subject matter.

Grace was a good deal more forthright, as was her custom. She was glad to know that his book was selling, even though it seemed to her "a doubtful honor" to have produced "one of the filthiest books of the year." Had her son ceased to be interested in loyalty, nobility, and honor? Surely he must know other words besides *damn* and *bitch*. It was hard for her to speak thus to her son. "But I could not keep silence any longer," she wrote, "if any word from me might help you to find yourself." Life to her was a wonderful boon; she had discovered a heaven on earth by learning to create things of beauty. If Ernest was in domestic difficulties or if drink had "got" him, he must throw off his shackles and rise up to be the man and writer that God had intended. Even before his conception he had been dedicated to God in the hope that he might make the world a better place. "I love you, dear," wrote Grace, "and still believe you will do something worthwhile. Try to find Him and your real work. God bless you." Ernest wrote back angrily that what his mother needed was a little shot of family loyalty. It might serve her as an anesthetic against all his so obvious disreputability.

But there were many on the other side. Fitzgerald wrote from Washington that he was delighted with the American reception of *The Sun*. "I can't tell you," he continued, "how much your friendship has meant to me during this year and a half—it is the brightest thing in our trip to Europe for me." John Peale Bishop had a drink with Ernest shortly before Christmas and showed him a letter just received from Edmund Wilson. Wilson had remarked to Bishop that *The Sun Also Rises* was the best novel by anyone of Hemingway's generation. Malcolm Cowley discovered that winter that Hemingway's "influence" was spreading "far beyond the circle of those who had known him in Paris." Girls from Smith College, coming to New York, "were modeling themselves after Lady Brett. . . . Hundreds of bright young men from the Middle West were trying to be Hemingway heroes, talking in tough understatements from the sides of their mouths." Thornton Wilder, then living in New Haven, reported that the Yale undergraduates were much impressed with *The Sun*, and that his own new novel contained a passage which he ardently hoped was Hemingwayesque.

The hundred days of the agreement with Hadley had stretched to a hundred and seven when Pauline's ship docked at Cherbourg. Ernest was there to meet her, ruddy from a week of skiing with Archie and Ada MacLeish. They stopped over in Paris long enough to pick up Pauline's sister Jinny to serve as a chaperone, and then went back to Gstaad for a long winter's holiday. They were still skiing among the Alps on January 27, 1927, the day that Hadley's divorce from Ernest became final.

26. MEN WITHOUT WOMEN

IN the early months of 1927 Ernest used loud bluster to conceal the remorse he felt at having lost his wife and child. He pretended, for example, to have heard a rumor that he had run off to Switzerland to avoid being murdered by various demented persons who thought they saw themselves in *The Sun Also Rises*. Harold Loeb, among others, was said to be out searching for him with a gun. Ernest's response, as he told it, was to send word around the Quarter that he could be found sitting outside Lipp's Brasserie between two and four on certain January afternoons. He took it as a sign of cowardice among his accusers that no bullets whistled.

He made a similar response to a New Year's letter from Chard Powers Smith, whom he had victimized in "Mr. and Mrs. Elliot." Smith had belatedly read the story in December, long after its appearance in both *The Little Review* and *In Our Time*. He wrote to say that Hemingway was a contemptible worm who had failed to bring off a typical cad's trick of character assassination. Ernest replied from Switzerland that Smith would not have dared to write him such a letter without knowing for sure that he was out of town. On his return to Paris, said he, he would take great pleasure in knocking Smith down a few times, or maybe only once, depending on his talent for getting up. He ended by expressing his hearty contempt for Smith, his past, his present, his future, and his epistolary style.

This capacity for contempt, already shown in dozens of other ways, was also apparent in his habit of accepting favors from people whom he then maligned behind their backs. He repaid a dinner invitation from Louis and Mary Bromfield by surreptitiously speaking of his host as "Bloomfield," impugning his gifts as a writer, criticizing the quality of the wine he served, and commenting satirically on Mary's pet cats, which he said swarmed over the dining table, stealing "what little fish there was" and then defecating in odd corners of the room. When Sherwood Anderson came to Paris, Ernest asked him out for a drink. In reporting the visit to Perkins, he said that Anderson was "not at all sore" about *The Torrents of Spring,* and that they had had a "fine time" together. Anderson took a somewhat different view of the incident. By his account, Ernest came knocking at his door, asking him out for a drink, talked for a few minutes, and then turned on his heel and strode rapidly away. Anderson said charitably that Ernest's "absorption in his ideas" had doubtless "affected his capacity for friendship."

His fame was clearly growing among the reading public. As Perkins had predicted, the novel kept its momentum well beyond the Christmas holidays.

Sales leaped from eight thousand in mid-January to twelve thousand early in February with no sign of abatement. This in turn helped to ignite the enthusiasm of magazine editors. Three stories were already in galley for publication in *Scribner's Magazine*. Alfred Kreymborg took "Alpine Idyll" for his *American Caravan,* and even the august *Atlantic Monthly* agreed to buy "Fifty Grand" for $350—the most that Ernest had yet been paid for a short story. Perkins's remark of January 25th summed up the situation: "The Sun has risen . . . and is rising steadily."

He was still at the Hotel Rossli in Gstaad, skiing and working on alternate days, when Perkins offered him a new goal in the form of a collection of stories to be issued in the fall. Ernest was enthusiastic. It would be his fourth published book in the United States and might go far towards cementing his reputation. He replied at once, suggesting a tentative title and a list of the stories he wished to include. One was "Up in Michigan," orphaned by Liveright from *In Our Time.* Two others were brand new, completed in early February. "A Pursuit Race" was a little sketch about a neurotic advance man for a burlesque show in Kansas City. The enquiry of "A Simple Enquiry" was made by a homosexual Italian officer to his young orderly. The tentative title, *Men Without Women,* was meant, Ernest explained, as an indication that "the softening feminine influence" was missing in all the stories, whether as a result of "training, discipline, death, or other causes." Perkins responded with his customary tactful eagerness, and plans for the book were set in motion.

Somewhat against Pauline's wishes, the wedding date was postponed until May. Ernest was in no great haste to remarry. He explained to Isabelle Godolphin that he and Hadley had "got in a jam" about his loving somebody else. Naturally, said Ernest, he didn't want to do anything about it, having been in that "splendid womanic state" for years. But Hadley had said he should get a divorce, and he had acted accordingly. He later told his father that even after the divorce he would have been willing to return to Hadley if she had wanted it. His feelings were not greatly mollified when Mike Strater wrote him that "all men of genius are immoral." Whether he married again or remarried Hadley or merely led "an old-fashioned immoral life" was not, said Mike, anyone's business but his own. But free-wheeling immorality held no temptation for Ernest. He continued to interest himself in Hadley's welfare, brought Bumby down to Gstaad for two weeks in January, and boasted to all his friends that he and Hadley were on "swell terms." Early in February he notified his parents that he and Hadley had separated in the fall. But he insisted that they were still "the best of friends," did not mention either Pauline or the divorce, and asserted that he was living a "monastic life."

Guy and Mary Hickok were watching over Hadley's welfare in Paris. Guy was eager to make a bachelor tour of Fascist Italy and twice asked Ernest to go along. Pauline opposed the idea; she had been too long separated from Ernest during her period of exile in Piggott. But Ernest agreed to go, despite his previous vow to stay clear of Italy as long as Mussolini was in power.

Early in March, he brought Bumby down to Gstaad for another ten-day visit. Pauline and Jinny took turns in supervising the boy's meals and naps while Ernest made three-mile ski runs each day in the high country above Wengen. At the end of the visit, he took Bumby back to his mother and set off with Guy one gray morning in the middle of March.

Guy's Ford was an experienced vehicle with dented running boards and a cracked windshield. But it carried them in reasonable comfort down through the farmlands of central France and out into the pale sunshine of the Riviera. By Sunday the 20th they were past Genoa and Rapallo, where Ernest met Don Guiseppe Bianchi, the priest who had anointed him while he lay wounded in the Piave valley in 1918. Afterwards they turned inland through wooded country, with the huts of charcoal burners visible among the trees and an old-fashioned smell of woodsmoke in the bracing air. At Carradano a young Fascist approached the car, carrying a battered suitcase and the inevitable brown-paper package. He demanded a ride to Spezia, and stood on the running board for twenty kilometers, holding onto a roof strut through the open window of the car. Outside Spezia he gathered his luggage and stood watching them suspiciously as they drove on into the town.

Mussolini had abolished brothels and driven their personnel into respectable occupations. Guy and Ernest found that the *ristorante* where they stopped for lunch was doing double duty. Hemingway was beside himself with delight when one of the waitresses, wearing nothing under her housedress, approached Hickok with a predatory gleam in her eye. But all his persiflage on this occasion was only a mask for his deeper feelings. The brief encounter with the priest had served to reawaken his religious sensibilities, and the end of his marriage to Hadley was still very much on his conscience. Outside Spezia he asked Guy to stop at a roadside shrine, where he knelt and prayed for what seemed a long time, returning to the car with tears on his cheeks.

They spent the night in Pisa and from there in the following week drove through Florence and over the hump of the Apennines to Rimini on the Adriatic. There they picked up mail at the post office, including several letters from Pauline. She was restive in Ernest's absence and mildly ironic about what she called this "Italian tour for the promotion of masculine society." She hoped that the trip would last him for a long time. When she became his wife, she was going to oppose all such separations. She and Jinny had been looking at apartments. The MacLeishes had told her of one at 6, rue Férou, a lanelike street near the Church of St.-Sulpice. It was large, clean, and newly redecorated. If Uncle Gus approved of it when he reached Paris, he would advance the money to pay the rent. She also reported having talked to a priest about the best way of getting married. Both of them would need certificates of baptism. Since Ernest had been baptized a Catholic in 1918, perhaps there was a record of it somewhere in Italy. The only other necessary document was a certificate of his marriage to Hadley, which had taken place outside the Church and would therefore be judged invalid. Pauline was eager to be married. If Ernest would only hurry back to her, he could have his own way all the time, she would cross him in nothing.

The travelers accomplished a wide northern loop through Forlì, Imola, Bologna, Piacenza, and so back to Genoa. Along the valleys of Tuscany and across the Emilian plain Ernest's praying and weeping sporadically continued. It was raining hard in Genoa and the street gutters stood ankle-deep in muddy water. The Mediterranean was gray as lead and covered with dirty foam. The restaurant at Sestri was damp and cold and the wine tasted strongly of alum. At the border of France they shrugged their way through the *douane* and slept the night at Menton. After ten days in Mussolini's Italy, the town seemed "cheerful and clean and sane and lovely." While the trip was still fresh in his mind, Ernest set down a series of sketches, derisory in tone, under the title of "Italy, 1927," and sent them off to Edmund Wilson for publication in the *New Republic*.

Hadley was now on the point of beginning her long-postponed trip to the United States. On April 16th Ernest saw her off on the boat train with Bumby and then turned back to his literary labors. The table of contents for *Men Without Women* was gradually established. The volume would include the long stories, "Fifty Grand" and "The Undefeated," and eight others composed at various times in the past year: "Today is Friday," "In Another Country," "The Killers," "A Canary for One," "A Pursuit Race," "An Alpine Idyll," "A Simple Enquiry," and "Banal Story." The last of these, which had appeared in *The Little Review* in the summer of 1926, was Ernest's final tribute to the matador Maera. On May 4th he added to this group the sketches of Fascist Italy which he had recently sold to the *New Republic,* and the Nick Adams story, "Ten Indians," completed in Madrid in May, 1926, and now tentatively retitled "After the Fourth." But even a round dozen did not seem to him to be enough. Within the next few weeks he brought the total to fourteen with "Now I Lay Me," and "Hills Like White Elephants." The first was a new story of Nick Adams, based on Hemingway's own experiences in Italy and including a flashback about Dr. and Mrs. Hemingway in Oak Park during his boyhood. The second, conducted almost wholly in dialogue, engaged the delicate topic of a man persuading his girl to have an abortion as they sat drinking beer outside a Spanish railway station in the Ebro Valley.

Ernest's growing reputation as a man of letters produced two new friendships during the spring. One was with Donald Friede, Horace Liveright's junior partner, who hurried across the ocean to try to persuade him back into the firm. Friede offered a new contract which would guarantee an advance of $3,000 on any novel, $1,000 on any book of short stories or essays, and straight 15 per cent royalties from the start. But Ernest was not tempted. He told Friede that he was "absolutely satisfied" to stay at Scribners and rejected out of hand a suggestion that Liveright should buy the rights to *The Torrents* and *The Sun* and reissue them, along with *In Our Time,* in a uniform edition.

The second new friendship was of far greater significance and duration. Waldo Peirce, a tall, untidy, bearded painter from Bangor, Maine, had read *The Sun Also Rises* with mounting enthusiasm and wanted to meet the man who had written it. Waldo was then forty-two, and had been a proud alumnus of Harvard for almost twenty years. Soon after graduation he had come abroad to follow a career in painting. He had driven ambulances around Verdun in 1916–17, and was already fluent in both French and Spanish. Large and gentle, always talking, given to writing and reciting long and often bawdy poems in three languages, Waldo was a man after Hemingway's heart. On learning that Ernest had a child named Bumby, Peirce made a whole series of bright, funny, cartoonlike drawings for the child's amusement. Like many others, Ernest found Waldo's ebullience irresistible, and was soon addressing him as *"Muy Caballero Mío."*

The date for the wedding with Pauline was now set at last. Late in April, she notified the numerous members of the Pfeiffer clan. They responded enthusiastically with gifts of money, including several $1,000 checks. Pauline's mother sent her blessings as well as a "financial contribution" to their happiness and well-being. The wedding was performed on the 10th of May under Catholic auspices in the Paris Church of Passy, with Jinny as her sister's attendant. The MacLeishes did not attend the ceremony, although Ada gave a small lunch afterwards. She was doing her best to swallow the disgust she felt over Ernest's efforts to persuade the Catholic Church that he had been "baptized in the faith by a priest who had walked between aisles of wounded men" in an Italian dressing station nine years earlier. She resented even more the implication that Hadley, as a nonbeliever, had therefore never been his wife and that their marriage in the Protestant church at Horton Bay had been invalid.

Whatever the duplicity Ernest practiced in order to bring his religious position into approximate accord with ecclesiastical regulations, he now regarded himself as at least a nominal Catholic. A few months later he sought, rather lamely, to explain his views to a Dominican father who had sent him an inquiry. For many years, wrote Ernest, he had been a Catholic, although he had fallen away badly in the period 1919–27, during which time he did not attend communion. But he had gone regularly to Mass, he said, during 1926 and 1927, and had definitely set his house in order (his phrase) in 1927. He felt obliged to admit that he had always had more faith than intelligence or knowledge—he was, in short, a "very dumb Catholic." He had "so much faith" that he "hated to examine into it," but he was trying to lead a good life in the Church and was very happy. He had never publicized his beliefs because he did not wish to be known as a Catholic writer. He knew the importance of setting an example—yet he had never set a good example. His fundamental program was simplicity itself: to try to lead a good life and to try to write well and truly. It was easier to do the first than the second.

The honeymoon lasted approximately three weeks and was spent at a small pension in Grau du Roi, a small fishing port five miles below Aigues Mortes at the extremity of the Rhône Delta. It was a warm and watery region, still largely unspoiled, and favored with a long, clean swimming beach where they disported themselves each morning. Aigues Mortes, said Ernest, was the finest walled town left in France. It pleased him also that Grau du Roi stood beside the canal which St. Louis had built as a launching place for his thirteenth-century Crusades. Pauline kept her promise to give Ernest his own way, and he flourished in a regimen of sea and sun, fishing and swimming, writing well with no sense of exertion, and finishing "Ten Indians" and "Hills Like White Elephants," both of which he mailed to Perkins from this spot on May 27th. The only bad luck was a cut foot, which became infected with anthrax. When they returned to Paris in June, he spent ten days in bed with swelling and fever.

The summer's trip to Spain was not greatly different from its predecessors except that Ernest had a new wife. After Pamplona, which he thought as wonderful as ever, they went to swim and rest in San Sebastian for a week before the big *feria* at Valencia. Ernest complained that he could not write, which was his usual situation while reading proof on a finished book. In Valencia, they stayed at the Hotel Inglés until the 31st, stopped in at the Aguilar in Madrid, and by the middle of August were settled in Santiago de Compostela, which Ernest called "the loveliest town in Spain." He watched the small hawks hunting in the deep shadows at the top of the nave in the cathedral and was amused when a peasant woman hurried up to him and asked where she should go to eat the body of Jesus. "Right over there, lady," said Ernest delightedly. On the first day of September they entrained for Palencia and the endless ride to Hendaye, a trip so fearsome that Ernest had extended his stay in Galicia longer than he had meant to do.

Hendaye Plage was as pleasant as ever during the fortnight of their stay. He took the occasion to write a long letter to his father, expressing his sorrow at having disappointed his parents over the break with Hadley. The letter was a mixture of truth and lies. For over a year, said Ernest, he had been simultaneously in love with two girls while remaining absolutely faithful to Hadley. When she decided on a divorce, the other girl was in America and Ernest had not heard from her in almost two months—a palpable lie when in fact Pauline had written him nearly every day. But he would never stop loving Hadley and Bumby, as well as Pauline, to whom he was now married. He concluded by saying that he was still angry at his mother for having accused him of pandering to the lowest tastes of the reading public.

That public could hardly be said to have neglected Ernest's novel. When *Men Without Women* appeared on October 14th, the sales of *The Sun Also Rises* had reached 23,000 copies, and there was still a good deal of fan mail, both negative and positive. Ernest read all the reviews and letters with care, and suggested that Perkins ought to procure some pictures of white-bearded New England worthies like John Greenleaf Whittier to be autographed and mailed out as portraits of Hemingway. He was greatly irritated by a front-page review of *Men Without Women* in the Sunday book section of the *New York Herald Tribune*. Virginia Woolf, the reviewer, called him courageous, candid, and highly skilled, but thought him too self-consciously virile, and said that his talent had contracted instead of expanding. All that Bloomsbury Group, said Ernest, had appointed themselves the saviors of the republic of letters, habitually imputing dishonest motives to young challengers on the way up. Mrs. Woolf's opinions upset him so much that he asked Perkins to save the others until Christmas, when he would be down in Gstaad. He was now working hard and found that the reading of reviews made him self-conscious and inhibited his writing.

The decision was wisely taken. Other reviewers referred to "the callous little world of Mr. Hemingway" and spoke of his preoccupation with "bull-fighters, bruisers, touts, gunmen, professional soldiers, prostitutes, hard-drinkers, [and] dope-fiends." His "vulgar people" were involved in "sordid little catastrophes." The flavor was that of cheap absinthe, even though the presentation was brilliant. The trouble with Hemingway was that he lacked a ruling philosophy. He was faithful, but only to surfaces. He was fundamentally a reporter whose facts stood out "with all the clearness and sharpness (and also the coldness) of pinnacles of ice."

Even before he read these judgments on his latest short stories, Ernest had begun work on a second novel. This was one of two notable beginnings that fall, the other being Pauline's pregnancy, which had revealed itself soon after their return to Paris from Hendaye Plage. Barely begun at Hendaye, the book had reached 30,000 words by the middle of October. Ernest spoke of finishing the first draft sometime that winter. By the week after Thanksgiving, he had done twenty chapters. He told Perkins that this was about a third of the whole, and described the book as a kind of modern *Tom Jones*. He was experimenting with third-person narration, having tired of the limitations imposed by the "bloody 1st person," which he had used in *The Sun Also Rises* and some of the short stories. It was beginning to be clear by this time that he could not finish by early winter, especially since he was looking forward to a couple of months of skiing in the neighborhood of Gstaad.

After that, said Ernest, he would go back to the United States to stay until the fall of 1928. One reason for the journey was that Pauline, like Hadley before her, preferred to have her baby on American soil. Yet Ernest had been longing to go home for more than a year. The breakup with Hadley had spoiled his plans for an American trip in the fall of 1926, and he had since been dreaming of finding some spot twelve or fifteen hours by train from New York City. There he would dig in and write, descending on the metropolis whenever a good prizefight came along, and having a few drinks with the boys in some of the better midtown speakeasies. His nostalgia for his homeland was further sharpened when Hadley and Bumby got back to Paris late in October. Though tired from the trip, Hadley looked beautiful to Ernest.

She had conquered her former tendency to tears and accepted the role of divorcée with seeming equanimity. She hinted that she had fallen in love with someone else. Her appearance was in marked contrast to that of Pauline, whose first pregnancy at the age of thirty-two was causing her some discomfort.

On a quick trip to the six-day bicycle races at the Sportspalast in Berlin, they met Sinclair Lewis, whom Ernest had known casually in Paris while he was still married to Hadley. Lewis had not heard of the divorce and remarriage and was shocked to discover, when they accepted his invitation to dinner, that this small, shy, rather gray-faced, and very silent woman was the new Mrs. Hemingway. The dinner took place in a small Rathskeller shaped like a Pullman car. The other guests were a jingoistic German woman called Agatha and a new friend of Lewis's named Ramon Guthrie, who taught French at Dartmouth College and had recently finished a novel. Agatha usurped the dinner conversation with a long monologue on the emptiness of all non-German painting through the time of Cézanne. Guthrie broke in at last to say that El Greco was the only painter she had not attacked. She had just opened her mouth to renew her monologue when Ernest banged his fist on the table. "El Greco," he shouted, "is a cock-eyed good painter." This shut Agatha's mouth and the dinner ended. Guthrie's great regret was that the lady's ruthless egotism had spoiled his chance to hear a conversation between two of America's most eminent novelists.

The year ended with a series of minor misfortunes. Jinny wrote from Gstaad that the early snow was all melted away. Ernest developed a sore throat and took to his bed in the rue Férou, convinced, as always, that it might turn into pneumonia or worse. When they set off on December 12th, the infection had settled in his chest and at Montreux, where they stopped overnight, bad luck again intervened. In the middle of the night Ernest gathered up his son to put him on the pot. Bumby sleepily stuck one finger into his father's right eye and the fingernail cut the pupil. The cut was only about the size of a small fishscale, but it was Ernest's one good eye and his vision was reduced to a weeping blur. Six days later he was still in bed with a fearsome combination of grippe, blindness, hemorrhoids, and an aching tooth. His only compensation was a beard which he described as "almost rabbinical."

He was further harassed by a copy of the *Oak Park News* containing a feature article about his mother. It was headlined LAUNCHES NEW CAREER AFTER RAISING FAMILY, and told of Grace Hall Hemingway's recent success as a landscape painter at the advanced age of fifty-two. "One might suspect," wrote the reporter, Bertha Fenberg, "the mother of Ernest Hemingway, author of *The Sun Also Rises,* to be something of a harsh realist, but this very jolly woman laughs at the pessimism of 'these young writers' and expresses the sane belief that the pendulum is swinging back to normal. 'God's in his heaven, all's right with the world' is her way of expressing her own happy life." No doubt, said Ernest sourly, Grace wished that her son Ernie were Glenway Wescott or some highly respectable Fairy Prince with an English accent and a taste for grandmothers.

At Ernest's bedside, Pauline had taken to reading aloud from Henry James's *The Awkward Age*. Ernest listened and squirmed. Why was it, he wondered, that whenever James was afraid that he would have to think about what his characters were doing the rest of the time, he bailed himself out with a drawing-room scene? His men, said Ernest, all talked like fairies except for a few caricatures of brutal outsiders. Was he as much of a fake as he seemed? He had a close knowledge of drawing rooms and a fine, easy way of writing, but very little else.

The one bright note as the year concluded was that a book called *Men Without Women*, written by a brutal outsider, had sold 15,000 copies a mere three months after publication.

27. GOING WEST

ERNEST'S misfortunes bracketed the new year and ran well downward into the spring of 1928. For the time being, most of them were minor irritations. Yet even after he regained full use of his eyes, he continued to be haunted by fear of blindness. What would he do? How could he revise his work? In a respectful letter to the semiblind James Joyce he said that for ten days he had had a very small taste of how things might be with Joyce himself. Even the cocaine wash the doctor prescribed had not erased the pain.

In January, MacLeish came to join him and they tried the famous run down the Saanersloch Fluh. But the tips of Ernest's skis kept slipping under the crust. During the descent he took ten bad spills, one of them a nose dive which buried his head and smashed the glass in his goggles. On the last day of the month Pauline and Bumby returned to Paris, leaving him to make one final trip to Lenk and Adelboden. Poor weather intervened to spoil it. Upon his arrival in Paris early in February he discovered that a cold snap had frozen and burst the pipes at the apartment in the rue Férou, leaving the whole house without heat for a week. He went to bed with an attack of the grippe.

He had just recovered from this affliction when he was felled yet again, early in March, by one of the most curious accidents of his career. He later denied that he was unduly accident-prone, but his poor eyesight and his physical awkwardness combined to cause a remarkable series of mishaps. On this occasion he had been to dinner with Ada and Archie MacLeish and had reached home about eleven. At two in the morning he entered the bathroom of his apartment. The place was very cold. Someone who had intended to pull the flushbox chain had instead yanked the cord that opened the skylight, cracking the glass in several places. As he fumbled sleepily with the cord, the whole decrepit skylight fell in upon his luckless head, gouging his forehead two inches above his right eye and felling him like a poleaxed steer. Pauline tried to stanch the flow of blood with layers of toilet paper, and then summoned MacLeish, who commandeered a cab. By this time, Ernest was giddy and half-delirious. They reached the American Hospital at Neuilly shortly before three. The intern on duty closed the gaping triangular wound with nine stitches.

He was now too famous to be ignored and the wire services picked up the story. Ezra Pound sent a message from Rapallo: "Haow the hellsufferin tomcats did you git drunk enough to fall upwards thru the blithering skylight! ! ! ! ! ! ! !" Perkins cabled Guy Hickok for an on-the-spot report: Hadley sent a letter of sympathy as soon as she heard: "You poor dear old thing! What rotten, rotten luck to have such a thing happen to a truly beautiful mitten like you! I expect you are both a bit discouraged about how life *is* one damn thing after another." Ernest's view of the situation could not have been more exactly summarized.

The worst of it was the adverse effect on his writing. In February he had tried a short story which had turned out to be "no bloody good." He complained to Perkins that his successive misfortunes—including three severe bouts with grippe, the anthrax infection from Grau du Roi, the cut in his eyeball in December, and now the skylight accident—had given his whole life and his head a hell of a time over the past year. You come back slowly, said he, yet you must never let the pack know that you have been away or wounded. His enthusiasm for the ongoing novel had cooled accordingly. At first it had seemed like a good idea: a kind of "modern Tom Jones." It now stood at twenty-two chapters and roughly 45,000 words. But he did not know enough to write it yet. He implied that his powers of invention had suffered as a result of the infections and the blow on the head. If the book failed to catch fire again, he proposed to drop it and go on to something else.

The something else, as it happened, was already in hand, though still in nascent form. He had begun it early in March before the skylight fell. At first he had thought of it only as a short story like "In Another Country." He had been trying for years to make fictional use of his war experiences of 1918. He wanted to tell a story of love and war, using as an epigraph the cynical lines from Marlowe: ". . . but that was in another country,/and besides the wench is dead." The other country could only be Italia, and the girl Agnes von Kurowsky. She was neither a "wench" nor was she dead. But the story ached to be told. The whole affair now lay ten years in the past, suffused with an aureate glow which none of the intervening visits to Italy had succeeded in expunging. Suddenly, like an unexpected annunciation, he had begun to get "a great kick" out of the war "and all the things and places." Whatever happened, the successor to *The Sun Also Rises* must be a first-rate novel. Perhaps this was it. Fitzgerald had almost extravagantly admired the opening sentence of "In Another Country": "In the fall the war was always there, but we did not go to it any more." Now in Ernest's desk in the study at 6, rue

Férou was a page of handwriting which spoke of another fall in that other country: "In the late summer of that year we lived in a house in a village that looked across the river and the plain to the mountains. In the bed of the river there were pebbles and boulders, dry and white in the sun, and the water was clear and swiftly moving and blue . . ."

Ernest's longing to return to America had finally come to focus on Key West. Dos Passos, who had once hitchhiked through the region, was enthusiastic about his "dreamlike crossing of the keys" aboard a train on the old Flagler viaduct. Key West "really was an island," said Dos.

It was a coaling station. There was shipping in the harbor. The air smelt of the Gulf Stream. . . . Cayo Hueso, as half the people called it, was linked by car-ferries with Havana. Cigar factories had attracted a part Cuban, part Spanish population. . . . The English-speaking population was made up of railroad men, old Florida settlers, a few descendants of New Englanders from the days when it was a whaling port, and fishermen from such allwhite settlements as Spanish Wells in the Bahamas.

A combination of roads and ferryboats had gradually made it attainable by car from the American mainland, and Pauline's Uncle Gus had promised to have a new yellow Ford runabout waiting for them when they arrived.

The purple scar on Ernest's forehead was still tender to the touch when he and Pauline embarked at La Rochelle on the Royal Mail Steam Packet *Orita* for an eighteen-day voyage to Havana. Ernest found to his displeasure that the *Orita* boasted neither gymnasium nor nursery, while his own small sleeping cell would have been better suited to a monk. Halfway across, he amused himself with a note to "Dear Miss Pfeiffer or may I call you Mrs. Hemingway" in which he satirized his monastic predicament. He had often wondered what he should do with the rest of his life; he was now convinced that it would be spent in an attempt to reach Cuba aboard the *Orita*.

In Havana they transferred to a C. and O. boat for the final hundred-mile run to Key West, arriving early in April. The island was hot and saltily humid each morning. In the afternoons and evenings it was cooled by trade winds off the Atlantic. They found a low-lying village, tropical, maritime, and relaxed, covered with flowering shrubs, coconut palms whose dry leaves rustled in the airstream, and half-paved streets of old white houses, many with comfortable porches and second-floor balconies. Dos Passos had described them as "faintly New England" in appearance. But it was New England down at heel, with a population that had shrunk from 26,000 to 10,000 in the years following the war.

Since they were going to be there for only six weeks at most, before going to visit Pauline's family in Piggott, they took rooms in the Trevor and Morris apartment building on Simonton Street. Ernest was out at once, exploring the

island, the banked yellow seaweed and washed-up Portuguese men-of-war
on South Beach, the unused Navy Yard, and the small Spanish restaurants.
The bars along Duval Street roared each night with rumba music and the
fistfights of merchant sailors. By day there was fishing off the wharves and
bridges. He enjoyed watching the constant parade of water traffic: commercial
power boats, cabin cruisers from up the coast, and the big gray wolflike Coast
Guard cutters coming and going in and out of the peaceful old harbor where
pirates like Henry Morgan had once flourished.

Ernest fell quickly into a work-and-fishing schedule precisely suited to his
temperament. Except for an occasional night on the town, followed by what
he always referred to as "gastric remorse," he rose and retired early. He
liked to write in the mornings while he and the day were both fresh, spending
most of the rest of his time in the open air, talking with anyone whose face
or occupation interested him, questioning them closely about their backgrounds, their families, and their professions. He was always a stickler for
detailed information, watching them narrowly through half-veiled brown
eyes, listening to their gossip and their yarns, and replying in kind with profane rough humor and the air of a man of the world. With the scar on his
forehead, he said, everyone took him for a Big Northern Bootlegger or Dope
Peddler, and nobody would believe that he had written books.

He soon met Bra Saunders, a professional fishing guide who knew every
shoal and key and mangrove swamp from Homestead to the Dry Tortugas.
There was also a tough little slab-faced man named Josie Russell who owned
the bar called Sloppy Joe's in Green Street, a small side street off Duval. It
occupied the whole ground floor of a white frame house. The place was dark
as a cave inside, with a long curving bar. Ernest greatly admired Josie's
colored bartender, a dignified man named Skinner. He was so smart, said
Ernest, that if he had been born in Africa he would have been a tribal chief.
Another of his favorites was an Irish machinist named J. B. Sullivan, who
had set up a machine shop two years earlier. Sully was then in his forties,
a baldheaded, chunkily built man from Brooklyn, New York, who had been
a construction worker on the Flagler Railroad across the keys in 1906. Sully
liked Ernest at once and thought him "a silent man, a deep man, who talked
slowly and very positively, always determined to have his information exactly
right." Except for his brains, said Sully, he might have been a Skid Row
character. But he was redeemed by his quick intelligence, his probing curiosity, and a warmth of personality which showed itself at once among non-
literary people like Sully.

His closest friendship was with Charles Thompson, a broad-shouldered,
brown-blond young man roughly his own age. Charles loved hunting and
fishing with something of Ernest's own passionate devotion. Pauline immediately took to his handsome wife, Lorine. The Thompson family ran a fish-
house, a cigarbox factory, a ship's chandlery, an icehouse, and a hardware

store and tackle shop. Almost nightly after Charles got off from work, he and Ernest went out fishing for amberjack, barracuda, red snapper, and tarpon. The Thompson fish market bought their catch for enough to pay for bait and gasoline. This was the kind of economy that made perfect sense to Ernest. Although *Men Without Women* had sold 19,000 copies by the middle of April, his income from writing was still sparse, and he did not want to be further beholden to Uncle Gus Pfeiffer than was strictly necessary.

Without Ernest's knowledge his parents had come to Florida. He did not learn of their presence in St. Petersburg until April 10th, when mail forwarded from Paris reached him at Key West. He telegraphed to invite them down, and was fishing off one of the piers when they entered the harbor. His farsighted father recognized him and gave the family bobwhite whistle. Ernest ran over to the C. and O. dock to welcome them and took them to meet Pauline. Grace looked vast and placid in a floor-length dress and a white felt hat. But the doctor was visibly ill. His hair and beard had gone gray and he was thin and nervous from his diabetic diet. He had grown uncertain about the wisdom of his heavy investments in Florida real estate and confided to Ernest a recent history of cardiac symptoms which he took to be associated with the diabetes. Even his neck had grown scrawny inside the wing collar he always wore. Grace loomed beside him, a picture of ruddy health. Ernest's heart went out to his father.

While the manuscript of his novel slowly approached the hundredth page, Ernest sent off enthusiastic invitations to his cronies to come and share in the delights of his newfound paradise. "Christ, this is a fine country," he wrote Mike Strater. "Viva d'America!" Dos Passos soon appeared, the restless nomad, wide-eyed with interest in scenes and people. Waldo Peirce's mother had just died, but he came along afterwards, a huge bearded man who reminded Dos of a Neptune on a baroque Roman fountain. Bill Smith stepped off the ferryboat from Boca Chica, slender and brown-faced, perpetually smoking, and calling Ernest by his boyhood nickname of Wemedge. They all put up at the Overseas Hotel, and spent long afternoons in Ernest's inimitable company, poling a skiff and bottom fishing among the nearer keys. At the closed-down Navy Yard they swam in the deep green waters of the inner basin, diving from the moss-covered stone steps, wary of the needle-fanged barracuda.

Ernest as always was intensely competitive, avid for championship, seldom able to conceal his envy of another man's success. They hired Captain Bra Saunders and his cabin cruiser for a trip to the Dry Tortugas. Ernest rowed off alone in the dinghy and put out a line, hooking a handsome sailfish which promptly broke the tip off his rod. He played it heroically, only to watch it throw the hook just as he brought it alongside. This was the trip on which Waldo, called Don Pico, hooked and lost seven good-sized tarpon. The eighth was a fighting monster six feet long that leaped high and reentered the sea with a sound, said Ernest, like William Howard Taft diving. Waldo played it for forty minutes before he boated it, his beard coiled in Tritonesque ringlets, his torso dripping with sweat and spray.

Captain Bra told them the story of the *Val Banera,* a Spanish liner blown off course in the hurricane of September 9, 1919. She had run aground in the quicksands south-southwest of Key West and foundered with all hands, including five hundred passengers. Bra was the first to find her, and nearly killed himself in successive vain attempts to crack open her portholes to get at the loot inside. He told about seeing a drowned woman, floating behind the glass with a small fortune in rings on one of her hands. Ernest listened carefully. This was a yarn direct from life, piratical in flavor, with its own intrinsic form. It was the kind of story he liked to know and tell—one man alone against the elements, strong and self-reliant, pitting his courage and endurance against great odds. Like Bra in 1919, many of Ernest's heroes were overcome by circumstances beyond their control. Like Bra, too, they often won a kind of Pyrrhic victory. The reward could not be measured in rings or gold bullion. It was simply the consciousness of having carried on with ingenuity and perseverance.

After such joys, the life in Piggott, Arkansas, seemed doubly dull. They arrived late in May. Ernest liked Pauline's mother immensely and immediately, but he was never entirely happy in the lap of domesticity—unless it was his own. He complained to Perkins that Piggott was a "Christ-offal place" and hinted to his father that he was homesick for northern Michigan and the scenes of his boyhood. Dr. Hemingway's reply was discouraging. While he and Grace would be very pleased to see Ernest and his wife at any time, the season in Michigan had been very cool and backward, and Pauline would do far better to have her baby in Kansas City or St. Louis rather than in Petoskey, where hospital facilities were limited.

Ernest capitulated and drove Pauline to Kansas City in the searing heat of midsummer. They stayed with Malcolm and Ruth Lowry in a large house on Indian Lane, across from the Country Club. While Pauline waited out her time, Ernest wrote in the mornings and followed a sporting life the rest of the day. He looked in at the nomination of Herbert Hoover at the Republican National Convention, retiring in disgust from the machinations of the politicians. But he liked the rich sportsmen, who did all the things the British did without their "bloody snobbery" or the English accents. He discovered an interest in polo and the locker-room bull sessions after the games where a man could smell a little sweat and cool off with bootleg Scotch. The yard of the Lowry house contained a swimming pool and good shade trees. At the end of the day Ernest customarily took a swim, had supper, and read Zane Grey's recent book on big-game fishing, which he had bought as a present

for Charles Thompson. By the middle of June his novel stood at 311 foolscap
pages and he was talking of going farther west to finish his first draft and
do some trout fishing. One of the Kansas City sportsmen had mentioned a
fisherman's paradise in Idaho. It was up on the Middle Fork of the Salmon
River, with no roads within fifty miles and the best fishing in the world. After
the baby's arrival he might go out there, or maybe to some place in Wyoming,
which could be reached by car in three days from Kansas City.

Pauline's labor pains began at last on June 27th, and she entered the
Research Hospital under the charge of Dr. Don Carlos Guffey. Her labor
lasted for eighteen hours and was terminated by Caesarean section on the
28th. The child was a nine-and-a-half-pound boy whom they named Patrick.
Pauline writhed for several days with postoperative gas pains. She could not
eat and milk was slow in coming. Dr. Guffey told Ernest that the wound
would take ten days to heal. She must then spend another week or ten days
in hospital, and must not become pregnant again for at least three years. Over
it all hung the Kansas City heat, with the thermometers steady at 92 degrees,
and the humidity at 96. By the time Pauline and the baby were ready to travel,
Ernest had finished the 478th page of his novel. He was already disgusted
with fatherhood. It took them twenty-one steaming hours to go by train from
Kansas City to Piggott and the baby cried most of the way. His son, said
Ernest, was built like a bull and bellowed like one. It was enough to drive a
man "bughouse." He could not understand why Waldo Peirce was so eager
to have children.

He got free of all this as soon as he could. On the night of July 25th he
caught the train back to Kansas City, where he picked up the Ford runabout,
met his old friend Bill Horne, and set off for Wyoming on the 28th. He had
given up the project of the Salmon River in Idaho, which could wait for
some later year. What he needed now, he wrote Waldo Peirce, was relief
from the heat of the prairie states, a little tranquillity in the head, and the
daily exercise of trout fishing in the Bighorn Mountains. They accomplished
the run of a thousand miles in three days and by the evening of the 30th
were signing the guest book at Folly Ranch on the eastern slope of the
Bighorns at an elevation of seven thousand feet. The place was being run as
a dude ranch, and Ernest found to his disgust that there were fifteen girls in
residence. He mooned about sullenly for a few days, writing in the mornings
and fishing in the afternoons. On August 3rd he rose at six, threw his bags and
his manuscript into the car, and left for Sheridan without saying good-bye.
At the Sheridan Inn he stayed four days, averaging nine pages a day; on the
8th he left for Eleanor Donnelley's Lower Ranch, which was empty of dudes
and quiet as a tomb. This time he ran his day's production to seventeen pages.
But he was so lonely by nightfall that he drank too much bootleg whiskey
and could do nothing next day. He was already longing for Spain. It was the
first time since 1923 that he had missed the fiesta in Pamplona, to say nothing

of the great *feria* at Valencia. He remembered the white-painted restaurants along the beach, and the black pans of seafood paella, and the trips back to town for ice-cold pitchers of beer and good meat melons.

By the time Pauline arrived in Sheridan on August 18th, Ernest was hoping to end his novel in two days more. She reported that Patrick weighed twelve pounds and looked like a Chinese woodchuck. The scar of her Caesarean still showed, but her strength was back. Ernest did not tell her that Catherine Barkley, the heroine of his novel, was about to die in childbirth at a hospital in Montreux. He took her to meet a French family who made and sold good wine in a neat frame house on Val Vista Street in Sheridan. Their names were Charles and Alice Moncini and they had two sons named August and Lucien. Charles was a trucker at the mines. Alice cooked and served meals. Ernest and Pauline sat on the vine-shaded back porch drinking cold home-brewed beer, with a view across the yellow grainfields, towards the distant brown mountains. They all spoke French together. Ernest listened intently, watching the faces and trying to remember all that was said. Whenever it suited him, he would put the Moncinis into a story, a character sketch full of cleanliness and order, a quiet account of simple people who made and drank the wine of Wyoming and wondered if a Catholique named "Al Schmidt" could be elected President on a platform which demanded an end to Prohibition.

About the end of August, Ernest finished the first draft of his novel. He was far too fatigued to be sure of the quality of what he had written. He thrust it aside until he was ready to start rewriting. A solid month remained before they would have to leave for Arkansas. They stayed at Willis Spear's Spear-O-Wigwam dude ranch, eight miles down the valley from Eleanor Donnelley's place. It lay at the foot of the Bighorns, not far from the Crow Indian Reservation. Ernest was eager to explore the country farther west, and they drove across to Lincoln County, south of Yellowstone Park near the border of Idaho. Ernest tried potting prairie dogs from the moving car with his Colt pistol. They stopped in at Shell to see Owen Wister, author of *The Virginian* and a loyal admirer of Ernest's fiction. They inspected the Grand Tetons and tried fishing in the Snake. At Moose near Jackson's Hole they called at a dude ranch run by Struthers Burt, a Princeton man and a Scribner author. Back in Sheridan they bagged nine prairie chickens on the Indian Reservation, and then headed south for Casper and the thousand-mile drive to Kansas City. Across Nebraska the wind blew half a gale, and the tumbleweed rolled crazily along the blacktop highway. Ernest drank whiskey to keep warm, besides eating most of a bag of new fall apples. By Sunday, September 23rd, they were back in Kansas City attending Mass. The pages of Ernest's manuscript numbered 600, exactly the number of trout he and Pauline had caught in a month of western fishing.

The month they spent in Piggott sharpened Ernest's desire to be somewhere else. He wanted to start rewriting his novel but he knew it was too soon. He put on a sweatshirt and long johns, jogging and sprinting along the back roads, and stopping to shadowbox under the trees. His weight dropped to 184, then 178. Being in training made him feel arrogant and he took to insulting the local yokels, whom he described as mean and bigoted. "You get damn few good guys in the Middle West," he told Waldo Peirce.

The roadwork made his legs "stiff as a board" and he sat on the front porch of Paul Pfeiffer's house typing letters to his friends and complaining about his homesickness for Wyoming, Zaragoza, Key West, and Paris. Paris, he thought, would be wonderful now, with the Stade Buffalo and the Parc du Prince and the Luxembourg littered with fallen leaves and the chance to ride his bike down the Champs Elysées from the Étoile to the Place de la Concorde. Still you'd just get over there when the good autumn weather would dissolve in rain and a man would be reduced to sitting outside the Deux Magots watching the fairies and the Lesbians pass by and wishing to hell he was destroying tarpon somewhere off Key West. Spain, though, would be good. He would like to have been born there so that he could write Spanish like a native instead of feeling always as if he were shooting on posted land or fishing out of season. Or he would like to go to New York to see some fights. He had a box with two praying mantises inside it, separated by a cardboard partition. He fed them live flies which they caught and ate, like barracudas stripping a live grunt. If he couldn't go to the Queensborough A.C., said he, he could always remove that partition from between his mantises and watch them fight like hell. In such ways he consoled himself for having to live with his in-laws.

Plans for the winter, hitherto amorphous, now rapidly congealed to a semblance of form. They would return to Key West while Ernest revised his novel. Lorine Thompson would find them a house. They would get a colored nursemaid for Patrick. Bumby would cross the Atlantic to stay with them until April, when they would all go to Paris. Ernest's sister Sunny would come down about Thanksgiving time to help with the children and with the typing of Ernest's final draft. Substantial sums of money were already in the offing, for Perkins, without having seen the new novel, was ready to guarantee $10,000 for the right to serialize it in *Scribner's Magazine* in the spring of 1929. Meantime, leaving Patrick with his grandmother and his aunt Jinny, Pauline and Ernest would go to Chicago, Conway, Massachusetts, and New York, returning to Piggott in mid-November to pick up Patrick and the car for the drive to Key West.

All this was accomplished. In Chicago during the last week of October the Hemingways stayed at the Whitehall, and paid a duty call in Oak Park— Ernest's first in five years. They also visited the Chicago Art Institute, where Ernest discovered (and vastly admired) the paintings of Winslow Homer. He had not been to Massachusetts since his boyhood visit to Nantucket with his mother, and the few days with the MacLeishes stretched to a week. In

New York he saw some prizefights, discussed his novel with Perkins, and enjoyed reunions with Strater and Peirce, who both agreed to come to Key West that winter.

On the 17th, the Hemingways and Mike Strater took a morning train from Penn Station to watch the Princeton-Yale game at Palmer Stadium. Scott and Zelda were already on hand at the Cottage Club on Prospect Avenue. Ernest walked over to Nassau Street to pay a call on Isabelle and Francis Godolphin. Princeton won the game, 12 to 2. Afterwards they took the special train for Philadelphia. Fitzgerald had behaved during the game, but was soon sophomorically drunk. His Buick was waiting in Philadelphia, driven by a former Paris taximan named Philippe. Scott was fast asleep long before they reached Ellerslie Mansion, his estate outside Wilmington. Next day, the Hemingways got aboard the Spirit of St. Louis for Chicago. Near Harrisburg, Ernest scrawled a thank-you note to Scott and Zelda. He was more than ever convinced of what he had recently told Max Perkins—that Zelda was her husband's evil demon. "I may be wrong," he had admitted to Max. But he did not really think so that night in November as the train rumbled westward through the mountains of Pennsylvania.

28. *A FAREWELL TO ARMS*

THE trip by car from Piggott to Key West with Pauline and Patrick occupied three hectic November days. Lorine Thompson had found them a large old white frame house at 1100 South Street in the residential district near the sandy swimming beaches on the Atlantic side of the island. They had barely moved in, and Sunny had only just arrived, when Ernest departed once more, this time to meet Bumby and to do some Christmas shopping in New York.

He was worried about his father, who had seemed more than ever depressed in spirits and gray in the face at Oak Park in October. On the northbound train he wrote him an encouraging letter, which he posted from Jacksonville. In New York he saw Lincoln Steffens, met Ring Lardner for the first time, and bought himself a harpoon gun at Abercrombie and Fitch. Bumby arrived on schedule, coming down the gangplank holding the hand of a stewardess. That Thursday afternoon they boarded the Havana Special at Pennsylvania Station. The train roared under the river and across the wintry wastes of the New Jersey flats. In the grimy station at Trenton there was a telegram for Ernest from his sister Carol in Oak Park. It said that his father had died that morning.

He telegraphed Perkins to send a hundred dollars to the North Philadelphia Station. The Pullman porter, whose name was McIntyre, agreed to watch over Bumby for the rest of the trip south. Ernest explained the situation to the child as well as he could. Bumby nodded. He was not worried. He had just crossed the Atlantic with other strangers. There was no reply from Perkins when Ernest left the train at North Philadelphia. He wired both Strater and Fitzgerald for loans. Money arrived from Scott shortly before eight o'clock. For the second time in three weeks Ernest rode the all-night train to Chicago.

In Oak Park he learned for the first time the manner of his father's death. The previous morning he had burned some personal papers in the furnace, climbed the stairs from the basement to his second-floor bedroom, and quietly closed the door. Some minutes later, his son Leicester, a boy of thirteen in bed with a cold, heard an astonishing sound: the single, sharp report of a gun in the silence of the house. Dr. Hemingway had shot himself behind the right ear with Anson Hemingway's worn old Smith and Wesson .32 revolver. The only others present in the dwelling besides the boy Leicester were Grace Hall Hemingway and the cook, Louise.

Ernest muttered darkly against his Uncle George, whom he blamed for having paid insufficient attention to the doctor's financial plight. The estate was relatively meager: a $25,000 life insurance policy, the two cottages at Walloon Lake, and the house in Oak Park, which was still encumbered with a $15,000 mortgage. The rest had been sunk in Florida real estate, which Ernest scathingly described as worthless. But Dr. Hemingway's real problems had been physical. Pain and persistent loss of sleep from diabetic disorders and angina pectoris had combined, said Ernest, to knock his father temporarily out of his head. What made him feel worst about the whole affair, as he wrote Max Perkins, was that his father was the one he really cared about. He was now the nominal head of a large family with many problems and debts. It was lucky that he had in hand a salable novel. He told the family that he had lately borrowed its title from that of a poem of George Peele's in *The Oxford Book of English Verse*. It was going to be called *A Farewell to Arms*.

Back in Key West he took up the task of revision, first with pencil, then with typewriter, working six hours a day and handing over each day's batch to his sister Sunny for final typing. The whole job took five weeks and was finished on January 22nd. With the end in sight, he urged Max Perkins to come down and collect it in person. Max wonderingly agreed. When he appeared on the first of February, Ernest set out to pack a whole month's fishing into the days of a single week. Each morning they were on the water by six and stayed out until late afternoon. Max read the typescript and pronounced it magnificent. But he shook his head over some of the soldierly language. Bridges, said he lugubriously, might not be able to serialize it after all. Back in New York after what he described as the best time he had ever had in his life, he found that his prediction about the language had been unduly pessimistic. Bridges shared his admiration completely, and Max wired Ernest an offer of $16,000, the largest sum *Scribner's Magazine* had ever yet paid for first serial rights.

Ernest had now begun to refer to his novel as "my long tale of transalpine fornication including the entire war in Italy and so to BED." Despite Perkins's approval and the sale of the serial to *Scribner's Magazine*, he was still uncertain of its quality and constantly sought reassurance from his other closest associates. One by one, as they straggled in to join him in the winter's program of fishing and drinking, he shyly brought out a carbon copy and nervously awaited their word that it was wonderful. Strater approved; Waldo Peirce gave it his imprimatur; and Dos Passos, whom Ernest had regarded as a bitterly severe and tough-minded critic ever since his adverse review of *The Sun Also Rises,* sent him into transports of joy when he agreed with the others that it was a splendid book.

Ernest had now begun to send his mother a hundred dollars each month as well as substantial tax payments on her real-estate holdings. He congratulated her for having decided to rent out rooms in the Oak Park house, advised her to sell the lots in Florida, and threatened to remove Uncle George's hide if he did not personally pay off the mortgage. He also suggested that Marce and Sterling Sanford should be called on for financial assistance, since they were "rich" and had always been great friends of the family, whereas he lived by his pen and had for some years been more or less an "outcast." He had paid Sunny's passage for the voyage to Europe and would continue to help out at home as long as he had money. He closed by saying that he had never written a novel about the Hemingway family because he had never wanted to hurt anyone's feelings. With the death of those he loved, however, a period had been put to this self-imposed taboo and he might be obliged to write such a book. In this way, apparently, he was seeking to get a whip hand over his mother.

Grace replied with a large crate addressed to Ernest. The house on South Street was cluttered with trunks and suitcases in various stages of being packed for the voyage to France in April, and the crate stood unopened for a week or two. Katy Smith was there for a visit, much admired by Dos Passos, who "couldn't think of anything but her green eyes." Katy, for her part, could not think of anything but the contents of the crate. "For heaven's sake, Ernest," she said one day, "haven't you opened your mother's box yet?" Ernest said no. He knew that it contained some of Grace's paintings which she wanted him to try to sell for her when he got back to Paris. At last Pauline got a hammer and pried it open. Inside were several of Grace's landscapes of the Garden of the Gods in Colorado Springs. There was also a large moldy chocolate cake which had leaked through the canvases, as well as the revolver that Dr. Hemingway had used on the morning of December 6th. At the time of the funeral Ernest had asked that the gun be sent to him as a historical keepsake. Grace was merely complying with his wishes.

In April Ernest shepherded his large family, including Bumby and Sunny, across the straits to Havana, where they boarded the North German Lloyd liner *Yorck* on the 5th. The ship docked at Boulogne on the 21st and they moved into the apartment at 6, rue Férou. Pauline had to go to bed with a septic sore throat which had begun before she left Key West. Patrick caught the infection and the household was too distraught for Ernest to get down to his writing, though he spent a good deal of time in correcting the proofs for the magazine publication of his novel. He was dissatisfied with the last three paragraphs in which he had loosely summarized the aftermath of Catherine's death and permitted himself a passage or two of pseudo-philosophical moralizing. Between May 8th and 18th he rewrote the conclusion several times in the attempt to get it exactly right. The domestic disorder, combined with worry over the proof sheets, made him uncommonly snappish. He exploded upon learning that Perkins had sent Owen Wister a set of galleys at Wister's request and that Wister, from his office in Philadelphia, had made several suggestions for revision. He was also deeply resentful when Robert Bridges tinkered with the text of the serialized version, which had begun to appear in installments in the May issue of *Scribner's Magazine.*

Ernest's old Toronto friend Morley Callaghan had just come to Paris with his wife Loretto. He had tried for some time without success to find out where Ernest was living. The problem was solved one noonday when the Callaghans heard a knock on the door of their hotel room and opened it to see Ernest standing there with Bumby. They dressed quickly and went along while Hemingway delivered his son to Hadley's flat in the rue Auguste-Blanqui. Afterwards they drank beer at a café near the Île de la Cité. Ernest was neatly attired in a dark gray suit and seemed to be pleased at having become a Catholic convert. The first time the Callaghans called at the apartment in the rue Férou, Ernest got out boxing gloves and insisted on a short sparring match. Satisfied with Morley's prowess, he made a date to meet him next day in the basement gymnasium at the American Club. He stood six feet and weighed two hundred pounds while Morley was four inches shorter and out of condition. But Callaghan discovered that he could hit Hemingway easily, having had a good deal of practice with fast college boxers. Ernest reported to Perkins on June 24th that he and Morley had already boxed five times. What he did not mention was a curious incident that marred their third encounter. Morley had worked out a routine, darting in and out with fast lefts to the head. "He knew what I was doing," wrote Morley. "His brown eyes always on me, he waited for a chance to nail me solidly. . . . It must have been exasperating to him that my left was always beating him to the punch. His mouth began to bleed. . . . His tongue kept curling along his lip, wiping off blood. . . . Suddenly he spat at me; he spat a mouthful of blood; he spat in my face."

Morley was so shocked that he stepped back and dropped his gloves. "That's what the bullfighters do when they're wounded," said Ernest solemnly. "It's a way of showing contempt." They had to stop boxing while Morley cleared his face of blood and spittle. He was "wondering out of what strange nocturnal depths" of Ernest's mind this "barbarous gesture" had come. But Ernest was jolly, lighthearted, and talkative. "As long as Morley can keep cutting my mouth," he told Jimmy, the bartender at the Falstaff, "he'll always remain my good friend."

Both Joan Miró and Scott Fitzgerald served on occasion as volunteer time-

keepers. Scott was along one day when Hemingway and Callaghan had agreed
to meet at five. Ernest lunched sumptuously at Prunier's on lobster thermidor
and white burgundy. Knowing that he would be deadly sleepy long before five,
he went round with Scott to persuade Morley to begin boxing at once. At the
American Club they put on the gloves and agreed on one-minute rounds with
two minutes of rest between. Scott took up a ringside position and started them
off. Counting on his ability to last a full minute in spite of his heavy lunch,
Ernest bored in fast and used up all his wind. Fitzgerald watched fascinated
while the round went on. At last Ernest leaped in with a desperate lunge.
Morley caught him squarely on the jaw and dumped him hard on his back.
"Oh, my God," cried Scott. "I let the round go four minutes." Ernest rose up
cursing and went off to wash the blood from his face. Scott was pale and
stricken. "He thinks I did it on purpose," he told Morley. "Why would I do
it on purpose?" Ernest came back looking grim and determined. He had now
fought himself clear of alcohol, as he put it, and managed to last out the remaining rounds. Afterwards, having a drink at the Falstaff, he was as jovial as
before. But Callaghan got the impression that Scott's pride had been shattered.
His negligence as timekeeper had caused Ernest to be knocked down. It was
like seeing your hero fall dead at your feet only to realize suddenly that you
yourself were still holding the smoking pistol.

By the end of the month Ernest was off for Pamplona, driving south with
Pauline in a new Ford roadster. As if to make up for the year he had missed,
he threw himself into the celebration with more than usual gusto. Ben Ray
Redman was paying his first visit to the fiesta. One day he saw Ernest deep
in talk at a café table. Redman gazed for some time at this famous young man,
"the author who had discovered Pamplona." Ernest wore a tweed jacket and
a loose necktie. One of his feet was thrust into a clumsy woolen carpet slipper
because he had somehow cut it the day before. Redman thought that with his
dark hair and mustache he would have been inconspicuous among the Spaniards except for his obvious "poise and strength"—a "pervasive and inescap-
able" force of personality that somehow made him stand out from the crowd.

After the fiesta, Ernest and Pauline slipped away to visit Joan Miró at
Montroig, a quiet Spanish village on a hill overlooking the sea. It made a
welcome interlude before the succession of bullfights at Huesca, Lérida, and
Tarragona, as well as the great annual *feria* at Valencia in late July. Ernest
was finding that he could write nothing but letters, one of which he signed "E.
Cantwork Hemingstein." Much of his correspondence dealt with the language
of *A Farewell to Arms*. He agreed only with great reluctance to the use of
dashes in place of the "dirty words," insisting that they had been used for
verisimilitude and that their shock effect would be absorbed by the context.
He resolved to dedicate the book to Uncle Gus, who had been named for
Gustavus Adolphus, and told Perkins that there couldn't be a less graceful
name or a much better man. It was Uncle Gus who had interceded with
Pauline's family in Ernest's behalf in 1926. According to Ernest, Pauline's

parents opposed their daughter's marriage to a man who had been married before and was widely known as a drunk with evil associates. Pauline had brought her uncle to meet Ernest at Gerald Murphy's studio. He had insisted on staying only ten minutes in order not to interfere with Ernest's writing. But the ten minutes had been enough. Uncle Gus had gone right off to a telegraph office and cabled the elder Pfeiffers that Pauline could not possibly marry a better or a finer citizen than young Hemingway.

Ernest had just celebrated his thirtieth birthday when he learned that Dos Passos had married Katy Smith in Ellsworth, Maine. He sent congratulations, along with best wishes for the success of Dos's new novel, *The 42nd Parallel.* Dos, said he, must keep money away from Katy, or vice versa. Money had been the ruination of too many of their friends. Don Stewart had taken up with Jock Whitney, to say nothing of selling his soul to Hollywood for a $25,000 contract. John Bishop's career had been spoiled by his wife's munificent income. The search for eternal youth had clearly sunk the Fitzgeralds. American capital was even ruining Spain. It was merely symptomatic of the general Americanization that chewing gum and Coca-Cola were being sold throughout the country. Ernest's bilious mood was not helped by the fact that prices were going up while the level of all the trout streams in the mountains near Santiago were steadily going down.

September was saved for Ernest by the advent of a new phenomenon named Sidney Franklin. Sidney came of Russian Jewish parents named Frumpkin and had been raised in Brooklyn, New York. Tall, sandy-haired, athletic, and talkative, he had borrowed his fighting name from Ben Franklin, served an apprenticeship in Mexico, and then made his Spanish debut in Seville that June, fighting as a *novillero.* During the summer his record had been impressive. Guy Hickok wanted to do a feature story about him for the *Brooklyn Daily Eagle,* and had asked Ernest to look him over. When the Hemingways left Santiago for Madrid on August 30th, this was Ernest's chief purpose. "Want to see Sidney Franklin," he wrote Perkins. "They say he's good."

Franklin impressed Ernest chiefly with his "cold, serene, and intelligent valor" as well as his artistry with the cape. He killed with so much sangfroid that Ernest urged him to dramatize it more. "He'd just go in and wham!" said he. "I told him not to make it look so easy." He quickly adopted Franklin and managed to be present at some of his major *corridas* in September. "I saw no reason to tell him that I had written any books," said Ernest, "and we passed many weeks in different parts of Spain together. Someone finally told him that I was a novelist and he found it very hard to believe. This I took as a compliment."

Following Franklin was something of an endurance contest. The new Ford developed rattles in every joint from being driven hundreds of kilometers over the potholed Spanish roads. Ernest complained that the heat was often intense enough to crack a man's head open. But he came to believe that Franklin's performance that fall was "a marvel and a miracle," while his life story was "better than any picaresque novel." Getting to know him was a compensation for an otherwise unproductive summer.

In spite of his own writing difficulties, Ernest played Dutch uncle to Fitzgerald, repeatedly urging him to get forward with *Tender Is the Night*. The only thing to do with a novel, said he, was to finish it. Scott's mood of depression was nothing but the Artist's Reward. Summer was anyhow a discouraging time to work: only in the fall, when the feeling of death came on, did you find "the boys" putting pen to paper. The good parts of a novel might be something a writer was lucky enough to overhear or they might be the wreckage of his whole damned life. The artist should not worry over the loss of his early bloom. People were not peaches. Like guns and saddles, they were all the better for becoming slightly worn. When a bloomless writer got his flashes of the old juice, he knew enough to get results with them. As always with Fitzgerald, Ernest managed to sound like a grizzled veteran of fifty rather than a comparative youngster of thirty whose second novel was not yet published.

The Spanish tour ended as usual with a "vacation" at Hendaye Plage across the border, and the Hemingways returned to Paris on September 20th, a week before the publication date of *A Farewell to Arms*. "FIRST REVIEWS SPLENDID," Perkins cabled on the 28th, "PROSPECTS BRIGHT." Percy Hutchinson, the *New York Times*'s Hemingway expert, said that "the story of the love between the English nurse and the American ambulance officer, as hapless as that of Romeo and Juliet, is a high achievement in what might be termed the new romanticism." Clifton Fadiman called it "the very apotheosis of a kind of modernism." Malcolm Cowley saw the title as symbolic of Hemingway's "farewell to a period, an attitude, and perhaps to a method also." His earlier books had virtually excluded ideas in favor of emotions. Now there were signs of a new complexity of thought, demanding "expression in a subtler and richer prose." The problem of "dirty" language which had agitated the Boston censors did not bother Henry Seidel Canby. "To object to it would be priggish," said he. "There is no decadence here, no overemphasis on the sexual as a philosophy." Altogether the reactions among the reviewers were the most positive in Ernest's career to date.

He had overeaten and overdrunk so much in Spain that he woke one September morning to find that the ends of his fingers were swollen like small balloons. He eliminated meat and alcohol from his diet and began drinking Vichy water. But he continued to drop in at his favorite cafés. On the 25th he ran into Morley and Loretto Callaghan at the Falstaff. They were about to leave for London without having paid a visit to Chartres. He insisted on driving them down next day, and was highly critical of Morley for concentrating on the stained glass while forgetting to genuflect before the high altar. Morley thought him oddly unaffected by the magnificence of the cathedral. But Ernest wrote Perkins next day that Chartres had seemed a "pretty cold proposition" to one who had spent most of August near the Cathedral of Santiago de Compostela.

A few afternoons later he was in Sylvia Beach's bookshop when he met for the first time a short and slender young man with a high domed forehead and a small brown mustache. This was Allen Tate, whose reviews of Ernest's books had been consistently laudatory. Tate was staying with his wife Caroline Gordon at the Hotel de l'Odéon nearby. The words of introduction were hardly out of Sylvia's mouth when Ernest began upbraiding Tate for having said that Defoe and Captain Marryat had influenced his work. When he learned that the Tates had been watching over Ford Madox Ford since his separation from Stella Bowen, Ernest asked if he knew that Ford was impotent. Tate grinned his sidelong grin and said in a soft Southern drawl that this did not concern him in the least, since he was not a woman. Ernest began expounding his views on male sexuality. A young man should make love very seldom, said he, or he would have nothing left for middle age. The number of available orgasms was fixed at birth and could be expended too soon. He was eager for Tate's opinion of *A Farewell to Arms* and brought round a copy to the hotel. Tate was in bed with the flu and Ernest refused to go in for fear of catching it. Next morning he was back to know how Tate had liked the book. On being told that it was a masterpiece, he ran down the stairs as pleased as a child.

By mid-October the novel had sold 28,000 copies. Ernest began to speak of using the early proceeds to set up a trust fund for his mother and the two younger children. When the stock market crashed, he was half sick with worry over the possible adverse effect on book sales. He had developed kidney trouble, which he attributed to fishing without waders in cold water in the Spanish mountains, and complained also of a torn muscle in his groin, the consequence of a minor mishap in Palencia. But he was encouraged to learn on November 12th that *A Farewell to Arms* was leading most of the bestseller lists. Its closest competitor was another war book, Remarque's *All Quiet on the Western Front.*

His Sundays that fall combined duty and pleasure—Mass at St. Sulpice with Pauline, followed by the six-day bicycle races at the Vélodrome d'Hiver. Colonel Charlie Sweeny was his regular companion until he learned that the races were fixed and refused to go anymore. Ernest then directed his contagious enthusiasm at Allen Tate, who began by thinking bike racing the most boring of sports and ended by becoming a somewhat sardonic high priest of the cult. Ernest liked a man who could learn that fast. He was soon telling John Bishop that Allen had real guts, moral guts. "So I was adjusted," said Tate, "to the Hemingway myth." In mid-November, accompanied by Guy Hickok, Ernest followed the bike racers to Berlin. On his return, he began to write a bullfight article for *Fortune,* Henry Luce's expensive and elegant new business magazine, which was ready to pay him a thousand dollars for 2,500 words. Archie MacLeish had taken an editorial job with *Fortune* in order to support his family. Ernest was scornful about "the romance of business," professed not to be able to understand how Archie had got mixed up with such an outfit, and took pride in his own position as a writer who had refused to compromise his artistic integrity.

All this aggressive behavior was the direct consequence of Ernest's growing conviction that he was a success. He launched a small campaign against those who he felt were seeking to destroy his reputation in the United States. One was Robert Herrick, whose article, "What Is Dirt?", in the November *Bookman,* had placed Hemingway among the purveyors of dirt for dirt's sake. Ernest composed an open letter in which he threatened the editor of *Bookman* with a physical spanking for having printed such trash. Even worse was the case of Bob McAlmon, his earliest publisher, whom he had recommended to Max Perkins as a potential Scribner author. Scott Fitzgerald came to dinner with Ernest and Pauline on December 9th. Towards the end of the evening, in his cups, he reported on the tales that McAlmon had relayed to Perkins and others during a visit to New York in October. One was that Ernest beat Hadley regularly and that Bumby had been born prematurely as a result of such a beating. Another was that Pauline was a Lesbian and Ernest a homosexual. Pauline said that it was Ernest's fault for ever having had anything to do with such swine. Ernest said that McAlmon was too pitiful to be beaten up, although he would have to go through with it because people of that ilk could respond only to physical correction.

Through this rank atmosphere, like a cannonball through a smokescreen, came the story that Morley Callaghan was claiming to have knocked out Hemingway during one of their boxing matches in June. The immediate source was Caroline Bancroft, a columnist for the *Denver Post,* whose yarn was given further currency by Isabel Paterson in the *New York Herald Tribune.* Callaghan, in Toronto, at once denied the rumor and Miss Paterson printed his retraction on December 8th. But Ernest, enraged, bulldozed Fitzgerald into sending a collect cable to Callaghan: HAVE SEEN STORY IN HERALD TRIBUNE ERNEST AND I AWAIT YOUR CORRECTION. Callaghan answered Fitzgerald with understandable heat, Hemingway wrote Callaghan to take the blame for the cable on himself, and Fitzgerald, in a kind of New Year's resolution, told Callaghan that the "stupid and hasty" cable had been a grave injustice. So the smoke of battle blew away in a small whirlwind of apologies.

Ernest was reminded of his father's suicide when the young expatriate Harry Crosby killed himself in New York City on December 11th. Harry was a hell of a good boy, said Ernest, and he was feeling awfully bad about losing him. Whatever the sincerity of his emotions about Crosby, with whom he had never been close, Ernest seems to have been in a *mea culpa* mood when he wrote a lengthy letter to Scott Fitzgerald the day after Crosby's death. It centered chiefly on the overtime round in the American Club basement. His own angry outburst as he left for the showers had meant nothing, he said, for

27. Ernest and Hadley, Schwarzwald, Aug., 1922.

28. Guy Hickok of the *Brooklyn Daily Eagle,* Paris, 1920 .

29. William Bird of Three Mountains Press, Paris, 1923.

30. Sylvia Beach of Shakespeare and Company, Paris, 1923. This and the portraits of Archibald MacLeish (31 R.) and Robert McAlmon (33 BELOW R.) were done by Paul-Emile Becat.

32. Henry Strater's "Boxer Portrait" of Ernest, 1922.

31

4. F. Scott Fitzgerald, Zelda, and Scottie, Paris, 1925.

35. Gertrude Stein and Alice B. Toklas in 1926.

6. Ernest Walsh, editor of *This Quarter*.

37. Waldo Peirce, 1929.

38. Niño de la Palma, Madrid, 1925.

39. Lady Duff Twysden, 1929.

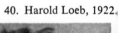
40. Harold Loeb, 1922.

41. John Dos Passos, in the 1920's.

42. Bill Smith at Horton Bay.

43. Ernest (in white pants) in the "amateurs," Pamplona, 1925.

44. ABOVE LEFT. Capt. E. E. (Chink) Dorman-Smith, Paris, 1924.

45. LEFT. Ernest in the courtyard of 113 rue Notre Dame des Champs, 1924.

46. Ernest and a sick steer, near Pamplona, 1927.

48. Strater's Rapallo profile of Ernest, 1923.

47. ABOVE. Vorarlberg, March, 1926: Frau Lent, Ernest, Dos Passos, Gerald Murphy.

49. With Bumby and Hadley, Schruns, spring, 1926.

50. The "dangerous summer" of 1926: the Murphys, Pauline, the Hemingways, and bootblacks, in Pamplona.

51. Near Gstaad, Switzerland, early 1927.

52. Pauline and Ernest at San Sebastian, 1927.

he had been around long enough to know that such errors of timing were common in amateur bouts. He recalled an occasion in the spring of 1925 when he had boxed with Jean Prévost, using Bill Smith as timekeeper. He was in such poor shape that he secretly asked Bill to stop the rounds whenever he seemed to be in trouble. Bill had stopped one two-minute round after only forty seconds. Prévost did not notice. When Ernest had recovered and was going well, Bill let the rounds exceed two minutes. That was the way it was. Fitzgerald's view of boxing was that of a man of honor and a gentleman. But Ernest said that he himself had been raised in a different and far rougher school, where dirty tricks were common in so-called friendly bouts. It was only in the context of McAlmon's lies that he had pushed Scott to cable Morley Callaghan. Now he had lost his good friend Harry Crosby. He was damned if he was going to lose such another good friend as Fitzgerald just because of some bloody squabble.

The pretense that his boyhood had been rough and dirty, the threatening stance of the tough guy in the face of those who had crossed him, and the assumption of the role of the maturing artist who had lost his early bloom and was now as worn as old saddle leather, were all facets of the public image that Ernest wished to project. It was a kind of tribute to his powers of self-dramatization that almost everybody, Pauline included, took him at his word. There were probably many times when he believed it himself.

29. THE ISLAND AND THE VALLEY

ERNEST'S affection for Paris had entered a temporary decline, and his nostalgia for Key West was correspondingly intensified. He booked passage aboard *La Bourdonnais* for January 10th and settled back to enjoy the holiday season as well as he could. When Dos Passos brought his bride Katy to Paris in mid-December, they all resolved to make another pilgrimage to Switzerland. The Murphys' son Patrick had developed tuberculosis and they had taken him to a hotel in Montana-Vermala in the hope that rest and good air might hasten his recovery. "We were all set on keeping the Murphys cheered up," said the goodhearted Dos Passos. One of those who helped was Dorothy Parker, who had never heard of Ernest's scurrilous poem about her, and had just brought out a silly and inaccurate, but also adoring, profile of Ernest in *The New Yorker* magazine. Ernest was quieter than the others, nursing a sore throat which he graphically described as "full of pus." He was hard put to it to muster up much of his former enthusiasm for life in the Alps.

Back in Paris for New Year's, he summoned enough energy to write the first book preface of his career. It was a loose piece of prose, though done with gusto and glittering with acute observations. Kiki of Montparnasse, a well-known artist's model and sometime courtesan, had set down her memoirs. Ernest's preface noted that she had dominated the era of the 1920s even more positively than Queen Victoria had done with the age that bore her name. He had found it pleasant, after work, to catch glimpses of Kiki's "fine face" and "wonderfully beautiful body." Her book was among the best he had read since Cummings's *The Enormous Room;* it even reminded him of Defoe's *Moll Flanders.* But Kiki's era was finished. Montparnasse had grown "rich, prosperous, brightly lighted, dancinged, shredded-wheated . . . [and] grapenutted" since he had first seen Kiki in 1921. As for Kiki, she had begun to look "like a monument to herself" at the age of twenty-eight.

La Bourdonnais stopped over for two days in New York en route to Havana. Ada MacLeish had just had an operation. Ernest rushed into her hospital room apparently bent on lifting her in his arms. Ada cried out, half afraid that his bear hug might break her in two. Ernest was much concerned for her welfare. He liked to say, grinning slyly, that there were two A. MacLeishes and that there was no doubt about which of them was his favorite. Afterwards he went to see Perkins and Strater, who both promised to come to Key West for the early spring fishing, and to join him in another trip to the Dry Tortugas. The ship took another six days to reach Havana. It was early February before they reached home. Lorine Thompson had found them a fine large house on Pearl Street out near the Casino.

Ernest wrote at once to urge Archie MacLeish to bring Ada down for a period of recuperation. He remembered their kindness during the breakup with Hadley, and how they had presented him with railway tickets to Gstaad at the time of the divorce. Now he proposed to stake them to a vacation on his island in the sun. But Ada was still too weak to make the trip, and Archie was too busy at *Fortune* magazine. Mike Strater appeared with a new fishing gaff big enough to spear the Woolworth Building, or so Ernest said. Mike painted his portrait, a clean-cut three-quarter-face bust in a blue shirt. Ernest would talk of nothing but the trip to Marquesas and Tortugas. He had rented a "fine tub" of a boat that would sleep four in great comfort. Max Perkins wrote that he would join them about the middle of March. John Herrmann and his wife Josie were wintering in Key West, and John agreed to make it a party of five. A man named Burge, a friend of Bra Saunders's, was going to serve as guide and navigator.

On the way down Max was newly impressed by the teeming wildlife in and above the varicolored waters. "Why don't you write about all this?" he asked Ernest. "Maybe sometime," said Ernest, pensively. "I don't know enough about it yet." A storm-beaten old pelican went flapping past. "Now look at him," said Ernest. "I don't even know what part he has in the scheme of things down here." He did know, thought Perkins, but it would not emerge in written form until it had marinated a long time in the depths of his subconscious.

Gray legions of mosquitoes drove them away from Cape Sable, and they trolled all the way to Marquesas. The world's record for kingfish with rod and reel was 57 pounds. Max Perkins, whom Ernest was now calling "Deadpan," delighted them all when he landed one that weighed 58. A faint smile could be seen playing over his features. They decided to camp for a while in the old shed at the end of the pier at Tortugas. They could at least stay until the Coast Guard drove them away. Some kind of weather was making up in the southeast, and the Gulf was slick with oily swells. When they chugged into the harbor, the sky was already clouding over. They were only 70 nautical miles from Key West, but they might have been in another world. The blank windows of old Fort Jefferson, where military prisoners had languished during the Civil War, stared down upon them as they strode ashore.

Then the big blow began. Everywhere they looked the waves were mountainous. They spread inflatable mattresses under the shelter of the weather-beaten shed, whose walls were carved with generations of names and initials. All they could do was cast plugs off the pier or venture out in the skiff for bottom fishing during the occasional lulls in the storm. Burge would not trust their tub of a boat for the run back to Key West. In the end they were storm-bound for seventeen days.

They raised piratical beards and feasted on all kinds of fish. Max kept talking about getting back to work, but it was clear that he was having the time of his life. They ran out of ice, then beer, then canned goods, then coffee, then liquor, then Bermuda onions, and at last everything but fish. Ernest did not care. He believed that a fish diet was good for the brain and would have been content to stay with it forever. He later said that he never ate or drank better in his life. Near the end of their stay, civilized luxury rediscovered them in the shape of an enormous white yacht which anchored inside the harbor. It was owned by a man named Eldridge Johnson who was an executive for the Victrola Company. Strater, who was thought to look most presentable, was sent as emissary to buy provisions. He returned with the news that they were all invited aboard for dinner. Some of them shaved for the first time in two weeks. They polished their shoes with candle tallow, dressed up as well as they could, and went. When they got back to Key West, all their wives were "worried sick" except Pauline. Ernest said proudly that she had never worried yet: it was a damned good trait in a woman to love you and not worry about you. Max wired his wife Louise that he was safely back on land, and sorrowfully departed for his desk in New York.

Although Ernest still had no use for Herbert Hoover, whom he scornfully referred to as "the Engineer in the White House," he was happy enough to learn that *A Farewell to Arms* had been added to the Presidential fiction library. The book he now turned to was not fiction at all, but rather the fulfillment of a five-year-old dream. In one of their earliest exchanges of letters, he had mentioned to Max a book on the Spanish bullfight—a "big book with wonderful pictures." He had made a small start on it with the article, "Bull-fighting, Sport and Industry," completed in Paris shortly before he sailed in January, and just published in the March number of *Fortune*. The article had turned his mind back to the major project and helped to end his long period of procrastination.

His other chief plan that spring was to go to Africa. Uncle Gus Pfeiffer had offered to finance a safari in Kenya and Tanganyika, which would be prodigiously expensive even in the midst of the Depression. Ernest turned for advice about guns to his old friend Milford Baker. They had met in Paris in 1918 and gone down to Milan together to drive ambulances, Ernest with Section 4 and Baker with Section 5. While Ernest was in New York just before his father's death, they had chanced to meet in the elevator at Abercrombie and Fitch. He soon discovered that Baker knew far more about rifles than he did. Baker had been collecting Hemingway first editions and had asked Ernest to autograph them. Now, fourteen months later, Ernest reopened the question of books and guns. The upshot was a new heavy Springfield rifle, to be custom made by Griffin and Howe under Baker's supervision. All through the spring letters went back and forth, each one bringing Ernest closer, at least in his imagination, to the hills and plains of East Africa.

It was already high summer at Key West when John and Katy Dos Passos arrived in mid-April. They had been in Madrid early in March when Sid Franklin was severely gored in the second bullfight of his second season. The news made Ernest feel "terribly badly," though he managed to assuage his sorrow with another trip to Tortugas, this time with Pauline and Dos Passos. He also consoled himself with a new drink, made by boring a hole in a fresh coconut, pouring in six or eight ounces of gin, and sipping the mixture through a straw. One night he got drunk on absinthe and threw knives at Pauline's piano. In May, working out with Charles Thompson's punching bag, he awkwardly cut open his right index finger from the root to the first joint, exposing the clean white bone, and requiring six stitches to close the wound. Along with the heat and humidity and a flying visit from Archie MacLeish, the torn finger held up his progress with the bullfighting book.

He summoned enough energy for various minor literary operations. One was an invitation from Cyril Clemens to be an honorary vice-president of the Mark Twain Society. Ernest accepted with "great pleasure." Another was a plea from Captain Louis Henry Cohn, a New York bookseller, who was putting together a bibliography of Hemingway's work and wanted to pay him $350 to write a foreword or an epilogue. Ernest said cautiously that he would have to see it first. Perkins asked for a new story for the August number of *Scribner's Magazine*. Ernest had already set down an account of the Moncini family of Sheridan under the title of "Wine of Wyoming." Pauline typed it and he sent it off with strong assurances to Max that it was an excellent story, despite the fact that it was nearly 6,000 words long and contained much dialogue in French. Max replied by return mail that the story was already in galleys and that Bridges was sending a check for $600.

Ernest was planning to get out of the humidity of Key West and back to the hills of Wyoming, partly to fish, partly to work on his bullfight book. Early in June Pauline took Patrick and his French nurse to Piggott. Ernest went to New York to meet Bumby's ship. One of his first acts on arrival was to find

Lewis Galantière, who was asleep in his room at a midtown hotel when Ernest telephoned. He wanted Lewis to read through "Wine of Wyoming," putting accent marks on the French words and checking for idiomatic usage. Lewis rather sleepily complied. It was the work of a few minutes. Afterwards Ernest fished from his pocket a small Spanish knife with a blade of Toledo steel and gave it to Lewis by way of compensation. Then, looking like a man who had solved a problem, he took the finished galley sheets off to Scribners. On the 23rd, he lunched with Milford Baker at the Harvard Club, and placed an order for a 6.5 mm Mannlicher to use in Wyoming and Africa. Next day he wrote Captain Cohn that he had decided against doing a foreword for the bibliography. A writer aged thirty, said he, should have nothing to do with such fancy projects. He wanted his writing to be judged on its merits rather than on anything he said or did as a man. Many who had met Gertrude Stein, for example, were so much impressed by her intelligence that they read the same qualities into her writings. On the other hand, some of the people who had met him personally were convinced by the experience that his books "must be, shall we say, shit." He took pride in his esthetic and financial integrity. In all other respects he felt that he had managed to make an ass of himself. Involvement with bibliographers might endanger the only probities he could rightly lay claim to. His wisest course was to stay clear. With this decision behind him, he gathered up Bumby at the French Line pier and set off on the long drive to Piggott.

They stayed in Arkansas only long enough to pick up Pauline. Patrick stayed behind in Piggott with his grandmother and his nurse. Ernest drove west with Pauline and Bumby through an immense heat wave. It was 108 in the shade all across Nebraska. Even in Sheridan it was bright and very hot. They asked about dude ranches and were directed to Simon Snyder's place on Sunlight Creek near Painter. The people there had never heard of Hemingway the novelist. When someone finally identified him, they "fell all over themselves to make him feel at home." Ernest disgustedly bundled his wife and son into the car and drove out to see another dude rancher named Nordquist. He owned a spread of land and cabins in a wide valley just inside the Wyoming state line some 12 miles from the old mining community of Cooke City, Montana. Nordquist was a big, dark-haired Swede in his early forties. He said that he had just the spot for them. It was a new double cabin in a stand of lodgepole pines with a view of tall mountains to the west. The Hemingways moved in on Sunday, July 13th.

What caught Ernest's eye was the river. The Clarks Fork Branch of the Yellowstone was a fast dark stream, teeming with trout and flowing easterly through the valley that shared its name. Half a mile back from the heavy plank bridge, which rumbled like thunder under the wheels of the car, stood the main lodge. It was flanked by a dozen cabins, made of chinked logs. The doors had old-fashioned rawhide latchstrings and handles fashioned from the tips of elk antlers. There was a large bunkhouse for the horse wranglers, and a corral with thirty-five head of saddle horses. Across the valley and the river to the east, the land rose in pale green terraces, dotted with sagebrush, studded with pines, and striped by the paths of descending streams. The really spectacular view was from the front porch of the Hemingways' cabin: the great dark peaks of Pilot and Index, 12,000 feet in elevation and rising more than 5,000 feet above the valley floor. Lawrence Nordquist had named the ranch the L Bar T from the first and last letters of his name.

Life at the ranch was free and easy. The high clear air was like a tonic and Ernest's appetite turned voracious. He always appeared early for breakfast at the main lodge, dousing his ham and eggs with heavy dollops of catsup, topping them with thick slices of Bermuda onion, and washing them down with coffee and half a bottle of red wine. He tried to work most mornings, sitting out on the cabin porch and leafing through a large pile of bullfight journals. Sometimes he walked to the corral after breakfast, leaning on the fence and watching Ivan Wallace saddling up the horses for the morning riders. "How about a little fishing this morning?" Ivan would say. "Can't do it," said Ernest. "Got to work." He would walk slowly back to his cabin, enveloped in his breakfast aura of wine and onions. Half an hour later he would reappear. "Ivan," he would say, "you've ruined the working day for me. Let's go fishing." He later told Floyd Allington, another of the wranglers, that the best fishing in the world was the Clarks Fork Branch of the Yellowstone.

The wranglers thought Pauline a "real good sport—a little dark-complected woman" in jeans and a boy's haircut. She seemed to be devoted entirely to caring for Bumby and shielding Ernest from interruption. In the afternoons and early evenings he often rode or fished alone. After dinner in the lodge he lingered awhile talking with the other guests, only to end by drifting down to the bunkhouse to visit with the hands. "I always learn something from you men," he told Ivan Wallace. "The dudes have nothing to teach me." Ivan was a redhead, who wore a big Stetson hat and stood about five feet four. Smokey Royce was a tall thin cowpoke who said he was from Texas and walked with a high-chinned swagger. Huck Mees was hard-drinking, slightly hunchbacked, adventurous, and foolhardy. Mun Wogoman was a blue-eyed Norwegian with a skin like saddle leather. Floyd Allington fished so well that Ernest wanted to try him out on kings and wahoos in the Gulf Stream. Apart from Ivan, the man that Ernest liked best was Leland Stanford Weaver, universally known as Chub. He had been raised in Red Lodge, but his built-in wanderlust had taken him to every state in the union and many of the ports of the Far East. After the first week or two they were all calling him "Pop" Hemingway, laughing at his eccentricities and admiring his prowess. Yarning, swearing, pontificating, or simply keeping his ears open for authentic bits of Americana, Ernest quickly established himself among these professional outdoorsmen, partly because he was a guest of Nordquist's but chiefly because they accepted him as a man.

August began wet. According to Ernest's fishing log, there were only two clear days between the first and the fifteenth. Cloudbursts, sometimes with hailstones, repeatedly muddied the river. Fishing alone on the first and the third, Ernest took only a dozen one day and seven the next. A complaint came through from Ed Simpson's ranch on the north fork of Crandall Creek that a bear was killing his cattle. Ernest and Ivan went up there and shot a horse for bait. "The best horse for a bear bait is a big horse," Ivan explained, "so there will be a lot of him. . . . You want to kill him where the sun will strike him so he will start to get high quick. If you kill him in the shade or if he gets rained on, he is liable to simply go sour and not come up at all. To bring him up faster you can build a fire on him. The smell of burnt hair and charred meat carries a long ways on the wind and the bear picks it up. You got to be careful not to burn clean through him because then he won't come up and also the ravens and magpies and eagles will get into him. Now the reason you want him to come up as quick as can be is so he will commence to put out. You always approach with the wind in his favor so as not to scare anything that is feeding on him and so you can judge how he is putting out as you approach."

They staked out the dead horse and came on down. Bill Horne and his bride Frances, called Bunny, were now spending a two-week vacation in the other half of the Hemingways' double cabin. The day after they arrived was the first good day in a week. Using McGintys and Gray Palmers, Bill and Ernest took forty-nine good rainbows and cutthroats in the canyon below the ranch where the water ran deep. Then the deluge set in once more. The stream ran high and very muddy, remaining so until the 21st when Bill and his wife, with Ernest and Pauline, took a final total of thirty.

The Hornes had just departed when Ernest met with another of his curious accidents. On the morning of the 22nd, riding a big and skittish bay named Goofy, he set out with Chub Weaver, Ivan Wallace, and Smokey Royce for the Crandall Creek grounds to see what had happened to their bear bait. Goofy was richly caparisoned with all Ernest's equipment, including his new Springfield rifle, a pair of Zeiss binoculars, his bundled raincoat, fishing rod and net, and a packet of lunch. They had just stopped to breathe the horses in a patch of timber when Goofy bolted. Ernest stayed on too long and was carried into thick woods, cutting his arms and legs and laying open a long jagged cut on the left side of his chin. Smokey larruped off to the ranch for the first-aid kit. But the face wound was too deep for amateurs. Ernest and Ivan rode over to the Crandall Ranger Station and rented a decrepit car from the ranger. His teen-aged daughter, Mary Williams, went along as driver. It was midnight when they got to Cody and roused Dr. Trueblood. He was a one-time veterinary who had changed subjects and earned his M.D. The only anodyne he used was a bottle of bootleg whiskey. When Ernest complained of its poor quality, Trueblood wrote out and promptly filled a prescription for a quart of Old Oscar Pepper Bourbon. After that the stitching went better.

They carried the bottle across the street to an all-night restaurant and had several drinks while Mary ate breakfast. On the way back to camp, whenever she got down to open and close the stock gates, Ernest and Ivan took a drink apiece for every gate. It was dawn when they turned in. They slept through the day and got out to the bear bait about dusk. The dead horse was good and high: they could smell it half a mile away. Feeding on the carrion was a big brown bear. Ernest killed him with one shot from the Springfield. "That bear," said Ivan, "has got about the biggest feet I ever seen on a bear." Skinning out the head was a problem because the bait was thick with maggots and the bear had fallen into it. But they finished off the whiskey and got the job done. Next day, back at the ranch, Ernest told Nordquist that he wanted to buy the horse called Goofy. Lawrence said that if he wanted a good saddle horse, there were a lot of better animals than that one. "I don't want to ride him," mumbled Ernest through his bandages. "I want to shoot him for bear bait."

Trueblood's stitches had pulled Ernest's face askew. He said that it made him look as if he were growling "the hell you say" at some adversary. But it did not cramp his style. In three days of fishing the Clarks Fork, he took a total of 92 trout, using a lure called the Professor and a hybrid of his own invention, a yellow bug with Royal Coachman hackles. On the 30th he took Bumby up for a look at the bear bait. A little fine snow had fallen and they shivered while they waited for a bear to appear. A large cow elk came crashing out of the timber. Bumby had never seen one that close. "Is it a camel, Papa?" he asked. They ate their lunch while they were waiting, and had almost decided to go home when they saw that a black bear had sneaked up on the bait. Again Ernest killed a bear with a single shot from the heavy Springfield. It was the second bear on the same bait in exactly a week.

The bullfight book progressed very slowly until Ernest conceived a character called the Old Lady. She broke into the seventh chapter with a whole battery of questions: "What is he saying? What is the young man saying?" When the young man asked how she liked the bullfights, she said that she liked them very much. The best thing of all was watching the bulls hit the horses. "Why did you like that?" asked the author. "It seemed so sort of homey," said the Old Lady. With such a one to talk to, Ernest's progress accelerated. By September 28th, even allowing for the delay caused by a two-week hunting trip after elk, mountain sheep, and bear, he had brought his manuscript close to two hundred pages.

The trip had begun on September 14th, the day after Pauline left with Bumby for New York. This time Ernest had a horse that he loved, a black mare named Old Bess with a white streak on her face. They went down to Squaw Creek and up over the steep trail to Timber Creek, a full day's ride. Next day they worked up the higher flanks of Pilot Mountain, crossing rockslides where the horses sought delicately for safe footing, following narrow ledges where one false step would have pitched horse and rider over the brink. This was the country of the mountain sheep. At midmorning they left the horses and began hiking. Ernest lay under a large rock and glassed the terrain yard by yard with his binoculars. Three miles off in a clump of green junipers he thought he could see the white rump of an old ram. He slid down into the valley, climbed up the other side, and sweated his way along a granite ledge to a spot where he could look down into a "grassy pocket cupped against the broken rock of the peak." One old ram and three younger ones were feeding among the junipers. "The old ram was purple grey, his rump was white, and when he raised his head you saw the great heavy curl of his horns." It was a downhill shot at 350 yards. Ernest adjusted the telescopic sight, aimed for a spot just behind the left shoulder, and squeezed off. The big ram leaped and crumpled. The young rams stood where they were, their heads turned, staring at the old leader, waiting for him to get up again. "They could not see you on that high ledge," said Ernest, "nor wind you, and the shot made no more impression on them than a boulder falling."

Another day, lower down, he got his first bull elk. He never forgot the deep high mounting whistle of the bull as he bugled, and the distant challenging answer that came, moments later, from another valley like a delayed echo. The bull was standing in a patch of timber beside a mountain meadow, and the two hunters had crawled so close that Ernest, peering excitedly through his binoculars, "could see his chest muscles swell as he lifted his head and still not see his head in the thick timber." When he came out to feed, dipping the proud head with the six-pointed antlers down to the tawny September grass, Ivan nodded and formed the words soundlessly: this was a first-class trophy. Ernest leveled the Springfield and dropped him with a single shot.

Dos Passos wired from New York that he would come out for a visit in October while Katy stayed with some of her relatives. The week before he was due to arrive, Ernest and Ivan rode up to Crandall Creek, where Ernest got his first sight of grizzly bear. Once more it was an event that he would long remember. "You heard a crash of timber," he wrote, "and thought it was a cow elk bolting, and then there they were, in the broken shadow, running with an easy, lurching smoothness, the afternoon sun making their coats a soft bristling silver." Then, just as suddenly, all three of them were gone, down below the rimrock into the valley beyond, and the place was as silent as if they had never appeared.

It was on this trip to Crandall Creek that Ernest first met John Staib. He and Ivan were walking along a trail when they saw a tall, heavyset man coming towards them. "There's John," said Ivan. "John Staib. How's your rifle? Is it clean? You watch. He'll want to see your gun." They waited while Staib came up, straight as a ramrod, coarse-featured, with very large feet and the heavy face of a deaf man. He had served in the Kaiser's army for three years before the First World War and still spoke with a thick German accent. They had just shaken hands when old John asked to see Ernest's gun, opened it, and sighted up at daylight through the bore. It was clean enough to suit him and he handed it back like a treasure. He told Ernest that it was a fine gun. But he must be sure to unload it every night. The thing you had to do was to give the springs a rest. When Staib stalked away down the trail, they knew he had not heard their good-byes.

Ernest met Dos Passos at Billings on the 21st of October. He looked pale from his season in New York, but he bubbled with anticipation of the new country and the animals. Back at the ranch he was struck by the way Ernest "already had the ranch hands under his thumb. They thought he was the most wonderful guy they had ever met." It occurred to Dos that Ernest would have made a first-rate chief of guerrilla fighters. There was something in his manner that made him a natural leader. Dos had bought an elk license and they were going to have a final week in the field before the long drive back east. They stayed overnight at the ranch and then set off for the high country. But Dos was too nearsighted for hunting. The one time he got near enough to an elk bull, he was carrying Ernest's new Mannlicher. He did not understand the principle of the set trigger, and while he was fooling desperately with the gun the elk galloped away. After that he contented himself with the scenery. It was more than enough to occupy him.

They lived high for ten days on venison and elk steaks, hunting Crandall and Timber Creeks and the wilderness section around Crazy Lakes. The roads were already frozen over when they packed the Ford for the drive around to Billings. Floyd Allington put on all his heaviest clothes and climbed into the rumble seat. He wanted to go along to Key West to try some of the fishing that Ernest had told him about. Ernest drove and Dos sat beside him, wedged in with sleeping bags and a quart of bourbon against the cold. On the morning of the 31st they rumbled over the plank bridge and set off up the Clarks Fork valley on the first lap of the long drive home.

30. DEATH IN THE AFTERNOON

ALL their plans were upset on the evening of November first. They spent the previous night in sleeping bags in Yellowstone Park, within earshot of the retching gurgle of a warm geyser. In the morning they left for Billings by way of Mammoth, Big Timber, and Columbus. At dusk they reached a point 22 miles west of Billings between Park City and Laurel. The road was two-lane flat gravel, with deep ditches on both sides. An oncoming car pulled out to pass, and Ernest was blinded by its headlights. "I had to pull over," he said afterwards, "and there wasn't enough road." The Ford turned turtle in the ditch, pinning Ernest upside down behind the wheel. When Floyd and Dos eased him out, they thought his legs were broken. But as he stood up, they saw that his right arm was hanging limp. A man and his wife who were heading for Shelby turned back and drove the victims to the hospital in Billings. It took a long forty minutes to cover the distance. Ernest sat in the back seat with his arm clamped between his knees.

St. Vincent's Hospital was operated and largely staffed by the Sisters of Charity of Leavenworth, a Catholic nursing organization. Ernest was placed in a private corner room with a fine view of Montana sunsets. Dos sent off a telegram to Pauline in Piggott. The doors of the car were sprung but the engine still ran and Dos drove it to Columbus for repairs. Ernest's condition was far more serious, an oblique spiral fracture, nearly compound, three inches above the elbow. The two ends of the bone had sheared off in such a way that they could not be kept in place by the usual forms of manipulation. A visitor named Earl Snook, a friend of the cowboy artist Will James, saw Hemingway in the midst of his pain, reporting that he was like a restless lion, pacing his room, gazing from the window, then resolutely turning his back on the great outdoors. Dos met Pauline's train on Tuesday, and waited through Thursday morning while the surgeon operated, binding the break with kangaroo tendons and sewing up the long incision. "I have never seen anyone behave so beautifully," wrote Pauline of her husband's stoical conduct.

After the first week, Ernest turned restive. He suggested ironically that Scribners could make money by insuring him against accident and disease. Since signing on with Perkins, he had suffered an anthrax infection, a cut in his right eyeball, a forehead gash from a skylight, congestion of the kidney, a sliced index finger, a torn chin, a branch run through his leg, and now a break in his chief professional tool, the right arm. He defiantly resolved to use his left hand to outwrite anyone to whom the news of his accident had been welcome. But this was bravura. He was clearly depressed by the disruption of two of his major plans. One was his expectation of finishing a first draft of the bullfight book by Christmas. At the time of the accident the manuscript stood somewhere between 235 and 250 pages. Pauline had offered to take down the rest by dictation, but Ernest knew that this would not work. Anything meant to be read by the eye, said he, must be written out by hand and checked by the ear and the eye in process. His "busted arm" made this a physical impossibility. The other plan was Africa. In September he had broached the subject to Archie MacLeish. They would make up a foursome with Charles Thompson and Mike Strater. They would all go out there and purify themselves with a little danger, said Ernest, pulling the trigger only when they got close enough to smell the lion's breath. This also was an unlikely feat for a man with a broken arm.

He could not even pace his room anymore. For nearly a month he lay immobilized in bed on doctor's orders. By the first of December the strain was beginning to be evident. "Ernest is really in pretty bad shape," wrote Pauline, "after pain all the time for a month, and not sleeping nights. He's had nothing to do but think, always lying in the same position, and he's pretty nervous and depressed from the pain and worry. . . . The mail's about the only thing that breaks the monotony."

Each night he listened to a portable radio. When one station signed off, as he later wrote, "you could go farther west and pick up another. The last one you could get was Seattle, Washington, and . . . when they signed off at four o'clock it was five o'clock . . . in the hospital; and at six o'clock you could get the morning revellers in Minneapolis." Nearly every station sooner or later carried the voice of Rudy Vallee the crooner, singing tunes like "Betty Co-ed has lips of red for Harvard" and "Little White Lies." These tunes ran through Ernest's head during the day, especially the one about Betty Co-ed, for which he evolved a parody that grew "steadily and increasingly obscene." He also amused himself with surly critiques of people he did not like, including Mr. Snook's friend Will James, the cowboy artist. Ernest said that he had met him once—a moth-eaten, shifty-eyed imitation of old C. W. Russell, who had been a *real* cowboy artist.

Another diversion was talking to a pair of sugar-beet workers, a Russian and a Mexican, who lay groaning across the hall. They had been wounded by an unknown assailant while drinking coffee in an all-night restaurant. A stray bullet meant for the Mexican had hit the Russian in the thigh. The Mexican, a small-time gambler, was shot twice in the stomach. He refused to identify the gunman, maintaining steadfastly that he had no enemies. The friends who came to see him also dropped in on Ernest, who conversed with them in demotic Spanish and rewarded their compassion with whiskey.

By all odds his favorite visitor was Sister Florence, a gentle nun who loved baseball and believed strongly that the Lord could be persuaded to intercede in human affairs. Her prayers had been answered during the World Series of October. Ernest loved to see her and to hear her breathless talk. Along with the Mexican gambler and the nighttime radio programs, Sister Florence became his chief consolation for the endless hours of lying in bed.

The period of imprisonment stretched to seven weeks while the broken arm swelled, burst, drained, and at last improved. He let his hair and beard grow long, and posed for pictures with his hospital tunic belted around his middle, looking like a wounded Cossack. In December, Archie MacLeish made the long rough flight out to see him. His reward for the effort came when Ernest, in a mood of dark suspicion, accused him of having made the trip only to be present at the death of Hemingway. The day MacLeish left, Earl Snook came back to check on Ernest's progress, and found him talking with the Mexican gambler. He was pale but outwardly cheerful, and they shared two bottles of Canadian beer. "This dry docking will affect his future writing," Snook predicted to Perkins. He did not know that Ernest was already meditating an autobiographical short story about the gambler, the nun, and the radio.

He was discharged in time for Christmas, which he and Pauline spent in Piggott. After the tree and the gifts, he went to bed in Paul Pfeiffer's house, still feeling "punk" from his long ordeal. He had just begun to walk around the town, wearing western clothes, full beard, long hair, and a sling to support his splinted arm, when an incident occurred which increased his former prejudice against Piggott. One day after grade school had reopened, he was limping through the schoolyard across Cherry Street. The children mistook him for a tramp. When they saw him heading for the Pfeiffer house, they became frenzied in their determination to protect the town's leading citizens from this rough-looking outlander. Some two dozen boys and girls pursued him, yelling "Tramp! Tramp!" and pelting him with snowballs. He was pale and shaken when he reached the Pfeiffers' front porch, and often mentioned it afterwards as a nightmare experience.

The accident and its aftermath soured his memories of 1930. So did Laurence Stallings's dramatization of *A Farewell to Arms,* which had opened in New York in September, only to close after three weeks. The failure of the play led to a victory in Hollywood, however. The sale of the movie rights brought in a substantial sum, of which Ernest's share was $24,000. Another event of the fall season fell midway between black and white. When Sinclair Lewis won the Nobel Prize for Literature, he took the occasion to congratulate Scribners on having published two of the "most superb" novels of recent years —*A Farewell to Arms* and Wolfe's *Look Homeward, Angel.* The deepening financial depression had seriously impaired the sales of both these books, and Lewis's boost was not unwelcome. But Ernest made it clear, at least privately, that he would have preferred to be boosted by someone else and in some other company. He was likewise irked by Edmund Wilson's introduction to the Scribner reissue of *In Our Time.* Covering Ernest's career to date, Wilson had described *A Farewell to Arms* as "a rather romanticized idyll." To Ernest this meant that Wilson was trying to make him out to be "a faking romanticist." In an aggressive comment to Perkins he boasted that he had not only met more people than Wilson had, but also that he knew a good deal more about the pleasures of sexual intercourse.

No one would have gathered from Ernest's bearlike growlings that Wilson's essay was easily the best short account of the first six years of Hemingway's writing. Wilson named "candor and coldbloodedness" as the watchwords of Ernest's vision of the world. Even in so idyllic a story as "Big Two-Hearted River," one still felt the implicit pain. "Every calm or contented surface," said Wilson, "still vibrated with its pangs." *In Our Time* was in fact a "key to the later and more ambitious books. Suffering and making suffer, and their relation to the sensual enjoyment of life" were the subject of all his work. "The undruggable consciousness of something wrong" invested the "green summer landscapes" of *The Sun Also Rises* with a curiously sinister quality. Finally, said Wilson, Hemingway had seen that "life, which we devour so voraciously for the very things about it which destroy us," was "always in the long run a losing game." Even in losing, "we must stick to the code of the sportsman and lose in a sportsmanlike way"—dying gamely in the end, like Manuel García in "The Undefeated."

All through the spring of 1931 in Key West, Ernest wrestled with the frustrations of his broken arm. As always, he surrounded himself with an ample company. They were now renting Fanny Curry's house at the corner of United and Whitehead Streets, where John and Josie Herrmann had lived the year before. Patrick, a chubby two and a half, still had his nurse Henriette and spoke mostly in French, though he had learned to ask, "Whatchasay, Papa?" in English. Ernest's sister Carol, a pretty girl of twenty with her brother's brown eyes and coloring, had entered Rollins College in Winter Park and was a frequent visitor. Ernest's mother appeared for two days, entertained chiefly by Pauline. Jinny Pfeiffer was also there. So was Chub Weaver, who had driven the Ford from Billings to Piggott to Miami, and was now living in a Key West boardinghouse, though spending most of his time in Ernest's company. Lawrence and Olive Nordquist went fishing with Ernest and Chub on Valentine's Day. John and Josie Herrmann returned from a tour of Russia to settle in Key West for the spring season. Even with a good right arm, Ernest's productivity might have been seriously limited by social engagements.

Except for a few letters laboriously scrawled with his left hand or pecked out on the typewriter at the rate of three words a minute, he did no writing at all. When Chub Weaver began reading one of his books, he took it out of his hands with the observation that it was meant to be sold, not read by his friends. Chub had secured an embalmer's license in Montana, and Ernest said that they would go to Spain and teach the Spaniards the art of embalming. "I've got to go over there this spring and finish my bullfight book," said he. "You come along and show them how to do it. Next to bullfighting, it's the highest paid profession in Spain." Chub grinned at him and said that he could not do it because he was not a Catholic. "Hell," said Ernest, "any man could become a Catholic for a million seeds." The nerve in his arm was rapidly regenerating and he gave the elbow a daily baking under a lamp. He boasted to MacLeish that he was again as strong and healthy as a pig, though his chest was black and blue from shooting off his shotgun lefthanded while holding the butt against his right shoulder. He seemed proud of his powers of rejuvenation. *"Dans la vie,"* he wrote, *"il faut (d'abord) durer."*

Max Perkins had now come to regard his Key West fishing expeditions as an annual institution. He appeared in March for a trip to Tortugas, this time in a large new boat belonging to Albert Pinder, commonly known as "Ole Bread." The other fishermen included Chub Weaver, John Herrmann, Burge, and a honeymooning couple named Pat and Maude Morgan. As in 1930, they soon ran out of Bermuda onions, a staple of Ernest's diet. He and Max went aboard a fishing smack to see if they could buy some. The cleanliness and order of the boat struck Ernest forcibly, and he took at once to the lean and laconic skipper, a Canary Islander named Gregorio Fuentes, who had followed the sea since boyhood. If Ernest ever realized his ambition of buying a boat of his own, Gregorio was just the kind of man he would have liked to employ to run it.

Max was obliged to leave before the expedition was over, and made his way back to Key West aboard another fisherman. The worst gale of the winter confined his companions to the old dock at Tortugas. Once more they ran out of supplies, chiefly ice, which they needed to keep three hundred pounds of fish from spoiling. John Herrmann and Burge went to Key West for a fresh supply, only to be held up for five days by engine trouble and rough water. When they got back, carrying John's wife Josie as supercargo, the fish had spoiled and Ernest made no secret of his rage.

He began to needle Herrmann about the long delay, and kept it up steadily on the way home. They were riding in Bread Pinder's boat, which Ernest was steering lefthanded. The sea was still rough, quartering waves slapped the hull, and Pinder began to fear for the welfare of the boat. Speaking loud enough so that Ernest could hear, he finally asked Herrmann to take over the wheel. Ernest surrendered it gruffly and turned to shooting booby birds, hurling insults at John over his shoulder. At last Josie decided that he had gone far enough. She took up a station behind him and said quietly, "Hem, if you don't stop talking that way, I'll take your gun and shoot you." Ernest at once unbuckled his piratical pistol belt, stowed it away with the pistol, turned on his redoubtable charm, and began to regale them with stories about his grandfather Hall's troubles with constipation on the ship that brought him from England in the 1850s.

By late April it had become clear that Pauline's second child would arrive in November. Ernest notified Dr. Guffey in Kansas City, and began to lay plans for the intervening months. By going to France in May and spending the period from June to September following the bullfights in Spain, he could work on his book and then bring Pauline back in plenty of time for her lying-in. They could then return to Key West for another winter, this time in a place of their own. There was an old stone house with balconies and iron railings opposite the lighthouse at 907 Whitehead Street. When Uncle Gus came down for his spring vacation, he went over the place with Pauline and Ernest. The roof leaked and some of the windows were broken, but it was one of the handsomest houses on the island and it would not cost much to put it in decent repair. The asking price was $8,000 and Uncle Gus was prepared to buy it as an outright gift to Pauline. One of their last acts before setting sail for the Spanish summer was the purchase of the place as their first permanent house in the United States.

The crossing was accomplished on separate ships. Pauline, with Patrick and the nurse, sailed for France from New York. Ernest took the *Volendam* out of Havana on May 4th in the company of seven Spanish priests who had been exiled from Mexico. They were apprehensive about the Republican revolution in Spain, where it was said that mobs had been burning some of the churches. The voyage was steady and dull—like a ride, said Ernest, in the ample bosom of Queen Wilhelmina. He left the ship at Vigo and headed straight for Madrid, hoping to arrive before the guillotines were set up in the Plaza Mayor. But the city was noisily and universally Republican. It was also clear that they were not going to let the revolution interfere with the bullfight season. Ernest reestablished connections with Sidney Franklin, who had come over in April. He was as flamboyantly egotistical as ever, though in poor health after a series of operations which had kept him in and out of hospitals for more than a year.

In Paris, Pauline was preparing to ship her furniture to Key West for installation in the new house. Ernest found the Left Bank writing clan much depressed by the *"crise des affaires"* brought on by the *"Krach américain."*

For himself, however, money was no problem. He and Pauline left Patrick and his nurse at Hendaye Plage for the summer, and went on to Madrid, staying at the Hotel Biarritz in the Calle Victoria, a down-at-heel establishment much frequented by matadors. He met and liked a Spanish painter, Luis Quintanilla, and listened carefully to Luis's quiet explanation of "the necessity of revolution" in Spain. He discussed the same matter with Jay Allen, a reporter for the *Chicago Tribune,* as well as with Hamilton Fish Armstrong and Elliott Paul. One night on the town with these companions, Ernest drunkenly assured Allen that he had been graduated from Princeton University. Allen had just got to bed in his hotel when a special messenger arrived with a note from Ernest apologizing for the lie. He had told it, said he, only because he had always envied Fitzgerald his college education. As a friend of Spain and a nominal Catholic, Ernest viewed with some cynicism the efforts of Don Jaime the Pretender to foment a new Carlist war in Navarre, using Pamplona as a command post. On Sunday, June 14th, some 23,000 rabid Carlists filled the Plaza de Toros in Pamplona, chanting "Viva Cristo Rey."

All the demonstrators had dispersed by the time of the fiesta of San Fermín, the seventh that Ernest had attended in the past nine years. After it was over, he finished the compilation of a glossary of bullfight terms for his book. It was his one experience in lexicography and he did it well. Many of the entries amounted to excellent short essays, learned, succinct, and often humorous. He had finished eighteen chapters of his text, inserting events from the current bullfight season in order to update the first draft he had brought over with him. Now there were only two chapters to go, one on the fine art of killing with the sword, including narrative portraits and personal reminiscences of a dozen of the most famous modern matadors, and the last—a kind of summary of all the impressions Hemingway had gathered in seven years of intermittent contact with the country and the people. The book was still unfinished when he returned to Paris in mid-September, but Ernest was reveling in the acquisition of an impressionistic painting of a guitar player by Juan Gris, which he had some thought of using as a frontispiece.

Going home on the *Île de France,* Ernest and Pauline were introduced to Jane Mason by Don Stewart and his wife. Mrs. Mason was the beautiful and lively wife of George Grant Mason, an official of Pan American Airways who lived and worked in Havana. Both Pauline and Mrs. Stewart were visibly pregnant and obviously uncomfortable, leaving Don and Ernest to squire Mrs. Mason during what Ernest described as a merry and drunken crossing. On a visit to the MacLeishes at Uphill Farm in Conway, Massachusetts, Ernest was standing before the fireplace when the MacLeishes' daughter Mimi came in to greet him. Something in his manner frightened her and she ran off to her bedroom. Ada found her crying and saying over and over that this was not the Hemingway she knew. Ernest spent nearly an hour talking to the child upstairs, and afterwards compared her to the child Ellie in "Disorder and Early Sorrow," the story of Thomas Mann's that he liked best after *Buddenbrooks.*

Next day Ernest and Archie drove to Cambridge to meet Waldo Peirce for a football game at Harvard stadium. They rooted loudly for the home team and drank a good deal of whiskey. Afterwards they strolled through the Yard, which Ernest had not seen since his sightseeing tour with his mother in 1910. MacLeish impulsively suggested a call on Charles Townsend Copeland, the famous Harvard teacher, and they knocked on the battered door of 15 Hollis Hall. Copey happened to be at home, an aging and rather querulous man for whom Ernest conceived an instant dislike. The meeting reminded Archie of a sudden confrontation between a precious housecat and the biggest and roughest dog on the block. Ernest was far more at home hunting partridge with Archie next day along the woods path at Uphill Farm.

Afterwards in New York, he turned over to Perkins the bullfight pictures that he had been at pains to gather during the Spanish summer; spent a drunken and boastful evening with a writer named Eric Knight, who came from Philadelphia and wanted to do an article on Ernest's life; and invited Captain Louis Cohn, the scholarly bookseller, to bring his bride Marguerite to dinner in the Hemingways' suite at the Brevoort. It was their first meeting after months of sporadic correspondence. Hemingway's latent distrust fell away as he talked with Cohn, a strapping six-footer with a neatly trimmed mustache and a record of distinguished service with the French army. Cohn told of having acquired, for a considerable sum, the corrected typescript of *The Sun Also Rises,* including the rejected opening pages about Brett Ashley, Mike Campbell, and Robert Cohn. A Scribner salesman had rescued it from an office wastebasket. Then it was time to go west to have the baby, and the Hemingways entrained on the Spirit of St. Louis at Pennsylvania Station.

While Patrick went on to Piggott with his new nurse Gabrielle, Pauline and Ernest settled in Kansas City, at first with the Malcolm Lowrys in the house on Indian Lane, and afterwards, when the Lowrys left for California, in the Riviera Apartments on Ward Parkway. Ernest had picked up somewhere a new piece of slang "ballroom bananas"—which he applied more or less indiscriminately to people and ideas which he regarded with suspicion. He was anxious to exclude all evidence of ballroom bananas from the manuscript of his bullfight book, which he cut extensively before going on to Chapters Nineteen and Twenty.

He was in the midst of these labors when Pauline's labor pains began. Dr. Guffey performed a Caesarean section on the morning of November 12th. Although Ernest had wanted a daughter, the child was a boy, nine pounds in weight, with blue-black hair. They named him Gregory Hancock, partly for several historic Popes, as Ernest explained, partly for Greg Clark of Toronto, and partly for Caroline Hancock Hall, Ernest's maternal grandmother.

On the first of December, with Pauline out of danger, Ernest went down to Piggott for a week of quail shooting in the bottomlands. By the time of his return to Kansas City, he had finished the "swell last chapter" of the bullfight book, a kind of coda, 3,000 words long. It constituted his apologia for having concentrated on the bullfight to the virtual exclusion of all his thronging memories of Spain since that first amateurish visit in the spring of 1923. He remembered the ride from Pamplona to Madrid when they all got drunk on wine samples and he had contrived to lose the railway tickets. He recalled the bull's ear, presented to Hadley by Niño de la Palma, and afterwards wrapped in Don Stewart's handkerchief for preservation; swimming the Irati near Aoiz, the water "clear as light," and the *fête champêtre* in the beech forest where the ancient trees were "like drawings in a child's fairy book"; the sick disappointment of the summer when loggers had spoiled the river and killed all the fish. From the summer of 1929 he remembered sweating out the torn muscle in his groin in the oven heat of a hotel room in Palencia; the visit to Miró in "Montroig, pronounced Montroych," where the cook cut the throat of a duck and stroked it gently while her small daughter caught the blood in a cup for the making of gravy, and the steaming splendor of the same duck that night, stuffed and roasted to be eaten with wine drawn from twelve-foot earthen jars, standing side by side in a dark room of the house. And from the summer just past, the storks wheeling in the sky above the tiled roofs of Barco de Ávila; the view from Luis Quintanilla's window in Madrid over the clay-white parade ground where the machine-gun cadets were marching, and far beyond them the summits of the Sierra de Guadarrama in serried ranks against the high Castilian sky; or the cookouts with the bullfighters and their whores beside the Manzanares along the Pardo road, where Bumby had practiced with the small cape and sword, made to his size and presented by Sidney Franklin. He would have liked to name over all the sights and sounds and smells, like a miser in his countinghouse: the wheat-colored fields of Navarre, the "small, careful stepping horses . . . rope-soled shoes . . . the loops of twisted garlics; earthen pots; saddle bags carried across the shoulder; wine skins; the pitchforks made of natural wood" with branches as tines; the tall papyrus grass along the littoral; the baked clay hills, red dust, white sand. The tinny sound of churchbells in the villages; the clop of mules and burros; the rustle of the sea-wind in the palms; the smells of olive oil and dust and hot paellas and of early morning in the freshly swept cafés. He would have liked to set down in words, as Goya did in paint, all that he had "seen, felt, touched, handled, smelled, enjoyed, drunk, mounted, suffered, spewed-up, lain-with, suspected, observed, loved, hated, lusted, feared, detested, admired, loathed, and destroyed." But he knew that "any part you make will represent the whole if it's made truly." And he knew, finally, that all books must end somewhere.

In bringing the book to an end, there were, of course, a few practical problems. When they moved into the house on Whitehead Street, Key West, on December 19th, the rooms were thronged with plumbers and carpenters, to say nothing of the huge packing cases of furniture shipped from France. Pauline took to bed from exhaustion, Patrick's new nurse Gabrielle fell sick, and Ernest came down with a sore throat. Young Patrick, one naptime, filled the mosquito sprayer with a mixture of tooth, talcum, and mosquito powder, liberally spraying the baby in his crib. When they asked whether he had meant to hurt his new little brother, he looked very frightened and said "yes." Ten days later he ate an ant-button containing half a grain of arsenic, and spent the next twenty-six hours vomiting.

The denouement of the long story of the composition of *Death in the After-noon* came at last in the midst of January:

FINISHED REWRITING BODY OF BOOK LAST NIGHT YOU CAN'T MISS HAVING IT FIRST OF WEEK PATRICK OK BEST—Ernest.

MANUSCRIPT HAS COME DELIGHTED TO GET IT—Max.

31. A PLACE TO COME BACK TO

THE house at 907 Whitehead Street was the first that Ernest had owned in ten years of married life. It was set back a hundred feet in a deep corner lot, planted with sago and date palms, palmettos, and banyan trees. Its architecture was roughly Spanish Colonial, with wrought-iron work on the upper veranda, rounded French windows equipped with green shutters, and thick stone walls to keep it cool. Seeing it from across the street, Ernest thought that it resembled Joan Miró's "The Farm" as it might have been painted by Utrillo. A squad of local artisans installed new water and electrical systems, repaired the leaking roof, and otherwise restored it from the ravages of eighty years. Before she left for Piggott, Jinny Pfeiffer supervised the uncrating and placement of the furniture from Paris, accomplishing miracles, as Ernest said, to make the place habitable. But habitation, for Ernest, was never synonymous with domestication. Over the dining-room fireplace he hung Waldo Peirce's painting of a brace of partridges and a shotgun, as if to signify the wide world that waited outside. "For guys like us," he wrote to Waldo, home was a place a man left behind him in order to come back to it afterwards. They were all getting older fast, and experience was always outside any four walls you could name.

Now that his arm was fully recovered, he reactivated plans for the trip to East Africa with Thompson, Strater, and MacLeish. Strater learned that it was possible to fly from Cairo to Nairobi, but Ernest declined the gambit. Suppose they cracked up and missed the hunting trip after all! He selected the guns he wanted to take: a 30.06 Mauser, the 6.5 Mannlicher, the 12-gauge pump shotgun for African birds, and the well-worn, well-loved Colt Woodsman pistol. Strater's informants said that an Englishman named Philip Percival was the best white hunter in Kenya. Three other able guides were Pat Aires, O. M. Rees, and A. J. Klein. They all charged the same: $1,000 a month. Klein's name made Ernest slightly suspicious. Germans were swell, said he, but "kikes" were not so good. The trip for four would be expensive. Besides round-trip transatlantic fares, deluxe accommodations from Marseilles to

Mombasa cost $400 each for a 19-day voyage. A Tanganyika guide named Konrad Schauer quoted a price of $9,500 for a two-month safari for four men with two white hunters, hunting licenses to cost an additional $550 apiece. Another named George Carey estimated the total cost of the trip at roughly $22,000. Ernest did not care. Uncle Gus was ready to put $25,000 into the venture. Ernest was as enthusiastic as a Boy Scout planning a Saturday hike in the woods.

All through the spring, he conducted a lively correspondence with Perkins about the format and illustrations for the bullfight book, which Ernest now proposed to call *Death in the Afternoon*. When Dos stopped in Key West on his way to Mexico with Katy, he called the book "hellishly good" and an "absolute model" of its kind. His only reservations came when "Old Hem" strapped on his long white whiskers and "gave the boys the low-down" on his personal philosophy. Ernest responded with a critique of *1919*, Dos's latest novel. He said that Dos must curb his desire for symbolic perfection and keep his characters human and full of faults. Symbolic characters were self-defeating. Joyce's Dedalus, for instance, was idealized beyond belief, whereas Leopold and Molly Bloom saved *Ulysses* by their common humanity. Dos must also avoid the stance of the "do-gooder." The only way a novelist could do good was to show things as they really were. If Dos felt drawn to Communism, that was his business. But he should not trust its promises. The human race was far older than any economic system, while all once-noble movements had eventually degenerated simply because they were run by human beings. Even the Founder of Christianity, said Ernest, had "yellowed out on the Cross": He was "only successful because they killed him." Dos had to remember that good management was synonymous with tyranny. As for Ernest himself, all forms of government were anathema to him.

He gave another epistolary lecture to Paul Romaine, a Midwestern bookseller who thought he could discern a leftward swing in American writing. Ernest said that he refused to follow fashions in politics. If some of the boys were swinging left, others would swing right, while some of the "yellow bastards" would go both ways. In writing there was neither right nor left, only good and bad. Dreiser's leftist tendencies were merely the pitiable attempt of an old man to save his soul. All the little punks were asking people to swallow Communism. Ernest said truculently that he was no god-damned patriot; he would be glad to machine-gun any political bastards who did not work for a living. When Romaine urged him to stop writing about Lost Generations and bulls, he answered that he had once spent six weeks writing a book about a few drunks, but had not since been preoccupied with this so-called (but not so-called by him) Lost Generation. As for bulls, he had found recreation and amusement for years in the bullrings of Spain. He had done the bullfight book to organize and keep all that he had learned. He was neither maladjusted nor apologetic, he counted himself a part of the world he lived in, and he knew how "lousily" the politicians were running their part of that world.

Romaine was gathering up some of Faulkner's early work for a small volume called *Salmagundi*. All but one of the poems and prose sketches came from the now defunct New Orleans *Double Dealer*. Romaine believed that it would enhance the value of his small limited edition if he could include Ernest's little poem, "Ultimately," on the back cover. Ernest agreed to the proposal, though he privately told his bibliographer, Captain Cohn, that the poem was bad enough to fit perfectly into a collection of Faulkner's "early shit." His opinions on Faulkner's later work were mixed. He told Owen Wister that he liked *As I Lay Dying*. *Sanctuary* struck him as "pretty phoney." But he sent Faulkner his best wishes by way of Romaine, adding that he seemed to be going well as a writer and that he sounded like "a good skate."

He was now experiencing what he called a big revival of belief in the short story. Besides "After the Storm," Bra Saunders's tale of the sunken Spanish liner, he had assembled six others for a new collection. Two of these had already appeared: "Wine of Wyoming" in *Scribner's Magazine,* and "The Sea Change" in Edward Titus's *This Quarter*. This curious story, a lesser twin to "Hills Like White Elephants," consisted almost entirely in a café conversation between a man and a girl. After a love affair with the man, the girl had suddenly developed a Lesbian attachment. Ernest later explained that the prototypes of his people were a couple he had once overheard in the Bar Basque in St.-Jean-de-Luz, though he was notoriously apt to conceal the actual origins of some of his stories with invented fibs.

Two of the other stories grew out of Ernest's friendship with Dr. Logan Clendening, a Kansas City doctor whom he had met at the time of Gregory's birth. Clendening conducted a syndicated medical column, and his daily mailbag was crammed with instances of human woe. He sent Ernest a sheaf of six letters from his correspondents, including one from a woman in Harrisburg, Pennsylvania, whose husband had contracted syphilis while serving with the United States Marines in Shanghai. She had asked the doctor whether or not it would ever again be safe for her to cohabit with her husband. Ernest edited the letter slightly, changing the date and the place-name, and adding a short introduction and conclusion. The result was "One Reader Writes"— probably the easiest short story he had ever devised. He drew on his remembrances of Kansas City in 1917 for the background of another story, an ironic Christmas tale called "God Rest You Merry, Gentlemen." It consisted in a conversation between two young ambulance surgeons about the case of a boy who had tried to persuade one of the doctors to castrate him and then mutilated himself with a razor in order to get rid of an "awful lust" which he took to be "a sin against purity." Once again, though less blatantly, Ernest had drawn on one of Dr. Clendening's letters, this time from a youth in West Englewood, New Jersey, who had spent many years worrying about the problem of sexual desire.

Ernest relaxed from his labors with fishing expeditions, including two to the Dry Tortugas in February and March. His great new fishing experiment began in April, when he crossed to Havana with Joe Russell, the owner of Sloppy Joe's Bar, for a maritime holiday. It was planned to last for two weeks but ended by running for more than two months. Russell, whose local nickname was Josie Grunts, owned a fast 32-foot cabin cruiser, the *Anita,* in which he had made more than one hundred fifty rumrunning trips from Cuba to the American mainland. He chose to count this one as a fishing vacation, and charged Ernest only $10 a day. Another two dollars a day paid for Ernest's room at the Ambos Mundos Hotel, with an extra half dollar when Pauline came over, as she did twice in May for a week at a time. He found the hotel room an ideal place for work. Between cruises, he read the proof sheets of *Death in the Afternoon* and deleted the equivalent of 4½ galleys of graybeard philosophizing, as Dos Passos had advised. When Pauline was there, they saw a good deal of Jane Mason, the friend of Don Stewart's whom they had met on the *Île de France* in the fall of 1931. Jane and her husband Grant lived in some style at Jaimanitas, just west of Havana. Jane was present for several days' fishing aboard the *Anita* early in May, and one entry in the log, not in Ernest's hand, read simply, "Ernest loves Jane."

But the supreme revelation of the Cuban trip was Ernest's discovery of the sport of marlin fishing. By the end of May he had caught nineteen with rod and reel. His admiration for these great fish knew no bounds. They were "fast as light," and "strong as bucks," with mouths like iron. They jumped higher and more often than tarpon, and weighed anywhere from 70 to 1,200 pounds. Ernest said jubilantly that fishing for marlin was completely and utterly satisfying as a sport, a living, a spectacle, and a form of exercise. His chief consultant on the habits of gamefish was a Cuban commercial fisherman named Carlos Gutiérrez. Carlos had begun going to sea with his father in 1884, when he was only six. Several times in the past fifteen years he had boated more marlin than any of the other commercial fishermen who worked out of Casablanca across the harbor of Havana, using a handline with baits cunningly lashed at various levels.

During his Cuban holiday Ernest completed "A Way You'll Never Be," the third of his Nick Adams stories of Italy in 1918, and a kind of nightmare sequel to "Now I Lay Me." He later explained his enigmatic title by saying that the heat of Havana had reminded him of the way it was on the lower Piave in the summer of 1918. At the same time, said he, he was watching a hell of a nice girl going crazy from day to day. He gave his story its title in order to cheer her up on the grounds that the "citizen" in the story, Nick Adams, had been "much nuttier" than this girl was ever going to be. The allusion was apparently to Jane Mason, who had been obliged to enter Doctors Hospital in New York for an operation on May 13th. The reference to her "going crazy" was a typical exaggeration, even considering Ernest's implication that her condition arose from a frustrated love for himself.

He was still in Cuba early in June when he decided to put off for a year the long-talked-of trip to Africa. Uncle Gus had hinted at the desirability of a postponement, Archie MacLeish had bowed out in April, Charles Thompson was willing to wait, and Mike Strater, though greatly disappointed, had no choice but to agree. Ernest's excuses for the delay included his eyesight, which had been troublesome all the spring, and his wish not to leave the United States "while so much was going on." But his actual reason seems to have been his eager determination to spend another summer and fall fishing and hunting at the Nordquist ranch in Wyoming. One more motivating factor was that he was seething with "damned good stories" that he wanted to tell. The long healthy days off the Cuban coast had given him a great access of "juice," his pseudo-biological term for creative energy. Perkins was greatly relieved at the postponement. "I hope to thunder you do put off that African trip," he wrote. "I never liked the idea of it anyhow."

Illness might in any case have compelled him to cancel the African safari. On the eve of his return to Key West after sixty-five days at sea, he hooked a large marlin and played it for over two hours, sweating mightily, only to have it throw the hook and escape just as he had brought it to gaff. He was so disappointed that he sat panting and cursing for half an hour while a sudden squall of cold rain chilled his overheated body. His respiratory system responded as it had always done to such sudden changes of temperature. A day or two later he steered home across the straits with a temperature of 102, and went to bed in the house on Whitehead Street with what the doctor diagnosed as a touch of bronchial pneumonia.

He was still convalescent, and still angry over his illness, when he took up once more his work on the galley proofs of *Death in the Afternoon*. Now for the first time he noticed something that angered him even more. At the top of each long sheet was a line of type which read:

4 Gal 80 . . 3404 Hemingway's Death 11½–14 Scotch

As he knew perfectly well, it was only typesetter's shorthand for the full title. But his irascibility was such that he chose to make an issue of it. "DID IT SEEM VERY FUNNY TO SLUG EVERY GALLEY HEMINGWAY'S DEATH," he wired Perkins, "OR WAS THAT WHAT YOU WANTED?" Next day he wrote that he would like to break the neck of the punk who was responsible. For one who was superstitious to start with, it was a hell of a damn dirty business to stare at those two words a thousand times while reading the proof. In the latest "filthy batch" some nameless nincompoop had even written out the offending words in red and purple ink! If he died in the midst of proofreading, Perkins's goddamned typesetter would be to blame.

He had only just got out of bed when he set off on July 2 for Piggott. His companion was his sister Carol, who was returning to Michigan to keep house for her brother Leicester until she left for further study at the University of Vienna. The car was a new V-8 Ford roadster, which so delighted Ernest with its speed and performance that he drove 654 miles in a single day and had to go to bed with fatigue as soon as he reached Piggott. The drive west with Pauline was a good deal more leisurely. The roads were crowded with migrant workers on foot or in ancient, chugging vehicles. Ernest was reminded of the "wild kids" of Russia when someone told him that there were 200,000 displaced workers looking for nonexistent jobs all over the country. He found it highly instructive to drive through familiar regions where everyone was now broke who had formerly been "lousy with cash." He felt no pangs of conscience at heading west in a new car with plenty of money in his pockets. After all, as he told Guy Hickok, he had had no share in the economic boom of the 1920s. This was not strictly true, of course, but Ernest had already begun to construct a little myth about the extremity of his poverty during the early days in Paris.

In Wyoming all was gold. On the afternoon of July 12th, Ernest and Pauline settled happily into Lawrence and Olive Nordquist's Cabin Number One. Pilot and Index rose black against the sunset and Ernest was up on the morning of the 13th in plenty of time to watch the sunrise over the range across the river. He was avid to recapture the sounds and smells of early morning: clatter of dishes in the ranch kitchen, drifting fragrances of bacon and coffee and trout, sun-warmed needles under the lodgepole pines, yarrow and clover and harebells and paintbrush and lupin bright in the dewy meadows, quiet murmur of the water in the narrow irrigation ditches angling through the property, the far roar of the plunging river, the clank of horsebells in the corral, stomp and whinny of the animals. He leaned on the weathered rails of the corral while Ivan saddled Old Bess for the morning ride, watched the tightening of cinches, the adjustment of stirrups, the small fierce dramas of horse wrangling.

When he felt like working, he strolled over to the Sidley cabin on the knoll near the river, sitting at the table inside, slowly covering the writing tablet with his down-slanting longhand, crossing out lines, building tiers of afterthoughts. In midmorning, when his eyes grew tired, Olive Nordquist would sometimes see him emerge from the door, wiping his glasses, squinting at the intense blue of the cloudless sky, gazing at Index as if he were trying to memorize its spectacular configurations, inflating his lungs with the clean air, and padding softly back in his moccasins for another hour at the desk. Somewhere he had acquired a black skullcap to wear while he was writing. He told Chub Weaver that it was "to keep his brains warm" and that whenever he wore it in New York, all the Jews followed him like a brother.

"We rode hard all summer," said Ernest. He remembered the screech of the corral gate as Ivan swung it open to let the riders pass through in Indian file, the worn familiar trail up the slope among the pines and quaking aspens, the horses stepping carefully over fallen timber and pausing at the first creek crossing to suck up the water with a whistling sound. The view of the ranch from the heights was rewarding as ever, with the thin smoke plume above the kitchen chimney and the cabins half-hidden in the flecked shadows of the trees. Pauline remarked how her horse kept its nose close to the swishing tail of Ernest's big mare, using it as a natural fly-whisk. Far off on a sloping spur a herd of elk was feeding. Ernest dismounted to breathe Old Bess and watch them through his binoculars, though the hunting season was still six weeks away. Going down the back trail, the horses trotted whenever the path was clear and burst into a gallop in the home stretch across the plashy meadow. Unsaddled, their withers dark with sweat, they rolled in the welcome dust, ready for the freedom of the pasture. The maid had left a bucket of ice in the cabin. Ernest sloshed Red Lodge moonshine into the waiting tumblers. The eastern ridge was still golden in the setting sun while the ranch buildings were already gray with the first shadows of the evening.

All of Ernest's activities that summer were overcast with a special sense of urgency. A year from now he would be on the point of leaving for Africa, and he could not tell whether he would ever see Wyoming again. The state had begun to build a road from Red Lodge up over Beartooth Pass and down to Cooke City. When it was done, as he sadly believed, it would destroy the hunting forever and drive all the animals into the refuge of Yellowstone Park. He fished with extra determination throughout July, taking nearly 150 trout, and noting with displeasure that a roadbuilder's dam, made for hauling sand, had dried up one whole fork of his favorite stream above One-Mile Creek. It was only with the greatest reluctance that he interrupted his fishing on July 26th to finish reading the final batch of page proofs for *Death in the Afternoon*.

The political world beyond his happy hunting-and-fishing grounds seemed more than ever inimical. He said that he liked the yowling of the coyotes in the hills far better than the mounting clamor of the Hoover-Roosevelt campaign speeches that came from his portable radio. Most of the West, he found, was "Hoovery," while Roosevelt, reputedly weak in the Northeast, was a veritable "Jesus" in Alabama, Georgia, and Florida. Since his favorite candidate was still Eugene Debs, he felt no elation at having to choose between "The Paralytic Demagogue" and "The Syphilitic Baby." But he took his religious duties more seriously than his political, driving Pauline to Powell, a round trip of nearly four hundred miles, so that she could attend the First-Friday Mass for August. If she were ever canonized, he jocularly told her mother, this feat should be recorded in the supporting documents, particularly as the crankcase on the Ford was smashed by a protruding rock fourteen miles short of home. But there were some nonreligious compensations. He took snapshots of four bears and four bull moose along the wilderness road, and they shot two dozen sagehens, some almost the size of turkeys, for Olive Nordquist to roast in a fragrant series.

He was out with Lawrence Nordquist on a pack trip to Crazy Lakes when Gerald and Sara Murphy arrived at the ranch for a vacation with two of their children, Baoth and Honoria. They all returned to the high country for a spell of fishing, and on September 9th Ernest took Gerald up Pilot Creek to instruct him in the art of shooting a mule for bear bait. Two days later he drove to Cody to meet Charles Thompson, who had come from Florida for a month of hunting. The season was open and he was restive to begin. He gave Charles only a day to become acclimated to the high altitudes before putting him astride a horse for a week's pack trip to the head of Pilot Creek. They hunted hard from dawn to dusk on four consecutive days, often in a wind so brisk that once Pauline lost a new Stetson hat over a tall precipice, and stalked nineteen rams over the roughest terrain that Charles had ever seen. But the game was so shy that they never got closer than 600 yards, and they returned empty-handed on the 18th.

Luck ran better on the second pack trip, this time to Timber Creek, a stiff 35-mile ride from the ranch. The Murphys were gone now and Pauline was to leave on the 22nd. Ivan Wallace and Chub Weaver built a cabin to shelter the hunters from cold and snow. The day Pauline left, Ernest and Charles were killing a horse for bear bait under Ivan's direction. They were on their way back to camp when Ivan saw a magnificent old bull elk half-hidden in a patch of timber. Thompson's bullet creased its back, Ernest hit it behind the shoulders, and the elk crashed into a gully. But when they came near, he sprang up again for one final dash to freedom. This time Charles was set and ready. He blew off one hind leg at the knee and the great animal toppled and died. Two days later, not to be outdone, Ernest killed an even larger bull elk with a single running shot through the lungs at a hundred yards. After such victories the larger game disappeared, and Ernest had to content himself with trapping a coyote near the carcass of the first elk and shooting a large eagle on the wing. At night by the fire in the cabin, he was full of talk and anecdotes. One evening, gorged with elk steaks and fortified with Red Lodge whiskey, he delivered a matter-of-fact discourse on suicide to Chub Weaver, repeating what he had said to Fräulein Glaser in the Vorarlberg six years earlier: he would never hesitate to kill himself if conditions were bad enough.

Death in the Afternoon had now appeared, and Ernest rode down to the ranch on October fourth to see if any reviews had arrived. There were only two, both disappointing. He put them aside and talked to Huck Mees about the bear-bait mule on Pilot Creek. Huck reported that the mule had been eaten entirely. All the larger bones were piled up neatly with the skull on top. Three bears had feasted there, including a grizzly with tracks eleven inches long. It had dug a foxhole beside the bait for protection while dining. Huck said that he had just shot a horse named Buster at the same site. When Ernest and Ivan got back to Timber Creek, riding all the way up in an early October blizzard, Thompson and Staib displayed a black bear they had shot in Closed Creek Valley. They hunted vainly next day among the snowy mountains, and on the tenth Ernest left the others for the return ride to the ranch. On the way down he saw a large bull moose some thirty yards away in an open meadow, but was obliged to let it alone because he had no license for moose. Instead he shot half a dozen fat grouse with the Colt Woodsman, while Old Bess stood trembling and blowing hard through her nostrils. Back at the ranch, he handed the birds to Olive Nordquist, made himself a whiskey sour, and sat down by the fire to read another batch of mail. There was a note from Perkins that the book had "started off very well indeed" despite the fact that business was terrible. "The reviews are good from the publisher's standpoint," said Max, "and there is much good in them from the author's standpoint, but I know there are things in them which you will hate."

Even the adverse reviews were less important than the fact that Charles Thompson had a bear while Ernest had none. On the afternoon of October 11th he rode up Pilot Creek with Lawrence Nordquist to the place where Huck Mees had shot Buster. Although the snow around the bait was already well trampled, it was not until dusk that a large black bear emerged from a thicket and began to tear at the frozen horsemeat. Ernest crawled to a range of seventy-five yards and drilled him through the shoulder. But the shot was too high and the bear "bawled like a bull" and ran. Even in semidarkness it was easy to trail him by the fresh blood on the snow. They were only twenty feet apart when Ernest's second shot brought him down. The hide was black as Ernest's beard and thick as a rug; he weighed five hundred pounds and measured eight feet from paw to outstretched paw, a good deal larger than the one Charles had shot the week before. Ernest's competitive spirit was satisfied at last.

That day and the next, Charles Thompson rounded out the season's bag with two buck deer and a small bull elk. They spent the last three days at the ranch in resting, packing, and feasting on elk and venison like Norse warriors in an earthly Valhalla. But when they left for home on the 16th it took them three days' driving to run out of a blizzard that pelted them with snow and ice all the way across Nebraska. Ernest rigged a candle in a tin can to help defrost the windshield for a few minutes at a time. It was, as he said, "a nightmare while it lasted." Key West, the Fortunate Island in the sun, seemed all the more a good place to come back to after two thousand miles of open road.

CHAPTER 6

Forms of Combat

32. WINNER TAKE NOTHING

BUMBY was on hand when Ernest reached Key West. He was now nine years old, tall and strong for his age, fluent as a native in French. After Christmas he was going to be tutored by Evan Shipman; meantime he was free to play in this tropical boys' paradise. The yard contained four pet raccoons, a possum, eighteen goldfish, and three peacocks. Swimming and fishing were less than a mile away. When Mrs. Pfeiffer discovered that Patrick and Gregory had whooping cough, Pauline went to Piggott to help with the care of her sons. Bumby was left alone with his father for the first time since the fateful railway journey which Dr. Hemingway's suicide had interrupted.

Ernest's pleasure in the reunion was somewhat flawed by the mixed reception of *Death in the Afternoon*. One reviewer called it childish "in its small-boy wickedness of vocabulary," and morbid "in its endless preoccupation with fatality." Others observed that his celebrated clarity of style had been vitiated with occasional obscurities, while his "he-mannish" posturing was becoming a bore. H. L. Mencken praised the expository writing while holding that Hemingway's determination to prove himself a naughty fellow often led him into banality. The one review that brought a public response from Ernest was that of Robert M. Coates in *The New Yorker*. Coates thought it a bitter book, the work of a romantic who refused to embrace the idea of death as "the end and complement of life." Sometimes, said he, the bitterness sank to mere petulance, as in the gibes at Faulkner, Cocteau, Aldous Huxley, and T. S. Eliot. Ernest admitted to rebuttals of Huxley and Eliot. Cocteau was a public figure and therefore "crackable." But Ernest said that he had plenty of respect for Faulkner and wished him all luck. That did not mean that he would not joke about him. "There are no subjects I would not jest about if the jest was funny enough," said Ernest, "just as, liking wing shooting, I would shoot my own mother if she went in coveys and had a good strong flight."

In November he set off with Bumby in the Ford roadster to join Pauline and the younger boys for Thanksgiving and Christmas in Piggott. As always, he found the American countryside "good to drive through and to see." While Bumby dozed beside him, he amused himself by trying to guess where in the passing fields coveys of quail would come to feed, where they would rise, how they would fly. The fall of the year was associated in his mind with both hunting and death. He had just heard of the death of his uncle Willoughby, the medical missionary, in Shansi Province, China. The fourth anniversary of his father's suicide was less than a month away. Then as now he had been traveling alone with Bumby. The germ of a story on the theme of fathers and sons was already taking shape in his mind.

The first film to be made from one of his books was now on the point of being released. It was Paramount's production of *A Farewell to Arms,* starring Helen Hayes, Gary Cooper, and Adolphe Menjou. Ernest thought it an abomination. He was distressed by the happy ending which the scriptwriters had devised as well as the attempts of the press agents to publicize his wartime heroism and his boxing ability. Soon after his arrival in Piggott, he sent Max Perkins a public statement in an effort to counteract the imaginative press releases which were then flooding the country.

Mr. Hemingway [he wrote], who is a writer of fiction, states that if he was in Italy during a small part of the late war it was only because a man was notoriously less liable to be killed there than in France. He drove, or attempted to drive, an ambulance and engaged in minor camp following activities and was never involved in heroic action of any sort. Any sane person knows that writers do not knock out middleweight champions, unless the writer's name happens to be Gene Tunney. While Mr. Hemingway appreciates the publicity attempt to build him into a glamorous personality like Floyd Gibbons or Tom Mix's horse Tony, he deprecates it and asks the motion picture people to leave his private life alone.

To escape the publicity, and the boredom he always felt in Piggott, Ernest took Max Perkins duck shooting shortly before Christmas. Great flights of ducks commonly descended on Arkansas to feed in the ricefields, and Ernest had accumulated 2300 shotgun shells to deal with them. He had also rented a houseboat which was anchored in the White River. Max was more excited by the scenery than the hunting, which was sparse because of a sudden cold snap. "I spent some of the coldest hours of my life doing it," he wrote afterwards. "There was just a powdering of snow on the steep banks . . . where we waited for ducks to drop to the water. It was just like the rivers in the *Harper's Weekly* Civil War pictures." The most memorable event of the trip for Max was the time they heard "a most terrific racket around a curve," followed by "a regular old-time Mississippi steamboat with two funnels, side by side, pouring out wood smoke. To Hemingway this was a commonplace, but to a Vermont Yankee it was like going back eighty or ninety years and coming into Mark Twain's world."

Back in Piggott, for reasons of privacy, and in order to give Ernest a place to work, the Hemingways had taken to sleeping in a remodeled barn "studio" behind the Pfeiffer house. They were at breakfast in the main house one wintry morning when the barn roof caught fire from an imperfectly insulated flue. The volunteer fire department quickly doused the blaze, but some of Ernest's books and typescripts were damaged by water. Otto Bruce, a young carpenter, and a young printer named Laud Payne helped repair the damage and dry out the soaked paper. On hearing of the episode, Ezra Pound wrote from Rapallo, "Waal, damn it awl, yew ole son, WHY live in a barn, and why not be there when it barns soz to tote out yr stuff?"

Ernest had lately been thinking of Pound, having been asked to contribute to a *Festschrift* arranged by Ford Madox Ford. It was a pamphlet designed to coincide with the publication of Pound's *A Draft of XXX Cantos* in January. "If one could cow the reviewers with authority," wrote Ford, "the cantos might receive decent attention." The notion of cowing reviewers appealed to Ernest, whose reply stated that

any poet born in this century or in the last ten years of the preceding century who can honestly say that he has not been influenced by or learned greatly from the work of Ezra Pound deserves to be pitied rather than rebuked. It is as if a prose writer born in that time should not have learned from or been influenced by James Joyce. . . . The best of Pound's writing—and it is in the Cantos—will last as long as there is any literature.

Shortly before the Hemingways were due to leave Piggott, Bumby came down with influenza. On learning that his temperature was 102, he turned pale, and could not seem to concentrate even when Ernest read aloud to him from Howard Pyle's *Book of Pirates*. Ernest went out quail shooting with a young Irish setter belonging to the Pfeiffers. When he came back, Bumby was still behaving strangely. His schoolmates in France had told him that no one could possibly survive with a temperature of 44. Since his own was more than twice that high, he was sure that he was going to die. He relaxed visibly when Ernest explained the difference between Fahrenheit and Centigrade. Once again, though he did not discover it for some years, Bumby had given his father an idea for a story.

All three of the boys were well enough by the first of the year to go back to Key West by train with Pauline. Ernest drove alone to Roanoke, Virginia, where he stored the car and went on to New York by rail. Tom Wolfe was in town. The two largest novelists in the House of Scribner had never met, and Perkins eagerly arranged to take them both to lunch. It was Ernest's first experience in literally looking up to a fellow writer. What struck him most, however, was Wolfe's childlike manner. As he later wrote to Perkins, geniuses of this kind were always like children, whom they resembled also in being one hell of a "responsability." Tom Wolfe, he thought, had a great talent, a very delicate fine spirit, and an obviously limited intelligence. He guessed privately that Max would have to be the brain behind most of Tom's future fiction.

A far less happy encounter during Ernest's two-week stay in New York was with a young man named John Gardner, who had fallen in love with Carol Hemingway while both were undergraduates at Rollins College in Winter Park, Florida. As nominal head of the family, Ernest fiercely assumed the responsibility of guarding Carol from all harm while she was following her studies at the University of Vienna. When Gardner appeared to ask his permission to marry Carol, Ernest not only refused, but also threatened to knock his teeth down his throat if he persisted. These histrionics merely strengthened the young man's determination. He took passage to Europe and hurried eastward to Vienna.

Between business conferences with Perkins and with his lawyer and agent, Maurice Speiser, Ernest spent parts of several days with Sidney Franklin, who was now all the more bumptious because Ernest had immortalized him in a special appendix to *Death in the Afternoon*. Ernest's anti-Semitism had begun to soften slightly under the influence of men like Sidney and Moe Speiser and the bibliographer, Captain Cohn. On the last day of his stay in New York, he went to see Cohn, who asked his permission to publish a limited edition of "God Rest You Merry, Gentlemen." Cohn was enraged at the adverse reviews of *Death in the Afternoon,* and wanted to spring to Hemingway's defense. But Ernest answered firmly that he would fight his own battles. He later declared, though not to Cohn, that he was far more interested in getting his work done, and in living his life to the hilt, than in being forcibly adopted by someone who wished to maintain the market value of his first editions.

It was at Cohn's place of business, The House of Books, that same day that Ernest first met a young Pennsylvania Dutchman named Arnold Gingrich. Gingrich was an ardent book collector who had written Ernest in December, asking him to autograph a copy of *Death in the Afternoon*. In a boastful reply, Ernest had advised Gingrich not to be "spooked" by the reviewers' criticisms of the book. Old "Papa," said he, still felt pretty good: even yet he had not reached the top of his form and he still expected to confound the critics with many more books and stories. Gingrich was currently editing a trade journal called *Apparel Arts,* with headquarters in Chicago. He thought Ernest "a swell guy," and was disappointed when he cut the interview short and rushed away to catch his train to Virginia.

From Roanoke he drove to Jacksonville, where Pauline met him for the rest of the journey to Key West. Evan Shipman the poet was now on hand to tutor Bumby. Insouciant and underfed as ever, full of nascent lyrics, talking incessantly of harness racing in his flat New England accent, Evan had not changed at all from the old days in Paris. In spite of his periodic difficulties in the regulation of his own life, he tried his hand at straightening out Ernest's bulging letter files, which included everything from old and insect-chewed fan mail to superannuated laundry bills and even an elk's tooth from Wyoming. Nothing, however, was to be thrown away. Ernest evidently supposed that he might sometime get around to answering dozens of letters from complete strangers which had lain in dusty bundles for months and often years.

The return to Key West once more released Ernest's literary energy. *Scribner's Magazine* had now accepted three more stories for publication in the spring: "A Clean, Well-Lighted Place," "Homage to Switzerland," and "Give Us a Prescription, Doctor." The last of these, later renamed "The Gambler, The Nun, and the Radio," drew directly on Ernest's experience in the Billings hospital while his broken arm was mending. "Homage to Switzerland" went back in time to Ernest's visit to Switzerland in 1927, just before his divorce from Hadley. It was a humorous and ironic three-part story about Mr. Wheeler, Mr. Johnson, and Mr. Harris in Montreux, Vevey, and Territet. Anyone acquainted with Ernest's marital history could easily recognize that all three men were himself, attempting to recover from the trauma of separation from his first wife, Hadley. "A Clean, Well-Lighted Place" was autobiographical only in the sense that it offered a brief look into the underside of Ernest's spiritual world, the nightmare of nothingness by which he was still occasionally haunted. All three were what Ernest called "safe" stories—safe, that is, for a family magazine like *Scribner's*. Its new editor, Alfred Dashiell, whom Ernest never tired of criticizing, had felt obliged to reject another called "The Light of the World," an ultra-tough story about a group of whores at a railroad station in a small town in northern Michigan. Dashiell believed, not without reason, that it was far too outspoken for the clientele his magazine served. Little did Dashiell know, said Ernest, how much concealed dynamite lay in the stories already accepted.

With three good stories in the works, Ernest's aggressive instincts came again to the fore, making him more than ever critical of nonproducers like Scott Fitzgerald. Scott's wife Zelda had done a little novel called *Save Me the Waltz,* which Ernest found unreadable. As for Scott, he felt that only two events could possibly redeem him: either Zelda must die or Scott must develop a stomach disorder severe enough to make him stop drinking. Why did he refuse to grow up? Why was he drunk whenever Ernest saw him? His "damned bloody romanticism" and his "cheap Irish love of defeat" were becoming tiresome. Ernest, on the other hand, said that he had a damned good time all the time. When he was able to work, he never felt low. He took great pleasure in living for 340 days out of every 365. He was always conscious, he said, of living not one life but two. One was that of a writer who got his reward after his death, and to hell with what he got now. The other was that of a man who got his everything now, and to hell with what came to him after death. Fame was anyway a strange phenomenon. A man might become immortal with ten lines of poetry or a hundred pages of prose. Or not, no matter how much he wrote, if he never had what it took. In his lifetime, a writer was judged by the sum total and average of his work. After he died, only the best mattered. He was convinced that human beings were probably "intended" to suffer. But his experience had shown him that a man could get used to anything as long as he refused to worry about bad luck before it happened.

He was planning another Cuban fishing trip for April. He wanted not only the sport but also the chance to gather material for a nonfiction book about the age-old mysteries of the Gulf Stream. Meantime he had begun work on a long short story, using the locales of Key West, Havana, and the waters that lay between. His hero, named for the famous pirate Henry Morgan, was modeled in part on his observations of Joe Russell, the rumrunning fisherman whose boat he had been renting for the Cuban fishing trips. By February 23rd, he was able to report to Perkins that he had finished three chapters and could see his way through to the end.

In March Ernest made another trip to New York, drawn by the prospect of a great deal of money. The film director Lewis Milestone was eager to make a documentary on Hemingway's Spain. It would follow up in celluloid the nostalgic closing chapter of *Death in the Afternoon,* and Milestone was hoping to record most of the footage on location in Spain in the coming summer. Sequences would be made in all the Spanish provinces, using nonprofessional actors. Ernest would serve as adviser and scout. On another day of his visit he went over to see the lion tamer, Clyde Beatty, in his dressing room at Madison Square Garden. Ernest gave him an autographed copy of *Death in the Afternoon,* and stayed to watch some of the rehearsal sessions. He was fascinated with Beatty's speed and agility, his masterly footwork, and his habit of working close to the animals. He remarked that Beatty's kitchen chair was as effective a means of control as a matador's cape in the bullring. The exact way in which the circus lions ran, crouched, and sprang was of special interest to him, since he expected to be hunting their wild counterparts in Africa before the end of the year.

His pride was twice irritated in the following weeks. On St. Patrick's Day, John Gardner cabled from Vienna that he would be married to Ernest's sister Carol in Kitzbühel before another week was out. Ernest sourly accepted the news of what he afterwards disgustedly called "the Miss Beefy business." He wrote Pauline's mother that the matter was finished. Never again would he mention the bride, the groom, or the marriage. A second blow came from Gertrude Stein, whose memoirs, openly disguised as *The Autobiography of Alice B. Toklas,* were about to be serialized in the *Atlantic.* Although her chapter dealing with Hemingway would not appear until summer, he knew already that she had changed radically since the days in Paris when she and Alice had stood up as godmothers for Bumby. But he was hardly prepared for some of her more outrageous statements. One of them said that she and Sherwood Anderson had virtually created Hemingway, and "they were both a little proud and a little ashamed of the work of their minds." Another held that he had picked up a good deal of information about the art of writing from serving as proofreader for *The Making of Americans* in 1924. Easily the worst of her assertions, from Ernest's point of view, was that he was "yellow," like some of the flatboat men in Mark Twain's account of old days on the Mississippi.

Ernest seethed with private anger. He told his closest associates that Gertrude had long since dropped him in favor of people whom he scornfully called her "feathered friends." She had suddenly become damned patriotic over sex about the time she reached her climacteric. The phenomenon had occurred in three stages. First, she had decided that nobody was any good who was not queer. Next she held that all queer people must be talented. Finally she managed to convince herself that anyone who was any good must be queer. Ernest remarked acidly that when he reached the point at which he could write nothing else, he would come out with some memoirs of his own. They would not try to prove anything, but they would be both accurate and funny.

Arnold Gingrich had lately written Ernest about a new men's magazine, as yet unnamed, which would begin publication in the fall. He wanted Ernest as a contributor, and would pay $250 apiece for short, nonfiction articles on hunting and fishing. The magazine would attempt to do for American men what *Vogue* was doing for American women. Gingrich said that Ernest need not worry about its quality. It was not going to be a sissy journal. It would have "ample hair on its chest and adequate cojones." When Ernest promised to do some articles, Gingrich sent him a stylish blue shirt and a leather jerkin, culled from the clothing made available to the editor of *Apparel Arts* by various advertisers. Ernest sent along his measurements—collar 17½, shoes 11–D, jackets 44–46, pants 34 by 34—and repaid Gingrich with a few items of personal history. One was that he liked Joyce as friend and writer, and had picked up a good deal of technical information from reading his work. He had gathered some other technical tips in conversations with Gertrude Stein and Ezra Pound. He had once been influenced by Sherwood Anderson, though not for long. Without having met D. H. Lawrence, he admitted to having learned from his writing a few tricks about describing landscape. In his youth he had gone through a period of imitating Ring Lardner. This, said he, had taught him nothing, largely because Lardner was an ignorant man. All he really had was a certain amount of experience of the world, along with a good false ear for illiterate speech.

When the moon filled in April, Ernest made the crossing to Cuba. He had chartered Joe Russell's *Anita* for another two-month stay, and secured the services of Carlos Gutiérrez as sea guide and fishing adviser. During the good weather of April and May, he averaged approximately a marlin a day. His pleasure was somewhat diminished by the fact that none of his special cronies was on hand to share the fun. Dos Passos, indeed, was in The Johns Hopkins Hospital in Baltimore with a fresh attack of rheumatic fever. When the news reached Ernest, he consulted a copy of *Black's Medical Dictionary,* which said that victims of this disease often developed temperatures of 106 and burning agony in all the afflicted joints. This would never do. He sold some of the common stock that Uncle Gus Pfeiffer had given him for the coming safari and sent Dos a check for $1,000. By the end of May, when Dos and Katy sailed to France to stay with the Murphys at Cap d'Antibes, Ernest had boated thirty-four marlin, including one that had jumped an incredible thirty-seven times. He was learning a lot, as he told Mike Strater, and some of it was true. He still stood in awe before the mysteries of the Gulf Stream and the habits of the wild life that lived in, on, or above the tropical seas.

By June, after two months in Cuba, he fixed at last upon a title for his new book of short stories. *Winner Take Nothing* contained just the hint of cynical acceptance of the human situation which he felt the stories embodied and illustrated. It was drawn, ostensibly, from an old book about gaming, though in fact Ernest had composed the passage in what he took to be the true seventeenth-century manner. "Unlike all other forms of lutte or combat," he wrote, "the conditions are that the winner shall take nothing; neither his ease, nor his pleasure, nor any notions of glory, nor, if he win far enough, shall there be any reward within himself." Finding the new title delighted him. The best that he had been able to do before was *After the Storm, and Other Stories.* The new one proved, as he told Perkins, that "old Papa" could be counted on to come through. It was the same as fishing. At the end of the first hour, the fish might be killing Hemingway. At the end of two hours, Hemingway killed the fish.

There were now fourteen stories. Ernest wanted to lead off with "The Light of the World," his tough yarn about a Michigan whore in love with a prize-fighter. Perkins dissuaded him from giving it such prominence. To put it first would play into the hands of his critics, who would again accuse him of using a "small-boy wickedness of vocabulary" simply for its shock effect. Perkins himself admired "A Clean, Well-Lighted Place" and suggested that "After the Storm," Bra Saunders's tale of the sunken liner, might prove to be the most popular story in the whole collection. Ernest capitulated, despite his continuing fondness for the great whore named Alice and his belief that what he had written was far better than *"La Maison Tellier"* of Maupassant. The final story, however, must certainly be "Fathers and Sons," based on his trip to Piggott with Bumby the preceding November and making fictional use, for the first time in Ernest's career, of his father's suicide. He was prepared to admit that *Winner Take Nothing* included things and people that the public might not care about. But he was convinced of the lasting worth of the collection. It represented another fourteen chapters in his declared program to make a picture of the whole world, or at least as much of it as he had personally seen.

Early in June a belated review of *Death in the Afternoon* appeared in the *New Republic.* The author was Ernest's old friend Max Eastman, and the title of the piece was "Bull in the Afternoon." Eastman half-humorously deplored the "unconscionable quantity of bull" which Hemingway had "poured and plastered" over his accounts of Spanish bullfighting. Why, he asked, did such a ferocious realist wrap himself in clouds of "juvenile romanticism" whenever he entered Spain? The reasons were not far to seek. Everyone knew, of course, that Hemingway lacked the "serene confidence" that he was "a full-sized man." Such doubts were not uncommon among those "delicately organized babies" called artists. It was characteristic of Hemingway to have overcome his own qualms by constantly reiterated assertions of his "red-blooded masculinity" and by developing "a literary style . . . of wearing false hair on the chest."

Eastman's remarks might have passed unnoticed but for Archie MacLeish. He took instant umbrage at what he thought to be a slur on Hemingway's sexual potency, addressed a letter of protest to Bruce Bliven as editor of the *New Republic,* and sent Ernest a copy of the article along with a carbon of his letter. Bliven was flabbergasted. So, apparently, was Eastman. They assured both Hemingway and MacLeish that no such implication had been intended. But Ernest was neither convinced nor mollified. Ignoring MacLeish's advice, he sent off an open letter in his best (or worst) humorous-sinister manner:

Sirs:

Would it not be possible for you to have Mr. Max Eastman elaborate his nostalgic speculations on my sexual incapacity? Here [in Havana] it would be read (aloud) with much enjoyment. Our amusements are simple and I would be glad to furnish illustrations to brighten Mr. Eastman's prose if you consider this advisable. Mr. Alexander Woollcott and the middle aged Mr. Eastman having both published hopeful doubts as to my potency is it too much to expect that we might hear soon from Mr. Stark Young?

The open letter, such as it was, did little to reduce Ernest's head of steam. If Eastman ever published that libel in book form, said Ernest to Perkins, it would cost his publisher plenty and put Eastman into jail. Swine like Eastman weren't worth writing for. Every phase of the reviewing racket was as disgusting as vomit. He accused Eastman of being a groper in sex and a traitor in politics. What he and his friends couldn't abide was the fact that Ernest was an indubitable man, that he could "beat the shit out of any of them," and finally, that he could write. That last was the hardest fact for them to swallow. But "old Papa" would make them like it—and so on for several pages more. Perkins tried to cool the lava flow with a whiff of fresh air. Eastman's article didn't really amount to anything at all, and would certainly not do Ernest any harm. "The reality," wrote Max, "is in the quality of what you write." Ernest's Vesuvian rumblings continued. A month later he reported that Eastman had written him a "kiss-ass letter" of apology and denial. But it would not serve to get him "out of the woods." Some time in the future Ernest would exact his vengeance.

It had been a rough season. Gertrude Stein, Max Eastman, and various reviewers of *Death in the Afternoon* had accused him of small-boy naughtiness, verbal license, stylistic lapses, banality, "he-mannish" posturing, anti-intellectualism, petulant gibes at fellow writers, sterility, cowardice, and (so he thought) sexual impotence. In his present mood, "Winner Take Nothing" might well serve as an epigraph, and perhaps even an epitaph, for the whole past year of his life, if not the whole first ten years of his writing career.

33. REVOLUTIONS

HEMINGWAY'S best antidote to the animadversions of the reviewers was big-game fishing. On the sea, at least, a man knew what he was up against. By the third week in July, he had spent a hundred days on the Gulf Stream. In that time he had killed upwards of fifty marlin and Joe Russell's boat *Anita* had been rammed so often by aggressive swordfish that it was beginning to leak.

Ernest loved it all, from morning to night. Many days that summer he was awakened by the sun, which rose over Casablanca peninsula and shone in through the window of his room at the Ambos Mundos. It was his custom to roll out of bed, take a quick shower, pull on khaki pants and a shirt, step into a dry pair of moccasins, pick up the morning papers at the hotel desk, and drop into the corner café for breakfast. On fishing days this meal was always slim—a piece of Cuban bread, a glass of vichy water and another of cold milk. He had hooked too many fish on a full stomach under that heavy sun to take any further chances.

He usually made up for his asceticism at lunch. Joe Russell and Carlos Gutiérrez saw to it that the *Anita's* icebox was well stocked with food and Hatuey beer, as well as fresh cerro mackerel and small kingfish for use as bait. Lunch commonly consisted of sandwiches and alligator pears which they seasoned with pepper and salt and freshly squeezed lime juice. On days when the fish were not running, they anchored off some deserted beach, went ashore for a swim, and paused long enough to cook a hot lunch.

Pulling away from San Francisco wharf in the early morning was always a time of magic. Over the side Ernest could watch the silver tarpon feeding and rolling in the slip. Each day there were dozens of small boats bottom fishing for red snapper or jigging for mackerel. Farther out were the commercial marlin fishermen, drifting for the fish that were traveling deep, with heavy handlines baited to tempt them at forty to seventy fathoms. When the northeast trades were blowing, the marlin surfaced and cruised with the wind, their scythelike tails knifing through the swells. Except for the erect curve of their tails, they looked like fast-cruising logs in the water. But on a strike their whole appearance miraculously changed. The dorsal fin came up, the wide blue pectorals spread out, and suddenly the marlin was transformed into some great undersea bird moving in for the attack.

Off Morro Castle on July 6th Ernest hooked a 750-pounder. The fight lasted an hour and a half and covered eight miles of ocean. Kneeling in the stern while Carlos alternately doused him with buckets of sea water or held him round the waist to keep him from being yanked overboard, he worked the marlin into a slow circling movement at the twenty-fathom level, gaining a yard or two of line in the course of each circuit. He had just got his second wind when the rod broke with a splintering crack and the fish was lost. Dripping with sweat and sea water, Ernest swore for a full half-hour. But his pride soon came bounding back. He had stayed with that fish long after a lesser sportsman would have cut the line and given up. "Poor old Hem, the fragile one," he crowed, thumbing his nose at Gertrude Stein, Max Eastman, and all the others who had called his masculinity in question.

Back in Key West two weeks later, he composed "A Cuban Letter" while the fishing was still fresh in his memory. It was the first of his articles for Gingrich's new men's magazine, which was going to be called *Esquire*. Ernest thought the name far too snobbish for a publication that was being launched in the bottom of the Depression. But he swallowed his reservations, sent off the article and some snapshots, and pocketed his $250 check. He was getting back to journalism for the first time in ten years. Gingrich had given him a free hand to say what he liked. It was a good opportunity to explain himself to a segment of the population who might share his love for the life of action. He called Gingrich's attention to the fact that his own sportswriting was far more practical than that of Zane Grey. All Grey wanted was that people should marvel at his skill. Ernest was ready with a thousand hints that would teach his readers how to fish or shoot or watch a bullfight or a revolution.

The first leg of the trip to Africa was now only two weeks off. Charles Thompson was the sole survivor of the original party of huntsmen. He was going to work all summer in Key West and join Ernest in Paris in the fall. MacLeish and Strater had both declined, partly because neither of them relished the prospect of spending two months on safari with a friend so competitive that he would make a death-struggle contest of each day's hunting. Ernest had long since booked passage aboard the *Reina de la Pacífica,* leaving Havana on August 7th. He would disembark at Santander to spend two months among the bullrings while Pauline and Jinny went on to deliver Bumby to his mother in Paris.

For the first time in six years Ernest was free of his feeling of responsibility for Hadley. Early in July she had been married to Paul Scott Mowrer in London. Mowrer, who had recently been divorced from his first wife, was European correspondent for the *Chicago Daily News,* and was on the point of returning to Chicago to take over the editorship of the paper. Jane Mason had also retired from Ernest's life, at least temporarily. Two accidents that summer had hurt her so severely that she was in bed in a cast at Doctors Hospital in New York. Jane was a damned beautiful woman, as Ernest told Max Perkins, and it was no fun to break one's back at the age of twenty-four.

When the Hemingways reached Havana on August 4th, the leftist revolution against the Cuban dictator, Gerardo Machado, was rapidly approaching its climax. During the spring and early summer, Ernest's fishing activities had kept him clear of the streetfighting, but Cuba was now in the grip of a general strike which had paralyzed most of the major cities. The Hemingways were safe enough at the Ambos Mundos, though Pauline and Jinny were reportedly fired on when they ventured into the streets. Ernest's sympathies lay with the Cuban people. He said privately that he hoped to Christ they would get rid of the "lousy tyrant" Machado. His ship was already under way on the 7th when crowds prematurely cheered news of Machado's resignation only to be mowed down in the streets by squads of the dictator's brutal *porristas.* On the afternoon of August 12th, the ship's radio brought news of the deposition and flight of Machado. Dr. Carlos Manuel de Céspedes, idealist and patriot, was the new provisional president of Cuba.

Ernest was less than happy over what had happened to the revolution in Spain during his absence. The peasants were as poverty-stricken as ever, but a huge new bureaucracy was spending the people's money like water. Ernest's private view was that all the idealists then in power were groping in the pie for ever-smaller plums. When plums and piecrust both were gone, a further revolution was in prospect. The first three years of the Spanish Republic had wavered uncertainly to a close. In spite of some bloodshed and a few proletarian outbursts, a strong conservative reaction was already setting in.

But his chief interests, as always, were extrapolitical. He went hunting wild boars in Estremadura with his revolutionary artist-friend, Luis Quintanilla. Around Madrid he noted with regret that the grimy old Café Tornos had been pulled down to make way for a new office building, and that a new place called the Aquarium disappointingly resembled "the last phase of Montparnasse." A modern bathing pavilion had been established beside the Manzanares out along the Pardo road where Ernest had formerly gone with Sidney Franklin and Bumby to swim and cook paellas over open fires. There was now "real sand, a big lagoon, and very cold and remarkably clean water." Nonswimming bathers watched with evident awe as Ernest kicked and snorted his way across the river and back. Among the Madrileños he noted that an athletic revolution was taking place. The new passion for outdoor exercise was making the girls both taller and thinner. It struck Ernest as a marked improvement. At the same time, bullfighting seemed to him to have fallen on evil days. Franklin was out of the running, faced with an intestinal operation to remedy the defects caused by a three-year-old rectal *cornada.* Among the new matadors, the "annual Messiah" was Felix Colomo, who had fought sensationally and been gored twice. Ernest was not much impressed.

Between trips to the bullring, Ernest read the final installment of Gertrude Stein's memoir, which he called a "damned pitiful book," and James Thurber's *My Life and Hard Times,* which he thought wonderful. He sent Thurber a jocular letter which stated that he was a far better autobiographer than Henry

Adams. "Even in the days when Thurber was writing under the name of Alice
B. Toklas," said Ernest, "we knew he had it in him if he could get it out."
Thurber was so happy with this observation that it was printed on the dust
jacket of his book. Ernest returned to his fast-moving action story of Harry
Morgan, which opened with an account of a morning streetfight between Cuban
revolutionaries and the henchmen of Machado. Except for the article on
marlin fishing for *Esquire,* it was his first literary use of Cuban materials.
Jinny Pfeiffer was so much convinced by its verisimilitude that she couldn't
believe it had not really happened. Since this effect was precisely what Ernest
had tried for, he was immensely flattered by the judgment of his sister-in-law.

When he reached Paris in the late fall, the city was as beautiful as ever.
But he had already begun to speak of it in the past tense. "A fine place to be
quite young in," he wrote. "A necessary part of a man's education." Montparnasse seemed all the gloomier because of the "perfectly calm way" in which
everyone accepted and took for granted the coming of another war. When it
came, said Ernest, the United States must keep clear. Paris had been the country of his youth. "But me," he wrote, "I now love something else. And if I
fight, I fight for something else." He meant his own country, from the remotest
tip of Florida to the highest peaks of Wyoming. He might even be prepared
to fight for his adopted country, Spain, though not for France, at least not
now. Ezra Pound had been lecturing on economics in Milan during the spring,
lauding the efficiency of Mussolini. Ernest was as bitter against Fascist Italy
as ever, though he had recently decided that Hitler was the one to hate. Von
Clausewitz had observed that war was the health of the state. Anyone with
Hitler's conception of the state, said Ernest prophetically, must use war to
keep his concept alive.

His autumnal gloom was deepened by a new outbreak of hostility among
the New York reviewers, whose reception of *Winner Take Nothing* carried
on where they had left off with *Death in the Afternoon.* "Wine of Wyoming"
and "After the Storm" were generally admired. But the new collection was
otherwise held to be the poorest and least interesting that he had yet placed
on view. T. S. Matthews recommended "A Day's Wait" to all enthusiasts of
Booth Tarkington's *Penrod and Sam.* But he chose to deplore Hemingway's
other subjects as "the kind of abnormalities that fascinate adolescence." Max
Perkins gingerly sent along a batch of reviews with the comment that most
of them were unsatisfactory and many "absolutely enraging." The rawness
of Ernest's wounds was somewhat palliated by a brisk sale that had disposed of
11,000 copies by mid-November.

Ernest chose to respond privately to Clifton Fadiman's review, which
had appeared in *The New Yorker* as "A Letter to Mr. Hemingway." It was
not enough, said Fadiman, that these stories were as honest and uncompro-
mising as ever. Ernest had developed his stories about sport and sudden
death to the saturation point. Why did he not now go on to something else?
Ernest's long reply mixed scorn and pride. He boasted that he had bred good

kids, enjoyed every woman he had ever wanted, been wounded and decorated "many times," and seen everything he genuinely believed in royally obscenitied to hell. With three collections of short stories, two novels, the "comic book" on Sherwood Anderson, and the treatise on the bullfight to his credit in the past nine years, he could not take seriously those who felt that "fragile old Papa" was slipping. He was resolved to "stick around" until his time came, writing so well and steadily that he would end by ruining each and all of the reviewers. Every two years he would break one "lousy critic's jaw," starting with Eastman and drawing his other victims by lot. His determination, he told Fadiman, was to write only once on a given topic, and to collect three more volumes of short stories on subjects that no one else had handled. He was also planning a very long study of the Gulf Stream and its migratory fish, using materials picked up during 185 days at sea in the past two years. His rule had always been simple: to study what interested him and to have a damned good time doing it.

His first public rejoinder to Gertrude Stein came in the form of a preface to an autobiography by Jimmy Charters, an engaging young Cockney bartender who had worked in Paris throughout the 1920s. Ernest based his remarks on the contrast between *saloons* like the Dingo and *salons* conducted by legendary women like Miss Stein. Jimmy Charters had "served more and better drinks than any legendary woman ever did in her salon." Even though Montparnasse had now become a dismal place, Jimmy had always managed to make it seem cheerful when he stood behind any of its bars.

The time of departure to Africa was now drawing close. Charles Thompson reached Paris and was given a tour of Ernest's ancient haunts. Solita Solano, a friend of Janet Flanner's, agreed to type out Ernest's Harry Morgan story and send it off to *Cosmopolitan*. Ernest went shooting in the Sologne with Thompson and Ben Gallagher, returning with a brace of pheasants and a haunch of venison. Next night, their last in Paris, the Hemingways invited the James Joyces to dinner. Joyce said that he feared his writing was "too suburban and that maybe he should get around a bit and see the world." His wife Nora agreed. "Jim," said she, "could do with a spot of that lion-hunting." But Joyce had no interest in lions. All that evening he kept quoting a beautiful passage about the survival of wildflowers down through the ages. It was the work of the nineteenth-century historian Edgar Quinet. Joyce had long since memorized it and even used it in his current work-in-progress, *Finnegans Wake*. The final phrase was the one that stuck in Ernest's mind: "fraîches et riantes comme aux jours des batailles." It might have stood as a description of the state of mind in which he was setting out for Africa.

34. HIGHLANDS OF AFRICA

AT high noon on November 22nd, the SS *General Metzinger* weighed anchor in Marseilles harbor and set her course for Port Said. All the way down the

Mediterranean, the weather held cold and rainy. As they approached the low Egyptian coast, the days turned fair and hot. At Port Said they went ashore for dinner, making a circuit of the native quarter and the public markets under the guidance of a dragoman. On the way through the Suez Canal, Ernest leaned on the rail for hours, gazing at the sandhills and watching the shore traffic. Once a soldier appeared on camelback, trotting his beast along the canal path, racing the ship. By December 2nd they had reached the southern end of the Red Sea and were about to enter the Gulf of Aden and the Indian Ocean. Ernest and Charles Thompson sat on deck playing checkers, scornful of the French crewmen who had lowered canvas storm curtains against the lethal effects of the tropical sun.

When they landed at Mombasa on December 8th, the heavy humidity of the coastal plain closed in like a Turkish bath. Arab dhows lined the waterfront below Fort Jesus, built by the Portuguese a century after Columbus discovered America. The narrow streets of the old island city reeked with the layered patina of four hundred years. On the mainland was the clean modern community of broad avenues and shade trees, where they spent the first weekend as guests of a young British couple, Charles and Katharine Fannin. Ernest's spirits rose on the 300-mile trip to Nairobi as the train climbed slowly through the dry bush country of the *nyika* and up to a high rolling region of hills and plains.

Nairobi sprawled in a saucerlike depression among surrounding hills— "a motley place," Karen Blixen called it, "with some fine new stone buildings, and whole quarters of old corrugated iron shops, offices, and bungalows, laid out with long rows of eucalyptus trees." At the New Stanley Hotel, they learned that Philip Percival would be free to serve as their white hunter within a few days. Meantime they were welcome to go down to his farm at Potha Hill in Machakos, twenty miles to the southeast among the Mua Hills. The delay would not be serious. They could begin hunting at once on the Kapiti Plains.

Ernest took at once to both the Percivals, but especially to the famous hunter, a rugged man of middle height with graying hair and rubicund face. His manners were courteous, his speech laconic, and his store of hunting stories as copious as John Staib's or Ivan Wallace's. Ernest immediately associated him in his mind with the Irish soldier Dorman-Smith. The chief difference was that Ernest learned something new from Percival each day, whereas with Chink it had been a matter of discovering the world together for years before their paths had finally diverged. Something in Ernest's wide smile and breadth of shoulder reminded Percival of Colonel Roosevelt as he had looked more than twenty years before. Although he saw at once that Ernest's eyesight was poor and that he was obliged to wear glasses while shooting, he found him acutely observant and quick to learn, with a memory that seemed to retain everything he saw or was told.

After more than two weeks at sea level, Ernest had difficulty in adjusting to the high altitude. Rising each morning at five and hunting all day on the Kapiti Plains, he was "dead pooped" by nightfall. They shot gazelles for meat, kongoni and impala for the heads, and enough guinea fowl to feed a regiment. Ernest's appetite and his admiration for the land were both enormous. He said repeatedly that none of the books he had read gave "any idea of the beauty of the country or the still remaining quantity of game." Even Montana and Wyoming paled by comparison. In all the thirty-four years of his life he had never known such a place as Africa.

The cavalcade for the Tanganyika trip was luxurious without being elaborate: a pair of lorries for the tents and other camping gear, and for the passengers a specially built, high-clearance vehicle, doorless and seating six, including the two gunbearers in the rear. Besides Philip and Charles, Pauline and Ernest, the only other white member of the group was a taciturn young man named Ben Fourie who served (in Philip's phrase) as "mechanic-cum-assistant-hunter." The Kikuyu driver, Kamau, was "a quiet man of about thirty-five" who managed to wear his patched and ragged hand-me-downs with an air of great elegance and dignity. The Hemingways' gunbearer was named M'Cola, which he himself pronounced M'Cora, a slender man past fifty with a "bald black skull" and "thin Chinese hairs at the corners of his mouth." His invariable costume consisted of shorts, a fuzzy woolen cap, an old U.S. Army tunic, and sandals cut from automobile tires. He had spent years in Philip's employ, and thought of himself as on loan to the newcomers. "I meant nothing to him," said Ernest. "He did not like me or dislike me." His manner towards Charles Thompson was "politely contemptuous." The one he really liked was Pauline, whose stature was comparable to his own, and whom he regularly defended as if the others "were simply a lot of people who interfered and kept Mama from shooting things."

On the morning of December 20th they set out for the day's run of nearly 200 miles due south from Nairobi on the Cape-to-Cairo Road. Against the morning sky to the west lay the Ngong Hills, where Karen Blixen had lived until she sold her coffee plantation and returned to Denmark to begin her career as a writer. They spent the night at the Athenaeum Hotel in the pleasant town of Arusha, with Kibo Peak of Mount Kilimanjaro like a stationary cloud on the northeast horizon. Next day they set up their first safari camp beside a clear stream at M'Utu Umbu within striking distance of Ngorongoro Crater. But they did not linger. Ahead lay the vast game preserve of the Serengeti Plain, where grazing animals numbered in the millions and where the lions who lived upon them raised their proud heads from every rocky eminence and almost every patch of shade.

For the first ten days the hunting went well. They took excellent heads of eland and roan antelope, Grant and Robertsi gazelle, bushbuck, waterbuck, and two fine leopards. But the new year had scarcely begun when Ernest felt the effects of amoebic dysentery. He could not tell whether to blame the dinner he had eaten at Port Said or the execrable food aboard the *General*

Metzinger. Refusing to surrender and still believing that he could last it out, he went hunting by car or truck on every day but two. But his whole view of the hunting through the first two weeks of January was unmistakably discolored by the physiological and psychological inroads of this most noisome of diseases, which made every victory a disappointment and converted every minor failure into a catastrophe. Nothing fitted his mood better than the slaughter of hyenas. He and M'Cola were agreed at least in this, that hyenas were "a dirty joke." So was the dysentery. After all his dreams of hunting in Africa, he could not avoid a recurrent sense of disenchantment with this sunbaked plain where the foul hyenas went loping out of range, looking back over their shoulders, "mongrel-dog-smart in the face."

One disappointment was the first lion they shot. It was supposed to be Pauline's. They came on it near sundown one day in early January, looking "yellow and heavy-headed and enormous" against the backdrop of a spindly tree. Pauline stepped from the car with Philip as second gun behind her. Ernest and Charles took up positions on the left and right flanks. At a word from Percival she knelt and aimed the little Mannlicher. There was an explosion and the lion was up and off to the left in a "strange, heavy-shouldered, foot-swinging" run. Ernest's Springfield roared and the lion somersaulted in the pale grass of a clearing. M'Cola refused to believe that Pauline had missed. "Mama hit," he said, positively. *"Mama piga simba."* He was the one who shouted the news ahead to the boys in the camp. They lifted Pauline to their shoulders, chanting the lion-song, and at last set her down gently before her tent. To Ernest, who knew for certain that he had shot Pauline's lion, the whole episode seemed slightly immoral, like a white lie badly lied.

His own lion pleased him well enough, though this adventure also had its darker side. He was out with Philip in the car when they saw a good darkmaned male, accompanied by his lioness, under a thorn tree near the edge of the plain. At a sign from Percival, Ernest stood up to shoot. The lion had paused and was looking back, his mouth wide open, his mane ruffled by the wind. There was a crack from Ernest's rifle and the great beast slumped. The lioness turned deliberately and vanished into the donga. They moved in on the kill. Blood showed bright in the thick hair of the mane. "You got him in the neck," said Philip. "Damned good shooting." But Ernest was torn between pride and shame. He was already watching the camel flies, busy in the blood at the site of the wound. He thought with a surge of pride that this was "a damned wonderful looking animal," the body long and smooth, the muscles still twitching like small electrical impulses under the tawny surface of the skin. The shame was that even in life, as now in death, this lordly creature should have had to contend with those swarming flies.

It was both different and disappointingly the same on the day when Charles and Ernest jumped three buffalo grazing in the open at the western extremity of the plain. They deployed for action with Philip in reserve. At the sound of the rifles, the huge bulls broke into a heavy gallop. Then two were down and there was only the third, bleeding from four wounds yet still galloping steadily through the dry scrub. Philip slammed in a shot with his favorite .450 and the bull went skidding muzzle down for a full five yards in the red earth. As with the lions, Ernest had expected a charge and the chance of some minor heroics. He admired and respected the bull's perseverance and his trucklike power. "But he was slow," said Ernest afterwards, "and all the while we shot I felt that it was fixed and that we had him."

The climactic event in Ernest's battle with dysentery came in mid-January. He was leaning rather weakly against a tree, shooting sandgrouse as they came towards a waterhole in a dry riverbed west of the Serengeti. Suddenly, he said afterwards, "I became convinced that . . . I had been chosen as the one to bear our Lord Buddha when he should be born again on earth. While flattered at this, and wondering how much Buddha at that age would resemble Gertrude Stein, I found . . . it difficult to take high incoming birds, and finally compromised by reclining against the tree and only accepting cross-shots." What had felt like childbirth was actually a prolapse of the lower intestine. When he staggered into camp with his bag of sandgrouse, Philip insisted that he must return to Nairobi for treatment.

A rescue plane was summoned by wireless from Victoria Nyanza. It appeared at last, a Puss Moth two-seater biplane, looking very tiny against the vast expanse of sky and plain. They had paced off a level area near the camp. When the plane appeared, the safari boys lit smudge fires at either end of the runway. The man who jumped down and came striding towards them in a tweed jacket, cord trousers, and an experienced brown felt hat was Fatty Pearson, a brilliant bush pilot and a friend of Philip's. Fatty, who was not fat at all, said that they had better get cracking. The morning was already well advanced, it was more than two hundred air miles to Nairobi, and they would have to make a refueling stop at Arusha.

Ernest settled painfully into the cramped seat behind the pilot's. The plane bumped away towards the farthest smudge fire, rising at last and circling the campsite. Everyone on the ground was waving. The low hills seemed to flatten out, the game trails took on the appearance of lines on a map, and the zebra and wildebeest looked to be climbing as they ran "in long fingers" across the yellow-gray plain, scattering in terror whenever the shadow of the aircraft overtook them. Pearson's flight plan took the plane over the Rift Escarpment and the Ngorongoro Crater. When it settled like a determined butterfly to the primitive airstrip at Arusha, Ernest got down to stretch his legs and locate a latrine. The second takeoff was smoother. The Moth droned steadily northwards for Nairobi. Far off to the east stood the bulk of Kilimanjaro, clothed in cloud and topped with snow, its highest peak unbelievably white in the afternoon sun.

After his fortnight of torture, Ernest found Nairobi a relief. Dr. Anderson put him to bed in the New Stanley Hotel and began a course of emetine injections. Six hours after the first of these, his condition began to improve.

Working on a lapboard, he wrote a piece for *Esquire*. It dealt with his illness and his first month of hunting. He dated it January 18th from Nairobi, and on the same day sent off some Graflex prints for use as illustrations, including one of himself kneeling proudly beside his black-maned lion. The mailbag contained a few welcome items from home. There was a month-old letter from Perkins which said that *Winner Take Nothing* had sold 12,500 copies up to the week before Christmas. There was also a cable from Harry Payne Burton of *Cosmopolitan,* praising "One Trip Across," the Harry Morgan story, and offering to buy it for $5,500, the largest sum Ernest had ever yet received for a short story.

When he rejoined the safari in the hill country south of Ngorongoro Crater about January 23rd, the period of plainsmanship was over and the trophies they now sought were rhinoceros, sable, and kudu. Philip had meantime acquired a local tracker whom Ernest nicknamed Droopy. He was about the same age as Kamau, "a real savage" with heavy-lidded eyes and "a great deal of style." He always carried a spear and wore only a red fez and a length of white cloth knotted over one shoulder. Ernest called him "a fine hunter and a beautiful tracker." There were tribal scars on his cheekbones "and others, symmetrical and decorative, on his chest and belly."

In contrast to the days on the Serengeti, the final week of January found Ernest in a state of euphoria.

This [he wrote], was the kind of hunting I liked. No riding in cars, the country broken up instead of the plains . . . and it was a pleasure . . . simply to walk, and to be able to hunt, not knowing what we might see and free to shoot for the meat we needed. Then, too, I liked Droopy and liked to watch him walk. He strode very loosely and with a slight lift, and I liked to watch him and to feel the grass under my soft-soled shoes and the pleasant weight of the rifle, held just back of the muzzle, the barrel resting on my shoulder, and the sun hot enough to sweat you well as it burned the dew from the grass. . . . I had been quite ill and had that pleasant feeling of getting stronger each day.

His pleasure in watching Droopy walk was matched by his delight in hearing Philip talk. One of the best parts of the day was the evening. Bathed, relaxed, and comfortable in pajamas, dressing gowns, and mosquito boots, they sat in camp chairs beside the fire, drinking whiskey and soda, rehearsing the adventures of the afternoon, or listening as Philip reminisced. To Ernest's mind, the most memorable of Philip's anecdotes were those that centered on the loss and recovery of nerve among his former clients. Ernest himself often discoursed on his favorite subjects of bravery and cowardice. Courage, he believed, was a matter of dignity and pride. "A coward said this pride was of no importance. Perhaps it wasn't but it was of great importance to whoever had it." A man without inner dignity was an embarrassment. Ernest knew from personal experience "what it was to be a coward and what it was to cease being a coward." Now, in the presence of actual danger, he found that he did not care what happened. "I knew it was better to live it so that if you died you had done everything that you could do about your work and your enjoyment of life up to that minute." Philip agreed that the moment of transition from cowardice to courage was a moving experience to watch. Ernest plied him with questions. This was a significant topic. So was Philip's story of the dried and frozen carcass of a leopard which a mountaineer named Reusch had found on the outer crater rim of Kibo Peak of Mount Kilimanjaro in the fall of 1926. Although Ernest said that no one seemed to know what the leopard was doing there, in fact he had been chasing a goat.

The fireside conversations always ended early so that Ernest could be up and away soon after dawn with Droopy and M'Cola. He gloried in the fresh mornings and breezy afternoons of this green hill country with its distant views of Lake Manyara and the brown Rift Valley. One afternoon they were loafing on a windswept hillside, sweeping the terrain with binoculars like elk hunters in Wyoming, when Ernest saw his first rhinoceros. It was "red colored in the sun, moving with a quick water-bug-like motion" down a grassy slope beside a tongue of forest. Three others soon appeared and two of them fought, small as beetles in the Zeiss lenses. Next day, hoping to impress his friend Droopy, he shot a reedbuck at a considerable range. *"Piga,"* said Droopy, smiling. *"Kufa,"* said Ernest. "Dead." But when they reached the buck, its heart was still beating strongly, and Ernest, using a penknife, managed to cut the large artery to bleed it to death. Afterwards, "still showing off to Droopy," he slit the body open and removed the liver and kidneys. Droopy asked for the knife. He would show Ernest a thing or two. Working deftly, he removed the stomach and turned it tripe side out, making a bag to carry the delicacies in. "It was a good trick," wrote Ernest, "and I thought I would show it to John Staib of Wyoming some time." John would "smile his deaf man's smile," and say, "By Godd, Urnust, dot's smardt."

Ernest's competitive spirit, which had helped to discourage Strater and MacLeish from making the African trip, had been kept in escrow through most of the shooting. But he could not avoid a small-boyish chagrin over the fact that Charles Thompson's trophies had almost invariably "dwarfed" his own, reversing the situation of the Wyoming hunt of 1932. The day Ernest got his rhino with a phenomenal shot at three hundred yards, he returned to camp only to discover that Charles had just bagged one far larger—a huge "marvel" whose lesser horn was longer than Ernest's greater. It was the same with Charles's buffalo, waterbuck, lion, and leopard, though Ernest soon salved his wounded spirits with another phenomenal kill on a buffalo at four hundred yards.

Something of his former antagonism towards the plains country came surging back when they left the rugged hills and descended into the "dried-up dustiness of the Rift Valley." He had been happy in the highlands. Shooting zebra for hides to give to friends at home, and oryx for specimens of their handsome black horns, struck him as the dullest of interludes. His gloom lasted into early February and a new location near Babati. "I never liked that camp," he wrote, "nor the [local] guides, nor the country." The tents were pitched under the trees in a forested flatland, and the adjacent hills were "steep, brushy, and very broken." The worst of it was the plague of tsetse flies, which swarmed through the camp in the heat of the day. Ernest feared and hated snakes, especially in the dark. But these flies were even worse than snakes. He spent his days swishing them away from his neck and arms with a leafy branch.

It was more than a relief when Philip said that they had better try a new region nearly two hundred miles away. From Babati they headed south once more on the Cape-to-Cairo Road, with long vistas of the yellow-brown Masai Steppes. In the well-kept town of Kandoa-Irangi they turned left at the crossroads, following the district highway eastward towards Handeni. In the farm village of Kibaya, Ben Fourie told of having sat in a haystack once, awaiting a kudu, while a lion stalked the hunter and nearly got him. This story seemed to confirm what they had been told: that kudu abounded in the rolling country between Kibaya and Kijungu, 65 miles away. The legend was that they were to be found at every saltlick. They came out into the open with their magnificent long backward-spiraling horns and stood broadside ready to be knocked over.

The campsite at Kijungu was a low plateau between two handsomely wooded mountains. While the tents were going up, Ben Fourie summoned the local guides. Two were naked citizens from the village. The other pair wore khaki pants and carried typewritten credentials. Abdullah was a short man with a thick nose. His tall companion was given to heroic posturing and dramatic gestures. Ernest disliked him at once and named him David Garrick. But Garrick surprised him that evening by guiding him unerringly to a saltlick five miles down the road. The soil of the lick showed fresh kudu tracks, and Ernest came back in a state of exaltation. It was, as they had said, only a question of standing there and shooting the better specimens. "I'll kill you two tomorrow on that lick," he boasted. "By God, I feel awfully good about tomorrow."

But it was Charles Thompson who got the first bull kudu. Ernest spent the morning with Garrick and Abdullah on a mountainside above the bowl-like valley where two kudu cows and a calf browsed peacefully in the distance. Once they heard the far-off boom of a hunter's heavy rifle. All they saw the rest of the day was a lone Masai warrior striding down the center of the valley and spooking whatever game there was. Back in camp Ernest stopped at the skinner's tent to see the kudu Charles had shot that morning. For once it looked like a beatable trophy: a freak head with coarse horns that slanted straight out like buck teeth. Still, it was a kudu, and Ernest had none. The time was getting short. In less than a week the rains would be moving up from Rhodesia, the roads would turn to quagmires in the February monsoon, and the hunting would be over.

While Thompson and Fourie went east after sable, Ernest continued his search for kudu. He spent the afternoon of Valentine's Day squatting in a dusty hollow inside a hunter's blind at the edge of a saltlick some forty miles west of camp. His companions were M'Cola, Abdullah, and Garrick. Four greater kudu bulls had left their heart-shaped tracks like African Valentines in the worn dirt of the saltlick. They would return at dusk if they came at all. The sun was just setting when the air resounded with the noise of an approaching truck, clanking and backfiring and frightening all the game for miles around. "It is finished," said Garrick, spreading his arms dramatically.

The noises of the truck diminished in the distance. They were halfway home when they saw it in a firelit clearing beside the road. A short, bowlegged man in a Tyroler hat and dirty *Lederhosen* was standing beside it in a crowd of natives. He said that his name was Hans Koritschoner. He spoke English with an Austrian accent. Astonishingly, he had heard of Hemingway, having read his bawdy poems years before in *Der Querschnitt*. He was full of questions and literary opinions. Ernest invited him to stop at Kijungu next day: perhaps one of Percival's mechanics could repair the truck.

The literary discussions resumed next day at lunch. Koritschoner had provided fresh butter. The table was set up under the green fly of the dining tent in the breezy shade. They ate green corn, mashed potatoes, and Grant's gazelle chops. The Austrian was a labor scout for a wealthy East Indian who ran a sisal plantation, but his avocation was ethnology. For years he had been making notes on tribal mores and languages. He showed them a native dance, shuffling round the lunch table. Ernest was only mildly interested. All this sudden social life was getting in the way of his kudu.

It was hot with a hint of oncoming rain when he woke from his siesta. The hunting car was already packed with food and beer. This time the goal was a saltlick 30 miles back towards Kibaya. All the way along the road they passed groups of natives heading westward away from the famine region around Handeni. They scouted two saltlicks without success and camped for the night beside the car in a steady drizzle. Their bad luck continued through the 16th. At lunch next day two natives arrived at the mess tent and asked to speak to Percival. One was an old man from the village, the other a dirty and skinny Wanderobo who stood on one leg like a crane. They were just back from three days in hill country less than a day's foot march from Kijungu, a region abounding in both kudu and sable.

Ernest set out at once with his entourage of five. Kamau drove the car across a yellow plain into a parklike country so beautiful that Ernest would have been content just to live there. They passed a Masai village where a crowd of young warriors came out to race the car. Some miles farther on they made camp in a corral-like enclosure, where three other natives joined them. It was after five when they set off after kudu. Within half an hour Ernest had shot two huge, beautiful kudu bulls. Their horns rose from their noble heads in great dark spirals, brown as walnut meats. Ernest was almost beside himself with boastful exuberance. He had beaten Charles Thompson at last.

The sable hunt next day was inevitably an anticlimax. He shot a cow sable by mistake and wounded a large bull with sweeping horns like scimitars. They trailed the bull all day without success. Ernest was sick at heart at the thought of the hyenas that would find and dispose of his prize. But his spirits revived as they drew near the corral camp that evening. All day he had given no thought to his kudu. Now he could see them again, with the head skins neatly salted and the great horns leaning tall as rifles against the log hut. They broke camp quickly and departed. At the Masai village Ernest opened tins of mincemeat and plum pudding as largess for the warriors, who swallowed it with relish. On the 55-mile drive back along the district road, he drank beer and dreamed of the future. All he wanted now was to get back to Africa. Seventy-two days were not enough. He was "hungry for more of it, the changes of the seasons, the rains with no need to travel"—even "the discomforts that you paid to make it real." He wanted to settle in, learn the language, take time, move slowly. Not this unseemly haste before the rains arrived.

He stayed awake while Kamau rammed the car across a long stretch of deeply rutted black cotton soil that would presently become impassable, and then dozed fitfully until the fires of the safari camp showed through the trees beside the road. He sounded the klaxon and fired a one-gun salute. They were all there to greet him, including Charles Thompson. M'Cola and Kamau unloaded the kudu horns and brought them forward into the firelight.

Then as in a nightmare he saw the latest trophy that Charles Thompson had brought back: "the biggest, widest, darkest, longest-curling, heaviest, most unbelievable pair of kudu horns" in all the world. "That's great," croaked Ernest while envy rose around him like a black tide. He knew that he was fooling nobody, least of all Charles. All night he writhed bitterly, but in the morning the envy was gone. Just before breakfast, he stood with Philip Percival comparing the heads. Side by side they all looked good.

"I'm glad you're feeling better," said Philip. "We have very primitive emotions. It's impossible not to be competitive. Spoils everything, though."

"I'm all through with that," said Ernest. "I'm all right again. I had quite a trip, you know."

"Did you not," said Philip.

35. THE LONG JOURNEY HOME

THE safari was all behind them when they reached the coast at Tanga. Only two weeks remained before they would have to embark at Mombasa to begin the long journey home. Ernest wanted to initiate Philip Percival into deep-sea fishing in the Indian Ocean. Young Alfred Vanderbilt was going to share expenses. By the end of the third week in February, they were luxuriously established at the Palm Beach Hotel in Malindi, overlooking a long white beach where the northeast monsoon blew cool and fresh through the palms at night.

The boat, chartered by wire, was called the *Xanadu*. The first day out they discovered that one of its engines was permanently disabled. The rings on the other were so badly worn and the valves so sticky that at best the boat could do no more than four miles an hour. Each time the motor died, the Hindu engineer removed the carburetor and blew into it lustily. Twenty minutes was the maximum time between breakdowns. They were sullenly drifting one day in a flat calm when they saw a strange red patch in the water. The sea was "alive with billions of worms, grey and red," spiraling rapidly in some kind of nuptial dance. Sharp-pointed at the ends, and about the size of large angleworms, they struck Ernest as a truly horrible sight. His snake-fear came up fast. Someone remarked that the ideal vengeance against the man who had rented them the boat would be to pitch him overboard into the horde of worms and let him swim a little.

In spite of the problems the fishing was good. They nailed a plank to the roof of the cabin in the stern, cut off the legs of two old chairs, fitted them with rod sockets, and spiked them to the plank. Vanderbilt and Percival occupied these thrones while Charles and Ernest maneuvered as well as they could in the narrow deck space below. They caught kingfish, amberjacks, a kind of hogfish, and two varieties of groupers, as well as dolphin and sailfish. Ernest began dreaming of setting up a camp on Mafia Island. There was a swift and narrow channel between the island and the coast through which all the migratory fish were said to pass. Some April, he told himself, he would fish the Red Sea and the Gulf of Aden from Port Sudan down, and then put in a full winter season off Zanzibar.

The *Gripsholm* was an immense improvement over the *General Metzinger* —"a tall, white, Swedish ship, comfortable, cool, and pleasant," equipped with a salt-water swimming pool. Vanderbilt and Baron von Blixen were now Ernest's boon companions, and they spent most of their time beside the pool. It took nine days to reach Haifa, where they went ashore to meet Charles's wife Lorine and made a short pilgrimage to the Sea of Galilee, pausing for lunch in the lee of an old stone wall. Galilee was calm and stagnant. Many grebes made spreading wakes in the water. Ernest sat idly, wineglass in hand, counting the birds and wondering why they were never mentioned in the Bible. He decided in the end that the ancient Jews could not have been naturalists.

They left the ship on March 18th at Villefranche and took the train from Nice to Paris, staying at the Paris-Dinard in the rue Cassette. The Thompsons sailed for home almost at once, but the Hemingways lingered for nine days more. Ernest was happy, relaxed, and full of generosity and personal charm. In November he had met and liked a thin, dark, serious young man named Ned Calmer, who worked for the *Paris Herald* and had written a good deal of fiction on the side. Calmer's wife Priscilla was a chronic invalid and they had a small daughter named Alden. On learning that she had not been baptized, Ernest volunteered to stand as godfather. After the ceremony, he took them to lunch at Weber's in the rue Royale. Ned's first novel was about to be published, but he could not afford the ship fare to go to New York for the occasion. Ernest shyly and quietly slipped him a check for $350, enough to pay passage for the whole family.

Another day he and Pauline asked Solita Solano and Janet Flanner to dinner at Michaud's. The third guest was James Joyce. Joyce spoke only in monosyllables while Ernest sat watching him in what seemed to Solita "a stupor of silent worship." By midnight Pauline and Janet had become extremely bored. When Ernest left for the lavabos, announcing that he was going to be sick, they quickly departed. Joyce reached an unsteady hand across the table. "Don't go," said he plaintively to Solita. Ernest, returning, wound up an old phonograph on the bar. Joyce wavered out to the middle of the room, seized the *patronne,* a tiny woman with dyed hair, and went into a kind of hopping waltz. "Gawd," said Ernest, "he'll kill himself." The waltzing grew wilder. At last Joyce staggered and fell back against a table. Ernest caught him, set him in a chair, and sent Solita for a taxi. He paid the bill and came out with Joyce over his shoulder like a half-empty sack. At Joyce's flat in the rue Galilée, Ernest carried the great man upstairs. When he came down, mopping his brow, he was almost sober. "No keys," he said. "Had to kick in the door." And then later, "Poor devil. At least he forgot the pain in his eyes."

On the 24th he paid a visit to Sylvia Beach's bookshop. She showed him a recent essay by Wyndham Lewis. It was called "The Dumb Ox," and dealt witheringly with Ernest's anti-intellectualism. He was so much enraged that he punched a vase of tulips on Sylvia's table. Overcome with contrition, he insisted on paying her 1,500 francs damages. It was also at Sylvia's one rainy evening that he met Katherine Anne Porter. The women were talking when he burst in, wearing an old raincoat and a battered hat pulled over his eyes. Sylvia introduced them. "I want the two best modern American writers to know each other," said she. When she went to answer the telephone, Ernest and Katherine Anne stood gazing at each other for a full ten seconds. Then Ernest turned and departed as rapidly as he had come in. Neither of them had said a word.

He behaved quite differently aboard the *Île de France* when the famous actress Marlene Dietrich entered the dining salon to join a dinner party already in progress. All the men rose to offer her their chairs, but she saw that she would make the thirteenth at the table and turned superstitiously away. Ernest stood in her path, saying gallantly that he would make the fourteenth. After dinner they made the circuit of the deck while she told him about her eight-year-old daughter Maria, who had taken to composing poetry. In New York he told the ship-news reporters that he was going to Key West for a "season of intensive writing" in order to get enough money to go back to Africa. The story was no sooner published than another famous lady asked him to tea. When he accepted, she told him that he need not wait to earn enough for another safari. She would provide the necessary money and go along with Pauline on the trip. As Ernest later told the story, he considered the lady's offer and politely declined.

Scott Fitzgerald was in town, having come up from Baltimore to celebrate the publication of *Tender Is the Night,* his first novel since *The Great Gatsby.* Max Perkins was sure that it would bolster Scott's flagging reputation, and told Ernest that finishing the book had done wonders for Scott's morale. But when Ernest met him, Scott was far too drunk for sensible conversation. Another disappointment to Ernest was the novel itself. Using Gerald and Sara Murphy as models for Dick and Nicole Diver, Scott had marvelously mimicked their manner of speech and perfectly described their life on the Riviera. But his failure, as Ernest saw it, was that he had reproduced their surface charm without comprehending their psychological complexities. Ernest thought Sara both lovely and strong—a regular pioneer mother. Scott had taken her image, merged it with Zelda's, made her into a psychopathic case, and ended by reducing her character to a cipher. Gerald in turn had been changed into a self-portrait of Scott. In Ernest's view, Scott had lacked the confidence to invent in the light of what he knew, and then compounded his failure by misunderstanding all that he reported.

At this moment of early April, Ernest was engaged with plans of far more importance to him than any literature except his own. Before leaving for Africa he had heard about the island of Bimini. It lay 45 miles east of Miami and was said to be a fisherman's paradise. But he needed a boat in order to get there. He knew exactly what he wanted: a diesel-powered 38-footer with twin screws, double rudders, ample bunk space, and proven seaworthiness. He had long since found such a craft illustrated in the catalogue of the Wheeler Shipyard in Brooklyn. The price was $7,500. Ernest had enough for a down payment of $3,300, which Arnold Gingrich gave him as an advance against his future contributions to *Esquire.* On the eve of going home, Ernest and Pauline took a cab to the shipyard and placed the order. Delivery was promised in thirty days, F.O.B. Miami, and Ernest rode back to the hotel in a state of rapture. He had already named his new cruiser. It would be called the *Pilar* in honor of the shrine and the *feria* at Zaragoza, and about equally for Pauline, who had chosen it as one of her secret nicknames when she first fell in love with Ernest.

After the seven-month absence, Key West looked better than ever. Many of their closest friends were there—Dos and Katy, the Murphys, Ada MacLeish, and the Thompsons. Dawn Powell and her husband came over from Havana to stay with Esther and Canby Chambers. Ernest rented Bra Saunders's new boat for every-other-day fishing expeditions. But he was restive to get back to serious writing. Except for the *Esquire* articles and the preface for Jimmy Charters, he had not set pencil to paper since completing the Harry Morgan story in Spain. By the end of April he had written fifty pages, only to find that thirty of them were so bad that he threw them away. Still he persisted. It was a story that had to be told. His working title was *The Highlands of Africa,* and the theme, summarized in the subtitle, was "Hunters Are Brothers." Brothers, he seems to have meant, in the shared experience of friendly rivalry, danger, and endurance, all of them matters very close to his heart.

He had determined to write the "true story" of the recent safari, not as a travelogue but rather as a narrative using all the familiar techniques of fiction: description, characterization, dialogue, action sequences, internal monologues, and even that special highland-lowland landscape device which he had discovered in *The Sun Also Rises* and developed in *A Farewell to Arms.* He wanted also to begin *in medias res* with the episode of the clanking truck which spooked all the game near the saltlick on Valentine's Day, 1934. He would then build to the climax of the kudu hunt by the use of structural devices such as flashbacks and the compression or extension of narrative time. It was a difficult organizational problem. The part he had saved from the first fifty pages told of his meeting with Hans Koritschoner and their opening conversation by the campfire, followed by the further talk next day at lunchtime in the safari camp near Kijungu. To give his story the air of fiction he had changed most of the names. Koritschoner became Kandisky, Pauline was P.O.M. (for Poor Old Mama), Charles Thompson was Karl, Philip Percival was Jackson Phillips or Pop, and Ben Fourie was Dan. Like the Michigan Indians in some of the early short stories, the native Africans bore their actual names: M'Cola, Kamau, Charo, Molo, Abdullah, or such humorous nicknames as Droopy and Garrick.

Although he planned to work at his story each day until it was done, he was already aiming towards another season of marlin fishing off the Cuban coast whenever the *Pilar* was delivered. He persuaded Dos Passos, who needed no urging, to make a quick preliminary trip to Havana to watch the May Day celebration, the first since Machado's overthrow, and to see how old friends like Carlos Gutiérrez and Manuel Asper were faring under the new regime. The travelers returned in mildly alcoholic melancholy. They had gone fishing twice, but the marlin were not yet down from the waters around Bimini. Gutiérrez and Asper were agreed that the Cuban political situation, in spite of the high hopes of the previous summer, was still "not so good."

On May 9th Ernest learned that his new cruiser had arrived in Miami. He commandeered Bra Saunders and hurried up to take possession. His brother Leicester was on hand in Key West the day the *Pilar* came riding like a queen into the harbor, resplendent, as Leicester said, in "new varnish and gleaming black paint." They all went aboard for a tour of inspection. One engine was a 75-horsepower Chrysler, the other a 40-horsepower Lycoming. Her gas tanks held 300 gallons and at full throttle she could do 16 knots in a flat sea. The cabin would sleep six, with room for two more in the cockpit. The galley was bright with chrome fittings. Ernest knew from the trip home that she was going to be a great little fishing machine. He could hardly wait to try her out on a shakedown run to Boca Grande.

All through May he alternated between fishing trips and daily progress with his African book, which reached the sixtieth manuscript page by the end of the month. In one passage, which he later deleted, he set down a sprawling list of things he loved and loved to do: seeing, hearing, eating, drinking, sleeping, and reading; looking at pictures, cities, oceans, fishes, and fighting; thinking and observing; being in boats and battles or on saddle horses with "guns between your legs." The list went on in a series of infinitives:

To watch the snow, rain, grass, tents, winds, changes of season . . . to talk, to come back and see your children, one woman, another woman, various women, but only one woman really, some friends, speed, animals, cowardice, courage, pride, co-ordination, the migration of fishes, many rivers, fishing, forests, fields, all birds that fly, dogs, roads, all good writing, all good painting, the principles of revolution, the practice of revolution, the Christian theory of anarchy, the seasonal variation of the Gulf Stream, its monthly variation, the trade winds, counter currents, the Spanish bull ring, cafés, wines, the Prado, Pamplona, Navarra, Santiago de Compostella, Sheridan, Casper, Wyoming, Michigan, Florida, Arkansas, Montana.

The list was too long and various. He crossed it out and tried again:

To stay in places and to leave, to trust, to distrust, to no longer believe and believe again, to care about fishes, the different winds, the changes of the seasons, to see what happens, to be out in boats, to sit in a saddle, to watch the snow come, to watch it go, to hear rain on a tent, to know where I can find what I want.

What he really wanted was a total immersion in the sensuous experience of living. The lists were nothing more than verbal talismans to help him achieve such an end.

Ada and Sara and Katy had now gone away—"damned nice women," said Ernest, fondly. Another of his departing favorites was the diminutive Dawn Powell. A crowd of well-wishers saw her off at the Key West station. She was secretly hurt that Ernest was not among them. But he came running along the platform just as the train pulled out, blowing enormous kisses and shouting unintelligible messages. She was no sooner out of sight when Archie MacLeish came down for a fishing holiday. Ernest had been nursing the shadow of a grudge against Archie for having declined to make the trip to Africa. Now he found, or invented, some grounds for belief that Archie had become too deeply involved in politics and economics. Archie, on his part, thought that fame was not sitting well with Ernest, and that his ego was too much like an overinflated balloon. They went out on the *Pilar* for kingfish, only to find that none were running. A bitter quarrel developed. "Ernest," said Archie, "took to shooting terns, taking one with one barrel and the grieving mate with the other. He was fed up with the world and I was fed up with him. . . . . It was a simple conflict of over-exposure. . . . He was a wonderful, irreplaceable, but an impossible friend; a man you couldn't get along with, a man you couldn't get along without." They had been good friends for ten years. Now Ernest grumpily told Waldo Peirce that he only liked the people he liked, not the bastards that liked him.

By the 20th of June his book had swelled to 150 pages. He was feeling good about it because he was managing to "get the old fourth dimension into the landscape again"—by which he meant the contrasting emotional atmospheres (disappointment and disease on the Serengeti, pursuit as happiness in the hills above Kijungu) that he had personally experienced. Things were going so well with his own writing that he reconsidered his earlier opinion of *Tender Is the Night,* deciding now that it was quite a sound book. He summed up his views in a long, frank, avuncular, and hortatory letter to Scott Fitzgerald. At first he had understated the book's virtues and overemphasized its shortcomings. Scott obviously had talent to burn, said Ernest, but he had "cheated too damned much in this one." His problem was that he had stopped listening long ago, except to answers to his own questions. This was what dried a writer up. The minute he started listening again, he would sprout like dry grass after a sozzling rain. He must also learn to forget his personal tragedy. Everyone was bitched from the start, anyhow, and it was clear enough that Scott had to be hurt like hell before he could write seriously. It was his obligation to use the damned hurt in his writing, not to cheat with it. Neither he nor Ernest was a tragic character: they were only writers who must write. Most good writers, including James Joyce, were rummies. But good writers could always make comebacks. Scott was twice as good right this minute as he had been at the time of *The Great Gatsby.* "Go on and write," said Ernest.

Scott's reply came by return mail, three times longer than Ernest's and just as serious. Scott said that his friend's "old charming frankness" had dispelled the "foggy atmosphere" that had grown up between them in recent years. "I think it is obvious," said he, "that my respect for your artistic life is absolutely unqualified, that save for a few of the dead and dying old men you are the only man writing fiction in America that I look up to very much. There are pieces and paragraphs of your work that I read over and over—in fact, I stopped myself doing it for a year and a half because I was afraid that your particular rhythms were going to creep in on mine by a process of infiltration."

It was a far cry from the misadventures of Dick and Nicole Diver on the Riviera to Ernest's adventures in Tanganyika. He was taking pardonable pleasure in the recollection of his behavior under stress in the heat and the cold, the sun and the rain, the difficulties and dangers of life on safari. He had lately written a passage of dialogue between himself and Pauline on the subject of his own and others' behavior in the face of danger. Pauline was made to say that Charles Thompson was a brave man. Ernest agreed.

"Why are you always so pleased when you're brave?" asked Pauline.

"I don't know," said Ernest. "I'm just always pleased."

"It's cute," Pauline said. "But it's sort of silly."

"Look," said Ernest. "The things that please me are very simple things. Most of them seem to have to do with natural reflexes and co-ordination. Like things that happen so quickly in trout-fishing, correcting from a cast already started in the hundredth part of a second in the air. When I was a kid every time I would do that I would be pleased. Now shooting and all the things that are made up of so many things to do and think at once all surrounding one central necessity please me."

The passage was a fairly exact analysis of Ernest's pride in doing difficult things well. As a small boy, he had been afraid of many things, including the dark. As an adolescent who had grown too fast, his muscular coordination had been seriously deficient. The victories of his maturity—particularly those involving physical courage, endurance, and quick reflexes— were therefore doubly pleasing to remember.

So was his freedom to live as he liked. In the past year he had fished in waters as far apart as the Caribbean Sea and the Indian Ocean. He had witnessed the start of a major Cuban revolution. He had crossed the Atlantic twice and gone from one end of the Mediterranean to the other. He had watched a season of bullfights in Spain, shot pheasant and deer in the Sologne, and made a memorable safari in Kenya and Tanganyika. He had brought out a new collection of short stories and achieved a tale of Harry Morgan of which he was justly proud. He had acquired a powerful black cruiser and come home again to take up the kind of life he loved and was built for—writing and fishing on his own schedule or, if he chose, on no schedule at all. Finally, he was deep in the heart of a book which he was beginning to think might turn into one of the best he had ever written.

36. *NOTES ON LIFE AND LETTERS*

WHEN Carlos Gutiérrez wrote in mid-July that the marlin were running at last, Ernest hurried down to Joe Russell's bar in Green Street to see if Joe would come along to Cuba as helmsman for the *Pilar*. But Joe could not come. Since the repeal of Prohibition his rumrunning business had disappeared, but Sloppy Joe's was doing well. He waved a hand towards the sailors on shore leave from the destroyers in the harbor. They were lined up three deep in front of the bar. "Not this year," he told Ernest. "I want to go just as bad as you do, Cap. But I've got to make it while I can."

"I know it," said Ernest, gloomily. "But we'll lose ten fish before anybody learns how to work them."

He was all the gloomier because his only employee aboard the *Pilar* was a landlubberly young man from Minnesota. His name was Arnold Samuelson, and he had hitchhiked all the way to Key West to interview Ernest about the art of writing. He was a farm boy who had worked as a newspaperman, an apprentice carpenter, a harvest hand, and a day laborer. Ernest nicknamed him Maestro because he could play the violin. The nickname was presently shortened to Mice, and Ernest once told him, "Mice, you certainly must be going to be a hell of a good writer because you certainly aren't worth a damn at anything else." At sea, according to Ernest, Mice was "slow where he should be agile . . . nervous under excitement, and with an incurable tendency towards sea-sickness and a peasant reluctance to take orders." This was the paragon who was going along as general helper when the *Pilar* crossed to Havana.

Ernest fixed Wednesday, July 18, as the day to start. Since the fishing holiday would interrupt his writing, he was at some pains to justify it. All his slaving in the "workhouse," he said, had made him go stale. Except for the trip to Miami to pick up his cabin cruiser, he had stuck to his book steadily since early April. By Bastille Day the manuscript stood at 201 pages. He stopped to write a chatty piece for *Esquire,* this one called "Defense of Dirty Words." It would help at least to reduce his $3,000 debt to Gingrich. He complained that all his writing life he had shied away from taking money from magazines for work to be done in the future. He did not like the idea of writing to order.

When the *Pilar* pulled in at the San Francisco docks the late afternoon of the 18th, Ernest sent for Carlos Gutiérrez and hired on a cook named Juan who could double as steersman. For the first two weeks, except for literary conversations with Arnold Samuelson, he spoke nothing but Spanish while they were afloat. The situation changed at the end of the month when two scientists came aboard at Ernest's invitation. They were Charles Cadwalader, a bluff and hearty man who was director of the Academy of Natural Sciences of Philadelphia, and his chief ichthyologist, Henry W. Fowler. They stayed at the Ambos Mundos and went out with Ernest each day. Fowler was a hardworking man, quiet and studious. In a month, helped by Ernest's "excellent knowledge of marlin and their habits," he gained enough new information to revise the classification for marlin for the whole North Atlantic. Cadwalader afterwards called it one of the finest holidays he had ever known. Grant and Jane Mason were often on board. An American reporter named Dick Armstrong was chief photographer and a Venezuelan sportsman, López Méndez, helped to run the boat. They made pictures of tuna and marlin specimens, recorded measurements, counted the number of spines on dorsal fins, and procured skins for mounting.

After the scientists had departed, Ernest befriended a Cuban painter, Antonio Gattorno, who lived in the suburb of Marianao. Although Gattorno's interest in fishing was limited, he made several trips aboard the *Pilar.* Ernest struck him as a man of notable contradictions, taciturn for hours, yet at other times bursting with funny anecdotes; alternately tough and tender; weeping with ease, yet accusing Gattorno of being a sissy when he deplored the slaughter of bulls in the ring. Once when Gattorno mentioned death, Ernest said that it was no worse than a knockout blow in boxing. Gattorno's tendency to seasickness was somewhat alleviated by the amount of alcohol that Ernest pressed upon him, beginning with vermouth over ice cubes at seven in the morning and progressing to endless Scotch-and-sodas by yardarm time.

The African manuscript was moving slowly forward. By August 20th, a month after his thirty-fifth birthday, Ernest had reached 23,000 words. His present subject was the shooting of his third buffalo in Droopy's green and hilly country. It was a pleasant memory but very hard to describe with accuracy, and Ernest's progress slowed to a crawl. In a letter to Pauline's mother he complained about the curious economics of writing. While he was engaged with a long book like this one, he could earn little or nothing, and the family intelligence service tagged him as a loafer. After the book was published and he *really* began to loaf, he was respectfully looked up to as the Supreme Money-Maker. It was, said Ernest, pretty darned ironic.

The September number of *Esquire* carried his "Defense of Dirty Words." It was inspired by a column of Westbrook Pegler's which pointed out that "Ring Lardner never wrote a dirty scene or line or even a dirty word," even though several of his stories contained some very unpleasant people. To all such arguments, Ernest had a standard reply: he used the words normally spoken by the people he was writing about. Whatever Heywood Broun or Alexander Woollcott might say about "small boys, back fences, and the walls of privies," Ernest declared that his own motives were pure. His purpose was verisimilitude, not gratuitous shock for the reader. In Lardner's work there was much to admire. But Ernest could not help regretting, for the sake of American literature, that Lardner had settled for mere "comic diction" rather than the real language of men.

Ernest went back to Key West early in September, leaving the *Pilar* in Havana for cleaning and overhauling. His book was now moving forward at the rate of five or six pages a day. In a great splurge of energy he completed twenty-two pages on the 10th, thirty on the 11th, and twenty on the 12th. Next evening he returned to Havana on the car ferry. The moon was filling and the marlin were hungry. The market fishermen out of Casablanca were averaging fifty big ones a day. If a man wanted to catch a monster, he must go where the monsters were, book or no book.

He did not leave in the best of humors. Gingrich had sent him a sheaf of newspaper clippings, including a sports column by Heywood Broun that branded him as a "phoney" on the subject of boxing. Ernest was ready to admit that he might be a phoney in the sense that every writer of fiction was: that is, he made things up. But oddly enough, said he, there were three subjects on which he was *not* a phoney: shooting, fishing, and boxing. If Gingrich doubted this, let him ask Philip Percival of Machakos, Kenya, how good a marksman Hemingway was. As for fishing, Gingrich could find out all he needed to know about Ernest's prowess on the Gulf Stream from Carlos Gutiérrez. In boxing, said Ernest, he could always make his opponents look bad defensively. After he tired, of course, he would have to take a beating from people whom he could otherwise make look foolish.

In Cuba he found that the fishing jinx that had plagued him all summer was still on. Juan was hospitalized with a ruptured appendix and it was necessary to hire on a substitute named Bollo to serve as cook. After one day at sea, the wind shifted into the south, the waves rose like demons, and the run fizzled out. By the 18th of October, though he fished nearly every day from dawn to dusk, he had caught only a dozen small marlin. There were compensations, of course, including the comradeship of his Cuban friends, the occasional presence of Jane Mason, and the simple pleasure of being captain of his own craft. One of the happier events of the fall was the arrival of large flights of tiny warblers. They had flown all the way from the mainland and were so exhausted that they took refuge on the floating island of the *Pilar*. Many stayed for several hours, gathering strength to go on. Ernest discovered that if no one was allowed to frighten them when they first appeared, they were surprisingly tame. To his fellow naturalist Cadwalader, he described the whole experience as "great fun."

Soon after lunch on another day, Carlos was startled by a sudden plume of water off the port bow. His first guess was that a Cuban or American gunboat might be lobbing shells into the area. Then he saw the black backs of a pod of whales gleaming through the swells. Ernest grabbed the binoculars and made a rough count. There were twenty, all told, and two or three of the largest looked to be seventy feet in length. He ran to unlimber the harpoon gun in the bow. They rigged a floating buoy with a bundle of lifebelts. Carlos nosed the *Pilar* between a pair that were swimming neck and neck. One of them spouted and drenched the deck. Ernest shook his head to clear his eyes and took aim at the wallowing back. There was a hollow boom and a puff of smoke. The harpoon lodged just behind the snout, and Ernest stood ready with the Mannlicher to kill the whale, if it breached, by a few well-placed rounds in the brainpan. But it was like waving a toy at a dinosaur. The harpoon pulled loose and the whales continued their lordly progress out to sea. It was the first and last whaling that Ernest ever tried. He was still talking about it in the early morning of October 26th when the *Pilar* weighed anchor and headed home for Key West.

Dos and Katy arrived early in November for another season in the benign salt air. Dos had spent the summer in Hollywood as a scriptwriter for *The Devil Is a Woman,* in which Marlene Dietrich was going to star. "Poor Dos got rich out there," said Ernest, churlishly. He made no attempt to conceal his displeasure at what he construed to be Dos's sacrifice of integrity. As old and easygoing friends, Dos and Katy did their best to keep him "kidded down to size." In their eyes he had become, a shade too conspicuously, "the famous author, the great sports-fisherman, the mighty African hunter." Yet they willingly played up to his special brand of princeliness. Whenever he had a sore throat, he would ostentatiously retire to bed before supper while the others brought him drinks and ate pickup dinners off trays in his master bedroom. "We called it the *lit royale*," said Dos, without rancor. "I never knew an athletic, vigorous man who spent as much time in bed as Ernest did."

Listening to the radio one of those November evenings, Ernest was astonished to hear the familiar voice of Gertrude Stein. It was like a distant echo from the tomb of a dead friendship. She had recently arrived in New York for a lecture tour, accompanied by Alice Toklas. After the program was over, Ernest called it "God-awful," and reflected briefly on the possibility of saying so in print. But he rejected the idea, as he told Gingrich, because it went against his digestion to take potshots at former friends. To attack her now would be like "socking" a dummy or a ghost. He had apparently forgotten a passage he had composed that summer for insertion in the African book. It repeated a conversation between himself and Pauline, one day on safari, in which Ernest complained of Gertrude's having called him "yellow." All her former talent, said he, had now degenerated to "malice and nonsense and self-praise." "Homme des lettres," he had written. "Woman of letters. Salon woman. What a lousy stinking life."

But he regularly sought to help others whose work he could respect—Prudencio de Pereda, who was trying to get his fiction published, and Ned Calmer, who had applied for a Guggenheim Fellowship. He encouraged Gattorno by purchasing some of his bright canvases, and urged Arnold Gingrich to buy and publish examples of the paintings of Waldo Peirce. He also collaborated in promoting a one-man show of the etchings of Luis Quintanilla at the Pierre Matisse Gallery in New York. Quintanilla was being held without bail in the Modelo Cárcel in Madrid on charges of having conspired against the Spanish government. The New York show opened on November 21st and attracted wide attention. Next day Pierre Matisse asked Ernest to sign and circulate a petition to help get Quintanilla out of jail. Ernest responded with enthusiasm. Luis, said he, was not only a damned fine artist but also one of the "best guys" he had ever known.

Lust for Life, Irving Stone's fictional biography of Vincent van Gogh, had just been published. He came to see Ernest and gave him an inscribed copy. They drank Irish whiskey and sat on an overturned skiff discussing their respective tasks. Stone said modestly that his job was the harder of the two. "I have to dig into the historic records for months and years," he said. "And I am fairly well bound to what I have found." Ernest remarked that there was no such thing as fiction. He talked of his "autobiographical short stories" and of the "combinations of characters," he had used to make up one character in a book. "He was making the point, and very forcibly, that there was no such thing as pure imagination in writing, that we simply did not pull ideas and characters and concepts out of left field. He intimated that his own novels could be called biographical novels rather than pure fictional novels because they emerged out of 'lived experience.' " When Stone asked him why he had never written a novel about life in America, Ernest replied that American life was too dull. Nothing important ever happened. Stone reminded him of Roosevelt's social and economic revolution. But Ernest shrugged off the suggestion. It was not, he said flatly, his kind of material.

His kind of material was embodied in the book on Africa. On the Friday morning of November 16th he completed handwritten page 492 and decided that the story was told. The book pleased him. In quality, he thought, it was more like "Big Two-Hearted River" than anything else he had ever done. First in 1924 and now in 1934 he had been concerned with what he called "landscape painting"—making country come alive. But the African book contained far more action and dialogue, and he was glad to say that it had form as well. His motive at the outset had been simply to recapture and record the way Africa looked and the way he had felt while he was there. As soon as he got into it, however, he discovered a natural structure embedded in the story, leading up to the climax of that "wonderful goddamned kudu hunt." It also had pace. In the past year, said Ernest, with the Harry Morgan story and now with this one, he had learned how to make a narrative move, so that it seemed short when it was really very long. He was also proud of his achievement in having written "absolutely truly—absolutely with no faking or cheating of any kind."

If Max agreed that the safari story could stand as the opening section in a new volume, *The First Fifty-four Stories,* they would be giving the reading public "super-value" for their money. After all, it was very likely the best thing that he had ever written. A narrative that combined true reporting, the excitements of action, and the quality of real literature was, Ernest thought, a pretty rare thing. First it all had to happen, and second the man to whom it happened had to be equipped to "make it all come true." This was as hard as "painting a Cézanne," and Ernest felt that he was "the only bastard right now" who was capable of such an achievement. It had been made possible by an immense accession of energy—so much "juice" that it was almost as "bad as a disease." He guessed that it might be associated with the inner urgencies of the autumn solstice, when a man felt that the old year was dying and was impelled to complete his work. On the Friday when he finished it, he found that he could not slow down. Next day he began a short story, and on Sunday composed yet another article for *Esquire.*

His title for the article was "Notes on Life and Letters." It was largely devoted to an assault on William Saroyan, whose first book of short stories, *The Daring Young Man on the Flying Trapeze,* had recently been published. Some of the stories had made bumptious references to Hemingway and Dos Passos, Faulkner and Joyce. Ernest replied with a shower of bullying epithets in the manner of a tough topkick berating an ignorant hayseed private. It was his usual method of letting off steam on the completion of a new long book.

But the piece was compounded of brutality and banality. It read like a verbal incarnation of Ernest the Bad.

Full of commiseration for Arnold Gingrich because he faced a tonsillectomy, Ernest the Good asked him down for a fishing trip aboard that "bloody marvel," the *Pilar*. It would cost him nothing but the plane fare, and Arnold would be sure to have a good time. When Gingrich proposed bringing Scott Fitzgerald along with him, Ernest agreed. But Scott declined, telling Gingrich that "he couldn't face Ernest again"—especially since "Ernest was such a success and he was such a failure." The story they devised for Ernest was that Scott's mother was seriously ill and that he could not take the chance of coming. When Gingrich arrived, they went out fishing for tuna and barracuda. Dos Passos did not much care for the editor of *Esquire*.

The man was in a trance [he wrote]. It was a world he'd never dreamed of. He was mosquitobitten, half seasick, scorched with sunburn, astonished, half scared, half pleased. It was as much fun to see Ernest play an editor as to see him play a marlin. Gingrich never took his fascinated eyes off Old Hem. Hem would reel in gently, letting his prey have plenty of line. The editor was hooked.

Dos had done a commentary on Luis Quintanilla's etchings designed for the *New Republic*. Ernest and Arnold tried to persuade him to sell it to *Esquire* instead. It was only after Gingrich had returned to Chicago that Dos, urged on by Ernest, wired his permission to let Gingrich go ahead with the Quintanilla piece. Old Hem, still playing his editor like a prize marlin, assured Gingrich that he and Dos both thought him a "very good guy" and the only trustworthy editor they had ever seen.

Ernest's African trophies had lately been sent down from the Taxidermy Studios of Jonas Brothers in Yonkers, New York. It had cost $750 to ship them from Mombasa to New York and $368.50 to mount them. The lion and the leopard had been converted into rugs, complete with open mouths and snarling fangs. There were also wall heads of his sable, a roan antelope, an impala, and an oryx. Another impala had been sent to ornament Gerald Murphy's apartment in New York. The firm of Jonas Brothers was still at work on the kudu and rhinoceros. Still, they were up there in Yonkers and he would have them soon, even if not for Christmas.

A week before Christmas, Ernest left Key West with Pauline and Patrick to make the 1,600-mile drive to Piggott in the open Ford runabout. He resented and regretted this interruption in his pursuit of life and letters, but the Pfeiffers were now growing old and Pauline believed that it meant a great deal to them to have the Hemingways in Arkansas for the holiday season. They spent the night of the 22nd at the Hotel Peabody in Memphis, and reached Piggott next day. The duck season was over, but Ernest hoped to shoot some quail, his invariable consolation for living with Pauline's parents. But the jinx that had operated on the Gulf Stream through that summer and fall had been at work in another way all over the American Middle West. A long drought had converted the whole region into a fearsome dust bowl. The quail had died off for lack of feed, and the shooting, if possible, was even worse than the Cuban fishing. The year that had begun so famously among the green hills of Africa came to an end in foul weather among the dried-up fields of Arkansas.

37. BIMINI DISCOVERED

THE weather in Piggott was the kind that Ernest abhorred. It rained steadily for seven of the ten days he spent there. He escaped as soon as decency allowed, driving downriver to New Orleans, where he ate and drank so much that he weighed 210 by the time he got back to Key West. A recurrence of African dysentery soon brought his weight down again. In letters to his friends he spoke of blood by the cupful, castor oil every two hours, and the effects of emetine, which caused his head to ring like the inside of a belfry and made it impossible to think sequentially.

When Max Perkins brought his wife Louise down for a visit in mid-January, Ernest showed him the fresh typescript of *Green Hills of Africa*. Max was characteristically enthusiastic, but also cautious about committing *Scribner's Magazine* to a high price for serialization. *Cosmopolitan* had offered to buy it if Ernest would cut it to 45,000 words. He angrily refused. He was dreaming of $10,000 or even fifteen or twenty. In response to Perkins's offer of a mere $4,500, he sent off an explosive night letter which summarized all he had done for Scribners since 1926. In the end he grumpily settled for $5,000.

He was now without question the most famous citizen of Key West. His house on Whitehead Street was even listed as one of the main tourist attractions. Visitors often pointed him out as he hurried down Simonton Street with his curious rolling gait, wearing dirty dungarees and bound for Thompson's hardware store or Sloppy Joe's Bar. He was studiously fascinated with Joe Russell's clientele. It now included not only the usual crowd of sailors and coastguardsmen on liberty but also a group of war veterans who came down from the work camps of the Civilian Conservation Corps on Upper and Lower Matecumbe Keys. They were building a road and bridges along the railroad right-of-way. Some were "husky, hardworking, and simply out of luck." Others were borderline pathological cases, punch-drunk and belligerent. Joe Russell showed Ernest a sawed-off billiard cue that he used to keep them in line. Ernest believed and echoed the persistent rumor that these men were an embarrassment to Roosevelt's New Deal, and that Harry Hopkins had shipped them to Florida to get them out of sight.

Ernest was already getting into shape for a fishing expedition to Bimini in the Bahamas. He planned to go in April as soon as the giant tuna appeared. Tourists took note of him as he stood at the wheel of his cruiser, barefooted, with his legs braced wide, wearing a green eye-shade, a tattered skivvy shirt, and white pants stained with grease and fish blood. A northerner named Sam

Bell went out with him several times, watching with admiration as Ernest jammed the rod butt into his considerable belly and pumped away at the reel with all his considerable might. The muscles in his right forearm were developed like those of a professional tennis champion. He was proud of them and pointed them out to Bell. It seemed to Bell that he radiated supreme self-confidence. Yet he also contrived to be "a shy and most pleasant fishing-companion." The inept Maestro Samuelson had gone home to Minnesota, and Ernest was training Bread Pinder as helmsman for the *Pilar*. He had also hired a tall and handsome Conch named Sacker Adams as cook and general helper. He was flattered by an invitation from Zane Grey, who wanted him as partner in a "giant world fishing cruise to make a picture." Grey believed, according to Ernest, that with personal appearances by himself and Hemingway, the project might gross half a million dollars. Ernest declined with pleasure. His private guess was that Grey was jealous of his fishing prowess and wanted to ride to fame on the reputation of Hemingway—the silliest of surmises.

He was out fishing with Dos Passos one Sunday in March when the news reached Key West that young Baoth Murphy had died of tuberculosis. It was not until the following Tuesday that he could bring himself to write a letter of sympathy. He had known the child since the days of Bumby's whooping cough on the Riviera. He told Gerald and Sara that it was not so bad for Baoth as it was for his survivors. Absolutely truly and coldly in the head, wrote Ernest, he knew that anyone who died young after a happy childhood had won a great victory, since he would be forever spared the discovery of what sort of place the world really is. Others must look forward to "death by defeat"— their bodies gone, their world destroyed. Baoth had "gotten it over with" while his world was still intact. Very few people were ever really alive anyhow. "Those that are never die," he wrote. "No one you love is ever dead." The task for all who had known Baoth was to live their lives a day at a time, being careful not to hurt one another. He proposed a simple metaphor: it was as if they were all aboard a boat which they knew would never reach port. Ahead lay all kinds of weather. They must keep the boat shipshape and go on being "very good to each other."

Early on the Sunday morning of April 7th, Ernest gathered up Mike Strater, Dos and Katy, Bread Pinder, and Sacker Adams. They weighed anchor for Bimini, 230 nautical miles to the northeast along the dark current of the Gulf Stream. There was a brisk south wind and the trolling was good. They had just sighted a large green turtle and were unpacking the harpoon gun to capture it when all the trollers got strikes almost simultaneously. Dos's was a dolphin and Ernest and Mike each hooked large sharks. As usual Ernest was the first to bring his fish alongside. With the gaff in his left hand and his Colt pistol in his right, he held the shark in position and began pumping bullets into its head. Suddenly the gaff broke with a loud crack and Ernest saw that his legs were covered with blood. He had somehow managed to shoot himself in both legs at the moment when the gaff broke.

Dos and Mike cut loose from their fish and Bread turned the *Pilar* back
for Key West. They cleaned the wounds with boiled water and antiseptic soap
and poured them full of iodine. Ernest vomited into a bucket. The pain had
not yet begun, but the accident was humiliating. Back in Key West, Dr. Warren gave him antitetanus, probed for the lesser splinters, and left the largest
piece to encyst inside the left calf. Instead of Bimini, Ernest went to bed. Katy
was "so mad she would hardly speak to him."

A week later they tried again. This time Charles Thompson went along in
place of Mike Strater, who planned to come over in May. Although still
limping, Ernest believed that he could recuperate better at sea than ashore.
The trip was accomplished without incident. Dos and Katy were delighted with
the tiny island. "There was a wharf," wrote Dos, "and some native shacks
under the coconut palms and a store that had some kind of a barroom attached, where we drank rum in the evenings, and a magnificent broad beach
on the Gulf Stream side." Ernest was equally enthusiastic. Except for the
Pan American seaplane and the sleek private yachts that came over from
Miami, Bimini might have been situated "at the end of the world." When
Pauline flew over late in April, she took one look at the splendid sea beach
and decided that it would be an ideal place to bring the children for the summer. Dos and Katy swam in the surf and collected shells, a hobby that Ernest
then scorned. He wrapped his head in a Turkish towel to ward off the heavy
sun and began trolling for tuna with Mike Strater.

The tuna came late. The first big one was hooked early one morning by
the caretaker from Cat Cay. It was afternoon when Ernest arrived in the
Pilar and took over the task of landing the fish. Dos and Katy presently came
out to watch the fun. By dusk, Ernest had begun to prevail, though his job
was made more difficult by a ring of spectator boats. It was already dark
when he brought the tuna alongside. The gaffman missed with his first lunge
and the fish made off once more. Threatening black clouds drove the small
boats back to harbor. Still Ernest kept on "doggedly reeling in." Then suddenly the sharks arrived, like torpedoes in the darkened waters. There was a
fearsome sound of clicking teeth and rending flesh, and the sea turned murky
with blood. When the tuna was finally hauled over the roller in the stern,
nothing of it remained but the backbone, the head, and the tail.

At the end of the battle, one large white yacht was still standing by. The
Moana belonged to an international sportsman named William B. Leeds.
Leeds's other prize possession was a Thompson submachine gun which he
used for killing sharks. It was clear to Dos and Katy that Ernest was itching
to own it, but they did not observe the transfer. Wet to the skin by the tropical
rainstorm, they spent the night aboard the *Moana*. Next morning they awoke
to find Ernest sprawled in the sunlight, with the tommy-gun "affectionately
cradled in the crotch of his arm."

The tommy-gun soon helped to produce a rift between Ernest and Mike
Strater. Mike was President of the Maine Tuna Club, having boated sixteen

giant tuna off the Maine coast between Ogunquit, where his summer place was, and the mouth of Saco Bay near Biddeford Pool. Fishing with Ernest one day in May, he hooked a 12-foot marlin. After an hour's fight, he had it moving towards the *Pilar* when the sharks came zeroing in. Ernest began plugging them with bursts from his tommy-gun on the pretext that he had to defend Mike's marlin from being mutilated. The effect was just the reverse. The water turned pink with blood and a whole ripping pack of sharks attacked Mike's prize. It took another hour to get the marlin aboard. What was left of it weighed 500 pounds. Ernest made things worse by writing an article for *Esquire* called "The President Vanquishes." He made no mention of his ill-timed intrusion with the tommy-gun. Strater pretended to like the article, but was in fact enraged. Ernest had helped to destroy the biggest marlin Mike had ever hooked.

Throughout the month of May, Ernest's behavior was often that of a bully. When Baron von Blixen flew over from Miami with his second wife, Eva, a handsome blond aviatrix, he invited them to bunk on board the *Pilar*. He was notably possessive towards von Blixen, whom he engaged in conversation about Africa, carefully excluding Strater. He also seemed resentful when the Baroness showed signs of preferring Strater to himself. He was immensely proud of his quick victory over a wealthy publisher named Joseph Knapp, who had come to Bimini aboard his yacht, the *Storm King*. By all accounts it was Knapp himself who picked the fight. Ernest leaped into action, clipping Knapp with two fast left hooks. When Knapp went into a clinch, Ernest clubbed him twice behind the left ear, and then backed off to throw his Sunday punch. Knapp's head banged hard against the planks of the dock. He was still unconscious when some of his crew carried him back aboard the *Storm King*. The members of a Negro calypso band celebrated Ernest's victory with an extemporaneous song about the "big slob" from Key West. On the last day of May, flushed with his various triumphs by sea and land, he flew back from Cat Cay to rejoin Pauline and the children and to catch up on six weeks of accumulated mail.

Letters from Gingrich and Perkins contained two curious bits of intelligence. Gingrich said that an impostor bearing the name of Ernest Hemingway had recently turned up in Chicago. He was a tall man with a mustache who had been following the ladies'-club public-speaking circuit from coast to coast, autographing copies of Ernest's books, and even spending some weeks at the Explorers' Club in New York, where, according to Ernest, he made a practice of taking young men to breakfast. He was said to be the son of an American admiral and was obviously a psychopathic case. The seemingly ineradicable myth that Hemingway himself was "a phoney and a buggar" could doubtless be traced, thought Ernest, to the nationwide operations of this scoundrel.

The second item was equally odd. Scott Fitzgerald had begun work on a historical novel of the Middle Ages, tentatively called *Philippe, Count of Darkness,* and covering the lifetime of a French nobleman from A.D. 880 to

950. Two installments had already appeared in Edwin Balmer's *Red Book,* and a third was scheduled for publication in August. Apart from the fact that the cultural historian of the Jazz Age had turned back to tenth-century France, the most surprising element was that the portrait of Philippe de Ville-franche was modeled on Hemingway as he might have existed in a medieval incarnation. "It shall be the story of Ernest," wrote Scott in one of his note-books. "Just as Stendahl's [sic] portrait of a Byronic man made *Le Rouge et Noire,* so couldn't my portrait of Ernest as Phillipe [sic] make the real modern man?" Max Perkins reported to Ernest that Scott had sworn off drinking: he had gone to Tom Wolfe's home town of Asheville, North Carolina, which he wittily referred to as "Gant's Tomb," and engaged in an abortive love affair with a young married woman. But he steadfastly declined to accept Ernest's invitation to come to Bimini, this time on the ground that he was not physically fit. In the future, as Perkins reported, Scott would like to go on a long trip with Ernest, "but only when he was in fine shape." Meantime it looked as if Scott were trying to exorcise the forever dominant bully-ghost of Hemingway by clapping him into medieval armor and making him leader of a rough and lawless band intent on recapturing the patrimonial acres of Villefranche from a rapacious pack of Norman barons.

Ernest flew back to Bimini on June 5th. He had not been there two weeks when he landed a giant mako shark after a thirty-minute fight. The shark jumped more spectacularly than any tarpon or marlin that he had ever seen, and weighed out at 785, only twelve pounds under the world's record. He began to boast that he had personally changed the "whole system" of big-game fishing around Bimini, and told Perkins that until he came along no one had taken a single tuna by rod and reel in four years' time. He cited the case of Tommy Shevlin, a wealthy young sportsman who had come over from Miami. Tommy had lost six good fish before he asked Ernest to come aboard and give him a few pointers. After the coaching, said Ernest, Tommy boated a 636-pound marlin that established a new Atlantic record.

The run of game fish tapered off late in June and Ernest had the *Pilar* pulled out on the ways for an engine overhaul and a copper-painting job on the bottom. He took advantage of the interval to issue a challenge. He would pay $250 to any Negro who could stay in the ring with him for three three-minute rounds, using six-ounce gloves. He had no fears about losing. The weeks of fishing had strengthened his shoulder and back muscles so much that his punch now packed the force of a mule kick.

The most formidable of his challengers was a big Negro named Willard Saunders, who worked for Julio Sánchez and was reputed to be able to carry a piano on his head. As Ernest later told the story, no doubt with some exaggeration, he was having a drink before supper with Mike Lerner, a mid-dle-aged executive and sportsman from New York. A messenger came aboard Lerner's yacht and said that there was a man on the dock who wanted to speak to Ernest. Willard Saunders was standing there respectfully.

"Mr. Ernest," said Willard, "I want to try you for the two-fifty."

"All right, Willard," said Ernest, "I'll try you in the morning before we go out to fish."

"No sir, Mr. Ernest," Saunders said. "I want to try you right here and now."

"All right," said Ernest, again. "I'll get the gloves."

"No," said the challenger, firmly. "I want to try you right here and now on the dock and without gloves."

The bout did not last long. Ernest cooled Willard in a minute and a half. Another contender met the same fate in two rounds, though not before he had connected with a right hook that paralyzed Ernest's face for half an hour. In all, he fought four times that month, twice bare-fisted and twice with gloves. The climax of the summer's boxing came when he sparred a few "exhibition" rounds with Tom Heeney, a heavyweight who had once fought Gene Tunney. Heeney was "way out of condition," as even Ernest admitted, but Ernest took great pride in the event, which loomed larger in his imagination every time he told about it.

His way of life on Bimini left little time for literature. His only effort in July was a piece for *Esquire* called "Notes on the Next War: A Serious Letter," which he mailed to Gingrich on the 17th. Ernest recalled the vow that he said he had made as he lay wounded in Italy in 1918. It was that if he managed to get through that night alive, he would do everything in his power to prevent a future war. Once a year now, said he, he tried to keep that vow, and the present article was the latest bit of evidence. He predicted that the second world war would come in 1937 or 1938. The United States would doubtless be brought into it by a combination of propaganda, greed, and the desire to cure "the impaired health of the state." Modern war, said Ernest, is always planned and waged by

demagogues and dictators who play on the patriotism of their people to mislead them into a belief in the great fallacy of war when all their vaunted reforms have failed to satisfy the people they misrule. And we in America should see that no man is ever given, no matter how gradually, or how noble and excellent the man, the power to put this country into a war which is now being prepared and brought closer each day with all the premeditation of a long-planned murder. For when you give power to an executive you do not know who will be filling that position when the time of crisis comes.

Reading proof on *Green Hills of Africa* made Ernest highly optimistic about its success. He predicted a sale of fifteen or twenty thousand. Why not? It was "absolutely true autobiography," as he told Perkins, presented with complete and admirable candor. It contained also the best writing he had ever done, as well as that "extra-dimensional quality" that he was always working for. Finally, it would have the effect of taking readers "bodily" into a region that they had never known or were likely to know. When Max proposed to assist in the proofreading by hiring an expert on Africa to verify linguistic details, Ernest hastened to say that he did not want his book "bug-gared up" with a lot of erudition. He had reproduced the Swahili exactly as it was spoken by members of the Wakamba, Kikuyu, Masai, and M'Bulu tribes, none of whom knew it as a native tongue. He would take his stand on precisely what he had written, pidgin-Swahili and all.

He was now telling his friends that the discovery of Bimini was a great event in his life: he liked it as well as any other place he had ever spent time in, and he was already eager to return to it, as he had been in Africa, even before he left it. But now, in the first week of August, its charm was beginning to fade. Hot weather had set in and he complained restively that his head was not functioning worth a damn. Neither was the *Pilar,* which was burning too much oil and needed new piston rings in both engines. She be-haved well enough on the trip back home, starting at midnight on the 14th, and reaching Key West twenty-six hours later. He had expected to spend a week putting her into shape before crossing to Cuba for a month of marlin fishing. The plan was to leave her there in the charge of Carlos Gutiérrez for the dura-tion of the hurricane season. But the engines turned out to be in worse shape than he had supposed. He reluctantly notified Carlos that he would not be coming, and settled in for a season in Key West, hurricanes or no.

38. *THE PERSUADERS*

THE leftist writers and critics of the middle 1930s were variously baffled, angry, and scornful over Hemingway's refusal to enter their camp. In the years of the Great Depression it struck them as reprehensible that a writer of his fame and stature should give his days to bullfighting, lion hunting, marlin fishing, and globe-trotting instead of joining them in the great task of saving the world.

None of them could say that he had not been forthright in stating his posi-tion. "The hardest thing to do," said he, "is to write straight honest prose on human beings. First you have to know the subject; then you have to know how to write. Both take a lifetime to learn, and anybody is cheating who takes politics as a way out. All the outs are too easy, and the thing itself is too hard to do." If a book was written "truly," it would contain "all the economic implications." And if it was a good book, and reading it over you saw that this was so, you could "let the boys yip." The noise would have "that pleasant sound coyotes make on a very cold night when they are out in the snow, and you are in your own cabin that you have built and paid for with your work."

Soon after his return from Bimini, the mail brought him an essay which he could not ignore. It was called "Ernest Hemingway: The Tragedy of Craftsmanship." The author was Ivan Kashkeen, who had translated two of Hemingway's short stories into Russian in 1934, and was familiar with everything else he had written up to and including the stories in *Winner Take*

Nothing. "You read the joyless tale of Hemingway's favorite hero," wrote Kashkeen, "ever the same under his changing names, and you begin to realize that what had seemed the writer's face is but a mask. . . . You imagine the man, morbidly reticent, always restrained and discreet, very intent, very tired, driven to utter despair, painfully bearing the too heavy burden of life's intricacies." The very mirthlessness of his spasmodic smile, said Kashkeen, betrayed the tragic disharmony inside Hemingway, a psychic discord that had brought him to the edge of disintegration. Kashkeen summed it up in an arresting phrase: *Mens morbida in corpore sano.*

In the very book that was currently being serialized in *Scribner's Magazine,* Ernest had sought to make it plain that he had long since overcome his former demons, including the fear of death. "I had been shot," he wrote, "and I had been crippled and gotten away. I expected, always, to be killed by one thing or another and I, truly, did not mind that any more." As for his obligations to society and democracy, he had fulfilled them long ago in his youth. Declining further enlistment, he had since resolved to make himself responsible only to himself. He had exchanged the "pleasant, comforting stench of comrades" for the lonely but pleasurable feeling that comes "when you write well and truly of something and know impersonally you have written that way."

Even in his self-imposed solitude, however, he wanted to be understood and appreciated by this man in another country who had read and written of his work. "Everyone," he told Kashkeen, "tries to frighten you now by saying . . . that if one does not become a communist or have a Marxian viewpoint one will have no friends and will be alone. They seem to think that to be alone is something dreadful; or that to not have friends is to be feared. . . . I cannot be a communist now because I believe in only one thing: liberty. First I would look after myself and do my work. Then I would care for my family. Then I would help my neighbor. But the state I care nothing for. All the state has ever meant to me is unjust taxation. . . . I believe in the absolute minimum of government."

"A writer," he continued, "is an outlyer like a Gypsy. . . . If he is a good writer he will never like the government he lives under. His hand should be against it. . . . He can be class conscious only if his talent is limited. If he has enough talent, all classes are his province. He takes from them all and what he gives is everybody's property. . . . A true work of art endures forever; no matter what its politics."

The news that his writings were popular in the Soviet Union made him both jubilant and boastful. He wrote Perkins that he was now outselling Dreiser, Dos Passos, Sinclair Lewis, and "several other guys" among Russian readers, and that they thought *Death in the Afternoon* was a "wow." This proved that people could like a man's writing regardless of his politics. Neither he nor his politics had changed. It was the same with economics. *They* (the nameless generic enemy) had now replaced religion with economics as the "opium" of the people. This gave the critics a new set of reasons for disliking Hemingway's work. But if a man could and would write, no critical system could hurt his "stuff" if it was good—or help if it was not. His popularity in Russia anyhow proved that "they" were not going to kill him off for a while yet. "Papa" was not only durable but also increasingly capable, in his own opinion, and learning new facts all the time.

Two weeks later, on the last night of August, a hot and sultry Saturday, Ernest carried a drink out to the back porch and sat down to read the evening paper. The moment he unfolded it and began to read, the reason for the sultriness became clear: a headline reported a tropical disturbance in the Bahamas. The hurricane season that he had feared because of the *Pilar* was now beginning. He went inside to find his September storm chart. It gave the dates and directions of forty major hurricanes since 1900. He computed that if the storm followed the usual pattern, it could not reach Key West before Monday noon at the earliest. That left roughly thirty-nine hours for getting ready.

His first concern was the *Pilar*. He spent most of Sunday making his boat as safe as possible. The harbormen refused to haul her out on the ways because there were too many others ahead. Ernest bought $52 worth of heavy new hawser from Thompson's hardware store and moored his craft in what he took to be the safest corner of the submarine base. On Monday, September 2nd, he moved the garden furniture and the children's toys into the house and nailed up the round-topped green shutters at all the windows. Everywhere in town others were doing the same. Large red warning flags with black squares whipped in the rising wind with noises like pistol shots. The barometer was falling steadily. He drove over to the submarine base to wrap his new hawser with canvas against the inevitable chafing. Unless the storm came in from the northwest through the mouth of the sub basin, he thought there was a good chance that the *Pilar* might ride it out. He waited with the crowd at the Weather Bureau until the ten o'clock advisory. It did not sound good, and he went home for a couple of hours of sleep, parking the car in the street because he did not trust the rickety garage.

By midnight the wind was howling, rain was roaring on the roof, and the barometer beside his bed read 29.55 and falling. He pulled on his clothes and jumped into the car. It would not start and he half-ran, half-trotted to the submarine base through a wilderness of falling wires and broken tree branches and palm fronds. His flashlight had shorted out in the wet and he was sick with worry. If his boat was lost, he told himself, he would never have enough money to get another. But the *Pilar* was still there, riding the foam-flecked surges. About half-past two the wind backed into the west and at four the glass steadied out and held the same pressure for an hour. By five, he decided that the worst was over and slopped back home in the faint gray morning light. A tree had fallen across the sidewalk and he knew from the "strange empty look in the front yard" that the large old sapodilla tree was also down. Inside the house he stripped off his wet clothes, toweled dry, drank down half a tumbler of whiskey, and fell at once into a dreamless sleep.

The nightmare came later. The hurricane had only grazed Key West. Out-riding winds had torn at Key Largo and the great mangrove swamp at the tip of the Florida peninsula. The full brunt of the storm's force had swept across Islamorada and Upper and Lower Matecumbe Keys. Besides native fishermen and tourist-trade people, nearly a thousand of the war veterans in the CCC camps had been caught and drowned.

Ernest was eager to go to the scene of the devastation. The survivors, if any, would need food and water. He offered to pay Bra Saunders if he would take him up in his boat, and asked J. B. Sullivan, the machinist, to make a third. The seas were still heavy when they left Key West harbor, and the water far from shore was filled with debris. The shorelines of the various keys were almost unrecognizable even to a veteran seaman like Saunders. A good-sized ship was beached near Alligator Pool Light, and an 85-foot tower on Lower Matecumbe lay fallen and twisted like something wrenched and cast aside by giant hands. When they went ashore, Saunders found a whole cache of slot machines half buried in tons of sand. He scraped away at some of them and came up grinning with a bushel of quarters.

This was a region, said Ernest, where there was not any autumn "but only a more dangerous summer." The whole island looked like the abandoned bed of a river. And then there were the dead. Among the massed bodies floating in the ferry slip was that of Joe Lowe, "the original of [Eddy Marshall] the rummy" in Ernest's Harry Morgan story. The railroad embankment had been swept away and the war veterans who had taken shelter behind it lay among the mangroves, all of them "beginning to be too big for their blue jeans and jackets." Altogether, as Ernest wrote Max Perkins, he saw more dead that day than he had seen since the summer of 1918. He thought of how it must have been while the men clung desperately to the rails in the screaming darkness until the enormous waves tossed them into the mangroves. Dead soldiers were to be expected. But the ultimate horror was the sight of the two women, "naked, tossed up into trees by the water, swollen and stinking, their breasts as big as balloons, flies between their legs." Someone identified them. They had been the two "very nice girls who ran a sandwich place and filling station three miles from the ferry."

Ernest was torn between fascination and anger. When Joe North wired to ask him for an article for the *New Masses,* he responded with 2,800 words in which he sought to fix the blame for the drowning of the veterans on the bureaucrats in Washington. He was quick to say privately that his willingness to write for the *New Masses* implied no change in his point of view towards those who ran it. They spent the year telling readers how worthless his writing was, only to wire him when they wanted the truth about the disaster. In fact, said Ernest, he had less respect for them than ever—especially including one

Robert Forsythe, who had done a piece about his extreme sensitivity to criticism. Ernest threatened to break his jaw the next time they met.

But many of those who read his article believed that Ernest was now making a swing to the left. An advance copy of the magazine fell into the hands of Charles B. Strauss, aged twenty-three, who had long been a Hemingway admirer. Strauss wrote him a letter of praise, hoping that his future work might be infused with a new sense of "brotherly purpose," portraying the sufferings of men "bound together in belief" rather than painting more portraits of isolatoes like Jake Barnes and Frederic Henry, "alienated and alone." Ernest replied kindly that he would like to get the concept of human brotherhood into his work. But if a man was capable of writing "truly," he did not have to take sides overtly. The right or wrong of the matter would clearly show up in what he wrote.

Green Hills of Africa was now a month short of publication. Ernest dedicated the book to Philip Percival, Charles Thompson, and J. B. Sullivan. The illustrations, which he admired and had labored to make as accurate as possible, had been done by Edward Shenton, a Philadelphia artist. Ernest wondered rather plaintively whether there was anyone among the New York reviewers who would give the book its due. But he was sanguine enough about it to risk a trip to New York in mid-September. The main attraction was the heavyweight bout between Joe Louis and Max Baer on the evening of the 24th. Ernest paid for the trip by covering the fight for *Esquire*. Gate receipts had reached the phenomenal level of a million dollars. Ernest's personal interest was heightened by the fact that Jack Dempsey, whom he had disliked for years, was going to serve as Baer's second at ringside.

He called it afterwards "the most disgusting spectacle" that he had ever seen. The fourth round was not yet over when Baer was counted out. During the first three he had been so visibly afraid of Louis that his fear had seemed to drift out across the ropes like a fog. Ernest's piece for *Esquire* said that he himself had often known fear. He still shuddered at the memory of the slippery ledges in Wyoming where he had crawled after mountain rams. His sudden "dread of eternity" the night he was blown up in Italy had dried up the springs of his courage for a whole month. But he still believed that fear was the best possible catharsis, especially if a man could control the dosage. On the other hand, Baer's performance in the presence of fear had been merely contemptible, even against an opponent like Louis, who seemed to Ernest "the most beautiful fighting machine" he had ever yet known.

Somewhat against his better judgment, he was back in New York in October, staying at the Westbury Hotel on East 69th Street. He was understandably nervous about the reception of *Green Hills of Africa*. There were several passages in the book that were bound to provoke attacks. He had gone out of his way to compare the general run of writers in New York to "angleworms in a bottle," trying to derive nourishment from daily contact with one another. He had defined critics as the lice that crawl on literature, and had cited the cases of two well-known writers who had actually been destroyed by adverse reviews.

Once again, as had happened so often since 1929, the reviews were mixed. Edward Weeks found the book absorbing in spite of his personal aversion to blood sports. Charles Poore called it the best-written story of big-game hunting that he had ever read. Carl Van Doren liked the "easy, intricate, and magical" prose as well as the portraits of the people. Apart from a few "butcher-shop details," Isabel Paterson enjoyed the book, not least because it provided "a complete summary of Hemingway, his talent and his limitations." Others, however, were not impressed. Lewis Gannett called it "just another safari," and Edmund Wilson thought it "the only really weak book" that Ernest had done. Bernard DeVoto said that it was "a pretty small book for a big man to write." T. S. Matthews was also disappointed. "I can remember the time," he wrote, "when he was just a big brother, and we thought his strong-arm stunts were swell. . . . We thought it was great stuff to have a he-man writer on our side. . . . What's the trouble now? . . . He thinks he can write a piece about anything and get away with it. He probably can, too. But it isn't the hot stuff he says it is."

After some rumination over these and other opinions, Ernest concluded that his book had been "ruined" by three mistakes, two of Scribners' and one of his own. Scribners had set too high a price on the book and failed to advertise it enough. He had made the mistake of daring the critics to attack and they had taken the dare, "ganging up" on his book and refusing to judge it on its merits. But he counted on the passage of time to prove the virtues of *Green Hills of Africa.* It pleased him that *Death in the Afternoon,* "once hailed as lousy," was now being spoken of with respect.

The persuaders on the left got in another lick at Ernest in December. Abner Green was a Hemingway admirer in his early twenties. Born in Brooklyn of immigrant parents, he was working as a writer of educational materials for the American Committee for the Protection of the Foreign Born. In a new literary magazine called *The American Criterion,* he addressed an open letter to Hemingway. It praised his fiction, deplored his *Esquire* articles as potboilers, and strongly implied that a leading American writer ought to be able to discover more important themes than the pursuit and dismemberment of animals and fish, no matter how big. Ernest read Green's letter and replied with one of his own, using many of the same arguments he had earlier used in writing to Ivan Kashkeen. A correspondence ensued in which Green attempted to arouse Hemingway to a new sense of social solidarity. Although he was plainly touched by Green's high-minded persistence, he continued to believe that the writer's basic obligation was to do well rather than to do good.

For all his lone-wolf fervor, however, such arguments as those of Kashkeen and Strauss and Green were beginning to take effect. This was fleetingly evident in his second Harry Morgan story, "The Tradesman's Return," completed and sent off to Gingrich on December 10th. The first Morgan story had shown the hero driven by economic necessity to such desperate measures as smuggling and murder. The second centered on his rum-running activities between Key West and Mariel on the Cuban coast. It began by emphasizing Harry Morgan's lonely independence, his stoical endurance, and his lack of pity for himself and others. By the end of the story, however, Harry and his Negro assistant Wesley were both so severely wounded that they barely made it back to a hidden channel on Woman Key. They had just begun to dump the sacked liquor over the side when a charter boat from Key West came chugging along the channel. The man at the wheel was a Key West fisherman called Captain Willie. His passengers were a couple of officious bureaucrats from Washington. They recognized Harry as a rum-runner and ordered Captain Willie to stop. But Willie had no such intention.

"Hey," he shouted to Harry, "dump your load and get into town. I got a guy here on board some kind of a stool from Washington. More important than the President, he says. He wants to pinch you. He thinks you're a bootlegger. He's got the numbers of the boat. I ain't never seen you so I don't know who you are."

"O.K.," came a shout from the booze boat. "Thanks, brother."

"That chap your brother?" asked one of the men from Washington.

"No, sir," said Captain Willie. "Most everybody goes in boats calls each other brother."

It was a gingerly engagement of the theme of working-class solidarity. It would hardly have proved convincing to men of Abner Green's background and convictions. "The Tradesman's Return" had nothing in common with the general run of proletarian fiction in the period of the Great Depression. Yet his leftist sympathizers could at least take comfort from the slender fissure, the thinnest of thin red lines, which had now appeared in the wall of Hemingway's resistance to persuasion.

39. THE SLOPES OF KILIMANJARO

THE second Morgan story was hardly out of Ernest's hands when he began a sequel, which carried his hero one step farther down the scale of economic desperation. It went along so well that he jubilantly wrote Fitzgerald twice in a single week, bawdy letters full of pre-Christmas cheer. But the cheer was mixed with bitter draughts, as if to confirm Arnold Gingrich's secret opinion that Scott's gloom always tended to "bring out the bully" in Hemingway. Ernest told Scott that he was like a brilliant mathematician who always came up with the wrong answers. Perhaps it was this realization, said he, that always made Scott get "stinking drunk" whenever he met his old friends. Why did he persistently confuse growing up with growing old?

Ernest's humor was on the macabre side. If Scott were really as depressed as he had sounded in his letter from Asheville, he had better insure himself heavily and fly south. Ernest would take him to Cuba and get him bumped off by a "nigger" revolutionist. His heart could then be sent to the Plaza Hotel, his liver to the museum at Princeton University, and a lung apiece to Perkins and George Horace Lorimer. Ernest would volunteer to carry the other trophies to Cap d'Antibes, where they could be ceremoniously hurled into the Mediterranean. Archie MacLeish would doubtless agree to write a mystical poem for the occasion. Ernest composed one of his own: "Lines to be Read at the Casting of Scott Fitzgerald's Balls into the Sea from Eden Roc," evidently a bawdy parody of a poem by Hart Crane.

All this banter left Fitzgerald unimpressed. The explanation reached Ernest shortly after Christmas when he opened an advance copy of the February *Esquire*. It contained a long confessional article of Scott's, called "The Crack-Up." Ernest was shocked. Scott, he felt, seemed almost to be taking pride in the shamelessness of his defeat. Why in God's name couldn't he understand that writers went through that kind of emptiness many times? Work was the thing that would save him if he would only "bite on the nail" and get down to it, honest work with honest fiction, a paragraph at a time. One of Scott's troubles was that he had never been able to think clearly. The thing to do with such a "marvelous talent" as his was to use it. Instead he had made the mistake of loving youth so much that he had jumped straight from there to senility without passing through manhood in between.

But all this tough talk was little more than a mask. In January Ernest himself went through a spell of insomnia and melancholia. It lasted three weeks and was dissipated only when he decided that it was being caused by insufficient exercise and worry over productivity. It was better, he concluded, to produce half as much and get plenty of action rather than to drive himself crazy in an attempt to speed up his work. After all, as he had told Kashkeen in August, he had "greater facility for action than for writing." In action, he did not "worry any more," whereas writing was something he could never do as well as he knew it ought to be done.

One of the recurrent foes of writing was visitors. Ernest complained loudly and bitterly that they were driving him nuts. This even applied to the film star Nancy Carroll. Paying a call on the Hemingways one February lunchtime, she was pursued by so many worshippers that Pauline locked the front gate to keep them from trampling the shrubbery. Hurrying out of the house after lunch, Ernest kicked the locked gate to open it and broke one of his big toes. He erupted like a volcano with anger and self-pity. His feelings were not helped by the fact that he had sworn off hard liquor for Lent.

When "good old Waldo" Peirce came down in February, accompanied by his young wife Alzira and his superactive twin sons, Ernest professed to be astonished at the degree of his domestication. He recalled a former occasion in a bar when two drunken sailors had made fun of Waldo's beard. Waldo had picked up one in each hand and cracked their heads together. But as a trainer of children, said Ernest fondly, Waldo was the "absolute bloody worst" in the world. While one of the twins whammed him over the head with a beer bottle and the other set fire to his beard, Waldo merely smiled and said, "Well, pretty soon they'll be in school." Ernest's views on parenthood were more austere. He took pleasure in answering his sons' questions and conducting them, though separately, on fishing trips aboard the *Pilar*. He thought that they were both good company, funny and smart. But he continued to take them in very small doses.

His spurt of writing kept on all through the spring. By the end of March, when Harry Payne Burton came down from *Cosmopolitan* to talk big money in a confidential voice, Ernest was ready with a new Spanish story. It was about a country boy named Paco, assistant waiter at a bullfighters' pension in Madrid. Like all his kind, Paco aspired to be a matador, only to bleed to death after a make-believe bullfight involving two meat knives and a dining-room chair. Burton told Ernest that he would pay $40,000 for the first serial rights to Ernest's new novel, $7,500 for long stories, and $3,000 for shorter ones. But he showed little interest in the tragic tale of Paco. Ernest sent it off to Gingrich as a substitute for another of his nonfiction articles.

He had not yet exhausted the material left over from his safari in Tanganyika. On April 19th he completed a story, tentatively called "The Happy Ending," which Harry Burton promptly bought for $5,000. It was a brilliant fusion of personal observation, hearsay, and invention. Ernest drew heavily upon his own experiences in shooting buffalo and lion. He also asserted, many years later, that he had drawn his portrait of Francis Macomber from a wealthy young international sportsman—a "nice jerk" whom he had known very well in real life. "He is just how he really was," said Ernest ambiguously, "only he is invented." Macomber's wife Margot was also invented from a living prototype. Handsome, well-kept, a society beauty with a nearly perfect oval face and a wealth of dark hair, she embodied all the internal qualities that Ernest detested among the wives of his wealthier friends. "I invented her complete with handles," said he, "from the worst bitch I knew (then) and when I first knew her she'd been lovely. Not my dish, not my pigeon, not my cup of tea, but lovely for what she was, and I was her all of the above, which is whatever you make of it." With some small show of gallantry, he added that this was as close as he could come to describing his earlier association with the lady.

Robert Wilson, white hunter to the Macombers, was based on Philip Percival, with his rubicund face, cool blue eyes, laconic speech habits, and his enviable combination of courage and judgment. Ernest later said that all he contributed to the invention of Wilson was to disguise Philip slightly for family and business reasons, and in order to keep him out of trouble with the Tanganyika Game Department. What he did not disclose was that the Macomber story was a much embroidered and wholly reconstructed version of a tale Philip had told him one night beside their safari campfire. Percival himself thought Ernest's yarn "devilishly clever." He had some fear that the people he had described to Ernest, including their white hunter, might recognize themselves in fictional disguise. Luckily, his own high standards of professional etiquette had prevented him from naming names, even to Ernest in private conversation. He took some comfort from the fact that Ernest had armed Wilson with a .505 Gibbs, a rifle never used by the white hunter in question.

Another topic of campfire talk was the fact that some white hunters had been known to sleep with their female clients. Unlike Wilson, who was said to carry a double-sized cot to accommodate such "windfalls," Percival himself drew the line at all such activities. But he had mentioned several cases in which one or another of his clients had lost their heads through fear. Ernest picked up this clue and exploited it by causing Francis Macomber to flee before a wounded and charging lion. The denouement of his story, in which Margot Macomber killed her husband while ostensibly trying to keep him from being gored by a wounded buffalo, was likewise one of Ernest's inventions. "As far as I know," said Philip Percival, "no client has ever succeeded in shooting her husband as EH describes."

While Ernest was busy with the Macomber story, Jane Mason had been in and out of Key West and back and forth from Miami. When he spoke of taking Joe Russell to handle the *Pilar* in Cuba in late April and early May, Jane volunteered to make the trip. Pauline was going to Piggott to give the Pfeiffer grandparents a "good dose" of Gregory. She proposed to join Ernest in Havana upon her return from Arkansas. Joe could not go until April 23rd. According to Ernest, Joe was the only one of his friends who seemed completely willing to go anywhere without his wife, while Jane was equally apt to go places without her husband.

A little before Easter, Hemingway's life was diversified by a regrettable incident. Wallace Stevens, a tall, gray man of portly build who was both an executive in a Hartford insurance company and one of the best poets then writing in the United States, had come to Key West for a short vacation. Stevens was a complete novice in boxing, besides being twenty years Hemingway's senior. For reasons that remain obscure, the poet seems to have baited the novelist into some sort of fight. Stevens emerged with a black eye and a badly bruised face. Waldo Peirce saw him next day, wearing dark glasses to conceal the damage. Stevens understandably asked Hemingway to say nothing publicly about the affair. Although Ernest complied, since he admired and respected Stevens as a poet, he could not resist an oblique and tantalizing reference in a letter to Dos Passos.

The trip to Cuba, accomplished late in April and lasting through the greater part of May, was a considerable letdown in comparison with those of former years. Marlin were extremely scarce, the *Pilar's* engines were behaving badly, and Ernest discovered that Carlos Gutiérrez, his expert gaffman, had become "¾ blind and quite deaf." After Josie Russell's return to Key West in the middle of May, the situation aboard the *Pilar* turned embarrassingly tense.

Never one to mince words when black anger overtook him, Ernest began to treat his old associate with a verbal roughness that witnesses found to be almost beyond belief. Bollo, the Cuban who had been aboard at the time of the whale hunt, took over the job of steersman. As the target of Ernest's ruthless barbs, Carlos was sometimes reduced to tears.

In spite of Carlos's disabilities, Ernest decided to carry him and Bollo along for the trip to the Bahamas in June, also signing on his son Patrick, as cabin boy. The boat's engine trouble had now been diagnosed as a cracked cylinder block. Ernest took her to Miami on the second of June and had the entire engine replaced. It was a wise move. When they left for Bimini two days later, they ran into the worst storm that the boat had weathered since the hurricane of 1935. Contrary winds piled up mountainous seas in all directions. Ernest steered northeast until daylight, his heart in his mouth, then set his course northwest, running down the backs of the billows as if the *Pilar* were a roller coaster, cursing helplessly while the water pumps sucked air and the cruiser's wide bows slapped thunderously into every trough. Patrick slept peacefully through most of the struggle, but Ernest was so frightened by the size of the waves that he found it impossible to keep his voice at normal pitch. Yet he stuck it out at the helm and ran through the storm, pulling into Bimini Harbor full of pride at his seamanship and his powers of endurance.

The island was populous with wealthy sportsmen in lustrous white yachts. Tom Shevlin was there with his wife Lorraine; the Kip Farringtons were both fishing vigorously in friendly competition; Colonel Richard Cooper came over from Miami; Nonie Briggs arrived with his pretty wife Margaret on a fishing holiday, often aboard the *Pilar;* Jane Mason chartered a boat in the hope of catching more fish than Ernest did. One day he learned that Marjorie Kinnan Rawlings, a handsome woman of forty who had been making a name for herself as a Scribner novelist, had come over as a guest of Mrs. Oliver Grinnell. He surprised them both by striding aboard the Grinnell yacht to pay a call. From her habitual reading of his works, Mrs. Rawlings had expected "a fire-spitting ogre." He destroyed the image at once by imprisoning her hand in his "big gentle paw" and telling her that he greatly admired her writings. He was, she gathered, a near-legendary figure among the islanders, equally popular with the wealthy anglers and the poverty-stricken natives. Everyone was still telling the story of his five-punch knockout of Joe Knapp, and the Negro musicians still sang the calypso song about the "big fat slob in Bimini Harbor."

Ernest was beginning to fear that his widening acquaintance among the rich might harm his integrity as a writer. He had already dramatized this fear in a story about a writer named Henry Walden, dying of gangrene on the plains of Africa and abusing his rich wife as a scapegoat for his own failure. He had completed a rough draft of the story shortly before the September hurricane and then put it away in his desk to settle and objectify until he was ready to finish it. While he continued to consort with the wealthy, he took some private care to disassociate himself from the values they seemed to stand for. When

Gingrich flew to Bimini for an editorial consultation, Ernest brought the matter up almost carelessly. "You and I are the only peasants here," he said one day, "with a hint of a wave of one hand" towards "the cluster of the rich and fashionable . . . who were in sight at the time." A few months later, he readily admitted to Mrs. Rawlings that these people were "awfully dumb"— except for Ben Finney, who was "quite a guy." He liked them all and got on well with them. But he felt that women who fished seriously were both the worthiest and the dullest bitches alive, while ninety percent of their men were the same, with an additional touch of oldmaidism.

During their literary conferences that month, Gingrich found Ernest surprisingly tractable, and even grateful for editorial opinions. He had brought along the first chapters of his third Morgan story—roughly 30,000 words, which he had not touched since early in the year—and asked Arnold's advice. By carrying it to full novel length and bringing out the previous Morgan adventures separately as part of a volume of collected stories to be published in the fall, he thought that he could make a comeback in fiction that would knock the New York crowd down into the gutters where they belonged.

Gingrich argued that this was a crazy idea. The Morgan stories belonged together. Ernest must carry through with Morgan Number Three, already so well begun, and then weld the whole together as a sort of trilogy in miniature. It would begin and end with Ernest's insights into the revolutionary politics of Cuba. Somewhere inside he could deal with the war veterans and the Matecumbe hurricane disaster. Josie Russell's place, disguised as Freddy's Bar, could serve as a focal point for Harry's business dealings on the American side. Finally, as they talked it out, the book could emphasize the theme of Harry Morgan's decline and fall, what Ernest called "the decline of the individual"—followed in the end by his reemergence. Ernest happily reported this change of plan to Max Perkins, with whom he had been corresponding about *The First Forty-Nine Stories,* successor to *The First Fifty-Four Stories* project. He also told Gingrich with almost childish gratitude that he was the "one guy" in all the world whom he trusted "completely, all the way around" for honest opinions about writing. Charles Thompson, J. B. Sullivan, and Josie Russell were men's men who could be depended on in all other ways, but Arnold was the man to turn to about literary matters.

The day before Marjorie Rawlings was due to return to Florida, Ernest hooked into a 514-pound tuna off Gun Cay and landed him, "still fresh as hell," way up off the Isaacs. The battle lasted almost seven hours and Ernest sweated away more than a pound for each hour. At the end of the third hour he was ready to faint with fatigue; then he got his second wind and the rest of the time went by like minutes. On the way home, by his own account, he filled up on beer and whiskey and soda, lay down to recuperate, and then found that he couldn't get up. But when the *Pilar* reentered Bimini harbor about 9:30 that evening, the whole population, including Marjorie Rawlings, turned out to see his fish, which was eleven and a half feet long. A fatuous old man with a new yacht and a young bride had arrived not long before, announcing that tuna fishing was easy. As the *Pilar* was made fast, Mrs. Rawlings watched in fascination as Ernest came surging up from belowdecks, "gloriously drunk, roaring, 'Where's the son of a bitch who said it was easy?' The last anyone saw of him that night, he was standing alone on the dock where his giant tuna hung from the stays—using it as a punching bag."

Mrs. Rawlings found Ernest a fascinating problem in paradox. She thought of the "big gentle paw" that had held her smaller one with so much tenderness at the time of their first meeting. Yet she could not help reflecting that this was the same paw with which he sporadically and mercilessly knocked people down. He seemed to her "so great an artist" that he did not need to be on the defensive, a man "so vast, so virile" that he had no reason to prove it with his fists. The clue to his character must lie, she thought, in some sort of "inner conflict between the sporting life and the literary life; between sporting people and the artist."

From her experience with Mrs. Grinnell during the visit to Bimini, she knew that when one was at sea, with the excitement of fishing, nothing else seemed valid. The sporting people were delightful companions. Yet whenever she was not with them she was overcome by the realization that as a literary person she was "worlds away from them." She knew things that they would never know. On the other hand, they wore an armor that she would never wear. It was not so much their money as their "reaction to living." They enjoyed life immensely, yet without being sensitive to it. "Hemingway," said Mrs. Rawlings, "is among these people a great deal, and they like and admire him—his personality, his sporting prowess, and his literary prestige. . . . Unconsciously, he must value their opinion. He must be afraid of laying bare before them the agony that tears the artist. . . . So, as in *Death in the Afternoon,* he writes beautifully, and then immediately turns it off with a flippant comment, or a deliberate obscenity. His sporting friends would not understand the beauty. They would roar with delight at the flippancy. They are the only people who would be pleased by the things in his work that distress all the rest of us."

When Mrs. Rawlings broached this hypothesis to Ernest himself, he explained that, after all, he had fished and hunted since boyhood and continued doing so because he got "an awful lot of fun and excitement out of it." Writing was for him a soul-searing process, accomplished indoors with the instruments of his trade, a self-imposed imprisonment. When it went well, nothing could match it for reward and enjoyment. When it did not, unless he wished to go crazy, he had no recourse but to take up the instruments of his second trade—the guns, the rods—and pursue the other satisfactions over the seas and through the forests. Nothing but writing could give him as much genuine pleasure as killing a bear, a buffalo, a kudu, a black-maned lion, or fighting to its death a huge and lordly marlin, a giant tuna, even a sperm whale if he could sink the harpoon deep enough in its flesh. Was this a conflict? He did not think so.

Soon after his return to Key West on July 16th, Ernest met a man named Harry Burns, a professor of English from the University of Washington in Seattle. With his genius for the invention of special names, Ernest whimsically rechristened his new friend Professor MacWalsey, and engaged him in marathon conversations that often lasted well past midnight. Burns was still there when the mails brought an advance copy of the August *Esquire*. It contained the final draft of Ernest's story about the writer dying of gangrene in Africa. During the months when it had languished untouched in his desk drawer, he had thought of it under its provisional title, "A Budding Friendship." Its new name was infinitely better: "The Snows of Kilimanjaro." Fortunately, also, he had chosen to call his protagonist by the simple name of Harry instead of Henry Walden, his earlier choice, with its Thoreauvian overtones.

Ernest later explained how he had arrived at the conception which governed his story. It all began, said he, with the rich woman who had invited him to tea in New York in April, 1934, and offered to stake him to another safari. Back in Key West that summer he had done some daydreaming about how things would have turned out if he had accepted her offer. The dying writer in the story was an image of himself as he might have been. Might have been, that is, if the temptation to lead the aimless life of the very rich had overcome his integrity as an artist.

It was his later boast that he had used up in this one story enough material to fill four novels. "I put all the true stuff in," said he, "and with all the load, the most load any short story ever carried," the story still was able to take off like a powerful airplane. Much of the "true stuff" went far back in Ernest's career. He recalled Grandpa Bacon's log house on Walloon Lake, the hilltop in Paris where he and Hadley had lived in 1922 and 1923, the fishing trip to the Black Forest that first summer. He romanticized and fictionized his journey to Constantinople. There were memories of Schruns and the ski instructor Walther Lent and the poker games at the Madlenerhaus, high in the Silvretta Range. He recalled the Nordquist ranch in Wyoming, with the "silvered gray of the sage-brush" on the hills across the river. For the climactic conclusion, in which Harry imagined the arrival of a small plane to carry him back to the hospital in Nairobi, Ernest drew upon his memories of his own flight out of the plains country for the treatment of his dysentery, and the distant view of the snow-capped western summit of Kilimanjaro. The epigraph at the head of the story mentioned the dried and frozen carcass of the leopard, about which Ernest had heard from Philip Percival. He later called it "part of the metaphysics" of his story. He knew well enough what it meant, said he, but he was under no obligation to explain.

The story not only embodied a good many of Ernest's personal memories, but its subject lay very close to his artistic conscience. He had told Kashkeen that a writer must be "an outlyer like a Gypsy." Had he in fact traded away some part of his gypsy's independence in exchange for the sporting life that he was living now? Like the story of the Macombers, "The Snows of Kilimanjaro" was filled with evidence of his growing hostility towards at least certain members of the international sporting set. One example was the group at Bimini whom Marjorie Rawlings had seen as a potential danger to Ernest's growth as a writer.

The story also reached out to involve Fitzgerald. The dying writer was made to remember "poor Scott Fitzgerald" and "his romantic awe" of that "special glamorous race" who had money. When Scott had discovered that they were not so glamorous as he had supposed, the realization "wrecked him just as much as any other thing that wrecked him." Ernest was determined not to follow Fitzgerald into the wreckage of a crack-up. As he had long ago told him, wreckage was made to be used by writers, even if it was the wreckage of one's whole damned life. If the rich were indeed the enemy, Ernest would use them as such in his fiction.

Ill and depressed among the green mountains of North Carolina, Fitzgerald was angered to see his name used in Ernest's story. He got off a curt note on the stationery of the Grove Park Inn in Asheville.

Dear Ernest: Please lay off me in print. If I choose to write de profundis sometimes it doesn't mean I want friends praying aloud over my corpse. No doubt you meant it kindly, but it cost me a night's sleep. And when you incorporate it [the story] in a book would you mind cutting my name? It's a fine story—one of your best—even though 'Poor Scott Fitzgerald, etc.' rather spoiled it for me. Ever your friend,

Scott

[P.S.] Riches have never fascinated me, unless combined with the greatest charm or distinction.

Ernest presently wrote Perkins that Scott's reaction was damned curious coming from a man who had spent all winter writing "those awful things about himself" in *Esquire*. His reply to Scott himself said ominously that for five years now he had not written a line about anyone he knew because he had felt so sorry for them. But all that was past. He was going to stop being a gentleman and go back to being a novelist, using whatever material he damned well chose.

The obtuseness of this reply astonished Fitzgerald, who thought it both crazy and conceited. Evidently, said Scott, Ernest had begun to think of himself as a "Great Writer." By what quirk of imagination had he concluded that the publication of the Crack-Up articles invited all comers to a "sort of open season" on Fitzgerald, as if he were a duck or a pheasant? Ernest seemed now to have "completely lost his head." He was like a "punch-drunk pug fighting himself in the movies." The thing to do was to avoid all further entanglement with him. For Ernest, said Scott, was every bit as "nervously broken down" as he was himself. It was only that the manifestations took different forms. "His inclination is toward megalomania," wrote Scott, "and mine toward melancholy."

What Ernest concealed from Scott, and from most of his other friends, was that the pendulum in his nervous system swung periodically through the full arc from megalomania to melancholy. Ivan Kashkeen had defined his affliction as *mens morbida in corpore sano.* One of the morbid aspects of Ernest's mind was the recurrent conviction that he might soon die without having completed his work or fulfilled his unwritten promise to his talents. At the time when he wrote the story of the dying writer on the plains of Africa, he knew very well that he had climbed no farther than the lower slopes of his personal Kilimanjaro.

CHAPTER 7

Loyalist

40. MOVING IN

DURING the last week in July, Ernest was busy preparing for another visit to the Nordquist ranch in Wyoming. This was also the week that marked the beginning of the Civil War in Spain. The Loyalists had just stormed the Montaña Barracks in Madrid when Ernest wrote his young friend Prudencio de Pereda that "we ought to have been in Spain all this week." But he did not seem to be in any great hurry to go. Nor did he show any outward signs of disappointment as he loaded the Ford car for a trip that would take him in exactly the opposite direction from Spain.

Besides Ernest, Pauline, and the two boys, Bumby and Patrick, Pauline's sister Jinny and Professor Harry Burns were riding along as far as New Orleans. It was hurricane weather and the drive to Louisiana was wet and sultry. Through Texas and Colorado heavy showers repeatedly drenched the car. Late in the afternoon of August 10th they crossed the echoing plank bridge into the L-Bar-T Ranch. The two boys leaped into action like colts let out to pasture. Next day, Ernest wrote Mrs. Pfeiffer that in the first twelve hours Patrick had stayed off his horse only long enough to eat.

Most of Nordquist's former staff had left for other jobs, though Chub Weaver agreed to come over from Red Lodge to serve as cook and general factotum during the hunting season. The Hemingways moved into the Sidleys' cabin on the knoll beside the river. It was larger than any of the others, and included a living room with a fieldstone fireplace and a spare bedroom that Ernest used to write in. The mailbag was filled with letters from people who had read and admired "The Snows of Kilimanjaro." Katy Dos Passos guessed that it had "made more people cry than anything since the Armistice." The same was true of the Spanish Civil War. "I never look for the Spanish news," she wrote, "without that sick cold feeling I only used to have about my personal affairs and miseries." Dos wrote that Luis Quintanilla had become an officer in the Spanish Republican Army. He had participated in the attack against the Rebel garrison at the Montaña Barracks on July 20th. Some of the wounded Rebels had been thrust into the very prison where Quintanilla had languished until Ernest and Dos had helped to secure his release.

In spite of his words to de Pereda, Ernest was still of two minds about going to Spain. He spoke longingly of another trip to Bimini and even of a second African safari. Yet the war troubled his conscience. At the end of September he told Max Perkins that he hated having missed "this Spanish thing" worse than anything in the world. He was still hoping to go if the fighting had not ended by the time he finished his novel. Premonitions of possible death struck him periodically like twinges of rheumatism. He confided to Marjorie Kinnan Rawlings his feeling that he would soon die, though he would much prefer to become a wise old man, wearing a white beard and chewing tobacco. Soon after setting down these sentiments, he sounded a more sinister note in a letter to MacLeish. He loved life so much, said he, that it would be a "big disgust" when the time came for him to shoot himself.

Tom and Lorraine Shevlin arrived early in September to be introduced to the wonders of the region. They made a fishing excursion to Granite Lake and another, after pronghorn antelope, to Nordquist's brother's ranch near Cody. On September 10th, Lawrence Nordquist put out baits for grizzly bear. In all his time at the ranch, Ernest had never shot one, and this was the season for an all-out drive. While they waited at the ranch for the mule carcasses to ripen, he somewhat shyly offered to let Tom Shevlin read the manuscript of his novel. Knowing his friend's sensitivity to adverse criticism, Tom reluctantly agreed. He admired Harry Morgan's prowess, but was not at all impressed by Ernest's portrait of Richard Gordon, a pseudo-proletarian novelist who had been introduced to serve as a counterfoil to Morgan. Nor did he care for the scenes involving the drunken CCC veterans in Freddy's Bar. Although "much too scared" to say so outright, he managed to intimate to Ernest that the overall effect was "lousy." Ernest angrily pitched the manuscript out of the window into a bank of early snow. Both men stubbornly waited for three wordless days until the baits were ripe and Ernest apologized for his loss of temper.

The Shevlins were already established in a camp on Timber Creek when the Hemingways joined them after seeing Bumby off to Chicago. Late that same afternoon, Ernest took Lorraine on foot up the trail towards the bear bait, while Tom stationed himself on a nearby hilltop to watch over the surrounding terrain. They were very high up, close to the timberline, when Lorraine and Ernest heard a heavy crashing in the woods. They took cover behind a rock and waited. In a matter of minutes, three grizzlies trotted from the edge of the timber, looking enormous in the waning light, their coats tipped with silver. They had heard but not winded the hunters. The largest came directly towards the spot where Ernest and the girl lay hidden. Ernest shooed Lorraine up the nearest tree and stood up to shoot. The grizzly reared up on its hind legs, forepaws akimbo, the rakelike talons showing. Ernest aimed for the left chest, the Springfield roared, and the bear bowled over sideways. The other two grizzlies ran back towards the forest and Ernest killed one of them with a slug behind the shoulder. The first now scrambled up, bleeding and bawling, and made for cover. Ernest ran to intercept it and killed it with a shot in the neck just as it lumbered up the bank of a stream.

Night had fallen when Nordquist completed the skinning out. The heavy hides gleamed thick and wet in the firelight, ready for salting. Ernest was exultant. Nor did he seem to be much let down when Shevlin killed a third grizzly two days later. He insisted on a lunch of bear steaks. Tom and young Patrick never afterwards forgot that meal. The meat was rank and stringy, cooked middling rare, and eaten in the form of sandwiches made from sourdough pancakes spread with orange marmalade. But Ernest consumed his portion with evident gusto, chewing long and appreciatively, his black beard glossy with bear fat.

He was still feeling exuberant on the long ride back to the ranch, though visibly jealous over the fact that Shevlin's grizzly had weighed and measured out as the largest of the three. The women and Patrick went ahead with Nordquist and the packhorses, which were laden down with the bear hides and the carcasses of two bull elk. It began to snow as Tom and Ernest rode down together. Five miles from the ranch, Ernest bet Tom $500 that he could beat him home. Tom was forty-five pounds lighter and fifteen years younger, but they galloped neck and neck on the downhill trail until they reached the flatland half a mile from the ranchhouse. There Tom's horse pulled two lengths ahead, plastering Ernest with such a barrage of mud that it cost Pauline and Lorraine four hours' work with trowels to remove it—or so Ernest said. The cost to himself was $500. When he tried to renew the rivalry with Shevlin in an evening crap game, he lost $900 more.

After the Shevlins left for California late in September, Ernest returned to his novel with renewed zest, hoping to complete the first draft sometime in October. He wrote Max Perkins that it was shaping up as a hell of a fine book, full of poor people, rich people, reactionaries, and revolutionaries. So far, except for the opening in Havana, all the action took place in and around Key West. The writing had been hard to do, but also the best kind of fun. He had brought the book along to the point where the whole course of its development stood forth clearly in his imagination.

Though the major action was invented, he had drawn directly on his own experience for innumerable supporting details. The Thompson submachine gun with which Harry killed the Cubans was a twin to the weapon Ernest had acquired from Leeds in Bimini and had been using ever since against marauding sharks. He also made good use of the Key West terrain, familiar now as the back of his hand after eight years of residence. The former submarine base at the Navy Yard where Harry stole back his boat was the very place in which the *Pilar* had ridden out the hurricane of September, 1935. Josie Russell was the prototype for Freddy Wallace, the owner of Freddy's Bar. Ernest even made him complain, as Josie had done that spring, about the way his legs ached from standing up all day behind the bar waiting on customers. Bee-lips, the lawyer with whom Harry did business, was drawn to the life from Georgie Brooks, a well-known Key West barrister and politician.

All through the weeks of writing, Ernest had behaved like a novelist instead of trying not to hurt the feelings of his friends. Shortly before Easter, he had amused Dos Passos with an account of their friend, Jack Coles. Jack had brought his "new squaw" to Key West. Ernest maliciously described her as a crop-haired woman with a bad complexion and the build of a lady wrestler. Now in his book, he continued to indulge his taste for personal satire with a scene in Freddy's Bar involving Harry Morgan and a Mr. and Mrs. James Laughton. The Laughtons were thinly disguised portraits of Jack Coles and his wife. A third tourist, who sported a rust-colored mustache and a green-visored sun hat, was a professor of economics named John MacWalsey. The professor spoke sardonically "with a rather extraordinary movement of his lips as though he were eating something too hot for comfort." This eccentric educator, who gradually evolved into a minor hero in the subplot of the novel, was based on a rough approximation of Professor Harry Burns and Arnold Gingrich.

While Hemingway flourished among the western mountains, Scott Fitzgerald was suffering the tortures of adverse publicity. A journalist named Michael Mok came to Asheville to interview him. The result appeared as "The Other Side of Paradise" on September 25th in the *New York Post*. Ten days later, *Time* magazine picked up the story. Scott wired Ernest: "IF YOU EVER WANTED TO HELP ME YOUR CHANCE IS NOW STOP A MAN NAMED MICHAEL MOCK [SIC] HAS TAKEN ADVANTAGE OF AN INTERVIEW TO SPREAD ME ALL OVER THE NY POST IN AN ABSURD POSITION STOP IT CUTS IN ON ME DIRECTLY AND INDIRECTLY. SCOTT." Ernest answered that he had not seen the interview but stood ready to do whatever he could. "WIRED UNDER IMPRESSION YOU WERE IN NEW YORK," came Scott's reply. "NOTHING CAN BE DONE AT LONG RANGE AND ON COOLER CONSIDERATION SEEMS NOTHING TO BE DONE ANYHOW THANKS BEST ALWAYS. SCOTT."

This vicarious reunion-via-Western-Union marked a temporary pause in the decay of their friendship. As Scott himself had said in his private notebooks, he had always longed to absorb into himself some of the qualities that made Ernest attractive, and to lean on him like a sturdy crutch in times of psychological stress. The passage of eleven years had made these attitudes so close to habitual that Fitzgerald had not thought twice before turning to Ernest for help in the Mok affair.

All this lay in the immediate background when Marjorie Rawlings paid a call on Fitzgerald in Asheville one Friday late in October. The inevitable topic soon came up. She found Scott far more forgiving than she herself would have been about Ernest's "crack" in "The Snows of Kilimanjaro." She told Scott that it must be some "sadistic maladjustment" that made Ernest "go around knocking people down." Scott told her about Ernest's violent letter at the time of the Crack-Up articles. He added that it was just as legitimate to "get one's grievances against life off the chest" by writing about them as it was to "give an uppercut to some harmless weakling." What evidently irked him most was the statement in "The Snows" that he was "ruined." He went out of his way in the talk of that afternoon to convince Mrs. Rawlings of his continuing resilience and courage.

Just as they were winding up their conversation in Asheville, Ernest was drinking an evening whiskey in the Sidley cabin on the Nordquist ranch. The very day that his fellow novelists were analyzing his character and personality, he was setting a steel muskrat trap to catch a packrat that had been keeping the family awake with its nocturnal gnawing. Next morning Pauline began packing for the return trip to Key West. Ernest's contribution to the preparations was to borrow a pair of Nordquist's hair clippers, which he dipped in alcohol and then used to shave off half his beard. As he assembled the pages of his book for the journey, he computed that since the middle of August he had written 352 longhand pages, roughly 50,000 words—"working like a bastard," as he put it.

The trip east included a brief stopover in Piggott and was accomplished without incident. Back in Key West he began to wrestle with the climactic scene of his novel, in which Harry Morgan lay dying in the captain's bunk of a Coast Guard cutter. For all Ernest's boastful words to Perkins and Gingrich that fall, the attempt to fashion a full-length novel by the attachment of a subplot to the three Morgan stories was giving him more trouble than he cared—or dared—to admit. After all the years of sturdy independence, the refusal to follow literary or political fashion, the repeated assertion of his own will and wilfulness, the fierce determination not to knuckle under, a counterforce was beginning to boil up from the depths. It was summarized in the dying words of Harry Morgan, who like Ernest had tried to stand by himself but was now less than certain that "one man alone" could survive in such a world as this. Maybe strength, or the renewal of strength, could be gained only through some kind of group action, such a united front as the Spanish Republic was seeking to forge against the Rebels under Franco.

Around Thanksgiving time, Spain came closer. A note in one of Walter Winchell's gossip columns said that Ernest would soon be going over for a look at the war. The mail presently brought Ernest a letter from John N. Wheeler, general manager of the North American Newspaper Alliance. Wheeler said that he had seen Winchell's statement, that his own organization serviced sixty leading newspapers, and that Ernest ought to think about the idea of covering the war for the NANA. Ernest replied cordially. This was the break he had been waiting for. Sidney Franklin, who was in Cuba, agreed to go along. Both Pauline and Max Perkins were much against the idea, though Pauline was somewhat mollified by the knowledge that Franklin would be at Ernest's side. He helped the Republican cause in a preliminary way by paying passage for two volunteers who were going to join the Loyalists. He also borrowed $1,500 to be paid in two monthly installments to the Medical Bureau of the American Friends of Spanish Democracy, pledging a like amount to be handed over on demand. The money was to be used to buy ambulances. Ernest's interest centered on the practical details of shipment. The cars would reach Le Havre in chassis form and be equipped with bodies after delivery in Spain. He strongly advised driving them down through France so that the engines would be broken in and they could be put to work immediately on arrival.

While Ernest continued his work on the novel, he made two new acquaintances among the winter visitors to Key West. They were James T. Farrell, author of the recently completed Studs Lonigan trilogy, and Rexford Guy Tugwell, a member of Roosevelt's Brain Trust. Farrell was a short and intense young man with unruly hair. He was much impressed by Ernest's generosity and kindness. Ernest immediately took him into his inmost confidence, or so Farrell thought, and even asserted during a wine-drinking session one evening that Faulkner was a far better writer than either himself or Farrell. A man named Jonathan Latimer had appeared in Key West. Farrell gave him a public tongue-lashing for putting on literary airs. Ernest, who was present, took Farrell aside. "Jesus Christ, Jim," he said, "don't do that. Those fellows have nothing but their writing. Take that away from them and they'll commit suicide." Tugwell did not share Farrell's admiration for Hemingway. "He was fascinated by the New Deal," wrote Tugwell in retrospect, "but not willing to undertake an understanding of its issues. He was puzzled by me—not a politician, but close to political affairs." When Tugwell tried to interest him in politics as a subject for fiction, Ernest shrugged his shoulders. "He would not take any trouble about it," said Tugwell. "He liked to live in such decaying places as Key West . . . to live a sporting life, and . . . to keep his subject matter primitive. . . . I thought then that he was getting himself into a situation with diminishing resources."

One day in December Ernest was sitting in Sloppy Joe's place, nursing a drink and talking with Joe Russell, when a trio of tourists wandered in. One was a handsome blue-eyed woman in her middle fifties. She was accompanied by a good-looking boy of college age and a tall girl whose bright blond hair reached to her shoulders. The older woman had just been sending a telegram at the Western Union office nearby and had come in with her son and daughter to look over the establishment with the curious name of Sloppy Joe's. It developed that they were on vacation from their home in St. Louis, that they had disliked Miami, and that on an impulse they had boarded a bus for a ride down the keys. The boy's name was Alfred, the girl was called Marty, and they addressed their mother as Omi.

The girl Martha looked askance at the large, dirty man in shorts and a grubby T-shirt. But Ernest turned on his charm, introduced himself in a shy mumble, and said that he had known St. Louis in the days of his youth. Both his wives had gone to school there, and so had Bill and Katy Smith. The blue-eyed lady said that she had lived there all her adult life. She was Edna Fischel Gellhorn, the recent widow of a gynecologist and obstetrician, Dr. George Gellhorn, an Austrian by birth. Her daughter Martha had been educated at the John Burroughs School, afterwards entering Bryn Mawr College in Pennsylvania. Both mother and daughter spoke with a recognizable Bryn Mawr accent.

Martha was restless and ambitious, determined to rise by her considerable talents, and already launched as a writer of fiction. Her first novel, *What Mad Pursuit,* had borrowed its title from Keats and its epigraph from Hemingway. *The Trouble I've Seen,* a collection of her short stories, had just been published in September, with an appreciative preface by H. G. Wells. She had lately been in Germany at work on a third book, and was very bitter about the rise of the Nazis. After this visit to her mother and brothers, she was planning to return to Europe.

The friendship with the Gellhorns ripened quickly. Ernest showed them around the island and invited them to meet Pauline. After her brother's return to school and her mother's departure for St. Louis, Martha stayed on for a while in Key West. Ernest was much in her company, sometimes taking her to a place called Penna's Garden of Roses or back to Sloppy Joe's. She spent so much time at his house that, as she presently told Pauline, she nearly became a fixture there, "like a kudu head." Subjective observers like Lorine Thompson began to think that Ernest was badly smitten by the bright-haired visitor. Pauline was far too perceptive not to notice, but she kept her counsel, at least publicly, in the apparent hope that nothing would come of it.

Ernest was meantime trying to finish his novel. He inserted a series of satiric passages on the private lives of the wealthy yachtsmen whose craft lay moored at the finger piers in the yacht basin. He also introduced a curious commentary on the once-wealthy suicides who had died of carbon-monoxide poisoning in locked garages, dived out of the windows of skyscrapers, or followed "the native tradition of the Colt or Smith and Wesson." His own chief worry now was the freedom with which he had exploited some of his friends and associates under thin disguises. Max Perkins spent the morning of December 8th at a lawyer's office with Tom Wolfe, who had been named defendant in a libel suit for $125,000. Ernest wrote Max that when his own book reached print, Scribners would have to insert an "air-tight" denial that any of the characters were based on actual people. As a preliminary safeguard, he summoned Gingrich from Chicago and Maurice Speiser from New York to look over the manuscript with libel suits in mind.

This process took most of a week, with afternoon interludes of fishing. Gingrich warned that the book clearly libeled Dos Passos through the figure of the novelist Richard Gordon, as well as Grant and Jane Mason, who in his view might be mistaken for the fictional Tommy and Helene Bradley. Being well acquainted with all of them, Gingrich thought that he could see "through every reference as through a screen door." The offending passages must be removed or reworked. But Ernest argued back, reminding Arnold that Jane Mason had been "flattered" when people said she was the model for Margot Macomber. Nobody would be likely to see any connection between the Masons and the Bradleys, anyway. Richard Gordon bore no real resemblance to Dos Passos, and if Dos should happen to object, Ernest was ready with a "neat stratagem." Knowing that Dos did not like Gingrich, he would merely tell Dos that Gingrich objected to a given passage. Dos would then be certain to approve it.

It was well into January when Martha Gellhorn left by car for Miami on the first leg of her trip back to St. Louis. She had no sooner departed than Ernest left with some deliberate haste on a business trip to New York. When they met in Miami, he took her to a restaurant for a steak dinner under the chaperonage of the boxer Tom Heeney. Afterwards they caught the same northbound train, parting company enroute and continuing to their respective destinations. Shortly before their train left, Gingrich wired Ernest, having heard a rumor that he was seriously ill. Between the lines of Pauline's reply, the merest hint of acerbity might have been detected: "SECONDHAND REPORT ABSOLUTELY BASELESS ERNEST IN MIAMI ENROUTE TO NEW YORK IN SHALL WE SAY PERFECT HEALTH THANKS FOR SOLICITUDE."

Her feelings, whatever they were, could not have been palliated by a letter from Martha in St. Louis several days later. She reported that St. Louis was wintry and damp. She longed to set sail for more exotic regions. She had enjoyed the steak dinner in Miami and admired Mr. Heeney. As for Ernest, whom she was now calling Ernestino, she had been reading his collected works with great admiration, and thought him a lovely guy. Whatever Pauline's opinion of this letter, it must have struck her as curiously reminiscent of some of those that she herself had sent to Hadley from Bologna in the spring of 1926.

41. CAPITAL OF THE WORLD

NEARLY every move that Ernest made in New York that January brought him one step closer to besieged Madrid. Some of the expenses of his trip were to be met through his first return to bona fide journalism since 1923. The contract he signed with John Wheeler called for $500 per cabled story, and $1,000 for those sent by mail up to 1,200 words. He also quizzed Jay Allen about conditions in Madrid, from which Allen had lately returned after resigning his post as Spanish correspondent for the *Chicago Tribune*. But the greater part of Ernest's time was given to working with the young novelist Prudencio de Pereda on a documentary film called *Spain in Flames*. Frankly propagandistic, the film included sequences on the siege of the Alcázar in Toledo, the Loyalist triumph in the Guadarrama Mountains, the destruction of defenseless towns by Fascist war planes, and the evacuation of the children of Madrid to escape Franco's relentless artillery bombardment of the center of the city. A previous but inept commentary accompanied the film. Ernest scrapped it and began afresh. Although he had returned to Key West before the world premiere at the Cameo Theatre in New York on January 28th, he wired a laudatory public statement to be used in advertising.

His position on the war was still largely humanitarian. Even if the "Reds" were as bad as they were rumored to be, he wrote Pauline's mother, they still represented the people of the country as over against the absentee landlords, the Moors, the Italians, and the Germans. He knew very well that most of the "Whites" were "rotten." Part of his purpose in going to Spain was to see how the lines of social demarcation were being drawn "on the basis of humanity." The struggle must affect all men because it was so plainly "a dress rehearsal for the inevitable European War." His intent in working for the NANA would be to serve as "anti-war war correspondent," seeking to keep the United States from becoming involved in the future conflict.

Although Ernest had wired Perkins early in January that his novel was finished, the statement was premature. Arnold Gingrich sent him a long letter filled with editorial advice: he was still troubled by the presence of a fictional character who he thought was based on Jane Mason. Ernest promised to reconsider the matter when he got to Paris, though he felt that Arnold's judgment was "slightly unsettled" on the point in question. He sent a rather high and mighty telegram to Gingrich, reminding him that he had been writing for many more years than Gingrich had been an editor. Arnold must remember, said Ernest, that at pro football games no pep talks were given or expected between the halves. But his real difficulty was that all the preparations for the trip to France and Spain left him no time to solve the problems that the novel still presented. He promised Perkins a completed typescript by June, though even this date remained problematical.

On his return to New York in February, he found Dos Passos engaged in fund raising for a second documentary film, designed like the first to acquaint American sympathizers with the plight of the Spanish people. It was to be directed by a gifted Dutch Communist named Joris Ivens, with John Ferno as cameraman. Archie MacLeish, Lillian Hellman, Dos, and Ernest formed a corporation called Contemporary Historians to help with the funding and eventually with the distribution of the completed film. Both now and later, Ernest disagreed with Dos Passos on matters of emphasis. Dos wanted to stress the predicament of the common people in the midst of civil war. Ernest was far more interested in the military aspects.

When he embarked at last aboard the liner *Paris,* his traveling companions were Sidney Franklin and the poet Evan Shipman. Each of the group behaved characteristically at dockside. Shipman vanished anonymously into the ship's bar. Franklin held audience for reporters in a noisy stateroom where his four handsome sisters were giving him a farewell party. Ernest submitted to an interview in which he said it was his purpose to make Americans aware of the new kind of war now being waged by Franco and his foreign allies. It was a total war, said he, in which there was no such thing as a noncombatant. A young reporter named Ira Wolfert carefully set down these views in his notebook, though his chief interest was in Hemingway's appearance and personality. "His chest," wrote Wolfert, "bulged through his coat like a parapet." Even at thirty-seven he looked extremely youthful. Behind his black mustache his round and rosy countenance beamed with health. He peered at his interlocutors through steel-rimmed glasses and spoke from the side of his mouth, answering questions with a "yop" or a "nope," and holding his large hands at waist level, as if prepared either to slap a friend on the back or to throw a punch at the jaw of anyone he did not like. His destination was Madrid, he explained, but he planned to visit all the nearby towns to find out what the war had done to the "little people"—waiters, cab drivers, cobblers, shoeshine boys. After that he would tour the front lines to "see what the boys are doing with the new toys they've been given since the last war."

He spent ten days in Paris, waiting vainly for the American State Department to grant Franklin a visa for Spain. He was often in the apartment of the leftist poet Robert Desnos, in the rue de Seine, where he met Ramon Guthrie, the Dartmouth French professor whom he had last seen in company with Sinclair Lewis ten years before in Berlin. Almost daily he had lunch or drinks with Janet Flanner and Solita Solano. Franklin was usually present, sitting gingerly on the edges of chairs because of a recent goring. They sometimes went to Franklin's dingy room at the Hôtel Montana in the rue St.-Benoît. Sidney forgot his discomfort whenever he unpacked his collection of matador costumes and swords and laid them out to be admired. All this finery made Solita dizzy. She could not discover how Ernest really felt about this "almost daily gloating" over the brilliant stuffs and the gold and silver embroidery. But his behavior varied little. For half an hour he would patiently admire Sidney's possessions. Then he would pick up a sword, hefting it, running his finger over the tarnished boss of the hilt, testing it for balance. Meantime Sidney spread his other treasures over the big double bed, the two chairs, and the single small table.

When Sidney's enthusiasm boiled over, he would suddenly seize a cape, cry out "Toro—huh—toro," and commence a series of veronicas. Ernest, grinning happily, would leap for the open space on the other side of the bed, lay his hands to his ears to simulate horns, and lunge at Sidney, who would perform with the cape while Solita and Janet watched from a corner of the room. The two men kept up a breathless commentary in the slang of the Spanish bullring, and it seemed to Solita that Franklin would have continued the game forever. But sooner or later the heavily sweating Hemingway always said, "Come on, youse guys, let's go get a drink," and carried the women away, while Sidney stayed behind, carefully brushing, folding, and repacking his collection, down to the last white stocking.

The seriousness of the situation in Madrid was brought home to Ernest when he met the painter Luis Quintanilla early in March. Since his release from jail, Luis had turned from a man of art to a man of action. Having begun at the Montaña Barracks in July, he had afterwards seen service in the Sierra de Guadarrama, Toledo, and the suburbs of Madrid. He said that a bomb had gutted his studio.

"And the big frescoes," said Ernest, "University City and the Casa de Pueblo?"

"Finished," said Luis. "All smashed."

"What about the frescoes for the monument to Pablo Iglesias?"

"Destroyed," Luis said. "No, Ernesto, let's not talk about it. When a man loses all his life's work . . . it is much better not to talk about it."

Ernest's fraternal feelings were deeply engaged. He had never forgotten the loss of his own early manuscripts at the Gare de Lyon in Paris. The fate of Quintanilla's work must now be classified among *los desastros de la guerra.*

The American Department of State remained adamant on the question of Franklin's visa. In the end Ernest invoked the aid of Quintanilla's superior, Luis Araquistain, Ambassador to Paris from Republican Spain, and went on alone to Toulouse, the staging area for flights south. Arriving on the 14th, he chartered a car and went to check the French border patrol. The car was twice stopped by mobile guardsmen with fixed bayonets. A police commissioner at the frontier said that only special visas from the French government could assure entry. It was one of the ironies of the time, thought Ernest, that 12,000 Italian troops had recently landed on the south coast as part of Mussolini's aid to Franco while the French continued to haggle over the passports of neutral observers. On the 16th he boarded an Air France plane which put down briefly at Barcelona and then continued south.

The scenery on the low-level flight down the coast did not suggest a nation at war. Small waves curled peacefully along the white beaches; trains chuffed over undamaged roadbeds; men were plowing the fields; factory chimneys sent up plumes of smoke. Not until Tarragona, where a Loyalist freighter lay heeled over at the water's edge, looking, Ernest thought, like a beached whale with smokestacks, was there any visible evidence of the conflict. Beyond the yellow sprawl of Valencia, the plane climbed briefly over a mountain range and settled to the "African-looking" shoreline of Alicante. Here the people were celebrating news of the Loyalist victory over the Italians at Guadalajara. Men and women sang and shouted, the streets resounded with guitar and accordion music, and pleasure boats with names like *Rosa de Primavera* cruised the bay, filled with lovers holding hands. There were queues before the recruiting stations. The fiesta atmosphere prevailed all the way up the coast to Valencia. Half asleep in the front seat of the car, Hemingway reflected that even the orange groves were celebrating, wafting rich perfume across the dusty roadway. He sat there drowsily, thinking of weddings.

At the press bureau in Valencia he secured official transport from Constancia de la Mora, a tall aristocratic woman in her early thirties, with the dark eyes, long neck, and oval face of a Modigliani model. The chauffeur assigned to him was called Tomás. He looked like a dwarf out of Velásquez modernized with a proletarian suit of blue denim. On the 20th they set out on the long drive out of the green Valencian plain and up through the arid gray mountains, with many wayside stops for warmth and wine. At length Ernest saw once again the yellow plateau of Castile, with the snow-crowned peaks of the Sierras to the north, and the city rising like a white fortress from the surrounding plain. "Long live Madrid," cried Tomás, "the capital of my soul." He sped down the Gran Vía to the Plaza de Callao and delivered his passenger to the grimy portals of the Hotel Florida.

Ernest was in a great hurry to visit the site of the victory at Guadalajara and Brihuega which had been so proudly hailed all over Republican Spain the day he flew in. He was already speaking of it as "the biggest Italian defeat since Caporetto." Now he wished to examine the terrain before the burial squads had completed their work. He paused in Madrid only long enough to register with the censor in the tall white building of the International Telephone and Telegraph Company, known locally as the Telefónica. Here he met a stiff-backed, Prussian-looking German Communist named Hans Kahle, who had fought in the Kaiser's war on the western front, fled Nazi Germany, and reached Spain in time to hold a command under Miaja in the winter's defense of Madrid.

Early in the morning of March 22, guided by General Hans and with Tomás at the wheel, Ernest was driven north through a mixture of gray rain and intermittent snow flurries. The weather prepared him for the evidence of disaster which they found on reaching the battlefields some fifty miles from Madrid. Here lay the mute debris of struggle and flight: abandoned machine guns, light mortars, piles of boxed ammunition, and a nightmare of tractors, trucks, and small tanks, stalled on the road shoulders, capsized in the ditches, or hub-deep in the fields. Tomás displayed little stomach for the war. On a muddy road which angled up a hill just below Brihuega, they met a Republican tank which had stalled on a hairpin turn with six others behind it. The target attracted three Rebel bombers, which plastered the wet hillside "in sudden, clustered, bumping shocks." From that time on, Tomás's handling of the car was notably inefficient.

On the heights above Brihuega, behind boulders where they had huddled for protection, they found the Italian dead, small and pitiful as forgotten dolls, their faces gray and waxen in the sullen rain. Once more Ernest noticed the curious abundance of letters and papers around them, as well as the entrenching tools with which they had tried vainly to dig foxholes in the rocky soil. Kahle said that the defeat of the Italians had destroyed Franco's hope of encircling Madrid. The city's climate might be atrocious, but its marvelous natural defense position more than made up for other deficiencies. Coming back, he pointed out that fortification had now progressed to a point where direct assault could no longer take the city. In order to win, Franco must drive through Teruel to the coast, separating Barcelona and Valencia. Meantime Republican forces in Castile were growing stronger each day. In a few months, as Ernest wrote in a despatch that drew heavily on Kahle's knowledge, the Loyalists could take the offensive.

Ernest was at dinner in the basement restaurant of the Gran Vía Hotel across the street from the Telefónica, when Martha Gellhorn and Sidney Franklin appeared. They had reached Valencia by widely different routes and driven up together. Ernest's greeting enraged Martha. In spite of her intrepid spirit, she was tired, dusty, and cold from the day's journey. "I knew you'd get here, daughter," said Ernest expansively, "because I fixed it so you could." Beyond a phone call or two he had in fact done nothing, and Martha resented the implication that she had needed help. The food in the restaurant was bad and the waiters were visibly distressed by the late arrivals. Martha's first meeting with Ernest since January could hardly have been accomplished under less romantic circumstances. His interest in her was still mainly that of a successful author for a younger aspirant, though they shared an idealistic concern for the plight of the common people. Rightly or not, Martha saw herself as more politically aware as well as more fiercely anti-Fascist than he was. Nor was she, strictly speaking, a war correspondent, though she carried a "fake letter" supplied by Kyle Crichton of *Collier's* magazine, and had used it to secure the necessary papers.

Next day Ernest took her to the Telefónica and introduced her to Arturo Barea and Ilsa Kulcsar, who together directed the office of censorship and provided newcomers with hotel rooms, petrol vouchers, and safe-conduct passes. This fantastically overworked pair stared in disbelief at the "sleek woman with a halo of fair hair, who walked through the dark fusty office with a swaying movement" which they associated with American film stars. Had she known of it, this opinion would have enraged Martha anew. She went north with Ernest on the 27th, the first warm spring day, to stand among the red hills of the Guadalajara sector and watch the scores of Rebel soldiers who moved like ants up a steep bluff across the narrow valley, fortifying their tableland against an expected Loyalist attack. The troops around Ernest and Marty smoked and laughed, "sunbathing and seam-picking" in the warm air. It was hard to imagine one's way back into the seven bitter days, much of it in foul weather, which had ended in the rout of three Italian divisions.

Now, at least, the situation was happier in the field than it was in the city. Franco's artillery on Garabitas Hill bombarded Madrid daily. Granite dust and the acrid fumes of high explosive lay everywhere. The morning after his return from the north, Ernest was awakened by the scream and boom of a shell in the square outside. In bathrobe and slippers he hurried down to see a middle-aged woman being helped into the lobby, bleeding from a wound in the abdomen. Not twenty yards from the hotel entrance was a great hole in the sidewalk and the body of a man covered with dust in a heap of rubble.

The noise from the University City sector, seventeen short blocks away, often kept up all night. Ernest tried to think of onomatopoetic words to describe the sound of small-arms fire: "tacrong, carong, craang" for rifles, and "rong, cararong, rong, rong" for machine guns.

Many of his wide acquaintance were converging on Madrid. He greeted Josie Herbst, the divorced wife of John Herrmann, as she came into the bleak lobby of the Florida, dragging a heavy knapsack and a typewriter, her shoes gritty with the granite dust. She was given a room some distance down the hall from the two-room suite that Ernest occupied with Franklin. Sidney's horn wound had not yet healed and he still had a cold from wading an icy river on the northern border, but he helped Ernest with great devotion. He was very fond of Pauline and resented Martha accordingly, complaining to Ilsa Kulcsar and others about Martha's effect on Ernest's character and conduct. Free breakfasts prepared by Franklin were offered each day. The main staircase at the Florida spiraled up the sides of a rotunda. As Josie Herbst and Dos Passos sat talking in the lobby, sipping morning tea and munching dried-out bread saved from the night before, delicious odors of percolating coffee and frying ham often assailed them. Soon Ernest or Sidney would yell down from the fourth floor, inviting them up. Since everyone was hungry most of the time, the temptation to go was strong. Josie often refused, only to hate herself for feeling virtuous in not accepting. Other visiting Americans sometimes resented Ernest's privileged status, since he never lacked transport or ready access to the limited supplies of gasoline. Far from sharing this view, Josie admired his air of exuberance. He was clearly enjoying his role as America's leading war novelist, and at the same time exploring new realms of experience, storing impressions as a battery stores power. Some of his ideas struck Dos Passos and Josie Herbst as naive. On the other hand, he could boast of inside knowledge from close association with responsible men like Hans Kahle, who were doing the actual fighting.

Dos and Ernest were continuing their debate about *The Spanish Earth*. Dos wanted to concentrate on the privations of everyday life in a typical village of Old Castile, where living conditions were almost incredible to foreign eyes. Ernest, while far from discounting the humanitarian aspect, wanted pictures of attacks, gun emplacements, bombardments, and destruction. Another cause of friction was Dos's determination to find out what had happened to José Robles Pazos, his Spanish translator and friend of twenty years. Robles had taught Spanish literature at Johns Hopkins University until the outbreak of the war, when he joined the Loyalists as a colonel. In the fall he had been advised to leave Spain because of powerful enemies, but had elected to stay. In December he had suddenly been arrested in Valencia. Government officials there had assured Dos in March that the charges against Robles were not serious and that he was in no danger. Ernest told Dos that he had the personal word of Pepe Quintanilla, the glib chief of counterespionage, that Robles would receive a fair trial. The trouble with this assurance was that Robles had already been executed after a drumhead court-martial. Josie Herbst, who had just learned the facts, told Ernest that Quintanilla was either a dupe or a liar, doubtless the latter. Ernest gaped with surprise, but at once assumed that Robles had been guilty. He said that he would break the news to Dos.

He chose the occasion of a group visit to the Castle of the Duke of Tovar, where foreign correspondents were bidden to lunch with some of the Russians. The news was an immense shock to Dos. Throughout the meal he sat gazing at his plate and saying almost nothing. Back at the Hotel Florida, Ernest waved and departed quickly. For him the case was closed. Fifteen months later, he attributed Dos's continued belief in Robles's loyalty to the good-hearted naïveté of "a typical American liberal attitude." The hauteur of this judgment reflected Ernest's pride in having been a confidant of the "in-group" of Madrid.

He made a point of frequent calls at the hotel called Gaylord's, the social center of operations for the Russian contingent. Once he was known there, he enjoyed the feeling of being able to wave familiarly to the sentries who guarded the porte-cochère with fixed bayonets, of striding through the marble entrance hall, and stepping unchallenged into the slow-moving elevator. At first, he did not like the place. Food and drink were too abundant, the appointments too luxurious for a besieged city. The talk struck him also as far too cynical. Yet he returned often, convinced that if he kept his ears open, he would be able to learn precisely how the war was being conducted. One immediate discovery was that many of the Spanish commanders had received thorough Soviet indoctrination. Enrique Lister from Galicia, who commanded a division, spoke Russian fluently. Juan Modesto of Andalusia, in charge of an army corps, had "never learned his Russian in Puerto de Santa María." El Campesino, ex-sergeant in the Spanish Foreign Legion, "with his black beard, his thick negroid lips, and his feverish staring eyes," was a fine brigade commander who talked far too much for one in his position. But Ernest was all attention.

His chief informant at Gaylord's was Mikhail Koltsov, correspondent for *Pravda* and *Izvestia,* a youngish intellectual with high-colored mobile features, horn-rimmed glasses, and a mop of crinkled hair. Koltsov knew, said Ernest, that his American friend had no leanings towards Communism. But since he believed in Ernest as a writer, he tried to show him how everything was actually run so that he could later provide a true account of it. One evening Ilya Ehrenburg found Ernest in Koltsov's suite, morosely drinking whiskey. After some preliminary exchanges, Ehrenburg asked in French if Hemingway cabled home only feature stories or sent spot news despatches as well. He was astonished when Ernest sprang up in a black rage and advanced menacingly upon him with a whiskey bottle. He had mistaken the word *nouvelles* for *novels.* Bystanders intervened and the incident ended in laughter. Even such behavior could not disguise from Ehrenburg the fact that Hemingway was basically a cheerful man, attached to life, eager to talk by the hour of hunting and fishing. He spoke seriously of the film he was going to make and the purposes he hoped it would serve. He was committed to the war, thought Ehrenburg, "attracted by danger, death, great deeds." He was daily seeing men who refused to surrender. "He was revived and rejuvenated."

These were exact terms for what was happening to Ernest that spring. He had returned to scenes not unlike those he had known in Italy long ago. He had lately spoken in *Green Hills of Africa* about the "pleasant, comforting stench of comrades," the happy interdependence of a brotherhood in arms. In the time between the wars, he had largely abandoned these in the pursuit of his lonely vocation. Now he was back in the breach. Difficulty and danger were elements in which he flourished. Fully, and for the most part unselfishly, committed to the Spanish people and their cause, he knew at the same time that this was the kind of experience by which he could grow, adding new dimensions to his stature as a novelist.

42. THE SPANISH EARTH

APART from Martha Gellhorn, Ernest's chief associates among the foreign journalists in Madrid were Herbert Matthews and Sefton Delmer. Both had been there far longer than he, Delmer since the start of the war in July and Matthews since November. Matthews was tall and slender, serious and studious in manner, with a thin ascetic face that reminded Ernest of Savonarola. Delmer, called Tom, was an Oxford graduate in his early thirties, six feet tall and weighing 220 pounds. In Ernest's eyes he might have passed for a "ruddy English bishop." Delmer was a good deal less enthusiastic than his companions about the way in which the Communists were directing the fortunes of the Spanish Republic. Nor did he fully share Matthews's conviction that these months in besieged Madrid were the "great days" of his life as a journalist, so much better than sitting at a desk in Paris rewriting official handouts from the embassies. Ernest's euphoria surpassed even that of Matthews. After his first two weeks at the Florida, he developed an impersonal feeling of freedom, as if he had neither wife nor children, house or boat, or any other domestic possessions or entanglements.

During April, he threw himself wholeheartedly into the preparation of the documentary film, which was going to be called *The Spanish Earth*. He was much in the company of Joris Ivens, the director, and John Ferno, the taciturn and businesslike cameraman. Ivens was a solidly built man of middle height, with thick brown hair and the look of a Left Bank intellectual, an artist and a Communist to his fingertips. He began functioning as Ernest's Political Commissar, convinced that his friend was ready at last to become part of a genuine collective movement.

The film-making was not easy. When they followed the Loyalist tanks and infantry through the broken gray hills in the Morata de Tajuña sector, the wind from the mountains showered them with dust, caking the moisture in their eyes and nostrils, and clouding the lenses of the cameras. On the 9th, after a carouse that continued past midnight, Ernest lay awake for hours listening to Rebel artillery pounding Loyalist positions around Carabanchel. Soon after six, Ivens knocked on his door, eager to make an early start on the work of the day. The Loyalists were starting an attack against the Rebel lines beyond the Casa de Campo, a broad open valley north and west of the city. With Hank Gorrell of the United Press and Ferno the cameraman, they left the hotel without breakfast and set out for brigade headquarters. Rebel artillery was shattering the ancient linden trees in the woodland near the old royal hunting lodge. They soon found that they had gone too far downgrade to get a clear view of the action, and climbed back, panting and sweating, to an eminence above the eastern edge of the woods.

From this point the whole battle was spread out before them. A thin line of infantry was advancing on a trench which angled down the opposing hillside. Three Loyalist bombers unloaded on the Rebel earthworks and the view from the ridge was blotted out in rising towers of dirt. But the exposed position of Ernest and his friends soon attracted enemy sniper fire. Ferno crawled away to find a location where the larger of the cameras, equipped with a telefoto lens, could be safely installed. The place he chose was a sort of grandstand seat in the row of apartment houses that fronted on the Paseo Rosales, commanding a long view westward into the valley. The buildings were ruined from five months of shelling, but one apartment on the top floor was intact enough to serve as a vantage point. Ernest nicknamed it "The Old Homestead," thinking of his grandfather Anson's house on North Oak Park Avenue. They camouflaged the camera with rags and spent the afternoon watching and filming the battle. It was too far off to film well. At a thousand yards, as Ernest said, "the tanks looked like small, mud-colored beetles bustling in the trees and spitting tiny flashes, and the men behind them were toy men who lay flat, then crouched and ran . . . spotting the hillside as the tanks moved on."

At twilight they carried the large camera down the stairs, removed its tripod, made three loads, and then sprinted, one at a time, across the dangerous corner of the Paseo Rosales into the lee of a stone wall. In the bare, cobblestoned Plaza de España, they hunched their shoulders and ducked low as a big German monoplane bombed the Loyalist batteries and then swept on in their direction. But the enemy crew had done their work and the plane roared away over the city.

Next day a large group converged on "The Old Homestead," including Dos Passos, Matthews, Sid Franklin, Tom Delmer, Martha Gellhorn, and Virginia Cowles. Delmer irritated Hemingway with scathing comments on the slow advance of the Loyalist tanks. Ernest was extremely careful "that no reflection from his or our binoculars should give away our hideaway and provoke a shell or two." He commented on the poor planning which caused the heaviest Loyalist attacks to come in the afternoon. The westering sun glinting on the camera lenses made them easily visible to the Moorish riflemen. "If you wanted to be properly sniped," said Ernest, "all you had to do was use a pair of [field] glasses without shading them adequately. They could shoot, too, and they had kept my mouth dry all day."

His liaison with Martha Gellhorn had only lately begun. Tom Delmer admired the "humorous indulgence" with which she treated Ernest, showing none of the "servile obsequiousness" with which his wants were commonly met by others. But Delmer was not aware that they had become lovers until a Rebel shell burst in the hotwater tank of the Hotel Florida. The steam that escaped made the place look like a corridor in hell. "All kinds of liaisons were revealed," said Delmer, "as people poured from their bedrooms to seek shelter in the basement, among them Ernest and Martha." He noticed particularly the French writer Saint-Exupéry, who had been hoarding a cartload of grapefruit in his room. "He stood with a basket at the staircase," said Delmer. As each woman passed, "he held out a yellow grapefruit with all the graciousness of an old-world French aristocrat and said, 'Voulez vous une pamplemousse, Madame?' "

But Ernest spent little time in the Hotel Florida. A succession of chauffeurs drove him to the various fronts around the outskirts of the city. After Tomás came one who made off with an official car and forty liters of petrol. Third was an anarchist boy named David from a village near Toledo. He spoke a language so inconceivably foul that Ernest's education in profanity entered a new orbit. David was passionately devoted to the idea of war until the day he saw a grocery queue of women hit by a Rebel shell near the Plaza Mayor. He soon left for the village of Fuentidueña de Tajo, where Ivens and Ferno were filming domestic scenes for *The Spanish Earth,* and did not reappear. His successor was Hipolito, tough, laconic, completely unromantic, and so capable that Ernest could easily imagine him as a sergeant of *conquistadores* in the heyday of Spain's colonial empire.

Ernest's military acquaintance broadened rapidly. Among his favorites were the American volunteer aviators Whitey Dahl, who was said to be wanted by the police of Los Angeles on a check-forging charge, and Frank Tinker, who came from De Witt, Arkansas, not far from Piggott. Another of his flying friends was Ramon Lavalle, whom he had known during Lavalle's boyhood in Paris. Still another acquaintance from the Paris days was Lieutenant Colonel Gustavo Durán, who had formerly been a student and composer of music. At the outbreak of the war he had held a reserve commission as second lieutenant, but had since risen rapidly in the Loyalist hierarchy and was now commanding the 69th Division at Torrejón de Ardoz and Loeches, east of Madrid. The lukewarm friendship of the Paris days now reached a new intensity. Like Luis Quintanilla, Durán was an artist turned soldier, and Ernest soon began to speak of him as one of his heroes.

He was a frequent visitor to the Eleventh International Brigade, largely composed of German Communists and commanded by Hans Kahle, with whom he had made the trip to Brihuega in March. Many of Kahle's men were veterans of the Kaiser's war, and all had had military training. For a time Ernest thought of doing a book on Kahle until he reflected that "we have too much together for me ever to risk losing any of it by trying to write about it." But it was the Twelfth Brigade which most engaged his affections, chiefly for the people and their *esprit de corps,* though also because they welcomed him with the respect due a creative artist while making him feel more like a soldier than a noncombatant. The commander, whose *nom de guerre* was General Lucasz, was a forty-one-year-old Hungarian who had written some short stories and a novel: "Short, chunky, jovial-looking, with pale blue eyes, thinning blond hair, and a gay mouth under a bristly yellow mustache," Lucasz delighted Ernest with his relaxed good humor. He was also much attracted to Werner Heilbrun, chief medical officer of the brigade, a gentle, efficient man who was a model of stoic fortitude and humanitarianism. "With his cap tilted sideways on his shock of black hair," Heilbrun moved among the wounded "like a weary beggar-monk," working day and night, "his deep-set eyes glowing with the sense of his mission." Lucasz's political commissar, Gustav Regler, was the third of Ernest's favorites in the Twelfth. A German Communist with a tawny complexion, a deeply lined forehead, and the jaw of a fighter, he had begun as a boy soldier in 1918. Since then he had been a persistent anti-Fascist and more recently a refugee from Nazi Germany.

Ernest's greatest hatred was reserved for André Marty, commander of the International Brigades at the crowded base in and around the city of Albacete, a large man, as Ernest described him, "old and heavy, in an oversized khaki beret," with "bushy eyebrows . . . watery gray eyes . . . and double chin." In Ernest's view Marty's "gray face had a look of decay" as if it had been modeled "from the waste material you find under the claws of a very old lion." Ernest was not alone in his prejudice. Ehrenburg found Marty "imperious, very short-tempered, and always suspecting everyone of treason." Regler stated flatly that Marty covered his inadequacy as a soldier "with an unforgivable, passionate spy-hunt." He quarreled publicly with many of his subordinates who disagreed with his neurotic or even psychotic decisions, including the heroically hardworking American, Louis Fischer, who served for a time as his Quartermaster General.

Although Ernest saw little of Marty, he formed a useful working acquaintance with a Polish officer whose real name was Karol Swierczewski. Like many other officers in the International Brigades, he fought under a pseudonym, in this case General Walter. Born in Warsaw, raised chiefly in Russia, he had served with the Red Army during the revolution, and was teaching military science and tactics at the Frunze Military Academy when the Spanish Civil War erupted. Since then he had commanded the Fourteenth Brigade during the battle of Coruña Road in December and January, moving on afterwards to the defense of Madrid. He greatly impressed Ernest, both by his military knowledge and by his singular appearance, "with his strange white face that never tanned, his hawk eyes, the big nose and thin lips and the shaven head crossed with wrinkles and scars."

The bombardment of Madrid continued all through April. The Gran Vía was so often strewn with broken glass that Ernest came to think of it as one would think of a hailstorm that happened every day. Ilsa Kulcsar's shoes were burned to cinders in her hotel room by a redhot chunk of shrapnel. One of the porters at the Florida was shot through the thigh by a stray machine-gun bullet. Another bullet made a neat round hole in a mirror in Martha's room while she was away. Food in the capital was in shorter supply than ever, though supplies from Valencia constantly rolled into Madrid, only to be inefficiently stored in locked warehouses until they rotted. Hungering for game, Ernest borrowed a shotgun and went hunting along the Pardo front on the morning of the 21st, returning with a wild duck, a partridge, four rabbits, and an owl whose silent flight he mistook for that of a woodcock.

That evening he wrote a news despatch, his first in ten days. Martha left it for Franklin to file, with a note:

Dear Sidney: I am going back to the Jarama front for the night. I have read and corrected [i.e. proofread] E's article. Will you please take all three copies to Ilsa, Room 402, in the Telefónica, and have her pass them. She keeps one copy, the other two should be sent to the addresses attached to them. I have no envelopes, but you can surely find some up there in the press room—401—or even ask Ilsa. Probably these should go tonight. E. wanted them to go in the diplomatic valise for the sake of speed; kindly tell Ilsa that, and tell her it is important as E. has not sent a story for some days and this is good for the cause . . . Thank you. Regler has bad fever again, and Bethune still thinks it is typhoid . . . All food is in my room, for his [Regler's] dinner. Gracias, Marty.

Next day Ernest left with Martha, and Hipolito as driver, for what he described as "ten hard days visiting the four central fronts." The itinerary included the 4,800-foot Sierra de Guadarrama, where they spent hours on horseback climbing to inspect the Loyalist positions. He was impressed by the smartness and the discipline of the seasoned mountain troops. Once they rode in an armored car up a road exposed to Rebel machine guns. Hunched in the dark interior, they listened to the sharp rivet-hammering of four separate bursts against the protective metal plates. Even such an experience seemed less dangerous to Ernest than daily life in Madrid. Upon their return they found the air gritty with granite dust, saw new jagged craters in the pavements along the Gran Vía, and reflected that beside this senseless shelling of the civilian population, the mountain front seemed almost idyllic.

Ivens wrote from Valencia late in April. Sidney Franklin and John Ferno were to finish the final scenes of *The Spanish Earth* in the village of Fuentidueña on the 28th and 29th, and Ivens asked Ernest to join them there. He himself was on the point of leaving for New York, and Ernest had been promised plane passage out of the country about the 6th of May. Dos Passos was still actively protesting the murder of his friend Robles, and had lately been to see the American ambassador in Valencia. Ivens hoped that Dos would eventually come to recognize "what a man and comrade has to do in these difficult and serious war times."

With the film footage for *The Spanish Earth* completed and boxed for shipment, Ernest was ready to go home. He filed his last despatch at the Foreign Ministry Building in the Plaza de la Cruz. The Telefónica, white in the morning sun, had become so good a target to Franco's artillery that Ilsa Kulcsar had asked and got permission to move the offices of censorship to the new location. Arturo Barea was close to a breakdown from overwork and the daily horrors of the bombardment. But Ernest, cheerful and hearty, knew nothing of this the day he said good-bye to Barea, standing on the flag-stones in the Ministry courtyard, laughing and joking in colloquial Castilian.

He was equally gay at the farewell party given in his honor by the Twelfth Brigade. It took place on the evening of May Day in the grounds of the ancient castle at Moraleja which served as their base hospital. Lucasz the commander was there, as well as Dr. Heilbrun and Gustav Regler. Ernest afterwards remembered how Lucasz had played "the tune he only played so, very late at night, on a pencil held against his teeth; the music clear and delicate like a flute." It was his final meeting with Heilbrun and Lucasz. But for a fluke of fortune, it might also have been his last with Gustav Regler.

43. AMERICAN INTERLUDE

ON Sunday, the 9th of May, Ernest reached Paris after forty-five days in Spain. Looking bronzed and healthy, he told reporters that he had not expected the war to last so long. He said that his purpose in returning to the United States was to revise the first draft of a novel. When this job was done and the book had been seen through the press, he would return to Spain for the "big war of movement" which he expected to begin during the summer.

After the interview with the reporters he spent four busy days in Paris, conferring with Luis Araquistain about the medical needs of the Loyalist Army, making a speech before the Anglo-American Press Club and another to the Friends of Shakespeare and Company at Sylvia Beach's bookshop. He stuttered and stammered through both the speeches, and his auditors got the impression that he would much rather be elsewhere. Joyce was present for the meeting at Sylvia's, huddled in a corner, fiercely uninterested in Spain and politics. Ernest assured the company that writing was very hard work. With the possible exception of *The Sun Also Rises,* he had never been wholly satisfied with any of his books. He spoke of these matters in an offhand fashion, and turned with evident relief to the reading of passages from his short story, "Fathers and Sons."

When he reached New York aboard the *Normandie* on May 18th, his immediate plans were to go to Key West, gather up his wife and children, and spend most of the summer at Bimini, revising the novel and fishing. Only two major interruptions confronted him. One was a speech he had agreed to deliver before the Second American Writers' Congress in New York early in June. The second was *The Spanish Earth*, which must now be cut, provided with a theme and a sound track, and then used for the all-important purpose of raising money for Loyalist ambulances. He was busily relaxing at Bimini on June 2nd when Joris Ivens wired from New York that President and Mrs. Roosevelt had agreed to see the film at the White House early in July. This important meeting had been arranged by Martha Gellhorn, a good friend of Eleanor Roosevelt's. Meantime, Joris sent along a statement of the theme of the film for Ernest's scrutiny and revision. "Our people," it said, "gained their position by a democratic election. Now we are defending our rights. We are forced to fight against the military clique and foreign intervention. The whole country is united in the fight. The peasants make better use of their own land, better than their former landlords. They bring forth the full potentialities of the Spanish Earth." Hemingway's version reduced Joris's six sentences to three: "We gained the right to cultivate our land by democratic elections. Now the military cliques and absentee landlords attack to take our land from us again. But we fight for the right to irrigate and cultivate this Spanish Earth which the nobles kept idle for their own amusement." As a summary of the causes of the war, both versions were somewhat simplistic. But they stated with economy the basic theme of the film.

On the 4th of June, Ernest flew from Bimini to keep his engagement with the Writers' Congress. Scott Fitzgerald was in town and they met briefly. Scott had "come back to life" in January, and was now working for Metro-Goldwyn-Mayer under a lavish contract. "I wish we could meet more often," he told Ernest. "I don't feel I know you at all." Once again, as so often in the past, he was impressed by Ernest's sanguine vitality. The program at Carnegie Hall was already well along when Ernest strode in. He stood in the wings, muttering that he was not a speechmaker. The huge auditorium was hot and filled with tobacco smoke. The orchestra and all the balconies and boxes were jammed with a capacity audience of 3,500, and another thousand had been turned away at the doors. Printed programs identified the sponsors as the League of American Writers, whose president was Donald Ogden Stewart. Besides Stewart, the speakers for the evening were Earl Browder, the Secretary of the Communist Party of the U.S.A., Joris Ivens with the still unfinished film, and finally Hemingway, with Archibald MacLeish as chairman and master of ceremonies.

Browder's paper was restrained and straightforward. The European dictators had shattered the Ivory Tower with their bombs; all writers must now address themselves to the life of the common people, "the source of all strength in art." Ivens introduced *The Spanish Earth,* which still lacked a sound track. "Maybe it is a little strange," said he, "to have at a writers' congress a moving picture, but I think it belongs here. . . . This picture is made on the same front where I think every honest author ought to be." Ernest sat through these speeches in the company of MacLeish and Martha Gellhorn. He was dressed too heavily for the hot weather, and clawed at his tie as if it were choking him. When MacLeish introduced him, the applause was thunderous. His glasses fogged, his tanned cheeks gleaming with moisture, he leaped up nervously and launched into his seven-minute speech before the ovation had died down.

A writer's problem [he said] does not change. He himself changes, but his problem remains the same. It is always how to write truly and having found what is true, to project it in such a way that it becomes part of the experience of the person who reads it. . . . Really good writers are always rewarded under almost any existing system of government that they can tolerate. There is only one form of government that cannot produce good writers, and that system is fascism. For fascism is a lie told by bullies. A writer who will not lie cannot live and work under fascism.

The rest of the speech was not especially notable for its internal logic. But its faults were far less important than the fact of Hemingway's willingness to speak at all. Paul Romaine, the bookseller from Milwaukee, was among the hundreds in the audience who watched and listened with undisguised fervor. "It was magnificent," said he, "as if everyone had taken him into their arms, truly a companion . . . in the fight against fascism. How could this fight be lost now, with Hemingway on our side?" Waves of applause swept the great hall as Ernest, "excited and wet, dashed into the wings not to appear again." His obvious sincerity, as well as "the strange power of his presence," had taken the place by storm.

On the way back to Bimini Ernest was smitten by a sudden brainstorm which reflected his continuing uncertainty about his unfinished novel. Instead of letting it stand by itself, it could be published as part of an omnibus volume containing a miscellany of prose pieces. These would include "The Snows of Kilimanjaro," "The Short Happy Life of Francis Macomber," the tragic tale of Paco, the boy waiter in Madrid, excerpts from the recent NANA despatches, the piece on the drowned veterans of Matecumbe Key, and the speech he had just given at Carnegie Hall. He had several possible titles in mind for the collection: *To Have and Have Not, The Various Arms,* and *Return to the Wars.* It was clear that he wanted the book to document in some fashion his recent reconversion to social consciousness. Max Perkins agreed to the proposal "except in small details," and set about assembling the various pieces to send to Ernest at Cat Cay.

The severest blow of the summer was the news on June 16th that Lucasz had been killed and Gustav Regler severely wounded by Rebel artillery on a country road near Huesca in Aragon. Regler survived only by a double miracle of will and luck. "A pound and a half of steel drove through Gustav's body from side to side," wrote Ernest, "making a hole in the small of his back which uncovered the kidneys and exposed the spinal cord." Next day the clean sweep of Ernest's friends in the Twelfth Brigade was tragically completed. Dr. Werner Heilbrun, full of grief at the loss of Lucasz and the wounding of Regler, set off alone in a staff car, driving towards the Pyrenees. A Rebel plane caught him in the open and killed him with a burst from its machine gun.

On the 19th, Joris Ivens cabled that he had finished editing *The Spanish Earth*. The remaining task was the preparation of the sound track. Orson Welles the actor had made a tentative version, but Prudencio de Pereda, the young novelist who had worked with Ernest on *Spain in Flames,* was determined that he should be asked to do the spoken narration. When Ernest dutifully appeared and set to work, de Pereda was almost beside himself with joy. In spite of the smothering heat, the long hours, and the multiple revisions, the task was gradually accomplished.

One almost incidental result of the visit to New York was Ernest's decision to go ahead with the publication of the Morgan novel under the title of *To Have and Have Not,* shelving the notion of bringing it out as part of a prose miscellany. Scribners at once placed the book on the fall list, and Max sent the typescript off to the printers, hoping for galley proof by the middle of July. Ernest had been back in Cat Cay only a few days when Joris Ivens cabled once more, this time with the schedule that he and Ernest would soon be following. On July 8th they would dine at the White House, afterwards showing the film to the President and Mrs. Roosevelt. On the 10th they would take the film to California to show it to the movie stars and gather money for ambulances.

Once again Ernest flew north to give assistance. Ivens and Martha Gellhorn were waiting when he reached New York, and they all went to Newark on July 8th to catch the afternoon plane. Martha surprised her companions by eating some sandwiches at the airport snack bar, explaining that the dinners at the White House were notoriously inedible. Washington was in the grip of a heat wave and the interior of the presidential mansion was like an oven. Harry Hopkins was present at the dinner, which was even worse than Martha had predicted. Ernest liked both Hopkins and Eleanor Roosevelt, whom he later described as enormously tall, thoroughly charming, and deaf as a post. It was otherwise with the President, whose "Harvardian" manner aroused Ernest's scorn. He thought Roosevelt "sexless" and even somewhat womanly in appearance, like a great woman Secretary of Labor. He later reported without sympathy on the amount of careful maneuvering that was required to get the paralyzed President from room to room or even into a chair. Both the Roosevelts were much moved by the film, although they believed that it needed more propaganda in order to make it fully effective.

Two days later, Ernest and Joris flew to California to enlist the financial support of the film colony in Hollywood. The campaign began well with a gathering under the sponsorship of Fredric and Florence March. Ivens ran off the film and Ernest read a speech that he had written out on fifteen sheets of hotel stationery. He pointed out that the film was visually exact even though the limitations of the medium made it impossible to re-create the total experience of living in wartime Spain. He spoke of the death of such friends as Lucasz and Heilbrun, the indiscriminate bombing of civilian populations, the killing and maiming of children, and the sufferings of the troops. He concluded by pointing out that $1,000 would send an ambulance to Spain. It would be "rolling, in action," four weeks from the time a donation was made. The combination of Ernest's fame, his obvious sincerity, and the effect of the film itself immediately brought in enough money to buy and equip twenty ambulances. Fitzgerald, who was present, was full of admiration. Next day he wired Ernest that "THE PICTURE WAS BEYOND PRAISE AND SO WAS YOUR ATTITUDE." The attitude itself, as Scott soon wrote Max Perkins, had "something almost religious about it." Ernest was keyed up to a kind of "nervous tensity" that sent him into and out of Hollywood "like a whirlwind," leaving thousands of dollars in contributions in his wake.

The galley proof of *To Have and Have Not* was waiting for him when he got back to New York. He registered at the Hotel Barclay with his usual open secrecy and galloped through the proofreading, eager to return to Bimini in time to celebrate his thirty-eighth birthday. His much-interrupted vacation ended on August 3rd when he brought the *Pilar* across to Miami, with Pauline and Bumby as crew. As a change from the Nordquist ranch in Wyoming, Sidney Franklin was going to take Pauline and the two older boys to a bull ranch in Mexico, while Gregory went to Syracuse with his nurse, Ada. Franklin had declined to return to Spain. He had done his stint, as Ernest put it, and was now more than ready to enter reserve status.

None of the family wanted Ernest to go. Pauline's mother sent him a long letter, urging him to change his mind. Ernest replied with understandable duplicity that in spite of Pauline's beauty and the happiness they shared, he had promised the Spaniards that he would come back. When the world was in such a bad way, it was simply egotistical to think of one's personal future. His first visit to wartime Spain had destroyed his belief in an afterlife, but it had also eliminated all his fear of death or indeed of anything else. When he appeared in New York on his way to Paris, he exuded self-confidence and well-being. He had seldom looked sartorially smarter than he did at a well-publicized dinner laid on by David Smart, publisher of *Esquire,* who was on the point of launching a sumptuous leftist magazine called *Ken.* Ernest sat affably in the place of honor at Smart's left, his hair cut and combed, his

silk tie neatly knotted, his double-breasted summer suit contrasting handsomely with his Florida sunburn.

His affability was quickly dissipated, however, on the afternoon of Wednesday, August 11th, when he strode into Max Perkins's office and found
Max Eastman sitting there. His resentment against Eastman for the "Bull
in the Afternoon" review had been rankling for upwards of four years. Although Perkins was apprehensive over what might happen, he affected a
matter-of-fact tone in saying to Eastman what he hoped was true: "Here's
a friend of yours, Max." The two men shook hands and exchanged minor
pleasantries. Perkins, relieved, had just settled back in his chair when Ernest,
grinning broadly, ripped open his own shirt to expose a chest which, as Perkins
said, was "hairy enough for anybody." Eastman laughed and Ernest, still
grinning, opened Eastman's shirt to reveal a chest "as bare as a bald man's
head." The contrast led to further laughter, and Perkins was just preparing
for a possible unveiling of his own when Ernest suddenly flushed with anger.

"What do you mean," he roared at Eastman, "accusing me of impotence?"

Eastman denied it. He was just going on to further explanations when he
caught sight of his own volume, *Art and the Life of Action,* which happened
to be lying on Perkins's desk. It contained a reprint of "Bull in the Afternoon"
and he thrust it at Ernest, saying, "Here. Read what I *really* said." Ernest
seized the book and began leafing through the pages, muttering and swearing.
"Let Max read it," said Eastman.

But Ernest, his face contorted with rising anger, smacked Eastman in the
face with the open book. Eastman instantly rushed at him, and Perkins, fearing that Eastman might be badly hurt, ran over to grab Ernest's arm. Just as
he came around the corner of the desk, the adversaries grappled and fell.
Perkins grasped the shoulders of the man on top, certain that it must be
Hemingway. Instead he found himself looking down into Ernest's upturned
face. He was flat on the floor and grinning broadly, having regained his temper
almost at once.

The newspapers broke the story three days later as Ernest was leaving
for France aboard the *Champlain.* Eastman believed, and had publicly stated,
that he had beaten Ernest fairly in a wrestling match. Ernest assured the man
from the *Times* that this was all poppycock. "He didn't throw anybody anywhere," said Ernest. "He jumped at me like a woman, clawing . . . with his
open hands. I just held him off. I didn't want to hurt him. He's ten years
older than I am."

The reporter pointed to the bump on Ernest's forehead, the result of his
skylight accident in 1928, and asked if it had anything to do with the Eastman fight. Ernest said no. He pulled off his jacket and rolled up his shirt
sleeve to show the scar on his right biceps from the broken arm of 1930.
"Eastman didn't do that to me, either," said he. "If Mr. Eastman takes his
prowess seriously, let him waive all . . . legal claims to damages, and I'll
put up $1,000 for any charity he favors or for himself. Then we'll go into

a room and he can read his book to me. . . . The best man unlocks the door."
After this manly challenge, Ernest strode up the gangplank of the liner, looking as bronzed and healthy as ever, and complacently convinced that his
offer would never be taken.

He was already back in Europe when Perkins sent Fitzgerald a play-by-play
account of the melee. Scott was torn between blame and shame. Ernest, he
thought, had done

exactly the asinine thing that I knew he had it in him to do. . . . The fact that
he lost his temper only for a minute does not minimize the fact that he picked
the exact wrong minute to do it. His discretion must have been at a very low ebb
or he would not have again trusted the reporters at the boat. He is living at the
present in a world so entirely his own that it is impossible to help him, even if
I felt close to him at the moment, which I don't. I like him so much, though,
that I wince when anything happens to him, and I feel rather personally ashamed
that it has been possible for imbeciles to dig at him and hurt him. After all you
would think a man who has arrived at the position of being practically his country's most eminent writer could be spared that yelping.

44. THE FIFTH COLUMN

THE war of movement that Ernest had predicted for the summer of 1937 had
moved mostly in the wrong direction. During his absence, none of the Loyalist
offensives had lifted the siege of Madrid or prevented the Rebel conquest of
the northern provinces. General Walter's attack on the Segovia front late in
May had begun well and then fizzled out. Bilbao had fallen to Franco on
June 18th. The bloody battle of Brunete in the blistering heat of July had cost
the Loyalists heavy casualties. The Basque provinces were conquered, and the
Rebel drive against Santander was launched on August 14th, the very day
Ernest had sailed from New York.

When he and Martha met Herbert Matthews at the Café de la Paix one
afternoon in early September, the news was still dark. Franco held two thirds
of Spain and a fresh assault on Madrid was daily expected. But when they
reached the Aragon front, the gloom lifted. A Loyalist offensive below Zaragoza had taken Belchite, and they went to explore the rubble and stench of
the ruined town. Ernest talked to some of the volunteers in the 15th International Brigade and learned of the tactics they had used at Belchite. Their
leader, Major Robert Merriman, had "bombed his way forward," in spite
of many wounds from hand-grenade splinters, and had refused to stop until
his men had reached and occupied the cathedral. Merriman immediately
entered Ernest's gallery of heroes.

Ernest, Martha, and Herbert Matthews were the first American correspondents to make a complete survey of the sector around Belchite. They
climbed steep, rocky trails on foot and horseback and followed raw new

military roads in trucks and borrowed staff cars. Food and lodging gave them the most trouble. The peasants provided bread and wine, and they cooked over open fires. They slept in an open truck equipped with mattresses and blankets from Valencia. Parked in roofed-over courtyards among chickens, cattle, sheep, and donkeys, they were awakened each dawn by a chorus of lowing, braying, and crowing. Snow had already fallen in the mountains and glacial winds blew in over the tailgate of the truck. Martha endured these hardships with typical courage and aplomb. For years afterwards, Ernest remembered and praised her conduct in those September weeks.

Madrid in late September was far quieter than it had been in April and May. Siege warfare still went on in Usera, Carabanchel, and University City, but whole days sometimes passed without shelling from the Rebel batteries across the Casa de Campo. Ernest and Martha moved into the Hotel Florida, this time without the jealous presence of Sidney Franklin. There were other changes. During the summer, Rubio Hidalgo had brought Constancia de la Mora from Valencia to replace Ilsa Kulcsar and Arturo Barea in the Censorship Bureau. On learning that they had been superseded, Ernest shook his head and frowned. "I don't understand the whole thing," he said, "but I'm sorry. It seems a lousy mess."

Early in October, Martha and Ernest went out with Matthews and Delmer to inspect the Brunete front. They peered down from the heights at Rebel soldiers walking in the streets, and were surprised to find most of the town not only intact but quiet. Delmer had mounted British and American flags on the front fenders of his Ford in token of neutrality. This nearly got them killed as they raced north towards Villanueva de la Canada. Rebel artillerymen mistook the Ford "for some sort of super-staff-car" and shells bracketed the road they were following. "Shells are all much the same," wrote Ernest. "If they don't hit you, there's no story, and if they do, you don't have to write it." Nevertheless, Delmer drove cautiously home through the blacked-out suburbs of Madrid. Constellations shone bright in the sky. Ernest and Herbert Matthews watched them from the back seat while Ernest discoursed learnedly on navigation by starlight in tropical latitudes.

His euphoria still persisted, though less markedly than it had done in the spring. His room at the Hotel Florida was a haven for men on leave from the International Brigades. One was Captain Phil Detro, a Texan well over six feet tall, who returned to the headquarters of the 15th Brigade near Albares with tales of Hemingway's hospitality—hot baths, ham and cheese, hard liquor, a blanket for crapshooting, a record player, and even now and then a girl. Ernest's meetings with the young Americans sometimes took place at Chicote's Bar, one of his favorite hangouts on the Gran Vía. It was here that he first met Milton Wolff, platoon commander in the Lincoln Machine-Gun Company. Wolff was twenty-two, as tall as Detro, with a large nose and a Lincolnesque build. He found Ernest in the company of a beautiful girl. "Hemingway bought the drinks," wrote Wolff, "and after a while I was alone with the girl. . . . Papa had fixed me up. Ten wonderful days in Madrid. I owe him that." Another visitor was Freddy Keller, a stocky boy with bright blue eyes who was Commissar for the Lincoln Machine-Gun Company, and had lately distinguished himself during the battle of Fuentes del Ebro. Fred appeared with a Greek named Johnny Tsanakis, a fierce anti-Fascist who had served with the Greek underground. Phil Detro introduced them to Hemingway, with whom they hit it off at once. Tsanakis had an amusing habit of holding forth with a monologue in Ernest's room, only to pause in mid-career, look around suspiciously, and ask, "These other guys in the party?" Ernest picked it up as a temporary watchword. During the visit, they went out to inspect the Usera front, which Ernest said was as important as the Casa de Campo and University City sectors. Martha bumped her head badly while climbing out of a dugout. After lunch that day, Hemingway as correspondent and Keller as Commissar were asked to review a march-past of some 800 members of the 36th Brigade.

Ernest was still busy in Madrid when *To Have and Have Not* appeared in mid-October in New York. As always, he followed the sales figures with worried concentration. Between October 30 and December 9, he cabled Perkins three times to learn how the book was going. By early November, Perkins was able to report that the book stood fourth among national bestsellers, with some 25,000 copies sold. Most of the reviewers, however, had displayed mixed feelings. Louis Kronenberger called the book confused or transitional or both. Despite Hemingway's success with Morgan and a handful of superb scenes, the book fell apart in the middle and displayed "shocking lapses from professional skill." J. Donald Adams thought that the Hemingway record would be stronger without the book, which struck him as distinctly inferior to *A Farewell to Arms*. *Time* magazine carried a cover story, reproducing Waldo Peirce's action portrait of Ernest in a blue-striped fisherman's jersey and a long-billed cap. The story itself held that Hemingway's writing method was now becoming dated, even though (under pressure from the political Left and the political Right) he had emerged into a new maturity of outlook. The Spanish Civil War, it was suggested, was mainly responsible for arousing his "hitherto well-hidden social consciousness." The reaction in England was somewhat more enthusiastic. The *Manchester Guardian*'s reviewer was moved by the relationship between Harry Morgan and his wife, but accused Hemingway of "loading the dice against the people of leisure." *The Times Literary Supplement* admired the dialogue of understatement and the excitements of the narrative; the book's deficiencies arose from the narrowness of the author's scale of values.

As always under adverse judgment, Ernest simmered, boiled, blew up, and subsided. But his memory retained a file of names of those who did not like the book. They were numerous enough to justify the term he had used before and would use again whenever any of his books failed to earn universal praise: once more, said he, there had been a "critical gang-up" obviously designed to put him "out of business." But the book was behind him and he was already well into another. All summer he had been thinking about a three-act play. It would seek to make dramatic use of materials that he had picked up from conversations with various Republican officials in Madrid the previous spring. Up to late July, he had conceived it as a long short story of counterespionage. During August and September, it had begun to take shape as a melodrama. When the lull on the fighting fronts seemed, in John Wheeler's words, "to obviate the necessity" of further NANA despatches, Ernest got to work.

He had long considered writing a play, without going any further than "Today Is Friday," the tasteless little account of the aftermath of the Crucifixion. As early as 1927, he had broached the subject of playwriting to Perkins, saying that he knew nothing about working for the stage, though it might be fun to try. Now, ten years later, he was as ready as he would ever be. Late in October he wrote Pauline that the play was done. On November 8th she sent the news along to Perkins. *The New York Times* presently broke the story, and interested theater people began badgering Scribners with phone calls, asking for further details. But Max Perkins was still very much in the dark about the title and contents: all he knew was that the play existed in rough typescript in Ernest's luggage at the Hotel Florida.

Those to whom Ernest had shown the play must have been struck by its autobiographical aspects. He had amused himself by giving his protagonist, Philip Rawlings, certain habits and qualities of his own. Rawlings had "big shoulders and a walk like a gorilla," commonly skipped breakfast, read all the morning papers, liked sandwiches made of bully beef and raw onion, drank regularly at Chicote's Bar, and protested that he was "not supposed to be a damned monk." His social behavior included much drinking and fighting, many irrational quarrels, frequent assertion of his manhood, and a determination not to surrender to the domination of women. In short, the figure of Philip Rawlings, a correspondent secretly engaged as a counterspy in besieged Madrid, was a projection of Ernest himself, based on his imagination of how it might feel to be an actual insider, working with someone like Antonio, a dramatic recreation of the thin-lipped executioner of Madrid, Pepe Quintanilla. With his passion for exactitude, he even used in some of the scenes a virtual replica of the room he was then occupying at the Florida, with the cretonne-covered chairs, the tall armoire where extra food was stored, the portable phonograph with Chopin records, and even a chambermaid called Petra. Further, since he was writing the play in the fall of the year, he introduced allusions to the recent capture of Asturias and to the signs of the coming winter.

The lady correspondent of the play, Dorothy Bridges, bore an unmistakable resemblance to Martha Gellhorn. She was a tall, handsome blonde with long smooth legs, a curiously cultivated accent, and a college degree. Like Martha, she disliked dirt, displayed a passion for making rooms homelike, and even owned a silver-fox cape. While she bore no physical resemblance to Pauline, she represented one more step in the gradual rejection of his second wife which Ernest had publicly begun in "The Snows of Kilimanjaro." When Philip scornfully named over the places to which he and Dorothy might go if he were not otherwise occupied, they were identical with those that Ernest had visited with Pauline in France, in Kenya, and in Cuba. All that, said Philip, was now behind him: "Where I go now I go alone, or with others who go there for the same reason I go." These were places where he went for duty's sake and in the company of men like Max, the broken-faced comrade who had spent his entire mature life in the fight against Fascism. The Moorish tart Anita told Philip that he was making a mistake in taking up with "that big blonde," Dorothy Bridges. Philip agreed that she was indeed "enormously on the make." But she was also beautiful, friendly, charming, rather innocent, and brave. "I'm afraid that's the whole trouble," said Philip to Anita. "I want to make an absolutely colossal mistake." There, in the midst of his play, was Ernest's curious characterization of his developing love affair with Martha Gellhorn.

In mid-November, Evan Shipman appeared, up from the Casa Roja in Albacete where he had been living and working since being discharged from the hospital. At Brunete in July he had been wounded in the right thigh by a machine-gun slug from a strafing Rebel plane. Pale and ragged as always, he was still profoundly cheerful, and made no complaints about the bad luck that had dogged his footsteps ever since April. The contingent of volunteers with whom he had tried to enter Spain had been caught and jailed by the police of Toulouse. On his release, he took a ship from Marseilles to Barcelona, and was serving as interpreter and runner for a French-Belgian battalion when he was hit. He had been in Madrid only a few days when he fell ill. He had just recovered when Ernest came down with a severe chest cold. Evan took care of him in Martha's absence, often squatting beside the bed, chain-smoking cigarettes made from pounded butts, and talking much of the night. He drove back to Albacete in the middle of December, only to fall ill again with grippe, which put him back into the hospital with a temperature of 104.

Ernest later reported that he himself was still "sick as a bastard" when he reached Barcelona on his way out of Spain shortly before Christmas. But he recovered quickly when he learned of a surprise Loyalist offensive which was being launched against the Rebel defenders of Teruel, reputedly the coldest town in Spain. On Friday the 17th, he drove down to Valencia with Delmer and Matthews. Early next day they reached the headquarters of Colonel Hernández Sarabia in a railway car parked in a railroad tunnel near Teruel. They breakfasted on oranges heated over open fires beside the tracks and set out to find Sarabia at a command post on a mountaintop. The weather, as promised, was "cold as a steel engraving" and the shrieking winds as "wild as a Wyoming blizzard." Crouching behind boulders, they watched the Loyalist advance upon the Muela, or "Tooth," one of several "odd thimble-shaped formations like extinct geyser-cones" which had been braced with concrete

and ringed with tank traps. The huge yellow hill called Mansueto, resembling
a battleship, had been bypassed by the attacking force in spite of roads that
were blocked with snowdrifts. Ernest spoke to a soldier, blue-lipped in the
raging wind, who was feeding a small fire and singing a song:

> I had an inheritance from my father:
> It was the moon and the sun.
> I can move all over the world now
> And the spending of it is never done.

Ernest was pleased. To win battles, said he, the Republic still needed infantrymen like this undaunted soldier.

They rushed back to Valencia, sent off their stories by courier to Madrid,
and by dawn of the 21st were back at Sarabia's railway tunnel. Later that
morning they reached the foreground of the action, taking up stations on a
flanking ridge which provided an excellent view but virtually no protection
from enemy machine guns. "All I wanted," said Ernest, "was a spade to make
a little mound to get my head under." He sprawled down beside a young
conscript whose rifle had jammed and showed him how to knock the bolt
open with a rock. After five days of cold and snow, the sky had turned blue
and the sun warm. All day the Loyalists advanced—over the railway, across
the Mansueto, where two dogs played innocently ahead of an attacking column, and on to the edge of the town, which stood out sharply in the evening
sun against the "fantastically eroded background of red sandstone." Just at
sunset two truckloads of dynamiters deployed and slipped quietly up the final
slope.

Ernest and his companions followed them into Teruel. "We had never received the surrender of a town before," he wrote. "When the civilians came
out of their houses, they asked me what they should do and I told them to
stay in the houses and not go into the street that night under any circumstances and explained to them what good people we reds were. . . . They
all thought I was a Russian and when I told them I was a North American
they didn't believe a word of it." The reception was fervent. "They embraced
us," wrote Matthews, "shook our hands until they ached, patted and prodded
and slapped us. . . . One woman brought out a pitcher of newly made wine,
dark-red and tangy, with a touch of the wineskin taste. And so the day ended."
During the mop-up of the town, which Ernest described as the most god-
wonderful house-to-house fighting that he had ever seen, he and the others
commuted daily from Valencia. On Christmas Eve they returned to Barcelona.
Ernest's second tour of duty in Spain was reaching an end. It had lasted for
twenty-three weeks.

While he and Martha celebrated a quiet Catalonian Christmas, Pauline
reached Paris alone and unannounced in a last-ditch attempt to save her
marriage. She had even let her hair grow in a long bob like Martha's although
she told Jay Allen that her purpose in coming to France was to understand the

causes of the war and to see why it meant so much to men like her husband. She asked Allen to intercede with the American Consul General to get her a visa for Spain. But Ernest was back in Paris before the visa was ready. He consulted the physician Robert Wallich for a severe liver complaint. Wallich put him on a regimen of Chophytol and Drainochol and forbade all further drinking. While they waited to embark for New York, Ernest and Pauline stayed on the top floor of the Hôtel Elysée Park at the Rond Point des Champs Elysées. Bill Bird paid a call on them, meeting Pauline for the first and last time. The atmosphere was gloomy. Bill heard afterwards that they were quarreling bitterly over Martha, and that Pauline had threatened to jump off the balcony of their hotel room.

They sailed for New York aboard the *Gripsholm* on January 12th. It was a far cry from the pleasant voyage they had made aboard the same ship out of Africa four years earlier. Gales harassed them all the way across, and the seas were still running high when Ernest went to Miami to bring the *Pilar* down to Key West. He was full of multiple angers, complaints, and self-pity, and much agitated by some stories in *Time* magazine which seemed to imply that Herbert Matthews had been the only newspaperman at the taking of Teruel. He wrote his first wife Hadley that he had personally arranged for Matthews and Delmer to accompany him to Teruel, and that he had persuaded Constancia de la Mora to accept their stories, even if it meant her losing her job as censor. He further boasted that he had scored a ten-hour newsbeat over Matthews, only to suffer from the enmity of the Catholics who manned the night desk at *The New York Times*. They had not only thrown away all his stuff, said he, but had even deleted his name from Matthews's despatches. Such arrant disregard of the truth was not unusual with Ernest in times of psychological stress. His upset liver contributed heavily to his bilious view of the world. His rejection of Pauline in favor of Martha stirred up the remorse that had remained quiescent ever since his rejection of Hadley in favor of Pauline. Without being precisely beside himself, he continued to be petulant, quarrelsome, and almost pathologically suspicious all through the early months of 1938.

In this condition of mind and body, everything was an irritant. Advance publicity from the new *Ken* magazine had named him as one of the editors. He sent Gingrich a statement to be printed in the first number: "Ernest Hemingway has been in Spain since *Ken* was first projected. Although announced as an editor, he has taken no part in the editing of the magazine or in the formation of its policies. If he sees eye to eye with us on *Ken* we would like to have him as an editor. If not he will remain as a contributor until he is fired or quits." Smart and Gingrich accepted the retraction, and Ernest composed a 1,600-word piece called "The Time Now, The Place Spain," which he airmailed to Gingrich on March 2. It was a very strong statement, as he aggressively told Gingrich, and there was plenty more where it had come from. The point was that if the United States would reverse its neutrality and sell the Loyalists the war materials they needed, Fascism could be beaten on Spanish soil. Otherwise and in the very near future, the United States would have to face far tougher people than the legions of Mussolini or the forces of General Franco.

Ernest was fighting a battle of his own between the urge to return to Spain and a determination, almost equally strong, to stay on in Key West to write some stories about his recent experiences in and around Madrid. It did not help his state of mind that the stories would not come. When Patrick and Gigi caught the measles, the household was disturbed and his surliness increased. He scolded Perkins for having failed to advertise *To Have and Have Not,* and when he read somewhere that Scribners had given a tea party for Max Eastman, he filled a page with angry mutterings about what he would do to Eastman if he ever caught him alone. When Perkins gently remarked that Tom Wolfe had recently been behaving like a manic depressive, Ernest answered that Wolfe was an enormous baby, adding that it must be very difficult to be a genius. Even Scott Fitzgerald's praise could not sweeten his rancor. Scott had described him, said Perkins, as the most dynamic personality in the world. Or was it only the United States? Max could not remember the geography of the compliment. Once more Ernest exploded irritably. He had never wanted to be dynamic. All he ever wanted to be was a writer, and by Jesus Christ that was what he was going to be.

Beneath these surface irritations, and in a way explaining them all, was Ernest's gnawing consciousness of his disloyalty to Pauline. Without going into detail, he told Max Perkins in early February that he was in such an unchristly gigantic jam of every bloody kind that it was practically comic. Comic it was not, except in a bitterly ironical fashion. He had not in fact wished to come home at all. Like that of Philip Rawlings in *The Fifth Column,* his future lay in other directions. He was too deeply committed both to Spain and to Martha to think of taking up his life again where he had left it only a single year ago.

45. THE BANKS OF THE EBRO

HE endured life at home in Key West as well as he could until the middle of March. On the evening of the 13th, he refereed an amateur boxing match which ended with a knockout in the final round. Ernest shooed the grinning victor into a neutral corner and began counting. The victim's handler threw a towel into the ring. Ernest kicked it away and went on counting. Overcome with emotion, the young handler climbed through the ropes and threw a punch at Ernest. Ernest clipped him once with a right hook and held him by the ear until a policeman led him away. "The kid lost his head," said Ernest.

The night in the ring was his last of the season. On the 15th he wrote Max Perkins that he could not sleep because he knew that he belonged in Spain.

His departure was precipitate. On the 17th he flew with Pauline from Miami to Newark and by Saturday the 19th he was aboard the *Île de France* on the way to Europe. He wrote Perkins from the ship to say that recent Loyalist reverses had left him no choice but to return to Spain. He was carrying a briefcase filled with the short stories which Scribners would publish that fall in a first collected edition. He would look them over and arrange them in order during his stopover in Paris. Copy for the book would reach Perkins in plenty of time to be set up in type.

On March 31st he entrained for Perpignan at the Gare d'Orsay in Paris. His companions were Vincent Sheean and Ring Lardner's son Jim, a long-legged young man with brown hair and horn-rimmed glasses. Ernest had a new six-week contract with NANA; Sheean and Lardner were both representing the *New York Herald Tribune*. In Perpignan, Ernest quickly arranged for a car to carry them to Barcelona. They arrived on the foggy evening of April 1st. The city had recently been bombed by the Italians, and disorder was everywhere. Ernest went to bed in an unkempt room at the Majestic without certain knowledge of the military situation on the banks of the Ebro. All he knew was that Franco's spring offensive in Aragon had opened on March 22nd, with the purpose of driving a wedge to the Mediterranean between Barcelona and Valencia to divide and then conquer the dwindling terrain still held by the Republic.

He was as eager as ever to be where the action was. On the morning of April 3rd he set off with Herbert Matthews for the long drive south to Tarragona. There the road forked inland towards Reus and Falset and the doomed village of Gandesa. The land looked serene and springlike with pink almond blossoms and gray-green olive orchards. But the war was close. Half a mile from Reus they had to dive for the ditch when a Rebel monoplane winged over as if to strafe them and then roared past to bomb the town ahead. Twenty miles farther inland they met the Loyalist refugees plodding for the coast, their carts piled high with household goods. Behind the civilians came retreating troops, followed by tanks and artillery pieces. Gandesa was gone, the said, fallen to the advancing Rebels.

At noon next day in the hills above Rasquera on the eastern bank of the Ebro, Ernest and Matthews met some of the survivors of the Washington-Lincoln Battalion, who had been surrounded on a hilltop outside Gandesa. They gave a hair-raising account of sneaking through the Rebel lines at night and swimming the Ebro in the cold dawn. "Nobody's got any social standing," said Ernest, "who hasn't swum the Ebro at least once." Captain Milton Wolff was there, looking far older than he had on furlough in Madrid in the fall. He had swum the river after two days of wandering alone through enemy territory. He wore long mustaches and a woolen hat, and his black cape was stained with red dust. Freddy Keller appeared, his blue eyes alert and undaunted despite a severe wound in the hip sustained at Gandesa. John Gates, Joe Hecht, and George Watt were in the group, wearing makeshift clothes

after having made a naked dash across the river near Miravet. Alvah Bessie
was on hand. He told Ernest that he had heard him speak at Carnegie Hall
in June. "Oh," said Ernest, "I'm awful glad to see you. I've read your stuff."
He pleased Bessie even further by handing him a full pack of Lucky Strikes.

On the 5th Ernest crossed the steel bridge at Tortosa and probed northwards along the west bank of the river as far as Cherta. Loyalist morale was
higher everywhere than the situation appeared to warrant, mainly because the
dog-tired defenders were being steadily refreshed by a stream of much-needed
armor. From there he went further north towards the foothills of the Pyrenees,
returning to report that the Rebels were overrunning strong Loyalist positions.
One sign of slack discipline was the number of rabbits the troops had taken
time to kill. Ernest stored the memory away for future use. He was encouraged by the fact that the defenders of Tortosa were still holding, though the
skies were full of German and Italian planes and two Italian divisions had
repeatedly attacked. Early in Easter week he stopped beside an antitank gun
on the west bank. Across the river was an old castle with two Rebel machine
guns in the towers and a tin can glinting in one of the windows. He was as
jubilant as a boy when the Loyalist gunners laid two shells through the yawn-
ing black doorway of the castle. He wanted them to try for the tin can in the
window, but was told that the shells were too valuable to waste.

This was the week when the Rebels first came within sight of the Mediterranean. Good Friday was a dark day for the Loyalists. A Rebel division from
Navarre under General Alonso Vega cut the Republic in two by taking the
fishing village of Vinaroz and wading exuberantly into the sea. Ernest and
Martha left Barcelona at dawn with Matthews and Delmer. By nine they were
past the shambles of Tortosa and across the steel bridge. They hurried south
to Ulldecona, a mere ten miles from Vinaroz. But Rebel units were even then
advancing in their direction and they withdrew to Santa Barbara, stopping for
lunch in a grove of olive trees where they were presently joined by Vincent
Sheean and Joe North. By the time they got back to Tortosa, the long steel
bridge was gone, a third of its central span wrecked in the brown river, the
work of Rebel bombers. Some yards downstream a crew of boys were nailing
boards across a narrow footbridge. Delmer inched the car across this makeshift structure in the wake of a mule-drawn peasant cart. Driving through
Tortosa, said Ernest, was like "mountaineering in the craters of the moon."
The rough road back to Barcelona seemed smooth by comparison.

The Rebel occupation of Vinaroz produced another pitiful stream of refugees who made their way north from towns like Alcanar and San Carlos de
la Rápita towards the comparative safety of Tarragona and Barcelona. On
Easter Sunday, Ernest met one of them, a tired old man of seventy-six, who
had come from San Carlos to a pontoon bridge which had been thrown across
the lower Ebro near Amposta. The old man was worried about the domestic
animals he had been obliged to leave behind him. From their brief conversation and his observation of the surrounding terrain, Ernest fashioned a short

story, his second of the war, which he sent out that night as a regular despatch. It was as compassionate as his group portrait of the Greek refugees at Adrianople many years earlier. This time, however, he knew enough about the art of synecdoche to make the old man at the bridge into a moving symbol of all those others whom the war had uprooted. By the next afternoon, the bridge was gone, the Rebel forces were in Amposta, and Ernest watched the Loyalist artillery blast the town they had just abandoned. This was also the day when Tortosa fell, virtually completing enemy domination of the lower Ebro valley.

The weather had now turned cold and bleak, and the long-delayed spring rains began to fall, blunting General Varela's drive, with three Rebel divisions, from reconquered Teruel down to the sea. Ernest busied himself with another article for *Ken* magazine, attacking Cardinal Hayes for having told a press conference in New York that he was praying for Franco's victory over the "radicals and Communists" on the Republican side. Along with Vincent Sheean, he also attempted to dissuade young Jim Lardner from enlisting in the International Brigade. All their arguments were unavailing, and Lardner joined up on April 24th, the last of the American volunteers.

Freddy Keller was recuperating from his wounds at the coastal hospital in Mataró north of Barcelona. Ernest drove up to see him with Herbert Matthews and Tom Delmer, who brought gifts of ham and cheese to Keller and the other wounded veterans of the Abraham Lincoln Brigade. Ernest had equipped himself with a military map, and quizzed Keller relentlessly about his movements and adventures during the Ebro campaign, including his capture by the Rebels, his escape from his guard, and his final crossing of the dangerously fast river. But the most memorable result of Ernest's visit to Mataró was his meeting with one of the nurses, a quiet and devoted Spanish girl named María, who struck all her charges as the very "soul of serenity." Early in the war she had been raped by Fascist soldiers. Like so much else that he had seen and heard in the past eighteen months, the case of María seized and held a permanent place in Ernest's memories of the Spanish War.

On the way back to Barcelona after a May Day trip to the Ebro delta, Ernest was riding with Joe North in Herbert Matthews's car when they came up behind a truckload of singing Spaniards. They waved to the correspondents and gaily brandished their fists in the Loyalist salute. But their gaiety was short-lived. At one of the sharp curves in the road the driver lost control and the truck somersaulted into the ditch, scattering its occupants among the boulders. The Americans leaped out to give such help as they could. Ernest was the first among the injured and dying, down on his knees in the new spring grass, applying bandages, mopping faces, trying to offer solace. North worked at his side through the scene of horror. Despite their political differences, North's regard for Hemingway's humanitarian instincts never cooled from that day forth.

Three days later Ernest flew to Marseilles to pick up his mail. It included a month-old letter from Perkins, who had read *The Fifth Column* and thought it "extraordinarily fine." "I was mightily impressed by it," said Max, "and moved too. It means plenty, and confirms what *To Have* showed, that you have marched forward into new fields, and large ones." Ernest replied next day that his hopes of seeing the play produced had been knocked down in March by the sudden death of Austin Parker, who had been planning to bring it to Broadway in the fall. But he was not greatly worried. He told Perkins that he was reveling in his first full day of rest since reaching Europe. He would like it to last a week. Instead, he must get up before dawn on the 6th and fly south to inspect the Castellón front above Valencia.

His contract with the North American Newspaper Alliance was about to expire. John Wheeler had not been sufficiently impressed by his cables to take whatever he sent without protest. *The New York Times,* which subscribed to Wheeler's service, had complained in April that Ernest's despatches often duplicated material sent in by their own correspondent, Herbert Matthews. Wheeler first tried to meet this objection by asking Ernest to confine his work to human-interest features rather than straight reporting, and then by asking him to restrict his reports to developments of vital importance. Without ever saying so, these instructions reflected adversely on Ernest's ability as a reporter. In fact his work for NANA was not noticeably superior to what he had done for the *Toronto Star* in the early 1920s. He could still summarize grand strategy with economy and force. He still displayed a keen interest in matters of terrain. He daubed his work with arresting similes and bright splashes of local color, and liked to include snatches of conversation with soldiers and civilians, though most of these were so heavily stamped with his personal mannerisms as to be of doubtful authenticity. Along with these mixed virtues went many faults, which were clear enough to men like Wheeler. There was a curious monotony in his stories of battles and bombardments. He liked to shock his readers with the sheen of blood on skin, the severed arm or leg hurtling through the air. He often hinted that he was alone when in fact he was usually with Martha Gellhorn, Matthews, and Delmer. He often struck a note of triumphant boastfulness, as if he wished his readers and his employers to be sure to recognize how near the front he was actually working. His eye for telling details and individual traits was not nearly so sharp as that of Dos Passos, nor did he commonly rise to the meticulous exactitude and inclusiveness which characterized the best work of Matthews and Delmer.

On the plane to Alicante he gazed down at Vinaroz and Benicarlo, now in enemy hands. "That brown range of hills," he wrote, "that slid down into the sea like a dinosaur come to drink was the line holding up Franco's advance toward Castellón." Alicante and Valencia both showed the effects of the war. All men of military age were now in uniform, and all the old luxuries were gone from the restaurants and the shops. Up the coast at Castellón, the townspeople had made an elaborate system of underground shelters into which they dived like prairie dogs each time the air-raid siren screamed. The Loyalist commander at Oropesa grinned at Hemingway and said that the period of panic was over. They would retreat down the coastline a foot at a time, giving where they had to, but battling the Rebels all the way.

Joe North was already in Madrid when Ernest drove up from Valencia for his first sight of the capital in five months. They met at the Bureau of Censorship and adjourned to the Hotel Florida in a heated political argument. "I like Communists when they're soldiers," cried Ernest, eying North like a bird dog, "but when they're priests, I hate them." North answered coldly that Ernest was making a false distinction. Communists made good soldiers precisely because of their priestlike qualities, their inward convictions, their sense of purpose. Ernest stood there in the hotel room, poised on the balls of his feet like a boxer, his long arms hanging at his sides, his stubbled chin thrust forward aggressively. Then he laughed suddenly, the invariable sign that he had had enough of argument. "Hell," he said, "I believe you're one of . . . the goddamn bishops. Here, *mi padre,* a libation."

Whatever their politics, he was too good a Loyalist not to believe in the soldiers of the Republic. "Discounting all optimism," he cabled John Wheeler,

this trip has been a revelation to this correspondent, flying in from the Catalonian Front. Each day and night, trenches and saps are being run out to outflank the enemy and eventually to relieve the siege of the city. Certainly there will be bitter fighting to relieve Castellón, and Franco will try to cut down from the Teruel sector between Castellón and Valencia. But there is a year of war clearly to be seen ahead where European diplomats are trying to say it will be over in a month.

46. PULLING OUT

BACK in Paris in the middle of May, Ernest and Martha found Evan Shipman, Freddy Keller, and Marty Hourihan established in the Hôtel Argonne across the street from Lipp's Brasserie. Keller and Hourihan, traveling together, had had great difficulties in getting out of Spain and were waiting to be vouched for by William Bullitt, the American Ambassador, on the triple recommendation of Martha, Sheean, and Matthews. Shipman had been arrested and imprisoned at Perpignan until friends secured his release. Ernest immediately took them under his wing, conducting them to the Longchamps racetrack, introducing them to Sylvia Beach at her bookshop, and buying them dinners at Lipp's. He even took Keller to hear a concert by the Austrian String Quartet, where he discoursed learnedly on the art of counterpoint, and urged his young friend to read Ulysses Grant's *Memoirs* and some of the novels of Romain Rolland.

Four American stowaways from the International Brigade were on board the *Normandie* when she docked in New York on Memorial Day. Ernest made no public comment about these men, merely telling reporters that he planned to return to Key West immediately to begin work on some short stories and a novel. When queried about the war, he said that he had become jaded with active reporting on the various fronts, though he might return to Spain if things "got warm over there." Franco, said he, was short of troops and handicapped by friction among the foreign elements in his army. The Loyalists were well organized and their chances of winning were good.

During his stopover in New York he went to see Jay Allen and his wife at their house in Washington Square. He seemed to be eager for information about Pauline, and very uncertain about her willingness to go on with their marriage. With an obtuseness that struck the Allens as somewhat curious, he blamed Pauline's sister Jinny for his strained marital relations, seeking to use her as a scapegoat instead of admitting that his love affair with Martha had always been the primary problem. Although the Allens were not reassuring, since they believed that Pauline had accepted the break as complete, Ernest went off to Key West almost as if nothing had happened, evidently resolved to brazen it out as well as he could.

Pauline's reception was cool but otherwise hospitable enough. Apart from fishing, Ernest divided his time almost equally between further articles for *Ken* and some short stories based on his recollections of Chicote's Bar in Madrid. David Smart had been accused of Red-baiting because (as he had frankly admitted to Ernest in March) the first issue had included "two cartoon cracks at Communism, as protective coloring." Merely because *Ken* was trying to make anti-Fascism respectable, said Smart, there was no reason for being labeled pro-Communist. Ernest took the position that if *Ken* had actually baited the Reds, its editor must be either a fool or a knave. Yet he continued his contract with the magazine throughout the summer, partly because Smart paid him a hundred dollars a week for whatever he chose to write, and partly because he wished to use the magazine as a weapon against Fascism. His sixth article denounced the alleged Fascists in the American Department of State for having done "their level, crooked, Roman, British-aping, disgusting efficient best" to end the Spanish War by "denying the Spanish government the right to buy arms to defend itself against the German and Italian aggression." Another piece condemned Dos Passos for political naïveté in the case of José Robles. Yet another denounced Neville Chamberlain and the French ministers for having betrayed England, France, and the Loyalists. Ernest called on Roosevelt to become a great president by opposing Chamberlain and supporting the Republic while there was yet time.

On June 22 he went to New York for the Louis-Schmeling fight. John Wheeler had offered him a paltry $250 for a pair of fight stories, one on the contenders, another "a colorful hairy description of the battle itself." He also proposed a lunch at the University Club, with Grantland Rice, Julian Street, and Gene Tunney. Ernest declined both proposals. Instead he was host to the same company at the St. Regis, and wrote for *Ken* a colorful hairy piece called "My Pal the Gorilla Gargantua." Gargantua was the name of a gorilla then being exhibited by the Ringling Brothers Circus. Gene Tunney had repeatedly asserted that a human heavyweight in prime condition could beat

Gargantua or any of his ilk. "If any man could, Gene could," wrote Ernest, "because he would not be afraid, because he can hit to the body, and because he is intelligent." Such an encounter would in any case be prettier to watch than the Louis-Schmeling fight, which was over almost as soon as it began, with Schmeling glassy-eyed on the ropes and Louis still "the fastest and hardest-hitting heavyweight" that Ernest had ever seen, Tunney and Gargantua included.

He returned to serious journalism with three more articles for *Ken*. In one he correctly predicted the outbreak of a general war in Europe for the summer of 1939 at the latest; in another he praised an insane Loyalist general named Mangada who had successfully held his sector in the Sierra de Guadarrama against repeated Rebel assaults by setting up command posts out ahead of his own front lines. A third article lambasted reporters who invented despatches without taking the trouble to distinguish truth from rumor, a topic Ernest had often discussed with his friend Matthews. Except for one last article which did not appear until the following January, Ernest's six-month association with *Ken* was now ended. His journalism of this period, unlike the sporting letters he had contributed to *Esquire,* was all of a piece. Whatever their limitations, his articles and despatches had centered on a single theme, fiercely espoused and constantly reiterated: the necessity of opposing the rise of Fascism in Europe before Hitler's Brown Shirts and Mussolini's Black Shirts overran the continent and precipitated a second world war. The Spanish conflict was clearly a prelude to the larger action. He had wanted the United States to help the anti-Fascist cause by selling arms to the Loyalists. This had not happened, nor (he felt) had any counterforce arisen to prevent the foreign ministers of England and France from selling out to political expediency and the empty promise of "peace in our time."

By the first of July, the volume of collected stories took final shape. Of the forty-eight stories which made it up, only one bothered Perkins, as it had long ago bothered Horace Liveright, the old *bête noire,* "Up in Michigan." Ernest defended it as sad rather than dirty. Its faults, he admitted, included some very wooden dialogue. Yet he believed that the seduction scene on the foggy dock marked the beginning of all the naturalness he had ever achieved. To the previous total he added the little story of the old man at the Amposta bridge on Easter Sunday, and settled on the long and rather awkward title of *The Fifth Column and the First Forty-Nine Stories.* He was counting on overwhelming the critics with riches, believing that it would be excellent strategy to hit them hard after the "gang-up" against *To Have and Have Not.* Nobody, as he told Perkins, could accuse him of egotism or persecution mania for saying that many of the reviewers hated him and would like to put him out of business, though he admitted that he was no doubt partly to blame: he had been "very snotty" sometimes in the past, and his victims still held this against him.

Only two major problems remained. One was the projected preface and the other, as yet unsettled, was whether or not to publish *The Fifth Column* as it stood. On August 3rd he said that he was heartily sick of his play. It had given him nothing but trouble for seven or eight months, and he wanted to get it behind him in favor of other projects. If he agreed to let someone else rewrite it for the stage, it might still earn some money. But its status was so "bloody unreliable" that it would doubtless be best to publish it as written, letting the production problem work itself out.

Key West had become too hot for working and he decided to drive his sons and Pauline out to Wyoming for a breath of mountain air. The expedition set off on August 4th, but they had gone no farther than Palm Beach when Ernest scratched the pupil of his bad left eye. The right eye was sympathetically affected, as had happened once before in Switzerland, and he spent two frustrated days in a motel room with the blinds drawn. When he emerged at last, with a patch over the bad eye and the other blearily weeping, he drove like a demon to get out of the heat and humidity. In Denver he ran out of money and wired Perkins for more. But by August 17th, while rain beat down steadily on the cabin roof under the lodgepole pines at the L-Bar-T ranch, he finished reading page proof on the stories and began work on the preface.

He paused long enough to write Pauline's mother with his customary mixture of boasting and bashfulness. Publishing the text of his play when he had counted on it to make a fortune on Broadway was, he thought, like sending a horse to the dogmeat cannery when you had expected it to win the Kentucky Derby. Still, in the past eighteen months, he had rewritten and published a novel, helped to make a moving picture, completed a play, done fifteen magazine articles, and filed some $15,000 worth of newspaper despatches. On the other hand, said he, if he had hired someone to run his life badly, he could hardly have done a worse job. In three trips to Spain he had neither been scared nor wounded. Possibly for this reason, he had been intolerant, self-righteous, ruthless, and cruel. The only way he could run his life decently was to accept the discipline of the Church. But the problem in Spain was that the Church had sided with the enemy. This fact bothered him so much that he had even quit praying: it seemed somehow "crooked" to have anything to do with a religious institution so closely allied to Fascism.

By August 20th the preface was finished and mailed—a thousand words of informal commentary in which, as in his letter to Mrs. Pfeiffer, he mixed pride and modesty. He concluded with a honing metaphor. In going where one had to go and doing what one had to do, a man dulled and blunted the instrument he wrote with. But it was far better to wear it down, knowing that it could be sharpened again, than to keep it locked up in a closet unused until the time arrived when its owner found that he had nothing left to say. A final detail was the dedication of the forthcoming volume. Ernest wrote it out in longhand: "To Marty and Herbert with love." In Paris, Barcelona, Valencia, Madrid, and even in New York, his liaison with Martha was well-known, but he had been careful until now to maintain the fiction that all was well at home.

Although this salute to Martha did not appear in the published book, he was willing at last to advertise in this way the new shift of allegiance.

Even Wyoming could no longer hold him. He met Perkins for breakfast at the Hotel Barclay in New York on the 30th, and sailed for France next day aboard the *Normandie*. In Paris, reunited with Martha, he set to work on the stories which he had blocked out in Key West before the heat drove him west. He relaxed from these labors by shooting pheasants with Ben Gallagher in the Sologne—wild, fast birds that rose like rockets through the autumn foliage. By October 22nd he was able to report that he had finished two stories and two chapters of a novel. One of the stories, "Night Before Battle," opened with an account of the Old Homestead, the ruined apartment in the Paseo Rosales where he had watched the Loyalist attack in April of 1937, and moved on to scenes in the Hotel Florida and the basement restaurant of the Hotel Gran Vía. He proudly mailed it off to Gingrich to be printed in *Esquire*.

Meantime the new book had appeared, a thick red volume of nearly six hundred pages, the longest of his works. Once more the reviews were mixed. Pauline, who was spending the fall in New York, gathered and sent a batch of the earliest. Ernest again bristled angrily, nor were his feelings much mollified when Perkins reported the sale of 6,000 copies in the first two weeks. Edmund Wilson called the stories "very fine" but cared nothing for the play. Clifton Fadiman agreed with Perkins that the play made "exciting reading," and described Ernest as "the best short-story writer now using English." Malcolm Cowley said that the figure of Dorothy Bridges kept the play from being "a tragedy or even a valid conflict between love and duty." Dorothy was merely "a Junior Leaguer pitching woo on the fringes of the radical movement." Ernest's preoccupation with violence had seemed excessive in the period between the wars; now, as the bloody decade of the 1930s neared its end, violence had proved to be the normal order of the modern world.

Ernest's act of withdrawal from Pauline was now coupled with a change in his attitude towards Spain itself. Late in October he told both Perkins and Gingrich that he had promised Pauline to stay clear of the fighting and had accordingly turned down an offer of a staff captaincy in a French outfit which was then being organized to help the Loyalists. But there were other reasons for staying away. With a mixture of sadness and scorn he spoke of "the carnival of treachery and rottenness on both sides" of the conflict, adding that he would make one final visit to Catalonia early in November. Then he would pull out and come home to work on his novel.

In Barcelona on November 4th, Matthews and Delmer brought him up to date on the fortunes of the Republic. The International Brigades had been pulled from the lines at the end of September, which happened to be the day after the disappearance and death of young Jim Lardner. The 15th Brigade, under Enrique Lister, was still holding a bridgehead on the far side of the Ebro. On the 5th, Ernest drove south to Tarragona and inland to Falset with General Hans Kahle, Henry Buckley, Matthews, Sheean, and

53. Ernest's house at 907 Whitehead Street, Key West, Fla.

54. Joe Russell, Ernest, and marlin, Havana, 1932.

55. RIGHT, *Pilar* under way.

56. BELOW. Ernest and Bra Saunders off Key West, 1928.

57. Lawrence and Olive Nordquist, owners of the L-T Ranch.

58. Pauline at the Nordquist Ranch, 1932.

59. Ernest during his hospitalization
in Billings, Mont., Nov., 1930.

60. Ranch hands Chub Weaver and Ivan Wallace, favorites of Ernest's, at Timber Creek, 1932.

61. Ernest and trophies at Nordquists', 1932.

62. Charles Thompson
and Pauline's Uncle Gus,
Dry Tortugas, 1932.

63. Ernest, Burge, Mike Strater, and Max Perkins, stormbound at
Fort Jefferson, Dry Tortugas, March, 1930.

64. The captain of the *Pilar* off Bimini, 1936.

65. Ernest boxing at Bimini, 1935.

66. Ernest and Pauline with Ernest's lion, Serengeti Plain, Jan., 1934.

67. Kudu and oryx trophies held by Ben Fourie, Charles Thompson, Philip Percival, and Ernest, Kijungu Camp, Tanganyika, Feb., 1934.

68. Ernest and his buffalo, Serengeti Plain, Jan., 1934.

69. Ernest as the NANA correspondent with Loyalist soldiers, Ebro River, April, 1938.

70. LOWER LEFT. Joris Ivens, Ernest, and Dr. Werner Heilbrun in trenches at University City, Madrid, April, 1937.

71. BELOW. General Enrique Lister with Ernest near Mora de Ebro, Nov., 1938.

72. LEFT. Patrick Hemingway at age 18 and the guide Taylor Williams, Sun Valley, Idaho, Oct., 1946.

73. BELOW. Pappy Arnold's picture of Ernest and Martha Gellhorn, Sun Valley, Nov., 1940.

74. LEFT. Ernest and son Gregory, then 10, in the Pahsimeroi, 1941.

75. BELOW. Otto Bruce and Tillie Arnold with Ernest, Sun Valley, Sept., 1940.

76. Working on *For Whom the Bell Tolls,* Sun Valley, Dec., 1939.

77. Hongkong, March, 1941, during his trip to cove the war in China.

78. The Finca Vigía, San Francisco de Paula, Cuba.

Bob Capa, the *Life* photographer. The Ebro was in flood, but General Hans found a boat and four men to row it, paying the fare in cigarettes. They climbed ashore and walked to Mora de Ebro, which was completely destroyed and empty except for tanks and trucks. The Fifth Army head-quarters was a whitewashed stone-and-stucco farmhouse on a rise of ground. They found General Lister both hearty and harassed. He was on the point of abandoning the bridgehead and withdrawing across the river, and asked Kahle to get the correspondents away. They piled in and shoved off in another small boat. Halfway across, the swift current caught and carried them towards the jagged ruins of the Mora bridge. Ernest seized an oar and rowed strenuously. It was only because of his skill that they all got safely ashore.

Next day he appeared with Matthews at the town of Ripoll, fifty kilometers south of Bourg Madame on the French border. The American volunteers from the International Brigades had been stationed there for ten days, await-ing final evacuation on December 2. In the street they met Alvah Bessie, whom Ernest had last seen in April on the Ebro.

"I'm glad to see you got out of this alive," said Ernest.

"I am, too," said Bessie.

"Because," Hemingway went on, "I always felt responsible for your being here."

Bessie looked puzzled.

"You heard the speech I made at the Writers' Congress?" asked Heming-way.

Bessie said that he remembered it well.

"I know that speech was responsible for a lot of guys' coming over," said Ernest.

The statement stuck in Bessie's mind. Could it have contained the merest hint of that curious megalomania which others had noticed at times during Hemingway's visits to wartime Spain?

That night in Barcelona, a large group gathered in the suite at the Majestic occupied by the *Pravda* correspondent, Boleslavskaya. Ernest attended, as did André Malraux. Ernest glowered at Malraux and drank whiskey. He believed that his rival had been at fault in having pulled out of the war in February, 1937, before the Loyalists had won any significant victories, in order to write huge "masterpisses" like *L'Espoir,* which had been published in Paris before the year was out. The company sang and danced until about midnight. Afterwards, Boleslavskaya's driver, a tall and dour man, suggested a moment of silence in memory of those who had died in defense of Madrid. Ernest stood quietly, holding his glass, his head bowed. Like the others in the room, he had lost many friends in the Spanish Civil War, including some like Dos Passos who were not killed.

What he had gained, however, was a new lease on his life as a writer. Refusing to waste the best of his materials in his newspaper despatches or his propaganda pieces for *Ken*, he had gathered and salted away a body of experience and information which he described to Perkins as "absolutely invaluable." Skilled and courageous commanders like Lister and Modesto could postpone for a few months the loss of the Spanish Republic. But Ernest believed that the politicians were treacherously at work behind the scenes and that the odor of corruption was increasingly evident. Now was the time to pull out. A writer's obligation was to write.

CHAPTER 8

East and West

47. SPOILS OF SPAIN

"WHAT I have to do now is write," declared Ernest. "As long as there is a war you always think perhaps you will be killed so you have nothing to worry about. But now I am not killed so I have to work. . . . Living is much more difficult and complicated than dying and it is just as hard as ever to write. . . . In stories about the war I try to show *all* the different sides of it, taking it slowly and honestly and examining it from many ways. So never think one story represents my viewpoint because it is much too complicated for that. We know war is bad. Yet sometimes it is necessary to fight. But still war is bad and any man who says it is not is a liar. But it is very complicated and difficult to write about truly. . . . In the war in Italy when I was a boy I had much fear. In Spain I had no fear after a couple of weeks and was very happy. Yet for me not to understand fear in others or deny its existence would be bad writing. It is just that now I understand the whole thing better. The only thing about a war, once it has started, is to win it—and that is what we did not do. The hell with war for a while, I want to write."

Apart from his despatches on the chauffeurs of Madrid and the old man at the Amposta bridge, the first result of Ernest's war experience was a series of short stories. He was still in Paris in mid-November when "The Denunciation" appeared in *Esquire*. It told of a waiter in Chicote's Bar who recognized a customer as a Rebel spy and turned him in with a telephone call to the secret police. Gingrich was also enthusiastic about a second story, "The Butterfly and the Tank," which was based like the first on an actual incident from the fall of 1937. Ernest had already summarized it briefly in *The Fifth Column*. A drunken citizen named Pedro took to squirting waiters in Chicote's with a flit gun of eau de cologne. Disgusted soldiers first beat and then shot him to death. When Steinbeck read it in the December number of *Esquire*, it struck him as "one of a very few finest stories in all time." To have seen it as a story was in itself a great thing, he wrote to Ernest. But to have written it so superbly was "almost too much."

Late in November Ernest returned to New York, spending a few days with Pauline and his sons at her apartment in East 50th Street. His chief concern was to settle the problem of *The Fifth Column*. The Theatre Guild, which had been lukewarm about it early in the year, had now taken an option on the play and proposed to hire a Hollywood screenwriter named Benjamin F. Glaser to adapt it for stage production. Glaser had earned the plaudits of the Guild for his successful translation of Ferenc Molnar's *Liliom*, and Ernest's attorney, Maurice Speiser, had already prepared a contract. It specified that Glaser should rewrite the play, point up the characterizations and the dialogue, and submit the results to Ernest's scrutiny. Ernest insisted that the new version should contain no adverse criticism of the Spanish Republic government or the Communist Party. The royalties, if any, were to be split half and half.

When Pauline's lease expired at the end of November, she and Ernest left separately for Key West, still keeping up the pretense that all was well between them. Ernest went fishing for sailfish and wahoo with Paul Willerts and continued to exploit his Spanish war experiences with yet another story called "Nobody Ever Dies," which he promptly sold to *Cosmopolitan*. Unlike its predecessors, this one was in his worst vein of tough sentimentalism— a tale of two young lovers wanted by the secret police of Cuba. Enrique, the hero, had been wounded in Spain exactly as Gustav Regler had been wounded at Huesca. The Cuban police murdered him and captured his girl, María. Ernest did his best to make her over as a latter-day Joan of Arc. He was inept enough to close his story with one last glimpse of the girl, sitting firm and straight in the car of her captors, "her face shining in the arc light."

By early January Glaser had completed a provisional adaptation of *The Fifth Column*. Ernest hurried up to New York only to discover that it was "absolutely appalling, stupid, childish, ignorant, sentimental, [and] silly." The "Jews," as he scornfully explained, had chosen to open the play with the high spots of Act III and then had nowhere to go from that point. He wrote two "new" acts from scratch in what he called an Old Testament nightmare of a fortnight's duration. The title, said he, should now be changed to *The Four Ninety-five Column Marked Down from Five*.

Glaser seemed willing to accept what Hemingway had done. By January 24th, when Ernest flew back to Key West, one character had even been cast: the sultry Lenore Ulric would play the role of Anita, the Moorish tart. There was tentative agreement that Lee Strasberg would direct, that Billy Rose might put up some of the money, and that Rose's friend Franchot Tone might play Philip Rawlings. At a dinner party with Scribner, Perkins, Glaser, and Speiser the night before he left, Ernest drank too much, and took to needling Glaser and Speiser with unseemly epithets. When Evan Shipman asked Perkins to attend tryouts for the play in New Haven early in February,

Max declined on the grounds that Ernest was by this date completely disgusted with plays, playwrights, producers, and even with life itself. It was true. He was now telling anyone who would listen that he ought to have written *The Fifth Column* as a novel.

In fact his head was filled with many nondramatic projects. The February number of *Esquire* contained his "Night Before Battle," which he had sent to Gingrich from Paris in October. He composed a free-verse poem "On the American Dead in Spain" for publication in the *New Masses,* donating the typescript of the poem and the manuscript of *The Spanish Earth* to be auctioned off for the rehabilitation fund of the Abraham Lincoln Brigade. He was already planning a new book of short fiction for the fall of 1939. Besides collecting the recent war stories from *Esquire* and *Cosmopolitan,* he wanted to write three more very long ones. Two would deal with Spain and the other with an old Cuban fisherman. The first, to be called "Fatigue," would try to recapture the battle of Teruel; the second would describe the storming of a pass in the Sierra de Guadarrama by a detachment of Polish Lancers. The third and most ambitious had been in his mind for several years. He had already outlined it in "On the Blue Water," published in *Esquire* in April, 1936. It would tell of an aged commercial fisherman out of Casablanca on the eastward side of Havana harbor. All alone in his skiff for four days and four nights he had fought a huge marlin, only to lose it to a pack of sharks because it was too big to get into his boat. The story would say everything that the old man did and thought during his long and lonely battle. Properly told, it could be "great," thought Ernest, and its presence in the new volume would "make" the book. He said that on his next trip to Cuba he hoped to go out in a skiff with old Carlos Gutiérrez to make sure that all his details were authentic.

His visit to Cuba was not long postponed. Beginning on February 14th he went there for a month. Each day he worked from eight to two, then played tennis, swam, or fished. He did not write any of the new stories he had proposed to Perkins. Instead he finished another called "Under the Ridge." The scene was a bleak hilltop in the Jarama sector where the 12th International Brigade had just made an abortive attack. The force of the tale came from the anger of a man from Badajoz, who resented the murderous disciplinary measures of the battle police, a pair of cold-faced Russians in black leather jackets.

But the major achievement of his Cuban visit was to make a start on his novel of the Spanish Civil War. It was a task so ambitious, as he told Perkins, that he had not expected even to attempt it for a long time. In Paris at the end of October he had mentioned having finished two chapters of a novel. But he personally counted March 1, 1939, as the real beginning. By the end of three weeks, it had grown to 15,000 words. He thought it twenty times better than "Night Before Battle," and his excitement rose as he became more deeply involved. Already he was beginning to get that old familiar feeling of being emptied out each day, yet ready to return to his task with renewed energy every morning.

Voices out of the past kept echoing through his workroom at the Ambos Mundos. One of them was Ford Madox Ford's. He was rather pathetically hoping to revive the *transatlantic review,* and wanted Ernest to write "a little note of souvenir" about the old days of 1924 in Paris. Another voice was that of Perkins, with news of Scott Fitzgerald. Was his career really over or would he make some kind of comeback? Ernest had recently reread *Tender Is the Night.* Its excellence "amazed" him; much of it was almost "frighteningly" better than the rest of his fiction; with improved integration, it could well stand as his masterpiece. Reading it again, with its distant echoes of the Murphys and the French Riviera, reminded him sharply of the years of their friendship. About Scott, said he, he had always felt a stupid and childish sense of superiority—like a tough, durable little boy sneering at another little boy who was talented but delicate.

He returned to Key West in the middle of March, largely to see Bumby, who was on spring vacation from school. The only trouble was that the Key West social season was then at its height. Pauline had made many new friends during Ernest's absence in Spain and France, and showed little disposition to shoo them away so that he could get on with his work. The Ben Gallaghers arrived from Paris, and Jinny Pfeiffer came down to drink and argue with Pauline and Ernest. Shipwreck Kelly appeared, eager to talk about a movie based on "The Short Happy Life of Francis Macomber." The new road down the keys, as Ernest complained, was like a tacit invitation to "every son of a bitch who had ever read a line" of Hemingway to come and be entertained. The small house where Ernest worked beside the swimming pool was constantly assailed with the sound of voices. When Tom Shevlin and Hugo Rutherfurd invited him to fish in a tuna tournament, Ernest bowed out. He was seething to get back to Cuba and his novel. Now, he knew, was the time of his career when he had to write "a real one."

On April 10th he crossed to Havana to resume his former life of writing, drinking, fishing, swimming, and tennis playing, though this time with the difference that he was presently joined by Martha Gellhorn. It was her first trip to Cuba and she came prepared to stay. Ernest had agreed to look for a house. But when she found him in the Ambos Mundos bar, although he seemed genuinely happy to see her, he had done nothing in the way of house-hunting. Martha soon located an old estate called Finca Vigía in the village of San Francisco de Paula some fifteen miles from downtown Havana. It was owned by a family named D'Orn and occupied a hilltop with distant views of the sea and the city. It had fallen into disrepair, smelt of drains, and could be rented entire for a hundred a month. When Ernest went out with Martha to see it, he was immediately scornful. It was too far gone, too far from Havana, and too expensive. He turned on his heel and departed to go fishing.

But Martha was persuaded that the house had possibilities. During his absence, and at her own expense, she hired artisans and employed servants to make the place cheerful and homelike. When he returned, she showed him the results. He liked it so well that he promptly moved in.

For the sake of appearances, he continued to use the Ambos Mundos as his mailing address. But by early May he had begun to mention to Perkins a "joint on the top of a hill" where there was always a breeze. His novel was progressing at the rate of 700 to 1000 words a day. He said that he was so happy with his work that it was sometimes 7:30 in the evening before he remembered to drink his usual three Scotches before dinner. He was now predicting that the book would be done by late July or early August. Beside that possibility, everything else seemed far away and completely unimportant.

Except for weekend fishing trips whenever he felt stale, he stuck steadily to his task. He had been in Cuba for a month when a polio epidemic broke out in Key West. He wired Perkins to send $500 to J. B. Sullivan, who promptly used it to ship Patrick and Gregory out of the danger zone. They would stay in New York through June and then spend July and August at a camp in Connecticut. As soon as the novel was finished, Ernest would take them away to Wyoming.

But the novel kept on expanding. When the manuscript reached 76,000 words and a logical stopping place in mid-August, Ernest decided to go west anyway. Pauline was abroad with Paul and Brenda Willerts. Ernest wrote Hadley that he had approved the trip. Pauline might as well have a good final fling before the lights began going out again all over Europe. For himself, Wyoming would do. He asked Otto Bruce to pick up the boys when their camp closed and to bring them by train to join him and Bumby at the Nordquist ranch. On the 27th he dropped Martha in St. Louis to stay with her mother and drove on alone from there.

Hadley had lately been much in his mind. At the time of his fortieth birthday in July, he had written her twice, signing the letters with his old nicknames of Tatie and Edward Everett Waxen. The more he saw of women, said he, the more he admired her. If heaven was something that people enjoyed on earth rather than after death, then he and she had known a good slice of theirs in the Black Forest and at Cortina and Pamplona in 1922–23. Hadley was on vacation with her husband Paul Mowrer at a ranch near Cody. When they returned from a fishing trip, they found another car parked near theirs. It was Ernest, listening to the radio while he waited for them to come back. He had not seen either of them for ten years. The meeting was quiet and cordial, centering chiefly on Bumby, who had already gone ahead to the Nordquist ranch to wait for his father's arrival. Once again Ernest was persuaded that Hadley's future was in the best possible hands.

His arrival at the L-Bar-T precisely coincided with the outbreak of the war in Europe. He stayed up most of the night listening to the newscasts on his portable radio. The war was hardly a surprise. He had been predicting it regularly in public and private for the past six years. But he felt about it just as he had felt about the onset of the Spanish Civil War in the summer of 1936. At that time, too, he had had a novel in progress, and had resolved to finish it before he thought of visiting the scene of the conflict. Now the pattern repeated itself. Although his letters of early September hinted at the commitments that the war might eventually bring, he was quite ready to gather his sons around him and bide his time. Europe, as he said, would be at war for many years to come.

He had scarcely settled in at the ranch when Pauline telephoned from New York. She had come back from Europe on the last day of August and was flying out to join him. But she arrived with such a bad cold that she was obliged to go to bed. Ernest later said that he cooked her meals and did his best to take care of her, though the cold weather and primitive living conditions made nursing so difficult that she got worse instead of better. Moreover, as he complained, he was very lonely at the ranch, with "nothing to do" when he had finished his work for the day. Whatever his excuses, he was at last determined to complete the break with his second wife. After what he regarded as a suitable interval he packed up his car, summoned Martha to meet him, and drove yet farther west to a new establishment called Sun Valley among the Sawtooth Mountains of central Idaho.

48. SUN VALLEY

SUN Valley was the name of a complete small village near the old mining town of Ketchum. It had been built in the midst of the Depression by Averell Harriman and the Union Pacific Railroad for the express purpose of making America ski-conscious. A publicity campaign was still in progress to celebrate its virtues as a year-round vacation resort, with skiing and skating in the winter, and fishing and hunting in the summer and fall. Ducks and pheasants abounded in the winding creeks and among the tawny hills. Famous visitors like Hemingway were much desired. Even now, late in 1939, the shops and restaurants, the hotels and the pseudo-Swiss chalets were thinly populated, and the road up the valley through Hailey and Picabo was still unpaved and hub-deep in dust. Ernest washed the dirt from his throat in the ultramodern bar at Sun Valley Lodge and moved with Martha into Suite 206, among the most luxurious of the twelve-dozen rooms at the Lodge.

Next morning, he had breakfast with two young Midwesterners who ran publicity for Sun Valley. Gene Van Guilder was a handsome and talented man in his middle thirties, a great rider and hunter who wore his western clothes with dash and style and spoke enthusiastically of painting and writing. His companion, Lloyd Arnold, was the chief photographer. They found Ernest friendly enough, but also wary and suspicious, as if fearful of being exploited for publicity purposes, as if he could not yet make up his mind what manner of men they really were. He was far more at ease with Taylor Williams, the chief guide at Sun Valley, a lean and caustic Kentuckian who was variously known as Beartracks or The Colonel.

His first suspicions vanished when he explored the country under the guidance of his new friends. His love of wing shooting and his appetite for game birds literally knew no bounds, and he settled happily into a rough pattern of work in the morning and play in the afternoon. By the end of October he had brought his novel to the middle of Chapter 18. He wrote Perkins that his story contained what people with Communist Party obligations could never write, what most of them could never know or—if they knew—allow themselves to believe. So far, said he, there were two wonderful women in the book. The locale was a Loyalist guerrilla camp in the Sierra de Guadarrama range northwest of Madrid. He was just now beginning to work on a flashback with scenes at Gaylord's, the Russian headquarters near the Prado, where he had talked so often with Koltsov, the *Izvestia* correspondent. Koltsov was already in the book, thinly disguised as Karkov. So were Valentín González, called El Campesino, ex-sergeant in the Spanish Foreign Legion; Enrique Lister, the Galician stonemason turned soldier; Juan Modesto from Andalucía; and Kleber, Lucasz, Hans Kahle, and Gustavo Durán—all the general officers Ernest had known that spring of 1937.

A tragic event interrupted his labors. Hunting ducks from a canoe one Sunday morning, Gene Van Guilder was instantly killed by a blast from a shotgun carelessly handled by one of his companions. Gene's widow Nin asked Ernest to write and deliver a graveside eulogy. Early in November he stood with the others in the small bare Ketchum cemetery and read firmly from a typescript. "Gene loved this country," said Ernest. "He saw it with the eyes of a painter, the mind of a trained writer, and the heart of a boy who had been brought up in the west. He loved the hills in the spring when the snows go off and the first flowers come. He loved the warm sun of summer and the high mountain meadows, the trails through the timber and the sudden clear blue of the lakes. . . . Best of all he loved the fall . . . with the tawny, and grey, the leaves yellow on the cottonwoods . . . and above the hills the high blue windless skies. . . . Now Gene has gotten through with that thing we all have to do. His dying in his youth was a great injustice. . . . But he has come back to the hills that he loved and now he will be part of them forever."

Ernest did not let his graveside sentiments blind him to the ironies of the funeral. Gene had died intestate and uninsured, with a bank balance amounting to seventeen cents, but his widow had insisted that all his hunting equipment must be buried with him, including an expensive silver-mounted saddle. As he left the cemetery with Pappy Arnold, Ernest muttered that he was glad they hadn't thrown in Gene's fishing rod and frying pan along with the rest.

Soon after the funeral Martha set off to cover the war in Finland for

Collier's magazine. Ernest made no serious attempt to oppose her plans, though he soon began to refer dramatically to the dark depths of his loneliness without her. After she left, he renamed Suite 206 "Hemingstein's Mixed Vicing and Dicing Establishment," and made it an evening haven for crap and poker games. One day he tried killing coyotes with a shotgun from a low-flying Piper Cub. Every fair afternoon he went hunting for pheasants, ducks, and jacksnipe with the novelist Christopher La Farge and a Philadelphia lawyer named Sturgis Ingersoll.

Another of his good companions was Clara Spiegel, who had come out with one of her sons to help Gene Van Guilder's widow through the early weeks of bereavement. Clara's husband Fred had driven ambulances with Ernest at Schio in 1918 and now owned a large mail-order business in Chicago. When she volunteered to help Ernest clean up his backlog of mail, he immediately accepted, dictated fifty letters, and rewarded her with various bits of wisdom on the art of writing. One misplaced word, said he, could be the tiny flaw that might open into a chasm five chapters later. "Don't say it, daughter, make it," he insisted. Whatever was merely stated was sure to be ephemeral; prose could last only if it were fully imagined and made whole and round. In conversation one evening, he brought up the topic of suicide and proposed that they enter into a pact. If either of them was strongly tempted, he must first let the other one know. Clara horrified him by refusing. Hitler's European Blitzkrieg was going too well. If the Nazis ever invaded the United States, said Clara, she would kill her sons and then herself. Ernest argued so strongly against this idea that she began to think of him as one of the three men she would turn to in time of distress. When she left for Chicago, she burst into tears and kissed him good-bye. He fumbled boyishly in his pocket and handed her a silver dollar. "For luck, daughter," he said.

He also admired Lloyd Arnold's wife Tillie, a small and courageous woman who excelled in cooking game birds. When the Arnolds spoke at length about their happy childhoods, Ernest looked glum and said that his own early years had been tragically unhappy. Once he slapped a large hand on Tillie's knee and told her that his mother was a bitch. Tillie scolded him soundly, her brown eyes snapping with anger. He heard her out with no sign of rancor or contrition. "Daughter," he said at last, "it's true about my mother, and I say it again at the risk of your respect for me."

In spite of his friendships he often spoke of being "stinko deadly lonely" in Martha's absence. It was like living in limbo, said he, with the additional problem of having to write good prose. Both Hadley and Clara asked him to Chicago for Christmas, but he declined on the ground that he was in the midst of the most exciting part of his novel. When he invited himself to Key West to spend Christmas with his sons, Pauline advised him that if he expected to come home only to leave after Christmas to rejoin Martha in Cuba, he had better not come at all. Ernest immediately complained to Hadley that Pauline's conduct was atrocious and unbearable. But if people thought only of themselves, he felt, this was all that could be expected. When Otto Bruce arrived to drive Ernest to Florida, he reported that Pauline was still determined not to see her husband again. She was leaving for New York with Patrick and Gregory to spend the holidays with her sister Jinny.

On December 12th, shortly before leaving Sun Valley, Ernest wrote at length to Pauline's mother. He said that he had counted on getting to Piggott with the children in October, only to have all his plans disrupted by Pauline's unexpected arrival at the Nordquist ranch. If he had been able to talk with Pauline's parents he was quite sure they would have found that he had changed far less than Pauline and Virginia. Virginia's version of his life and conduct was very fantastic. But she had spread it sufficiently and at the right time to break up Ernest's home. The true version was far different, of course, and he wanted the elder Pfeiffers to know it. He would continue to look after Pauline's material interests as though they were his own, and would also take good care of the children, with whom he got along very well. His time of working on the book had been a lonely one. He hoped that it was going to come out well. So far, extraordinarily enough, there was not a single bad word in it. He closed by wishing them all a good Christmas. If it was not a merry one this year, future Christmases might be.

Mrs. Pfeiffer laboriously typed a reply. All this trouble and misunderstanding between Ernest and Pauline was beyond her comprehension. She and her husband were both deeply grieved. Ernest had belonged to the family for so many years that she had come to regard him as one of her very own. This was the saddest Christmas she had ever known. A broken family was a tragic thing, particularly when children were involved. She would always remember Ernest in her prayers, and she hoped that they would meet again in a fairer clime upon a farther shore.

A week later Ernest and Otto were back in Key West. As Pauline had promised, she and the children were gone and the house was empty. On the day after Christmas a man in Phoenix, Arizona, wired Ernest's publishers to ask for his current address. Next day Scribners telegraphed a reply: "HEMINGWAYS ADDRESS KEY WEST FLORIDA." But it was not. From that date onwards his address was Finca Vigía, San Francisco de Paula, Cuba.

49. FOR WHOM THE BELL TOLLS

WHEN Martha returned from Finland in the middle of January, 1940, she found that "The Pig," as she fondly called Ernest, was working wonderfully. She had been home only a few days when he completed Chapter 23. As advance evidence of the quality of the book, he sent Perkins two samples— the opening paragraphs of the first chapter and Pilar's story of the massacre of the Fascists in Pablo's Ronda-like native village. A spell of cold weather drove him back to his old habit of writing in bed to keep warm. In this man-

ner he completed Chapter 24, though he said that it was unlucky for verisimilitude to be shivering while trying to write about a hot morning in June,
1937.

He advised Perkins not to show the massacre chapter to any of the
"ideology boys," including Alvah Bessie. He would sooner make cracks
about religion to a nun than deprive the leftists of their ideology. But the
trouble with Bessie's brigade had been too much ideology and not enough
military training and discipline. Too much ideology, said Ernest, was a ring
in the brain like a ring through the nose-gristle of a bull. If the leftists wanted
to go on thinking that the Loyalists never killed anybody, let them bask in
their illusions. As for himself, he had accepted the Communist discipline in
Spain because it was "the soundest and sanest for the prosecution of the
war." Now that it was over, he had reverted to being a writer—not a Catholic
writer or a Party writer or even an American writer, but only a writer trying
to tell the truth as he had personally learned it.

When the weather turned fine in February, his days settled into a pattern
of reasonable contentment, with work every morning, one drink before a two
o'clock lunch, and a little reading at siesta time. In the afternoons he often
played tennis with Martha and a group of exiled Basques who had fought for
the Loyalists and were now supporting themselves as professional pelota
players in Havana. After a few hard-fought sets, they all drank and sang.
Ernest tried to pick up a smattering of their language by listening carefully to
the words of the Basque songs. He bought some roosters from his friend
Mayito Menocal, and joined a cockfighting club. His other relaxations included
shooting live pigeons at the Club de Cazadores, hunting game birds in the
back country, and spending at least one gaudy night each week in Havana,
drinking deep at the Floridita, betting on the jai alai games at the Fronton,
and afterwards returning to his seat at the bar for four or five hours of drink
and talk. He explained the nights of drinking as a necessary counterforce to
the daily bouts of writing which left him as whipped, wrung out, and empty
as a used washrag. But they were the only aspect of his life in Cuba that
really enraged Martha. One Sunday in mid-February he felt obliged to take
her to the movies to make amends for having stayed out with the boys until
three that morning. He had begun with absinthe, continued at dinner with a
bottle of good red wine, shifted to vodka before the jai alai games, and then
settled down to whiskey and soda for the rest of the evening. He felt well
enough afterwards, though not well enough to work. He continued to cherish
his unscientific conviction that a few sets of "terrific tennis" with Ermua
Aretio and the brothers Ibarlucia would boil the alcohol out of his system.
On Sunday nights he went to bed early, took some sleeping pills, and rose at
dawn on Monday to start his work afresh.

He had planned a far shorter book than this one was turning out to be.
By the end of Chapter 28 he complained of feeling restive after so many
months of solid work. Yet he knew that he must not become panicky and

try for greater speed. He told Perkins that if he chose to write as sloppily as Sinclair Lewis, he could do 5,000 words a day year in and year out. His own practice was the opposite: constant daily control to avoid the necessity of complete rewriting when he was done. His work, as he explained to Charles Scribner, was a disease, a vice, and an obsession. To be happy, he had to write, which made it a disease. He also enjoyed it, which turned the disease into a vice. Since he wished to write better than anyone else had ever done, the vice quickly became an obsession.

In order to reassure himself of the quality of what he was doing, he kept showing parts of the novel to a variety of close friends—Joris Ivens, Esther Chambers, Christopher La Farge, Otto Bruce, and of course Max Perkins. They all responded so ecstatically that he decided to risk a reading by Ben Finney, whom he revered as a veteran of the Marine Corps and a fearless bobsled pilot. Finney read through all that Ernest had written in a marathon bout that lasted from four one afternoon to four the next morning. He tried to make Ernest admit that he had personally experienced the action described in the novel. "Hell, no," said Ernest, vastly pleased. "I made it up." Despite such assurances, he still had moments of doubt. Pauline now hated him so much, he said, that she had refused to look at the book. This was a damned shame because she had the best literary judgment of any of them.

But the novel was still far from finished. At the end of the first week in April he completed Chapter 32, the twelfth that he had done since his return from Sun Valley. One of these was the superb account of El Sordo's last stand on the hilltop. Another was María's harrowing story of having been raped by Fascist soldiers. Chapter 32 was a cynical interlude at Gaylord's Hotel in which Ernest could hardly contain his anger at both the warring sides. For all his Loyalist sympathies, he had never been able to swallow the program of propaganda which had elevated Dolores Ibarruri, a Communist peasant woman from the Basque provinces, into La Pasionaria (The Passion Flower), a kind of leftist saint. "Dolores always made me vomit always," he emphatically told his friends. He took pleasure in painting a travesty portrait of the First Lady of Republican Spain, allowing his nausea to spill over into Robert Jordan's bilious reflections on other "flowers of Spanish chivalry" from Cortés to the present day. "There is no finer and no worse people in the world," said Jordan.

Many of his friends appeared in the book, sometimes under their actual names, sometimes in thin disguises. He had lately been corresponding with Gustavo Durán, the Loyalist commander who had fled to London in 1939. Durán appeared by name, as did Petra, Ernest's chambermaid at the Hotel Florida. General Lucasz of the 12th International Brigade was described with loving precision. So was the Polish general Karol Swierczewski, known to his troops as General Walter, and in the novel as General Golz. Koltsov the journalist stalked through Gaylord's under his fictional name of Karkov. María, the heroine, bore the name of the nurse whom Ernest had met at

Mataro in the spring of 1938, although her physical characteristics, including the blond hair "like a wheatfield in the wind," were evidently designed as a secret tribute to Martha Gellhorn. Robert Jordan, the professor from Montana, owed at least something to the courageous figure of Major Robert Merriman of the 15th International Brigade, the one-time professor of economics from California. Like most of Ernest's heroes, however, Jordan shared many of the personal characteristics and opinions of his creator. Jordan's parents were clearly modeled on Dr. and Mrs. Hemingway. The elder Jordan had shot himself to death with a Smith and Wesson Civil War pistol. His son was made to reflect on his father's cowardice ("the worst luck any man could have") and his mother's aggressiveness ("because if he wasn't a coward he would have stood up to that woman and not let her bully him"). Ernest even gave Jordan one of his own most prominent traits—a "red, black, killing anger" that spread scorn and contempt as widely and unjustly as a forest fire spreads ruin, only to die away and leave his mind as quiet and empty-calm as a man might be after "sexual intercourse with a woman he does not love."

Early in April he interrupted his progress in order to write a preface for *The Great Crusade,* Gustav Regler's autobiographical novel about the 12th International Brigade. To escape visitors and get the job done, Ernest went down to Mayito Menocal's sugar and rice plantation at Camagüey, Oriente Province, some three hundred miles from Havana. The preface was not the first favor he had done for Regler, having already sent him a substantial gift of money and arranged to have him released from a French internment camp in nominal custody of Colonel Charles Sweeny, the aging soldier of fortune. Although Ernest's novel was largely invented, whereas Regler's followed fact, Ernest said that "there are events which are so great that if a writer has participated in them his obligation is to write truly rather than assume the presumption of altering them with invention." It gave him pleasure to recognize the figures of General Lucasz and Werner Heilbrun, as well as Regler himself, the sole survivor of the original triumvirate. Despite severe wounds, imprisonment, poverty, and exile, said Ernest, Regler had continued to display "the same bravery and immunity to personal suffering that a fighting cock has, which, wounded repeatedly, fights until it dies."

Having finished the preface, he came down with an illness which lasted five days. By April 20th he threw it off, finished Chapter 35, and began to think about a title. Of some twenty-six possibilities, *The Undiscovered Country* was his favorite, though he was still not wholly satisfied. By his own account he worked two whole days with the Bible and Shakespeare before turning to *The Oxford Book of English Prose.* Leafing through the extracts from the works of John Donne, he came on a passage which caught his eye. In images derived from geography and from the funeral customs of seventeenth-century London, Donne had set down a little parable about the interdependency of all human beings. Ernest saw with delight that the passage pointed up the theme of tragic loss and human solidarity which he had been developing in the story of Robert Jordan. It concluded with the statement that "any man's death diminishes me, because I am involved in Mankinde; and therefore never send to know for whom the bell tolls; it tolls for thee."

Throughout the rest of April and May, Ernest complained to Perkins that Pauline was trying to put him "out of business." She did not like to face the fact that he was writing a hell of a good book while living with someone else. She had been "shelling" him "plenty, plenty." He had tried growing armor plate to no avail. It had become a point of pride with him to write so well now that any book he ever wrote in Pauline's company would seem slight by comparison. In parting from her he had agreed to pay $500 a month for the support of Patrick and Gregory, but he told Perkins that in case he died these payments were to stop immediately. His mother wrote to say that she had heard he was doing a novel and hoped that for once it might contain "something constructive." Ernest answered coldly. Who could say? Perhaps the book might indeed turn out as she wished.

By Memorial Day Ernest believed that the end of his novel had come into view, though still far off—like a heavenly city. As if to signalize this apocalyptic moment, the living-room ceiling fell down, covering everything with plaster dust which the leaking rains soon converted to a hard white coating. When Patrick and Bumby arrived for a short visit, the living room looked to Martha like a wading pool. This was a blow to her sense of neatness, but she was even more upset by the noises from the American mainland, including false political speechmaking, the threat of increased taxation, and the constant waste of federal funds. Twice a day she fell into "paroxysms of rage" over the state of the nation and the world. She would have liked to go to Europe to see if anything could be done, and her itch at least to get away from the isolation of the Finca was becoming intolerable. When Ernest, preoccupied with his own work, became profanely critical of her social interests, Martha picked up and left to spend a month in New York.

When she returned late in June, bringing her mother for a visit, Ernest assured her that he was nearly done. He had sworn not to have a haircut until the novel was finished and his appearance was notably unkempt. He had found the blowing of the bridge almost unbearably exciting. After it was over he felt, as he said, nearly as limp and dead as if he had been there himself. He professed to be reluctant to kill his hero after having lived steadily in his company for seventeen months. On July 1, however, he decided that the end was near, and sent Perkins a cable: BRIDGE ALL BLOWN AM ENDING LAST CHAPTER. It was time at last for a visit to his barber in Havana.

He was padding down the sidewalk in the old city when he caught sight of Joe North and a man named Douglas Jacobs whom he had first met at Jay Allen's. He let out a whoop and seized North in a bear hug. He said that he was eager to tell Joe all about the new novel before Joe read it and got angry at it. They arranged to meet for lunch at the Floridita. Despite the profound differences of political opinion between North and Hemingway,

the lunch went so well that they were still deep in talk at four o'clock. Suddenly
the door of the bar swung open and Martha stalked in. "She was obviously
in a rage," said Jacobs, "and made little effort to hide it." Ernest had promised
to meet her and her mother at two. He mumbled an apology which Martha
shrugged off. "You can stand me up," she cried, "but you can't do that to
my mother." Ernest paid the bill, excused himself, and sheepishly followed
her out.

In spite of his ceremonial haircut, the forty-third and final chapter continued to give him trouble. By July 13th, Jordan was lying prone beneath a
tree, watching the approach of the Fascist Lieutenant Berrendo. The book
could obviously end there, yet Ernest was still vaguely dissatisfied. He spent
the final week before his forty-first birthday in composing a kind of epilogue,
two short chapters designed to knit up every dangling thread as neatly as
possible. One part told of a meeting between Karkov and General Golz
after the failure of the Segovia offensive, and of their driving together back
to Madrid, discussing Jordan's blowing of the bridge and his subsequent disappearance. The short final chapter described Andres and his visit to the
abandoned camp of Pablo and Pilar, where he stood for a moment gazing
at the wrecked bridge in the gorge below. It was evidently necessary for
Ernest to write these anticlimactic sections in order to find out that they were
neither necessary nor desirable.

He waited anxiously until the manuscript was typed and then carried it to
New York. A late July heat wave covered the whole eastern seaboard and the
train was like an oven. In the poor light of the parlor car he worked over
the typescript until his eyes gave out, and staggered out at Pennsylvania
Station feeling like "a blind sardine in a processing factory." His room at
the Hotel Barclay was only a few blocks from Scribners, and he began to
deliver the book piecemeal by runner boy at the rate of 200 pages a day.
Calling at his hotel a few days later, Bob Van Gelder of the *New York Times
Book Review* found him wearing an unbuttoned pajama jacket and surrounded by a lively company. One of his companions was the exiled Loyalist
commander, Gustavo Durán, who had recently married an American girl
named Bonte Crompton and moved to the United States. Durán listened
politely to the talk between Hemingway and Van Gelder, and Ernest occasionally paused to translate for his benefit. When Durán left the room to make
a phone call, Ernest explained in a whisper that he had often longed to get
information from him while he was writing his novel. But Durán had now
assured him that the story as written was perfectly sound. When Durán left
for his bride's summer home in New Hampshire, Ernest asked him to read
the galley proofs to make sure that the Spanish was correct. Ernest observed
modestly that he himself was obviously unqualified to do a book on Spain, the
Spaniards, the movement, or the war, and was moreover acutely embarrassed
to ask Durán, a native Spaniard who was also his "God damn hero," to read
what he had written. Durán complied, partly out of curiosity. He was not

much impressed by the quality of Ernest's Spanish. On the other hand, with some reservations, he thought the book surprisingly effective.

On August 26th Ernest airmailed from Havana the first 123 galleys of his book. He had been uncommonly docile about revising to meet the objections of Perkins and Scribner, and had carefully rewritten a passage of onanism to make one of the love scenes less offensive. But he argued back vigorously against their view that Pilar's disquisition on "the smell of death to come" was not in good taste. It was harsh all right, said he, but to delete it would be like removing the bass viol or the oboe from his symphony orchestra merely because they sounded ugly when played alone. The passage was meant to be horrifying, but not gratuitously obscene: he had needed to get across the earthy vulgarity of the gypsies he had known in Madrid. They were a very strange people. He had not wanted to "pretty them up" any more than he had done with the Michigan Indians in the Nick Adams stories.

Finally, and most importantly, he had decided to remove his epilogue. His original motive, he explained, was like a good sailor's determination to have everything knitted up and stowed away shipshape. But now he saw that the novel really stopped when Jordan lay on the pine-needled floor of the forest just as he had lain sixty-eight hours earlier in the opening sentence of the first chapter. This was all the rounding out that the novel required.

50. REWARDS

ERNEST had begun 1940 by asking Perkins for another thousand-dollar advance on his half-finished novel. Perkins complied, with the hope that this would be a big year. With the combined income from the Broadway play, which was now launched and doing well, and the publication of the novel, it was certain that Ernest's royalties would exceed the $6,000 he had earned in 1939. Perkins's hope was fulfilled late in August when the Book of the Month Club chose the novel for October, and proposed a first printing of 100,000 copies. Scribners was planning to match this figure in the regular trade edition. Ernest wrote wryly to Arnold Gingrich, computing what *For Whom the Bell Tolls* had cost him—the loss of one wife and of a year and a half out of his life. But he made no attempt to conceal his pride in the novel, which contained no loose writing and was all of a piece, with "every word depending on every other word" straight through the grand total of forty-three chapters.

He now planned a vacation in Sun Valley with Martha and his sons, who would assemble from diverse points of the compass during early September. Martha alerted Clara Spiegel to the complex arrangements, asking her to keep an eye on the boys until their father arrived. After more than three years of what Martha called "living in contented sin," she and Ernest were planning to be married as soon as Pauline's divorce became final. Martha secretly entertained some doubts about the wisdom of the move, but said nothing about them to Clara. "Maybe," she wrote, "you'll be a flower girl at our nuptials, darling?"

She flew from Jacksonville to visit her mother in St. Louis while Ernest, sharing the driving with Otto Bruce, set out on September 1 for another of the long cross-country treks that he loved. On reaching Sun Valley he set to work almost at once, completing proofreading and sending final corrections to Perkins in a series of long telegrams. One undated page labeled "DON'T LOSE THIS FOR CHRIST'S SAKE" gave the printer a checklist of Spanish spellings and accents together with the dedication: "This book is for Martha Gellhorn." Lloyd and Tillie Arnold helped him with the final batch of proofs. When they gathered from their reading that Ernest's father had shot himself, Ernest confirmed the guess and spoke with some eloquence on what he called the "common sense view of suicide." If things got bad enough, said he, suicide was always permissible. He carefully explained to Martha the technique of using a shotgun, springing the trigger with a bare toe.

Getting rid of the proofsheets made him so exuberant that he told Charles Scribner that he had not drawn an even semisober breath since sending them off. After Bumby's return to school he took the younger boys and Martha on a jackrabbit hunt. Patrick and Gregory killed eighty each, and Ernest and Martha swelled the total to almost four hundred. A spell of rainy weather made Ernest irascible and he wrathfully exploded on learning that the publication date of the novel had been put off until October 21. This was great news, he moaned, when he had worked himself blind in twenty-four-hour stretches to meet the deadline and bankrupted himself wiring final corrections. He was sick of being the only one in the organization who respected dates and worked through weekends while the Scribner editors stayed away from the office from Friday to Monday. He wished to Christ he were a gentleman instead of a professional writer who kept his promises—and so on through another page and a half of seething prose.

Although she had now stopped calling him "The Pig," Martha could not help comparing Ernest's appearance with that of Gary Cooper, who had come to Sun Valley with his wife Rocky for a shooter's vacation. According to Ernest, Martha kept urging him to emulate Cooper by wearing smart clothes and being handsome. Although he made no attempt to comply, he called Coop a fine man—as honest, straight, friendly, and unspoiled as he looked on the screen. If the novel were taken by Hollywood, said Ernest, Coop would make an excellent Robert Jordan. He was also a better rifleshot than Ernest, who excused his deficiency as the result of too much drinking for too many years. To even things up, he ached to box with Cooper, hoping that weight and experience would count heavily in his favor. His chief pleasure lay in needling the actor about his sartorial splendor and his limited ability with the shotgun.

When the weather was bad, Ernest did a good deal of reading, ordering dozens of books from the Scribner bookstore. One list included Wolfe's posthumous novel, *You Can't Go Home Again*. Ernest noted laughingly that Harper was advertising it as "a work of mature power." He was not much impressed by Wolfe's portrayal of Maxwell Perkins as Foxhall Edwards, and boasted that he could get Perkins straighter in 1,000 words than Wolfe had done in 10,000. Tom was wonderful and unsurpassable on his home town of Asheville, North Carolina. All the rest, said Ernest, was overinflated journalese.

His hope of selling *For Whom the Bell Tolls* to the movies came closer to fulfillment early in October with a long-distance call from Donald Friede, who had first known Ernest in the 1920s while serving as business partner to Horace Liveright, and was now a story editor for Myron Selznick. Friede asked if Hemingway had a Hollywood agent. Ernest said no and promptly invited him to Sun Valley. Friede flew to Salt Lake City, boarded a train, descended at Shoshone at three in the morning, and reached Sun Valley Lodge at six. Ernest was already up and waiting. Had he read the book? He had not. Ernest gave him breakfast and a copy of the typescript. Friede spent the day reading it. He was overcome with enthusiasm. On October 7th, homeward bound, he wired Scribners to rush twenty-five copies of the book by air express to Myron Selznick's address in Beverly Hills. So began the final phase of Ernest's first real success story since *A Farewell to Arms*.

To escape an overdose of company which included Dorothy Parker and her husband as well as the Gary Coopers, Ernest conducted Martha on a week's pack trip into the wild Middle Fork region of the Salmon River. Martha gamely carried on, sustained by a competitive spirit nearly as strong as Ernest's. Upon their return, however, she took to her bed with some form of grippe, aching all over and plunged, as she said, into a veritable cesspool of gloom. But she observed with pleasure that all Ernest's outdoor activity served as a restorative for him, if not for her. He had even cut back considerably on his drinking, always "a sign of things quieting down and becoming solid once more." He was so tractable that she felt no pang in flatly ignoring his suggestion that she write under the name of Martha Hemingway. After less than a month in Sun Valley, she had begun to urge *Collier's* to send her to cover the war in China.

With the approach of publication day, Perkins kept up a reassuring postal barrage about the book's probable reception. But Ernest was too nervous to wait for the first shipment of reviews, and telephoned Jay Allen in New York to ask him to read some of them aloud. Jay kept protesting that the phone call was too expensive, but Ernest did not care. His responses were like those of a small boy. "Did he really say that?" he would ask. Or, "That guy is just digging his grave as a critic." He was pleased with John Chamberlain's opinion that the novel had "the bracing quality of brandy" and with J. Donald Adams's conviction that this was "the fullest, the deepest, and the truest" of Hemingway's novels. Adams found the love scenes between Jordan and María the best in American fiction, far beyond those in *A Farewell to Arms* and infinitely preferable to the "casual couplings" of *The Sun Also Rises*. Bob Sherwood in the *Atlantic* called the book "rare and beautiful," containing "strength and brutality," but also "a degree of delicacy" which proved that "this fine writer, unlike some other fine American writers," was "capable of self-criticism and self-development." Clifton Fadiman in *The New Yorker* likewise emphasized the principle of growth: the book expressed and released the adult Hemingway, "whose voice was first heard in the groping *To Have and Have Not*." In the *Nation*, Margaret Marshall said that the bad taste left in the mouths of readers by *The Fifth Column* was now dissipated, and that Hemingway had set himself a new standard in characterization, dialogue, suspense, and compassion for the human being faced with death. While the novel did not embody "the deeper social meanings of the Spanish Civil War," it provided "as moving and vivid a story of a group of human beings involved in that war as we are likely to have."

Like any author with much at stake, Ernest accepted the praise as his just due and was indignant about the adverse comments. But when Donald Friede advised from Hollywood that he was holding out for a figure of $150,000, Ernest cannily urged him to sell the book for $100,000 "plus ten cents a copy for each copy sold including Book of the Month." Since the Book of the Month organization had now contracted for 200,000 copies, and Scribners had printed another 160,000 copies, Ernest stood to gain $136,000 from the film sale alone, apart from royalties on Book of the Month printings and the regular Scribner trade edition. He thought it wise to settle matters with Paramount Pictures during the first flush of victory. There was no telling when a counterattack might come. By the end of October the sale was completed on these terms. It struck Ernest as "bloody wonderful." In fact it was, since Friede had secured the highest price ever yet paid for film rights to a book.

The triple business triumph sharpened Ernest's hunger for further hunting. The bad weather of September was gone and the clear fall days were ideal for duck and pheasant shooting. Early in November he led a troop of marksmen over the hills behind a small farm near Dietrich. When they returned with the day's bag of pheasants, the farmer's wife provided a large chicken dinner. The family had thirteen children and a truck with which they had hauled milk until the clutch gave out. Ernest asked Pappy Arnold if the truck was worth repairing. On being told that it was, he gathered up $85 in bills, rolled the money into the semblance of a cork, thrust it into the top of a half-empty bottle of wine, and left it on the front seat of the truck with a note urging the farmer to finish the wine and get his truck fixed.

News of his final divorce from Pauline reached Ernest over the Associated Press wire from Miami on November 4th. The uncontested decree was based on charges of desertion and Pauline was given custody of her sons. Ernest showed no outward sign of contrition at the end of a marriage which had lasted thirteen years, during which he had produced seven books, acquired the *Pilar* and the house in Key West; and enjoyed an African safari, frequent visits to Europe, many sporting vacations in Montana and Wyoming, and the freedom to spend two years in warring Spain. In leaving Hadley for Pauline he had suffered remorse for at least three years. Something inside his association with Pauline had finally served to cauterize his conscience. In "The Snows of Kilimanjaro" he had obliquely blamed her for being wealthy. A good deal later he attributed the failure of his second marriage to sexual maladjustment growing out of Pauline's ardent Catholicism and the fact that she could not safely bear more children. Somewhere among his motivations in giving up Pauline for Martha lay the hope of having a daughter. Pappy Arnold took some handsome prenuptial pictures of Martha and Ernest, sun-bronzed, healthy, and gazing westward into the sunset, and they left Sun Valley on November 20th with plans to be married in Cheyenne, followed by a honeymoon at the Hotel Barclay in New York and Christmas at the Finca.

A justice of the peace performed a quiet civil ceremony next day in the Union Pacific Railroad dining room at Cheyenne. Ernest found it "wonderful to be legal" after four years of association, and proudly drove Martha to New York. Bumby wired Perkins from the Storm King School to ask where his father was, and Ernest invited him in for two weekend visits, starting him on a course of boxing lessons at George Brown's gymnasium, and buying him some clothes and a good weekend bag. The long-suffering Perkins was also approached by Harold Peat, lecture agent for H. G. Wells, who said that Mr. Wells was staying at the Columbia University Club and was most anxious to meet Hemingway. Martha had known Wells for some years and he came to tea in their suite at the Barclay along with Gustavo Durán. A little man afflicted with diabetes, Wells sat happily in a hotel chair with his feet barely touching the floor, charmed by all the hullabaloo, the incessant ringing of the telephone, and the coming and going of Bob Capa, George Brown, and other visitors. The tone and flavor of the meeting, said Martha, was "The Boys' Book of Adventure by Sea and Land."

The editors of *Collier's* had now agreed to send Martha to cover the war in China. Her idea of fun, as Ernest said, was to celebrate the rest of their honeymoon on the Burma Road. Somewhat against his better judgment, he spent an afternoon with Ralph Ingersoll and emerged with an assignment of his own for a series of despatches to Ingersoll's new liberal tabloid, *PM*. He and Martha made reservations for the trip to Hong Kong and then left for home. During a stop-over in Key West, Ernest happened to meet Sinclair Lewis, who was there on his way to Havana. They got along fairly well, and parted in amity.

Ernest's Christmas gift to himself and Martha was the purchase of the Finca Vigía. Fearing that the news of his recent successes with *For Whom the Bell Tolls* would raise the asking price, he empowered Otto Bruce to conduct negotiations without revealing the buyer's name. Bruce concluded the arrangements on December 28 at $12,500. To celebrate the event, Ernest went quail shooting in Pinar del Río Province, romantically returning under starlight to the house he now owned and meant to occupy for the rest of his life.

His pleasure in the new house was marred by the leftist counterattack on his new novel. Although he had expected and predicted it, he was not prepared for the virulence of the assault. Mike Gold used one of his "Change the World" columns in *The Daily Worker* to assail Hemingway as "limited, narrow . . . mutilated by his class egotism . . . [and] the poverty of his mind." The novel merely proved, said Gold, that an unprincipled man who understood neither democracy nor communism was able to join in the Spanish Civil War for various personal reasons and to maintain an appearance of loyalty for a few years. When the cause seemed lost and democracy defeated, he chose to desert—as Frederic Henry had done in *A Farewell to Arms*—"leaving a trail of alibis, whines, and slanders."

Alvah Bessie's review in the *New Masses* was both fairer and better informed. As a veteran of the Lincoln Brigade, he had twice seen Ernest in Spain and began his long and thoughtful analysis with a tribute to Ernest's intimate participation in the struggle. Yet he found the novel very deficient both in depth of understanding and breadth of conception. "He has yet to expand his personality as a novelist," said Bessie, "to embrace the truths of other people everywhere; he has yet to dive deep into the lives of others, and there to find his own." But Bessie was also the author of a long open letter to Ernest, dated November 20, and forwarded to *The Daily Worker* over the signatures of Milt Wolff, National Commander of the Veterans of the Abraham Lincoln Brigade, Freddy Keller, New York Post Commander, and Irv Goff, Acting Secretary-Treasurer. Hemingway had "mutilated" the cause for which so many brave men had fought and died. He had maligned La Pasionaria and slandered André Marty. He had misrepresented the attitude of the Soviet Union towards the Spanish Republic. Worst of all, he had failed to show the relevance of the war in Spain to the world of 1940, where Fascism still ran rampant. In sum, his friends repudiated Ernest's work as false, distorted, slanderous, and undemocratic.

He was still defending his position the day before Christmas. He had heard from Hans Kahle, former commander of the XVth Brigade and the 45th Division, that *For Whom the Bell Tolls* was a great and true book. Gustavo Durán, who had participated along with General Walter in the very Loyalist attack on Segovia that appeared in the book, had also praised it. So had Mirko Markovich, commander of the Washington Battalion, and Steve Nelson, the battalion's political commissar and perhaps the best-liked member of the International Brigades. Such an array looked formidable, Ernest thought, against such people as Alvah Bessie, Mike Gold, and David McKelvey White.

He said that he had once been asked by André Malraux when he planned to write about the Spanish Civil War. His answer was that he would wait until he could write truly about that son of a bitch Marty without harming the Loyalist cause. If only Marty were not such a bloody symbol, Ernest believed, they would have shot him long ago.

When Milt Wolff made the mistake of writing him a private letter accusing him of having been a mere "rooter" for the Loyalists and a part-time "tourist" in Spain, Ernest was hurt enough to answer with an angry blast:

Dear Milt: I won't try to explain how concieted [sic], confused and stupid your letter was. Will only take up one point. So I was just a rooter in Spain. O.K. Did it ever occur to you that there were 595,000 some troops in the Spanish army beside the 15th Brigade and that the entire action of my book took place and was over before you personally had ever been in the line and before Alvah Bessie had ever left America? While Mike Gold, that other heroic denouncer hasn't reached Spain yet. I guess he is saving himself for the next movement there. At the time the book deals with you did not know Marx from your ass and neither did Freddy [Keller]. I know because I remember the date on which I advised him to do some reading. . . . O.K. scientist given what experience I have and what talents I may possess what would you like me to have done to aid the cause of the Spanish Republic that I did not do? So I was a rooter because I did not command a battalion of the 15th International Brigade. O.K. Scientist. Have it as you want it. But we are not friends anymore after that letter which will doubtless be a relief to you as you can believe any kinds of lies you hear about me now and even work up some special personal denunciations of your own. . . . I have never seen you after you have been wounded. It takes guys different ways. So don't talk too snotty about the things you haven't done yet. And scientist old pal I was in wars, commanded troops, was wounded etc. before you were dry behind the ears. So don't give me the old soldier talking to the non-combatant. . . . You have your Marty and I've married my Marty and we'll see who does the most for the world in the end. And I'll keep right on trying to get you out of jail and one thing and another and you'll keep on denounceing [sic] me every time you are ordered to. It's all fine. After your letter I think you are a prick if that makes it any easier for you to knife your friends in the back. . . . Does that make you feel better? Hemingstein.

Ernest's big year ended solemnly enough with a letter from Max Perkins, who had just returned from Scott Fitzgerald's funeral. "I thought of tele-graphing you," said Max, "but it didn't seem as if there were any use in it, and I shrank from doing it. Anyhow, he didn't suffer at all, that's one thing. It was a heart attack and his death was instantaneous." Scott's final letter to Ernest in November had thanked him for an inscribed copy of *For Whom the Bell Tolls,* calling it a better novel than anyone else could have done. "I envy you like hell and there is no irony in this," Scott had said. "I envy you the time it will give you to do what you want." The envy was justly directed. At the time of Scott's death, *For Whom the Bell Tolls* had sold 189,000 copies.

51. TO THE EAST

MARTHA and Ernest completed preparations for the Far East during a return trip to New York in January. They stayed at the Lombardy, a favorite hotel of Martha's, reentering the customary whirl of social engagements. A Union Pacific representative from Sun Valley persuaded Ernest to attend a party given by Colin Miller, who had been reared in Oak Park. Miller had been present at the high-school assembly in 1919 when Ernest had made his speech and exhibited his shrapnel-torn uniform. But the meeting of the fellow townsmen was not a success, and Ernest strode angrily away when Miller, as a joke, asked him to autograph a set of Mark Twain.

Other engagements went better. Gustavo Durán and his wife Bonte came in from Rye and Bonte was charmed with her first sight of Ernest. Dancing with her at the Stork Club, he confided his opinion that Gustavo was a great man and a war hero. She was overwhelmed with pride and happiness, visualizing a lifetime of friendship in an aura of gold. Ernest spoke repeatedly of securing a post for Gustavo as technical adviser to Paramount in the filming of *For Whom the Bell Tolls,* and both Duráns were struck by the seeming inexhaustibility of his largess. So was Solita Solano, who had fled Paris when it fell to the Nazis in 1940 and was living in Washington Square. Solita asked Ernest down for a drink and spoke movingly of Margaret Anderson, former editor of *The Little Review,* who was now stranded and starving. Ernest immediately volunteered a contribution of $400 to pay Margaret's passage to the United States, and told Solita that she must never worry: as long as any of them had money, it would be shared by all.

He was levitated and joyous. Donald Friede approached him one night when he and Durán were attending a performance of Olsen and Johnson's *Hellzapoppin* at the Winter Garden, and handed him a check for $100,000. It was the most money he had ever seen in one lump, and they went into Lindy's Bar to celebrate. When he flourished the check under the bartender's nose, the word quickly spread, and the company was electrified. Congratulatory hands whacked his broad shoulders and the sweaty good will of *Hellzapoppin* blossomed along the bar.

Typhoid shots put him to bed at the Lombardy, aching in every joint. Earl Wilson, the *New York Post* columnist, found him leaning against rumpled pillows, wearing blue polka-dot pajamas and a green eyeshade. They spoke of the art of interviewing. Ernest, who denied ever taking notes, discoursed on his habits of observation. Around boxing rings he would remember the sound of the fighters' shoes on the resined canvas, or in ball parks the way an outfielder tossed his glove aside after an inning, never looking to see where it landed. The talk turned to Cuba. Ernest said that he had been driven there by the curious hordes who descended on Key West. He spoke of Mayito

Menocal and the cockfighting club, and gave an inexact but stirring account of how he had composed *For Whom the Bell Tolls.*

At this point Martha entered breezily, dropping a bundle of magazines on the foot of Ernest's bed. "Should I tell Earl how I went busted," said Ernest, "and how you went to Finland to make some more money so I could go on?"

"No," said Martha, curtly. She had heard all this before and disappeared into an adjoining room.

When Ernest recovered, Bumby came down for a weekend visit from Storm King School. They went to a Saturday-night show and worked out twice with boxing lessons at George Brown's gymnasium. Ernest reported the visit to Hadley. His tones were once more exuberant. Bumby was in great shape and *For Whom the Bell Tolls* was still selling like frozen daiquiris in Hell. The New York vacation ended when Ernest and Martha took an American Airlines plane for Los Angeles on January 27th. The Coopers met them at the airport, bearing them off for a two-day visit to Hollywood. Ernest still hoped that Cooper would play Jordan, but the role of María was not yet filled. Ingrid Bergman was on a skiing holiday at June Lake on the Nevada border 600 miles away. Donald Friede asked David Selznick to summon her for a meeting with the Hemingways. She drove most of the night of January 30th, caught a plane from Reno to San Francisco, and lunched with Ernest and Martha at a restaurant in Sacramento Street. They discussed the romantic picture which was yet to be born. Ernest warned her that she would have to crop her hair to play the part and asked to see her ears, which would of course be exposed. Like everything else about her, they struck him as remarkably photogenic.

The second leg of the trip to the Far East was smoothly accomplished aboard the SS *Matsonia.* Ernest's aunt Grace met them with the usual leis, reporters asked questions and took pictures, and they settled in at the Halekulani Hotel Cottages in Waikiki. Ernest reluctantly agreed to be guest of honor at a hastily assembled luncheon meeting on Fisherman's Wharf with half a dozen professors from the University of Hawaii. The young men had been waiting hungrily for more than an hour when Ernest appeared with the host, Professor Gregg Sinclair. Sinclair never drank, no drinks were offered, and Ernest squirmed unhappily until he spied some bottles of Chianti. "There," said he, "that's the stuff we need." A few glasses loosened his tongue without wholly overcoming his air of discomfort. At one point he stumbled over the word "periphery" and became acutely embarrassed. Thereafter he began to pretend that he was virtually illiterate, speaking in tones of such self-abasement that some of his listeners thought him either "neurotically modest" or "frantically insecure." He spoke bitterly of the leftist attack on *For Whom the Bell Tolls,* and defended his metaphor of the moving earth in Jordan's love scenes with María. When one of the teachers said that his students were reading *A Farewell to Arms,* Ernest advised against it. "That's an immoral book," said he. "Let them read *The Sun Also Rises.* It's very moral." After two hours he looked outside and saw that some of his relatives were waiting for him in a car. "You can't get away from your family," he said. It was clear enough as he left that he was glad to get away from the college professors.

He was again the uneasy guest of honor at a luau on an estate near the Oahu Country Club. He drank a good deal and conversed at length with Charles Bouslog, a professor who had been present at the lunch on Fisherman's Wharf. Mrs. Bouslog hovered near, constantly replenishing Ernest's glass until Martha objected. Ernest waved her aside with imperious gestures and kept on drinking. In the course of the evening he came close to a fight with a tall free-lance writer named Bishop who had been needling him with insulting remarks. Ernest removed his jacket, laid it carefully on the porch railing, and beckoned Bishop to accompany him into the shadows of the yard. But Bishop vanished unscathed and Ernest reentered the general conversation, speaking volubly now in what sounded like a recording from the lips of his fictional heroes. Was this, Bouslog wondered, the final disaster of success when a man came to sound like his own idea of himself?

The first month of the Chinese tour was spent in the British Crown Colony of Hong Kong, where the Hemingways occupied a luxurious suite in the Repulse Bay Hotel. Although the war was now four years old and the Japanese were moving freely in and out of the international city, Ernest found little evidence of tension. In general, said he, "morale was high and morals were low." Some five hundred Chinese millionaires had brought thousands of beautiful girls from all parts of China, while the troops along that part of the coast had attracted an immense swarm of prostitutes. The atmosphere was gay, like a "continuous circus," said Martha. Food was still abundant and excellent. The Happy Valley racetrack was open and thriving. There were rugby and cricket matches nearly every day, and association football on weekends.

Soon after his arrival Ernest met another soldier of fortune to add to his gallery of eccentric heroes. This was General Morris Abraham Cohen, a British expatriate who had come out to China in the 1920s as bodyguard to Sun Yat-sen. Cohen afterwards served as Chief of Police in Canton until it fell to the Japanese in 1938. He was a short and forthright man, heavily built and invariably armed with a pistol in a shoulder holster. He was fluent in Cantonese and other Chinese dialects, though his English had retained traces of childhood Cockney. He regaled Ernest with stories of Chiang Kai-shek, whom he disliked, and of the warlord general from Canton whom he was then serving as intelligence agent in Hong Kong. Cohen introduced Ernest to the widow of Sun Yat-sen, and it was perhaps under Cohen's influence that Ernest privately described her as the only "decent" Soong sister. Cohen's worldliness and insider's knowledge so much impressed him that he spoke half-seriously of writing a book about him.

When the charm of Hong Kong at last wore thin, he made plans to go where the fighting was. Cohen advised him to choose a war zone like the 7th where Chiang Kai-shek's regulars, the Army of the Kuomintang, were actively engaged with a strong Japanese salient. Early in March the Hemingways flew to Namyung and were taken in a very old car over roads deep in yellow mud to the 7th War Zone Headquarters at Shaokwan. They lunched next day with the commanding general and Ernest began to study the military situation. Although Martha complained very little at first, conditions were primitive and she was soon unnerved by the cold and filth, as well as a stubborn fungus infection on her hands and feet. Her gorge rose when she was introduced to the Army's snake wine, a drink made from rice, with small snakes coiled in the bottom of the bottles, and a variant called bird wine, which contained a brace of sodden cuckoos. Ernest began to praise snake wine as a cure for falling hair, with which he was beginning to be troubled, though he continued to favor Scotch as the sovereign remedy for almost everything else. A long time later he told a friend that Martha was sickened by Chinese squalor, dirt, and signs in hotel rooms asking guests not to mash bugs on the walls because it would spoil the wallpaper. "Papa," said she, "if you love me, get me out of China."

But Ernest, though with reservations, found the country both "wonderful and complicated," and pretended to be surprised that he had not discovered it before. The 7th War Zone covered an area about the size of Belgium. They inspected troop dispositions on foot, and descended the North River in a decrepit motorboat and a succession of sampans. On shore they rode tough little Mongolian ponies that did not seem much larger than dogs. The weather was generally foul: for one stretch of nearly two weeks, they never managed to get wholly dry. But Ernest drank rice wine and studied maps with the officers, whom he found to be "extraordinarily frank, straight-talking, intelligent, and articulate." The atmosphere at the front was as different from that of a British staff meeting in Hong Kong "as the locker room of the Green Bay Packers professional football team would be from even such a good prep school as Choate." The Chinese general asked him what the British thought of the Chinese infantry. Under the stimulus of "numerous cups of rice wine" Ernest aped the British manner of speaking:

"Johnny's all right and a very good fellow and all that. But he's absolutely hopeless on the offensive, you know. . . . We can't count on Johnny."

"Johnny?" asked the General.

"John Chinaman," said Ernest.

"Very interesting," the General said. "Let me tell you a Chinese story. Do you know why the British staff officer wears a single glass in his eye?"

"No," said Ernest.

"He wears a single glass in his eye so he will not see more than he can understand."

"I will tell the officer when I see him."

"Very good," the General said. "Tell him it is a little message from Johnny."

The first green of April was beginning to show along the banks of the Yangtze when Ernest and Martha flew on to the "terraced, gray, bomb-spattered, fire-gutted, grim stone island" of Chungking, China's wartime capital, with its steep streets, persistent fogs, forbidding walls, and flights of wet stone steps. In contrast to their life in the field, they found the hotels excellent, with abundant food and ample hot water. Martha luxuriated in the nearly forgotten pleasures of keeping clean, and they began a series of interviews with the leaders of the Chinese government.

One was a three-hour afternoon meeting with Chiang Kai-shek, with Madame Chiang as interpreter. Ernest concluded that the Generalissimo was fundamentally a military leader who was merely going through "the motions of being a statesman." His objectives had always been those of a soldier. Ernest found little evidence of democratic thinking: no country at war, said he, "remains a democracy for long. War always brings on a temporary dictatorship." The fact that any vestiges of democratic thought still remained gave evidence, Ernest thought, that China was a country to be admired.

Chinese rice wine, with or without snakes and birds, could do little to slake Hemingway's persistent thirst. One day in Chungking he heard that a young Navy lieutenant named Lederer was hoarding two cases of whiskey, bought "blind" at a Chinese auction. Brandishing a roll of bills, Ernest hurried over to the dock on the Yangtze where the gunboat *Tutuila* was moored. Lederer had not even opened his treasures: he was soon to be transferred and was saving the whiskey for a farewell brawl. This, said Ernest, was very shortsighted. "Never delay kissing a pretty girl," he advised, "or opening a bottle of whiskey. . . . I'll give you anything you want for half a dozen." Lederer thought fast. "Okay," he said, "I'll swap you six bottles for six lessons on how to become a writer."

After each of his lessons, Lederer congratulated himself on having exchanged a few bottles of booze for the "hard-earned literary secrets of the best writer in America." The sixth lesson was climactic. "Bill," said Ernest, "before you can write about people, you must be a civilized man. To be civilized, you must have two things: compassion and ability to roll with the punches. Never laugh at a guy who has had bad luck. And if you have bad luck, don't fight it. Roll with it—and bounce back." Finally, as if by afterthought, Hemingway advised him to go home and sample his whiskey.

Back at his cache, Lederer opened one of the bottles. It contained lukewarm tea. So did all the rest: the auctioneer had been a fraud. Hemingway had known the truth for nearly a week. Yet he had neither laughed at the victim nor evaded his part of the bargain. Lederer salted his story away for twenty years. From that day in Chungking he always remembered Hemingway as a civilized man.

Ernest and Martha discussed the Soviet intervention in Sino-Japanese affairs at lunch with Madame Chiang. Nelson Johnson, an old China hand who was then serving as American Ambassador, irritated Ernest with his bland assumption that "China can do anything that China wants to do." But when Ernest flew up to Chengtu, where Chiang Kai-shek maintained a military academy, he began to think that Johnson was right. The Officer's Club was modern and efficient, with a strong Prussian atmosphere.

Outside in the dusty streets of the old high-walled city, the camel caravans were still coming down from Tibet as they had been doing for centuries, slow, inexorable, and imperturbable, and almost forcing the observer to think in millennial terms. The impression of China's ability to achieve the impossible was strengthened for Hemingway when he watched an army of eighty thousand workers building, mainly by hand, an airfield capable of accommodating the huge four-motored Flying Fortresses. It gave him such a feeling as he might have had in Egypt in the time of the Pharaohs if he had "ridden some early morning up from the south out of the desert and seen the great camp and the work that went on when men were building the pyramids." But the Chinese workers dragging the huge ten-ton rollers across the runway did not behave like Egyptian slave laborers. Ernest could hear them singing in a steady undertone "as of surf breaking on a great barrier reef."

In mid-April the Hemingways set out along the road to Mandalay. They flew to Kunming, the Chinese terminus of the Burma Road, and from there south to Lashio across the Mekong River. The Japanese were bombing Kunming daily and Ernest observed that their air attacks had knocked out a few bridges along the Burma Road. But the indefatigable Chinese quickly rebuilt the bridges and had developed an ingenious ferry system for the times between. The trip from Lashio to Mandalay was accomplished by car. In Rangoon, Ernest gazed sourly at the golden spire of the Shwe Dagon Pagoda, unimpressed by yet another British colonial city, smaller than Hong Kong and twice as hot, with a temperature that often climbed to 103. This was where the honeymooners parted, Martha going on to Jakarta, and Ernest returning to the fleshpots of Hong Kong.

A meeting of the Advisory Board on Pulitzer Prizes was meantime taking place at Columbia University, far away in New York. The judges unanimously chose *For Whom the Bell Tolls* as the best novel written by an American and published in 1940. But the Chairman of the Board had other ideas. "I hope," said Dr. Nicholas Murray Butler, president of Columbia, "that you will reconsider before you ask the University to be associated with an award for a work of this nature." The Board, which included Arthur Krock of the *New York Times*, heard this veto with dismay. But the "few feeble murmurs" around the table died quickly away, and Hemingway, who had never won a major literary prize, was denied this one by an act of Olympian intercession. In Manila some days later, he learned that there would be no Pulitzer Award in fiction for the year 1940.

With 18,000 miles behind him, Ernest did not look forward to the 12,000 that still lay between Hong Kong and home. He was fatigued and irascible during his final week in Kowloon across the harbor, venting his spleen upon

Max Perkins for not having written oftener, particularly about the sales of his book. Although he wrote her frequently, he evidently resented Martha's continued absence in Java, and later told a story, probably invented, of a night spent with three beautiful Chinese girls who he said were sent to his suite by Cohen's Cantonese warlord. Not knowing what to do with three, he suggested that they all take a shower. After that, still baffled by procedural problems, he turned out the light and learned as well as he could.

By one of those coincidences that often happen to far travelers, Ernest met Ramon Lavalle, whom he had last seen in Madrid during the Civil War. Lavalle had married a Spanish girl and was now living in a house on a hilltop in Kowloon. They had a baby son and a four-year-old daughter named Gwendoline Pasionaria, but called Wendy. Seeing Wendy for the first time, Ernest was greatly smitten. He held the child tenderly in his arms and told Ramon that he had always wanted a daughter. Although he later assured Ralph Ingersoll that Hong Kong was well defended, this was only public propaganda. His private opinion was that the British garrison had no chance. "They'll die trapped like rats," he told Lavalle. Hundreds were killed when the city fell to the Japanese on the following Christmas Day. Ernest did not learn until much later that the child Wendy was among the victims.

For the past three years Lavalle had been smuggling merchandise through the Japanese lines into the hinterlands beyond Canton by bribing Japanese sentries with Scotch whiskey. During his final week on the mainland, Ernest accompanied him on one such mission. It took them thirty miles outside the New Territories. They bypassed enemy lines and spent several hours with a group of Chinese guerrillas. Lavalle was fluent in Cantonese and gained intelligence of a heavy concentration of fresh Japanese troops outside Canton. Apart from this adventure, however, Ernest's final days in Hong Kong were mainly social. He dined alone with Madame Kung, the Prime Minister's wife, and briefed James Roosevelt, the President's son, on conditions in Chungking. None of this served to dissipate his gloom, which was increased by news from Perkins that Sherwood Anderson and Virginia Woolf had both died. He observed that members of the writing clan were dying like flies. With Ford Madox Ford and Wolfe in 1938–1939, Fitzgerald in 1940, and now two more in 1941, the shades were closing in. He would not miss Virginia Woolf but it was a damned shame about old Sherwood, who had always liked living very much. Pretty soon, thought Ernest, nobody would be alive but Edith, Osbert, and Sacheverell Sitwell.

His mood was still gloomy when the Lavalles saw him off on the 6th of May for the flight to Manila. The plane was crowded and the prospect of island-hopping from Manila to Guam to Wake to Midway to Hawaii was not inviting. On the 11th he attended a "ghastly" dinner given by the Philippine Writers' Association where everyone's attempt to be gaily informal bored him so much that he got too drunk to care. Of his six scheduled articles for Ingersoll's *PM,* he had written three in Hong Kong, typing them out on thin paper and concealing them in his shoes to avoid censorship. In Manila he made a few more notes and explored some of the Spanish bars of Intramuros. Otherwise his sole gain from the Philippine stopover was a good short summer haircut.

The rest of the trip was not much better. In Guam, which he called a "dump," his only pleasure was a meeting with Bernt Balchen, who was returning to the United States after flying bombers in China. Ernest admired Balchen for having fought in Norway and Finland, flown over both Poles, and conquered the Atlantic with Admiral Byrd. Delayed at Guam by adverse winds, they went fishing together on the 15th, though it got them nothing but an overdose of tropical sun. More sunburn at Wake made Ernest's nose peel and swelled his ankles. The flight to Midway was long and nasty. Ernest strode off the plane at Honolulu convinced that crossing the Pacific by Clipper was the longest bore on earth. He afterwards remembered the day he reached San Francisco as supremely bright and clear. It was the end of May and the Bay area was still green with spring and blazing with flowers. He would have been glad to see the Golden Gate even in a fog. His long "bastard" of a trip was almost over and he was back in what he more than half-seriously called the land of hope and glory.

52. THE WOUND AND THE BOW

WHILE he waited for Martha to join him in New York, Ernest gave an afternoon's audience to Ralph Ingersoll, who came up to his suite at the Barclay. A secretary kept shorthand notes of the long interview while Ernest pontificated on the China-Burma situation. The floor was strewn with the maps he had brought back from Hong Kong, Chungking, and Rangoon. Ingersoll subsequently dictated a lengthy account of the meeting to serve as an introduction to Ernest's feature articles.

On the way south, Martha and Ernest stopped over in Washington to report their findings to the military. Colonel Charlie Sweeny took them to see Colonel John W. Thomason, Jr., at the Office of Naval Intelligence on Constitution Avenue. Thomason was a firm-lipped Texan, aged forty-eight, a Marine Corps veteran of twenty years' service. He was also a skilled artist, a biographer of Jeb Stuart, and the author of innumerable short stories and longer works, many of them illustrated by himself. The fact that he had won the Silver Star and the Navy Cross for valor in France in 1918 immediately endeared him to Ernest, who struck him in turn as "very sensible and decent." He also liked Martha's critique of the inadequate British defense system at Singapore. Both Sweeny and Thomason discoursed learnedly on Japan's future conduct in the Pacific. Ernest disagreed but did not argue back. Like Sweeny in the past, Thomason might well be useful to him in the future.

In Key West Ernest was reunited with his younger sons before they left for a summer with Pauline in California. When Pauline wired from San Francisco some days later that they had arrived safely, Ernest replied that he still missed her in spite of all their fights. He signed his letter "with love"—though Pauline's telegram had concluded only with "regards." His nostalgia for the old haunts in Key West was sharpened by news of the recent death of Joe Russell, owner of Sloppy Joe's and partial prototype of Harry Morgan. Joe had died suddenly after an emergency operation in Havana. It was typical of his lifelong preference for the uncommon common man that he missed Josie more than any of the literary people who had died in the past two years. On hearing of the death of Ford in the summer of 1939, he had merely shrugged and quoted Joe Russell: "People dying this year that never died before."

Like the late Tom Wolfe he was involved in a plagiarism suit. On his last day in New York a playwright named John Igual de Montijo had filed an action in Los Angeles, alleging that Hemingway had taken parts of *For Whom the Bell Tolls* from a film script called *Viva Madero*. On the morning of June 27th Ernest grumblingly appeared before Raoul F. Washington, American Vice-Consul in Havana, to make a deposition. He denied that he had been present in February, 1939, at a gathering on North Argyle Street, Hollywood, when Montijo read his play aloud to Eddie Kay, Virginia Kay, Lou Fisher, and Alex Flashberg. "I have been in California only three times in my life," said Ernest. "One was in July of 1937. I did not return to California . . . until January of this year on my way to the Orient. I passed through California in May of this same year, 1941, on my return from the Orient. In February of 1939, I was living in the Sevilla Biltmore Hotel in Havana." Although the suit was thrown out of court eight months later, Ernest was deeply agitated on learning in August that the thousand-dollar bill for legal fees had been debited against his royalty account. He complained bitterly that Charlie Scribner should know better than to cut steaks out of his racehorses, adding that he would rather commit hara-kiri than submit to further robbery. Next day, typically, he cabled an apology. Charlie must disregard his angry nightletter.

Max Perkins warned him repeatedly that the "infernal revenue agents" were hungrily watching his recent earnings. Ernest's well-worn maxim about losing in St. Louis what you had won in Chicago was about to be confirmed once again. He computed his income tax at roughly one hundred thousand dollars, the amount of his entire first payment from Paramount. All that he and Martha had made from their "bastardly" trip to China would swell the government's take to 75 per cent. It was of course ridiculous, as he pointed out, that he had barely been able to afford a $60 outlay to buy a new skiff for an old Havana fisherman who had been starving to death for lack of equipment.

He was therefore rather sardonic when Pauline wrote from San Francisco in mid-July that Ernest was not giving enough time to Patrick and Giggy. "It is a pity you can't be with them," said she. "Can't you arrange that?" Ernest explained patiently that he was trying to save on his income tax by maintaining a six-month nonresident status. The trip to the Far East had covered three months; he must now stay in Cuba from June 15 to September 15. Otto Bruce might be able to bring the boys to Sun Valley to wait for their father's arrival. But he reminded Pauline that her $6,000 in annual alimony was actually costing him $21,000 before taxes. In spite of the blood money, he wished her a happy forty-sixth birthday on July 22nd, the day after he turned forty-two.

During the summer he saw a good deal of his friends at the American Embassy in Havana. One of the First Secretaries was Robert P. Joyce, who had come to Cuba in January with his handsome wife Jane. Joyce was a Foreign Service officer of wide experience, urbane, efficient, and down-to-earth. He and his wife formed the habit of dropping in at the Finca on Sunday afternoons, often staying for dinner and late evening talk, and the two couples became fast friends. Ellis O. Briggs had returned as ranking officer in July. He shared with Ernest a passionate interest in skeet-trap and live-pigeon shooting at the Club de Cazadores del Cerro, and they often went further afield, flying to Cienfuegos to shoot ducks in the marshes, or driving to Pinar del Río Province after *yaguasas*.

Late in September, having completed the three-months' residence in Cuba, the Hemingways returned to Sun Valley and a further reunion with Ernest's Idaho family of Taylor Williams, the Arnolds, and the Atkinsons. Before settling down to ducks and pheasants, he wanted to make another expedition after antelope. Williams suggested the valley of the Pahsimeroi over beyond the Lost River Range north of Arco. Mt. Borah loomed 12,000 feet above the 40-mile-long valley, where small mining towns were the only mark of civilization. The Indian name of the valley meant "water and one place of trees." It pleased Ernest, and he kept repeating it during the long and dusty drive with Colonel Williams, Pappy Arnold, and the three Hemingway boys.

Each night the youngsters bedded down in the car. The others slept in a bug-ridden cabin belonging to an unwashed sourdough whom they knew only as the Old Timer. He emphasized his advanced age by calling Williams "young man" and addressing Ernest as "kid." He said that he personally recalled the summer day in 1876 when the Sioux licked Custer on the ridge above the Little Bighorn, and even claimed to have been around the premises at the famous Wagon Box fight of 1867 when twenty-eight soldiers from Fort Phil Kearny stood off three thousand Sioux warriors under Chief Red Cloud.

They mounted up on a Saturday morning and rode to the top of the range, with a distant northward view across the "loveliest" of mountains towards the Middle Fork of the Salmon River. The antelope were abundant enough, grazing in herds a mile away but always disappearing with the speed of an express train the moment their scouts honked the signal. Sunday was a duplicate of Saturday except that now the herds stayed even farther off and constantly flashed the white ruff on their rumps as they spooked and departed. With Pappy Arnold snapping unposed pictures, the hunters climbed again to the top of the range, blocking and then turning all the likely draws, crawling on hands and knees up dozens of ridges, and sweeping the country with field glasses. Back at the cabin that night, empty-handed and saddlesore, they drank whiskey sours and heard the Old Timer tell about the hanging of a frontier desperado.

Once more on Monday they climbed to the high, rolling country, working all the draws and pockets and ridges. Ready to hand in his gun bucket just back of the mare's withers was Ernest's scarred old Springfield .30-06. It stayed there most of the day until they wearily began the descent and suddenly, happily, jumped a good-sized herd feeding in a cul de sac with one wide exit. Ernest slid from his horse, yanked out his Springfield, and ran hard for the spot they would have to pass. "When they came streaming over the hump," said he, "I picked the biggest buck and swung ahead of him and squeezed gently and the bullet broke his neck. It was a very lucky shot."

A year later, Taylor Williams was still astonished. "I saw Ernest jump from his horse, cover a hundred-yard dash on foot, and drop a running antelope at two hundred and seventy five yards with a single shot. That's rifle shooting, if you ask me." This and other hunting adventures with Ernest had long since convinced the Colonel of his prowess. He was the easiest man to travel with that Williams had ever met, never complaining, planning every move and working out every detail like a very alert infantry officer, liking equally the lingo, the regularity, and the responsibility. The rougher and harder it was, the better he seemed to like it.

After the Old Timer's cabin on the Pahsimeroi, Sun Valley seemed superlatively luxurious, with clean beds, heated swimming pool, late afternoons at the roulette wheel in Ketchum, and nights in the chi-chi bar of the Ram restaurant. Gary and Rocky Cooper were back for another season. Coop looked worn and pale with making too many pictures and was anxious to improve his skill with the shotgun. Ernest was little drawn to Robert Taylor, who had come for a vacation with his wife Barbara Stanwyck, but he spent some hours urging the director, Howard Hawks, to hire Evan Shipman as technical adviser for a trotting-horse film that Hawks was planning to make.

His equally loyal attempt to get a Hollywood job for Gustavo Durán was finally frustrated by Paramount's fear of Communism. Although neither Hemingway nor Durán had the least inclination towards Party membership, Sam Woods, the director, was ultrasensitive to the Red Menace. Ernest sent Gustavo a $1,000 check (which was promptly returned) and advised him to accept a post offered by Nelson Rockefeller, who was then working under Roosevelt to improve cultural relations with Latin America. For a time Donald Friede sought to circumvent Woods's prejudices by persuading David Selznick to buy *For Whom the Bell Tolls* from Paramount and to appoint Howard Hawks as director. This project also came to nothing. But Cooper was more than ever anxious to play Robert Jordan. He told Ernest that the picture might become a powerful instrument in the continuing war against Fascism.

Ernest had been reading Edmund Wilson's *The Wound and the Bow,* which included a long essay called "Hemingway: Gauge of Morale." In Wilson's view Hemingway had begun well only to slip gradually downhill to the failure of craft which spoiled *To Have and Have Not* and made *The Fifth Column* a mere "small boy's fantasy." He had now entered a phase in which he was "occupied with building up his public personality," posing for handsome photographs with open shirt and outdoor grin and bearing an "ominous resemblance to Clark Gable." This was the Hemingway of the "loose disquisition, arrogant, belligerent, and boastful." Wilson likewise found in several of the more recent stories "a growing antagonism to women," which he thought might be traced to Hemingway's implicit fear that "the woman will get the man down." It was this kind of fear, Wilson suggested, which had caused him to invent such an "amoeba-like" little heroine as María in *For Whom the Bell Tolls.* The love affair in a sleeping bag completely lacked "the kind of give and take that goes on between real men and women." It displayed, perhaps compensatorily, "the all-too-perfect felicity of a youthful erotic dream." Such opinions did not exactly arouse Ernest's admiration for Wilson's critical powers. He told Max Perkins that he was unable to discover just what Wilson thought his "Wound" was: homosexuality, impotence, or just plain meanness. As to the "Bow," said Ernest, he still had a hell of a good one and that was what Wilson could not forgive: some day, when he wrote his personal memoirs, he would notch up an arrow and shoot Bunny with it.

He was more than a little concerned to know what Wilson was going to do with Fitzgerald's posthumous *The Last Tycoon,* which appeared that fall under Wilson's editorship. On reading the book, which also contained a selection of Scott's stories, he had little to say about Wilson himself except to condemn his taste in fiction. "The Rich Boy" was silly, and "A Diamond as Big as the Ritz" was simply trash. Yet both of them were better than *The Last Tycoon,* which did not move at all. Scott had managed to suggest something of Irving Thalberg's business acumen and personal charm, but the women struck Ernest as preposterous and the book itself was simply dead—like a slab of bacon when the mold has cut too deep to be removed. The supreme irony of Scott's career, said Ernest, was that he had lost his "juice" just when he had begun at last to learn what life was all about. All the dust had left the butterfly's wing, even though the wing had continued to move spasmodically until the butterfly was dead. In spite of its faults, *Tender Is the Night* was still Scott's best, tragic and magic at once, with wonderful description and atmosphere.

Ernest was cheered by the fact that his own novel had now sold well over half a million copies. The Limited Editions Club had decided to award it their triennial Gold Medal. Sinclair Lewis, as chairman of the editorial committee, sent Ernest a "damn nice letter" and was planning to make the presentation speech at a ceremony on November 26th. Ernest declined to attend. He had had enough of New York that year and invented the excuse that he had already promised Martha a trip elsewhere. But he was bursting with curiosity to know what Lewis would say, and asked Scribners to send a stenographer to take it all down in shorthand.

The southbound trip that Ernest had "promised" Martha took them through the Arizona Indian country. They left Sun Valley on December 3rd and reached Grand Canyon the following afternoon. At a trading post in the Navaho reservation Ernest was much amused by an example of Indian humor. The little town was filled with dusty and disreputable-looking tribesmen. Martha, blond and chic, stood at the counter with what Ernest called her best Bryn Mawr manner and said rather imperiously, "Have you any beads? I want to see some beads." Leaning on the showcase nearby was an ancient Indian with long hair and wrinkled face. He groped in his pocket and pulled out a single bead about the size of the head of a pin. "Here bead," said he, solemnly handing it to Martha. "Now you see bead."

They were crossing the Texas border on the way to San Antonio when news of the Pearl Harbor disaster reached them by radio. Ernest reacted explosively. Both Charlie Sweeny and John Thomason had been fatally wrong in Washington in June about the prospects of war with Japan. The myth of the matchless American Navy had been destroyed, while Frank Knox should have been relieved as Secretary of the Navy within twenty-four hours after the debacle, and the American generals and admirals on Oahu should have been promptly shot.

His bloodthirsty mood extended itself to Max Perkins and Charles Scribner. Despite his telegraphed request, they had failed to appoint a stenographer to take down Lewis's speech at the Gold Medal ceremony. Lewis had spoken from notes and his laudatory sentiments had vanished into thin air. This, said Ernest heatedly, was the most careless and callous action he had ever met with in civil life. He planned to present the Gold Medal to Scribners as a reminder of their unforgivable ineptitude. He never wanted to see the medal, ever! For the moment, as he dashed off this angry communiqué in his suite at the Saint Anthony Hotel in San Antonio, the loss of the speech bulked as large in his mind as the loss of the capital ships at Pearl Harbor and the planes on Hickam Field. As always after such outbursts, his sanity soon reasserted itself. The world war had now reached out to embrace the United States, and he knew something about its probable consequences.

53. IMPROVISATIONS

To Hemingway, January looked like the beginning of a "new strange bad year" in which both he and the nation would have to start a long slow climb out of the depths, improvising as they went. For himself it began at ground level with the problem of meeting his income tax obligations. His earnings in 1941 had amounted to $137,357.01. Although he had sequestered $85,000 in a special tax account, he saw that even this would not suffice, and applied to Scribners for a personal loan of $15,000. He did not find it possible to take the matter lightly. A man, he said, worked all his life and finally made a fortune only to have the government take it all to pay for the idiocy, conceit, and sloth which had precipitated the nation into yet another war.

Although he occasionally spoke of getting on with a book of short stories, his literary productivity during 1942 was slender. Early in March he was approached by Nat Wartels from Crown Publishers in New York. Crown was planning an elaborate anthology of war writing and Wartels wanted to reprint the Caporetto and El Sordo sequences from *A Farewell to Arms* and *For Whom the Bell Tolls*. He also hoped to induce Hemingway to edit the volume with an introduction. Max Perkins was enthusiastic and Ernest presently agreed, although in making the selections he planned to lean heavily on the editorial and military experience of Perkins, John Thomason, and Charlie Sweeny.

Another of his preoccupations during the spring was the script which Dudley Nichols had prepared for the film version of *For Whom the Bell Tolls*. Donald Friede was proud of having secured Nichols as Hemingway's screenwriter, but Ernest, having examined the treatment, was highly critical. His novel, he suggested, had attracted half a million book buyers because it offered a unified action sequence, a credible love story, and a persuasive demonstration of what men and women were willing to die for. With some exceptions, Nichols had handled the action very well indeed. But his script failed utterly in communicating the power of Pilar's political convictions in uniting the whole guerrilla band, nor did it begin to explain Jordan's willingness to die for the Republican cause. Nichols's love scenes struck Hemingway as astonishingly inept, while his picturesque conception of the appearance of the Spaniards could only have been derived from fourth-rate productions of Bizet's *Carmen* or the banal cinematic effusions of Rouben Mamoulian, whose very name stirred Ernest's ire. In place of the red bandannas prescribed by Nichols, the actors must all wear grays and blacks, and the whole emphasis must be on the native dignity of the Loyalists. Ernest did not volunteer his own editorial services. Instead he threatened to publicize his opposition unless changes were made. But he was elated to learn that Ingrid Bergman was going to play María.

While he managed to persuade himself that both the film and the anthology could do something to help the American war effort, he was already longing for a more active role. Other writers might lend their talents to propagandizing, as John Steinbeck had done for the Air Force with *Bombs Away*. Ernest said emphatically that he would rather cut three fingers off his throwing hand than write such a book. He was willing to go to the war himself, or send his sons as they came of age, or contribute such money as he could command. But he was unwilling to write anything official unless it could be "absolute truth"—a manifest impossibility in wartime. His application to John Wheeler to report the war for the North American Newspaper Alliance had met with a tactful rebuff. Wheeler explained that at this nadir of the war, the armed forces did not yet want any reporters on the fighting fronts. Ernest therefore began to cast about for a program of action nearer home.

He found his opportunity soon after coming back from a holiday in Mexico City, where he and Martha spent two weeks as guests of a wealthy young American named Nathan Davis. The scheme was to set up a counterintelligence organization in Havana to meet the infiltration of Cuba by Nazi fifth columnists. They were gaining entry to the island with forged passports, helped by some of the 3,000 Falangist sympathizers in and near Havana. Many of the large Spanish clubs were openly anti-American and pro-Axis. Cuba's most influential newspaper, *Diario de la Marina,* was owned and edited by a wealthy Spaniard whose sentiments were as overtly critical of the United States as he dared to make them. The arrival of foreign spies was especially dangerous because of the wolf-pack of German submarines which was then preying on Allied tankers and cargo ships throughout the Caribbean.

Ernest's chief liaison men were Ellis Briggs and Bob Joyce at the American Embassy. Ernest told Joyce, stretching the truth considerably, that he had helped to form a private intelligence network in Madrid in 1937 and that a similar organization was badly needed in Cuba. His motives were clear enough: patriotism, pleasure in secret planning, and a love for commanding "inside" operations, especially if they involved firearms and possible personal danger. Joyce interceded with Briggs and they both approached Spruille Braden, the new Ambassador, who had recently come to Cuba from Colombia. Early in May Ernest was invited to present his case. He explained the need for the operation and outlined his qualifications for running it. His mastery of Spanish was more than adequate and the range of his acquaintance was wide. All he needed from the American government would be minor supplies and small arms. He would arrange and pay for the rest, using the small guest house in the Finca grounds as headquarters. Braden discussed the question with the Cuban Prime Minister, and Ernest was empowered to proceed.

He managed to get it going about the middle of May, drawing heavily on the membership of the Basque Club of Havana, for whom he had long been a special kind of hero. But his recruits covered a wide social spectrum, ranging from his friends among the jai alai players to Don Andrés Untzaín, a Catholic priest who had served as machine gunner for the Loyalists. There were also waiters from the Floridita and other Havana restaurants, a number of Cuban fishermen, some anti-Fascist Spanish noblemen then living in voluntary exile in Cuba, and a sprinkling of wharfrats and bums. According to the Ambassador, the informal code name for this group was the *Crime Shop,* but Ernest was soon calling it the *Crook Factory.* As might have been expected, the organization was somewhat loose. It was held together by the force of Ernest's personality and liberal infusions of wine, spirits, and pesos. Reports came in by word of mouth or in writing. These were funneled through the Finca, where Ernest translated and processed them for transmission to Joyce at the Embassy. Ernest himself was the bearer. About once a week he drove into Havana, entered the building through a business establishment on the ground floor, and then climbed the four flights of stairs to Bob Joyce's office.

During Martha's absence in St. Louis on a visit to her mother, Ernest simultaneously directed the Crook Factory and began a running controversy with Wartels at Crown on the contents of the *Men at War* anthology. Much of the book had already been set up in galleys, but Ernest's convictions about truth and falsehood in war stories made him a formidable adversary, while his long list of recommendations for additions and deletions helped to run Crown's printing bills to staggering levels. Among the deleted items were a "phony story" by Ralph Bates about women machine gunners at Brunete, a selection from Arthur Guy Empey's *Over the Top,* and an account of young Winston Churchill by Richard Harding Davis. On the other hand, Ernest wanted to include Stendhal's Battle of Waterloo from *The Charterhouse of Parma,* the Battle of Shiloh from Lloyd Lewis's life of General Sherman, the Battle of the Somme from Frank Richards's *Old Soldiers Never Die,* and Frank Tinker's story of the Italian debacle at Guadalajara and Brihuega.

All this reading of war literature sharpened his longing to do some fighting of his own. One of the selections for the anthology was an account of the sinking of a German transport off the coast of Norway by the small British submarine *Sturgeon.* Ernest had also read, though he did not reprint, the story of the exploits of Count Felix von Luckner of the German Navy, who had disguised a sailing ship to look like a Norwegian fishing boat and used it to prey on Allied shipping. The German submarines in the Caribbean were rumored to be sinking as many as thirty-five Allied ships each week. Native fishermen, plying their trade along the edges of the Gulf Stream, brought back tales of enemy submarines which surfaced, boarded their vessels, and demanded supplies of fresh water, fish, or vegetables.

May was not yet over when Ernest appeared at the Embassy with another proposal. This was to equip the *Pilar* as a Q-boat, with a well-trained crew and a supply of bazookas, grenades, short-fuse bombs, and two or three .50-calibre machine guns. Under Ernest's command they would cruise along the north coast as far as Cayo Confites at the eastern extremity of the Old Bahama Channel, pretending that they were scientists gathering specimens for the American Museum of Natural History. If and when halted by a Nazi submarine, they would wait until the enemy boarding party had emerged on deck and the craft had closed with the *Pilar* to a distance of fifty yards. Then, on signal, Ernest would rev up his motors, close the gap to twenty yards, and begin shooting. The heavy machine guns would mow down deck personnel while Ernest's crewmen, trained for the purpose, would lob grenades down the conning tower, and if possible arm and heave one of the short-fuse bombs into the sub's forward hatch. Ernest told Braden that he could find the right men. All he needed to make his romantic dream come true was good radio equipment, arms and ammunition, and official permission.

He discussed the plan with Colonel Thomason, who had been helping him with the war anthology and was now Chief of Naval Intelligence for Central America. "Ernest," said John, "you are certainly going to have to improvise." He seemed so dubious about the wisdom of proceeding that Ernest began to call him "Doubting Thomason." No submarine commander would be so foolish, said he, as to let Ernest's men throw "bean bags down his hatch." But the Ambassador, an imaginative man, believed that in spite of certain elements of super-bravado the idea was not necessarily impractical, and he broke all regulations to procure the necessary equipment.

Ernest immediately assembled a crew of eight from among his most trusted confederates. The code designation for the scheme was *Friendless,* the name of one of his favorite cats at the Finca. As his executive officer he chose Winston Guest, a large millionaire athlete who had recently been staying at the Finca. Colonel Thomason recruited a Marine master sergeant from the American Embassy to serve as gunner. His name was Don Saxon and he could field-strip and reassemble a machine gun in the dark in a matter of seconds. The others were all non-Americans: Juan Dunabeitia, a tall, thin, merry-eyed Basque who knew the sea so well that he was called Sinbad the Sailor, later shortened to Sinsky; Paxtchi, one of the jai-alai-playing Ibarlucia brothers, who had frequented the Finca for years and often vanquished Hemingway at tennis; the Canary Islander Gregorio Fuentes, Ernest's veteran mate and cook aboard the *Pilar;* Fernando Mesa, an exiled Catalan who had once been a waiter in Barcelona; a heavyset, pale-faced Spanish Cuban named Roberto Herrera, whose elder brother Luis had been a surgeon for the Loyalists; and a silent man, known only as Lucas, whose origins remain obscure.

A shipment of grenades arrived and was carried aboard in egg crates. Machine guns were disassembled and sneaked on in people's pockets. A sensitive radio was installed, and for emergencies there was a collapsible rubber boat, equipped with aluminum oars, and colored bright orange so as to be easily spotted from the air. Patrolling began in June, but Ernest was disappointed to discover that the sub-sinking business was anything but brisk. The *Pilar's* log reflects the usual range of activity at this period.

June 12, 1942: Patrolled to Puerta Purgatorio. . . . Return 5:30.
June 13: Watch from 2 A.M. to 7. Out before daylight, patrolled 12 miles out until dark. In at 8 P.M. Win Guest went to Bahia Honda in auxiliary.
June 14: Watch from 4 A.M. Out at daylight, 7:20. Patrolled until 1 P.M., then anchored inside at 4 P.M. with supplies.

These, of course, were practice runs which could at any moment of day or night have decoyed the enemy into range. Ernest held occasional drills, demanded regular field-stripping and cleaning of the guns, and sometimes permitted the lobbing of grenades at bits of flotsam. He was quite prepared to sacrifice his beloved vessel in exchange for the capture or the sinking of an enemy, and never doubted (throughout what he called "the boat-time") that his occupation was "completely worthwhile"—an opinion shared both by his crew members and his superiors ashore. Yet, although a watch was always posted at sea and the radio often crackled with shortwave conversations between U-boat officers in recognizable German, the *Pilar* attracted no submarines in her early months of work.

When Patrick and Gregory appeared in mid-July for a vacation with their father, Martha wryly referred to herself as the "only unadjusted member of the group." She was afflicted with a kind of claustrophobia, and was eager to get back to journalism by taking a six-week fact-finding cruise through the Caribbean on assignment for *Collier's*. Although she liked and got on well with the boys, her relations with Ernest were becoming strained. His constant goings and comings on subhunting errands were often followed by noisy drinking parties at all hours. Furtive individuals employed by the Crook Factory appeared and disappeared among the shrubbery, and Ernest sometimes tried to carry over his habits of seagoing command into household affairs. Martha resented most of this, and her longing to return to journalism, though certainly genuine, was one way of fighting back.

Leaving Ernest to keep bachelor quarters with his sons, Martha eventually set out in a thirty-foot sloop with three Negro retainers. It was the first time since before the Spanish Civil War that Ernest had had his younger sons all to himself for an extended period, and he wished to make the most of it before the war closed in. He began to take the boys as apprentice crew members on the *Pilar's* antisubmarine patrols, believing that the experience would give them the same sort of education that cabin boys had profited by on British men-of-war in Captain Marryat's time. To the boys it was a great lark. But Ernest, in the long night watches, reflected now sullenly, now satirically, on Martha's frequent absences from his bed and board. As he had done on leaving Pauline for Martha, he often allowed sentimental memories of his first marriage to fill his mind. On the night of the day following his forty-third birthday he lay awake for a long time, remembering such matters as the battered old *Leopoldina* on which he and Hadley had crossed to Vigo, the races at Enghien, the first Pamplona fiesta, the summer in the Schwarzwald, and (not least) the out-of-season fishing at Cortina d'Ampezzo.

54. MEN AT WAR

ALL through that blazing tropical summer, Ernest continued his supervision of the Crook Factory and his Q-boat cruising. Constant exposure to heavy sunlight at sea made his face so tender that he gave up shaving entirely. People began to praise the luxuriance of his beard—"the effect," said Ellis

Briggs, "was terrific"—although his social contacts at the Embassy were made somewhat difficult by his aversion to getting dressed up. "His customary garb around Havana," said Briggs, "was a pair of faded blue bathing trunks" with a "sweaty guayabera shirt" and he often went barefoot even in downtown Havana at such places as the Floridita Bar and El Patio.

He was like a timid boy in the presence of Mrs. Braden, a Chilean aristocrat who managed to treat him graciously without being able to hide a trace of coolness at his unkempt appearance. His idea of fun was far different from hers. He boxed with Winston Guest, knocked out Shipwreck Kelly, and even suggested that the Ambassador, a strongly built and broad-shouldered man, might enjoy putting on the gloves with him. His manner in Braden's presence was courteous, modest, and deferential. When the Ambassador and his wife came to dine at the Finca, they were nearly overcome by the abundance and variety of the drinks. Ernest commonly began with absinthe drops. Besides red and white table wines, there was always much champagne at dinner, and afterwards a seemingly endless succession of Scotch highballs. If the evening lasted long enough, Ernest sometimes rounded it off with more absinthe. At such times he seldom appeared to be drunk, though he often developed what he called "mastodon hangovers" and did little work the following day.

Sunday afternoons at the Finca were always gay and populous. "Ernest's taste in people was extraordinarily catholic," said Briggs, "and he attracted all kinds. His personality was so powerful that few were unaffected by it." On a typical Sunday, besides the ever-present jai-alai players and other ex-patriate Basques, one often found a visiting sportsman or a writing friend from the north, a scattering of Spanish priests, men of wealth like Winston Guest or Tom Shevlin, Ellis Briggs with his wife and two children, Bob and Jane Joyce, the two Braden daughters, and sometimes Nancy Oakes and her husband, "Count" Freddy Marigny. Ernest's ability to combine paternalism and boyishness made him popular with the younger guests, to whom he listened sympathetically with no attempt at domination. "When he spoke of something that interested him, he chose his words with precision and not infrequently with diffidence." His friends observed a special clairvoyance in his social relations, and Briggs called him the most perceptive person he had ever met. "In a group of people, if two of them were antagonistic to each other, Ernest felt it at once, as accurately as if they wore printed placards." Although among friends he did not unduly exploit this power, now and again a streak of cruelty appeared as he relentlessly prodded "tender areas of the spirit" in people whose presence he resented.

Even the closest of his associates sometimes felt the weight of his wit, which covered the whole range from the deft to the elephantine. One day when Winston Guest roared up beside the *Pilar* with a load of supplies, something in the way the light hit his face reminded young Gigi of Lon Chaney, Jr., in a horror film called *The Wolf Man*. Guest accepted the nicknames of Wolfer and eventually Wolfie with his customary good humor, and continued to function as Ernest's executive officer through the waning summer. They sighted several enemy subs, but came close only once. They were out in the Gulf Stream near a kind of atoll called Megano de Casigua when a U-Boat suddenly surfaced far offshore. "Papa," said Wolfie, "she looks like an airplane carrier." Ernest passed the word to up anchor and set off in pursuit. But the sub ignored them and soon vanished over the horizon to the northeast.

Late in August Ernest completed and sent off his introduction to the *Men at War* anthology. It was a highly personal and discursive essay of 10,000 words, written, as he said, by a man with three sons to whom he was in certain ways responsible "for having brought them into this unspeakably balled-up world." If the book could render patriotic service, it would be by acquainting American youth with the nature of war from the beginning of human history up to now. Although the volume contained both fiction and nonfiction, Ernest's chief criterion was always verisimilitude: he wished the selections to show what war was really like rather than how it was supposed to be. Each July, on the approximate anniversary of his wounding at Fossalta di Piave, he reread Frederick Manning's *The Middle Parts of Fortune,* or *Her Privates We,* "the finest and noblest book of men of war" to be found anywhere. His purpose was always the same, to remind himself of how "things" had really been so that he would never lie to himself or to others in anything he might choose to write about men in battle.

He told of the destruction of his "illusion of immortality" on the Italian front. The experience had given him a very bad time until he reflected that "nothing could happen to me that had not happened to all men before me. Whatever I had to do men had always done. If they had done it, then I could do it too, and the best thing was not to worry about it." He gave an account of a conversation with his son Bumby in May in which he had advised the boy not to worry, and recalled the occasion in Milan in 1918 when Dorman-Smith had introduced him to the passage about dying in Shakespeare's *Henry IV*. The words were still framed in gold at the back of his mind, a better protection than a St. Christopher medal.

Ernest's family dwindled still further when Patrick left early in September to enter Canterbury, a Catholic school for boys in New Milford, Connecticut. Martha was still away. Having concluded her Caribbean cruise, she was now exploring the jungle behind Paramaribo in Dutch Guiana, and would go from there to see Eleanor Roosevelt in the White House. Ernest consoled himself as well as he could with pickup baseball games at the Club de Cazadores with Cuban friends like Cucu Kohly, Rodrigo Díaz, and Mungo Pérez, or officers on shore leave from the "Hooligan Navy," including Tom Shevlin and Bill Ching. Between drinks Ernest liked to pitch a few innings, and took pleasure in ribbing Ching about having depth-charged a school of grouper fish that he had mistaken for a Nazi submarine.

The *Men at War* anthology and the Limited Editions Club reprint of *For Whom the Bell Tolls* both appeared in October. Sinclair Lewis's preface was a slightly more formalized version of his remarks at the Gold Medal breakfast ceremony in New York. Ernest's childish disappointment in having missed the speech was now pacified, especially since the preface praised the same three aspects of the novel that he had pointed out: the love story, the adventure story, and Jordan's willingness to die for a cause. The anthology was respectfully but not enthusiastically received. Herbert Gorman, in a lead article in *The New York Times Book Review,* found it "always impressive, sometimes frightening, and occasionally almost unbearably touching." The narratives relating to the present war seemed far more frank and truthful than those that dealt with the First World War, which seemed to Gorman a notable gain. Vincent McHugh, writing in *The New Yorker,* criticized Hemingway's choice of work by professional writers as over against the "plain words of ordinary soldiers" which might have been gathered from unpublished letters and diaries. The preface irked several reviewers. Howard Mumford Jones found its air of self-righteousness intolerable and said that the contents of the book had been unwisely chosen to support Hemingway's continuing obsession with death and "how to die." The military analyst, Walter Millis, described the preface as "angry, chaotic, rambling, and pointless."

Ernest had now made up his mind to relinquish his directorship of the Crook Factory. He told Bob Joyce that "a real pro" was needed to receive and correlate the reports of the clandestine operatives. His failure to find a Hollywood job for Gustavo Durán had lately set him dreaming about the possibility of bringing him to work in Cuba. Joyce cleared the matter with Braden and Briggs and then wrote a secret letter to the State Department. Durán was vacationing in New Hampshire when the project was broached to him. Although it would mean a temporary separation from his wife, she urged him to accept. Naturalization proceedings were set in motion. He became an American citizen on November 3rd, was issued a passport on the 9th, and on the 12th flew to Havana.

Despite his pleasure at being reunited with Hemingway, who greeted him at the airport with a bear hug, Gustavo was less than eager to command the counterespionage operation. He was unmoved by the more melodramatic aspects of cloak-and-swordsmanship, and thought it merely childish when Ernest insisted that he keep a loaded revolver under the pile of clean shirts in the dresser beside his bed in the guesthouse. Reading through the first batch of reports from Ernest's operatives, he found nothing which he thought would seriously inconvenience foreign spies, and was distinctly ill at ease in the role which Ernest had brought him to fill.

Martha had now returned to the Finca for what Ernest ironically called "a spot of domesticity" after her travels through the jungles of Surinam and Manhattan. She was much preoccupied with finding enough quiet to carry on with her writing, and did not approve of Gustavo's decision to bring his wife to Cuba. For once, Ernest agreed. On the morning of Bonte's arrival he drove Gustavo to the airport, but he had neither washed nor shaved for the day, and Bonte was hurt and puzzled by the grubbiness of her reception. All of Ernest's former affection was gone—replaced by a kind of harshness which she found mysterious in one who had danced with her at the Stork Club and praised her husband's heroism in Spain.

Two other incidents widened the breach. A favorite cat disappeared from the Finca and Ernest feared that the dogs in the village had killed it. He blamed the distraught household servants for their carelessness and told Bonte of an occasion when he had intentionally "gut-shot" a peasant's cur for having torn one of his cats to pieces. It had taken the dog three days to die and Ernest seemed to be asking Bonte's approval of his action. Instead she burst into tears and called it a monstrous piece of cruelty. Her rapport with Ernest was never the same again. The second incident might have been comic except for its consequences. The Duráns were returning to the Finca after a long evening at a dance with friends from the Embassy when the driver of the car awakened Martha by inadvertently honking his horn under the window of her room. She had to take sleeping pills and could not work well that day. Ernest was again upset. "I don't know who your friends were," he told Gustavo, "but if I'd had a gun I would have shot them." This was the final blow. The Duráns left that morning for the Ambos Mundos Hotel, followed at an interval by a propitiatory bouquet of roses from Martha to Bonte.

At the Embassy, however, Gustavo was an immediate success. He was "personable, articulate in three languages, with an attractive wife," and Old World *hidalgo* manners. The Duráns throve in Havana society, while Gustavo's natural and acquired skills in speechwriting and the handling of people made him extremely useful to Ambassador Braden and Ellis Briggs. Caught up in this network of responsibilities, he grew even less happy with his Crook Factory assignment and the time soon arrived when he declined a duty which Hemingway believed he should have accepted. At an Embassy luncheon with Briggs and Joyce, Ernest attacked Gustavo "with all the savagery of which he was capable. Gustavo took that bitter tongue-lashing, turning first red and then white." It was an attack like those that Ernest had unleashed on Donald Ogden Stewart, John Dos Passos, and Archibald MacLeish on occasions in the past—so harsh and extreme as to end all possibility of continuing friendship. After Durán had left the room, Ernest asked Briggs whether he had borne down too hard. When Briggs said yes, Ernest merely shrugged. He soon began to spread the story that his former war hero had gone soft, an accusation quite contrary to fact, yet precisely in line with other episodes when Ernest's black rage overcame his judgment.

Ernest's domestic affairs were showing signs of strain. He liked to refer in these days to the great unending battle between men and women, and it was clear to the Hemingways' friends that such a battle had been joined within the walls of the Finca. They knew that Ernest could not have been easy to keep house for and that, as one of them put it, "Martha's talent was often at odds with Ernest's genius." His hours were unpredictable; his associates were innumerable, noisy, and often unwashed; his personal untidiness was more than matched by a "ghastly collection of in-bred cats" which roamed the Finca's interior at will and left their filth in odd corners. "It was fun to be a guest there," said Ellis Briggs, "and Ernest could be the kindest and most considerate of hosts, but it must have been undiluted hell to try to have any organized life with him."

Martha was convinced, after five years' association with him, that his egotism often carried him far beyond the call of genius. Her travels of the summer and fall had been undertaken in part to resist his evident determination to own her completely. He was full of self-dramatization, much given to lying to her about his adventures, and almost neurotic in his conviction that life was stale and weary without manufactured glamour. One night in Havana he scolded her publicly for lack of generosity in Christmas gifts to the Finca servants, and then drove the Lincoln home alone, leaving her to fend for herself. On another evening, when she insisted on driving because he had been drinking, he slapped her with the back of his hand. She braked his well-loved Lincoln to a safe ten miles an hour and deliberately drove it through a ditch and into a tree, leaving him there and walking back home.

The *Pilar's* patrols were now beginning to seem more than ever like an amateur enterprise, with ample armament and manpower and nothing at all to sink. One blustery day late in the year, Jane Joyce and Martha were allowed on board to make what was described as a practice run. Except for the rough water, which soon turned the women queasy, this little voyage had a somewhat bathetic air. The destination was a buoy well out in the Gulf Stream where the crew was to practice grenade throwing and the machine guns were to be fired. The *Pilar* circled the buoy several times while Ibarlucia hurled grenades. Among the whitecaps their explosions were scarcely visible. Winston Guest complained to Mrs. Joyce about the failure of his repeated attempts to enlist in the armed services, and quoted some poetry of his own composition. The appearance of a dilapidated British freighter put an end to the practice session, and the *Pilar* pitched and rolled through the teeth of a norther back to her home port of Cojimar.

The accusation of amateurism was also lodged against the Crook Factory, which was still vaguely in operation. Rivalries among the various intelligence services in Cuba were making coordination of their efforts ever more difficult for Bob Joyce, whom the Ambassador had charged with this duty. To meet this and similar problems elsewhere in Latin America, President Roosevelt ordered the entire counterespionage organization transferred to the Federal Bureau of Investigation. The sixteen special FBI agents assigned to Havana were scornful of the slapdash methods of the Crook Factory. Ernest angrily called them "Franco's Iron Cavalry," on his personal theory that since some of them came of Irish Catholic ancestry they were therefore susceptible to Fascist influence. One of them, as it turned out, had indeed been in Spain as a newspaperman assigned to the Rebel side. Ernest complained to Joyce, who interceded with the Ambassador. The man in question was recalled to Washington by his superiors and Ernest reveled in his victory. But the Crook Factory was finished. The faithful operatives were disbanded and the curtain was rung down on Hemingway's earliest contribution to the American war effort.

55. DANGLING MAN

MARTHA believed from the bottom of her heart that Ernest should go to the wars. She had refused to take the Crook Factory seriously, and now enraged him by suggesting that the *Pilar's* Q-boat patrols were only an excuse to get rationed gasoline so that he and Winston Guest could go on fishing while the rest of the civilized world fought, suffered, and died. Young Mayito Menocal was present at some of the arguments on this subject. He was a grandson of the general who had been President of Cuba during and after the First World War, and the son of Ernest's close friend. In January, 1942, he had been expelled from Cornell University and believed that his father regarded him as "a worthless character." Ernest received him as a member of the Finca family—he was just Bumby's age—and consoled him by saying that he, too, had once been rejected by his parents as "a worthless." During the boy's temporary visits to the Finca, he was an unwilling witness to some of the "terrible fights" between Martha and Ernest. This embarrassed him so much that he formed the habit of waiting down by the swimming pool until the fireworks had died out.

One result of Ernest's recurrent quarrels with Marty was his return to serious drinking. He could often be found at the Floridita while the tall daiquiris came and went in seemingly inexhaustible supply. He was ready to pay the check for almost anyone with fresh war news from Europe, where he half believed that he should go, though he dangled uncertainly as to when, where, and for what purpose. His behavior showed a strong strain of self-aggrandizement, coupled with the most preposterous lies. He began treating his close friends like members of the press or the reading public, as if they could somehow help to perpetuate the Hemingway legend for practical business purposes. At first they were surprised and even dismayed, not knowing that truth stretching had been among his leading avocations since boyhood. They noticed that he seldom lied when he was sober, and they were convinced that he would never lie about really serious subjects. Young Mayito eventually excused him on the grounds that he was a professional writer of fiction, a liar by trade: there was no reason to expect him "to turn his gift of invention off and on like a faucet" merely because he was among close friends.

Among the other signs of change that they thought they noticed was Ernest's increasing pleasure in assuming the role of Papa. This again had been going on for years. His children called him Papa and even Marty, who was not much given to flattery, sometimes half-humorously spoke of "Poppa." But it was the social extension of the term that bothered Mayito. Ernest reveled in Winston Guest's admiration and secretly called him "the ideal subaltern." He was so well-disciplined, said Ernest, that if he said, "Wolfie, jump out of this airplane; I know you have no parachute but one will be provided on the way down," Wolfie would merely say, "Yes, Papa," and go diving through the door. "Yes, Papa" was a phrase widely used among the members of the Club de Cazadores, and soon spread from there to his favorite bars in Havana. Mayito and other Cubans continued to call him Ernesto. "Yes, Papa" suggested a subservience which they thought was bad for Ernest. It brought out the less admirable traits in his character, not least his curious liking for obsequious behavior among those who basked in his ambience.

Marty's refusal to knuckle under puzzled and hurt him. "Ernest, you're dirty," she told him once aboard the *Pilar*. "Why don't you take a bath more often?" She aroused his anger by letting him make elaborate plans for long fishing trips "only to hire a car and return to the Finca from the first port they touched." He could not understand why she was unwilling "to tag along and like it," as Hadley and Pauline had usually done. Even Pauline had changed. He began to complain that she had been behaving "really wickedly" whenever he wanted to see Patrick and Gigi. The alimony payments irked him all the more in the light of her family's wealth. He said that he admired Colonel Sweeny's way with women. If they caused him any trouble, he gave them "the old tone of command." Any man who allowed himself to suffer from women, said Ernest, had a disease as incurable as cancer. He cited Fitzgerald and Evan Shipman as instances of men who had married "sick wives." It was being sick that made them so mean, said he, and it was because they were sick that they couldn't be handled as they should have been. According to his theories, the first great gift for a man was to be healthy. The second, almost equally important, was to fall in with healthy women. A man could always trade in one healthy woman for another—the mistake was to start with a sick one. Pauline had been "a hell of a fine girl" before she turned sour. Perhaps, he thought, a man ought to shoot any woman he planned to leave, even if it got him hanged. A less drastic solution would be to "get so" that no one could hurt you. But by that time, as a rule, you were dead.

Marty continued to harp on Ernest's European obligations. His own view, as in 1936, was that there would be plenty of war to go to for a long time, and that there was no special hurry. Still she persisted. What had happened to his patriotic pride? Everyone else was getting into it. Max Perkins's letters were full of news about the military activities of Ernest's friends, among others John Herrmann, Evan Shipman, and Colonel Thomason. Bumby had left Dartmouth College for Officer's Candidate School, and would soon be sent overseas. Yet Ernest still lingered on at the Finca, reluctant to leave the "good mob" aboard the *Pilar,* the excellent home cooking, the Capehart record player, the brood of beloved cats, the tennis court and swimming pool, the quail and wild guinea hens, the bass fishing in a nearby stream, the pigeon shooting at the Club de Cazadores, and not least the parade of tall daiquiris at the Floridita.

Archie MacLeish wrote out of the blue to ask Ernest's opinion of the recent activities of Ezra Pound, who had taken to broadcasting his eccentric economic theories from Mussolini's radio stations in Fascist Italy. Ernest replied that Ezra was obviously crazy, though he might eventually be brought to trial as a traitor. He probably should have shot himself after the publication of Canto Number Twelve. As for himself, said Ernest, he had decided not to worry about such matters. Instead he would go on doing his duty with the patrols aboard the *Pilar*. He told Archie that he was glad to be friends with him again. He still regretted the "self-righteous bastardry" of his Spanish Civil War period, when he had managed to alienate all the old pals that he had failed to alienate during his "son-of-a-bitching" epoch of 1934. He had missed them all "like hell" ever since, including Dos Passos as he had used to be before the Loyalists shot his skilled but worthless translator Robles.

He told MacLeish that he would like to live long enough to write one more novel. In the past seventeen years he had managed to embody four hard-won ideas, one to a book. Promiscuity-no-solution was the theme of *The Sun Also Rises*. A passage from Marlowe's *The Jew of Malta* was the "idea" in *A Farewell to Arms*. Morgan's dying words about "one man alone" summed up the point of *To Have and Have Not*. In *For Whom the Bell Tolls,* it was "no man is an island." Since 1940, said he, he had discovered two or three fresh ideas, though he did not name them. One of them might some day find its way into a new novel. But he did nothing to bring the book to birth, saying that nobody could write anything good in wartime unless he was a superman.

The world premiere of Paramount's *For Whom the Bell Tolls* took place in New York on July 10th. Two and a half years had gone by since Ernest had signed the contract. Only recently he had been attributing the long delay to Hollywood's fear of General Franco. Perkins went to see the film and was greatly impressed, though he told Ernest that he preferred the performances of Katina Paxinou as Pilar and Akim Tamiroff as Pablo to those of Ingrid Bergman and Gary Cooper. On his return to Cuba after fifty-eight days at sea, Ernest read Max's report and found it depressing. Hollywood, said he, had flunked again, as they had done with *A Farewell to Arms*. He said that he hoped he would never be compelled to see the damned film.

He was somewhat offhanded in his reaction to the news that his old friend Harold Stearns was being treated for terminal cancer of the throat. He said that Harold had had so many fatal illnesses that it was hard to believe in this one. No man's stomach could take what Harold had given his in the old days in Paris. In spite of occasional warnings to the contrary, Ernest still believed that his own insides were impervious to corrosion. As young Mayito observed, he could go aboard the *Pilar* after a bout of heavy drinking, leave off liquor for a few days, and become his normal self once more. On the other hand, he often drank at sea. Once he stood on the flying bridge, steering through a tremendous thunderstorm and swaying, not with the motion of the boat but from the effects of tequila, which he called "steering liquor" and kept in a rack beside the wheel. Drunk or sober, he took pride in steering for hours on end. It was another instance of his carefully cultivated stoicism.

He celebrated his forty-fourth birthday with a shooting match at the Club de Cazadores, winning it by acclamation. The party shifted at sundown to the Finca, where a whole pig was roasting, a birthday gift from the fishermen at Cojimar. They all drank *definitivos* and sat at their ease singing folksongs around a table under the great ceiba tree. When the pig was brought in, Don Andrés Untzaín asked the blessing and the jai-alai players pelted one another with hard rolls. For a while Ernest watched paternalistically. Then he called a halt by saying that on his birthday no one was allowed to throw rolls until dessert.

Martha had now finished her novel. She was determined to see it through a final revision in New York and then to go to England as a war correspondent for *Collier's*. With Patrick and Gigi returning to school and Ernest leaving for what he expected to be a three-month cruise on the *Pilar*, she saw no reason to stay on at the Finca, alone with the servants and harassed by her longing to be where the fighting was. She got away at last on October 25th, traveling by way of Lisbon, and arrived in London early in November.

With Martha and his sons away, Ernest complained that the large and empty Finca was lonelier than limbo. He had trained the cats Boise and Uncle Wolfer to take stations on the pillars of the front porch like lions in a circus. Of the last six shoots at the Club de Cazadores he had won five, and he was betting on Ermua in all the jai-alai games. Bob Joyce had left the Embassy to join the OSS, and there had also been some changes in the crew of the *Pilar*, though Wolfie Guest, Paxtchi, Sinbad, and Gregorio remained among the regulars. Ernest congratulated Patrick on the success of his third-string football team at Canterbury. Evidently, said he, the Mouse was carrying on the great pigskin tradition of Papa, who had been known at Oak Park High as Droopy-Drawers, the Sagging All-American, and of Bumby, The Spavined Mule of the Hudson at Storm King School. Behind them all stood the stalwart figure of Clarence E. Hemingway, who could run both ways with equal ease while carrying the ball, and was always accompanied by a teammate with a compass to tell him which goal line to cross.

Wild north winds made navigation difficult through much of November. On the 9th the *Pilar* managed to rescue Thorwald Sánchez's schooner, which had broken her moorings with no one aboard and was drifting onto the rocks. The servant Juan from the Finca brought the mail to Bahía Honda, and Ernest, the wind whipping his beard, sat down in the cockpit to reply to Patrick's letters, wearing two sweaters and a coat and blowing on his fingers to keep them warm. It was Old Taylor's Hot Toddy weather, said he, and the icy surf was breaking over the bar all across the harbor entrance. The cats at the Finca were probably cold, too, and if the hard weather held he would go home to see them. He missed the cats and his younger kids. It was no use to miss Marty and Bumby because they were too far away.

Christmas was less fun than usual in spite of brief visits from Patrick and Gregory. Bumby was gone overseas in command of a platoon of Negro military police. Although Ernest was immensely proud of his son's military achievement to date, he bitterly complained to Ellis Briggs that Bumby had been given a policeman's assignment. He was the first soldier in the family since Abe Lincoln's time but also the only Hemingway in three generations to be on that side of the law. Martha's absence continued to gnaw away at his sense of injustice. He complained that he was "sick-lonely" without her, and told Hadley that on his return from difficult cruises he had only his cats and dogs for companionship. He had engaged several secretaries, but none of them had lasted long, and his correspondence piled up unanswered in two large wooden boxes. Housekeeping at the Finca had deteriorated. Stumbling home with fatigue after weeks on the water, he drank a few drinks, listened to records on the Capehart player, and then fell asleep on the floor while the cats hunted mice in his luxuriant beard. Such, at any rate, was the self-portrait he painted to engage Hadley's sympathy as the long year drew to an end.

Whatever his complaints, neither his reputation nor his income had suffered much in 1943. *For Whom the Bell Tolls* had now sold 785,000 copies in the United States, and in England another 100,000—more than any other American novel of recent years except *Gone With the Wind*. On the other hand, he had written nothing since the introduction to *Men at War* in August, 1942. He assured Perkins that he was not to be thought of as either a rummy or a problem writer run dry. Sometimes the urge to write was so strong that it was worse than being in jail. His consolation was that all these vital new experiences were going to give him plenty to write about after the war was over. Then he proposed to cool out and start biting on the nail.

CHAPTER 9

Another War

56. *PURSUIT TO LONDON*

IN the bars of Havana during the early months of 1944, Ernest took to announcing that he would soon saddle his horse and ride off in pursuit of Martha. Since he had married her as a wife and not as a distant ideal, he had almost resolved to follow her across the Atlantic, "kick her ass good," and tell her that she must either stay home or go to military school. He complained that since 1941 he had worked extremely hard and written nothing, that he had had no wife since September 1943, and that the machinations of the politicians kept him continuously angry, like a fire under a boiler. Amid all this bluster, he spoke now and then of going to New York to arrange for passage across the Atlantic. Yet he did not seem to be in any great hurry to depart. On the last day of January, he wrote his wife that he still had no special interest in Europe. He merely felt like an old horse being saddled for the jumps by an unscrupulous owner.

Martha flew home in March to take decisive action. She felt that Ernest had postponed his departure for the wars long enough and that the time had come to blast him loose from Cuba. She had been talking with Roald Dahl, Assistant Air Attaché at the British Embassy in Washington. Dahl said that it was impossible to obtain air passage for people not engaged in priority war business. But the Air Ministry in London would allocate Ernest a plane seat if he would undertake to report on the heroic activities of the Royal Air Force in some one of the American magazines. When Ernest agreed to this proposition, a contract was quickly arranged with *Collier's* magazine, and the Hemingways set off for New York to await passage.

Ernest enjoyed himself in his customary New York fashion. Dahl spent an evening at the Hotel Gladstone with the Hemingways and the boxing coach George Brown. They spooned caviar from a two-kilo tin and drank champagne. Ellis Briggs also saw him briefly, noticing that "his luggage consisted of a toothbrush and comb, no change of clothing, but innumerable two-ounce bottles of Angostura bitters, Ernest having heard somewhere that his

British friends could no longer obtain bitters because of submarine depredations in the Caribbean." Vincent Sheean, who had shared his Ebro adventures in 1938 and was now in New York on a week's leave from the Army Air Force, spent many hours in his company. Ernest spoke of John Steinbeck, who had praised "The Butterfly and the Tank" story in 1939. Sheean and his wife obligingly brought them together for dinner under the James Thurber murals in Tim Costello's bar-restaurant on Third Avenue. Mrs. Steinbeck was also present, and the party was later joined by John Hersey. Standing at the bar in the front room was John O'Hara. He had brought along his walking stick, a gift from Steinbeck, an excellent piece of blackthorn, though very old and rather brittle. On seeing the cane, Ernest bet O'Hara fifty dollars that he could break it over his own head. O'Hara took the bet and Ernest, holding the stick by both ends, pulled it down against his skull until it cracked. He threw the pieces aside with a scornful comment. It was no great achievement, though he behaved as if he thought it was. O'Hara lost fifty dollars as well as the cane. Steinbeck was disgusted.

Martha shipped out on May 13 as the only passenger aboard a ship with a cargo of dynamite. Ernest stayed on, waiting for plane space. On Sunday the 14th, which happened to be Mother's Day, he telephoned Dawn Powell the novelist and invited himself to breakfast at her apartment on East Ninth Street. He arrived bearing gifts, a bottle of Scotch and a jar of Bahamian mustard. Esther Chambers, another old friend from his Key West days, was also of the party. When Esther left about noon, Ernest was stretched out on the sofa, apparently immovable. They nibbled at ham sandwiches and cheese ("and all our friends," said Dawn) and drank occasional highballs until six o'clock. Dawn's cat took to hiding behind a curtain and peering out at the large, bushbearded interloper. She said, laughing, that the beast looked and acted like a house detective. Ernest scolded her. "Never laugh at a cat," he said firmly, bobbing his head for emphasis. "Dogs like it because they want to be pals with you. Cats don't want to be pals; they must be kings and queens." He said that he was still angry at Martha for having left the Finca without troubling to say good-bye to her own special cat. In midafternoon, Dawn suddenly remembered Mother's Day, and telephoned a telegram to her mother-in-law. "Jesus," said Ernest, sitting up, "is it Mother's Day? Then I'll have to send the old bitch a wire, too."

The flight orders came through for May 17. Ernest was traveling light, with only a valpack, a musette bag, and two large flasks. His companions included the actress Gertrude Lawrence, who was carrying a dozen fresh eggs for her English friends, and a group of naval personnel: Rear Admiral Leland Lovette, in charge of public relations for the Navy; his aide, William Van Dusen; Lt. Henry W. R. North, a nephew of the Ringling Brothers and a graduate of Yale; and Lt. (j.g.) Michael Burke, a former All-American football star from the University of Pennsylvania. North and Burke were in the OSS and expected to parachute into France. The Navy men all wore mufti out of deference to the neutrality of Eire, where they were to change planes. The takeoff was preceded by dinner at the 21 Club. During the flight in the Pan American boat-plane, all of Gerty's eggs were smashed, staining her skirt and eliciting bawdy comments. Van Dusen was carrying a quantity of buckwheat flour. Ernest proposed that they use it on some future occasion for a pancake breakfast at the Hotel Dorchester, where he was going to stay. When the plane put down at last on the River Shannon, most of the passengers sat down to a full Irish breakfast at Foynes, but Ernest, who often skipped breakfast, treated North and Burke to a "liquid repast" before the connecting flight to London.

It was Ernest's first visit to the city which he persisted in calling "dear old London town." Since he came of English stock on both sides, he took his arrival as a homecoming of sorts. After nearly five years of war, the Dorchester, commonly called "The Dorch," still managed to keep its sense of luxurious comfort. Trees were in fresh leaf in Hyde Park across the way from Park Lane, and there was a pleasant smell of English greensward in the air. Ernest advised the Air Ministry that he wished to accompany some of the pilots on their missions to the Continent. George Houghton, who was then in charge of some three hundred correspondents accredited to the RAF, was asked to visit Hemingway personally at his hotel and to arrange a suitable program. He arrived at the Dorchester late one morning with a young Flight Lieutenant, John Macadam, who was to serve as Ernest's conducting officer. They knocked on the great man's door for some minutes before a gruff voice invited them in. Ernest was still in bed, but "insisted on getting up, despite the fact that he was completely naked, because, as he said, he made it a point always to stand at attention when speaking with an officer who had gold braid on his hat." He telephoned for drinks, and they began to plan his RAF program.

The Allied invasion of the Continent was said to be coming any day now. In the period of waiting, Ernest's room at the Dorchester became a mecca for old friends and new associates. Martha was still somewhere on the Atlantic but London was full of girls, in and out of uniform. Ernest's only complaint was that his huge beard scared them away. Fred Spiegel appeared, who had driven ambulances with him in Italy twenty-six springs ago. Gregory Clark of the Toronto *Star* dropped in for a visit. Ira Wolfert, correspondent for the North American Newspaper Alliance, was often in Ernest's company. Lewis Galantière, the first friend he had made in Paris in December, 1921, came in one morning to find a champagne party in progress with Ernest as host. One of the guests was Lael Tucker Wertenbaker, whose husband Charles was head of the London Bureau of *Time, Life* and *Fortune*. Bob Capa, the photographer, was a frequent visitor, along with an attractive girl with whom he occupied a penthouse in Belgrave Square. So was Ernest's younger brother Leicester, who belonged to a documentary film unit. One of the other privates in his unit was William Saroyan, who had traded insults with Ernest in 1935. Although they met and chatted briefly at a party given by the literary critic

Cyril Connolly, Saroyan was not among the courtiers who flowed in and out of Hemingway's room, with its wide foyer, tiled bath, rug-sized bath towels, and its air of hospitality unlimited.

Shortly after his arrival in London, Ernest met a diminutive blonde from northern Minnesota. Her name was Mary Welsh and she had just turned thirty-six. During the Spanish Civil War, after five years on the *Chicago Daily News,* she had come to England to work as a feature writer for Lord Beaverbrook's *Daily Express.* She was married to Noel Monks, an Australian reporter for the *Daily Mail.* At the time of the Blitz in 1940, she had transferred to the London Bureau of *Time, Life,* and *Fortune.* Except for an interlude in New York in 1942, she had been in London throughout the war. She lived in a penthouse apartment at 31 Grosvenor Street, near the American Embassy and the Dorchester Hotel. During Noel's frequent absences on assignment, she worked on political and economic studies which served as background for articles in all three of the Luce magazines. It seemed to her that economics and politics were far closer to the realities of the world than fiction and poetry.

Her manner of life in the early months of 1944 is suggested by entries in her diary. January 1: "Home early by myself. Lonely for Noel—and was the only person in the office today—everybody much hung over. Intended going dancing with Bill—but we stayed home instead and talked about Massillon, Ohio, and how people aren't as they think they are. . . . Pleasant and quiet." January 3: "Bought gorgeous gold earrings and felt ashamed by my extravagance. Worked at home." January 31: "Made my first lemon pie and it was divine." February 14: "The raids are getting me down." February 29: "Noel seems so far away. [Irwin] Shaw is entertaining—says I'll manage all right if I stay in Europe." May 21: "To Lucy and Alan [Moorehead's] with Noel for lunch. . . . Boys [the invasion armada] expect to leave London this week." May 22: "Noel anticipates a Nazi invasion of Eire—airborne. . . . Walked home alone through the [Green] Park, in my new Jaegmar suit, feeling I've had the best of my life and made little of it—no children, . . . and feeling at times a stranger to Noel."

Along with thousands of others, she had read of Hemingway's arrival. It meant little enough to her until the week following her Sunday lunch with the Mooreheads. One noonday she put on a suit and a sweater and went to lunch with Irwin Shaw at the White Tower in Soho, a restaurant much frequented by military and foreign press personnel. Shaw belonged to the same documentary film unit as Ernest's brother Leicester. When Mary slipped out of her suit jacket in the overwarm and crowded restaurant, Shaw whistled softly and remarked that her appearance in the sweater would bring men round their table like bees to a queen. One of those who stopped and stood looking down admiringly was the heavily bearded Hemingway. Shaw made the introduction, and Ernest soon began to behave like a predatory swain. He was more than a little concerned with the increasing thinness of his hair.

One day Roald Dahl dropped in to see him at the Dorchester. He was busy with an eyedropper and a bottle of hair-growing lotion.

"Why the eyedropper, Ernest?"

"To get the stuff through the hair and onto the scalp."

"But you don't have much hair to get through."

"I have enough," said Ernest, firmly.

Everyone wanted to give him a party. One day there was a phone call from Jimmy Charters, the little Cockney bartender whom he had known in Paris. Nina Hamnett the painter, presiding queen of a Soho pub called Fitzroy's, had read that Ernest was in town and urged Jimmy to organize a reunion of the old Montparnasse crowd, with Ernest as guest of honor. The date was set for Friday the 26th at the Bricklayers' Arms. He had already accepted another invitation for the evening of the 24th. Capa and his girl were laying it on in their Belgrave Square apartment. She had saved up ten bottles of Scotch and eight of gin. Capa added a case of champagne, soaked some peaches in brandy, and scoured the West End for party food.

Ernest spent most of the evening in a corner, talking to Peter Gorer, a tall, hawk-nosed doctor from Guy's Hospital, and his wife, a blond German refugee who spoke little English. He proudly showed them a photostat of a testimonial letter from Ambassador Spruille Braden. It thanked Hemingway and his crew for valuable and hazardous operations in two years at sea. That, said Ernest, explained his beard. Overexposure to the sun on the water had given him a benign skin cancer. Dr. Gorer, a cancer specialist, found the yarn highly dubious. Towards ten o'clock, Ernest spotted a stalwart, tow-haired man. He was alone and gazing from the window at the slow movements of the barrage balloons, moored like lazy giants above the ancient buildings. Ernest sidled over and introduced himself. The man said he was Bill Walton. He was a journalist with the London Bureau of the Luce magazines, and had once shared a cubicle with Mary Welsh at the home offices in New York. He was wearing the insignia of a paratrooper. He had just completed a rigorous training program with the 82nd Airborne. When the invasion came, he was going to jump into France. Ernest mistook Walton's pensive demeanor for gloom, which he was now calling "black ass." The term was new to Walton. When he denied the affliction, Ernest was visibly pleased.

Sometime after midnight, Ernest led his brother Leicester and Peter Gorer out to Capa's kitchen. "Come on, kid, let's box," said he. "We need some exercise." They set down their drinks and sparred vigorously, large and sweat-soaked in the small room. Afterwards they invited the fragile Dr. Gorer to hit them in their tensed stomach-muscles, a boyish game which had delighted Ernest for years. When Gorer desisted, nursing his fist, others stepped in with their best punches.

The party broke up around three o'clock on the murky morning of the 25th. Dr. Gorer and his wife volunteered to drive Lael Wertenbaker and

Ernest back to the Dorchester. Lael declined, a decision she never regretted. Gorer had been drinking since ten o'clock, and the streets were blacked out. He started the motor and drove down the street, feeling his way as well as he could. They had gone less than half a mile when the car banged head on into a steel water tank. Ernest's head smashed the windshield. His face and beard were a mass of blood from a deep wound in his scalp, and he had to be lifted from the wreckage. The Gorers, though badly cut by broken glass, were able to walk clear. They were all taken to St. George's Hospital at Hyde Park Corner, two blocks from the Hotel Dorchester. Ernest had a severe concussion and both his knees were swelling rapidly from collision with the dashboard. He was conscious but irritable when Leicester reached his side a few hours later. Leicester noticed that beneath the bandages his brown eyes were still lively and that he was eager to read of his latest exploit in all the morning papers. He was soon "tidied up" in surgery and later reported that the doctors had needed two and a half hours to put in fifty-seven stitches. He was left with a huge bandage and a headache that would torture him for months.

Martha's ship now docked at Liverpool. The voyage had been harrowing. Blackout regulations had been strict and smoking forbidden. For two weeks the ship had zigzagged interminably through the gray waters. She sighed with relief as she stepped ashore. Reporters asked for her views about her husband's accident. It was news to her. They explained that it had happened after an all-night party. Ernest was now recovering in the London Clinic. Martha was angry. Such roistering in wartime, though doubtless common, struck her as contemptible. She checked in at the Dorchester and went over to see Ernest. He lay there, huge in the bed, his hands clasped behind his broken head. His beard covered half his chest, and the bandage, like a turban, swathed his forehead. If he had expected compassion, he was disappointed: Martha burst out laughing. He was much hurt. For months thereafter he complained about his wife's "silly inhumanity." When she deplored the partying which had brought him to this pass, and began to deprecate his reputation as a great fighting man, he could only, and rather lamely, repeat the already hoary joke that he had never had a WAC shot out from under him. He later told friends that her sense of humor must have suffered some alarming deterioration, for after the WAC joke she left the room in anger.

In succeeding days Ernest's room at the Clinic attracted many well-wishers, among them Jimmy Charters, whose plans for the Montparnassian reunion had been spoiled by the accident. "He stretched out his hands to welcome me," said Charters, "roaring away his usual greetings as if he had only been scratched. He would not let me dwell on his accident. Instead he forced me to talk of old times in Montparnasse. . . . Fame and fortune had not changed him. . . . He had me laughing like mad before long, and were it not for the bandages, I would have forgotten that he was ill." When they discovered that they had both been born in 1899, Ernest cried, "Jimmy, you and I are getting to be an old pair of so-and-sos," and handed his friend a pile of pound notes as a parting gesture.

North and Burke, the young Navy men with whom he had flown the Atlantic, likewise found him contemptuous of his injuries. He was only worried that his condition might prevent his making the invasion trip, which was said to be close. Again, as with Charters, he turned the conversation quickly away from his accident and spoke of his skill in commandeering London taxis. Because of his beard and his build, said he, he so much resembled the immortal cricket-hero, W. C. Grace, that cabbies appeared as if by magic to do his bidding. Burke had brought along a half-bottle of Scotch as a get-well present only to find that Ernest was already amply supplied. "So," said Burke, "he took my half bottle and gave me a full bottle in exchange. A generous friend." He was generous also in the dissemination of fatherly advice to all young warriors. A young British paratrooper was introduced and asked him for advice about jumping into occupied France. "Just keep your bowels open," said Ernest heartily, "and remember there's some corner of a foreign field that is forever England."

He left the London Clinic on May 29th. Though forbidden alcohol because of the concussion, he soon began drinking whiskey again, and on the first of June was up and dressed when Leicester reached the hotel in the morning. His head was throbbing so loudly that he thought it must be audible throughout the room. But he insisted on a walk outdoors. He wanted to see Houghton and Macadam about his postponed flights with the RAF. Once in motion, he was hard to stop. Wishing to open a checking account in Barclay's Bank, he asked North and Burke to go along in Navy field dress and side arms, explaining that the pompous bank manager would be impressed by such stalwart bodyguards. Afterwards he entertained his friends at a pub called Frisco's, run by an American Negro whom he had known in Paris. Frisco had a scratchy collection of American jazz records and excellent whiskey. Ernest paid the bill with the first cheque drawn on his new Barclay account, and then turned to the organization of Hemingstein's Bearded Junior Commandos, with himself as leader and North and Burke as his staff, "drilling" them in a language which he identified as Turkish.

His odd combination of benignity, gaiety, and boorishness did not make him universally popular during these early weeks in London. Some of his acquaintances believed that he was acting a part. Although he had immense charm when he chose to use it, and often when he did not, there were other occasions when he behaved childishly. To Charles Wertenbaker, an *aficionado* of twenty years' standing, he was very possessive about bulls and bullfighting, as if he had staked out a personal claim which others could invade at their peril. The poet John Pudney, an RAF Public Relations officer, found his behavior curiously offensive. "To me," said Pudney, "he was a fellow obsessed with playing the part of Ernest Hemingway and 'hamming' it to boot:

a sentimental nineteenth-century actor called upon to act the part of a twenti-
eth-century tough guy. Set beside . . . a crowd of young men who walked
so modestly and stylishly with Death, he seemed a bizarre cardboard figure."

His boorish behavior was most noticeable in his dealings with Martha,
whom he continued to blame for her "cruel neglect" since the time of his
accident. Ira Wolfert, the NANA correspondent, was an unwilling witness
to one of Ernest's acts of vengeance, in which Ernest telephoned Martha,
whose room was on the floor above, and asked her to dinner. Just before
her arrival he went into the bathroom and undressed. When she appeared at
the door, he made as if to attack her. She withdrew in angry tears. Wolfert
scolded Ernest, who telephoned to apologize. After some persuasion, Martha
agreed to go to dinner if they would call for her at her room. They were
headed in that direction when they met Mary Welsh in the corridor. Ernest
at once commandeered Mary, leaving Wolfert to take Martha to dinner.

57. CROSS-CHANNEL OPERATIONS

ERNEST'S broken head postponed his planned tour of duty as observer with
the Royal Air Force. Well before D-Day, however, he was issued a blue uniform with a shoulder flash marked "Correspondent," and a regulation escape
kit containing a map on a silk handkerchief, money, pills, a compass, and
chocolate, enough to last three days in the event of being shot down. He also
met, through John Pudney, a husky six-foot-four Group Captain named Peter
Wykeham Barnes. Wykeham Barnes was a veteran of nearly five years' combat
flying in North Africa, the Middle East, and lately in England, where he was
in command of an attack wing of Mosquitoes based at Gravesend. When they
met again shortly after the accident, Ernest explained his head bandage with
a cock-and-bull story about having stumbled into the Dorchester's ornamental
concrete fountain at dawn after a riotous all-night party at the RAF Club in
Piccadilly.

D-Day was now at hand. On the weekend of June 2nd, along with hundreds
of other war correspondents, Ernest was briefed and borne off to the south
coast where the long-expected invasion flotilla was about to move. On the
drizzly night of June 5, he limped aboard the attack transport *Dorothea L.
Dix.* The commander was a bluff-faced Irishman named W. I. Leahy. Ernest
cornered him at once and asked about the plans for Tuesday morning. Was
this a diversion in force to fool the German defenders while the main Allied
landings took place somewhere else? Or were they really going ashore? Ashore,
said Leahy. During the first half-hour the minefields would be swept clear
and the landing craft would zip in through the newly opened lanes. Ernest
went to inspect the huge nets that were rigged amidships down the sides of
the *Dix.* His knees were still swollen from the accident twelve days before,
and he was worried about having to clamber down. By two in the morning

the huge flotilla was slowly churning through the choppy waters of mid-channel. When the order came to change ships, Leahy took no chances of another accident with Hemingway. He was lowered overside in a bosun's chair and lifted into the stern of a lurching LCVP to be delivered to another transport, the *Empire Anvil,* some distance to the rear. This time he insisted on climbing the net with the others, and by five o'clock, when it was time to enter the landing craft that would take them ashore, he laboriously descended the same ropes.

It was first light now. A northwest wind cut the tops of the billows and hurled the spray aboard. The boat resembled a coffin. Sheets of green water drenched the helmeted troops, packed shoulder to shoulder "like medieval pikemen" in the open hold. From his place in the stern beside Bob Anderson, the commander, Ernest looked back at the silhouettes of cruisers, low on the horizon, and the incredibly delicate maneuverings of the huge battleships, the *Texas* and the *Arkansas,* as they swung broadside to the French coast, hurling salvos from their fourteen-inch guns "like railway trains thrown skyward." Inside his jacket was an old pair of miniature Zeiss binoculars, wrapped in a woolen sock. Spray fogged their lenses, but he watched the shoreline as well as he could.

The nearer they got the more hostile it looked. The long sandy beach with the bluffs behind it was littered with the debris of battle. Two tanks burned fiercely at the edge of the tide. The dead from the first six assault waves lay like bundles as far as the eye could see. The seventh was ashore or going ashore. A pair of German machine guns in a concrete pillbox and a ruined house were laying down a deadly crossfire. A wilderness of iron stakes, hung with contact mines, was still to be negotiated before the ramp could be lowered and the men put ashore. Leahy's prediction had been overoptimistic. The wonder was that six waves of assault boats had already got through the murderous defenses. Aboard Hemingway's LCVP there was much discussion about landmarks, the steeple of the church at Colleville, the line of steep cliffs at the other extreme. But Ernest, drying his lenses with the woolen sock, was sure that this was the place: Fox Green Beach sector of Omaha Beach at 0700, Tuesday, 6 June, 1944.

Destroyers were now running in "almost to the beach and blowing every pill-box out of the ground with their five-inch guns." As Hemingway watched, a three-foot piece of a German defender with an arm attached sailed "high up into the air in the fountaining of one shellburst." Or so he wrote it, adding, in the old Grand Guignol manner of his despatches from Madrid, that it reminded him of a scene from *Petroushka.* Lieutenant Anderson helped rescue the survivors from another landing craft foundered and awash among the mine stakes. A destroyer took on the wounded. "There was no reason for anyone to stay out now," wrote Ernest. "We ran in to a good spot we had picked and put our troops and their TNT and their bazookas and their lieutenant ashore and that was that." That was that for Hemingway, as well.

Anderson raised his ramp, cleared the beach, and roared away to find the transport *Dix* and put Ernest back aboard.

Martha made the Channel crossing on a hospital ship which stood offshore through the night of June 6th taking on wounded. Unlike Ernest, she managed to get ashore, an achievement he never forgave her. On disembarking in England, she met Bill Van Dusen, the Naval A-D-C who had flown the Atlantic with Ernest in May. Bill said that Ernest was already back in London. Martha wrote a little note, which Van Dusen agreed to deliver. She was delighted at his safe return; she would be leaving shortly for Italy on a "hopeless Cook's Tour." But at least she would be seeing some action. "I came to see the war," she said, pointedly, "not live in the Dorchester." The note eventually reached Ernest, who amused himself by annotating it with acidulous marginalia. But Martha, as it turned out, saw him before he saw her note. When she reached the Dorchester to prepare for her Italian journey, Ernest was in her room with a girl. He continued at the Dorchester, receiving visitors, carrying on his courtship of Mary Welsh, and writing the first of his articles for *Collier's*. One day shortly after Martha's departure, Roald Dahl found him alone at his typewriter, finishing a piece about the invasion. Dahl asked to see it. He thought it very bad indeed. "But Ernest," said he, to mask his true opinion, "you've left out that marvelous bit you told me about the expression on the man's face as he tried to get out of a burning tank." "My God," said Ernest, "you don't think I'd give that to *Collier's,* do you?"

June was half over when the Germans opened their buzzbomb campaign. These flying V1 bombs—also known as doodlebugs and robots—were launched from scores of so-called "ski-sites" in France and designed to fall haphazardly and in great numbers all over the southeastern shires and as far north as London. Ernest described them as large metal darts with removable wings and white-hot bungholes. They were capable of carrying a one-ton warhead up to 200 miles at speeds in excess of 400 miles an hour. The noise they made was ugly in the extreme, like "a lorry in low gear followed by a backfiring motorcycle." Ernest had been back in England about ten days when he made the first of his moves to gather material on the Royal Air Force. Their chief weapon against the buzzbombs was a squadron of Typhoons working from an airstrip near Stonehenge on Salisbury Plain. From four in the morning until midnight, the pilots flew endless missions in the attempt to intercept and shoot down the flying bombs. Ernest went down one day to have a look.

He was immediately enthusiastic about the Typhoons, which he mistakenly called Tempests, large gaunt planes that looked as tough as mules, and even more so about the laconic young officers who flew them. The Wing Commander was short and cocky, with a "tough bad tongue" and a good deal of style. One Squadron Leader was a Free Belgian with the hard, dark face of a six-day bicycle racer. The other was a tall, shy-spoken Englishman. He had the purplish-red complexion of one whose face had been burned away and afterwards repaired by skin grafting. Under urging, he described in some detail "how it had been" the first time he succeeded in shooting down a buzz-bomb. "You can't just say exactly where you'll shoot them down," said the Squadron Leader quietly. "They go very fast, you know." Ernest had a burning desire to be accepted as an equal by these young heroes. He later told of early morning visits to the local pubs in their company, and of having stopped at Salisbury Cathedral to pray for the souls of his English ancestors.

He also paid a visit to headquarters of the 98th Squadron, under the command of Wing Commander G. J. C. Paul. This unit consisted of about 25 B-25s, based at Dunsford, eight miles south of Guildford in Surrey and some forty miles in from the coast. He was in the Officers' Mess on the afternoon of June 15 when a V1 passed close to the airfield and exploded not far from the perimeter. On learning what had happened, the correspondents all ran "off like a flash," Ernest among them, to get a close-up view of the damage. They reached the scene in time to have "a thorough look round" and to pick up some bomb fragments. This was strictly forbidden and the local police soon appeared at the office of C. R. Dunlap, commander of the Wing, to report the theft. "Hemingway," said Dunlap, "had just arrived at the bar of the Officers' Mess and had taken up his favorite position when the police came in. As he had either been recognized or accurately described by witnesses, he received first attention. The police took a dim view of the whole proceedings and made no bones about it. Hemingway was quick to appreciate the situation and, looking like a small boy who had been caught with his hand in the cookie jar, went in company with the police to his room to give up the pieces—as in due course did all the other culprits."

Another buzzbomb figured prominently in the long-postponed pancake breakfast, which took place in Ernest's room at the Dorchester on the Sunday morning of June 18th. Bill Van Dusen brought the buckwheat flour and Rear Admiral Lovette provided the bourbon. Among the others in attendance were North and Burke, Hemingstein's Bearded Junior Commandos. North found the pancakes leathery, Burke thought them delicious. But the center of interest lay outside: a nauseous batch of buzzbombs "were sailing up the river to London with some regularity that morning." Ernest calmly described his favorite theory that no one was in danger unless he was being shot at personally. Buddy North, who was peering from the open window, pointed to one that seemed to be headed directly for the room they occupied. But the bomb fell far short of the Dorchester. It had just crossed the Thames when it stopped, wobbled uncertainly, and then went plummeting down upon the famous old Chapel of the Horse Guards near Westminster Abbey. The Chapel was destroyed, with a heavy loss of life among the Sunday morning worshippers. The pancakes cooled in their syrup while North and Burke raced down through the Green Park to offer their services in getting out the survivors. The others returned to Admiral Lovette's whiskey.

British intelligence had long known of the buzzbomb launching platforms. In the past six months, the RAF had flown 4,710 sorties against these targets.

Their code name was "No-Ball," a term applied both to the platforms and "their storage and manufacturing centres." Among the pilots, they were known as ski-sites. Since they were heavily protected by antiaircraft guns, 41 aircraft had been shot down and more than 400 others variously damaged. The planes used by the RAF for this work were Mitchell twin-engine medium bombers. Unlike the Typhoon interceptors, they were capable of carrying observers. Late in June, Ernest appeared once again at the headquarters of the 98th Squadron at Dunsford and asked permission to go along on one of the strikes.

The chosen day was clear, with good visibility. Ernest wore his steel-rimmed glasses and buckled the chin strap of his helmet behind his beard. In his RAF uniform, leather jacket, and parachute equipment, he looked like a giant as he beamed down at Wing Commander Alan Lynn of the 139th. After the publicity pictures, he climbed into the copilot's seat beside Lynn. The bombardier-navigator was a Hollander named C. Waardenburg Kees, whose disembodied voice kept up a steady barrage of directives over the intercom. About midday they took off in two "boxes" of six planes apiece. In less than five minutes they had left the land behind. The Channel appeared far below, a waste of gray-blue water, wrinkled like elephant hide. Then they were suddenly close to the target area, a patch of woods in a mosaic of tilled fields at Drancourt. Hundreds of bomb craters pockmarked the ground on all sides of the ski-site. Flak burst blackly all around them as they leveled out for the run. When the bay of another Mitchell flapped open and the bombs dropped clear, Ernest thought of a great cat "having eight long metallic kittens in a hurry." The voice of Kees intoned steadily: "Bombing, bombing, bombing . . ." Then all six planes heeled over in a wide-sweeping evasive arc and scurried back to Dunsford as fast as they had come. Ernest was disappointed: everything had happened too fast. He asked Lynn if they could return to the target area so that he could see what had happened. Lynn refused. The flak was too heavy and the risk too great. He had already heard in his headphones that they had lost the leading plane in the second box.

Ernest made no more flights until about ten days after his adventure in the Mitchell. He later reported that an RAF flight surgeon had grounded him because of his broken head. "Laddy," said the doctor, "you can have one more week. But I ought to be shot for giving it to you." In the interim he occupied his time by writing a poem to Mary Welsh. Their love affair was proceeding to his complete satisfaction, and he said that he wanted to prove to her that his head was good enough to write with, if not to fly with.

The poem was called "To Mary in London." Like his other verse of this period, it was a curious blend of complaint and longing, of sentimentality and tough resolution, accomplished in flat lines of prosaic free verse. What structure it had depended on a contrast between his former life in Cuba and his new life in London. After two years of submarine hunting, he had come to this strange foreign city, "shy from too long on the water." He thought of the *Pilar*, riding at anchor far away, her crew dispersed, her armament returned to the proper authorities. He remembered the long nights when he had steered on the flying bridge, coursing through tropical seas, listening to the crackle of the static in his headphones. He mentioned the day they sighted the enemy submarine and set the course that would enable them to close with her. In that hour they were all "dry-mouthed but happy," while Wolfie Guest, "the muscles jumping in his cheeks," stood there saying, "Papa, it's all right with me. Don't worry for a moment, Papa. It's all right with me." In London, however, he was "homesick and lonely" for the sea and his people. A trunk-back turtle had eaten his heart and all his hopes were sunk forever in "a shoal where the Red Groupers spawned a month ago." In place of his good companions aboard the *Pilar,* all he had now was that dark brother, his enormous headache. But his dark brother was faithful and true, never leaving him except for those brief interludes in airplanes when he shifted the headphones "selfishly" for respite from the pulsing beat of pain, or those other times when Mary Welsh came quietly to the door of his room at the Dorchester,

> Opening softly with the in-left key,
> Saying, "May I come in?"
> Coming small-voiced and lovely
> To the hand and eye
> To bring your heart back that was gone,
> To cure all loneliness.

The strain of self-pity was occasioned partly, no doubt, by the perpetual headache, and partly by his hurt feelings over Martha's failure of sympathy at the time of the car accident. One day at the hotel, his brother Leicester found him gazing sadly from the window and murmuring that Marty had come to see him only twice while he was "laid up and hurting." The mood continued for some months. In a letter of the following September, he observed that while he was flying in medium bombers he did not care about living. But the more he flew at 12,000 feet through the dark blossoms of dangerous flak, the more he wished to survive, while by the end of June, when he went on missions in Mosquito fighters, his memory of Martha had dwindled to a bad joke.

June was nearly over when Hemingway accepted one of Group Captain Wykeham Barnes's repeated invitations to visit Mosquito Attack Wing 140. The buzzbomb campaign had driven the unit out of Gravesend to RAF Station Thorney Island, near Portsmouth. From there they were making continuous day and night attacks on German lines of communication behind the Normandy bridgehead. On June 28th, John Pudney escorted Hemingway to the tented camp on Thorney Island. Ernest wore "extremely inferior RAF battledress, very hairy and ill-fitting, in which he looked like a blue-grey bear." He was much interested in the recent speciality of Wing 140: attacks on Gestapo headquarters in various parts of occupied Europe. These assignments had been so brilliantly carried out, often at a treetop level with bombs skittering through front doors, that Wykeham Barnes's name stood high on the Gestapo's "Special List" in the event of his capture. Hemingway posed a long string of questions on the technique of low-level, pinpoint attacks by day and night, and indicated that he was eager to fly once more.

On the afternoon of the 29th, Wykeham Barnes obligingly took him up for a trial run in his own Mosquito, "EGX." The Mark VI Mosquito, light and fast, was strictly a two-seater plane in which the pilot and the navigator sat shoulder to shoulder. Since Wykeham Barnes was even bigger than Hemingway, they were extremely crowded. It resembled, as Hemingway said, the attempt of a grizzly bear to enter an Austin. "The flight was laid on," said his host, "to give him some experience in riding in the navigator's seat, and he urged me to roll the Mosquito and throw it around quite considerably." The pilot complied, and it may have been this afternoon ride out over the sea and back again which caused Ernest to invent the *Ad Astra Ad Nauseam* motto for the squadron.

Shortly before midnight they took off again. "It was a pitch-black night with no moon," said Wykeham Barnes.

I had been told I must not take Ernest over enemy territory, and indeed I could not go far, at night and low-level, without a proper navigator. So we meant to run around the English Channel and see if we could pick up anything interesting. Sure enough, we found ourselves in a stream of V1s, fired against Portsmouth.

Towards the end of its flight from its French launching-base, the V1 was doing better than 400 miles an hour, a good 30 mph faster than my Mosquito's top speed. Intercepting one at night was very difficult indeed. The first one we tried for, getting above and ahead and diving as it passed under us, was too near the Portsmouth guns, and before we could get in a shot we were having a bad time from the full-scale AA barrage. I fired one short burst at the V1, and then pulled away before we reached the barrage balloons. Ernest seemed to love the fireworks bursting all round us, and urged me to press on and make sure of the V1.

We patrolled around, and ten minutes later sighted another V1. I was already in a state familiar to those who tangled with Ernest—I was acting against my better judgment. My wing had no responsibility for destroying V1s. I knew I could not catch one except by a fluke, I knew there were proper night fighters after them and I was getting in the way, and I knew I was supposed to keep Ernest out of trouble. If you did blow one up, particularly at night, it was touch and go for yourself, also.

We dived even more steeply on the second V1, and got nearer to it. I really had to drive the old airplane to her limit, even to hold on for a while. I reckoned it was in range and gave it two long bursts. I thought I saw a flash a bit off-centre of its fuselage, and then we were in the Portsmouth barrage again. I pulled away in a confusion of searchlights and intensive flak. As we winged over, there was a huge flash behind us, and the aeroplane danced around like a leaf in a whirlwind. Someone got the V1, but not us. We patrolled some more and then landed. Ernest seemed to have loved every moment.

I seldom went to bed until my last aircraft had landed, around dawn. As usual I sat up that night, in the operations tent, but what was unusual was that I had

Ernest to talk to. He had a great deal to say on mental stress and strain, on courage and fear, traditional Hemingway topics, and though he was as intelligent as one might expect (I had read all his books, and told him frankly how much I admired them), he tended to take a tougher and brawnier line than that acceptable to us worn-out old veterans (4½ years non-stop). I remember criticising the Americans for harsh action in cases of combat nerves or combat fatigue. I quoted the case of a Fortress captain who was busted down to private and put to work, the next day, cleaning the Fortress he had captained. Ernest kept up the tough line, and we told him that he'd have to get some service in; that the bravest men were the newest in action, and so on. It was all very good-humoured.

We parted at dawn to go to our tents. I was all in, and asleep in ten minutes. I met Ernest at midday in the mess tent. He looked terrible. I asked him if he had slept, and he said no, he had been at his typewriter ever since we parted. He said he liked to get it down fresh, and I felt the warm admiration one has for a true professional. But he never told me what he wrote that night.

Conditions in Normandy were steadily improving. Shortly before Ernest's Mosquito flights, two of his fellow correspondents had established themselves in a commodious white stone house in Cherbourg. One was Ernest's new friend, Bill Walton, who had parachuted into Normandy as planned at one o'clock on D-Day morning. The other was Charles Collingwood of the Columbia Broadcasting System, aged twenty-six, who had landed on Utah Beach with an underwater demolition team as part of the second wave on June 6th. Three weeks later, meeting by chance in Cherbourg, they had moved into the house with a mustached British major named John Palfrey. All things considered, it was an almost luxurious arrangement. A married couple served as butler and cook. The establishment immediately became a sort of wayfarers' hotel for correspondents, including Bob Sherwood, Bill Paley, Bob Capa, and Charles Wertenbaker.

Ernest had yet to set foot on Norman soil, though he had been in England for six weeks. One of his new friends in London was Wertenbaker's cousin George, who had just been promoted full colonel at age twenty-seven. His Fighter Group of P-47s was now based in Isigny, and had a small twin-engine light aircraft in which they were allowed to carry war correspondents back and forth to England. Early in July, Ernest hopped a ride across the Channel and appeared, beaming and beardless, at the Walton-Collingwood villa in Cherbourg. He explained the loss of his beard by saying that his London doctor had at last consented to let him shave, and surprised Walton even further by bringing him a whole month's accumulation of mail. "We had a memorable bash in honor of his arrival," wrote Collingwood. "It was lubricated with compass fluid (pure alcohol) obtained by the Navy, plus some booze we had come across in captured German submarine stores deep in a cliff overlooking the harbor. . . . The festivities were enlivened by a group of Irish deepsea divers who were engaged in clearing the harbor of the fiendish . . . mines and other destructive devices the Germans had sown. They stayed up most of the night drinking and singing, slept it off for a couple of hours on the floor, and then . . . disappeared beneath the surface of the most dangerous body of water in the world. Very tough characters."

For a week Ernest stayed with his compatriots in Cherbourg. He was full of his recent exploits in Wykeham Barnes's Mosquito and characteristically ebullient about his rough time with the other units of the Royal Air Force. He joined in the drinking and singing as if he had not a care in the world— as indeed for the moment he had not. Each morning the correspondents left their comfortable villa to cover the war down the road, returning at nightfall to further sessions with the compass fluid. Although Ernest dutifully scribbled notes about the armor and the infantry, he made no visible effort to write them up. After a week of this, he departed as quietly as he had come, returning to the Dorchester and the further pursuit of his love affair with Mary Welsh. On July 17th he took her to a farewell lunch at the White Tower, the place of their first introduction. "Wonderful lunch with Hemingway," she wrote in her diary, "though I terribly sleepy." Then he made his way across the Channel once again, and the London chapter of his life came to a close.

58. *RETURN TO NORMANDY*

WHEN Hemingway got back to Normandy on July 18th, he first checked in with one of Gen. George Patton's armored divisions. The dust they raised was a constant irritant to his eyes and his always sensitive throat. He made a short entry in a small pocket diary. "This was the summer of the dust and the mud. The metal fighter strips would be ankle deep in dust and huge clouds of dust would billow, blinding and chokeing you, as the P-47s . . ." This was as far as the entry went, but there were other irritants besides Patton's armor and the fighter planes. One was a fellow correspondent called Nemo Canaberro Lucas, a Brazilian for whom Ernest conceived an almost instant dislike. On his forty-fifth birthday, July 21, Ernest was suffering more than usual from the combination of heat, dust, and noise. As the afternoon waned, he consoled himself with the thought of a cool bath and a long drink. At the press camp, he found that only enough of his whiskey remained to make one drink. He poured it lovingly into a tumbler, added water to make it last longer, placed it on the arm of his camp chair, took off his combat boots, and sat back relaxed. He was not prepared for Nemo Canaberro Lucas, who was just coming in from a day of note-taking, covered with sweat and streaked with dust. As he passed Ernest's chair he saw the drink, picked it up, and drained it in one gulp. Then he fixed Hemingway with a stare and said, as if deeply aggrieved, "It had water in it!" Ernest nearly shot him, and there were times afterwards when he wished that he had done so. Before his first week was up, he had had enough of Patton's dusty armor; he called the experience an "abortion" and set about looking for an outfit better suited to his tastes.

The organization he chose was the 4th Infantry Division. On July 24th he appeared at the divisional press camp and asked to meet the commanding general. He was taken to the trailer where Gen. Raymond O. Barton was at work. Barton, known since his West Point days as Tubby, was a thickset, strongly built man with a military mustache and a troublesome ulcer. The only thing he could remember about the man Hemingway was that he had once been a sports reporter and that he had had a fistfight with some prominent person. In any case, Barton had little time to spare. His division was on the eve of a large-scale offensive designed to carry the invading forces out of the present bridgehead with a breakthrough at St.-Lô. Ernest left for the lay-out which Barton maintained for correspondents and was taken in charge by Capt. Marcus Stevenson, a divisional public relations officer. A Texan who had served as A-D-C to the late Gen. Theodore Roosevelt, Jr., Stevenson was regarded by Barton as "a natural for herd-guarding Ernie"—especially since he shared Hemingway's liking for action and front lines. He sported a pair of mustaches that made Ernest think of a Texas sheriff.

Under Stevenson's guidance, Ernest set out to meet the officers in Barton's command. On the 28th, three days after the breakout operation had been launched, he went with Ira Wolfert to pay a morning call on the 22nd Regiment in a small farmhouse near the crossroads hamlet of Le Mesnil-Herman. The military situation was still fluid and confused. American and German troops were often separated by little more than a hedgerow or a patch of timber. The previous day's advance had covered more than ten miles, three hundred prisoners had been taken, infantry patrols probed constantly to the south, the July dust choked the green hillsides, and the restless fever of attack was in the air. Lieut. Col. E. W. "Lum" Edwards, operations officer, was "awfully busy" when the tall, grizzled man and his shorter companion appeared and asked to see Col. Charles Trueman Lanham, who was equally busy in the front room of the farmhouse where his operations maps were posted. The tall man mumbled his name and occupation. Colonel Edwards took the message.

Buck Lanham had commanded the 22nd for almost three weeks. He was a short, wiry, brown-eyed West Pointer from Washington, D.C., intense and dynamic, explosive and profane. Lum Edwards told him of the visitors. One was a war correspondent; the other, he understood, was a Colonel Colliers from Washington. "Our respect for visitors diminished," Lanham later said, "in direct proportion to the level of their echelon above our own. A visitor from Washington was therefore at the bottom of the scale. I told Colonel Edwards to show the gentlemen in and went back to my maps."

Lanham was completely unprepared for the gigantic figure of a man who presently shouldered his way through the narrow farmhouse door. "Colonel Colliers?" said he, cocking his head and holding out his hand.

"I'm no colonel," the visitor said. "I'm a correspondent for *Collier's*. My name is Hemingway."

"Ernest, no doubt," said Lanham.

"Yes. My name is Ernest."

Lanham briefed his visitors on the day's operations. He was surprised by the speed and astuteness with which Hemingway absorbed military information. He seemed to have a built-in battle sense and an almost professional instinct for terrain. His questions were intelligent and his manners quietly deferential. The discussion went so well that Lanham ended by asking his visitors to lunch. He was himself an experienced writer and sometime poet. During the meal he tried to turn the conversation to literature. Hemingway was "simple, direct, gentle, and unaffected." But he fended off the literary questions. His purpose, it was plain, was to talk about the war.

For the next nine days Ernest stayed with his adopted division as it moved steadily southward through La Denisière, Villebaudon, Hambye, Villedieu-les-Poêles, and St.-Pois. He was clearly in his element. All his diffidence had dropped away. He called it "a tough fine time with the infantry." He wrote back to Mary Welsh in London that the life he was leading was surprisingly jolly, full of shooting and fighting over small hills, along the dusty roads, in and out of hedgerows and wheatfields, with burned-out enemy tanks, wrecked *Kraftwagens,* captured 88s, and the "deads" from both sides. He found a Spanish-speaking sergeant in one of Colonel Lanham's platoons and they were soon fast friends. Sometimes they did not even stop to eat. Sleep was snatched in the rain, on the ground, in barns, in farm carts. Rising before dawn, he would "scrub good all over" with soap and washrag. Then at first light, stealing a look at his face in a pocket mirror, he would find the dust already so thick on his eyelashes that he thought he resembled a well-ginned debutante who had cried into her mascara.

At Villebaudon on the 31st he acquired a captured German motorcycle equipped with a sidecar, and a Mercedes-Benz convertible with badly mangled wiring and a bullet through the steering column. General Barton assigned him a driver from the division motor pool. Pvt. Archie Pelkey was twenty-nine, a grade-school dropout from Potsdam, New York, who had been working for Alcoa Aluminum in Massena before his induction. He had red hair and china-blue eyes. One of his front teeth had been broken off in an accident. He repaired the Mercedes and drove Ernest back to the motor pool to get the car repainted. When they passed Barton's trailer, the general appeared in the doorway, waving and smiling over the new acquisition. The first of August was clear, with a good breeze, Ernest's favorite weather. After supper he sat barefoot beside a table, writing to Mary, while a small flop-eared dog chewed happily on his toes. He joined for a while in the evening poker game. By the time he got back to his letter, the dark had settled down. He tried to convey to Mary the far-off sound of machine pistols—*trrut, trrut*—"like a kitty-cat purring, but hard and metallic."

After such peaceful interludes, he returned almost hungrily to the noise of battle. On the morning of August 3rd he appeared with Pelkey at the northern extremity of Villedieu-les-Poêles, a sizable market town locally known as the

City of Stoves. They were aboard the motorcycle and carried a supply of grenades. Artillery from both sides was pounding the main street. Snipers were active. Many of the buildings were on fire, walls were collapsing, aid men were busy with the wounded, and the fighting moved slowly from house to house. As the Americans progressively occupied the town, Ernest talked to some of the natives. One of them said that a cellar full of SS men had been bypassed by the advancing infantry and offered to show him where the place was. He armed himself and Pelkey with grenades and followed the guide to the house in question. He yelled down the cellarway in French and German. The hidden men must come out with their hands up. There was no answer. He yelled again with the same result. He pulled the pins from three grenades and tossed them down. "All right," he said. "Divide these among yourselves." There is no certain indication that German troopers were actually in the cellar. If they were there, Ernest could boast, as he later did, that he had killed "plenty" Nazis. But the tide of the battle was rolling on, and he did not go down to inspect the results of his work.

The French were convinced that he must be an officer. They took him to see the mayor of the town, who ceremoniously presented him with two magnums of champagne. He had just returned to his motorcycle when Colonel Lanham came streaking down the main street in a jeep with a mounted machine gun. He had finished his business in the town and was on his way back to his command post half a mile away. Something about the grizzled figure on the sidewalk seemed familiar. It was the correspondent he had had to lunch the week before. He ordered his driver to stop and asked Ernest what the hell he thought he was doing there. Hemingway grinned and waved. From one of his saddlebags he took a magnum of champagne and presented it to Lanham. Then he told him the story of the SS men in the cellar. Blowing up Germans was not the proper business of a war correspondent, but Lanham was too busy to care. As he drove off in his jeep, cradling the champagne in the crook of his arm, Ernest still stood on the street corner, poised like a boxer on the balls of his feet, watching the liberation of the City of Stoves.

He boasted to Mary Welsh that General Barton counted on him for reconnaissance missions in forward areas, fondly describing Ernest's motorcycle as "irregular cavalry," and supplying him with arms and ammunition. At least once, near the end of a day when Barton was dog-tired and gnawed with the pain of his ulcer, he and Ernest stretched out on the same blanket while Ernest filled him in with the "gen" on German troop movements in the country just ahead. "Mostly," said Ernest, "I talk French and say where they are and whether they have left or not and how it is ahead. Sometimes in very quiet whispers." Two days after the taking of Villedieu-les-Poêles, these scouting activities nearly got Barton's irregular cavalry into serious trouble.

The division had by now swung southeast into the hilly farm country around St.-Pois. The three regiments were deployed on a wide front and temporarily more or less inactive, though the German rearguard sent occasional patrols to probe Barton's forward defenses. Bob Capa, the *Life* photographer, was attached to General Patton's Fourth Armored Division near Granville, twelve miles away. Ernest asked Barton's permission to send the Mercedes to bring Capa over for the weekend. When he arrived, riding in style, he was transferred to the pillion of the motorcycle, sitting behind Pelkey, with Ernest in the sidecar. They set off to find Colonel Lanham's command post.

The village of St.-Pois was a huddle of gray Norman houses with black roofs. There was a manor house called Château de St.-Pois, and a single church with a damaged spire. The main street was an unpaved country road leading south among enfolding hills. Lanham's command post lay somewhere off to the right, and could be reached by a lane leading off the main road. Somehow they missed the turning and came larruping around a curve at the bottom of the hill directly into the path of a German antitank gun.

Pelkey slammed the motorcycle to a halt and they all leaped for the ditches. Ernest landed so hard that he banged his head on a boulder and his back on another. The Germans opened up with a machine gun on the abandoned motorcycle while the Americans hugged the ditches. For almost two hours they listened to the German patrol talking back and forth through the hedgerows, ready with machine pistols in case of any move to escape. Dusk was falling when the antitank gun withdrew. Ernest and his companions crept backward around the curve and set off to find Lanham's regiment. Capa and Hemingway were arguing furiously. Ernest had accused Capa of lying in wait in the ditch across the road, out of the German line of fire, just to make certain of getting the first picture of a famous writer's dead body.

The account that Ernest sent back to Mary Welsh next day said that all the jolly future that they had been planning had been placed temporarily "on the bum." He was "knocked down by a tank shell," said he, and then fired on by the tank's machine gun as well as by two soldiers with machine pistols, who were talking on the other side of the hedge only ten feet away. They spoke very disrespectfully of Mary's big friend, whom they considered to be dead. After the tank withdrew, Ernest had rescued the motorcycle, though it was so badly shot up that they had to tow it home. He said that he had hurt his back and that he had been urinating blood. But the worst aspect of the affair was the new bump on his head. He had only recently recovered from the headaches that resulted from his concussion in May. Now they returned with a vengeance. He spoke of double vision, and even maintained later on that the St.-Pois incident left him impotent for several months. Whatever the truth of the matter, it seems clear that he was trying to impress his new love Mary Welsh with the splendor of his exploits, nurturing the germs of truth in his private laboratory until they grew far larger than lifesize.

On the quiet Sunday morning following this incident, Ernest drove across with Willie Walton for a short holiday at Mont St.-Michel. General Barton flattered him at leavetaking by presenting him with a bottle of bourbon and assuring him that he would be much missed, both personally and officially.

Ernest's plan, as he told Mary Welsh, was to hole up and write for a few days in "this old hang out of Henry Adams." With the welcome smell of the sea in his nostrils once again, he crossed the narrow causeway. The tide was out and the enormous waste of sandflats lay golden-gray in the August sunlight, which gilded the turrets and towers of the old monastery at the top of the small mountain. Recently liberated by Patton's westbound forces, the island was off limits to all but general officers and war correspondents. But the officers were busy with the conquest of Brittany and the correspondents had the place largely to themselves. The souvenir shops and most of the hotels along the steep cobblestoned street of the village were closed and desolate. Hemingway and Walton moved into the one that was open, the Hôtel de la Mère Poularde, among a company which included Wertenbaker and Wolfert, Helen Kirkpatrick and A. J. Liebling, Charles Collingwood, and Bob Capa.

Young Collingwood called it an extraordinary interlude. Liebling, an inveterate gourmet, was "more or less in charge of the cuisine." Hemingway chose the wine, paying "gallant attentions to the *patronne,* Madame Chevalier," who brought out "all sorts of marvelous bottles hidden from the Germans *derrière les fagots.*" There were many two-hour lunches with the middle-aged Madame Chevalier and her happily hospitable husband. After the liberation of Rennes, Collingwood and Wertenbaker discovered a practical-joke shop. It was intact and well-stocked and they "brought back half the gadgets," booby-trapping Ernest's dinner plate and driving him to distraction with a lefthanded corkscrew. They also inserted a lifelike worm in Liebling's stewed pear. Everyone waited to see what he would do. He calmly lifted it aside and went on eating.

As they had done at Cherbourg, the correspondents went out daily to cover the war down the road. Buck Lanham's 22nd Infantry Regiment was now stationed near Juvigny and Mortain, south of St.-Pois and some fifty kilometers east of Mont St.-Michel. When Ernest drove over at the beginning of the week, he found that Lanham had established his command post in something far handsomer than the farmhouses he had used until then: a handsome Norman castle, Château Lingeard, on a rise of ground dominating a wide valley. The kitchen staff was planning a special dinner in celebration of Lanham's twentieth wedding anniversary, with a menu that included roast goose and a large cake. But Ernest declined to attend. He seemed nervous and restive. Something spooked him about Lanham's command post. He drove back in the evening to Mont St.-Michel.

Next day all hell broke loose. German armor broke through the Mortain gap in a mighty counteroffensive back to Avranches. The correspondents stayed where they were, watching the battle through binoculars from the roof of the monastery at the top of the little mountain. Over to the east, the Château Lingeard came under heavy fire from German artillery. Shells crashed through the roof and into the cobblestoned courtyard. Several officers were killed and many were wounded, including Colonel Lanham. The anniversary dinner was canceled. On the 10th the regiment was ordered to a new position thirty miles to the south. The counteroffensive was soon contained and the Germans withdrew to the east. When Ernest drove out again to find the 22nd Regiment, Lanham reminded him of his restive behavior at Château Lingeard. Why had he refused the dinner invitation and left in such a hurry? "The place stank of death," said Ernest. Somewhere in his subconscious he had felt a premonition.

His favorites among his fellow correspondents were Bill Walton, whom he always called Willie, and Ken Crawford. Walton's pleasure in having made the drop into France on D-Day morning struck Ernest as rather touching, while his attitude towards Ernest himself seemed consistently "kind and loveing." With Ira Wolfert it was a different matter. Ernest described him as a brilliant but omnivorous reporter who unconsciously appropriated and promptly cabled whatever anyone told him, whether or not he had personally seen it. When Ernest pointed out such small martial ironies as a wounded cow suckling her calf or a farm dog that barked aggressively at bombers, Wolfert was sure to have it all in the papers next day. Yet Ernest himself performed in a similar fashion. Virtually everything he wrote for *Collier's* that summer was a melange of personal observation and materials gleaned from a wide variety of other sources. None of his despatches was completely accurate. He seemed to be far more concerned with the feel of things than with the facts. As a lifelong purveyor of fiction, he could not resist the temptation to fictionalize. He invented dialogue like a novelist. As in his NANA despatches from Spain, he often omitted the names of his companions, leaving the impression that he was alone in feats of derring-do. He sometimes contrasted his own modest conduct with the infamous behavior of others. He was always compressing, foreshortening, overdramatizing. During his stay at Mont St.-Michel he wrote an article called "The General," based in part on his friendship with General Barton, but well-laced with invented dialogue and other fictional devices. As he had shown his D-Day article to Roald Dahl in London, so now he rather diffidently approached Charles Collingwood for an opinion about "The General." "In those days," said Collingwood, "I was a very young and very brash war correspondent, and made the mistake of thinking he really wanted to know. . . . So I told him it read to me like somebody's parody of Ernest Hemingway. I don't think he spoke to me again until we got to Paris."

But nothing could keep Ernest from a genuine enjoyment of the war in France. His view was not far removed from that expressed in Evelyn Waugh's *The End of the Battle*. "Even good men thought that their private honor would be satisfied by war. They could assert their manhood by killing and being killed. They would accept hardships in recompense for having been lazy and selfish. Danger justified privilege." The ever-present danger of forward combat positions did indeed justify for Hemingway the privileges he laid claim to—rather modestly in the presence of the professional warriors whose skills and courage he admired and revered, and a good deal less modestly as his adventures receded into retrospect, assuming ever more heroic outlines. "I love combat," he often said within the closed circle of his bosom friends, though he usually felt obliged to add that it was a "rotten" admission to make. Still there was something about the killing of an enemy that appealed to his sense of manhood, especially if he himself were in danger at the time. As a passionate exponent of blood sports in Tanganyika and Wyoming, he had known all his adult life the "aesthetic pleasure and pride" that came of "killing cleanly." Not for nothing had he watched the destruction of 1,500 bulls in the ten years before the publication of *Death in the Afternoon*. In that book he had even asserted that "when a man is still in rebellion against death he has pleasure in taking to himself one of the Godlike attributes: that of giving it." Among those who enjoyed the act of killing, this pleasure was the "most profound" of them all. It was associated in Ernest's mind with pride— "a Christian sin and a pagan virtue." During the war, it was also associated with hate, another of the seven deadly sins. Some years later, Ernest told Bernard Berenson that to love killing was doubtless a sin, even when his victims were Germans. He was "not a Jew," despite his nickname of Hemingstein. He had not personally suffered at the hands of Hitler or Mussolini. Yet he had hated the Nazis and the Fascists so much that he had actually enjoyed killing them. His main job in France, Belgium, and Germany—as he saw it —was to provide information on the disposition of enemy forces far enough in advance to help save the lives of his own compatriots. This he had done well enough, he felt, so that his conscience never bothered him about the killing, whether it was done by others or, as he liked to hint, by himself.

59. THE ROAD TO PARIS

THE next order of business was going to be the liberation of Paris. During the third week in August, Hemingway detached himself from the 4th Infantry Division and was driven south by Red Pelkey in the jeep which General Barton had placed at his disposal. On the afternoon of Sunday, August 20th, Col. David Bruce of the OSS found him at the command post of the 5th American Infantry Division outside Chartres. They arranged to meet that evening at Rambouillet, a pleasant village in the rolling countryside farther along the fateful road to Paris.

Ernest had already spent a night in Rambouillet after a busy weekend of advance scouting. On the 18th he had come down from Écouché to the town of Maintenon, halfway between Chartres and Rambouillet. The 5th Infantry Division was said to be leaving and the 7th Armored moving in. Ernest was eager to know which of these would be advancing to the relief of Paris so that he could attach himself to one of the columns. He could not find out. Next morning he and Pelkey located the 2nd Infantry Regiment of the 5th Division in a patch of woodland outside Maintenon. They were directed to a regimental outpost near Épernon, a few kilometers closer to Paris. Here for the first time Ernest met two truckloads of Free French fighters under a tired-looking "commander" named Tahon Marceau. His men were stripped to the waist in the August heat, and armed with two Sten guns and Luger pistols. They assured Hemingway that German infantry had abandoned Rambouillet, the next town closer to Paris, before dawn that morning. They warned him, however, that the enemy had left a roadblock of felled trees, as well as a minefield, at the southern extremity of the town.

He accompanied the partisans along the smooth macadam road towards Rambouillet. As they had said, the roadblock was there beside the high wall of an estate. Large plane trees had been felled across the road. Two smashed jeeps and a wrecked truck showed where an American patrol had been killed. The seven victims had been buried in a nearby field. Parts of their uniforms lay in the bed of the truck. Squatting in the ditches were two German tanks, "fitted with wire controls which ran back to gun pits so as to hit an approaching column in front and in flank." Among the fallen tree trunks the Germans had sowed forty American mines taken from the ambushed truck.

Tahon Marceau was sure that the enemy had pulled back toward Chevreuse and Trappes and that the 2nd Regiment should extend to Rambouillet. A stocky, cheerful lieutenant named Irving Krieger, of the 2nd's Antitank Company, now began the systematic clearing of the minefield. The half-naked irregulars clothed themselves in the American fatigues found in the truck, and Hemingway "ordered" a patrol into the town. They prowled the streets and scouted the roads beyond without finding any Germans. But the country people reported a substantial enemy force within easy striking distance: 800 men, 4 field guns, 8 antitank guns, and 15 tiger tanks. Ernest advised Krieger to resow the minefield in case the Germans decided to double back.

The prospect of spending the night in Rambouillet with only eight lightly armed irregulars against such a German force held little appeal. Ernest returned to divisional headquarters in an attempt to procure from General Red Irwin some machine guns for use in the defense of the town. He returned empty-handed, angry, and more than ever determined to hold Rambouillet. Fortunately, in the course of the evening, the 5th Reconnaissance Troop under Lieut. M. S. Peterson moved into the center of the village. Patrols fanned out along the roads to the east with instructions to engage enemy infantry but to fall back before German armor. But they made no contact with the Germans. On the morning of the 20th Ernest went back to the 2nd Infantry's positions to get fresh supplies for Peterson. "This time he got cooperation and enough arms to take care of his irregulars."

He also located a command post. Just where the road from Épernon described a slow leftward curve into the town of Rambouillet stood a handsome, four-square, three-storied structure of gray stucco with a slate roof and a good country weathercock. This was the Hôtel du Grand Veneur. Behind it was an apple orchard where bees hummed in the honeysuckle. The *patron* had managed to preserve an excellent cellar of wines as well as a proper French respect for the quality of the food he served. Here, on the morning of the 20th, Ernest established himself in two rooms, and continued his attempt to serve as liaison between the loosely functioning partisan patrols and divisional headquarters farther south.

When Colonel Bruce arrived that day, he found Ernest in nominal command of ten partisans. "We were enchanted to see him," wrote Bruce. "Agents and patrols kept rushing in with reports, some of them contradictory, but all indicating that the Germans were laying mines down the road toward us about eight miles away, with a force of approximately 150 men. As there were no American troops in Rambouillet, Hemingway and the French had become more or less convinced the Germans would retake the town [that night]. We grilled the only Boche prisoner we could find. He either knew nothing or was a good actor, so we turned him back to the French, who he was firmly convinced intended to execute him."

As ranking officer in town, Colonel Bruce prepared a plan for its defense, procuring a supply of German hand grenades from the American regiment in Maintenon, and securing a promise from the Resistance leader that thirty to forty men would be sent along to help. He held a discussion with Major James W. Thornton. The total manpower at their disposition was some thirty Americans, including two drunken AWOL paratroopers, ten Resistance people, and fourteen gendarmes. There were also a few machine guns. Thornton arranged to patrol the roads leading towards Paris, reporting any German movements. Ernest volunteered to assist. Since the Geneva Convention prohibited correspondents from bearing arms, he asked Colonel Bruce for a handwritten order to justify his assuming command over the partisans. Thornton and Hemingway then disposed the available forces at two positions on the outskirts. During the heavy rains that night there were several small alarms. A German patrol made contact with Thornton's position, but came no closer. Bruce had arranged a password—"France-Orléans"—which everyone hissed at everyone else.

Word had now spread that Generals Eisenhower and Bradley had diplomatically assigned the job of taking Paris to the 2nd French Armored Division under General Jacques Leclerc. A crowd of war correspondents converged on Rambouillet to find Hemingway solidly entrenched at the Grand Veneur and in apparent command of a group of partisan fighters. Since he was not visibly filing despatches, and since he often worked in shirtsleeves, leaving his correspondent's insignia pinned to his tunic in the hotel, many of his fellow reporters were convinced that he was flagrantly violating the Geneva agreement. The few who managed to glance inside his rooms reported that one of them contained a small arsenal of grenades, mines, tommy guns, and pistols. Ernest was not above giving some of them the impression that everyone but himself should have stayed at home. When Bruce Grant, a six-footer from Chicago, complained loudly in the crowded hotel dining room that Ernest was hogging hotel space, punches were thrown until someone pulled the large antagonists apart. But Ernest did not care. With Bruce's handwritten orders and a black notebook buttoned inside his shirt, he was concentrating now on gathering all the information that he thought would be of use to General Leclerc in the forthcoming drive on Paris.

Although the Grand Veneur continued to be crowded, Colonel Bruce's diary entry for Monday, August 21, said that "our local army disintegrated rapidly today. Having decided that the American troops were not going directly to Paris by this route, the correspondents and specialists are haring off in all directions. Hemingway and ourselves are holding this position, and sending out small patrols along all the roads. It is maddening to be only thirty miles from Paris, to interrogate every hour some Frenchman who has just come from there and who reports that even a very small task force could easily move in, and to know that our Army is being forced to wait and for what reason? Yesterday, the Resistance people, hearing we were in Versailles and were moving onto Paris, rose prematurely and are said to have suffered considerable losses."

Ernest later boasted that his scouting operations were "straight out of Mosby," and once made the incredible assertion that by August 23, he had learned the "entire Kraut MLR"—including the positions of all roadblocks, minefields, radar, antiaircraft, antitank, and artillery between Rambouillet and the southern purlieus of Paris. He also knew the numbers and locations of all tanks, with corrections being plotted every half hour. Despite the exaggeration, he seems to have performed capably at Rambouillet. "Ernest liked to dramatize himself," wrote Bruce, "and indeed he had good reason to do so. In military affairs, he was a real expert, especially in regard to guerrilla activities and to intelligence collection. Although entirely brave, he was cautious enough to imagine and to take precautions against unexpected and unorthodox manners in which an enemy might behave. He had a true scout's instinct. . . . After a few days the ranks of Ernest's irregular band were swollen by itinerant recruits to whom we passed out grenades and a few Sten guns. They were active and fearless, sometimes purveyors of valuable intelligence, but the best intelligence was that furnished by natives of villages and of the countryside between Rambouillet and Paris."

On the afternoon of the 21st, Colonel Bruce moved into a room at the hotel to begin a series of interrogations. From an intelligence standpoint, the most important person with whom he dealt in those days was Michel Pasteau, whose code name was Mouthard, a tall, blue-eyed, hollow-chested man with receding red hair who had spent some years in Abyssinia and French Somaliland, and had now become "a trusted agent of Colonel Passy's clandestine organization." Bruce and Pasteau had met by chance after the taking of Chartres, and Pasteau had readily agreed to associate himself with Colonel Bruce's activities. He was an engineer by training, highly educated and articulate, and had read some of Hemingway's books, liked him, and got on well with him, though as a professional intelligence officer he was not "enthusiastic about the slapdash methods of the partisans in evaluating information."

Both Bruce and Pasteau found Hemingway extremely skillful both in interrogation and in the evaluation of what was learned. That afternoon they listened together to a man who had the exact location of a minefield which he had watched the Germans laying the night before. Another had taken part in yesterday's insurrection in Paris. A third had spent the preceding night in Trappes. Two Alsatian women accused of sleeping with Germans were ushered in. Someone denounced a woman walking in the hotel garden as the former mistress of an important Gestapo officer in Paris. A Frenchman and his wife drove up with three German prisoners stiffly erect in the back seat, guarded by a youngster with a Sten gun. "A very young Pole deserted from the German tank unit ahead of us. He buried his uniform and his submachine gun and filtered through the lines in his underwear and a pair of trousers he had found in a shelled house. He brought good information and was put to work in the kitchen of the hotel." One old man picked up by Ernest's jeep six miles north of town purveyed complete information on a minefield and antitank emplacement on the road beyond Trappes. Since he was too old to be risked outside again, "he joined the Polish child in protective custody." These and others were interrogated by Hemingway and the "tireless and resourceful Mouthard." When Gene Currivan of *The New York Times* "pretty damn near bled to death from a can-opener wound," Ernest rushed him upstairs and applied first aid. That evening, after an exhausting day, Ernest and the OSS officers enjoyed a fine dinner, including "paté de foie gras stuffed abundantly with truffles." Word of parachute drops of munitions reached them at dusk. Bruce, Hemingway, Mouthard and some of the others went out to find the material and returned with a welcome accession of bazookas, grenades, and rifles for the arsenals they maintained in the upstairs rooms.

During the patrol operations at this period, Red Pelkey constantly amused Hemingway. Until D-Day he had never spoken a word of French. Now, ten weeks later, he asserted that he had forgotten his English entirely. He also preferred the nickname Jim, given him by the irregulars, to his given name of Archie, which he disliked. North of Rambouillet, wearing an appropriated sergeant's uniform and a gap-toothed smile, he chanted the outfit's marching song:

> *Dix bis Avenue des Gobelins,*
> *Dix bis Avenue des Gobelins*
> *Dix bis Avenue des Gobelins,*
> That's where my Bumby lives.

It dated from 1925 when Ernest and Hadley had taught it to their small son, so that if lost he could be conducted back to the apartment of Marie Rohrbach, his sometime nursemaid. The partisans were all spoiling for what they called *Paname*. The term puzzled Pelkey, who did not know that it was Devil's Island argot for Paris. He was intent only on reaching the Avenue des Gobelins, a mystical point beyond the northern horizon.

The major question was still when the grand march would begin. On the 22nd, Colonel Bruce entered some of the current facts and speculations in his diary. General Patton's Third Army had been in a position to take Paris for several days. Two of his divisions were across the Seine and moving north. It was rumored in some quarters that the liberation awaited the arrival of President Franklin Roosevelt who would personally enter the city. Others held that Gen. Bernard Law Montgomery, unable to get through the territory assigned to his forces, would swing through American-held sectors and thus lead a triumphal march to the Place de la Concorde. The location of General Leclerc's 2nd Armored Division was in doubt. "Like the Scarlet Pimpernel," wrote Bruce, "it is said to have been seen here, there, and everywhere." Around lunchtime on the 22nd, however, an advance guard of Leclerc's was found in a wheatfield near Nogent-le-Roy; Bruce and Mouthard briefed its commanding officer on the disposition of German armor between Rambouillet and Paris. The correspondents were furious with Leclerc because he would not reveal his plans. He in turn was angry with them because they were merely looking for a story while he had the responsibility of "capturing the capital."

Signs of change set in on Wednesday the 23rd when a small patrol from Leclerc's division passed through Rambouillet in the direction of Versailles. Despite precise intelligence from Bruce's organization, the patrol was back an hour later, having run into enemy ambush which cost them two killed, two wounded, and a vehicle destroyed. The lieutenant in charge had been shot in the back, an arm, and a leg, but he gaily helped drink a bottle of champagne. "While we were talking to him," says Bruce, "General Leclerc arrived in a three-star jeep. He is tall, spare, handsome, stern-visaged, and a striking figure. All his people were in light vehicles and went into the Park of Rambouillet. I was presented to the General there, and asked by him to give all the intelligence I could to his G-2, Commander Repiton. This, with the assistance of Hemingway, Mouthard and [John] Mowinckel, I did."

Ernest characteristically dramatized the encounter. Leclerc's greeting, said he, would live in his ears forever. "*Buzz off, you unspeakables,* the gallant general said, in effect, in something above a whisper, and Colonel B[ruce], the resistance king, and your armored-operations correspondent withdrew." Ernest carefully planted a vengeful statement in his next despatch to *Collier's*: "A rude general is a nervous general." Until this stiff-backed professional soldier died some years later in a plane crash, Ernest's name for him in conversation and letters was "that jerk Leclerc."

On the morning of the 24th the drive to liberate Paris began. Rain had fallen in the night and continued intermittently throughout the day. An hour outside Rambouillet everyone in open vehicles was thoroughly wet. With some thought of stealing a march on Leclerc's slowly moving armored columns, Hemingway and Pelkey slithered along a back road from St.-Rémy to Courcelle only to decide that it would be wiser to rejoin the French armor at Toussus le Noble. Colonel Bruce's party left Rambouillet about eight, passing through Dampierre to St.-Rémy, where they took cover behind a wall, only to discover that the shelling was from friendly guns. The rain limited visibility and the column proceeded with caution along the winding highway. Nine kilometers from Versailles, they halted at a crossroads, entered an adjoining farmyard, and were soon "eating an omelette and drinking a bottle of wine . . . snugly ensconced in a warm kitchen." Hemingway, meanwhile, had run into a concentration of German tanks and 88s near Buc. While French mechanized artillery disposed of the stoppage, he and Pelkey entered a ruined café called Clair de Lune. Inside they found an Army historian, Lt. Col. Sam Marshall, with his driver-escort, Lieut. John Westover. Marshall was a firm-jawed and rather saturnine newspaperman from Detroit. Westover bore a distant resemblance to the young F. Scott Fitzgerald. They had spent the night in a woodland near Cernay-la-Ville, and were even wetter than Hemingway and Pelkey. They had just encountered a Spanish girl whose man was in the Irregulars. She was eighteen, with olive-green skin, stringy hair, and protruding front teeth. Hemingway's account of his arrival was typical of his tongue-in-cheek reportage. "I took evasive action . . . and waded down the road to a bar. Numerous guerrillas were seated in it singing happily and passing the time of day with a lovely Spanish girl from Bilbao. This girl had been following wars and preceding troops since she was fifteen."

By Marshall's account, Hemingway appeared in the door of the ruined café yelling, "Marshall, for God's sake, have you got a drink?" Westover returned to their jeep for a hidden fifth of Scotch, which the Americans were busily drinking when they were joined in turn by Michel Pasteau. "What about the girl?" asked Ernest. "She wants to find her husband, and she has been on the lam ever since we lost the Spanish Republic. I've talked to her and know she is OK. She may be a little bit pregnant." He turned to Marshall. "Can she go in your jeep?" Marshall and Westover agreed, with the result that she accompanied her newfound friends all the way into *Paname*.

Colonel Bruce, who had emerged from the farmhouse breakfast to find Hemingway, Mouthard, Pelkey, and the others on the road to Paris once more, was now pleased to discover that the French, by relying on intelligence gathered at Rambouillet, were bypassing most of the positions where determined enemy resistance could be expected. At Villacoublay they turned into the high road for the capital. Except for frequent barricades of ancient motor cars and long avenues of felled trees, the last major obstacle was a "blocklong German ammunition dump" where "stacked shells were already blowing sky-high" and converting the area into an inferno. "The crackle of small arms ammunition, tracer bullets, and the heavy roar of the larger stuff exploding," wrote Bruce, "was not only annoying but quite dangerous, as missiles were whizzing in every direction. We finally passed within a few yards of the edge of the dump and I, for one, found this part of the journey terrifying." Marshall and Westover ran the gauntlet of searing heat and flying metal without damage. Pelkey laughed merrily at the Fourth of July display. "Sure is popping off, Papa," he shouted above the din, every freckle on his face completely happy.

"As we went down the hill toward the Seine about five o'clock in the afternoon," wrote Bruce, "the streets were lined with people. All houses were gay with flags, and the population almost hysterical with joy. Our progress was extremely slow, and there were many long halts as road blocks were cleared, or small points of enemy resistance eliminated. During these stops we were mobbed by the bystanders. . . . When they knew we were Americans, that seemed to increase their enthusiasm. . . . The French flag was everywhere—often it had the Cross of Lorraine imprinted on it." Westover drew from his pack a wrinkled American flag. Affixed to a pup-tent pole and held aloft, this emblem soon filled the American jeeps with more wine, fruit, and flowers than the occupants knew what to do with. Everyone went hoarse with shouting "Vive la France." During the afternoon, said Bruce, they were offered enough drinks to wreck a normal constitution: beer, cider, white and red Bordeaux, champagne, rum, whiskey, cognac, Armagnac, and Calvados.

When night fell that Thursday, they were still a mile away from the Pont de Sèvres. French tanks were meeting strong resistance in a factory below the bridge. An artillery duel was in progress between German batteries in the Longchamps racetrack and Allied tank destroyers along the riverbank. Vehicles were bivouacked along the sidewalks. Michel Pasteau found a house in which the Americans distributed themselves, eating cold rations and some of the fruit which the liberated Parisians had forced upon them. The triumphal crossing of the bridge had to be delayed until noon of the following day.

After nearly a week of sticking his neck out, said Ernest, his only present war aim was "to get into Paris without being shot." He barely achieved it. Shortly after noon on the 25th, according to Colonel Marshall, the column stopped suddenly in a large square near the Bois de Boulogne. Rifle fire erupted, and "an artillery shell out of nowhere struck and felled a chestnut tree on the parkway, so that it fell as a screen between the jeep and the nearest apartment building" thirty yards away. Hemingway and Colonel Bruce scuttled for the buildings across the traffic circle. Marshall, Westover, and the Spanish girl took cover behind the fallen tree trunk. Then, with "a roar and a rattle" six halftracks and five tanks entered the square, peppering the nearby building with bursts of machine-gun fire. As the armor swept away, they heard a man's voice as from a great distance. Then they saw someone in a running crouch on the third-floor balcony of an apartment building on the far side. Westover remarked on the resemblance to Lon Chaney haunting Notre Dame de Paris. But it was Hemingway, shouting something in French. "What's

he saying?" they asked the girl. "That the Germans are in the building behind us," she answered. "We have to get out. The French are bringing up
artillery." While Ernest covered their escape route with a carbine, they scurried for a doorway while a tank sent a few shells into the unfortunate house.
Marshall reflected saturninely that a dozen hand grenades would have done
the job better. "But that would have been poor theater."

According to Colonel Bruce they were stopped again when three German
tanks were signaled ahead. "We then turned off and, under the guidance of
a Spahi lieutenant, raced through the side streets until we emerged just
behind the Arc de Triomphe on Avenue Foch where we parked the cars."
Marshall and Westover ran into a hail of gunfire along the rue de Presbourg.
The target area this time was an apartment house said to contain a sinister
group of Orientals. But it was only one small Tonkinese laundryman, whose
shoulder had been grazed by a bullet. Marshall and Westover bandaged him.
They also prevented a Frenchwoman from being shorn by a crowd of her
compatriots who accused her of consorting with the Germans. The Spahi
lieutenant, resplendent in a red cloak, now took notice of the girl in the jeep.
"Get that woman out," he cried. *"On fait pas la guerre avec les femmes."*
Marshall reacted explosively. "Since when?" he roared. "Go away, young
man, and study a little military history." But the girl needed no further hint.
"Without a word she slipped away to join her lover," said Marshall, "and we
never saw her again."

We walked across [wrote Bruce] to the Tomb of the Unknown Soldier. It was
being guarded by six veterans, standing at attention, and a mutilated ex-soldier,
seated in a wheelchair. They had been there all during the fracas at the [Hotel]
Majestic [which was on fire]. The French Captain in charge asked us if we
wanted to ascend to the roof of the Arc. We did so and were greeted by a squad
of Pompiers standing at attention. For some reason, their Commander presented
me with a pompier's medal. . . . At the end of the Champs Élysées a vehicle
was burning in the Place de la Concorde and behind, in the Tuileries Gardens, it
looked as if a tank was on fire. Smoke was issuing from the Crillon Hotel and,
across the river, from the Chamber of Deputies. Snipers were firing steadily into
the area around the Arc de Triomphe, and French were firing back at them. . . .
The view [from the top] was breathtaking. One saw the golden dome of the Invalides, the green roof of the Madeleine, Sacré-Cœur, and other familiar landmarks. Tanks were firing in various streets. Part of the Arc was under fire from
snipers. A shell from a German 88 nicked one of its sides.

On many later occasions, Ernest asserted that he had personally liberated
the Travellers Club. What actually happened, after an interlude of champagne
drinking, was that Hemingway, Bruce, and Pelkey, finding the Champs
Élysées completely bare of traffic, drove at breakneck speed down the broad
avenue and pulled up at the Club door. All the rooms were closed except
the bar, where the Club president, an elderly Frenchman, was stationed with
a number of the Old Guard. Since the Americans were the first outsiders to

reach the Club, a testimonial bottle of champagne was quickly opened and toasts offered. As they drank, a sniper began to fire from an adjoining roof. Pelkey shouldered his rifle and made for the roof, but was balked in his attempt to deal with the sniper.

According to the Hemingway tradition, the next great step in the liberation of Paris took place at the Hôtel Ritz in the Place Vendôme. Bruce, Hemingway, Pelkey, and several of the irregulars made another dash through small-arms fire from the Travellers Club to the Café de la Paix. They found the Place de l'Opéra filled with "a solid mass of cheering people." The Bruce-Hemingway party lost a carbine by theft and were roundly kissed by what seemed thousands of men, women, and babies. When they could move their vehicles again, they escaped to the Ritz, which had been open and doing business throughout the German occupation. They found the hotel completely undamaged and entirely deserted "except for the manager, the imperturbable Ausiello," who gravely welcomed the wayfarers at the door. They requested and were given lodging in the hotel, and quarters were found nearby for the "Private Army." When asked what else they needed, they answered that they would like to have fifty martini cocktails. The bartender could not be found and the cocktails were mediocre. But Ernest was finally in nominal possession of the Ritz.

He made no attempt to cover the formal surrender of Dietrich von Choltitz, the German commandant of Paris, to General Leclerc near train gate 33 at the Gare Montparnasse, though he magnanimously lent his typewriter to Joe Driscoll of *The New York Times* so that he could write a liberation story. Alan Moorehead, the British historian, found Ernest and his cronies drinking Perrier-Jouet in the Ritz Bar on the rue Cambon side, and later in the evening there was a dinner at which Ernest entertained seven uniformed American officers. Besides Colonels Bruce and Marshall and Lieutenant Westover, these included Comm. Lester Armour of the OSS, Bruce's assistant G. W. Graveson, Brig. Gen. Edwin L. Sibert, J. F. Haskell, and Capt. Paul Sapiebra. Sapiebra had been present at the ceremonial of surrender across the river. The diners exchanged signatures on the Ritz menus as souvenirs. "None of us," said Ernest, "will ever write a line about these last twenty-four hours in delirium. Whoever tries it is a chump." He continued his entertaining on Saturday with a lunch at the Ritz for Helen Kirkpatrick, Ira Wolfert, John Reinhart, Charles Wertenbaker, and Irwin Shaw. Over the brandy Helen said that she and Reinhart were going to see the victory parade in its march towards Notre Dame. Ernest tried to argue her out of it. "Daughter," said he, "sit still and drink this good brandy. You can always watch parades but you'll never again celebrate the liberation of Paris at the Ritz." The brandy was better than the food, which even at the Ritz was poor and expensive.

After four years of German rule, Paris showed few outward signs of change. This struck Ernest as so improbable that he felt as if he had died and returned to stalk happily through some post-mortem dream. He was hospitably received when he went to "liberate" the Nègre de Toulouse, as well as Lipp's Brasserie on the Boulevard Saint-Germain, where his bearlike enthusiasm was rewarded with a bottle of Martell brandy. There was also a joyous reunion with Sylvia Beach at the bookshop in the rue de l'Odéon. Sylvia had learned from Helen Kirkpatrick that Ernest was back in Paris, and he posed in uniform for pictures. The *Franc-Tireur* published an account of the occasion the following week, stating that M. Hemingway had given an impression of "invulnerability and power." Sylvia still had the copy of *Winner Take Nothing* which he had inscribed for her on his return from Spain in the spring of 1937. He seized a fountain pen, added to his old inscription the words, *"Lu et approuvé,"* and affixed a new date: "Paris, August 25, 1944," though it was in fact the 26th.

He was not at all averse to having his exploits mentioned in the French press, whose working members were delighted to spread the Hemingway "liberation legend." One curious result of the publicity was a letter from M. Chautard, lumberman, sawyer, and owner of the apartment building in the rue Notre Dame des Champs where Ernest had lived with Hadley and Bumby after their return to Paris twenty years ago. His wife was dead, said Chautard, but he wished that Hemingway would do him the honor of coming to lunch. Ernest politely declined, pleading the pressure of military duties. As for his old enemy, the macaw-voiced Madame Chautard, he observed that if she were crossed with his mother, the combination would win a blue ribbon at the all-time international bitch show.

He wrote Mary Welsh, who was actually in Paris at the time, an account of his "strange" adventures on the road from Rambouillet to the Ritz. Having thrown away the book somewhere the other side of Chartres, said he, he had found a group of maquis near Rambouillet. Probably because he was so old and ugly-looking, they had insisted on placing themselves under his command. He had clothed them with uniforms from a dead cavalry recon outfit and armed them from Division. When American recon was withdrawn from Rambouillet, he had taken the town and defended it (though "very scared twice,") against fifteen Kraut tanks and fifty-two German cyclists. He had also run patrols, many of them more frightening than Grimm's fairy tales, in order to furnish the "gen" for the advancing French. He had "fought the outfit" several times in what he cavalierly called "chickenshit operations." They performed well and were "very fine peoples" whom Mary would like. Luckily for the record, the Army's official war historian, Sam Marshall, had been "with us" during one phase of the advance. They entered Paris by the Étoile and the Place de la Concorde. Since the liberation, he had behaved well and quietly, taking no advantage of other correspondents because of his own participation in various military actions, and carefully explaining to them whatever he knew of the way in which victory had been achieved.

60. *UNDER THE WESTWALL*

IN the last warm days of August, Ernest held court to many visitors in his room at the Ritz. The most important of these, from his point of view, was Mary Welsh, who had earlier hitched a ride on an airplane from England to a field near Le Mans, reached Paris by jeep in the confusion of the liberation and subsequently covered General Leclerc's victory march down the Champs Elysées on the 26th. Although she was working nearly around the clock, she saw Ernest in his room at the Ritz as soon as she could. He received her at the door with a "welcoming merry-go-round bear-hug" and led her inside to meet "his mob." There was a GI stove in the fireplace, and Mary noticed that the floor was bare. Ernest's uniform was equally bare of insignia except for the 4th Infantry Division's shoulder patch of four green ivy leaves.

Other visitors often found him in the company of a few of the partisans who had scouted for him on the road from Rambouillet. Two of his favorites were Onesime and Marcel. The most important of the group was, however, a dark-haired man of thirty-three named Jean Décan. His hatred for the Nazis was fanatical. He had been in the French underground for nearly two years and had twice been arrested and tortured by the Gestapo in the horror chambers of the rue des Saussaies. His first encounter with Hemingway at the Grand Veneur in Rambouillet had quickly developed into a master-and-man relationship. On the 25th he had fought a skirmish against a detachment of Germans in the Tuileries and then tried vainly to enlist in the French Army. Since that time he had become Ernest's personal bodyguard.

Ernest's French translator, Marcel Duhamel, was serving as his confidential secretary. He was responsible for a visit from one of Ernest's leading rivals. It was a story that Ernest loved to tell afterwards, and it got better with each passing year. He was sitting with his "worthless characters" on the "nice delicate old furniture" in his room. They were field-stripping and cleaning weapons. Ernest had his boots off and was wearing "one of the two shirts" he owned. He was not prepared for the resplendent figure who came striding through the door. It was André Malraux in the uniform of a colonel, with gleaming cavalry boots.

"*Bonjour,* André," said Ernest.

"*Bonjour,* Ernest," Malraux replied. "How many have you commanded?"

Hemingway's answer was typically modest. "*Dix ou douze,*" said he, with studied insouciance. "*Au plus, deux cent.*"

Malraux's thin face contracted in the famous tic. "*Moi,*" he said, "*deux mille.*"

Hemingway fixed him with his coldest stare and said in level tones, "*Quelle dommage* that we did not have the assistance of your force when we took this small town of Paris." Malraux's reply is not on record. But one of the partisans presently beckoned Ernest into the bathroom. "Papa," he whispered, "*on peut fusiller ce con?"* No, said Ernest, it would not be necessary to shoot the man. Offer him a drink and he would leave without bloodshed. So they offered him a drink and went on with their soldierly work in the sunny room, leaving their distinguished visitor to preen, jerk, and twitch until he rose to depart. This, at any rate, was Ernest's version of the event.

Another of Ernest's visitors at this time was a young, dark-haired sergeant in a CIC outfit. His name was Jerome D. Salinger and he was much impressed with his first sight of Hemingway. Salinger was a writer of short stories, twenty years Ernest's junior. At twenty-five, he had already sold some of his work to *Story* magazine and the *Saturday Evening Post.* He found Hemingway both friendly and generous, not at all impressed by his own eminence, and "soft"— as opposed to the hardness and toughness which some of his writing suggested. They got on very well, and Ernest volunteered to look at some of his work. Salinger returned to his unit in a state of mild exaltation.

While Ernest was following the literary life in liberated Paris his friends of the 4th Division were occupied in hot pursuit of the enemy north and east of the capital. By nightfall on August 31st, Colonel Lanham's Double Deucers had secured a bridgehead across the Aisne. In the next three days they crossed the Oise north of Guise near the Belgian frontier. The region was flat farmland, intersected with slow streams and barge canals. Much of the action took place inside a quadrangle formed by the towns and villages of Wassigny, Le Cateau, Landrecies, and Pommereuil. The temporary task force of which the 22nd was a part achieved a series of remarkable victories in heavy fighting, during which they destroyed large quantities of German armor, captured an ammunition dump, and took 2,000 prisoners.

On the first of September a cryptic message was delivered to Ernest at the Ritz. "Go hang yourself, brave Hemingstein," wrote Buck Lanham. "We have fought at Landrecies and you were not there." It was an updated version of King Henry IV's joyous taunt to the Duke of Crillon after a victory at Arques. Although Ernest believed that he had used up all his luck in the march on Paris, this was too great a challenge to ignore. He resolved to try, as he put it, to pass a couple more times with the dice. Early next morning, armed to the teeth and driven by Décan, he left the Place Vendôme in his jeep and headed north.

It was the most foolhardy of his wartime adventures. The region he crossed was crawling with pockets of German troops and armor which had been bypassed in the swift Allied "rat-race" for the Belgian border. Most of them were desperately trying to cross south of Liège into the comparative safety of the Westwall and the well-fortified bunkers of the Siegfried Line. Much of Ernest's itinerary remains obscure. His rough notes on the trip, scrawled on two pages in his War-Diary, do little more than suggest the route he followed. "Trip out," he writes. "Puncture at Le Bourget—Follow Div to above Compiègne—The night in the narrow field under sky—the wind in the trees as fall weather came—The five V2's—Thought were night fighters—Sept. 3—

6 a.m. at Div headquarters—Start for Vic Sur Aisne—Lose column with puncture—nail—another puncture—3rd puncture—The MP's the 3000 Germans 15 FFI's out of sixty back—Column stalled at Fère—Bridge out—we reconnoitre bridges—The reparable bridge found by bicycle—John's man escapes—Recon in advance of 50 cyclists. Recon to ———— 2 Germans at X-roads—42 cyclists—Right turn into ———— Horsedrawn soldiers—The 2 escape routes across road—4 prisoners in X—6 more at station—The three tanks at Mézières—3 more in bushes by windmill—On into ————— The fight to our left and below at St. Quentin———"

It would appear that he and Décan followed the regular route north from Paris through Senlis to Compiègne, where they spent the night of September 2 in a field and saw the five German V2s, supersonic successors to the clumsy buzzbombs, swooping high overhead for England. Next morning they turned eastward for Vic-sur-Aisne on the road to Soissons, only to be so much delayed by punctures that they lost the column and did not catch up with it again until they found it stalled at La Fère, above Laon. It is possible, though unlikely, that they got as far east as Mézières, and much more probable that they followed the back road through Crécy to Guise, within easy striking distance of Lanham's regiment. In any case, the dice he had mentioned continued to roll in his favor.

Near the village of Wassigny about ten miles from Guise, Ernest and Jean ran into trouble. Or so he said. By his account their presence attracted more than a dozen local volunteers. A reconnaissance group discovered that the short road between Wassigny and the considerable town of Le Cateau was cut off by German armor, making a roundabout detour advisable. The major obstacle was an enemy antitank gun so situated down a side road as to be able to interdict the main route. Anxious to remove it, one of the Wassigny volunteers came up to Hemingway, saying, *"Mon capitaine, on ne battre pas?"* No, said Hemingway. American infantry was in the area and would eventually take care of the threat. When the young man spat on the ground in what looked like an insolent manner, Ernest flew into one of his rages. He told the youthful gallant that if he thought he could knock off a gun like that, it was all his. The attack lasted an awful four minutes, leaving the German gun intact, but killing six of the French and wounding two others. All this occurred, said Ernest, because he had lost his temper.

He caught up with Lanham at Pommereuil on September 3rd. Lanham told him he was lucky to have arrived in one piece. But "brave Hemingstein" had proved his point: that he was not afraid. The temporary task force was disbanding and there was no need to stay. He hurried back to the sanctuary of Room 31 at the Ritz. His reunion with Mary was highly successful. They lived, by her account, "on little besides Lanson Brut champagne and the wonder of being together again." She had left Paris shortly before the Germans moved in four years earlier, and they went to see her old flat behind the Invalides. They sat in the sunlight on the quai at the Île St.-Louis, where Ernest had read

stories for Ford's *transatlantic review* twenty years earlier. He entered a few
details in his diary. "Lunch at Lavigne's—Rode up to Boule Mich, stopped
in bookstore, and then walked to [Café] Flore, dined hotel, slept till early."
Wishing to make Ernest's room at the Ritz homelike, Mary bought colored
prints of pictures that he liked and hung them on the walls. One was Van
Gogh's painting of well-worn workman's boots, which reminded her of Ernest's
army boots, bearing the wrinkled impress of his character and his wartime experience. The only trouble with the reunion was its brevity. "Pickle," wrote
Ernest some days later, "did we not have a lovely time for such a short im-
permanence?"

The fast-moving 4th Division was already eighty-five miles inside Belgium
on the morning of September 7th when Ernest once more left Paris, this time
in a cavalcade of five vehicles: two cars, a motorcycle, and two jeeps. Besides
Ernest and Red Pelkey, the group included Jean Décan and the two other
irregulars named Marcel and Onesime, Capt. Marcus Stevenson, Peter Lawless
of the London *Daily Mail,* and the Brazilian, Nemo Lucas, who had stolen
Ernest's drink in July. "The Brazilius" had not changed: he still talked volubly in broken English, and would borrow anything from a typewriter to a
toothbrush.

The country reminded Ernest of the Schwarzwald in the summer of 1922.
He took special notice of all the trout streams. But he discovered that his
clothes were not warm enough. Across the plateau of Villers-Cotterêts to
Soissons a strong gale was blowing. He was deadly sleepy after Paris and as
they moved eastward into the Ardennes, he felt the symptoms of a cold in
his chest. Black storm clouds were massed above the pine forest. But no rain
fell and that night they slept beside the vehicles on the brown-needled floor of
the woods. The wind blew high and cold, tossing the tops of the pines as it
used to do in that season when he was a boy in Michigan. So, he told Mary
Welsh, there was no need to feel cheated out of the fall, as one often felt
when living in a strange city or in countries whose climates were different.

Throughout the trip Ernest was impressed by the curious mixture of peace
and war. When they stopped in Libin in southern Belgium to spend the
second night, he admired the forest behind the château. A few deer and wild
boar had managed to survive the years of occupation under the eye of the
gamekeeper, who also ran the local pub. Yet all around them were signs of the
delaying action of the Germans, who harassed the flanks of the advancing
American columns, sowed mines, rigged booby traps, set up ambushes, and
sought to capture vehicles to help them in their flight. Delayed by blow-
outs, the little column progressed to St.-Hubert, where Red and Jean cooked
beef tenderloins butchered from cows killed in a pasture near Hatrival. It
was very cold and Ernest slept soundly in a bedroom beside the courtyard.
While the townspeople sauntered to church on the morning of the tenth,
Jean and Red made a Sunday breakfast of bacon and eggs. Ernest commented
in his journal about the excellence of the jams in the ration kits. The hotel

charged them nothing for the rooms, the wine, the cooking they had done in the kitchen, or the fact that Jean had slept the night with the *patronne's* tall daughter.

The morning air was still "lovely" when they set off once more. They could hear the sound of tanks and heavy machine guns along the Bastogne road. "Ah," said the Brazilius, "that is the cheers of our troops as she advances." Ernest was already calling him the Brazil Nut. Outside Compagne they interviewed four prisoners. One was a Hitler Jugend, very frightened; another a silent boy of eighteen; the third was an older man from a Security Regiment who groveled politely in guttural French; but the fourth was an SS man, tough, young, and very blond, who gave "complete information as if he were speaking to a fellow military student." The 22nd Infantry was in the region. They managed to find Colonel Lanham in a patch of forest near Bertogne. They went on to Mabompré and watched a German attack on the crossroads below, pausing for lunch during the fight.

That afternoon they reached the western extremities of the Belgian village of Houffalize, sixty kilometers southeast of Liège. From the hilltop overlooking the valley, they could see the rolling forested country stretching towards the German frontier. Lanham deployed a platoon of tank destroyers in hull defilade. They were firing at German armor as it raced across the village bridge and out of town. The Brazilius, driven by curiosity, wandered towards the TDs, exposing himself on the skyline of the hill, inviting fire from the German batteries beyond the village, and endangering all his companions. Hemingway had just yelled to him to get down when one of the tank destroyers, maneuvering into a better firing position, ran over a mine and knocked itself out of action. When the dust settled, the Brazilius still stood upright as a sore thumb. Hemingway ran crouching to his side, hurled him to the ground, and threatened to kill him if he got up again. Shocked and hurt, the Brazilius scrambled to his knees only to be rudely dumped once more by the enraged Hemingway.

The bridge in the midst of the town was essential to the eastward passage of Lanham's vehicles. A local Belgian guided him along a goatpath over the high ground that flanked the village on the right. Ernest and the others took the main road down the hill. It was a poor choice. The retreating Germans had left roadblocks of tree trunks, all of them well-mined and booby-trapped. They had also fixed a heavy charge of TNT under the bridge. Lanham's jeeps were just entering the main square when the bridge went up in a blast so huge that several nearby houses were also destroyed.

When Hemingway and Lawless got there, Lanham was surrounded by villagers bearing gifts—cakes, baskets of eggs, and bottles of wine and brandy. He was consulting some of them on the question of replacing the bridge, since the regimental engineers were far back in the column. The citizens of Houffalize set to work at once. Lanham and Hemingway perched on a fence to watch. Some of the bystanders, noting Hemingway's size and martial appearance, began to address him as a general. But Ernest said modestly that he was only a captain. How did it happen, they asked, that at his age he had not progressed beyond the rank of captain? "Alas," said Ernest sadly, "it is because I never learned to read and write."

During this interlude, the artisans of Houffalize were digging out the debris, snaking timbers, building buttresses, hauling and nailing planks, and making a bridge capable of carrying all vehicles up to heavy tanks. Incredibly, the task was accomplished within a single hour. When it stood complete, the colonel and his quasi-general crossed the river on the echoing planks which had not been there an hour earlier and returned to the regimental command post. That night Ernest was too tired to eat and went to bed early, partly to escape the society of the Brazilius. "If Carmen Miranda tires you," he wrote in his diary, "this Brazilian would slay you dead. Slept well once he was out."

The clear, blue September weather reminded him of hunting days in his boyhood and he spoke of the region around Houffalize as Indian country. The forest they had traversed on the 10th was as thick, he wrote his son Patrick, as the stand of lodgepole pines behind the Nordquist ranch in Wyoming. One recent command post had been a hunting lodge with mounted heads above the fireplace. Deer tripped flares in the nighttime woods, while foxes, hares, and coveys of wild pigeons could be started up from almost any thicket. In the irony familiar to soldiers down the ages, nature went on naturing even in the midst of war.

Ernest reflected that the days since mid-August had been the happiest of his life, without loneliness, disappointment, or any disillusionment. Nothing was false; all problems were clear and well-defined. He was proudly aware that Lanham now thought better of him than ever before, and jotted down notes on a staff conference of Lanham's in the "little polyglot town" of Beho on the German frontier.

The twelfth was a fine wild day of chasing and shooting. German armor was fleeing towards the protection of the Westwall, and Lanham was driving on to occupy the high ground above Hemmeres. Hemingway's group went with the northern half of a pincer column, following a tank and some halftracks through Schirm and Maspelt. Once they fell behind and Jean had to do an Indian scouting job to find their route at a crossroads. Far ahead, Ernest watched a half-track scuttle like an animal out of the forest edge and back again. Two planes, their bombs gone, strafed below tree level on the left. But over the highest hill that they climbed they came suddenly upon a scene as welcome to them as the Pacific was to Balboa. "There," wrote Hemingway, "was Germany spread out before us."

Behind a haycock just below the ridge they stopped to watch two German tanks racing up the road beyond the village, with American artillery blasting white-yellow clouds of smoke and road dust in their path. Then they went down a forest trail to the river. The railroad bridge was only a tangle of timber and iron. They crossed at a ford ("water brown over brown mossy stone") to watch the first American tanks enter Germany. It was 4:27 P.M., Tuesday, September 12, 1944.

In the town of Hemmeres "ugly women and squatty ill-shaped men" came sidling towards them with bottles of schnapps, drinking some themselves to show that it was not poisoned. Other villagers held up their hands in token of surrender. All the houses were deserted, and in one they found the still warm fragments of an officers' meal. Amid the hammering sound of heavy machine guns and the boom of artillery on the right, Lanham's combat team passed beyond the village to secure the high ground to the eastward.

Ernest requisitioned a deserted farmhouse on the edge of the village, immediately adopting and feeding the cat and the dog, and sending Jean to find villagers who could milk the complaining cows. Then he asked Colonel Lanham and his staff to dinner. He shot the heads off a small flock of chickens with his pistol, and set a German woman to plucking and fricasseeing them. About dusk, Lanham arrived with Colonel Ruggles, his three battalion commanders, and his personal staff officers. They began with a staff conference, reviewing orders and outlining plans for the 13th. Hemingway, Lawless, Stevenson, and the Brazilius listened in and poured the drinks. "All our booty drunk up," wrote Hemingway in his War-Diary. "Teague sends for some wine. Supper of chicken, peas, fresh onions, carrots, salad, and preserved fruit and jelly for dessert."

The Brazilius, whom Ernest was now calling The Pest of the Pampas, had volunteered an exposition of his "theory of the rear azimuth." When the moment arrived, he leaped to his feet, waving a borrowed compass, and began to describe his "rear-ass theory of pursuit." The whole company dissolved in laughter. "No one," said Lanham, "had the remotest idea what he was talking about." To Lanham, in far retrospect, the dinner in the farmhouse seemed the happiest night of the war.

The food was excellent, the wine plentiful, the comradeship close and warm. All of us were as heady with the taste of victory as we were with the wine. It was a night to put aside the thought of the great Westwall against which we would throw ourselves within the next forty-eight hours. We laughed and drank and told horrendous stories about each other. We all seemed for the moment like minor gods, and Hemingway, presiding at the head of the table, might have been a fatherly Mars delighting in the happiness of his brood.

Early next morning Ernest was awakened by the clack of Lawless's typewriter, and the prowling and whining of Brazilius, who wanted to borrow the machine, having left his own behind. He continued so obstreperous throughout the day that Ernest lost his temper just before dinner and cursed him to his face. The victim took the bawling-out with his customary air of injured innocence. But after dinner, his rage dispelled and his stomach happily filled with steak, German onions, and *Brandwein,* Ernest wrote Mary that he was beginning to purr like an old jungle beast. Across the table, Captain Stevenson was also writing to his girl, pausing occasionally to read significant excerpts aloud, and receiving Ernest's mature counsel in return.

The fine autumn weather now dissolved in cold rain. Ernest somehow lost his Burberry, got wet through, and began to cough and sneeze. He boasted to his son Patrick that he would have been taken prisoner several times daily if he had not learned to use his head and those two egg-shaped glands located elsewhere. But this was some more of his romantic pretending. When the combat team launched its attack on the Westwall, he was back at Divisional headquarters bedded down with a severe cold. It was a good place to be. The high ground that the 22nd Regiment faced was a wooded ridge, extending for miles northeast-southwest and called the Schnee Eifel. All along the ridge lay strongly fortified bunkers, built of reinforced concrete, camouflaged against attacks from the air, manned in part by SS troops, and dominating the broad valley to the west. All the approaches were strewn with antipersonnel and Teller mines. Heavy artillery was deployed along the heights. This was the impregnable Westwall against which the American attack took form at 1000 hours on September 14th.

When Ernest got back on the 18th, he found the regiment established in the town of Schweiler between Mütxenich and Winterscheid. He was as eager as a boy to find out what had happened in his absence. Lanham took him on tour of the contested ground. Casualties had been heavy but the Westwall had been breached. Ernest interviewed Capt. Howard Blazzard, who filled him in on some of the details of the attack. He concluded that the worst liar in Hollywood could not begin to invent what Lanham and his team had accomplished. When the 3rd Battalion had bogged down in the assault on the heights, Lanham had gone forward, armed only with a Colt .45, to rally his men. "Let's go get these Krauts," said he. "Let's get up over this hill now and get this place taken." In the end the tank destroyers had worked behind the German bunkers, firing point-blank at doors and embrasures. "You never saw such a mess," said Blazzard. "Every one of [the Germans] was wounded in five or six different places, from pieces of concrete and steel. . . . All the time inside there was the most piteous moaning and screaming." Besides thirty "reasonably good Krauts," the Americans who entered the first bunker captured several cases of sardines and several more of excellent brandy.

In the tiny village of Buchet on the hillside above the rolling plain, Ernest established himself in a farmhouse which he named Schloss Hemingstein. It was here, in the following week, that Captain Stevenson arrived one rainy evening with John Groth, the artist. Groth was a slim and gentle man whose cartoons and sketches had been a staple of *Esquire* magazine for years. He was much impressed by his first sight of Hemingway, who was seated in the farmhouse living room surrounded by admirers, including Jean Décan and the photographer Kimbrough. Beside him on the table was a half-filled glass and a clutch of grenades. In one corner stood a demijohn of cognac, recently filched from a grocer at Bleialf on the plain below. Groth accepted a glass and fell to sketching Ernest by the light of the oil lamp. When he grew sleepy, Ernest gave him a couple of the grenades, with instructions to drop them from his window in case the Germans counterattacked. Groth dozed fitfully and fully clothed in a dirty featherbed upstairs, until the roar of artillery roused him before daylight. Peering down the stairwell into the room below, he saw Hemingway still awake, his tommy-gun in his lap. He was reading a pocket-sized magazine.

Later that morning they lay in underbrush with an observer, watching American artillery pound the village of Brandscheid. That night, along with a dozen others, they were guests at a steak dinner in Lanham's command post.

The meat had just been served [wrote Lanham], when an 88 crashed through the wall which Hemingway was facing. It went out the other side without exploding. . . . The 88 traveled at almost exactly the speed of sound, so there was never any warning of its approach. In a matter of seconds my well-trained people had disappeared into a small potato cellar. . . . I was the last one to get to the head of the stairs. I looked back. Hemingway was sitting there quietly, cutting his meat. I called to him to get his ass out of there into the cellar. He refused. I went back and we argued. Another shell came through the wall. He continued to eat. We renewed the argument. He would not budge. I sat down. Another shell went through the wall. I told him to put on his goddamned tin hat. He wouldn't, so I removed mine. We argued about the whole thing but went on eating. He reverted to his favorite theory that you were as safe in one place as another under artillery fire unless you were being shot at personally. I pointed out that this was precisely what was being done and that he was beginning to sound like the Brazilius. We continued to argue, to drink, and to eat. And perhaps to feel the drinks a little. The firing presently died down and the rest of the group came back up. The food was reheated and the dinner continued.

On Saturday the 23rd, Ernest wrote Mary that he had fully expected to be back in Paris by this date. The story of the assault on the Westwall was stowed away now in his memory. He would have liked to set it down in the luxury of the Ritz. Both in the letter and eventually in the article itself, he managed to give the impression that he had been personally present during the assault on the 14th and 15th. It had been weirdly Wagnerian, said he, among the Dragon's Teeth of the Siegfried Line, and the Dragon had swallowed up many of the finest people. He did not indicate that he had not been present. He confessed to wishing desperately to get out of this "hawk and cough and spit area" and into a proper house with Mary Welsh. He had seen her in hotels like the Dorchester and the Ritz, but never yet in a house of their own. He wanted to be where he could wash his head and even own a pile of clean shirts instead of the one experienced rag that he had been wearing for so long.

There were persistent rumors at Divisional headquarters that he might be in trouble over his scouting work at Rambouillet. The "liars" and the "phonies" and the "ballroom bananas" were evidently trying to make something shameful of a piece of work in which he took great pride. In retrospect he thought of it as an emergency, where he had simply done his duty. Suppose a rule forbade journalists from jumping into the Seine. If someone were drowning, who would comply? He was sure that his friends would support him to the hilt. One was Joe Driscoll of *The New York Times,* to whom he had lent his typewriter on liberation day. General Barton and Colonel Lanham could likewise be counted on to assist him in time of need.

Next morning the rains swept in again, at first hard and sharp, then soft and driven by the wind. Enemy shelling was heavy. He would have to stay at Buchet a while longer. It was not fair to pull out when the going was tough. He began to compose a poem:

> Loseing the three last night,
> Takeing them back today,
> Dripping and dark the woods . . .

But there was too much talking in the small living room at Schloss Hemingstein. He abandoned his verse-making with the comment that it sounded anyway like "chickenshit Hiawatha." Today, though only forty-five, he was feeling old. Not funny and good and nice like Mary's friend Sam Boal. Not charming like "our fine brother," Willie Walton. Instead he was like an aged steeplechase horse, ugly and misshapen but at least back in training. With the rain and the wind and the current impasse in western Germany, everything in the Big Picture looked bad. In the Small Picture, luckily, he had thrown off the cold in his head and chest. Although it sounded dirty to say so, he was very happy in this war.

61. IM HÜRTGENWALD

THE message that Ernest had been dreading arrived one morning in October. "You will proceed," it said, "by military aircraft and/or Government motor transportation on or about 4 October from present station to Headquarters, Inspector General Third Army (Rear) to carry out the instructions of the A.C. of S., G-2, Supreme Hq. AEF." The purport was not mentioned, but he knew it well enough. He was to be interrogated about his activities in and around Rambouillet during August 18 to 25, 1944. He went by jeep to Nancy and walked through the moonlight to the hotel where the Inspector General worked.

The officer assigned to his case was Colonel Park. The allegations were numerous. War Correspondent Hemingway had removed his correspondent's insignia in order to assume command of FFI forces in Rambouillet. He had helped to defend the town on August 19–20; he had been either a colonel or a general officer with the FFI, and in this capacity had persistently run patrols. The correspondents who brought the accusations likewise stated that they had found in his room a stock of antipersonnel and antitank grenades, as well as mines, German bazookas, and sundry small arms. They further alleged that he had maintained a "map room" in Rambouillet, that a full colonel had acted as his chief of staff, and that he had declared to a fellow correspondent that he was no longer writing despatches. The penalty, if any of these charges were proved, would be Hemingway's loss of accreditation as a war correspondent and his prompt return to the United States. "In the morning," said Colonel Park, "I will question you and take your statement under oath." Hemingway turned in after midnight to get such sleep as he could.

Next morning, Ernest admitted that he might have doffed his tunic with insignia owing to the warm August weather—but only momentarily and for purposes of "sanitation." He asserted that he had never commanded troops, though repeatedly asked to do so by Resistance groups who finally agreed to accept his advice in lieu of actual leadership; that he had merely served as adviser to Major Thornton in disposing defensive troops at the outskirts of the town; and that those who addressed him by military titles did so simply in affectionate terms. He pointed out that anyone who owns a dory along the New England coast is automatically addressed as Captain; all residents of Kentucky are natural-born Colonels; and any Chinese who has served in uniform the requisite number of years is customarily regarded as a General. The weapons and ammunition were stored in his room solely as a convenience to irregular troops operating under the command of duly constituted authorities. While he owned maps and went on patrols, this was done only to gather material for his magazine articles. Instead of having a full colonel as his staff officer, he merely served as liaison man for the colonel, transmitting his orders to the irregulars because his French was fluent and the chances of misapprehension accordingly fewer.

There seems to have been only peripheral discussion of whether Hemingway had actually fought with the 4th Division after the liberation of Paris during the "rat-race" across France and Belgium. Hemingway disposed of this idea by assuring Colonel Park, who nodded approvingly, that he had been accompanied at all times by Captain Stevenson, the Division's Public Relations Officer, who would bear personal witness to Hemingway's innocence. To the malicious charges by various backbiters that Hemingway had persistently impeded the progress of the armies by trying to act like a character out of his own fiction, he answered that he could produce character and conduct testimonials from General Barton and Colonel Lanham which would indicate the contrary.

Colonel Park concluded the interview by advising Hemingway to set his mind at rest. On the way back to Paris, it was very cold, with a hint of impending snow. Ernest checked to see if Mary was in the hotel. She was not there and he "walked through the long alley where all the things were that you did not have the money to buy and admired them in their glass cases." Next to Mary, what he wanted most was a drink in the crowded bar on the rue Cambon side in order to forget, if possible, that for the first time in his life he had committed perjury.

Full exoneration was shortly forthcoming. "The rap," as he said exuberantly, was beaten. He was more anxious than ever to rejoin the 4th Infantry Division, which had now been ordered into the region around Murringen and Krinkelt for rest and retraining. On Sunday the 8th he sent summary accounts of the Nancy affair to General Barton and Colonel Lanham. Despite his relief at being cleared, he felt bitter at having held Rambouillet under orders, only to be accused of "being a show-off and a horse's ass." Had he admitted the truth of the charges, he could have gone home "a lousy hero," waiting in comfort for a suitable medal to be struck off by the Key West Chamber of Commerce or the Havana Pigeon Shooters' Club. Instead he had "covered" for all his former associates, denying his part in the most useful, successful, and cheapest-run military action of his entire life. Bitterness, however, was a piece of baggage he could not afford. His chief emotion was shame at having a rear-echelon address like the Hotel Ritz. He wanted nothing more than to rejoin his friends where the fighting was.

His estranged wife was at the moment closer to the fighting than he. On the 14th, at the forward division headquarters of the 82nd Airborne in Nijmegen, she met Lieut. John Westover, who had helped Ernest "liberate" the Ritz. Westover wrote home to his wife that Martha wore "lots of perfume" and was "very pretty, very charming." He told Martha that he had entered Paris in Hemingway's company, though he supposed that she must long since have heard that story. "Yes," said Martha, "he said something about it. I'd just gotten into Paris from Italy and he came back from the Fourth Division. We talked for about two hours and he said he had some drinking to do and I had some friends to see, so I haven't seen him since." It struck Westover as a curious way to run a marriage.

Ernest was still bitter and still at the Ritz on the 17th of October when he wrote to thank Lanham for his generous character testimonial. His "celebrated case" now bored him, said he, but so did several chairborne officers he had lately met. One was a four-striper Navy captain whom the other correspondents all seemed to revere, although he had never fought, never been to sea, and knew nothing of navigation. Ernest did not mention his own antisubmarine exploits. But he believed that the captain somehow suspected him of having been to sea and hated him accordingly. In entering the same room, said Ernest, he always tried to do it in such a way as to make the captain feel that "things were not so good as they had been up to that time." This was of course a practice at which he excelled. There was also a colonel with an amputated arm who had been extremely and pointedly rude on several occasions. Contrary to his usual attitude towards those whom war had mutilated, Ernest considered various counter insults, such as recommending quietly that the colonel acquire an artificial arm, or even hinting that the amputation had resulted from a self-inflicted wound. In the end, however, he kept his mouth shut. It was one form of behavior that the war had taught him—more or less.

Hemingstein's Bearded Junior Commandos joined him frequently for breakfast in his room at the Ritz. The Vosges Mountain region where Mike Burke had been working with the partisans had recently been overrun. He had returned to Paris and found Ernest at the Ritz Bar. Ernest quizzed him repeatedly about the fire fights between the Free French and the Germans. "Where were they?" he would ask, as he had done along the banks of the Ebro six years earlier. "Where were you? What weapons did you have?" Burke said that he had reread *For Whom the Bell Tolls* "while waiting for the proper moon period to be dropped into France" and that he had often thought of both Hemingway and his book while "wandering around in the mountains of Eastern France." Ernest was delighted. He read aloud to North and Burke excerpts from some of his poems, of which he seemed inordinately proud. Another of his inventions was the Valhalla Club, in which the Junior Commandos were to be charter members. As commander in chief of the armed forces, the President of the United States was to be responsible for all bar bills. An elephant, supplied by Buddy North's family circus, was to be retained as club bouncer. These ideas were developed at length in afternoon sessions at the Ritz Bar.

But the seances were not limited to mornings and afternoons. One evening Ernest conducted his young friends and Mary on a guided tour of the bars of Montmartre. Here, wrote Burke, "Papa began to make modest claims of having been an outstanding tackle on the Oak Park High School football team when it was coached by the great Bob Zuppke. I chided him about his exaggerated abilities as a gridiron hero and he allowed that no skinny, swivel-hipped Pennsylvania All-American could get past him. This . . . led to an informal football game in the Place du Tertre, me carrying a bottle of wine as a football and Papa lined up on the other end of the square looking like an earnest Sam Huff in steel-rimmed glasses. . . . The patrons of the bistro . . . poured out into the street to watch this contest." Burke leaned low and took off, while Ernest reared his huge bulk and went in for the tackle. Burke found it no great feat "to execute a crossover step and a stiff-arm" which dumped Ernest onto the cobblestones. But he bounced up again "like a rubber ball, glasses undamaged, uniform slightly torn, and full of laughter."

In such ways as this he spent the month of October in Paris, partly because his adopted regiment was relatively static in Belgium, but chiefly because of Mary Welsh. His nickname for her had recently changed from "Small Friend" and "Pickle" to "Papa's Pocket Rubens." He wrote his son Patrick that if she got any thinner she would be promoted to "Pocket Tintoretto." In any case, she was a very fine girl. Along with Bob Capa's girl, she had been awfully good to him at the time of his London accident, looking after him in what he now recalled, not without self-pity, as the worst time he had ever had.

He was writing her another poem, a rough pastiche of free verse and freer prose. He put it together on several mornings between September 28 and October 9, largely in the lavatory adjoining her room at the Ritz. Outside the window the leaves were beginning to change color in the garden of the Ministry of Justice. Inside, Ernest was trying to achieve a kind of counterpoint with the classic ingredients of love and war. Here, at "home," as he put it in the poem, was his new true love, "Mary Welsh of the quick eyes, the concaved lovely face (the cheeks from the Ming Dynasty) and the lovely breasts" that were "the figurehead of all [his] ships." And there, beyond the horizon, in Belgium and along the western frontier of the Reich, was the war to which he would return whenever an attack was to be mounted.

There also was the realm of death. He paid bitter tribute to the men of the 22nd Infantry Regiment who had died between the two midnights of September 13 and 14, 1944. The casualty reports for the day named six officers and sixty-one enlisted men killed in action among the bunkers of the Siegfried Line. "Now sleeps he with that old whore Death who yesterday denied her thrice," the poem began. "Do you take this old whore death for thy lawful wedded wife? Repeat after me. I do. I do . . . Sixty-seven times."

Later assembled from the various scraps of paper on which he had scribbled it, the poem covered nearly eight pages of typescript. He began carrying it in his uniform pocket. He took it to a party at Sylvia Beach's bookshop in the rue de l'Odéon. David E. Scherman was doing a story on Sylvia for *Life* magazine, and had asked her "to have a few friends around as in the old days" of the 1920s. The group included Janet Flanner, the brilliant Paris correspondent for *The New Yorker* magazine, as well as Valéry, Vercors, Scherman, and others. They all listened respectfully.

Marlene Dietrich had taken a room at the Ritz to serve as a pied-à-terre while she traveled to various fronts as USO entertainer for the troops. Once or twice at the Ritz Bar she read the poem aloud in her throaty voice, inducing tears among those at the table, Ernest included. "Papa," she would say, gazing at him with her large and melancholy eyes, "I don't care what you do since you wrote that poem." So encouraged, he began to think aloud in the same imagery. He told Buck Lanham that he now knew death as well as he knew the oldest whore in Havana. Although he might buy her a drink, he would never go upstairs with her. Yet *never* was a big word. He knew very well that whatever we say we will never do, we are sure to do sooner or later.

Along with the poems, Ernest had begun to meditate a "wonderful" novel based on his war experiences—at sea hunting submarines, in the air with the RAF, and over the land with the 4th Infantry Division. He wrote Max Perkins that he had been on the verge of starting the part about the sea when he left Cuba for New York in April. If his luck held and he returned safely from the ETO, he said that he would be a very valuable literary property to Scribners. He had hit some excellent pay dirt on his last prospecting trip to the Schnee Eifel.

Another such trip was imminent. He had been back at the Ritz for more than six weeks when he learned that a new offensive was about to be launched by the 4th Infantry Division. Its mission was to clear a wide pathway through some fifty square miles of thickly forested hill country west of the Rhineland city of Düren. The assignment looked nearly impossible. Streams were icy and turbulent, the mud deep and viscous. The Germans were well dug in. Mines were buried everywhere. Mortars and machine guns defended every slope and defile. Heavy artillery lay within easy range. The farming villages of the region, Brandscheid and Gey, Kleinhau and Grosshau, had been converted into virtual fortresses. One other small community had given its name to the dark and dripping woodland. This was the Hürtgenwald.

Late in the afternoon of November 15th, Lieut. Col. Tom Kenan looked up from his battalion command post, which was located in a deep hole in a small clearing on the western extremities of Hürtgen Forest. Peering somewhat nearsightedly down at him through steel-rimmed glasses was a tall man in olive-drab trousers, combat boots, a knitted helmet liner, and a steel helmet. His bulk, already sizable enough from Kenan's perspective, was further accentuated by a white leather jacket, lined with sheepskin. Kenan recognized it as the kind the Germans had been using for camouflage among the early winter snows in the Schnee Eifel. By contrast, the spectacles astride his nose seemed "pitifully small and inadequate." He was carrying a Thompson submachine gun. This was Kenan's first sight of Hemingway, who had arrived in a jeep a few hours earlier, cold and weary, driven by his bodyguard, Jean Décan, and accompanied by Bill Walton.

Until very late that night Lanham and Hemingway sat talking in the regimental trailer, drinking up some of the whiskey Ernest had brought, and filling in the gaps between letters. Ernest spoke of his son Bumby, who had been missing in action since October 28th, and of Martha's recent request for a divorce. Lanham talked of his wife Mary, his only daughter, and his small new house in Arlington, Virginia, the first he had ever owned. Ernest told of the recent hurricane, which had blown down many trees in the grounds of the Finca, and of the loyalty of Gregorio Fuentes, who had stayed aboard the *Pilar* throughout the storm.

Lanham's plywood trailer, the scene of many talks between Ernest and the staff of the 22nd, was a masterpiece of rolling architecture, drawn from place to place by weapons carriers or 2½-ton trucks. It contained two bunks, a stove, a drop-leaf table, a washstand, two settees, and a field telephone. There was also a German helmet, extravagantly decorated with flowers by "Big Hawk" Hawkins, a staff officer, and presented to Lanham for use as a chamber pot. Despite such amenities and the presence of his civilian friend, Lanham felt gloomy that night. At one point he said that he had a feeling that he might not survive the Hürtgen campaign. Ernest exploded. He was sick of "all this shit" about premonitions. The great Ernie Pyle was always having them. You heard about them all the time, but they meant nothing. But even as he spoke, he knocked on wood. Whatever he might say to the contrary, he was as superstitious as a medieval peasant.

The attack next day was scheduled for 1245 hours. German artillery was active all morning. With Ernest in tow, Lanham went out early to inspect battalion positions and check orders. The acting commander of the First Battalion, a major, had established his post in a carefully prepared dugout of earth and logs. He was a "little gray sort of man" of whose capacities as leader Lanham was not wholly convinced. On the way back to the trailer in the jeep Lanham mentioned his doubts to Hemingway: in a day or two he might have to relieve the major. Ernest listened silently. "Buck," he said, after a moment, "you won't ever have to relieve him." Lanham characteristically bristled. "Why?" he asked. "He won't make it," said Ernest. "He stinks of death."

When the jeep reached the regimental command post ten minutes later, it was stopped by Lieut. Col. John F. Ruggles, the executive officer. "Colonel," said Ruggles, saluting, "the major has just been killed. Who takes the First Battalion?"

A shell fragment had ripped between the logs of the dugout, killing the major instantly. Ernest made no comment and walked on to the trailer. At the Operations Center, Lanham ordered Maj. George Goforth to replace the dead man and reviewed plans for the day's attack. When he got back he found Ernest sitting in the trailer with a drink in his hand. "How the hell did you know that?" asked Lanham. But Hemingway only mumbled that he could not say. Here, inside Germany, was the same curious stench that he had smelled at the Château Lingeard in Normandy three months earlier.

In the eighteen days of the Hürtgen campaign, casualties mounted steadily. German artillery and mortar fire was intense, incessant, and accurate. "The tangled forest," said Lanham, "was itself a formidable enemy." The dense growth of conifers made artillery barrages doubly dangerous when shells burst among the limbs and metal fragments scattered widely in so-called "tree bursts." Antipersonnel mines were all over the place. The weather remained insufferable. "You can't see," said George Morgan, a T-5 in Goforth's battalion. "You can't get fields of fire. Artillery slashes the trees like a scythe. Everything is tangled. You can scarcely walk. Everybody is cold and wet, and the mixture of cold rain and sleet keeps falling. Then we attack again and soon there is only a handful of the old men left."

From the point of view of his associates among the hard-driven officers of the regiment, Hemingway's behavior was still as exemplary as it had been at the Westwall in September. During the day he would roam around, driven by Jean Décan, and staying, as Colonel Lum Edwards said, "out of our hair." But at night, "after things were buttoned up, he would drift into the S-3 section where he and I, and often Colonel Lanham, would talk and tell stories. One evening he got on the subject of the mating antics of African lions and wound up demonstrating how a male lion acted. On other occasions we would talk about courage and the proper reactions to fear and duty. He was contemptuous of the psychiatric view that each individual had a breaking point and could take just so much for so long. He rejected the idea that there should be no more criticism of the mental breaking point than the physical one. He seemed to believe that 'guts' were something a man had or didn't have, and that fear in combat was simply the test. Yet he was not impressed by reckless bravado. Rather, he admired the man who could see clearly what was necessary to do and had the courage to do it, regardless of the percentage of risk involved. He never admired raw courage unless it was the only way of getting the job done. I never saw him act foolishly in combat. He understood war and man's part in it to a better degree than most people ever will. He had an excellent sense of the situation. While wanting to contribute, he knew very well when to proceed and when it was best to wait awhile."

He was notably cynical on the topic of war and religion. The Division Chaplain was a small and deeply sincere man, so fascinated by Ernest's opinions that he kept coming back for more. Ernest once asked him if he believed the widely quoted statement from Bataan that there were no atheists in foxholes. "No sir, Mr. Hemingway," the chaplain said, "not since I met you and Colonel Lanham." The reply delighted Ernest, who added it to his growing collection of martial anecdotes.

His lifelong scorn of "head doctors" reappeared in his maltreatment of a divisional psychiatrist named Major Maskin. One night the doctor invited himself into Ernest's billet and began to ask his probing, subtle questions. Ernest put on a sober face, saying that he needed Maskin's advice. He was troubled about his cats at Finca Vigía. He had twenty or thirty and kept getting more. "The little bastard was fascinated," said Ernest. "His eyes were bugging out." Many people liked cats, said the doctor. That was no problem. "With me it is," said Hemingway. "My problem is that I can't seem to stop having intercourse with them."

Ernest gloried in the role of senior friend and counselor to both officers and men. Sometimes he called himself "Old Ernie Hemorrhoid, the Poor Man's Pyle." Many of the battalion and company commanders were in fact only slightly over half his age. His bulk and appearance contributed to their sense that he was more experienced than they were, both in combat situations and in life itself. Lum Edwards, George Goforth, Swede Henley, John Dowdy, and Tom Kenan were all at this time about twenty-seven years old. In talking with them, Ernest sought to remain as unobtrusive as his size would permit, but they could not help feeling that he was observing them narrowly and perhaps even sizing them up as fighting men. When some of Kenan's subordinates "began to use rather exaggerated verbiage to describe the bitterness of the [German] defense, Hemingway responded mildly and uncritically that he had not observed quite that intensity" in enemy operations. He was careful to be calm and friendly, speaking with a shy but obviously sincere smile.

Another of Lanham's battalion commanders, a humorous South Carolinian named Swede Henley, was impressed by Hemingway's fearlessness. "He stayed with me for several days," says Henley, "in my command post in the front lines in the rain, sleet, and snow. He was always right in the thick of the heaviest part of the fighting, looking for something to write about. He carried two canteens—one of schnapps, the German equivalent of southern corn whiskey, and the other of cognac. He always offered you a drink and he never turned one down. One of the things that amused me was how he always put the canteen in the corner of his mouth and gulped it down."

Despite bad weather, poor rations, severe casualties, frequent deaths, and other deprivations, these infantry officers enjoyed their locker-room gossip. Ernest was as completely accepted in their circle as any of the military. Like Swede Henley, they were all "impressed by the fact that, of his own free will and volition, he had elected to remain well forward in the combat zone." Several of the battalion commanders had read *For Whom the Bell Tolls* during their ten-day voyage to England the winter before, and they joked with him now about the sleeping-bag scenes between Jordan and María. He responded with good humor, but modestly and with a trace of shyness.

Even potentially lethal moments could be endured with laughter. After several days of hard fighting, a small clearing was uncovered in the forest. It was part of a firebreak and even boasted an unmined access road. Lanham ordered his trailer brought forward and his staff dug in around the periphery. Day after day, Ernest occupied one of the leatherette seats while Lanham conducted his command. Now and again Lanham would open the trailer door to check by ear the location of small-arms fire. If a shell landed while he was peering out, as happened often, he would leap back and slam the flimsy plywood door, as though it could offer protection. This impractical gesture always set both men off in gales of schoolboy laughter.

The Hürtgenwald was far too dangerous to permit such scouting operations as Ernest had conducted in France. Except for one emergency, he was content to watch and listen. But when the time came, he was more than equal to it. Lanham's command post in the forest clearing had been closely watched for two days by a German platoon hidden in a bunker a hundred yards away. On the morning of the 22nd they came out shooting. Lanham's headquarters commandant, Captain Mitchell, was killed at once. Hemingway moved in fast with his tommy-gun. In the face of brisk small-arms fire, Décan valiantly tried to go to the aid of Captain Mitchell. The attack was soon repulsed, the surviving Germans were taken prisoner, and a troublesome mortar was knocked out of action—all by quick action in which Ernest had been an active participant.

But there were other times when he had the good sense to lie low. One morning American artillery fell short with a barrage. Many soldiers in forward positions were killed. Among the victims was Lanham's "striker" or orderly, an eccentric Regular Army man known as Eightball Watkins. When the bombardment ended, Ernest accompanied Lanham to the Operations dugout where some of the dead had been brought. "Do you know what old Eightball would say if he could?" asked one of the bystanders. "He'd say, 'By God, Colonel, it took our own artillery to get me!' " Ernest was visibly moved. Watkins had been a familiar figure around Lanham's trailer. Like many of the others, he agonized over such meaningless losses. For years to come they would form the substance of his nightmares.

Other horrors implanted themselves in his memory, not least those that he saw in the destruction of Grosshau—a "potato village," as Lanham called it, that "was in fact part of the integrated defenses of the Siegfried Line," with walls built underground that were often three to five feet thick. Repeated poundings by artillery of every caliber, attacks by heavy bombers, and flaming seas of white phosphorus had failed to dislodge the defenders of Grosshau. It did not fall until the 22nd Regiment swarmed into it and cleared it out in hand-to-hand fighting. The "butcher bill" for this all-out assault was tremendous. Even after it fell, the town continued under steady barrage from German artillery and at least one huge railway gun firing from the western outskirts of Düren.

Ernest was boiling to enter Grosshau. On November 30th he set off with Bill Walton through mud and slush. German shellfire often compelled them to take cover in the ditches, many of which had been cleared neither of mines nor of the dead. One American soldier, lying in the road, had been so flattened by the passage of many vehicles that he was hardly recognizable as human. Even worse was the spectacle of a German corpse at the edge of the town, roasted with white phosphorus, and the half-starved dog that was feasting on the flesh. Such visions and smells could sear their way into any observer's memory. Ernest never forgot them.

During the Grosshau visit, Hemingway and Walton were constantly under fire. Lieut. James McLane, leader of one of Lanham's companies, had set up his C.P. in the basement of a ruined house. Just as the barrage outside suddenly increased in intensity, he looked up to see Hemingway's great bulk swing over the edge of the cellar hole and drop down, followed immediately by the slighter Walton. McLane had to duck quickly to avoid a collision. Afterwards he remembered with admiration the cool calm of both his visitors. So did Walton himself. During the whole Hürtgen Forest campaign, he found Hemingway at his absolute best, intent upon sharing all the hazards of war with his friends in the regiment. Though Walton was ten years younger than Hemingway, he was never conscious of any discrepancy in their ages. Ernest seemed gay of heart, without internal conflict, happily free of the complications of women.

After the reduction of Grosshau, it remained to take the town of Gey and move out of Hürtgen into the Cologne plain, where the attack would fortunately be downhill. "At this time," said Lanham, "my mental anguish was beyond description. My magnificent command had virtually ceased to exist. . . . These men had accomplished miracles. . . . My admiration and respect for them . . . was transcendental. My anguish centered on the thought of what would happen if the Germans threw a counterattack. Division Headquarters ignored my apprehensions. . . . And so I began to put together the personnel at regimental headquarters, the signal people, the clerks, the drivers, the mechanics—two rough companies. . . . I would alert them by day and by night. I made them keep their weapons and ammunition with them at all times in case an attack should come."

One finally came at 3:30 in the morning. Two of the three tanks were knocked out at once. The battalion commander who flashed the word to Lanham was shooting Germans with his free hand while the other held the field phone. German assault waves seemed to be everywhere. Lanham formed his reserve unit and they moved off at dogtrot towards the sound of the fight. Then he called Hemingway. "I'll be right there," said Ernest. "Wait for me." When he arrived, Lanham's ragtail reserve had just swarmed into the fight. The German advance began to falter. A company commander managed to conduct a small group into the rear of the attacking force. The one remaining tank moved to the right flank and began to cut loose. The crisis passed and the Germans surrendered by dozens. At Lanham's elbow throughout, Hemingway listened to a blow-by-blow account of the infantry's latest travail. Once more it lodged permanently in his memory. He had been there. He knew exactly how it was.

Lanham's regiment had now been virtually decimated. Between November 16th and December 3rd, it sustained 2,678 casualties, including 12 officers and 126 men killed in action, 184 missing, 1,859 wounded, and nearly 500 nonbattle casualties. On the morning of December 4th, when the division was at last pulled out of line to a rest billet near the city of Luxembourg, Ernest told Willie Walton that they must go to say good-bye to the departing survivors. The morning was cold, with a heavy ground fog and a low ceiling. Their battered jeep was moving slowly down a mud-slimed road when they heard a strange ripping sound. Only Ernest recognized it. The Luftwaffe, short of aircraft, was using an obsolete plane of a type he had known in Spain. "Jump," he yelled, and they leaped for the ditch. Out of the dirty sky came a low-flying German plane, strafing the road and stitching the jeep down the middle. Ernest and Willie stayed where they were. The ditch was mined and the plane might return. But Ernest, huge and muddy in his sheeplined jacket, maintained a monumental calm that Walton found impressive. Presently he unhooked a canteen from his web belt and offered Walton a drink. It was a premixed martini. It tasted of metal. But Walton had seldom enjoyed anything more. For him, as for Ernest, it marked the end of the terrible eighteen days in Hürtgenwald.

62. PARIS COMMAND POST

WHEN Hemingway got back from Hürtgen Forest at the end of the first week in December, he had had enough of the war. He began to negotiate for a return flight to the United States. The winter weather in western Germany had given him a severe cold in the head and the chest. Ernest went to bed although, as usual, he held court for a variety of visitors, including Jean-Paul Sartre, a short and voluble man in thick glasses, and Simone de Beauvoir. Sartre was curious about his opinion of William Faulkner. Ernest magnanimously admitted that Faulkner was a better writer than he. When Simone asked how ill Ernest really was, he kicked off the bedclothes and waved one muscular leg in her direction. "Healthy as hell," said he. For the moment, at least, he seemed to be on top of the world. But he later asserted that he had often "coughed the toilet at the Ritz full of blood." His brother Leicester, who occasionally dropped in, recalled the pallor of his face beneath the ragged beard, and the way he staggered back to bed after one of these bouts of retching, holding onto the furniture for support.

Another chance for heroic behavior was presently thrown into Ernest's lap. About nine o'clock on the morning of the 16th the German high command launched a huge mechanized drive against the American First Army's slender defense line in Luxembourg. It was their first major counterattack since the Avranches offensive in August, and had been planned by their best remaining strategist, General Kurt von Rundstedt. General Barton's 4th Division took the first impact on the left flank, where Colonel Bob Chance's regiment, with piecemeal reinforcements from other units, met and bore the brunt of the battle.

Pulling all available wires, Ernest managed to get through by telephone to General Barton's headquarters. According to Barton, he explained that he was sick and on the way home. "But he wanted to know if there was a show going on which would be worth his while to come up for. . . . For security reasons, I could not give him the facts over the telephone . . . so I told him in substance that it was a pretty hot show and to come on up." By early morning of the 17th, Ernest had managed to procure a jeep and driver through General Red O'Hare. He later said that he was still running a temperature, and sweating so much that he had to change his shirt four times between getting out of bed and leaving the hotel. He wore two fleece-lined coats, one given him by an American flyer and the other the Kraut jacket he had used at Hürtgen.

By the time he reached Luxembourg, the worst of the German offensive had been contained. At Divisional headquarters, Barton told him that "Bob Chance was carrying the ball for the 4th Division." He asked Ernest to make sure that "Bob and his outfit" got a "good publicity play." But Ernest, for the moment, was much too ill to comply. Along with Bill Walton, he accepted Buck Lanham's invitation to move into his command post near Rodenbourg, where the two correspondents shared a large double bed with their own bedrolls. At Lanham's insistence, the regimental doctor dosed Ernest heavily with sulfa pills and ordered him to stay quiet. The house was that of a priest who was said to have collaborated with the Germans. Ernest rummaged around until he found a store of sacramental wine. He took an almost maniacal delight in drinking the contents and then carefully urinating the bottles full again. He later explained that the bottles had served him in lieu of a chamber pot, since the thermometer stood at zero and he did not want to risk his life "with the fever and all" by going to the latrine downstairs. One further elaboration was that he labeled the bottles "Schloss Hemingstein, 1944" and made the mistake of sampling one in the dark, thus proving the contention of the Biblical preacher that "all is vanity."

On the morning of the 22nd he returned to circulation, though still weak and afflicted with periodic sweating. Colonel Jim Luckett was in charge of a small task force near Breitweiler. Ernest joined him on a hilltop to watch what Luckett satirically called "a magnificent display of force" by a regiment of the 5th Division. "They were dressed in snow camouflage made from sheets," said Luckett, "and went across the plateau two or three miles conducting marching fire. What they were shooting at I don't know. Ernie and I had a pleasant time joking about it." Back at Division, with the help of Colonel Jack Meyer and his staff, Ernest worked for the next day and a half gathering data on what was now being called the Battle of the Bulge. According to Ernest, Charles Wertenbaker used this material for two long articles in *Life* magazine.

Ernest's marriage to Martha was now approaching dissolution. She appeared about noon on the 24th for what Ernest ungallantly called her "big Christmas counterattack." Unaware of the situation, Colonel Ruggles invited her to spend Christmas Eve and Day with the 22nd Infantry and sent a jeep to Luxembourg city to bring her to the command post at Rodenbourg. "It was my intention to surprise Ernest pleasantly," said Ruggles, "but I'm afraid it was otherwise." Since Martha had already broached the subject of divorce in November, Ernest did nothing to alleviate the strain.

That evening he attended a stag dinner in General Barton's mess, a schoolhouse in Luxembourg. Although it was the ailing general's fifty-fourth birthday, he had planned the dinner to honor Colonel Chance. Among the guests were Gen. H. W. Blakely, who was about to succeed Barton as commander of the Division; Brig. Gen. Rodwell, Barton's second in command; the saturnine Colonel Luckett; and the guest of honor, Colonel Chance. One notable absentee was Colonel Lanham, who had quarreled bitterly with Barton and Rodwell during the Hürtgen campaign, and had been ordered to take temporary command of the 12th Regiment, as well as his own, so that Chance could attend the festivities. They drank NAAFI rations of Scotch and gin, the local brandy, and much champagne. The Christmas turkey, with mashed potatoes and cranberry sauce, seemed almost homelike. The feast had been in progress for two hours when Colonel Luckett became so outspokenly critical of the divisional command that Barton ordered him out. He left with Ernest for a champagne party with the 70th Tank Battalion. Ernest later appeared with Martha at Barton's billet where they drank brandy and talked for a while around Barton's Christmas tree. But Martha and Ernest soon drove away to Rodenbourg. Unlike Ruggles, Lanham already knew of the parlous state of their marriage. Nonetheless, he gave them his bedroom and shivered through the frosty night in his unheated trailer.

Next morning they made a holiday tour of Lanham's battalion command posts. Ernest sat in front with the driver, behaving, as Martha thought, with supreme arrogance. Unaware of Lanham's competence in the language, she began to scold Ernest in French. Lanham sat silently, watching the back of Ernest's neck, which grew redder by the minute. At last Ernest turned around. "In case you don't know it," he told her, cuttingly, "Buck speaks much better French than you do." Lanham ignored the altercation as well as he could. The roads around Luxembourg were extremely dangerous. Fighter planes from both sides habitually strafed moving vehicles. Buck was more than usually alert, having barely escaped death on the 24th from an attack by American P-47s. Although no attack occurred that morning, they did see an astonishing sight: a thin, white vapor trail like a chalk line drawn with incredible speed across the sky. It was a German V2 rocket, successor to the buzzbombs, heading for its target at supersonic speed. Lanham ordered the driver to stop while they watched. Martha took note of the time and place. "Remember this, Ernest," Lanham heard her say. "That V2 is my story, not yours." Ernest said nothing until the tour was over, when he told Martha with bland assurance that she had now been as close to the real front lines as she was ever likely to be. Since she had been to many fighting fronts since 1939, she found the remark especially irksome. It was made no better by his public use of her private nickname, Mooky.

His program of harassment reached a new low on New Year's Eve. Bill Walton had just checked into the Luxembourg hotel where the Air Force was quartered when he met Martha for the first time. The tall girl with honey-colored hair and well-fitting tan slacks struck him as very attractive. She accepted his invitation to dinner and they spent the afternoon coasting on a hillside with dozens of apple-cheeked Luxembourg children. When Walton got back to the hotel, he found Ernest sitting in his room. "I've just been coasting with your wife," Walton told him, "and I'm going to take her to dinner." Ernest grinned savagely. "And me, too," said he. "I'm coming along."

It was not a happy occasion. Ernest berated his wife at great length and in a loud voice. Walton soon gave up his attempt to turn the talk into less acrimonious channels. It was not until Martha had gone and they were back in Walton's room that he began to scold Ernest for his unseemly conduct. "Willie," said Ernest, "you can't hunt an elephant with a bow and arrow." But he was still not through. Some minutes later he stripped off his uniform, found a mop and bucket in the chambermaid's closet, put the bucket on his head for a helmet, laid the mop on his shoulder like a lance, and marched off down the hall in his long johns to lay siege to Martha's room.

Apart from the contretemps with Martha, the Von Rundstedt offensive was the last battle of the war in which Ernest participated. Early in January he returned to the Ritz, taking up his former life as father-in-residence to officers and men of the 4th Infantry Division who came to Paris on leave. He later reported, with what truth it is impossible to say, that one of his visitors was the famous George Orwell, whom he had last seen in Barcelona. Orwell looked nervous and worried. He said that he feared that the Communists were out to kill him and asked Hemingway for the loan of a pistol. Ernest lent him the .32 Colt that Paul Willerts had given him in June. Orwell departed like a pale ghost. Another encounter was with William Saroyan. He was just outside the bar on the lower level of the Hôtel Scribe when he saw Hemingway in the midst of four or five war correspondents. One of them waved at Saroyan, who approached the group. "Here's Bill Saroyan," said his friend. "Where's Bill Saroyan?" said Ernest. Saroyan said, "In London you had a beard, but even without it I haven't forgotten you. Did shaving it off make you forget me?" Ernest turned away and resumed his talk with the fawning newspapermen. Saroyan found their sycophancy "embarrassing to witness" and went off about his business.

Some nights later Ernest took vengeance. Group Captain Peter Wykeham Barnes of the RAF was on temporary leave in Paris, and happened to meet Ernest at the Scribe. "After taking in quite a quantity of grog," he wrote, "we adjourned to the George V for dinner. We went down to a lower floor to eat, and everything was ringing like bells when Ernest espied William Saroyan sitting two tables away. . . . This worked on him like a powerful injection. . . . He started by stating, 'Well, for God's sake, what's that lousy Armenian son of a bitch doing here?' The more . . . I tried to hush him, the worse it got. . . . Finally, Saroyan's companions . . . began to come back at Ernest. I'm not too sure how it developed, but shortly afterwards I was in a full-scale brawl, rolling about under the tables and banging the heads of total strangers on the wooden floors. I got the impression that someone bit my ankle. . . . The management arrived, reinforced I think by gendarmes, and the whole lot of us were thrown out *up* the stairs and into the Paris black-out. The two factions separated . . . Ernest was laughing like a hyena."

It was about this time that Ernest learned through channels that his son Bumby was safe, or at least alive, in a German POW compound. Ever since his return from the Hürtgen campaign, he had been "sweating out" the absence of trustworthy knowledge about Bumby's welfare. In the "Second Poem to Mary" he had defined the phrase as "that which one must suffer without any possibility of changing the result." Inside his head he kept hearing the words, "Missing in Action." The story was dramatic enough, even for Ernest. Lieut. John H. Hemingway had joined the OSS in July and parachuted into France at Le Bosquet d'Orb, fifty kilometers north of Montpellier. His assigned task was the training of partisans to infiltrate enemy positions. Late in October he was making a daytime reconnaissance along the Rhône valley with Capt. Justin Green and one of the French partisans. They heard digging inside a patch of woods. Green crawled in to reconnoiter. It was a bad mistake. The enemy opened up with rifles and grenades. Green was wounded in one foot and Bumby in the right arm and shoulder by grenade fragments and six rounds from a high velocity carbine. The Frenchman was hit in the belly and later died. Under interrogation, the Americans discovered that their captors were an Alpenjäger unit. The officer in charge was an Austrian who pricked up his ears when Bumby gave his name and serial number. He had been in Schruns in 1925 and had known Ernest, Hadley, and the two-year-old boy who now stood before him, aged twenty-one, and bleeding badly from his wound. The officer rapidly ended the interrogation and shipped Bumby off to a hospital in Alsace. A team from the 4th Armored Division subsequently liberated him from a POW camp near Hammelburg, but he was recaptured four days later, and taken to Stalag Luft III in Nuremberg.

Late in January Mary left for London. She was back in Paris by Valentine's Day. Ernest was talking about a coming visit from Buck Lanham and Bob Chance, who were soon to reach Paris from their command posts in western Germany—the first leave that either of them had had since D-Day. They checked in at the Crillon, spruced up a little, and went off through wet and gloomy weather to Ernest's command post at the Ritz. Here for the first time they both met Martha's successor Mary, and Lanham, as a special gift, presented Ernest with a pair of German machine pistols. When mounted on stocks they were roughly the equivalent of light machine guns. Buck had also brought a substantial supply of ammunition for the weapons. Ernest was so much excited by the gift and by the reunion with two such eminent comrades-in-arms that he got, by his own subsequent admission, "a little wild." He was in fact so far along with his drinking that he insisted upon walking about in the room with one of the guns fully loaded under his arm—something he would never have done under ordinary circumstances. Although Lanham and Chance both thought it a risky business, they protested only mildly. Such an experienced gun handler as Ernest could presumably be trusted.

He presently picked up a portrait photograph of Mary's husband, Noel Monks. Over Mary's protests, he showed the picture around among the guests, made some unkind remarks about its subject, who had been "faintly difficult" about the idea of giving Mary a divorce, and then set the picture up in the fireplace. He was just squaring off to give it a burst with his new machine pistol when Lanham grabbed his arm. A ricochet might have killed or wounded the people in the room, to say nothing of innocent bystanders in other parts of the hotel. Ernest lowered the gun, seized the picture, and retired into the lavatory, closing the door behind him.

Not two minutes later, the group in the room were astonished to hear two short, ugly bursts of fire. They hurled open the bathroom door to find him howling with laughter. He had carefully mounted the picture of Monks on the toilet, shot it to tatters, and of course destroyed the toilet bowl completely. The bathroom floor was flooded. People tried to sop it up with bath towels. A delegation of worried managers appeared. There were leaks in the rooms below. The air filled with Gallic expostulations.

Ernest was determined to make the most of this dramatic moment. He took his stand on the bidet like a Fourth of July orator. *"Messieurs,"* he said, *"je regrette profondément le malheureux incident. Messieurs, permettez-moi de vous présenter mon ami, le Colonel Lanham, qui sera bientôt général. C'est un soldat de ligne formidable qui a été sous le feu de l'ennemi sans arrêt depuis les débarquements de Normandie, et n'a eu depuis repos ni distractions. Il est venu ici pour nous rendre visite, à Madame et moi-même. Il nous a dit qu'il désirait utiliser les toilettes. Quand il s'assit pour se soulager, Boum!*
. . . Et vous pouvez vous-mêmes, Messieurs, vous rendre compte des résultats. Nous n'avons plus de temps à perdre. Il me faut une nouvelle toilette immédiatement, avant le matin."

Whatever the management thought, they professed sympathy at this strange accident. They clucked their tongues amiably and sent for the plumbers. Ernest thought it all very funny indeed. But Mary was so furious that she seriously considered ending their relationship then and there. Buck Lanham, she told Ernest, had called it an adolescent trick. "Hope so," Ernest mumbled. "Hope so. But a lot of people in grown-up jobs think of this adolescent as Papa."

Lanham returned next morning to find Ernest, Mary, and Marlene Dietrich expecting him. The room was well stocked with hard liquor, champagne, and cocktail food. When Ernest and Mary departed to do some errands, as they said, it dawned on Lanham that this was a planned conspiracy of Ernest's to leave the brave warrior in the company of the beautiful actress. He found the thought embarrassing, and was considerably relieved when Miss Dietrich made no attempt to be seductive. She was nursing a bad cold and drinking champagne to cure it. She spoke at length of her adventures on the USO tours, and mentioned the fact that Gen. George Patton, one of her ardent admirers, had given her a set of his pearl-handled pistols. When Mary and Ernest reappeared in the middle of the afternoon, Lanham had begun to share Hemingway's often-reiterated admiration for "the Kraut."

Ernest took pride in showing off both Mary and Marlene to visiting officers, and boasted that his room was the Paris command post for all veterans of the 22nd Infantry Regiment. When Bill Walton was assigned a room at the Ritz, he soon discovered that it was on the same floor as Miss Dietrich's. He had bought a rather extravagant hat, ornamented with black cock feathers, as a present for his friend Content Peckham in the New York office of *Time*. Marlene modeled it around the corridors, even wearing it on one occasion when she sat on the toilet in Walton's room, talking to him while he shaved. Ernest discoursed at length on Marlene's excellence as a woman, carefully explaining to Walton that they had never been lovers.

They had a party for Bill Walton before he left for home. He had scarcely gone when Ernest (typically enough) began to criticize the piece Walton had written for *Life* magazine about the Hürtgen Forest campaign. According to Ernest, Bill's four pages of good intentions were like giving your best bird dog a copy of Aeschylus and supposing that he would read it instead of chewing it up. Such backbiting also went on with General Barton. While continuing to address flattering letters to him, Ernest privately called him "our lost leader," and composed a little parody of Browning's poem, beginning, "Just for a hooker of bourbon he left us/—For a Ballroom Banana to stick on his coat."

Although he said repeatedly that he missed his life with the 4th Division and the 22nd Regiment, he now renewed his plans for going home. His heart, he told Lanham, counseled him to stay on through the end of the war; but his head kept advising him to take up his own private fight, which was to return to Cuba, get himself in shape to write after a lapse of nearly four years, and take care of his own regiment, which consisted now of Mary Welsh and his three sons. That would be far harder than staying on in Europe; it was therefore what he must do.

He had also been tortured recently by a return of the headaches which he attributed, probably with reason, to four major concussions in two years' time. The last days of February and the first of March were especially bad. But at three on the morning of March 2 he awoke to find the headache gone. He attributed the relief to a "miracle of the waters": he had taken a hot bath before going to bed.

He used the afternoon of March 2 in "shopping for transport" to New York. Spring vacation for his schoolboy sons Patrick and Gregory would begin March 14, and he wanted to have them with him in Cuba. After the social life of Paris, he longed for the privacy of the Finca. He had lately sent home $3,-000 to repair the house and grounds. Perhaps he could keep away from perpetual drinking, conversations with well-wishers, and even the veterans of the 12th Brigade in the Spanish Civil War whom he had been supporting, by his own account, since 1939.

His shopping expedition yielded space aboard a returning bomber with Gen. Orville Anderson, leaving for the United States on Tuesday the 6th. On the eve of his departure he scrawled a farewell note to Mary, his "dearest Pickle." He would love her always. Now he would go to get their life together started. Every minute they were apart he would be truly faithful: in his heart, in his head, and in his body. And he signed it: "Your loveing husband, Mountain." During a stopover in London he looked in briefly on Martha, who was in bed with grippe at the Hotel Dorchester. But he did not linger. That phase of his life was over.

CHAPTER 10

Returnings

63. *THE VIEW FROM THE FINCA VIGÍA*

ALTHOUGH Ernest spent much time and money in restoring the house and grounds against Mary's arrival, and once signed himself "E. Hemingway, Writer and Farmer," the farming was far more extensive than the writing. He was also discovering that he missed the war. He compared his loneliness in being away from Mary to that of a soul in Limbo or Purgatory. Trying to reduce his drinking by ninety per cent as a homecoming present for her made him feel righteous. But it was a poor substitute for having two cold bottles of Perrier-Jouet Brut 1937 in his room at the Ritz, with Marlene Dietrich to talk to while he shaved, and afterwards a luncheon date with Mary. In wartime Paris, said he, his nonproductivity as a writer had not given him guilt feelings. He was proud of his association with the military and felt fully justified in having as much fun as possible when he was not in or near the front lines. Home again, yet still unable to settle into the old patterns, he felt useless.

His flight across the Atlantic in the bomber had been boringly uneventful. During a week's stopover in New York, he had busied himself with long-distance calls to relatives of his military friends, including Buck Lanham's wife, Pete. He enjoyed a brief reunion with Morris Abraham Cohen, the general from Hong Kong, and a long publisher's lunch with Max Perkins. Then he collected his younger sons, Patrick in New York and Gigi in Florida, and took them away to Cuba to spend their spring holidays.

After the boys had departed, he was plunged once more into the "black lonelies." He ran a large domestic staff, including a Chinese cook, a butler, a maid, a chauffeur, and two small boys to run errands to the village. He also employed four gardeners to repair the damage left by the hurricane of 1944, and to thatch the roof of the patio beside the swimming pool. Indoors he cleaned out his desk and destroyed unanswered mail. Most of the nights were hard to get through. To get tired enough to sleep, he drove to Havana on April 10th to walk through the old part of the city. His resolution to return home in good season broke down when he passed the *frontón*. He dropped in on the last of the jai-alai games and then drank frozen daiquiris until two in the morning. The Floridita was still the best of anodynes against his recurrent nightmares, which were now peopled with blank-faced German infantry. He was too gregarious or too haunted, or both, to enjoy being alone unless he was writing, as he was still unable to do. He told Mary that he was planning to read Thoreau, who always reveled in solitude. His own problem, however, was that he did not wish to live by himself. He was not impatient for Mary's arrival, said he: he was merely desperate.

She telephoned at last on the morning of the 13th, having reached New York after a stormy trans-Atlantic passage. Her first obligation was to go to Chicago to explain to her parents why she was leaving Noel Monks in order to marry Ernest. He listened to her slow and sultry voice and said that he could not possibly wait two more weeks without seeing her. But he resolved to use the intervening time to improve her "mountain property" (himself) which had fallen into considerable disrepair during the winter of war in Europe. In this he was making progress. His chest had recovered and the headaches were farther apart. He no longer drank in the mornings, waiting until noon for his first Tom Collins and taking only a quarter bottle of wine with lunch. He did not propose to give up drinking, but only to learn to dominate his thirst.

Next day Dr. José Luis Herrera, the voluble surgeon, came out for lunch by the pool. Ernest described the adverse effects of his two wartime concussions: terrible headaches, slowness of thought and speech, loss of verbal memory, a tendency to write syllables backwards, sporadic ringing in the ears, and partial impairment of hearing. The doctor was dismayed to learn that he had spent only four days in bed in London after the blackout accident. He said also that the Calvados and bad gin that Ernest had drunk in France and Belgium had been the worst possible treatment for subdural hematoma. The inflammatory effect, as Ernest explained to Mary, accounted for those occasions in Paris when he had behaved badly because he was "not himself." Now in Cuba the prognosis was good. Herrera advised gradual retraining of the injured brain, with limited intellectual activity each day.

Ernest took pride in his powers of resilience. On Saturday the 14th he dined with Graciella Sánchez and stayed out until two in the morning at a waterfront café. Next day he won $38 shooting pigeons at the Club and on Monday permitted himself a lunch in Havana where he "lorded it" ever so lightly over some of the twenty marksmen he had beaten the day before. Tuesday he ran the *Pilar* as far as the cove at Bacuranao, wearing only a jockstrap and a rod-butt-rest in order to get well-tanned for Mary's arrival. On the 19th he talked to Mary again by long distance, finished thatching the pool shelter, sorted books for a new bookcase, swam ten laps, did seventy-five lifting exercises, shot a match with Alvarito Villamayor in which he killed nineteen out of twenty pigeons and won $30, and concluded the day with three sets of tennis and a few more laps in the pool. Such a program was necessary, as he told Mary, in order to write "good," love and cherish his new wife, think straight, fight when necessary, and enjoy "truly" and with all five senses his one and only life while he was still able to live it. Once in condition, he would get back into the swing of writing, first with personal letters, then with simple short stories, then with complex short stories, and at last with a novel.

He made no attempt to conceal his scorn for those who had not been in uniform. One of these was Gustavo Durán, whom he had first idolized as a hero of the Spanish Civil War and then vilified at the time of the Crook Factory. At an Embassy cocktail party, Ernest was leaning drunkenly against the stone balustrade on the terrace when Gustavo approached to greet him. His eyes were cold as they shook hands, but he asked politely about the health of the Duráns' child. They had meantime had another and Gustavo mentioned it. "Oh," said Ernest in his most cutting tone, "you managed quite well to keep out of the war, didn't you?" The insult was obvious. Durán bowed and turned away.

Except for frequent letters from Buck Lanham, who had been promoted to brigadier general in March, Ernest now sought to force the war temporarily into the middle distance. He took diffident notice of the sudden death of Franklin Roosevelt, whom he had never liked, and refused to join in the widespread mourning. Others, said he, might speak of FDR's martyrdom in the same breath with a mention of Easter, but nobody had in fact ever been anywhere who had not been with the infantry from Normandy onwards. He explained that although he had wished to stay with the 22nd Combat Team until V-E Day, he had felt obliged to come home as soon as he knew that the Germans were beaten. Otherwise he would have "ended up" as a bum. He justified his return to Cuba for the sake of his sons and Mary Welsh. As soon as Mary came to join him, life could begin once more.

When she arrived, on the second of May, Ernest went to the airport in the Lincoln and bore her triumphantly home for her first sight of the Finca. She found him in far better shape than he had been when he left Paris in March. His stomach was flatter, he ate and drank like a sound and happy gourmet, he was "marvelous" with the servants and the pets, and he volunteered to attend to the affairs of the household until she could learn enough Spanish to assume command. As Martha had done in 1939, Mary settled happily into the new situation. She took visible pleasure in the tropical climate, and Ernest discovered that she liked his cats, loved the ocean, fished and swam well, and was handy aboard the *Pilar*. He soon wrote Lanham that she was brave, kind, unselfish, adaptable, and "beautifully tanned."

Although her presence banished his earlier loneliness and his feelings of uselessness, he found that he could not—indeed did not want to—forget about the war. The most heartening news of the spring season was that Bumby had at last been liberated, and that he was coming to recuperate at the Finca after more than six months of living on nothing but soup in a succession of German prisoner-of-war camps. He arrived early in June, along with Gregory and Patrick. Bumby was gay and gregarious as ever, but badly in need of rest and change. Ernest doted on his record as a soldier and proudly told his friends that the wound in his right shoulder was still big enough to put one's fist through. Jack happily ate Gregorio's cooking aboard the *Pilar,* consumed frozen daiquiris with his father at the Floridita, and (like his younger brothers) immediately accepted Mary Welsh, as they had accepted Martha, as the new mistress of the Finca Vigía.

He was still there on June 20th when Ernest set out to drive Mary to the airport to fly to Chicago. It had rained that morning for the first time in eight months. On a hilltop along the Mantilla Road outside Havana, trucks had been hauling clay and the grade was as slippery as if it had been soaped. Although Ernest was cold sober and driving slowly, he lost control of the Lincoln when it skidded. The car leaped a ditch and crashed into a tree. He banged his head against the rearview mirror, cracked four ribs against the steering wheel, and sustained a synovial hemorrhage of the left knee when it hit the dashboard. Mary was covered with blood from a deep cut in her left cheek and many lesser abrasions across her forehead. In spite of nervous shock she took it bravely and remembered with admiration that "Papa carried me into the first-aid joint against his stove-in chest with his bad-hurt arm, walking on his bad-hurt knee." He immediately secured the services of a plastic surgeon to save her "lovely mobile face" from a permanent scar.

The period of recuperation postponed arrangements for her divorce from Noel Monks. Her father and mother had now accepted Ernest, and T. J. Welsh sent him three religious books as a first gift. In reply, and to clear up from the beginning his own position on religious matters, Ernest offered a short history of the changes his faith had undergone in three wars. In 1918, said he, he had been very frightened after his wounding, and therefore very devout. He feared death, believed in personal salvation, and thought that prayers to the Virgin and various saints might produce results. These views changed markedly during the Spanish Civil War, owing to the alliance between the Church and the Fascists. He then decided that it was selfish to pray for his own benefit, though he missed the "ghostly comfort" as a man might miss a drink when he was cold and wet. In 1944, he had got through some very rough times without praying once. He felt that he had forfeited the right to any divine intercession in his personal affairs, and that it would be "crooked" to ask for help, no matter how frightened he might be. For him, as for Pauline, though for different reasons, the Spanish Civil War had been the turning point. Deprived of the ghostly comforts of the Church, yet unable to accept as gospel the secular substitutes which Marxism offered, he had abandoned his simplistic faith in the benefits of personal petition and turned, like his hero Robert Jordan, to embrace a doctrine of "life, liberty, and the pursuit of happiness."

Some months later he pointed out to Mary that together they had willingly bypassed Mary Baker Eddy's Christian Science, to which her parents subscribed, and his own Congregationalist deity ("God and his beard") as well as various Puritanical misconceptions about human conduct. The substitute he proposed was hedonistic and sentimentally humanistic. He and Mary must evolve their own rules of behavior, said he, believing in each other. This would require only the care that a good gardener would give to a good garden with good soil. They must try to be considerate and understanding and decent: to fight for what they thought was right, to make good children who would do the same, to write books that would give lasting pleasure to others, to leave the world a better place, and finally to be happy. Ernest hoped that his words did not sound too much like Dr. Hemingstein and his Inspirational Prose at a country camp meeting, and predicted that he would probably backslide now and again.

Over the summer his general health improved steadily. The headaches sometimes came back and he half ruefully adapted a cigarette slogan to describe the state of his brain: "Something new has been addled." But he was more or less ready to get back to writing when Vanguard Press sent him galley proofs of John Groth's *Studio: Europe,* for which he had agreed to write an introduction. One chapter, "Schloss Hemingway," recalled the time, eleven months ago, when Stevie Stevenson had brought Groth forward from Division to Ernest's farmhouse "command post." "When you like someone as much as we liked John," wrote Ernest, "and respect his courage, good humour, and sound humanity, you should not be asked to write an introduction to his book and his drawings. . . . John's drawings . . . have some kinship with the illustrations for Grimm's Fairy Tales. Since the Schnee Eifel was supposed to be where many of those fine stories happened, there may be some sense in that. Reading his account of our home-life in that same district, it seems only slightly less fantastic than if Grimm had written it. I do not remember it that way. But nobody ever remembers it the way it was."

At the end of August, Mary flew to Chicago to accomplish her divorce. Ernest declined to go, chiefly because his own divorce from Martha required six months of continuous residence in Cuba, but also because he could not face the prospect of paying a call on his aged mother in River Forest, Illinois. In Mary's absence, Ernest wrote to General Barton, who was now hospitalized with gastric ulcers at Fort McClellan, Alabama. Under his command, said Ernest, the 4th Infantry Division had been one of the greatest in American military history. He was proud to have given it some of the recognition it deserved by relaying information back to other correspondents, including Hank Gorrell of the United Press, Ira Wolfert of NANA, and Charles Wertenbaker of *Time* and *Life.* This shepherding and wet-nursing of others had been necessary, said Ernest, both to keep them from being killed and also to get into print quickly with news of the Division's exploits instead of holding it up for six weeks until it could appear in *Collier's.* He was also proud of having given "that jerk Leclerc" all information on the disposition of German forces between Rambouillet and Paris, though still bitter at having had to deny it all before the Inspector General of the Third Army. It was only later, said he, that he had been told by the head of OSS in the ETO (Colonel Bruce) that he could expect a decoration for his work at Rambouillet.

Whether or not Barton took these remarks as a hint, he soon wrote Hemingway that one of his last acts before retiring had been to recommend him for an ETO ribbon and a Bronze Star. "I based the letter," said Barton, "on your invaluable assistance in getting and giving me information (not in violation of the Geneva Convention). Your putting me in contact with the Maquis in Paris and the rat race across France is included. I left out certain grenade assaults in St. Pois. Personally I would like to see you get a DSM but don't know how we could tie up any other American decorations and the Bronze Star."

Ernest had just received General Barton's letter, and Mary was still in Chicago, when General Buck Lanham and his wife Pete accepted Ernest's invitation to take a Cuban holiday. On the morning of September 22nd they arrived at the Finca for a two-week visit. Lanham had only recently returned from Europe to become Chief of the Information and Education section of the War Department. Ernest now met Mrs. Lanham for the first time, finding her "nice, charming, frank, sincere, brave, and understanding." Her real name was Mary and she was about Mary Welsh's size, though her hair was prematurely gray. They went to the fights in Havana, spent an evening at the *frontón*, dined at the Floridita and the Chinese restaurant, shot pigeons at the Club de Cazadores, and fished from the *Pilar* and her auxiliary, the *Winston*.

Buck took to these activities with characteristic enthusiasm. Ernest was outwardly embarrassed but inwardly touched by Lanham's praise of his wartime conduct. He led their conversations repeatedly to discussions of former associates in the regiment and the division, and also to the topic of world politics, the Japanese surrender, the position of Russia, and the atomic bomb, about which he was now having second thoughts. When Lanham said that he had never read *The Torrents of Spring,* Ernest brought out a copy and stood peering over his friend's shoulder as he read, laughing at examples of his own wit. Buck thought the wit somewhat elephantine and the satire ill-conceived, but he knew enough about Ernest's sensitivity not to make an issue of these opinions. During the lengthy luncheons, which were fortified with an admirable Spanish claret, Ernest reminisced about his boyhood, mentioning an episode in which he had tried to impress a girl by pretending to have composed a march, though he had actually stolen the tune from *Pomp and Circumstance*.

After lunch, Lanham usually took a siesta while Ernest and Pete went on talking. Pete was a frank and forthright woman of firm views. She engaged him in arguments about the cruelties of bullfighting and the probable presence of poisonous snakes in the Cuban underbrush. Ernest soon began to bridle, complaining in letters to Mary that frontal attacks of this sort were not to his liking. Mrs. Lanham, for her part, soon decided that he was a temperamental misogynist. He frankly condemned his mother as a domineering shrew who had driven his father to suicide. He was also highly critical of Martha Gellhorn. It occurred to Mrs. Lanham that Martha and Grace were the only two women in his life who had ever stood up to him and defied him. He was scornful towards Martha's demand that he return her flat silver, which had been a gift from her mother. "Look at this," said he, picking up a handsome teaspoon. "Just because she had it before we were married, she wants it back. Can you imagine such a thing?" Mrs. Lanham found no difficulty in agreeing with Martha, and tactfully suggested that he would hardly wish to keep articles engraved with Martha's monogram.

But Ernest only shook his head and launched into an account of his previous marriages. He said frankly that Pauline had stolen him away from her good friend Hadley. Pauline had had the wealth that Hadley lacked and that he had needed at the time. When Pauline, in her turn, had protested against his falling in love with Martha, he had simply told her that "those who live by the sword must die by the sword." He said rather blandly that he was to blame for the breakup of all his marriages except the one to Martha. His thoughtless treatment of Hadley had been his responsibility alone. Mrs. Lanham managed to hold her tongue, and a kind of armed truce prevailed between them until shortly before the end of the visit. Mary was now back from Chicago, and Ernest was speaking of Russia's place in world politics. Some of his arguments reminded Mrs. Lanham of Chamberlain and his famous umbrella. "Ernie," said she, "where's your umbrella? What you're saying sounds like straight appeasement to me." Ernest leaped to his feet, his eyes blazing and his face flushed, and for a moment seemed on the point of hurling his wineglass into Pete's face. When she left Cuba, Pete was convinced that she had been admitted into that large company whom Ernest abominated— the female part of the world's population. The exception, however, was Mary Welsh.

Several times during the Lanhams' visit, Ernest's headaches returned. He attributed them to feelings of frustration over wanting to write while anxious to see that his guests enjoyed themselves. But he was deceiving himself. He had always found difficulty in getting back to writing after returning from any war. Fighting and lovemaking too easily replaced creativity. He blamed the "cauterizing" of his "delicate equipment" on his labors with the Crook Factory, the Q-Boat command, the RAF, the 4th Infantry Division, and the combined effects of "alcohol and ruthlessness." Yet his three years of adventuring, he felt, had hardboiled him only temporarily. He was not really that way inside, where the old desires to be kind, honest, delicate, and straight still remained. In place of the scabbed-over scars of cauterization, he wanted all things to be clean, attractive, and good—"like early morning." Nothing could match a writer's satisfaction in making a new piece of the world and knowing that it would stand forever. Writing was what he had come on earth to do. It was his true faith, his church, his politics, his command. His think-machine, he believed, was now working fairly well. He was busy grinding valves and inserting new rings in the other two machines, one for narrative and one for invention. He hoped that they would soon be fixed and running.

Meantime he tried his hand at another brief introduction, this time for an anthology called *A Treasury for the Free World*. "Now that the wars are over and the dead are dead," he wrote, "we have come . . . into that more difficult time when it is a man's duty to understand his world." In war, men needed "obedience, the acceptance of discipline, intelligent courage, and resolution." In peace, their duty was "to disagree, to protest, even to revolt and rebel" while still working always "toward finding a way for all men to live together on this earth." The United States had come out of the war as the strongest of the powers. It was important that she did not also become the most hated. Among other achievements, American armed forces had prob-ably "killed more civilians of other countries than all our enemies did in all the famous massacres we so deplore." The atomic bomb was the sling and the pebble which could destroy all the giants, including ourselves. We must avoid any trace of the mentality of the Fascist bully. Nor should we fall into the fatal errors of hypocrisy, sanctimoniousness, or vengeance. Instead we must educate ourselves to appreciate the "rights, privileges, and duties of all other countries."

Soon after he had set down these views, Ernest enjoyed his first postwar business success, selling two of his short stories to the movies for a sum greater than he had realized from the sale of *For Whom the Bell Tolls*. "The Killers" brought $37,500 and "The Short Happy Life of Francis Macomber" another $75,000. One irony of the situation was the relative ease and brevity of his labors in writing these stories as against the seventeen months he had spent on the novel. Another was that while his special tax account contained $24,-000, his personal check stub showed a current balance of $499.38.

Just before Christmas he received a pleading letter from his former scout and driver, Jean Décan. He had been denounced as a collaborationist and needed a testimonial to prove that he had hated and fought the Germans throughout the war years. "You'll be very kind," he wrote, "if you send me that testification. That must be the last German trick. Have one arrested by his own men." Ernest immediately sprang to Jean's defense, emphasizing his constant usefulness and courage from Rambouillet through the Battle of the Bulge, and persuaded General Lanham to do the same. The injustice made him boil and burn. A good man was wasting his first postwar Christmas in a French jail because the evil that the Germans had done still worked on in France like a cancer. Even the arrival of his sons to spend a belated Christmas could not wholly dissipate his anger and his gloom.

64. THE NETTLE AND THE FLOWER

THE Christmas holidays of 1945 marked the approximate close of Ernest's "cooling-out" period from the bumps and rigors of the war. When Martha officially divorced him on December 21st, he took the act as a Christmas gift. He was almost touchingly eager to elaborate and spread abroad the legend of his wartime hardihood on land and sea and in the air. He publicly commended General Lanham as "one of the finest, most skillful, and most intelligent infantry officers" he had ever known. In the same statement he was careful to claim credit for having been at Lanham's side during "several weeks of bitter fighting in September, November, and December of 1944."

The Finca was busy throughout January and February with arrivals and departures. Bumby ended a three-month visit with his father and went west to resume his college career, this time at the University of Montana. Tom Shevlin and Wolfie Guest both returned from military duties in the Pacific and lost no time in calling on Ernest. The list of visitors included the Richard Coopers, the Gene Tunneys, and Charles Ritz of the Paris Ritz. Howard Hawks's wife Slim accompanied the Hemingways to Megano de Casigua, where the crew of the *Pilar* had once given chase to the German submarine. Ernest had now renamed it Paraíso.

Mary and Ernest formalized their marriage in Havana on March 14th. For various reasons she found it less impressive than their informal troth-plighting ceremony at the Ritz in Paris in the fall of 1944. The scene this time was a lawyer's office in an old-fashioned house with high ceilings and heavy dark furniture. The lawyer rapidly read the Spanish text of the lengthy documents, based on the Napoleonic Code and much concerned with goods and chattels. When the principals were called on to supply the names and birthplaces of all ancestors for three generations, Mary was obliged to telephone her parents in Chicago to unweave the genealogical web. Besides a number of Cuban friends, the witnesses included Ernest's younger sons and Winston Guest. After the first session, they all adjourned to the Floridita for lunch and what Ernest called "a cup of hemlock." The second visit to the lawyer was followed by a champagne-and-caviar reception at the flat of the Richard Coopers in Vedado. The wedding day ended at the Finca with a violent verbal battle, begun by Ernest over some triviality. This so angered Mary that she packed her bags and would have left at once but for fatigue and the aftereffects of champagne. Peace was restored next morning, the mildest time in Ernest's day, and their marriage resumed its normal course, although Ernest felt that he had lost status with his wife.

In the early months of 1946, Ernest got back to fiction with a strange new novel called *The Garden of Eden*. It was an experimental compound of past and present, filled with astonishing ineptitudes and based in part upon memories of his marriages to Hadley and Pauline, with some excursions behind the scenes of his current life with Mary. For his opening chapters he chose the locale of the seaport village of Le Grau-du-Roi at the foot of the Rhône estuary. This was the place in which he had spent his honeymoon with Pauline in May, 1927. Like Ernest at that time, the hero, David Bourne, had been married only three weeks and was the author of a successful novel. His wife Catherine fiercely shared his hungers and his pleasures. He devoted his days to her fanatical desire to tan her body by lying naked on hidden beaches. Their nights were given to experiments with the transfer of sexual identities in which she assumed the name of Pete and he the name of Catherine.

Another set of lovers, living in the Latin Quarter of Paris, were Nick Sheldon, a young painter, and his wife Barbara. Their dingy flat was clearly modeled on the place in the rue du Cardinal Lemoine where Ernest and Hadley had set up housekeeping in 1922. Like Hadley, Barbara had thick, red-gold hair; and like Catherine Bourne she was so deeply immersed in a dream of absolute marital unity that she even wished to resemble her husband. Nick had allowed his Indian-black hair to grow for five full months. To celebrate the occasion when she first trimmed it to look like hers in all but color, Nick took her to lunch at Lipp's Brasserie. They ate *choucroute garni* and admired themselves in the wall mirrors, afterwards returning to their frigid flat for lovemaking. Barbara closed the day with an interior monologue obviously indebted to Molly Bloom's soliloquy at the end of Joyce's *Ulysses*. Meantime, the amatory episodes between David and Catherine Bourne at Le Grau-du-Roi continued with one in which Catherine surprised her husband by having her hair shaped to the contours and colors of his own.

Although he kept his close friends abreast of his rapid progress with his novel, which by his own account stood at 400 longhand pages in mid-February, 700 by the end of April, and 1,000 in mid-July, his plans for the work were singularly inchoate. He confessed to Lanham that he could never stick to a preconceived pattern, but invented as he went from minute to minute without knowing what was going to happen next. Except to assert that he took pleasure in writing about fornication, he revealed nothing specific about the contents of his book, though now, as later, he said that he was spurred to effort by a "big impending sense" that he would die within a year. He seems to have intended, sometime after page 1,000, to write about his good friends in the 22nd Infantry Regiment, including Buck Lanham, Art Teague, Swede Henley, George Goforth, and Tom Kenan. In fact, said he, he had accumulated enough material in 1944 to spend the rest of his life doing fictional accounts of the Regiment, the 4th Division, and the Royal Air Force. But this part of his book still lay in the future.

In June and again in July, Ernest composed letters which spread abroad the story of his wartime exploits. One was sent to the Russian novelist, Konstantin Simonov, who was making an American tour. "I was at sea for about two years in a difficult job," wrote Ernest, "then went to England and flew with the RAF as a correspondent before the invasion, accompanied the Normandy invasion, and then spent the rest of the time with the 4th Infantry Division. The time with the RAF was wonderful but useless. With the 4th Infantry Division and with the 22nd Regiment of Infantry I tried to be useful through knowing French and the country and being able to work ahead with the Maquis. . . . I would like you to have known our Colonel of the 22nd Infantry (now General Lanham) who is my best friend, and the commanders of the 1st, 2nd, and 3rd battalions." There was much more of the same. Ernest closed with the wish that Simonov could read *For Whom the Bell Tolls*. "It isn't about war as we knew it the last few years," he wrote. "But about small hill war it is all right and there is one place where we kill the fascists you would like." Simonov replied cordially from Boston. He said that although *For Whom the Bell Tolls* was not yet published in the USSR, he had read it twice in typescript in a Russian translation. It was one of the three or four books in his library that he really loved. The "small hill war" was nothing against it. All wars were fought by small groups, including the epic defense of Stalingrad. As for Ernest's translator, Ivan Kashkeen, he was still alive, still red-headed, and still full of love and understanding for the works of Hemingway.

In July Ernest provided Milton Wolff with another account of his adventures of 1944. On Liberation Day (so he said) he "went in [to Paris] ahead of anybody." Things "only got bad when we busted the Siegfried Line on Sept. 14 and then had a long bad time in the Schnee Eifel. . . . Later Hürtgen Forest was very bad. Big fight too at the time of the Von Rundstedt offensive. . . . Was a hell of a summer, fall, and winter." There was more of the same. His performance in the war had been such that he did not need to misrepresent it by implying that he had beat everyone else into Paris or that he had been personally present at the "busting" of the Siegfried Line.

When Mary learned in July that she was going to have a baby, Ernest began arrangements to take her to Sun Valley. The establishment had been used by the Navy during the war as a rest haven and was just being turned back to civilian use. He sent the Lincoln to West Palm Beach to be reconditioned, and summoned his sons, who were in California with Pauline, to join him in Idaho in August. He had accumulated 10,000 shotgun cartridges as well as 2,000 rounds of rifle ammunition, and was eager to get into action. The trip west began early in August. Except for the misbehavior of the reconditioned Lincoln, all went well through the night of the 18th, which they spent at the Mission Motor Court in Casper, Wyoming. Next morning at seven, while Ernest was packing the car for an early start, Mary awoke in agony. Her pregnancy had been ectopic and the left Fallopian tube had suddenly ruptured. The chief surgeon of the Memorial Hospital of Natrona County was away on a fishing trip. Mary hovered all day on the brink of death until at last her veins collapsed, her pulse faded, she lost consciousness, and the intern, pulling off his gloves, advised Ernest to take final leave of his wife.

But the man who had once written a fictional scene about "saying goodbye to a statue" flatly refused to take death as an answer. Hurrying into a surgeon's gown and a face-mask, he made the intern probe for a vein, cleared the feedline of a bottle of plasma, inserted the needle, and stayed at Mary's side until her pulse resumed, her respiration returned to normal, and the surgeon appeared. Four more bottles of plasma, two blood transfusions, and a week inside an oxygen tent brought Mary back to safety. So remarkable an escape from imminent death proved, said Ernest, that it never paid to quit. For weeks he continued to be fascinated by this proof that "fate could be fucked" rather than submitted to. Mary's courage impressed him deeply. She was equally affected by his action in saving her from "Boot Hill," and for years continued to assert that he was "a good man to have around in times of trouble."

As always in emergencies, Ernest behaved admirably, drinking little and doing his best to be kind and cheerful. Ten days had gone by before he complained of being "faintly fed up" with the "gay life" he was leading at the Mission Motor Court. His sons had been waiting in Ketchum and he met them in Rawlins on the 29th, bringing them to Casper for a week's stay. The boys drove out each day to fish the North Platte River in Black Canyon seventy miles away. After Mary's illness, Ernest worried constantly about the possibility of further accidents. It gave him, said he, a mechanical cold feeling in the lower belly and sudden prickling at the top of his scalp. But nothing happened and by early September he was able to move his wife to Sun Valley.

He was ecstatic as ever with the vales of Idaho. The air was bracing and the hunting excellent. From mid-October onwards they dined on game nearly every night, with mountain sheep, elk and venison steaks, pheasants and ducks. After the departure of his brothers, Patrick, who was spending the year out of school, bagged a fat buck for the table. Bumby returned in October to fish for steelhead trout and celebrate his twenty-third birthday. The occasion was marked by a private showing of *The Killers,* produced by Mark Hellinger and starring Burt Lancaster and Ava Gardner. It was the first film from any of his work that Ernest could genuinely admire. Colonel Sweeny came over from Salt Lake City with Mrs. Dorothy Allen and her brother, Clarence Bamberger. Gary and Rocky Cooper arrived for their first Sun Valley visit since 1941. Another welcome visitor was Slim Hawks. Mary's recuperation continued steadily. It seemed to Ernest that her trust in him had been greatly increased by his conduct during the Casper emergency. He thought of Hotspur's famous metaphor in Shakespeare's *Henry IV:* "Out of this nettle, danger, we pluck this flower, safety." His modification of it, sent in an exuberant letter to Lanham, was: "Out of this fucking nettle, danger, we pluck this good old flower of confidence and faith in a guy."

Hotspur's maxim was soon proved again. On the last day of October, Ernest and Mary went out after pheasant in the company of Slim Hawks and Patrick. At the end of the afternoon they were back at the car unloading the guns.

Ernest had just leaned down to unlace his boots when Slim accidentally discharged her 16-gauge automatic so close to his bent head that it singed the hair on the back of his skull. He rose up pale and furious and took the gun away from her. She was so horror-stricken at the nearness of her miss that he quickly swallowed his anger and dismissed the episode as lightly as he could. But within a week he had described it in detail in letters to Lanham, Perkins, and Otto Bruce.

The stay in Sun Valley ended on November 10th in order to allow for visits to Salt Lake City and New Orleans and a three-week stay in New York. Mrs. Allen and Colonel Sweeny were their hosts in Utah. Mary's parents came down to New Orleans for their first and only meeting with their new son-in-law. On the 26th, Patrick took the train for New York, followed by Ernest and Mary two days later. They arrived on December 1st, and stayed in an ornate suite at the Sherry Netherland by courtesy of Mark Hellinger and Universal Pictures as a special dispensation to the author of *The Killers*.

One leading purpose of the visit to New York was Ernest's second postwar reunion with Gen. Buck Lanham. Ernest had promised his friend a week of shooting on the private preserves of Gardiners Island, a domain of three thousand acres a few miles off Montauk and Orient Points at the eastern extremity of Long Island. The Gardiner family had owned it exclusively since the seventeenth century. There was a large old manor house in the midst of vast reaches of fields and woods, abounding in pheasants, black ducks, wild turkeys, and herds of deer. Winston Guest had a year's lease on the island and the Hemingways, with Buck and Patrick, expected to have this offshore Garden of Eden all to themselves. The very rich, said Ernest happily, were not his people, but he entered their country like any other foreign realm.

General Lanham came up from Washington on the 2nd, nursing a bad cold and bearing an eiderdown coat as a gift for Ernest. In the opulent suite at the Sherry Netherland he found his friend in conversation with the science writer, Paul de Kruif. Lanham observed somewhat sourly that Ernest was talking in his choppy, pseudo-Indian style, as if verbal primitivism could somehow shield him from the incursions of urban civilization. The primitivism extended also to his clothing: tight western pants, felt bedroom slippers, and a shirt from which several buttons were missing. Ernest bear-hugged Lanham and said that they would shortly dine at the Stork Club as guests of Sherman Billingsley. As the time drew near, he made no move to shave or change his clothes. Lanham lent him a tie, persuaded him to shave, and got Mary to replace the buttons. At the Club they found the *New York Post's* gossip columnist, Leonard Lyons, who was dining with his wife, and Damon Runyon, who was spending his last free evening before entering the hospital for treatment of throat cancer. The party went well until early morning when Ernest spied Ingrid Bergman at supper with Charles Boyer. As he had done with Saroyan in Paris, he began to direct a barrage of insults at Boyer, leaning towards Lanham to ask loudly whether or not he should give that small green-faced character the back of his hand. The Lyonses, as well as Lanham and Mary, tried vainly to change the subject, and both the actors did what they could to placate Ernest's aggressive behavior, but he continued his bullyboy tactics until the party disbanded.

Ernest later described the promised shoot at Gardiners Island, to which they flew next day, as a *fracaso,* failure's saddest form. In place of happy hunting, with opportunities for long conversations on quiet evenings, they found what Ellis Briggs called "an excessively confused operation," with people constantly arriving by airplane "to play bridge, argue, shoot, and drink." Ernest assured Lanham that they were eating damned well, that Wolfie was a gracious host, and that many of the other guests were splendid people. But the weather was unseasonably warm for December, the hunting was poor, and the week ended with Ernest's abortive attempt to stalk deer with bow and arrow.

Two further fiascos rounded out the New York visit. One was Ernest's trip by cab to the offices of the *Daily Worker* in an old loft building at 35 West 12th Street. In a recent column, Mike Gold had renewed his attacks on Hemingway as one of the "hollow men" of American literature. Ernest took the elevator to the eighth floor and told the girl receptionist that he wished to see Gold. She answered that he was out and offered to take a message. "OK," said the hulking visitor, "tell Mike Gold that Ernest Hemingway says he should go fuck himself." Had he known it, Mike Gold would have greatly relished the second episode, for the scene was again the Stork Club, which Gold had repeatedly condemned as a foul nest of Fascist reactionaries. On this evening Ingrid Bergman was dining with Michael Blankfort, Hollywood scriptwriter and author of a successful novel, *The Brave and the Blind,* about the siege of the Alcázar in Toledo. Years earlier, Blankfort had resented Ernest's description of his novel as "phony"—an adjective chosen on no better grounds than that Blankfort had not been personally present at the siege itself. He was therefore unpleasantly surprised to hear a voice intrusively suggesting that he and Ingrid might like to share another table. He recognized Hemingway and promptly refused the invitation. When asked why, he explained the reasons for his resentment. Ernest at once turned on all his charm. This matter, he said, had been on his conscience for six years. He had actually found Blankfort's novel magnificent, even fearing that it was a better book than *For Whom the Bell Tolls.* Turning to Ingrid Bergman, he assured her that Blankfort was one of the best writers in America and that he was deeply ashamed not to have praised his work publicly in 1940. Blankfort's acerbity dissolved in this torrent of melted butter. He was even happier when Ernest promised to review his latest book, a biography of Evans Carlson, for *The New York Times.* Blankfort's publisher duly sent a review copy to the Finca Vigía. But Ernest neither acknowledged its receipt nor did he ever write the promised review.

65. EDEN INVADED

MORE than a hundred pages of *The Garden of Eden* were now in typescript, with nine hundred pages still in longhand. The theme of the book was slowly taking shape on the horizons of Ernest's imagination. It was not strictly new to his vision of human life, having been implicit in *A Farewell to Arms* and *For Whom the Bell Tolls,* as well as several short stories. Even now another year would have to pass before he recognized and stated it: "the happiness of the Garden that a man must lose."

For a time in the early months of 1947 there were no serious invasions of his Cuban domain. The Basques in charge had kept the Finca well, his younger sons were on hand for the year-end holidays, Mary was in good health once more, while Mark Hellinger the producer and Maurice Speiser the attorney were discussing a Hollywood royalty arrangement that would guarantee Ernest a substantial income for some years to come. After Gigi's return to school, Patrick stayed on with his father and stepmother—a warmhearted and companionable boy who wanted to go to Harvard and was getting ready for his College Board examinations.

It was not until April that the bad time came. On a visit to Pauline, Patrick and Gregory were involved in the wreck of a small car. Gigi's knee was injured, but recovered in a few days. "On the surface," wrote Pauline, "Patrick had only a cut on his chin. He complained of a headache . . . [and] talked in a rather excited manner. He then went back to Cuba where the headache got worse." Ernest diagnosed the problem as a neglected concussion. On the afternoon of the 11th he had Patrick review his French and then played him a set of tennis. Next day in Havana, the boy bravely took his College Board tests. Except for math, he did fairly well. Ernest took him to lunch between sessions and squired him through the day. But by the morning of the 14th he was feverish and delirious. That night he turned violent.

To make matters worse, Mary was called to Chicago, where her father had fallen ill with prostatic cancer. Ernest quickly converted the Finca into a hospital, organizing Juan Dunabeitia, Roberto Herrera, and the servant René into a team of male nurses, and taking the midnight-to-dawn watch as his own, snatching catnaps on a mattress outside the sickroom door. Pauline flew over on the 16th. "I hope you do not mind," she wrote Mary. "I was very worried about Patrick. . . . This is the first real trouble I have ever had. . . . I am glad you are not here in this gloomy house." She stayed until May 10th, planning meals and managing the domestic staff. Ernest reported that she was behaving admirably. She had heard many noisome stories about him—that he drank excessively, chased women, gambled, and loafed. Now she pleased him by saying that she knew they were all lies.

Ernest reported every nuance of his struggle in long letters to Mary, composed on a clipboard in the quieter watches. Like David Bourne in his new novel, he amused himself by urging Mary to have her hair bleached to a smoky silver or rinsed to a rich auburn. One night in May, elated because Patrick had eaten a steak after a month of rectal feeding, Ernest experimented on his own hair so successfully that it turned to the color of a new copper penny. Next day he explained to the people at the Finca that he had accidentally picked up a bottle of shampoo left over from Martha's time.

Mary returned on the 18th, exhausted by her own struggle in Chicago. When Pauline reappeared five days later, the two Mrs. Hemingways surprised Ernest by liking each other, and amused him with some girlish banter about their attendance at Hemingway University. Although Mary praised Ernest as "a very durable guy," he was showing signs of nervous strain, chiefly from lack of sleep. It was doubtless this condition which caused him to explode with wrath on reading in the papers that William Faulkner had called him a coward.

This, at any rate, was the construction he chose to put on Faulkner's words. In talking to some students at the University of Mississippi, Faulkner had named Wolfe, Dos Passos, Erskine Caldwell, Hemingway, and himself as the best modern novelists, and had then laid down his doctrine of "splendid failure." Wolfe had made the "best" failure because his courage was greatest. He risked clumsiness and even dullness in order to "shoot the works, win or lose and damn the torpedoes." Dos Passos had sacrificed some courage to the demands of style. Hemingway stood last on the list because he lacked the courage to get out on a limb of experimentation, as the others had done to varying degrees. Faulkner's opinion was plainly newsworthy and the Associated Press picked it up.

Ernest was deeply insulted. He sent the newspaper clipping to General Lanham and asked him to write Faulkner the truth about his behavior under fire in 1944. Lanham loyally gave Faulkner a long account of Ernest's war record, concluding with the statement that he was "without exception the most courageous man I have ever known, both in war and peace. He has physical courage, and he has that far rarer commodity, moral courage." Faulkner replied with a letter of explanation to Lanham and one of apology to Hemingway. "I'm sorry of this damn stupid thing," he wrote Ernest. "I was just making $250. I thought informally, not for publication. . . . I have believed for years that the human voice has caused all human ills and I thought I had broken myself of talking. Maybe this will be my valedictory lesson. I hope it won't matter a damn to you. But if or when or whever [sic] it does, please accept another squirm from yours truly."

Although Ernest privately believed that he rated the Distinguished Service Cross, he was glad enough to accept a Bronze Star on June 13th at a small ceremony at the Embassy in Havana. The citation said that he had performed "meritorious service" as a war correspondent "from 20 July to 1 September and from 6 November to 6 December, 1944, in France and Germany." During these periods "he displayed a broad familiarity with modern military science, interpreting and evaluating the campaigns and operations of friendly and enemy forces, circulating freely under fire in combat areas in order to obtain an accurate picture of conditions. Through his talent of expression, Mr. Hemingway enabled readers to obtain a vivid picture of the difficulties and triumphs of the front-line soldier and his organization in combat."

He had barely got his medal back to the Finca when Max Perkins died suddenly on June 17th. Charles Scribner sent Ernest an account of Max's last days, concluding with the statement, "I never had a better friend." It was a view that Ernest shared. He cabled sympathy and followed it up with a letter calling Perkins one of his best and most loyal friends and wisest counselors in life as well as in writing. He was also, said Ernest, "a great, great editor" who had never cut a paragraph of Hemingway material or asked him to change one. This last was not completely true, though in the few changes he had recommended, Max had always chosen to handle Ernest with a judicious mixture of tact and flattery. But nothing could bother Max now. No longer, said Ernest, would he have to wrestle with the executorship of Tom Wolfe's "chickenshit estate" or fight to keep women writers from building nests in his hat. The fact that he had used up all his resistance by refusing to take vacations was, Ernest thought, a lesson for all men.

He sent Mary to Key West to stay with Pauline and recuperate from a siege of intestinal illness. Patrick was much improved by the time she returned in July, and for a time the run of bad luck seemed to be over. Pauline came over again for a joint birthday celebration with Ernest, and Mark Hellinger, producer of *The Killers,* indicated that he was ready to buy four more short stories at $75,000 each, with an additional guarantee to the author of 10 per cent of the profits of each picture over one million dollars.

In August, however, a fearsome new specter appeared. Inside his head Ernest began to hear a strange buzzing and humming, like the sound made by telephone wires along country roadsides. Dr. Herrera found that his blood pressure had risen to 215 over 125. He was badly overweight at 256 pounds, and the doctor advised a strict diet. Ernest kept the news secret from everyone but Mary, hoping that the air and exercise in Sun Valley would help put him in shape again. He set off in September in a new Buick Roadmaster with Otto Bruce as driver. They varied the usual itinerary in order to pay a call at Windemere on Walloon Lake, which was now in charge of Ernest's sister Sunny. Crossing the great plains afterwards, he regaled Otto with stirring tales of boyhood escapades, probably about half true. On the road from Billings to Beartooth Pass, they stopped in Red Lodge to see Chub Weaver, Ernest's old friend from the days at the Nordquist Ranch. Late in the evening of the 29th they reached Sun Valley and were given a suite at the Lodge.

Mary and Pauline stayed behind at the Finca, Pauline to help Patrick through the final weeks of convalescence, and Mary to supervise a major construction job. She sketched the design for a three-storied tower with a commanding view of the sea and the distant city, and had it built by a local

79. RAF Correspondent Hemingway with Wing Commander Alan Lynn before taking off to bomb a V-1 launching platform, late June, 1944.

80. Air Marshal Sir Basil Embry with Group Captain Peter Wykeham-Barnes.

81. At the Hotel de la Mère Poularde, Mont-St.-Michel, Aug., 1944: Bill Walton, Mme. Chevalier, Ernest, an Army Signal Corps photographer, M. Chevalier, Bob Capa.

82. General Barton's Christmas dinner, Luxembourg, 1944.

83. Rambouillet, Aug., 1944: Correspondent Heming with Michel Pasteau, questioning a Free French scout

84. Gen. R. O. Barton (LEFT), Ernest, and Col. Robert Chance in Luxembourg, Dec., 1944.

85. LEFT. Ernest reading one of his war poems to Janet Flanner, Deux Magots, Paris, late fall, 1944. LIFE photograph by David Scherman © Time Inc.

86. BELOW. With Col. Charles T. Lanham and a captured German 88 after the breaching of the Siegfried Line, Germany, Sept. 18, 1944.

87. Mary Hemingway at the Club de Cazadores,
Aug., 1945.

88. RIGHT. Ernest in Cuba, 1952. LIFE photograph by Alfred Eisenstadt © Time Inc.

89. At the Floridita with Gen. Buck Lanham and
Mayito Menocal the younger, Sept., 1945.

90. Ernest with his namesake nephew in a picture taken by EH's sister Sunny at the Finca in 1947.

. Adriana Ivancich.

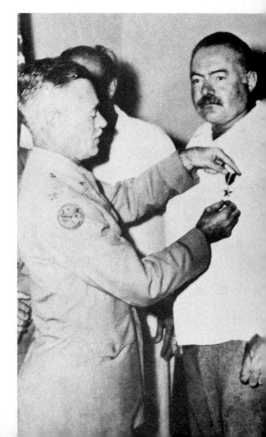

92. Ernest receiving Bronze Star medal, Havana, June 16, 1947.

93. On safari, 1953: Philip Percival, Ernest, Richard Percival. LOOK Magazine. Copyrig
1954, Cowles Communications, Inc.

94. Mary and her Grant's gazelle. LOOK Magazine. Copyright 1954, Cowles Communicatio
Inc.

95. Antonio Ordonez, Madrid, 1959. LIFE photograph by Loomis Dean © Time Inc.

96. LEFT. Ernest with Juanito Quintana and the photographer Cano, Pamplona, July, 1959.

97. BELOW. Ernest's sixtieth birthday party at La Cónsula, July 21, 1959.

98. The Topping house,
Ketchum, Idaho,
across Big Wood River.

99. Ernest in Ketchum,
Christmas, 1959.

stonemason. Its purpose was to give the pet cats a room of their own, Ernest a quieter place for working, and Mary herself a private situation for sunbathing. Ernest continued to be astonished at how "marvellously" his second and fourth wives got on together, and told Charles Scribner that he was well equipped to write a book on the subject. He did not know whether to be amused or hurt when Mary, having joined him at Sun Valley, soon set off to spend Thanksgiving week in California with Pauline, Bumby, and Patrick.

He stuck to his diet so well that by the end of the year he had lost 28 pounds and driven his blood pressure reading down to 150 over 104. He reported that the doctor had been "obviously spooked" at his condition when he got there. He himself was spooked by a whole series of deaths, beginning with Max Perkins, and continuing with the decapitation of Katy Dos Passos in a terrible motor accident on September 12th. Two of his former associates in Spain also died, Gen. Hans Kahle of natural causes, and Gen. Karol Swierczewski by political assassination. Even Ramón, the cook at the Finca, appeared on the roster, having died suddenly of a heart attack. These were enough, said Ernest, to suggest that "our Heavenly Father" must be dealing off the bottom of the deck. The bad news of the holiday season was the sudden death of Mark Hellinger at the age of forty-four. He had already paid Ernest half of the first $50,000 guarantee; the balance was withheld pending settlement of the estate. Ernest borrowed $12,000 from Charles Scribner to build up his current tax account, and complained that although Hellinger's film of *The Killers* had made three million dollars, the author's contract had been so drawn that he had received a mere $50,000. After the long history of bad luck with *The Fifth Column,* he might have been forgiven for being superstitious about the adaptation of his writings to dramatic form. But he continued to count on the business acumen of Maurice Speiser, who had engineered the agreement with Hellinger.

Shortly before Christmas a girl named Lillian Ross telephoned from Mexico, where she had been gathering materials for a *New Yorker* profile—her first—on Sidney Franklin. When she explained that she wished to consult Hemingway about his friendship with Sidney, he invited her to stop over in Ketchum. She reached the MacDonald Cabins about seven o'clock on the morning of December 24th. Her first sight of Ernest won her over completely. "He was standing," she wrote, "on the hardpacked snow, in dry cold of ten degrees below zero, wearing bedroom slippers, no socks, Western trousers with an Indian [actually German] belt that had a silver buckle, and a lightweight Western-style sports shirt open at the collar. . . . He had a graying mustache . . . [and] looked rugged and burly and eager and friendly and kind."

His progress on *The Garden of Eden* had been interrupted a week earlier by the arrival of Juan Dunabeitia and Roberto Herrera, whom he had promised an Idaho vacation as a reward for their loyalty during Patrick's illness. The atmosphere in the two cabins they all occupied was about as conducive to writing, Ernest said, as Buck Lanham's trailer command post in the fall of 1944. Besides Juan and Roberto, the three Hemingway boys, Mary and Ernest, there was "a crowd from Salt Lake and scores of other people." Mary cooked duck, pheasant, and venison dinners every night, with pies for the children and endless chocolate cakes, which they finished off at breakfast. She also became so enthusiastic about skiing that they postponed their departure for two extra weeks.

After the events of 1947, Ernest was not very sanguine about 1948. "Daughter," he told Ingrid Bergman at a New Year's Eve party, "this is going to be the worst year we have ever seen." When they left on February 1 for the long drive to Florida, they managed to escape being caught in a whole series of blizzards only by heading south as far as the Rio Grande. Ernest came home to his first sight of the new tower. He admired the view from his workroom but found great difficulty in working there. "He missed our household noises," wrote Mary, "—René sweeping the fiber rug of the sitting room, subdued clatter and chatter from the kitchen, well-known footsteps hurrying." They had brought back a new dog from Idaho, a springer spaniel named Blackie or Black Dog, who shortly became Ernest's most loyal retainer.

Contrary to Ernest's prediction, the spring went smoothly and well. Malcolm Cowley, whom Ernest called the best critic then working in the United States, came down in February with his wife and son for a two-week session of interviews in preparation for a long article on Hemingway's career to be published in *Life* magazine. Ernest had also begun to correspond with Lillian Ross, the profile-writer for *The New Yorker,* his recent visitor in Ketchum. He was already addressing her as "Daughter." Cowley and Miss Ross were to become the first chroniclers of his life to operate with his personal blessing. He said that talking about himself made him almost physically sick. After Cowley left Cuba, Ernest wrote him that their biographical sessions had destroyed his ability to write for a whole week.

The interviews with Cowley had helped, however, to lay the groundwork for the perpetuation of the Hemingway legend. Ernest virtually guaranteed this result by urging Cowley to consult General Lanham about the events of the war. In notifying Lanham that Cowley would shortly come to see him in Washington, Ernest said that whatever Lanham thought about him, good or bad, might be relayed to the interviewer. It all ran for history, said he, assuming that his adventures were important in history, as he was now sure they were. He knew very well from Lanham's letter to Faulkner that the General's loyalty and friendship would make him speak of Hemingway in the most glowing terms, with considerable emphasis on his bravery under fire.

All through the spring he continued his correspondence with Cowley and Miss Ross, throwing out helpful hints about his personal history and beliefs. He told Cowley of his Bronze Star medal, his membership on the governing board of the International Game Fishing Association, of his having once shot thirty-six straight doubles against Ronnie Tree and Bill Astor of England while returning from Spain aboard the *Normandie,* of boxing with Tom Heeney at Bimini in 1935, and of besting the big Negro challenger Willard Saunders. He described his submarine hunting in the Caribbean and boasted that he had bedded every woman he had ever wanted and some that he hadn't. He said that his hatred of his mother was non-Freudian, that she was an all-time, All-American bitch, and that the first big psychic wound of his life had come when he discovered that his father was a coward. He even offered a detailed account of Dr. Hemingway's suicide.

The letters to Miss Ross were filled with good will and humorous anecdotes. He indicated his disgust with Sidney Franklin's "lies" about their former association, and suggested suitable subjects for her future profiles in *The New Yorker,* among them Jimmy Cannon the sportswriter, Trujillo the Dominican dictator, and Arturo Suárez, the Cuban newspaper columnist. He said disarmingly that he had early taught himself to walk dangerously so that people would leave him alone. He provided Lillian with a list of his personal heroes, including Peter Wykeham Barnes of the RAF; Michel Ney, Napoleon's rearguard commander on the retreat from Moscow; his wife Miss Mary for her refusal to die on the operating table in Casper long after pit bulls would have quit; and his son Patrick, who had now completed a successful year at Stanford University and was about to leave on a vacation trip to Europe. The names of Gustave Flaubert and James Thurber rounded out his list of heroes.

The editors of *Cosmopolitan* now sent one of their staff members to Havana on a special assignment. His name was Aaron Edward Hotchner, an Air Force veteran in his middle twenties. He had been an admirer of Hemingway's work since his high-school days in St. Louis, Missouri, and was awed by the prospect of meeting the master, though full of doubt about his assignment, which was to ask him to write a piece on "The Future of Literature." Ernest met him at the Floridita, treated him to a bewildering series of frozen daiquiris, talked with him about everything but the future of literature, and took him out fishing next day aboard the *Pilar.* When they shook hands in parting on the sidewalk in front of the Hotel Nacional, Ernest half-promised to write the article that Hotchner had come to get, and the young man flew home filled with nascent hero-worship.

In June Ernest pridefully declined an invitation to become a member of the American Academy of Arts and Letters, and sent Charles Scribner a series of letters full of down-to-earth family gossip, including the statement that he always had to ease off on making love when he was working hard because the two things were run by the same motor. Later in the month, as a parting gesture for Patrick, he arranged a ten-day cruise to Cay Sal, the Anguillas, and the Bahama Banks, with Mary, Mayito Menocal, and Elicio Arguelles. Gigi and Patrick came over from Key West, and the whole company slept each night aboard Menocal's newly refurbished yacht, the *Delicias,* using the *Pilar* and the *Winston* for fishing by day. A heavy east wind made the currents too strong for bottom fishing in twenty fathoms, but their success with trolling was phenomenal. During three five-hour stretches, by Ernest's account, they averaged one fish every three minutes, including marlin, wahoo, albacore, amberjack, three kinds of grouper, yellowtail, kingfish, mackerel, and 120 barracuda. They also captured three large turtles. The ice bins of the *Delicias* and the *Pilar* were filled with almost a full ton of game fish.

Part of Ernest's introduction for the new illustrated edition of *A Farewell to Arms* was done during this voyage. Four days after his return, on June 29th, it stood complete, a loose remembrance of things past, stressing his difficulties and joys in writing the novel. He was less than happy with Rasmusson's illustrations, especially those of Catherine Barkley. In fact, said he, consulting the mirrors of his memory, she had resembled the youthful Marlene Dietrich. All such girls, with naturally lovely faces, looked best when they cried or were about to cry, swelling slightly around the eyes and lips instead of getting the pinched-up Mother Superior look of Rasmusson's portrait of Catherine Barkley on the bed. He did not believe in illustration. There was an inevitable gap between the author's and the artist's conception of things and places and people. If Ernest wrote a book about the Bahamas, he would like it to contain pictures—not illustrations—by Winslow Homer; if he were Guy de Maupassant, pictures by Toulouse-Lautrec or Renoir would suit the books he wrote. But no mere illustrator could avoid disappointing the author of a novel; almost by definition he was an outsider: the "someone else who was not there."

Another long cruise in July was carefully planned to include his forty-ninth birthday. Having recently completed the preface to *A Farewell to Arms,* he now said that he always thought of himself as just "going on thirty"—exactly the age he had attained when that novel was finished. His fellow voyagers this time were Mary, Sinsky, Gregorio, Gigi, and Manolito, the young son of the owner of a small café at Cojimar. Ernest was much taken with Manolito, who loved the ocean, never got seasick, helped Gregorio, and worshipped Gigi. The whole cruise went well and the birthday itself was a special delight to Ernest. Mary had gone to a good deal of trouble, buying and wrapping "wonderful presents," many of them bearing presentation cards from the cats and dogs of the Finca. There was also a half pound of fresh caviar and a cake with icing and candles. The Hemingways' wine merchant in Havana had presented a case of champagne. Ernest and Sinsky broke it out at six o'clock in the morning and drank it steadily until after nightfall. Ernest affirmed his joy and pride at having attained the age of forty-nine and said that he was looking forward to his fiftieth, when all the world would damn well have to respect him. But his forty-ninth was also memorable. He told Lillian Ross that he had been "just stink happy all day long."

His mood of euphoria lasted through most of the summer. He helped Roberto make up a birthday purse for "Leopoldina," the aging Havana prostitute, and said that he was thinking seriously of giving his Thompson submachine gun to a museum as a memento of his wartime adventures: it would be as valuable as one of Hawthorne's shoes or a comma left over from the works of Henry James. He also began planning a trip to Europe, his first since the war. He convinced himself that Sun Valley was becoming "cluttered up" with too many people, and that a change of pace and place would benefit both Mary and himself. He wanted to board a slow boat from Havana early in September, going through the Northwest Providence Channel in the Bahamas, through the Sargasso Sea, and then straight across, with stops at Funchal, Lisbon, and Gibraltar, and debarkation at Cannes. The ship would be small enough so that he hoped to troll all the way across. Gregorio was already preparing a Hardy rod for the purpose.

In the midst of these plans came the disturbing news that his lawyer, Maurice Speiser, was gravely ill. A young assistant named Alfred Rice was acting in his stead. Ernest reminisced fondly about his first meeting with Speiser in Hendaye twenty years earlier. The words were scarcely out of his typewriter when a cable from Rice notified him that Maury had died on August 7th. Although he had often been highly critical of Speiser's conduct of his business affairs, Ernest mourned his death as yet another in the long series of deprivations which he had endured in the years since 1944. It seemed to prove his contention to Ingrid Bergman that 1948 would be another bad year. Many "perfectly OK people" who had thought that "Papa was dumb" were now dead. He took satisfaction in having proved that he could outlast them. Yet from time to time in the darker moods of his fiftieth year, he could hear the cold wind sighing around the gateposts of Eden.

66. PAST AND PRESENT

THE romantic days of his youth in Italy were much in Ernest's mind when the *Jagiello* docked at Genoa, the port from which he had sailed homewards thirty years before. Except for the postwar tours with Hadley in the early 1920s and the quick trip with Guy Hickok in 1927, he had not set foot inside the country since 1918. As soon as the Buick was unloaded, he hired a chauffeur and drove off with Mary for Stresa while past and present, the imagination and the reality, contended within him for mastery.

"Christ, Buck, this is wonderful country," he told Lanham. Mary, the newcomer, was enchanted by the profusion of fall flowers and the violet-colored mists in the valleys; Ernest reveled in a homecomer's euphoria. The North Italians treated them both "like royalty." Alberto Mondadori, one of his two Italian publishers, assured him that his books had outsold those of any other author in Italy since the war. Everyone was reading him, from common sailors to the sporting families of the Italian nobility. His pleasure mounted as they drove from Stresa through Como, Bergamo, and up the winding road to Cortina d'Ampezzo. Although the village itself had grown, the contours of the pink and red peaks had not changed since Ernest and

Hadley and Renata Borgatti had wintered there in 1923. Most wonderful of all, said Ernest, forgetting his intermediate trips, was the chance to rediscover the North Italian countryside, which he had seen before only from crowded military camions or through the dust goggles he had worn while driving the Fiat ambulance. Count Federico Kechler and his wife Maria Luisa were on holiday in the village. He came to the hotel to ask Ernest to join him in trout fishing. It was a far cry from the old days with the down-at-heel guide "Peduzzi." Kechler was a member of the Friulian nobility who had served in the Navy during the war—a thin man with a high forehead, prominent eyes, and cadaverous cheeks. Ernest's Italian was rusty, but it came back gradually in conversation with the Kechlers. Federico's English was so impeccable that he might have been mistaken for a retired officer of the Royal Navy.

From Cortina late in October they drove down through Belluno and Treviso to the magical city of Venice. If you cared anything about history, said Ernest, Venice was absolutely god-damned wonderful. The fact that he and Mary were "very popular characters" among the Venetians did nothing to diminish his pleasure. He was presented with a scroll which made him Cavaliere di Gran Croce al Merito in the Knights of Malta, and rejoiced with Lady Mary in the solid comforts of the Gritti Palace Hotel and Harry's Bar. The whole city, he now believed, belonged to him personally. He even managed to persuade himself that he had twice helped to defend it in his youth. Out of his dreams arose a romantic image of himself standing chest-deep in the salt marshes of the lagoon at Capo Sile, fighting side by side with other defenders of the city. It was, of course, a complete invention, but in his own mind it had the force of fact.

The old war was so much in his mind that he made a special trip to the site of his wounding thirty years before. From the much rebuilt, redestroyed, and dingy town of Fossalta, he drove out along the sunken road that gave the place its name. The miles of old earthworks along the riverbank had long since been filled in and grassed over in a complex of protective dikes. Reeds rustled in the wind along the edges of the river. In the valley behind one of the dikes stood a long, low, yellow house that had been there in 1918—perhaps the same that Ernest had recalled and used in "A Way You'll Never Be." He came upon what he took to be the very crater ("like a designed depression in a golf-course") which was all that remained of the dugout where the trench-mortar projectile had exploded. He would have liked to accomplish a ceremonious defecation. Finding this impossible, he dug a small hole with a stick and inserted a 1,000-lire note. This homemade symbolism was meant to indicate that he had contributed both blood and money to the Italian soil. That evening he returned to Venice, as Mary said, "wizer and jubilant."

Ernest spent most of November, partly with Mary and partly alone, at the Locanda Cipriani, a pleasant inn on the island of Torcello, an hour's boatride north of Venice in the Lagoon. There he settled into a loose schedule of work in the mornings and duck shooting in the afternoons. He was charmed by the flaming logs of beech and birch in their open fireplace as well as by the eleventh-century church nearby. From the church tower, on clear days, it was possible to see the marshland around Capo Sile and, with the aid of binoculars, the town of Fossalta beyond. What could exceed the romance of such a situation, where a man could almost literally look back over thirty years? On the plea that he hated sightseeing, at least of that sort, he declined to accompany Mary on a motor trip to Florence and Fiesole, and stayed behind to write "The Great Blue River," a piece about the Gulf Stream for *Holiday* magazine. Mary returned late in the month, full of her adventures, which had included frequent visits to the Florentine galleries in the company of her British friends, Lucy and Alan Moorehead, and even a meeting with Bernard Berenson, the art historian, in the garden of his Villa I Tatti near Fiesole—a neat little white-bearded wisp of a man, aged eighty-three, with a towering intellect.

They were going to winter in Cortina, having engaged a chalet called the Villa Aprile in the southern outskirts of the village. Early in December Ernest went partridge shooting with Count Carlo Kechler, the brother of Federico, and appeared next day at a shooting preserve south of Latisana on the lower Tagliamento, the property of the Barone Nanyuki Franchetti. The only woman present that rainy Saturday afternoon was Adriana Ivancich, a friend of Nanyuki's. She had never shot before and by the close of the day she was tired, wet through, and thoroughly disgusted at having been whacked in the forehead by the empty shell cases ejected from her gun. When the huntsmen gathered to warm up with whiskey and discuss the day's events, she was in the kitchen before an open fire, drying her hair and longing for a comb to straighten it with. Ernest spoke kindly to her: he was sorry, he said, that she was the only girl there. She was struck at once by his evident sympathy and by the alacrity with which, on learning that she wanted a comb, he broke his own in two and handed her half of it.

Adriana was a *jeune fille bien élevée* only a month short of nineteen. The family Ivancich had anciently come from Lussinpiccolo on the island of Lussino off the Dalmatian coast. Shortly before 1800, they had established themselves in Venice. Their palazzo stood in the Calle de Rimedio, a narrow little thoroughfare just east of the Piazza San Marco. Adriana had been educated at a Catholic girls' day school in Venice and was still leading a sheltered life under the watchful eyes of her widowed mother, Dora. She was of medium height, with a slender girlish build and a narrow pale face that went shadowy under the cheekbones. Her eyes were hazel, her ancestral nose was slightly hooked, and she had capable hands with which she was always drawing small cartoons and sketches. Ernest liked her soft voice, her rather ardent feminine manner, the evidences of her devout Catholicism, the fact that she was superstitious, and (not least) her dark beauty. Standing at ease before the fire, he chatted amicably for some time while she combed out and arranged her black hair. When he asked her to lunch to meet Mary, she carried along her scrap-book, full of girlish cartoons and even such keepsakes as the wrapper from the first bar of chocolate that she had been allowed to eat. He added his auto-graph to her collection. He was already calling her "daughter."

With the back of the car full of the birds he had shot, Ernest drove up to Cortina. He and Mary spent a quiet Christmas, with a fir tree cut from the mountain forest and a pitcher of Bloody Marys at noon. His chief Christmas present was the sale of "My Old Man" to Twentieth Century Fox for $45,000. As the year closed, he mentioned his novel about the land, sea, and air, telling Charles Scribner that he was now at work on the part about the sea. It was the hardest of the three parts, since it covered the years 1936–44, whereas he had been with the RAF only two months and with the infantry another seven. He assured Scribner that he was working slowly for two reasons. One was the constant bad ringing in his ears, which had required him to take a nauseous medicine every four hours for the past fifteen months. The other was that this time he was determined to write better than he had ever written before.

He was now reading two novels, *The Young Lions* by Irwin Shaw and *In Sicily* by Elio Vittorini. He thought the first a disgraceful and ignoble book, and called its author an opportunistic coward who had never fired a shot in anger. He believed that Shaw had portrayed Mary Welsh as a fictional girl named Louise, Leicester Hemingway as a ne'er-do-well named Keane, and himself as a character called Ahearn. He read *In Sicily* in galley proof and wrote a short preface for the American edition. Vittorini was an original writer with "rain" in his works, unlike those reviewers in New York who fed "on the dried manure of schism and the dusty taste of disputed dialectics." Ernest defined *rain* as

knowledge, experience, wine, bread, oil, salt, vinegar, bed, early mornings, nights, days, the sea, men, women, dogs, beloved motor-cars, bicycles, hills and valleys, the appearance and disappearance of trains on straight and curved tracks, love, honor . . . porcupine quills, cock-grouse drumming on a bass-wood log, the smell of sweet grass and fresh-smoked leather, and Sicily.

Malcolm Cowley's "A Portrait of Mister Papa" had just appeared in *Life* magazine. It was the first biographical study that Ernest had authorized, it made much of his adventures in the war, and he read it avidly. Although it was "not awfully accurate," as he told Lanham, it was continuously interesting. He praised Cowley's scrupulous honesty in having withheld data which he had been forbidden to use, and soon wrote to assure the author that he had found the article "OK." But he retreated hastily when Cowley raised the question of going on to a full-length biography. As he later explained to Lillian Ross, his new friend on *The New Yorker* magazine, it seemed "sort of chicken" to permit himself to be thus embalmed while still alive. If he were ever to be "mounted," the people for the job were Jonas Brothers of Yonkers, the finest taxidermists in the land.

Mary, who had lately taken to calling herself "the short happy wife of Mr. McPappa," took issue with Cowley's implication that Ernest had not been a star athlete in his days at Oak Park High School. With some heat, she wrote to Cowley that he clearly did not know enough about Ernest to become his biographer. Her husband was in fact a remarkable athlete. But Ernest followed up her letter with one of his own in which he admitted his limitations as a football player. On the other hand, he said with some pride that he had been good with rifle, shotgun, and fishing rod since age twelve, and that he had often shot cigarettes out of Bill Smith's mouth around Horton Bay. Shooting and fishing, yes; team sports, no.

Both the Hemingways were shortly in trouble—Mary with a broken anklebone from a skiing accident in soft snow, and Ernest with a severe chest cold that kept him in bed for two weeks in February. But the worst physical problem came in March, some weeks after Mary had emerged from her plaster cast. An infection from a small scratch in the corner of his left eye began to spread rapidly across his face. The doctors in Cortina diagnosed erysipelas, a contagious disease of the subcutaneous tissue. Ernest believed that the trouble had begun with a dust particle which had lodged in his eye while riding in the open Buick over unpaved secondary roads. A more romantic story was later given out that the injury had originated from a fragment of wadding from a shotgun shell during one of his duck-shooting expeditions. When the doctors at Cortina expressed fear that the infection might spread to the brain, Ernest entered a hospital in Padua. Massive doses of penicillin reduced the fever and arrested the disease. By this time, his whole face was covered with what he called "crut," his eyes were swollen shut, and his discolored beard thrust up through the dark ointment like stubble in a muddy field.

Sinclair Lewis had now reached Venice and taken a suite at the Gritti. As Ernest later reported it, Lewis took the occasion of his absence to "nail" Mary with a three-hour diatribe on the theme of "I love Ernest, but . . ." His chief objections were that Ernest was a snob, that his productivity as a writer was niggardly, and that he had never responded in kind for Lewis's generous praise of *For Whom the Bell Tolls*. Lewis concluded by expressing his sympathy for Mary in her role as wife to a genius, and left her to pay for all the drinks. When Ernest returned from Padua with the ravages of erysipelas still evident on his face, he indulged the snobbery of which Lewis had accused him by telling the headwaiter at the Gritti that Lewis was nothing but a Baedeker-bearing bastard with a complexion that resembled the mountains of the moon.

Adriana Ivancich's older brother, Gianfranco, had just returned from an extended trip to New York, and Ernest had them both to lunch at the Gritti. Gianfranco was twenty-eight, a short, lively, brown-haired, brown-eyed man whose war record at once endeared him to Ernest. He had served as an officer in an Italian armored regiment at the battle of El Alamein in 1942 under the command of General Erwin Rommel. He was soon afterwards wounded and then evacuated on the last Red Cross ship to leave North Africa before it fell to the Allies. Following months of recuperation in various Italian hospitals, he joined the American OSS, serving as chief of partisan activity in the Veneto. In the confusion of enmities at the end of the war, he was captured by criminal elements and driven for several miles with a cocked pistol held coldly at the base of his skull. Meantime the family's country estate at San Michele al Tagliamento had been inadvertently destroyed by American medium bombers whose target was a nearby bridge. On the 12th of June, 1945, Gianfranco had found the body of his eminent father, Gr. Uff. Dott. Carlo Ivancich, murdered by hands unknown, lying amidst the rubble of an alley in San Michele. The family had ever since been struggling to recover from the tragic events of 1944–45. Ernest's romantic view of Adriana, as well as his admiration for the manly and stoical Gianfranco, was enhanced by all he heard of their recent history.

Ernest now left off his desultory work on the sea sections of his long novel in order to attempt a shorter one. At first it was only a story about shooting ducks before dawn in the chilly waters of the Lagoon. But it quickly expanded in his imagination to a far more ambitious effort in which he drew on various other aspects of his recent months in northern Italy. He was at least enough of a snob to want to make fictional use of his new friendships with the families of Franchetti, Di Robillant, Kechler, and Ivancich. He had a perfect setting in the hospitable interiors of Harry's Bar and the Gritti Palace Hotel, as well as the seascapes and cityscapes of Venice in winter. He wanted a structure which would dramatize the confrontation between two spots of time thirty years apart. In the first, like himself, his hero would be a boy of nineteen severely wounded on the Basso Piave within distant eyeshot of Venice. Over against this would be laid the attitudes and experiences of the same man revisiting the region in his forty-ninth year and looking back on his youth with characteristic nostalgia. Such a structure would enable him to include some of his personal recollections of the war as he had known it in France, Belgium, and Germany.

The book was still little more than a duck shooter's story when the Italian visit ended and the Hemingways boarded the *Jagiello* at Genoa on April 30th for the circuitous voyage back to Havana. He was still uncertain of the novel's direction or its final dimensions. When the ship docked at Cristobal in the Canal Zone on May 22, he declined to discuss his work beyond saying to a reporter that it was still in progress. Further progress was delayed by the usual mountain of unanswered mail. To deal with it, he hired a part-time secretary named Juanita Jensen from the American Embassy in Havana. Nita had been forewarned that his language might on occasion become a little rough. She was both pleasantly surprised and slightly disappointed when her new employer turned out to be the "most polite perfect gentleman" that she had ever met. For several weeks he dictated with the utmost regard for her sensibilities. Then one day he said, "Would you mind if I call you daughter?" "Not at all," said the girl. As if encouraged, he began to use somewhat less decorous language than before and at last reached the climactic moment when he uttered a four-letter word. At this he stopped dictating and fixed Nita with a fatherly eye. "You must forgive me, daughter," said he, "for using this language, but I find that it is absolutely necessary." "Go right ahead," the girl said. "Please feel free to say whatever you like." The effect was almost miraculous. "From then on," she said, "I noticed a terrific change in his dictation. He was more at ease, he said whatever came into his mind, and I don't think he withheld anything."

Early in June his progress with the novel was interrupted again with a fishing trip to the Bahamas. Nanyuki Franchetti came over from Venice, Buck Lanham flew down from Washington, and Gigi arrived from Key West. The weather was rough; Gregorio Fuentes had a bad chest cold; a Cuban fisherman named Santiago, hired as an engineer, soon showed that he knew little about engines; and Gigi had to be rushed to Key West in a Navy crashboat for an emergency appendectomy.

Ernest spent the next month anticipating his fiftieth birthday. Like the Army colonel in his book, he kept repeating that he was half a hundred years old. It seemed to please him as much as the inward conviction that he was still twenty-five. The only irksome aspect of the day was that none of his American admirers sent a congratulatory cable, though there were flattering messages from one or two foreign publishers. He spent the afternoon of the 21st with five companions aboard the *Pilar,* drinking up a case of champagne. There were many birthday presents, he felt like a youngster, his weight was down to 200, and the word count on his novel for the week was 3,199.

On the following Saturday, he and Mary took his new secretary, Nita Jensen, for a weekend fishing trip along with Ray Rarick, an assistant air attaché at the Embassy. Nita and Ray had just swum ashore from the boat when Gregorio shouted that they must come back for lunch. As they waded in to obey, an enormous shark went coursing between them and the *Pilar.* "I wasn't about to step foot in that water," said Nita. "I looked around to see how far the road was from the beach. I was barefooted, I just had my bathing suit on, and of course no money to use for busfare. . . . So we stood there and yelled, at least I did, and finally got the word across to Papa that there was a shark. . . . His reaction was amazing. He grabbed his huntingknife and stuck it between his teeth, took his glasses off and dived overboard. He swam all the way to shore to get me and accompany me back to the boat and to reassure me that the shark wasn't the killer type. I don't think I ever swam so fast in my life, and I made it to the *Pilar* in record time. Afterwards, Gregorio told me that it was just a cat-shark, and that they were more afraid of humans than humans were of them. Papa was just as sweet and sympathetic as he could be. In fact, afterwards, I thought he was a little disappointed that he didn't get the chance to use that knife or to fight the shark."

The book was now going along so well that Ernest allowed himself a bout of bragging to Charlie Scribner. "Jeezoo Chrise," he wrote, "you have to have confidence to be a champion and that is the only thing I ever wished to be." His novel was very likely going to be a better book than any other son of a bitch alive or dead could write. Each day he stood before his typewriter, listening to the morning crowing of his fighting roosters in the yard and rejoicing in the fact that he had been born to write. He had now reached the stage of looking for titles. One of his favorites was *The Things That I Know*. Another was *A New-Slain Knight,* from the medieval ballad of "The Twa Corbies." He had secretly treasured it since 1926. Now, perhaps, was the time to use it.

From the boastful mood it was only a step to one of dark rage. A woman at *McCall's* magazine had been trying to get an interview with his aging mother in River Forest, Illinois. Grace was now seventy-seven and was being cared for by Ruth Arnold. Lately, he had been "playing the role" of a devoted son. But the truth, Ernest said, was that he hated his mother's guts precisely as she hated his. Sometime in the Depression, when Ernest had ordered her to sell the worthless Florida real estate, she had warned him never to threaten her: his father had tried it once when they were first married, and he had lived to regret it. Now Ernest took a firm stand. If she ever granted an interview to that bitch from *McCall's,* he would cut her off without a penny. He had found a new generic phrase for such situations: "How do you like it now, gentlemen?" It applied not only to his decision about his mother, but also to the case of a German soldier he said he had killed sometime during the "rat-race" of the summer and fall of 1944. In his capacity as self-appointed intelligence officer he was interrogating several of the enemy. One was so arrogant that Ernest threatened to kill him unless he revealed the proposed German escape route. "You will not kill me," said the soldier, "because you are afraid and because you are a race of moral degenerates, and besides it is against the Geneva Convention." Ernest fixed him with a cold eye. "What a mistake you made, brother," he said, and shot him three times in the belly and once more in the head, so that his brains came out through his nose as he fell over. This at any rate was his boast to his gentlemanly publisher, Charles Scribner. Like so many of his war stories, it was either invented or picked by hearsay from someone else. Yet the mere telling of it was a way of getting rid of the gall that rose in his throat whenever he thought of the woman at *McCall's* and his poor old mother in River Forest, Illinois.

But he was a man of many moods. In one of them he sent a tactful letter to the octogenarian Bernard Berenson, thanking him for having been so kind to Mary during her visit to Fiesole in November, and assuring the old man that he was "one of the [few] liveing people that I respect most." He hoped it was not heretical to say that he did not care for Firenze, being "an old Veneto boy" himself. A man had only one virginity to lose, and there his heart would ever be. Such a statement might sound "slightly wet," but it admirably expressed how he felt about all parts of the Veneto, including even Pordenone. He was already talking of another trip to Italy, leaving in November on the *Île de France,* calling in at the Ritz in Paris, and then descending to the Veneto, where he could revise the book on weekdays and shoot ducks on Sundays. Once finished, the novel would be serialized in *Cosmopolitan* magazine, largely because of Ernest's liking for young Aaron Hotchner, whom he now called "one of the nicest kids I have ever met." Hotch was coming to Cuba with his wife for a vacation early in September. He touched Ernest's heart by insisting on staying at Varadero to avoid interrupting the master at his work. When he arrived on the fifth, Ernest lost no time in getting him aboard the *Pilar* and handing him the early chapters of the novel. As he had done with Buck Lanham in 1945, he leaned over Hotchner's shoulder while the reading went on, breathing into his ear, offering marginal comments, and laughing heartily at some of the passages which he thought were witty. Hotchner found it hard to concentrate, and covered his embarrassment by asking to take the pages away to be read at greater leisure. The upshot of the visit was happy enough, since Hotchner virtually became Ernest's agent in the negotiations for serialization with the senior editors of *Cosmopolitan.*

A week after Hotchner's departure, Ernest settled at last on a title: *Across the River and into the Trees,* a slightly abbreviated version of the dying words of Gen. Stonewall Jackson. He borrowed $10,000 from Charles Scribner and sent Mary off to see her aging parents in Chicago as well as to buy a mink coat—"to make up to her," he explained, "for how shitty I have been when jamming in the stretch." The racetrack metaphor was fairly just: he computed his wordage at 13,441 between Sept. 5th and 29th, in spite of time off for two fishing trips. While Mary was away, he did his best to keep his bad-boy reputation. A new whore whom he nicknamed Xenophobia had recently appeared in Havana and he sent his retainer, Roberto Herrera, to bring her out to the Finca for dinner. Some days later he paid a nonprofessional call on Leopoldina, who was just his age. They exchanged the local gossip and told each other what Ernest described as "sad stories of the death of kings." Afterwards he set Roberto to counting the words of the manuscript. There were roughly 45,000 and Ernest believed that another 15,000 would finish the job. "Am trying to knock Mr. Shakespeare on his ass," he told Scribner. "Very difficult."

When Mary got back early in October, Ernest was already talking of completing the novel by November 1. All the time he had ever spent in Italy, he wrote Buck Lanham, was now "paying off doubled and redoubled." He said that his hero Cantwell was a composite portrait of three men: Charlie Sweeny, the former soldier of fortune; Lanham, the hard-driving West Pointer; and most of all himself as he might have been if he had turned to soldiering instead of writing. What he wanted to get was a picture of a highly intelligent fighting man deeply embittered by experience. The background, as always, was love and death. In the foreground stood the embattled hero, the eternal type of "one against the world." The fighting in the book, said he, was "all offstage as in Shakespeare." It included some remarks on the taking of Paris, and some more on his experiences in the Ardennes, the Schnee Eifel, and Hürtgen Forest. He said that his struggle to finish the novel was worse than Hürtgen—a considerable exaggeration. But then, he was in an exaggerating mood. He said that he had now decided to expend all he knew about the land war instead of saving out some of it for his big, triple-decker novel on the Land, the Sea, and the Air. It was the kind of operation he had performed in "The Snows of Kilimanjaro" in the middle thirties: condensing the materials of several novels into the flashbacks of a single short story. The mood of reckless spending was upon him.

He was right in asserting that he had borrowed much from his recent visit to Italy. He not only sent his Colonel past the bombed-out country estate of the Ivancich family at San Michele al Tagliamento, but also provided him with a romanticized duplicate of his own ceremonial visit to the dikes of Fossalta. He gave him a distant view from the tower of the ancient church on Torcello and lodged him at the Gritti Palace in Venice. He introduced him to an American novelist whose face was "as pockmarked and as blemished as the mountains of the moon seen through a cheap telescope." He provided him also with an estranged wife whom the Colonel, like Ernest, had "cauterized . . . and exorcised" in the intervening years. Finally, he gave him such real-life friends of his own as the headwaiter at the Gritti Palace, Cipriani of Harry's Bar, and Nanyuki Franchetti.

In evolving the figure of Renata, the fifty-year-old Colonel's nineteen-year-old inamorata, Ernest followed a line not unlike that of the mythical sculptor Pygmalion, who fashioned the image of a woman so beautiful that he promptly fell in love with his creation. As Renata's prototype, he chose the black-haired, nineteen-year-old Adriana Ivancich, for whom he had broken his comb near Latisana in December, and with whom he had had lunch in Venice in April. Adriana was not a countess like Renata, nor was she (except in a remote and schoolgirlish fashion) in love with Ernest. The relationship could best be described as sentimentally Platonic. He was at pains not to reveal what he was doing to her fictional counterpart, Renata, when he sent her the first of many letters early in October. He called her "daughter" and saluted her as "My Dear Adrianna." He told her that his son Gigi, who had met her on a recent trip to Venice, had called her the loveliest girl he had ever seen. He said that he was coming to Paris in November; if she would come, too, they could have fun betting on the races at Auteuil. He would be "quite rich from the book" so that they need not worry if they lost money on the horses. He hoped that she was well and happy; he knew that she was beautiful but he would rather have her well. He urged her to write to him in Italian, and closed the letter, "With much love, Mr. Papa."

What this romantic paternalism did not reveal was that in the figure of Renata Ernest was attempting a poetic metaphor of greater complexity than he had ever tried before. He wished to surround her with a Venus-like aura, like a goddess risen from the sea to become the presiding spirit of the ancient city of Venice. He had borrowed her name from the Renata Borgatti whom he and Hadley had befriended at Cortina in 1923, but was fully conscious that the name itself meant "reborn." What he wanted her to represent was the spirit of youth, reborn in the mind of his fifty-year-old Colonel. She could stand for the freshness, innocence, courage, and idealism that both Ernest and Colonel Cantwell had enjoyed in the days before war had aged and embittered them. In the passage of lovemaking under an O.D. blanket in a windswept gondola, Ernest was indulging himself in the same sort of vicarious eroticism which he had followed in *A Farewell to Arms*. Adriana had never been—would not in fact ever be—alone in a gondola or in his room at the Gritti Palace Hotel with Ernest. But this did not prevent him from dreaming his dreams.

Apart from the symbolic meanings he was seeking to convey, the relationship between Renata and the Colonel was curiously comparable to that of the lovers in *The Garden of Eden,* Ernest's long and emptily hedonistic novel of young lovers in the old days at Grau-du-Roi and the Costa Brava: page after page of their talk was filled with inconsequential commentary on the color and condition of their hair, the food and drink they were always consuming, and the current state of their suntanned skins. Something of this carried over into the food-drink-and-lovemaking passages in *Across the River*. The atmosphere was darkened, however, by a strange psychological malaise, as if Ernest were using the pages of his novel as the equivalent of a psychiatrist's couch. Even the bold talk in his letters about knocking Mr. Shakespeare across the ring and into the front seats might have been construed as more of the same: an exercise in self-assurance to restore his flagging courage.

The gall inside him came out in various ways, most notably in the mocking remarks which he dictated to Nita Jensen for the Roosevelt Birthday Memorial Concert to be held at the Waldorf Astoria Hotel in New York on January 30, 1950. Averell Harriman had written to ask his assistance. Ernest benignly promised to help if his work on the novel allowed him to do so. But it was a promise he meant to ignore. The "dedication," which happily was never sent, spoke with the utmost scorn of the rich and spoiled paralytic who had changed the world and then died of overwork.

By November it was clear that Ernest would not finish his novel before leaving for New York and Paris. Nita Jensen typed out some of the opening chapters for Hotchner to show to Herbert Mayes, the new editor in chief at *Cosmopolitan*. Ernest was already promoting a trip to France for his young friend. "Wish we had him on our team," he wrote. "Maybe we have." Lillian Ross had lately suggested doing a profile of Ernest. "I probably couldn't talk good enough to make it worthwhile," he told her. "But it would be fun to do it if you did it." On the eve of departure, the usual air of mild desperation overhung the Finca. Mary saw to the packing of fourteen pieces of luggage.

Adriana's brother Gianfranco, who had now come to Havana, worked all hours over Nita's typescript, correcting the spelling of Italian place-names and the errors of geography. Mary wrote Bernard Berenson that the push to complete his novel had turned Ernest into "a vial of seething chemicals, dangerous to meddle with." But the corrosives had simmered down by the time Ernest cabled Lillian Ross that they would fly up next day, reaching Idlewild airport late in the afternoon of November 16th. The book was not done but the end was in sight. Less than six months after his return aboard the *Jagiello,* he was going abroad once more. The holiday mood was already upon him.

67. ACROSS THE RIVER

LILLIAN ROSS was on hand to meet the plane. She found Ernest standing at one of the gates, hugging a well-scuffed briefcase and waiting for Mary, who was assembling the luggage. His graying hair needed cutting and his face was covered with a ragged white beard half an inch long. A wad of paper eased the pressure of his steel-rimmed glasses on the bridge of his nose. His brown tweed jacket was too tight in the shoulders and too short in the sleeves. As if he were expecting cold weather, his shirt, tie, sweater-vest, and slacks were all of wool, and his brown loafers were as scuffed as the briefcase. He said that he was in good shape physically but royally pooped from jamming with his book. People didn't appreciate the "terrible responsibility of writing." All they saw was the irresponsibility that came afterwards, when the writer was relaxing from his work, as he was now.

New York did not impress him. "This ain't my town," he said. "It's a town you come to for a short time. It's murder." It was now Wednesday evening and the *Île de France* was sailing Saturday. In the suite at the Sherry Netherland, he shucked his jacket and tie, called the Plaza to ask Marlene Dietrich to supper, and ordered champagne and caviar. When the wine appeared, he handed a glass to Miss Ross and said that his new war novel was a better book than *A Farewell to Arms* because he had meantime disposed of youth and ignorance. "How do you like it now, gentlemen?" he asked, wearily. But it was only a rhetorical question. Miss Dietrich's arrival interrupted his monologue. Like Mary, she owned a full-length mink coat. She accepted a glass of champagne, opened her purse, and passed around snapshots of her infant grandson. "Everything you do, you do for the sake of the children," she said. "Everything for the children," Ernest agreed.

The supper party was presently swelled by the arrival of Charles Scribner, a serious and rather shy man with neatly parted yellow-white hair; George Brown, the gentlemanly athlete in whose midtown gymnasium Ernest had often boxed; and Virginia Viertel, called Jigee, a svelte woman of about Mary's age who was going to cross the ocean with the Hemingways. When Aaron Hotchner came in, Ernest led him into the bedroom and began to paint a glorious picture of all that he would miss if he stayed behind while the others were in Paris. He had hit upon a subterfuge which he thought might work. Hotchner would return to Herbert Mayes with part of the manuscript and the promise that Hemingway would submit the rest from Paris. Mayes would then insist that Hotchner ride herd on Hemingway, with an expense account from *Cosmopolitan,* until the whole book was in hand. Ernest's grin was conspiratorial. The racetrack at Auteuil would be an ideal spot for manuscript conferences. He also wanted to walk his new friend all over the Left Bank to show him the scenes of his former triumphs.

When Lillian Ross arrived at Ernest's suite late Thursday morning, she found him wearing a plaid bathrobe and drinking champagne. He said that he had been up since dawn working on his book, and launched at once into further autobiographical reminiscences, heavily larded with boxing terminology. It was fun to be fifty and about to defend his title again. He had won it in the twenties and defended it in the thirties and forties. Now here he was coming into the ring once more. "I am a strange old man," he murmured, as if to himself. But he knew that Miss Ross was listening. The program for Friday morning was a visit to the Metropolitan Museum. When Lillian arrived for her third interview session, Patrick had come down from Harvard, Ernest was wearing his new Abercrombie and Fitch topcoat, and they set off in a taxi through the rainy streets. The Breughel room was closed for repairs, but Ernest was in his element with El Greco's "Toledo"—which he called "the best picture in the Museum"—and particularly with the Cézanne collection. He stood for some minutes before "Rocks—Forest of Fontainebleau" and told Lillian that he had learned to make landscapes from his study of Cézanne during the old days in Paris.

Crossing on the *Île de France,* he spent his time working on the book, though not much, exercising in the gymnasium, drinking at the bar, and renewing old friendships with members of the crew. He sent Lillian a shipboard letter, thanking her for a parting gift of tequila and for having refused to "crowd" him during the interview sessions. She had his permission to write any god-damn thing she wanted to write, though she must be sure to spell the names correctly, and avoid libelous statements about the people he had mentioned to her. They docked at Le Havre in gray November weather, drove to Paris, and were given Mary's old wartime room at the Ritz. Marlene had caused it to be filled with red roses. Hotchner flew across and stayed at an unpretentious hotel where he had been quartered during the war. Ernest began to talk excitedly about the fall steeplechase meeting at Auteuil: he and Hotch would form a syndicate in the Little Bar on the rue Cambon side of the Ritz, gathering each day at noon to drink Bloody Marys and study the racing forms.

Amidst these joys, Ernest finished the first draft of his book. He immediately began telling his friends that he was "beat to the wide"—a phrase he had resurrected from Duff Twysden's vocabulary of 1925. He was proud of the final scene in which Colonel Cantwell climbed into the back seat of his

"god-damned, over-sized luxurious automobile" and died of a heart attack.
Mary, Hotchner, Virginia Viertel, and even Madame Le Gros, the elderly
woman who was typing the manuscript, were all in tears, or so Ernest said,
and he rode the crest of their emotion. His letters of the fortnight before
Christmas were almost incredibly boastful. He had "won again" and asserted
that he had finished the job in a burst of energy, writing for twenty-two to
twenty-four hours a day for several days, revived only by catnaps in his chair.
He had sold the serial rights for $85,000, and expected trade-book sales to
reach or exceed 500,000 copies. He professed to be "all mixed up" in his
fatigue "with womens and horses." He was letting his beard grow, and he
thought that he resembled Flaubert beachcombing. Still, said he, it was a
damned good beach.

The weather was rainy and windy with occasional bursts of sun; gales agitated the Channel and swept in to strip the leaves from the trees in the Luxembourg and the Tuileries. Ernest tramped the streets with Hotchner, who
impressed him more each day as "straight, honest, intelligent, conscientious,
and fast." He told him elaborate tales of war and peace, usually based on fact
but tending to rise into realms of fantasy which were described in such realistic detail that Hotchner took them for truth. On clear afternoons they played
the horses at Auteuil. The day the meeting opened, they posted four winners,
none of them a favorite. The horse craze spread to Don Andrés, the Basque
priest, who arrived on the 13th on his way to the Vatican. On the 21st he
eagerly joined the Hemingstein Squadron, along with Aaron Hotchner and
half the staff of the Ritz Bar, in laying money on the nose of Bataclan II. For
a few hundred yards, Bataclan led the pack, only to lose ground so steadily
that he was far behind at the final jump. Then luck intervened. One of the
leaders stumbled and fell, the other joined the pileup, Bataclan leaped the
other side of the hedge and came galloping home the winner by six lengths.
The board showed a payoff of 232 for 10. Hotchner was dispatched to collect
the winnings, half a bushel of 10,000 franc notes which Ernest stuffed into
his pockets for distribution to members of his Squadron.

The month in Paris ended on Christmas Eve when the Hemingways and
the Viertels set off for the south of France in a large rented Packard. "We . . .
piled in Hotch at the last minute," wrote Ernest, who sat beside the driver,
discoursing on the passing scene. They spent the first night at Saulieu, ate
Christmas dinner near Valence, and presently emerged into a patch of Indian
summer weather that lasted all through Provence. Ernest continued his informal lectures from the front seat, pointing out the beauties of Avignon and
the medieval wonders of the old fortified town of Aigues-Mortes. At Le Grau-
du-Roi, he told them the story of St. Louis, King of France, and his use of the
port as a jumping-off place for his last two Crusades. The lectures continued
across the Camargue and the Arlesian countryside to Aix-en-Provence. But
his enthusiasm waned when they struck the "damned built-up Riviera," with
its look of Gallic suburbia. At Nice, the Viertels and Hotchner caught the

night train for Paris and Ernest unlimbered his typewriter to catch up on correspondence until the weather cleared for the trip to Venice.

During the first week of January, 1950, Ernest and Mary were much in the company of their aristocratic friends. Nanyuki Franchetti came down from Cortina, his leg still in a cast from a skiing accident, to initiate them into a new sport—shooting statues on the grounds of the estate with an elephant gun. When Ernest said that he doubted the wisdom of cutting loose on statuary with a .477, Nanyuki's mother said that she was sick of the statues and wanted them destroyed. Mary shot "beautifully" with the heavy guns and played small tunes on the chapel bell with a .22. Afterwards they spent two days at Carlo Kechler's establishment in Codroipo, near Udine. Carlo had sold his Alfa Romeo and many of his horses in order to buy a "really excellent Goya" and a "better than fair El Greco." Ernest had brought a tin of gray caviar and two bottles of Gordon's gin, and they all sat before a fire of mulberry roots drinking gin and Campari. Listening to the wild wind of the Veneto roaring outside, Ernest felt that he was in his proper element. "I corrupt easily," said he, "but in that sort of life I corrupt very fast." Beside his bed at night were two bottles of dry red wine. The reading lamp had been adjusted to the proper angle, his boots had been polished and his hunting clothes cleaned and laid out for the morrow. Even the Goya and the Greco had been taken down from the walls and leaned against chairs in the bedroom so that they would be the first objects his eyes would see when he awoke at dawn.

Life in Venice was far more hectic. The headwaiter at the Gritti introduced Ernest to a local tavern where they could drink and sing in the evenings. He and Mary took to entertaining their friends at sumptuous luncheons on Torcello. One of them was in honor of the ubiquitous priest, Don Andrés. The guest list, by Ernest's account, included the Princess Aspasia, mother of King Peter of Yugoslavia, Nanyuki Franchetti and his wife, and "the three most beautiful girls" in Venice, one of whom was Adriana Ivancich. Although Ernest called her "daughter" and strove to keep the relationship politely paternalistic, he continued to confuse her with the Renata of his novel, and his gaze in her direction was often moony. Mary recognized his problem and spoke of it sympathetically, but she was not overjoyed, and believed that Venetian society was filled with predatory females. The Princess Aspasia once declared herself mad for Ernest, and offered to build him a special house in her garden if he would come and live there.

On the night of the 28th, a foot of snow descended on the roofs and piazzas of Venice and Mary said that she wanted to see Cortina again. When they drove up for a weekend early in February, the snow lay so temptingly on all the slopes that they ended by staying two weeks. It was the height of the season and the bars were crowded. Ernest renewed his ancient custom of writing in bed for privacy and warmth, while Mary skied over the same terrain where she had cracked her anklebone the year before. In the midst of their stay Ernest developed another skin infection. He had been shooting with a new Italian automatic shotgun with a fast and simple blowback, and the doctors decided that his face must be allergic to gunpowder. He was put on a sustaining dose of a million units of penicillin a day, supplemented by aureomycin and ichthyol ointment.

On getting back to Venice he described himself as "full of beans and penicillin" and ready to begin working over the first 238 pages of his typescript. His spirits were somewhat dampened both by the condition of his face and by a letter from Hotchner which said that he had been fired from his job at *Cosmopolitan.* Mary had just gone back to Cortina to resume skiing when she fractured her left ankle, virtually duplicating her feat of 1949. It meant three weeks in a cast and several more of therapy and massage. Ernest was doleful. Mary herself was apologetic but cheerful when she rejoined him at the Gritti on March 5th. She gracefully presided over a dinner party for the Mondadoris on Torcello while sitting on a couch. Mondadori pleased Ernest by saying that his name was next in line for a Nobel Prize, though Stockholm continued silent. To obviate a possible scandal involving living people, Ernest forbade Italian publication of *Across the River* for at least two years. But he pointed with evident pride to Adriana's designs for the dust jacket of the American edition—a stylized perspective of a Venetian canal.

The exchange of his "warm and lovely" Venice for a Paris that was cold and wet struck Ernest as an anticlimax. He promptly came down with a bronchial cold. There was also a disturbing letter from Ezra Pound's friend, Miss Olga Rudge. She pointed out that Ezra had been languishing for five years at St. Elizabeth's Hospital in Washington. His friends were salving their consciences with "tributes to his literary worth"—but precious little else. "I know," she concluded, "you are allowing your 1923 article to be republished in the English tribute for E's 65th birthday—but—forgive my bluntness—what else have you done for E?"

The knowledge that he had in fact done nothing else did not lighten Ernest's gloom. But he gaily performed his duties as host when Charles Scribner and his wife Vera reached Paris next day, and seemed positively rejuvenated by the arrival of Adriana Ivancich and "another lovely girl" named Monique de Beaumont. "The children," as he called them, helped Mary with the packing and went along to Le Havre to see the Hemingways off on the 22nd aboard the *Île de France.* The leavetaking plunged Ernest into further depths of melancholy, and he extravagantly complained that it was like having his heart fed into a meat grinder. The homeward voyage was both stormy and dull. He gazed with surly distaste at the skyline of New York—the damned "chickenshit cement canyon town" which he had left so exuberantly four months earlier.

The social life in the Hemingways' suite at the Sherry Netherland was active as before. Patrick appeared from Harvard; Marlene Dietrich came to dinner, full of praise for the early chapters of *Across the River* and pretending to be jealous of Renata. Ernest had lunch with Colonel Sweeny, coffee with Harold Ross of *The New Yorker,* and breakfast with Buddy North, who also took them to the circus. Evan Shipman came in, reminding Ernest that it was just twenty-five years ago this coming October that he had first climbed the dark staircase to the apartment in the rue Notre-Dame-des-Champs, under the erroneous impression that he was about to meet Gorham B. Munson. Ernest showed him the "First Poem to Mary," composed in London in 1944. What impressed him more forcibly, however, was something in Ernest's manner which hinted that he was "more than ordinarily unhappy." Lillian Ross spent as much time as possible in Ernest's company. Her profile was partly done, and he answered her probing questions with his usual mélange of truth and fiction.

The happiest event of the pause in New York was a totally unexpected reunion with Chink Smith, who had come over on a speechmaking tour for the Irish government. He had now succeeded to his ancestral heritage in County Cavan, changed his name to Dorman-O'Gowan, and retired from the British Army as Lieutenant-General, after having served as Chief of Staff to Auchinleck against Rommel in the African desert. He was a distinguished soldierly figure with that cheerful look in the eyes that never failed to arouse Ernest's admiration. The degree to which Ernest had "bleached and bloated" in twenty-five years surprised him, but he was quick to suggest that he ought to join the Irish Army as "The O'Hem, a mythical figure from the American underworld." Having read an installment of *Across the River,* he delighted Ernest by calling it "devilish good." How did Ernest know things that were known only to retired army officers? "You understand sorrow," he wrote. "Why didn't you tell me?"

Ernest was certain that he understood sorrow in all its forms. It returned in billows when they reached the Finca on April 7th and he found three letters from Adriana. He replied that he had missed her every minute since Le Havre. Gianfranco, who met them at the pier, had just lost his job with a shipping company, and Ernest promised Adriana to look after his welfare. He also busied himself by sending Lillian Ross a series of autobiographical reminiscences which he felt might tone up her forthcoming profile, and did his best to bother Mary with various bits of irresponsible behavior. On May 5th, for example, he kept her and her elderly lady cousin waiting for lunch at the Club Náutico for the best part of an hour. When he appeared at last he brought the whore he had nicknamed Xenophobia. Mary's cousin thought that it was all "quite funny and jolly, as it was meant to be," but Mary was "god-damned mad." Ernest excused the lapse by explaining to his friends that he was dead-tired from working on the galleys of his novel, while Xenophobia was not only crisp, fresh, and young, but also hungry for the lunch he had promised her. In his Dr. Jekyll moods, he continued to behave like a sober citizen, accepting with grace the honorary presidency of the local PTA. As Mr. Hyde, however, he told Lillian Ross that while he would not bring Xenophobia to the Yacht Club again, he hoped that he would do something worse.

The talk of the town around New York was Lillian Ross's profile of Ernest, published on May 13th and widely if not universally regarded as "devastating." This attitude astonished Miss Ross, who prided herself on her objectivity. She had tried to present only what she had seen and heard in Ernest's presence on November 16–18, 1949, leaving implicit her "feeling of affection and admiration" for the man and his work. Ernest did not wholly share her view. On reading the profile in galley proof two weeks earlier, he had predicted to Charles Scribner that it would make him "plenty good new enemies." Despite Miss Ross's good intentions, she had managed to present both Scribner and Hemingway as "horses' asses." Still, they were "well intentioned H.A.'s," and people would doubtless remember nothing but the fact that their names had been in the paper. As he had done after the publication of Cowley's "Portrait" in *Life,* he wrote the author kindly that it was a "good straight OK piece." It was losing him no more than one friend a day. She must not worry about such losses. People always got things mixed up. He did not suppose for a moment that she had been trying to "put him out of business."

He was still sinking almost daily into sentimental dreams of Venice. He said that it was no sin to love both Mary and Adriana, but merely a form of hard luck. The literary benefits were obvious. True creativity, he felt, came to full flowering only from being in love. Apart from his nostalgia he continued to behave according to his inclinations. On June 10th he went to Havana, "checked with a couple of old whores," got home for lunch two hours late, and was "bawled out" by his wife. Next day he wrote Scribner that *Across the River* was to be dedicated "To Mary With Love." He worked most of that morning on a piece called "The Shot" which was mainly about his antelope hunt in the Pahsimeroi with Taylor Williams and Pappy Arnold in 1941. Next day he set out with Mary on a trip down the coast in the *Pilar* and the *Tin Kid,* visiting the sea Indians and spending two nights each at Bahía Honda and Megano de Casigua.

At sea again on July 1st, he had another of his odd accidents. He and Mary, with Roberto and Gregorio, were starting a three-day fishing trip to celebrate completion of the page proofs. A heavy sea was running. They were coming into Rincón to anchor. Ernest was climbing to the flying bridge when Gregorio turned the *Pilar* broadside to an oncoming wave. The boat lurched just enough to throw Ernest off balance. He slipped on the wet deck and fell heavily, banging his head against one of the large clamps that held the gaffs in place. He managed to hold onto the rail and to pass his unbroken glasses down to Gregorio. But when he touched his hand to the top of his head, it came away bright with arterial blood. Roberto was following in the *Tin Kid.* He hurried aboard and stanched the bleeding, although it was some time before they could get Ernest home. It was a deep scalp wound, down to the bone but not through it. Dr. Herrera closed it with three stitches. Next morning Ernest was up and about by six, though his head ached badly and there was a lump on his spine the size of a golf ball. Two surgeons assured him that only the thickness of his skull had saved his life. Perhaps, he said wryly, that was a form of literary criticism.

All through the summer he kept up a barrage of letter-writing to close friends and strangers. In moods of loneliness, of which he professed to have many, letters enabled him to be gregarious. Dorman-O'Gowan was back in Ireland and Buck Lanham was still in Europe. He spoke much of war, including the new one in Korea, where he said he would gladly serve under Lanham. To Adriana he sent praise and protestations of his love, as well as a running account of the fortunes of Gianfranco. He had done two children's fables about Venice for *Holiday* magazine, and she was going to make the illustrations. He had struck up a friendship with Harvey Breit of *The New York Times*, to whom he wrote frequently and knowingly about baseball and boxing. To Lillian Ross, who had gone to California to gather profile material on the making of the film of *The Red Badge of Courage*, he sent anything that came into his head, an amusing gallimaufry of news, complaints, philosophic observations, advice, and wit. He suited his tone to the temper of his recipients, writing with great politeness to a young teacher named Fraser Drew, who had sent some of his books to be autographed. On the other hand he was capable of almost incredible savagery, as in his reply to a letter from Miss Kathleen Sproul, who had taught his sister Carol during her days as a student at Rollins College in Florida. Since Carol had first met her husband while they were undergraduates at Rollins and married him against Ernest's wishes, he still had a deep-seated grudge against the college. When Miss Sproul addressed him as "Ernie" and commiserated with him over the "tragic" reviews of a book of his that she had not read, he exploded in wrath. His blast called her presumptuous and impertinent, and he sent her three dollars to buy the book in question. If she found it too sad for her tastes, she was instructed to give it to some young person who might appreciate it more.

As his tone suggested, he was often highly irritable, partly from headaches which had reappeared after the accident of July 1st, partly from feelings of frustration over Adriana. He said that he needed no psychiatrist's couch to understand the causes of his depressed moods. They were boredom, pride, and disgust. All of them were curable—if not one way, then another. He even hinted at the possibility of suicide, not without some incidental histrionics. He told Lillian Ross of a long deep dive he made on the 23rd of August far out in the Gulf Stream where the water was a mile and a half deep. By his own account he went "way down," letting out all the air. It was awfully nice down there and he was tempted to stay. Then he reflected on the need of setting a good example to his children, and his pride came surging back. If "they" wanted him, they would have to come and get him. He told himself that he would not stay down there—"not for nobody nor for nothing." He swam and kicked his way to the surface, red-faced and blowing, and climbed back aboard the *Pilar*. Or so he said, though perhaps it was only self-dramatization taking over.

68. *SLINGS AND ARROWS*

IN spite of Ernest's high hopes and preliminary vauntings, *Across the River* was received that September with boredom and dismay. The American reviews bristled with such adjectives as disappointing, embarrassing, distressing, trivial, tawdry, garrulous, and tired. Many said that the book read like a parody of his former style. The reception was about the same in England. Like some of the RAF pilots in 1944, a reviewer in the London *Observer* thought that Hemingway's implicit attitude was out of fashion. The familiar "posture" of his heroes—"despair held bolt upright by courage and virility"—now looked somewhat démodé, while the author's stature had seemingly shrunk to that of an "eccentric of the rustic American type, with an original though limited literary talent."

Mary had just crossed to the mainland to resettle her aging parents in Gulfport, Mississippi. Ernest wrote her that the reviewers fell into two groups: those who saw him as a bum, hanging punch-drunk on the ropes, and those who were finding "the best prose ever written" in the pages of his book. The second group was small indeed, though it did exist. Elliot Paul and Charles Poore both defended it; the reviewer in the *London Times Literary Supplement* compared its swan-song mood to that of Sophocles in *Oedipus at Colonus* or of Shakespeare in *The Tempest*. The name of Shakespeare was likewise invoked by John O'Hara, who called Ernest a champion to be reckoned with and "the most important author since the death of Shakespeare." This was the review that Ernest sent to Adriana Ivancich, with the observation that the *New York Times Book Review,* where it appeared, was the most important in the country.

One curious result of the publication of the book was the news from Venice that Afdera Franchetti, the pretty schoolgirl sister of Nanyuki, had begun telling her friends that she was the model for Renata. *Europeo* magazine printed a picture of Adriana and Afdera over the statement that Renata was a composite portrait of both. But Afdera went further: Ernest was desperately in love with her, she said. She had twice visited him in Cuba and they had recently spent a month together in Paris, winning millions of francs at Auteuil. Ernest found all this highly amusing, and wrote Adriana that Afdera must not be scolded for her little-girl fantasies: it was no sin to indulge them so long as they did no harm.

He was beginning to be troubled with severe pains in his right leg. They did not seem to be psychosomatic. By his account, the right foot was cold as ice, and swollen like "an elefant in the circus." Dr. Herrera tried electrical diathermy and massage until an X ray revealed several fragments of encysted metal dating from 1918, doubtless jarred loose by the tumble of July 1st, and causing the pain and the edema by pressure on nerves and veins. An operation was considered and rejected. "May try sea-bathing and ignoring the whole thing," said Ernest with a show of stoicism.

He agreed to write a short preface for a checklist of his published work to be prepared by Lee Samuels, a tobacco importer who often made trips between New York and Havana and had spent years gathering a Hemingway collection. At the same time he gently fended off a request from Harvey Breit to undertake the writing of his biography. It was too early to write anything definitive, said Ernest; too many "womens" were still alive, including his mother and his wives. His job was not to think about himself but to concentrate on his work, his family, and his daily problems. The only way to achieve his goal of living forever *"in his work"* was to enter wholeheartedly into every book he wrote. If he began thinking and talking about himself, it might, he feared, choke out everything else.

His behavior at home was becoming increasingly difficult. He was still angry over the reviews and irritable from the pain in his leg. Into this atmosphere poked the banal radio voice of the gossip columnist, Louella Parsons. She said that the Hemingways' marriage was breaking up because of an Italian countess, who was now living openly with Ernest at the Finca. Ernest identified it for what it was, a twisted version of Afdera's fantasies. After Mary's return from Gulfport, he subjected her to various forms of childish behavior, insulting her in the presence of guests at the Finca, setting his freshly served dinner plate on the floor beside his chair, using abusive language, and complaining about her actions in private letters to his friends. He had not acted in this way since his tantrums in Paris in 1945, and Mary now, as then, half suspected that a general disintegration of his personality was taking place. Like most such eruptions, this one presently simmered down. Ernest invented several scapegoats to blame for the poor reception of his book. One was the Lillian Ross profile: he believed that *Time* magazine's "shoddy" review had been strongly influenced by it. A second was the photograph of the author on the back of the dust jacket: he thought it made him look like "a cat-eating Zombie." He also held that the time lag between the end of the serialization in *Cosmopolitan* and the publication of the book had played into the hands of those "critics" who had been trying for years to put him out of business.

But business, as such, was not bad. *Across the River* was steadily climbing towards the top of the bestseller lists, while the fan mail indicated that many of his admirers had been deeply moved by the story. He was touched and encouraged by laudatory letters from three generals: H. W. Blakely, who had taken command of the 4th Infantry Division at Christmas, 1944; Dorman-O'Gowan, who was still writing frequently from Ireland; and Lanham, who praised the military aspects of the novel and congratulated Ernest for having had the guts to attack such sacred cows as Bernard Law Montgomery. Another consolation was Hollywood's interest in buying his story. He said, probably with some exaggeration, that he had turned down an offer of $250,000 for an outright sale. After his experience with *A Farewell to Arms,* he preferred to hold out for a "leasing agreement." This would pay dividends to his heirs whenever a new version of the film was made.

The best consolation of all came on October 28th, with the arrival of Adriana, chaperoned by her mother Dora. In the company of Gianfranco, Roberto, and Gregorio, Ernest and Mary met the ship outside Morro Castle. They helped their guests through immigration, and then took them to lunch at the Club Náutico. It seemed to Ernest that he was happier while they were there than he had ever been, although this was a characteristic illusion. Each morning he woke in the setting that he loved best in all the world—the old house on the hilltop, with the *Pilar* only fifteen minutes away in the Bay of Havana, and the pigeon-shooting club a mere three kilometers from the front drive of the Finca, and the Floridita exactly fourteen kilometers distant along the old Camino Real. At first light, the Guernsey cow and the heifer could be seen grazing in the misty meadow below the house, the beloved cats and dogs roamed the domain as if they owned it, tropical fruits hung ripening on the trees. Over in the guest house, still asleep beside her mother, was the girl with the "loveliest name there ever was."

He took pains to avoid any breath of scandal, keeping clear of the guest house at all times, taking care not to dance with Adriana or give any outward sign of his feelings about her. When she worked on her drawings in the room at the top of the tower, he usually stayed downstairs. He told her that they were equal partners in a firm called White Tower, Incorporated, and that when he saw her it made him feel that he could do anything, including writing better than he could possibly write.

All through their stay, as Adriana told Charles Scribner, she and her mother had a "wonderful time" doing "all sorts of interesting and amusing things" with those "lovely people," the Hemingways. They shot pigeons, shopped in Havana, and late in November were stormbound aboard the *Pilar* at Puerto Escondido. They returned on the 27th to celebrate Thanksgiving one week late. Mary gave a large party for them on December 9th. Ernest continued to behave in a manner both paternal and avuncular, though inwardly he was telling himself that Adriana was fresh as a young pine tree in the snow of the mountains, strong as a good colt, and lovely as the first rays of the morning sun among the Dolomites.

Early in December his writing ability suddenly blossomed. He later told Adriana that it came about because she was there. He was neither the first nor the last of the romantics to elevate a pretty girl to the status of a muse while managing to remain in love with his wife. His "huge working streak" lasted unbroken through the first three weeks of the month, and on Christmas Eve he declared that one of his three books about the sea was "finished." His tentative titles were *The Sea when Young, The Sea when Absent,* and *The Sea in Being.* He said rather mysteriously that he had not touched *The Sea when Young* since 1947, and there is a strong presumption that he was referring to his cut-down version of the abortive *Garden of Eden.* The one he had just finished was *The Sea when Absent.* Its hero was an American named Thomas Hudson. In appearance, manner, and personal history, he was clearly based on Ernest himself. His former wife, who appeared prominently in the story, was much like Hadley, while their eldest son, whose death the book recorded, bore a superficial resemblance to Bumby. Part 3, *The Sea in Being,* had been taking shape in his mind for sixteen years, but none of it had yet been set down.

The "completion" of *The Sea when Absent,* incomplete though it was, combined with the presence of Adriana to make "a lovely Christmas." Patrick was there with his new wife Henny; Gigi appeared with a girl whom Ernest did not like. There was a constant stream of visitors, including Winston Guest, Tom Shevlin, Gary Cooper, and Patricia Neal, who had all come over from Palm Beach for some midwinter pigeon shooting. Even the news that Faulkner had been awarded the Nobel Prize for Literature could not dampen Ernest's holiday enthusiasm. "Cabled him as soon as I heard," he told Harvey Breit in a New Year's Day letter, adding that Faulkner was a nice guy and deserved the prize. If it should ever be offered to *him,* said Ernest, he would be strongly tempted to thank them politely and then refuse to appear for the ceremony.

After the holiday hubbub, the early mornings were cool and quiet and his urge to write returned with a rush. He began to tell the story of the old Cuban fisherman and the giant marlin that Carlos Gutiérrez had told him in 1935. He presently wrote Harvey Breit that he had been afraid to tackle it for ten years, though in fact he had put it off for sixteen. By January 17th, his manuscript stood at 6,000 words, about a quarter of the whole. The old man, whose name was Santiago, had drunk his morning coffee, said good-bye to the youth Manolo, "left the smell of the land behind, and rowed out into the clean early morning smell of the ocean." On the 18th, Ernest added 808 words, knocked off for lunch with Gene Tunney and his wife, went to the cockfights with Tunney and Gigi, stood around drinking until the middle of the evening, and at dawn next day returned to his story with renewed vigor. On February 6, he wrote Harvey Breit that he had been working like a bulldozer, averaging a thousand words a day for sixteen days—a remarkable record for one whose normal daily complement was five hundred. That afternoon he attended the cockfights again. His entry won in less than a minute, using its natural spurs. It seemed a happy augury.

He needed the consolation of winning, for this was the day when Adriana and her mother boarded the plane from Havana airport. Mary went with them to take them on a guided tour of Florida before they caught the train from Jacksonville for New York and a homeward voyage starting on the 23rd. Ernest complained of great loneliness just after they had gone, though he was in fact too firmly in the grip of his novel to think of much else. By February

17th it stood virtually finished. The old man had caught his great marlin, lashed it alongside his skiff, and then lost it to the sharks on the way back to Havana. Nothing now remained but to take him up the hill and into his shack, where he would sleep the sleep of absolute exhaustion until the boy Manolo awakened him on the morning after.

Ernest could never afterwards quite express his astonishment at the speed and ease with which the story of Santiago had spun loose from the cocoon where it had lain waiting for sixteen years. Nor could he fully comprehend the parabolical quality which this seemingly simple story of profit and loss, perseverance and durability, somehow managed to convey both to himself and to those whom he allowed to read it in typescript. Seven years earlier, in the introduction to an anthology which really initiated the study of Hemingway's work in depth, Malcolm Cowley had called Ernest much more than a naturalistic descendant of Theodore Dreiser and Jack London. Instead, Cowley held, he had from the first shown kinship with those "haunted and nocturnal writers" who dealt in "symbols of an inner world." He was thus able to endow many of the activities of his heroes "with a curious and almost supernatural value." It was this quality, more than any other, which he had now managed to bring to his portrait of Santiago.

He was gradually becoming aware of a whole series of critical studies of his life and writing. Besides the portraits by Cowley and Miss Ross, there had been a volume called *Ernest Hemingway: The Man and his Work,* edited by J. K. M. McCaffery and published almost simultaneously with *Across the River.* It included a short profile by Johnny Groth, extracts from Gertrude Stein's autobiography, and Cowley's *Life* portrait. There were also eighteen critical essays by Kashkeen, Alfred Kazin, Edmund Wilson, Edgar Johnson, and others. The only one of these that Ernest liked was Edward Fenimore's stylistic study of English and Spanish in *For Whom the Bell Tolls.* He found the rest of the articles unreadable, and in none of them could he recognize either "the man" or his "work."

Part of the reason for his antipathy was well described by McCaffery in an editorial preface. "If there is one common denominator of this collection," wrote the editor, "it is the striking fact that . . . the personality of the subject has made a profound impact on the critic and has, in almost every case, affected the tone of the criticism." There can be little doubt that Ernest took notice of this point. It made him doubly wary and suspicious when he learned early in 1951 that two people had begun books about him. One was a young man at Yale University, who was already investigating his early journalism and had written to ask his help. This was Charles A. Fenton, who wanted to know if Ernest had saved any copies of the *Cooperative Commonwealth* for 1920–21. Ernest replied breezily that none had survived, and gave Fenton a brief history of his connection with that journal. A few weeks later there was another letter, this time from a Princeton professor named Carlos Baker, who was planning a full-length study. Ernest replied politely that he did not want his biography written while he was alive. He had already dissuaded Cowley and Breit, and he was resolved to impede in every way, including the legal, the publication of anything biographical. When Baker replied that his study was going to be critical, not biographical, Ernest answered that he would gladly help with information about his writings. As for his life, it was "no more important than my body will be when I am dead."

He now argued that the right of privacy was essential to an author. If he chose to "invent" fictional people based on real ones, he laid himself open to libel suits whenever the investigator ferreted out their real-life prototypes. Lies about what he was doing were always appearing in print. If he took time to deny each one, he would have no time left for anything else. Any researcher, bumbling about among truths, half-truths, conjectures, and lies, would soon emerge with a snarl of misinformation which would cost the subject both time and energy to untangle. Ernest did not want dates and hotel registers and such data uncovered because too many people were involved. With almost bewildering frankness, he said that he had been obliged to practice coitus interruptus with Pauline after the two Caesarean births because further children would endanger her life, and birth control was barred by her religion. Then came Martha. Then came "lots of stuff" that he did not want to remember, "and whores and nice girls and whores" again until he met Mary. The simplest way to avoid all this was to forbid biography.

Towards the end of April, he heard of the existence of yet another book, this time by a young professor at New York University. His name was Philip Young and he had first written it as a doctoral dissertation in 1948. An editor named Thomas Bledsoe had read it for Rinehart and Company and advised Young that if he would "clean the thing up so as to get the Ph.D. stink off it," Rinehart would gladly publish it. Young revised extensively and the new typescript was sent to Malcolm Cowley for evaluation. Cowley wrote Hemingway about the book. He thought it began and ended well. The middle was rather "flabby" in that it seemed to confuse Hemingway with his fictional heroes. Ernest's reply reached Cowley on May 19th. He reiterated his determination to stop all biographical studies, and said that he had already fended off Cowley, Baker, Breit, and a character named Sammy Boal. If Young's book was biographical, he would purge it along with the others. When Cowley conveyed these views to Bledsoe, Bledsoe replied that Young's book was critical, not biographical. By this time, however, Cowley had had enough. On June 8th, he wrote Ernest that he was bowing out of an embarrassing situation.

While the professorial interpreters moved on with their interpretations, Ernest turned to a new segment of his book about the sea. On March 5th he began to tell a story based on his sub-hunting adventures in 1942–43. As in the story he had finished (though not polished) before Christmas, the hero was Thomas Hudson. The story told of his pursuit of the crew of a sunken German submarine in the Caribbean, and closed with Hudson's death. He later said, somewhat overdramatically, that he had "dreaded" to write it and had even hoped at one time that he would never have to set it down. The reason for his dread was not entirely clear. Perhaps he meant only that it was so hard a task that he doubted his ability to bring it off. But there was a hint in what he said that the story was a true one—indeed, one might have inferred from his words that it had actually happened to him.

As he watched his pile of manuscript building up each day, Ernest was struck by a heartening sense of accomplishment. It was partly engendered by the fact that several of his pieces were now appearing in magazines. The March number of *Holiday* contained "The Good Lion" and "The Faithful Bull," the Venetian fables he had written in January, 1950, for Adriana's small nephew, Gherrardo Scapinelli, and for the daughter of Carlo Di Robillant. *True* magazine for April included "The Shot," his account of the pronghorn antelope hunt in Idaho. His introduction to Lee Samuels's checklist of his works was already in proof sheets at Scribners and scheduled for publication in July. He had done yet another preface which was now in print, this one for François Sommer's picture book of African animals, *Pourquoi Ces Bêtes Sont-elles Sauvages?*

All these, of course, were minor items. The major achievement of that spring, as he well knew, was the Santiago story. It had leveled out finally at 26,531 words. As he had done with other work, he began testing its effect on his friends, assuring and reassuring himself that they would find it as moving as he did. When they came down for a visit late in February, he handed it to Charles and Vera Scribner, and also to Hotchner, who had flown over to discuss his proposal to make some free-lance money with a ballet version of "The Capital of the World." Among the other readers were his sister Ura and her husband, Air Marshal Lord Tedder and his lady, Alfred Rice the attorney, and Ernest's wartime friend Bill Walton. They all agreed, as he put it, that the book contained a "mysterious quality" not visible in his other work. In April he handed a copy to his Norwegian publisher, Harald Grieg, and sent off another to Baker, the Princeton professor. Baker obeyed his instructions to read and return it without showing it to anyone else, and told Ernest that Santiago reminded him of King Lear. Ernest said that *Lear* was indeed a wonderful play, but added that the sea was already "quite old" when Lear was king.

He was almost as enthusiastic over his current novel about the pursuit and near capture of the Nazi submarine crew. On May 17th, after two and a half months of work, he declared it finished. It followed chronologically the novel he had finished on Christmas Eve and contained many of the same characters. He told Charlie Scribner that it was similar in quality to the story of Santiago, although the action was very fast and the dialogue very exact. At 45,000 words it was also nearly twice as long. To celebrate its completion and the arrival of a substantial royalty check from Jonathan Cape, he ordered "three big wonderful steaks from the posh American food place" in Havana, and drank two bottles of Pommard. Mary, who had now seen the completion of four novels since her marriage to Ernest, three of them in the past five months, was "too excited to eat."

Ernest thought his careful diet of rye crisps, raw green vegetables, peanut butter sandwiches, and occasional glasses of wine was partly responsible for his recent success. He explained his dietary beliefs at length to Charlie Scribner. Everyone's metabolism was different. He himself never ate sweets or starches; his daily alcoholic intake gave him enough sugar. Each morning since 1939 he had taken six B-1 Combex capsules. He was never really hungry as a horse except when he was in the mountains or cruising at sea. Then his preferences turned to "good fresh fish, grilled" or good steaks with the bone, cooked very rare, or lamb, also rare. He liked elk, mountain sheep, venison, and antelope in that order, and among game birds, grouse, young sage hen, quail, teal, canvasback, and mallards, served with mashed potatoes and gravy. All kinds of fruits, including his home-grown mangoes and alligator pears, appealed to him, while his favorite vegetables were Brussels sprouts, Swiss chard, broccoli, and artichokes with sauce vinaigrette. So, lovingly, he named over the delicacies he had denied himself while writing his recent books.

Refreshed by a weekend holiday and several victories in the annual marlin tournament, he returned to the "long first section" of his sea book. The original three-part plan had now expanded to four. He hoped to make each section an independent unit. Later he would accomplish the welding job that would unify the whole. He judged the present length of Part 1 at 85,000 words, though he was characteristically vague about its content. The parts he regarded as really finished were 3 (the sea chase) and 4 (Santiago and the marlin). In his judgment, they were "impregnable to criticism" and proved how fallacious was the view that he was "through" as a writer. A *Cosmopolitan* editor named Jack O'Connell came down from New York to talk business. O'Connell was so enthusiastic over what Ernest showed him that he proposed to publish the Santiago story complete in one issue. After a pause of three months, he would bring out the sea-chase story in two consecutive numbers. For a time the question of serialization looked settled. But when Ernest learned that they were willing to pay only ten thousand for the first and twenty for the second, he cooled off rapidly and turned the offer down.

In the midst of these negotiations came news of the death of his mother, aged seventy-nine, in Memphis, Tennessee. Ernest wrote Baker that the news had made him recall how beautiful Grace had been when she was young before "everything went to hell in the family," and also how happy they had all been as children before it all broke up. On the day she was buried in Forest Home Cemetery in Illinois, the bell in the village near the Finca Vigía began tolling at dawn. He explained that his mother had not lately been well enough to live in her own home in River Forest even with Ruth Arnold as a companion, and that his sister Sunny had been looking after her. He added that he did not believe that she had had "the grace of a happy death." For the time being, at any rate, he seemed willing to forget the withering words that he had so often used to describe her, both in private letters and public fiction.

On July 5th, Mary left Havana airport for New Orleans, first to see her parents in Gulfport and then to fly north for a reunion of her high-school class in Minnesota, followed by a visit to her cousin in Michigan. Ernest wrote her almost daily. His letters were filled with complaints about the emptiness of their bed, the impossible cooking of her maid, Clara, and the pressure of domestic details. He had resolved to spend his fifty-second birthday aboard the *Pilar* once again, anchoring out of the heat and humidity in the "natural icebox" of Puerto Escondido. Lee Samuels borrowed a microfilm unit and copied 1,600 pages of Ernest's manuscript so that he could safely take the originals with him on the trip. He wrote Charlie Scribner that if anything happened to him, Scribner could safely publish "the old man and the sea" as one small book. It was the first time he had used the phrase which ultimately became the book's title, having now evidently dropped the idea of calling it *The Sea in Being*. He also assured Scribner that Parts 2 and 3, the story of Thomas Hudson from before the war until his death at sea, were "in shape to publish"—though this was a hopeful exaggeration. But it would require much time and labor to rewrite the opening section, which he was tentatively calling *The Island and the Stream*. It contained "wonderful parts" that he hated to cut out, but he was now clear that it must be reshaped to the style and tempo of the other three sections.

In the end he decided not to take his manuscript with him on the birthday trip. Instead he would fish, swim, read, sleep, shoot iguanas with his Colt pistol, and recondition his wind and legs with short hikes along the shore and up the nearby hillocks. It was turning into the hottest July he had ever known in Cuba. Although Puerto Escondido was only about fifty miles from Havana, it was usually ten degrees cooler. Gregorio Fuentes was cheerful, the *Pilar* was in good running order, and the morning sky was full of silky cirrus clouds. Ernest hoped to bring back "lots of good fresh fish for the deep-freeze." As had happened to him a thousand times before, his appetites and his resilient enthusiasms were rising up refreshed and eager for action.

69. *PEOPLE IN PAIN*

ERNEST returned from Puerto Escondido into bad weather and bad luck. The trade winds had failed in May and remained quiescent. The atmosphere was humid as Rangoon. Shoes and clothes in the closets sprouted gray-green fur; small Japanese gardens of fungus appeared on the walls; the spines of the books in his library "grew penicillin overnight." Mary had just got back from her north-country vacation when word came that her father's cancer had recurred. He had undergone surgery in 1947, but lately had given up medical treatment for Christian Science. Ernest was as scornful of this sect as his father had been before him. Believers, said he, "are always cheerful until it hurts." Mary flew off to Gulfport on the 9th of August to be of such help as she could. She returned on the 20th, having got her father into a hospital and persuaded him to renew hormone therapy. As an only child, she had spent many hours of her girlhood in her father's company. Now that he was eighty-one, thin and ill, she liked to remember him as he had been in his younger days. Meantime there was Ernest's welfare to be considered. Mary told Charlie Scribner that his temper had been fine and even for quite a long time now. This was important "because, as he says, a good half of his work is done in the subconscious. . . . It has to happen there before it can go on paper." When the subsurface work could go on in tranquillity, his writing was invariably better.

Yet tranquillity was hard to achieve. Some people were in pain, like Evan Shipman, who had had several cancer operations, and Jean Décan, Ernest's wartime bodyguard, who was languishing in a French prison. Others, especially his fellow novelists, often ruffled Ernest's temper until he exploded. Nothing could match the vehemence with which he condemned James Jones, author of *From Here to Eternity,* for behaving like a "whiner" and a "Battle-Fatigue type." He indulged himself further by describing Tom Wolfe as a one-book glandular giant with the guts of three mice, and Fitzgerald as a rummy and a liar with the inbred talent of a dishonest and easily frightened angel. He inveighed against the second chapter of Mailer's *The Naked and the Dead* (which he never finished) by calling it "poor cheese pretentiously wrapped." His first ungrudging reaction to Faulkner's Nobel Prize was spoiled by his assertion that he was proud of not writing like the author of the latest installment of the "Octonawhoopoo" story in the *Partisan Review.* He was enraged by Dos Passos's novel, *Chosen Country,* which was based in part on information about the lake country of northern Michigan that Dos had derived from his late wife Katy. Ernest's chief objection was the portrait of himself as he had been in Michigan before the war and in Chicago in 1920–21. His fictional name was George Elbert Warner; he appeared first at the lake as an Indian-like boy with dirty fingernails, and afterwards as a Marine Corps veteran newly returned to the city. Ernest wrote Bill Smith that the Finca Vigía supported a pack of fierce dogs and cats trained to attack one-eyed Portuguese bastards who wrote lies about their friends.

The death of his mother and the illness of Mary's father had served to sharpen his consciousness of death, which was never far below the surface. Deaths came in bunches, he recalled, and usually with dire results for himself. The cable and the long-distance telephone had come to seem like instruments of the devil, since the incoming news was almost invariably bad. These views were confirmed on September 30th when Pauline cabled from San Francisco, where she had gone to see her sister Jinny, that Gigi was in some sort of trouble in Los Angeles. She would fly down, discover the facts, and telephone Ernest. Her call came through after midnight on the first of October. The Los Angeles problem was serious but not insuperable. She said that she would write him the details next day.

Ernest heard nothing more until noontime, when a cable arrived from Jinny. Pauline had died at four o'clock that morning, a few hours after having entered St. Vincent's Hospital in Los Angeles. Jinny would telephone, the cable said. Ernest waited vainly all the afternoon and called her in the evening. She said that she had forgotten about her promise to telephone, and hung up in the middle of a brief and cold conversation. Her response was understandable, even to Ernest. They had been enemies since the beginning of his affair with Martha. He swallowed his wrath and began to think back on his life with Pauline. As in the case of his mother, his mounting sorrow over the death of a woman he had once loved and then rejected came like "a wave" hitting a boat in a harbor. For a time he falsely supposed that Gigi's problems had hastened Pauline's death. In fact, however, she had been ill for some time, with such symptoms as accelerated heartbeat, high blood pressure, and severe headaches, the consequences of an undiagnosed tumor of the adrenal medulla. Now she was dead, aged fifty-six.

The continued imprisonment of Ezra Pound rose to accost Ernest once again. The South American poet Gabriela Mistral had conceived a scheme for his release from St. Elizabeth's Hospital. A hundred winners of the Nobel Prize would be asked to sign a petition to President Truman, asking dismissal of the charges against Pound. T. S. Eliot had advised caution when approached in the spring. Pound was said to believe that "Elifunt's" letter should be ignored, while Gabriela described Eliot as "un hombre muy tímido." She advised the Pound scholar D. D. Paige to approach Hemingway, who was known to scorn timidity, though he had not yet won a Nobel Prize.

Ernest replied on October 22nd. While the Mistral scheme was brave and noble, the practical aspects could not be overlooked. Eliot's letter had been sound, not timid. Many valorous people had tried to free prisoners, only to lose them in the process. President Truman, moreover, was approaching an election year. The government was already under attack for favoring Communists, and the hue and cry might equally embrace proponents of Fascism. Pound the great poet and Pound the generous friend were not legally the same, said Ernest, as the Pound who had broadcast over Mussolini's radio in wartime. If he were ever declared sane, he would have to stand trial for treason. The Mistral plan was accordingly unworkable.

To the three critical studies of his work that were now in various stages of advancement there was now added a fourth by a British journalist named John Atkins. Once again Ernest forbade biography and sent along a few bits of information designed to show that he was not an ogre. Having heard about it only from Malcolm Cowley, he continued to regard Philip Young's book as "some sort of sneak thing," evidently supposing that Young was writing biography disguised as criticism. He conceived the sly notion of heading it off by denying Young permission to quote from his novels and short stories. Young himself was understandably puzzled, since he had given years of work to the preparation of a legitimate critique and had no hint as to why Hemingway was so strongly opposed to it. But to Ernest the problem was plain. He told Charlie Scribner that he had had far more publicity than was good for him. He wanted "more and truer stuff" written about his work, and fewer lies, myths, "phony anecdotes," misquotations, and distorted facts about his life. He thought that the situation had now reached the point at which people were beginning to wonder how a bumbling, Choctaw-speaking, punch-drunk wreck like himself could earn a million dollars a year with his writing.

The sudden death of Dean Christian Gauss of Princeton, reported in a letter from Baker, confirmed his dark view of the year 1951. Just before Thanksgiving, the Basque sea captain Juan Dunabeitia was taken with a third heart attack as his ship was clearing Cárdenas. He was again brought to the Finca to recuperate under Ernest's watchful eye. Even the rugged priest Don Andrés had cardiac symptoms. Ernest reported that he was "afraid to die" and set himself the task of cheering him up. The early death of Harold Ross of *The New Yorker* gave yet another indication that the shades were closing in. If every year were like 1951, said Ernest, they would all be dead before they knew it.

He was a little ashamed of having worked so well in so bad a year. Besides the completion of three sections of his book about the sea, he had been cutting and revising the fourth, *The Island and the Stream*. In the first month he had reduced 485 pages to 305. Although his statistics were often contradictory, he said in mid-September that he had removed some 30,000 words, with 76,-000 remaining. He continued to take every opportunity to test the Santiago story on visitors to the Finca. One of these was Harry Burns, the eccentric professor from the University of Washington, who arrived unannounced one humid day to be joyously hailed as the original Professor MacWalsey, and invited to stay at the guesthouse. Ernest showed him the typescripts of the Santiago and the sub-chasing stories, and Burns made evident, "not too fulsomely," his appreciation of the chance to read them. There was also a sheaf of some thirty poems. Burns thought them inferior to his prose, but contrived to be tactfully noncommittal.

Mary was unhappy over Burns's visit, having entertained a mild prejudice against university professors ever since her undergraduate days at Northwestern. Ernest's own antiprofessorial feelings were engaged in December, when he heard from Philip Young's editor, Tom Bledsoe. He reiterated his determination to prevent biographies, and said that if he had known that Young was writing a critical study of his work, he would have been happy to provide him with facts about his fiction. One example of what Young might have learned was the "whole genesis" of *The Sun Also Rises*. After Ernest's wound at Fossalta, he explained, the surface of his scrotum became infected from bits of uniform cloth which had been driven into it by the concussive explosion of the mortar shell. Ernest had accordingly met "other kids with genito-urinary wounds." This in turn set him to wondering what a man's life would be like if his penis had been lost while testicles and spermatic cord remained intact. He said that he had known a boy wounded in this fashion. Using him as a model, he had tried to imagine his way into the boy's problems. By such examples, said he, he could have helped Young immeasurably. As it was, however, he still stuck to his refusal to let Young quote from his works.

He concluded sardonically that it must have been a hell of a lot more fun in the old days when there were more writers and fewer critics—a questionable historical generalization. This set him thinking that he might become a critic himself. He broached the idea to Charlie Scribner. He was sure that he could do "a modest scholarly introduction" which would state why and how his stories had been written and tell what they were "really" about. This ought to help the college kids a lot more than the guff that the college professors were always handing out. Maybe he could write the introduction and then get Charlie to hold it for posthumous publication. But it was only an idea. "Some collegiate character" would probably have to do the job. His own obligation was to write the stories and leave the interpreting to the interpreters.

He closed the year as he liked to do, outdoors in the crisp and lucid air, hunting wild guineas on the upland farm that Gianfranco had lately bought. He walked a long way, climbing many stone fences erected by hands long dead, and passing the ruins of old cane mills, overgrown with briars and the brown tangle of winter grass. He was reminded of the ancient Portuguese ruins he had seen in 1934 among the coastal jungles between Mombasa and Lamu. Sometime he would go back there, as he had returned to the Veneto in 1948. After all his hard work, he needed a vacation. Even New York might do: he could stay at the Barclay incommunicado and work out daily in George Brown's place. He might sail to Europe on the *Île de France* or the *Liberté,* boxing in the ship's gymnasium and swimming in the indoor pool. Mexico was out, but there might be good shooting in Arizona north of Nogales. So he dreamed, and so another year ended.

A blue norther sprang up in January, making it cold enough, as he said, to sleep with both a wife and a blanket. But the year was not yet a month old when the house was agitated by the suicide of Mary's maid, Clara. To shake loose from this affair, the Hemingways set off in the *Pilar* and the *Tin Kid* for an "austerity vacation" along the Cuban coast. Even one day on the water recharged Ernest's batteries and he was hoping to spend all of February at sea. For a week the trip was idyllic, with clear, breezy weather. They rose with the sun, fished all morning, swam and read in the afternoons, and got to bed by 9:30. Ernest slept well, ate voraciously, cut back on his drinking, and exuded wit and good cheer. On the 16th, Mary went ashore with Gregorio to get ice at a village called La Mulata on the northwest side of the island. She took the occasion to telephone the Finca to see if all was well.

It was not. Soon after their departure a cable had come with the news of yet another death. On the morning of February 11th, Charles Scribner had died suddenly of a heart attack. The day they learned of it there was a huge electrical storm, "like in the Bible," said Ernest. He listened to the surf pounding dolefully against the reef outside their mooring place. Next day there was a brisk north wind. They turned in its teeth and came home to the port of Cojimar. Ernest wrote to Vera Scribner that with the death of his dear and good friend there was no longer anyone to trust or confide in or to make rough jokes with. The loss was irreparable.

The contretemps with Philip Young had lately entered a new phase. In a paper read at the annual meeting of the Modern Language Association in Detroit just after Christmas, Young had presented a psychological interpretation of some of Hemingway's writings. When someone told Ernest about it, he advised Tom Bledsoe that a copy of the paper, together with a note from Young himself, might help to clarify the situation. Young accordingly wrote Ernest for the first time, explaining his position as well as he could. The letter was waiting at the Finca when Ernest got back from his trip down the coast, but he delayed for two weeks before drafting a reply. He said that he had been shocked by the way in which Young had lightly used serious medical terminology without being medically qualified. He added that the whole business had caused him nothing but worry, annoyance, and severe interruptions of his work. Then he said that if Young would state unequivocally that his book was not biography disguised as criticism, Young could go ahead and quote from his works. There, for the moment, the matter rested.

Happier problems awaited his attention. One was what to do with the story of Santiago and his marlin, which was still in typescript a year after its completion. The problem was solved, at least provisionally, by Leland Hayward, who had come down to Havana on vacation with his wife, the former Slim Hawks. Hayward believed that the book should be published in full in a single number of *Life* magazine. His enthusiasm was so great that Ernest sent a copy of the story to Wallace Meyer, a quiet and scholarly man who was now his point of editorial contact with Scribners. He told Meyer that he would not try to point out the story's "virtues or implicaciones." All he knew was that it was the best he had ever done in his life. It could well stand as an epilogue to all his writing and to all he had learned, or tried to learn, while writing and trying to live. The brevity of the book caused him some concern. Perhaps Scribners would find it impossible to publish so short a story as a complete novel. Yet he knew that, in the history of publishing, many books of this length had enjoyed extraordinary sales: *The Story of the Other Wise Man,* for example, or *A Christmas Carol,* or *The Man Without a Country.* He was sick and tired of not publishing anything. Other writers published short books; there was no reason why he should be considered a bum for not producing a *War and Peace* or a *Crime and Punishment.* People might even enjoy handling a good non-overweight book where a man had shown what a human being could do, and something about the dignity of the human soul.

He set off with Mary on March 10th to take up the austerity vacation that Scribner's death had interrupted. On the 16th, while the *Pilar* lay at anchor off Pinar del Río province, he wrote Meyer that he was still wondering about the title. As soon as he got home to the source books where all the titles were, he would try again. Usually he had a list of fifty or more. When he woke at night aboard the boat, new ones kept popping into his head, only to burn away afterwards "like morning mist" on the ocean. Some days later, still at sea, he confessed that he had not improved on his first idea. *The Dignity of Man* was correct but pompous. He did not wish to retain his working title, *The Sea in Being*. But it was in any case a worthy book. He told Meyer that he had done the first draft of *The Sun* in six weeks at age twenty-six; at twice that age he had completed *The Old Man* in eight weeks. He had been obliged to rewrite his first novel completely. But he had learned enough in twenty-five years so that he didn't have to rewrite *The Old Man* at all.

Except for Fulgencio Batista, who had seized power in Cuba early in March with a military coup, all went well throughout the month of April. Wallace Meyer reported that the editors at the Book of the Month Club had read and liked *The Old Man and the Sea*. Leland Hayward talked to the editors at *Life* magazine and sent Ernest an optimistic cable. Ernest was jubilant over the prospect of finding 5,000,000 readers for his novel. This, said he, was sounder, healthier, and more honorable than winning the Nobel Prize. Meantime he enjoyed a reunion with Herbert Matthews, who had come down to study the latest phase of the Cuban revolution for *The New York Times,* and wrote Adriana Ivancich that he was hoping to make some real money at last. He said that he had begun a short story "about Michigan long ago." He called it inwardly complex but outwardly "very simple." It was simple enough, certainly, and based on the heron-shooting episode at Mud Lake in his high school days. He presented the game wardens as arrant and loose-mouthed villains, drinking and camping out at Windemere Cottage while they waited to nab Nick Adams for the crime of poaching. Nick and his sister, who was plainly based on Ernest's sister Sunny, evaded arrest by penetrating deeper and deeper into the northern wilderness. It was a curious throwback to the time of his boyhood both in style and in substance, but it was enough of a change from what he had recently been writing to make him happy. He told Adriana that he was trying to keep his New Year's resolution to write better, stay healthy, be kind to his neighbors, and avoid rudeness, egotism, and needless worry.

His program was succeeding pretty well. On the 30th of April he gave away the bride when Nita Jensen was married to Walter Houk, first secretary at the American Embassy. Ernest spoke much of his companion, Black Dog, who retired with him to the pool after each day's stint of writing. Ernest drank a mixture of gin and coconut milk while the dog hunted the small lizards that sunned themselves on the masonry. The water of the pool had warmed with the advancing spring. Ernest and Mary often swam naked in the quiet noons. Her rose garden was flourishing and so were the nasturtiums she had planted under the ceiba tree. She was elated over the luxuriance of the shrubs —frangipani and bougainvillea, colonia and jasmine—and not least over the fact that Ernest was as tranquil and as mild as a good day in May.

70. THE OLD MAN AND THE SEA

MOST of Ernest's time from May to December was given to *The Old Man and the Sea*. Cables from Leland Hayward and Alfred Rice told him early in May that *Life* magazine had agreed to publish the entire text in a single number during the first week of September. This was a triumph, since *Life* had never before made such an experiment. It would also pay well. Things looked so good that Ernest could not help worrying. Perhaps there was some hidden catch. Wouldn't the Book of the Month Club have to notify its membership that the book would appear first in a magazine? Could they then make a guarantee and stick to it? He feigned a triumphant manner and bought a tin of caviar to make the feigning easier. Yet still he worried.

By the middle of the month his fears were set at rest. Rice cabled that the money from *Life* had been received and deposited, though much of it would have to be set aside in the special tax account. The Book of the Month Club officers reassured him about the guarantee. Ernest made it plain to Wallace Meyer that advance publicity for the novel must not depict him as a curiosity or a controversial figure. He wished to be "dignified with this book": he must be judged as a writer and nothing else. If necessary, the critical free-for-all could start again with the next novel. The dust-jacket designs from Scribners did not please him and he cabled Adriana to try her hand. She soon airmailed a set of designs to New York. The choice was a stylized down-hill view, in white, blue, and brown, showing five shacks, three fishing-boats, and beyond them the sea, stretching out towards infinity. Ernest was delighted. He wrote that he had never been prouder of her. *Viva El Torre Blanco,* he cried. *Viva! (Un Momento de Silencio). Viva!* The question of the portrait of the author for the back of the dust jacket was solved by Lee Samuels, who snapped thirty-five pictures of Ernest sitting beside the pool. Ernest was sure that one of them would do. All he wanted was not to look like a zombie. He told Meyer that he was truly not vain about his face and body, adding that when he *had* been good-looking, he had not known it.

This time, for once, there would be no need for a disclaimer about the identities of his fictional characters. The old man and the fish, as Ernest pointed out, were both dead long since. The sharks would not be likely to bring libel suits. He did not seem to be worried over difficulties with Manolito, the young son of the café-owner at Cojimar, who had probably served him as a rough model for Manolo, the boy in the story. He was momentarily agitated when Carlos Baker wrote to remind him of an old letter to Max Perkins in which he had mentioned Carlos Gutiérrez as one distant prototype of Santiago. But he solved that problem by asking Baker not to mention the connection. Sitting by the pool in the heavy heat of May 30th, he decided that the book would be dedicated "To Mary and to Pilar." But it was Memorial Day and he began to think of friends who had died. That evening he told Mary that he wanted to inscribe the book "To Charlie Scribner and to Max Perkins." She magnanimously agreed. Nothing now remained but the proof sheets, which he corrected on a long holiday at Paraíso.

He had meantime resolved the contretemps with Philip Young, who had written to say that his academic future depended on publication of the book he had spent five years in preparing. He offered to rewrite once more, remove all quotations, and state in a foreword that Hemingway had been unwilling to grant the customary permission. Ernest capitulated in a letter and a cable. "IF IT MEANS YOUR JOB IF NOT PUBLISHED INFORM WALLACE MEYER AT SCRIBNERS YOU HAVE MY FORMAL PERMISSION TO QUOTE. HOPE YOURE HAPPY. HEMINGWAY." Young replied that while not entirely happy he was truly grateful, and the way seemed clear at last.

In June, however, Ernest began wrangling with another of his critics, Charles Fenton of Yale, who was still at work on his doctoral dissertation about Hemingway's journalistic apprenticeship. Rumors had reached Ernest that Fenton was probing into his private life, and he hotly protested that it was like being tailed by the FBI—or even the OGPU or the Gestapo. Fenton replied in anger and Ernest tried a softer line. He had once had a wonderful novel to write about Oak Park, he explained, but had never written it for fear of hurting people. All he had ever wanted was to be a good writer. Now he knew that jackals, laundry-listers, and hyenas would be chewing away at his corpse the minute he died. Once more Fenton's answer was an angry one, and on the night of July 13th Ernest beat out a letter in which he said that he was going to enclose a check for $200 to pay Fenton's way to Cuba and back. If Fenton dared to come down, Ernest would like nothing better for a fifty-third birthday present than to get Fenton alone in any enclosed place. Fenton replied patiently, explaining his position once again, and Ernest quieted down with a long letter in which he pointed out the flaws of fact and interpretation that appeared in an article Fenton had sent about the early days in Kansas City.

During the severe heat of mid-June, with the thermometer at 92 in the shade, Alfred Eisenstadt came down to make color portraits of Ernest for the *Life* magazine cover, as well as pictures of fishermen and boats to guide Noel Sickles, who was going to illustrate *The Old Man and the Sea*. Ernest contracted a severe headache from sitting in the sun for several hours while Eisenstadt worked, and discoursed on his hatred of illustrations. Eisenstadt hired the eighty-year-old fisherman Anselmo Hernández to walk up the hill at Cojimar as a stand-in for the fictional Santiago. Anselmo made such a touching picture as he toiled stoically through the heat that Ernest could not stand it, and quietly told Eisenstadt that the photography must stop.

Harvey Breit of the *New York Times Book Review* had now conceived the ingenious notion of asking William Faulkner to review *The Old Man and the Sea*. When Faulkner reached New York on his way back from Europe, Breit put the question. Faulkner said that he wouldn't know how to tackle such a thing, and went off to Mississippi. But he presently surprised and delighted Breit by sending along a "statement" in praise of Hemingway. "A few years ago," it began, ". . . Hemingway said that writers should stick together, just as doctors and lawyers and wolves do. I think there is more wit in that than truth or necessity either, at least in Hemingway's case, since the sort of writers who need to band together willy nilly, or perish, resemble the wolves who are wolves only in pack, and, singly, are just another dog." There was a good deal more, in Faulkner's characteristic style, praising Hemingway's integrity as a writer and indicating that of all men he was least in need of the protection of the pack.

But when Breit mailed Ernest a copy, he discovered that he had stirred up a hornet's nest. Ernest pored over Faulkner's syntax and foolishly concluded that the same man who had called him a coward in 1947 was now describing him as "just another dog." Faulkner had never acknowledged his congratulatory cable at the time of the Nobel Prize. Meantime, said Ernest, he himself had written a novel that was better and straighter than Faulkner's Nobel Prize oration, and it had all been done "without tricks nor rhetoric." Why hadn't Faulkner merely refused to review *The Old Man and the Sea* and let it go at that? And so on through a long letter. By this time the seat of Harvey Breit's pants was on fire. "Listen, I'm damn sorry," he told Ernest. His innocent purpose had been "to sow friendship, not discord."

Midway of these maunderings it dawned on Ernest that he might have misunderstood Faulkner's meaning. He admitted that perhaps he was just a soreheaded and touchy bastard, but still he continued to worry the "statement" as a dog worries a squirrel. Great writing contained a "mystery" that could not be dissected out and stayed valid forever. A real writer could make this mystery with a simple declarative sentence. Maybe he was being too hard on Faulkner. But he was not being as hard on him as he had always been on himself. He would soon be fifty-three, and in all those years he had tried to write well. Old Faulkner could have his "Anomatopoeio County." As for Ernest, he felt cramped in a county—any county. His domain was the Gulf Stream, and his fish was the fighting marlin. All that Faulkner knew about was the lowly catfish.

None of this, luckily, reached the ears of Faulkner, who presently sent in a short review of *The Old Man and the Sea* to the little magazine *Shenandoah*. He called the novel Hemingway's best. "Time may show it to be the best single piece of any of us," he wrote, "I mean his and my contemporaries. This time, he discovered God, a Creator. Until now, his men and women had made themselves, shaped themselves out of their own clay; their victories and defeats were at the hands of each other, just to prove to themselves or one another how tough they could be. But this time, he wrote about pity: about something somewhere that made them all: the old man who had to catch the fish and then lose it, the fish that had to be caught and then lost, the sharks which had to rob the old man of his fish; made them all and loved them all and pitied them all. It's all right. Praise God that whatever made and loves and pities Hemingway and me kept him from touching it any further."

If Ernest saw this review of his novel, he gave no sign. But in letters of this period he repeatedly discoursed on what a "strange damn story" it must be that could profoundly affect so many people, himself included. His Italian translator wrote that she had been weeping all afternoon over the book. This and similar reactions from other readers confirmed him in his conviction that he had achieved an effect "way past what I thought I could do." The esthetics behind it was outwardly simple and inwardly complex. "The emotion was made with the action," he said proudly. He rejected the notion that he had set out to portray the malignity of nature. It was of course true that the ocean could trap you by seeming so fair and attractive; but a man was a fool who allowed himself to be trapped. He also denied that he had employed "what they used to call Naturalism." A naturalistic treatment could easily have been a thousand pages long, filled with the history and sociology of Santiago's village and all its people, the dinghy races, the bootlegging activities, the revolutions, and all the day-to-day aspects of rural life. His task, on the other hand, had been to convey Santiago's experience so exactly and directly that it became part of the reader's experience, freighted with all the implications that the reader could bring to it—inside or outside the frame the book provided.

As the time of publication drew near, Ernest's boyish excitement mounted. Dan Longwell of *Life* told him of a "whispering campaign" which had attained national proportions. Six hundred extra sets of galleys of the *Life* edition had been distributed for promotional purposes. Each man who read it had boasted of his inside track to a dozen others. Meantime, the bookstores, fearful of losing sales because of the serial appearance, were bootlegging the book to their customers. The ironic aspect of all this quiet furor was that Ernest had been obliged to sequester for his special tax account $24,000 of the $40,000 that *Life* had paid him, while the Book of the Month Club guarantee would just suffice to pay off the $21,000 he had borrowed from the late Charles Scribner to meet past tax bills. This left him $16,000 in the black. "You can't win, General," he told Buck Lanham.

Apart from the tax problems, the publication of *The Old Man and the Sea* produced nothing but pleasure. *Life* sold 5,318,650 copies within forty-eight hours. Advance sales on the regular American edition ran to 50,000 and settled thereafter into a brisk weekly sale of 3,000. In London, advance sales reached 20,000 and continued at 2,000 a week. A cable from Jonathan Cape predicted a total sale in excess of 100,000. These statistics were impressive enough, but Ernest was struck even more, if possible, by the effect the book was making on readers. All kinds, he said, kept telephoning congratulations. Those who saw him personally thanked him and often burst into tears. It was "worse than Pagliacci," said Ernest happily. American reviewers were mostly ecstatic. Harvey Breit called the book "momentous and heartening." Joseph Henry Jackson had nothing but praise for this "miracle-play of Man against Fate." *Time* found "none of the old Hemingway truculence" and judged the book a masterpiece of craftsmanship. The letter columns of *Life* blossomed with laudatory epithets. Rabbis and ministers began preaching sermons on Ernest's text. For three weeks, Ernest himself averaged eighty to ninety letters a day from well-wishers: high-school kids, boys in the service, various professors, columnists in New York, old pals from Italy, Montana, and Bimini, and many strangers.

Bernard Berenson earned his gratitude with a letter of praise. Ernest and Mary both wrote to thank the old man. The secret about the novel, Ernest explained, was that there wasn't any symbolism. Sea equaled sea, old man was old man, the boy was a boy, the marlin was itself, and the sharks were no better and no worse than other sharks. He called Berenson a "wise old man," and wondered whether he would be willing to write a sentence or two about the book for Scribners to quote in their advertising. He assured Berenson that he was the only critic that he could respect and said that if he really liked the book, and were willing to say so, it would jolt some of the less respectable critics. He closed with an apology for having made the request, but did not rescind it. Berenson speedily responded from the Casa al Dono in Vallombrosa with "a few lines about this little masterpiece." "Hemingway's *Old Man and the Sea*," he wrote, "is an idyll of the sea as sea, as un-Byronic and un-Melvillian as Homer himself, and communicated in a prose as calm and compelling as Homer's verse. No real artist symbolizes or allegorizes— and Hemingway is a real artist—but every real work of art exhales symbols and allegories. So does this short but not small masterpiece."

Ernest lost no time in relaying this statement to Wallace Meyer, suggesting that it be used as a blurb in advertisements for quarterlies like the *Hudson* and the *Partisan* reviews, evidently with some notion of confounding the fusty intellectuals. He told Meyer that Berenson had cleared up the symbolism business pretty well and let in a breath of fresh air. In thanking Berenson, and seeking to impress the old man with the power of his historical imagination, he said that he sometimes had the feeling that he had lived in all times and all countries. He knew, for example, exactly how the various types of body armor felt and where they chafed. Flaubert's historical novel of ancient Carthage, *Salammbô,* had always bored him because he knew just how things had *really* been in those days along the shores of the Mediterranean. Novelists, said he, were superliars who could make their lies truer than the truth. He was personally proud of having such good and wide knowledge to make his lies out of.

Although he said privately that he disliked living under the new Batista dictatorship, he accepted a Medal of Honor from the Cuban government "in the name of the professional marlin fishermen from Puerto Escondido to Bahía Honda." But he declined to go to New York to celebrate his success. There had been too damned much publicity anyhow. Drunks kept wanting to hit him (so he said) for having double-crossed Scribners by letting *Life* publish the book first. Sober people praised his story with tears in their eyes. Both reactions were now wearing his temper thin. Having books published, he believed, was even more destructive than making love too much. If he went to New York, he would only have to drink with various wits of the town, and doubtless it would end by his having to knock someone out. Mary could go in his place and taste the taste of triumph. He would stay in Cuba and fight the giant marlin. By the end of September he had caught twenty-nine and was hoping for a thirtieth. "The leaving of the water and the entering into it of the huge fish," he told Berenson, "moves me as much as the first time I ever saw it." Perhaps he thought that the curious style of such sentences was in some way comparable to Homer's. A Havana paper reviewed *The Old Man and the Sea* with much emphasis on the hidden symbolism. A local fisherman (so Ernest said) was puzzled by the term. "Ernesto," he asked in Spanish, "what is symbolism? In the paper it said that the sharks were the critics." Ernest smiled: "Symbolismo," he said sententiously, "es un truco nuevo de los intellectuales." It amused him to keep up this anti-intellectual and antisymbolic pose.

One of Ernest's projects at this time was his determination to help Gianfranco Ivancich, who had been trying unsuccessfully to sell his Cuban farm, and whose future still remained uncertain. He was only three years older than Bumby, and Ernest looked upon him half as brother and half as son. He needed the loyalty and devotion that Gianfranco displayed—like Sinsky, Roberto, Gregorio, and Don Andrés, but with greater intelligence, delicacy, and "mystery" than the others. It was well that he was on hand for another reason. Gigi had lately taken to quarreling with his father by mail, blaming him for his treatment of Pauline and condemning *The Old Man and the Sea* as sentimental slop. It was only, or mainly, a young man's declaration of spiritual independence on having reached the age of twenty-one, but it served to darken one of the corners in the back of Ernest's mind.

Another project reached the boiling point in December, when Leland Hayward came down to see Ernest about a film version of the novel. Ernest respected Hayward for having persuaded *Life* to serialize the book, and also as the producer of such hits as *South Pacific, Oklahoma,* and *Call Me Madam.* Hayward suggested that Spencer Tracy and a younger actor should read aloud from the book in a series of one-night stands across the country, as Charles Laughton had been doing with Shaw's *Don Juan in Hell.* This would soften up the public for a film, directed by Vittorio de Sica, narrated by Tracy, and using "local people on a local ocean with a local boat" as the actors. They could begin major shooting in a year and a half. Meantime Ernest could film the shark sequences off Punta Purgatorio, a reef near Paraíso, lashing baitfish alongside a skiff and mounting cameras on the flying bridge of the *Pilar*.

Ernest approved the idea in principle, but the notion which really appealed to him was that of another shooting safari in Africa. Patrick was now in Kenya with his wife, and his reports to his father were highly enthusiastic. Ernest got out a Lonsdale Library volume called *Shooting Big Game in Africa* so that Mary could do some advance homework on the edible and the hostile beasts. Darryl F. Zanuck's film of *The Snows of Kilimanjaro* had recently opened with much fanfare in New York. Ernest said that he was oiling up his old .577, which was good for rhino, buffalo, and lightly armored vehicles. On arrival at Mombasa, he would put the gun on his shoulder, head for Mount Kilimanjaro, climb Kibo Peak, and start "a search for the Soul of Zanuck."

CHAPTER 11

A Matter of Life and Death

71. *YEAR OF THE HUNTERS*

MOST of Ernest's thoughts were now of Africa. The pending business with Leland Hayward delayed his departure all through the spring of 1953, and he chafed at the postponement. For nearly three years, as he told Berenson, he had labored steadily at sea level. Now he was eager to "get up into the hills." He sharpened his shooting eye with quail-hunting expeditions into the back country, and banged away at pigeons in the Club de Cazadores.

When the circus came to Havana, he established close friendships with two bears named Okie and Katya under the watchful eye of their pretty blond trainer, Herta Klausser. Okie was a large Malayan bear with teeth like a four-year-old lion. He kissed Ernest's face and even permitted some holding of paws. Ernest jocularly proposed to take Katya to the Floridita, maintaining that all bears were rummies by nature. He wrote a little essay for the Ringling Brothers Program. The circus, he said, was the only remaining spectacle that had the quality of a "truly happy dream." The big cats did things that no cat would ever do. The bears rode bicycles and danced, and would all have gotten drunk if the Klausser family had allowed it.

Among his unplanned preparations for the African trip was a manhunt. In the small hours of January 17th he was dozing in Mary's bed at the other end of the house when he heard furtive noises in his own bedroom. He sprang up "fast and barefoot," seized his .22, and blazed away in the darkness. The three burglars fled, but not before one of them had been wounded. There was further bloodletting in the following week. Gianfranco was preparing to sail for Venice to become director of a steamship line. They were helping him pack one evening when a taxi disgorged a large young man from Connecticut. He announced that he had come to be Ernest's pupil and to stay at the Finca, but it soon became clear that he wanted to fight. Ernest angrily threw a dozen hard left hooks at his head and face. The young man fell bleeding. Ernest paid the cab driver and told him to deliver the boy to one of the small whorehouse hotels in Havana, and to wash him up.

He was almost equally disgusted when he read the critical studies of his work by John Atkins and Philip Young. The first struck him as a well-intentioned hodgepodge, and the second as excessively confused. He rejected Young's assertions that "Out of Season" was indebted to Scott Fitzgerald, and "The Killers" to Stephen Crane; that the basic symbols in "The Snows of Kilimanjaro" were derived from Flaubert and Dante; that there was an implication of homosexuality in his portrait of the Negro in "The Battler"; and (most horrendous) that he had been portraying *himself* in the account of Francis Macomber. The academic critics, he now concluded, were all trying to fit his works "to the procrustean bed of their isms and dialectics," and, what was worse, behaving like gossip columnists rather than scholars.

This last point was evidently the most irksome of all. In February he heard from his old friend Dorothy Connable that Charles Fenton had approached her for information about the early days in Toronto. Ernest told Dorothy that it was a miserable thing to have people writing about his private life while he was alive. Those days in Toronto belonged to the Connables and himself. The only way to stop these FBI buzzards was to tell them *absolutely nothing*. When given the truth, they rejected it for something more sensational or something that fitted the theory into which they were trying to cram his life. Dorothy's letter and Valentine had set him to recalling the wonderful dry cold of the Toronto winters, his love and admiration for Mrs. Connable, and the decency with which the "good, fine, lovely, beautiful Dorothy" had treated the callow youngster from Oak Park.

There was the even stronger argument against the scholarly interlopers, that they were trespassing on materials that he might one day wish to include in his own memoirs. He had spoken earlier of setting down his recollections of Paris in the twenties, and lately had given out several of the more lively anecdotes in letters to correspondents. One was the story of Fitzgerald's false belief that his sexual organs were inadequate to the purpose. Another concerned a Lesbian conversation between Gertrude and Alice which Ernest said he had once overheard. Who could tell what the boys would steal while sneaking down back stairways, swathed in the cloak of criticism? As he had first done with Philip Young, he now instructed Scribners to deny Fenton the right to quote from his works.

For one fortnight in late January and early February, he began to fear a recurrence of the bad year of 1951. A cable from his sister Sunny in Memphis said that her husband had died suddenly of a heart attack. Ernest set about doing what he could by long-distance telephone. Mary came down with a fever, sore throat, and stiff neck which kept her in bed for a week. Another unhappy event of this period was Gianfranco's departure aboard the *Andrea Gritti* on January 26th. It was worse than having somebody dead, said Ernest, because a man could always reconcile himself to the "deads" more easily than to the temporary departures of the living. Yet both he and Mary were almost beside themselves with sorrow when the cat called Willie was hit by a car, and came crawling up through the grounds of the Finca with both his right legs broken. The case was hopeless and Ernest shot the cat, weeping hot tears at the loss of a pet he had loved for eleven years.

The bright spring weather brought many visitors to the Finca—"the usual Cirque d'Hiver," Mary called it—filling every bed in the house, to say nothing of drinking glasses and ashtrays. Kip La Farge spent several weeks in the Little House, joined there on March 7th by Evan Shipman, who was thinner than ever and very ill with cancer of the pancreas. Next day Mary wrote Gianfranco an account of the hubbub. "After I got the mob breakfasted and off fishing this morning," she said, "I wandered around the Finca and went to the pool. Sunbathed all morning . . . and watched the leaves and tiñosas [buzzards] gliding so high in the sky they were mere specks. It is the first Sunday I've had all alone here since you left, and in a way I am enjoying it, feeling free." Twice in March she went with Ernest for extended visits to Paraíso, with Gregorio and the boy Felipe as mate and able seaman. Ernest browned to a color he called "Indio tostado." Mary swam, searched for shells, and was "very happy." They got back home on the evening of April 2, just in time to prepare for the long-awaited arrival of the Haywards and Spencer Tracy.

Ernest was pleasantly surprised with Tracy, who seemed both modest and intelligent. Under the guidance of his host, he went to inspect the small port of Cojimar, and even had the good luck to see old Anselmo Hernández asleep in his shack after having fished all through the night before. Tracy was a teetotaler who endeared himself to Ernest by getting up each morning at 6:30, whereas the Haywards customarily slept until noon. It was the Easter weekend, which struck Ernest as a poor time for business transactions. It soon became clear that Tracy would not be free to make the picture until 1955. Easter Sunday was Mary's birthday, and she spent an hour alone in the sun on the tower, happy in the conviction that this seventh year of their marriage had been the best of them all in harmony and good friendship.

On the first Monday in May they were fishing the reefs off Pinar del Río when they heard Ernest's name on the six o'clock news broadcast. *The Old Man and the Sea* had won the Pulitzer fiction prize for 1952. He tried not to look as pleased as he felt. It was the only Pulitzer he had ever won, though he had come close in 1940. He began calling it the Pullover Prize and the IgNoble Prize, and signed over the award check to Bumby, for whom it represented five months' jump pay at a hundred a month. Ernest could afford the gesture. The arrangements just concluded with Hayward guaranteed him a $25,000 advance royalty for the use of his novel, and an equal amount for his services in supervising the photographic work with the sharks in the Caribbean and the giant marlin off Peru. In the middle of May a group of editors from *Look* magazine came down to offer Ernest substantial payments for a series of articles on his forthcoming safari. He promptly bought Mary a yellow Plymouth convertible and began "staffing out" the African trip.

Before setting sail for Mombasa he was hoping for another visit to the fiesta of San Fermín in Pamplona. The problem was that Franco was still in power and that Ernest was universally known to have been a staunch Loyalist. But when he talked with his friends about a stopover in Spain, they agreed that he might honorably return, provided that he did not recant anything that he had written and kept his mouth shut about politics. The time of departure was chosen with this plan in mind. Ernest and Mary booked passage aboard the *Flandre* for June 24th and arranged with Gianfranco to meet them at Le Havre on the 30th. From there they could proceed leisurely to Pamplona in the Lancia, moving on afterwards to Madrid and Valencia and then to Paris before sailing from Marseilles for Mombasa. In Nairobi they would meet their Cuban friend Mayito Menocal, who would fly in to join them on safari with Philip Percival as white hunter.

Ernest said good-bye to Black Dog, whom he did not expect to live until he got back, and set off with Mary for Key West and New York. During the voyage he kept in training by eating little, working out daily in the *Flandre's* gymnasium, drinking Vichy water every evening after dinner, and winning all the trapshooting matches. Apart from shipboard letters, his only literary involvement was with Charles Fenton's doctoral dissertation. Alfred Rice had handed him a copy of the typescript in New York. He read it in mid-ocean and wrote Fenton that if he died in Africa, the book could be published. Otherwise, emphatically not.

"If you want to travel gaily, and I do," said Ernest, "travel with good Italians." He meant Gianfranco, who met them at Le Havre, and a cheerful, dark-haired, deferential man named Adamo, a funeral director from Udine who had come along to serve as chauffeur. They passed quickly through Paris, paused at Chartres, and put up at Poitiers. Down through the valley of the Loire, which Gianfranco had never seen before, Ernest amused himself by imagining that he was a medieval knight riding his horse along the riverbank. The notion stayed with him all the way south through Dax and St.-Jean-de-Luz to Hendaye, where he had worked long ago on the first draft of *The Sun Also Rises*.

The frontier crossing at Irún was accomplished without incident, though Ernest, with his love of melodrama, later boasted that it had required great *cojones* to reenter Franco's Spain and pretended that he had been in danger of being shot by the border guards. On arrival in Pamplona they discovered that all the hotel space was solidly booked. They took rooms instead at Lecumberri, 33 kilometers to the north, a pleasant Basque town nestled in a green valley. The Hotel Ayesterán was starkly clean in the best North Spanish style, with oaken bedsteads and scoured wooden floors.

Next day they rose before dawn for the drive to Pamplona. Waiting for them in the main square was Ernest's old friend, Juanito Quintana, who had lost his hotel there during the civil war. He was now sixty-three, a short man with narrow shoulders and a manner at once dignified and winsome. Also waiting was Rupert Bellville, a tall Englishman who had first met Ernest on shipboard in 1937 while they were both on their way to Spain to take opposite sides in the war. The company breakfasted on strong coffee, tied on red kerchiefs, and hurried over the cobblestones to the bullring in time to watch the breathless arrival of the *encierro*. At lunch they were joined by a veritable "salade"—(as Ernest called it)—including Tom and Durie Shevlin, Peter Viertel, and a large young Princeton graduate named Peter Buckley, who said that he had known Bumby when they were both small boys in Paris. Buckley was full of praise for a brilliant new matador named Antonio Ordóñez, son of that Niño de la Palma whose exploits Ernest had celebrated under the name of Pedro Romero in *The Sun Also Rises*. Ernest was well pleased with his reception in Pamplona, being treated, as he said, "like local boy makes good." He pretended that his purpose in having come was to get the "gen" for an appendix to *Death in the Afternoon* on the evolution and decline of the modern bullfight. But Antonio soon convinced him that *decline* was too strong a word. After a notable corrida one afternoon, he walked over to the Hotel Yoldi to meet the new hero, a slender, dark-haired young man of great personal dignity and charm. Ordóñez, Ernest concluded, was far better than his father had been on his father's best day.

After the joyous beginning, as had happened before in Ernest's experience, the fiesta dissolved in heavy rains. Mary caught a bad cold, as Hadley had once done under similar circumstances, and the trips back and forth to Lecumberri were loud with the sound of the showers on the roof of the Lancia. In the end Gianfranco drove Bellville to Biarritz while Ernest and Mary turned south for Burgos and Madrid with Adamo at the wheel.

They made detours off the main route, first to Sepúlveda and again to Segovia and San Ildefonso, so that Ernest could show Mary the site of his imagined guerrilla hideout in the Sierra de Guadarrama. It was a region of granite rock, forested with oak and pine, and punctuated with the dark openings of caves. A mountain torrent rushed under a small stone bridge. Ernest, gazing happily at the passing landscape, said that this was the country of *For Whom the Bell Tolls*. Although the bridge was not a precise duplicate of the steel-girdered structure that Robert Jordan had dynamited in the novel, Ernest was satisfied to discover that he had described the terrain exactly as it was.

Madrid was full of other ghosts, and Ernest called it "sort of spooky." But he was determined to occupy the same room in the Hotel Florida where he had lived in the fall of 1937. He told Buck Lanham that he knew by built-in radar that the Spaniards would regard this as the correct thing for him to do. In the same letter, he strongly implied that he had actually fought with the Loyalists in 1937, urinating into the water jackets of the Maxim machine guns when they became overheated, and smelling the boiled urine smell in the dust of the naked gray terrain ("worse than Hürtgen") where he and his comrades had held off the fifth counterattack by Franco's rebels.

The pictures in the Prado were "as solidly etched" in his "head and heart" as if they had hung on the walls of the Finca in all the years since he had last seen them. He pored over Goya, Breughel, and Hieronymus Bosch, and stood long before Andrea Del Sarto's "Portrait of a Woman," with whose face he had fallen in love years before. He found them all even more enjoyable than ever. It was the best possible birthday gift, though there were several others: news that the Korean war was over, news that Batista had honored him with the Order of Carlos Manuel de Céspedes, and even a hatchet-burying poem from Archie MacLeish.

They rounded out the Spanish tour with a call on Ordóñez and his brother-in-law, Luis Miguel Domínguin, at the Villa Paz ranch near Saelices, and then moved on to Valencia. Mary went sightseeing with Juanito Quintana and Peter Buckley, and they all saw several bullfights. Then it was time to hurry back to Paris and a room at the Ritz until the morning of August 4th, when they left for Marseilles with Adamo in the Lancia, stopping over at Aix-en-Provence, and going aboard the *Dunnottar Castle* for the voyage to Mombasa.

The weather was better and the ship far cleaner than either had been in 1933. Four days out, a cold wind blew off the northern mountains, like a breath of winter in the midst of August. Egypt and the Suez were hot and windless until the desert cold settled down late at night. The sky was full of clear stars, and the lights of passing ships looked bright and warm. They amused themselves with trapshooting as long as the weather allowed. But in the Red Sea the heat closed in with a vengeance, accompanied by heavy monsoon winds that raised twenty-foot waves.

That Friday there was a dance at the tourists' end of the ship. A young British sailor named Clive Cookson had been changing a gin block amidships and was just going forward to clean up when he came upon Hemingway leaning on the rail and gazing out to sea. He was wearing a white nylon shirt and flannel pants. Gray stubble covered his chin and he was sweating heavily, his face and nose pink in the heat. His chest bulged through the shirt and he seemed to tower over Cookson. The young man said that he had liked the story of Malcolm Macomber. "It's *Francis* Macomber," said Hemingway, fiercely. Cookson blushed and stammered. He had heard rumors that Hemingway was going to Mombasa to write a novel or direct a film. "Damn the rumors," said Ernest. "Bloody rumors." He fell silent and Cookson felt dismissed. But Ernest was not through. "I'm carrying a lot of weight lately," he said, pointing to his stomach. "It's not big at all," lied Cookson. The flattery seemed to anger Hemingway, but his rage quickly subsided. "Wait a minute," he said. "I'll get Mary."

When she came, they spoke of the stars. Ernest said that he had made a mistake about the star that Santiago saw in *The Old Man and the Sea*. Seven people had written him about it. The old man could not have seen Rigel in that part of the world at that time of year. "They were so good to write," said Ernest, magnanimously. He insisted on lending Cookson Mary's expensive book on stars. The young man kept it overnight, returning it next day out of fear that some of his shipmates might steal it. The sea and the heat had turned Hemingway philosophical. "You know," he told Cookson, "we're kicking our way into adolescence from the minute we're born. Gradually you form your own ideas of how you should lead your life. It's strange, but when you get hurt—really hurt, I mean—you're willing to throw those ideas aside for another set that now make sense to you and calm your hurt." Perhaps he was dreaming of Italy in 1918. But Cookson did not ask him and he never said.

It was raining when they reached Mombasa. Cookson leaned on the rail watching the Hemingways' departure. They were in a Land Rover with a colored driver. Ernest was fishing in his pocket for papers and glaring furiously at the African policeman who guarded the gates to the dock. But he was all smiles when Philip Percival appeared. The passage of twenty years, as well as a recent bout with tick typhus, had aged him noticeably without in the least diminishing his cheerful outlook. Mary fell in love with him at once. Mayito Menocal had already flown into Nairobi, only to be hospitalized by severe arthritis. But he emerged in good spirits to join the others at the camp on Philip Percival's Kitanga Farm. The photographer from *Look* also appeared, a pleasant man named Earl Theisen, much preoccupied with his camera equipment.

They spent the closing days of August luxuriously encamped in nine tents on the green-and-brown hillside at Kitanga Farm in the Mua Hills near Machakos, making several trips to Nairobi for supplies, hunting clothes, and final safari arrangements. Before breakfast on the second day, Philip came to say that Kilimanjaro had emerged from its cloudbank a hundred miles to the southeast, and they all piled into the car for a look from the crest of Potha Hill. Ernest was jubilant to learn that they were to be allowed to spend the month of September as sole hunters in the Southern Game Reserve in the Kajiado District forty miles south of Nairobi. The region had just been reopened to hunters and was said to be teeming with game. They picked up their hunting licenses in Machakos, paid a thousand shillings each and two hundred more for an extra lion, lunched on cold lesser bustard, fresh tomatoes, and beer, and set off in a small cavalcade, prepared for instant action.

They did not have to wait long. A few miles down the road they were hailed by a young and dusty game ranger named Denis Zaphiro, who had parked his Land Rover at the roadside and stood there smiling. "You want to shoot a rhino?" he asked. "Yes," said Ernest. "Well, come along," Zaphiro said. "He's just in here." Ernest and Mary, Mayito and Theisen climbed into the Land Rover. The ranger swerved off the road into deep grass, and stopped when the rhino came into sight, standing beside a thorn bush. Zaphiro had been tracking him since late morning; someone had shot him and he was dragging one foot. The men went forward, leaving Mary to watch. Dusk was falling. She was slightly nervous: it seemed to her that Ernest was getting too close. He closed the gap to twelve paces before he raised the sixteen-pound .577. The heavy rifle roared and the rhino spun around. He fired again and the beast ran off among the thorn clumps. They followed the blood spoor while the light lasted and gave up only when it was too dark to see. In their absence the boys had set up the camp, which looked cheerful when they came to it by firelight. Seven tents stood under a huge thorn tree beside the Salengai River, a wide dry bed with a trickle of water down one side. Denis Zaphiro said that many elephants might pass in the night on their way to the watering places: they would sound like giants wearing galoshes. A curious lion might even peer into the tent.

The night passed, however, without visitations. Next morning at dawn Ernest and Zaphiro went in search of the rhino. They found it dead near where they had stopped the evening search, and left the carcass untouched in the hope of attracting hyenas, which Ernest was eager to destroy. Zaphiro and Ernest were already good friends when they got back to the camp for breakfast. He was a Londoner, aged twenty-seven, nearly as tall as Ernest but slenderly built. During the war he had been in the British Army and afterwards had served with the Equatorial Corps in some of the finest game country in Africa. For the past three years he had been a ranger with the Kenya Game Department—an ardent and articulate conservationist who had pioneered in the use of light aircraft for locating the moving herds of game. It was he who had just secured permission to open the Southern Game Reserve for hunting.

The Salengai River region swarmed with birds and beasts. Ernest indulged his love of wing shooting on great flocks of doves, sandgrouse, and guineas. There were also many maribou storks standing solemnly and woodenly in the glades, and reminding Mary of weak-legged old professors of algebra. According to Denis, the district harbored four hundred elephant, ten rhino, and some twenty lion, but there was an enormous variety of lesser game. Mary's first "beastie" was a gnu and Ernest's a gerenuk. Masai warriors drifted in, wearing rusty-pink tunics, striking their spears into the ground, saying "Jambo," and giving firm, dry handshakes. On the fifth of September, driving eastward towards the village of Sultan Hamud, they stopped at a Masai settlement, where Ernest showed off for the natives with his .22, shooting cigarettes out of hands and plugging pennies and half-dollars.

When the Masai complained to Zaphiro of marauding lions, he put out zebra carcasses to serve as baits. Ernest and Mary left at dawn on September 6th with Zaphiro, Earl Theisen, and the gunbearers. As they approached the first bait, they heard a noise of breaking branches. "There's something big in there," said the mild-mannered Theisen. "How right you are," whispered Ernest in glee. Just beyond the thin brush thirty yards off the road, seven elephants were feeding. The hunters sneaked past to the bait, trying to walk like

Indians. Nothing remained of the zebra but a small fragment of rib bone. As they turned away, three more elephants appeared at the edge of the clearing. Denis was serving as rearguard for their return to the Land Rover when one of the young bulls saw him. In a kind of hurried shamble the whole herd crossed the road—great hulks stained with red dust and many cows with their young. Ernest counted fifty-two, which soon grew to seventy-two in the dramatic letters he was writing to Lanham, Berenson, and Breit. It was he who quickly made a camp joke of Theisen's remark, "There's something big in there."

The week on the Salengai gave everyone a chance to get acquainted. Mayito Menocal's white hunter was Roy Home. Mary's gunbearer was Charo, well past seventy, even smaller than she, and still only vaguely aware that Ernest had immortalized him in *Green Hills of Africa*. N'Gui, aged thirty, was Ernest's gunbearer. After a few quick questionings he persuaded himself that N'Gui was the son of M'Cola, his late blood brother from 1933. Denis Zaphiro got on so well with Ernest and Mary that Philip Percival asked him to serve as their white hunter. Ernest fondly nicknamed him "Gincrazed," a term soon shortened to "G.C." The arrangement, as Denis said, "had the blessing of the Game Department in Nairobi." The hope was that a good article by Hemingway might encourage people to come to Kenya in spite of the bad publicity occasioned by the Mau Mau Emergency.

In the early morning of their last day at Salengai, Ernest got his first lion. Despite his subsequent boasting, it was not a good show. The sky was drizzle-gray when they left in the Land Rover. Two lions were feeding on the bait. "Papa shot one at 200 yards," wrote Mary. "We heard the whock, but he didn't fall and he didn't roar." All he did was vanish. Percival and Menocal came to swell the posse for a search. In half an hour Denis found the wounded lion and finished him off with two quick shots. Ernest also shot twice. At the skinning out, the Hemingways each took a raw tidbit of meat to chew on.

The gesture was meant in part for luck. Mayito Menocal was consistently outshooting Ernest, while modestly attributing his good fortune to the yellow scarf he wore. If it was luck, it showed clearly two days later in the Kajiado District, near the Kimana River and Swamp. The move southward was accomplished in four hours, and the camp was pitched under tall trees beside a dusty but parklike plain. On the 11th Mayito shot a black-maned lion, nine feet from tail tip to nose and weighing 500 pounds. In marked contrast to Ernest's experience with the lion at Salengai, Mayito had shot only once. Ernest's difficulties reappeared when he and Mary penetrated Kimana Swamp with Denis. A large herd of buffalo was grazing there, their ebony backs showing above the tall reeds. When Ernest shot at one of the bulls, Denis assured him that the bullet had connected. But they were able to find neither buffalo nor blood spoor.

In an attempt to recoup, Ernest unpacked the old Springfield that he had used so unerringly in 1933. At first it worked well: on two successive days he killed a zebra and a gerenuk with one shot apiece. Then he began missing again—two zebras, a warthog, a lion, a lioness, and a baboon—all in two weeks of hunting around Kajiado. But he continued to be a good wing shot and seized every opportunity to go out after birds. The walking was good for him. His weight fell off to 190 despite his strong appetite, and his letters always reported that he was having a wonderful time. Except for his difficulties with the rifle, it was true. The cook N'Bebia fed them well, and the dishes were so abundant and exotic that Ernest's appetite for game began to fall off. He renewed his western-ranch-style breakfasts with sandwiches of fried egg, ham, sliced onion, ketchup, Worcestershire sauce, and mustard pickle.

They broke camp on September 19th, returned to Salengai for three days, and by the 24th had reached a new region which the Game Department had named Figtree Camp. It lay west of Magadi and north of Lake Natron beside a clear creek called the Oleibortoto that flowed out of the western edge of the Rift Escarpment. Mary was enchanted with the place. It was a few miles south on a hillside that Mayito got a fine male leopard and Mary soon afterwards a lesser kudu buck with a single shot in the neck.

Theisen left for Nairobi and the long trip home on the first Sunday in October. Mayito and Roy Home set off for Tanganyika, while Ernest and Mary stayed on for another ten days at Figtree Camp, still hoping that Mary would get a lion. On October 13th they broke camp, drove back to Nairobi, met Tom Shevlin, and returned to Percival's Kitanga Farm for a hilarious dinner. Mary stayed on there to write an article on Spain while Ernest flew down to Tanganyika to see Patrick, whose new 3,000-acre farm lay near a place called John's Corner among high wooded hills and mountain meadows. Ernest had shaved off all his hair. The scars from his various head wounds showed and he pointed them out proudly to Patrick and Henny. He took the occasion to write Gianfranco, praising Mary's "ideal" behavior throughout the safari.

Although they both assured their friends at home that they had never had a better time in their lives, the third month of shooting produced much bad luck. Their trip to Ibohara Flats in the Usangu District was a failure. Game was scarce and daytime temperatures often reached 114 degrees. Back in Kajiado they spent a week in Denis's new house, where Bill Lowe, the *Look* editor, joined them for ten days of generally unsatisfactory hunting. Rounding a sharp curve, Ernest tumbled out of the Land Rover, cutting his face and spraining a shoulder. Mary learned sorrowfully of the death of Baa, her pet gazelle. Henny was ill and Patrick came down with a bad case of malaria.

Ernest had been showing signs of wanting to go native. At dinner one night he told Mary that she was "depriving him of his new wife"—a Wakamba girl named Debba from a shamba near the village of Laitokitok. Mary, who had long since elected to believe that boys will be boys, observed helpfully that the problem could easily be met, though Debba ought first to have a much-needed bath. Ernest quickly subsided, saying that it was not the time to discuss it. For a couple of weeks thereafter nothing much happened. On the 12th Mary flew to Nairobi for Christmas shopping with a bush pilot named Roy Marsh, who had been bringing the mail to the Kimana camp and taking the hunters for joyrides over the swamp and the Chulu Hills. When she returned on the 16th, she found that Ernest had been going native with a vengeance. He had dyed his suede jackets and two shirts "into various shades of the Masai rusty pink ochre," and taken up hunting with a spear. On the 14th, he had gone out leopard hunting. He knocked a leopard out of a thorn tree and followed it into heavy bush. Ten feet away they found a splash of blood and a piece of the leopard's shoulder blade. When N'Gui handed Ernest the bone fragment, he popped it into his mouth like a savage talisman. The leopard took refuge in a clump of thorn. Ernest had to throw in six rounds with the Winchester pump gun before the animal stopped roaring and died. Ernest celebrated the event western style with five bottles of beer, only to be awakened in the evening by the arrival of Debba and some of her friends. He took them into Laitokitok and bought them dresses for Christmas. Back at the camp, as Mary wrote, the celebration soon became so "energetic" that they broke her bed. But when one of the safari servants warned that Debba's aunt might cause trouble, Ernest wisely desisted and sent or took the girls back to the shamba.

They kept the holidays African style, celebrating Christmas morning with a decorated thorn tree and gifts for the safari servants. For Christmas noon, Ernest had arranged a special Ngoma. Debba, chaperoned by her aunt, was among the crowd of Wakamba and Masai who came for the show. Ernest delivered a solemn speech. The safari scouts performed a dance, decked out in dyed ostrich plumes. They marked New Year's Eve quietly with tea and mince pies, brought down by the Percivals.

"Now at the fire we're happy," wrote Mary in her diary on January 2nd, "thinking what a marvelous year it has been."

Ernest sat rubbing his shaven head. "I'm not a phony but I'm a terrible braggart," he said.

"No," thought Mary, fondly. "Just full of joy."

"We were smart kittens to come to Africa," said Ernest.

72. *UGANDA AND AFTER*

At a quarter past six on the Friday evening of January 8, 1954, the Hemingways were at peace in the familiar surroundings of their camp at Kimana. Not many such evenings now remained. In a couple of weeks they would be starting from Nairobi on a vacation trip to the Belgian Congo. Roy Marsh was going to fly them in a Cessna 180 as a belated Christmas gift for Mary. As plans now stood, they would leave Kimana on the 15th, spend one night at the Amboseli Reserve and a few more with Denis in Kajiado, and then move on to Nairobi for what Ernest called regrouping.

Meantime there was Ernest's job. Denis had engineered his appointment as

Honorary Game Warden for the Kimana Swamp region in the midst of the Mau Mau Emergency. Although the basic intention was "to give him the feeling that he was involved in the wildlife of Africa," he had full powers of arrest, search, and prosecution. Few amateurs could have carried out the assignment with such a mixture of gaiety, responsibility, and personal pride. When leopards or marauding lions attacked the Masai livestock, or when elephants trampled their cornfields, he responded to the complaints, surveyed the damage or the half-eaten carcasses, and prescribed suitable courses of action. Sometimes he was out half the night prowling with a spear. He said that it was like pitching big-league ball six or seven days a week, and pretended to have taken up chewing tobacco as a spur to his confidence.

Between patrols among the shambas, he often dropped in on the stores and bars of the villages, and in particular the establishment of a Hindu named Singh, who owned a *ducca* or small store and a sawmill in Laitokitok. Shortly before they were to leave, Singh's wife served up a delicious meal of curried chicken and noodles. Afterwards, at one of the shambas, Ernest gathered six small boys into the front seat of the hunting car and gave them driving lessons, backing and turning, sounding the klaxon, and giving mock chase to the solemn-faced Masai donkeys.

On the 21st, as planned, they took off from West Nairobi airport in the Cessna with Roy Marsh at the controls. Roy was a slender and confident young man with a small black mustache. The flight plan was circuitous. They flew southwest to Figtree Camp, where they dropped a note for Denis Zaphiro, explored the Rift Escarpment from the air, and marveled at the color of Lake Natron, pink with immense flocks of flamingoes. That afternoon they turned west over Ngorongoro Crater and the Serengeti Plain. Ernest pointed out the campsite of December, 1933, and the spot where Pauline had killed her lion. They set down briefly at Mwanza to refuel, and by sundown had reached Kivu, the most beautiful lake that Mary had ever seen. Bukavu, surnamed Costermansville, sheltered them overnight.

Next day they turned north, threading the chain of Lakes Edward, George, and Albert, and descending that evening at Entebbe on the northwest shore of Victoria Nyanza. Mary had made hundreds of pictures: Natron and the flamingoes, the great herds at Ngorongoro and Serengeti, color shots of Kivu, native villages under thatch, fishermen in dugout canoes, elephant and buffalo grazing side by side, hippo bathing along the lake shores. On the third day they saw the White Nile curling like a ribbon across the green landscape, and detoured eastward along the Victoria Nile so that Mary could photograph Murchison Falls, where the river plunged roaring down a series of spectacular cataracts.

Roy circled the falls three times, winging over for the picture taking. Somewhere in the third circle a flight of ibis suddenly crossed the path of the plane. As he dived to avoid them, Marsh struck an abandoned telegraph wire which stretched across the gorge. It nicked the propeller and raked the tail assembly.

He angled away from the falls, cleared the shelving bank, fought for altitude, lost it steadily, and looked for a place to come down. They were three miles southwest of the falls when the land rose up to meet them. The plane crunched down with a clash of rending metal among rough clumps of thorn. "Let's get out quickly," said Marsh. The Hemingways jumped clear, setting foot for the first time in their lives upon the rocky soil of Uganda.

After the roar of the plane it seemed deathly quiet. Roy straightened the radio antenna. They could hear his voice inside the cabin. "Mayday, mayday, mayday. Victor Love Item down three miles south-southwest of Murchison Falls. Nobody hurt. Awaiting overland rescue." He repeated the message and switched to reception. There was no answer. In the thick scrub around them they could hear the sounds of animals. Mary was in shock and they made her lie down. For some minutes Ernest could get no pulse at all; when it returned at last, it was 155 to the minute. Her chest ached sharply and Ernest had sprained his right shoulder at the moment of impact. Otherwise, as Marsh had said, they were unhurt.

As soon as they could, they climbed a hill where empty telegraph poles stood out against the sky. The afternoon waned and Ernest gathered firewood. From the knoll they could see the river, where hippos and elephants came down to wade and drink. That night, Mary slept fitfully under a sweater and a raincoat, while Ernest and Roy dozed beside the fire.

As soon as it was light, Roy left for the falls to make a large arrow pointing to the fallen plane. Ernest was ranging for firewood when he saw an amazing sight—a large white boat was coming down the river. He and Mary waved their raincoats to attract attention. There was no sign from the boat that they had been seen. The elephants were too close to allow for a run to the riverbank. They watched in desperation while the boat tied up at a small landing and people began sauntering ashore. They waved and shouted again and this time they were seen. A group of natives set off to climb the hill. Ernest stayed behind to wait for Roy while Mary went down to the boat.

The name on its bows was the *Murchison*. The man in charge was an East Indian who doubted the desirability of taking another party aboard. The boat had been chartered for the day by Ian McAdam, a British surgeon from Kampala, who had already left with his wife and son to look at the Falls. When Ernest and Roy arrived, the Indian insisted on collecting extraordinary fares of a hundred shillings apiece. He was accustomed to wealthy Americans, having rented the *Murchison* to John Huston and his company during the filming of *The African Queen*.

It was late afternoon when they reached Lake Albert and followed the eastern shore towards Butiaba. A bush pilot named Reggie Cartwright was waiting for them at the dock with a policeman named Williams. They had spent the day searching. The word was out that the Hemingways had been killed. A BOAC Argonaut, crossing near the falls, had reported the wreckage, with no sign of survivors. Cartwright's plane, a twelve-seater De Havilland

Rapide, was refueled and ready at the Butiaba airport, and he proposed to fly them to Entebbe.

Night was closing in when they reached the airstrip. The Rapide looked vaguely airworthy, but the runway resembled a badly plowed field. Ernest and Mary and Marsh climbed aboard with some reluctance, watching the ground ahead while the plane went bumping over the furrows, roaring and creaking, lifting and banging down again. Suddenly the plane stopped and burst into flames.

Fire was swirling outside Mary's window as she unhooked her seatbelt. It seemed an age before she could find the door on the port side. It was jammed shut. Up forward Roy Marsh had kicked out one of the windows. He and Mary got through it and ran clear, with Cartwright following. Ernest appeared on the port wing, having butted his way through the jammed door with his hapless head and his damaged shoulder. He leaped down staggering and wavered off in the flickering light. Twice in two days, they had crashed and come out alive.

But not unscathed. In smashing clear of the cabin Ernest had broken his head. His scalp was bleeding and clear liquid was seeping down behind his left ear. Mary was limping badly with the pain of a damaged knee. They climbed in with the policeman Williams and his wife for the 50-mile ride to Masindi. Ernest said afterwards that it was the longest ride of his life, and it could hardly have seemed short to Mary. At the Railway Hotel in Masindi there was neither food nor quiet. Several bush pilots appeared to join the celebration. Like Cartwright, they had all been combing the country for some sign of the wreckage. As soon as possible, the Hemingways retired to their room and nibbled at some sandwiches. Neither of them was in the least hungry and Ernest could not seem to stop coughing.

Next morning Mary cabled her parents. All over the world people were learning from newspapers and radios that they had survived. A doctor appeared with bandages, and they set off for Entebbe in a rented car with a driver. It was more than a hundred miles over dusty roads. They were given a corner room at the Lake Victoria Hotel. Representatives from East African Airways were waiting for a firsthand report on the crashes. Afterwards, Ernest talked woozily to the press, although he was seeing double and his hearing came and went like a radio in a thunderstorm. "My luck," he told them, "she is still good." That night Stuart Cloete sat with them while they dined. In Ernest's eyes he looked like twins.

He got through the rest of the week on gin and raw courage. His lower intestine had collapsed, there was something wrong with one kidney, he vomited often, his lower backbone felt like a redhot poker, and he carried his broken head like an egg. Patrick flew in Tuesday noon on a chartered plane from Dar es Salaam. He had 14,000 shillings and a quiet authority which pleased and touched his father. On Thursday Roy Marsh brought a Cessna 170 to take Ernest to Nairobi. Patrick and Mary followed next day by commercial airline. It was only nine days since the start of the trip, but it seemed like a thousand years. Congratulatory cables poured in from both hemispheres. Sitting up in his tousled bed, Ernest read them all. Afterwards came the premature obituaries, which had appeared in newspapers all over the globe, together with hundreds of statements from all kinds of prominent people who had been asked for them when it had seemed certain that Hemingway was dead. These he gobbled up with what Mary called "immoral zest," though he could not help supposing that some of the people had welcomed the news of his death.

He was still in danger of dying. Apart from the full-scale concussion, his injuries included a ruptured liver, spleen, and kidney, temporary loss of vision in the left eye, loss of hearing in the left ear, a crushed vertebra, a sprained right arm and shoulder, a sprained left leg, paralysis of the sphincter, and first degree burns on his face, arms, and head from the plane fire. With his customary pose of invulnerability he had told reporters that he had never been better. The truth was that he had never been worse. Early in February there even were times when his concussion seemed to make him maudlin. He wrote Bernard Berenson that if he ever wished to adopt a really bad boy, Ernest would be glad to be his "pup." He added that Berenson was his hero for having achieved such a lovely and fragile old age. He assured Adriana that both times he had "died" his only regret had been that it would make her sad, and made sentimental allusions to Petrarch and Laura, Héloïse and Abelard. He told Harvey Breit that he had twice inhaled fire before he got out of the second crash, and that this had never helped anybody except Joan of Arc.

Before the accidents they had chartered a fishing boat and arranged to keep the truck and the hunting car, as well as the safari servants, so that they could set up a new camp at Shimoni on the Kenya coast. While Mary went down to Mombasa to see to the arrangements, Ernest stayed on in Nairobi, dictating a 15,000-word article for *Look* magazine, which had promised him $20,000 for what he called a true and humorous account of the late unpleasantness in Uganda. What came out was mainly true, though written with much verbosity, many comic circumlocutions, and Ernest's customary exaggerations. The most surprising thing about the article was not that the prose was faulty, but that a man in his condition had been able to do it at all.

The camp at Shimoni was already in operation when Ernest flew down on Washington's Birthday with Roy Marsh, landing on the sea beach a few miles north. Patrick and Henny and the Percivals were already on hand, and Ernest spoke enthusiastically of his plans for fishing. But though the rest of the party went out nearly every day, he seldom joined them. The injury to his spine kept him in constant pain and he moved with great difficulty. In the midst of these problems, a bad brushfire sprang up near the camp, and he was foolhardy enough to try to help the other firefighters. His physical condition was so poor that he stumbled and fell into the flames. On being pulled out, his clothes smoldering, he groggily discovered second degree burns on his legs, abdomen, chest, and lips, and third degree burns on his left hand and right forearm. This was too much, and he stayed aboard the fishing boat in Mombasa harbor until it was time to board the *Africa* for the voyage to Venice.

During the voyage he stayed in his cabin until the ship reached Port Said, and then got up for an hour or two each day to exercise his legs. He had lost twenty pounds and felt weak from internal bleeding. When the ship docked in Venice late in March, he went to bed at the Gritti Palace Hotel. He wrote Berenson that he had had some notion of making a long-deferred pilgrimage to Florence, but had now thought better of it. Maybe, instead, he would go out to Torcello and just lie in his bedroom before a fire of beech logs. But he stayed where he was, receiving the usual stream of visitors. They were all shocked at his appearance. He told them that he was curing his burns with lion fat. But this romantic touch did not prevent him from collecting dozens of urine-samples in bottles and glasses in the bathroom of the suite, and he paid many visits to the Clinica for X rays and other examinations. His right kidney was badly ruptured and two of his lumbar vertebrae were crushed. But throughout April, which was cold and wet that year, he maintained an outward show of good cheer under the pall of worry and pain.

He still insisted that Venice was his town, and took pleasure in contrasting his personal habits with those of Henry James. James, he told Adriana, was a great American writer who came to Venice, looked out of the window, smoked his cigar, and thought. Apart from the cigar, his own case was not greatly different. He managed a trip to Torcello, and another to Codroipo at the invitation of Federico and Maria-Luisa Kechler. For the rest, he spent much of his time reading in his room, wearing steel-rimmed glasses, an eyeshade, wrinkled pajamas, and a rumpled bathrobe. Colonel Jim Luckett and his wife found him holding court in a T-shirt, an old gray sweater, ragged pajama bottoms, and carpet slippers. He kept up a lively monologue about the Battle of the Bulge and his recent battle with fate in Uganda. He dressed up for lunch with David and Evangeline Bruce, but returned to his bed soon afterwards, "beat to the wide," as his phrase was, and gobbling pills by the handful. Whenever possible he saw Adriana, who was now twenty-four, and kept telling her that he hoped she would soon marry the finest man in the world. Yet while deferring to her mother's concern for Adriana's reputation, he continued with many little secret jokes about their partnership in White Tower, Incorporated. He told her proudly that the American Academy of Arts and Letters had given him an Award of Merit, which they wanted to present to him in New York in May. But he added that he had no intention of going. His plan was to go to Madrid for the San Isidro bullfights and then sail from Genoa on a slow boat for Havana.

The arrangements for the visit to Spain were complex as always. In mid-April, Mary went off to Paris and London, afterwards driving to Seville with Rupert Bellville to attend the *feria* of the week after Easter. Adamo came down from Udine to drive Ernest to Spain in the Lancia. Aaron Hotchner, whom Ernest's letters called "Hotch (darling)," was summoned from Holland to make the trip as companion and listener. He arrived on May 2, glorying in yet another opportunity to travel with his benefactor. Ernest gave him an affectionate *abrazo,* joked with him about his freckled face and gangster slouch, put him up at the Gritti Palace, and fed him attentively at Harry's Bar. Hotch was a fine companion, he told Adriana, with "such a loveing and learning mind." On the evening of May 5 he took Hotch along to the Ivancich palazzo for a dinner of hamburgers, American style. Afterwards there was a farewell party in Ernest's suite at the Gritti.

Next day they set out for Milano along the Autostrada. It was nothing like the romantic view of northern Italy that Ernest had been longing to see. The banked advertising billboards along the route struck him as "vulgar and awful." He stuffed a pillow behind his aching back and was assailed by waves of nausea whenever he shifted position. But he regaled Hotchner all the way with fictitious anecdotes and a great variety of other misinformation about his past. At the Hotel Principe in Milano, they paid a call on Ingrid Bergman, who was currently appearing as Joan of Arc at the Teatro Scala. She received Ernest with affectionate regard, and he reciprocated as well as his pains would permit. But he was barely polite to her consort, Roberto Rossellini, a short man with a fringe of untidy hair and a sad Italian face whom Ernest scornfully described as a "22-pound rat."

The second day's drive through the Piedmont by way of Torino and Cuneo and down to Nice was more to Ernest's liking. He gazed with pleasure at the May-time green of the valleys and the snow-covered Alps. But he barely escaped being crushed by a crowd of worshippers at Cuneo, where a salesgirl recognized him while he was buying a bottle of Scotch. He got back to the car with the help of a squad of soldiers, badly shaken by the experience. When they reached the Hotel Ruhl on the Promenade des Anglais in Nice, he got a barber to disguise him by shaving off his beard. On the 9th of May, Adamo, wearing one of Ernest's Masai-pink jackets, sent the Lancia whistling to Aix-en-Provence, and on the 10th to Carcassonne. The weather was cold and foggy through Biarritz to San Sebastian, where they paused to pick up Juanito Quintana. He was working for a wine company and living in penury in a walk-up flat, and was happy to join them for the drive to Madrid. Again they stopped briefly at the cathedral of Burgos, where Ernest knelt down painfully and bowed his head in prayer. At a stone bridge outside the city they drew up while Ernest solemnly assured Adamo that this was the famous bridge of *For Whom the Bell Tolls.*

Madrid was crowded for the San Isidro festival, but Ernest had a reservation at the Palace Hotel, which was at least as sumptuous as the Ritz in Paris. When Mary and Rupert Bellville arrived from Seville, he insisted on attending the bullfights despite the wretched weather. He talked with a tall thin young man named George Plimpton, who was beginning work on an interview to add to a series which had been appearing in *The Paris Review.* On May 18th, the first day of warm sun, he drove out in a small cavalcade to a bull-breeding ranch near El Escorial, where he lounged on a spread-out cape, and watched Luis Miguel Dominguín work with some yearling calves. He also posed for pictures with Dominguín and Ava Gardner, pleasurably capti-vated to be photographed in the distinguished company of a famous film actress and "the best bullfighter alive." But he admitted afterwards in private that even bullfighting seemed anticlimactic to a man who had just come out of Africa.

The crash at Butiaba and the fire at Shimoni had, in fact, left him no more than a shadow of his former vigor. During the stopover in Madrid he was obliged to consult Dr. Juan Madinaveitia, who listened to his history, gave him another physical examination, and advised continued rest, a careful diet, and a greatly reduced intake of alcohol. He followed the prescription as well as he could during the final week in Madrid and the drive to Genoa in the Lancia. The long voyage to Havana on board the *Francesco Morosini,* though "boring as hell," was also "restful and healthy." When the ship reached Funchal, Madeira, he was heartened by a surprise letter from Adri-ana, to which he responded the same day with suitable endearments. For the rest, he ate sparingly, and gave his days to reading, dozing, and watching the colors of the sea. He did not feel like doing much else. Even the writing of a single letter was enough to induce fatigue. Back home once more, after an absence of nearly thirteen months, he placed himself in the hands of Dr. Herrera, and continued his recuperation with "work-outs" in the swimming pool and a board beneath his mattress to ease his back. Uganda or no, he did not propose "to run as King Lear," and he kept saying that he was al-ready homesick for the far-off hills of Africa.

73. THE BOUNTY OF SWEDEN

For all his Lear-like outbursts and his snowy beard, Ernest was only just turning fifty-five, and determined to fight his way back to health, both physical and mental. He told the aged Berenson that there was, after all, nothing like youth, nothing like loving "who you loved," nothing like waking each day not knowing what the day would bring, but knowing that it would bring something. Fame as a writer was one thing, and he was on record as wanting to write books that would last forever. But he had had enough of that other thing called publicity. All the plane-crash business, he said, had only re-placed the old and false tough-guy mythology with a new legend of inde-structibility that was equally false. What interested him in his serious times was fiction, the roughest of trades. It meant the ability to seize the impalpable and make it seem not only palpable but also normal. Since this was an obvious impossibility—like the action of the alchemist who turned base metal into gold—people valued it wherever they found it. Yet too much adulation was bad for a writer. His true reward lay within himself—in the consciousness of having written to the top of his ability and then beyond it.

Rumors were abroad that his name was up for the Nobel Prize. Having heard them before, he was skeptical, though he said that if he ever got his hands on that much tax-free money, he would buy a Cessna 180 and have some real fun. Otherwise, the award might be dangerous. He had a sour-grapes theory that "no son of a bitch that ever won the Nobel Prize ever wrote anything worth reading afterwards." The case seemed to be proved by Faulkner's *A Fable,* published in August. It struck Ernest as false and contrived: all a man needed, in order to do 5,000 words a day of that kind of stuff, was a quart of whiskey, the loft of a barn, and a total disregard of syntax.

Summer and fall went by with the usual mixture of good and bad luck. On his fifty-fifth birthday he appeared at the International Yacht Club to receive the Order of Carlos Manuel de Céspedes, announced a year earlier. Mary had just returned from Gulfport, where she had placed her parents in a nursing home. Philip Percival was in London for a cancer operation. Gianfranco, hard at work on his *finca,* was courting a girl named Cristina Sandoval whom Ernest disliked. Ava Gardner and Dominguín appeared for a visit. Ernest was cheered by overtures from Gregory, patching up their three-year-old quarrel. He talked incessantly about a documentary film on African wildlife, but angrily withdrew his name when those in charge announced the arrangements prematurely.

For a time in the summer, he could write nothing but letters. As fall approached he began a series of stories based on his recent experiences in Africa. One of them expanded so steadily under his hand that he thought it might become a novel. In fact it was more like a slightly fictionized day-to-day diary of the safari, almost completely formless, filled with scenes that ranged from the fairly effective to the banal. He and Mary and Denis Zaphiro were in the foreground, and the safari servants and other Africans moved in and out as the occasion required. He made much of N'Gui and Charo, whom he called by their actual names, while the Wakamba girl Debba appeared several times—short-haired, hard-handed, and impudent, but otherwise, as he had told MacLeish, "just like Prudy Boulton," the Indian girl at Walloon Lake. In mentioning the story to Buck Lanham, a native of Washington, D.C., he said that he thought Buck would like the story—unless he was prejudiced against the theme of miscegenation.

Lanham had recently returned from Europe to the Armed Forces Staff College in Norfolk, Virginia. Bored by inaction, he resolved to enter the hospital for repair of a long-standing hernia. One day in late October, a nurse appeared. "General," said she, "you have a long-distance call." The voice on the other end was unmistakably Ernest's.

"Buck, I just called to tell you I got that thing."

"That thing? What thing?"

"That Swedish thing. *You* know."

"You mean the Nobel Prize?"

"Yeah," said Ernest. "You're the first one I called."

"God-damned wonderful," Lanham said. "Congratulations."

"I should have had the damn thing long ago," said Ernest. "I'm thinking of telling them to shove it."

"Don't be a jackass. You can't do that."

"Well, maybe not," said Ernest. "There's thirty-five thousand dollars. You and I can have a hell of a lot of fun with thirty-five thousand dollars. The big thing I called about, Buck, is I want you to come down here and handle me. Everybody's going to be banging on the door of the Finca. Buck, how about it?"

Lanham mentioned his day-old hernia operation.

"Hell, Buck," said Ernest, "that's not serious. Come on down. Can't those docs fix you up?"

"They did," said Lanham. "They did it so well I walked all the way down this goddam corridor holding my gut in my hand to answer your phone call."

"Well, Buck," said Ernest, "I tell you truly, I'm not going over there. I'll write something for them to read. What would you say if *you* were getting the Nobel Prize?"

By October 28th, the day of the official announcement, Ernest had decided to be polite and even sententious. In the midst of the crowded celebration at the Finca, Harvey Breit telephoned from New York for an interview.

"Would you care to name any writers who lived before [the establishment of] the Nobel Prize in 1901 that you, as a judge, would give the award to?" asked Breit.

"Well," said Ernest, "as a Nobel winner I cannot but regret that it was never given to Mark Twain, nor to Henry James, speaking only of my own countrymen. Greater writers than these also did not receive the prize. I would have been happy—happier—today if the prize had gone to that beautiful writer Isak Dinesen, to Bernard Berenson, who has devoted a lifetime to the most lucid and best writing on painting that has been produced, and I would have been most happy to know that the prize had been awarded to Carl Sandburg. . . . Since I respect and honor the decision of the Swedish Academy I should not make any such observation. But anyone receiving an honor . . . must receive it in humility."

"Hem," said Harvey Breit, "I think that does it."

"Think that's okay, eh?"

"I think it's very okay," said Breit. "It's wonderful and I love you, Hem."

Ernest cradled the phone, wiped his sweating brow, and returned to the celebration. He later explained that he had wanted to be graceful and generous that morning, and that he was pleased to have given recognition and personal happiness to three people who had "worked hard all their lives." It was not too small a thing to have made three people happy in a single day, especially since all of them were elderly.

He was displeased by the official citation from the Nobel Prize Committee. It praised his "powerful, style-making mastery of the art of modern narration." But it also described his earlier writings as "brutal, cynical, and callous" —and therefore at variance with the rule that an award must be given for "a work of ideal tendencies." Still, the citation had spoken of the "heroic pathos" which formed "the basic element of his awareness of life," as well as his "manly love of danger and adventure," and his "natural admiration for every individual who fights the good fight in a world of reality overshadowed by violence and death." All in all, the little paragraph had the air of something prepared by a committee, and Ernest grumblingly accepted it as such.

Two days after the award announcement, he observed to young Charles Scribner that the "damn thing" was now fortunately over with. It had interrupted his work, invaded his privacy, and produced much "distasteful publicity." Still, the $35,000 check would help him pay off some of his debts, especially a long-overdue loan from Lee Samuels. As for the elegant gold medal, he was uncertain what to do with it. Yeats had called it "The Bounty of Sweden," and Ernest wished to be bounteous. He considered giving it to Ezra Pound, but thought better of it. For a time he hid it in the secret jewelry drawer at the Finca. In the end he presented it to the Virgen of Cobre, Cuba's national saint, to be kept in the shrine of Our Lady at Santiago de Cuba.

In November he heard from the American Embassy in Stockholm. The Ambassador, John Cabot, had learned from the newspapers that Mr. Hemingway's health would not allow him to appear personally to receive his prize. If this were true, the Ambassador would accept it in his behalf. Minister Stahle, Director of the Nobel Foundation, had expressed the hope that Mr. Hemingway might send along a brief statement to be read at the ceremonial banquet.

Ernest complied by recording the following speech:

Members of the Swedish Academy, Ladies and Gentlemen: Having no facility for speechmaking nor any domination of rhetoric, I wish to thank the administrators of the generosity of Alfred Nobel for this prize. No writer who knows the great writers who did not receive the prize can accept it other than with humility. There is no need to list these writers. Everyone here may make his own list according to his knowledge and his conscience. It would be impossible for me to ask the Ambassador of my country to read a speech in which a writer said all of the things which are in his heart. Things may not be immediately discernible in what a man writes, and in this sometimes he is fortunate; but eventually they are quite clear and by these and the degree of alchemy that he possesses he will endure or be forgotten. Writing, at its best, is a lonely life. Organizations for writers palliate the writer's loneliness but I doubt if they improve his writing. He grows in public stature as he sheds his loneliness and often his work deteriorates. For he does his work alone and if he is a good enough writer he must face eternity, or the lack of it, each day. For a true writer each book should be a new beginning where he tries again for something that is beyond attainment. He should always try for something that has never been done or that others have tried and failed. Then sometimes, with great luck, he will succeed. How simple the writing of literature would be if it were only necessary to write in another way what has been well written. It is because we have had such great writers in the past that a writer is driven far out past where he can go, out to where no one can help him. I have spoken too long for a writer. A writer should write what he has to say and not speak it. Again I thank you.

"I'm naturally proud to have a prize," he told Robert Manning, who appeared on November 17th to interview him for a *Time* cover story, "but I was writing very good when it came along and I don't want to win a prize if it means losing a book." In reply to a letter of congratulation from General Dorman-O'Gowan, he said that he was completely unimpressed by this "Swedish business." All the incidental publicity, following so close upon that of the plane crashes, had given him a bellyful. "I don't like any of it," said Ernest. To escape further interruptions, he took Mary down the coast in the *Pilar* as soon as he could get clear. Back at the Finca shortly before Christmas, he found that the "Swedish gong" was still sounding and that all manner of people were still eager to invade his privacy with their unwanted congratulations. On the 22nd he was busily cutting up green turtles and fish to package for his deep freeze when he was subjected to a visitation from the Portuguese and Chinese consuls general. "I took what pleasure there was," said Ernest, "in shaking them by the hand with a turtle-smeared hand and wishing them God Speed."

All through the first five months of 1955, Ernest's theme song stayed the same: a dirge about being besieged by people and by pain. It began with the new year. He went to bed early on December 31st, having drunk nothing, and awoke next morning with a heavy rash on his face and chest which looked at first like a return of erysipelas. Two weeks later he told Charles Scribner that his health was still "not so hot." The pain in his back was a constant irritant a whole year after the airplane crashes, and he told Adriana somewhat romantically that he was writing in part to keep from going crazy with pain. When Mary's father died in the middle of February, her absence in Gulfport merely added to Ernest's gloom. The rest of his difficulty was pressure from people. When he was through work for the day, all he wanted was to let the "juice" run back in; he did not want to explain or argue about anything, or to stand on exhibition "like an elephant in a zoo."

About ten in the morning of April 6th, four Princeton sophomores appeared at the front door while he was at work. He explained that he had to earn his living by writing, and asked them to wait down by the swimming pool until he was through for the day. He sent René down with some beer and tried to return to his work. But it was "upset for keeps," so he put on a shirt and went down to joke with the boys. About three that afternoon they departed in a state of exaltation. They had not been gone four hours when another undergraduate appeared, unloaded his suitcase and his topcoat, thrust a bundle of manuscript into Ernest's hands, and stayed until almost midnight. He was a member of John Ciardi's creative writing course at Rutgers. Ernest read and criticized three short stories, disagreed with Ciardi's written comments on the stories, gave the boy a lecture on writing, and lent him $25 to get home with.

Two days later came a young professor from Buffalo, this time by invitation. His name was Fraser Drew and he had been a Hemingway collector for years. Juan the chauffeur picked him up at the Ambos Mundos and Ernest greeted him on the terrace. "EH is a huge man," wrote Drew, "dressed in khaki shorts and an old shirt, with gray hair and a gray beard and a ruddy complexion. He shakes hands and welcomes me and seems shy at first, as if I, not he, were the important man." He showed Drew the first floor of the house and then walked with him to the swimming pool. By this time he had lost his shyness and was speaking freely—"a very easy person to be with," Drew thought, "slow-moving and slow-speaking, and with a gentle manner." He was "very kind and modest" and his voice was "quiet and low." They spoke of the critical studies of his work by Atkins, Baker, Fenton, and Young. "He is very kind about them all," wrote Drew, "but feels that books should not be written about living men. He is amazed at Atkins' writing his book in Khartoum, far from libraries and even primary sources. . . . EH did not like Young's book at all, for his major thesis was that the Hemingway books all derive from trauma. . . . EH admires Carlos Baker and Baker's big book. . . . But it is a hard book and makes too much, as many critics do, of the symbolism. . . . No good writer ever prepared his symbols ahead of time and wrote his book around them, but out of a good book which is true to life symbols may arise and be profitably explored if not over-emphasized. . . . The Fenton book EH also finds overdone. Fenton is a disappointed creative writer and a disappointed FBI investigator."

It was Good Friday and Drew mentioned the fact that he was a Catholic. "I like to think that I am," said Ernest, "insofar as I can be. I can still go to Mass, although many things have happened about divorces and remarriages." He mentioned the Basque priest, Don Andrés. "He prays for me every day," Ernest said, "as I do for him. I can't pray for myself any more. Perhaps it is because in some way I have become hardened."

By this date Ernest was badly overweight from enforced lack of exercise. To get back into shape and avoid further visitors he took Mary on a trip down the coast aboard the *Pilar*. When they returned on May 4th, he had brought his weight down to 230, and felt such an influx of energy that he was able in the next three weeks to push the number of pages in the book on Africa to a new total of 446. But his back continued to hurt when he was tired, and he complained of poor sight in his left eye and deafness in his left ear. He said nothing of these afflictions to Leland Hayward and Peter Viertel, who arrived on June 1 to reactivate plans for the film of *The Old Man and the Sea*. As he had done with Spencer Tracy, he took Viertel on a tour of Cojimar and tried to give him some insight into the art of fishing by catching three white marlin. Viertel proposed to complete the film-script by September 1, when the camera crews would arrive to make the preliminary fishing sequences. After the departure of Viertel and Hayward, Ernest discovered that he had lost another four pounds. His blood-pressure reading had dropped to 158 over 68, and he was feeling better than he had at any time since Africa.

Yet he was never able to count on a life free of adversity. On St. John's Day came the sudden death of Don Andrés, who had suffered with a bad heart for two years. A week later Ernest crossed to Key West with Mary to see to the repair and rental of the house on Whitehead Street. Aaron Hotchner flew down for the Fourth of July to discuss his latest scheme, a series of dramatizations of Ernest's short stories. He was shocked to see how much Ernest had aged since their last meeting in Madrid in 1954. So were Bill Walton and Gianfranco Ivancich, who helped Ernest celebrate his fifty-sixth birthday. "Shit-maru, how the years go," he wrote Patrick next day. "But we have good fun and that is more than most people have."

In August the cameramen and technicians arrived to make some fishing sequences for *The Old Man and the Sea*. Ernest's strength was apparently restored and his arrangements were elaborate. He hired four "old-style" small boats from Cojimar, and used the *Pilar* and Mayito's *Tensi* to converge on the smaller boats whenever there was a strike. They worked every fair day for the first two weeks in September, though the sea was extremely rough. On the first day Ernest boated two large marlin, and took pride in long steering sessions on the flying bridge, fortifying himself with sips of tequila. It was a large operation, with fourteen men in the camera crew, besides Ernest, Gregorio, and Mayito's cousin, Elicín Argüelles, a tireless sportsman. Ernest supplied ice, bait, and fishing gear. observing gleefully that it was like organizing a safari on the sea.

As his trainer for this strenuous venture, he imported his old friend and boxing coach, George W. Brown. Brown gave him postoperative rubdowns and delighted him with unfailing solicitude. "Did they hurt you, Ernie?" George would say. "How's the back? Lie down like you were going to sleep. Make him a drink, René. What kind of liquor going to hurt you, boy? Hold it up to his mouth, René. Drink it slow, Ernie. Just relax good, and let me get the legs loosened up." Ernest reveled in such treatment, and called on George to be one of the witnesses to his will, which he laboriously wrote out in blue ink on a sheet of onionskin paper and dated September 17th. It gave his whole estate to Mary, who was also named executrix. The fourth clause stated that "I have intentionally omitted to provide for my children now living or for any that may be born after this will has been executed, as I repose complete confidence in my beloved wife Mary to provide for them according to written instructions I have given her."

The three sons were prospering, each in his own way. Bumby had left the army for a business career, and pleased his father by coming to the Finca for a two-week vacation in October. Both the other boys were in Tanganyika, where Gigi was doing some hunting and where Patrick had lately finished his apprenticeship as a white hunter, a fact of which his father could hardly have been more proud. He said that he was luckier in fatherhood than James Joyce, citing the undistinguished career of Joyce's son Giorgio as proof.

In times of mental stress that fall, Ernest took out his ill temper by potting buzzards from the top of the tower, sometimes pretending that they were people he did not like. These included Bernard DeVoto, whose death in November he made no pretense of regretting. Ernest's sharpest shooting was reserved for Faulkner—"Old Corndrinking Mellifluous," as he named him. His hunting tales had just been collected in a handsome volume called *Big Woods*. Through Harvey Breit, Ernest sent Faulkner a message that the stories were very well written and delicately perceived, but that Mr. Hemingway would have been more moved if Mr. Faulkner had ever hunted animals that ran both ways.

His interest in bullfighting was revived by Dominguín and Ordóñez, who came to Havana on the way to winter engagements in Central and South America. Now that his sprawling African book was approaching page 700, he began to talk of taking Mary for a week in Caracas, where Spain's leading matadors were to fight between November 27th and December 4th. But the plan did not work out. On November 17th he unwisely went in person to receive the Order of San Cristóbal at ceremonies in the Havana Sports Palace. After sweating for two hours in the hot glare of television lights, he caught a cold in the cool night air. Two days later his right foot swelled "like a football" and a severe infection developed in his right kidney. The other kidney and the liver were soon involved, with symptoms denoting nephritis and hepatitis. He stayed in bed from November 20th to January 9th, though well enough by November 30th to resume occasional work on his African book, and to do a good deal of incidental reading. It was now almost two years since the African plane crashes. He had caught up with Faulkner by winning the Nobel Prize, and made some progress towards physical rehabilitation. But his internal problems were by no means solved, as the present illness proved.

74. LOOKING BACKWARD

HE was still in bed at the beginning of 1956. His red corpuscle count was well below normal, and Mary had a persistent anemia of her own. Another form of anemia afflicted the film of *The Old Man and the Sea*. For all their labors in September, they had not been able to get adequate action shots of any giant marlin. The talk now was of flying to Cabo Blanco, Peru, where the marlin were said to average a thousand pounds and to behave with something of the lordly grandeur of the one in Ernest's novel.

In preparation for the trip, which was planned for late April, Ernest tied cellophane around his large African manuscript and laid it away. Although the prospect of days without writing made him feel savage, he wryly remarked that he hoped to get through the spring without killing anyone, himself included. When Leland Hayward appeared in March with Fred Zinneman, the director, Ernest was highly critical of the casting. The boy they had picked for the part of Manolo looked to him like a cross between a tadpole and Anita Loos. As for Spencer Tracy, who had put on weight since his last trip to Cuba, the early rushes made him resemble "a very fat, rich, and old" though still competent actor. Even worse were the temperamental squabbles among the people involved, not least Tracy himself. After two weeks of watching from the sidelines, Ernest wrote Wallace Meyer that he would never again have anything to do with motion pictures.

He flew to Peru as planned in the company of Mary, Gregorio, and Elicín Argüelles, and they fished in very rough water from early morning to late afternoon each day. For two weeks they saw no marlin at all. Coming back empty was too great a strain and they began fishing for fun in the lee of the desert cliffs along the windy coast. Once they saw a condor walking backwards along the beach, carrying a large dead pelican as if it weighed nothing. In the evenings Ernest sampled the good Peruvian wines and a drink called pisco, which was like tequila fortified with vodka. Although the ocean stayed rough, they were luckier in the second two weeks. Ernest and Elicín each boated two giant marlin, though none of the four was a thousand-pounder. Ernest's back stood up surprisingly well, and he was pleased to bring a 680-pound fish alongside in eight minutes flat before he slacked off the line to let it perform a dozen good jumps for the cameramen.

He came home late in May asserting that his weight was down to a healthy 217 and that he now planned "to live a long time and have plenty of fun." Apart from that and Mary's health, which had also apparently improved, he said repeatedly that the trip had been a waste of time. The damned movie people had destroyed three or four months of his "one and only life." The only compensation was another sizable payment from Warner Brothers, which seemed to prove that at least he could always make money. *Look* magazine offered him $5,000 for 3,000 words of text and picture captions to accompany some pictures that Earl Theisen had made during a recent visit to the Finca. Reluctant at first, and much inclined to argue with Bill Attwood, the emissary from the magazine, Ernest ended by whipping through the assignment in a day and a half. But his article quoted approvingly a remark of Cyril Connolly's that "all excursions into journalism, broadcasting, propaganda, and writing for the films" were pure folly, "since thereby we condemn good ideas, as well as bad, to oblivion."

During the week of his fifty-seventh birthday he managed to be both generous and highly irascible. He sent Ezra Pound a check for $1,000 "on the old Chinese principle . . . that no one possesses anything until they have given it to another." But he was anything but generous four days later when he assured a correspondent that William Faulkner was "a no-good son of a bitch." His most readable books, in Ernest's judgment, were *Sanctuary* and *Pylon.* "The Bear" was worth attention, and some of the Negro "stuff" was good. But *A Fable,* he said, was not even worthy of a place at Ichang, where they shipped the night soil from Chungking.

Part of his irritability could no doubt be traced to the fact that his own writing was going only fairly well. The African manuscript stayed untouched in its cellophane cocoon while he spent most of the summer on short stories. "A Room on the Garden Side" was an anecdote of the Ritz Hotel just after the liberation of Paris. "The Cross Roads," also called "Black Ass at the Cross Roads," was a realistic fictional account of an ambush of fleeing Germans on the road to Aachen in early September, 1944. "The Monument" and "Indian Country and the White Army" were about the firefight at Houffalize, Belgium. Although all these stories of the war were rough and unfinished, and often rambling and pointless, the worst of the summer's crop was "Get Yourself a Seeing-Eyed Dog"—a sentimental episode about an American gone blind in Venice, an idea probably suggested by Ernest's bout with erysipelas in 1949.

In August he put his work aside and began planning a trip to Europe. Mary's anemia had stubbornly continued and he was hoping that a change of climate would effect a permanent cure. They spent the last two weeks of the month in New York, having borrowed Harvey Breit's house at 116 East 64th Street in order to avoid too much publicity in a hotel. Buck Lanham flew up from Washington for an evening's reunion. Ernest handed him a typescript of the war stories, saying expansively that he had "immortalized" Lanham, as well as the 22nd Infantry Regiment and the 4th Division. Although Lanham read them through with understandable interest, he did not find them impressive enough to suggest immortality.

When the *Île de France* sailed, the Hemingways managed to get aboard without being seen by reporters. But Ernest was recognized at once by his old acquaintance Irving Stone, who was taking his wife to Italy in order to begin writing *The Agony and the Ecstasy.* "I've been watching you kids," said Ernest, bluffly. "You've done all right." Stone pointed out with some amusement that the ship's bookstore was displaying nine of his books and only three of Ernest's. Ernest flushed angrily. Next morning the display had been changed to six by Hemingway and six by Stone. One of the shipboard films was Stone's *Lust for Life.* Ernest left in the middle of the showing, first leaning down to ask Stone's pardon. "It takes me at least three sittings to get through one of my own pictures," he whispered. Later he told Stone of his outrage at the waste of time in making the film version of *The Old Man and the Sea.*

Mario Casamassima, a lean and sardonic friend of Gianfranco's, was the replacement for Adamo as their driver for the trip to Spain. It began in Paris at the Ritz and was accomplished in two hops on September 17th and 18th. On the way to Madrid, they stopped at Logroño to watch Ordóñez dispose of several bulls. This time, for reasons of peace and quiet, they stayed outside Madrid at the Gran Hotel Felipe Segundo on the hillside overlooking the vast pile of San Lorenzo del Escorial. With Mario at the wheel, they were only half an hour from Madrid; the hotel offered out-of-season rates and easy access to the places that Ernest wanted to see. Unlike Paris, where the weather had been rainy, the fall days in Spain were so beautiful, as he wrote Berenson, that he felt as if he had already died and gone to heaven.

The major event of the fall season was the end-of-the-season *feria* of Pilar at Zaragoza—four days of celebration and bullfighting beginning on October 12th. As at Logroño in September, Ordóñez was the leading matador. He had fought sixty-six times that season and been gored three times, once seriously. The clan that gathered to watch him included Peter Buckley, the young photographer, who was on the point of writing a book about the bull-fight, illustrated with his own pictures; Rupert Bellville and a pretty American woman; the Maharajah of Cooch Behar; and Aaron Hotchner, just in from Rome. On the *Île de France* Irving Stone had noticed that Ernest was over-drinking. "What can I do?" said Mary to Mrs. Stone. "He didn't marry a policeman. It's better if I let him alone." Now in Zaragoza, Hotchner noticed the same thing. Mary repeated her previous sentiments: she did not like it, but she refused to nag her husband. Despite these sessions with the bottle, he was always in condition for the *corridas* in the afternoon, and was greatly touched when two bulls were dedicated to him on successive days. The crowd stood up and roared its plaudits. Hundreds of people brought him bullfight tickets to be autographed, and he reveled in these signs that he was still revered by the Spaniards.

The aged doctor-novelist, Pío Baroja y Nessi, was already on his death-bed when Ernest went to pay a call, bringing socks and a sweater and a bottle of Scotch to warm the old man's bones. Dr. Baroja had continued writing through his eighty-first year, and Ernest told him flatly that he ought to have won the Nobel Prize. When Baroja died two months short of his eighty-fourth birthday, Ernest went to the funeral. The day was misty with sunlight break-ing through. On the way to the cemetery the streets were banked with flowers for All Souls' Day. Only a handful of mourners appeared. The plain pine coffin had just been painted and some of the black came off on the faces, hands, and clothing of the pallbearers. Ernest was moved and touched.

He was eager to introduce Ordóñez to the pleasures of hunting in Africa. Shortly before Baroja's funeral, he had booked passage to Mombasa and begun arranging a six-week safari with Patrick as white hunter. Complications soon developed when Nasser closed the Suez Canal. This meant that the SS *Africa* would have to round the Cape of Good Hope, delaying their arrival in Mombasa by several weeks. Another problem was the parlous state of the Hemingways' health. Although Mary's anemia had improved, she came down in November with gastritis and colitis, and was obliged to place herself in the hands of Dr. Madinaveitia. On seeing Ernest, the doctor insisted on examining him, as well. He was puffy around the eyes and troubled by nose-bleeds. The examination showed that his blood pressure (210/105) and his cholesterol count of 380 were both dangerously high. His liver was functioning badly, and the fluoroscope seemed to indicate an area of inflammation around the aorta, which Ernest attributed to his fishing activity in Peru.

Madinaveitia put him on a strict diet, eliminating fats, reducing alcohol intake, and forbidding sexual intercourse. He told Ernest that a trip to Africa was out of the question. Ernest said defiantly that he would go anyway. It might be his last, but he had fooled the doctors before. He was not "running as a hypochondriac," and could last for "one trip more." His defiance continued through November 14th, when he learned that the Canal was finally blocked. The hunting he had to settle for was a day of partridge shooting at a ranch near El Escorial. Although it was fun, it was a poor substitute for Salengai and the Kimana Swamp and the back room at Singh's in Laitokitok. On the 17th, with Mario at the wheel and Ernest seated glumly beside him, they set off in the Lancia to spend the rest of the year at the Ritz in Paris.

The Ritz, as it turned out, had been harboring a Hemingway treasure trove for more than twenty-five years. When the porters had finished stacking the huge pile of luggage in Suite 56, they reminded Ernest of two small moldering trunks with his name on them which had apparently been in the Ritz basement since 1928. The contents included whole sheaves of typed fiction, blue and yellow notebooks full of Ernest's clear longhand, old newspaper clippings, books and sweatshirts and sandals, the musty remains of his early years in Paris. He took immense pleasure in this backward look. "It's wonderful," he told Mary. "It was just as hard for me to write then as it is now." He bought two new trunks and got a hotel valet to help him repack his treasures for the homeward voyage.

Yet he was still far from well. On November 30th he had to summon Dr. Louis Schwartz to handle his case. "It was a sunny day," wrote Dr. Schwartz, "and I remember well the elation I felt . . . at meeting a man I admired. I remember well also the enormous trunks which obstructed the entrance to his apartment. There he was in bed, smiling faintly, his short white beard haphazardly clipped, putting me at ease, telling me his story with some hesitation in his voice, Mrs. Hemingway correcting him from time to time on some details. He submitted like a well-behaved old child to my medical routine . . . accepting without discussion all the laboratory tests and without serious complaint a strict diet. . . . I saw him about once a week for a good month."

Betweentimes Mary did her best to keep Ernest in action. After her return from a week's holiday in London, they went to Auteuil almost daily, or crossed to the Left Bank to browse in bookstores or knock down cardboard ducks in shooting galleries. François Sommer had them out to Mursan to hunt wild boar in the Forest of Ardennes. Ernest took Leonard Lyons the columnist to see the armor and tapestries in the Musée Cluny. They entertained at lunch for the customary parade of friends and acquaintances, but usually dined alone in their suite at the Ritz. Mary wrote Patrick that Ernest was bored with his diet and the minor joys of Paris in midwinter, and also indignant that "his body should have done this traitor-type thing to him." Black Dog had died at the Finca and Ernest turned more morose than ever at the "dull fight" he was having to make. He stuck to his diet even on Christmas Day, though he complained to Meyer that this method of keeping him from blowing a gasket was making him nervous, hungry, and irritable.

He had just heard from Archie MacLeish, who was doing his best to secure Pound's release from St. Elizabeth's Hospital. The present scheme was to ask the Attorney General to nol pros the original indictment, thus disposing of the treason charges and remanding the case to the doctors. MacLeish had composed a letter to this end. T. S. Eliot and Robert Frost had already agreed to back it up. Ernest had been waiting for just such a practical approach. "Sure I signed it," he told Lenny Lyons. "Pound's crazy. All poets are. . . . They have to be. You don't put a poet like Pound in the loony bin. For history's sake we shouldn't keep him there."

Late in January on the *Île de France* Ernest became a willing patient of Dr. Jean Monnier, who gave him large injections of vitamins, and medicines to reduce the cholesterol count. In the six days of the crossing his blood pressure fell to the lowest level in months. He decided to stay aboard the ship for its West Indian cruise, since Matanzas in Cuba was one of the ports of call, and persuaded George Brown to come along as his "trainer." During the two-day stopover in New York there was the usual whirl of activity in their suite at the Savoy Plaza. Ned Calmer and his daughter went with Mary to see Ernest off at the pier. Mary took the train to Minneapolis, where her mother was ill in a nursing home, and then flew home before Ernest and George arrived.

All through the spring of 1957, Ernest continued in a depressed state. "The protagonist," as Mary wrote Berenson, was "his poor, long-suffering liver." He told Wallace Meyer in May that it was "a bore not to drink, and very hard to take bores without something to drink." When the *Atlantic Monthly* asked him for a contribution to their forthcoming centenary number, he began a memoir of his early association with Scott Fitzgerald—"how I first met him and how he was." He found it easy to remember and hard to write. In the end, however, he got to thinking how the friends of Dylan Thomas had "betrayed" him with anecdotes after his death. This feeling of incipient treason was so strong that he put the Fitzgerald piece aside. In its place he wrote a short story called "A Man of the World," about a malodorous old bum named Blackie who had been blinded in a tavern brawl in Jessup, Wyoming. "I think it is a good story," said Ernest. If he really thought so, his judgment was slipping.

During the summer the movement to quash the treason charges against Ezra Pound made a significant forward stride. When MacLeish returned from London in June, he reported to Ernest that he had talked to both Eliot and Frost. Frost had agreed to go to Washington in Pound's behalf. MacLeish asked Ernest to meet him there. Ernest excused himself on grounds of illness, though he sent Frost a long and eloquent letter outlining the reasons for releasing Pound, who had never been "a dangerous traitor" but only a "crack pot." Should the Department of Justice consent to nol pros the indictment, Ernest was prepared to contribute $1,500 to resettle Ezra in Italy with his daughter. Armed with this letter, and accompanied by MacLeish, the aged Frost journeyed to Washington in the dank heat of July 19th, and paid a visit to the Department of Justice. Ernest had just turned fifty-eight when MacLeish sent him an interim report. The results looked encouraging, though MacLeish foresaw that various complications might delay Ezra's release for as much as a year.

In other respects, 1957 was turning out to be the "son of a bitch of a year" that Ernest had predicted. Four months of spring rains had been succeeded by a long summer siege of heat and humidity. Bumby had hardly begun work as an investment counselor in Havana when he came down with hepatitis and spent two months in bed. He was just on the mend when his half-brother Gregory fell ill in Florida and was in and out of the Miami Medical Center throughout the fall. Mary's mother was under intensive nursing care in Minnesota. Even the Gulf Stream was flat and empty. When Denis Zaphiro came from Africa for a Cuban holiday, the fishing was the worst in twenty years, and he was able to boat only two fair-sized black marlin.

Although Ernest was too fearful of government censorship to say much in his letters about political conditions in Cuba, he complained to Berenson that the former charm of the coast was gone, the beaches dug up to make cement for skyscrapers, a four-lane highway cut through the hills near the Finca. Havana itself was beginning to look like a combination of Barcelona and Caracas. At four o'clock one morning in August, the rougher side of politics came uncomfortably close when a government patrol entered the grounds of the Finca, looking for a fugitive from the rebel underground, and killing Ernest's new dog Machakos. With an effort he kept silent, but it was one more instance of the perils of living under a dictatorship.

Even the holiday trip to New York that September was a disappointment. They stayed at the Westbury, hung around Toots Shor's restaurant, watched a dull fight between Sugar Ray Robinson and Carmen Basilio, and attended two ball games at the Yankee Stadium. One evening while Mary and Denis went to the theater, Ernest squired Marlene Dietrich to dinner at the 21 Club. But the old magic was gone: Ernest remarked somberly that something had happened to the city, and called it "a strange trip." It cost him a ten-pound gain in weight and a further setback with his liver. He was supremely disgusted to learn on coming back to Cuba that his income-tax bill was going to amount to a staggering $41,000.

He could not rid himself of a sinister feeling of imminent change. As if to signalize it, Mary's aged mother died quietly in Minnesota on New Year's Eve. From early December onwards, the Cuban weather turned "wild" and "strange." Arctic air broke through in norther after norther. Daily temperatures rarely rose above fifty degrees. Violent storms rolled in from the south and the fish seemed to have disappeared from the sea. In the pueblo of San Francisco de Paula there was hunger and unemployment. At the same time, Havana was coming to look more than ever like Miami Beach. "I do not know where to go," said Ernest plaintively.

Yet, for the time being, the Finca was still a good place for work. Through the fall of 1957 and the spring of 1958, he moved forward steadily with a brand-new book. It was a series of sketches centering on his life in Paris from 1921 to 1926. He said that it contained "the true gen on what everyone has written about and no-one knows but me." In 1933 he had boasted to Max Perkins that his ultimate memoirs would be damned good because he was jealous of nobody and owned a "rat-trap memory." In 1949 he had re-opened the subject with Charles Scribner. Now in 1957, having come into possession of the musty documents from the Ritz basement, he was moved at last to action. The first sketch, on his early friendship with Fitzgerald, had been started and laid aside in May, 1957. Now he was moving along with a dozen others. His memory was no longer so sharp as it had once been: some of the names had slipped away and he was careless with dates. Although he was not now jealous of his old associates, many of whom were dead and out of it, his ancient scorn was still much in evidence—scorn of drunks and wastrels, of posing and poseurs, and of the predatory rich (including Pauline and the Murphys) whom he blamed for the dissolution of his first marriage. Along with the scorn came infusions of love—for Hadley and their son, for the streets and hills of Paris, for the swift gray river between its high banks, for the two winters when they had escaped to the dry cold and clean snow of the Austrian mountains. Through all the sketches moved the observant figure of Ernest himself—the sardonic hero, appetitive and enthusiastic, full of virtue, though capable of error. It was his portrait of the artist as a young man.

According to Mary, the first three sketches were finished by December. One was an account of Ernest composing "The Three Day Blow" in a café on the Place St.-Michel in January, 1922, just before he and Hadley left for their first holiday in Switzerland. The next two dealt with Gertrude Stein after their return, and with Ford Madox Ford three years later. An early version of the piece on Ford had been deleted from *The Sun Also Rises* before its publication in 1926. It told of Ford's snobbish rejection of a man he identified as Hilaire Belloc, who later turned out to be the diabolist, Aleister Crowley. Ernest rewrote it with amusing elaborations.

When he handed Mary the first three sketches, she was disappointed. "It's not much about you," she told him. "I thought it was going to be autobiography." He was working by *remate,* said Ernest, borrowing the jai-alai term for a double-wall rebound. Through the spring of 1958 he kept on steadily. By July 31, he asserted that the book was virtually done. He was "still trying to figure out the best way to handle it"—by which he doubtless meant the order in which the sketches would appear. By now the number had swelled to eighteen, including two more on Gertrude Stein, and one apiece on the esthete Harold Acton, the poet Ralph Cheever Dunning, and the editor Ernest Walsh. Like the portrait of Ford, most of these were limned in acid. But there were kind ones, too: Sylvia Beach, the painter Pascin, Ezra Pound, Evan Shipman. He was still considering the addition of two more chapters that he had begun, bogged down with, and set temporarily aside. Altogether, counting the first trial flight about his meeting with Scott Fitzgerald, the book had occupied him for more than a year.

In the intervals of work on his sketchbook, he had also been rewriting his long novel, *The Garden of Eden,* begun ten years earlier and partly used in the development of *Across the River and into the Trees.* By the end of June he had revised twenty-eight chapters, and at the end of July he predicted that it would be done in three weeks' time. It was still incomplete, though "close to the end," by mid-September, and he computed its length at 160,000 words. In fact, however, it ran to forty-eight chapters and more than 200,000 words. It had none of the taut nervousness of Ernest's best fiction, and was so repetitious that it seemed interminable. Apart from the landscape and the food and wine, he was trying to embody certain secret phases of his sexual life with Mary and to insert, as flashbacks, some of the material from the second African safari. Much of the narrative proceeded by dialogue, though it was notably lacking in the wit and concision of the passages of talk in his sketches of Paris.

He was clear in his own mind that the Paris book must come first. Among its gentler chapters was the humorous story of Ezra Pound's energetic devotion to the welfare of his fellow writers. It was a timely tribute. On April 18th, after the better part of thirteen years, the charges against Pound had been dismissed. He was now back in Italy, living with his daughter at Schloss Brunnenberg in Merano. As for Ernest, it had taken him twenty-two months to get the better of his own internal disorders. The cholesterol problem was the first to be resolved, his once-inflamed aorta was now pumping "strong and true" at fifty-four to the minute, his blood pressure had come down, and his weight stood at 207. The liver complaint had lasted longest, but even that was called "cured" by the end of September. In a cheerful letter to Gianfranco,

Mary reported that Ernest's brain was once more working as sharply as it had done before the crash at Butiaba. But she was more sanguine than the facts warranted.

75. *A MAN OF SIXTY*

IN his sixtieth year Ernest was determined to have some fun. The fifty-ninth had been so rigorous with the disciplines of writing and dieting that he now spoke of it as a time of "all work and no play." To have fun was not necessarily to give up writing. The "appalling" world situation convinced him daily that writing was the "only positive thing" a man could do. He was spurred on, moreover, by a feeling that his time was growing short and that he could not waste even an hour. But Cuba no longer seemed suitable for either work or play. He said that he would never spend another summer there if he could help it. After the strange and stormy winter, a prolonged heat wave had moved in. The sea lay flat and oily, the days were like electric ovens, and the nights were hardly cooler than the noons.

He longed again to sniff the bracing air of the western mountains. Lloyd Arnold found a house that could be rented in Ketchum, and Ernest invited Betty and Otto Bruce to go along for the ride. Mary and Betty flew to Chicago, where their husbands met them early in October. The car was crammed with luggage and Ernest was enthralled by the appearance of the countryside. All across Iowa, Nebraska, and Wyoming, he counted and identified every bird he saw and kept a running record of the wild animals. He insisted on stopping at grocery stores in the smaller towns to buy apples, cheese, and pickles, which he washed down with Scotch and fresh lime juice. They listened to the World Series on the car radio. When the national anthem was played, Ernest always removed his cloth cap and held it unostentatiously against his chest in a comic gesture of patriotism. Bulletins about the dying Pope Pius XII frequently interrupted the broadcasts. Each time this happened, Ernest quietly made the sign of the cross. In Iowa they made a point of driving through Parkersburg, Pauline's birthplace, and Dyersville, where Ernest's great-grandfather, Alexander Hancock, had settled in 1854.

At a small town in Nebraska, they stopped for a steak dinner in the only restaurant. The waitress said that the manager's children had spotted the big bearded stranger as a famous man. "Who am I?" asked Ernest. "Burl Ives," said the children. He was only mildly amused. Next morning at breakfast he told them who he was and graciously autographed menus for the waitress and the children. In Sheridan, Wyoming, they entered a saloon to prepare for the trip over the Bighorns to Cody. All the men along the bar were watching the World Series on television. One of them looked around. "Well, look who thinks he's Hemingway," he said, in a voice filled with ridicule and challenge. But Ernest had overcome such challenges before. In two minutes he was surrounded by a backslapping, handshaking crowd of admirers. In Cody that night they pulled up at a motel which looked clean and comfortable. Ernest balked. Something about the place spooked him; he stuck to his suspicion so firmly that they had to go to another.

They were warmly received by their friends in Ketchum: Taylor Williams, Pappy and Tillie Arnold, Clara Spiegel, Chuck and Flossie Atkinson, Forrest MacMullen, Don Anderson, and Dr. George Saviers. Old Colonel Williams was in poor health and deafer than ever. Dr. Saviers had been stationed for five years at Sun Valley Hospital, and Don Anderson, a tall quiet man of thirty-six, was in his fifth year as sports director at Sun Valley Lodge. The Atkinsons had established a new shopping center and motel on the site of the old gamblers' haven, the Christiania Casino. Nearby, in the center of town, stood the log house that the Arnolds had found for the Hemingways. They settled in to await the opening of the shooting season. Ernest complained of fatigue from the trip, and they were all shocked by the change in his appearance and manner. But his spirits revived during one of Tillie Arnold's chicken dinners. He shucked off his jacket, picked up their large Siamese cat, waltzed it around the room, and amused the company by singing off-color parodies slightly off-key. He was in no hurry to get to work and he was still being careful about his diet. But he presently said that the clear dry air was making him feel "like the best of the old days."

After the Bruces had gone, he began to hunt every day. For two years after the Butiaba crash he had not been able to swing with a bird. Now his reflexes were fast and his shooting eye vastly improved. With Don Anderson, whom he still called "The Kid," and Forrest MacMullen ("The Duke"), he spent dozens of hours stalking birds in the meadows and along the watercourses. Don was more certain than ever that, except for Taylor Williams, Ernest was the best field shot he had ever seen. By Thanksgiving, he had achieved six doubles and two triples on green-head drakes. Although it was widely said that the spring bird hatch had been excellent, neither of the Hemingways was prepared for the great abundance of pheasants, Huns, and chukars. They were as thick, said Ernest exultantly, as the quail used to be in the flats around Piggott.

Despite his contentment with his Ketchum "family," he welcomed three visitors in November. One was his Polish translator, Bronislaw Zielinski, to whom he took at once, calling him "Old Wolf" and "The Magnetic Pole." The upshot of his visit was Ernest's offer of a $1,000 prize and the royalties from the Polish translation of *Green Hills of Africa* to the Pole who wrote the best novel in 1959. A second visitor was Aaron Hotchner, who was adapting *For Whom the Bell Tolls* for television. While he was there, Ernest worked most mornings and took his friend afield in the afternoons, teaching him the rudiments of wing shooting. They drove down to Hailey so that Ernest could answer questions about his writing before a group of Catholic schoolchildren. Hotchner kept notes of what Ernest said and sold them some months later to *This Week* magazine. The third visitor was Gary Cooper, still a devotee of Sun Valley after twenty years. One day of heavy snow, he brought over a smoked goose, and they spent an afternoon of quiet talk before the fire, eating the goose and drinking Chablis. Cooper said that he had yielded to his wife's persuasion and become a Catholic. Ernest was sympathetic. He had done the same thing thirty years earlier, and he still "believed in belief."

The situation in Cuba was a constant worry. He tried to forget it by rewriting parts of the Paris sketchbook and revising three chapters of *The Garden of Eden*. But fears filled his mind that his adopted island might soon be gripped by civil war. He was greatly relieved early in January when Fulgencio Batista fled to Ciudad Trujillo while the forces of Fidel Castro took over the capital. Herbert Matthews wrote to say that the Finca was safe. René Villeréal, reached by telephone, said that all was well, though food was very scarce. A munitions explosion at Guanabacoa had broken a few of the Finca windows and damaged part of the roof. Jaime Bofils, a small and smiling Cuban whom Ernest had known for years, telephoned reassuringly to say that he had been appointed to the new provisional government and that he was personally protecting the estate. Another welcome piece of news was that Dr. Herrera had known Fidel Castro during his medical-school days, and the officer in command of the Havana garrison was a native of San Francisco de Paula who had formerly played on the village ball team when Ernest was pitcher.

There was, of course, much bloodshed. A dozen young men from San Francisco de Paula and the neighboring village of Cotorro had been arrested, murdered, and cast into ditches by Batista's secret police. On the other hand, the Batista sergeant who had shot the dog Machakos in August had been hanged in November "with the usual mutilation" by some of the boys from Cotorro. As an old student of revolutions, Ernest took the position that any change in Cuba was better than none. Batista's gang had looted the rich island naked, and Ernest estimated that he had made off with $600 to $800 million. If Castro could run a straight government, it would be great, but he was up against a hell of a lot of money. Some of the United States interests like United Fruit were well and responsibly administered; others had made "terrific deals" with Batista and were "very un-OK." "I wish Castro all luck," said Ernest. "The Cuban people now have a decent chance for the first time ever." His only regret was that he had not been on hand to see Batista pull out.

When their lease on the Heiss house expired in mid-December, they moved to another owned by a family named Whicher. It was still unfinished, with a tarpaper exterior and plywood floors, but the wealth of housekeeping gadgets delighted Mary: baseboard heating that kept them warm even in subzero weather, a deep-freeze unit which they promptly filled with game birds, and a large television set that hung from the ceiling. All the Ketchum family began dropping in to watch the Friday-night fights and the professional football games on Saturdays. Ernest liked it so well that he began to look for a house to buy. The best one then available was a two-story chalet made of poured concrete, the property of Bob Topping. It stood at the end of a gravel road on a sage-brush-covered hillside a mile northwest of the center of town. There was a large living room paneled in yellow oak and a master bedroom of the same size upstairs. A smaller back bedroom, finished in black walnut, would do for Ernest's study. The views were magnificent—of tent-shaped mountains north and south, and through the large eastern windows a double bend of the Big Wood River, flanked with tall aspens and cottonwoods. Chuck Atkinson thought that Ernest could get the furnished house and seventeen acres of land for something like $50,000.

Across the valley through the leafless trees lay the grass-green oblong of the Ketchum cemetery. This was where they had buried Van Guilder in 1939, and where they now held another funeral for Taylor Williams, who had died suddenly on February 18th. This time Ernest pronounced no oration. After the mourners had dispersed, he and Don Anderson stayed behind to fill the grave. He remarked quietly that funerals were antiquated paganism, and to be got through with as quickly as possible. The dead were dead. For the living, Ernest favored the use of a quart of good whiskey. But it made him morose in retrospect. His old friend Charlie Sweeny had recently come from Salt Lake City to pay him a call. He had no sooner returned home than he telephoned Ernest that he had just had another stroke. "I have very little depth on the bench in friends," said Ernest.

Just after the funeral, he completed arrangements to spend the summer in Spain, largely at the estate of a wealthy American expatriate, Nathan (Bill) Davis, whom Ernest had known off and on for twenty-five years. His establishment, La Consula, was close to the village of Coín near Málaga on the Costa del Sol. It would provide Ernest with a quiet place for writing and a home base for resting up between bullfights. Antonio Ordóñez was going to perform a series of *mano a mano corridas* against his brother-in-law, Dominguín, and Ernest wanted to see them all. His health was better than it had been at any time since the plane crash at Butiaba, his kidneys and liver had ostensibly recovered, his blood pressure and cholesterol count were both back almost to normal. "It looks like a wonderful summer," he told Bill Davis. His enthusiasm was more like that of a boy than of a man in his sixtieth year.

They left Ketchum in mid-March in a rented car, with Aaron Hotchner to help with the driving as far as New Orleans. At Phoenix Ernest paused to write out a check for $50,000 to buy the Topping house in Ketchum, and in Tucson he enjoyed a garrulous reunion with Waldo Peirce the painter and his wife Ellen. Ernest took over the driving between New Orleans and Key West, where they turned in the car and flew across to Havana on Easter Sunday. He thought that the Castro revolution was "very pure and beautiful" so far, and comparable to what had been hoped for when the Spanish Republic was first set up. Castro was planning an American tour for April. Although Ernest felt that the cards were heavily stacked against him, he hoped that Castro would be able to keep his temper and reap some benefits from well-wishers on the mainland.

A characteristic interlude during Ernest's brief stay at home was his meeting with the playwright, Tennessee Williams. It was engineered by Kenneth Tynan, who had come down to interview Castro, and made an incidental luncheon date with Ernest at the Floridita. Williams joined them belatedly, having heard the fearsome rumor that "Hemingway usually kicks people like me in the crotch." His fears went unrealized, even when he told Ernest that he had recently met Ordóñez in Spain and described him as "a lovely boy, very friendly, very accessible." Williams went on to say that he had been introduced to Pauline in Key West. He inquired into the causes of her death. "She died like everybody else," said Ernest, "and after that she was dead." Things went better when the conversation turned to Ernest's plane-crash injuries. "You can survive on one kidney," he told Williams, "but if your liver gives out, you're through." The novelist and the playwright then parted in amity, linked at last, as Tynan said, "by medicine and mortality."

The conversation with Williams marked the beginning of the "dangerous summer" of Ernest's sixtieth year. By early May the Hemingways were in residence at La Consula, having flown to New York, crossed on the *Constitution,* disembarked at Algeciras, and driven along the potholed coastal road in a rented pink Ford, with Bill Davis at the wheel. The estate reminded Ernest of the Finca, except that it was larger and older. Davis defended his privacy with two gates, each manned by a pair of servants. The large white house had been built in 1835. There were well-kept formal gardens and a sixty-foot swimming pool, The handsome interior was everywhere ornamented with Davis's collection of paintings and prints. He was a tall gray-eyed man of fifty-two, prematurely bald. He had been living there for some years with his wife Annie and their two children. Ernest and Mary were given adjoining bedrooms on the second floor. Ernest's was a large corner room, opening onto a wide balcony and overlooking the courtyard on the garden side. There was a stand-up desk and a table for his papers. "Anyone who couldn't write here couldn't write nowhere," he said. Early in May he began the first of his writing assignments for the summer, a preface for a new school edition of his short stories.

By the 13th he had roughed out a first draft, which he put aside in order to drive up to Madrid for the San Isidro bullfights. They stayed at the Suecia, a new hotel in the center of the city where the management treated them like visiting royalty. Whatever his complaints to the contrary, Ernest was not averse to publicity. He knew very well that his white-bearded figure was world-famous, and gloried in being recognized as the bosom friend of Ordóñez, in whose career he was assuming a proprietary interest. One instance of his powers was visible to thousands on May 24th in the new Plaza de Toros. The sensation of the afternoon was a youngster named Segura, whose work with the cape and muleta was brilliant and whose kill was quick and sure.

The crowd saluted him with a sea of waving handkerchiefs, but there was no official recognition of his performance until Ernest rose, faced the President, and solemnly waved one of his own. At once the President complied, awarding Segura both ears of his bull.

Between the 26th and the 31st, Antonio's schedule called for fights at Córdoba, Sevilla, Aranjuez, and Granada. Bad weather in Madrid had given Mary a severe cold and fever, and she was neither willing nor able to keep up with Ernest's impossible pace, which called for endless kilometers in the "lousey pink Ford" with Bill Davis driving. But Ernest took the journeying in stride. On the afternoon of the 30th he was in Aranjuez, south of Madrid. "The rain was gone," he wrote, "and the town was new-washed in the sun. . . . We went to the old café-restaurant under the shade of trees and watched the [Tajo] river and the excursion boats." One of his companions was John Crosby of the *New York Herald Tribune,* who joined him for a feast of strawberries. Afterwards they watched Ordóñez in a heroic performance. It ended when his second bull of the day gored him in the left buttock. Bleeding badly and taut with anger, he killed the bull before he collapsed. Ernest stayed with him for the first fifty hours to make sure that the wound would not become infected. A week later Antonio flew down to Málaga to recuperate under his friend's compassionate care.

Having now witnessed thirteen bullfights, Ernest returned to his preface. Antonio's wound would prevent his fighting further until the end of June, and Ernest's mornings could be given over to writing. But he found difficulty in concentrating on anyone or anything besides Antonio, whom he described as brave, smart, fast, "loveing," incorruptible in a corrupt sport, and "the best guy you'll ever meet." He hurried through revision of his preface in order to visit Antonio's bull ranch near Medina Sidonia, north of Tarifa. The whole Costa del Sol charmed him so much that he spoke of buying a tract of land at Conil near Cape Trafalgar. As for his preface, it "dressed out" finally at 5,800 words, and was designed "to counter the lies and formulas" of the critics. The big thing in writing, said he, was "the struggle between the living thing you make and the dead hand of the embalmer."

When Antonio resumed his schedule late in June, Ernest followed him once more: Zaragoza one afternoon, Alicante the next, then Barcelona, then Burgos. He boasted, and evidently believed, that it made a big difference to Antonio to have him there—wishing him luck before each fight, talking it over afterwards, sharing the wine and the late Spanish dinners when the squadron of short, dark-haired men piled out of the Mercedes and swaggered into some fortunate restaurant along the highway. For another man of sixty, such a program would have been a boring impossibility. But Ernest told himself that it was "a lot more fun than sitting on my ass in Cuba taking Cuban politics seriously." By the time of the San Fermín fiesta at Pamplona on July 6th, he had seen twenty bullfights and was spoiling for more.

Pamplona, as he wrote afterwards, was "rough as always." For a week they "averaged something over three hours' sleep at night to the pounding of the war-drums of Navarre." Antonio was there, though only as a celebrant. Juanito Quintana was down from San Sebastian. Annie Davis and Mary came up from Málaga. Aaron Hotchner had caught up with Ernest at Alicante on June 28th. Dr. Saviers and his wife Pat had come over from Sun Valley as Ernest's guests. A nineteen-year-old girl named Valerie Danby-Smith introduced herself into the group as a journalist. During one night of revelry, Ernest and Antonio, accompanied by Hotchner, "captured" two pretty American girls, who dutifully accepted "imprisonment" next day at Ernest's table in the Bar Choko.

Part way through the fiesta, the group began picnic and swimming trips to the Irati River above Aoiz, the magical region that Ernest had discovered in 1924. He feared that it would be "all cut up and destroyed" like so many other places he had loved. Instead he found that "the last great forest of the Middle Ages" was still intact, with a stand of tall beeches and a "century-old carpet of moss." Sipping vin rosé and nibbling at the picnic lunch, he sat with his back to one of the trees, "as happy as I had ever been." He did not seem much concerned that Mary was obliged to hobble painfully with a cane, having broken a toe on the slippery stones of the riverbed. In fact his behavior at Pamplona and in the weeks that ensued was aggressively adolescent. Evidently believing, as earlier with Adriana, that a miraculous renewal of youth could be achieved by association with a nineteen-year-old girl, he adopted Valerie Danby-Smith as his secretary, insisting on having her at his elbow during meals, at the bullfights, and in the car. During one of his stopovers in Madrid, Dr. Madinaveitia had given him a clean bill of health, and he seemed to be determined to make the most of it.

His sixtieth birthday coincided with Carmen Ordóñez's thirtieth. Mary had spent more than a month in planning a gala celebration at La Consula. "We had a great mixture of people," she wrote afterwards, "everybody from David Bruce and Evangeline and Miguel Primo de Rivera and Buck Lanham to pretty American girls, an Englishman who's a champion guitar-player of calypso, Millais by name . . . and Spaniards of various ranks." Among those she did not name were Gianfranco and his wife Cristina, who drove in with Ernest's brand-new Lancia; Carmen and Antonio; the Maharajah of Cooch-Behar and his red-headed lady; Dr. Saviers and his wife; Peter Buckley and his wife; Valerie Danby-Smith; and Aaron Hotchner. There was an elaborate dinner on the wide balcony on the second-floor front, with a cake and gifts and many toasts. An orchestra played and there were flamenco dances. A small shooting gallery was erected in the grounds, and later there were fireworks. The party lasted all night, and the last celebrants left after breakfast on the 22nd.

But the occasion was not altogether golden. Dr. Saviers was treating Ernest for a kidney disorder which had developed in Pamplona, and his bedroom at La Consula was filled with glasses and bottles containing urine samples.

His behavior had been somewhat odd for several days. Buck Lanham had flown in from Madrid on the evening of the 18th. In the course of a late dinner, he had presented Ernest with the history of the 22nd Infantry Regiment, a mimeographed volume of nearly two hundred pages. On reading Lanham's inscription, Ernest burst into tears and left the room until he recovered. Two nights later, he presided at a dinner at the Hotel Miramar. Among the guests were Ambassador and Mrs. Bruce, the Davises, Valerie, and Hotchner. Late in the evening, having danced with Mrs. Bruce, Lanham passed behind Ernest on his way back to his seat. He put his hand fleetingly on Ernest's shoulder in a gesture of friendship and remarked that it was only a mere twenty minutes until July 21st and the birthday. As he turned away, part of his left arm grazed the back of Ernest's head. Ernest winced as if he had been burned, and said in a loud clear voice that nobody was permitted to touch his head. White with anger, Lanham departed. A while later, Ernest caught up with him, apologetic and weeping. He explained that he was bald and that he had combed his white, curly back hair forward in a bang in order to hide the baldness. If Lanham would forgive him, he said that he would go to the barber next day and have his "goddamned hair" cut short like Lanham's. Lanham told him to stop talking like a jackass, though he was still angry enough to add that the only reason he was not leaving that night was that there were no flights out of Málaga. It was the only quarrel they had ever had. Lanham felt sorry for him but could not forgive him.

Lanham was also sorrowfully struck by Ernest's unhealthy nostalgia for his young manhood and the astonishing obscenity of his language. In spite of Mary's labors in organizing the birthday party and her unremitting attention to his welfare, Ernest seemed to be going out of his way to be cruel. He complained that she had spent all his money on the festivities, when in fact she had paid for most of it with the proceeds of an article she had done for *Sports Illustrated*. He ridiculed her limping and even sought to bulldoze Dr. Saviers into saying that her toe was not actually broken. These and worse indignities were more than Lanham could take, and he said so. But Ernest seemed lost to all exhortation.

Before flying back to Washington, Lanham accompanied Ernest and his "mob" to the *feria* at Valencia. The group had now dwindled to nine—Lanham, Gianfranco and Cristina, Bill and Annie, Valerie and Aaron, and the Hemingways. Ernest could not escape the feeling that a pattern of destruction was imminent. At the first *corrida* the skies turned dark and the wind rose. Both Antonio and Luis Miguel were apprehensive. "Ernesto," said Antonio, "this wind is terrible." It did not subside. The afternoon grew dark and the lights were on when Dominguín's last bull charged in. On the ninth pass, the wind swept the muleta aside and the bull threw Dominguín onto the sand. Before Antonio could interfere, the animal gored Dominguín in the groin. Three days later, both matadors were hospitalized at the Sanatorio Ruber in

Madrid. The jinx had caught up with Antonio, who had been gored at Palma de Majorca.

The *mano a mano* contests between Antonio and Luis Miguel were grist to Ernest's mill. He had contracted to do a bullfight article for *Life* magazine, and was keeping notes for the purpose. The climax of the duel was reached at Málaga in the middle of August when both matadors ignored their bandages in a magnificent display of skill and courage. Then bad luck returned. A week later in Bilbao, Dominguín was gored so seriously that he was obliged to retire for the rest of the season. He was back in the Sanatorio Ruber once again when Antonio, fighting at Dax across the French border, sustained a foot injury serious enough to put him in the hospital at San Sebastian.

Ernest stayed by his friend's side until the worst of the pain was gone. Then he bade him a tender good-bye and set out for Madrid in the new Lancia, with Valerie beside him and Davis driving. Just outside Aranda de Duero south of Burgos the right front tire blew out. The car mowed down five stone slabs along the shoulder of the road. No one was hurt, but the whole front of the car was demolished. They left it in Madrid and flew back to Málaga. Next day Ernest admitted sadly that he had had enough of spectator sports; he had become too much involved in the fortunes of Antonio: it was as nerve-shattering as "being married to an alcoholic." Mary was glad to have her husband back again unharmed. "Papa Sportif" could be amusing. But she preferred him when he was "quiet, contemplative, and my friend."

The revels, such as they were, had now come to an end. Antonio was debarred for a month after a dispute with bullfight officials. Aaron Hotchner wrote to say that he had concluded a big deal with Buick and CBS for several 90-minute shows adapted for television from Ernest's short stories. Author and adapter would again split fifty-fifty. Mary was eager to get home to Cuba. She had suffered all summer with everything from bad colds to humiliation. But Ernest seemed determined to stay on at La Consula through the middle of October. Nothing would serve but that he must begin his bullfighting article while he was still inside the magical borders of Spain. It was October 10th before he got down to work. Except for the short-story preface, he had written nothing all summer beyond a few letters dictated to Valerie. On his opening day, he produced 541 words and 845 the next. He was recalling the magical days of 1953 when he had come back to Spain for the first time since Franco's victory in 1939. By October 15th he had done 5,000 words and was only just begun.

Over in Italy, Ezra Pound stood uncertainly upon the brink of his seventy-fourth birthday. "In happier days," he wrote Ernest, "I had yr monumental cheque sunk in plexiglass as a token of yr magnanimous glory. Now too damn valuable as souvenir to leave on the table for paper-weight as intended." Ezra was feeling the effects of advancing years. "Old man him tired," said he. But Ernest at sixty was already spoiling for more fun. Antonio and Carmen had agreed to come to Ketchum for the end of the duck-shooting season. "I want to get some exercise and get in shape," said Ernest.

76. JOURNEY DOWN

ERNEST's point about getting into shape was a point well taken. The summer of 1959 had been more dangerous to him than he was ready to recognize. During a brief stopover at the Ritz in Paris, he developed a bad cold from sitting in a draft. He feared that it would settle in his infected kidney and was still gulping pills when he got aboard the *Liberté*. He had bought Mary a diamond pin as partial recompense for the summer of neglect, but he was still rather childishly resentful about her view of his own conduct. He enumerated the adjectives which he said she had applied to him: heartless, thoughtless, selfish, basically stupid, spoiled, unperceptive, and on the skids from egotism and publicity seeking. In one way or another he had earned most of these, but he showed no disposition to admit it.

He spent much of the rough voyage nursing the cold in his stateroom. He was running a slight fever and his head felt "stuffed and stupid." A note was delivered to him from a man named Andrew Turnbull, who had been in Paris gathering material for a life of Scott Fitzgerald. Turnbull asked whether Mr. Hemingway would be willing to talk about his memories of Scott. Ernest's worn briefcase contained the manuscript of his Paris sketchbook, which included three chapters on Fitzgerald. He was not disposed to reveal his trade secrets to any stranger and did not reply until the last day of the trip. On October 31st he dressed for lunch, had a drink at the bar, and agreed to talk. Although Turnbull shared the view of another passenger that there was something "staged and put on" about Hemingway, he could not help feeling that "a great dignity flowed from his tall lurching frame and his sad mask of a face." Like many others at this time, he was struck by the "meagerness" of the bare forearms, the "delicacy" of the features "above the froth of beard," and the whites of his eyes, which were veined with red. His conversational manner was shy and wistful, he was not very helpful about Fitzgerald, and his eyes flicked over Turnbull with "a kind of grazing diffidence."

· In New York he was met at the gangplank by Aaron Hotchner, who bore him away to an apartment that Ben Finney had borrowed for Ernest's use. Hotchner found him oddly querulous and much concerned about whether Mary would like the diamond pin. She had asked Finney, as well as George Brown, George Plimpton, and Hotchner, to help find a decent apartment which would insure privacy whenever they chose to come to New York. They had located one on the fourth floor at 1 East 62nd Street, across from the Knickerbocker Club, with a sidelong view of Central Park. Ernest called it excellent, "a safe place" in the spy-thriller sense of the word. But it was Mary's idea, not his. He wanted to get back to his old house in Cuba and then to show Antonio his new one in Ketchum. On November 3rd he delivered the manuscript of his Paris sketchbook to Charles Scribner, with instructions to forward it to Ketchum for his final revisions. Then he collected Antonio and Carmen Ordóñez and flew south to join his wife.

A crowd with banners had gathered at Havana airport to welcome him home. Reporters asked what he thought of the increasing American coldness towards Castro. He deplored it, saying that after twenty years' residence he considered himself a true Cuban. To prove it, he kissed the hem of a Cuban flag. The gesture was too fast for the photographers. They asked him to do it again. "I said I was a Cuban, not an actor," he grinned. He was visibly relieved at Mary's affectionate greeting. She had completed repairs to the Finca, and stood ready to put the Ketchum house into shape for the reception of Antonio and Carmen. But she did not propose to continue forever as a cook and a drudge. This time she would take the servant, Lola Richards. Ernest kept his mouth shut. He wanted to take Antonio hunting. Nothing must spoil his plans.

The trip west began very well and ended in disappointment. Showing the American landscape to Antonio and Carmen was a glorious experience. Despite much snow and cold weather, Ernest described the journey as "unbelievably wonderful." The final day's run covered 800 miles from the southern rim of the Grand Canyon west to Las Vegas and north through Hailey on the old familiar Route 93. Antonio liked Las Vegas, but Ernest was more impressed by a new "town" called Jackpot, a handful of roadhouses and slot machines on the Nevada-Idaho border. Mary was ready and waiting when they crossed the railroad tracks and the bridge and came surging up the gravel driveway. The disappointment came almost at once. Antonio's sister in Mexico was nearly hysterical over some domestic crisis, and he felt obliged to go to her assistance. When Carmen and Antonio had gone, the Hemingways were alone together for the first time since April.

Their bliss was short-lived. On November 27th, they went out hunting with George Saviers. Mary brought down a pintail with a beautiful overhead shot. But she was standing in down timber and lost her balance, falling to the frozen ground and shattering her left elbow. Saviers performed a two-hour operation and put the arm in a cast. The pain was intense and the prognosis uncertain. Ernest took it hard, complaining that it had smashed all his plans for a hunting vacation, just when he wanted to get into shape for work on the *Life* article and the Paris sketchbook. Most of his mornings were given to running errands and attending to Mary's needs at Sun Valley Hospital. He growled that he was doing the things the servants did at the Finca. His blood pressure was rising and he was not sleeping well. But the weather was the kind he liked. "It is very beautiful here today after three days of snowing," he wrote Bill Davis on January 13th, "sharp and cold and high clear mountain sky and the

snow squeaks when you walk on it. From the window of the big bedroom
you can watch a pair of mallards feeding on water cress at the big pool just
below the house."

He had lately been reading Harold Loeb's autobiography, *The Way It Was*.
He found it "very touching and sad" because of Loeb's "search for how he
wished things to have been." Ernest was also concerned with might-have-beens
in his own "autobiography," the Paris sketchbook—particularly in the concluding chapter about the winter of 1925–26 in Schruns, when Pauline and
the Murphys and the "pilot-fish" Dos Passos had invaded his private Austrian
Eden and destroyed it. But he made no overt connection between Loeb's book
and his own. On being told that Loeb was suffering from angina pectoris, the
same affliction which had beset Ernest's father before his suicide in 1928, he
said that he wished Loeb could have "the grace of a happy death." His mood,
in fact, was elegiac. For here, in the dramatic juxtaposition of Loeb's youthful dreams and his present pain, was one more proof of the sentiments Ernest
had early conveyed to his father: "And how much better to die in all the
happy period of undisillusioned youth, to go out in a blaze of light, than to
have your body worn out and old and illusions shattered."

The train trip back to Miami was accomplished in mid-January. Mary
stayed in her berth most of the time, her aching elbow supported by pillows.
It was no comfort to find that the Finca was like an icebox from a whole
succession of bleak northers. But Ernest was eager to resume work on his
bullfight article, untouched since Málaga. To save him time, Mary agreed to
his proposal that Valerie be brought over as his secretary. The Hemingways
did their best to stay clear of Cuban politics. The Russians had begun their
flirtation with Castro. Anastas Mikoyan came out to the Finca with his entourage, presenting Russian translations of several of Ernest's books. Herbert
Matthews appeared in March, still enthusiastic about the revolution. Mary
called him the "national hero" of Cuba. They were privately agreed that 75
per cent of the people supported Castro, particularly because of his determination to give them decent food, education, and medical care.

By April Fool's Day, "working like a steam engine," Ernest had brought
his bullfight article to 63,000 words. "Am tired of skinning all those dead
horses," he said, "and they can take bull fighting . . . and put it where they
found it." Although he complained that his contract with *Life* had been nothing but a headache, he seemed to have forgotten that they had asked for only
10,000 words. He alone had insisted on expanding it. By May 28, he declared
it finished at 120,000 words. The pressure of working at it from late January
to late May had exhausted his eyes, but most of all his head. The worst of
it, as he wrote in Spanish to Juanito Quintana, was that all the forced labor
(*trabajando forzado*) had confused his brain—if not something more serious.
In this manner, on June 1, 1960, came his first hint that he might be losing
his reason.

Three weeks later he summoned Aaron Hotchner to help him cut the type-script. The heat was relentless and there were heavy rains each afternoon. With infinite labor, they managed to delete some 50,000 words. Hotchner carried the abridged version back to New York. Even the abridgment was more than twice too long, but Ed Thompson, the managing editor, agreed to buy a selection of it for $90,000, with another $10,000 for reprint rights in the Spanish language edition. It was now called "The Dangerous Summer," in allusion to the *mano a mano* combats of 1959. Although the piece was ostensibly finished, Ernest convinced himself that he must return to Spain to gather up loose ends and participate in what remained of Antonio's grueling schedule. "Antonio wants me with him all the time," he said, "as we are a winning combination." Having to leave him the preceding October had been "rough." Now he wanted to "hook up" with his hero once again.

The season was far advanced when he resolved to go. Hotchner prepared the apartment on 62nd Street for Mary's occupancy. Late in July, with Valerie, the Hemingways crossed to Key West, staying at the Santa Maria Motel in rooms secured by Otto Bruce. They had brought along most of Ernest's manu-script material, and Bruce shipped it to Ketchum. Ernest was almost psychoti-cally concerned about Valerie's alien status, since she had come to Cuba in February on a temporary American visa and had not bothered to renew it. He pestered the Office of Immigration in Key West with assurances that she was only a visitor. Then he flew on to New York, leaving the women to come by train.

In marked contrast to his sixtieth, Ernest's sixty-first birthday came and went like a shadow. He seldom left the apartment, and set up a card table in a corner of the living room to serve as an office. Charles Scribner conferred with him there. Among his few visits outside were a trip to an eye doctor and a lunch at Toots Shor's with Lenny Lyons, Jimmy Cannon, and Hotchner. Hotchner had been negotiating with Twentieth Century Fox for a film play, *The World of Nick Adams,* based on his television adaptations of some of the stories, strung together in a pseudo-biographical sequence. Ernest was dis-satisfied with the preliminary offer of $100,000 and insisted that Hotchner hold out for $900,000. If this figure suggested delusions of grandeur, the de-pressive phase was very close. On July 31st he wrote his son Bumby that he was not in good shape and that his eyes were bothering him badly. He added that he wished he did not have to go to Spain at all.

He did not need to go and he should not have gone. But he kept insisting that Antonio needed him. After several postponements, he got aboard the overnight TWA jet for Lisbon and Madrid. His seat companion was a Chicago attorney named Luis Kutner, with whom he had once corresponded about the release of Ezra Pound. Like Turnbull in October, Kutner was astonished to discover that this unsure and quiet man was not the "robust, virile, aggres-sive" hero of popular legend. When the plane reached Madrid, Ernest was fatigued and upset by the sudden change in time zones. He conferred briefly with Bill Lang, the Paris representative of *Life* magazine, and then drove off with Bill Davis for two days' rest at La Consula.

The Davises had seen him in most of his moods, but none like this. He showed the symptoms of extreme nervous depression: fear, loneliness, ennui, suspicion of the motives of others, insomnia, guilt, remorse, and failure of memory. He had been in Spain only ten days when his letters to his wife complained of cramps and nightmares. At the end of two weeks he said flatly that he feared a "complete physical and nervous crack up from deadly overwork." It had been his lifelong habit to awaken cheerfully. Now each day seemed like a nightmare seventy-two hours long. "Woke bad today," he said on the 19th. Although he spoke of being lonely, new faces made him nervous. The whole bullfight business seemed "corrupt" and "unimportant." Everybody in it was "as egotistical as Sinsky at his worst." He even suspected that Dominguín was secretly conspiring against Antonio. Yet he was much worried that his *Life* article had been unfair to Dominguín. When the first installment of "The Dangerous Summer" reached him by airmail early in September, he recoiled in anguish at the grinning cover portrait, calling it a "horrible face." He felt "ashamed and sick" to have done such a job, and was full of remorse at having made "such a mess." He wrote Mary repeatedly, calling her "poor blessed kitten," and saying that he now realized why she had hated Spain so much in the summer of 1959. He wished that she were with him now to keep him from "cracking up."

At his urgent request and at the invitation of Annie Davis, Mary sent Valerie over to help him with his mail. She arrived calm and cheerful to find him at the opposite extreme. Antonio had sustained a concussion when a bull dumped him at Bilbao, and Carmen had had a miscarriage. Ernest said that he was sick of it all to the marrow of his bones: the only reason he stuck it out was that every time he had been this bad before he had managed to rise out of it into a "belle époque" of writing. He was still hoping to repeat the process, and could not bring himself to face the fact that never before in his life had he been half so "bad" as he was now.

Valerie and the Davises were distraught. When Aaron Hotchner joined them in Madrid early in October, the atmosphere in Ernest's suite at the Suecia was like that of a wake. It was clear that he had delusions of persecution. He explained to Hotchner that Bill Davis had tried to kill him by wrecking the Lancia in 1959, and was now trying again. His kidneys were troubling him, or so he thought. He was irascible beyond belief. He exploded at the waiters in the Callejón restaurant and stalked out angrily before lunch was over. Back at the Suecia he took to his bed for four days, finding many reasons for postponing his homeward flight. At last his friends managed to get him aboard a midnight plane for Idlewild. It was like saying good-bye to a stranger.

Mary's worst fears were confirmed when she saw him. As in July, he stayed in the apartment. He was worried about Valerie in Spain, Hotchner in London, his houses in Cuba and Idaho, his income taxes, and the condition of his kidneys. After a week of this, it required all Mary's organizational and persuasive powers to get him aboard the train for Idaho. They reached Shoshone on October 22nd and were driven home by Dr. Saviers. Even in the bosom of his Ketchum family, Ernest could not summon up the semblance of good cheer. One day he grazed another car while backing out of a parking slot in Ketchum. He was greatly upset, feared that the sheriff might arrest him, took down the license number, and got into touch with the owners. Even when they assured him that the damage was slight, his worries continued unabated. He told Mary that they would have to give up the Topping house because he could not afford to pay the taxes on it. She tried to alleviate his fears by telephoning his New York bank, where his balance was very substantial. Even this assurance failed to console him.

He continued to be haunted by the delusion that the Federal Bureau of Investigation was after him because of Valerie's immigrant status. She had now come to New York to enroll as a student at the American Academy of Dramatic Arts. He sent a check to cover her tuition, using Hotchner as entrepreneur. In mid-November, he summoned Hotchner to Idaho, driving to Shoshone with Forrest MacMullen to meet the train. All the way home he was certain that the "Feds" were on his trail. In Ketchum two employees were working late in the bank across from Chuck Atkinson's Christiania Motor Lodge. Ernest was convinced that government agents were auditing his account as part of a program of personal harassment.

Innocent of Ernest's condition, two professors of English from Montana State University came to ask him to lecture at Missoula. Like everyone else who had seen him close up, Seymour Betsky and Leslie Fiedler were shocked by his appearance. "The only resemblance to the man we had imagined," wrote Betsky, "was in the fullness of the face. And even the face was pale and red-veined, not ruddy or weather-beaten. We were particularly struck by the thinness of his arms and legs. . . . He walked with the tentativeness of a man well over sixty-one. The dominant sense we had was of fragility." They were equally surprised by his apparent inability to talk. He "spoke in spurts of a few words, hardly ever in sentences. . . . He didn't want to talk about his own writing at all, and we didn't press him." After ninety minutes of this, they were relieved when he asked them to drop him off in Ketchum on their way home. Driving back to Missoula, they agreed that he had been "enormously considerate, almost gentle, a man with Old World manners, down to the ritual pouring of a small glass of wine." Only severe illness, they felt, could account for the gap between the public image of Hemingway and the man they had met.

Well before Thanksgiving it was clear that he must be hospitalized. The ·crucial questions were where and how soon. Both the establishment of the Menninger brothers and that of the Mayo brothers were discussed. Dr. Saviers observed that when Ernest's work was going well, his blood pressure was normal, while anxiety could shoot it up to dangerous levels. In the last week of November, it stood at 250/125. The chief problem, however, was psychological. With Mary's authorization, Hotchner described Ernest's recent behavior to an eminent psychiatrist in New York. "My limited knowledge of the patient," said this doctor, "led me to formulate a symptomatic diagnosis and a treatment program that included organic facilities followed by a psychotherapeutic program based on a working hypothesis of contributing causes." In spite of the difficulties of long-range diagnosis, the doctor took "a very central role in arranging hospitalization" for the patient at the Mayo Clinic in Rochester, Minnesota. On November 30th, in the utmost secrecy and in the company of Dr. Saviers, Ernest was flown from Hailey to Rochester in a Piper Comanche, piloted by Larry Johnson. It was a pleasant trip in good weather, with one refueling stop at Rapid City, South Dakota. Ernest was in good spirits and discoursed happily about the history of the American West. In Rochester he entered St. Mary's Hospital under the name of George Saviers. Mary followed by train, registering at the Hotel Kahler as Mrs. Saviers.

Dr. Hugh R. Butt, a specialist in diseases of the liver, was Ernest's physician for the organic disorders. The "psychotherapeutic program" was in charge of Dr. Howard P. Rome, one of the two senior consultants in the Section of Psychiatry. "Our Dr. George Saviers at Sun Valley couldn't get Papa's blood pressure to stay down," wrote Mary a few days later. "So we came here where the Mayo Clinic people are giving Papa what they call a general examination —but which is intense, microscopic, minute, and thorough. . . . The good news is that most of the tests and laboratory reports so far have optimistic conclusions. . . . I have confidence that they will not only find but exorcize the source of Papa's trouble." Apart from the hypertension, which had troubled Ernest since 1947, the organic tests were "essentially negative." A glucose tolerance test, however, did reveal "mild diabetes mellitus." Dr. R. G. Sprague of the Metabolic Section thought that Ernest's weight of 175 pounds was "ideal," and that within reason he could eat whatever he wished so long as that weight level was maintained. Dr. Butt found a "palpable left lobe of the liver . . . with a round edge." The diabetic symptoms, together with the enlarged liver, the result of heavy ingestion of alcohol over many years, suggested to Butt that Ernest "might possibly have a very rare disease called hemachromatosis." Since this would have required a biopsy for definitive diagnosis, he decided not to investigate it further at the time.

His blood pressure continued to rise in times of anxiety. In the early weeks of treatment, according to Dr. Butt, "it ranged as high as 220 systolic and 150 diastolic." The doctors believed that some of his depression symptoms resulted from the drugs he had been taking to control the hypertension, and recommended that he avoid further use of them unless it became "absolutely necessary." But his depressions were sufficiently severe so that Dr. Rome prescribed and administered a course of electric shock treatments at the rate of two a week through the rest of December and early January. Except for headache

and the usual temporary aphasia, Ernest seemed to respond well. He befriended his doctors and nurses, ordered sets of his books sent to them from
Scribners, and paid many visits to the home of Dr. Butt, saying that "he got
tired of the hospital and liked to go to a house where there were many books."

On one occasion early in December, he came wearing a hat, which he removed carefully, combing his hair forward to conceal his baldness. He was
extremely shy until a few drinks started him talking. He spoke with some
animation of the African plane crashes, but nearly wept with frustration when
he could not recall the name of the Kimana Swamp game preserve. They knew
that his inability to remember was a result of the shock treatments. But all
his delusions had not been erased: he told them seriously that someone was
trying to rob him in spite of the fact that he had no money. He was very gay
at a Christmas Eve dinner with Dr. and Mrs. Butt and their four children.
He and Mary sang snatches of folk songs in Spanish, French, and German.
He happily reported on another dinner early in January, when Dr. Butt allowed him to drink Sancerre, Muscadet, and Haut-Brion in small amounts.
He also went target shooting with Butt and his son in an old quarry out near
the Mayo estate, shattering 27 clay pigeons in a row, and unerringly smashing wine bottles with a .22 pistol at a range of 110 feet.

His presence in Rochester remained a well-kept secret until January 11th,
six weeks after his arrival. The announcement that he was there brought a
flood of mail from well-wishers, both friends and strangers. The letters from
his friends were like a spectrum of the periods and the places of his past: the
Thompsons in Key West, Tom Shevlin of the days in Bimini, Milton Wolff
from the Spanish Civil War, and Ellis Briggs, to whom he sent a happy letter
about stag parties in Havana with Spruille Braden and Winston Guest during
the spy and sub-hunting days after Pearl Harbor. There were warm letters
from the infantry officers Buck Lanham and Jim Luckett with whom he had
proudly formed friendships in 1944, and another from Philip Percival, who
reported that he had shot two cattle-killing lions on his seventy-sixth birthday.
Ernest's replies, which he dictated to a medical secretary named Patricia Mc-
Quarrie, showed that his memory, at least for distant events, was almost back
to normal, while the tone of what he wrote was tinged with some of the old
exuberance.

He was visibly delighted on January 12th to receive a telegram from President-elect John F. Kennedy, who invited the Hemingways to the inauguration
ceremonies on the 19th and 20th. Ernest's reply next day said that "Mrs.
Hemingway and I are greatly honored . . . and wish the administration all
success in their cultural projects and in all things. Unfortunately when we
leave here after treatment for high blood pressure I must restrict certain activities and therefore we will be unable to attend the inaugural ceremonies but
wish to extend our thanks to the President and Mrs. Kennedy and our warm-
est personal congratulations." On the 20th, he and Mary watched the wind-
whipped ceremonies on television. Afterwards, perhaps a shade gratuitously,

he sent the President a second message. "Watching the inauguration from Rochester there was happiness and the hope and the pride and how beautiful we thought Mrs. Kennedy was. Watching on the screen I was sure our President would stand any of the heat to come as he had taken the cold of that day. Each day since I have renewed my faith and tried to understand the practical difficulties of governing he must face as they arrive and admire the true courage he brings to them. It is a good thing to have a brave man as our President in times as tough as these are for our country and the world."

Bad weather and a head cold kept him in Rochester until January 22nd, when he was discharged from St. Mary's Hospital. It was the fifty-third day since his arrival, and seven years to the day since he had taken off with Roy Marsh from the West Airport of Nairobi on the first leg of the ill-fated flight to Uganda. This time no problems arose. Larry Johnson flew the plane due west along the now familiar route. They crossed the Wind River range and the Craters of the Moon and landed at Hailey without incident eight hours after takeoff.

"Working hard again," said Ernest three days later. "Have blood pressure licked." For a time it seemed to be true, though the work consisted chiefly in an attempt to arrange the sketches of his Paris book into the best possible sequence. Each morning he rose at seven, began work at eight-thirty, and stopped "dead tired" about one. After lunch and a nap he walked the snowy roads for exercise, sometimes alone, a too-slender figure in checked cap and heavy boots, pausing to wave to the schoolchildren on their way home. Mary worked out a scheme in which they drove north on Route 93, parked the car, and hiked over a different section of the road each day. Ernest was trying hard to follow the doctors' advice, avoiding hard liquor and drinking only a little claret with his meals. One day he bought a jigger cup at Chuck Atkinson's market to measure his daily intake. "Try to only think from day to day," he wrote early in February, "and work the same, but things have been rough and are rough all over." He missed his Cuban library and asked Scribners for copies of the King James Bible and the *Oxford Book of English Verse,* where he hoped to find a title for his Paris book.

Charles Scribner sent him a message of encouragement, reminding him of his lifelong maxim: *"Il faut (d'abord) durer."* Ernest was touched. He sent back the word that he had "sure tried." Each morning he stayed for hours in the back bedroom, standing at his high desk before the window, shifting papers back and forth, yet "hardly lifting his eyes," as Mary said, to the magnificent panorama of mountains to the north. As February waned, he behaved more and more like a recluse. No longer did he invite his friends to watch the Friday-night fights on television. His visits to Ketchum and Sun Valley dwindled to none. When he emerged from his room upstairs, padding down to the living room in his Indian moccasins, he had little to say. There was a curious distance behind his eyes. Sometimes he stood gazing from the wide front windows across the river towards the Ketchum cemetery through the boughs of the leafless cottonwoods. He seldom spoke of what he saw, if indeed he was seeing anything.

Except for very occasional letters, he wrote nothing. In February he was asked to contribute a sentence for a presentation volume to President Kennedy. Mary bought some paper, cut it to size, and he began to work at the living-room desk. There he labored all day, pausing only for lunch, covering scores of sheets, utterly unable to get it right. The feeling of tension spread through the house. Mary waited as long as she could stand it and then went out for a walk. When she returned, he was still at his work. One of the few people he wanted to see was George Saviers, who appeared almost daily to take his blood pressure, by whose ups and downs Ernest's whole life seemed to be governed. They usually sat side by side on the couch under the window at the north end of the living room. Ernest would sit there, the gray apparatus around his arm, saying pitifully that he could not write—it just wouldn't "come any more." Tears went coursing down his cheeks.

Through March the tension steadily mounted. Ernest worried constantly about weight, blood pressure, and diet. Chuck Atkinson had recently had a skin cancer removed from his face. When he dropped in to see how Ernest was getting along, Ernest said that he feared his own weight loss was due to cancer. He was also much concerned about the possibility of lawsuits in connection with his Paris book. One day he telephoned his first wife, Hadley, who was wintering with her husband on a dude ranch in Arizona. She was struck by the utter mirthlessness of his voice. He had forgotten the names of the man and the woman who had exploited young writers in Paris in 1925. Hadley suggested Ernest Walsh and Ethel Moorhead, but was unable to recall the circumstances. He asked who would know. She named Sylvia Beach, Bill Bird, and Ezra Pound. Ernest said that Sylvia was too inaccurate. Pound might or might not respond. Ernest and Bill Bird were not on good terms. He mentioned a recent visit to Ketchum from Bumby and his family. The conversation ended. But Hadley could not forget the tone of his voice.

Mary saw, but could not halt, the great sadness that had come upon him. When the Harriman Cup Races were held on Baldy Mountain, Don Anderson invited them to watch. Mary was finally induced to go along with Clara Spiegel, but Ernest declined. Bud Purdy came back from a hunting trip in Africa, bringing pictures of Patrick, Henny, and their small adopted daughter. Ernest wrote in praise of the growing family but soon lapsed into complaint. "Things not good here," he wrote, "nor about the Finca and am not feeling good, but mailing this may make feel better." Early in April, nervously distraught with her long siege, Mary walked in her sleep and fell headlong down the stairs, gashing her head and spraining a foot. Reduced to hobbling with a cane, she did her best to keep cheerful. The spring was advancing, the sagebrush was turning green, juncos and larks went flashing past the window, the snow was gone from the slopes of the mountains. But Ernest had eyes for none of this, locked as he was in the cage of his despair.

Towards eleven one April morning, Mary limped downstairs. Ernest was standing in the corner of the living room near the foyer where the gun rack was. He was wearing the red Italian bathrobe which they always called "the Emperor's robe." In his hands was a shotgun and on the windowsill were two shells. Mary began to talk to him quietly. She knew that Dr. Saviers was due at noon to take his blood pressure, and her desperate purpose was to hold out until he came. She said that Ernest must not give up. He still had much to do. She praised his courage and reminded him of his sons. He had written a note, but not to her. It seemed to be scribbled over with figures. He put it into the pocket of the bathrobe and she never saw it again. The minutes ticked past. She went on talking in a low voice. He stayed sullen and silent, staring blankly through the south window at the April landscape or sitting in a chair holding the gun. After an eternity of fifty minutes she heard a car in the driveway. It half-circled the house and stopped at the back door beside the cinder-block guesthouse. Footsteps clomped through the kitchen and down the two steps into the living room. It was George Saviers, as welcome as any angel. He talked to Ernest quietly, quietly, persuading him to hand over the gun. Then he took him off to the Sun Valley Hospital and put him under heavy sedation.

There was no choice but to secure his readmission to Mayo Clinic. Larry Johnson was alerted to be ready to fly Ernest back to Rochester in the Piper Comanche four-seater. Don Anderson and Joanie Higgons, a nurse at Sun Valley Hospital, were detailed to bring Ernest back home to pick up some clothes. At the back door they got out of the car. With a curious foxy smile, Ernest said that Don and Joanie needn't bother to come in. He knew where the stuff was and it wouldn't take long. But Don answered quietly that they were required to stay with him. Ernest made a beeline through the kitchen where the cleaning woman was at work, hurried down the steps into the living room, and crossed to the gun rack. In spite of the fact that Don was almost at his heels, he managed to grab a shotgun, ram home two shells, snap it shut, and point the muzzle at his throat. "No, Papa," said Don, trying to wrestle the gun from Ernest's grip. In spite of his size and strength, he could not get it loose. Joanie said afterwards that the look on Ernest's face was ferocious. Still wrestling, Don managed to open the breech and asked Joanie to remove the shells. Then he forced Ernest onto the settee. He sat with glazed eyes, silent and sullen, even when Mary came down from her bedroom and began to talk to him as she had done before. Joanie summoned George Saviers, who rushed over at once. He and Don drove Ernest back to the hospital and he was put to bed again.

On April 25th, two mornings later, Saviers and Anderson took him to Hailey for the 1100-mile flight. Ernest insisted on writing Mary a note. It seemed to Don that he spent all of fifteen minutes scrawling with a stub of pencil on a scrap of paper, using the wing as a desk. He gave the note to Larry Johnson's wife for delivery to Mary. Then he and Don got into the back seats, with Larry and George up front. The plane rose, climbed high, and crossed the mountains. The weather was perfect. Below them lay the black lava beds and the broad brown plain stretching eastward. But Ernest would not look. He sat there gloomily, his eyes straight ahead. Don tried talking about a new duck-shooting area, but Ernest only grunted. He kept fussing with his belt. He had lost so much weight that it did not fit. Don made a joke of it. Surely his pants would not fall down while he was sitting still. But Ernest kept squirming until Don offered his own belt. In the narrow seat it was hard to get off. When he handed it over, Ernest promptly whipped out a long clasp knife and cut the belt to size. There was another struggle to get it through the waist loops before he settled down. The plane droned eastward through the bright morning. Ernest sat muttering that he was being shanghaied.

It was late morning when they landed for fuel at Rapid City, 550 air miles from Hailey. The magnetos did not check out before takeoff and they taxied to the repair hangar to have one of them replaced. Ernest got down, ostensibly to stretch his legs. Don stayed doggedly at his heels while he made a hurried tour of the hangar section of the airport. He was looking for a gun, and pawed through drawers and tool chests in the sheds, murmuring that they often kept guns in such places. He even checked the glove compartments in some of the parked cars. When the Comanche was ready to go, he saw another plane taxiing down the ramp and walked straight towards its whirling propellers. He and Don were no more than thirty feet away when the pilot cut the engines and Ernest lost interest.

He was a little better on the final leg of the flight. They reached Rochester airport about three in the afternoon. Dr. Butt and an orderly were on hand to meet him. He was apparently delighted to see Dr. Butt again. But he seemed surprised that his friends were going to leave immediately. He turned rather wistfully to Don Anderson. "Kid," he asked, "you're not going back now, are you?" When Don said they would have to go, Ernest said no more, and walked off with Dr. Butt to the waiting limousine.

As he had done in December and January, Ernest submitted to the daily routine and a further series of shock treatments. There was a scrawled note from Dos Passos in Baltimore: "Hem, Hope this isn't getting to be a habit. Take it easy there. Best of luck. Dos." Gary Cooper and his wife sent a sympathetic wire: "WHATS THERE TO SAY EXCEPT THAT YOU HAVE OUR LOVE?" In Cuba, the abortive Bay of Pigs invasion passed almost unnoticed. So did Castro's May Day speech proclaiming the formation of a socialist state. Dr. Rome put Ernest on his honor not to attempt suicide. Although he said that he could always use a lightcord or a coat hanger, he did not try.

Mary had been advised to stay at home in Ketchum. She had locked all the guns in the storage room in the basement, but the two threats of suicide made her more doubtful than ever that Ernest was receiving proper treatment in Rochester. In mid-May she told Betty and Otto Bruce that she was so exhausted with worry that she would like to spend a month in cold storage. But real rest was out of the question. Late in May she went to New York to consult with the eminent psychiatrist who had arranged for Ernest's first admission to Mayo Clinic. She had been there less than a week when she was called to Rochester at Ernest's request. He had been complaining that he had no girl at the hospital. But the visit was not a success. She had made a list of questions to ask Dr. Rome. His answers did not satisfy her. Ernest presented one front to the doctors and quite another to her. She was dismayed to learn that Dr. Rome thought him ready to be discharged. Back in New York, she tried to arrange his transfer to a psychiatric institute in Hartford, Connecticut. The Mayo Clinic advised against the move. Ernest's old paper, *The Kansas City Star,* reported on May 31st that his condition was improving. Mary knew otherwise but was powerless to act. The impasse dragged on into the month of June.

There were still ways of getting to him. A man named Herbert Wellington had written a fisherman's guide to the waters of the Yellowstone. Charlie Scribner sent Ernest a copy. He read it avidly and asked Scribner to send another copy to Bumby in San Francisco. It set him dreaming of the old days at the Nordquist ranch beside the Clark's Fork of the Yellowstone. Scribner also reported that all of Ernest's books were selling very well. This, said Ernest, made him "feel very good." Work was his life. He was hoping soon to return to Ketchum and start to work again.

Dr. Saviers's nine-year-old son Fritz was hospitalized in Denver. He was suffering from nonspecific myocarditis and the prognosis was poor. George said that a note from Ernest might help to cheer him up. "Dear Fritz," wrote Ernest, "I was terribly sorry to hear this morning in a note from your father that you were laid up in Denver for a few days more and speed off this note to tell you how much I hope you'll be feeling better. It has been very hot and muggy here in Rochester but the last two days it has turned cool and lovely with the nights wonderful for sleeping. The country is beautiful around here and I've had a chance to see some wonderful country along the Mississippi where they used to drive the logs in the old lumbering days and the trails where the pioneers came north. Saw some good bass jump in the river. I never knew anything about the upper Mississippi before and it is really a very beautiful country and there are plenty of pheasants and ducks in the fall. But not as many as in Idaho and I hope we'll both be back there shortly and can joke about our hospital experiences together. Best always to you, old timer, from your good friend who misses you very much./Mister Papa./"

The talk of returning to Idaho was not a dream. Ernest had convinced his doctors that he was fit to be discharged. When Mary reached Rochester, she knew that an enormous mistake was being made. But Ernest was eager to be off and she felt that she must comply. She telephoned George Brown in New York. He flew to Rochester to drive them home to Ketchum. Mary rented a Buick from Hertz and they set off on the morning of June 26th. Ernest sat beside George in the front seat, watching the road. The first day all went well. They covered 300 miles and spent the night at a motel in Mitchell, South Dakota. On the 27th, however, Ernest's delusions returned. Mary had bought some wine so that they could have a picnic lunch along the way. He kept worrying that state troopers would arrest them for carrying alcoholic beverages. By noon he began to talk of where they would spend the night. Such problems had never bothered him before. Mary must call ahead to make a reservation. Each day thereafter he was so insistent that once or twice she dropped coins into telephones to simulate calls she never made. They often stopped for the day at two or three in the afternoon. It took them five days to cover 1700 miles.

They reached Ketchum on Friday, June 30th. Mary slept in the front bedroom and Ernest in the back. George Brown stayed in the cinder-block guesthouse beside the parking area outside the kitchen door. Next morning Ernest and George drove out to the hospital to see George Saviers. George said that Fritz had been pleased with Ernest's letter. The child had been spending a few days at home but that night George would have to take him back to Denver on the train. Ernest walked over to see Don Anderson at his Sun Valley office. Don was not there and they drove home. In the afternoon, Chuck Atkinson came over to see Ernest, and they talked for an hour, standing out on the front porch. Clara Spiegel wanted them to come to dinner. Ernest refused. He invited Clara for Sunday dinner instead. Ernest and Mary took George Brown to the Christiania Restaurant beside Chuck Atkinson's motel. Ernest sat in a corner facing the room. He said little but did not seem morose. The restaurant filled with Saturday-night diners. They left early and returned to the house. Almost at once Ernest began to prepare for bed. He was brushing his teeth in the bathroom adjoining his bedroom when Mary suddenly remembered a gay Italian song: *"Tutti Mi Chiamano Bionda"*— "They all call me blond." She sang it to Ernest and he joined her in the closing line. He put on his blue pajamas and snapped on the reading light beside his bed. Mary went to sleep in the big front room.

Sunday morning dawned bright and cloudless. Ernest awoke early as always. He put on the red "Emperor's robe" and padded softly down the carpeted stairway. The early sunlight lay in pools on the living-room floor. He had noticed that the guns were locked up in the basement. But the keys, as he well knew, were on the window ledge above the kitchen sink. He tiptoed down the basement stairs and unlocked the storage room. It smelled as dank as a grave. He chose a double-barreled Boss shotgun with a tight choke. He had used it for years of pigeon shooting. He took some shells from one of the boxes in the storage room, closed and locked the door, and climbed the basement stairs. If he saw the bright day outside, it did not deter him. He crossed the living room to the front foyer, a shrinelike entryway five feet by seven, with oak-paneled walls and a floor of linoleum tile. He had held for years to his maxim: *"il faut (d'abord) durer."* Now it had been succeeded by another: *"il faut (après tout) mourir."* The idea, if not the phrase, filled all his mind. He slipped in two shells, lowered the gun butt carefully to the floor, leaned forward, pressed the twin barrels against his forehead just above the eyebrows, and tripped both triggers.

Sources and Notes

Debts and Credits

Index

Sec. 1. The Country and the Town

SOURCES

Books and documents: A set of five volumes, kept for EH by his mother, 1899–1917 (unpublished); Marcelline Hemingway Sanford, *At the Hemingways,* 1962; Leicester Hemingway, *My Brother, Ernest Hemingway,* 1962. **Author's interviews and correspondence:** with Marcelline Sanford, Dec., 1962 and Feb., 1963; with Mrs. E. J. Miller (née Madelaine Hemingway), July, 1964; with Sterling S. Sanford, July, 1964; with Mrs. Wesley Dilworth and her daughter, Mrs. Maxine Davis, July, 1964. From Sterling S. Sanford, Apr. 12, 1968.

NOTES

EH's ancestry and immediate family: his maternal grandfather, Ernest Hall, was born in Sheffield, England, in 1840, the son of Charles and Mary Miller Hall, and educated at St. Saviour's Grammar School in London. In 1855 he followed his family to Dyersville, Iowa. About 1857 he left home, worked his way down the Mississippi, and settled in Louisiana. On his return home in 1861 he served as corporal with Troop L, First Iowa Volunteer Cavalry. In 1865 he married Caroline Hancock of Dyersville, who bore him two children: Grace (EH's mother), born in Chicago, June 15, 1872, and Leicester Campbell, born 1874. Ernest Hall died in Oak Park, May 10, 1905, aged sixty-five. Caroline Hancock was born near Liverpool, England, Sept. 18, 1843, of Alexander and Caroline Sydes Hancock. On the death of his wife in January, 1853, Captain Hancock took his three children around Cape Horn in the bark *Elizabeth* with the intention of homesteading in Australia. But he returned from Sydney to the United States, settling his family in Dyersville, Iowa, in 1854. His other children were Charlotte Sydes Hancock (1842–52); Annie Sydes Hancock (1845–1937); and Benjamin Tyley Hancock (Feb. 29, 1848–1937). Caroline Hancock Hall died Sept. 15, 1895 in Oak Park.

EH's paternal grandfather, Anson Tyler Hemingway, was born in Plymouth, Connecticut, Aug. 26, 1844. His earliest American ancestor was Ralph Hemingway, who came from England about 1633, married Elizabeth Hewes, and became a member of the Roxbury, Massachusetts, church. In 1854, Anson came west with his father, Allen, a wholesaler of clocks, who was reputedly associated with Seth Thomas. He enlisted as a private in Company D, 72nd Regiment, Illinois Infantry, on July 28, 1862, and eleven months later was stationed near Vicksburg, Mississippi. On Jan. 1, 1865 he was a first lieutenant, B Company, 70th US Infantry, at Natchez, and at the end of the year was at St. Joseph, Louisiana. His diary entry for Apr. 9, 1866 reads: "Got home from the Army today." He matriculated at Wheaton College, Illinois, a Congregationalist institution, where he met his wife-to-be, Adelaide Edmonds, who was some years older than he. They were married Aug. 27, 1867, and moved to Oak Park, occupying a small house at the corner of Oak Park Avenue and Superior Street, later pulled down and replaced by the much larger house that EH knew in his boyhood. Anson's real-estate office was at 189 La Salle Street, Chicago. They had six children: Anginette Blanche, called Nettie, afterwards second wife of Frank B. Hines of Albion and Carbondale, Illinois; Clarence Edmonds, father of EH, born Oak Park, Sept. 4, 1871; George R.; Willoughby, born April 1, 1874; Alfred Tyler, born Dec. 4, 1877; and Grace. Anson died in Oak Park, Oct. 7, 1926, aged eighty-two. Adelaide Edmonds was born Aug. 17, 1841 on a farm near Rock River, Illinois, worked her way through Wheaton College by teaching school, and died in Oak Park Feb. 5, 1923. She was the only grandmother EH knew. Children of Clarence E. and Grace Hall Hemingway: Marcelline, born Jan. 15, 1898; Ernest Miller, born July 21, 1899; Ursula, born April 29, 1902, and named for Ursula March, heroine of Dinah Maria Mulock's didactic novel, *John Halifax, Gentleman* (1856); Madelaine, called Sunny, born Nov. 28, 1904, and named for Grace's cousin, Madelaine Board; Carol, called Beefy or Beefish, born July 19, 1911; Leicester Clarence, born April 1, 1915.

EH's favorite "Birds of Nature": published serially, Jan.–June, 1898 and June–Dec., 1899, ed. by C. C. Marble and published by A. W. Mumford, Chicago, 1900. EH owned these volumes in his lifetime; they were given on his death to the Key West Public Library.

Dilworth family of Horton Bay: James Dilworth married Elizabeth Buell in January, 1886. Their son Wesley was born in 1890. On July 12, 1915, he married Kathryn Kennedy, born in 1895. She had been graduated in 1914 from high school in Boyne City. Wesley died of cancer in 1951. EH's story, "Up in Michigan" contains an exact description of Horton Bay in paragraphs 4 and 5.

EH's memory of leaving his grandfather Hall's house in 1905: "Now I Lay Me," in *The Fifth Column and the First 49 Stories,* NY, 1938, p. 463.

Sec. 2. Arts and Sciences

SOURCES

Letters of EH: to his father, Oct. 19, 1908. To author, Aug. 27, 1951. **Other letters:** Dr. C. E. Hemingway to EH, July 8, 1907; Dr. Hemingway to EH, Oct., 1910 (postcard); Dr. Hemingway to EH, March 8, 1925. **EH's work: (a) Unpublished:** "My First Sea Vouge," Apr. 17, 1911; "The Opening Game," Apr. 12, 1912; untitled "African Book," 1954–55; untitled fragment on Nick Adams and the Indians, date of composition uncertain. **(b) Published:** "Sepi Jingan," *Tabula,* Vol. 23 (Nov., 1916); "The Doctor and the Doctor's Wife," *First 49 Stories,* 1938, pp. 197–201; "Fathers and Sons," *First 49 Stories,* pp. 586–597; "Remembering Shooting Flying," *Esquire,* Vol. 3 (Feb., 1935). **Books:** Grace Hemingway's Albums, Vols. 3–4 (unpublished); Marcelline H. Sanford, *At the Hemingways,* 1962; Leicester Hemingway, *My Brother, Ernest Hemingway,* 1962. **Author's interviews and correspondence:** with Marcelline Sanford, Dec., 1962; with Mrs. E. J. Miller and Sterling Sanford, July, 1964. From Frank B. Hines, June 21, 1963; from Margarette Hines, Jan., 1964.

NOTES

Twelve quarts of milk: EH's "African book," MS. unpublished, composed in 1954–55.
EH's memories of his father: "Fathers and Sons," *First 49 Stories*, NY, 1938, p. 594.
Dr. Hemingway shoots tomcat: Clarence E. Hemingway to EH, July 8, 1907, preserved in Grace's album, Vol. 3.
EH's memories of the path to Bacon's farm: "Fathers and Sons," p. 590.
EH to his father in New Orleans, Oct. 19, **1908:** Album, Vol. 3.
EH's gift books of 1909: information supplied by Mrs. Ernest Hemingway, who catalogued the inscribed copies of his books in storage in 1961. EH was also an inveterate reader of *St. Nicholas*, the children's magazine.
EH and mother to Nantucket: EH to author, Aug. 27, 1951, says that his mother was trying to civilize him by exposing him to some of his fancier relatives, and that she was a great snob, bowdlerizing everything in the family history into a wonderful respectability, and substituting the Elysian Fields for the actual Tyburn Hill.
Dr. Hemingway's postcard to EH, Oct., 1910: Album, Vol. 3.
EH's first extant short story: Album, Vol. 4. Tyley Hancock, born Feb. 29, 1848, was still in his fourth year at the death of his mother on Jan. 9, 1853.
Visit from Dr. Willoughby Hemingway: Willoughby had married Mary Williams in Oxford, Ohio, Oct. 1, 1903, with Marcelline as flower girl, and had since been a medical missionary for the American Bible Society at T'ai Ku, Shansi, China.
The Indians near Bacon's farm: account from an untitled and unpublished 4-page fragment about Nick Adams. It centers on the deaths and departures among the Indians of Walloon Lake and Horton Bay. The tall Indian killed by the train may have been an invention of EH's (see his high-school story, "Sepi Jingan") but the rest of the account was confirmed by his sister, Mrs. E. J. Miller, in interviews with author, July, 1964. Description of Nick Boulton and Billy Tabeshaw: "The Doctor and the Doctor's Wife," *First 49 Stories*, pp. 197–199. When Dr. Hemingway read this story in March, 1925, he recognized the occasion and dated it as belonging to the summer of 1911. "That was when you were 12 yrs. old and Carol was born that summer," he wrote to EH. "I got out the Old Bear Lake book and showed Carol and Leicester the photo of Nic Boulton and Billy Tabeshaw on the beach sawing the big old beech log." (C. E. Hemingway to EH, March 8, 1925). If the doctor resented the implication that Dr. Adams is a coward in having been faced down by Boulton in the argument, he said nothing of it in this letter. The likelihood is that EH invented this incident while recalling the rest. It will be noted that the story speaks of Dick Boulton, rather than Nick, since EH's boy protagonist was called *Nick* Adams.
Portrait of Simon Green of Horton Bay: from unpublished fragment mentioned above.
The Hines family of Albion, Ill.: Frank B. Hines, Jr., to author, June 21, 1963, and Miss Margarette Hines to author, Jan., 1964. Some account of this trip appears in EH's article, "Remembering Shooting Flying," *Esquire*, Vol. 3 (Feb., 1935), pp. 21 and 152.

EH's poem, "The Opening Game": Grace Hemingway's Album, Vol. 4.
Eating a porcupine: Harold Sampson, quoted in M. H. Sanford, *At the Hemingways*, Boston, 1962, p. 81.

Sec. 3. Juvenilia

SOURCES

Letters of EH: to his parents, ca. Sept. 6, 1913; to his mother, Sept. 8, 1914; to his mother, July 31 and Sept. 16, 1915. To Charles Scribner, July 19, 1950; to author, Feb. 24, 1951; to Charles A. Fenton, Sept. 23, 1951.
Other Letters: Dr. Hemingway to EH, July 19, 23, and 31, 1915; Grace Hemingway to Dr. Hemingway, July 30, 1915; Lewis Clarahan to EH, Aug. 8, 1915; Harold Sampson to EH, Aug. 14, 1915; Dr. Hemingway to Grace and Marcelline Hemingway, Apr. 4, 1917; Lloyd Harter to EH, June 14, 1917.
Books: Grace Hemingway's albums, Vols. 4–5; Charles A. Fenton, *The Apprenticeship of Ernest Hemingway*, 1954; Warren Browne, *Titan Versus Taboo: The Life of William Benjamin Smith*, 1961; Marcelline H. Sanford, *At the Hemingways*, 1962; Leicester Hemingway, *My Brother, Ernest Hemingway*, 1962.
EH's work: (a) Unpublished: Diary of a hike to Walloon Lake, June 10–21, 1916; deleted portions of "Big Two-Hearted River," composed 1924; early draft of "Ten Indians," composed ca. Sept. 27. 1925; untitled short story based on the heron episode, composed April, 1952. **(b) Published:** contributions to Oak Park High School *Tabula* and *Trapeze*: see listing in Audre Hanneman, *Ernest Hemingway, A Comprehensive Bibliography*, 1967, pp. 125–129; "Remembering Shooting Flying," *Esquire*, Vol. 3 (Feb., 1935), pp. 21 and 152; "Ten Indians" and "Fathers and Sons," *First 49 Stories*, 1938.
Author's interviews and correspondence: with Lewis Clarahan and Mrs. Susan Lowrey Kesler, Jan., 1962; W. B. Smith, Jr., April, 1962; Mrs. E. J. Miller, Mrs. Kathryn Dilworth, Mrs. Maxine Davis, and Sterling S. Sanford, July, 1964. From W. B. Smith Dec. 6, 1961, Jan. 15 and Feb. 1, 1962, April 3, 1964; from Mrs. Kesler, Feb. 15, 1962; from Gordon Shepherd, March 12, 1963; from Lewis Clarahan, Sept. 19, 1964, July 12, Aug. 21, and Aug. 22, 1967.

NOTES

EH's poor eye-sight: M. H. Sanford, *At the Hemingways*, pp. 156–157.
First hike to Walloon Lake: Clarahan to author, Sept. 19, 1964. Grace Hemingway's album, Vol. 5, has an entry: "They did not walk much of the way." EH later made a marginal note: "That is bunk. We walked 130 miles. EH."
Date of Wesley Dilworth wedding: Mrs. Kathryn Dilworth to author, July, 1964. All the Hemingways were present.
EH shoots first cock pheasant: "Remembering Shooting Flying," *Esquire*, Vol. 3 (Feb., 1935). One of EH's companions on this trip was Philip White, a classmate. "I was with him when . . . we shot a pheasant on the [game] farm, and Ernest covered it under his

shirt to prevent being arrested for poaching, or trespass, or burglary, as he was guilty of all three and so was I." Philip M. White to Otto McFeely, July, 1948. McFeely sent an account of his interview with White to Malcolm Cowley, July 19, 1948.
EH's boxing enthusiasm: Grace's album, Vol. 5. **He knocks out Clarahan:** Clarahan to author, Sept. 19, 1964.
EH boasts of fighting with professionals in Chicago: EH to Scribner, July 19, 1950, and EH to Charles Fenton, Sept. 23, 1951, are representative examples.
The Smith family: the father of the family was Dr. William Benjamin Smith, b. Oct. 26, 1850 in Stanford, Kentucky; Kentucky University, A.B., 1870; A.M., 1871; Ph.D., University of Göttingen, 1879. He taught mathematics at Central College, Fayette, Mo., and married Katharine Drake Merrill, Oct. 25, 1882. Before her death on June 12, 1899, she had borne him four children: Merrill Neville (1883), Yeremya Kenley (1885), Katharine Foster, b. St. Louis, Oct. 26, 1891, and W. B., Jr., b. St. Louis, Aug. 20, 1895. Mrs. Smith's sister, then Mrs. Foster, took over the care of the children in the summer of 1899. In 1902 she married Dr. J. W. Charles. They bought the farmhouse at Horton Bay in the summer of 1912. Yeremya's name was a variant spelling of Jeremiah, but he was commonly called Kenley or Y. K. Mrs. Charles was often alluded to by EH as "the Madame," or sometimes Aunty. She bore a grudge against Dr. Smith, whom she blamed for her sister's untimely death.
EH and Prudence Boulton: Two of EH's stories mention Prudence. The most explicitly sexual is "Fathers and Sons," where Nick recalls the forest ground on which he and Trudy (here modified from Prudy) discovered the pleasures of intercourse. "She did first what no one else has ever done better" with her "plump brown legs, flat belly, hard little breasts, well holding arms, quick searching tongue, the flat eyes, the good taste of the mouth." The same girl, this time called Prudy, appeared in "Ten Indians." Dr. Adams there reported to Nick that he had seen Prudy and Frank Washburn "thrashing around" in the woods while Nick was away in Petoskey with the Garners (Bacons) on a Fourth of July trip. The first draft of this story, composed in Chartres, France, ca. Sept. 27, 1925, had a different conclusion. Prudy came to Nick's window in the middle of the night and asked him to come out. Her family had returned drunk from Petoskey, and she had fled the house to complain of it to Nick. When Nick kissed her, her cheeks were wet with tears. Unpublished, untitled early version in light-brown notebook "L'Incroyable" with EH's name and the place and date.
Dr. Hemingway's sexual advice: "Fathers and Sons."
EH and Frances Coates: documented in Grace's Album, Vol. 5. Mrs. Frances Grace (née Coates) to author, Feb. 14, 1966.
Second hike to Walloon Lake: EH's Diary of the trip (unpublished) and Lewis Clarahan to author, July 12, Aug. 21, and Aug. 22, 1967.
EH's awkwardness in football: Gordon Shepherd to author, March 12, 1963.
EH's exemplary writings: Mrs. Kesler to author, Feb. 25, 1962. Besides his short stories,

EH contributed two poems to the *Tabula,* one a football rhyme, which parodied stanza 7, Longfellow's "A Psalm of Life," and the other, "The Worker," about a ship's stoker. This was EH's earliest excursion into the life of the proletariat.
Hoax attack on EH's camp: Mrs. Kesler to author, Feb. 25, 1962. Mrs. Kesler supplied copies of two newspaper clippings about the episode, and believed that the account in the *Trapeze* "was *surely* written by Hemingway although not signed by him." EH also selected the apothegm ("Which not even critics criticize") that accompanied Susan's name and picture in the Senior *Tabula.* She was the author of his: "None are to be found more clever than Ernie."
EH's speech at First Congregational Church: a printed program survives in Grace's Album, Vol. 5. The date was June 17, 1917.

Sec. 4. The Enormous Room

SOURCES

Letters of EH: EH to Charles A. Fenton, Jan. 12 and July 29, 1952.
Books and articles: Charles A. Fenton, *The Apprenticeship of Ernest Hemingway;* Marcelline H. Sanford, *At the Hemingways; Stylebook of the Kansas City Star,* revised edition, 1956; Theodore Brumback, "Hemingway's War Days Recounted by Friend," North American Newspaper Alliance feature, Dec. 19, 1936; Paul W. Fisher, interview with EH, Kansas City *Times,* Nov. 26, 1940.
EH's work (a) Unpublished: Undated sketch on Nick Adams's train trip to Kansas City and first sight of Mississippi River; undated character sketch of Lionel Moise. **(b) Published:** Vignette on Hungarian thieves, *in our time,* Paris, 1924; "A Pursuit Race," *Men Without Women,* NY, 1927; "God Rest You Merry, Gentlemen," *Winner Take Nothing,* NY, 1933; *For Whom the Bell Tolls,* NY, 1940.
Author's interviews and correspondence: with William B. Smith, April, 1964; with Mrs. E. J. Miller and Owen White, July, 1964; with Dale Wilson, Oct., 1966. From C. G. Wellington, Dec. 20, 1950; from Sally Carrighar, April 24, 1962; from Russel Crouse, Aug. 15, 1963; from Dale Wilson, Oct. 31, 1966.

NOTES

Carl Edgar's interest in Katy Smith: EH to Fenton, July 29, 1952; the same information appears in the deleted portion of "Big Two-Hearted River."
EH's interview with Trumbull White: Owen White (son) to author, July 12, 1964. Another acquaintance of EH's from Bay View in the summer of 1917 was Bill Grundy of Louisville, Ky. Grundy appeared no more in EH's life until the first draft of *The Sun Also Rises,* where EH borrowed his name for Jake Barnes's fishing companion at Burguete, but changed it to Bill Gorton in the final version. A third summer resident at Bay View was Sterling S. Sanford, then a senior engineering student at the University of Michigan, who married Marcelline Hemingway in 1923.

Incident of the purloined canoe: Mrs. E. J. Miller to author, July, 1964.
EH thinks of shooting his father: W. B. Smith to author, April 3, 1964. A similar episode appears in "Fathers and Sons," *First 49 Stories*, pp. 594–595.
Dr. Hemingway's farewell to EH on departure for Kansas City: fictional version quoted from *For Whom the Bell Tolls*, NY 1940, pp. 405–406.
EH's first sight of the Mississippi River: from an unpublished, untitled sketch, possibly belonging to the period 1920–1921 or perhaps earlier. The day of the trip is established as Oct. 15 by internal evidence in the sketch, which says that it is the last day of the World Series. Chicago won the first two games (2–1, 7–2) at White Sox Park, Chicago, Oct. 6–7, 1917. New York won at home (2–0, 5–0) on Oct. 10–11. Chicago won the fifth game in Chicago (8–5) on Oct. 13th, and the final game (4–2) on Oct. 15th in New York. Happy Felsch played center field for Chicago and Slim Sallee pitched for New York in the first and fifth games. Both players are mentioned in the sketch, as well as Mark Twain, Huck Finn, Tom Sawyer, and La Salle.
Alfred Tyler and Arabella Hemingway (EH's uncle and aunt) and their house on Warwick Blvd.: Sally Carrighar to author, April 24, 1962.
The Kansas City "Star" and its chief editors in 1917: Dale Wilson to author, Oct. 31, 1966.
EH at the movies: Sally Carrighar to author, Apr. 24, 1962. I have not been able to identify the Fairbanks film they watched. Possibilities are *The Good Bad Man, Reggie Mixes In,* or *Manhattan Madness*, all issued in 1916, or *The Man from Painted Post,* 1917.
EH moves into Edgar's apartment: Fenton, *Apprenticeship,* p. 36.
EH in Hotel Muehlbach pressroom bathtub: EH to Fenton, Jan. 12, 1952.
EH's "short-stop" run on the "Star": quoted from interview with Paul W. Fisher, *Kansas City Times,* Nov. 26, 1940, and from EH to Fenton, 1952, printed in Fenton, *Apprenticeship,* NY, 1954, p. 35.
EH's training on the "Star": C. G. Wellington to author, Dec. 20, 1950. Fenton, *Apprenticeship,* p. 31. *The Stylebook of the Kansas City Star,* revised edition, 1956, p. 3, repeats the directions to reporters from the edition in use when EH read it in 1917. The author is indebted to Messrs. Dale Wilson and Inghram D. Hook for a copy of the *Stylebook*.
EH rides city ambulances: Wellington to author, Dec. 20, 1950.
EH's pieces on the smallpox victim, the municipal doctor, and the Kansas City whores: EH to Fenton, Jan. 12, 1952.
EH's "sad story" about the whore in love: Fenton. *Apprenticeship,* p. 46. Another piece, probably by EH, has been identified and reprinted by Donald Hoffmann of the *Star*: "Kerensky, The Fighting Flea," *Kansas City Star,* Jan. 28, 1968, Section D, p. 1. See also Mel Foor, *Kansas City Star,* July 21, 1968, Section D, pp. 1–2.
Kansas City in 1917: Dale Wilson to author, Oct. 31, 1966.
EH's character sketch of Moise: from an undated, unpublished holograph MS. Fenton, *Apprenticeship,* pp. 38–42, leaves the impression that Moise and Hemingway were closer

than in fact they were. He quotes Wesley Stout, who later became editor of the *Saturday Evening Post,* that it "was from Moise, whose footsteps he dogged" that EH learned how to write. Russel Crouse seems also to have been misinformed. EH's "great pal in Kansas City," wrote Mr. Crouse, "was . . . named Lionel Moise and I've always thought that Moise was the guy Ernie eventually used as the basis of his [personal] 'character.' The two of them were rough and tough but the only erudite rough and tough guys I ever knew. They could clean out a bar and then quote Shakespeare to the bartender." (Russel Crouse to author, Aug. 15, 1963). But EH makes clear his very slight acquaintance with Moise in EH to Fenton, July 29, 1952. He calls Moise a "primitive force" with a great relish for drink and women. I have found no confirmation for EH's story of the stabbing on Lincoln Highway, and he leaves a mistaken impression of the geography of that highway. According to Dale Wilson, the highway's closest approach to Kansas City would be near Council Bluffs, Ia., some 150 miles to the north.
EH's chief associates among "Star" staff: Dale Wilson to author, Oct. 31, 1966.
EH's short stories using Kansas City locales: the site of the shooting of the Hungarians at 15th Street and Grand Avenue was near the *Star* building; a tire company and the Street Railway Company were located there. "God Rest You" alludes to the Woolf Brothers Saloon, which did not exist, EH having borrowed the name from Kansas City's largest men's store. (Inghram D. Hook to Dale Wilson, Oct. 26, 1966.)
EH blames poor eyesight on his mother: M. H. Sanford, *At the Hemingways,* pp. 156–157.
History of Theodore Brumback: Fenton, *Apprenticeship,* pp. 47–49.
Decision to apply to ambulance corps: Fenton, pp. 48–49.
EH moves out of Edgar's apartment to one of his own: Theodore Brumback, "Hemingway's War Days," North American Newspaper Alliance feature, Dec. 19, 1936.

Sec. 5. The Schio Country Club

SOURCES

Letters of EH: to Dale Wilson, May 18, 1918; to his parents, ca. May 27, July 21, Aug. 18, and Sept. 11, 1918; to his former *Star* associates (postcard), ca. June 6, 1918; to Maxwell Perkins, Feb. 19, 1927 and May 30, 1942; to Malcolm Cowley, Sept. 5, 1948.
Other letters: Theodore Brumback to Dr. and Mrs. Hemingway, ca. July 18–19, 1918, with a postscript by EH; W. D. Horne, Jr., to Malcolm Cowley, Aug. 7, 1948; Horne to Harold Loeb, Aug. 31, 1961; Horne to M. H. Sanford, ca. Sept. 1961.
Books and articles: *Report of the Department of Military Affairs, Jan., 1918–Feb., 1919,* Rome, 1919; Theodore Brumback, "Hemingway's War Days Recounted by Friend," North American Newspaper Alliance feature story, Dec. 19, 1936; *Ciao* (Section Four newspaper), issue of June 18, 1918.
EH's work: (a) Unpublished: fragment of novel, *Along with Youth* about the crossing

on the *Chicago,* dated June 15, 1925. **(b) Published:** *A Farewell to Arms,* NY, 1929; *Death in the Afternoon,* NY, 1932; "Now I Lay Me," *First 49 Stories,* NY, 1938.
Author's interviews: with Messrs. W. D. Horne, Howell Jenkins, Frederick Spiegel, Jerome Flaherty, and Lawrence T. Barnett, Jan., 1962; with John Dos Passos, April, 1962; with Mrs. M. H. Sanford, Dec., 1963; with Miss Frances Pailthorp, July, 1964; with Mr. and Mrs. Archibald MacLeish, March, 1965; with Pio Bertoli and Paolo Altamura of the Lanerossi Mills in Schio, and with various aging citizens at Fossalta-di-Piave, Oct., 1965; with Dale Wilson, October, 1966.

NOTES

War as game: EH to Perkins, May 30, 1942.
EH in New York: Horne to Sanford, ca. Sept., 1961, and Horne to author, Jan., 1962. The certificate of EH's medical examination was dated May 9, 1918, signed by Dr. D. M. Dunn of the Life Extension Institute, 25 W. 45th Street, NYC, and mailed to Oak Park on May 14. Letters from EH about New York are EH to Dale Wilson, May 18, 1918, and EH to his parents, ca. May 27, 1918. EH had seen Mae Marsh in *The Birth of a Nation* in 1917. He boasted to Wilson that she had asked him to dinner on May 19, and had confessed she was in love with him. When he suggested marriage at the Little Church Around the Corner, "she opined as how ye war widow appealed not to her." She was sure he would become a great newspaperman. Gee, she was a wonderful girl, too good for the likes of Hemingstein. But news of EH's betrothal must be kept out of the K.C. *Star.* When queried on this matter by Dale Wilson in October, 1966, Miss Marsh said she had never met EH but wished that she had. Dale Wilson to author, Oct. 10, 1967.
Crossing on "Chicago": EH to parents, ca. May 27, 1918. On June 15, 1925, EH told part of the story of the crossing as the substance of a fragment of a novel, which he then abandoned. It consisted mostly of boyish conversations on drinking and sex among Nick Adams, Leon Chocianowicz, and Howell Jenkins, called The Carper.
Bordeaux, Paris, and train ride to Italy: Horne to Loeb, Aug 31, 1961; Horne to M. H. Sanford, ca. Sept., 1961; and Brumback, "Hemingway's War Days." Dec. 19, 1936.
Munitions-plant explosion: EH to former associates on *Star* (postcard) ca. June 6, 1918, printed in K.C. *Star,* July 14, 1918, p. 5A. EH's later account is in *Death in the Afternoon,* NY, 1932, pp. 135–136.
Stopover in Milan: Horne, Jenkins, Spiegel, and Flaherty to author, Jan., 1962. The roll of officers and drivers appears in *Report of the Department of Military Affairs,* pp. 42–50.
Section Four Barracks in Schio: Horne et al. to author, Jan., 1962.
Quotations from "Ciao": issue of June 18, 1918, the only one to which EH contributed. *The Report . . . of Military Affairs* shows that Section Four was the least active of the 5 ARC sections. They carried 1500 stretcher cases and 9000 sitting wounded, making 1200 trips and covering 75,000 kilometers. Section Three carried 54,000 wounded on 4500 trips and drove nearly 400,000 kilometers.

EH meets Dos Passos: Dos Passos to author, May 28, 1962.
Austrian offensive on the Basso Piave: "Our Part in the Big Drive," *Ciao,* June 18, 1918.
EH's restiveness: Brumback, "Hemingway's War Days," and Frederick Spiegel to author, Jan., 1962.
Red Cross Canteens: *Report . . . of Military Affairs,* pp. 17–20.
EH volunteers for canteen service: Horne to Sanford, ca. Sept., 1961, and Horne to Cowley, Aug. 7, 1948.
Silkworm house at San Pedro Norello: Horne to Cowley, Aug. 7, 1948, and Horne to Sanford, ca. Sept., 1961. EH's story, "Now I Lay Me," *First 49 Stories,* NY, 1938, pp. 461 and 465. "You'll read it far better than I can tell it," Horne told Mrs. Sanford, "if you'll reread the first paragraphs of 'Now I Lay Me.' "
EH befriended by priest: According to Romualdo M. Zilianti O.S.B., Abbot-General of the Abbanzia Monte Oliveto Maggiore, Chiusure(Siena), the name of the priest who befriended EH was Cappellano Don Giuseppe Bianchi, who later took the name of Father Gerardo and served as a Benedictine priestmonk of the Abbey of Monte Oliveto until his death in 1965 (Zilante to author, Sept. 11, 1968).
EH calls self a camp follower: EH to Perkins, Feb. 19, 1927.
EH's wounding: the most trustworthy account is EH's own, contained in a letter to his parents, Aug. 18, 1918. The substance of that letter is followed here. EH describes the Austrian trench mortar in a letter to Cowley, Sept. 5, 1948. In this same letter, he vouches for the autobiographical accuracy of the passage on the wounding of Frederic Henry in *A Farewell to Arms,* NY, 1929, p. 58.
EH's thought of suicide in the roofless shed: reported by him in 1919 to Miss Frances Pailthorp of Petoskey, Michigan, and by her to author, July 9, 1964.
EH's meeting with the wounded soldier at the distribution center in Fornaci: this account originally formed part of EH's story on Mayor Church of Toronto at the boxing match, *Toronto Star Weekly,* March 13, 1920. The Italian material was deleted before publication in the paper, but retained by Miss Dorothy Connable, who generously supplied a copy to author.
EH baptized by the Italian priest: this event is confirmed by the testimony of Mrs. Archibald MacLeish to author, March 1965.
EH's train trip to Milan: the route seems to have been the same as that followed by Lieutenant Henry in *A Farewell to Arms,* NY, 1929, pp. 82–83. It is likely that some details of the trip as described in the novel were also autobiographically accurate, but it seemed best not to reproduce them here because it is impossible to be certain.

Sec. 6. Milano

SOURCES

Letters of EH: to parents, July 21, Aug. 18 (publ. *Chicago Evening Post,* Oct. 23, 1918), Sept. 11, Oct. 18, 1918 (publ. *Oak Parker,* Nov. 16, 1918, pp. 6–7); to Charles Scribner, April 8, 1942, and July 9, 1950; to Bernard Berenson, Oct. 14, 1952; to John Atkins, Dec. 28, 1952.

Other letters: Agnes von Kurowsky to EH, Sept. 26, Oct. 16, 17, 22–23, 24, and 29, 1918; Nov. 2, 3, 5–6, 7, 22, 25, 28, and 30, 1918; Dec. 4, 8, 10, 15, 16, 19, 1918; Theodore Brumback to Dr. and Mrs. Hemingway, ca. July 18–19, 1918 (postscript by EH); Rev. William E. Barton to EH, Oct. 16, 1918; Lieut. Leon Chocianowicz to EH, Oct. 18, 1918; Capt. James Gamble to EH, Dec. 11, 1918; Elsie Macdonald to EH, Nov. 2, 1926, Dec. 14, 1926, Jan. 20, 1928, Oct. 20, 1929; John Miller to EH, Nov. 16, 1926; Carl Hugo Trik to EH, March 13, 1933; Mrs. Agnes Stanfield to Jack Buck, May 27, 1957. W. D. Horne to Mrs. Sanford, ca. Sept. 1961 and Oct. 23, 1961.
Books and articles: *Report of the Department of Military Affairs,* Rome, 1919; *Burke's Landed Gentry of Ireland,* 4th ed., London, 1958; M. H. Sanford, *At the Hemingways,* 1962. **Unpublished:** Diary of Carl H. Trik, Christmas, 1918; Memoir by Maj. Gen. E. E. Dorman-O'Gowan.
EH's Work: (a) Published: *A Farewell to Arms,* 1929, esp. chapters 13, 17, 20, and 35; *Men at War* introduction, 1942.
Author's interviews and correspondence: with W. D. Horne, Jr., Jan., 1962; with Mrs. William H. Stanfield, Jr. (née Agnes von Kurowsky), March 29, 1965. From Henry Villard, Feb. 1, 1962; from Mary Welsh Hemingway, March 5, 1962; from Jack Buck, April 16 and 24, May 4 and 23 and June 5, 1957; from Maj. Gen. E. E. Dorman-O'Gowan, Feb. 24, 1962; from George W. Pay, Oct. 16, 1963.

NOTES

EH's arrival in Milano: see Chapter 13, *A Farewell to Arms;* EH to parents, July 21, 1918.
Nurse Macdonald: based on contemporaneous snapshots, her letters to EH of Nov. 2, 1926, and Oct. 20, 1929, and Mrs. Agnes Stanfield to author, March 29, 1965.
EH in hospital: Brumback to Dr. and Mrs. Hemingway, ca. July 18–19, 1918, with postscript by EH. Letter printed in full in Sanford, *At the Hemingways,* pp. 161–163.
Captain Sammarelli: EH to his father, Sept. 11, 1918.
EH's comments on hospital and wounds: EH to parents, July 21, 1918, and Elsie Macdonald to EH, Jan. 20, 1928.
Agnes von Kurowsky: born Jan. 5, 1892, in Germantown, Pa. Father: Paul Moritz Julius von Kurowsky, naturalized American citizen of Polish, Russian, and German ancestry. Came from Königsberg about 1890. Mother: Agnes Theodosia Holabird of New York City, whose father, Samuel B. Holabird, was Quartermaster General to the U.S. Army during the Reconstruction period. Agnes was raised in Washington, D.C., where she worked in the Public Library until 1914, when she entered Nurses' Training School, Bellevue Hospital, NYC, graduating April 24, 1917. Then attached to School of Nursing, Long Island College Hospital, Brooklyn. The author is indebted for most of the foregoing to Jack Buck.
Character of Agnes: Henry Villard to author, Feb. 1, 1962.
Captain Enrico Serena: Mrs. Agnes Stanfield to author, March 29, 1965, identified him as the probable prototype of Captain Rinaldi in *A Farewell to Arms.*

EH's operation: dated Aug. 10, 1918, in Villard's diary. Mrs. Stanfield told Mrs. Mary Welsh Hemingway that her date with Serena took place on the evening of that day: Mrs. Stanfield to Mrs. Hemingway, Feb., 1962, forwarded to author by Mrs. Hemingway on March 5, 1962.
Elsie present for operation: Elsie Macdonald to EH, Dec. 14, 1926.
EH's pride in his fame: EH to parents, Aug. 18, 1918. Letter published in full in *Chicago Evening Post,* Oct. 23, 1918: OAK PARK BOY SHOT TO PIECES—JOKES ABOUT IT—ERNEST HEMINGWAY SUFFERS 227 WOUNDS WHILE IN RED CROSS SERVICE. Reprinted in Sanford, *At the Hemingways,* pp. 166–169.
EH holds court in hospital room: Villard to author, Feb. 1, 1962.
Removing fragments with penknife: Mrs. Stanfield to author, March 29, 1965.
Scolding Elsie: Elsie Macdonald to EH, Jan. 20, 1928.
Bill Horne's visits: W. D. Horne, Jr., to author, Jan., 1962. Several excellent pictures of EH in bed, with service cap and lips pursed in a whistle, were made by Herbert Darling, an ARC ambulance driver of Section One.
EH's attractive qualities: Mrs. Stanfield to Mrs. Hemingway, Feb., 1962; Mrs. Stanfield to author, March 29, 1965; Elsie Macdonald to EH, Nov. 2 and Dec. 14, 1926, Jan. 20, 1928, and Oct. 20, 1929.
EH in love with Agnes: Mrs. Stanfield to Jack Buck, May 27, 1957 and to author, March 29, 1965. Elsie Macdonald to EH, Dec. 14, 1926. Many letters from Agnes to EH (cited above) testify to the nature and extent of the affair. The letter in which she says she misses him, though not as "wildly" as he misses her, is dated Oct. 16, 1918. Agnes told the author that her transfer to Florence in mid-October marked the beginning of the end of the romance, which suggests a duration of two months, ca. Aug. 15 to Oct. 15, though correspondence continued four months more. Agnes denied to author that her relations with EH were overtly sexual, as in the Barkley-Henry relationship in *A Farewell to Arms.* Henry Villard, who was in the hospital from Aug. 1 to about Sept. 1, told the author (Feb. 1, 1962) that "Ernie's incipient romance with Agnes had not developed to an extent that called for comment." On reading *A Farewell* in 1929, he recognized Agnes in the portrait of Catherine Barkley, except for the sexual aspects. As for these, he thought that "Ernie must have dreamed a good part of the story during his tedious stay in the hospital."
EH's recuperation and promotion: EH to his father, Sept. 11, 1918.
Visit to San Siro track: one such occasion may be dated in mid-September from a surviving letter from Agnes to a friend, Sept. 28, 1918. Confirmed in George W. Pay to author, Oct. 16, 1963. See also *A Farewell to Arms,* Ch. 20. There were doubtless several visits.
Visit to Stresa: Agnes to EH in Stresa, Sept. 26, 1918. John M. Miller, Jr., to EH, Nov. 16, 1926.
Meeting with Count Greppi: Mrs. Marcelline Sanford, *At the Hemingways,* following p. 180 prints a picture of EH and some relatives of Count Greppi outside the Hotel Stresa. She dates it as of Nov. or Dec., but it should be September. EH to John Atkins, Dec. 28, 1952,

mentions his meeting with Greppi. EH to Charles Scribner, July 31, 1950, says it was Greppi who brought him up politically, and calls him "opposite number to Metternich" among Italian statesmen. *A Farewell to Arms*, Chapter 35, introduces Count Greffi, aged ninety-four, "a contemporary to Metternich" who "had been in the diplomatic service of both Austria and Italy" and whose birthdays "were the great social event in Milan." I am indebted to Count Giacomo Lechi for the information that EH's account in the novel, apart from the slight change in the name, is entirely accurate. Count Giuseppe Greppi was born March 25, 1819, and died May 8, 1921, at the age of 102. During a distinguished diplomatic and political career, he served both Austria (until 1859) and afterwards Italy (until 1889). By the time EH met him he had long been retired but retained a sharp continuing interest in international politics.

EH's return from Stresa: Agnes to EH, Nov. 2, 1918, recalls the occasion.
EH's Spagnolini uniform: Horne to Mrs. Sanford, ca. Sept., 1961.
Agnes transferred to Florence: Agnes to EH from Florence, Oct. 16, 17, 22–23, 24, and 29, 1918.
Letters from friends: Rev. William Barton to EH, Oct. 16, Lieut. Leon Chocianowicz to EH, Oct. 18, 1918.
EH in newsreel: Sanford, *At the Hemingways*, p. 171.
EH on heroism and death: EH to parents, Oct. 18, 1918. Publ. in *Oak Parker*, Nov. 16, 1918, pp. 6–7.
EH to Bassano: W. D. Horne to Mrs. Sanford, ca. Sept., 1961 and Oct. 23, 1961.
Start of Vittorio-Veneto Offensive: *Report of the Dept. of Military Affairs*, pp. 9–11.
EH's jaundice: Horne to Sanford, ca. Sept., 1961; EH to Scribner, Apr. 8, 1942; Agnes to EH, Nov. 2, 3, 5–6, 1918. **Fictional account:** *Farewell to Arms*, 1929, p. 154.
EH meets Dorman-Smith: Maj. Gen. Dorman-O'Gowan, Memoir, sent to author, Feb. 24, 1962. Eric Edward Dorman-Smith was born July 24, 1895 and educated at Uppingham and the Royal Military College, Sandhurst. In 1949 he reassumed his original family name of Dorman-O'Gowan. His military career is outlined in *Burke's Landed Gentry of Ireland*, London, 1958, p. 538. The Shakespeare quotation is from *Henry IV, Part II*, Act III, scene ii, lines 253–258. EH quotes it in *Men at War*, 1942, introd., p. xiv.
Agnes and Elsie Jessup: Mrs. Stanfield to author, March 29, 1965, said that memories of Miss Jessup helped color EH's portrait of Catherine Barkley, and that she warned EH against Gamble's offer.
Agnes to Treviso: letters to EH of Nov. 22, 25, 28, 30, Dec. 4 and 8, 1918. The last of these anticipates EH's visit. Another letter, Dec. 10, proves that he came to Treviso on the 9th. Her letter of Dec. 15 discourses on his character; that of Dec. 19 regrets she cannot be in Milan for Christmas.
EH at holiday parties: Dorman-O'Gowan, Memoir; Carl H. Trik to EH, March 13, 1933, provides further details and quotes the Christmas entry in Trik's diary: "Milano. Cova. New friend name of Hemingway. Red X dance. With EH to party afterwards. Charades, Headache. Pia. Mass."

Gamble invites EH- to Taormina: Gamble to EH, Dec. 11, 1918. The letter said that he had just rented "a little house and garden belonging to an English Artist. . . . Now the only thing lacking is company and I only hope that you will take care of that. . . ,"
EH's erotic sojourn in Sicily: Dorman-O'Gowan's Memoir.

Sec. 7. *Soldier's Home*

SOURCES

Letters of EH: to Howell Jenkins, June 15, July 15, July 26, ca. Sept. 15, and Dec. 20, 1919; to Edwin Balmer, Aug. 3, 1934; to Malcolm Cowley, Aug. 19, 1948; to author, Nov. 9, 1951.
Other letters: Agnes von Kurowsky to EH, Jan. 6, 12, 15–16, Feb. 3 and 15, and March 1, 1919, and Dec. 22, 1922; W. D. Horne to Mrs. M. H. Sanford, ca. Sept., 1961.
Books and articles: (a) Newspapers: *Yonkers Daily News*, Dec. 20, 1918; *New York Sun*, Jan. 22, 1919; *The Oak Parker*, Feb. 1, 1919; O.P.H.S. *Trapeze*, March 21, 1919; *Detroit Free Press*, June 18, 1963. **(b) Books:** *The Messages and Papers of Woodrow Wilson*, 2 vols., N.Y., 1924; M. H. Sanford, *At the Hemingways*, 1962; Leicester Hemingway, *My Brother, Ernest Hemingway*, 1962; Constance C. Montgomery, *Hemingway in Michigan*, N.Y., 1966.
EH's work: (a) Unpublished: "The Passing of Pickles McCarty or The Woppian Way," composed ca. spring, 1919; deleted portion of "Big Two-Hearted River," composed 1924. **(b) Published:** *Toronto Star Weekly*, April 10, April 24, and Aug. 28, 1920; "Up in Michigan," "The End of Something," "The Three-Day Blow," "A Very Short Story," and "Soldier's Home."
Author's interviews and correspondence: with Mrs. M. H. Sanford, Dec., 1962; with Messrs. W. D. Horne, Jr., Howell Jenkins, Albert Dungan, and Gordon Shorney, Jan., 1962; with W. B. Smith, Jr., April, 1964; with Mrs. Kathryn Dilworth and Mrs. Maxine Davis, July, 1964; with Mrs. William H. Stanfield, March 29, 1965. From Dr. Guy C. Conkle, May 2, 1962; from Lawrence T. Barnett, June 20, 1963; from Mrs. James P. Hulley to Maj. Gen. C. T. Lanham, April 26, 1964; from Mrs. Dorothy Reynolds Heckendorn, Oct. 5, 1964; from W. B. Smith, Jr., Sept. 17, 1965; from Waring Jones, Oct. 12, 1966.

NOTES

EH's dockside interview: *NY Sun*, Jan. 22, 1919, p. 8.
Meeting with Horne: Horne to author, Jan., 1962. Mr. Horne was uncertain whether Ann's last name was Sage or Trowbridge.
Horne's departure from war and return home: Horne to M. H. Sanford, ca. Sept. 1961, and article in *Yonkers Daily News*, Dec. 20, 1918.
EH's homecoming: *At the Hemingways*, pp. 176–177.
Letters from Agnes: Jan. 6 and 12, 1919. The letter of the 6th told of seeing President and Mrs. Wilson at the Palazzo Reale in Milan on Jan. 5. The President made four speeches at Milan. See *The Messages and Papers of Woodrow Wilson*, NY 1924, I, 604–608.

EH's first months at home: *At the Heming-ways*, pp. 178–188.
Roselle Dean interview: *Oak Parker*, Feb. 1, 1919, p. 12.
The little girls' Valentine: Dorothy R. Heck-endorn to author, Oct. 5 1964.
EH's loneliness: see fictional portrait of Har-old Krebs in "Soldier's Home," *First 49 Sto-ries*, 1938, pp. 243–251.
Further letters from Agnes: Jan. 15–16, Feb. 3 and 15, and March 1, 1919.
Italian parties: *At the Hemingways*, pp. 185–188.
EH lectures on war: according to Gordon Shorney, EH lectured at the First Baptist Church, the Lamar Theatre, and the Southern Club on Kenilworth Avenue. The high-school assembly speech of March 14 was reported by Edwin Wells in the *Trapeze*, March 21, 1919, p. 1.
EH's opening remarks on relation between fear and salivation: Mrs. James P. Hulley to General Lanham, April 26, 1964.
Visit to YMCA pool: Albert Dungan to au-thor, Jan., 1962.
Agnes rejects EH: Mrs. William Stanfield to author, March 29, 1965, said her letter pointed out the differences in their ages and indicated that their plans would not work out. The let-ter has not appeared. It is possible that EH destroyed it, though he kept most of her other letters. "A Very Short Story" sketches the love affair and the breakup, and summarizes the content of the letter of rejection. As first printed (Sketch No. 10, *in our time*, Paris, 1924), the story used the locale of Milan and the name of "Ag." Later, from fear of libel, EH changed the locale to Padua and the name to Luz.
EH's dismay: *At the Hemingways*, pp. 188–189.
EH's complaint to Elsie Macdonald: Agnes and Elsie had quarreled in Milan (Agnes to EH, Jan. 6, 1919). When Agnes reached NYC on the SS *Re D'Italia* in July, 1919, Elsie read aloud to her from EH's "very biting letter." (Agnes to EH, Dec. 22, 1922). The date of Agnes's letter of rejection is established as sometime in March by a letter from John Miller to EH, April 4, 1919, in reply to one by EH in which he talked of Agnes and the rejection.
EH boasts of cauterizing wound with booze and women: EH to Howell Jenkins, June 15, 1919.
EH has dates with Kathryn Longwell: *My Brother, Ernest Hemingway*, pp. 57–59.
EH gives cloak to Miss Longwell: M. H. San-ford, to author, Dec., 1961.
Visit from Bill Smith: EH to Jenkins, June 15, 1919; Smith to author, April 3, 1964, and Sept. 17, 1965. During the talk about Parisian girls on the El coming home from Chicago, Bill asked, "Boid, how old are the French women?" EH remembered the question and used it as an epigraph in the Paris edition of *in our time*.
"The Passing of Pickles McCarty": copy pro-vided author by Waring Jones. Date of com-position is conjectural. The quality of the prose and frequent echoes of EH's high-school lecture in March argue for the spring of 1919.
EH at Horton Bay: EH to Jenkins, June 15, 1919; Dr. Guy C. Conkle to author, May 2, 1962.

Cigarettes, liquor, and Lieut. Caracciolo: EH to Jenkins, June 15, 1919.
EH and Smith at Pine Barrens: EH to Jenkins, July 15 and 26, 1919.
Grace's new studio and her estimate of her son: *At the Hemingways*, pp. 193–198.
EH's conference with Balmer: recalled in EH to Balmer, Aug. 3, 1934. The original type-script of "Pickles McCarty" has the list of magazine editors on the back of p. 1 in Bal-mer's hand. For Balmer's career, see *NY Times* obituary, March 22, 1959.
Second trip to Pine Barrens and street-light episode: EH to Jenkins, July 15 and 26, 1919; Lawrence T. Barnett to author, June 20, 1963; EH to author, Nov. 9, 1951.
Trip to Seney: EH to Jenkins, ca. Sept. 15, 1919. EH drew on this trip for two articles in *Toronto Star Weekly*, Apr. 24, 1920, p. 13, Aug. 28, 1920, p. 21.
On being crippled: EH to Malcolm Cowley, Aug. 19, 1948. Seney began about 1885 when two capitalists from Detroit built a railroad between St. Ignace and Marquette. Way sta-tions were named for company officials, in-cluding George L. Seney of New York. The freight was lumber and Seney was a haven to hundreds of lumberjacks. A famous local character named P. J. (Snap Jaw) Small bit off the heads of live frogs and snakes in ex-change for drinks in the saloons. Between 1891 and 1895 Seney was twice destroyed by forest fires. By 1919 it was a virtual ghost town. In 1924, EH used the locale for "Big Two-Hearted River," although the river at Seney is the Fox. Big Two-Hearted River is an actual stream farther north and east; EH borrowed its name for poetic and symbolic purposes. Sheridan Baker was the first to identify the Fox as the river in the story. See *Michigan Alumnus Quarterly Review*. Vol. 65 (Feb. 28, 1959), pp. 142–149. A short history of Seney appeared in *Detroit Free Press*, June 18, 1963, p. 4B.
Rainbow trout in Lake Charlevoix: EH, *To-ronto Star Weekly*, Apr. 10, 1920.
EH's friendship with Marjorie Bump: Kathryn Dilworth to author, July 10, 1964. For auto-biographical aspects of "The End of Some-thing" and "The Three-Day Blow," see Mont-gomery, *Hemingway in Michigan*, NY, 1966, pp. 128–140. Marjorie's sister Georgianna, called Pudge, sometimes accompanied her sister and EH.
Origin of "Up in Michigan": Mrs. Kathryn Dilworth and Mrs. Maxine Davis to author, July 10, 1964. They said that the girl got a hemlock sliver in her bottom the night of the seduction. EH's story accurately portrayed Horton Bay as he knew it, mentioning the dock and one of the warehouses, long since pulled down. EH borrowed the first names of Jim and Liz Dilworth for his lovers, Jim Gilmore and Liz Coates, and made Gilmore a blacksmith, as Dilworth was. Liz's last name may have come from the Coates House, a reputable hotel in Kansas City, or from Frances Coates, whom EH had admired in high school. In the story, Jim took his meals, and Liz Coates waited on table, at D. J. Smith's, an eating establishment clearly mod-eled on Dilworth's. Before the seduction, Jim went hunting deer in the Pine Barrens, where EH had himself seen deer in July, 1919.

Sec. 8. North Country

SOURCES

Letters of EH: to Howell Jenkins, Dec. 20, 1919; to Grace Quinlan, Jan. 1, 1920; to Dorothy Connable, Feb. 16, 1920; to Mrs. Ralph Connable, June 1, 1920; to his mother (postcard), June 24, 1920; to Grace Quinlan, Aug. 1 and 8, 1920; to Howell Jenkins, Sept. 16, 1920; to Grace Quinlan, Sept. 30, 1920.
Other letters: Marcelline Hemingway to Sterling Sanford, Oct. 14, 1919; Edwin Balmer to EH, Feb. 1, 1920; Dr. Hemingway to EH, March 18, 1920; Grace Hemingway to EH, March 18, 1920; Dr. Hemingway to EH, April 19, 1920; Dr. Hemingway to his wife, June 28, July 18, 21, 26, and 28, 1920; Dr. Hemingway to EH, July 22, 1920; Grace Hemingway to EH, July 24, 1920; Dr. Hemingway to his wife, Sept. 2, 15, and 19, 1920; Grace Hemingway to EH, Oct. 4, 1920; Dr. Hemingway to his wife, ca. Oct. 6, 1920.
Books and articles: J. H. Cranston, "Hemingway's Early Days," *Midland Free Press Herald,* Oct. 19, 1945; J. H. Cranston. *Ink on My Fingers,* 1953; Charles A. Fenton, *The Apprenticeship of Ernest Hemingway,* 1954; M. H. Sanford, *At the Hemingways,* 1962; Leicester Hemingway, *My Brother, Ernest Hemingway,* 1962; Ross Harkness, *J. E. Atkinson of the "Star,"* 1963; Constance C. Montgomery, *Hemingway in Michigan,* 1966.
EH's work: Unpublished: "Wolves and Doughnuts," composed ca. Dec., 1919.
Author's interviews and correspondence: with Miss Hazel Potter, Edwin G. Pailthorp, Mrs. E. J. Miller, and Mrs. Irene Gordon, July 8–12, 1964; Toronto group interview, Jan. 12, 1965; with Miss Dorothy Connable, Feb., 1964 and July, 1964. From Dorothy Connable, April 17, 1964.

NOTES

EH's brief visit to Oak Park: "Ernie is with us again," wrote Marcelline, "but only for a week. He drove down with Bill Smith last Monday [Oct. 6, 1919] and expects to return to Horton Bay for the whole winter. . . . I fear he will freeze, but he desires to write— to create immense quantities of literature. . . ." Marcelline Hemingway to Sterling Sanford, Oct. 14, 1919, quoted in *At the Hemingways,* p. 199.
EH rents room at Mrs. Potter's: Hazel Potter to author, July 10, 1964; see also Montgomery, *Hemingway in Michigan,* pp. 159–171.
EH's friends in Petoskey: E. G. Pailthorp to author, July 10, 1964; Mrs. Irene Gordon to author, July 8 and 12, 1964; Montgomery, *Hemingway in Michigan, loc. cit.*
EH's "Wolves and Doughnuts": The quoted fragment appears on the back of a letter, EH to Howell Jenkins, sent from Petoskey, Dec. 20, 1919. Possible prototypes of the Café Cambrinus are the Venice Café, 520 S. Wabash Ave., run by David Vigano, and the Subway Restaurant, 448 N. Franklin St., run by J. Armenali.
EH's yarns about Italy: Pailthorp to author, July 10, 1964.
EH speaks in Petoskey Public Library: Dorothy Connable to author, April 17, 1964, and

Montgomery, *Hemingway in Michigan,* pp. 160–161.
Connables invite EH to Toronto: Dorothy Connable to author, April 17, 1964; EH to Jenkins, Dec. 20, 1919.
EH's holiday in Oak Park and Chicago: EH to Jenkins, Dec. 20, 1919; EH to Grace Quinlan, Jan. 1, 1920; Irene Gordon to author, July 10, 1964. EH told Grace Quinlan that he might return to the K.C. *Star* or write advertising for Firestone Tires in their "Ship by Truck" campaign, but he kept his promise to the Connables instead.
Connable household in Toronto: Dorothy Connable to author, Apr. 17, 1964. **Tennis-court hockey-rink:** Ernest Smith to author, Toronto group interview, Jan. 12, 1965, transcript, p. 22. According to Dorothy Connable, EH wrote a piece about a supercilious British visitor called "The Young Englishman and the Girl Who Could Skate." If it appeared in the *Toronto Star Weekly,* as she believed, it has not been located.
EH introduced to "Toronto Star": Toronto group interview, transcript, pp. 4–5; J. H. Cranston, *Ink on My Fingers,* 1953; Fenton, *Apprenticeship,* 1954, pp. 77–81.
EH seeks help from Edwin Balmer: Balmer to EH, Feb. 1, 1920; "I'm very glad you sent me those stories. My opinion remains precisely what I said last summer."
EH receives news and comment from Oak Park: Dr. Hemingway to EH, and Grace Hemingway to EH, March 18, 1920.
EH's social life in Toronto: Pailthorp to author, July 10, 1964; Toronto group interview, transcript, pp. 9–10.
EH's talks with Harriet and Dorothy Connable: Dorothy Connable to author, Apr. 17, 1964.
EH's behavior at "Star" offices: Cranston, "Hemingway's Early Days," *Midland Free Press Herald,* Oct. 19, 1945, p. 2; Toronto group interview, transcript, p. 5; Roy Greenaway to author, Feb. 24, 1965; Ross Harkness, *J. E. Atkinson of the "Star,"* U. of Toronto Press, 1963. Harkness is not fully reliable on EH.
EH's contributions to the "Star Weekly": for a listing, see Audre Hanneman, *Ernest Hemingway, A Comprehensive Bibliography,* Princeton University Press, 1967, pp. 130–131.
EH's plans for summer and fall of 1920: EH to Mrs. Ralph Connable, June 1, 1920.
EH's competitive spirit: W. B. Smith to author, April 3, 1964; Mrs. Irene Gordon to author, July 8, 1964.
EH's neglect of family obligations: EH to his mother (postcard), June 24, 1920; Dr. Hemingway to his wife, June 28, July 18, 21, 26, and 28, 1920, quoted in *My Brother, Ernest Hemingway,* pp. 64–66; Dr. Hemingway to EH, July 22, 1920.
Midnight picnic at Ryan's Point: Mrs. E. J. Miller to author, July 8, 1964; EH to Grace Quinlan, Aug. 8, 1920.
Grace's criticism of EH's recent behavior: Grace Hemingway to EH, July 24, 1920.
EH on his mother's letter and his trip to Black River: EH to Grace Quinlan, Aug. 1 and 8, 1920.
Dr. Hemingway's prayers for EH: Dr. Hemingway to his wife, July 26, 28, and 30, 1920, and Sept. 2, 15, and 19, 1920. Quoted in

My Brother, Ernest Hemingway, pp. 65–69.
EH at Horton Bay and Charlevoix (September, 1920): EH to Jenkins, Sept. 16, 1920; EH to Grace Quinlan, Sept. 30, 1920; Grace Hemingway to EH, Oct. 4, 1920.
EH's indeterminate plans for future: EH to Jenkins, Sept. 16, 1920; Dr. Hemingway to his wife, ca. Oct. 8, 1920, quoted in *My Brother, Ernest Hemingway,* p. 70

Sec. 9. Hadley

SOURCES

Letters of EH: to Grace Quinlan, Nov. 16 and Dec. 1, 1920; to his mother, ca. Dec. 22, 1920 and Jan. 10, 1921; to Bill Smith, ca. Feb. 15, 1921 and ca. May 15, 1921; to Grace Quinlan, Aug. 7 and 19, 1921; to Hadley Richardson, late Aug., 1921; to Y. K. Smith, Oct. 1, 1921; to author, Oct. 7, 1951; to Charles A. Fenton, Jan. 12, 1952; to Bernard Berenson, Oct. 4, 1955.
Other letters: Hadley Richardson to EH, Jan. 1, 9, 15, and 23; March 5, 7, 8, 15, and 29; April 1, 21, 22, 24, 25, and 27; May 5, 12, ca. May 15, 22; June 3, 6, 10, 18, 22, 24, and 30; July 2, 7, 14, 17, 21, and 24; Aug. 6, 8, 10, 13, 17, 18, 20, 21, 22, and 23, 1921. James Gamble to EH (telegram), Dec. 27, 1920. Grace Hemingway to Marcelline Hemingway, Aug. 18 and 28, 1921. Y. K. Smith to EH, Oct. 2, 1921. Sherwood Anderson to Lewis Galantière, Nov. 28, 1921. Sherwood Anderson to Gertrude Stein, Sylvia Beach, and Ezra Pound, Dec. 3, 1921.
Books and articles: H. Rappaport, *The Nation,* Vol. 113 (Oct. 19, 1921); *Memoirs of Sherwood Anderson,* 1942; *Letters of Sherwood Anderson,* 1953; M. H. Sanford, *At the Hemingways,* 1962; Leicester Hemingway, *My Brother, Ernest Hemingway,* 1962; *Mercure de France,* Fall, 1963.
EH's work: (a) **Unpublished:** two fragmentary sketches, undated, on Nick Adams dressing to be married, and going to the honeymoon cottage with his wife, Helen. (b) **Published:** for a listing of his contributions to the *Toronto Star Weekly* and one by-lined article in the *Cooperative Commonwealth* in 1920–21, see Audre Hanneman, *Ernest Hemingway, A Comprehensive Bibliography,* 1967, pp. 131–132.
Author's interviews and correspondence: with Hadley R. Mowrer, July, 1962; with W. D. Horne, Dec., 1962; with W. B. Smith, April, 1964; with Mrs. Irene Gordon, July, 1964; with Mrs. Isabelle Simmons Godolphin, Feb., 1965; with Y. K. Smith, Aug., 1965. From Mrs. Ruth Bradfield Gay, Oct. 20, 1962; from Mrs. Hadley R. Mowrer, Jan. 15, 1967.

NOTES

Death of Florence Richardson and Hadley's Chicago visit: Hadley R. Mowrer to author, July, 1962; William B. Smith to author, April, 1964; Y. K. Smith to author, August, 1965.
Hadley's first impressions of EH: Hadley to EH, Jan. 9 and 23, 1921. Y. K. Smith's apartment was then at 100 E. Chicago Ave.
EH unemployed: W. D. Horne to author, Dec., 1962; EH to Grace Quinlan, Nov.

16 and Dec. 1, 1920. Horne and Hemingway lived at 1230 North State Street in November and December.
EH employed by "Cooperative Commonwealth": EH to his mother, ca. Dec. 22, 1920 and Jan. 10, 1921; EH to Bill Smith, ca. Feb. 15, 1921; EH to Charles A. Fenton, Jan. 12, 1952.
EH moves to "The Belleville" at 63 E. Division Street: EH to his mother, Jan. 10, 1921. He moved about Jan. 3, 1921.
EH's correspondence with Hadley and news of his activities: details drawn from Hadley to EH. Jan. 1, 9, and 15, 1921, and EH to Bill Smith, ca. Feb. 15, 1921. **Jim Gamble's invitation:** AM SAILING FOR ROME SS ROCHAMBEAU JAN. 4TH WILL STAY UNTIL JUNE COME ALONG HAVE WRITTEN: Gamble to EH (wire), Dec. 27, 1920.
EH visits St. Louis and Hadley returns the visit (March): recalled in Hadley to EH, Aug. 20, 1921.
Account of EH at Y. K. Smith's: Mrs. Ruth Bradfield Gay to author, Oct. 20, 1962. Other details in Hadley to EH, March 5, 7, 8, 15, 29 and 30; April 1, 21, 25, and 27; ca. May 15, 1921.
EH meets the Sherwood Andersons: Y. K. Smith to author, Aug., 1965.
EH tours German restaurants: EH to Bill Smith, ca. May 15, 1921; Y. K. Smith to author, Aug., 1965.
EH and Horne on Memorial Day visit to Hadley: Horne to author, Dec., 1962; Hadley to EH, May 12 and 22; June 3, 6, and another (undated) letter of June, 1921.
EH comment on rivers versus girls: EH to Bill Smith, ca. May 15, 1921.
EH camps on roof: Y. K. Smith to author, Aug., 1965.
Y. K. Smith returns to 100 East Chicago Avenue: Hadley to EH, June 10, July 5, and July 17, 1921. These letters also reflect her views on the forthcoming marriage.
EH afflicted with low spirits: Hadley to EH, Apr. 22, 1921.
Hadley's July visit and gift of typewriter, EH's poem and short story, "A Divine Gesture": Hadley to EH, July 8, 13, 16, 19, 21, 23 and 26, 1921.
Wedding plans: The engagement was formally announced in June at a tea given by Helen Breaker. The Social Items column in the St. Louis *Post-Despatch* stated erroneously that Mr. "Hemmingway" had attended the University of Padua after his war service. Hadley produced gales of laughter by saying that Ernest had been the first American killed in Italy. (Hadley to EH, June 6, 1921.) The wedding invitation was from Mr. and Mrs. Roland Green Usher, and named Saturday afternoon, Sept. 3, 1921, at four o'clock in the First Presbyterian Church, Horton Bay, as the time and place. (Copy sent by Hadley to EH, Aug. 18, 1921.) Further details on the plans are in Hadley to EH, Aug. 8, 10, 13, 17, 18, 21, 22, and 23, 1921; EH to Grace Quinlan, Aug. 19, 1921; and Grace Hemingway to Marcelline Hemingway, Aug. 18 and 28, 1921.
Wedding day: Hadley R. Mowrer to author, July, 1962; Horne to author, Dec., 1962; Ruth Bradfield Gay to author, Oct. 20, 1962; Edwin G. Pailthorp to author, July, 1964; two

unpublished Nick Adams sketches by EH, undated, one on getting dressed for the wedding, the other on going by car and rowboat to Windemere.
Honeymoon and return to Chicago: Hadley R. Mowrer to author, July, 1962.
Quarrel with Y. K. Smith: Y. K. Smith to author, Aug., 1965; EH to Y. K. Smith, Oct. 1, 1921; Y. K. Smith to EH, Oct. 2, 1921.
EH learns of imminent collapse of Cooperative Society of America: EH to Hadley, late Aug., 1921. **EH resigns job with Cooperative Commonwealth:** Hadley R. Mowrer to author, July, 1962.
EH writes satire on wedding gifts: *Toronto Star Weekly*, Dec. 17, 1921, p. 15. (This was published after he had sailed for Europe.)
Anderson volunteers letters of introduction: Anderson to Lewis Galantière, Nov. 28, 1921; Anderson to Gertrude Stein, Dec. 3, 1921. See *Letters of Sherwood Anderson*, ed. Howard Mumford Jones and Walter B. Rideout, Boston, 1953, pp. 82–85. Anderson to Sylvia Beach: *Mercure de France*, Fall, 1963, p. 102. A duplicate of the letters to Miss Stein and Miss Beach was sent to Ezra Pound.
EH gives Anderson canned goods: *Memoirs of Sherwood Anderson*, NY, 1942, p. 473.

Sec. 10. One True Sentence

SOURCES

Letters of EH: to his parents, Dec. 8 and 20, 1921; to Bill Smith, ca. Dec. 21, 1921; to Mr. and Mrs. Sherwood Anderson, ca. Dec. 24, 1921; to Howell Jenkins, Dec. 26, 1921, Jan. 8, 1922, March 20 and ca. March 25, 1962; to Sherwood Anderson, March 9, 1922; to his father, May 2, 1922.
Other letters: Hadley to Dr. and Mrs. Hemingway, Jan. 4, 1922; E. E. Dorman-Smith to EH, Jan. 13, 1922; Bill Smith to EH, Feb. 19, 1922; John R. Bone to EH, Feb. 2, Feb. 20, and March 22, 1922.
Books and articles: George Seldes, *World Panorama*, 1932: Gertrude Stein, *The Autobiography of Alice B. Toklas*, 1933; George Slocombe, *The Tumult and the Shouting*, 1936; Paul Scott Mowrer, *The House of Europe*, 1945; Charles A. Fenton, *The Apprenticeship of Ernest Hemingway*, 1954; Richard Ellmann, *James Joyce*, 1959; Max Eastman, *Great Companions*, 1959; David Cecil, *Max, A Biography*, 1965; George Seldes, "Pages from a Genoa Diary" (unpublished).
EH's work: (a) Unpublished: untitled poem sent to Bill Smith, ca. Feb., 1962; "Paris, 1922," six one-sentence prose sketches. **(b) Published:** *Toronto Star Weekly*, Feb. 4 and 18, March 4 and 18; April 10, 11, 13, 24, and 25, 1922; "A Divine Gesture" (fable), *The Double Dealer*, Vol. 3 (May, 1922); "Wanderings" (six poems), *Poetry*, Vol. 21 (Jan., 1923); *A Moveable Feast*, 1964.
Author's interviews and correspondence: with William Bird, June, 1962; with Hadley R. Mowrer, Dec., 1962; with Lewis Galantière, March, 1963; with Mrs. Guy Hickok, May, 1963; with William B. Smith, May, 1964; with Y. K. Smith, Aug., 1965. From George Seldes, Feb. 1962; from Mr. and Mrs. Paul Scott Mowrer, April 4, 1965.

NOTES

Arrival in New York: EH to parents, Dec. 8, 1921.
Crossing on the "Leopoldina": EH to Bill Smith, ca. Dec. 21, 1921.
Calling at Vigo: *Star Weekly*, Feb. 18, 1922, p. 15; EH to parents, Dec. 20, 1921; EH to Bill Smith, ca. Dec. 21, 1921; Hadley to Dr. and Mrs. Hemingway, Jan. 4, 1922; Hadley R. Mowrer to author, Dec., 1962.
Arrival in Paris: EH and Hadley to the Sherwood Andersons, ca. Dec. 24, 1921; EH to Howell Jenkins, Dec. 26, 1921; Hadley to Dr. and Mrs. Hemingway, Jan. 4, 1922.
Meeting with Galantière: Lewis Galantière to author, March, 1963.
74, rue du Cardinal Lemoine: EH to Jenkins, Jan. 8, 1922; Hadley R. Mowrer to author, Dec., 1962; *A Moveable Feast*, 1964, pp. 3–7.
"One true sentence": *A Moveable Feast*, p. 12.
Chamby, Switzerland: EH to Jenkins, Jan. 8, 1922; *Toronto Star Weekly*, Feb. 4, 1922, p. 3; March 4, 1922, Feature Section, p. 25; March 18, 1922, p. 15. E. E. Dorman-Smith to EH, Jan. 13, 1922.
Return to Paris: *A Moveable Feast*, pp. 11–13.
EH's scorn of false artists: Charles A. Fenton, *The Apprenticeship of Ernest Hemingway*, 1954, p. 102; *Toronto Star Weekly*, March 25, 1922, p. 15.
Meeting with Pound: Hadley R. Mowrer to author, Dec., 1962. **EH's satire on Pound:** Galantière to author, March, 1963. **Boxing with Pound:** EH to Anderson, March 9, 1922, and EH to Jenkins, March 20, 1922; Galantière to author, March, 1963.
Meeting with Gertrude Stein: *Autobiography of Alice B. Toklas*, 1933, pp. 260–271: *A Moveable Feast*, pp. 13–15.
EH on Joyce: EH to Anderson, March 9, 1922, printed in part in Richard Ellmann, *James Joyce*, 1959, p. 543; *A Moveable Feast*, p. 56.
EH on Sylvia Beach: *A Moveable Feast*, pp. 35–36.
EH meets Guy Hickok: Hadley R. Mowrer to author, Dec., 1962; Mrs. Mary Hickok to author, May, 1963.
EH's writing for "Toronto Star": for listing of articles see Audre Hanneman, *Ernest Hemingway, A Comprehensive Bibliography*, Princeton, 1967, pp. 132–133.
John Bone's approval: Bone to EH, March 22, 1922.
Quarrel with Bill Smith: Bill Smith to EH, Feb. 19, 1922. Unpublished poem, "Blood is thicker than water," composed ca. Feb., 1922.
Trip to Genoa: George Slocombe, *The Tumult and the Shouting*, 1936, p. 68; William Bird to author, June 2, 1962; Hadley R. Mowrer to author, April 7, 1962; George Seldes, *World Panorama*, 1932, p. 199 and "Pages from a Genoa Diary" (unpublished), a copy given to author, Feb., 1962; Paul Scott Mowrer, *The House of Europe*, 1945, p. 416.
EH wounded by water heater: *Toronto Daily Star*, May 2, 1922, p. 5; William Bird to author, June 2, 1962.
EH on famous statesmen: for EH's articles from Genoa see Audre Hanneman, *Ernest Hemingway, A Comprehensive Bibliography*, Princeton, 1967, pp. 134–135.
EH meets Eastman and Steffens: *Toronto*

Daily Star, Apr. 24, 1922, p. 1; Max Eastman, *Great Companions,* 1959, pp. 45–46; George Seldes to author, Feb., 1962; Slocombe, *The Tumult and the Shouting,* 1936, p. 204.
Visit to Beerbohm: Slocombe, pp. 175–176; Eastman, pp. 42–45; David Cecil, *Max, A Biography,* 1965, p. 396.
"A Divine Gesture": *Double Dealer,* Vol. 3 (May, 1922), pp. 267–268.
Poems, "Mitrailliatrice" and "Along with Youth": quoted from *Poetry,* Vol. 21 (Jan., 1923), pp. 193–195.
"Paris, 1922": unpublished one-sentence sketches, probably composed ca. late May, 1922.

Sec. 11. Going Back

SOURCES

Letters of EH: to his father, May 2, 1922; to his parents, May 24, 1922; to Howell Jenkins, ca. March 25 and June 14, 1922; to W. D. Horne, July 17, 1923.
EH's work: *Toronto Daily Star,* June 10, June 24, and July 22, 1922; *Toronto Star Weekly,* Nov. 17, 1923 and Jan. 12, 1924; *Green Hills of Africa,* 1935; *A Moveable Feast,* 1964.
Author's correspondence: from Maj. Gen. E. E. Dorman-O'Gowan, Feb. 24, 1962; from Hadley R. Mowrer, April 4, 1962.

NOTES

Springtime trips out of Paris: Enghien race track and hike to Compiègne: EH to his father, May 2, 1922; *A Moveable Feast,* pp. 51–52; Hadley R. Mowrer to author, April 4, 1962.
Visit to Mildred Aldrich: EH to Howell Jenkins, ca. March 25, 1922.
Reunion with Dorman-Smith at Chamby: EH to his parents, May 24, 1922; *Toronto Daily Star,* June 10, 1922; *Toronto Star Weekly,* Nov. 17, 1923; *Green Hills of Africa,* pp. 279–280; *A Moveable Feast,* p. 54. Hadley R. Mowrer to author, April 4, 1962.
Crossing the Pass of St. Bernard to Aosta: *Toronto Star Weekly,* Jan. 12, 1924. General Dorman-O'Gowan's Memoir of EH. Hadley R. Mowrer to author, April 4, 1962. *A Moveable Feast,* p. 53.
Return to Milan: Hadley R. Mowrer to author, April 4, 1962. *A Moveable Feast,* pp. 53–54. According to Hadley, they also paid a call on the Duc d'Aosta's brother, and were shown through the family mausoleum.
EH interviews Mussolini: *Toronto Daily Star,* June 24, 1922, pp. 5 and 16. Hadley R. Mowrer to author, April 4, 1962.
Return to Schio and Fossalta: EH and Hadley to Howell Jenkins, June 14, 1922; EH to W. D. Horne, July 17, 1923. *Toronto Daily Star,* July 22, 1922.

Sec. 12. Black Forest, Black Sea

SOURCES

Letters of EH: to his parents, May 24, 1922; to Harriet Monroe, July 16, 1922; to his father, Aug. 25, 1922; to Gertrude Stein, ca. Sept. 27, 1922; to John Bone, Oct. 27, 1922.
Other letters: John Bone to EH, Apr. 8, 1922;

Frank E. Mason to EH (cables), Oct. 1, 4, and 6, 1922; John Bone to EH (cable), Oct. 6, 1922; Bone to EH, Nov. 8, 1922. Hadley to Dr. and Mrs. Hemingway, Oct. 21, 1922.
EH's work: (a) Unpublished: "Schwartzwald" (poem). **(b) Published:** *"Ultimately"* (poem), *Double Dealer,* Vol. 3 (June, 1922). *Toronto Star Weekly,* Aug. 12, 1922, Nov. 17, 1923; *Toronto Daily Star,* Aug. 26, Sept. 1, 5, 9, 19, 30; Oct. 4, 9, 16, 18, 19, 20, 24, 25, 28; Nov. 3 and 14, 1922. "Minarets" story and "The Snows of Kilimanjaro," *First 49 Stories,* NY, 1938, pp. 195 and pp. 150–175.
Books: John Dos Passos, *The Best Times,* NY, 1966.
Author's interviews and correspondence: with Lewis Galantière, March, 1963; with William Bird, June, 1963. From Hadley R. Mowrer, April 7, 1962.

NOTES

EH's writing, summer of 1922: For his articles in the *Toronto Star* at this time, see Audre Hanneman, *Ernest Hemingway, A Comprehensive Bibliography,* Princeton, 1967, pp. 135–136. "Ultimately" appeared in *Double Dealer,* Vol. 3 (June, 1922), p. 337.
Baum, Dos Passos, and the Bal Musette: Hadley R. Mowrer to author, April 7, 1962; Dos Passos, *The Best Times,* NY, 1966, p. 141.
Bastille Day music: *Toronto Star Weekly,* Aug. 12, 1922, p. 11. One curious sidelight of this period is EH's refusal to go to Russia for the *Star,* as Bone had asked him to do (Bone to EH, Apr. 8, 1922). In May Bone advanced him a check for $465 to cover expenses, with a promise of two months' salary at $75 a week. When EH wrote Harriet Monroe on July 16, he enclosed a Notes-on-Contributors item which said that he was "at present in Russia as staff correspondent for the *Toronto Star.*" The original is stamped as received in Chicago, July 29, 1922. According to a note dated Sept. 7, 1962 (Roy Greenaway to William L. McGeary), EH later told Greenaway that he had rejected the Russian assignment because Russian hotels were notoriously poor and comfortless.
Flight to Strasbourg: *Toronto Daily Star,* Sept. 9, 1922, p. 8.
Black Forest: *Toronto Daily Star,* Sept. 1, p. 23; Sept. 5, p. 6; Sept. 19, p. 4; *Toronto Star Weekly,* Nov. 17, 1923, p. 11; Hadley R. Mowrer to author, April 7, 1962; Lewis Galantière to author, March, 1963; William Bird to author, June, 1963. EH alludes to the rented trout stream and a bankrupt hotelkeeper in Triberg who committed suicide in "The Snows of Kilimanjaro," *First 49 Stories,* NY, 1938, pp. 166–167.
"Schwartzwald": The poem was probably composed in August or September, 1922. EH to Harriet Monroe, July 16, 1922, alludes to her acceptance of the six poems he had sent her in the winter. They appeared under the title "Wanderings" in *Poetry,* Vol. 21 (Jan. 1923), pp. 193–195.
Visit to Dorman-Smith at Cologne: The Hemingways followed the Rhine to Frankfurt and went by boat past Coblenz and Bonn to Cologne.
Incident of the murdered policeman: *Toronto Star Weekly,* Sept. 30, 1922, p. 16.
EH goes to Constantinople: Hadley R. Mow-

rer to author, April 7, 1962. There is an allusion to the EH-Hadley quarrel in "The Snows of Kilimanjaro," *First 49 Stories*, NY, 1938, p. 162. Postcard to Gertrude Stein from Sofia, ca. Sept. 27, 1922. EH's secret pact with INS is evidenced in Frank Mason to EH, Oct. 1, 4, and 6; John Bone to EH, Oct. 6; and EH to Bone, Oct. 27, 1922. In this last letter, EH made up a cock-and-bull story to explain why his story on the Thracian refugees had been "pirated" (his word) by INS before it reached the *Star*: when he wrote the cable in Adrianople, his funds were low; he knew he could use the INS charge account to send it to Paris, where it would be transmitted to Somerville at the *Star*'s London office. But INS stole the story. EH reported that he had lately gone to Mason and "had it out" with him; Mason told him that he had put the story on the wire only after making sure that no Canadian papers subscribed to INS EH's account of the affair was supremely disingenuous, since he had been working for INS as well as the *Star* at this time. Bone replied to EH's explanation on Nov. 8, 1922. **EH's observations on Constantinople:** for a list of his *Star* articles on this trip, see Audre Hanneman, *Ernest Hemingway, A Comprehensive Bibliography*, Princeton, 1967, pp. 136–137. See especially *Toronto Daily Star*, Oct. 28, 1922, p. 17. The memories of the city by the dying writer in "The Snows of Kilimanjaro" are mainly erotic fantasy and hearsay. Like EH, Harry and his wife quarreled before he left Paris. Unlike EH, Harry "whored the whole time," fought a British gunner subaltern for a "hot Armenian slut," and "turned up at Pera Palace with a black eye" next morning. There is no evidence that Ernest behaved even remotely in such a fashion. On Anatolia, he derived his information from a Captain Wittal of the Indian Cavalry. "Their own artillery had fired on the troops and the British observer had cried like a child." The reference is to a British artillery major named Johnson. EH met Johnson and Wittal, who were acting as liaison officers with the press in Constantinople. Wittal told EH that Johnson had cried at the spectacle of Greek artillery bombarding their own infantry. (*Daily Star*, Nov. 3, 1922, p. 10.) This commentary provides insight into EH's customary use of material. He knew something about the terrain, had observed British troops frequenting bawdyhouses in Galata, and talked with some British officers about Anatolia. He wove these materials together and made them part of Harry's biography.
EH to Muradli: *Toronto Daily Star*, Nov. 3, 1922.
EH and Greek refugees in Adrianople: *Toronto Daily Star*, Oct. 20, p. 17 and Nov. 14, 1922, p. 7. See also "Minarets" story, *First 49 Stories*, NY, 1938, p. 195.
Return to Paris: Hadley to Dr. and Mrs. Hemingway, Oct. 21, 1922.

Sec. 13. Lausanne

SOURCES

Letters of EH: To Harriet Monroe, Nov. 16, 1922; to Hadley, Nov. 24 and 25 (telegrams) and Nov. 28, 1922; to Isabelle Simmons, early Dec., 1922 to W. D. Horne, July 17, 1923; to Edmund Wilson, Nov. 25, 1923; to author, Apr. 1, 1951.
Other letters: Ezra Pound to Dr. William Carlos Williams, Aug. 1, 1922; Frank E. Mason to EH (telegrams), Nov. 24, 25, 27, 28, and 29, 1922; Agnes von Kurowsky to EH, Dec. 22, 1922; E. E. Dorman-Smith to EH, Dec. 15, 1923.
EH's work: (a) Unpublished: account of Henry Strater, composed probably late spring, 1923; character sketch of Dave O'Neil, composed probably spring, 1923; deleted portion of " Big Two-Hearted River,' composed 1924. **(b) Published:** *Toronto Daily Star*, Jan. 27, 1923, Feb. 10, 1923; "They All Made Peace. What Is Peace?" *The Little Review*, vol. 9 (Spring, 1923); *Toronto Star Weekly*, Jan. 12, 1924; "Old Newsman Writes," *Esquire*, Vol. 2 (Dec. 1934); "a.d. Southern Style," *Esquire*, Vol. 3 (May, 1935); "The Malady of Power," *Esquire*, Vol. 4 (Nov., 1935); *A Moveable Feast*, 1964.
Books: Lincoln Steffens, *Autobiography*, 1931; Edmund Wilson, *The Shores of Light*, 1952.
Author's interviews and correspondence: with William Bird, June, 1963; with Henry Strater, July, 1964; with Mrs. Isabelle Simmons Godolphin, Oct., 1964. From Hadley R. Mowrer, April 7, 1962 and Sept. 8, 1965.

NOTES

Pound's "inquest": Pound to Dr. W. C. Williams, Aug. 1, 1922.
Bird's Three Mountains Press: Bird bought the place soon after his return from Germany. The seller was a French journalist, Roger Dévigne. Bird got the idea for the name of his company while poring through D. B. Updike's *Printing Types: Their History, Form and Use*. Vol. 1, plate 117 reproduced the Vulgate text of Psalm 121 from a large-letter edition in the Vatican Library, and Bird took special notice of the sentence: *"Levavi oculos meos in montes."* The three mountains of Paris—Montmartre, Montparnasse, and St. Geneviève—could serve as colophon, embodying Bird's initials. The triple peaks formed the W and the framework made the B. (William Bird to author, June 2, 1963).
EH notifies Harriet Monroe: EH to Miss Monroe, Nov. 16, 1922.
Meeting with Strater: Henry Strater to author, July, 1964. Other details from EH's unpublished sketch of Mike and Maggie Strater. Bill Bird was to use the "boxer portrait" as the basis for a woodcut which served as frontispiece for the Three Mountains Press edition of *in our time* (Paris, 1924).
Advice for Sylvia Beach; melon from Gertrude Stein: EH to Harriet Monroe, Nov. 16, 1922.
Writing "My Old Man": date of composition probably early November, 1922. EH sent it to Steffens at Lausanne sometime between Nov. 22 and Dec. 16, 1922.
Death of Parfrement: quotation from deleted portion of "Big Two-Hearted River" (1924).
EH's dislike of Walsh and Ford: *A Moveable Feast*, pp. 83 and 123. EH did not ac-

tually meet Ford until early 1924. Comment on Walsh in EH to Harriet Monroe, Nov. 16, 1922. EH had first met Walsh in June or July: EH to Harriet Monroe, July 16, 1922.

Dave O'Neil: from EH's unpublished sketch. The children of David and Barbara O'Neil were George, Horton, and Barbara. (Hadley R. Mowrer to author, Sept. 8, 1965.) George (once called Gidge) appears in "Cross-Country Snow" as Nick Adams's skiing companion.

Clemenceau interview: William Bird to author, June 2, 1963. EH mentions the interview and his story on it in "a.d. Southern Style," *Esquire*, Vol. 3 (May, 1935), p. 25.

Lausanne Peace Conference: *Toronto Daily Star*, Jan. 27, 1923.

EH's work for Hearst wire services: EH to author, April 1, 1951. Further details in Frank Mason to EH (telegrams), Nov. 24, 25, 27, 28, and 29, 1922; and in EH's articles, "Old Newsman Writes," *Esquire*, Vol. 2 (Dec., 1934), pp. 25-26 and "The Malady of Power," *Esquire*, Vol. 4 (Nov., 1935), pp. 31 and 198.

Illnesses of Hadley and EH: EH to Hadley (telegrams), Nov. 24 and 25, and letter of Nov. 28, 1922. The letter mentions EH's visit to the Gangwisch pension on Nov. 26 to reserve rooms for himself and Hadley, Dorman-Smith, and Isabelle Simmons. The pension was called Chalet Chamby.

Steffens admires EH stories: Steffens, *Autobiography*, NY, 1931, pp. 834-835.

W. B. Ryall: "The Malady of Power," *Esquire*, Vol. 4 (Nov., 1935), pp. 31 and 198. The exploding cigar incident is here, as well as EH's account of boxing with G. Ward Price, a British journalist who regularly trounced him—an unusual admission for EH.

EH's revised view of Mussolini: *Toronto Daily Star*, Feb. 10, 1923. EH still admired the one-eyed, bald-headed, fifty-nine-year-old Gabriele D'Annunzio, Prince of Monte Nevoso, a native of the Abruzzi. He combined a soldier's and a writer's life. EH had given a copy of his *The Flame* to Dorothy Connable in 1920. Although EH thought D'Annunzio "a little insane," he was still "a divinely brave swashbuckler." He was also, unhappily, a Fascist.

Loss of manuscripts: EH to author, April 1, 1951; Hadley R. Mowrer to author, April 7, 1962; *A Moveable Feast*, pp. 73-74, also tells of his return to Paris.

"They all made peace": Composition of poem described in EH to Edmund Wilson, Nov. 25, 1923: "I wrote it in the *wagon-restaurant* going back to Lausanne. Had been at a very fine lunch at Gertrude Stein's and talked there all afternoon and read a lot of her new stuff and then drank a big bottle of Beaune myself in the dining-car. Facing opening the wire again next morning I tried to analyze the conference." Letter printed in Wilson, *The Shores of Light*, NY, 1952, pp. 56-57, with EH's permission. The poem appeared in *The Little Review*, Vol. 9 (Spring, 1923), pp. 20-21.

Christmas holidays in Chamby: EH to Isabelle Simmons, early Dec., 1922; EH to W. D. Horne, July 17, 1923; *Toronto Star Weekly*, Jan. 12, 1924, p. 20; E. E. Dorman-Smith to EH, Dec. 15, 1923.

Fourteen avalanches: *Toronto Star Weekly*, Jan. 12, 1924, p. 20.

Sec. 14. Rapallo and Cortina

SOURCES

Letters of EH: to Gertrude Stein, ca. Feb. 11 or 18, 1923; to his father, March 26, 1923; to Ernest Walsh, ca. Sept., 1925; to F. Scott Fitzgerald, ca. Dec. 20, 1925; to author, April 1, 1951.

Other letters: Hadley to EH, telegram, March 24, 1923; Dorman-Smith To Whom It May Concern, April 8, 1923.

EH's work: (a) Unpublished: undated five-page holograph manuscript fragment, "The Bull Ring: Outline 1st Chapter"; undated account of Mike Strater; undated fragment on sheets, Rapallo, Feb., 1923; undated fragment on cats, Rapallo, Feb., 1923. **(b) Published:** articles on the Ruhr, *Toronto Daily Star*, April 14, 18, 21, 25, and 28; May 1, 2, 5, 9, 12, and 16; "Cat in the Rain," *In Our Time*, 1925; six miniature sketches, first published in *Little Review*, and afterwards collected in *in our time*, Paris, 1924; *A Moveable Feast*, 1964.

Books: Robert McAlmon, *Being Geniuses Together*, 1938; Robert E. Knoll, *McAlmon and the Lost Generation: A Self-Portrait*, 1962.

Author's interviews and correspondence: with Henry Strater, July, 1964; from Hadley R. Mowrer, Apr. 7, 1962 and June 29, 1966; from Gen. E. E. Dorman-O'Gowan, Feb. 24, 1962.

NOTES

Going to Rapallo: from holograph MS., "The Bull Ring."

EH's disappointment with Rapallo: EH to Gertrude Stein, ca. Feb. 11 or 18, 1923; undated fragment on sheets, ca. Feb., 1923; account of Strater, unpublished; Henry Strater to author, July, 1964.

Portraits of Hadley and EH: Strater to author, July, 1964.

Hadley compares EH's hair to that of Balzac: Hadley R. Mowrer to author, Apr. 7, 1962.

Meeting Edward O'Brien: *A Moveable Feast*, 1964, pp. 73-74.

Meeting Robert McAlmon: McAlmon, *Being Geniuses Together*, London, 1938, pp. 154-155. Robert E. Knoll, ed., *McAlmon and the Lost Generation*, Lincoln, Nebraska, 1962, pp. 11, 88-89, 107-108, 144-148; 184-185.

EH echoes "The Waste Land"; notes for "Cat in the Rain": Fragment on cats, Rapallo, 1923. Identification of EH and Hadley with the persons of the story is my surmise. EH denied to Fitzgerald (letter of ca. Dec. 20, 1925) that the story was autobiographical, asserting that the innkeeper was modeled on a hotel manager in Cortina, and that the young husband and wife were drawn from a "Harvard kid" and his girl whom EH had met in Genoa. These statements should probably be regarded with suspicion.

Walking tour with the Pounds: EH to author, April 1, 1951; Hadley R. Mowrer to author, April 7, 1962, and June 29, 1966.

Cortina d'Ampezzo: EH to Ernest Walsh, ca. Sept., 1925; Hadley R. Mowrer to author, Apr. 7, 1962 and June 29, 1966.

EH composes miniatures for "Little Review": EH to author, April 1, 1951, confirms that the Mons stories were from Dorman-Smith, as

does the Dorman-O'Gowan Memoir of EH, sent to author, Feb. 24, 1962. Gertrude Stein and Henry Strater were EH's only friends who had seen Spanish bullfights before March, 1923, except Dos Passos, whom he had seen only once. The Greek cabinet ministers were executed for treason on Nov. 28, 1922: Gounaris, Stratos, Baltatzes, Theotokes, Protopadakis, and Hadjianestes. I have been unable to discover the source of the first miniature about the kitchen corporal.
Ruhr assignment from Bone: Hadley to EH, telegram from Cortina to Paris, March 24, 1923; EH to his father, March 26, 1923. EH's Ruhr articles, *Toronto Daily Star*, Apr. 14, p. 4; Apr. 18, p. 4; Apr. 21, pp. 1 and 7; Apr. 25, pp. 1–2; Apr. 28, pp. 1–2; May 1, p. 28, continued May 2, p. 1; May 5, pp. 1 and 34; May 9, p. 17; May 12, p. 19; May 16, p. 19. EH's safe-conduct from Capt. Dorman-Smith is dated April 8, 1923.
EH returns to Cortina: Hadley R. Mowrer to author, Apr. 7, 1962.
EH composes "Out of Season": *A Moveable Feast*, 1964, p. 75. EH later told Fitzgerald that the story was an almost literal transcription of what happened. He and Hadley had had a row. When he came in from an unproductive fishing trip, he wrote the whole story right off on the typewriter without punctuation. It was meant to emphasize the tragedy of the drunken guide, who hanged himself in the stable after EH reported him to the hotel manager and got him sacked. EH said that he left out the hanging because he wanted to write one tragic story that did not contain violence. EH to Fitzgerald, ca. Dec. 20, 1925.

Sec. 15. Iberia

SOURCES

Letters of EH: to Gertrude Stein, June 20, 1923; to Isabelle Simmons, June 24, 1923; to W. D. Horne, July 17, 1923; to Robert McAlmon, Aug. 5, 1923; to F. Scott Fitzgerald, ca. Dec. 20, 1925.
Other letters: William Bird to Ezra Pound, Sept. 17, 1923; William Bird to R. E. Knoll, May 23, 1958 and Sept. 30, 1961.
EH's work: (a) Unpublished: undated sketch on housework, composed ca. mid-July, 1923; undated sketch on Henry Strater's map of Spain, composed ca. fall, 1923. **(b) Published:** *Toronto Star Weekly*, Sept. 15 Oct. 20, and Oct. 27, 1923; *Death in the Afternoon*, 1932.
Books and brochures: Lincoln Steffens, *Autobiography*, 1931; Malcolm Cowley, *Exile's Return*, 1951; Robert E. Knoll, editor, *McAlmon and the Lost Generation*, 1962. McAlmon's undated brochure for Contact Editions, 2 pp., issued spring, 1923; two undated broadsides from the Three Mountains Press, issued spring, 1923.
Author's interviews and correspondence: with William Bird, June, 1962; Toronto group interview, Jan., 1965. From Hadley R. Mowrer, April 7, 1962.

NOTES

EH's plans for first trip to Spain: William Bird to R. E. Knoll, May 23, 1958, quoted in Knoll, *McAlmon and the Lost Generation,*

Lincoln, Nebraska, 1962, pp. 225–226. Undated and unpublished sketch of Strater as mapmaker, composed by EH, ca. fall, 1923. **Train trip to Bayonne:** *McAlmon and the Lost Generation*, p. 230.
EH sees first bullfight, in Madrid: Bird to author, June, 1962; EH to W. D. Horne, July 17, 1923.
EH watches McAlmon's behavior in Seville: *Death in the Afternoon*, 1932, p. 496.
EH gets proofsheets of Three Stories and Ten Poems: EH to McAlmon, Aug. 5, 1923, used by courtesy of Professor Norman Holmes Pearson.
Pound's parting admonition to Hadley: Hadley R. Mowrer to author, April 7, 1962.
EH in Seville, Ronda, and Granada: Bird to Knoll, Sept. 30, 1961, used by courtesy of Professor Knoll. *McAlmon and the Lost Generation*, p. 231.
McAlmon announces EH's forthcoming short stories: undated two-page Contact Editions brochure, issued spring, 1923.
Bird announces forthcoming book by EH: two undated broadsides issued by Bird, spring, 1923. Further details from William Bird to Ezra Pound, Sept. 17, 1923, and Bird to author, June, 1962.
EH plans to take Hadley to Spain: EH to Gertrude Stein, June 20, 1923, and EH to Isabelle Simmons, June 24, 1923.
EH and Hadley in Pamplona: EH to Horne, July 17, 1923; Hadley R. Mowrer to author, Apr. 7, 1962. *Toronto Star Weekly*, Oct. 27, 1923, p. 33.
EH admires Villalta and Maera: *Death in the Afternoon*, 1932, pp. 70, 77–82, 86, and 161. EH's article on Pamplona in the *Toronto Star Weekly*, Oct. 27, 1923, does not mention Villalta, but gives considerable space to Maera and Algabeno.
Hadley's illness and EH's complaints: from a one-page typed sketch, unpublished, composed mid-July, 1923.
Birth-control story: Steffens, *Autobiography*, 1931, p. 835. Hadley's severe cold was contracted at Pamplona after a deluge of rain which interrupted the bullfights in the middle of the week. It was apparently in late July or August, after their return to Paris, that EH first met Malcolm Cowley at Ezra Pound's. Cowley, *Exile's Return*, NY, 1951, p. 120.
EH derives sketch about the King of Greece from anecdote by Shorty Wornall: See *Toronto Star Weekly*, Sept. 15, 1923, p. 15.

Sec. 16. The Bearing of the Young

SOURCES

Letters of EH: to Gertrude Stein, Oct. 11 and Nov. 9, 1923; to Sylvia Beach, Nov. 6, 1923; to Edmund Wilson, Nov. 11 and Nov. 25, 1923; to his parents, Dec. 18, 1923 and Jan. 12, 1924; to John Bone (2 letters) ca. December 26, 1923.
Other letters: John Bone to EH, Aug. 18, 1923; Gregory Clark to EH, Aug. 31, 1923; Hadley Hemingway to Dr. and Mrs. Hemingway, Sept. 15, 1923; William Bird to Ezra Pound, Sept. 17, 1923; Ezra Pound to EH (Bird's letter with Pound's postscript) ca. Sept. 20, 1923; Hadley Hemingway to Isabelle Simmons, Oct. 12, 1923; Hadley Hemingway to Sylvia Beach,

Nov. 27, 1923; Grace Hemingway to EH, Dec. 26, 1923.
EH's work: (a) Unpublished: sketch about Cedarvale Mansions apartment, ca. Oct. 15, 1923; sketch on Reade and Clark, Oct. or Nov., 1923. **(b) Published:** *Toronto Daily Star,* Sept. 25, Oct. 4, 5, 6, 8, 1923; *Toronto Star Weekly,* Sept. 15, Oct. 20 and 27, Nov. 3 and 17, 1923; *Three Stories and Ten Poems,* late August, 1923; *transatlantic review,* Vol. 2 (October, 1924).
Books: Edmund Wilson, *The Shores of Light,* 1952; Charles A. Fenton, *The Apprenticeship of Ernest Hemingway,* 1954; Morley Callaghan, *That Summer in Paris,* 1963; Ross Harkness, *J. E. Atkinson of the "Star,"* 1964.
Author's interviews and correspondence: with William Bird, June, 1962; with Hadley R. Mowrer, Aug., 1962, with Dorothy Connable, July, 1964; with Sterling S. Sanford, July, 1964; with Isabelle Simmons Godolphin, Oct., 1964; from Hadley R. Mowrer, Aug. 12, 1962; from W. L. McGeary, various communications 1962–68; from Ernest Smith, April 28, 1964; from James A. Cowan, Feb. 15, 1965; from Roy Greenaway, Feb. 16, 1965.

NOTES

EH welcomed home by Bone and Clark: Bone to EH, Aug. 18 and Clark to EH, Aug. 31, 1923. Bone had indicated his interest in EH's return to Canada in letters of Feb. 20, Aug. 30, Nov. 2, and Dec. 13, 1922. EH had evidently promised to come back as early as Feb., 1923, while he was in Rapallo. Bone's reply of March 7, 1923, says: "Delighted to know from your last paragraph that you expect to be in Toronto ready for work in September. That will be splendid."
Harry Hindmarsh's treatment of EH: Ross Harkness, *J. E. Atkinson of the "Star,"* p. 164; Morley Callaghan, *That Summer in Paris,* pp. 22–24. Charles A. Fenton, *The Apprenticeship of Ernest Hemingway,* pp. 244–256.
EH's living quarters: Hadley to Dr. and Mrs. Hemingway, Sept. 15, 1923; unpublished sketch by EH, ca. Oct. 15, 1923. When the Murphy bed was let down, it blocked the way to the sunroom, which served as a living room. When Ernest Smith and Arthur Dunstan came to call on EH, bringing a bottle, they had to crawl over Hadley's feet as she lay half asleep. EH introduced them to her in the process. (Ernest Smith to author, Apr. 28, 1964.)
Bird's plans for "in our time": Bird to Pound, Sept. 17, 1923, forwarded by Pound to EH with a postscript, ca. Sept. 20, 1923.
EH in Sudbury: EH's articles on Sudbury appeared in *Toronto Daily Star,* Sept. 25, 1923, p. 4 (two stories). EH's account of reading Conrad is in the Joseph Conrad Supplement, *transatlantic review,* Vol. 2 (Oct., 1924), pp. 341–342.
EH in New York: EH to Gertrude Stein, Oct. 11, 1923.
Asks Isabelle Simmons to interview Megan Lloyd George: Isabelle Simmons Godolphin to author, Oct. 22, 1964. EH's despatches on Lloyd George appeared in *Toronto Daily Star,* Oct. 4, p. 12, unsigned; Oct. 5, p. 14; Oct. 6, pp. 3 and 17, and Oct. 8, p. 14; *Star Weekly,* Oct. 6, pp. 1–2.

EH scooped on Hulbert speech: Ross Harkness, *J. E. Atkinson of the "Star,"* p. 164.
Birth of John H. N. Hemingway: EH to Gertrude Stein, Oct. 11, 1923; Hadley Hemingway to Isabelle Simmons, Oct. 12, 1923; Dorothy Connable to author, July, 1964.
EH's household before and after baby's homecoming: unpublished sketch by EH, ca. Oct. 15, 1923; EH to Gertrude Stein, Nov. 9, 1923.
EH activates review by Edmund Wilson: EH to Wilson, Nov. 11 and 25, 1923, printed in *The Shores of Light,* 1952, pp. 55–57. Rascoe's column mentioning *Three Stories and Ten Poems* appeared Oct. 21, 1923, and may be the first public mention of EH's book in the U.S.
EH's dislike of Canada and journalism: EH to Sylvia Beach, Nov. 6, 1923, printed in *Mercure de France,* Autumn, 1963, pp. 105–107. EH to Gertrude Stein, Nov. 9, 1923. On Nov. 27th, Hadley wrote Sylvia Beach that coming to Toronto was "the first big mistake" that she and EH had made.
EH on suicide: EH to Gertrude Stein, Nov. 9, 1923. This is one of his earliest references to suicide. The note recurs in times of stress throughout his life.
Meeting Morley Callaghan: Callaghan, *That Summer in Paris,* pp. 27–29.
EH's views on Clark and Reade: Unpublished sketch, fall, 1923.
Clark's views on EH: Gregory Clark, Toronto group interview, Jan., 1965, transcript, p. 19. It is curious that three out of four of EH's wives were unable to recall his slight speech impediment, which was still faintly perceptible in tape recordings made towards the end of his life.
EH's passion for writing: James A. Cowan to author, Feb. 15, 1965; Callaghan, *That Summer in Paris,* pp. 29–30.
Spoiled copies of "in our time": William Bird to author, June, 1962. Edmund Wilson did a combined review of *Three Stories and Ten Poems* and *in our time* in *Dial,* Vol. 77 (Oct., 1924), pp. 340–341.
EH's trip to Oak Park: EH to his parents, Dec. 18, 1923 and Jan. 12, 1924; Grace Hemingway to EH, Dec. 26, 1923; Sterling Sanford to author, July, 1964. Uncle Tyley Hancock was then seventy-six. Sanford was an engineer with Detroit Edison. It was he who took the snapshot of EH and young Leicester standing on the snowy lawn. Marcelline Sanford had ordered a dozen copies of *in our time* for use as Christmas presents. Bill Bird filled the order. On reading the book, Marcelline decided that its contents were too gamy for Christmas purposes and sent the books back to Paris. (William Bird to author, June, 1962.)
EH resigns from "Star": Two undated memoranda from EH to John Bone, one typed, one holograph, undated, ca. Dec. 26, 1923. The typed copy is signed "Ernest" and the other is a much worked-over first draft from which the final version was evidently made, if indeed it was actually sent. There is a persistent tradition among EH's former *Star* colleagues that he typed out a long list of his grievances against Hindmarsh, pasting the pages end to end and posting the long screed on the office bulletin board. Hindmarsh ignored it and EH took it home to show to Hadley.
Lease-jumping at Cedarvale Mansions: James A. Cowan to author, Feb. 15, 1965. Cowan

was married to Grace Williams in the nearly empty apartment in mid-January, 1924. The infant John was tethered to the piano leg during the brief ceremony.
Departure from Toronto: Mary Lowrey Ross, Toronto group interview, Jan., 1965.

Sec. 17. Carpenter's Loft

SOURCES

Letters of EH: to Auguste Fabiani, Aug. 29, 1923; to George Breaker, ca. Oct. 15, 1923; to Gertrude Stein, Nov. 9, 1923; Feb. 17, 1924; ca. late June, 1924; ca. July 10, 1924; July 13, 1924; to Sylvia Beach, July 24, 1924; to Frank Crowninshield, ca. Aug., 1924; to George Breaker, Aug. 27, 1924; to Howell Jenkins, Nov. 9, 1924; to Horace Liveright, June 18, 1925; to Malcolm Cowley, Aug. 25, 1948; to author, April 1, 1951; to Bernard Berenson, March 20–21 and Apr. 13, 1953.
Other letters: George Breaker to Hadley (wire) Oct. 17, 1923. Hadley to Breaker, ca. Oct. 20, 1923; Breaker to Hadley, Oct. 27, 1923, and Jan. 12, 1924; Hadley to Breaker, March 26, 1924; Hadley to Grace Hemingway, Apr. 10–11, 1924; William Bird to Bernard J. Poli, Nov. 10, 1961.
EH'S work: (a) **Unpublished:** original opening of "Indian Camp," composed ca. Feb., 1924; sketch of Ford and Stella, composed ca. May or June, 1924; "The Art of the Short Story," composed June, 1959. (b) **Published:** "Indian Camp," *transatlantic review,* Vol. 1 (April, 1924); "Chronique: And Out of America," *transatlantic review,* Vol. 2 (July, 1924); *Toronto Star Weekly,* Sept. 13, 1924; *Death in the Afternoon,* 1932; *A Moveable Feast,* 1964.
Books and articles: Ford, "Chroniques: Plymouth, June," *transatlantic review,* Vol. 2 (July, 1924); Sisley Huddleston, *Paris Salons, Cafés, Studios,* 1928; Lincoln Steffens, *Autobiography,* 1931; Ford, introduction to *A Farewell to Arms,* Mod. Lib. edition, 1932; Ford, *It Was the Nightingale,* 1933; Robert McAlmon, *Being Geniuses Together,* 1938; Donald C. Gallup, "The Making of *The Making of Americans,*" *New Colophon,* 1950; William Carlos Williams, *Autobiography,* 1951; Sheridan Baker, "Hemingway's Two-Hearted River," *Michigan Alumnus Quarterly Review,* Vol. 65 (Feb. 28, 1959); Harold Loeb, *The Way It Was,* 1959; John Dos Passos, *The Best Times,* 1966; Bernard J. Poli, *Ford Madox Ford and the "transatlantic review,"* 1967.
Author's interviews and correspondence: with John Dos Passos, April, 1962; with Walter Johnson, April, 1962; with William Bird, June, 1962; with Hadley R. Mowrer, August, 1962; with Isabelle Simmons Godolphin, Oct., 1964. From Donald Ogden Stewart, Feb. 20, 1951; from Margaret Anderson, March 31, 1962; from Hadley R. Mowrer, April 7, 1962; from Frank Hines, June 21, 1963; from Kitty Cannell, Oct. 13, 1963, and May 11, 1964; from Mrs. William Carlos Williams, Aug. 3, 1965; from Harold Loeb, June 6, 1964 and Dec. 27, 1965.

NOTES

EH in New York: Margaret Anderson to author, March 31, 1962; Walter Johnson to author, April 5, 1962; Isabelle Simmons Godolphin to author, Oct. 22, 1964.

EH's new apartment at 113, rue Notre Dame des Champs: Hadley to Dr. and Mrs. Hemingway, April 10–11, 1924; Hadley R. Mowrer to author, April 7, 1962. The latter also describes the Chautards, the naming of Bumby, and the Rohrbach family. EH quotes Mme. Rohrbach on working hours in "The Snows of Kilimanjaro," *First 49 Stories,* NY, 1938, p. 168.
EH as subeditor of "transatlantic": EH to Gertrude Stein, Nov. 9, 1923, mentions Pound's invitation to return to Paris and help edit the *transatlantic review.*
Ford's editorial quarters at 29, Quai d'Anjou: William Bird to Bernard J. Poli, Nov. 10, 1961, excerpted in Poli, *Ford Madox Ford and the "transatlantic review,"* Syracuse, NY, 1967, p. 26.
Ford's first meeting with EH: *It Was the Nightingale,* Philadelphia, 1933, pp. 295–296. Another account is in Ford's introduction to Modern Library edition of *A Farewell to Arms,* NY, 1932, pp. x–xiv. EH described his task as a *corvée* (drudgery) in EH to author, Apr. 1, 1951, and gave permission to quote at that time. EH also portrays Ford in *A Moveable Feast,* NY, 1964, pp. 83–84.
EH meets Harold Loeb: Loeb, *The Way It Was,* NY, 1959, pp. 190–194. Loeb was born Oct. 18, 1891, and was graduated from Lawrenceville School and Princeton (Class of 1913). He tried his hand at business, spent two years as an army sergeant during the war, and then invested half his patrimony to buy a partnership in a New York bookstore called The Sunwise Turn. In 1921, he separated from his wife, the former Marjorie Content, sold his partnership, went to Paris, founded *Broom,* and met Kitty Cannell. She introduced him to Ford, whom she had known in London before the war. Details on Loeb's life are from *The Way It Was.* He there misdates his first meeting with EH as of the fall of 1923, when EH was in Toronto.
Kitty Cannell resents EH's neglect of Hadley: Kitty Cannell to author, Oct. 13, 1953.
Hadley's investments: George Breaker of St. Louis, entrusted with Hadley's securities, had advised selling some $19,000 worth of United Railway 4 per cent bonds for $10,802.56. The money was deposited with his broker, Mark C. Steinberg. Breaker indicated that he had bought securities subject to Hadley's approval, but he did not name them. On Jan. 12, 1924, he said that he and his wife Helen were coming to Paris about Feb. 15 and would discuss the matter then. But they had not appeared by the end of March. These details are recorded in EH to Breaker from Toronto, ca. Oct. 15, 1923; Breaker to Hadley (wire) Oct. 17, 1923; Hadley to Breaker, ca. Oct. 20, 1923; Breaker to Hadley, Oct. 27, 1923; Breaker to Hadley, Jan. 12, 1924; Hadley to Breaker, March 26, 1924.
EH persuades Ford to publish "The Making of Americans": Gertrude Stein, *The Autobiography of Alice B. Toklas,* N.Y., 1933, pp. 264–265. EH to Gertrude Stein, Feb. 17, 1924, quoted in Donald C. Gallup, "The Making of *The Making of Americans,*" *The New Colophon,* New York, 1950, pp. 58–59. Ernest later recalled that Gertrude "disliked the drudgery of revision and the obligation to make her writing intelligible. . . . The book

began magnificently, went on very well for a long way with great stretches of great brilliance and then went on endlessly in repetitions that a more conscientious and less lazy writer would have put in the waste basket. . . . For publication in the [*transatlantic review*] I had to read all of Miss Stein's proof for her as this was a work which gave her no happiness." (*A Moveable Feast,* N.Y., 1964, pp. 17–18.)
Reviews of EH's first two books: *Three Stories and Ten Poems* reviewed by K.J., and *in our time* reviewed by M. R. [Marjorie Reid] in *transatlantic review,* Vol. 1 (April, 1924), pp. 246–248.
"Indian Camp" published: *transatlantic review,* Vol. 1 (April, 1924), pp. 230–234. EH's original unpublished opening of the story covered eight handwritten pages.
Bumby christened: Hadley to Grace Hemingway, April 10–11, 1924; EH to Bernard Berenson, April 13, 1953. EH's leanings towards Catholicism, initiated by the Italian priest in 1918, were now in abeyance. Hadley never saw him attend Mass or perform any acts of worship during the period 1921–26. (Hadley R. Mowrer to author, August, 1962.)
EH and Ford discuss EH's fame: Hadley to Grace Hemingway, April 10–11, 1924. **Ford likes EH's prose:** *It Was the Nightingale,* Phila. 1933, p. 323. **Ford describes EH's way of speaking:** Introduction to *A Farewell to Arms,* Mod. Lib. ed., NY, 1932, p. xvii.
EH's domestic mornings: *A Moveable Feast,* NY, 1964, p. 96. The cat, Mr. F. Puss, had been rescued in 1923 by Harold Loeb from a pit near the Trajan Column in Rome. It was on the verge of a nervous breakdown from cold and hunger. Loeb to author, June 6, 1964.
EH's activities around the Quarter: boxing with professionals (EH to Berenson, March 20–21, 1953); **buying pesetas** (EH to Breaker, Aug. 27, 1924); **boxing with friends** (Loeb to author, June 6, 1964; and Loeb, *The Way It Was,* NY, 1959, p. 216); **bicycle races with Ward** (*A Moveable Feast,* pp. 64–65); **tennis** (Williams, *Autobiography,* NY, 1951, p. 218). Dr. Williams and his wife went to supper with the Hemingways at the sawmill apartment on June 3, and then attended the prizefights. Next morning, Dr. Williams examined Bumby, who was two pounds underweight but otherwise sound. He retracted the baby's foreskin, causing him to cry, much to EH's chagrin (Mrs. William Carlos Williams to author, Aug. 3, 1965); **prizefights** (Sisley Huddleston, *Paris Salons, Cafés, Studios,* NY, 1928, pp. 121–123). EH and Larry Gains: Gains was a Negro boxer from Toronto who reached Paris about July 1, 1923 and was introduced to Louis Anastasie of 136, rue Pelleport, a boxing promoter who immediately signed Gains to a three-year contract. Gains knew no French, but was assured by Jack Walker, another Negro boxer, that the contract was "all right," even though Walker himself knew only a "little sporting-paper French." The contract gave Anastasie absolute supervision of Gains and a 25 per cent cut on his earnings. EH wrote an eleven-page letter on the boat train to Cherbourg before the *Andania* sailed Aug. 17, 1923. The letter recommended Gains to Maître Auguste Fabiani of 5, Place Edouard, Paris. Gains was to deliver the letter to Fabiani. Guy Hickok had recommended the move to EH and had also named Fabiani.

EH meets Donald Ogden Stewart: Stewart to author, Feb. 20, 1951.
Dos Passos's visits: Dos Passos to author, April, 1962 and Dos Passos, *The Best Times,* NY, 1966, pp. 141–142.
EH exhorts Ella Winter: Lincoln Steffens, *Autobiography,* NY, 1931, p. 835.
EH writes "Big Two-Hearted River": EH to Malcolm Cowley, Aug. 25, 1948. **Omits reference to Nick Adams's wounds:** *A Moveable Feast,* 1964, p. 76. **EH's comment on name of river:** "The Art of the Short Story," 1959. See Sheridan Baker, "Hemingway's Two-Hearted River," *Michigan Alumnus Quarterly Review,* Vol. 65 (Feb. 28, 1959), pp. 142–149, for identification of the river in the story as the Fox.
EH on Ford and Stella: unpublished sketch, composed ca. May or June, 1924.
F. M. Ford's trip to New York: Bernard J. Poli, *Ford Madox Ford and the "transatlantic review,"* Syracuse, New York, 1967, pp. 98–99. It would appear that Ford left Paris late in May, stopped over briefly in England, sailed for New York early in June, and did not return until July 3, when his ship docked at Cherbourg. This left EH to see the July number through the press and to assemble the contents of the August number by about the first of July, before Ford's return. Ford's announcement of his appointment of EH as pro-tem editor was headed, "Chroniques: Plymouth, June," and appeared in the July number (Vol. 2, pp. 94 ff). EH's account of his reluctance to take over the editorship in Ford's absence was given about a year later in EH to Horace Liveright, from Paris, June 18, 1925.
EH's satirical editorial: EH's "Chronique: And Out of America" in *transatlantic review,* Vol. 2 (July, 1924), pp. 102–103. In the same number was Donald Ogden Stewart's story "Fragment IV," which was identified as part of Stewart's novel, *John Brown's Body* (pp. 116–120).
Frank Hines's visit: Frank Hines to author, June 21, 1963.
EH and Hadley in Spain (1924): EH to Gertrude Stein, two postcards showing Gitanillo in action, sent from Spain, late June, 1924; *Toronto Star Weekly,* Sept. 13, 1924, p. 18 (EH's final article to the *Star*); EH to Gertrude Stein, ca. July 10 and July 13, with a further postcard of July 13, 1924; EH to Sylvia Beach, postmarked July 24, 1924; EH to Frank Crowninshield, ca. Aug., 1924; Donald Ogden Stewart to author, Feb. 20, 1951. **On attitudes of Dorman-Smith and Sally Bird to bullfights:** *Death in the Afternoon,* NY, 1932, pp. 496–497.
First visit to Burguete: Dos Passos to author, April, 1962; William Bird to author, June, 1962; R. McAlmon, *Being Geniuses Together,* London, 1938, pp. 212–217; Dos Passos, *The Best Times,* NY, 1966, pp. 156–157.
EH's admiration for Spain and Spaniards: EH to Howell Jenkins, Nov. 9, 1924.

Sec. 18. Transatlantic

SOURCES

Letters of EH: to Gertrude Stein, ca. Aug. 2 (note) ca. Aug. 5 (letter), Aug. 9 and 15, Sept. 14, and Oct. 10, 1924; to George Breaker,

Aug. 27, 1924; to Edmund Wilson, Oct. 18, 1924; to McAlmon, Nov. 20, 1924; to author, Aug. 26, 1952.
Other letters: Ford to Gertrude Stein, Sept. 18, 1924.
EH's work: (a) Unpublished: deleted conclusion to "Big Two-Hearted River," composed early August, 1924; **(b) Published:** "Mr. and Mrs. Elliot" (first called "Mr. and Mrs. Smith") in *The Little Review,* Vol. 10 (Autumn-Winter, 1924–25); "The Soul of Spain with McAlmon and Bird the Publishers," *Querschnitt,* Vol. 4 (Autumn, 1924, and November, 1924); "The Lady Poets with Foot Notes," *Querschnitt,* Vol. 4 (Nov., 1924); "The Age Demanded," *Querschnitt,* Vol. 5 (Feb., 1925); "Big Two-Hearted River," *This Quarter,* Vol. 1 (May, 1925); "The Doctor and the Doctor's Wife," *transatlantic review,* Vol. 2 (Dec., 1924); "Cross-Country Snow," *transatlantic review,* Vol. 2 (Jan., 1925); *A Moveable Feast,* 1964.
Books and articles: Ford's editorial comments on EH, *transatlantic review,* Vol. 2 (August and November, 1924); Edmund Wilson, "Mr. Hemingway's Dry-Points," *Dial,* Vol. 77 (Oct., 1924); Burton Rascoe, *We Were Interrupted,* 1947; Edmund Wilson, *The Shores of Light,* 1952; Donald Gallup, ed., *The Flowers of Friendship,* 1953; Harold Loeb, *The Way It Was,* 1959; Richard M. Ludwig, ed., *Letters of Ford Madox Ford,* 1965; Bernard J. Poli, *Ford Madox Ford and the "transatlantic review,"* 1967.
Author's interviews and correspondence: with Edmund Wilson, January, 1953; with Harold Loeb, Oct., 1959; with W. B. Smith, April, 1964; from Kitty Cannell, Oct. 13, 1963.

NOTES

News items of early August, 1924: EH to Gertrude Stein undated note and letter of ca. Aug. 2 and 5, and letters of Aug. 9 and 15, 1924. Mme. Chautard's stuffed dog reappears in a drunken colloquy between Jake Barnes and Bill Gorton in Ch. VIII of *The Sun Also Rises.* Identification supplied by W. B. Smith to author, April, 1964.
EH's quarrel with Ford: Ford's critique of EH's August number appeared in *transatlantic,* Vol. 2 (Aug., 1924), p. 213. Since Ford had reached Cherbourg on his homeward trip on July 4, he was back in Paris in time to insert this critique in the August number before it went to press. EH was then in Spain, and it is doubtful if he saw Ford's remarks until his return to Paris early in August. EH reported on the crisis in letters to Gertrude Stein, ca. Aug. 5, Aug. 9, and Aug. 15, 1924.
EH secures help of Krebs Friend: EH to Gertrude Stein, Aug. 15, 1924. Nathan Asch's description of Friend is quoted in Poli, *Ford Madox Ford and the "transatlantic review,"* Syracuse, NY, 1967, p. 117. According to EH, the arrangement with Friend called for a monthly grant of $200 for six months. Friend would then have the option of buying Ford out or continuing the monthly grants for another six months. At first, according to EH, Ford climbed his highest horse, demanding more money and different arrangements, and calling Friend a businessman and a foe to all artists. But he soon accepted the terms.

EH tells Gertrude Stein about having finished "Big Two-Hearted River": EH to Gertrude Stein, Aug. 15, 1924, from *The Flowers of Friendship,* ed. Donald Gallup, N.Y., 1953, pp. 164–165. Some of Ernest's tentative literary judgments were also in the deleted portion of "Big Two-Hearted River." He repeated his recent praise of E. E. Cummings's *Enormous Room* as "one of the great books." Next to Cummings, Don Stewart "had the most." It sometimes appeared in his books about the Haddocks. "Ring Lardner maybe. Very maybe." McAlmon had something. Young Nathan Asch, who had shown Ernest some of his stories that spring, also "had something but you couldn't tell. Jews go bad quickly." Then there were the "old guys like Sherwood" Anderson and the "older guys like Dreiser." None of these statements was a reasoned literary judgment, which would not in any case have been relevant to Ernest's story of Nick's ruminations beside the Fox River on a summer afternoon.
EH's esthetic views: from deleted portion of "Big Two-Hearted River," composed Aug., 1924.
His comment on the difficulty of writing: EH to Gertrude Stein, Aug 15, 1924 from *The Flowers of Friendship,* ed. Donald Gallup, NY, 1953, pp. 164–165.
EH's new stories: "The Doctor and the Doctor's Wife" was recognized by Dr. Hemingway as based on the log-sawing episode of the summer of 1911 (Dr. Hemingway to EH, March 8, 1925). "Soldier's Home" changed the home-town locale from Oak Park to Oklahoma; the protagonist was Harold Krebs, a name probably compounded from the first names of Harold Loeb and Krebs Friend. "The End of Something" and "The Three-Day Blow" both used the first name of Marjorie Bump of Petoskey, and the first name of Bill Smith, and the locale was Horton Bay (called Hortons Bay) and "The Point" at the western end of the Bay below the Dilworths' Pinehurst Cottage. See Constance C. Montgomery, *Hemingway in Michigan,* NY, 1966, pp. 128–140. "Cross-Country Snow" was plainly related to EH's skiing with George O'Neil near Chamby-sur-Montreux in late December, 1922 and January, 1923. Hadley was called Helen in the story, and Nick Adams said that she was pregnant, as Hadley was at this time. "Cat in the Rain" has already been discussed in "Rapallo and Cortina," above. The original typescript of "Mr. and Mrs. Elliot" is in the Jane Heap Collection at the University of Wisconsin Library in Milwaukee, and plainly shows that the first title was "Mr. and Mrs. Smith." That EH meant the story to relate to Mr. and Mrs. Chard Powers Smith is proved by an interchange of letters between EH and Smith (Smith to EH, Jan. 1, 1927 and EH's reply, undated but written "several weeks" later).
EH sends book manuscript to Stewart: EH to George Breaker, Aug. 27, 1924, says he will have his first full-length book ready in two weeks and that Dos Passos will take it to New York. EH to Edmund Wilson, Oct. 18, 1924, says that the book was finished and sent to Don Stewart at the Yale Club, NYC, "about three weeks ago." This would make the date of transmission ca. Sept. 28, 1924, or some two weeks after the date predicted in the letter to Breaker.

Loeb's interest in EH's book: *The Way It Was*, NY, 1959, pp. 216–219.
Kitty Cannell's forebodings: Kitty Cannell to author, Oct. 13, 1963.
Episode with Leon Fleischman: Loeb, *The Way It Was*, NY, 1959, pp. 225–227 and Kitty Cannell to author, Oct. 13, 1963.
EH finds outlet in "Der Querschnitt": for listing of his poems published in this magazine, see above (Sources).
EH on Flechtheim: EH to author, Aug. 26, 1952. In *A Moveable Feast*, p. 71, EH repeated his personal misremembrance that he sold some stories at this time to the *Frankfurter Zeitung*, although in fact none of his prose appeared there until 1927. Flechtheim did, however, publish the first short story of EH's to appear in Germany. "The Undefeated" appeared in 2 parts in *Der Querschnitt*, Vol. 5 (Summer, 1925 and July, 1925), pp. 521–535 and 624–633, with the title "*Stierkampf.*"
Wilson reviews EH's first two books: Edmund Wilson, "Mr. Hemingway's Dry-Points," *Dial*, Vol. 77 (Oct., 1924), p. 341.
EH's letter of thanks: EH to Wilson, Oct. 18, 1924, printed in Wilson, *The Shores of Light*, NY, 1952, pp. 59–60.
EH's acidulous gossip: Asch-Shipman fight (EH to McAlmon, Nov. 20, 1924); Eliot's *Criterion* (EH to Gertrude Stein, Aug. 9, 1924); Eliot vs. Conrad (EH in *transatlantic review*, Vol. 2, Oct. 1924, pp. 341–342); Pound's "nervous breakdown" (EH to Gertrude Stein, Oct. 10, 1924). EH continued this early habit in *A Moveable Feast*. Among his victims there were Natalie Barney (pp. 110–111) whom he also attacked in EH to Gertrude Stein, ca. Aug. 5, 1924; Wyndham Lewis (pp. 108–110), and Ralph Cheever Dunning (pp. 143–146). Ford published 12 of Dunning's poems in *transatlantic*, Vol. 2 (November, 1924), pp. 485–486. EH to McAlmon, ca. Nov., 1924, called one of them "pretty near the god-damndest poem" he had ever read. It was probably the one called "Wind of Morning."
EH writes sketches on a fat girl and on the Hartmans: unpublished sketches, composed ca. fall, 1924.
EH on Ford's blundering: EH to Gertrude Stein, Sept. 14 and Oct. 10, 1924. **Ford's complaint of being kicked around:** Ford to Gertrude Stein, Sept. 18, 1924 in *Letters of Ford Madox Ford*, ed. Richard M. Ludwig, Princeton, NJ, 1965, p. 162. **Ford's apology for EH's attack on Eliot:** *transatlantic review*, Vol. 2 (Nov., 1924), p. 550. **EH's surly rejection of Ford at the Bal Musette:** Burton Rascoe, *We Were Interrupted*, Garden City, NY, 1947, pp. 184–186.
EH impugns ability of Krebs Friend: EH to Gertrude Stein, Oct. 10, 1924.

Sec. 19. To the Eastern Kingdom

SOURCES

Letters of EH: to Isabelle Simmons, June 24, 1923; to Howell Jenkins, Nov. 9, 1924; to his father, Nov. 20, 1924; to McAlmon, ca. Nov., 1924, Nov. 20, Dec. 10, and ca. Dec. 15, 1924; to Gertrude Stein, Dec. 29, 1924; to Harold Loeb, Dec. 29, 1924 and Jan. 5, 1925; to Ernest Walsh and Ethel Moorhead, ca. Jan., 1925; to Gertrude Stein, Jan. 20, 1925;

to George Horace Lorimer, Jan. 21, 1925; to Bill Smith, Jan. 27, 1925; to Jenkins, Feb. 2, 1925; to Robert McAlmon, ca. early February, 1925; to Bill Smith, Feb. 12, 1925; to Walsh and Moorhead, Feb. 13, 1925; to Gertrude Stein, Feb. 13, 1925; to Loeb, Feb. 27, 1925; to Horace Liveright (cable) March 5, 1925; to Walsh, March 27, 1925, and ca. April 1, 1925; to Liveright, March 31, 1925; to F. Scott Fitzgerald, ca. Dec. 20, 1925; to author, Feb. 1, 1953.
Other letters: Dr. and Mrs. Hemingway to EH, Nov. 16, 1924.
EH's work: "Homage to Ezra," *This Quarter*, Vol. 1 (May, 1925); *A Moveable Feast*, 1964.
Author's interviews and correspondence: with Ada and Archibald MacLeish, March 9, 1965; with Herr Josef and Frau Auguste Nels (son and widow of Paul Nels), Oct. 28, 1965; from Hadley R. Mowrer, July 12, 1962, and Jan. 17, 1966; from Josephine Herbst, July 3, 1963; from Janet Flanner and Solita Solano, Dec. 27, 1966.

NOTES

EH's liking for snow and mountains: EH to Isabelle Simmons, June 24, 1923.
EH's hedonism: EH to Jenkins, Nov. 9, 1924;
EH's low funds: blue MS. notebook with entries in EH's hand, Nov.–Dec., 1924.
Plans for Schruns: Hadley R. Mowrer to author, July 12, 1962 and Jan. 15, 1966; EH to McAlmon, Dec. 10, 1924; Herr Josef Nels to author, Oct. 28, 1965. EH's computation reads:

$$\begin{array}{r} 235{,}000 \text{ a day pension and heat} \\ 10{,}000 \text{ baby's milk} \\ \underline{50{,}000 \text{ bonne for baby}} \\ 295{,}000 = \text{Day} \\ \underline{\quad 7 \quad} \\ 2{,}065{,}000 \text{ Kroner per week.} \end{array}$$

EH meets the MacLeishes, John Herrmann, and Josephine Herbst: Ada and Archibald MacLeish to author, March 9, 1965; Josephine Herbst to author, July 3, 1963.
EH talks to Walsh about "This Quarter": EH to McAlmon, ca. Nov., 1924. **Walsh's interest in poetry:** *A Moveable Feast*, 1964, p. 123.
EH and Janet Flanner: memoir of EH by Janet Flanner and Solita Solano, sent to author, Dec. 27, 1966.
EH completes "The Undefeated": EH to McAlmon, Nov. 20, 1924.
EH sends "Soldier's Home" to McAlmon: EH to McAlmon, Dec. 10, 1924, where EH called it (perhaps for propaganda) the best story he had yet written.
EH removes original conclusion from "Big Two-Hearted River" and so instructs Stewart: EH to McAlmon, ca. Nov., 1924.
Arrival in Schruns: Paul and Auguste Nels to author, Oct. 28, 1965; EH to Gertrude Stein, Dec. 29, 1924, Jan. 20 and Feb. 18, 1925.
First weeks in Schruns: EH to Harold Loeb, Dec. 29, 1924, and Jan. 5, 1925. While EH waited for news about his book manuscript in New York, he sent Walsh "Big Two-Hearted River" for the first number of *This Quarter*. Count von Wedderkop accepted "The Undefeated" for a future number of *Der Querschnitt*. On Jan. 21, EH sent two typescripts of "The Undefeated," one to Lorimer at the *Saturday Evening Post*, and the other

to Scofield Thayer at the *Dial*. Three weeks later, still waiting, he made an entry in one of his blue notebooks:

MS received The Undefeated
from Spike Hunt
Jan. 20, Vanity Fair MS Feb. 5
B.F.

MS sent out The Undefeated
Dial, Sat. Eve.
Post, Jan. 21
1925, Should hear
March 1, 1925

To be published—accepted
Big Two-Hearted River—This Quarter
(March 1)
Bull Ring—Der Querschnitt (Feb. 1)

EH's covering letter to Lorimer, Jan. 21, spoke of his wish to write about bullfighting as it actually was, based on his own observations while living in the bullfighters' pension on the Calle San Jerónimo in Madrid. He expressed some concern about the use of technical terms in the story, but felt that the context explained them. This letter, not examined by author, was summarized in Parke-Bernet Catalogue of March 31, 1964, Sale 2268, Item 71, p. 19.
Life in Schruns: EH to Gertrude Stein, Dec. 29, 1924, and Jan. 20, 1925; EH to Loeb, Dec. 29, and Jan. 5, 1925; EH to Bill Smith, Jan. 27, 1925; EH to Howell Jenkins, Feb. 2, 1925; Frau Auguste Nels to author, Oct. 28, 1965. *A Moveable Feast*, 1964, pp. 198–206.
EH receives "This Quarter" prospectus and sends advice: EH to Ernest Walsh and Ethel Moorhead, ca. Jan., 1925, Feb. 13, and ca. Apr. 1, 1925; EH to McAlmon, ca. early Feb., 1925. **EH sends prospectus to Miss Stein:** Jan. 20, 1925.
First trip to Madlenerhaus: This seems to have occurred Jan. 17–19, inclusive: EH to Gertrude Stein, Jan. 20 and Feb. 13, 1925; *A Moveable Feast*, p. 205.
Second trip to Madlenerhaus; poker winnings: EH to Bill Smith, Feb. 12, 1925.
Vermuntgletscher trip: EH to Loeb, Feb. 27, 1925.
Liveright accepts "In Our Time": EH to Loeb, Feb. 27, 1925. **Required revisions:** EH to Liveright, March 31, 1925.
On finishing "The Battler": EH to Ernest Walsh, Feb 13, 1925
On real-life originals of Ad Francis and Bugs: EH to author, Feb 1, 1953. Some bad luck went with the good. The people who had sublet the Hemingways' Paris apartment skipped out without paying the rent. George Breaker of St. Louis made a $2500 down payment on his debt to Hadley with a check which the bank returned stamped "insufficient funds." (EH to Harold Loeb, Feb. 27, 1925.)
EH heals rift with Bill Smith: EH to Bill Smith, Jan. 27, 1925; EH to Jenkins, Feb. 2, 1925. EH's first idea was to get Bill a job at 1500 francs a month working as secretary-librarian to Sir William Johnston Gordon, a British baronet, father of EH's friend, the Honorable Dorothy Johnston, called Dossie. Dossie came to Schruns that winter to ski in the company of Josephine Bennett and Alma Estelle Lloyd.

EH writes laudatory essay on Pound: "Homage to Ezra," *This Quarter*, Vol. 1 (May, 1925), pp. 221–225.
EH discovers meaning of Österreich: EH to F. Scott Fitzgerald, ca. Dec. 20, 1925.

Sec. 20. This Quarter

SOURCES

Letters of EH: to Ernest Walsh and Ethel Moorhead, March 18, 24, 27, 28, 30, and 31; Apr. 1, 4, 10, 12, and 19, 1925; to Horace Liveright, March 31, 1925; to Maxwell Perkins, Apr. 15, 1925; to John Dos Passos, Apr. 22, 1925; to Perkins, June 9, 1925; to Sherwood Anderson, May 23, 1925; to F. Scott Fitzgerald, ca. Dec. 20, 1925.
Other letters: Fitzgerald to Perkins, ca. Oct. 18, 1925; Maxwell Perkins to EH, Feb. 21 and 26, 1925; Sherwood Anderson to Gertrude Stein, ca. early March, 1925.
EH's work: (a) Unpublished: fragment on revolutions, composed ca. June 15, 1925; fragment of novel, *Along with Youth*, composed late June, 1925. **(b) Published:** "Notes on Life and Letters," *Esquire*, Vol. 3 (January, 1935); *A Moveable Feast*, 1964.
Books and articles: H. M. Jones and W. B. Rideout, eds., *Letters of Sherwood Anderson*, 1953; Harold Loeb, *The Way It Was*, 1959; *Burke's Peerage*, 1959; Andrew Turnbull, ed., *The Letters of F. Scott Fitzgerald*, 1963; William Wasserstrom, "Hemingway, the *Dial*, and Ernest Walsh," *South Atlantic Quarterly*, Vol. 65 (Spring, 1966).
Author's interviews and correspondence: with John and Maria Rogers, Jan., 1962; with William B. Smith, Apr., 1964; with Karl Pfeiffer, Sept., 1967; with Laud Payne, Sept., 1967; from Dean Christian Gauss, Dec. 26, 1950; from Donald Ogden Stewart, March 2, 1962; from Nancy Cunard (via Solita Solano) March 4, 1962; from Kitty Cannell, Oct. 13, 1963; from Duncan Chaplin, Jan. 22 and Feb. 6, 1964; from Marianne Moore, Jan. 20, 1966; from Laud Payne, Sept. 21, 1967.

NOTES

Loeb congratulates EH: *The Way It Was*, 1959, p. 246.
EH and Hadley meet the Pfeiffer sisters; Pauline's first reaction to EH: Kitty Cannell to author, Oct. 13, 1963.
EH's work for Walsh with Herbert Clarke: EH to Walsh and Moorhead, March 18, 24, 27, 28, 30 and 31; Apr. 1, 4, 10, 12, and 19, 1925. I am indebted to the Alderman Library, University of Virginia, for copies of these letters.
EH and the "Dial": This transaction took two months. EH's covering letter, sent with the MS. Jan. 21, 1925, is in the Yale Collection of American Literature, where the records of the *Dial* are deposited. Dr. James Sibley Watson, Jr., was publisher and Scofield Thayer chief editor. "The Undefeated" was the only work of EH's which Miss Marianne Moore was asked to read during her time with the *Dial* in 1924–25 (Marianne Moore to author, Jan. 20, 1966). EH's belief that Gilbert Seldes was involved in rejecting the story was false, but helps to account for his gratuitous attack on

Seldes in *Esquire*, Vol. 3 (Jan., 1935), p. 21. Much later, in preparing *A Moveable Feast*, EH brought the name of Ernest Walsh into association with the *Dial*. The matter was discussed by William Wasserstrom, "Hemingway, the *Dial*, and Ernest Walsh," *South Atlantic Quarterly*, Vol. 65 (Spring, 1966), pp. 171–177. But there is some reason to believe that in preparing the typescript of *A Moveable Feast* for publication, EH's widow, Mary Welsh Hemingway, and the late L. H. Brague, Jr., EH's editor at Scribners, somehow allowed material to be transposed on p. 125 of *A Moveable Feast*, so that EH seemed to be saying that Walsh was one of the editors of the *Dial*, whereas the reference to "this quarterly" (line 11) was actually to *This Quarter*, of which (as EH well knew) Walsh was "one of the editors." I am indebted for this suggestion to Dr. David Jeffrey. For further information, see Nicholas Joost, *Ernest Hemingway and the Little Magazine*, Barre, Mass., 1968.
Walsh accepts "The Undefeated": EH to Walsh, March 27, Apr. 1, and Apr. 4, 1925.
EH resigns as unpaid subeditor: EH to Walsh, Apr. 4, 1925.
EH recommends Bill Smith and is rebuffed: EH to Walsh, Apr. 19, 1925. The story had a curious aftermath. Following Walsh's death, EH's letters to him and Miss Moorhead reached the Rare Book Department of Scribners. Perkins sent them to EH. Some bore annotations by Miss Moorhead. On that of Apr. 4, 1925, she wrote: "Hemingway was very insistent about our giving a friend of his a job . . . at 1000 francs a month. E.W. repeatedly told him we could not. I of course agreed with E.W." To this comment, EH added one of his own: "You will see from the correspondence that I suggested they hire someone to do the work I was doing for nothing."
EH's views on "In Our Time" and "The Battler": EH to Liveright, Mar. 31, 1925. Liveright asked Sherwood Anderson to write a blurb for EH's book. Anderson was in New Orleans, and wrote Gertrude Stein that he liked all of EH's stories. (*Letters of Sherwood Anderson*, ed. Jones and Rideout, NY, 1953, p. 136.) EH wrote Dos Passos to thank him for his part in urging Liveright to take *In Our Time*. He repeated his judgment of "The Battler" as a hell of a swell story about a "busted down pug" and a "coon." It was better than "Up in Michigan," although EH had always liked the story of Jim "yencing" Liz. Others of course, did not like it. If he had called it "Way Out in Iowa" and changed the yencing to a community corn roast, H. L. Mencken might have published it. (EH to Dos Passos, Apr. 22, 1925.)
Perkins writes EH: Perkins first wrote Feb. 21, with a follow-up letter Feb. 26, enclosing a copy of the first. Fitzgerald's advice to Perkins to approach EH came ca. Oct. 18, 1924. (Andrew Turnbull, *The Letters of F. Scott Fitzgerald*, NY, 1963, p. 167.)
Bill Smith reaches Paris: Smith to author, Apr. 3, 1964; Loeb, *The Way It Was*, NY, 1959, p. 247. EH to Dos Passos, Apr. 22, said he was working like a son of a bitch starting at seven each morning in spite of "gastric remorse" from drinking all night. He spoke of plans by *Der Querschnitt* to publish a book of his "dirty poems" illustrated by Pascin. This plan came to nothing.
Loeb's passion for Duff Twysden: *The Way It Was*, 1959, pp. 247–257; Kitty Cannell to author, Oct. 13, 1963. Robert Cohn in *The Sun Also Rises* is said to like Hudson's *The Purple Land;* Loeb's favorite Hudson novel was, however, *Green Mansions*.
Duff Twysden's background: *Burke's Peerage*, 1959, p. 2269. Other details from Nancy Cunard (Feb., 1962) forwarded to author by Solita Solano, March 4, 1962; Mr. and Mrs. John Rogers to author, Jan., 1962; Donald Ogden Stewart to author, March 2, 1962; W. B. Smith to author, Apr. 3, 1964.
EH meets Fitzgerald: *A Moveable Feast*, 1964, pp. 152–155. EH mistakenly identified Fitzgerald's athlete friend as Duncan Chaplin. Chaplin was not present (Duncan Chaplin to author, Jan. 22 and Feb. 6, 1964).
Second meeting with Fitzgerald and trip to Lyon: *A Moveable Feast*, 1964, pp. 156–176. My brief summary does not do justice to this amusing story, which should be read in EH's version.
Discussions with Gauss: Dean Christian Gauss to author, Dec. 26, 1950.
EH starts novel, "Along with Youth": This and a brief fragment on plotting by revolutionists at the Café Rotonde on the Boulevard Raspail appear at opposite ends of a blue notebook dated June 15, 1925. The story of the revolutionists occupies three pages and part of a fourth. *Along with Youth* breaks off on unnumbered p. 27.

Sec. 21. The Sun Also Rises

SOURCES

Letters of EH: to Bill Smith, Feb. 14 and 17, 1925; to Maxwell Perkins, Apr. 15; to John Dos Passos, Apr. 22; to Harriet and Dorothy Connable, May 3; to Harold Loeb, June 21; to Ernest Walsh, June 25; to F. Scott Fitzgerald, July 1; to Loeb, July 13; to Gertrude Stein, July 15; to Sylvia Beach, Aug 3; to Barklie McK. Henry, Aug. 12; to Howell Jenkins, Aug. 15; to his father, Aug. 20; to Gertrude Stein, Aug. 20, 1925. To author, Apr. 1, 1951.
Other letters: Duff Twysden to EH, ca. late June, 1925. Duff Twysden to Harold Loeb (2 letters), ca. late June, 1925.
EH's work: (a) Unpublished: fragment of an opening for *Fiesta*, a novel, composed early July, 1925; first 1½ chapters of *Fiesta*, composed between July 23 and Aug. 3, 1925, and later deleted; first draft of *The Sun Also Rises* in seven *cahiers*, dated July 23–Sept. 21, 1925. **(b) Published:** *Death in the Afternoon*, 1932; preface to illustrated edition of *A Farewell to Arms*, 1948; *A Moveable Feast*, 1964.
Books and articles: George Plimpton, editor, "The Art of Fiction XXI: Ernest Hemingway," *Paris Review*, No. 18 (Spring, 1958); Harold Loeb, *The Way It Was*, 1959.
Author's interviews and correspondence: with William Bird, June, 1962; with Hadley R. Mowrer, Aug. 1962; with W. B. Smith, Apr., 1964; from Donald Ogden Stewart, Feb. 20, 1951 and March 2, 1962; from Kitty Cannell, Oct. 13, 1963.

NOTES

EH anticipates third visit to Pamplona: EH to Bill Smith, Feb. 14 and 17, 1925.
Plans for Burguete and Pamplona: EH to Loeb, June 21, 1925.
The bullfight book for Flechtheim: EH to Dos Passos, April 22, 1925 and EH to Harriet and Dorothy Connable, May 3, 1925. This book may have been in EH's mind when he wrote Perkins on April 15 about a bullfight book comparable to Doughty's *Travels in Arabia Deserta*. EH did not complete the assignment for Flechtheim.
Loeb and Duff at St. Jean-de-Luz: *The Way It Was*, 1959, pp. 259–283. Duff's letters to Loeb are included in this account. The note from Duff to EH survives among his papers. It is undated and my placement of it is conjectural. Brett's trouble was probably lack of money. The remark about the Spanish fairies is in EH to Loeb, June 21, 1925.
EH's last editorial act for Walsh: EH to Walsh, June 25, 1925.
Loggers' destruction of streams: EH to his father, Aug. 20, 1925; W. B. Smith to author, Apr., 1964. In a letter of July 1, EH sketched his idea of heaven for Fitzgerald. It must contain a bullring and a private trout stream. In the town EH would maintain two houses, one for his wife and children and the other for nine beautiful mistresses; in the country, he would have a bull ranch, Hacienda Hadley. When a messenger appeared with the news that a notorious monogamist named Fitzgerald was approaching at the head of a band of strolling drinkers, EH would send Bumby to lock chastity belts on his nine mistresses.
Pamplona fiesta: *The Way It Was*, pp. 285–287 and photographs facing p. 279. **Account of Ordóñez:** *Death in the Afternoon*, 1932, pp. 88–89. **EH's comments on reactions to bullfight of Stewart, Bill Smith, and Duff Twysden:** *Ibid.*, pp. 497–498. EH there refers to Duff as an "alcoholic nymphomaniac."
Loeb's view of the bullfights: *The Way It Was*, p. 289. **Stewart's disappointment with the fiesta; views of Bill Smith on EH and Duff:** Stewart to author, Feb. 20, 1950, and March 2, 1962; Smith to author, Apr., 1964.
EH and Loeb quarrel: *The Way It Was*, pp. 292–297. **EH's apology:** EH to Loeb, undated, handwritten note [July 13, 1925]; see *The Way It Was*, p. 297.
End of fiesta and departures of principals: W. B. Smith to author, Apr., 1964.
EH and Hadley by train to Madrid: EH to Gertrude Stein, July 15, 1925.
Ordóñez honors Hadley: *Death in the Afternoon*, p. 89; Hadley R. Mowrer to author, Aug., 1962.
EH's first attempt to tell the fiesta story: quotations from a fragmentary typescript of first two scenes, undated, but possibly set down in Pamplona as early as July 6–12, 1925. This one begins, "It was half-past three . . ." Another typescript of thirty-eight pages begins "I saw him for the first time in his room at the Hotel Quintana in Pamplona." Yet another single sheet starts in the same way but changes the real Hotel Quintana to read Montoya. My view that these trial drafts precede the main draft is conjectural. A scene like this one appears in the published version, Chapter XV.

Going to Valencia: EH to Sylvia Beach, Aug. 3, 1925.
EH starts second draft of "Fiesta, A Novel": EH to author, Apr. 1, 1951; EH to George Plimpton, interview, *Paris Review*, No. 18 (Spring, 1958). Both these communications state that he began the novel on his 26th birthday, July 21. The MS. notebooks, however, show a starting date of July 23. This is not important, except as one more piece of evidence of EH's habit of personal mythmaking. The MS. draft of what became *The Sun Also Rises* appears in seven small *cahiers*, dated as follows: (1) Valencia, July 23–Aug. 3; (2) Valencia, Aug. 3; Madrid, Aug. 5–6; San Sebastian, Aug. 8–9; Hendaye, Aug. 10–12; (3) [Hendaye], Aug. 12–17, Paris, Aug. 19–20; (4) Paris, Aug. 20–29; (5) "Finished Paris, Sept. 9"; (6) "Sept. 9 Paris"; (7) "The End. Paris—Sept. 21—1925."
Jake Barnes's personal history: EH is evidently following rather closely the history of Bill Bird, who had moved to Paris in 1920 as European manager of the Consolidated Press, with offices at 19, rue d'Antin. Bird's partner in Washington (who served as model for Barnes's partner, Robert Graham) was David Lawrence. Bird had known him since his college days in 1909. This borrowing by EH is made clear in Bird's unpublished autobiography, of which he generously permitted the author to read two chapters on June 1, 1962.
Barnes's friendship with Cohn: EH's longer first-draft account was eventually cut to begin with the sentence: "Robert Cohn was once middleweight boxing champion of Princeton."
EH's account of progress with novel: During August, 1925, he spoke of his progress to Sylvia Beach, Aug. 3; Barklie Henry on the 12th; Howell Jenkins, 15th; his father, 20th; and Gertrude Stein, 20th.
Mme. Chautard's surprise: EH to Gertrude Stein, Aug. 20, 1925. **Sweeny and the Riff Rebellion:** same letter.
Friendship of Smith and Loeb: Smith to author, Apr., 1964; EH to his father, Aug. 20, 1925.
Farewell dinner for Loeb and Smith: Loeb, *The Way It Was*, p. 300; Kitty Cannell to author, Oct. 13, 1963.
EH finishes first draft of "Fiesta": MS. Notebook No. 7.

Sec. 22. Double-Crossings

SOURCES

Letters of EH: to Barklie Henry, Aug. 12; to Howell Jenkins, Aug. 15; to Ernest Walsh, ca. Aug. 20 and ca. late Sept.; to his father, Sept. 24; to Walsh, Nov. 30; to Horace Liveright, Dec. 7, 1925.
Other letters: Duff Twysden to EH, ca. late Sept., 1925; Dr. Hemingway to EH, Dec. 2 and 9, 1925.
EH's work: (a) Unpublished: "Foreword. The Lost Generation: A Novel," composed ca. Sept. 27, 1925; "Ten Indians," early draft, composed ca. Sept. 27, 1925; "The Art of the Short Story," composed June, 1959. **(b) Published:** "Fifty Grand," composed ca. Oct.–Nov., 1925; *In Our Time*, publ. Oct. 5, 1925; *Torrents of Spring*, composed ca. Nov. 23–30, 1925, and publ. May 28, 1926; introduction to

Clement Greenberg, ed., *Joan Miro*, 1948; introd. to illustrated edition of *A Farewell to Arms*, 1948; *A Moveable Feast*, 1964.
Books and articles: Max Eastman, *Great Companions*, 1959; Andrew Turnbull, ed., *Letters of F. Scott Fitzgerald*, 1963; John Dos Passos, *The Best Times*, 1966; Dan Daniel, "Leonard's Foul Punch," *The Ring*, Vol. 35 (Jan., 1957); Calvin Tomkins, "Living Well Is the Best Revenge," *New Yorker*, Vol. 38 (July 28, 1962); P. G. and R. R. Davies, "Hemingway's 'Fifty Grand' and the Jack Britton-Mickey Walker Prize Fight," *American Literature*, Vol. 37 (Nov., 1965).
Author's interviews and correspondence: with Henry Strater, July, 1964; from Hadley R. Mowrer, Feb. 16, 1964; from Clinton King, March 18, 1964.

NOTES

EH's exhaustion after completing first draft: EH to father, Sept. 24, 1925; introduction, illustrated edition of *A Farewell to Arms*, NY, 1948, p. viii.
Swimming in Seine and comments on Italy: EH to Ernest Walsh, ca. Aug. 20 and ca. late September, 1925. The latter refers to the torn ligament.
EH's trip to Chartres: dated by holograph inscription on brown *cahier*: "Ernest Hemingway. Chartres. Sept. 27, 1925."
EH considers naming novel "The Lost Generation": from an unpublished foreword in the same *cahier*, which includes anecdote about Miss Stein and the garagekeeper. The anecdote was much altered in later retelling: see *A Moveable Feast*, 1964, pp. 29–31.
Duff Twysden seeks EH's help: undated holograph note among EH's papers.
Duff's conversation recorded: from an undated purple *cahier* like the one dated Sept. 27, 1925. "It's sort of what we have in place of God" appears in *The Sun Also Rises*, Chapter XIX. Duff later told her next husband, Clinton King, that she had no sexual affair with EH: Clinton King to author, March 18, 1964.
EH's inhibitions about extramarital sexual intercourse: EH takes this position when offered one of Pascin's models as partner (*A Moveable Feast*, 1964, pp. 101–104). Max Eastman, *Great Companions*, NY, 1959, p. 50, tells of meeting EH at the Dôme one day in 1925. He was remorseful after having spent most of the night on Montmartre, and told Eastman that he couldn't help wanting some of the girls in the dance halls, but always came home disgusted with himself for having had such feelings. His numerous later boasts about sexual conquests seem to have been mostly invented.
EH writes "Ten Indians" and "Fifty Grand": An early draft of "Ten Indians" appears in the dated *cahier*, Sept. 27, 1925. A good account of the Britton-Leonard fight is that of Dan Daniel, "Leonard's Foul Punch," *The Ring*, Vol. 35 (Jan., 1957), pp. 8–9 and 48. P. G. and R. R. Davies, "Hemingway's 'Fifty Grand' and the Jack Britton-Mickey Walker Prize Fight," *American Literature*, Vol. 37 (November, 1965), pp. 251–258, seeks to establish the Britton-Walker fight, Madison Square Garden, Nov. 1, 1922, as the one on which EH bases his story.

Fitzgerald advises omission of anecdote about Britton and Leonard: EH, "The Art of the Short Story," unpublished preface, composed June, 1959.
Gerald and Sara Murphy: Gerald Murphy (Yale, 1911) was the son of Patrick Murphy of Boston, who owned the leather-goods store of Mark Cross. Sara Murphy (née Wilborg, of Cincinnati) was presented at the Court of St. James's in 1914 and married Gerald in 1916. Their careers are the subject of a profile by Calvin Tomkins, *The New Yorker*, Vol. 38 (July 28, 1962), pp. 31–69. See also Dos Passos, *The Best Times*, NY, 1966, pp. 141–151.
EH buys Miro's "The Farm": EH, introduction to Clement Greenberg, ed., *Joan Miro*, NY, 1948, and Dos Passos, *The Best Times*, NY, 1966, p. 144.
Send-off for "In Our Time": EH to Barklie Henry, Aug. 12 and EH to Howell Jenkins, Aug. 15, 1925.
Publication of "In Our Time": Boni and Liveright, NY, Oct. 5, 1925.
Early reviews of "In Our Time": *New York Times*, Oct. 18, 1925, p. 8; H. S. Gorman, *New York World*, Oct. 18, 1925, p. 7; Herschel Brickell, *Literary Review of the New York Evening Post*, Oct. 17, 1925, p. 3.
EH writes "The Torrents of Spring": composed in seven to ten days at the end of November, 1925. EH to Ernest Walsh, Nov. 30, 1925. Hadley was sick in bed for a week, ca. Nov. 23–30, 1925 and this was when EH got most of the work done. The lunch with Dos Passos and the nocturnal visit by Fitzgerald are jocosely mentioned in the book, NY, 1926, pp. 107–108 and 119.
Fitzgerald's apology: Fitzgerald to EH, Nov. 30, 1925 in Andrew Turnbull, ed., *Letters of F. Scott Fitzgerald*, NY, 1963, p. 295.
Opinions of "Torrents of Spring" among EH's intimates: Hadley R. Mowrer to author, Feb. 16, 1964 gives her own and Pauline's views. Dos Passos, *The Best Times*, NY, 1966, p. 158. Gertrude Stein's view: *A Moveable Feast*, NY, 1964, p. 28. Henry Strater to author, July 2, 1964.
EH sends "Torrents" to Liveright: EH to Horace Liveright, Dec. 7, 1925.
Dr. Hemingway on "In Our Time": Dr. Hemingway to EH, Dec. 2 and 9, 1925.

Sec. 23. Year of the Avalanches

SOURCES

Letters of EH: to Sylvia Beach, ca. Dec. 14; to his mother, Dec. 14; to Howell Jenkins, Dec. 14; to Fitzgerald, Dec. 15, ca. Dec. 20, and Dec. 31, 1925; to Fitzgerald, Jan. 1, 1926; to Isabelle Simmons Godolphin, Feb. 10 and Feb. 25; to Louis and Mary Bromfield, ca. March 5; to Maxwell Perkins, March 10, Apr. 1, Apr. 8, and Apr. 24, 1926.
Other letters: Hadley to Sylvia Beach, ca. Dec. 15, 1925; Louis Bromfield to EH, ca. Dec. 15, 1925; Horace Liveright to EH, Dec. 30, 1925; Pauline Pfeiffer to EH and Hadley, Jan. 14 and 16, 1926; Pauline to Hadley, ca. Feb. 1, 1926.
EH's work: (a) Unpublished: entries on reading in Chartres *cahier*, ca. Sept. 27, 1925; entries in EH's buckram notebook, ca. March

6–26, 1926. **(b) Published:** *Death in the Afternoon*, 1932; *A Moveable Feast*, 1964.
Books: R. Knoll, ed., *McAlmon and the Lost Generation*, 1962; John Dos Passos, *The Best Times*, 1966.
Author's interviews and correspondence: with Mr. and Mrs. T. O. Bruce, March 29, 1965; with Miss Rosalind Wilson, July 21, 1966; from Kitty Cannell, Oct. 13, 1963; from Hadley R. Mowrer, Feb. 16, 1964; from Dawn Powell, May 12, 1965; from Edward Hattam, June 4, 1966.

NOTES

Second trip to Schruns: EH to Sylvia Beach, ca. Dec. 14; EH to his mother, Dec. 14; EH to Jenkins, Dec. 14, 1925.
EH reads "Torrents" aloud to the Murphys: EH to Fitzgerald, Dec. 15, 1925.
Fräulein Glaser: Edward Hattam to author, June 4, 1966. Hattam's information came from Herr Erich Freund, who had known Herr Lent and Fräulein Glaser, 1924–26.
Avalanche at Lech: *A Moveable Feast*, 1964, pp. 203–204.
EH's reading at Schruns: listed in part in EH's *cahier* dated from Chartres, Sept. 27, 1925, and in EH to Fitzgerald, Dec. 15, 1925, where he recommends also Knut Hamsun's *Growth of the Soil* and Dos Passos's *Three Soldiers*. At this time Hadley told Sylvia Beach of a visit to the Hotel Adler at Tschagguns, near where one hundred chamois came down at noon each day to be fed: Hadley to Sylvia Beach, ca. Dec. 15, 1925.
EH on best subjects for fiction: EH to Fitzgerald, Dec. 15, 1925.
EH's winter recreations: EH to Fitzgerald, Dec. 15, ca. Dec. 20, and Dec. 31, 1925.
Pauline at Schruns: Kitty Cannell to author, Oct. 13, 1963.
Liveright rejects "Torrents": Liveright to EH, cable, Dec. 30, 1925, quoted in EH to Fitzgerald, Dec. 31, 1925.
Publishers' interest in EH: EH to Fitzgerald, Dec. 31, 1925. EH here quotes letter from Bromfield to EH, lately received.
EH plans trip to New York: EH to Fitzgerald, Jan. 1, 1926.
Liveright's letter of rejection: Liveright to EH, Dec. 30, 1925.
Pauline and EH: *A Moveable Feast*, 1964, pp. 209–210.
Pauline's chatty letters: Pauline to EH and Hadley, Jan. 14 and 16, 1926.
EH sees Pauline in Paris: Pauline to Hadley, ca. Feb. 1, 1926.
EH sees publishers in New York: EH to Isabelle Godolphin, Feb. 10, 1926; EH to Louis and Mary Bromfield, ca. March 5, 1926.
EH's social life in New York: EH to Isabelle Godolphin, Feb. 10 and 25, 1926; Dawn Powell to author, May 12, 1965. The author is indebted to Rosalind Wilson (July 21, 1966) for a description of Miss Powell. Herrmann's *What Happens* is discussed in R. Knoll, ed., *McAlmon and the Lost Generation*, Lincoln, Nebraska, 1962, p. 234.
EH back in Paris: EH to Louis and Mary Bromfield, ca. March 5, 1926; EH to Perkins, March 10, 1926.
His developing liaison with Pauline: *A Moveable Feast*, 1964, p. 210. The clause ("and where we went and what we did, and the un-

believable wrenching, killing happiness, selfishness and treachery of everything we did gave me such a terrible remorse,") was edited out before publication, but appears in EH's original typescript.
Dos Passos and the Murphys at Schruns: *A Moveable Feast*, pp. 207–210; Dos Passos, *The Best Times*, 1966, p. 158.
EH's plans for picaresque novel on Red Ryan: buckram notebook MS. entry, ca. late March, 1926.
EH's discourse on death and suicide: buckram notebook MS. entry, ca. late March, 1926.
Discussions of avalanches with Fräulein Glaser: buckram notebook MS. entry, ca. late March, 1926.
Finishing revision of "The Sun Also Rises" in avalanche time: *A Moveable Feast*, 1964, pp. 204 and 211; EH to Perkins, April 1, 1926.

Sec. 24. The End of Something

SOURCES

Letters of EH: to Fitzgerald, ca. Apr. 23 and May 4; to Maxwell Perkins, May 5; to Sherwood Anderson, May 21; to Perkins, June 5; to Henry Strater, ca. July 24; to Perkins, Aug. 26, 1926; to Bernard Berenson, Oct. 14, 1952.
Other letters: Perkins to EH, May 18; T. H. Ward to EH, May 18; Gerald Murphy to EH, May 22; Perkins to Charles Scribner, May 27; Fitzgerald to EH, ca. early June; Perkins to EH, June 14; Murphy to EH, July 14; Pauline to EH and Hadley, July 15, 1926; Guy Hickok to EH, Feb. 2, 1927.
EH's work: Published: "Alpine Idyll"; "A Canary for One"; "The Killers."
Books and articles: James Schevill, *Sherwood Anderson*, 1951; George Plimpton, *Paris Review*, No. 18 (Spring, 1958); Calvin Tomkins, *New Yorker*, Vol. 38 (July 28, 1962); Edward Hattam, Hemingway's "An Alpine Idyll," *Modern Fiction Studies*, Vol. 12 (1966).
Author's interviews and correspondence: with Hadley R. Mowrer, Aug., 1962; with Juanito Quintana, Oct., 1965; from Donald Ogden Stewart, March 2, 1962; from Hadley R. Mowrer, Feb. 16 and March 25, 1964.

NOTES

The Loire valley trip and the confrontation: Hadley R. Mowrer to author, August, 1962. EH later wrote Bernard Berenson that he was in bed with a "no-good girl" when Hadley returned earlier than expected. He had to get the girl out onto the roof, change the sheets, and get down quickly to open the door at the bottom of the stairs. This letter placed the incident in the fall of 1925 before the second visit to Schruns. If it happened, as is unlikely, it was in the spring of 1926. EH to Berenson, Oct. 14, 1952. This was a time when EH's inhibitions about lying were well cauterized with scar tissue.
EH writes "Alpine Idyll": EH to Perkins, May 5, 1926. Edward Hattam, Hemingway's "An Alpine Idyll," *Modern Fiction Studies*, Vol. 12 (1966), pp. 261–265, discusses the connection between EH's story and the typical mortuary lore of the Austrian peasants.

EH plans to go to Spain: EH to Fitzgerald, ca. Apr. 23 and May 4, 1926.
EH in Madrid: first days (EH to Fitzgerald, May 15), EH on Pauline's elaborate departures (*A Moveable Feast,* MS. version, passage deleted before publication).
EH's productive Sunday, May 16: (EH to George Plimpton, *Paris Review,* No. 18, Spring, 1958, pp. 79–80). This account was deceptive, since EH had already done first drafts of "Ten Indians" and "The Killers." He rewrote both in Madrid, instead of beginning *de novo,* as his remarks to Plimpton implied.
Hadley and Bumby to the Riviera: Hadley R. Mowrer to author, Aug., 1962. Before leaving Paris, Hadley had dismissed the Austrian nursemaid, Mathilde Braun, whom she had brought back from Schruns. The tearful girl was put aboard the train for home by Mike Ward. (T. H. Ward to EH, May 18, 1926.) Gerald Murphy wrote EH his reason for insisting that Bumby be quarantined. Healthy children were "no encumbrance"; sick ones were "hell to be with." He and Sara did not want to go through weeks of whooping cough with their own three children. (Murphy to EH, May 22, 1926.)
EH explains motivations behind "Torrents of Spring": EH to Anderson, May 21, 1926. EH had praised Anderson's autobiography in *Ex Libris,* Vol. 2 (March, 1925), p. 176. See Ray Lewis White, ed., *A Story Teller's Story,* Cleveland, 1968, p. xix.
EH rejoins Hadley: EH to Perkins, June 5, 1926; *A Moveable Feast,* 1964, pp. 185–186.
Fitzgerald at the Casino: Calvin Tomkins, *The New Yorker,* Vol. 38 (July 28, 1962), pp. 60–61. This party took place on June 4.
Fitzgerald's critique of opening of "The Sun Also Rises": Fitzgerald to EH, ca. early June, 1926. This long letter advised EH to make a number of cuts in the first 1½ chapters of the novel, to eliminate the sneers, the irrelevancies, and the "elephantine facetiousness." It was excellent criticism and EH immediately complied with it. EH to Perkins, June 5, from the Villa Paquita, Juan-les-Pins, says he had decided to start the book with what is now p. 16 in the MS. There was nothing there that was not explained later, and the book would move faster because of the omission.
Perkins praises "The Sun Also Rises": Perkins to EH, May 18 and June 14, 1926. Although he said nothing of it to Hemingway, Perkins had met some opposition to the book among other editors at Scribners. He took the line that the firm had a reputation for ultra-conservatism which would simply be confirmed if they declined to publish EH's novel. John Hall Wheelock backed him in this view and their arguments prevailed. (Perkins to Charles Scribner, May 27, 1926.) Perkins told EH that he would have to change a few forthright references to the appendages of the bulls, but these changes could wait for galley proof.
Typical reviews of "Torrents of Spring": Harry Hansen, *New York World,* May 30, 1926, p. 4. "W.Y." *New York Evening Post,* June 12, 1926, p. 9. T. L. Masson, *Literary Digest,* Oct., 1926, p. 667. L. S. Morris, *New Republic,* Vol. 48 (Sept. 15, 1926), p. 101. Allen Tate, *The Nation,* Vol. 123 (July 28, 1926), p. 89. Ernest Boyd, *Independent,* Vol. 116 (June 12, 1926), p. 694. *New York Times,*

June 13, 1926, p. 8. **Anderson's Views:** James Schevill, *Sherwood Anderson,* Denver, Colorado, 1951, pp. 226–228.
Pauline visits EH and Hadley at Juan-les-Pins: Hadley R. Mowrer to author, Aug., 1962, Feb. 16 and March 25, 1964. Guy Hickok later traced the breakup of EH's marriage to Pauline's visit at this time. "Somebody looking for a [Ph.D.] degree," he said, "ought to trace the influence of whooping-cough in history." (Hickok to EH, Feb. 2, 1927.)
Hemingways, Murphys, and Pauline to Pamplona: Hadley R. Mowrer to author, Aug., 1962, and March 25, 1964; Juanito Quintana to author, Oct., 1965; Calvin Tomkins, *The New Yorker,* Vol. 38 (July 28, 1962), pp. 56–57; Gerald Murphy to EH, July 14, 1926.
Pauline writes of her desires: Pauline Pfeiffer to EH and Hadley, July 15, 1926.
Murphy praises the Hemingway marriage: Gerald Murphy to EH, July 13, 1926.
EH hints at imminent breakup: EH to Henry Strater, ca. July 24, 1926.
Murphys and Stewarts learn of separation: Donald Ogden Stewart to author, March 2, 1962. The trip to Paris from the Riviera was closely described in EH's story, "A Canary for One." This observation confirmed by Hadley R. Mowrer to author, Feb. 16, 1964.
EH's dedication for "The Sun Also Rises": EH to Perkins, Aug. 26, 1926.

Sec. 25. The Hundred Days

SOURCES

Letters of EH: to Perkins, Aug. 21 and Sept. 7; to Fitzgerald, ca. late Sept.; to Pauline Pfeiffer, Oct. 12 and ca. Oct. 14 or 21; to Perkins, Oct. 25; to Hadley, Nov. 18; to Perkins, Nov. 22; to Fitzgerald, ca. mid-November; to Pauline, Dec. 3; to Perkins, Dec. 7 and 21, 1926. To his parents, Feb. 5, 1927; to Fitzgerald, ca. Sept. 15, 1927. To author, Apr. 1, 1951.
Other letters: L. E. Pollinger to Charles Scribner, Aug. 31; Gerald Murphy to EH, Sept. 4; Perkins to EH, Sept. 8; Dr. Hemingway to EH, Sept. 21; Pauline Pfeiffer to EH, Sept. 24, 25, and 28 (cables), Sept. 25 and 29; Oct. 4 (2 letters), 5, 6 (cable); Dr. Hemingway to EH, Oct. 7; Pauline to EH, Oct. 8 (2 letters), 11 (2 letters), 12 (2 letters), 14, 16, 19, 23, 26, and 30; Grace Hemingway to EH, Oct. 31; Pauline to EH, Nov. 2; Robert Bridges to EH, Nov. 11; Hadley to EH, Nov. 16 and 19; Pauline to EH, Nov. 18, 27 (2 letters), 28, 30 (2 letters); Dec. 1, 2, 4 (2 letters); Grace Hemingway to EH, Dec. 4; Robert Bridges to EH, Dec. 4; Pauline to EH, Dec. 8 and 12; Perkins to EH, Dec. 10; Dr. Hemingway to EH, Dec. 13; Pauline to EH, Dec. 13 and 17; Perkins to EH, Dec. 18; Pauline to EH, Dec. 22; Fitzgerald to EH, Dec. 23; Pauline to EH, Dec. 25 and 27; Dr. Hemingway to EH, Dec. 31, 1926. Edmund Wilson to EH, Jan. 27, 1927; Thornton Wilder to EH, Feb. 15, 1926; MacLeish to EH, ca. mid-June, 1927; Evan Shipman to EH, Jan. 17, 1944.
EH's work: (a) Unpublished: sketch of life with Bumby, composed ca. Nov. 16–18, 1926; deleted passage from *A Moveable Feast,* composed ca. 1958; **(b) Published:** "Today Is Fri-

day," "A Canary for One," "In Another Country." *The Sun Also Rises,* 1926; *A Moveable Feast,* 1964.
Books: Malcolm Cowley, *Exile's Return,* 1951; John Dos Passos, *The Best Times,* 1966.
Author's interviews and correspondence: with Mrs. Mary Hickok, May, 1962; with William Bird, June, 1962; with Hadley R. Mowrer, Aug., 1962; with Harold Loeb, Oct., 1962; with W. B. Smith, Apr., 1964; with Archibald and Ada MacLeish, March 9, 1965; with Karl Pfeiffer, Sept. 26, 1967. From Donald Ogden Stewart, Feb. 20, 1951 and March 2, 1962; from Kitty Cannell, Oct. 13, 1963; from Hadley R. Mowrer, Jan. 27, 1964; from Laud Payne, Sept. 21, 1967.

NOTES

Hadley's hundred days agreement: This document survives among EH's papers.
Pauline's cables and letters on board "Pennland": Pauline to EH, Sept. 24, 25, and 28 (cables), Sept. 25, 29, Oct. 4 (2 letters), 1926.
Pauline in New York: Pauline to EH, Oct. 4 (2 letters), 5, 6 (cable), 8 (2 letters), 11 (2 letters), 1926. Gerald had told Dos Passos of the separation of EH and Hadley. One Tuesday night, on a tour of Harlem jazz joints with Dos and the Murphys, Pauline explained the situation to Dos Passos.
Murphy's gift to EH: Gerald Murphy to EH, Sept. 4, 1926. It was this letter which led Ernest more than thirty years later to make his terrible and unjust attack on the Murphys in the manuscript version of *A Moveable Feast,* where they are called "the rich." Certainly, he wrote, "the rich never did anything for their own ends. They collected people then as some collect pictures and others breed horses and they only backed me in every ruthless and evil decision that I made. . . . It wasn't that the decisions were wrong although they all turned out badly finally from the same fault of character that made them. If you deceive and lie with one person against another you will eventually do it again. *I had hated these rich because they had backed me and encouraged me when I was doing wrong.* But how could they know it was wrong and had to turn out badly when they had never known all the circumstances? It was not their fault. It was only their fault for coming into other people's lives. They were bad luck for people but they were worse luck to themselves and they lived to have all of their bad luck finally; to the very worst end that all bad luck could go." (Quoted from the MS. version of "There Is Never Any End to Paris," the final sketch in *A Moveable Feast,* passage deleted before publication. Italics supplied.)
Pfeiffer family of Piggott: Paul M. Pfeiffer (1867–1943) and his wife Mary Downey (1869–1952) were born in Cedar Falls, Iowa. Paul had seven brothers and two sisters. He began business as owner of a drugstore in Parkersburg, Iowa, where Pauline was born July 22, 1895, and her brother Karl in 1900. The family lived in St. Louis 1900–12, and moved to Piggott in 1913. Paul acquired timberlands nearby at prices ranging from 70 cents to $4 an acre, and at one time owned

60,000 acres, from which two hundred men cleared trees, pulled stumps, and later planted cotton, corn, wheat, and soybeans. Virginia Pfeiffer was born in St. Louis in 1902, and Max Pfeiffer (who died young) was born in St. Louis in 1906. The family house at the corner of Cherry and 10th streets stood on a rise of land, the beginning of Crowley's Ridge, which runs from Missouri down through the eastern part of Arkansas. The rest of the country is alluvial plain some forty miles west of the Mississippi River. (Laud Payne to author, Sept. 21, 1967 and Karl Pfeiffer to author, Sept. 26, 1967.) Pauline reached home Oct. 15, 1926.
Pauline's praise of EH: Pauline to EH, Nov. 1, 1926.
EH's personal hell: EH to Fitzgerald, ca. late September, 1926.
EH's literary successes: L. E. Pollinger of Curtis Brown to Charles Scribner, Aug. 31, 1926; EH to Perkins, Aug. 21 and Sept. 7, 1926; Perkins to EH, Sept. 8, 1926. George Platt Lynes, Edith Finch, and Adlai Harbeck published EH's "Today Is Friday" as No. 4 of The As Stable Pamphlets (125 Engle Street, Englewood, N.J.) in an edition of 300 numbered copies, 1926.
Pauline in Piggott; enroute by train: Oct. 12 and 14; **at home:** Oct. 16, 19, 23, 26, 30, 1926.
EH's close friendship with the MacLeishes: Archibald and Ada MacLeish to author, March 9, 1954. This period was recollected in MacLeish to EH, June 15, 1927.
EH's attack on Dorothy Parker: Donald Ogden Stewart to author, March 2, 1962.
EH's self-pity and Pauline's reply: EH to Pauline, Oct. 12, 1926; and ca. Oct. 14, 21 or 28, 1926. Pauline to EH, Nov. 30, 1926. Pauline's "mad-house depression" came on Oct. 24: Pauline to EH, Oct. 29, 1926.
EH sells "A Canary for One" and submits "In Another Country": "A Canary for One" was enclosed with EH to Perkins, Oct. 25, 1926, and accepted in Robert Bridges to EH, Nov. 11, 1926. "In Another Country" was sent to Perkins Nov. 22 and accepted in Bridges to EH, Dec. 4, 1926.
EH moves furniture for Hadley: Hadley R. Mowrer to author, Aug., 1962. There were other losses at this time. Dr. Hemingway wrote EH on Oct. 7, 1926 that his eighty-two-year-old father Anson had died at seven that morning. EH's grandmother Adelaide had died in 1923, and their son Tyler in 1922. "We like to think," wrote Dr. Hemingway, "of the happy reunion of Mother and Father and Tyler." He was hoping to sell the old house on North Oak Park Avenue, which he called "The Old Homestead."
Hadley in Chartres and EH with Bumby: Hadley to EH, Nov. 16, 1926. EH's unpublished sketch of life with Bumby. ca. Nov. 16–18, 1926. Bumby's joy in life with father: EH to Perkins, Nov. 23, 1926. EH to his father, Dec. 1, 1926, reports on Bumby's welfare.
EH's praise of Hadley: EH to Hadley, Nov. 18, 1926. Although EH said that he had made over the royalties to her on this date, he waited to do so until Dec. 21. (EH to Perkins, Dec. 21, 1926.)
Hadley agrees to divorce: Hadley to EH, Nov. 19, 1926.
EH's self-criticism among friends: William

Bird to author, June, 1962; EH to Fitzgerald, ca. Nov. 20, 1926.
Sales of "The Sun Also Rises": Max Perkins to EH, Dec. 10 and Dec. 18, 1926.
Reception of novel by reviewers: H. S. Gorman, *New York World* (Nov. 14, 1926), p. 10; C. B. Chase, *Saturday Review of Literature*, Vol. 3 (Dec. 11, 1926), p. 420; L. S. Morris, *New Republic*, Vol. 49 (Dec. 22, 1926), p. 142. **Objections to the characters in "The Sun":** *New York Times*, Dec. 5, 1926, p. 5; *Springfield Republican*, Nov. 28, 1926, p. 7. Ernest Boyd, *Independent*, Vol. 117 (Nov. 20, 1926), p. 594.
EH's views on the meaning of his novel: EH to Fitzgerald, May, 1926 and EH to Perkins, Nov. 16, Nov. 19, and Dec. 7, 1926. EH to author, Apr. 1. 1951, accused Gertrude Stein of "splendid bombast" in her "lost-generation" statement and denied that he had ever thought of his generation as "lost"—but only "beat-up."
Identification of characters in "The Sun Also Rises": William Bird to author, June, 1962; Mary Hickok to author, May, 1962. Perkins asked EH to change the name of a minor character, Roger Prescott, since it was too close to Glenway Wescott, EH's model. EH changed it to Roger Prentiss. Shipman's observation on Harold Stearns is from Shipman to EH, Jan. 17, 1944. Donald Ogden Stewart to author, Feb. 20, 1951, recognized himself in the figure of Bill Gorton. But EH also borrowed elements from Bill Smith (W. B. Smith to author, April, 1964), and from Dos Passos. Dos had discovered Mme. Lecomte and her restaurant on the Île-St.-Louis during his days with the Norton-Harjes Ambulance. In the novel Bill and Jake dine there and Mme. Lecomte makes a "great fuss" over seeing Bill Gorton for the first time since the war (*Sun Also Rises*, Ch. 8). See also Dos Passos, *The Best Times*, N.Y. 1966, p. 58. One curious slip occurs in the first Modern Library edition of *The Sun* (NY, 1930, p. 91) when Jake introduces Bill to Robert Cohn as "Bill Grundy." Bill Grundy was a Kentuckian whom EH had met in Northern Michigan in the summer of 1917.
Reactions of Kitty Cannell, Harold Loeb, and Duff Twysden: Kitty Cannell to author, Oct. 13, 1963; Harold Loeb to author, Oct., 1962; Duff's attitude described in EH to Fitzgerald, ca. Sept. 15, 1927.
Reactions of EH's parents: Dr. and Mrs. Hemingway read the novel about the time they began hearing rumors of EH's domestic difficulties. "Dear boy," wrote Grace, "we have heard rumors of the cooling off of affection between you and Hadley" (Grace to EH, Dec. 4, 1926). Dr. Hemingway wrote to EH on the same subject, Dec. 13 and 18, 1926. Dr. Hemingway's cautionary remarks about the novel are in his letters to EH of Dec. 13 and 31, 1926. Grace's attack on EH's subject matter is in her letter to EH of Dec. 4, 1926. EH's remark on his mother's need of family loyalty is in EH to parents, Feb. 5, 1927.
Praise from fellow writers: Fitzgerald to EH, Dec. 23, 1926. **EH reports on Bishop's letter from Wilson:** EH to Perkins, Dec. 21, 1926. Edmund Wilson himself wrote EH that the book was a "knockout": Wilson to EH, Jan. 27, 1927. **Cowley's comment on social effects of the novel:** *Exile's Return*, NY, 1951, pp.

225–226. Wilder on book's popularity at Yale and his own "imitation": Thornton Wilder to EH, Feb. 15, 1927.
Pauline's return: Archibald and Ada MacLeish to author, March 9, 1965; Pauline Pfeiffer to EH, Dec. 25, 1926.
Date of divorce: Hadley R. Mowrer to author, Jan. 27, 1964.

Sec. 26. *Men Without Women*

SOURCES

Letters of EH: to Perkins, Jan. 20, 1927; to Chard Powers Smith, ca. Jan. 24; to parents, Feb. 5; to Perkins, Feb. 14; to Isabelle Godolphin, March 5; to Fitzgerald, March 31; to Perkins, Apr. 16, Apr. 25, May 4, and May 27; to Mr. and Mrs. Paul Pfeiffer, ca. June 10; to Perkins, June 10 and June 24; to Barklie Henry, July 14; to Waldo Peirce, July 22; to Barklie Henry, ca. Aug. 7; to Perkins, Aug. 17; to MacLeish, Aug. 29; to Fitzgerald, ca. Sept. 15; to Perkins, Sept. 15 and ca. Oct. 15; to Father Donavan, ca. Nov. 24; to Perkins, Nov. 24; to Isabelle Godolphin, Dec. 5; to Fitzgerald, ca. Dec. 15 and Dec. 18; to Waldo Peirce, late Dec., 1927; to Frances Thorne, Feb. 12, 1929; to Charles Scribner, Aug. 3, 1949; to Philip Young, June 23, 1952.
Other letters: Chard Powers Smith to EH, Jan. 1, 1927; Hickok to EH, ca. Jan. 15 and Feb. 2; Perkins to EH, Jan. 14 and Feb. 4; Henry Strater to EH, Feb. 16; Perkins to EH, Feb. 21, Feb. 28, and March 9; Pauline to EH, March 15, 17, 18, 19, 20, 22, and 23; Perkins to EH, Apr. 30; Mrs. Paul Pfeiffer to EH and Pauline, ca. May 1; Hickok to EH, June 7; Perkins to EH, July 14, 1927.
EH's work, Published: "My Own Life," *The New Yorker*, Vol. 2 (Feb. 12, 1927); "Nothemist Poem," *Exile*, No. 1 (Spring, 1927); "Italy, 1927," *New Republic*, Vol. 50 (May 18, 1927); *Men Without Women*, NY, Oct. 14, 1927; "Valentine," *Little Review*, Vol. 12 (May, 1929).
Books: L. H. Cohn, *A Bibliography of the Works of Ernest Hemingway*, 1931; Vincent Sheean, *Personal History*, 1935; Robert McAlmon, *Being Geniuses Together*, 1938; Sherwood Anderson, *Memoirs*, 1942.
Author's interviews and correspondence: with Hadley R. Mowrer, Aug. 1962; with Mrs. E. J. Miller, July, 1964; with Ada MacLeish, March, 1965; with Donald Friede, May, 1965; with Waldo Peirce, June, 1966; from Miss Andrée F. Hickok, June 28, 1966.

NOTES

Instances of bluster and backbiting: Waiting at Lipp's: EH to Fitzgerald, March 31, 1927. **Scolding by Chard Smith:** Smith to EH, Jan. 1, 1927 and EH to Smith, ca. late Jan., 1927. **Backbiting Bromfield:** EH to Fitzgerald, March 31, 1927. **Mollifying Anderson:** EH to Perkins, Jan. 20; *Memoirs of Sherwood Anderson*, NY, 1942, pp. 475–476. At this time, EH contributed a humorous piece to *The New Yorker*, Vol. 2 (Feb. 12, 1927), pp. 23–24. A loose parody of Frank Harris's autobiography, it consisted of a series of short episodes, each with a subtitle beginning, "How I Broke With . . ."

Spread of EH's fame: Sales of "The Sun Also Rises": Perkins to EH, Jan. 14, Feb. 4, Feb. 21, and March 9, 1927. **Sales of "Alpine Idyll" and "The Killers":** EH to Perkins, Jan. 20, 1927. Some few voices rose against *The Sun*. The *Dial*, already in EH's black books for having rejected "The Undefeated," said that the characters in the novel were "as shallow as the saucers in which they stack their daily emotions," and that EH had contented himself with a mere "carbon copy of a not particularly significant surface of life in Paris" (*Dial*, Vol. 82, Jan., 1927, p. 73). **Plans for "Men Without Women":** Perkins to EH, Jan. 28 and Feb. 28, and EH to Perkins, Feb. 14, 1927. EH later gave a long, facetious account of his search for a title in a letter to Fitzgerald of ca. Sept. 15, 1927. He said that he was up in Gstaad and went to all the bookstores trying to find a Bible in order to get a title out of it. But all the stores offered for sale were small carved wooden bears, and he came near calling the book *The Little Carved Wood Bear*, which would have given the critics a wonderful chance to make profound explanations. At last Pauline managed to borrow a Bible from a Church of England clergyman who was vacationing in Gstaad. Ernest "looked all through that Bible" for a suitable title, finding that practically every good one had already been "swiped" by others, principally Kipling. So he was driven back upon the title *Men Without Women*, hoping that it would have a large sale "among fairies and old Vassar Girls."
EH's further comments on his marital situation: EH to his parents, Feb. 5 and EH to Isabelle Godolphin, March 5, 1927. **Strater's comment:** Henry Strater to EH, Feb. 16, 1927. **Hickok proposes Italian tour:** Guy Hickok to EH, ca. Jan. 15 and Feb. 2, 1927.
EH brings Bumby to Switzerland for another visit: EH to Isabelle Godolphin, March 5, 1927.
Italian tour with Hickok: EH, "Italy, 1927," later retitled "Che Ti Dice La Patria." When the account of the lunch in Spezia appeared in the *New Republic*, Vol. 50 (May 18, 1927), pp. 350–353, Guy Hickok was soon badgered with clippings in which the incident of the prostitute was underscored in red pencil. "I understand now," he told EH, "why everybody you use in your stuff goes out and gets a gun. I feel like Duff [Twysden]. . . . Come in this week. I keep my gun here in my desk." (Hickok to EH, June 7, 1927.) The praying and weeping episodes are attested in a letter from Hickok's daughter Andrée to author, June 28, 1966.
Pauline writes EH poste restante: Pauline to EH, March 15, 17, 18, 19, 20, 22, and 23, 1927.
Hadley takes Bumby to the U.S.A.: EH to Perkins, April 16, 1927; Perkins to EH, April 30, 1927. Hadley stayed for a time with an adopted aunt, Mrs. Constance Rapallo, enjoying a round of party and play-going in New York. On the 28th she called on Perkins, who supplied funds, and then left for St. Louis to stay with her sister. She made a side trip to Oak Park with Bumby, whom none of the Hemingways had seen. Dr. Hemingway was both solicitous and proud, though Ernest's parents were still much shocked over the divorce. Following another stay in St. Louis,

Hadley went to Carmel, California, for the summer (Hadley R. Mowrer to author, August, 1962).
Stages in the planning of "Men Without Women": EH to Perkins, Feb. 14, ca. April 25, May 4, May 27, June 10, and Aug. 17, 1927, along with matching letters from Perkins to EH during the same period. For a time, it looked as if a long bullfight story called "A Lack of Passion" might get into the volume (EH to Perkins, May 4, 1927; Perkins to EH, July 14, 1927) but on August 17 Ernest wrote that it had grown to about the size of a novel and would not "come right." It was dropped. So was the idea of including "Up In Michigan" —possibly because of Ernest's recognition of the fact that it would not fit very well under the *Men Without Women* title. The abortion story, "Hills Like White Elephants," was evidently in process of being written as early as March, 1927. The third page of Ernest's letter to Fitzgerald of March 31 contained a sentence, "We sat at a table in the shade of the station." Ernest explained its presence there with the notation: "this the start of something or other." It is of some interest to see that he began the story in the first person. But third-person narration is the mode of the final version, and the original opening sentence has become, "The American and the girl with him sat at a table in the shade, outside the building" and has become the fourth sentence of the opening paragraph. According to Robert McAlmon, the seed of the story had been planted in Ernest's memory four years earlier in conversation. "One night in Rapallo [in February, 1923] the lot of us were talking of birth control, and spoke of the cruelty of the law which did not allow young unmarried women to avoid having an unwanted child. Recalling an incident of college days I told a story of a girl who had managed to have herself taken care of. Her attitude was very casual. 'Oh, it was nothing. The doctor just let the air in and a few hours later it was over.' . . . Later Hemingway informed me that my remark suggested the story." R. McAlmon, *Being Geniuses Together*, London, 1938, p. 159.
EH meets Donald Friede: EH to Perkins, May 27, 1927; Friede, *The Mechanical Angel*, NY, 1948, p. 28; Friede to author, May, 1965.
EH meets Waldo Peirce: Waldo Peirce to author, June 1, 1966; EH to Waldo Peirce, July 22, 1927.
EH marries Pauline: On the place of the wedding, Miss Virginia Pfeiffer (via Dr. Gregory Hemingway) to author, March 17, 1966. Mrs. Paul Pfeiffer to EH and Pauline, ca. May 1, 1927. **Ada MacLeish's wedding luncheon and her views on EH's "Catholicism":** Ada MacLeish to author, March 9, 1965.
EH attempts to explain his Catholicism: EH, penciled draft of a letter to the Dominican Father, V. C. Donavan, at the Priory of St. Vincent Ferrer, 869 Lexington Ave., New York City. Father Donavan was a friend of Donald Ogden Stewart's, and had presumably asked Hemingway for a statement about his religious beliefs. The draft is undated, but appears to have been done about November 24, 1927. Pauline's letter to Ernest of March 19, 1927, while he was in Italy with Guy Hickok, mentions his baptism by the priest in 1918. The story that EH was converted to Catholicism in

Italy was confirmed by his sister Sunny (Mrs. Ernest Miller to author, July 1964). Ernest wrote his father on May 23, 1926, that he had attended Mass in Madrid that morning and would go to the bullfights that afternoon. Hadley stated that Ernest never attended Mass while she lived with him (September 3, 1921–September, 1926), at least so far as she was able to observe (Hadley R. Mowrer to author, August, 1962). EH's "Nothoemist Poem" appeared in Pound's *Exile*, No. 1 (Spring, 1927), p. 21. The original version was much longer than the two lines that Pound published: "The Lord is my shepherd, I shall not want him for long." EH later wrote Capt. L. H. Cohn that his intended title, "Neothomist Poem," referred to the "temporary embracing of church by literary gents" (L. H. Cohn, *A Bibliography of the Works of Ernest Hemingway*, NY, 1931, p. 89). Even later he wrote Philip Young that his poem was meant to "kid" Jean Cocteau, who had then just switched from opium to Neo-Thomism. He added that the poem did not express his own personal beliefs (EH to Philip Young, June 23, 1952). **EH and Pauline on honeymoon:** EH provided accounts of Grau du Roi in EH to Perkins, May 27, 1927, and EH to Miss Frances Thorne (later Mrs. W. D. Horne), Feb. 12, 1929. He mentioned his infected foot in EH to Perkins, June 24, 1927, and later told Isabelle Godolphin that he had nearly died of anthrax: EH to Isabelle Godolphin, Dec. 5, 1927. Pauline returned from the trip in blooming health: EH to Mr. and Mrs. Paul Pfeiffer, ca. June 10, 1927. **EH and Pauline summering in Spain:** EH to Barklie Henry, July 14 and ca. Aug. 7; EH to Waldo Peirce, July 22; EH to MacLeish, Aug. 29, 1927. **EH's lies about Hadley and Pauline:** EH to his father, Sept. 9–14, 1927. **EH on his fan mail:** EH to Perkins, Sept. 15 and ca. Nov. 1, 1927. **EH irritated by Virginia Woolf:** EH to Perkins, ca. Nov. 1, 1927; Miss Woolf's review appeared in *NY Herald Tribune Books*, Oct. 9, 1927, p. 1. Another British judgment, by Cyril Connolly, called the stories "a blend of Gertrude Stein's manner, Celtic childishness, and the slice of life . . . redeemed by humor, power over dialogue, and an obvious knowledge of the people he describes." *New Statesman*, Vol. 30 (Nov. 26, 1927), p. 208. **Further irritating reviews:** Lee Wilson Dodd, *Saturday Review of Literature*, Vol. 4 (Nov. 19, 1927), p. 322; Joseph Wood Krutch, *The Nation*, Vol. 125 (Nov. 16, 1927), p. 548; Percy Hutchinson, *New York Times Book Review*, Oct. 16, 1927, p. 9. EH took vengeance on Dodd and Krutch in a poetical "Valentine" beginning, "Sing a song of critics, pockets full of lye," and echoing some of the phrases they had used in their reviews. This poem appeared in the final number of *The Little Review*, Vol. 12 (May, 1929), p. 42. **EH's second novel:** EH to Perkins, Sept. 15, ca. Oct. 15, and Nov. 24, 1927. He later told Charles Scribner of having written 40,000 words on a novel about Oak Park shortly after finishing *The Sun Also Rises*. He abandoned it, he said, because he did not know enough to finish it. EH to Charles Scribner, Aug. 3, 1949. **EH's hope of returning to the U.S.A.:** EH to

Barklie Henry, ca. **Aug. 7,** 1927; EH to Perkins, ca. Oct. 15 and Nov. 24, 1927. **Hadley's return from American visit:** She sailed from New York for Cherbourg aboard the *Lancastria* on Oct. 22 (EH to Fitzgerald, ca. Sept. 15, 1927; Hadley R. Mowrer to author, Aug., 1962). **EH and Sinclair Lewis in Berlin:** Professor Ramon Guthrie to author, August, 1965; Vincent Sheean, *Personal History*, NY, 1935, p. 280. EH later discussed El Greco in *Death in the Afternoon*, 1932, p. 205. **EH's year-end miseries:** EH to Isabelle Godolphin, Dec. 5, 1927; EH to Fitzgerald, ca. Dec. 15 and Dec. 18, 1927. The article on Grace Hemingway's paintings appeared in the *Oak Park News*, Nov. 8, 1927. **EH's views on Henry James's "The Awkward Age":** EH to Waldo Peirce, late Dec., 1927.

Sec. 27. Going West

SOURCES

Letters of EH: to Perkins, Jan. 15 and 30, 1928; to James Joyce, Jan. 30; to Perkins, Feb. 12 and March 17; to Pauline, ca. late March; to Perkins, Apr. 21; to Strater, May 13; to Dorothy Connable, May 14; to Perkins, May 31; to his father, June 1; to Perkins, June 7; to Waldo Peirce, June 17; to Mrs. Paul Pfeiffer, July 2–3; to Strater, ca. July 4; to Peirce, July 23 and Aug. 9; to Hickok, Aug. 18; to Peirce, ca. Aug. 22; to Hickok, Sept. 27; to Perkins, Sept. 28; to Peirce, ca. Oct. 1, ca. Oct. 15, and ca. Oct. 23–30; to Perkins, Oct. 11; to Fitzgerald, Nov. 18, 1928. To Peirce, Apr. 15, 1932; to Charles Scribner, July 4, 1951. **Other letters:** Pound to EH, March 11, 1928; Hadley to EH, ca. March 11; Dr. Hemingway to EH, June 4; Owen Wister to Waldo Peirce, Aug. 31, 1928. **EH's work: (a) Unpublished:** Unfinished "Tom Jones" novel; sketch of Fitzgerald during and after Princeton-Yale game, composed perhaps ca. 1958, deleted from *A Moveable Feast*. **(b) Published:** "Wine of Wyoming," *Scribner's Magazine*, Vol. 88 (Aug., 1930); "After the Storm," *Cosmopolitan*, Vol. 92 (May, 1932). **Books and articles:** Marcelline Sanford, *At the Hemingways*, 1962; Leicester Hemingway, *My Brother, Ernest Hemingway*, 1962; Virginia Spear Edwards, "Willis M. Spear," *Men of Wyoming Territory*, Vol. 3 (1965); John Dos Passos, *The Best Times*, 1966. **Author's interviews and correspondence:** with Mr. and Mrs. W. B. Horne, Dec., 1961; W. B. Smith, Apr., 1964; Mr. and Mrs. Archibald MacLeish, Mr. and Mrs. T. O. Bruce, Mr. and Mrs. Charles Thompson, and J. B. Sullivan (all in March, 1965); Nathaniel Burt, Nov., 1965 and April, 1968. From Olive Nordquist, March 23 1965; from Elsa Spear Byron, Sept. 23, 1965; from Mrs. Anthony Ulchar, Apr. 25, 1967.

NOTES

EH's bad physical luck: EH to James Joyce, Jan. 30, 1928; EH to Perkins, Jan. 15, Jan. 30, and Feb. 12, 1928. **Skylight accident:** EH to Perkins, March 17, 1928; Archibald and Ada MacLeish to author, March 9, 1965. **Comments by friends:** Ezra

Pound to EH, March 11, 1928. Hadley to EH, ca. March 11. Several photographs show EH with his scar, one with Sylvia Beach before the bookshop, and several portrait studies by Helen Breaker, who was now trying to earn her living in Paris as a photographer.
EH's new novel on the "Tom Jones" model: EH to Perkins, Feb. 12 and March 17, 1928.
Inception of "A Farewell to Arms": EH to Perkins, March 17, speaks of having begun the novel that became *A Farewell* "two weeks ago," or about March 3, 1928. "It goes on and goes wonderfully," he said on March 17.
Account of Key West: John Dos Passos, *The Best Times*, NY, 1966, pp. 198–199; Charles and Lorine Thompson to author, March 28, 1965.
Passage to Havana: EH to Dorothy Connable, May 14, 1928; EH to Pauline *en voyage*, ca. late March, 1928.
Living quarters in Key West: Lorine Thompson to author, March 28, 1965.
EH's Key West friends: EH to Perkins, Apr. 21, 1928; Charles Thompson to author, March 29, 1965; J. B. Sullivan to author, March 30, 1965. Other friends included Jakey Key, a gnarled Conch who spent much of his time fishing from the city dock, and George Brooks, Assistant District Attorney. Eddie Saunders, called Bra, was born in Green Turtle Key, Bahamas, Feb. 27, 1876. He married Julia Bethel March 27, 1901, and died at home (614 Grinnell St., Key West) Jan. 14, 1949. (Mrs. Anthony L. Ulchar [daughter] to author, Apr. 25, 1967.)
Charles and Lorine Thompson: Thompson was born in Key West, Nov. 24, 1898. The family name was Norberg (Swedish), changed to Thompson by Charles's grandfather. Charles was educated in New York and at Mt. Pleasant Military School in Ossining-on-the-Hudson, and joined the Army in 1919. In 1920 he worked for the Mallory Steamship Company and held various other jobs in Key West. His wife-to-be came from Richmond, Ga. They met in 1922 while she was teaching school in Key West and were married Sept. 6, 1923. Charles and Lorine Thompson to author, March 28, 1965.
Dr. and Mrs. Hemingway in Key West: EH to Perkins, Apr. 21, 1928; Charles Thompson to author, March 28, 1965; Marcelline Sanford, *At the Hemingways*, Boston, 1962, p. 227.
EH invites friends to Key West: EH to Strater, May 13, 1928; EH to Perkins, June 7, 1928; EH to his father, June 1, 1928; John Dos Passos, *The Best Times*, NY, 1966, p. 199; William B. Smith to author, Apr., 1964.
Bra Saunders's story of the "Val Banera": Mr. and Mrs. T. O. Bruce to author, March 22, 1965; Charles and Lorine Thompson to author, March 28, 1965. "After the Storm," Hemingway's version of the story, written four years later, was published in *Cosmopolitan*, Vol. 92 (May, 1932), pp. 38–41 and 155. Ernest mentioned it to Waldo Peirce (EH to Peirce, April 15, 1932) as a story they had heard from Bra Saunders: "You probably remember when Bra told it to us first."
EH's opinion of Piggott, Ark.: EH to Perkins, May 31, 1928.
EH suggests visit to Walloon Lake: EH to his father, June 1, 1928. Dr. Hemingway's reply of June 4 is mostly quoted in Leicester Hem-

ingway, *My Brother, Ernest Hemingway,* Cleveland, 1962, pp. 107–108.
EH and Pauline in Kansas City: EH to Waldo Peirce, June 17, 1928.
Birth of Patrick Hemingway: EH to Mrs. Paul Pfeiffer, July 2–3, 1928. EH to Strater, ca. July 4, 1928.
Train trip home to Piggott: EH to Waldo Peirce, July 23, 1928.
EH and Bill Horne to Wyoming: EH to Waldo Peirce, Aug. 9, 1928: Mr. and Mrs. W. D. Horne to author, Dec., 1961. The Hornes own a privately printed *Log of Folly Ranch* for 1928. It shows that EH was officially in residence July 30–Aug. 18. Bill was there July 30–Aug. 11 and Frances Thorne (the future Mrs. Horne) July 20–Aug. 23, 1928.
Pauline joins EH in Sheridan: EH to Guy Hickok, Aug. 18, 1929. For the identity of the Moncini family, the author is indebted to Mrs. Elsa Spear Byron. EH's "Wine of Wyoming" story was written in 1930 and published in *Scribner's Magazine,* Vol. 88 (August, 1930), pp. 195–204. It follows almost exactly the events of late August and early September, 1928, while EH and Pauline were in and around Sheridan.
EH and Pauline at Spear-O-Wigwam Ranch: Mrs. Elsa Spear Byron to author, Sept. 23, 1965. Virginia Spear Edwards, "Willis M. Spear: Wyoming Pioneer," in *Men of Wyoming Territory,* Vol. 3, 1965, pp. 15–22, gives an account of Mrs. Byron's father. EH to Perkins, Sept. 28, 1928, says it is one month since he finished his novel.
Final month's adventures in Wyoming: EH to Waldo Peirce, ca. Aug. 22, and Sept. 23, 1928; Elsa Spear Byron to author, Sept. 23, 1965; Olive Nordquist to author, March 23, 1965; Nathaniel Burt to author, November, 1965, and April, 1968. Owen Wister to Waldo Peirce, Aug. 31, 1928. EH to Charles Scribner, July 4, 1951.
EH's month in Piggott and his longing for France and Spain: EH to Guy Hickok, Sept. 27, 1928; EH to Waldo Peirce, ca. Oct. 1 and ca. Oct. 15, 1928.
EH and Pauline on eastern tour: EH to Perkins (wire) Oct. 23, 1928; EH to Waldo Peirce, ca. Oct. 23–30, 1928.
Princeton football game: Isabelle Godolphin to author, Oct. 22, 1964; unpublished sketch on Fitzgerald during and after the game, deleted from *A Moveable Feast.*
EH's thank-you letter: EH to Fitzgerald, Nov. 18, 1928.
EH's opinion of Zelda: EH to Perkins, Oct. 11, 1928.

Sec. 28. *A Farewell to Arms*

SOURCES

Letters of EH: to Perkins (2 wires), Dec. 6, 1928; to Pullman Porter McIntyre, ca. Dec. 7; to Perkins, Dec. 9; to Fitzgerald, Dec. 9; to Mrs. Paul Pfeiffer, Dec. 13; to Strater, Dec. 22, 1928. To Waldo Peirce, Jan. 4 and ca. Jan. 7, 1929; to Perkins, Jan. 8; to Hickok, Jan. 9; to Perkins, Jan. 11; to Peirce, Jan. 15 and 18; to Perkins, Jan. 22 and 23 (wire); to Perkins, March 11; to his mother, March 11; to MacLeish, March 26; to Robert Bridges, May 8; to Thornton Wilder, May 26; to Perkins, June 7 (2 letters); to Peirce, Owen

Wister, and Perkins, all June 24; to Wilder, July 18; to Perkins, July 26 and 31; to Wister and Fitzgerald, both late July; to Sylvia Beach, Aug. 18; to Mrs. Pfeiffer, Aug. 22; to Perkins, Aug. 28; to Peirce, Aug. 29; to Fitzgerald and Dos Passos, both Sept. 4; to Perkins, Sept. 9; to Fitzgerald, Sept. 13; to Perkins, Sept. 27 and Oct. 4; to Carol Hemingway, ca. Oct. 5; to Perkins, Oct. 20–21, 22, 31, Nov. 19 and 30; to MacLeish, Dec. 1; to Perkins, Dec. 7–10; to Fitzgerald Dec. 12, and ca. December, 1929. To Lillian Ross, Feb. 24, 1952; to Bernard Berenson, Oct. 14, 1952.
Other letters: Carol Hemingway to EH, Dec. 6 (wire); Fitzgerald to EH, Dec. 28, 1928. Perkins to EH, Jan. 15 and 25, 1929; Feb. 13 (wire and letter); Hickok to EH, May 5; Robert Bridges to EH, May 8; Perkins to EH, May 24, 28, 29 (cable), 31, and June 12; Hickok to EH, July 26; Perkins to EH, Oct. 15 (cable), and 22; Callaghan to Isabel Paterson, Nov. 26; Isabel Paterson to Callaghan, Dec. 3; Fitzgerald to Callaghan, Jan. 1, 1930.
EH's work: Published: *A Farewell to Arms*, Sept. 27, 1929; *Death in the Afternoon*, 1932.
Books and articles: Ben Ray Redman, "Spokesman for a Generation," *Spur*, Vol. 44 (Dec. 1, 1929); Sidney Franklin, *Bullfighter from Brooklyn*, 1952; Marcelline Sanford, *At the Hemingways*, 1962; Leicester Hemingway, *My Brother, Ernest Hemingway*, 1962; Morley Callaghan, *That Summer in Paris*, 1963; Lillian Ross, *Reporting*, 1964; John Dos Passos, *The Best Times*, 1966.
Author's interviews and correspondence: with Mrs. E. J. Miller and Sterling Sanford, July, 1964; with Mr. and Mrs. T. O. Bruce, Mr. and Mrs. Archibald MacLeish, J. B. Sullivan, and Mr. and Mrs. Charles Thompson (all in March, 1965). From Allen Tate, Apr. 2, 1963; from Dawn Powell, May 10, 1965; from John Dos Passos, May 15, 1965.

NOTES

Piggott to Key West: EH to Mrs. Paul Pfeiffer, Dec. 13, 1928.
Rented house on South Street: Lorine Thompson to author, March 28, 1965.
EH meets Ring Lardner: Fitzgerald to EH, Dec. 28, 1928: "Ring thought you were fine. He was uncharacteristically enthusiastic."
Dr. Hemingway's suicide: Carol Hemingway to EH (wire), Dec. 6, 1928; EH to Perkins (2 wires), Dec. 6; EH to Pullman Porter McIntyre of Car E–72, ca. Dec. 7; EH to Fitzgerald, Dec. 9; EH to Perkins (on southbound train near Corinth, Miss.), Dec. 9; EH to Mrs. Paul Pfeiffer, Dec. 13; EH to Henry Strater, Dec. 22, 1928; EH to Bernard Berenson, Oct. 14, 1952. The letter that EH had sent his father from Jacksonville was delivered on the morning of Dec. 6, but left unopened by Dr. Hemingway. Grace opened it and learned that EH was in New York meeting Bumby. She wired Scribners to ask them to communicate with EH. Carol wired EH aboard the southbound train. Arrangements were nearly complete when EH reached Oak Park. The coffin was placed in Grace's music room. The funeral was held on Saturday, Dec. 8, at the First Congregational Church. Half the town attended. The Cook

County police impounded the suicide weapon, subsequently returning it to Grace, who sent it to EH at his request. Information from Mrs. E. J. Miller and Sterling Sanford to author, July, 1964; other details from Marcelline Sanford, *At the Hemingways*, 1962, pp. 231–234, and Leicester Hemingway, *My Brother, Ernest Hemingway*, 1962, pp. 110–111.
EH revises "A Farewell": EH to Waldo Peirce, Jan. 4, ca. Jan. 7, Jan. 15, and Jan. 18, 1929; EH to Perkins, Jan. 8, 10, 22, and 23 (wire).
Perkins comes to Key West: Perkins to EH, Jan. 15 and 25.
Sale to "Scribner's Magazine": Perkins to EH, letter and wire, Feb. 13, 1929.
"Transalpine fornication": EH to Hickok, Jan. 9, 1929.
Approval of novel by Strater, Peirce, and Dos Passos: EH to Perkins, March 11, 1929.
EH's aid and advice to his mother: March 11, 1929.
Grace's crate of paintings: Dawn Powell to author, May 10, 1965; John Dos Passos to author, May 15, 1965; Leicester Hemingway, *My Brother, Ernest Hemingway*, 1962, p. 111.
Crossing to Paris and work on end of novel: EH to MacLeish, March 26, 1929; Guy Hickok to EH, May 5; Robert Bridges to EH, May 8; Perkins to EH, May 24, 28, 29 (cable), and 31; EH to Thornton Wilder, May 26; EH to Perkins (2 letters), June 7; Perkins to EH, June 12; EH to Peirce, June 24, 1929.
Boxing with Callaghan: Callaghan, *That Summer in Paris*, NY, 1963, pp. 91–112, 125–127, 166–167. EH to Perkins, June 24, 1929.
Fitzgerald's long round: *That Summer in Paris*, pp. 211–221; EH to Perkins, Aug. 28, 1929. There are some discrepancies between EH's contemporaneous account and that of Callaghan many years later. Callaghan did not mention EH's vinous lunch at Prunier's, probably because he did not know of it. He also said that the rounds were supposed to last three minutes, with a minute's rest between, whereas EH told Perkins that the rounds were to last one minute each, with two minutes rest "on acct. of my condition." Morley said that he caught EH on the jaw, spinning him around. EH said that he "slipped and went down once and lit on my arm and put my left shoulder out in that first round and it pulled a tendon so that it was pretty sore afterwards" with the result that they did not get a chance to box again before he and Pauline left for Spain. EH may have believed this version of the incident. As late as August 28th, running his tongue along the inside of his lower lip, he could still feel the "big scar" where he had been hit. Yet two sentences later he told Perkins that Morley could not hit hard; otherwise he "would have killed me."
EH and Pauline in Pamplona: EH to Peirce, Aug. 29, 1929; Ben Ray Redman, "Spokesman for a Generation," *Spur*, Vol. 44 (Dec. 1, 1929), pp. 77 and 186.
Summering in Spain: EH to Wilder, July 18; EH to Owen Wister and Fitzgerald, both late July; EH to Perkins, July 26 and 31, 1929. About July 22, which was her thirty-fourth birthday, Pauline had her hair dyed blond as a gesture of sexual independence and a surprise for EH (Hickok to EH, July 26, 1929; Ada MacLeish to author, March, 1965). Much is made of this gesture in EH's later unpublished novel, *The Garden of Eden.*

Dedication to G. A. Pfeiffer: EH to Perkins, July 26 and 31, 1929.
Dos Passos marries Katy Smith: Dos Passos, *The Best Times,* 1966, p. 202; EH to Dos Passos, Sept. 4, 1929, with a warning on the corrupting effects of money.
Americanization of Spain: EH to Sylvia Beach, Aug. 18; to Mrs. Paul Pfeiffer, Aug. 22; to Waldo Peirce, Aug. 29, 1929.
EH meets Sidney Franklin: Guy Hickok to EH, July 26, 1929. EH to Lillian Ross, Feb. 24, 1952. Sidney Franklin, *Bullfighter from Brooklyn,* NY, 1952, pp. 170–180. Lillian Ross, "Sidney Franklin: El Único Matador," *Reporting,* NY, 1964. Miss Ross's article, which first appeared as a profile (her first) in *The New Yorker* magazine discussed Hemingway's association with Franklin at some length with Hemingway during a visit to Ketchum, Idaho, just before Christmas, 1947. Ernest gave the wrong date for his first meeting with Franklin. He remembered it as August 15th, but the contemporaneous letter to Perkins from Santiago on August 28th clearly indicates that it could not have been earlier than September 1. EH's statement that he spent "many weeks" in Franklin's company is an exaggeration. His account of Franklin appears in *Death in the Afternoon,* 1932, pp. 503–506. Their first meeting is chronicled in Lillian Ross, *Reporting,* NY, 1964, pp. 182–183.
EH's advice to Fitzgerald: Sept. 4 and 13, 1929. Fitzgerald told EH on Sept. 9 that his "analysis of my inability to get my serious work done is too kind in that it leaves out dissipation."
Reviewers' reception of "A Farewell": excerpts are from Percy Hutchinson, *New York Times Book Review,* Sept. 29, 1929, p. 5; Clifton Fadiman, *The Nation,* Vol. 129 (Oct. 30, 1929), p. 497; Malcolm Cowley, *New York Herald Tribune Books,* Oct. 6, 1929, p. 1; H. S. Canby, *Saturday Review of Literature,* Vol. 6 (Oct. 12, 1929), p. 231.
EH's swollen fingers and trip to Chartres with the Callaghans: EH to Perkins, Sept. 27, 1929. The trip is described in *That Summer in Paris,* pp. 231–238, where the month is wrongly given as October.
Meeting with Allen and Caroline Tate: Tate to author, Apr. 2, 1963; EH to Perkins, Oct. 4, 1929. In denying the influence of Defoe and Captain Marryat, EH did not mention the fact that *Robinson Crusoe* had been one of his favorite books in boyhood and that he had strongly recommended *Peter Simple* to Fitzgerald during his first winter in Schruns.
Early sales of "A Farewell"; EH's worries and pride: Perkins to EH, Oct. 15 (cable), and Oct. 22, 1929; EH to Perkins, Oct. 20–21, 22, 31, and Nov. 19, 1929.
EH's activities in November and December: EH to Perkins, Oct. 20, Nov. 19, and Dec. 16, 1929; EH to Peirce, ca. Nov. 19; EH to MacLeish, Dec. 1; EH to Fitzgerald, ca. Dec., 1929; Allen Tate to author, Apr. 2, 1963.
EH's threats to the "Bookman" editor and Robert McAlmon: EH to Perkins, Nov. 30, enclosed the letter; EH to Perkins, Dec. 7–10, discussed McAlmon's allegations.
Contretemps with Callaghan: The "Turns with a Bookworm" column by Isabel Paterson which first enraged Hemingway was published in *New York Herald Tribune Books* on Sunday, Nov. 24, 1929. Callaghan's denial was sent to Miss Paterson on Nov. 26. She replied on Dec. 3 to say that she was printing his correction on Sunday, Dec. 8, as she did. The texts of these letters and of Fitzgerald's collect cable to Callaghan are printed in *That Summer in Paris,* NY, 1963, pp. 242–243. He also includes accounts of the letters of apology from Fitzgerald (Jan. 1, 1930) and Hemingway (Jan. 4, 1930), and interprets the incident at length on pp. 241–251.
EH on his bout with Prévost (1925) and on Crosby's suicide: EH to Fitzgerald, Dec. 12, 1929.

Sec. 29. The Island and the Valley

SOURCES

Letters of EH: To Barklie Henry, Dec. 2, 1929; to Perkins, Dec. 15; to MacLeish, Dec. 31, 1929. To Perkins, ca. Jan. 8, 1930; to Peirce, Feb. 7; to Peirce, ca. Feb. 8; to Milford Baker, Feb. 12; to Perkins, ca. Feb. 14; to Strater, Feb. 18; to Perkins, March 10; to Baker, March 14; to Peirce, Apr. 6; to Cyril Clemens, Apr. 6; to Baker, Apr. 8; to Perkins, Apr. 15; to Baker, Apr. 15; to Capt. L. H. Cohn, Apr. 23; to Mrs. Paul Pfeiffer, Apr. 23; to Perkins, ca. April 30; to Baker, May 5 and 17; to Hickok, ca. early May; to Strater, May 20; to Perkins, May 31; to Peirce, June 1; to Strater, ca. June 5 and June 20; to Hickok, ca. June 6; to Baker, June 20 (wire and letter) to Capt. Cohn, June 24; to MacLeish, June 30; to Perkins, July 10 (wire); to Strater, Aug. 25; to MacLeish, ca. Sept.; to William D. Horne, Sept. 12; to Perkins, Sept. 28, 1930. To Charles Scribner, ca. Aug. 15, 1940.
Other letters: Perkins to EH, Dec. 9, 1929; Feb. 14 and 28, 1930; Milford Baker to EH, Feb. 17; Charles Kingsley to Perkins, March 19; Jonathan Cape to Perkins, March 24; Baker to EH, March 28; Perkins to EH, Apr. 8; Perkins to Cape, Apr. 11; Baker to EH, Apr. 16 and 30, May 14, 15, and 22, June 2 and 4; Perkins to EH, June 3; Baker to EH, June 20 (wire). Perkins to Earl Wilson, Jan. 30, 1941; Perkins to EH, June 6, 1941.
EH's work: (a) Unpublished: undated fragment on bootleg whiskey in Montana and Wyoming. **(b) Published:** "Bullfighting, Sport and Industry," *Fortune,* Vol. 1 (March, 1930); introduction to *Kiki's Memoirs,* Paris, 1930; *Death in the Afternoon,* 1932; "The Clark's Fork Valley, Wyoming," *Vogue,* Vol. 93 (Feb., 1939).
Books and articles: Dorothy Parker, "The Artist's Reward," *The New Yorker,* Vol. 5 (Nov. 30, 1929); John Dos Passos, *The Best Times,* 1966.
Author's interviews and correspondence: With Lewis Galantière, Feb., 1963; with Henry Strater, Olive Nordquist, Ivan Wallace, L. S. Weaver, and Floyd Allington (all July, 1964); with Lorine Thompson, March, 1965. From Josephine Herbst, July 3, 1963; from Milford Baker, Feb. 20, 1966.

NOTES

Swiss Holiday: EH to Perkins, Dec. 15, 1929; Dos Passos, *The Best Times,* 1966, p. 203. Dorothy Parker's profile of EH had appeared in *The New Yorker* for Nov. 30. Sales of

A Farewell to Arms passed 60,000 while EH was in Switzerland. Barklie Henry gently chided EH for having used both parts of his name in the book—Catherine Barkley and Lieut. Henry: EH to B. McK. Henry, Dec. 2, 1929. The Swiss holiday ended Dec. 31, when EH wrote MacLeish from Paris to say he had just returned.

"Kiki's Memoirs": EH's introduction appears on pp. 9–14 of this book, which was translated by Samuel Putnam, illustrated with photographs of Kiki and of her paintings, printed in Dijon by Darantière, McAlmon's printer, and published in Paris at the Black Manikin Press at 4, rue Delambre near the Dingo Bar. Putnam persuaded EH to do the introduction.

House on Pearl Street, Key West: Lorine Thompson to author, March, 1965; EH to Peirce, Feb. 7, 1930. This house was later pulled down.

EH invites the MacLeishes to Key West: EH to MacLeish, ca. Feb. 8, 1930.

EH's plans for Tortugas: EH to Strater, Feb. 18; EH to Perkins, ca. Jan. 28, ca. Feb. 14, and March 10; Perkins to EH, Feb. 14 and 28, 1930. These letters allude to two other matters of some literary interest. The Fox Film Corporation appropriated EH's *Men Without Women* title to use for a film about the crew of a submarine. Although both Max and EH believed that it set a poor precedent, they accepted Fox's courtesy payment of $500. Early in March, a rare-book dealer named Jacob Schwartz in High Holborn, London, put up for sale at £30 the copy of *Three Stories and Ten Poems* which Hemingway had inscribed to Ernest Walsh in 1924, as well as the personal letters which he had then sent Walsh while getting together the first number of *This Quarter* magazine. Scribner's London representative, Charles Kingsley, bought these items for transmission to Perkins. (Kingsley to Perkins, March 19, 1930.)

Tortugas trip: Herrmann as crew member: Josephine Herbst to author, July 3, 1963; **Perkins and EH on wildlife:** Perkins to Earl Wilson, Jan. 30, 1941; **Cape Sable and Perkins's fishing triumph:** EH to Peirce, Apr. 6 and June 1, 1930. **Further details:** Strater to author, July, 1964; Perkins to EH, Apr. 8, and Perkins to Jonathan Cape, Apr. 11, 1930.

"A Farewell to Arms" in Hoover's library: EH to Mrs. Paul Pfeiffer, Apr. 23, 1930.

EH's bullfighting article: *Fortune*, Vol. 1 (March, 1930), pp. 83–88.

Plans for safari and for purchase of Springfield rifle: Milford Baker to Mrs. Ernest Hemingway, Feb. 3, 1966, forwarded to author, Feb. 20, 1966. EH to Milford Baker, Feb. 12, March 14, Apr. 8, April 15, May 5, May 17, and June 20, 1930. Milford Baker to EH, Feb. 17, March 28, April 16, April 30, May 14, May 15, May 22, June 2, June 4, 1930. The gun was in the blueing by April 21, and was expressed to EH by Baker on June 2, 1930. "Rifle absolutely splendid," said EH's telegram of June 20, 1930. He was as pleased with his gun as a small boy with a shiny new bicycle. He wrote Mike Strater that it was the damnedest, classy, simple, easy-to-shoot-with thing he had ever seen. It came up as naturally as pointing a finger, had less kick than a 16-gauge shotgun, and packed immense power: one shot with the 220-grain bullet

into an 18-inch-thick palm tree tore out a place the size of his head and shoulders. Not the least of its virtues was a telescopic sight, as easy to mount as shoving a shell into the chamber. (EH to Henry Strater, between June 5 and 20, 1930.)

Dos Passos in Key West: Dos Passos, *The Best Times*, p. 204.

News of goring of Franklin: EH to Mr. and Mrs. Paul Pfeiffer, Apr. 23, 1930, and EH, *Death in the Afternoon*, 1932, p. 505.

Tortugas trip with Dos and Pauline: EH to Perkins, ca. Apr. 30, 1930.

New and old drinks: EH to Hickok, ca. early May.

EH cuts finger: EH to Strater, May 20; EH to Peirce, June 1, 1930.

EH becomes officer in Mark Twain Society: EH to Cyril Clemens, Apr. 6, 1930.

Captain Cohn's bibliography: EH to Cohn, Apr. 23, 1930.

"Wine of Wyoming" sent to Scribners: EH to Perkins, May 31; Perkins to EH, June 3, 1930.

EH in New York: Conversation with Galantière: Galantière to author, Feb., 1963.

Arrangements with Milford Baker: EH to Baker, June 20 and 29, Baker to EH, June 20, 1930.

EH on Cohn's bibliography: EH to Cohn, June 24, 1930.

Driving west: EH to MacLeish, June 30, 1930; EH to Perkins, July 10 (wire); Mrs. Olive W. Nordquist, transcript of L Bar T Ranch Guest Book for 1930, provided to author, March, 1965.

Nordquist Ranch: Olive Nordquist to author, July, 1964, when Mrs. Nordquist conducted author on a tour of the ranch, long since sold to others.

Ranch personnel: Mrs. Olive Nordquist, Floyd Allington, Ivan Wallace, and L. S. Weaver to author, July, 1964. *Olive* in 1930 was still in her late twenties, short, blond, sturdy, and hardworking, an excellent cook and ranch supervisor, much in love with Wyoming. She had been married to Nordquist for eight years. They had owned the ranch since 1925. *Ivan Wallace* was twenty-nine, born in Alberta of Nebraskan parents who brought him back to the U.S.A. at age two. They settled in Red Lodge, Montana, over the Beartooth Range from Cooke City. Until age twenty-five, Ivan trapped around Crandall Creek (pine marten, red fox, otter, and coyote). *Leland Stanford Weaver*, called Chub, had been raised in Red Lodge. He went to school for a time in St. Paul, Minn., then hopped a freight train to New York, where he cooked and washed dishes for a living. After that he "went all over" the U.S.A. and shipped out of California as cook on various freight steamers. He was almost exactly EH's age and height, but thin and wiry; like EH he had lost his father in 1928. He returned to Red Lodge and was working at a mountain camp near Beartooth Lake when Nordquist hired him for the L Bar T. He appears in *For Whom the Bell Tolls*, 1940, p. 337.

EH's fishing: EH's Fishing Log, Summer, 1930.

Setting out bear bait: Ivan Wallace, quoted in EH to Charles Scribner, ca. Aug. 15, 1950.

Visit by Bill and Bunny Horne: EH to Mr. and Mrs. W. D. Horne, Sept. 12, 1930; Olive Nordquist's Guest Book, 1930.

Accident with Goofy and trip to Cody: Ivan Wallace and L. S. Weaver to author, July, 1964; EH to MacLeish, ca. Sept., 1930; EH to Mr. and Mrs. W. D. Horne, Sept. 12, 1930. The accident is also alluded to in Olive Nordquist's Guest Book.

Bootleg whiskey: Burt Wallace, Ivan's uncle, used to pack in fortnightly supplies of wine and whiskey from Red Lodge, coming over Beartooth Gap (Ivan Wallace to author, July, 1964). EH wrote a short fragment (unpublished and undated) on attempts to age and mellow Montana whiskey in charcoal kegs. Red Lodge, at this time, was a one-street town in the valley of the swift-running Rock Creek under the shadow of the Beartooth Range. The elevation was 5,555 feet and the population was about the same. It was something of a boom town, with two coal mines in the immediate vicinity and several more within a few miles' radius. It was also notable for bootlegging. Whiskey stills dotted all the nearby hills, and whole carloads of grapes and sugar came in from Billings sixty miles away to be used in the making of wine. One of the vintners was Mary Francone, whose wines probably reached EH's palate, though it cannot be established that they ever met. Once an especially noisome keg of whiskey came over Beartooth Pass on muleback. They left it to age in a cabin on Crandall Creek. A year later, John Staib went up to fight a fire and was asked to check on its progress. It was still too raw, so he took a 5-pound bag of sugar that had hardened into a loaf, poured whiskey over it, and set it out in a pan to see if a bear would drink it and get drunk. When he returned next day, the pan was licked clean but the bear had disappeared to sleep it off. (L. S. Weaver to author, July 21, 1964.)

Shooting brown and black bears: Ivan Wallace to author, July, 1964; EH to MacLeish, ca. Sept., 1930; EH's Hunting Log for Aug.–Oct., 1930. *"J'ai tué un ours avant hier qui a mangé douze vache"* [sic] (EH to Strater, Aug. 25, 1930). EH loved to pretend that the predatory animals he killed had been a danger to the local cattle owners. He continued to use this kind of statement through 1953–54 in Africa.

Progress with bullfight book: EH to MacLeish, ca. Sept., 1930; EH to Perkins, Sept. 28, 1930. In August and early September, EH reluctantly took time out to go over the text of *In Our Time*. Horace Liveright had finally sold it to Scribners and a reissue was in prospect, with an introduction by Edmund Wilson. Besides Wilson's introduction, there was also one by Hemingway, a "miniature" later entitled "On the Quai at Smyrna." The book appeared on October 24, 1930. But Ernest in Wyoming remarked that tinkering with the text after the lapse of five years was like skinning dead horses.

Hunting on Timber and Crandall Creeks: EH to Perkins, Sept. 28, 1930; EH, "The Clark's Fork Valley, Wyoming," *Vogue*, Vol. 93 (Feb., 1939), pp. 68 and 157.

EH meets John Staib: Ivan Wallace to author, July 19, 1964. Staib lived alone in a mountain cabin with his dog and his horse. According to Wallace he was very neat: the floors of his cabin were always scrubbed as clean as a ship's deck. His only dirty habit was tobacco chewing. When asked to a meal, he removed his chaw, placed it on the windowsill, and afterwards resumed it. Staib is alluded to in *Green Hills of Africa*, 1935, p. 54.

Dos Passos visit: *The Best Times*, 1966, pp. 204–205; Olive Nordquist's Guest Book; Ivan Wallace and L. S. Weaver to author, July, 1964.

Starting for home: Olive Nordquist's Guest Book; Olive Nordquist and Floyd Allington to author, July, 1964.

Sec. 30. Death in the Afternoon

SOURCES

Letters of EH: to Perkins, Aug. 12, 1930; to MacLeish, ca. Sept., 1930; to Perkins, Oct. 28, Nov. 14 (wire), ca. Nov. 15, and Nov. 24 (wire); to MacLeish, Nov. 22; to Perkins, Dec. 1; to Hickok, Dec. 5; to Owen Wister, Dec. 26; to MacLeish, Dec. 28, 1930. To MacLeish, Jan. 14, 1931; to Mrs. Pfeiffer, Jan. 28; to Perkins, March 12 (wire); to MacLeish, March 14; to Perkins, Apr. 12; to MacLeish, Apr. 19; to Dr. Guffey, Apr. 27; to Peirce, Apr. 30 (wire) and May 4; to Mrs. Pfeiffer, May 13; to Peirce, May 14; to Hickok, June 16; to Dos Passos, June 26; to MacLeish, June 29; to Hickok, July 15; to Perkins, Aug. 1; to Mrs. Pfeiffer, Aug. 31; to Peirce, Oct. 5 (wire); to Eric Knight, Oct. 10; to Hickok, Oct. 14; to Eric Knight, ca. Nov. 6; to Peirce, ca. Nov. 11; to Mrs. Pfeiffer, Nov. 12 (letter and wire); to Perkins, Nov. 12–25; to Mrs. Pfeiffer, Nov. 14, 16, and 23; to Captain Cohn, ca. Nov. 13 or 14; to Peirce, Nov. 17; to Perkins, Dec. 9; to Strater, Dec. 10; to Perkins, Dec. 26, 1931. To Perkins, Jan. 5, 1932, and Jan. 14, 1932 (wire). To Perkins, June 10, 1943.

Other letters: Perkins to EH, Aug. 18 and Sept. 11, 1930; Milford Baker to EH, Sept. 24; Perkins to EH, Oct. 3; Perkins to Jonathan Cape, Nov. 1; Pauline to Perkins, Nov. 7 (wire); Pauline to MacLeish, Nov. 9; Perkins to EH, Nov. 13; Pauline to Perkins, Dec. 1 and ca. Dec. 15; Earl Snook to Perkins, ca. Dec. 12; Perkins to Strater, ca. Dec. 15; Ford Madox Ford to Hugh Walpole, Dec. 16, 1930. Perkins to EH, Jan. 20, 1932 (wire).

EH's work: Published: *In Our Time* (reissue), 1930; *The Torrents of Spring* (reissue), Dec. 1931; *Death in the Afternoon*, 1932.

Books: Edmund Wilson, introduction to *In Our Time*, 1930; Sidney Franklin, *Bullfighter from Brooklyn*, 1952; Caresse Crosby, *The Passionate Years*, 1953; J. Donald Adams, *Copey of Harvard*, 1960; Warren V. Bush, ed., *The Dialogues of Archibald MacLeish and Mark Van Doren*, 1964; Richard M. Ludwig, ed., *The Letters of Ford Madox Ford*, 1965.

Author's interviews and correspondence: with Mrs. Marguerite Cohn, Dec., 1961; with John Dos Passos, Apr., 1962; with Olive Nordquist, Sister Conceptor, L. S. Weaver, and Floyd Allington, July, 1964; with Mr. and Mrs. Archibald MacLeish and Mr. and Mrs. T. O. Bruce, March, 1965; with Waldo Peirce, June, 1966. From Donald Ogden Stewart, Feb. 20, 1951; from Jay Allen, March 6, 1963; from Josephine Herbst, July 3 and Aug. 19, 1963; from Archibald MacLeish, Jan. 31, 1965; from Charles Scribner, Jr. Apr. 18, 1968.

NOTES

EH in car accident: Pauline Hemingway to Archibald MacLeish, Nov. 9, 1930; EH to Perkins, ca. Nov. 15; EH to Hickok, Dec. 5, 1930. John Dos Passos to author, April, 1962. Floyd Allington to author, July 20, 1964. Dos Passos escaped with a stiff neck; Allington was thrown clear, dislocating his right shoulder.

EH hospitalized in Billings: Pauline to MacLeish, Nov. 9; EH to Perkins (dictated), ca. Nov. 15; Perkins to EH, Nov. 13, 1930. Dos Passos to author, April, 1962. Sister Conceptor to author, July 20, 1964. EH's room was 422. The hospital was a four-story yellow brick structure with 200 beds. **EH's operation:** Pauline to Perkins, Nov. 7, 1930 (wire). **EH summarizes recent accidents:** EH to Perkins, ca. Nov. 15, 1930.

Dislike of dictated writing: EH to Owen Wister, Dec. 26, 1930.

EH on plans for Africa: EH to MacLeish, ca. Sept., 1930.

EH's condition on December 1: Pauline to Perkins, Dec. 1, 1930.

Radio as anodyne: EH to MacLeish, Nov. 22, 1930, and EH's short story, "The Gambler, The Nun, and The Radio."

On Will James: same letter to MacLeish. **On the Russian and the Mexican:** same letter. They appear also in the story.

Sister Florence: Sister Conceptor to author, July 20, 1964. She identified Sister Florence as the prototype of Sister Cecilia, the nun in EH's story. EH made other changes, such as placing the hospital in Hailey, Idaho, Ezra Pound's birthplace; calling his protagonist Frazer; and giving him a broken leg instead of a broken arm.

Visit by MacLeish: MacLeish to author, Jan. 31, 1965; Pauline to Perkins, ca. Dec. 15, 1930. EH tried to make up to MacLeish for accusing him of necrophilia by urging Perkins to publish MacLeish's *Conquistador,* a long poem on Cortés in Mexico, saying that Perkins could not possibly have a better poet or a better guy for Scribners' spring list. EH to Perkins, Dec. 28, 1930. MacLeish stayed with Houghton Mifflin.

Visit by Earl Snook: Snook to Perkins, ca. Dec. 12, 1930, extract sent by Perkins to Henry Strater, ca. Dec. 15, 1930.

Release from hospital: Sister Conceptor to author, July 20, 1964. EH was discharged Dec. 21, 1930 after fifty days.

Arrival in Piggott: EH to MacLeish, Dec. 28, 1930.

Tramp incident: T. O. Bruce to author, March 29, 1965. "I hear Hemingway has broken his arm whilst hunting exotic beasts in Montana, so the race is always a little precarious, even to the strong": Ford to Hugh Walpole, Dec. 16, 1930, in Richard M. Ludwig, editor, *The Letters of Ford Madox Ford,* Princeton, 1965, p. 198.

Failure of Stallings dramatization of "A Farewell": Perkins to Jonathan Cape, Nov. 1, 1930. Milford Baker saw the play and told EH that it was "an awful mess" (Baker to EH, Sept. 24, 1930). According to EH, his agent Reynolds had received and rejected an offer of $15,000 for film rights to *A Farewell* in 1929. The final sale in the fall of 1930 netted $80,-000 of which EH received $24,000. It was an outright sale, a fact which EH regretted many times later (EH to Perkins, ca. Nov. 15, 1930).

Sinclair Lewis's praise of EH's novel: EH was disgusted to learn that Lewis had won the Nobel Prize for Literature. It was certainly a filthy business, said EH, that the prize went to Lewis instead of Ezra Pound or James Joyce. Possibly Lewis had won because his novels presented the best aspects of Swedish life in America. In any event, the award had eliminated the Dreiser menace, though of two bad writers, Dreiser deserved the prize a hell of a lot more than Lewis did. But EH did approve the awards to W. B. Yeats and Thomas Mann (1922 and 1929) both of which made him "damned happy." EH to Guy Hickok, Dec. 5, 1930.

EH angered by Wilson's introduction to "In Our Time" reissue: EH received and read Wilson's introduction sometime between Nov. 24 and Dec. 1, 1930 (EH to Perkins [dictated], Dec. 1, 1930). He had originally recommended Wilson for the job: EH to Perkins, Aug. 12, 1930, and exchanged letters with Perkins in the interim (Perkins to EH, Aug. 18, Sept. 11, and Oct. 3, 1930, and EH to Perkins, Oct. 28). He grew suspicious while hospitalized and twice wired Perkins (Nov. 14 and 24, 1930) asking to see the introduction. Wilson, introduction to *In Our Time,* Scribners, 1930, pp. ix–xv.

EH in Key West: L. S. Weaver to author, July 21, 1964; Olive Nordquist to author, July 22, 1964; Josephine Herbst to author, July 3, 1963; EH to MacLeish, Jan. 14, 1931; EH to Mrs. Paul Pfeiffer, Jan. 28, 1931.

Conversation with Chub Weaver on embalming and books: Weaver to author, July 21, 1964.

Boasting to MacLeish: March 14, 1931. This letter contains EH's remark about the necessity of lasting. Charles Scribner, Jr., later translated the phrase into an epigram: "First: last" (Scribner to author, April, 1968).

With Perkins to Tortugas: Perkins to EH, March 11, 1931 (wire); EH to Perkins, March 12 (wire). EH's report on rest of trip after Perkins left: EH to Perkins, Apr. 12, 1931.

First meeting with Gregorio Fuentes: recalled in EH to Perkins, June 10, 1943. By that date Gregorio had been working for EH as mate and cook on the *Pilar* for about five years.

EH needling Herrmann: Josephine Herbst to author, Aug. 19, 1963.

EH alerts Dr. Guffey to Pauline's second pregnancy: EH to Guffey, Apr. 27, 1931.

Plans for Spain: EH to Peirce, May 4, 1931; EH to MacLeish, Apr. 19 and June 29, 1931.

Purchase of house on Whitehead Street: J. B. Sullivan to author, March 30, 1965. EH alludes to the purchase in EH to Peirce, May 4, 1931, and EH to MacLeish, June 29, 1931.

Crossing to Spain: EH to Peirce, Apr. 30 (wire), May 4 and 14, 1931; EH to Mrs. Paul Pfeiffer, May 13, 1931.

EH in Madrid and Paris: EH to MacLeish, June 29, 1931; EH to Mrs. Paul Pfeiffer, Aug. 31, 1931. Sidney Franklin, *Bullfighter from Brooklyn,* NY, 1952, p. 204.

EH meets Luis Quintanilla, Jay Allen, and others: Jay Allen to author, March 6, 1963.

EH on the Carlist uprising in the north: EH to Hickok, June 16, 1931. Late in June, EH and Pauline went to the Sierra de Gredos to fish. He admired Barco de Ávila, where the

villagers had just killed a marauding wolf, and where a bear's paw was nailed to the door of the church: EH to Dos Passos, June 26, 1931 and EH, "Fishing Log for 1931."
EH at Pamplona: EH to Hickok, July 15, 1931. Caresse Crosby, widow of Harry Crosby, met EH and Pauline in San Sebastian after the fiesta, and watched Bumby practicing capework with Sidney Franklin. See Caresse Crosby, "An Open Letter to Ernest Hemingway," in *The Torrents of Spring*, Crosby Continental editions Number 1, Paris, Dec., 1931. See also her autobiography, *The Passionate Years*, NY, 1953, p. 284. EH's account of Bumby's behavior at his first bullfight (under "J.H.") appears in *Death in the Afternoon*, NY, 1932, p. 495. Another of Bumby's reactions is sketched on pp. 227–228.
EH's progress with glossary: EH to Perkins, Aug. 1, 1931.
Voyage home: EH to Hickok, Oct. 14, 1932.
Meeting Jane Mason: Donald Ogden Stewart to author, Feb. 20, 1951.
Visit to the MacLeishes: Archibald and Ada MacLeish to author, March 9, 1965.
Harvard game and visit to Copeland: MacLeish to author, March 9, 1965; Waldo Peirce to author, June 1, 1966. See also J. Donald Adams, *Copey of Harvard*, Boston, 1960, p. 142.
Hunting with MacLeish: MacLeish in *The Dialogues of Archibald MacLeish and Mark Van Doren*, ed. Warren V. Bush, NY, 1964, p. 85. Before leaving Conway, EH wired Peirce in Bangor, Maine, Oct. 5, 1931.
EH in New York: EH to Eric Knight, Oct. 10, 1931; Marguerite Cohn to author, Dec., 1961.
EH in Kansas City: EH to Perkins, Oct. 16 (wire); EH to Eric Knight, ca. Nov. 6; EH to Peirce, ca. Nov. 11, 1931.
Birth of Gregory Hemingway: EH to Mrs. Paul Pfeiffer, wire and letter, Nov. 12; EH to Perkins, Nov. 12–25; EH to Mrs. Pfeiffer, Nov. 14, 16, and 23; EH to Capt. L. H. Cohn, ca. Nov. 13 or 14; EH to Peirce, Nov. 17, 1931.
EH to Piggott: EH to Perkins, Dec. 9, and EH to Henry Strater, Dec. 10, 1931.
EH's memories of Spain: *Death in the Afternoon*, Chapter Twenty. EH did not provide dates, which are here sorted out by the author. The Goya quotation is from *Death in the Afternoon*, p. 205. Bumby's small cape and sword are also mentioned in Franklin, *Bullfighter from Brooklyn*, NY, 1952, p. 204.
Household problems in Key West: EH to Perkins, Dec. 26, 1931, and Jan. 5, 1932.

Sec. 31. A Place to Come Back To

SOURCES

Letters of EH: to Strater, ca. Apr., 1931; to Hickok, Dec. 12, 1931. To Mrs. Pfeiffer, Jan. 5, 1932; to Paul Romaine, Jan. 15; to Perkins, Jan. 21; to Owen Wister, Jan. 30; to Strater, Feb. 9; to Perkins, Feb. 24; to Dos Passos, March 26; to Capt. L. H. Cohn, March 28; to Peirce, Apr. 15; to Strater, May 14; to Dos Passos, May 30; to Perkins, June 2; to Peirce, June 6; to Strater, June 10; to Perkins, June 27 (wire) and June 28; to Romaine, July 6; to Strater, July 14; to Romaine, Aug. 9; to Mrs. Pfeiffer, Aug. 12; to Strater, Oct. 14;

to Hickok, Oct. 14 and 29, 1932. To Clifton Fadiman, Nov. 26, 1933.
Other letters: Evan Shipman to EH, Jan. 22, 1932; Strater to EH, Feb. 1, 19, and 24, 1932; Dos Passos to EH, ca. Feb. 21, 1932; Jane Mason to EH, May 10, May 11, and June 6 (wires); Perkins to EH, June 11; Charles Thompson to Lorine Thompson, Sept. 19; Pauline to Perkins, Sept. 21; Charles Thompson to Strater, late Oct., 1932.
EH's work: Published: Poem, "Ultimately," reprinted on back cover of Faulkner's *Salmagundi*, Jan., 1932; "After the Storm," *Cosmopolitan*, May, 1932; "A Paris Letter," *Esquire*, Feb., 1934.
Books: Roger Asselineau, ed., *The Literary Reputation of Hemingway in Europe*, 1965.
Author's interviews and correspondence: with W. D. Horne, Dec., 1962; with Olive Nordquist, L. S. Weaver, Ivan Wallace, and Mr. and Mrs. Robert Cox, July, 1964; with Charles Thompson, March, 1965. From G. Grant Mason, Aug. 13, 1965 and Feb. 10, 1966.

NOTES

907 Whitehead Street: EH to Mrs. Pfeiffer, Jan. 5, 1932; EH to Waldo Peirce, Apr. 15, 1932. The deed to the house was dated Apr. 29, 1931.
Plans for Africa: Henry Strater to EH, Feb. 1, 19, and 24, 1932. EH to Strater, Feb. 9, 1932.
Dos Passos reads MS of "Death in the Afternoon": Dos Passos to EH, ca. Feb. 21, 1932. William Lengel, as emissary from Harry Payne Burton of *Cosmopolitan*, had read the MS in January. EH told Perkins on Jan. 21 that Lengel was "all wildly steamed up" about serializing excerpts from the book, but EH decided on *Scribner's Magazine*. Lengel offered a dollar a word for short stories. EH sold him "After the Storm" for $2,700 (EH to Hickok, Oct. 14, 1932). The story appeared in *Cosmopolitan*, Vol. 92 (May, 1932), pp. 38–41 and 155. It was EH's first story published by the Hearst organization.
EH's advice to Dos Passos: March 26 and May 30, 1932.
EH on politics and literature: EH to Paul Romaine, July 6 and Aug. 9, 1932.
EH grants Romaine right to reprint "Ultimately" in Salmagundi: EH to Paul Romaine, Jan. 15, 1932. The volume is dated Jan., 1932, a 53-page pamphlet in an edition of 525 numbered copies. EH's poem is on the back cover. The rest is Faulkner's, taken from *The Double Dealer*, June, 1922 through April, 1925. The exception is the poem, "*L'Aprés-midi d'un Faune*," first published in the *New Republic* for Aug. 6, 1919.
EH on Faulkner's novels: EH to Owen Wister, Jan. 30, 1932.
EH on Faulkner's early work: EH to Capt. L. H. Cohn, March 28, 1932. Evan Shipman wrote EH from Paris, Jan. 22, 1932, that translations of *The Sun Also Rises* and *A Farewell to Arms* by a Princeton professor named Maurice Coindreau were making money for Gallimard as well as a name for EH among French readers, while Caresse Crosby's paperback edition of *The Torrents of Spring* was selling briskly in Paris and the provinces. On EH's French reputation, see Roger As-

selineau, ed., *The Literary Reputation of Hemingway in Europe*, NY, 1965, esp. pp. 39–72.
EH's revival of interest in short stories: EH to Perkins, Feb. 24, 1932. On Feb. 7th, EH told Perkins that he had finished three fine stories. By Feb. 24, the number had risen to seven, with two more said to be in progress. One of the new ones was "A Natural History of the Dead," soon to appear in *Death in the Afternoon*. EH revised it for publication as a short story by omitting the dialogue between the Old Lady and the Author, and added part of a sentence on dying of Spanish influenza. His alleged real-life source for "The Sea Change" is mentioned in his unpublished preface, "The Art of the Short Story," 1959.
EH's debt to Dr. Clendening's letter file: copies of six letters from patients to Clendening remained in EH's files and were kindly given to author by Waring Jones. EH wrote Hickok (Dec. 12, 1931) that Clendening was a hell of a fine guy. A native of Kansas City (1884–1945), he earned his M.D. at University of Kansas, 1907, and taught internal medicine there for years. His *The Human Body* (NY, 1927) sold 500,000 copies, and his column of medical advice, "Diet and Health," was syndicated in hundreds of newspapers. The author is indebted to Dr. Paul Benton for a detailed account of his career. Names of Dr. Clendening's correspondents have been withheld.
EH's spring fishing at Tortugas: W. D. Horne to author, Dec., 1962. Mr. and Mrs. Horne, along with EH's sister Carol, made the trip in February. In March, EH went again with Strater, MacLeish, and Uncle Gus Pfeiffer (EH to Waldo Peirce, Apr. 15, 1932).
To Cuba with Joe Russell: EH to Strater, May 14; EH to Dos Passos, May 30; EH to Peirce, June 6, 1932.
EH and the Masons: G. Grant Mason to author, Aug. 13, 1965 and Feb. 10, 1966. "Ernest loves Jane" entry appears in the log of the *Anita*, which opens Apr. 23, 1932.
EH discovers marlin fishing: EH to Strater, May 14, and EH to Dos Passos, May 30, 1932.
EH meets Carlos Gutiérrez: EH to Strater, July 14, 1932. Gutiérrez was born in 1878 and was fifty-four when EH met him. He lived then at 31 Zapata, Havana. Since 1912 he had kept a written record of all his catches, with weights and dates. He described to EH how he caught a 450-pound tuna in 1931: having hooked it well, he kept the line taut for hours, hauling in slack, and letting the fish pull him along in his skiff until it was exhausted. Compare Santiago in *The Old Man and the Sea*.
EH explains origin of "A Way You'll Never Be": EH to Clifton Fadiman, Nov. 26, 1933. Jane Mason wired EH from Jacksonville, May 10, 1932, on her way to New York. On May 11, she wired from New York that her "show" at Doctors Hospital was scheduled for the 13th. On June 6, she wired EH at the Ambos Mundos from her parents' house in Tuxedo Park, New York, saying she would reach Havana on June 11 and wanted to go fishing with EH on the 12th. EH to Strater, May 14, 1932, asks him to telephone MacLeish about Jane Mason and suggests they both go to see her in the hospital, as she is a hell of a fine girl.
EH postpones African trip: EH to Perkins,

June 2, 1932; EH to Strater, June 10, 1932; Perkins to EH, June 11, 1932.
EH's pneumonia: EH to Perkins, June 28 and EH to Strater, July 14, 1932.
EH angered by typesetter: EH to Perkins, June 27 (wire) and letter of June 28, 1932.
EH to Wyoming: EH to Strater, July 14, and EH to Hickok, July 14, 1932.
Summer on Nordquist ranch: EH to Hickok, Oct. 14, 1932. L. S. Weaver, Olive Nordquist, and Mr. and Mrs. Robert Cox to author, July, 1964; EH's fishing log for July, 1932. The complaint about the new road from Red Lodge over Beartooth appears in EH to Strater, Apr., 1931. The highway opened in 1934. EH's complaint about the dry fork is in his fishing log for July 26th, 1933.
EH on presidential campaign of 1932: EH to Hickok, Oct. 14 and 29, 1932.
EH and Pauline to Powell, Wyoming: EH to Mrs. Pfeiffer, Aug. 12, 1932.
Arrival of the Murphys: Olive Nordquist's Ranch Guest-Book, 1932. The Murphys left on Sept. 16.
Arrival of Charles Thompson: Thompson to author, March, 1965. Thompson reached Cody Sept. 11 and EH brought him to the L Bar T next day.
Departure of Pauline: Pauline drove east with Mrs. Eleanor Cochran and her two daughters on Sept. 22. She went to Key West to supervise repairs on the house. Bumby disembarked early in October in New York. His ship was met by the Murphys, who put him aboard the train for Key West.
Hunting mountain rams: Charles to Lorine Thompson, Sept. 19, 1932; EH to Strater, Oct. 14, 1932; Ivan Wallace to author, July 19, 1964.
Hunting bear and elk: EH to Strater, Oct. 14, 1932; Charles Thompson to Strater, late Oct., 1932; L. S. Weaver to author, July 20, 1964.
EH talks of suicide: Weaver to author, July 20, 1964.
EH returns to ranch to read reviews: EH, Hunting Log for Oct. 5, 1932. Olive Nordquist's Ranch Guest-Book for 1932; EH to Strater, Oct. 14, 1932; EH, "A Paris Letter," *Esquire*, Vol. 1 (Feb., 1934), p. 2.
Perkins's report on reviews: Perkins to EH, Sept. 28, 1932.
Final days of hunting: EH to Strater, Oct. 14, 1932. Pauline reported to Perkins just before leaving Wyoming in September that she and Ernest had had a superb summer, and that EH was in "noble" condition, "galloping about on a large black horse with a big black beard" (Pauline to Perkins, Sept. 21, 1932).
Drive home to Key West: Charles Thompson to Henry Strater, late Oct., 1932. EH, "A Paris Letter," *Esquire*, Vol. 1 (Feb., 1934), p. 2.

Sec. 32. *Winner Take Nothing*

SOURCES

Letters of EH: to the editors of *Hound and Horn*, Aug. 27, 1932; to R. M. Coates, Oct. 5, 1932; to Perkins, ca. Oct. 28 and Nov. 15, 1932; to Ford Madox Ford, Nov. 21; to Strater, Dec. 4, 1932; to Perkins, Dec. 7, 1932 (wire). To Perkins, Jan. 4, 1933 (wire and letter); to Perkins, Jan. 7 (wire); to Alfred Dashiell, Jan. 26; to Perkins, Eric Knight, and Arnold Gingrich (all on Jan. 31); to Perkins,

ca. late Jan.; to Perkins, Feb. 10; to George Albee, Feb. 16; to Perkins, Feb. 23; to Gingrich, March 13; to Dos Passos, ca. March; to Mrs. Paul Pfeiffer, March 23; to Gingrich, Apr. 3; to Janet Flanner, Apr. 8; to Gingrich, Apr. 9; to Dos Passos, ca. May 15; to Gingrich, June 7; to Samuel Putnam, June 9; to Perkins, June 11; to the editors of *New Republic*, June 12; to Perkins, June 13, ca. July 15, ca. July 25, and July 31 (cable); to Perkins, Aug. 31 and Sept. 18, 1933. To author, Nov. 22, 1951.
Other letters: Carol Hemingway to EH, Sept. 12, 1932; Gerald Murphy to EH, ca. Sept. 30 (wire); Ford Madox Ford to EH, Nov. 6; Mary Garden to EH, Nov. 30; Perkins to EH, Dec. 3 and 12, 1932. Ezra Pound to EH, Jan. 15, 1933; Arnold Gingrich to Helene Richards, Jan. 22; Alfred Dashiell to EH, Jan. 30; Gingrich to EH, Feb. 24; John Gardner to EH, March 17 (cable); Evan Shipman to EH, ca. May 12; MacLeish to Bruce Bliven, May 31. Perkins to Marjorie K. Rawlings, Jan. 5, 1950, and to Ann Chidester, July 15, 1943.
EH's work: Published: contents of *Winner Take Nothing*, publ. Oct. 27, 1933. "Wine of Wyoming," "A Clean Well-Lighted Place," "Homage to Switzerland," and "Give Us a Prescription, Doctor," had previously appeared in *Scribner's Magazine*, and "After the Storm" in *Cosmopolitan*. For dates and references to magazine publications, see Audre Hanneman, *Ernest Hemingway: A Comprehensive Bibliography*, Princeton, 1967.
Books and articles: Margaret Anderson, *My Thirty Years' War*, 1930; Lawrence Leighton, "An Autopsy and a Prescription," *Hound and Horn*, Vol. 5 (July–Sept., 1932); Aldous Huxley, *Music at Night*, 1932; Ford Madox Ford, ed., *The Cantos of Ezra Pound: Some Testimonies*, 1933; Gertrude Stein, *The Autobiography of Alice B. Toklas*, 1933; Max Eastman, *Art and the Life of Action*, 1934; John Hall Wheelock, ed., *Editor to Author: The Letters of Maxwell E. Perkins*, 1950; David Dow Harvey, ed., *Ford Madox Ford: A Bibliography*, 1962; Clyde Beatty, *Facing the Big Cats*, 1965; Andrew Turnbull, *Thomas Wolfe*, 1967.
Author's interviews and correspondence: with Edmund Wilson, Jan. 1953; with John Gardner, Aug., 1960; with John H. Hemingway, Aug., 1964. From Clyde Beatty, Apr. 15, 1965.

NOTES

Return to Key West; backyard pets: EH to Janet Flanner, Apr. 8, 1933.
Whooping cough: EH to Perkins, Nov. 15, 1932 and EH to Strater, Dec. 4, 1932. The Murphys agreed to meet Bumby's ship in NYC: the Murphys to EH, ca. Sept. 30, 1932 (wire).
Adverse reviews of "Death in the Afternoon": R. M. Coates, *The New Yorker*, Vol. 8 (Oct. 1, 1932), pp. 61–63; H. L. Mencken, *American Mercury*, Vol. 27 (Dec., 1932), pp. 506–507; R. L. Duffus, *NY Times Book Review*, Sept. 25, 1932, pp. 5 and 17; Edward Weeks, *Atlantic* (Nov., 1932), p. 437; *Forum*, Vol. 88 (Nov., 1932), p. ix; *London Times Literary Supplement*, Dec. 8, 1932, p. 936. The English edition was published Nov. 15, 1932, and the American on Sept. 23. **Laudatory reviews** included Herschel Brickell, *NY

Herald Tribune Books, Sept. 25, 1932, pp. 3 and 12; Ben Ray Redman, *Saturday Review*, Vol. 9 (Sept. 24, 1932), p. 121; Malcolm Cowley, *New Republic*, Vol. 73 (Nov. 30, 1932), p. 76. The famous singer, Mary Garden, wrote EH a letter of praise from the Ritz Tower, NYC, Nov. 30, 1932. Perkins reported to EH on Dec. 3 that Allen Tate liked the book.
EH's reply to Coates review: Dated Oct. 5, 1932 from Cooke City, Mont., and printed in *The New Yorker*, Vol. 8 (Nov. 5, 1932), pp. 74–75. The slurs on Eliot, Faulkner, and Huxley for which Coates scolded EH were in *Death in the Afternoon*, pp. 139, 173, and 190. EH was rebutting Huxley's essay, "Foreheads Villainous Low" from *Music at Night*, London, 1932, pp. 201–202. The letter to Coates was EH's second in six weeks. The lead article in *Hound and Horn*, Vol. 5 (July–Sept., 1932), pp. 519–539, was "An Autopsy and a Prescription" by Lawrence Leighton, who called the fiction of EH, Dos Passos, and Fitzgerald "repulsive, sterile, and dead." EH's bawdy reply, dated Aug. 27, 1932, from Cooke City, Mont., was published in *Hound and Horn*, Vol. 6 (Oct.–Dec., 1932), p. 135.
Driving west with Bumby: This was the trip on which EH drew for the setting of "Fathers and Sons." He later told Edmund Wilson that they stopped in northern Mississippi on the final night of the journey. Only as he signed the hotel register did he realize that he was in Faulkner country. Coates's review of *Death in the Afternoon* had accused him of making petulant gibes at Faulkner. Worried about the fact that Faulkner might be resentful, EH said that he sat up all night in a chair in the hotel bedroom, a shotgun on his knees, guarding Bumby. Edmund Wilson to author, Jan. 10, 1953.
Duck shooting with Perkins: EH's invitation of Dec. 7 was accepted by Perkins on the 12th. He reached Memphis on the 14th in the midst of a wave of arctic cold. The houseboat was called the *Walter Adams* and was owned by a man named Wilkins. Ducks were scarce. Two days after they left, a thaw set in and the ducks came in huge flocks. Wilkins offered EH a week's free shooting to make up for the scarcity of mid-December (EH to Perkins, Jan. 4, 1933). Perkins recalled the trip in several letters; two are quoted here: Perkins to Marjorie Kinnan Rawlings, Jan. 5, 1940, and to Ann Chidester, July 15, 1943. Both are printed in *Editor to Author: The Letters of Maxwell E. Perkins*, ed. John Hall Wheelock, NY, 1950, pp. 151 and 233. EH later told Charles Scribner that Perkins had that "awful puritannical [sic] thing" that made him give up anything as soon as he had fun doing it (EH to Scribner, Dec. 1, 1951).
Barn fire in Piggott: T. O. Bruce to author, March, 1965; Laud Payne to author, Sept., 1967. Ezra Pound to EH, Jan. 15, 1933.
Testimonial for Pound: Ford Madox Ford to EH, Nov. 6, 1932. EH to Ford about Pound, Nov. 21, 1932. Ford's little *Festschrift* was published as *The Cantos of Ezra Pound: Some Testimonies by Ernest Hemingway, Ford Madox Ford, T. S. Eliot, Hugh Walpole, Archibald MacLeish, James Joyce, and Others*, New York, Farrar and Rinehart, 1933. See David Dow Harvey, *Ford Madox Ford: 1873–1939: A Bibliography of Works and Criticism*,

Princeton, N.J., 1962, pp. 99–100. EH wrote Arnold Gingrich (March 13, 1933) that he had read every line of Pound's work, and that he would stand or fall as poet by his Cantos, which contained some "Christ-wonderful" poetry, though weighted down with stale jokes and "quite a lot of crap."

Bumby's influenza: This attack gave EH his story, "A Day's Wait." This surmise confirmed by John H. Hemingway to author, Aug., 1964.

EH's return to the east: EH to Perkins, wire and letter from Piggott, Jan. 4, 1933, and wire from Knoxville, Tenn., Jan. 7, 1933.

EH meets Thomas Wolfe: EH to Perkins Jan. 31, 1933. An account of this meeting appears in Andrew Turnbull, *Thomas Wolfe*, NY, 1967, p. 194.

EH's threat to John Gardner: Gardner to author, Aug., 1960. On March 16, 1932, Gardner's mother had written Grace Hemingway from Orlando, Fla., giving an account of the Gardner family's distinguished history. On Sept. 2, 1932, Carol had written EH from Bristol, N.H., saying that she had been seeing Gardner at Lake George, N.Y.

EH on his meetings with Franklin and Speiser: EH to Eric Knight, Jan. 31, 1933.

EH on conversations with Captain Cohn: EH to Arnold Gingrich, Jan. 31, 1933.

Gingrich on EH: Gingrich to Helene Richards, Jan. 22, 1933. EH left NYC by train for Roanoke, Va., on the afternoon of Jan. 20, after a stay of thirteen days.

EH returns to Key West: EH to Eric Knight, Jan. 31, 1933. Evan Shipman's winter visit is covered in Shipman to EH, ca. May 12, 1933.

"Scribner's Magazine" takes three stories: EH returned proof on "A Clean, Well-Lighted Place" and "Homage to Switzerland" to Dashiell on Thurs., Jan. 26; receipt acknowledged Jan. 30 by Dashiell, who hoped for a 3rd story for the May number. The third story was "The Gambler, The Nun, and the Radio," then called "Give Us a Prescription, Doctor."

EH on "safe" stories and concealed dynamite: EH to Eric Knight, Jan. 31, 1933.

EH on the Fitzgeralds: on Zelda: EH to Perkins, ca. Oct. 28 and Nov. 15, 1932. **On Scott:** EH to Perkins, ca. late Jan., and Feb. 23, 1933.

EH on life, fame, and immortality: EH to George Albee, Feb. 16, 1933.

EH on the necessity of suffering: EH to Perkins, ca. late Jan., 1933.

EH plans book on Gulf Stream: EH to Perkins, Feb. 10, 1933.

EH begins Harry Morgan novel: EH to Perkins, Feb. 10 and 23, 1933; EH to Mrs. Paul Pfeiffer, March 23, 1933.

EH's trip to NY (March): conference with Milestone: EH to Arnold Gingrich, Apr. 3, 1933. **Meeting Clyde Beatty:** Beatty, *Facing the Big Cats*, NY, 1965, pp. 15–16 and 161; Beatty to author, Apr. 15, 1965.

Carol marries John Gardner: the marriage occurred March 25, 1933. Gardner to EH, March 17 (cable) notified EH of the coming marriage. EH to Mrs. Pfeiffer, March 23, 1933, vowed to reject the Gardners.

Gertrude Stein attacks EH: *The Autobiography of Alice B. Toklas*, NY, 1933, pp. 265–270. **EH's comment:** EH to Dos Passos, ca. March, 1933. Margaret Anderson had earlier lampooned EH as a pink and white rabbit with soft brown eyes: *My Thirty Years' War*, NY, 1930, pp. 258–260. EH to Dos Passos, letter cited, attributes both attacks to the menopauses of the Misses Anderson and Stein.

EH agrees to write articles for Gingrich: Gingrich to EH, Feb. 24, 1933; EH to Gingrich, March 13, Apr. 3 and 9, 1933.

Crossing to Cuba: EH to Strater, March 10 and May 27, 1933; EH to Janet Flanner, Apr. 8, 1933.

Dos Passos's illness: EH to Dos Passos, ca. May 15, 1933. EH to MacLeish, May 14, 1933, congratulated him on winning a Pulitzer Prize for *Conquistador* and composed a little quatrain for the occasion, parodying W. B. Yeats's "To a Young Beauty." I owe the identification of this parody to Professor A. W. Litz. EH named *Conquistador*, Dos Passos's *1919*, and Edmund Wilson's *The American Jitters* as the three best books of 1932 (EH to Samuel Putnam, June 9, 1933).

EH chooses "Winner Take Nothing" title: EH to Perkins, June 11, 1933 (cable). EH later said that he had composed the epigraph himself (EH to author, Nov. 22, 1951).

EH on his ability to endure: EH to Perkins, ca. July 25, 1933.

Order of the Stories in "Winner Take Nothing": EH to Perkins, July 31, 1933 (cable) and Aug. 31, 1933; Perkins to EH, Aug. 2, 1933. Several letters of EH compare "The Light of the World" to *"La Maison Tellier."* One of these is EH to Gingrich, June 7, 1933. EH's title is probably derived from Holman Hunt's famous picture, "I am the Light of the World." It depicts Jesus crowned with thorns, wearing a richly brocaded mantle, holding a starry lantern, and knocking at a cottager's door. Copies of this picture were widely distributed in EH's youth. One was Number 93 in a series called Wilde's Bible Pictures. Grace used a copy as frontispiece to Vol. 4 of her series of scrapbook albums which she kept for EH 1899–1917. EH to Perkins, Sept. 18, 1933, differentiated between "reported" and "invented" stories. In the first category are "Wine of Wyoming," "One Reader Writes," "A Day's Wait," and "After the Storm," which EH now stated was "word for word" as Bra Saunders had told it in 1928. Among the invented stories were "The Killers," "The Undefeated," "Hills Like White Elephants," "The Sea Change," and "A Simple Enquiry." EH told Gingrich on June 7, 1933, that "The Mother of a Queen" was a true story about the bullfighter Ortiz. Although he did not say so, one may surmise that he had learned the story from Sidney Franklin. EH told Perkins that "Fifty Grand" was completely invented, though in fact it was based on the Benny Leonard-Jack Britton fight of 1922. Rejected titles for "Fathers and Sons" included "Tomb of a Grandfather," "Indian Summer," and "Long Time Ago Good."

Quarrel with Max Eastman: "Bull in the Afternoon" appeared in *New Republic*, Vol. 75 (June 7, 1933), pp. 94–97. MacLeish saw an advance copy. His letter of protest to Bliven was dated May 31. EH's open letter to the editors was dated June 12. That same day MacLeish cabled EH in Havana that his friends advised against submitting the letter to the magazine. EH replied that it was perfectly sound to go ahead. On June 28, 1933, p. 184 the *New Republic* printed a letter from Eastman denying personal innuendoes against EH. EH's threats appear in EH to Perkins, June 13 and ca. July 15, 1933. Perkins's reply was dated June 16, 1933. When Eastman reprinted his essay in *Art and the Life of Action*, NY, 1934, pp. 87–101, he revised the offending statement. "It is of course a commonplace," he then wrote, "that anyone who too much protests his manhood lacks the serene confidence that he *is* made of iron. . . . But some circumstance seems to have laid upon Hemingway a continual sense of the obligation to put forth evidences of redblooded masculinity."

Sec. 33. Revolutions

SOURCES

Letters of EH: to Arnold Gingrich, June 10, 1933; to James Charters and Morrill Cody, June 20; to Strater, July 7; to Perkins, ca. July 15 and July 26; to Strater, ca. late July; to Gingrich, Aug. 1; to Perkins, Aug. 10, Aug. 31, and Sept. 18; to Mrs. Paul Pfeiffer, Oct. 16, 1933. To Morrill Cody, Jan. 2, 1934.
Other letters: James Charters to EH, June 1, 1933; Morrill Cody to EH, June 2; Perkins to EH, July 6; Jane Mason to EH and Pauline, Sept. 2; Cody to EH, Oct. 5; Jane Mason to EH and Pauline, Oct. 28 and Nov. 1; Ivan Opfer to EH, Nov. 10; Cody to EH, Dec. 26, 1933. Charters to EH, Jan. 26, 1934.
EH's work: Published: *Winner Take Nothing*, Oct. 27, 1933; "Marlin off the Morro: A Cuban Letter," *Esquire*, Vol. 1 (Autumn, 1933); "The Friend of Spain: A Spanish Letter," *Esquire*, Vol. 1 (Jan., 1934); "A Paris Letter," *Esquire*, Vol. 1 (Feb., 1934); "One Trip Across," *Cosmopolitan*, Vol. 96 (April, 1934); preface to James Charters, *This Must Be the Place*, July, 1934.
Books: Edgar Quinet, *Introduction à la Philosophie de l'Histoire de L'Humanité*, 1857; James Joyce, *Finnegans Wake*, 1939; Richard Ellmann, *James Joyce*, 1959; James Thurber, *The Years with Ross*, 1959.
Author's interviews and correspondence: with Mr. and Mrs. Paul Scott Mowrer, Aug., 1962; with Patrick Hemingway, Dec. 16, 1965. From Solita Solano, Feb. 18, 1962; from Morrill Cody, Sept. 18 and Dec. 12, 1962, and Oct. 19, 1966; from Grant Mason, Feb. 10, 1966; from Mrs. James Thurber, ca. Nov. 20, 1966; from Raymond Harwood, Dec. 14, 1966.

NOTES

EH's fishing exploits: "Marlin off the Morro: A Cuban Letter," *Esquire*, Vol. 1 (Autumn, 1933), pp. 8, 39, and 97. EH to Strater, July 7 and ca. late July, 1933.
EH's objections to the name "Esquire": EH to Gingrich, ca. June 10, 1933.
Remarks on Zane Grey: EH to Gingrich, Aug. 1, 1933.
Plans for summer: EH to Perkins, July 26, 1933.
Hadley's remarriage: Paul Scott Mowrer was born in Bloomington, Ill., July 14, 1887, married Winifred Adams in 1908, became Paris correspondent for the *Chicago Daily News* in 1910, and was named editor of the *Daily News* soon after his marriage to Hadley in

London on July 3, 1933 (Hadley and Paul Mowrer to author, Aug., 1962).
Jane Mason's accidents: Mrs. Mason was involved in an automobile accident near the Havana airport that summer. Patrick and Bumby Hemingway were riding in her car and they were talking about some snapshots that she had spread in her lap. A gust of wind scattered the pictures. When she leaned to retrieve them, she lost control of the wheel. The car somersaulted into a deep gully, landing rightside up. The small boys were not hurt, but Jane was severely bruised. According to her former husband, Grant Mason, the damage to her back was the result of "jumping out of our home in Jaimanitas at an altitude, all of her friends agreed, which would be reasonably impressive as an effort at suicide but not high enough to cause death or serious injury. As I remember it, she went off a second story balcony. . . . I do not think the accident was directly related to anything currently happening with Ernest or me or with anyone else but just one of her changeable fits of elation and depression. In case she tried another such stunt, I arranged for constant nurse attendance and then shipped her to New York on a Ward Line vessel with special bars on the portholes." (G. Grant Mason, Jr. to author, Feb. 10, 1966.) Perkins wrote EH about Mrs. Mason on July 6, 1933. EH's reply to Perkins was written ca. July 15, 1933. Further details on the car accident: Patrick Hemingway to author, Dec. 16, 1965, and Grant Mason to author, Feb. 10, 1966. Jane wrote EH and Pauline on Sept. 2, 1933, that she had been in a cast for three months. On Oct. 28 she was discharged from the hospital. In the interim, Cuban revolutionists had burned the Masons' house in Jaimanitas, and Jane took an apartment at 455 East 57th Street, New York. (Jane Mason to EH and Pauline, Nov. 1, 1933.)
EH on Cuban terrorism: EH to Perkins, Aug. 10, 1933.
EH on crossing to Santander: EH to Perkins, Aug. 31, 1933.
EH's unhappiness over changes in Spain: "The Friend of Spain: A Spanish Letter," *Esquire*, Vol. 1 (Jan., 1934), pp. 26 and 136; EH to Perkins, Sept. 18, 1933; EH to Mrs. Paul Pfeiffer, Oct. 16, 1933. These letters also mention Sidney Franklin's surgical operation, which EH paid for.
EH's reading of Gertrude Stein's and Thurber's autobiographies: EH to Perkins, Aug. 31, 1933. The letter to Thurber has disappeared. Thurber mentions it in *The Years with Ross*, Boston, 1959, pp. 157–158. I am indebted for assistance in the search for EH's original letter to Thurber to Mrs. James Thurber and to Raymond C. Harwood and B. W. Hagen of Harper and Row.
EH renews work on Harry Morgan story: EH to Perkins, Sept. 18, 1933. EH's high opinion of the story is evident in EH to Mrs. Pfeiffer, Oct. 16, 1933. It was first published as *"One Trip Across"* in *Cosmopolitan*, Vol. 96 (April, 1934), pp. 20–23 and 108–122. It is my surmise that this was the "novel" (then fifty pages in length) which EH mentioned to various correspondents in April, 1933. He seems to have brought the MS. to Spain and finished it by mid-September. His only other literary work at this time was the editing and

rewriting of Sidney Franklin's translation of a romantic bullfight novel, *Currito de la Cruz*, by Alejandro Pérez Lugín, a "trashy job" in which he persevered until it was done. EH to Perkins, Aug. 31, 1933.
EH's gloom over changes in Montparnasse: "A Paris Letter," *Esquire*, Vol. 1 (Feb., 1934), pp. 22 and 156. The article also discusses his views on the coming war.
EH on Hitler: EH to Perkins, Sept. 18, 1933.
Reviewers' reception of "Winner Take Nothing": summarized from Horace Gregory, *New York Herald Tribune Books*, Oct. 29, 1933, p. 5. William Troy, *Nation*, Vol. 137 (Nov. 15, 1933), p. 570. Louis Kronenberger, *New York Times*, Nov. 5, 1933, p. 6. H. S. Canby, *Saturday Review of Literature*, Vol. 10 (Oct. 28, 1933), p. 217. T. S. Matthews, *New Republic*, Vol. 77 (Nov. 15, 1933), p. 24.
Fadiman's open letter and EH's reply: "A Letter to Mr. Hemingway." *The New Yorker*, Vol. 9 (Oct. 28, 1933), pp. 74–75; EH to Fadiman, Nov. 26, 1933.
EH's preface for Charters's "This Must Be the Place": Charters to EH, June 1, 1933, and Morrill Cody to EH, June 2, 1933. Cody, an American newspaper correspondent who had known EH since the days of the Anglo-American Press Club luncheons in 1924, had made a first draft of the book out of materials dictated by Charters, together with some memories of his own. EH replied from Havana, June 20, 1933, directing his letter to Charters, with a postscript to Cody. Cody to EH, Oct. 5, 1933, said that the book was in shape. Ivan Opfer, who was to illustrate the English edition of the book, wrote EH about it on Nov. 10. EH to Cody, ca. Nov. 11, suggested meeting Cody and Charters at Sylvia Beach's bookshop that afternoon. EH to Cody, Nov. 20, promised to write the preface on the way to Mombasa. Cody to EH, Dec. 26, 1933, was still hoping for the preface. EH sent the preface to Cody from Nairobi, Kenya, Jan. 2, 1934. Cody to EH, Jan. 26, 1934, suggested minor editorial changes. Charters to EH, Jan. 23, 1934, said he was proud and flattered to be a friend of EH's and that he was eager to read the preface "in which I will be a thousand times more proud of than the whole book." The book appeared in London in July, 1934, and in the U.S. in 1937. **Other details:** Cody to author, Sept. 18 and Dec. 12, 1962, and Oct. 19, 1966.
Solita Solano takes charge of "One Trip Across": Solita Solano to author, Feb. 18, 1962. EH wrote Miss Solano from Marseilles Nov. 22, 1933, enclosing a letter to *Cosmopolitan* to be forwarded with the typescript. He had fixed finally on the title, "One Trip Across." EH's note was daubed in some way. The daubs, he explained, meant that he was drunk.
EH shooting with Ben Gallagher and sharing the game with James and Nora Joyce: *Green Hills of Africa*, NY, 1935, p. 195.
Joyce's fear that his work was suburban and Nora's view that he should go to hunt lions: anecdote from EH in *Time*, Vol. 54 (Dec. 13, 1954), p. 75.
Joyce quoting Quinet: *Green Hills of Africa*, p. 71. EH misquoted Joyce's quotation, for in *Green Hills* the line appears as *"fraiche et rose comme au jour de la bataille."* [sic] The original passage is quoted at length by Richard

Ellmann, *James Joyce*, NY, 1959, p. 676. Quinet said of certain flowers, *". . . leurs paisibles générations ont traversé les âges et sont arrivées jusqu'à nous, fraîches et riantes comme aux jours des batailles."* (Quinet, *Introduction à la Philosophie de l'Histoire de l'Humanité, Œuvres Complètes*, Paris, 1857, II, p. 367.) Joyce parodied the passage throughout *Finnegans Wake*, and quoted it *in extenso* in the schoolroom episode, the second section of Part II, which he had begun in this year, 1933. The passage, which in many ways embodied Joyce's view of history, had become almost obsessively entangled in his thinking. I am indebted for most of this information to Professor A. Walton Litz.

Sec. 34. Highlands of Africa

SOURCES

Letters of EH: to Clifton Fadiman, Nov. 26, 1933; to Patrick Hemingway, Dec. 2; to Perkins, Dec. 3; to Gingrich, Dec. 19, 1933. To Perkins, Jan. 17, 1934; to Gingrich, Jan. 18, 1934. To Lillian Ross, June 16, 1950.
Other letters: Perkins to EH, Dec. 12, 1933; Harry Payne Burton to EH, Dec. 23, 1933 (cable) and letter of Jan. 19, 1934; Katharine Fannin to EH, Jan. 30, 1934. Hans Koritschoner to EH, Dec. 22, 1938. Richard Reusch to John Howell, July 5, 1968.
EH's work: (a) Unpublished: deleted passage from holograph MS. of *Green Hills of Africa*. **(b) Published:** "a.d. in Africa," *Esquire*, Vol. 1 (April, 1934); "One Trip Across," *Cosmopolitan*, Vol. 96 (April, 1934); "Shootism versus Sport," *Esquire*, Vol. 2 (June, 1934); "Notes on Dangerous Game," *Esquire*, Vol. 2 (July, 1934); *Green Hills of Africa*, 1935.
Books and articles: Dr. R. Reusch, "Mount Kilimanjaro and its Ascent," *Tanganyika Times*, Feb. 10, 1928; Isak Dinesen, *Out of Africa*, 1937; Philip Percival, unpublished autobiography.
Author's interviews and correspondence: with Charles Thompson, March, 1965. From Philip and Richard Percival, Feb. 2, 1964; from Addison Southard, March 23, 1967; from Marcus Smith, Jan. 19, 1968; from G. S. Child to Richard Bevis, Feb. 12, 1968, copy forwarded to author by Marcus Smith, Feb. 1968; from John M. Howell, July 12, 1968.

NOTES

Marseilles to Mombasa: EH to Clifton Fadiman, Nov. 26; EH to Patrick Hemingway, Dec. 2; EH to Perkins, Dec. 3, 1933. EH's unpublished diary of the voyage covers the period Nov. 27 (Port Said) to Dec. 2 (approaching Djibouti). The letter to Perkins asked him to send copies of *A Farewell to Arms, Men Without Women*, and *Death in the Afternoon* to Addison Southard, American Minister to Addis Ababa, whom EH met in the course of the voyage.
Weekend in Mombasa: Mrs. Katharine Fannin to EH, Jan. 30, 1934. Charles Thompson to author, March 28, 1965.
Arrival in Nairobi: The party checked in at the New Stanley Hotel Dec. 10th, and got in touch with J. F. Manley, treasurer of Tanganyika Guides, Ltd., of which Baron von Blixen, divorced husband of Karen Blixen,

was Director for Tanganyika and Philip Percival for Kenya. The organization was formed in 1930. (Philip and Richard Percival to author, Feb. 2, 1964.) Von Blixen had brought his wife to Kenya in 1917 and by 1933 was world-famous as a white hunter. The description of Nairobi is from Isak Dinesen (Karen Blixen), *Out of Africa*, NY, Modern Library, 1952, pp. 10–11. She had given up her plantation in the Ngong Hills in 1931, but had not yet written *Out of Africa*, which first appeared in 1937.

First days at Potha Hill: EH to Arnold Gingrich, Dec. 19, 1933. Young Alfred Vanderbilt was there, a friend of Grant and Jane Mason's. He had come out in November with Winston Guest, who had bagged two elephants and was homeward bound. EH urged Vanderbilt to write race-track pieces for *Esquire*, and recommended him to Gingrich.

Philip and Flora Percival: Both Percivals were then forty-nine and were natives of Somersetshire. Philip had come out in 1905 to join his brother Blayney, who was game warden for the district. In 1908 he returned to England to marry Flora Vivien Smith-Spark, who followed him out in 1909, and set up housekeeping at Potha Hill. Poisonous ticks soon drove them to Limuru, where they raised coffee and wattle for three years before returning to Potha Hill. Ex-President Theodore Roosevelt and his son Kermit helped determine Percival's future when they came out on safari and lived at Kitanga, adjoining Potha Hill. R. J. Cunningham was the Roosevelts' white hunter, with Percival as chief assistant. Percival later established a guide service, using the proceeds to support his farm. They raised ostrich for the plumes, bred cattle and horses, and grew coffee, wheat, and citrus fruits. Details from Percival's memoir (unpublished), examined by author, Oct., 1963, and from Philip and Richard Percival to author, Feb. 2, 1964. See also "a.d. in Africa," *Esquire*, Vol. 1 (Apr., 1934), p. 19.

Percival reminds EH of Dorman-Smith: *Green Hills of Africa*, NY, 1935, pp. 280–281. A canceled passage in the holograph MS. of the book spoke of EH's oldest friends, Dorman-Smith, Guy Hickok, and Mike Ward. Charles Thompson was "a damned good guy." Dos Passos was "brave as a damned buffalo." Hickok was one of the best and most intelligent. Fitzgerald was called "a coward of great charm." The passage then went on about courage and cowardice:

A brave man had a certain pride. A coward said this pride was of no importance. Perhaps it wasn't but it was of great importance to whoever had it. . . . A man without inner dignity is an embarrassment. The cowards had the charm though. Not all of the charming ones were cowards. Look at [Gene] Tunney. There was a very brave man and he had great charm. . . . My father was a coward. He shot himself without necessity. At least I thought so. I had gone through it myself until I figured it in my head. I knew what it was to be a coward and what it was to cease being a coward. Now, truly, in actual danger I felt a clean feeling as in a shower. Of course it was easy now. That was because I no longer cared what happened. I knew it was better to live it so that if you died you had done

everything that you could do about your work and your enjoyment of life up to that minute, reconciling the two, which is very difficult.

Tanganyika itinerary: Charles Thompson to author, March 28, 1965. The camp at M'Utu Umbo is described in *Green Hills*, p. 123. Also spelled Mto Wambu and Mto Wa Mbu, it means Mosquito Creek.

Hunting Serengeti Plain, Dec. 23, 1933 to Jan. 16, 1934: "a.d. in Africa," *Esquire*, Vol. 1 (April, 1934), p. 19.

Onset of dysentery: EH to Perkins, Jan. 17 and EH to Gingrich, Jan. 18, 1934. In *Green Hills*, p. 283, EH blames the "dirty boat out from Marseilles." See also the article, "a.d. in Africa."

Pauline's lion: *Green Hills*, pp. 40–41.

EH's lion: "Shootism versus Sport," *Esquire*, Vol. 2 (June, 1934), pp. 19 and 150. Besides the two males, Pauline's and his own, EH shot a lioness, breaking her neck with a 220-grain solid at 30 yards. See "a.d. in Africa," pp. 19 and 146.

Shooting buffalo bulls: *Green Hills*, p. 115 and "Notes on Dangerous Game," *Esquire*, Vol. 2 (July, 1934), p. 94.

EH's intestinal prolapse: "a.d. in Africa," p. 19. The dysentery is alluded to only in passing in *Green Hills*, pp. 46, 51, 55, and 283. EH to Lillian Ross, June 16, 1950, echoes the statement made in *Green Hills*, p. 283.

Flight to Nairobi: EH to Perkins, Jan. 17, 1934 says that it took place "yesterday" (Jan. 16), passing over Ngorongoro Crater and the Rift Escarpment to Arusha. EH states further that he has had dysentery two weeks (i.e., since about Jan. 1).

Identity of Fatty Pearson: Philip and Richard Percival to author, Feb. 2, 1964; they confirm the fact that the flight was substantially as described in "The Snows of Kilimanjaro," *First 49 Stories*, NY, 1938, pp. 173–174.

EH writes "a.d. in Africa": EH to Gingrich, Jan. 18, 1934. The picture of EH and his lion appeared as an illustration for "Shootism versus Sport," *Esquire*, Vol. 2 (June, 1934), p. 19.

Sales of "Winner Take Nothing": Perkins to EH, Dec. 12, 1933.

Sale of "One Trip Across": Burton to EH, Dec. 23, 1933 (cable) and letter of Jan. 19, 1934. Actual date of purchase was Feb. 14, 1934. The story appeared in *Cosmopolitan*, Vol. 96 (April, 1934), pp. 20–23 and 108–122.

Hunting hill country with Droopy: *Green Hills*, pp. 46–55.

Percival's campfire conversation: *Green Hills*, pp. 190 and 197, and "Notes on Dangerous Game," *Esquire*, Vol. 2 (July, 1934).

The leopard carcass on Kibo Peak of Kilimanjaro: Philip and Richard Percival to author, Feb. 2, 1964. Marcus Smith to author, Jan. 19, 1968 says that the Rev. Dr. R. Reusch found the frozen leopard in Sept., 1926, and saw it again in July, 1927. His account of the discovery (*Mt. Kilimanjaro and Its Ascent*) was printed in *Tanganyika Times*, Feb. 10, 1928, and in *Ice Cap* (Bulletin of the Kilimanjaro Mountain Club), No. 1 (1932). G. S. Child (College of African Wildlife Management, Mweka) to Richard Bevis, Feb. 12, 1968, states that in 1952 signs of the leopard skeleton were still visible near Leopard Point on Kibo's outer crater rim. "Ice and snow had been receding on the mountain and the leopard has presumably thawed out and then been consumed by the ravens which are found right up to the summit." According to Dr. Reusch to John Howell, July 5, 1968, the leopard froze while resting after chasing a goat.

EH on courage: canceled passage, holograph MS of *Green Hills,* p. 467. The bearing of EH's fireside conversations with Percival on "The Short Happy Life of Francis Macomber" should not be overlooked.

EH sees rhino and shoots reedbuck: *Green Hills,* pp. 50–54.

Rivalry between EH and Thompson: *Green Hills,* pp. 63, 76, 83–84.

EH's discontentment in Rift Valley and Babati camp: *Green Hills,* pp. 124–134, 136–142.

EH's fear of snakes: *Green Hills,* p. 58.

Move to Kijungu camp: *Green Hills,* pp. 143–144.

Meeting Garrick and Abdullah: *Green Hills,* pp. 162–166.

Thompson's freak kudu: *Green Hills,* pp. 170–174.

Meeting Hans Koritschoner: *Green Hills,* pp. 2–31. Koritschoner appears as Kandisky in the book. His identity is established by his letter to EH, Dec. 22, 1938, from Bukoba, Tanganyika. "It was in Tanganyika Territory," he wrote, ". . . where you found one day a man with a broken down motor car, who was a reader of the *Querschnitt.* . . . You pulled this man out of his awkward situation, he spent 2 days in your camp in Kijungu. . . . It was not a main road where we met." In the intervening years, he had become a government ethnologist, collecting figurines and other symbolic objects from the East African Bantus. He asked EH's financial help. EH's reply, if he made one, is lost.

EH hunting kudu, Feb. 15–16, 1934: *Green Hills,* pp. 34–36, 176–184, 188–189.

Bagging two kudu bulls, Feb. 17, 1934: *Green Hills,* pp. 216–244.

Sable hunt and return to camp, Feb. 18–19, 1934: *Green Hills,* pp. 246–294.

EH's dream of returning to Africa: *Green Hills,* pp. 73 and 282–285.

Sec. 35. The Long Journey Home

SOURCES

Letters of EH: to Gingrich, March 20 (cable), March 24, and Apr. 12, 1934; to Perkins, Apr. 16 and Apr. 30; to Lester Ziffren, May 18; to Gingrich, May 25; to Peirce, ca. May 26; to Fitzgerald, May 28; to Perkins, June 30; to Gingrich, June 21; to Edwin Balmer, Aug. 3, 1934. To Gen. C. T. Lanham, Jan. 1, 1947.

Other letters: Katharine Fannin to EH, Feb. 22, 1934; J. F. Manley to EH, March 14, 1934; Fitzgerald to EH, June 1, 1934; J. F. Manley to EH, Dec. 24, 1934.

EH's work: (a) Unpublished: various passages deleted from the holograph MS of *Green Hills of Africa.* **(b) Published:** "Notes on Dangerous Game," *Esquire,* Vol. 2 (July, 1934); "Sailfish off Mombasa," *Esquire,* Vol. 3 (March, 1935); *A Moveable Feast,* 1964.

Books and articles: Leicester Hemingway, *My Brother, Ernest Hemingway,* 1962; Andrew Turnbull, ed., *The Letters of F. Scott Fitz-*

gerald, 1963; Warren V. Bush, ed., *The Dialogues of Archibald MacLeish and Mark Van Doren,* 1964; Marlene Dietrich, "The Most Fascinating Man I Know," *This Week* Magazine, Feb. 13, 1955; K. A. Porter, "Paris: A Little Incident," *Ladies' Home Journal,* Vol. 81 (Aug., 1964).

Author's interviews and correspondence: with General Charles T. Lanham, June, 1963; with Charles Thompson, March, 1965; with Gen. John F. Ruggles, Feb., 1966. From Ned Calmer, Feb. 18 and March 5, 1963; from Archibald MacLeish, Jan. 31, 1965; from Dawn Powell, May 10, 1965.

NOTES

Fishing in the Indian Ocean: "Notes on Dangerous Game," *Esquire,* Vol. 2 (July, 1934), p. 94; "Sailfish off Mombasa," *Esquire,* Vol. 3 (March, 1935), pp. 21 and 156. Further details from Charles Thompson to author, March, 1965. The party went from Tanga up the coast road to Moa, back into Kenya and thence through Shimoni and Tiwi to Mombasa. There they met Vanderbilt and continued to Malindi. The rental agent for the boat was named Bemister: J. F. Manley to EH, Dec. 24, 1934.

Voyage on the "Gripsholm": The ship left Mombasa March 3, reaching Port Sudan on the 9th, Suez on the 11th, and Haifa on the 12th. The itinerary was given in Katharine Fannin to EH, Feb. 22, 1934. The voyage was mentioned in "Sailfish off Mombasa," *Esquire,* Vol. 3 (March, 1935), p. 156.

Lunch by the Sea of Galilee: *Green Hills,* p. 294.

From Nice to Paris: Charles Thompson to author, March, 1965, and Solita Solano to author, Feb. 18, 1962. From Paris, EH sent Gingrich two more African articles: EH to Gingrich, March 20 (cable), and letter of March 24, 1934.

EH and the Calmers: Ned Calmer to author, Feb. 18 and March 5, 1963. Between March 26 and April 30, EH lent $1,155 to fellow writers: EH to Perkins, Apr. 30, 1934.

Dinner with Joyce at Michaud's: Solita Solano to author, Feb. 18, 1962.

EH breaks Sylvia Beach's vase: holograph note by Sylvia Beach, dated March 24, 1934, in the Sylvia Beach Collection, Princeton University Library. EH's vengeful remarks on Lewis appear in *A Moveable Feast,* 1964, p. 108.

EH meets Katherine Anne Porter: Miss Porter, "Paris: A Little Incident in the Rue de l'Odéon," *Ladies' Home Journal,* Vol. 81 (August, 1964), pp. 54–55. Miss Porter adds that EH "seemed to me then to be the walking exemplar of the stylish literary attitudes of his time. . . . He paid heavily, as such men do, for their right to live on beyond the fashion they helped to make, to play out to the end not the role wished on them by their public but the destiny they cannot escape because there was a moment in their lives when they chose that destiny."

EH meets Marlene Dietrich: Miss Dietrich, "The Most Fascinating Man I Know," *This Week* Magazine, Feb. 13, 1955. According to Mary Hemingway, the actual author of the article was A. E. Hotchner. After the first meeting, Miss Dietrich and EH began to correspond in a desultory fashion. She soon began to save his letters in a fireproof strong-box. EH kept two dozen of hers, all for the period 1950–61. She said that she never made him into a father-image or called him Papa (this was not true, for she often called him Papa in the letters) but regarded him as a "warm-hearted oracle" who listened sympathetically and often replied with words of wisdom that when laid end to end constituted a working philosophy of life.

EH's comments to ship-news reporters: *New York Times,* Apr. 4, 1934, p. 18.

Story of wealthy woman who offered to pay for another safari: EH to Gen. Charles T. Lanham, Jan. 1, 1947. During the war EH had described this event both to Col. Lanham and to Col. John F. Ruggles. He explained that "The Snows of Kilimanjaro" was based in part on his imagination of what would have happened had he accepted the woman's offer. (Lanham to author, June, 1963, and Ruggles to author, Feb., 1966.)

EH in New York: EH saw Waldo Peirce (EH to Peirce, ca. May 26, 1934), Sidney Franklin (EH to Lester Ziffren, May 18, 1934), and his old friend Edwin Balmer (EH to Gingrich, Apr. 12, 1934). EH recalled Balmer's early generosity to him in EH to Balmer, Aug. 3, 1934. Balmer had invited EH to submit stories for *Red Book.* Contents of Balmer's cable are quoted in J. F. Manley to EH, March 14, 1934.

EH meets Fitzgerald in New York: EH to Fitzgerald, May 28, 1934.

Buying the "Pilar": Wheeler Shipyard brochure mailed to EH July 14, 1933. Invoice for purchase was dated May 5, 1934, and bore inscription, "Rec. May 12" with the signature of Charles Johnson, Wheeler representative. It reflected a down payment of $3,000, the sum advanced by Arnold Gingrich. The name *Pilar* (Nuestra Señora del Pilar, Our Lady of the Pillar) refers to the image of the Blessed Virgin on a pillar of porphyry in the shrine and church at Zaragoza, and also to the *féria* held in her honor on Oct. 12 or 13. See *Death in the Afternoon,* 1932, p. 514. I am indebted to Professor Raymond S. Willis for information about Pilar.

Return to Key West: EH to Perkins, Apr. 16, 1934. EH's fishing log for Apr. 15–21 names many of the friends who fished with him.

EH begins "The Highlands of Africa": EH to Perkins, Apr. 30, 1934. Working title and subtitle appear in the holograph MS. at the University of Virginia Library.

May Day trip to Havana: EH to Perkins, Apr. 30; to Lester Ziffren, May 18; and to Gingrich, May 25, 1934.

Arrival of the "Pilar": EH to Gingrich, Apr. 12 and May 25, 1934; Leicester Hemingway, *My Brother, Ernest Hemingway,* 1962, pp. 147–149. The Baron, as EH called his brother, was at this time nineteen, much inclined to ape EH. He and Al Dudek, a Petoskey friend, had spent most of April beating their way across the Gulf of Mexico in a boat that Leicester had built in Alabama that winter.

Progress with African book: EH to Peirce, ca. May 26, 1934.

EH's list of earthly pleasures: Holograph MS., *Green Hills,* pp. 29 and 29-insert.

Departure of Mesdames MacLeish, Murphy, and Dos Passos: EH to Peirce, ca. May 26, 1934.

Good-bye to Dawn Powell: Dawn Powell to author, May 10, 1965.

EH's quarrel with MacLeish: EH to Peirce, ca. May 26, 1934; Archibald MacLeish to author, Jan. 31, 1965. The quarrel is alluded to in *The Dialogues of Archibald MacLeish and Mark Van Doren,* ed. Warren V. Bush, NY, 1964, pp. 86–87. The anecdote in Leicester Hemingway, *My Brother, Ernest Hemingway,* 1962, p. 190, which says that EH intentionally marooned MacLeish on an uninhabited key, is denied by Mr. MacLeish as apocryphal.

EH's "4th dimension" in African book: EH to Perkins, June 20, and EH to Gingrich, June 21, 1934.

EH and Fitzgerald exchange letters: EH to Fitzgerald, May 28, and Fitzgerald to EH, June 1, 1934. Fitzgerald's letter appears in Andrew Turnbull, ed., *The Letters of F. Scott Fitzgerald,* NY, 1963, pp. 308–310.

Dialogue on courage and allied powers: deleted passage from holograph MS. of *Green Hills of Africa,* p. 86.

Sec. 36. Notes on Life and Letters

SOURCES

Letters of EH: to Everett R. Perry, ca. Feb. 25, 1933; to Charles Cadwalader, Apr. 5, 6, and 9, 1934 (wires); to Prudencio de Pereda, Apr. 13, 1934; to Gingrich, July 14 and 15, 1934; to Antonio Gattorno, ca. July 15; to Edwin Balmer, Aug. 3; to Mrs. Pfeiffer, Aug. 20; to Charles Cadwalader, Sept. 6; to Perkins, Sept. 10 (wire); to Gingrich, Sept. 13; to Perkins, Oct. 5; to Cadwalader, Oct. 18; to Gingrich, Oct. 18; to Ned Calmer, Oct. 24; to Gingrich, Oct. 25; to Gingrich and Perkins (both Nov. 16); to Perkins, Nov. 20; to Gingrich, Nov. 19, Nov. 21, Nov. 26 (wire), and Nov. 27; to Peirce, Nov. 29; to Ned Calmer, Dec. 8; to Gingrich and Cadwalader (both Dec. 13); to Perkins, Dec. 14 and 28; to Gingrich, Dec. 28, 1934.

Other letters: Everett R. Perry to Scribners, Jan. 12, 1933; Charles M. B. Cadwalader to EH, March 6, Apr. 5, and July 12, 1934; John E. Brown to Morgan Hebard, July 25; Cadwalader to Hebard, Aug. 28; Cadwalader to EH, Aug. 31 and Sept. 11; Perkins to EH, Sept. 15 and Oct. 1, 1934; Lester Ziffren to EH, Nov. 1; Dos Passos to Pauline Hemingway, Nov. 7 (cable); Mary Hoover to EH, ca. Nov. 7; Gilbert Seldes to Gingrich, Nov. 12; Jay Allen to EH, Nov. 13; Pierre Matisse to EH, Nov. 22; Fitzgerald to EH, Nov. 26; Waldo Peirce to EH, ca. Dec. 1 (wire); Dos Passos to Gingrich, Dec. 7 (wire).

EH's work: (a) Unpublished: undated holograph note on Dos Passos and the Murphys; deleted passage from holograph MS. of *Green Hills of Africa.* **(b) Published:** "Defense of Dirty Words," *Esquire,* Vol. 2 (Sept., 1934); "Genio after Josie," *Esquire,* Vol. 2 (Oct., 1934); "Notes on Life and Letters," *Esquire,* Vol. 3 (Jan., 1935); "Monologue to the Maestro," *Esquire,* Vol. 4 (Oct., 1935); "There She Breaches," *Esquire,* Vol. 5 (May, 1936).

Books and articles: Edwin Balmer, "Our Literary Nudism," *Esquire,* Vol. 2 (Sept., 1934); William Saroyan, *The Daring Young Man on the Flying Trapeze,* 1934; Donald Gallup, ed.,

The Flowers of Friendship, 1953; Andrew Turnbull, ed., *The Letters of F. Scott Fitzgerald,* 1963; John Dos Passos, *The Best Times,* 1966; Arnold Gingrich, "Scott, Ernest, and Whoever," *Esquire,* Vol. 66 (Dec., 1966). **Author's correspondence:** from Milton H. Altman, Apr. 14, 1962; from Antonio Gattorno, Sept. 8, 1964; from William Saroyan, Dec. 20, 1965.

NOTES

EH asks Joe Russell to Cuba: "Genio After Josie," *Esquire,* Vol. 2 (Oct. 1934, pp. 21–22.
EH hires Arnold Samuelson: "Monologue to the Maestro," *Esquire,* Vol. 4 (Oct., 1935), pp. 21, 174A, 174B.
EH justifies Cuban vacation: EH to Gingrich, July 14 and 15, 1934. These letters show EH's mood of depression, and are filled with complaints. But he proudly notes his progress with the African book.
Arrival in Cuba: "Genio After Josie," *Esquire,* Vol. 2 (Oct., 1934), pp. 21–22. "Genio" was Gutiérrez's term, the rough equivalent of "talking it up" among ballplayers. Josie was the nickname for Joe Russell.
Cadwalader and Fowler as EH's guests: Cadwalader to EH, July 12, 1934, asks permission to come down. John E. Bowers to Morgan Hebard, July 25, says Cadwalader and Fowler are fishing with EH; Cadwalader to Hebard, Aug. 28, says he has "recently returned from Cuba." Cadwalader to EH, Aug. 31 thanks him for hospitality. EH describes his work for Cadwalader in EH to Cadwalader, Sept. 6; Cadwalader's reply is dated Sept. 11, 1934.
EH and Gattorno: Gattorno to author, Sept. 8, 1964.
EH's notes on progress with book and economics of writing: EH to Mrs. Pfeiffer, Aug. 20, 1934.
EH's "Defense of Dirty Words": *Esquire,* Vol. 2 (Sept., 1934), pp. 19, 158B, and 158D. He had already set forth similar arguments in EH to Everett R. Perry, Los Angeles City Librarian, ca. Feb. 2–5, 1933. For a copy of this letter I am indebted to M. H. Altman, Apr. 14, 1962. Perry had first complained about EH's gamy language to Scribners, Jan. 12, 1933. Another complaint, signed by Walter Whitney, brought a reply from Alfred Dashiell (May 5, 1934) which quoted *in extenso* EH's letter to Perry. "Our Literary Nudism," by Edwin Balmer, appeared in the same number of *Esquire* with EH's piece. EH to Balmer, Aug. 3, 1934, apologizes to Balmer for taking a different point of view, and gratefully recalls Balmer's early help with EH's short stories.
EH returns to Key West: documented in EH to Cadwalader, Sept. 6 and EH to Perkins, Sept. 10 (wire).
EH's progress with African book (September) and his defense of sporting interests: EH to Gingrich, Sept. 13, 1934.
EH's autumn fishing and arrival of warblers: EH to Cadwalader, Oct. 18, 1934.
EH's whale hunt: EH to Cadwalader, Oct. 18, 1934. EH later elaborated and fictionized this adventure in "There She Breaches," *Esquire,* Vol. 5 (May, 1936), pp. 35, 203–205. He makes a lively story of it while handling the facts as earlier reported to Cadwalader with considerable poetic license.

EH critical of Dos Passos: EH complained of Dos Passos's work in Hollywood in EH to Ned Calmer, Oct. 24, 1934. Dos and Katy returned to Key West about Nov. 8 or 9, 1934 (Dos Passos to Pauline, Nov. 7, cable from Havana when his ship had docked there after coming through the Panama Canal). Dos Passos describes EH's surliness in *The Best Times,* NY, 1966, pp. 215 and 219. An undated holograph note of EH's, written on the back of the last page of Evan Shipman's long poem *Mazzepa* [sic] reads as follows: "Marx the whimpering bourgeois living on the bounty of Engels is exactly as valid as Dos Passos living on a yacht in the Mediterranean while he attacks the capitalist system." The reference, and a very unfair one it is, is doubtless to Dos Passos's visit to the Murphys in the early summer of 1933, when Dos was just recovering from another severe attack of rheumatic fever.
EH on Gertrude Stein's radio broadcast: EH to Gingrich, Nov. 16, 1934. The Misses Stein and Toklas reached New York on Oct. 24th, 1934, and stayed in the United States until May 4, 1935 (Donald Gallup, editor, *The Flowers of Friendship: Letters Written to Gertrude Stein,* NY, 1953, pp. 288 and 299). EH's attack on Gertrude Stein appeared eventually in *Green Hills of Africa,* NY, 1935, pp. 65–66. The quotations here used come from the holograph MS., p. 87. EH deleted the passage beginning, "Homme des lettres," perhaps on the grounds that he had already condemned salonkeepers, and Miss Stein by implication, in his introduction to James Charters's *This Must Be the Place.*
EH helps de Pereda, Calmer, Gattorno, and Quintanilla: EH to de Pereda, Apr. 13, 1934, offers to read and judge his fiction; EH to de Pereda, Nov. 20, 1935 mentions having liked one of his stories. EH to Ned Calmer, Dec. 8, 1934, quotes the recommendation EH had written for Calmer's Guggenheim application; Gattorno to author, Sept. 14, 1964; EH to Gattorno, ca. July 15, 1934. Accounts of Quintanilla in Madrid reached EH from Lester Ziffren, Nov. 1 and from Jay Allen, Nov. 13, 1934. Mary Hoover, a Quintanilla disciple, brought the etchings to New York, and wrote EH about them, ca. Nov. 7, 1934. One of her fears was that Quintanilla's jailing would keep him from doing the Pablo Iglesias frescoes, which he had been commissioned to do.
The international petition to secure Quintanilla's release: Pierre Matisse to EH, Nov. 22, 1934. EH's catalogue statement on Quintanilla was reprinted in *Esquire,* Vol. 3 (Feb. 1935), pp. 26–27.
EH meets Irving Stone: Stone to author, June 27, 1966.
EH finishes "Green Hills": EH to Perkins and Gingrich, both Nov. 16, 1934.
EH's literary energy: EH to Perkins, Nov. 20, 1934.
EH attacks Saroyan: EH took issue with two passages in *The Daring Young Man on the Flying Trapeze.* On p. 34, Saroyan spoke of "a great philosophical work on tennis, something on the order of *Death in the Afternoon,*" which he called "a pretty fine piece of prose," adding that even when EH was a fool, he was "at least an accurate fool." On p. 57, he asserted that "if I felt inclined, I could

write like John Dos Passos or William Faulkner or James Joyce." Before the piece appeared Gingrich offered to pay Saroyan for a public rejoinder. Saroyan declined and wrote directly to Hemingway instead. Ernest replied "cordially," urging his young friend "to get in there and knock the critics for a loop" with his second book. Saroyan then "thanked him for his kind advice" and an armed truce ensued. (Saroyan to author, Dec. 20, 1965.) EH's article also attacked Gilbert Seldes in order to avenge himself for an insulting letter which (he said) Seldes had written him ten years earlier, advising him to stick to reporting instead of trying serious fiction. Seldes sent Gingrich a letter on Nov. 12, 1934, seeking to discover the grounds for Hemingway's attack. The original rumor which said that Seldes had written Hemingway an insulting letter about his story submitted to the *Dial* had first appeared in a gossip column in the *Graphic*. Dorothy Parker's profile of Hemingway in *The New Yorker* had elaborated on the story, hinting that Seldes had advised Hemingway to stick to newspaper work. On reading this, Seldes wrote Hemingway. Ernest professed ignorance. "What was it all about?" he asked. Seldes had sent him a denial but not the accusations. He himself had never made any accusations. He had read Dotty Parker's piece in *The New Yorker* and saw no reference to Seldes. "It all sounds like ballroom bananas to me," said Ernest. "Best to you always." But Ernest had been preoccupied with ballroom bananas on October 18, 1934, when he told Gingrich flatly that he had a letter from Seldes, which he had fortunately kept, in which Seldes as editor of the *Dial* had turned down Chapter Six of *in our time* and sought to dissuade Hemingway from further serious writing. Upon being queried by Gingrich as to where the Seldes letter was, Ernest replied that it was locked up with his papers in Paris. The knowledge that it was there gave him a certain damned fine feeling of superiority because he knew he could finish off Seldes whenever he wished but refrained from doing so. He had had Seldes worried about that letter for a long time now and was planning to keep him worried. (EH to Gingrich, Nov. 16, 1934.) He had no quarrel with people unless they lied about questions of fact or repeated old lies. But, said Ernest, "when I lie myself its Hokay." (EH to Gingrich, Oct. 25, 1934.)
Gingrich's visit to Key West: EH to Gingrich, Nov. 19 and 21, 1934. EH's wire of Nov. 26 says it will be "swell to see you and Scott." Fitzgerald to Perkins, Nov. 26, 1934, says, "Your suggestion to go to Key West is tempting as hell but I don't know whether it would be advisable on either Ernest's account or mine." Fitzgerald says nothing about his mother's illness. (Fitzgerald to Perkins, Nov. 26, 1934, in *The Letters of F. Scott Fitzgerald*, ed. Andrew Turnbull, NY, 1963, p. 256.) Gingrich's account of the trip to Key West is in "Scott, Ernest, and Whoever," *Esquire*, Vol. 66 (Dec., 1966), p. 186. Dos Passos's account is in *The Best Times*, NY, 1966, p. 216.
EH's African Trophies: Cost of shipping trophies from Mombasa to New York: EH to Gingrich, Nov. 27, 1934. **Cost of taxidermy:**

Invoice from Jonas Brothers, dated Dec. 1, 1934. The Murphys' apartment was at 439 East 51st St.
Christmas trip to Piggott: The Hemingways leave for Piggott: EH to Perkins, Dec. 14, 1934.
The night in Memphis: Hotel Peabody bill for Dec. 22–23, 1934.
Foul weather and poor quail hunting: EH to Perkins and EH to Gingrich, Dec. 28, 1934.

Sec. 37. Bimini Discovered

SOURCES

Letters of EH: to Gingrich, Jan. 15, Feb. 4, and Feb. 11, 1935; to Perkins, Feb. 18 (wire) and Feb. 22; to Gingrich, March 1; to Gerald and Sara Murphy, March 19; to Perkins, March 30, ca. Apr. 5, Apr. 14, May 1, June 3, and June 4; to Gingrich, June 4; to Perkins, June 19; to Alfred Dashiell, June 30; to Perkins, July 2 and July 4; to Gingrich, July 17; to Perkins, July 30 and July 31; to Gingrich, July 31 and Aug. 7; to Perkins, ca. Aug. 15; to Gingrich, Aug. 26, 1935. To General Charles T. Lanham, March 30, 1947.
Other letters: Perkins to EH, Jan. 15 (wire), Feb. 4, Feb. 15, and Feb. 19, 1935 (wire); Father G. A. Whipple to EH, March 2; Thornton Wilder to EH, March 13; Perkins to EH, Apr. 21 and Apr. 25; Baron von Blixen to EH, May 6 (cable); Dr. Lawrence Kubie to Jane Mason, May 7; Jane Mason to Dr. Kubie, May 12; Arnold Samuelson to EH, May 15; Perkins to EH, May 21 and June 5; Baron von Blixen to EH, June 13, June 24, and June 28 (cable); Jane Mason to EH, June 29; Strater to EH, Sept. 14, 1935.
EH's work: Published: "On Being Shot Again," *Esquire*, Vol. 3 (June, 1935); "The President Vanquishes," *Esquire*, Vol. 3 (July, 1935); "He Who Gets Slap Happy," *Esquire*, Vol. 4 (Aug., 1935); "Notes on the Next War," *Esquire*, Vol. 4 (Sept., 1935); "There She Breaches," *Esquire*, Vol. 5 (May, 1936); "Gattorno: Program Note," *Esquire*, Vol. 5 (May, 1936).
Books: Leicester Hemingway, *My Brother, Ernest Hemingway*, 1962; Andrew Turnbull, ed., *The Letters of F. Scott Fitzgerald*, 1963; Arthur Mizener, *The Far Side of Paradise*, 2nd edition, 1965; John Dos Passos, *The Best Times*, 1966; Robert Sklar, *F. Scott Fitzgerald: The Last Laocoön*, 1967.
Author's interviews and correspondence: with Henry Strater, July, 1964. From Samuel Bell, Jan. 16, 1963; from Dr. Lawrence Kubie, June 28, July 16, and Aug. 2, 1963; from Josephine Herbst, July 3, 1963; from Richard H. ("Sacker") Adams, Sr., Apr. 14 1967.

NOTES

Piggott, New Orleans, and home: EH to Gingrich, Jan. 15, 1935.
Recurrence of dysentery: EH to Gingrich, Feb. 4 and 11, 1935.
Perkins's visit: Perkins to EH, Jan. 15 (wire) and letter of Feb. 4, 1935.
Offer from "Cosmopolitan": EH to Gingrich, Feb. 4, 1935.
Sale to "Scribner's Magazine": Perkins to EH, Feb. 15; EH to Perkins, Feb. 18 (wire); Perkins to EH, Feb. 19 (wire), 1935.

War veterans from Matecumbe Keys: "He Who Gets Slap Happy," *Esquire,* Vol. 4 (August, 1935), p. 19. "Who Murdered the Vets?" *New Masses,* Vol. 16 (September 17, 1935), p. 9. Besides these articles, EH wrote of these veterans in Chapter twenty-two of *To Have and Have Not,* NY, 1937, pp. 193–202, where the pseudo-novelist, Richard Gordon, spends part of an evening at Freddy's Bar, a fictional representation of Joe Russell's place. Even Josie's sawed-off billiard cue appears in this chapter.
EH's plans for Bimini: EH to Gingrich, March 31, 1935.
EH's seagoing appearance: Samuel Bell to author, Jan. 16, 1963.
Departure of Arnold Samuelson: EH to Gingrich, Feb. 4, 1935.
EH hires Albert Pinder and Richard Adams: EH to Gingrich, March 1, 1935. EH always misspelled Adams's nickname as "Saca." Richard Adams to author, Apr. 16, 1967.
Death of Baoth Murphy: EH to Sara and Gerald Murphy, March 19, 1935. A copy of this letter kindly supplied by Archibald MacLeish. It will be noted that EH says nothing of the consolations of religion. He was still known, however, as a practicing Catholic. In February, he had contributed $25 to the Jesuit Seminary Missionary Fund of New Orleans, Louisiana, through a Father Maureau. On March 2, Father Whipple wrote belatedly to thank him for the gift. "We are very deeply grateful indeed for this goodness on your part," said he. "I will remember your good self very fervently in my Masses. . . . I note from Father Maureau's letter that you are anxious to enroll the whole family. You, yourself, are already a PERPETUAL member, so I will make out the enrollment certificate for the Hemingway Family, instead of Mr. Hemingway and Family. You will find the certificate enclosed. It means that our Jesuit Fathers laboring in God's Vineyard throughout the South will offer up for the new members of the Association 611 special Masses. GOD BLESS YOU AND YOURS AND KEEP YOU ALWAYS. Very, very cordially in Christ. Griswold A. Whipple, S.J." Father Whipple's letter is dated from New Orleans, March 2, 1935.
EH's leg wounds: "On Being Shot Again," *Esquire,* Vol. 3 (June, 1935), pp. 25, 156–157. Further details in EH to Gingrich, April 8 and April 14 and EH to Perkins, April 14, 1935. In John Dos Passos, *The Best Times,* NY, 1966, p. 210, the weapon is erroneously said to be a rifle. EH later told Sam Bell that he had plugged the wounds and gone on fishing (Samuel Bell to author, Jan. 16, 1963), which was of course a lie.
Arrival at Bimini: EH to Perkins, April 14, 1935, says that they are leaving "tomorrow morning" (Monday, April 15th). John Dos Passos, *The Best Times,* NY, 1966, pp. 210–212. EH to Perkins, May 1, 1935. Henry Strater to author, July 2, 1964. The "bar" that Dos Passos mentions was called "The Compleat Angler," run by Mrs. Helen Duncombe. She also had a few cottages for rent.
EH's tuna and the tommy gun: John Dos Passos, *The Best Times,* 1966, pp. 212–214. According to EH, the tommy gun was lent to him by a friend: "He Who Gets Slap Happy," *Esquire,* Vol. 4 (Aug., 1935), p. 182.

Strater's marlin and the tommy gun: "The President Vanquishes," *Esquire,* Vol. 3 (July, 1935), pp. 23 and 167. When Strater read this article, he wrote EH, "You sure did me proud" (Strater to EH, Sept. 14, 1935). But he told the author (July 2, 1964) that EH had destroyed his marlin by foolish use of the tommy gun.
Visit of von Blixen: Henry Strater to author, July, 1964. Von Blixen to EH, May 6, 1935: "CAN EVA AND SELF VISIT YOU THURSDAY REPLY HOUSEBOAT AMBASSADRESS ROYAL PALM DOCK MIAMI?" During the visit EH asked him to correct the Swahili in *Green Hills of Africa* (EH to Perkins, June 3, 1935). Blix wrote EH on June 13, 1935, that it would be a mistake to include any Swahili.
EH's fight with Knapp: EH to Gingrich, June 4, 1935. According to EH, there was a horde of witnesses, including the boat captains Howard Lance and Bill Fagen, as well as Ben Finney, an ex-Marine and sportsman from New York.
EH flies back to Key West: EH to Gingrich, June 4, 1935.
Hemingway impostor: EH to Gingrich, June 4, 1935. The man's visit to Chicago in May had been called to Gingrich's attention by Miss Georgia Lingafelt, a collector of Hemingway's work. Leicester Hemingway, *My Brother, Ernest Hemingway,* Cleveland, 1962, pp. 135–136, recalls that the same man came to the front door of Grace Hemingway's house in Oak Park in the spring of 1933, and went away on being told by Leicester that his mother was lying down with a headache. Hemingway to author, Feb. 17, 1951, discussed this "phony" at length.
Fitzgerald's medieval story: Accounts of Fitzgerald's *Philippe, Count of Darkness* appear in Arthur Mizener, *The Far Side of Paradise,* 2nd edition, NY, 1965, pp. 280 and 392; Andrew Turnbull, editor, *The Letters of F. Scott Fitzgerald,* NY, 1963, pp. 263 and 282–283; and Robert Sklar, *F. Scott Fitzgerald: The Last Laocoön,* NY, 1967, pp. 299–300. Pertinent letters are Perkins to EH, April 25, May 21, and June 5, 1935, that of May giving Fitzgerald's reason for not joining EH in Bimini, and that of June reporting on the state of Fitzgerald's health.
EH's mako shark: EH to Perkins, June 19, and EH to Alfred Dashiell, June 30, 1935.
EH coaches Tom Shevlin: EH to Perkins, June 19, 1935.
"Pilar" overhauled: EH to Alfred Dashiell, June 30, 1935.
EH's fights on Bimini: EH to Perkins, July 30 and EH to Gingrich, July 31, 1935.
On Willard Saunders: EH to Charles T. Lanham, March 30, 1947.
Sparring with Tom Heeney: EH to Perkins, July 30, 1935. Leicester Hemingway, *My Brother, Ernest Hemingway,* Cleveland, 1962, pp. 191–192, misdates this sparring match as belonging to 1936. His elaborate account says that it took place before sunrise on the deserted western beach of North Bimini. Ernest looked up suddenly to see that a "long line of watchers" had appeared. "Listen, Tommy," he said, "we've got to quit now. Here we are giving a free show when any charity would be begging for a chance to pass the hat." When Heeney agreed, they shed their gloves "and dived in for a swim." I have been unable to

establish the truth of this anecdote as to time, place, spectators, or Ernest's terminal statement.

EH predicts general European war: "Notes on the Next War," *Esquire*, Vol. 4 (Sept., 1935), pp. 19 and 156.

EH's vow against war: EH to Gingrich, July 17, 1935.

EH's predictions and comments on "Green Hills of Africa": EH to Perkins, July 2, July 4, and July 31, 1935. Perkins's suggestion of hiring an expert on Africa had come as a result of the fact that Baron von Blixen was somewhat dilatory in returning the proof sheets with his own corrections.

EH returns to Key West: EH to Gingrich, Aug. 7 and EH to Perkins. ca. Aug. 15, 1935.

EH gives up plans for Cuba: EH to Gingrich, July 17 and Aug. 26, 1935.

Sec. 38. The Persuaders

SOURCES

Letters of EH: to Fanny Butcher (unfinished; unsent?), Dec. 25, 1934. To Perkins, Feb. 19, 1935; to Perkins, ca. Aug. 15, 1935; to Ivan Kashkeen, Aug. 19; to Perkins, Sept. 7 and Sept. 16; to Gingrich, Sept. 15 (wire): to Charles B. Strauss, Sept. 17; to Gingrich, Dec. 8 and Dec. 9 (letter and wire); to Fitzgerald, Dec. 16; to Perkins, Dec. 17 and ca. Dec. 30, 1935. To Ivan Kashkeen, Jan. 12, 1936.

Other letters: William Saroyan to EH, Dec. 16, 1934 and Jan. 2, 1935; Ivan Kashkeen to EH, Dec. 8, 1935.

EH's work: Published: "Old Newsman Writes," *Esquire*, Vol. 2 (Dec., 1934); "Who Murdered the Vets?" *New Masses*, Vol. 16 (Sept. 17, 1935); "Million Dollar Fright," *Esquire*, Vol. 4 (Dec., 1935); "The Tradesman's Return," *Esquire*, Vol. 5 (Feb., 1936). *Green Hills of Africa*, Oct. 25, 1935. EH's letter to Kashkeen, *Soviet Literature*, Vol. 11 (1962). **Books and articles:** Ivan Kashkeen, "Ernest Hemingway: The Tragedy of Craftsmanship," *International Literature*, Number 5 (May, 1934); Robert Forsythe [Kyle Crichton], "In This Corner, Mr. Hemingway," *New Masses*, Vol. 13 (Nov. 27, 1934). Harry Carlile, *The Legacy of Abner Green*, 1959; Deming Brown, *Soviet Attitudes Toward American Writing*, 1962; Ilya Ehrenburg, *Memoirs, 1921–1941*, 1964.

Author's interviews and correspondence: with Charles Thompson and J. B. Sullivan, March, 1965. From Charles B. Strauss, July 4, 1962.

NOTES

EH's views on economics and politics in relation to serious writing: "Old Newsman Writes," *Esquire*, Vol. 2 (December, 1934), pp. 25–26.

Kashkeen on Hemingway: *International Literature*, Number 5 (May, 1934); reprinted in *Ernest Hemingway: The Man and His Work*, ed. John K. M. McCaffery, Cleveland, Ohio, 1950, pp. 76–113. Kashkeen noted that EH's Mr. Frazer echoed the Marxist view that religion is the opiate of the people (Mr. Frazer said *opium*). But Frazer, in a long internal monologue, listed many other opiates, including music, economics, patriotism, sexual

intercourse, drink, the radio, gambling, ambition, our daily bread, and "belief in any new form of government." (Closing section of "The Gambler, The Nun, and the Radio"). Kashkeen introduced EH to Russian readers with "Dve novelly Khemingueya," *Internatsionalnaya Literatura*, Number I (Jan., 1934). EH's rise to popularity in Russia was henceforth rapid. By 1937, nine out of fifteen Russian writers named him their favorite non-Russian author. *The Sun Also Rises* appeared in 1935 and *A Farewell to Arms* in 1936. Kashkeen wrote EH on Dec. 8, 1935, to say that "to you along with this letter we are sending the translation of your *The Sun Also Rises (Fiesta)*. The translator Vera M. Toper is a member of my group. . . . In the Russian edition of your Selected Stories she made 'An Alpine Idyll,' 'Cross-Country Snow,' and 'A Natural History of the Dead.' *A Farewell to Arms* is being translated by another member of our group and is to appear in summer." See Deming Brown, *Soviet Attitudes Toward American Writing*, Princeton, 1962, pp. 297–315.

EH's self-defense at being a lone wolf: *Green Hills of Africa*, NY, 1935, pp. 148–149.

EH's letter to Kashkeen: published in *Soviet Literature*, 11 (1962), pp. 160–163. The remark in EH's first postscript about "some writers' congress" appears to invalidate the assertion by Ilya Ehrenburg, *Memoirs 1921–1941*, NY, 1964, p. 302, that EH cabled greetings to the Congress of Writers in Moscow in 1935, along with Joyce and Dreiser.

EH boasts of his popularity in Russia: EH to Perkins, ca. Aug. 15, 1935. His views on the new school of economic criticism of literature appear in his unfinished (and perhaps unsent) letter to Fanny Butcher of the *Chicago Daily Tribune*, begun at Piggott, Dec. 25, 1934.

The hurricane of Sept. 2, 1935, and EH's trip to Matecumbe: EH, "Who Murdered the Vets?" *New Masses*, Vol. 16 (Sept. 17, 1935), p. 9. Charles Thompson to author, March 29, 1965; J. B. Sullivan to author, March 30, 1965; EH to Perkins, Sept. 7, 1935.

EH critical of the "New Masses": EH maintained that the editors had double-crossed him by naming his piece, "Who Murdered the Vets?" instead of using his own title, "Who Killed These Men?" Yet the text of his article had posed such questions as, "Who sent the vets down there to live in frame shacks during the hurricane season?" and "Why were they not evacuated?" and "What's the punishment for manslaughter?" —so that the double-cross was only a matter of degree. (EH to Perkins, Sept. 16, 1935). Robert Forsythe, whose ideas EH impugns in the letter to Perkins, had incurred EH's wrath with a hard-hitting article called "In This Corner, Mr. Hemingway," *New Masses*, Vol. 13 (Nov. 27, 1934), p. 26. As to Malraux, whose novel EH had praised in his recent letter to Kashkeen, Ernest told Strauss that leftist critics like Max Eastman, Granville Hicks, and Robert Forsythe would long since have nailed Malraux's hide to the wall if he had been "coming up" in the United States instead of establishing his reputation in France.

Strauss writes EH: C. B. Strauss to author, July 4, 1962. Strauss here summarized the content of his letter to EH. EH's reply to Strauss was dated Sept. 17, 1935.

Dedication, decoration, and expectations of reception for "Green Hills of Africa": EH to Perkins, ca. Sept. 16, 1935. The illustrations by Edward Shenton, who also illustrated Faulkner's story "The Bear," were based in part on Shenton's study of three reels of movie film supplied by EH and showing the kudu country, the Masai warriors, the Roman, and the histrionic Garrick: EH to Perkins, Feb. 19, 1935.

EH's September trip to New York: EH to Gingrich, Sept. 15, 1935 (wire) stated that he would be leaving Wed., Sept. 18, by car. His passengers were Pauline, Bumby, and Patrick. They left the car in Columbia, S.C., because of a polio epidemic in the Carolinas, and took the train for New York, where Bumby left for Chicago to begin seventh grade. EH to Fitzgerald, Dec. 16, 1935, said he thought of detouring to Asheville to pay him a call. In New York EH spent an evening with Ilf and Petrov, two visiting Russians. Kashkeen to EH, Dec. 8, 1935, called them "our twin humourists." EH talked about false teeth until he noted that one of them was wearing a set, which covered him with confusion. Recovering, he offered to "let them shoot a nigger" if they came to Key West, or even to shoot one for them if they had scruples. (EH to Kashkeen, Jan. 12, 1936.)

EH's account of the Louis-Baer fight: "Million Dollar Fright," *Esquire*, Vol. 4 (Dec. 1935), pp. 35 and 190B.

EH's October visit to New York: EH to Gingrich, Oct. 17, 1935.

EH's attacks on literati: *Green Hills of Africa*, pp. 21–24.

Mainly laudatory reviews of "Green Hills of Africa": Edward Weeks, *Atlantic Bookshelf*, Vol. 156 (November, 1935), p. 30. Charles Poore, *New York Times Book Review*, Oct. 27, 1935, p. 3. Carl Van Doren, *NY Herald Tribune Books*, Oct. 27, p. 3. Isabel Paterson, *NY Herald Tribune Books*, Nov. 3, 1935, p. 18. Mencken's *American Mercury* followed its time-honored custom of reviewing EH in its "Briefer Mention" column (Vol. 36, December, p. 503), which disgusted Hemingway, though the short notice praised the book highly. In a conversation with Mencken about this time, Sara Mayfield found that "The Sage" was "incapable of understanding the chronic disorder" of Scott Fitzgerald's life or his "long alcoholic eulogies" of EH. "Being a man whose domestic life was well-ordered, happy, and decorous . . . and whose love of *wein, weib, und gesang* was tempered with moderation and good taste," writes Miss Mayfield, Mencken was convinced that EH's "battle, bottle, bitch formula" was destined to be shortlived. Sara Mayfield to author, spring, 1965.

EH's manner offends some reviewers of "Green Hills": Carl Van Doren, *New York Herald Tribune Books*, Oct. 27, 1935, p. 3. *Forum*, Vol. 95 (January, 1936), p. v. Fanny Butcher, *Chicago Daily Tribune*, Oct. 26, 1935. Lewis Gannett, *New York Herald Tribune*, Oct. 25, 1935, p. 17. T. S. Matthews, *New Republic*, Vol. 85 (Nov. 27, 1935), pp. 79–80. Matthews accuses EH of borrowing a literary reference and passing it off as his own. When EH shot the buffalo in Droopy's

country, Pauline was made to say: "It was wonderful when we heard him bellow. It's such a sad sound. It's like hearing a horn in the woods." (p. 119). Matthews quotes the French: "Dieu, que le son du cor est triste au fond du bois." The source is the closing line of "Le Cor" by Alfred de Vigny. Other reviews mentioned are by Edmund Wilson, *New Republic*, Vol. 85 (Dec. 11, 1935), p. 135 and Bernard DeVoto, *Saturday Review*, Vol. 12 (Oct. 26, 1935), p. 5.

EH's complaints over "Green Hills" reviews: EH to Perkins, Dec. 17 and ca. Dec. 30, 1935.

Abner Green and EH: Harry Carlile, *The Legacy of Abner Green: A Memorial Journal*, issued by the American Committee for the Protection of the Foreign Born for the 27th National Conference, Dec. 19–20, 1959. The open letter to Hemingway, entitled "Please, Mr. Hemingway" and written by Green under a pseudonym, is quoted in part in this journal, as is the sentence from one of EH's letters to Green.

EH finishes "The Tradesman's Return": EH to Gingrich, Dec. 8 (letter) and Dec. 9 (letter and wire), 1935. The story first appeared in *Esquire*, Vol. 5 (February, 1936), pp. 27, 193–196. It subsequently became Part II (Harry Morgan. Fall) in *To Have and Have Not*, NY, 1937, pp. 67–87. EH briefly considered calling the story "White Man, Black Man, Alphabet Man," but dropped the idea. EH to Gingrich, Dec. 9, 1935.

Sec. 39. *The Slopes of Kilimanjaro*

SOURCES

Letters of EH: to Gingrich, Aug. 26, 1935; to Fitzgerald, Dec. 16, 1935; to Perkins, Dec. 17, 1935; to Fitzgerald, Dec. 21, 1935; to Perkins, ca. Dec. 30, 1935. To Dos Passos, Jan. 13, 1936; to Mrs. Paul Pfeiffer, Jan. 26; to Perkins, Feb. 7; to Gingrich, Apr. 4; to Dos Passos, Apr. 12; to Harry Saltpeter. Apr. 16; to Perkins, Apr. 19; to Dos Passos, June 10; to Margaret and Nonie Briggs, July 7; to Dos Passos, July 18; to Gingrich, July 21; to Margaret and Nonie Briggs, July 21; to Perkins, July 23; to Strater, Aug. 11; to Marjorie Kinnan Rawlings, Aug. 16, 1936.

Other letters: Perkins to EH, Feb. 11 and Feb. 27; Thomas Shevlin to EH, Feb. 22 (cable); Pauline Hemingway to Dawn Powell, Feb. 28; Jane Mason to EH, March 7; Perkins to EH, Apr. 8; Marjorie Kinnan Rawlings to Perkins, June 18; Pauline to Margaret and Nonie Briggs, July 7; Fitzgerald to EH, July (before the 23rd); Marjorie Kinnan Rawlings to EH, Aug. 1; Fitzgerald to Beatrice Dance, Sept. 15; Fitzgerald to Perkins, Sept. 19, 1936. Samuel Bell to Alfred Putnam, Dec. 12, 1962.

EH's work: (a) Unpublished: "Lines to Be Read, etc.," poem, composed Dec., 1935; "The Art of the Short Story," 1959. **(b) Published:** "The Tradesman's Return," *Esquire*, Vol. 5 (Feb., 1936); "The Horns of the Bull," *Esquire*, Vol. 5 (June, 1936); "The Snows of Kilimanjaro," *Esquire*, Vol. 6 (Aug., 1936); "The Short Happy Life of Francis Macomber," *Cosmopolitan*, Vol. 101 (Sept., 1936); Introduction, *Men at War*, 1942.

Books and articles: Three Fitzgerald "Crack-Up" articles, all in *Esquire*, Vol. 5, "The

Crack-Up," (February); "Pasting It Together," (March); "Handle With Care," (April); Vivienne de Watteville, *Speak to the Earth*, 1935; Harry Saltpeter, "Rabelais in a Smock," *Esquire*, Vol. 5 (July, 1936); Edmund Wilson, ed., *The Crack-Up*, 1945; Leicester Hemingway, *My Brother, Ernest Hemingway*, 1962; Andrew Turnbull, ed., *The Letters of F. Scott Fitzgerald*, 1963; Arnold Gingrich, "Horsing Them in with Hemingway," *Playboy*, Vol. 12 (Sept., 1965); Broadcast on Wallace Stevens, "Perspective from Two Worlds," WGBH (FM), Boston, Massachusetts, Jan. 18, 1966; Arnold Gingrich, "Scott, Ernest, and Whoever," *Esquire*, Vol. 66 (Dec., 1966).
Author's interviews and correspondence: with Waldo Peirce, June, 1966. From Harry H. Burns, Apr. 29, 1963; from Philip and Richard Percival, Feb. 2, 1964; from General S. L. A. Marshall, March 23, 1966.

NOTES

EH begins third Morgan story: EH to Perkins, ca. Dec. 30, 1935.
EH's bawdy letters to Fitzgerald: Dec. 16 and Dec. 21, 1935. In EH to Perkins, Dec. 17, EH refers to having received a "dull and gloomy" letter from Fitzgerald.
EH shocked by Fitzgerald's "Crack-Up" articles: EH to Dos Passos, Jan. 13 and EH to Perkins, Feb. 7, 1936. The articles appeared in *Esquire* for Feb., March, and April. EH read them all, but commented especially on the first. Perkins to EH, Feb. 27, 1936, agreed that it was "absurd" of Scott to have "given up" at the youthful age of forty.
EH's patch of melancholia: EH to Mrs. Paul Pfeiffer, Jan. 26, 1936.
EH's broken toe: Pauline Hemingway to Dawn Powell, Feb. 28, 1936. The accident happened about Feb. 14. It is described also in General S. L. A. Marshall to author, March 23, 1966. Marshall was in Key West for the benefit of his invalid wife, Iva. He was an old friend of Miss Carroll's.
Waldo Peirce and family: EH to Perkins, Feb. 7, 1936. Some of EH's stories about Peirce are in Harry Saltpeter, "Rabelais in a Smock," *Esquire*, Vol. 5 (July, 1936), p. 22. These were largely drawn from EH to Saltpeter, Apr. 16, 1936.
Harry Payne Burton at Key West: EH to Gingrich, Apr. 4, 1936. The letter states that EH had written the story of Paco "about two months ago" in early February. EH had several titles: The Capital of Illusion; Outside the Ring; The Start of the Season; A Boy Named Paco; To Empty Stands; The Judgment of Distance; and The Sub-Novice Class. It appeared in *Esquire*, Vol. 5 (June, 1936), pp. 31 and 190–193, as "The Horns of the Bull," and finally in the collected stories (1938) as "The Capital of the World."
EH completes "The Short Happy Life, etc.": EH to Perkins, Apr. 19, 1936. EH mentions real-life prototypes of the Macombers in "The Art of the Short Story," unpublished preface, composed ca. June, 1959. The same document identifies Percival as the model for Robert Wilson. The hearsay aspects of the story are discussed in Percival's unpublished autobiography, which he generously allowed the author to read in Oct., 1963. Further testimony on the origins of the story in Philip and Richard Percival to author, Feb. 2, 1964. Wilson's Shakespeare quotation, "A man can die but once, etc.," is from *Henry IV*, Part 2, Act III, sc. ii, lines 253–258. EH owed this to Dorman-Smith from 1918. EH's introduction to *Men at War*, NY, 1942, p. xiv, quotes the passage. "That is probably the best thing . . . in this book," says EH, "and with nothing else, a man can get along all right with that."
EH on his trip to Cuba with Joe Russell and Jane Mason: EH to Dos Passos, Easter (Apr. 12), 1936. One of Mrs. Mason's letters to EH (March 7, 1936) notifies him that she is coming from Miami to Key West.
Hemingway-Stevens fight: EH to Dos Passos, Apr. 12, 1936. Waldo Peirce to author, June, 1966; "Perspective from Two Worlds: Wallace Stevens, Poet and Businessman," Radio Broadcast, Station WGBH/FM, Jan. 18, 1966. Wilson Jainsen: "One of Stevens's pleasures was to go down to Key West. . . . Stevens and Hemingway had much in common, including convivial evenings. . . . I have a hazy recollection of Mr. Stevens having a shiner at one time." Manning Heard: "He had a shiner and a broken hand, and he didn't comment about it, but enough to say further that it was the result of a brawl . . . with Ernest Hemingway."
Problems in Cuba: EH to Strater, Aug. 11, 1936, which mentions Gutiérrez's disabilities.
On EH's ruthless treatment of Carlos: Leicester Hemingway, *My Brother, Ernest Hemingway*, 1962, pp. 192–193. See also EH to Margaret and Nonie Briggs, July 7, 1936.
On the "Pilar's" engine trouble: EH to Perkins, Apr. 9, 1936 says the engine is running beautifully. But Sam Bell personally replaced all the spark plugs one day about that time before the *Pilar* could even leave the dock. Samuel Bell to Alfred Putnam, Dec. 12, 1962.
Storm on the way to Bimini: EH to Dos Passos, June 10, 1936.
Sportsmen at Bimini: EH to Margaret and Nonie Briggs, July 7, 1936.
EH calls himself and Gingrich "peasants": Arnold Gingrich, "Scott, Ernest and Whoever," *Esquire*, Vol. 66 (Dec., 1966), p. 189. Gingrich discusses EH's character and behavior also in "Horsing Them in with Hemingway," *Playboy*, Vol. 12 (Sept., 1965), pp. 123 and 256.
EH speaks scathingly of Bimini sporting set: EH to Marjorie Kinnan Rawlings, Aug. 16, 1936.
EH confers with Gingrich on the Morgan stories: EH to Perkins, July 11, 1936.
EH's praise of Gingrich's critical judgment: EH to Gingrich, July 21, 1936.
EH's 514-pound tuna: EH to Dos Passos, July 18, 1936. Mrs. Rawlings's account of EH's conduct and her analysis of his character: Marjorie Kinnan Rawlings to Perkins, June 18, 1936.
Mrs. Rawlings tells EH of her views: Marjorie Kinnan Rawlings to EH, Aug. 1, 1936. EH replied to her on Aug. 16, 1936.
EH meets Harry H. Burns: Burns to author, Apr. 29, 1963.
EH explains origin of "The Snows": EH, "The Art of the Short Story," 1959. EH originally had two epigraphs for the story. The canceled one was from Vivienne de Watteville, *Speak to the Earth: Wanderings and Reflections Among Elephants and Mountains*, London,

1935. Miss de Watteville was the daughter of Bernard de Watteville, a Swiss naturalist from Berne, mauled to death by a lion when Vivienne was twenty-four. She was with him when he died and wrote a book, *Out in the Blue*, based on her diaries. *Speak to the Earth* deals with her second safari, four years after the first. EH found the quoted passage on p. 129. The original typescript bears the marginal notation, "Better out—EH" beside the de Watteville quotation. According to Arnold Gingrich, the deletion was made at his suggestion.

EH's reference to Fitzgerald in "The Snows": EH's story says Fitzgerald once began a story with, "The rich are very different from you and me." When someone replied, "Yes, they have more money," Fitzgerald was not amused. The "someone" was EH, as is proved by the revised typescript of "The Snows," as well as by an entry in Fitzgerald's Notebook E, which reads, "They have more money (Ernest's wisecrack)." See Edmund Wilson, ed., *The Crack-Up*, NY, 1945, p. 125.

Fitzgerald objects to the use of his name: Fitzgerald to EH, July (before the 23rd), 1936. The letter is printed by Andrew Turnbull, *The Letters of F. Scott Fitzgerald*, NY, 1963, p. 311. Mr. Turnbull misdates the letter as belonging to August, 1936. EH to Perkins, July 23, mentions having already received and answered it.

EH on Fitzgerald's letter of objection: EH to Perkins, July 23, 1936. An entry in Fitzgerald's Notebook E says he liked EH until "we began trying to walk over each other with cleats." Edmund Wilson, ed., *The Crack-Up*, NY, 1945, p. 147.

Fitzgerald on EH's megalomania: Fitzgerald to Beatrice Dance, Sept. 15, 1936 and Fitzgerald to Perkins, Sept. 19, 1936. These letters are printed in Turnbull, *The Letters of F. Scott Fitzgerald*, NY, 1963, p. 267 (to Perkins) and p. 543 (to Dance). I have been unable to find the original of EH to Fitzgerald. Fitzgerald discussed it with Mrs. Rawlings when she came to call on him on Oct. 23, 1936. He also showed it to Gingrich, who thought it "brutal," using language "that you'd hesitate to use on a yellow dog." Gingrich, "Scott, Ernest, and Whoever," *Esquire*, Vol. 66 (Dec., 1966), pp. 186–187.

Sec. 40. Moving In

SOURCES

Letters of EH: to Dos Passos, Apr. 12, 1936. To MacLeish and Gingrich, both July 21, 1936; to Prudencio de Pereda, July 23; to Lawrence Nordquist, July 25; to Mrs. Paul Pfeiffer, Aug. 11; to Henry Strater, Aug. 11; to MacLeish, Aug. 16; to Marjorie Kinnan Rawlings, Aug. 16; to Gingrich, Sept. 16; to Perkins, Sept. 26; to Gingrich, Oct. 3; to Perkins, ca. Nov. 8, Dec. 2, and Dec. 15; to Roger Chase, Dec. 16, 1936 (wire). To Roger Chase, Feb 11, 1937. To Charles Scribner, June 23, 1950.

Other letters: Thomas Shevlin to EH, July 24, 1936; Lorraine Shevlin to EH, ca. July 24; Arnold Samuelson to EH, July 27; Mrs. Rawlings to Perkins, July 31; Jane Mason to EH, Aug. 27; Dos Passos to EH, Sept. 15; Kate Dos Passos to Pauline Hemingway, Sept. 15;

Fitzgerald to EH, Sept. 28 and ca. Sept. 29 (wires); Perkins to EH, Oct. 1; Pauline to Harry H. Burns, Oct. 24; Mrs. Rawlings to Perkins, Oct. 25; John N. Wheeler to EH, Nov. 25; Perkins to EH, Dec. 9, 1936. Pauline to Gingrich, Jan. 11, 1937 (wire); Martha Gellhorn to Pauline, Jan. 14, 1937.

EH's work: Published: *To Have and Have Not*, publ. Oct. 15, 1937.

Books and articles: Michael Mok, "The Other Side of Paradise," *New York Post*, Sept. 25, 1936; Edmund Wilson, ed., *The Crack-Up*, 1945; Hugh Thomas, *The Spanish Civil War*, 1961; James T. Farrell, "Ernest Hemingway," *Nugget*, Dec., 1961; T. S. Matthews, *O My America*, 1962; Arnold Gingrich, "Scott, Ernest, and Whoever," *Esquire*, Vol. 66, Dec., 1966.

Author's interviews and correspondence: with Thomas Shevlin, Oct., 1963; with Harry H. Burns, Oct., 1963; with John N. Wheeler, Nov., 1963; with L. S. Weaver and Olive Nordquist, July, 1964; with Mr. and Mrs. T. O. Bruce and Lorine Thompson, March, 1965; with Patrick Hemingway, Dec., 1965. From H. H. Burns, Aug. 3, 1963; from Thomas Shevlin, Oct. 10, 1963, and Jan. 10, 1964; from Olive Nordquist, Sept. 9, 1964; from James T. Farrell, July 24 and 25, 1966; from Rexford G. Tugwell, July 19, 1967.

NOTES

Plans for trip west: EH to Gingrich and EH to MacLeish, both written on July 21, 1936, his thirty-seventh birthday.

Mention of outbreak of Spanish Civil War: EH to Prudencio de Pereda, July 23, 1936. EH to Lawrence Nordquist, July 25, 1936, advised Nordquist that EH proposed to leave Miami with Pauline and the two boys on the morning of July 27th, that the trip would take two weeks, and that they would move on somewhere else if there was no room for them at the L-Bar-T. Although Cabin No. 1, where the Hemingways usually stayed, was booked, Lawrence and Olive Nordquist assigned them to the Bill Sidley place. It would be a "nice working-out," thought Olive, "having the cabin for writing away from ranch activities, except when they wished to come for meals and association." Olive Nordquist to author, September, 1964.

Trip to New Orleans: Harry H. Burns to author, Aug. 3, 1963. Pauline wrote Burns Oct. 24, 1936, recalling this phase of the trip. Jinny Pfeiffer had flown in from Bimini to join them (Thomas Shevlin to EH, July 24, 1936), and took a plane from New Orleans to Arkansas. In New Orleans EH amused himself by calling Burns MacWalsey. The name seems to have originated in Bimini. Lorraine Shevlin thanked EH for a gift of books with the comment that it proved him to be the "highest type of McWalsey": Lorraine Shevlin to EH, ca. July 24, 1936. EH also spoke of Gingrich as MacWalsey: EH to Gingrich, July 21, 1936.

New Orleans to the ranch: EH to Mrs. Pfeiffer, Aug. 11, 1936 and Pauline to H. H. Burns, Oct. 24, 1936.

Settling in at the Nordquist ranch: EH to Strater, Aug. 11; EH to MacLeish, Aug. 16; EH to Mrs. Rawlings, Aug. 16. L. S. Weaver to author, July, 1964, and Olive Nordquist to author, Sept., 1964.

Praise for "The Snows of Kilimanjaro": Arnold Samuelson to EH, July 27, 1936; Marjorie Kinnan Rawlings to Perkins, July 31, 1936; Jane Mason to EH, Aug. 27, 1936; Kate Dos Passos to Pauline Hemingway, Sept. 15, 1936.

John and Kate Dos Passos on the Spanish Civil War: Kate to Pauline, Sept. 15 and Dos Passos to EH, Sept. 15, 1936.

Attack on Montaña Barracks: Hugh Thomas, *The Spanish Civil War*, NY, 1961, p. 156.

EH dreams of return to Bimini and Africa: EH to Marjorie Kinnan Rawlings, Aug. 16, 1936.

EH's hope to go to warring Spain: EH to Perkins, Sept. 26, 1936. Perkins was much impressed by stories of the siege of the Alcázar, lifted by the arrival of a Franco column on Sept. 27th: Perkins to EH, Oct. 1, 1936. EH later told Perkins that Franco was a good general but also "a son of a bitch of the first magnitude": EH to Perkins, Dec. 15, 1936.

EH on death and suicide: EH to MacLeish, Sept. 26, 1936.

Visit of the Shevlins: EH to Gingrich, Sept. 16, and EH to Perkins, Sept. 26, 1936. Thomas Shevlin to author, Oct. 3, 1963, describes the quarrel with EH over the Morgan novel.

Grizzly-bear hunt: EH to Perkins, Sept. 26 and EH to Gingrich, Oct. 3, 1936.

Bear-steak sandwiches: Thomas Shevlin to author, October 10, 1963 and Patrick Hemingway to author, Dec. 9, 1965. Ernest told Perkins (Sept. 26, 1936) that he could have killed all three grizzlies on the afternoon of the 17th but that they were so "damned handsome" he felt sorry at having killed more than one. Tom Shevlin said that he "was on a nearby hill glassing the bait and had seen the grizzlies leave the bait and start down the trail that Lorraine and Papa were following on foot to get a close-up of the bait. I couldn't warn them and was very nervous when I heard all the shooting. Papa could shoot a 30.06 like a machine-gun." Thomas Shevlin to author, January 10, 1964.

Race with Tom Shevlin: EH to Charles Scribner, June 23, 1950. EH said that he had "ruined" Tom fishing at Cat Cay, but that Tom had ruined him in this race.

EH's crap-game losses: Shevlin to author, ca. Nov. 26, 1963.

EH reports progress on his Morgan novel: EH to Perkins, Sept. 26, 1936, and ca. Nov. 8, 1936; EH to Gingrich, Oct. 3, 1936. His mention of the word count is puzzling, since in the letter of Sept. 26 he gave the count as 55,000, while in that of Oct. 3, it was said to be 43,000. He may have meant by the first figure an overall count, including approximately 15,000 words of the first two Morgan stories, already published. The figure of 43,000 represents the number of words written between his arrival at the ranch in August and the date of the letter of Oct. 3rd.

Fitzgerald and the Mok interview: Michael Mok, "The Other Side of Paradise," *New York Post*, Sept. 25, 1936. *Time* picked up the story in Vol. 28 (Oct. 5, 1936), p. 54. Fitzgerald's wires to EH were sent Sept. 28 and ca. Sept. 29. EH to Gingrich, Oct. 3, 1936, quotes the contents of these wires. Fitzgerald's private views on EH appear at various places in his notebooks. Typical entries

appear in *The Crack-Up*, ed. Edmund Wilson, NY, 1945, pp. 79, 169, and 181.

EH's eccentrics in the Morgan novel: Bee-Lips Simmons and George Brooks (Mr. and Mrs. T. O. Bruce to author, March 22, 1965). Mr. and Mrs. Jack Coles as prototypes of Mr. and Mrs. James Laughton: a surmise based on EH to Dos Passos, April 12, 1936. Harry Burns and Arnold Gingrich as prototypes of John MacWalsey: elements of the description fit both men as they looked in the summer of 1936. EH later apologized to Burns for having introduced the character of MacWalsey: Harry H. Burns to author, Aug. 3, 1963.

Rawlings-Fitzgerald interview in Asheville: Marjorie K. Rawlings to Perkins, Oct. 25, 1936.

The Hemingways leave the ranch: Pauline to Harry H. Burns, Oct. 24, 1936.

Stopover in Piggott on the way home: EH to Perkins, ca. Nov. 8, 1936.

Morgan's dying words: *To Have and Have Not*, Chapter Twenty-three.

John Wheeler invites EH to report on Spanish War: Wheeler to EH, Nov. 25, 1936.

EH's plans for Spain: EH to Perkins, Dec. 2, 1936 mentions Franklin's willingness to go. On Dec. 9, Perkins urged EH not to go.

EH pays passage for volunteers: EH to Perkins, Dec. 15, 1936.

EH pledges support for Medical Bureau, American Friends of Spanish Democracy: EH to Roger Chase, Dec. 16, 1936 (wire). **His interest in ambulances:** EH to Chase, Feb. 11, 1937.

EH meets Farrell and Tugwell: EH to Perkins, Dec. 2, 1936; Farrell to author, July 24 and 25, 1966; Tugwell to author, July 19, 1967. See also Farrell, "Ernest Hemingway," *Nugget*, Dec., 1961, pp. 64–65.

EH meets the Gellhorns: Lorine Thompson to author, March 28, 1965. Mrs. George Gellhorn is admiringly portrayed in T. S. Matthews, *O My America*, NY, 1962, pp. 12–15.

Martha's kudu reference: Martha Gellhorn to Pauline, Jan. 14, 1937.

EH attacks rich and discourses on suicide: *To Have and Have Not*, Chapter 24.

EH discusses libel with Gingrich and Speiser: Arnold Gingrich, "Scott, Ernest, and Whoever," *Esquire*, Vol. 66 (Dec., 1966), pp. 189, 322–324. The libel suit against Wolfe is discussed in Perkins to EH, Dec. 9 and EH to Perkins, Dec. 15, 1936.

Martha Gellhorn's journey home: Martha to Pauline, Jan. 14, 1937.

Pauline's message to Gingrich: Pauline to Gingrich, Jan. 11, 1937 (wire).

Sec. 41. Capital of the World

SOURCES

Letters of EH: to Perkins, Jan. 2, 1937 (wire); to Howell Jenkins, Jan. 19 (wire); to Tom Brandon, Jan. 29 (wire); to Will Richard, Feb. 1; to Francis H. Low, ca. Feb. 1; to Capt. Donald Campbell, ca. Feb. 1; to Richard Cooper, ca. Feb. 2; to Leicester Hemingway, ca. Feb. 2; to John A. Read, ca Feb. 2; to John Peale Bishop, ca. Feb. 2; to Gingrich, Feb. 7 (wire); to Mrs. Paul Pfeiffer, Feb. 9; to Roger Chase, Feb. 11; to Lester Ziffren, Feb. 15; to Perkins, Feb. 16; to Roger Chase,

Feb. 22 and Feb. 23, 1937 (wires). To Bernard Berenson, Oct. 14, 1952.
Other letters: Perkins to Pauline Hemingway, March 2; Pauline to Perkins, March 6, 1937.
EH's work: Published: NANA despatches, March 12, 16, 18, 23, and 28, 1937; "The Chauffeurs of Madrid," May 22, 1937; "Treachery in Aragon," *Ken,* Vol. 1 (June 30, 1938); "Three Prefaces" for *All the Brave* by Luis Quintanilla, Apr., 1939; preface to *The Great Crusade,* by Gustav Regler, 1940; *For Whom the Bell Tolls,* 1940.
Books and articles: Ira Wolfert, NANA despatch on EH, Feb. 28, 1937; John Dos Passos, *Journeys Between Wars,* 1938; Constancia de la Mora, *In Place of Splendor,* 1939; Virginia Cowles, *Looking for Trouble,* 1941; Arturo Barea, *The Forging of a Rebel,* 1946; Josephine Herbst, "The Starched Blue Sky of Spain," *Noble Savage,* Vol. 1, March, 1960; Daniel Aaron, *Writers on the Left,* 1961; Ilya Ehrenburg, *Memoirs, 1921–1941,* 1964.
Author's interviews and correspondence: with John Dos Passos, April, 1962; with Ramon Guthrie, Sept., 1965. From Solita Solano, Jan. 17, 1962; from Jay Allen, March 6, 1963; from Ilsa Barea, Aug. 7 and Aug. 15, 1963; from Josephine Herbst, Aug. 19, 1963; from Prudencio de Pereda, Aug. 29, 1964, and June 2, 1967; from Herbert Matthews, Jan. 15, 1967.

NOTES

EH in New York (January): EH to Mrs. Pfeiffer, Feb. 9, 1937, outlines his contract arrangements with Wheeler.
Talks with Jay Allen: Allen to author, March 6, 1963.
EH's work on "Spain in Flames": Prudencio de Pereda to author, Aug. 29, 1964. **His public praise of the film:** EH to Tom Brandon, Jan. 29, 1937 (wire). EH also became nominal head of the ambulance corps committee, American Friends of Spanish Democracy, announced by Saul Carson, *NY Times,* Jan. 12, 1937, p. 4.
EH's humanitarian interest in Spain: EH to Mrs. Paul Pfeiffer, Feb. 9, 1937.
EH's premature announcement of finishing his Morgan novel: EH to Perkins, Jan. 2, 1937 (wire).
EH on Gingrich's critique of his novel: EH to Gingrich, Feb. 7 (wire). EH admitted that the novel needed more work in EH to Perkins, Feb. 16, 1937, noting especially his concern over "the Bradley part."
EH in New York (February): Dos Passos to author, Apr., 1962, mentioned his own fund-raising activities and the formation of Contemporary Historians.
EH sails for France: Ira Wolfert, NANA despatch on EH, Feb. 28, 1937.
EH in Paris: Ramon Guthrie to author, Sept. 1, 1965.
Franklin's bullfight finery: Solita Solano to author, Jan. 17, 1962.
EH meets Luis Quintanilla: EH, "Three Prefaces" for *All The Brave,* by Quintanilla, NY, Apr., 1939.
EH's flight to Alicante and return to Valencia: EH, NANA despatches, March 12, 16, and 18, 1937.
EH from Valencia to Madrid: "The Chauffeurs of Madrid," NANA despatch, May 22, 1937. Background material in Dos Passos, *Journeys Between Wars,* NY, 1938, pp. 330–360; Con-

stancia de la Mora, *In Place of Splendor,* NY, 1939, p. 290; Virginia Cowles, *Looking for Trouble,* NY, 1941, pp. 3–14.
EH visits Brihuega-Guadalajara sector: EH, NANA despatch, March 23, 1937; EH, preface to Gustav Regler, *The Great Crusade,* NY, 1940, p. viii; Arturo Barea, *The Forging of a Rebel,* NY, 1946, p. 643.
Arrival of Martha Gellhorn and Sidney Franklin: source wishes to remain anonymous.
Arturo Barea and Ilsa Kulcsar: Barea was a native Castilian, aged forty, of middle height, thin and intense. He had participated in the Montaña Barracks attack, and owed his position to Rubio Hidalgo, Chief of Press and Propaganda. Ilsa Kulcsar, christened Ilse Wilhelmine Elfriede Pollak in Vienna, was thirty-five, an economist and sociologist by university training, married at nineteen to the Viennese Leopold Kulcsar. Imprisoned in Hungary under Horthy and afterwards in Austria under Dollfuss in 1933, she escaped to Czechoslovakia in 1935, and became editor of a socialist magazine. This brought her to the notice of Luis Araquistain and hence to Spain. She was plumpish, sturdy, 5 feet 3, with brown hair, green eyes, and a husky voice. She and Barea were then living together at the Hotel Gran Vía.
EH revisits Brihuega sector: EH, NANA despatch, March 28, 1937.
Arrival of Josie Herbst: Ilsa Barea to author, Aug. 7, 1963; Josephine Herbst to author, Aug. 19, 1963. Josephine Herbst, "The Starched Blue Sky of Spain," *Noble Savage,* Vol. 1 (March, 1960), pp. 76–117.
EH and Dos Passos disagree about documentary film: Dos Passos to author, Apr., 1962; Arturo Barea, *The Forging of a Rebel,* NY, 1946, p. 653; Ilsa Barea to author, Aug. 15, 1963.
The case of José Robles Pazos: EH, "Treachery in Aragon," *Ken,* Vol. 1 (June 30, 1938), p. 26. Dos Passos was induced to write about the matter by a review of his novel, *Adventures of a Young Man,* by Malcolm Cowley, *New Republic,* Vol. 99 (June 14, 1939), p. 163, in which Cowley followed EH's line. Dos Passos's reply, *New Republic,* Vol. 99 (July 19, 1939), pp. 308–309, gave the other side of the story, as did another letter (same issue, pp. 309–310) by Milly Bennett, Mrs. Hans Amlie. The Dos Passos–Hemingway disagreement is summarized in Daniel Aaron, *Writers on the Left,* NY, 1961, p. 344. Josephine Herbst to author, August 19, 1963, provides the anecdote about the breaking of the news to Dos Passos. It is of some interest to note that Robles had written to Hemingway from Baltimore, Dec. 8, 1931, proposing that he should translate *A Farewell to Arms* into Spanish. The proposal was not accepted.
EH at Gaylord's: *For Whom the Bell Tolls,* NY, 1940, pp. 228–230. Ilya Ehrenburg, *Memoirs, 1921–1941,* quoted from version published in *Odyssey Review,* Vol. 2 (Dec., 1962), pp. 52–56. The phrasing differs somewhat in the book version, Cleveland and New York, 1964, pp. 383–387.
EH and Koltsov: Arturo Barea, *The Forging of a Rebel,* NY, 1946, pp. 584–585. EH to Bernard Berenson, Oct. 14, 1952, provides an interesting sidelight on Koltsov discussing Arthur Koestler with EH, although EH's testimony may not be trustworthy.

Sec. 42. The Spanish Earth

SOURCES

Letters of EH: to Mrs. Paul Pfeiffer, Aug. 2, 1937. To Bernard Berenson, Oct. 14, 1952. **Other letters:** Martha Gellhorn to Sidney Franklin, Apr. 22, 1937; Joris Ivens to EH, Apr. 26 and May 3 or 4, 1937 (wire); Herman Shumlin to EH, Jan. 28, 1939. **EH's work: Published:** NANA despatches, Apr. 9, 11, and 22, May 2, May 22, and Dec. 23, 1937. "The Heat and the Cold," essay published with *The Spanish Earth,* 1938; "Night Before Battle," *Esquire,* Vol. 11 (Feb., 1939); preface to Gustav Regler, *The Great Crusade,* 1940; *For Whom the Bell Tolls,* 1940. **Books and articles:** Herbert Matthews, *Two Wars and More to Come,* 1938; John Dos Passos, *Journeys Between Wars,* 1938; Frank G. Tinker, *Some Still Live,* 1938; Virginia Cowles, *Looking for Trouble,* 1941; Arturo Barea, *The Forging of a Rebel,* 1946; Gustav Regler, *The Owl of Minerva,* 1959; Hugh Thomas, *The Spanish Civil War,* 1961; Jerzy R. Krzyzanowski, "For Whom the Bell Tolls: The Original of General Golz," *Polish Review,* Vol. 7, 1962; Ilya Ehrenburg, *Memoirs, 1921–1941,* 1964; Arthur H. Landis, *The Abraham Lincoln Brigade,* 1967. **Author's interviews and correspondence:** with Ramon Lavalle, Dec. 1961; with Gustavo Durán, Feb., 1962; with John Dos Passos, April, 1962; with Louis Fischer, April, 1965. From Alvah C. Bessie, Feb. 28, 1962; from Ilsa Barea, Aug. 15, 1963; from Vincent Sheean, Aug. 22, 1965; from Sefton Delmer, Feb. 9, 1966; from Ramon Lavalle, March 24, 1966.

NOTES

Matthews and Delmer: Matthews, *Two Wars and More to Come,* NY, 1938, p. 291; Sefton Delmer to author, Feb. 9, 1966. EH on Matthews and Delmer, NANA despatch, Dec. 23, 1937.
EH's euphoria: EH to Mrs. Paul Pfeiffer, Aug. 2, 1937.
Joris Ivens: Ilsa Barea to author, Aug. 15, 1963. Martha Gellhorn called Ivens a "wonderful, wise, good man." He had left the U.S.A. Dec. 26, 1936, and was in or around Madrid until early May, 1937.
Making "The Spanish Earth": EH, NANA despatch, Apr. 9, 1937. The budget for *The Spanish Earth* ran to approximately $13,000. Investors included Ward Cheney, Dashiell Hammett, Lillian Hellman, Ralph Ingersoll, Archibald MacLeish, Gerald Murphy, Dorothy Parker, Herman Shumlin, and The North American Committee for Spain. Most of these put up $500 each. The North American Committee contributed $4,000. EH's investment was at least $2,750 and probably a good deal more, to say nothing of the time he gave to the actual filming and to composing and narrating the commentary. Herman Shumlin to EH, Jan. 28, 1939.
"The Old Homestead": EH, NANA despatch, Apr. 9, 1937. EH, "Night Before Battle," *Esquire,* Vol. 11 (Feb., 1939), p. 27; Dos Passos, *Journeys Between Wars,* NY, 1938, pp. 367–368; Matthews, *Two Wars and More to Come,* NY, 1938, pp. 282–284; Sefton Delmer to author, Feb. 9, 1966.

Martha and EH: Sefton Delmer to author, Feb. 9, 1966.
EH's chauffeurs: "The Chauffeurs of Madrid," NANA despatch, May 22, 1937, written in New York.
Fuentidueña de Tajo: This village lies not far from Tarancón along the main Madrid-Valencia highway, some 54 kilometers southeast of the capital. Dos Passos describes it well in *Journeys Between Wars* (p. 385): a poor village of several hundred houses on a shelf of land above the river, with a crumbling old Moorish castle on the hill behind it, and cave houses, which are common in the region, cut into the marl of the terraced slopes, good natural shelters in case of air raids. The cash crop of the local peasants was wine, made from dark purple grapes. In 1937 an irrigation project for raising tomatoes was being tried, which pleased the humanitarian Dos Passos far more than accounts of military strategy.
EH's flying friends: Whitey Dahl: EH to Bernard Berenson, Oct. 14, 1952. **Frank Tinker:** see his *Some Still Live,* NY, 1938, earlier serialized in the *Saturday Evening Post,* vol. 210. Dahl and Tinker are both discussed in Arthur H. Landis, *The Abraham Lincoln Brigade,* NY, 1967, pp. 126–128. **Ramon Lavalle:** Ramon Lavalle to author, March 24, 1966.
Friendship with Gustavo Durán: Durán to author, Feb., 1962. EH first went to see him in April, bringing American cigarettes and bourbon whiskey. Others in the party included Bob Capa, the *Life* photographer, Lillian Hellman, Dos Passos, and Rafael Alberti and his wife.
EH's attachment to the 11th and 12th Brigades: EH, preface to Gustav Regler, *The Great Crusade,* NY, 1940, p. viii; Regler, *The Owl of Minerva,* NY, 1959, pp. 296–298. The description of Lucasz is from *For Whom the Bell Tolls,* NY, 1940, p. 358; that of Heilbrun is from EH, "The Heat and the Cold," published with *The Spanish Earth,* Cleveland, Ohio, 1938, p. 57 and from Regler, *The Owl of Minerva,* pp. 287–289. Two further remarks on EH's military associations at this time are relevant here. Sefton Delmer to author, Feb. 9, 1966, says that he did not care for EH's anxiety to show off to himself, and possibly to others. "As, for instance, when he insisted on carrying, all by himself, duffle bags loaded with tinned food up the 7 flights of stairs to the flat Matthews and I shared, an unnecessary feat of strength. Or when he wanted to cross Arganda Bridge in range of enemy guns. At the time I thought this was showing off. . . . It has, however, since occurred to me that he may have been trying to find out for his novelist purposes what it felt like crossing the bridge." Vincent Sheean to author, Aug. 22, 1965, comments on EH's later implication that he led troops during this war. Meeting Pauline in San Francisco in 1940, Sheean was amazed to learn that she thought EH had been in combat. "But, Pauline," said Sheean, "he was a correspondent for the North American Newspaper Alliance and that is all." Pauline replied with "tolerant wisdom" that this was what he pretended to be while in fact holding a high combat command with the Loyalists. "This legendary, mythogenic quality," adds Sheean, "was not Ernest's fault; it was intrinsic to his character; he created such stories as unthinkingly as others breathe."

Others simply called EH "a romantic liar."
EH on André Marty: *For Whom the Bell Tolls*, NY, 1940, pp. 416–417. See also Ehrenburg, *Memoirs, 1921–1941*, 1964, p. 397; Regler, *The Owl of Minerva*, NY, 1959, p. 292; and Hugh Thomas, *The Spanish Civil War*, NY, 1961, pp. 300–302, 348, 377, and 444. Alvah C. Bessie to author, Feb. 28, 1962, comments on Marty's almost pathological hatred of newspapermen.
EH and General Walter (Karol Swierczewski): *For Whom the Bell Tolls*, NY, 1940, p. 8. See also Hugh Thomas, *The Spanish Civil War*, NY, 1961, pp. 299, 347–348, 444, 460, 472, 475, 511, and 622–623, and Jerzy R. Krzyzanowski, "For Whom the Bell Tolls: The Origin of General Golz," *Polish Review*, Vol. 7, New York, 1962.
Conditions in Madrid, late April: EH, NANA despatch, Apr. 22, 1937; Dos Passos, *Journeys Between Wars*, NY, 1938, pp. 361 ff., and Arturo Barea, *The Forging of a Rebel*, NY, 1946, p. 646.
EH's trip to the Sierra de Guadarrama: EH, NANA despatch, May 2, 1937. See also Virginia Cowles, *Looking for Trouble*, NY, 1941, pp. 38–39. She describes a battalion commander nicknamed El Guerrero who may have served EH as a rough working model for either Pablo or El Sordo in *For Whom the Bell Tolls*.
Completion of "The Spanish Earth": Joris Ivens to EH, from Valencia, Apr. 26, 1937; Ivens to EH, from Paris, May 3 or 4, 1937 (wire).
Change of location of censorship bureau; Barea's illness; and EH's parting with Barea: Barea, *The Forging of a Rebel*, NY, 1946, pp. 648, 654–656, and 664.
Farewell party, 12th Brigade: EH, "The Heat and the Cold," in *The Spanish Earth*, Cleveland, 1938, p. 58.

Sec. 43. American Interlude

SOURCES

Letters of EH: to Perkins, June 10, 1937; to S. Dinamov, ca. July 21; to Mrs. Paul Pfeiffer, Aug. 2, 1937.
Other letters: Fitzgerald to Corey Ford, Apr., 1937; Luis Araquistain to EH, May 12, 1937; Joris Ivens to EH, June 2, June 15, June 16, June 19, and June 29 (cables); Fitzgerald to C. O. Kalmer, June; Fitzgerald to EH, June 5, and July 13 (wire): Fitzgerald to Perkins, ca. July 15; Perkins to EH, July 18 and July 28; Ivens to EH, Aug. 5 (wire); Perkins to Fitzgerald, Aug. 24; Fitzgerald to Perkins, Sept. 3, 1937.
EH's work: Published: Carnegie Hall speech in *The Writer in a Changing World*, ed. by Henry Hart, 1937; preface to Gustav Regler, *The Great Crusade*, 1940.
Books and articles: NANA despatch on EH, May 10, 1937; Henry Hart, ed., *The Writer in a Changing World*, 1937; Richard Ellmann, *James Joyce*, 1959; Gustav Regler, *The Owl of Minerva*, 1959; Andrew Turnbull, ed., *The Letters of F. Scott Fitzgerald*, 1963; David C. Mearns and John McDonough, *LC Information Bulletin*, Vol. 22 (Oct. 7, 1963); Arthur Mizener, *The Far Side of Paradise*, second ed., 1965.
Author's interviews and correspondence: with John Dos Passos, April, 1962. From George

Seldes, Dec. 2, 1961, and Feb. 3, 1962; from Francis G. Smith, Jr., Nov. 26, 1962; from Paul Romaine, Feb. 4, 1963; from Prudencio de Pereda, Aug. 29, 1964.

NOTES

EH reaches Paris: NANA despatch on EH, May 10, 1937; Luis Araquistain to EH, May 12, 1937, refers to their recent conference on emergency needs in the fields of medicine and sanitation. Araquistain resigned his post on May 16 after the fall of Largo Caballero as prime minister. EH reached Paris May 9 and sailed for New York on the 13th.
EH speaks to Anglo-American Press Club: Francis G. Smith, Jr., to author, Nov. 26, 1962. "The only speaker I ever felt sorrier for," wrote Smith, "was Edmund Wilson." After the speech, EH went to the Ritz Bar with Smith, Franklin, and Percy Phillips of the *NY Times*, then president of the club.
EH speaks at Sylvia Beach's bookshop: Francis G. Smith, Jr., to author, Nov. 26, 1962. After his reading of "Fathers and Sons," EH inscribed and dated the copy of *Winner Take Nothing* that he had used. It is in the Sylvia Beach Collection, Firestone Library, Princeton University. He added a postscript to the inscription after the liberation of Paris in August, 1944. On Joyce's dislike of mixing literature and politics, see Richard Ellmann, *James Joyce*, NY, 1959, pp. 716–717. One evening after dinner at the Select with Webb Miller, Robert Desnos, and George and Helen Seldes, EH told Seldes, "I had to go to Spain before you liberal bastards would believe I was on your side."
EH at Bimini: EH made arrangements to bring Joris Ivens to Bimini late in May. But Ivens did not go. On June 2, he wired EH from New York about the meeting with the Roosevelts. It was at this time also that Ivens and EH collaborated on the statement of the theme of *The Spanish Earth*.
EH meets Fitzgerald in New York: Fitzgerald to EH, mailed from Washington, D.C., on June 5, 1937, from a southbound train, wished EH good luck on his second trip to Spain. Fitzgerald's "return to life" is discussed in Fitzgerald to Corey Ford, Apr., 1937, and Fitzgerald to C. O. Kalman, June, 1937, in *The Letters of F. Scott Fitzgerald*, ed. Andrew Turnbull, NY, 1963, pp. 549–550. See also Arthur Mizener, *The Far Side of Paradise*, 2nd ed., Boston, 1965. p. 301.
EH speaks at Carnegie Hall: George Seldes to author, Feb. 3, 1962; Dos Passos to author, April, 1962; Paul Romaine to author, Feb. 4, 1963. EH's speech was printed in *The Writer in a Changing World*, ed. Henry Hart, NY, 1937, pp. 69–73. This book contains a full report on the Congress and prints sixteen of the speeches delivered on June 4–6. A summary report of the meeting appeared in *Time*, Vol. 29 (June 21, 1937), pp. 79–81. After EH's speech, he went to a bar with Sidney Franklin, Joseph North, Henry Carlile, Thornton Wilder, and Paul Romaine.
EH proposes a prose miscellany volume: EH to Perkins, June 10, 1937.
Death of Lucasz and Heilbrun: Joris Ivens to EH, June 16, 1937 (cable) first notified EH of this loss. An eyewitness report on the events of June 11–12 near Huesca is in Gustav Reg-

ler, *The Owl of Minerva*, NY, 1959, pp. 311–312.

EH on wounding of Regler: EH, preface to Regler, *The Great Crusade*, NY, 1940, p. ix.

EH works on "The Spanish Earth": Ivens and de Pereda to EH, June 15 and June 19, 1937 (cables); Prudencio de Pereda to author, Aug. 29, 1964.

EH at White House: EH to Mrs. Paul Pfeiffer, Aug. 2, 1937. A second source wished to remain anonymous.

EH in Hollywood: The flight took place July 10, 1937. EH and Ivens stayed at the Hollywood Plaza Hotel. EH wrote out his speech on hotel stationery. The holograph MS. of this speech was presented to the Library of Congress on July 26, 1963 by Mrs. Frederic March. See David C. Mearns and John McDonough, *LC Information Bulletin*, Vol. 22 (Oct. 7, 1963), pp. 533–534. Fitzgerald's congratulatory wire was sent to EH July 13. See also Fitzgerald to Perkins, ca. July 15, 1937, in *The Letters of F. Scott Fitzgerald*, ed. Andrew Turnbull, NY, 1963, p. 274.

EH reads galley proof of "To Have and Have Not": Perkins to EH at the Barclay, July 18, 1937; Perkins to EH, June 28, 1937.

EH returns to Bimini and Cat Cay: EH to S. Dinamov, ca. July 21, 1937. The letter was printed in *Soviet Literature*, Number 11 (1962), pp. 158–159.

EH returns to Key West: EH to Mrs. Paul Pfeiffer, Aug. 2, 1937. This letter outlines plans for Pauline and the children, as well as EH's comments on his personal philosophy and his reasons for wishing to return to Spain.

EH attends dinner to launch "Ken" Magazine: picture and story in *Time*, Vol. 30 (Oct. 18, 1937), p. 81.

Hemingway-Eastman tussle: Maxwell Perkins to Fitzgerald, Aug. 24, 1937, provides a detailed eyewitness account. A good satire on the affair appeared in *The New Yorker*, Vol. 13 (Aug. 28, 1937), p. 7. EH's account of the fight appeared in *New York Times*, Aug. 13, 1937, p. 15. Fitzgerald's views are in Fitzgerald to Perkins, Sept. 3, 1937, in *The Letters of F. Scott Fitzgerald*, ed. Andrew Turnbull, NY, 1963, p. 275.

Sec. 44. The Fifth Column

SOURCES

Letters of EH: to John Wheeler, July 27, 1937. To Arnold Gingrich, Jan. 30 and Jan. 31, 1938; to Hadley R. Mowrer, Jan. 31; to Perkins, Feb. 1 and ca. Feb. 9; to Gingrich, Feb. 26, Feb. 28 (wire), March 3, March 10, March 13, and March 14 (wire), 1938. To Ivan Kashkeen, March 23, 1939.

Other letters and documents: Louis Aragon to EH, Sept. 18, 1937; Mrs. Paul Pfeiffer to EH, Oct. 3; Frank Tinker to EH, Oct. 8; Evan Shipman to EH, Oct. 21; Pauline Hemingway to Maxwell Perkins, Nov. 8; John Wheeler to EH, Nov. 24; passport issued to Pauline Hemingway, Dec. 13, 1937. Dr. Robert Wallich, prescription for EH, Jan. 3, 1938; Perkins to EH, Feb. 3 and Feb. 4, 1938; Evan Shipman to EH, March 14, 1938.

EH's work: Published: NANA despatches, Sept. 14, Sept. 23, Sept. 30, Oct. 7, Dec. 19 and Dec. 23, 1937. "The Time Now, The Place Spain," *Ken*, Vol. 1, Apr. 7, 1938;

"Dying Well—or Badly," *Ken*, Vol. 1, Apr. 21, 1938; *The Fifth Column and the First Forty-nine Stories*, 1938; introduction, *Men at War*, 1942.

Books and articles: Profile of Robert Merriman, *The Volunteer for Liberty*, Dec. 13, 1937; Herbert Matthews, *Two Wars and More to Come*, 1938; Virginia Cowles, *Looking for Trouble*, 1931; Herbert Matthews, *The Education of a Correspondent*, 1946; Arturo Barea, *The Forging of a Rebel*, 1946; Mikhail Koltsov, *Ispanskii Dnevnik*, 1957; Hugh Thomas, *The Spanish Civil War*, 1961; Ilya Ehrenburg, "Memoirs, 1921–1941," *Odyssey Review*, Vol. 2 (Dec., 1962); Milton Wolff, "We Met in Spain," *American Dialog*, Vol. 1, Oct.–Nov., 1964; Arthur H. Landis, *The Abraham Lincoln Brigade*, 1967.

Author's interviews and correspondence: with John Dos Passos, Apr., 1962; with William Bird, June, 1962; with Fred Keller, May, 1966. From Jay Allen, March 6, 1963; from Katherine T. Norris, Aug. 8, 1963.

NOTES

Bad news from Spain: Herbert Matthews, *Two Wars and More to Come*, NY, 1938, pp. 299–312.

EH meets Major Robert Merriman: Killed in action six months later, Merriman was an American Communist in his early twenties. The son of a lumberjack, he had worked his way through the University of Nevada, including an ROTC course. He had then served briefly as Lecturer in Economics at the University of California, followed in 1936 by a visit to the Soviet Union to gather materials for a monograph on collective farming. He was among the first American volunteers in Spain, commanding the Lincoln Battalion at the battle of Jarama in Feb., 1937. While convalescing from a wound, he helped train the Mackenzie-Papineau Battalion. When EH met him, he was chief of staff to the 15th International Brigade, but continued active fighting until his death. I owe Cecil D. Eby some of the foregoing information. See also EH, NANA despatch, Sept. 14, 1937; Hugh Thomas, *The Spanish Civil War*, NY, 1961, pp. 380, 461, 472, and 519; and Arthur H. Landis, *The Abraham Lincoln Brigade*, NY, 1967, p. 33. Eby argues convincingly that Merriman served as prototype for Robert Jordan in *For Whom the Bell Tolls*.

EH on Aragon front with Martha and Matthews: EH, NANA despatch, Sept. 23, 1937. On the 28th, EH swam in a small river near Cuenca. It was said to be dominated by Rebel machine guns, but EH saw only a number of four-pound trout which he fed with grasshoppers (NANA despatch, Sept. 30, 1937).

Return to Madrid: EH, NANA despatch, Sept. 30, 1937; Arturo Barea, *The Forging of a Rebel*, NY, 1946, pp. 663–664 and 685.

EH on Brunete front with Martha, Matthews, and Delmer: EH, NANA despatch, Oct. 7, 1937.

Persistence of EH's euphoria: Mikhail Koltsov, *Ispanskii dnevnik*, Moscow, 1957, p. 561, quoted in Jerzy Krzyzanowski, *Polish Review*, Vol. 7, 1962. But EH could no longer forget the world outside so successfully as he had done in March and April. Louis Aragon wrote him on Sept. 18 that he had been unanimously elected to the Presidium of the Association Internationale des Écrivains pour la Défense de la Culture, but EH declined the honor. The Second Congress of this organization had met June 25 in Madrid while EH was in Bimini. Aragon had cabled him an invitation on June 16. Hugh Thomas errs in stating (*The Spanish Civil War*, NY, 1961, pp. 495–496) that EH attended. Pauline's mother wrote EH Oct. 3, urging him to come home. Pauline had just left for New York with her sister Jinny, and Mrs. Pfeiffer reported that she was restless and visibly worried about EH's welfare. Frank Tinker had lately been in Piggott, still gun-shy from his service as a volunteer aviator with the Loyalists.

EH's hospitality to American volunteers: Fred Keller to author, May, 1966; Milton Wolff, "We Met in Spain," *American Dialog*, Vol. 1 (Oct.–Nov., 1964), p. 8. Many entries on Keller, Wolff, and Detro appear in Arthur H. Landis, *The Abraham Lincoln Brigade*, NY, 1967.

Reception of "To Have and Have Not": Reviews quoted or paraphrased are from *New York Times Book Review*, Oct. 17, 1937, p. 2; *Time*, Oct. 18, 1937, pp. 79ff; *Nation*, Vol. 145 (Oct. 23, 1937), p. 439; *Manchester Guardian*, Oct. 15, 1937, p. 7; *London Times Literary Supplement*, Oct. 9, 1937, p. 733.

EH writes "The Fifth Column": EH's earlier expression of interest in the drama appeared in EH to Perkins, Nov. 24, 1927. Mikhail Koltsov mentions *The Fifth Column* as a comedy in his diary entry for Nov. 6, 1937, *Ispanskii dnevnik*, Moscow, 1957, p. 561. Pauline Hemingway to Perkins, Nov. 8, says EH advises that the play is done. Its existence is noted in *New York Times*, Nov. 15, 1937.

Philip Rawlings and EH: parallels noted are from *The Fifth Column and the First Forty-Nine Stories*, NY, 1938, pp. 4–5, 15–16, 24, 44, 49, 50, 55, 60, 67, 69, 96–98. On reading the play, Virginia Cowles recognized the portrait of Pepe Quintanilla, with whom she and EH once had lunch at the Gran Vía restaurant. *Looking for Trouble*, NY, 1941, pp. 30–31.

Visit from Evan Shipman: Shipman to EH, Oct. 21, 1937, and March 14, 1938; EH to Maxwell Perkins, ca. Feb. 9, 1938. EH, introduction to *Men at War*, NY, 1942, pp. xxviii–xxix. Herbert Matthews, *Two Wars and More to Come*, NY, 1938, pp. 228–229.

EH at Teruel with Matthews and Delmer: Ilya Ehrenburg, "Memoirs, 1921–1941," *Odyssey Review*, Vol. 2 (Dec., 1962), p. 57; EH, NANA despatches, Dec. 19 and Dec. 23, 1937; EH to Ivan Kashkeen, March 23, 1939; Herbert Matthews, *The Education of a Correspondent*, NY, 1946, pp. 96–106.

Pauline reaches Paris: Jay Allen to author, March 6, 1963. Pauline's passport for this trip was issued Dec. 13, 1937, and shows her long hair.

EH's liver trouble: Robert Wallich's prescription has been preserved among EH's papers.

EH's marital trouble: William Bird to author, June, 1962.

Return voyage on the "Gripsholm," Jan. 12–17, 1938: EH to Hadley R. Mowrer, Jan. 31, 1938.

"Time" magazine on Teruel: *Time*, Vol. 31 (Jan. 3, Jan. 10, and Jan. 17, 1938).

EH's anger at not being mentioned in "Time" stories: EH to Hadley R. Mowrer, Jan. 31, 1938.

EH's denial of editorship of "Ken": EH to Gingrich, Jan. 30 and Jan. 31 (wires), Feb. 26 (letter), and Feb. 28, March 3, March 13, and March 14, 1938 (wires).

EH's first article for "Ken": "The Time Now, The Place Spain," *Ken*, Vol. 1, Apr. 7, 1938. On the 14th he sent off a second article, "Dying Well—or Badly," which appeared in *Ken* on the 21st. It was chiefly a commentary on pictures of dead Loyalists. EH espoused, though unwittingly, Yeats's theme in "The Second Coming"—that "the best lack all conviction while the worst are full of passionate intensity." As EH put it, "The fascist nations act while the democratic nations talk, vacillate, connive, and betray."

EH's irritations: EH to Perkins, Feb. 1 and ca. Feb. 9, 1938; EH to Gingrich, March 10 and 13, 1938; Perkins to EH, Feb. 3 and Feb. 4, 1938. According to Katherine T. Norris, EH sustained a black eye in a February Saturday night brawl at a Duval Street saloon in Key West. Next day he was closeted with David Smart, who had flown down to discuss the first issue of *Ken*. Miss Norris and a friend called on Pauline that afternoon. They were being shown the yard when they heard a noise above their heads and glanced aloft. There was EH, hurrying along the runway that joined the main house to the pool house, shielding his black eye with one hand, and peering down at them as he ran. (Katherine T. Norris to author, Aug. 8, 1963.)

EH complains of being in a gigantic jam: EH to Perkins, ca. Feb. 9, 1938.

Sec. 45. The Banks of the Ebro

SOURCES

Letters of EH: to Maxwell Perkins, March 15, March 17 (wire), March 19, and May 4, 1938. To Bernard Berenson, Oct. 14, 1952.

Other letters: Vincent Sheean to EH, Feb. 24, 1938; John Wheeler to EH, Apr. 24, 1938 (cable).

EH's work: Published: NANA despatches, Apr. 3, 4, 5, 10, 15, 17, 18, and 29, and May 8, 1938. "The Cardinal Picks a Winner," *Ken*, Vol. 1, May 5, 1938. EH's description of Capt. Milton Wolff is in Jo Davidson, *Spanish Portraits*, 1939. Three Prefaces to Luis Quintanilla, *All the Brave*, 1939.

Books: Alvah C. Bessie, *Men in Battle*, 1939; Vincent Sheean, *Not Peace But a Sword*, 1939; Herbert Matthews, *The Education of a Correspondent*, 1946; Alvah C. Bessie, editor, *The Heart of Spain*, 1952; Joseph North, *No Men Are Strangers*, 1958; Hugh Thomas, *The Spanish Civil War*, 1961.

Author's interviews and correspondence: with Fred Keller, May 1966; with Joseph North, June, 1966. From Herbert Matthews, Jan. 15, 1967.

NOTES

EH referees Negro prizefight: *NY Times*, March 14, 1938, p. 17.

EH leaves on third trip to Spain: EH to Perkins, March 15, March 17 (wire), and March 19 (en voyage), 1938. EH's decision to leave was so sudden that he asked Perkins to secure passage for him on the *Île de France* on less than two days' notice.

EH leaves for Perpignan with Sheean and Lardner: Vincent Sheean, *Not Peace But a Sword*, NY, 1939, pp. 235–243. Sheean had

outlined his problems in getting a newspaper assignment in Sheean to EH, Feb. 24, 1938.
EH leaves Barcelona for the Ebro: EH, NANA despatch, Apr. 3, 1938. Herbert Matthews, *The Education of a Correspondent*, NY, 1946, pp. 123–129.
EH interviews American survivors of Gandesa: EH, NANA despatch, Apr. 4, 1938. Herbert Matthews, "Breakthrough," Apr. 4, 1938, in *The Heart of Spain*, ed. Alvah C. Bessie, NY, 1952, pp. 267–270. EH's view of Milton Wolff is in Jo Davidson, *Spanish Portraits*, NY, 1939. EH's meeting with Alvah Bessie is described in Bessie, *Men in Battle*, NY, 1939, pp. 135–136.
EH surveys west bank of the Ebro to Cherta: EH, NANA despatch, Apr. 5, 1938. This despatch concluded with the words: "PLEASE CABLE MY WIFE KEYWEST AM OK MUCH LOVE."
EH swings north and returns to watch Loyalist gunnery on Ebro: EH, NANA despatch, Apr. 10, 1938. Sheean, *Not Peace But a Sword*, NY, 1939, pp. 74–75, praises EH's ability to size up a whole military position at once, as a professional soldier would.
Events of Good Friday: Herbert Matthews, *The Education of a Correspondent*, NY, 1946, pp. 132–135; Vincent Sheean, *Not Peace But a Sword*, NY, 1939, pp. 72–78; EH, NANA despatch, April 15, 1938. On the way back to Barcelona after leaving Tortosa, EH reported that they passed a column of trucks filled with crated pictures from the Prado. EH prayed silently that they would not be bombed or strafed by the circling Rebel planes. He later told Bernard Berenson that the Loyalists were wrong in evacuating the pictures over an exposed highway. The slogan in Madrid the previous spring, he said, had been: "Respect anything you do not understand. It may be a work of art." EH to Bernard Berenson, Oct. 14, 1952. See also Hugh Thomas, *The Spanish Civil War*, NY, 1961, p. 530.
Events of Easter Sunday: EH, "Old Man at the Bridge," NANA despatch, Apr. 17, 1938. This was printed in *Ken*, Vol. 1, May 19, 1938 as EH's fourth contribution.
Events of Easter Monday: EH, NANA despatch, Apr. 18, 1938. Back in Barcelona that night EH wrote part of a preface for a book of drawings by Luis Quintanilla. He had begun it in Key West on March 10 and tried unsuccessfully to enlarge it while crossing the Atlantic. Modern Age Books had just cabled him, threatening to cancel the contract unless he sent them 1,000 words. Working by candlelight during a failure of electricity, he beat out another 800 words in the loose and chatty style he sometimes affected. "Everything except the Ebro seems very unimportant tonight," he wrote, and yanked the paper from the typewriter. But he held what he had written two more weeks, adding a final segment before he sent it off. It appeared in Quintanilla's *All the Brave*, NY, 1939, pp. 7–11.
Enlistment of Jim Lardner: Vincent Sheean, *Not Peace But a Sword*, NY, 1939, pp. 244–270 describes his own and EH's efforts to dissuade Lardner from joining the International Brigade. John Wheeler relayed to EH a message from the boy's widowed mother, asking him to try to get him a propaganda job (Wheeler to EH, cable, Apr. 24, 1938). He also asked for a short interview with Lardner,

giving his reasons for enlistment. EH does not seem to have complied with the second request.
EH visits Keller at Mataro: Fred Keller to author, May, 1966. Keller said at this time that EH clearly drew on his memories of the girl María in portraying her namesake in *For Whom the Bell Tolls*. When Keller's daughter was born some years later, EH urged him to name her María. A good account of Keller's adventures in the Ebro sector around Gandesa is in Arthur H. Landis, *The Abraham Lincoln Brigade*, NY, 1967, p. 467. Col. Gen. Haji-Umar Mamsurov claimed to have known a 12-year-old girl named Maria who was raped by Fascist soldiers, and to have influenced *For Whom the Bell Tolls* in many other ways. See Yegor Yakovlev, "Can You Say For Whom the Bell Tolls?" *Soviet Life*, Number 7 (July, 1968), pp. 52–55.
May Day truck accident: Joseph North, *No Men Are Strangers*, NY, 1958, p. 142. North's account stressed the youth of the victims. According to Herbert Matthews, however, they were of all ages. "I remember," he wrote, "a young woman weeping for her father, who died as we watched." Matthews to author, Jan. 15, 1967.
EH in Marseilles: EH to Perkins, May 5, 1938. The letter from Perkins, which he read at this time, was dated April 7th.
EH in Alicante, Valencia, and Castellón: NANA despatch, May 8, 1938, marked as sent by courier from Castellón to Madrid. See also Hugh Thomas, *The Spanish Civil War*, NY, 1961, pp. 451–452.
EH's political argument with North: Joseph North, *No Men Are Strangers*, NY, 1958, pp. 143–144.
EH predicts another year of war: EH, NANA despatch, May 10, 1938, from Madrid.

Sec. 46. Pulling Out

SOURCES

Letters of EH: to Perkins, May 5, 1938; to Gingrich, June 28; to Perkins, July 12, Aug. 3, and Aug. 17; to Mrs. Paul Pfeiffer, Aug. 18; to Perkins, Aug. 20; to Gingrich, Oct. 22; to Perkins, Oct. 28. To Perkins, May 10, 1939.
Other letters: David Smart to EH, March 10, 1938; John Wheeler to EH, June 2, June 20, and June 28, 1938.
EH's work: Published: Contributions to *Ken*: "United We Fall Upon Ken," June 2, 1938; "HM's Loyal State Department," June 16; "Treachery in Aragon," June 30; "Call for Greatness," July 14; "My Pal the Gorilla Gargantua," July 28; "A Program for U.S. Realism," Aug. 11; "Good Generals Hug the Line," Aug. 25; "False News to the President," Sept. 8; "Fresh Air on an Inside Story," Sept. 22, 1938. EH's final article in *Ken* was "The Next Outbreak of Peace," Jan. 12, 1939. *The Fifth Column and the First Forty-Nine Stories*, published Oct. 14, 1958. "Night Before Battle," *Esquire*, Vol. 11, Feb., 1939, pp. 27–29, 91–92, 95, and 97.
Books: Vincent Sheean, *Not Peace But a Sword*, 1939; Herbert Matthews, *The Education of a Correspondent*, 1946.
Author's interviews and correspondence: with Fred Keller, May, 1966. From Alvah Bessie, Feb. 19 and Feb. 28, 1962; from Jay Allen, March 6, 1963.

NOTES

Stopover in Paris: Fred Keller to author, May, 1966.
Arrival in New York: *New York Times,* May 31, 1938, p. 12.
EH's views on his marriage: Jay Allen to author, March 6, 1963.
Smart's anti-Communist cartoons: David Smart to EH, March 10, 1938. EH's reply was in "United We Fall Upon Ken," *Ken,* June 2, 1938.
EH attacks Dos Passos, Neville Chamberlain, and the U.S. Department of State: "HM's Loyal State Department," *Ken,* June 16; "Treachery in Aragon," *Ken,* June 30; and "Call for Greatness," *Ken,* July 14, 1938.
EH at Louis-Schmeling fight: EH "My Pal the Gorilla Gargantua," *Ken,* July 28, 1938. John Wheeler to EH, June 2, June 20, and June 28, 1938. In sending the Louis-Schmeling piece on June 28, Hemingway asked Gingrich to insert a box saying that he was on vacation *from* Europe. This would silence well-wishers who were sure to start bellyaching that he had abandoned serious considerations for sports writing. EH to Gingrich, June 28, 1938.
EH's final contributions to "Ken": EH "A Program for U.S. Realism," *Ken,* Aug. 11, 1938; "Good Generals Hug the Line," *Ken,* Aug. 25, 1938; "Fresh Air on an Inside Story," *Ken,* Sept. 22, 1938. Hemingway returned to his allegation that fascists in the U.S. State Department were fooling President Roosevelt about the true situation in Spain in an article called "False News to the President," *Ken,* Sept. 8, 1938.
Preparations for "The Fifth Column and the First Forty-Nine Stories": Perkins to EH, July 1 and EH to Perkins, July 12 and Aug. 3, 1938. The letter of Aug. 3 says that EH has completed two stories about Chicote's Bar, 3,000 and 4,200 words in length, both "imperfect."
Heat and humidity in Key West drive EH to Wyoming: EH to Perkins, Aug. 3, 1938, and May 10, 1939. According to EH, the temperature in the small house by the swimming pool where he worked reached 105. By insulation and air conditioning, it could be brought down to 87.
EH's scratched pupil and drive west: EH to Perkins, Aug. 17 and EH to Mrs. Paul Pfeiffer, Aug. 18, 1938. The letter to Mrs. Pfeiffer also summarizes his record as a writer and his views on the Church's alliance with Franco.
EH writes preface for his collected stories: EH to Perkins, Aug. 20, 1938, is the covering letter. Here also EH gives his plans for arrival in New York.
EH sails for France: *New York Times,* Sept. 1, 1938.
EH in Paris: EH to Gingrich, Oct. 22, 1938. "Night Before Battle," sent to Gingrich at this time, appeared in *Esquire,* Vol. 11 (Feb., 1939), pp. 27–29, 91–92, 95, and 97.
Publication and reception of the play and the collected stories: Publication date was Oct. 14, 1938. Sample reviews quoted are Edmund Wilson, *Nation,* Vol. 147, Dec. 10, 1938, pp. 628 and 630; Clifton Fadiman, *The New Yorker,* Vol. 14, Oct. 22, 1938, p. 6. Malcolm Cowley, *New Republic,* Vol. 96, Nov. 2, 1938, pp. 367–368. EH's complaints about its reception

are in EH to Perkins, Oct. 28, 1938. Perkins's reports on sales are in Perkins to EH, Oct. 27, 1938. One of the best reviews was that of Lionel Trilling, "Hemingway and His Critics," *Partisan Review,* Vol. 6, Winter, 1939, pp. 52–60. Trilling said that the play was by the man, and the stories by the artist; the man was self-conscious, the artist conscious; the man was naive, the artist innocent.
EH's plans for fourth visit to Spain: EH to Gingrich, Oct. 22 and EH to Perkins, Oct. 28, 1938. These letters contain hints of his disaffection with the course of the Spanish conflict. The one to Perkins includes sympathy at the death of Thomas Wolfe, who had died Sept. 15th.
EH in Barcelona and Mora de Ebro: Vincent Sheean, *Not Peace But a Sword,* NY, 1939, pp. 328–338; Herbert Matthews, *The Education of a Correspondent,* NY, 1946, pp. 138–139.
EH meets Bessie at Ripoll: Alvah Bessie to author, Feb. 19 and Feb. 28, 1962.
The party at Boleslavskaya's suite: Sheean, *Not Peace But a Sword,* pp. 339–340.
EH's prejudice against André Malraux: EH to Perkins, May 5, 1938.

Sec. 47. Spoils of Spain

SOURCES

Letters of EH: to Pauline Hemingway, Jan. 4 and Jan. 20, 1939 (wires); to Hadley Mowrer, Jan. 27, 1939; to Mrs. Paul Pfeiffer, Feb. 6; to Perkins, Feb. 7; to Ivan Kashkeen, March 23; to Perkins, March 25; to Thomas Shevlin, Apr. 4; to Perkins, May 13; to Ralph Ingersoll, May 20; to Perkins, May 20; to his mother, May 26; to Perkins, May 30, July 10, and ca. July 24; to Hadley Mowrer, July 15 and July 26; to Mr. and Mrs. Paul Pfeiffer, July 28; to Perkins, Aug. 27 and Sept. 3; to Mrs. Paul Pfeiffer, Dec. 12, 1939.
Other letters: John Gassner to Theatre Guild Board, Jan. 28, 1938; Harold Clurman to EH, Feb. 5; Thornton Wilder to EH, March 1; John Wheeler to EH, June 28, and July 20; John D. Williams to EH, Oct. 4 and Oct. 11; Ralph Rueder to EH, Nov. 28; Hans Koritschoner to EH, Dec. 22, 1938. John Steinbeck to EH, Jan. 23, 1939; Herman Shumlin to EH, Jan. 28; Evan Shipman to EH, Feb. 8; Ralph Rueder to EH, March 1; Ford Madox Ford to EH, March 14; Joe Losey to Ralph Ingersoll, March 24; Perkins to EH, Apr. 27; Perkins, office memorandum, Aug. 28; T. O. Bruce to Perkins, Aug. 28, 1939.
EH's work: Published: "The Denunciation," *Esquire,* Vol. 10 (Nov., 1938); "The Butterfly and the Tank," *Esquire,* Vol. 10 (Dec., 1938); "On the American Dead in Spain," *New Masses,* Vol. 30 (Feb. 14, 1939); preface to Joseph North, *Men in the Ranks,* March, 1939; "Night Before Battle," *Esquire,* Vol. 11 (Feb., 1939); "Nobody Ever Dies," *Cosmopolitan,* Vol. 106 (March, 1939); "Under the Ridge," *Cosmopolitan,* Vol. 107 (Oct., 1939).
Books: none.
Author's interviews and correspondence: with Paul Scott Mowrer, Aug., 1962. From John Gassner, March 3, 1966.

NOTES

EH on writing about war: EH to Ivan Kashkeen, March 23, 1939. This letter was published in *Soviet Literature*, No. 11 (1962), pp. 163–164.

"Esquire" accepts two short stories for publication: "The Denunciation," *Esquire*, Vol. 10 (November, 1938), pp. 39 and 111–114; "The Butterfly and the Tank," *Esquire*, Vol. 10 (December, 1938), pp. 51, 186, 188, and 190.

Steinbeck praises "The Butterfly and the Tank": Steinbeck to EH, Jan. 23, 1939.

EH returns to New York: EH to Hadley Mowrer, Nov. 28, 1938, dated from Pauline's apartment at 147 E. 50th Street.

EH signs contract for Glaser's adaptation of "The Fifth Column": The contract was dated Dec. 1, 1938. The history behind this decision was chequered. John Gassner, chairman of the Play Department of the Theatre Guild, read and reported on the play, then called *Working, Do Not Disturb*, in Jan., 1938. His objections centered on characterization, motivation, and mismanagement of entrances and exits. Harold Clurman soon afterwards read and criticized it for the Group Theatre, again rather negatively. On March 1, Thornton Wilder advised EH to beware of Jed Harris and to place the play with the agents Brandt and Brandt. Three weeks later came the sudden death of Austin Parker, who had wanted to produce the play in September. Joe Losey of 1600 Broadway took a three-month option at $1,000. When this lapsed, John Wheeler of NANA urged EH to give the play to John Golden. In October, John D. Williams described it as "very human, very fine, because untheatrical," and said he hoped soon to talk business with EH. When nothing came of that, the Theatre Guild again entered the field, with the result that Glaser's services were retained. John Gassner to author, March 3, 1966. Gassner's report was dated Jan. 28, 1938. Harold Clurman to EH, Feb. 5, 1938; Thornton Wilder to EH, March 1, 1938; Joe Losey to Ralph Ingersoll, March 24, 1938; John Wheeler to EH, June 28 and July 20, 1938; John D. Williams to EH, Oct. 4 and Oct. 11, 1938; EH to Ralph Ingersoll, May 20, 1939.

EH returns to Key West: EH to Hadley Mowrer, Nov. 28, 1938, said he would leave NYC no later than Friday, Dec. 2. Pauline was leaving Nov. 29 or Nov. 30 when her lease expired. The children left on the night of the 28th.

EH sends "Nobody Ever Dies" to "Cosmopolitan": The story appeared in Vol. 106, March, 1939, pp. 29–31 and 74–76. It is by far the weakest of his stories of this period, possibly because it was invented rather than observed.

EH dislikes Glaser adaptation: EH to Pauline, Jan. 4 and Jan. 20, 1939 (wires); EH to Hadley Mowrer, Jan. 27, 1939; EH to Mrs. Paul Pfeiffer, Feb. 6; EH to Perkins, Feb. 7, 1939. Evan Shipman to EH, Feb. 8, 1939.

EH sends "The American Dead in Spain" to the "New Masses": the poem appeared in Vol. 30 (Feb. 14, 1939), p. 3. EH sent the MSS. for auctioning to Ralph Rueder, in reply to Rueder's request of Nov. 28, 1938. Rueder to EH, March 1, 1939, said that the

sale of the two items produced $150. EH also did a foreword for Joseph North's propaganda pamphlet, *Men in the Ranks*. He said that all the veterans had now come home except those still "stranded on Ellis Island, or in Franco's prison corrals, or those who made their permanent homes in Spain in plots of ground six feet long . . . with a fine view of the grass roots" (North, *Men in the Ranks*, NY, March, 1939, pp. 3–4). Herman Shumlin advised EH that $2,500 remained from the proceeds of *The Spanish Earth*. Since the North American Committee was now in desperate need of funds for Loyalist refugees, Shumlin suggested that original investors might relinquish rights to their shares in favor of the Committee (Shumlin to EH, Jan. 28, 1939). EH agreed at once, scribbling his telegraphed answer on the back of Shumlin's letter.

"Esquire" publishes "Night Before Battle": Vol. 11, Feb., 1939, pp. 27–29, 91–92, 95, and 97. The story had been submitted in a letter to Gingrich, Oct. 22, 1938.

EH's short-story plans: EH to Perkins, Feb. 7, 1939. "On the Blue Water" appeared in *Esquire*, Vol. 5 (April, 1936), pp. 31 and 184–185.

EH writes "Under the Ridge": EH to Perkins, March 25, 1939.

EH begins his war novel: EH to Perkins, March 25, 1939.

Ford asks EH for a memoir: Ford to EH, March 14, 1939.

EH's estimate of Fitzgerald: EH to Perkins, March 25, 1939.

Social season in Key West: EH to Thomas Shevlin, Apr. 4, 1939. At this time EH sold *To Have and Have Not* to Howard Hawks for what he called a "derisory" amount, as reported in EH to Hadley Mowrer, July 26, 1939.

Renting Finca Vigía: EH to Perkins, May 10, 1939. Another source wishes to remain anonymous.

EH's progress with his novel: EH to Perkins, May 10, May 13 (cable), May 30, July 10 and ca. July 24, 1939. EH to Grace Hall Hemingway, May 26, 1939, contains further details.

EH's plans and departure for Wyoming: EH to Hadley Mowrer, July 15 and July 26, 1939; EH to Mrs. Paul Pfeiffer, July 21, 1939. In July EH heard from Mrs. Pfeiffer that Frank Tinker, the Arkansan who had flown for the Loyalists, had killed himself. EH said that he would have tried to dissuade Tinker if he had known about it. He had often enough argued himself out of suicidal impulses. He told Hadley that the important thing was not to let discouragement tempt you into taking the easy way out, as both her father and his own had done. EH to Mr. and Mrs. Paul Pfeiffer, July 28 and EH to Hadley, July 26, 1939.

EH meets Hadley and Paul Mowrer: Paul Scott Mowrer to author, Aug., 1962. The recent nostalgic letters to Hadley were those of July 15 and 26.

EH joined by sons and T. O. Bruce at Nordquist ranch: Perkins, office memorandum, Aug. 28; T. O. Bruce to Perkins, Aug. 28; and EH to Perkins, Sept. 3, 1939.

Pauline's arrival and illness: EH to Mrs. Paul Pfeiffer, Dec. 12, 1939.

Sec. 48. Sun Valley

SOURCES

Letters of EH: to Perkins, Oct. 27 and Nov. 12, 1939; to Arnold Gingrich, Nov. 18; to Perkins, Nov. 21; to Hadley Mowrer, Nov. 24 and Dec. 1; to Clara Spiegel, Dec. 9; to Mrs. Paul Pfeiffer, Dec. 12; to Perkins, Dec. 17 (wire); to Hadley Mowrer, Dec. 19, 1939. **Other letters:** Perkins to EH, Nov. 21, 1939; Mrs. Paul Pfeiffer to EH, ca. Dec. 17; Perkins to EH, Dec. 19; Charles Scribner to Mc-Call Corporation, Dec. 20, Scribners to Macfarland Barker, Dec. 27, 1939 (wire). **EH's work: Published:** eulogy for Gene Van Guilder, *Boise Statesman,* Nov. 2, 1939. **Books:** none. **Author's interviews and correspondence:** with Mr. and Mrs. Lloyd Arnold, July, 1964; with Mrs. Clara Spiegel, July, 1964; with Charles Atkinson, Aug., 1964. From R. Sturgis Ingersoll, March 28, 1963; from Lloyd Arnold, Nov. 30, 1965.

NOTES

EH reaches Sun Valley: Lloyd Arnold to author, July 30, 1964 and Nov. 30, 1965. **EH's new friends in Sun Valley:** EH to Perkins, Oct. 27, 1939. Charles Atkinson to author, Aug., 1964. Lloyd Arnold to author, Nov. 30, 1965. Chuck Atkinson and his wife Flossie ran a restaurant and grocery store in Picabo. EH also befriended an assistant guide at Sun Valley named Ray (Pop) Mark. One of the best duck-hunting grounds was Silver Creek in an east-west valley south of Ketchum. Nearby lived Clarence Wold, whom Ernest nicknamed The Stutter Man. The best pheasant grounds lay farther south near Richfield and North Shoshone. **EH's progress with his novel:** EH to Perkins, Oct. 27, 1939. **EH's eulogy for Van Guilder:** printed in *The Boise Statesman,* Nov. 2, 1939. Further details from Lloyd Arnold to author, July 30, 1964. **Martha leaves for Scandinavia and Finland:** EH to Perkins, Nov. 12, 1939. This letter also speaks of the Vicing and Dicing Establishment. Perkins declined EH's invitation to come out and try it: Perkins to EH, Nov. 21, 1939. Further details in EH to Hadley Mowrer, Nov. 24, 1939, and R. Sturgis Ingersoll to author, March 28, 1963. **EH's friendship with Clara Spiegel:** Clara Spiegel to author, July 31, 1964. One of the letters she typed for EH was a sarcastic one to Gingrich, dated Nov. 18, 1939. It implied that Gingrich was becoming too lordly. **EH's association with the Arnolds:** Mr. and Mrs. Lloyd Arnold to author, July 30, 1964. **EH declines Christmas invitations:** EH to Hadley Mowrer, Dec. 1 and EH to Clara Spiegel, Dec. 9, 1939. Martha was now at the Finnish front, but would be back in Sweden by mid-December and home by Pan-American clipper early in January. **EH complains of Pauline's "selfish" conduct:** EH to Hadley Mowrer, Dec. 1, 1939. **Pauline goes to New York:** EH to Hadley Mowrer, Dec. 19, 1939. **EH explains his marital position:** EH to Mrs. Paul Pfeiffer, Dec. 12, 1939. Mrs. Pfeiffer's undated reply was sent ca. Dec. 17th.

EH's departure for Cuba: EH to Hadley Mowrer, Dec. 19, 1939. Quoted telegram is from Scribners to Macfarland Barker, Dec. 27, 1939.

Sec. 49. For Whom the Bell Tolls

SOURCES

Letters of EH: to Perkins, Dec. 8, 1939. To Perkins, ca. Jan. 13, Jan. 18, ca. Feb. 13, and Feb. 18, 1940; to Charles Scribner, Feb. 24; to Patrick Hemingway, Feb. 26; to Perkins, March 1 and March 3; to Malcolm Cowley, ca. March 13; to Perkins, Apr. 6; to Jay Allen, ca. Apr. 8; to Perkins, ca. Apr. 20, ca. Apr. 22, Apr. 22 (cable), and Apr. 30; to his mother, ca. May 12; to Perkins May 13 and May 31, July 1 (cable) and July 13; to Gustavo Durán, Aug. 13 and ca. Aug. 26; to Perkins, Aug. 26, 1940. To Malcolm Cowley, ca. late Jan., 1941. To Charles Scribner, Jan. 28, 1946. **Other letters:** Perkins to EH, Jan. 18, 1940; Martha Gellhorn to Clara Spiegel, Jan. 29; Martha Gellhorn to Hadley Mowrer, Apr. 9; Martha Gellhorn to Clara Spiegel, May 30; Perkins to EH, Aug. 1, 1940. **EH's work: Published:** preface to Gustav Regler, *The Great Crusade,* 1940; *For Whom the Bell Tolls,* 1940. **Books and articles:** A. Quiller-Couch, ed., *The Oxford Book of English Prose,* Oxford, 1900; Robert Van Gelder, "Ernest Hemingway Talks of Work and War," *New York Times Book Review,* Aug. 11, 1940. **Author's interviews and correspondence:** with Gustavo Durán, Feb., 1962. From Douglas M. Jacobs, March 5, 1964; from Mario G. Menocal y de Almagro, Oct. 17, 1964.

NOTES

Martha returns to live at the Finca: Martha Gellhorn to Clara Spiegel, Jan. 29, 1940. **EH sends Perkins samples of his writing:** receipt acknowledged in Perkins to EH, Jan. 18, 1940 (wire). EH to Perkins, ca. Jan. 23, mentions writing in bed to keep warm. From Sun Valley on Dec. 8, 1939 he had warned Perkins about the "ideology boys." He repeated the advice in EH to Perkins, ca. Jan. 13. His particular mention of Alvah Bessie was the result of the fact that Bessie had criticized "Under the Ridge" for questionable ideology because it showed the resentment of the native Spaniards against the Russian battle police. Perkins had relayed Bessie's opinion to EH. Many of EH's political views were expressed in the internal monologues of his hero Robert Jordan. Compare especially *For Whom the Bell Tolls,* NY, 1940, pp. 163 and 305. **Pattern of EH's days:** EH to Perkins, ca. Jan. 28, ca. Feb. 13, Feb. 18, 1940, and EH to Patrick Hemingway, Feb. 26, 1940. One of Ernest's medical theories held that there was a one-for-one correspondence between allergies and sexual abstinence. His evidence was that when he was a small boy, and fornicating very little except for an occasional Indian girl in the Michigan woods, eating strawberries always gave him hives. With the multiplication of sexual experiences in Italy in 1918 he discovered that he could eat all the

strawberries he wanted without ill effects. He advised Perkins, a chronic hay-fever sufferer, to conduct a series of experiments to see whether he, too, might develop immunity. (EH to Perkins, March 3, 1940.)
EH on his working methods: EH to Perkins, ca. Feb. 13 and March 1, 1940.
Writing as disease, vice, and obsession: EH to Charles Scribner, Feb. 24, 1940.
EH shows parts of MS. to friends: EH to Perkins, ca. Jan. 13, 1940. His account of Ben Finney's reading is in EH to Perkins, ca. Apr. 22, 1940.
EH's dislike of Dolores Ibarruri: EH to Jay Allen, ca. Apr. 8, 1940. Jordan's views appear in *For Whom the Bell Tolls*, NY, 1940, pp. 309 and 354–355. Among many allusions to La Pasionaria in Hugh Thomas, *The Spanish Civil War*, NY, 1961, see especially p. 8.
EH's use of friends in "For Whom the Bell Tolls": Durán is referred to on pp. 246, 335, and 340; Petra on p. 347; Lucasz on pp. 233 and 358; General Karol Swierczewski (General Walter) as Golz, pp. 4–8; Koltsov, pp. 234–240.
Autobiographical aspects of "For Whom the Bell Tolls": Smith and Wesson pistol, pp. 336–337; Dr. and Mrs. Hemingway, p. 339. EH alludes to Chub Weaver, his friend from the old days at the Nordquist ranch, on p. 337, and to the mare Old Bess on the same page. In a discourse on friends (p. 381) Jordan mentions Chub Weaver, Charles Thompson, Guy Hickok, and Mike Strater. In a conversation with María and Pilar, p. 116, EH has Jordan describe a lynching in Ohio, using information derived from his sister Marcelline. The account of Jordan's anger is on p. 370.
EH writes preface to Regler's "The Great Crusade": This preface is dated from Camagüey, 1940; it was written in early April, as shown in EH to Jay Allen, ca. Apr. 8, 1940. Mario G. Menocal to author, Oct. 17, 1964, describes the 16,000-acre estate, with rice and cane mills, and a commodious ranchhouse where EH worked.
EH's assistance to Regler: EH to Malcolm Cowley, ca. March 13, 1940.
EH picks title: EH to Perkins, Apr. 21 and cable of Apr. 22, 1940. See John Donne's Devotion, *Oxford Book of English Prose*, ed. by Arthur Quiller-Couch, Oxford, 1900, p. 171. EH later told Cowley (ca. late Jan., 1941) that a Cuban named Mike Terafa was present the day he found the title. So were the Basque pelota players. They all became delirious with joy, running around and crying, "Ernesto has got a title!" Then they all had a celebration and went to a jai alai game.
EH critical of Pauline's behavior: EH to Perkins, Apr. 6, May 13, and May 31, 1940.
EH angry at his mother: EH to Grace Hall Hemingway, ca. May 12, 1940.
Fall of the living-room ceiling and Martha's departure for New York: Martha Gellhorn to Clara Spiegel, May 30, 1940. A further source wishes to remain anonymous.
EH tells Perkins that the novel is done: EH to Perkins, July 1 (cable) and letter of July 13, 1940.
EH meets North and Jacobs: Douglas M. Jacobs to author, March 5, 1964. Jacobs also describes Martha's arrival at the Floridita.
EH writes epilogue: the account of these final

sections appears in a typed editor's note, evidently prepared by Perkins.
EH carries MS. to New York: Letters to him at the Hotel Barclay came from Perkins on July 31 and Aug. 1. EH describes his hot train trip in EH to Charles Scribner, Jan. 28, 1946.
Van Gelder interviews EH at the Barclay: "Ernest Hemingway Talks of Work and War," *New York Times Book Review*, Aug. 11, 1940, p. 2. Gustavo Durán to author, Feb., 1962, describes his visit to EH at this time. EH had helped him through his first weeks of exile with a small grant, and had now insisted on his coming to New York. Durán found EH's solicitude almost paternal. They occupied twin beds and EH rose early, breakfasting on tea well laced with gin, and tiptoeing barefoot around the suite in order not to awaken his friend.
EH asks Durán to correct Spanish in "For Whom the Bell Tolls": EH to Durán, Aug. 13 and ca. Aug. 26, 1940.
EH mails first 123 galleys to Perkins: EH to Perkins, Aug. 26, 1940. This letter also contains his comments on changes made at the suggestion of Perkins and Scribner, and mentions his decision to delete the epilogue, which he said was like the return to the dressing room after a prizefight or a ball game, or like his original conclusion to *A Farewell to Arms*, where Lieutenant Henry followed the body of Catherine Barkley (EH made a slip and spelled it Barclay like the hotel) to the Swiss cemetery.

Sec. 50. Rewards

SOURCES

Letters of EH: to Perkins, Jan. 3 and ca. early Feb., 1940; to Clara Spiegel, Aug. 23; to Gingrich, Aug. 27; to Perkins, Aug. 27 and Aug. 28 (wire); to Charles Scribner, Aug. 29; to Perkins, Aug. 30 and Sept. 2 (wires), Sept. 9 (3 wires), Sept. 10, and Sept. 12 (wire); to Charles Scribner, Sept. 12 and Sept. 21; to Perkins, ca. Oct. 1; to Scribner, ca. Oct. 10; to Perkins, ca. Oct. 12, Oct. 29, Nov. 12, and Nov. 20 (wire); to Irving Fajans, Dec. 24; to Hadley R. Mowrer, Dec. 26; to Charles Scribner, Dec. 29, 1940; to Milton Wolff, ca. Jan., 1941.
Other letters: Perkins to EH, ca. Jan. 10, 1940; Martha Gellhorn to Clara Spiegel, Sept. 1, 1940; Donald Friede to William Weber, Oct. 7 (wire); Donald Friede to Charles Scribner's Sons, Oct. 7 (wire); Perkins to EH, Oct. 11 and Oct. 31; Fitzgerald to EH, Nov. 8; John H. Hemingway to Perkins, Nov. 28 (wire); Harold Peat to Perkins, Dec. 3 (wire); Perkins to EH, Dec. 28 and Dec. 31, 1940.
EH's work: Published: *For Whom the Bell Tolls*, Oct. 21, 1940.
Books and articles: Arthur Quiller-Couch, ed., *The Oxford Book of English Verse*, 1900; Hugh Thomas, *The Spanish Civil War*, 1961; Mark Schorer, *Sinclair Lewis*, 1961; Andrew Turnbull, ed., *The Letters of F. Scott Fitzgerald*, 1963; *American Dialog*, Vol. 1 (Oct.–Nov., 1964).
Author's interviews and correspondence: with Gustavo Durán, Feb., 1962; with W. B. Smith, Apr., 1964; with Mr. and Mrs. Lloyd Arnold,

July, 1964; with Clara Spiegel, July, 1964; with Mr. and Mrs. T. O. Bruce, March, 1965. From Alvah Bessie, Jan. 7 and Dec. 19, 1962; from Lloyd Arnold, Nov. 30, 1964.

NOTES

Perkins predicts "big year" for EH: Perkins to EH, ca. Jan. 10, 1940.
EH's novel chosen by Book of the Month Club: EH to Arnold Gingrich, Aug. 27, 1940.
Plans for Sun Valley: EH to Clara Spiegel, Aug. 23, 1940; Martha Gellhorn to Clara Spiegel, Sept. 1, 1940. Bumby was camping and fishing in the west. His half brothers were in California. Bumby met their train at Ogden, Utah, and conducted them to Sun Valley. EH and Martha took the *Pilar* to Key West on Aug. 29. There they met T. O. Bruce, who drove them to Jacksonville. Martha took a plane from there to St. Louis before joining EH in Idaho.
EH reads final proofs on his novel: EH to Perkins, Aug. 27, Aug. 28 (wire), Aug. 30 (wire); Sept. 2 (wire), Sept. 9 (3 wires), Sept. 10, Sept. 12 (wire), and ca. Oct. 1, 1940. EH to Charles Scribner, Aug. 29, Sept. 12, and Sept. 21, 1940.
EH talks of suicide: Lloyd Arnold to author, July 30, 1964, and Nov. 30, 1965. Another source wishes to remain anonymous.
EH on rabbit hunt: EH to Charles Scribner, Sept. 21, 1940. EH said solemnly that on returning from the rabbit hunt they added a horse to the day's slaughter. It ran directly into the path of the brand-new car and its head shattered the windshield, though by a miracle none of the occupants was hurt. EH said it was all very lucky: he would certainly have hated to be killed by an animal as stupid as a horse. But the whole story was his own invention, concocted to dismay Scribner, who liked horses.
EH explodes at delay in publication of his novel: EH to Perkins, ca. Oct. 1, 1940.
EH meets Gary and Rocky Cooper: EH to Scribner, Sept. 21, 1940; Martha Gellhorn to Clara Spiegel, Oct. 23, 1940; EH to Perkins, ca. Oct. 12, 1940; Mr. and Mrs. Lloyd Arnold to author, July 30, 1964; Clara Spiegel to author, July 31, 1964; Lloyd Arnold to author, Nov. 30, 1965.
EH on Wolfe's "You Can't Go Home Again": EH to Perkins, ca. Oct. 12, 1940.
EH orders books from Scribner Bookstore: undated memorandum to Perkins, ca. Sept. 12, 1940. Among the volumes ordered was a new edition of *The Oxford Book of English Verse.* This was evidently meant to supplement, not replace, an earlier edition which he had acquired from Sylvia Beach's Shakespeare and Company, whose bookplate it bore. This was the edition of Oct., 1900, ed. by Quiller-Couch. EH's copy contained a few annotations in his own hand. On page 39 he called *The Nut-Brown Maid* "wonderful but too damned long." On page 142, beside George Peele's *A Farewell to Arms,* EH wrote: "Made title of book from this EH." On page 174, beside *Her Reply,* by Christopher Marlowe, EH made a marginal note: "This man was in love with Queen Elizabeth and when she ordered him to be beheaded he wrote a fine poem and

touched the edge of the axe and said, very cheerfully, 'It is a sharp medicine but it cures all diseases.' How do you like it now, Gentlemen?" EH confused Marlowe with Sir Walter Raleigh on the occasion of his execution on October 29, 1618. On page 388, he underscored the lines in Andrew Marvell's *To His Coy Mistress:* "But at my back . . . eternity" and "The grave's a fine and private place . . . embrace." The date of these annotations does not appear, but the remark beside the Marlowe story, "How do you like it now, Gentlemen," suggests that his note was made sometime in 1949 or 1950 when Hemingway, writing *Across the River and into the Trees,* took these seven words as a kind of slogan. The annotated copy, owned by Gianfranco Ivancich, was examined by the author in Venice in October, 1965.
Friede visits Sun Valley: Donald Friede to author, May, 1965; Friede to William Weber and Friede to Charles Scribner's Sons, Oct. 7, 1940 (wires).
EH and Martha on Salmon River trip: Martha Gellhorn to Clara Spiegel, Oct. 23, 1940. According to the Arnolds, Martha went riding with Tillie one day after recovering from her grippe. "What the hell am I knocking myself out with hunting for?" she murmured.
EH asks Allen to read him advance reviews: Jay Allen to author, March 6, 1963. Reviews quoted in text are by John Chamberlain, *Herald Tribune Books,* Oct. 20, 1940, p. 1; J. Donald Adams, *New York Times Book Review,* Oct. 20, p. 1; Robert E. Sherwood, *Atlantic,* Vol. 166 (Nov., 1940); Clifton Fadiman, *The New Yorker,* Vol. 16 (Oct. 26, 1940), p. 82; Margaret Marshall, *The Nation,* Vol. 151 (Oct. 26, 1940), p. 395. EH was much incensed by Edmund Wilson's review, *New Republic,* Vol. 103 (Oct. 28), p. 591. "Old Bunny," said EH, was no longer interested in good writing but only in sectarian politics. Wilson's disbelief in the character of María also angered EH. He scornfully recalled Wilson's statement of 1929 that Lieutenant Henry could not possibly have rowed Catherine Barkley to Switzerland against the wind for thirty miles. In fact, said EH, Henry had sailed with the wind, using the umbrella as a sail, and the distance was only sixteen miles. EH to Perkins, Oct. 29, 1940.
Settlement of contract with Paramount Pictures: EH to Perkins, Oct. 29 and Perkins to EH, Oct. 31, 1940. Donald Friede to author, May, 1965.
EH's farm-family benefaction: Lloyd Arnold to author, July 30, 1964.
Pauline's divorce becomes final: Mr. and Mrs. Charles Thompson to author, March, 1965. The circuit judge was Arthur Gomez.
EH explains reasons for leaving Pauline: EH to author, Feb. 17, 1951.
EH marries Martha Gellhorn: *New York Times,* Nov. 21, 1940. Another source wishes to remain anonymous.
EH and Martha in New York: EH to Perkins, Nov. 20, 1940 (wire); John Hemingway to Maxwell Perkins, Nov. 28 (wire); Harold Peat to Perkins, Dec. 3 (wire); EH to Hadley Mowrer, Dec. 26, 1940. Gustavo Durán to author, Feb. 26, 1962; William B. Smith to author, Apr., 1964.
EH meets Sinclair Lewis in Key West: for an

account of this visit, see Mark Schorer, *Sinclair Lewis*, NY, 1961, pp. 671–672. Schorer states that Lewis and the Hemingways crossed to Havana together.
EH returns to Cuba and buys Finca Vigía: Mr. and Mrs. T. O. Bruce to author, March 22, 1965.
EH celebrates with quail shooting: EH to Charles Scribner, Dec. 29, 1940.
Leftist counterattack on "For Whom the Bell Tolls": Michael Gold, *Sunday Worker*, Dec. 8, 1940; Alvah Bessie, *New Masses*, Vol. 37 (Nov. 5, 1940), pp. 25–29. Open Letter to EH, *Daily Worker*, Nov. 20, 1940. Harry Hansen reviewed the open letter in his column in the *New York World Telegram*, placing beside it a laudatory comment by Ralph Bates which had appeared in the December number of *Common Sense*. Hansen took EH's part in the controversy: he was not a social historian but an imaginative writer who had effectively dramatized his theme of human interdependence. The debate continued on Dec. 2, when Hansen printed a long letter from Bessie, who associated himself with the VALB open letter of Nov. 20 (which he had in fact written) and defending André Marty. Two weeks later, for balance, Hansen printed a letter by Morris Maken, secretary of the Veterans of the International Brigade, a lesser rival of the VALB. Maken found the novel powerful and authentic, said that the Kremlin had exercised a sinister influence in Spain, and called André Marty "a menace." Bessie replied to Maken, attacking his veracity on personal grounds, and calling him a "malingerer, a deserter, a sorehead, and a coward." Hansen did not print Bessie's reply, having decided that the main issues had already been raised. Harry Hansen's columns, *New York World Telegram*, Nov. 27, Dec. 2, and Dec. 16, 1940. Alvah Bessie to author, Jan. 7, 1962, and Dec. 19, 1962.
EH counterattacks: EH to Irving Fajans, Dec. 24, 1940.
EH's quarrel with Milton Wolff: EH's letter to Wolff is printed in full in *American Dialog*, Vol. 1 (Oct.–Nov., 1964), p. 11. Some weeks later EH "took back" his obscenity, apologized for his "tough letter," and wished Wolff luck. Seven months later he lent Wolff $425 to buy a chicken farm. See further letters in *American Dialog*, cited above.
Perkins advises EH about death of Fitzgerald: Perkins to EH, Dec. 28, 1940. Fitzgerald had praised EH's novel in a letter of Nov. 8, 1940. See *The Letters of F. Scott Fitzgerald*, ed. by Andrew Turnbull, NY, 1963, pp. 312–313.
Sales record of "For Whom the Bell Tolls" to mid-December: Perkins to EH, Dec. 28, 1940. Perkins was elated over the "wonderful seven pages of pictures" in *Life*, Vol. 10 (Jan. 6, 1941), pp. 49–55. This double feature showed EH and sons hunting in Idaho and also printed a selection of Robert Capa's pictures of the Spanish Civil War. Front matter on p. 12 stated that Capa so much resembled EH's conception of the gypsy Rafael in the novel that EH had half-seriously asked him to play the part in the film version. Perkins to EH, Dec. 31, 1940, contains his comments, along with further remarks about Scott Fitzgerald.

Sec. 51. To the East

SOURCES

Letters of EH: to Solita Solano, Jan. 26, 1941; to Hadley Mowrer, Jan. 26; to Perkins, ca. late Feb. and April 29; to Martha Hemingway, May 2, 7, 12, 13, 14, 15, 16, and 18, 1941. To Charles Scribner, May 10 and Sept. 3 or 4, 1950. To Bernard Berenson, March 6, 1953.
Other letters: Earl Wilson to Maxwell Perkins, ca. Jan. 8, 1941; Eleanor Roosevelt to Martha Hemingway, Feb. 28, 1941.
EH's work: Published: for a listing of EH's contributions to *PM*, see Audre Hanneman, *Ernest Hemingway: A Comprehensive Bibliography*, Princeton, 1967, p. 161.
Articles: *Los Angeles Examiner*, Jan. 28, 1941; *Life*, Vol. 10 (Feb. 24, 1941); Martha Gellhorn, *Collier's*, Vol. 107 (June 7, 1941); Ralph Ingersoll, *PM*, June 9, 1941; Martha Gellhorn, *Collier's*, Vol. 107 (June 28, 1941); W. J. Lederer, *Reader's Digest*, Vol. 80 (March, 1962); Arthur Krock, "In the Nation," *NY Times*, May 11, 1962.
Author's interviews and correspondence: with Mr. and Mrs. Gustavo Durán, Feb., 1962; with W. B. Smith, Apr., 1964; with Mr. and Mrs. Lloyd Arnold, July, 1964; with Donald Friede, May, 1965. From Solita Solano, Apr. 4, 1962; from Carl Stroven, Oct. 24, 1962; from Marshall W. Stearns, Nov. 24, 1962; from Charles R. Bouslog, Nov. 26, 1962; from Ramon Lavalle, Feb. 26, 1963; from W. L. Bond, July 31, 1963; from Colin Miller, Aug. 2, 1964; from Lloyd Arnold, March 23, 1966; from Ramon Lavalle, March 24, 1966; from W. L. Bond, Apr. 15, 1966; from Mrs. Jasper Jepson, Apr. 18, 1966; from W. J. Lederer, May 11, 1966; from Addison Southard, May 17, 1967.

NOTES

EH in New York, Jan., 1941: Colin Miller to author, Aug. 2, 1964; Mrs. Gustavo Durán to author, Feb. 26, 1962; Solita Solano to author, April, 1962. EH to Solita Solano, Jan. 26, 1941. W. B. Smith to author, Apr., 1964.
EH's payment from Paramount: Gustavo Durán to author, Feb., 1962; Donald Friede to author, May, 1965. *Hellzapoppin* was already well into its third year on Broadway, and offered an evening of bangs and boffola, heckling by stooges, and an anarchic atmosphere of sweaty good will. According to Friede, EH next took his check to the Stork Club and asked Sherman Billingsley to cash it. Billingsley's actual response was "Wow!" which struck Friede as unworthy of the occasion. He invented and circulated a story that Billingsley, keeping a poker face, said that it was still too early in the evening. He would cash it when the night's receipts were in.
EH in bed from typhoid shots, interviewed by Wilson: Earl Wilson to Maxwell Perkins, ca. Jan. 28, 1941, with a typescript of the interview.
Bumby's visit: EH to Hadley Mowrer, Jan. 26, 1941.
EH and Martha with the Coopers: *Los Angeles Examiner*, Jan. 28, 1941.

Meeting with Ingrid Bergman: *Life,* Vol. 10 (Feb. 24, 1941), p. 48, and Donald Friede to author, May 12, 1965.

EH and Martha reach Hawaii: Mrs. Jasper Jepson (née Ursula Hemingway) to author, Apr. 18, 1966. EH's aunt Grace (Mrs. Chester Livingston) was then living in Hawaii, as was EH's nephew, Anson H. Hines. Mrs. Jepson and her husband had not yet moved there.

EH at Hawaiian luncheon and luau: Carl Stroven to author, Oct. 24, 1962; Marshall W. Stearns to author, Nov. 24, 1962; Charles R. Bouslog to author, Nov. 26, 1962. On being complimented for his wonderful title, *For Whom the Bell Tolls,* EH said carelessly that he had read Donne for years—on Sundays. This was an invention to impress the professors.

Arrival in Hong Kong: EH to Ralph Ingersoll, interview in *PM,* June 9, 1941; Martha Gellhorn, *Collier's,* Vol. 107 (June 7, 1941), p. 13.

EH meets General Cohen and Sun Yat-sen's widow: EH to Charles Scribner, Sept. 3 or 4, 1950, and Ramon Lavalle to author, March 24, 1966. EH met all three Soong sisters: Soong Ai-ling, born 1888, and married to Dr. H. H. Kung, the prime minister; Soong Ching-ling, born 1890, married to Sun Yat-sen in 1915, and widowed in 1925; and Soong Mei-ling, born 1896, and married to Chiang Kai-shek in 1927.

EH flies to War Zone 7: Ernest talked transport with W. L. Bond, a gray-haired aviation official with a flaming red mustache who lived near him at the Repulse Bay Hotel. Bond explained that Pan American Airways operated the China National Aviation Corporation under a joint-ownership arrangement with the Chinese Central Government at Chungking. The only difficulty, aside from getting reservations, was that "the Japanese had developed the unpleasant habit of shooting down [these] planes whenever they could." Ernest immediately went to the CNAC offices and bought tickets to Namyung for Martha and himself. He was enraged a few hours before flight time to learn that his reservations had been canceled in favor of two important Government officials. Although the ticket agent said that he and Martha could go on the freight plane that same night, Ernest strode back to the hotel and angrily accosted Bondy Bond. For a moment the two men stood eyeball to eyeball, Bond calm, Ernest breathing hard. Then Bond explained that the freight plane took only fifteen minutes longer than the passenger flight. If the famous tough guy objected to sitting on a box instead of a cushion, Bond would be completely disillusioned. Ernest's pugnaciousness departed. "Swell," he said, grinning broadly. "Let's have a drink." (W. L. Bond to author, July 31, 1963, and April 15, 1966).

Life around Shaokwan: EH to Charles Scribner, May 10, 1950; Lloyd Arnold to author, March 23, 1966; and see especially the report by Martha Gellhorn, *Collier's,* Vol. 107 (June 28, 1941), pp. 16–17. Martha was a little consoled by a letter of Feb. 28 from Eleanor Roosevelt, who wished her happiness in her marriage and hoped soon to know EH better. EH's praise of the country occurs in EH to Perkins, ca. late Feb., 1941.

EH and John Chinaman: EH's *PM* despatch, June 10, 1941. After a month in the war zone, EH and Martha went to Kweilin, where hundreds of miniature limestone mountains lined the riverbank and stood like pyramids in the surrounding fields. This was a civilized interlude in their journey. See Ingersoll's interview with EH, *PM,* June 9, 1941, p. 7.

EH in Chungking: EH despatch, *PM,* June 15, 1941, p. 6 and Ingersoll's interview with EH, *PM,* June 9, 1941, p. 7.

EH meets Lieutenant Lederer: W. J. Lederer, "What I Learned from Hemingway," *Reader's Digest,* Vol. 80 (March, 1962), pp. 207–208, and W. J. Lederer to author, May 11, 1966.

EH interviews with Madame Chiang, Nelson Johnson, et al.: EH, despatches in *PM,* June 10, 1941, p. 4 and June 18, 1941, pp. 16–17.

EH returns to Hong Kong: EH to Martha, May 2, 1941. The flight back was troubled by heavy air turbulence. At Kunming, the Douglas aircraft picked up a full load, including a missionary with a broken back on a stretcher. Everyone was airsick, EH included. He told Martha that the "vomitage" was carried on in five different dialects. Over Hong Kong the ceiling was very low. The British pilot, Captain Pott-Smith, made three attempts to land before the one that worked, and was rewarded by EH with a drink at 2 a.m.

"For Whom the Bell Tolls" rejected for Pulitzer Prize: Arthur Krock, "In the Nation," *NY Times,* May 11, 1962.

EH splenetic in Hong Kong: EH to Perkins, Apr. 29, 1941.

EH and the Chinese girls: EH to Bernard Berenson, March 6, 1953. According to Lloyd Arnold, the story was often repeated to EH's friends in Sun Valley that fall, with Martha gaily joining in.

EH's social life in Hong Kong: EH stayed at the Peninsular Hotel in Kowloon. Among his reunions was one with Addison Southard and his wife Lucy, whom he had first met on the voyage to Africa in 1933 while Southard was American Minister to Addis Ababa. They had already met Martha in Paris before her marriage to EH, and had given a large dinner party for EH and Martha on March 1. EH also attended a Chinese-style party given by Mrs. Elsa Stanton at Fan Ling on the mainland; drank cocktails with Charles Boxer of the British Intelligence; and lunched with Carl Blum, general manager of the U.S. Rubber Company for the Far East. (Addison Southard to author, May 17, 1967.) EH's reunion with Lavalle and his first meeting with Wendy (who was to die of dysentery just short of her 5th birthday) are described in Ramon Lavalle to author, Feb. 26, 1963, and March 24, 1966. At Lavalle's house EH participated in a drinking marathon with Lavalle, Rewi Alley (a New Zealander he had known in Madrid), and Alberto Pérez-Sáez, the Peruvian consul.

EH learns of death of Sherwood Anderson and Virginia Woolf: EH to Perkins, Apr. 29, 1941.

EH's homeward Clipper flight: EH to Martha, May 7, 12, and 13 (Manila), 14 (enroute to Guam), 15 (with an early morning postscript of May 16 on Guam), and 18 (Halekulani, Honolulu).

Sec. 52. The Wound and the Bow

SOURCES

Letters of EH: to P. A. Bartlett, Aug. 11, 1939. To Pauline, June 9, 1941; deposition to Raoul F. Washington, June 27; to Pauline, July 19; to Perkins, Aug. 26; to Scribner, Aug. 31 and Sept. 1 (cables); to Perkins, Sept. 12; to Gustavo Durán, Nov. 4 (wire), Nov. 6, and Nov. 7 (wire); to Perkins, Nov. 15 and Dec. 12, 1941, and Feb. 22, 1942; to author, Feb. 17, 1951.
Other letters: Perkins to EH, May 15, 1941; Col. John W. Thomason to Perkins, June 4; Pauline to EH, July 16; Donald Friede to Gustavo Durán, Oct. 30; George Macy to Perkins, Oct. 31; Martha Gellhorn to Clara Spiegel, Nov. 10; Charles Scribner to EH, Nov. 24, 1941 (wire).
EH's work: Published: "The Shot," *True,* Vol. 28 (Apr., 1951).
Books and articles: Elsa Spear, *Fort Phil Kearny, Dakota Territory, 1866–1868* (1939); Ralph Ingersoll, interview with EH, *PM,* June 9, 1941; Edmund Wilson, *The Wound and the Bow,* 1941; Edmund Wilson, ed., Fitzgerald's *The Last Tycoon,* 1941; "Bob Davis Reveals," *New York Sun,* Oct. 1, 1942; Col. Roger Willock, *Lone Star Marine,* 1961.
Author's interviews and correspondence: with Gustavo Durán, Feb., 1962; with Mr. and Mrs. Robert Joyce, Nov., 1963; with Lloyd Arnold, July, 1964. From Ellis O. Briggs, Feb. 27, 1964.

NOTES

EH's interview with Ingersoll: *PM,* June 9, 1941, p. 6.
Stopover in Washington: Col. John W. Thomason to Perkins, June 4, 1941. The interview had taken place on June 3. For details of Thomason's career, see Col. Roger Willock, USMC, *Lone Star Marine,* privately printed, Princeton, NJ, 1961, esp. pp. 137 and 175–185.
EH sees Patrick and Gregory in Key West: EH to Pauline, June 9, 1941.
EH sends love to Pauline: Same source as above.
Death of Joe Russell: same source. EH said that he had been "riding it out" with Josie, at least in spirit, and indicated that it was a great loss. Another informant, who wishes to remain anonymous, doubts the genuineness of EH's grief, saying that he mourned his friend "for all of five minutes." EH's comment on Ford's death was made in EH to P. A. Bartlett, Aug. 11, 1939.
Montijo plagiarism suit: filed in Los Angeles, June 2, 1941. EH's deposition to Raoul Washington, June 27, 1941. **EH's complaints on being charged for legal fees:** EH to Perkins, Aug. 26, and EH to Scribner, Aug. 31 (cable). **EH's apology:** EH to Scribner, Sept. 1, 1941 (cable).
EH on income tax: EH to Perkins, Aug. 26, 1941.
EH's exchange with Pauline on money matters: Pauline to EH, July 16 and EH to Pauline, July 19, 1941.
EH's friendship with Joyce and Briggs: Mr. and Mrs. Robert Joyce to author, Nov. 17, 1963; Ellis O. Briggs to author, Feb. 27, 1964.

EH returns to Sun Valley: Lloyd Arnold to author, July 30, 1964.
Pahsimeroi antelope hunt: EH, "The Shot," *True,* Vol. 28 (April, 1951), pp. 25–28; Taylor Williams, quoted in "Bob Davis Reveals," *NY Sun,* Oct. 1, 1942.
Background of the Old Timer's yarns: Elsa Spear, *Fort Phil Kearny, Dakota Territory, 1866–1868,* Sheridan, Wyoming, 1939.
EH consorts with film people at Sun Valley: EH to Perkins, Nov. 15, 1941.
EH attempts to secure job for Gustavo Durán: Donald Friede to Durán, Oct. 30, 1941 (wire); EH to Durán, Nov. 4 (wire); EH to Durán, Nov. 6; EH to Durán, Nov. 7 (wire); and Gustavo Durán to author, Feb. 26, 1962.
EH's reaction to Wilson's "The Wound and the Bow": EH to Perkins, Aug. 26, 1941. Wilson's Hemingway essay appeared in this volume (Boston, 1941), pp. 214–242.
EH's views on Wilson edition of "The Last Tycoon" and on Fitzgerald: EH to Perkins, Nov. 15, 1941.
EH's gold medal award: George Macy to Perkins, Oct. 31, 1941. Charles Scribner wired EH on Nov. 24, 1941 that Perkins had declined to attend the ceremony and asked EH to telegraph something to be read to the group.
Martha and the Indian beads: EH to Perkins, Feb. 22, 1942.
EH's reaction to Pearl Harbor disaster: EH to Perkins, Dec. 12, 1941; EH to author, Feb. 17, 1951. Although EH was now scornful about the predictions made by Thomas and Sweeny in June, he had not done much better. "There is an excellent chance," he had stated at about the same time, "that Japan will not try to move south this year at all, but will try to defeat China by two great final drives. . . . It looks as though Japan will not risk war with England and America until she sees a possibility of England and the U.S.A. being so occupied that they cannot oppose her adequately." But Japan fooled many others besides EH.
EH's anger at Scribners' failure to transcribe Lewis's speech: EH to Perkins. Dec. 12, 1941.

Sec. 53. Improvisations

SOURCES

Letters of EH: to Gustavo Durán, Dec. 30, 1941. To Perkins, early Jan. and Jan. 20, 1942; to Hadley Mowrer, Jan. 21; to Perkins, March 3; to Donald Friede, March 3, March 16 and Apr. 21; to Perkins, May 8 (cable) and May 30; to Hadley Mowrer, June 12; to Perkins, July 8; to Hadley Mowrer, July 23; to Donald Friede, Aug. 13; to Perkins, Aug. 27 and Sept. 7, 1942. To Malcolm Cowley, Apr. 9 and June 28, 1948.
Other letters: Perkins to EH, Jan. 9, 1942; Martha Hemingway to Clara Spiegel, July 8, 1942.
EH's work: Published: Introduction to *Men at War,* 1942.
Books: Ellis O. Briggs, *Shots Heard Round the World: An Ambassador's Hunting Adventures on Four Continents,* 1957.
Author's interviews and correspondence: with Robert Joyce, Apr., 1964; with Spruille Braden, Jan., 1965; with T. O. Bruce, March,

1965; with Winston Guest, June, 1965. From Robert Joyce, Nov. 9, Nov. 17, and Nov. 29, 1964.

NOTES

EH views 1942 with foreboding: EH to Perkins, early Jan., 1942.
EH's income-tax problems: Perkins to EH, Jan. 9, 1942; EH to Perkins, Jan. 20, 1942; EH to Hadley Mowrer, Jan. 21, 1942.
Wartels invites EH to edit war anthology: EH to Perkins, March 3, 1942.
EH's discontent with movie script of "For Whom the Bell Tolls": EH to Donald Friede, March 3, March 16, Apr. 21, and Aug. 13, 1942.
EH longs for active role in war effort: EH to Perkins, Jan. 20, March 3, and May 30, 1942.
EH plans counterespionage: first hinted at in EH to Gustavo Durán, Dec. 30, 1941. Robert P. Joyce to author, April, 1964, and Nov. 9, 17, and 29, 1964; Spruille Braden to author, Jan. 30, 1965. At this time in May, EH's son Bumby flew to Cuba. He was now a freshman at Dartmouth. He had wanted to enlist in the Marine Corps, but EH dissuaded him on the grounds that he would be a better officer with more education. EH talked with him about his future. See EH, Introduction to *Men at War*, NY, 1942, p. xxvii.
EH's problems with Crown Publishers: EH to Perkins, May 30, 1942.
EH makes "Pilar" into Q-Boat: Robert and Jane Joyce to author, Apr., 1964; Spruille Braden to author, Jan., 1965; Winston Guest to author, June, 1965; Ellis O. Briggs, *Shots Heard Round the World*, NY, 1957, pp. 55–73. EH to Malcolm Cowley, Apr. 9 and June 28, 1948. It was decided that EH would serve under the joint command of two Marine colonels, both friends of Thomason's: John Hart, Air Attaché, and Hayne D. Boyden, Naval Attaché, affectionately known as Cuckoo. The only senior officer who knew of the project was Admiral Butch Weyler, Commander of the Naval Base at Guantánamo. Count von Luckner (1881–1966) commanded the *See Adler*, an American windjammer fitted up as a raider, which sank 15 Allied ships in 1916–17.
EH begins patrols in June: Robert and Jane Joyce to author, Apr., 1964; fragment of the log of the *Pilar*, June 12–14, 1942; EH to Malcolm Cowley, June 28, 1948; Ellis O. Briggs, *Shots Heard Round the World*, NY, 1957, pp. 55–73.
Arrival of Patrick and Gregory: EH to Hadley Mowrer, June 12 and July 23, 1942.
Martha's claustrophobia: Martha Hemingway to Clara Spiegel, July 8, 1942.
Martha's Caribbean tour and EH's sour reflections: EH to Perkins, July 8, Aug. 27, and Sept. 7, 1942.
EH's sentimental recollections of Hadley: EH to Hadley Mowrer, July 23, 1942.

Sec. 54. Men at War

SOURCES

Letters of EH: to Hadley Mowrer, Sept. 15, 1942; to Patrick Hemingway, Oct. 7, Oct. 15, Oct. 20, and Oct. 23; to Hadley Mowrer, Nov.

28, 1942. To Lillian Ross, July 2, 1948, and June 3, 1950.
Other letters: John Hemingway to Patrick Hemingway, Oct. 15, 1942.
EH's work: Published: Introduction to *Men at War*, 1942.
Books: *For Whom the Bell Tolls*, Limited Editions Club reprint, with an introduction by Sinclair Lewis, Oct., 1942.
Author's interviews and correspondence: with Mr. and Mrs. Gustavo Durán, Feb., 1962; with Mr. and Mrs. Robert Joyce, April, 1964; with Spruille Braden, Jan., 1965; with Dr. Gregory Hemingway, March, 1965. From Ellis O. Briggs, Feb. 27, 1964; from Robert Joyce, Nov. 9, Nov. 17, and Nov. 29, 1964.

NOTES

EH's new full beard: Ellis O. Briggs to author, Feb. 27, 1964.
EH as host and guest: Gustavo Durán to author, Feb., 1962; Ellis O. Briggs to author, Feb. 27, 1964; Spruille Braden to author, Jan. 30, 1965.
Winston Guest nicknamed Wolfie: Dr. Gregory Hemingway to author, March, 1965.
Pursuit of German submarine: EH to Lillian Ross, June 3, 1950; Spruille Braden to author, Jan., 1965. EH used the incident in his poem, "To Mary in London," written in June, 1944. He afterwards nicknamed Megano de Casigua the "Aberdeen Proving Grounds," though nothing was proved there.
EH writes preface to "Men at War": *Men at War*, NY, Crown Publishers, Oct. 1942, pp. xi–xxxi. EH had used the Shakespeare quotation in "The Short Happy Life of Francis Macomber," placing it in the mouth of the white hunter Wilson, who had always lived by it, as had EH himself.
Patrick to Canterbury school: EH to Patrick, Oct. 7, 15, 20, and 23, 1942; John Hemingway to Patrick Hemingway, Oct. 15, 1942; EH to Hadley Mowrer, Sept. 15 and Nov. 28, 1942.
Pickup baseball games: EH to Lillian Ross, July 2, 1948.
Lewis's introduction to "For Whom the Bell Tolls": Limited Editions Club reprint, Princeton University Press, Oct., 1942.
Reviews of "Men at War": Those quoted were by Herbert Gorman, *New York Times Book Review*, Nov. 8, 1942, p. 1; Vincent McHugh, *The New Yorker*, Vol. 18 (Oct. 24, 1942), p. 80; Howard Mumford Jones, *Saturday Review of Literature*, Vol. 25 (Dec. 12, 1942), p. 11; Walter Millis, *New York Herald Tribune Books*, Oct. 25, 1942, p. 3.
Gustavo Durán and the Crook Factory: Mr. and Mrs. Gustavo Durán to author, Feb. 26, 1962; Robert P. Joyce to author, Nov. 17, 1964.
Martha's return: EH to Hadley, Nov. 28, 1942.
EH attacks Durán: Ellis O. Briggs to author, Feb. 27, 1964.
Domestic strain at the Finca: EH to Perkins, Aug. 27, 1942; Gustavo Durán to author, Feb., 1962; Ellis O. Briggs to author, Feb. 27, 1964. Another source wishes to remain anonymous.
Jane Joyce and Martha as "guests" aboard "Pilar": Jane Joyce to author, Apr., 1964.
FBI agents supersede Crook Factory: Robert P. Joyce to author, April, 1963, and Nov. 9,

17, and 29, 1963. "My own impression of the Crook Factory," wrote Ellis O. Briggs, "was that it was remarkably professional, even though the attention that it engaged on the part of a number of operatives was accorded out of affection for Ernest as much as patriotic ardor for the Cause of the Free World." Ellis O. Briggs to author, Feb. 27, 1964.

Sec. 55. Dangling Man

SOURCES

Letters of EH: to MacLeish, Apr. 4, 1943; to Perkins, Apr. 4 or 11, Apr. 7, and Apr. 15; to MacLeish, early May; to Perkins, May 13 and 18; to MacLeish, June 30; to Otto Bruce, July 7; to Perkins, ca. July 18, Aug. 2, and August 10; to MacLeish, Aug. 10; to Perkins, ca. Sept. 15; to Patrick Hemingway, Oct. 30 and Nov. 10; to Charles Scribner, Nov. 24; to Hadley Mowrer, Nov. 25; to MacLeish, Dec. 25 and Dec. 26; to Hadley Mowrer, Dec. 26, 1943.
Other letters: Perkins to EH, Feb. 10, March 19, and Apr. 2, 1943; Whitney Darrow, Scribner interoffice memorandum, May 13; Martha Hemingway to Patrick Hemingway, May 15; Perkins to EH, July 20; Gregory Hemingway to Patrick Hemingway, Aug. 9; Perkins to EH, Sept. 23; Scribner to EH, Nov. 12; Perkins to EH, Dec. 6, 1943.
EH's work: Published: none.
Books: Ellis O. Briggs, *Shots Heard Round the World*, 1957.
Author's interviews and correspondence: with Gustavo Durán, Feb., 1962; from M. G. Menocal, Oct. 1 and Oct. 17, 1964; from Archibald MacLeish, Jan. 31, 1965.

NOTES

EH's quarreling, drinking, and lying: Mayito Menocal to author, Oct. 1 and Oct. 17, 1964.
Importance of being Papa: Menocal to author, as above.
EH on handling women: EH to Perkins, ca. Sept. 15, 1943; EH to Hadley Mowrer, Nov. 25, 1943. Behind EH's opinions on this subject lay his ideas about his mother, with whom he continued to exchange polite notes. On July 7, 1943, he reported to Otto Bruce that Grace was still alive, though increasingly guided by divine voices.
Military activities of EH's friends: Perkins to EH, Feb. 10, March 19, and Apr. 2, 1943.
EH's reluctance to leave Finca Vigía: EH to Perkins, Apr. 4 or 11, Apr. 7, Apr. 15, and May 13, 1943.
EH on Pound: EH to MacLeish, Apr. 4, early May, June 30, and Aug. 10, 1943.
EH on quarreling with former friends: EH to MacLeish, Apr. 4, early May, and June 30, 1943.
EH on his "ideas" in four novels: EH to MacLeish, early May, 1943.
Release of "For Whom the Bell Tolls" film: Whitney Darrow, Scribner interoffice memorandum, May 13, 1943; EH to Perkins, May 13 and ca. July 18, 1943; Perkins to EH, July 20, 1943.
EH's remarks on Harold Stearns: Perkins to EH, July 20; EH to Perkins, Aug. 2, 1943.
EH's steering-liquor and stoicism: *M. G.* Menocal to author, Oct. 17, 1964.

EH's forty-fourth birthday: Ellis O. Briggs, *Shots Heard Round the World*, NY, 1957, pp. 55–73; Gustavo Durán to author, Feb., 1962; Gregory Hemingway to Patrick Hemingway, Aug. 9, 1943.
Martha's departure: Perkins to EH, Sept. 23; EH to Patrick, Oct. 30; EH to Scribner, Nov. 24, 1943.
EH alone: EH to Patrick, Oct. 30 and Nov. 10, 1943.
Thanksgiving and Christmas at Finca Vigía: EH to Scribner, Nov. 24; EH to Hadley, Nov. 25; EH to MacLeish, Dec. 25 and Dec. 26; EH to Hadley, Dec. 26, 1943.
EH's year-end situation: Scribner to EH, Nov. 12; EH to Scribner, Nov. 24; Perkins to EH, Dec. 6, 1943.

Sec. 56. Pursuit to London

SOURCES

Letters of EH: to Perkins, late Sept., 1943; to Charles Scribner, Nov. 24, 1943. To Dawn Powell, Jan. 31, 1944; to Martha Gellhorn, Jan. 31; to Ramon Lavalle, Feb. 2; to Mrs. George Gellhorn, Sept. 21, 1944. To Charles Scribner, Aug. 29, 1950 and April 11, 1951.
Other letters: George Houghton to W. M. Mills, Sept. 6, 1965.
EH's work: none.
Books, articles, and other documents: Mary Welsh's diaries, 1943–45 (unpublished); Robert Capa, *Slightly Out of Focus*, 1947: Joe McCarthy, "Costello's: The Wayward Saloon," *Holiday*, Vol. 26 (Oct., 1959); John O'Hara, Letter to the Editor, *Holiday*, Vol. 26 (Dec., 1959); James Charters, "Jimmy the Barman Remembers," transcript of BBC broadcast, Summer, 1961; Leicester Hemingway, *My Brother, Ernest Hemingway*, 1962; Constantine Fitzgibbon, *The Life of Dylan Thomas*, 1965.
Author's interviews and correspondence: with Ira Wolfert, Nov., 1961; with Frederick Spiegel, Dec., 1961; with Mary Hemingway, Apr., 1962; with Lewis Galantière, March, 1963; with William Walton, Apr., 1964; with Mary Hemingway, Aug., 1964; with John H. Hemingway, Aug., 1964; with Gregory Clark, Jan., 1965; with the archivists of St. George's Hospital and the London Clinic, Nov., 1965; with Lael Tucker Wertenbaker, Jan., 1966. From H. W. R. North, Apr. 12, 1963; from Ellis O. Briggs, Feb. 27, 1964; from Dawn Powell, May 12, 1965; from Roald Dahl, July 28, 1965; from Vincent Sheean, Oct. 31, 1965; from George Houghton, Dec. 5, 1965; from William Saroyan, Dec. 20, 1965; from John Pudney, Dec. 26, 1965; from Michael Burke, Dec. 30, 1965; from John Hersey, Jan. 30, 1966; from Lael Tucker Wertenbaker, March 27, 1966; from John O'Hara, June 7, 1966.

NOTES

EH's complaints over Martha's absence: EH to Perkins, late Sept., 1943; EH to Scribner, Nov. 24, 1943; EH to Dawn Powell, Jan. 31, 1944; EH to Martha Gellhorn, Jan. 31, 1944; EH to Ramon Lavalle, Feb. 2, 1944.
Martha persuades EH to go to Europe: Roald Dahl to author, July 28, 1965. A second source wishes to remain anonymous.
EH in New York (April–May): Roald Dahl

to author, July 28, 1965. Ellis O. Briggs to author, Feb. 27, 1964.

Cane-breaking incident: Vincent Sheean to author, Oct. 31, 1966; John Hersey to author, Jan. 30, 1966; John O'Hara to author, June 7, 1966. Although Costello's Bar later moved to new quarters one number further down Third Avenue, the management brought Thurber's murals and the broken blackthorn cane. The author inspected the cane, which was then kept behind the bar along with two shillelaghs. Joe McCarthy, "Costello's: The Wayward Saloon," *Holiday,* Vol. 26 (Oct., 1959), pp. 108–115, summarizes the incident. So does John O'Hara in a letter to the editor, *Holiday,* Vol. 26 (Dec., 1959), p. 4. O'Hara, who misremembers the date according to other witnesses, adds that when he returned home he sent EH a check for $50. EH promptly returned it, but O'Hara sent it back again. EH said he would replace the broken cane, but did not do so. Steinbeck brought another back from Ireland as a birthday present for O'Hara on Jan. 31, 1956. John Steinbeck reports that EH said derisively, "What kind of a stick is that?" O'Hara said it was a blackthorn. "That's no blackthorn," said EH. "Let me see it." He then broke it on his head and threw it aside saying, "You call that a blackthorn?" Steinbeck adds that "it was a very old blackthorn, well over a hundred years old and it was brittle and had lost its sap. I know because I gave it to John. It wasn't nice." John Hersey, who arrived late, heard the story at second hand from Tim Costello. It is probably impossible to relate the story exactly as it happened. Mr. Hersey calls it "a beautiful example of Tolstoi's dictum that as soon as an event has taken place, it becomes as many events as it had witnesses, for they all tell different stories."

EH at Dawn Powell's: Dawn Powell to author, May 12, 1965.

EH's flight to London: H. W. R. North to author, Apr. 12, 1963; Michael Burke to author, Dec. 30, 1965.

EH meets RAF representatives: George Houghton to W. M. Mills, Sept. 6, 1965; George Houghton to author, Dec. 5, 1965.

EH's hospitality: Frederick Spiegel to author, Dec., 1961; Lewis Galantière to author, March, 1963; Gregory Clark to author, Jan., 1965; William Saroyan to author, Dec. 20, 1965; Lael Tucker Wertenbaker to author, Jan. 7, 1966. Robert Capa, *Slightly Out of Focus,* NY, 1947, pp. 137–138; Leicester Hemingway, *My Brother, Ernest Hemingway,* Cleveland, 1962, pp. 229–233.

EH meets Mary Welsh: Mary Hemingway to author, April 4, 1962, and Aug. 3, 1964. Supplementary details from her unpublished diaries, 1943–45.

EH and the hair tonic: Roald Dahl to author, July 28, 1965.

Charters-Hamnett invitation: James Charters, "Jimmy the Barman Remembers," BBC broadcast, Summer, 1961, copy of text kindly provided by Morrill Cody. On Nina Hamnett, see Constantine Fitzgibbon's lively portrait in *The Life of Dylan Thomas,* Boston, 1965, pp. 151–152.

Capa's party: Robert Capa, *Slightly Out of Focus,* NY, 1947, pp. 137–138; Lael Tucker Wertenbaker to author, Jan. 7 and March 27, 1966. William Walton to author, April, 1964.

Leicester Hemingway's biography also alludes to it on pp. 236–237.

EH's accident in Gorer's car: Lael Tucker Wertenbaker to author, Jan. 7, 1966; Michael Burke to author, Dec. 30, 1965; interview with archivist at St. George's Hospital, Nov. 15, 1965. Far off in Algiers, EH's son Bumby heard a broadcast that his father had been killed. It was the heaviest blow of his life and he drank steadily for three days until the truth came through. (John H. Hemingway to author, Aug. 2, 1964.) The news of Bumby's reaction to his supposed death touched Ernest deeply and he never tired of boasting about it to his friends. See also Leicester Hemingway, *My Brother, Ernest Hemingway,* p. 237. EH mentions the accident in EH to Charles Scribner, Apr. 11, 1951. Further details from the archivists of St. George's Hospital, Nov. 15, 1965, and The London Clinic, Nov. 16, 1965, and from Roald Dahl to author, July 28, 1965.

Martha and others visit EH in the London Clinic: H. W. R. North to author, Apr. 12, 1963; EH to Mrs. George Gellhorn, Sept. 21, 1944; Michael Burke to author, Dec. 30, 1965; EH to Charles Scribner, Aug. 29, 1950; and James Charters, BBC broadcast, Summer, 1961.

EH emerges from London Clinic: H. W. R. North to author, Apr. 12, 1963 and Michael Burke to author, Dec. 30, 1965. See also Leicester Hemingway's biography, p. 239.

Instances of boorish behavior in EH: Lael Tucker Wertenbaker to author, Jan. 7, 1966; John Pudney to author, Dec. 26, 1965; Ira Wolfert to author, Nov. 15, 1961.

Sec. 57. Cross-Channel Operations

SOURCES

Letters of EH: to Mrs. George Gellhorn, Sept. 21, 1944. To Lillian Ross, Sept. 18, 1949; to Charles Scribner, June 26, July 21, and Oct. 11, 1950, and April 11, 1951.

Other letters: Martha Gellhorn to EH, June 7, 1944.

EH's work: (a) Unpublished: short story on London and the RAF, date of composition uncertain. **(b) Published:** "Voyage to Victory," *Collier's,* Vol. 114 (July 22, 1944); "London Fights the Robots," *Collier's,* Vol. 114 (Aug. 19, 1944); "To Mary in London," (poem), *Atlantic,* Vol. 216 (Aug., 1965).

Books and articles: Air Marshal Sir Basil Embry, *Mission Completed,* 1957; Leicester Hemingway, *My Brother, Ernest Hemingway,* 1962; William Van Dusen, "Hemingway's Longest Day," *True,* Feb., 1963; David Irving, *The Mare's Nest,* 1965.

Author's interviews and correspondence: with William Walton, Apr., 1964; with Air Commodore G. J. C. Paul, Nov., 1965; with Charles Collingwood, Nov., 1965. From H. W. R. North, Apr. 12, 1963; from Roald Dahl, July 28, 1965; from Charles Collingwood, Aug. 9, 1965; from Air Marshal Sir Peter Wykeham, Aug. 30, 1965; from Air Marshal C. R. Dunlap, RCAF, Dec. 21, 1965; from John Pudney, Dec. 26, 1965; from Michael Burke, Dec. 30, 1965; from Air Commodore G. J. C. Paul, Jan. 10, 1966; from H. J. E. van der Kop, Jan. 13, 1966; from Col. George Wertenbaker,

March 1, 1968; from Alan Lynn, March 8, 1968; from Mary Hemingway, July, 1968.

NOTES

EH meets Group Capt. Peter Wykeham Barnes: Air Marshal Sir Peter Wykeham to author, Aug. 30, 1965; John Pudney to author, Dec. 26, 1965.
EH's D-Day crossing: EH to Charles Scribner, Apr. 11, 1951, and EH, "Voyage to Victory," *Collier's,* Vol. 114 (July 22, 1944), pp. 11–13 and 56–57. The statements by Leicester Hemingway (pp. 242–243) and William Van Dusen, "Hemingway's Longest Day," *True* (Feb., 1963), pp. 55 and 62, indicating that EH actually went ashore and helped boot scared infantrymen up the slope out of the murderous fire on the beach, seem to be without foundation.
Martha Gellhorn on D-Day: Martha Gellhorn to EH, June 7, 1944, delivered by the hand of William Van Dusen. Another source wishes to remain anonymous.
Dahl reads EH's invasion article: Roald Dahl to author, July 28, 1965. When Dahl brought round his first slim volume of short stories, *Over to You,* EH kept it two days and then returned it. Dahl asked how he had liked the stories. "I didn't understand them," said EH, striding away down the corridor.
EH visits RAF fighter wing on Salisbury Plain: EH, "London Fights the Robots, *Collier's,* Vol. 144 (Aug. 19, 1944), pp. 17, 80–81.
EH prays at Salisbury Cathedral: EH to Scribner, Oct. 11, 1950.
EH in error in aircraft identification: Air Commodore Paul states that "there were no Tempests in the Allied Expeditionary Air Forces prior to 6th July, 1944, when No. 56 Squadron in No. 85 Group received them. There were, however, very many Typhoons, which differed from the Tempest in having a liquid-cooled 24-cylinder Napier engine." Air Commodore G. J. C. Paul to author, Jan. 10, 1966.
EH steals V1 fragments at Dunsford: Air Marshal C. R. Dunlap, RCAF, to author, Dec. 21, 1965.
The buzzbomb and the pancakes: H. W. R. North to author, Apr. 12, 1963; Michael Burke to author, Dec. 30, 1965.
RAF bombing of buzzbomb launching sites: Air Marshal Sir Basil Embry, *Mission Completed,* London, 1957, pp. 255–257; David Irving, *The Mare's Nest,* Boston, 1965, *passim.* Additional details, including code designations, from Air Commodore G. J. C. Paul (CB, DFC) in interview with author, Nov. 18, 1965; and H. J. E. van der Kop to author, Jan. 13, 1966.
EH's flight to Drancourt and back: Alan Lynn to author, March 8, 1968. Lynn enclosed a marked map, showing entry over enemy territory above Cayeux-sur-Mer, penetration to Drancourt, followed by a quick turn over Pinchefalise and the Canal de la Somme to escape the heavy concentration of flak around Abbeville. EH describes the flight in "London Fights the Robots," *Collier's,* Vol. 114 (Aug. 19, 1944), pp. 17 and 80–81. He later told Gen. R. O. Barton that he flew as copilot, sitting at Lynn's right.
EH forbidden further flying: EH to Scribner, July 21, 1950. He also told Scribner that dur-

ing 1944 he flew in almost every type of aircraft including the gliders Hengist and Horsa, named for fifth-century Jute warriors. There is no supporting evidence for this statement, which appears in EH to Scribner, June 26, 1950. The observation on the first poem to Mary appears in EH to Lillian Ross, Sept. 18, 1949.
EH's first poem to Mary: "To Mary in London," *Atlantic,* Vol. 216 (Aug., 1965), pp. 94–95. About the time EH finished this poem, his former executive officer, Winston Guest, was finishing officers' training at Parris Island and earning his commission in the U.S. Marine Corps.
EH moons over alleged neglect by Martha: Leicester Hemingway, *My Brother, Ernest Hemingway,* Cleveland, 1962, p. 240. EH speaks of desire for death while flying in medium bombers and the gradual return of his wish to survive while flying in Mosquitoes: EH to Mrs. George Gellhorn, Sept. 21, 1944. There is a possibility that EH did not send this letter, a copy of which exists among his papers. It clearly implies more than one mission in medium bombers, though he made only one.
EH's Mosquito flights: Air Marshal Sir Peter Wykeham to author, Aug. 30, 1965, and EH, unpublished short story on London and the RAF.
Collingwood and Walton in Cherbourg: Charles Collingwood to author, Aug. 9, 1965, and interview, Nov. 16, 1965. William Walton to author, interview, Apr. 2, 1964.
Celebration of EH's arrival in Cherbourg: Collingwood to author, Aug. 9, 1965. EH's explanation of the loss of his beard: EH to Mrs. George Gellhorn, Sept. 21, 1944. EH's first meeting with Col. George Wertenbaker had occurred at the Dorchester. EH regaled him with an account of the automobile accident, speaking of "holding his head wound together with one hand while helping his companion with the other." According to Colonel Wertenbaker, EH appeared at Isigny on a wet and foggy night, "laden down with wine and cheese (typical)." After a time he began to write war poetry, handing Wertenbaker two pages to read. Wertenbaker asked if he could keep the pages, and EH agreed. But he tore them up before he left that night. As to the plane rides across the Channel, Wertenbaker recalls that EH "was always the first to say he would rather swim over than take a seat from an infantry man." Col. George Wertenbaker to author, March 1, 1968.

Sec. 58. Return to Normandy

SOURCES

Letters of EH: to Mary Welsh, July 1, Aug. 1, and Aug. 6, 1944. To Maj. Gen. Raymond O. Barton, Sept. 3, 1945. To Malcolm Cowley, June 28, 1948. To Lillian Ross, Sept. 18, 1949. To Charles Scribner, Apr. 11, 1951. To Bernard Berenson, May 27, 1953.
Other letters: none.
EH's work: Published: "The G.I. and the General," *Collier's,* Vol. 114 (Nov. 4, 1944).
Books: Robert Capa, *Slightly Out of Focus,* 1947; A. J. Liebling, *Normandy Revisited,* 1958; Evelyn Waugh, *The End of the Battle,*

1961; General Charles T. Lanham, *Memoir,* 1963 (unpublished).
Author's interviews and correspondence: with Maj. Gen. Charles T. Lanham, USA, Ret., Apr., 1962 and June, 1963; with William Walton, Apr., 1964; with Charles Collingwood, Nov., 1965; with Gen. John F. Ruggles, Feb., 1966; with Archie Pelkey, Oct., 1966. From Col. E. W. Edwards, Feb. 5, 1962; from Maj. Gen. Raymond O. Barton, March 20 and July 13, 1962; from Col. Thomas A. Kenan, June 25, 1962; from Charles Collingwood, Aug. 9, 1965; from Helen Kirkpatrick, Jan. 25, 1966; from Maj. Gen. C. T. Lanham, March 14–22, 1968.

NOTES

EH's temporary tour with General George Patton: EH to Lillian Ross, Sept. 18, 1949, describes his time with Patton's armor as an "abortion."
Nemo Lucas and the stolen drink: Col. Thomas A. Kenan to author, June 25, 1962.
EH's transfer to 4th Infantry Division: General Barton to author, March 20, 1962. EH described Stevenson as "a wonderful contact man, a very brave and charming Joe [who] did a terrific job as host and helper to correspondents" (EH to Barton, Sept. 3, 1945). General Roosevelt had died of a heart attack in his sleep, July 13, 1944. According to General Lanham, EH always said afterwards that his abrupt departure from Patton's army came about because Patton was a "phony and a fraud." Dust was furthermore a universal problem. "Every outfit was loaded with transportation, wheeled and tracked. At the end of a day, everybody would have qualified for a minstrel show." Lanham's regiment, the 22nd, was detached from the 4th Division at this time, and teamed with CC-A of the 2nd Armored Division under Brig. Gen. Maurice Rose to make the initial penetration just below St.-Lô. The regiment was given a Distinguished Unit Citation for this action. Lanham to author, March 14–22, 1968.
EH meets Colonel Lanham: Col. E. W. Edwards to author, Feb. 5, 1963. Gen. Lanham, *Memoir,* pp. 1–2.
EH with 4th Infantry Division, July 29–Aug. 1: EH to Mary Welsh, July 1 and Aug. 1, 1944. There are two letters for Aug. 1. General Lanham, *Memoir,* and Archie Pelkey to author, Oct., 1966.
EH in Villedieu-les-Poêles: General Lanham, *Memoir.*
EH's reconnaissance duties: EH to Mary Welsh, Aug. 1 and Aug. 6, 1944.
EH and the German patrol at St.-Pois: EH to Mary Welsh, Aug. 6, 1944; Robert Capa, *Slightly Out of Focus,* NY, 1947, pp. 167–168; General Barton to author, June, 1963. All these accounts differ markedly, but the substance is roughly as summarized in the text. EH told General Barton on Sept. 3, 1945, that the encounter with the German patrol came about because of "bad gen" from Col. Jack Meyer. This may have been an exaggeration, as his account to Mary Welsh, Aug. 6, 1944, certainly was. EH told Charles Scribner, Apr. 11, 1951, that the tank shell lifted him and dropped him on his head, producing a big concussion and double vision. On June 28, 1948, he told Cowley that this experience made

him "impotent" for four months. Exaggeration is again evident in EH's account. The German vehicle was not a tank, but an antitank gun. According to Lanham, EH "came to my C.P. immediately after this incident, recounted the details, did not mention any injury to the head (none was evident), [and] did not blame Jack Meyer for missing the road but himself for not following the telephone wire that ran to my C.P." (General Lanham to author, March 14–22, 1968.)
EH at Mont St.-Michel: EH to Mary Welsh, Aug. 6, 1944. William Walton to author, Apr. 2, 1964. Charles Collingwood to author, Aug. 9, 1965 and interview of Nov. 16, 1965; A. J. Liebling, *Normandy Revisited,* NY, 1958, p. 154. EH later told Walton that he had helped Mme. Chevalier with a money-changing operation.
EH spooked by Château Lingeard: General Lanham, *Memoir,* pp. 5–6.
Avranches counteroffensive: Helen Kirkpatrick to author, Jan. 25, 1966.
EH's views on Walton, Crawford, and Wolfert: EH to Mary Welsh, Aug. 1, 1944.
EH writes "Collier's" article called "The General": published in *Collier's,* Vol. 114 (Nov. 4, 1944), p. 11 as "The G.I. and the General." In 1945, EH forwarded the original typescript to Barton, inscribed "For Major General Raymond O. Barton USA with affection, admiration and respect." His covering letter said that the story was written just after Barton took St.-Pois and before the German counteroffensive. "The day it referred to was one before we took St. Pois." Photostat of original typescript and covering letter kindly provided to author July 13, 1962, by the late General Barton. EH asks Collingwood's opinion of his article: Charles Collingwood to author, Aug. 9, 1965.
Evelyn Waugh on men at war: *The End of the Battle,* Boston, 1961, p. 305.
EH on the profound pleasures of killing cleanly: *Death in the Afternoon,* NY, 1932, pp. 232–233.
EH's joy in killing Nazis and Fascists: EH to Bernard Berenson, May 27, 1953. There is some reasonable doubt as to how many Nazis (if any) EH actually killed. Gen. John F. Ruggles to author, Feb., 1966, said he had no doubt that EH killed a few German soldiers.

Sec. 59. The Road to Paris

SOURCES

Letters of EH: to Mary Welsh, Aug. 27, 1944; to Perkins, Oct. 15, 1944; to Hadley Mowrer, Apr. 24, 1945; to General R. O. Barton, Sept. 3, 1945; to Malcolm Cowley, July 5, 1948; to Lillian Ross, Aug. 9, 1950; to Bernard Berenson, March 21, 1953.
Other letters: John G. Westover to his wife, Oct. 15, 1944; Gene Currivan to EH, Jan. 8, 1959.
EH's work: Published: "Battle for Paris," *Collier's,* Vol. 114 (Sept. 30, 1944); "How We Came to Paris," *Collier's,* Vol. 114 (Oct. 7, 1944).
Books and articles: Col. David Bruce, Diary for Aug. 20–25, 1944 (unpublished); *Le Franc-Tireur,* Aug. 30, 1944; Robert Capa, *Slightly Out of Focus,* 1947; S. L. A. Marshall,

"How Papa Liberated Paris," *American Heritage,* Vol. 13 (April, 1962); Andy Rooney, "One Eye on the War, One on Paris," *Overseas Press Bulletin,* Aug., 1964; Françoise Gilot and Carlton Lake, *Life with Picasso,* 1964.

Author's interviews and correspondence: with Charles Ritz, Nov., 1965. From Ambassador David Bruce, Dec. 13, 1965; from Mrs. Robbins Milbank (Helen Kirkpatrick), Jan. 25, 1966; from Gen. S. L. A. Marshall, Feb. 16 and March 23, 1966; from John G. Westover, May 12, 1966.

NOTES

EH approaches Rambouillet: Col. David Bruce, diary entry for August 20, 1944. Hemingway, "Battle for Paris," *Collier's* 114 (Sept. 30, 1944), pp. 14, 65–67. Brig. Gen. S. L. A. Marshall to author, Feb. 16, 1966. Just before leaving for Maintenon, Ernest had paid a brief visit to the headquarters of the 2nd French Armored Division under Leclerc at the village of Ecouché near Argentan. A mixed company of American correspondents and minor French officials was bivouacked in an apple orchard at the edge of town. Among them were Helen Kirkpatrick of the *Chicago Daily News,* Irwin Shaw, a French film star named Claude Dauphin, Perry Miller, Emlen Etting, and Elizabeth de Miribelle, General DeGaulle's "girl Friday." They enjoyed "a banquet in mess tins with food bought from French peasants." There was a "lively argument" as to whether or not the lettuce should be washed, in which Hemingway served as arbiter. Helen Kirkpatrick washed it. (Mrs. Robbins Milbank to author, Jan. 25, 1966.)

Events of Aug. 19–20, 1944: EH, "Battle for Paris," *Collier's,* Vol. 114 (Sept. 30, 1944), pp. 14, 65–67. Gen. S. L. A. Marshall to author, Feb. 16, 1966.

Defense of Rambouillet: Col. David Bruce, diary entry for August 20, 1944. There are some discrepancies in contemporary testimony. According to an unpublished document by Major Thornton, dated 2 Oct., 1944, from SHAEF, IS 9 (WEA) G-2 Div., he had entered Rambouillet with a contingent of paratroopers on the 19th. On the 20th he advised Colonel Bruce that he might retire his men back to Jouy near Chartres, but Bruce dissuaded him. On the other hand Gen. S. L. A. Marshall speaks of "about fifteen American and Canadian paratroopers who had just been wandering around." Marshall to author, Feb. 16, 1966. According to Bruce's diary, "Major Thornton was most helpful and, with the French and Major Neave (a British officer), arranged to patrol the roads leading toward Paris. . . . Between Hemingway, Thornton, Neave, Gravey [G. W. Graveson], and myself, there was constant contact." EH's later report was that he said to Colonel Bruce: "Dave, I'm liable to get in an awful jam. [Please] give me a written order from you as head of OSS justifying me having these [Maquis] and taking them into Paris." Bruce scrawled an order in pencil, which Hemingway carried in his shirt pocket. Later he tore it up in Bruce's presence. EH to Malcolm Cowley, July 5, 1948. Bruce's password: diary entry, Aug. 20, 1944.

EH's room at the Grand Veneur: Ambassador David Bruce to author, Nov. 23, 1965. According to Bruce, he never saw EH carry or use a weapon. But "carbines and grenades were always close at hand" while the rooms occupied by both Bruce and EH "resembled portions of an arsenal." This was "because there was no other place safely to store these accumulations."

Arrival of correspondents at Rambouillet: Bruce, diary entry, Aug. 20, 1944; Robert Capa, *Slightly Out of Focus,* NY, 1947, pp. 168–169.

Antipathy of correspondents towards EH: Andy Rooney, "One Eye on the War, One on Paris," *Overseas Press Bulletin,* Aug., 1964. Rooney got the impression that EH "knew more about German gun and tank placements than any of the military assigned to the task."

Departure of correspondents: Col. David Bruce, diary entry for Aug. 21, 1944.

EH's later boasts about his Rambouillet operations: EH to Perkins, Oct. 15, 1944; EH to Gen. R. O. Barton, Sept. 3, 1945. Colonel Bruce's views appear in David Bruce to author, Dec. 13, 1965.

Interrogation of prisoners: Col. David Bruce, diary entry for Aug. 21, 1944. EH, "Battle for Paris," *Collier's,* Vol. 114 (Sept. 30, 1944), pp. 14, 65–67. Gene Currivan to EH, Jan. 8, 1959. Currivan added that his can opener wound was the only one he got "in the whole damn war except for wrenched knees" in a jeep accident in the Saar.

EH's marching song and Archie Pelkey: EH to Bernard Berenson, March 21, 1953.

Encounter with Leclerc: Col. David Bruce, diary entries for Aug. 22–23, 1944; EH, "How We Came to Paris," *Collier's,* Vol. 114 (Oct. 7, 1944), p .14.

Enroute to Paris: EH, "How We Came to Paris," *Collier's* 114 (Oct. 7, 1944), pp. 14, 65–66. S. L. A. Marshall, "How Papa Liberated Paris," *American Heritage,* Vol. 13 (April, 1962), pp. 94–95. Col. David Bruce, diary entry for August 24, 1944. There is some question as to whether the girl's name was Elena (Marshall) or Irene (Westover). EH to Lillian Ross, Aug. 9, 1950.

Entering Paris: Colonel Bruce's diary entry for August 25, 1944. Marshall, *op. cit.,* 101, whose account of the Spahi officer confirms that of Hemingway, except for the rank. Marshall calls him a major. Hemingway to Lillian Ross, Aug. 9, 1950. There are many discrepancies between Colonel Bruce's and Colonel Marshall's remembrances of the afternoon, as is not to be wondered at.

Inside Paris: Col. David Bruce, diary entry, Aug. 25, 1944. Charles Ritz to author, Nov. 12, 1965. EH to Malcolm Cowley, July 5, 1948. According to Marshall, he and Westover had meantime "taken over the [Hotel] Claridge" and "arrived at the Ritz" before the others in the party. They were met at the door by Charles Ritz himself, who presented Marshall with a Dunhill pipe. Marshall was having a drink when Westover came to him and said, "Ernest is here, just came in. Imagine, this morning I was just a lieutenant of artillery and tonight I introduce Hemingway to Ritz of the Ritz." (General S. L. A. Marshall to author, March 23, 1966.)

Celebrations and reunions: Gen. S. L. A. Marshall, "How Papa Liberated Paris," *American*

Heritage, Vol. 13 (Apr., 1962), p. 5. Mrs. Robbins Milbank to author, Jan. 25, 1966. EH to Mary Welsh, Aug. 27, 1944; EH to Hadley Mowrer, Apr. 24, 1945. *Le Franc-Tireur,* Aug. 30, 1944, p. 5. Inscribed copy of *Winner Take Nothing,* Princeton University Library, Sylvia Beach Collection.
EH hears from M. Chautard: EH to Hadley Mowrer, Apr. 24, 1945. There is another pleasant story, unfortunately apocryphal, that EH called on Picasso in the rue des Grands Augustins, only to find him absent. The concierge suggested that EH might like to leave a small gift for the master. EH returned with a box of hand grenades, marked "To Picasso from Hemingway." As soon as she had deciphered the stenciling on the box, the concierge ran away, refusing to return until the box had been removed. (Françoise Gilot and Carlton Lake, *Life with Picasso,* NY, 1964, p. 61.) In denying the truth of this story, Mary Hemingway added, "We saw Picasso a couple of times and I did a piece for *Time* on all the work P. had done during the war—big departures from previous work—about which the U.S. knew nothing. Once or twice we dined with him and Françoise in his local café." Mary Hemingway to author, July, 1968.
EH describes his exploits for Mary's benefit: EH to Mary Welsh, Aug. 27, 1944.

Sec. 60. *Under the Westwall*

SOURCES

Letters of EH: to Mary Welsh, Sept. 8, 1944; to Patrick Hemingway, Sept. 10; to Mary Welsh, Sept. 11, 13, and 15; to Patrick Hemingway, Sept. 15; to Mary Welsh, Sept. 23 and Sept. 24, 1944. To Gen. Charles T. Lanham, July 23, 1945. To Perkins, Nov. 7, 1946. To Malcolm Cowley, Apr. 13, 1948. To Lillian Ross, Sept. 18, 1949. To Gen. E. E. Dorman-O'Gowan, Nov. 10, 1950. To Bernard Berenson, Feb. 17 and March 21, 1953.
Other letters: J. D. Salinger to Whit Burnett, Sept. 9, 1944.
EH's work: (a) Unpublished: War-Diary, Sept. 2–18, 1944; short story, "A Room on the Garden Side," probably composed ca. 1956. **(b) Published:** "War in the Siegfried Line," *Collier's,* Vol. 114 (Nov. 18, 1944).
Books and articles: Voltaire, *Henriade,* in Works, ed. by Louis Moland, Vol. 8 (1881); John Groth, *Studio: Europe,* 1945; John Groth, introduction to reissue of *Men Without Women,* 1946; *Le Soir* (Brussels), Sept. 10, 1950; William S. Boice, *History of the 22nd Infantry Regiment,* ca. 1959; Gen. Charles T. Lanham, *Memoir* (unpublished), 1962–63; Cyrus Sulzberger, *The Resistentialists,* 1962; Mary Hemingway, Album Note to *Ernest Hemingway Reading,* Caedmon Record, TC 1185, 1965.
Author's interviews and correspondence: with Gen. Charles T. Lanham, June and Sept., 1965. From Gen. John F. Ruggles, Feb. 24, 1966; from General Lanham, March 14–22, 1968.

NOTES

EH and Mary reunited: Mary Hemingway, Album Note to *Ernest Hemingway Reading,*

Caedmon Record TC-1185, 1965; EH to Mary Welsh, Sept. 8, 1944.
EH's bodyguard, Jean Décan: Cyrus Sulzberger, *The Resistentialists,* NY, 1962, pp. 19–20.
EH's visit from André Malraux: account based on EH's unpublished short story, "A Room on the Garden Side [of the Hotel Ritz]" and EH to Bernard Berenson, Feb. 17, 1953.
EH meets Jerome Salinger: J. D. Salinger to Whit Burnett, Sept. 9, 1944.
Activities of 22nd Infantry Regiment, Aug. 31–Sept. 3, 1944: W. S. Boice, *Regimental History,* pp. 40–46.
Lanham's message to EH: General Lanham, *Memoir,* p. 9. Later allusions to it appear in EH to Lanham, July 23, 1945 and EH to Cowley, Apr. 13, 1948. The French King Henry IV had raised the siege of Arques against the armies of the Catholic League in 1589. His taunt (*"Pends-toi, brave Crillon; nous avons combattu à Arques et tu n'y étais pas"*) was made much of in Voltaire's *Henriade* (*Works,* ed. Louis Moland, 1881, Vol. 8, p. 204).
EH's cross-country trip after Lanham: EH, War-Diary, entries for Sept. 2–3, 1944, and EH to Lillian Ross, Sept. 18, 1949. EH's story of the encounter with the antitank gun may be true but was more likely invented. "Frankly," wrote General Lanham to author, March 14–22, 1968, "I doubt much of EH's account of this trip because he recounted nothing of this sort to me when he checked into my C.P. If any man—particularly an EH—had just been through such a series of events they would spill out when he got to his destination and saw the man [Lanham] who had prompted the trip. . . . I was particularly eager to know if he had encountered any Krauts of significance (in terms of numbers) behind us or along our route. He had not. He had seen what he thought were small bodies of Germans (couldn't be sure) far off on the horizon one or two times but had had no trouble making the run." In the fall of 1965, the author examined the entire road, a distance of roughly nine kilometers, and found only one place which could provide the sort of concealment which EH describes. This was a side road running southwest just outside Le Cateau near a railroad bridge, so situated as to command the bridge but not the rest of the road to Wassigny. EH told Bernard Berenson another story which seems to belong to this period and also to lack authenticity. It concerned a Frenchman named Boursier who had carefully emplaced a machine gun and wished to stay with it. *"Écouté, Boursier,"* said EH. *"Il faut retirer."* *"Merde,"* said Boursier. *"Je me trouve trés bien ici. Ma flanc est protégé par une colline. J'ai le mittrailleuse bien placé. Je me trouve enormement bien ici et je reste."* The dialogue reads like something Hemingway might have invented. Put into Spanish, it could easily have been said by someone like Primitivo in *For Whom the Bell Tolls.* It reflected, in any case, EH's admiration for the courage of the simple warrior, and he put into Boursier's mouth the "word of Cambronne" which echoed constantly, whether in French or English, through his own wartime utterance. EH later told E. E. Dorman-O'Gowan (Nov. 10, 1950) that running his gang of Free French fighters was just like playing cops and robbers. "They

used to call us the 60-day Indians and then the 90-day Indians and finally we were the D plus 105 Indians and then we were none."
EH leaves to rejoin 4th Infantry Division: EH, War-Diary, p. 5. Private Archie Pelkey had now been allowed to return as Hemingway's driver. After the liberation of Paris, he had been sent back to the motor pool. Thereupon he was smitten by despair, kept to himself, and wept often. He would neither work, obey orders, salute, nor say Sir. Even the divisional psychiatrist was helpless before his melancholia. Pelkey said that his whole life had been changed by his experiences with the French Forces of the Interior. If he could not be back with Papa, he had no wish but to die. So, at least, Hemingway recalled in a letter to Berenson, March 21, 1953. But Pelkey himself was surprised to learn of it when queried by the author.
EH in the Ardennes: EH, War-Diary, pp. 5–7; EH to Mary Welsh, Sept. 8, 1944.
EH in southern Belgium: War-Diary, pp. 10–15.
Arrival at Houffalize: General Lanham's *Memoir*, pp. 9–10. EH's War-Diary, pp. 15–17.
EH mistaken for a general: Lanham, p. 10. EH was never one to let go of a good story. He had used this one in a recent despatch (*Collier's*, Sept. 30, 1944, p. 67) identifying his interlocutor as a partisan at Rambouillet. Leicester Hemingway, *My Brother Ernest Hemingway*, Cleveland, 1962, pp. 254–255 says that the questioner was a staff officer of General Leclerc's. EH to Patrick Hemingway, Sept. 10; EH to Mary Welsh, Sept. 11 and Sept. 13, 1944.
Rebuilding of the bridge at Houffalize: EH, War-Diary, p. 17. Lanham, *Memoir*. The bridge served the American armies well for many weeks. A large part of the First Army crossed it from east to west, and traffic was heavy in both directions up to the Battle of the Bulge in December, when the structure was once more destroyed. Before leaving Houffalize at dawn on the 11th, Colonel Lanham thanked the citizens by letter, through their mayor, for the expeditious job. Six Septembers later, while serving as Chief of the Military Assistance Advisory Group for Belgium and Luxembourg, Lanham, then a general, was surprised and touched to open a Belgian newspaper which contained a story about a new bridge in Houffalize. A plaque on its parapet quoted Lanham's letter of September 11, 1944: "*Aux Citoyens de Houffalize. Avant l'arrivée des ingénieurs, vos adroits artisans ont construit un pont en quarante-cinq minutes.*" (*Le Soir*, Brussels, Sunday, September 10, 1950).
EH in Schirm and Maspelt: EH, War-Diary, pp. 20–21.
EH in Hemmeres: EH to Mary Welsh, September 13, 1944, Letter I. EH's War-Diary, pp. 21–24. William S. Boice, *History of the 22nd Infantry Regiment*, pp. 48–49. Lieut. Col. Arthur Teague was commander of the Third Battalion of the 22nd Regiment. Gen. (then Lieut. Col.) John F. Ruggles called Teague "the outstanding troop leader in the Fourth Infantry Division." General Ruggles to author, Feb. 24, 1966. General Lanham to author, March 14–22, 1968, calls him "the finest Battalion C.O. I had and perhaps the best I ever knew."

EH's chicken dinner: EH, War-Diary, pp. 24–25. EH to Mary Welsh, Sept. 13, 1944, Letter 1. General Lanham, *Memoir*, p. 14.
EH and the Brazilius: EH, War-Diary, pp. 26–27.
EH boasts of intelligence and "cojones": EH to Patrick Hemingway, Sept. 15, 1944.
EH misses attack on Westwall: General Lanham to author, Sept., 1965.
Terrain of Schnee Eifel: *22nd Regimental History*, pp. 50–51: General Lanham's *Memoir*; personal inspection by author.
Assault on the Westwall: EH, War-Diary, pp. 28–52. This concluding section of the diary is largely given over to EH's interview with Blazzard, which gave him the substance of his final article for *Collier's*, "War in the Siegfried Line," Vol. 114 (Nov. 18, 1944), pp. 18, 70–73. Back at Division, EH wrote about the assault on the basis of preliminary reports: EH to Mary Welsh and EH to Patrick Hemingway, both dated Sept. 15, 1944. EH's "Second Poem to Mary," written in Paris some weeks later, made much of the casualties of the 22nd Infantry Regiment in this engagement.
Groth reaches Schloss Hemingstein: Groth, "A Note on Ernest Hemingway," used as a preface to EH's illustrated edition of *Men Without Women*, Cleveland, 1946. A much longer account is in Groth's *Studio: Europe*, NY, 1945, pp. 202–238. This version is profusely illustrated with sketches by Groth dated September 23, 24, and 25, 1944. EH told Perkins that Groth behaved very well in the Schnee Eifel sector, proving himself honest, unselfish, and kind: EH to Perkins, Nov. 7, 1946.
Steak dinner interrupted by German 88: Lanham, *Memoir*, pp. 15–16; Groth, *Studio: Europe*, p. 214. The steaks, like all others enjoyed in combat zones, had come from an "artillery cow." It was always held to have stepped on a mine, cut its throat on barbed wire, or been killed by artillery. Hemingway jocosely told his son, Patrick, that he had the eye of an eagle for the fall of such a cow. If you marked the place on the map with coordinates, you could return the next day and butcher out the tenderloin. (EH to Patrick Hemingway, September 10, 1944.)
EH gives Mary Welsh the impression that he was present during the assault on the Westwall, and longs to be with her again: EH to Mary Welsh, Sept. 23, 1944. In his *Collier's* article he employed a similar approach: "We passed the unmanned old-fashioned pillboxes . . . and got up into good high ground that night. The next day we were past the second line of concrete fortified strong points . . . and that same night we were up on the highest of the high ground before the Westwall ready to assault in the morning. . . . Ahead of us was the dark forest where the dragon lived. . . . We were hitting it on the point that the Germans had chosen to prove, in sham battles, that it was impregnable." He could perhaps have justified the first person plural as an editorial "we" or as a reference to "our" American troops. Yet no one reading his letter or the article would have doubted that he was personally present during the assault. See "War in the Siegfried Line," *Collier's*, Vol. 114 (Nov. 18, 1944), p. 18.
EH hears rumors of possible investigation of

his activities at Rambouillet: EH to Mary Welsh, Sept. 23, 1944.
EH tries verse on battle in forest and characterizes self: EH to Mary Welsh, Sept. 24, 1944.

Sec. 61. Im Hürtgenwald

SOURCES

Letters of EH: to Col. C. T. Lanham, Oct. 8, 1944; to Gen. R. O. Barton, Oct. 8; to Perkins, Oct. 15; to Lanham, Oct. 17; to Patrick Hemingway, Nov. 19, 1944. To Gen. Charles T. Lanham, Jan. 20, 1946. To Malcolm Cowley, Aug. 25, 1948, and Feb. 10, 1949; to Lillian Ross, Sept. 18, 1949.
Other letters: Capt. H. J. Swanson to EH, Oct. 4, 1944; Grace Hall Hemingway to Scribners, Oct. 11; Lieut. John Westover to Mrs. Westover, Oct. 15; Martha Hemingway to EH, Nov. 3, 1944.
EH's work: (a) Unpublished: short story on EH's interrogation at Nancy, probably composed ca. 1956; *The Sea Chase*, composed 1951. **(b) Published:** *Across the River and into the Trees*, 1950; "Second Poem to Mary," *Atlantic*, Vol. 216 (Aug., 1965).
Books: William S. Boice, *History of the 22nd Infantry Regiment*, ca. 1959; Cyrus Sulzberger, *The Resistentialists*, 1962; General Lanham's *Memoir* (unpublished), 1962–63.
Author's interviews and correspondence: With William Walton, Apr., 1964; with John H. Hemingway, Aug., 1964. From Col. Earl W. Edwards, Feb. 5, 1962; from C. M. Henley, March 9, 1962; from Col. Thomas A. Kenan, June 25, 1962; from Col. James S. Luckett, Nov. 8, 1962. From H. W. R. North, Apr. 12, 1963; from Gen. Charles T. Lanham, Sept. 25, 1963; from Michael Burke, Dec. 30, 1965; from Lael Tucker Wertenbaker, Jan. 7, 1966; from David E. Scherman, March 18, 1966; from John Westover, May 12 and May 23, 1966; from Gen. John F. Ruggles, June 22, 1966; from Gen. C. T. Lanham, March 14–22, 1968; from Mary Hemingway, July, 1968.

NOTES

EH's interrogation orders: Capt. H. J. Swanson to EH, Oct. 4, 1944.
Investigation of EH by Inspector General, Third Army: EH to General Barton and EH to Colonel Lanham, both dated Oct. 8, 1944. A later letter to Lanham is dated Jan. 20, 1946. An unpublished and untitled short story by EH tells of lunch with General Patton before departing for Nancy, the interview with Colonel Park, and the return to Paris. Although EH did not know it, his mother wrote Scribners on Oct. 11 to ask for his address in the ETO: she wanted to send him a Christmas box.
Martha at Nijmegen: Lieut. John Westover to Mrs. Westover, Oct. 15, 1945; Westover to author, May 12 and May 23, 1966.
EH's bitterness: EH to Lanham, Oct. 17, 1944.
EH and his Bearded Junior Commandos: H. W. R. North to author, April 12, 1963. Michael Burke to author, December 30, 1965. Ernest's singular pride in his poems at this period is also attested by David Bruce, who

watched Hemingway drink himself into a state of unconsciousness one night in Paris. As he approached the blackout stage, he began to extract soiled and crumpled scraps of paper from his pocket, identifying them as his "pomes." Bruce said that he had not known Ernest was a poet. Ernest said that in fact he was a damned good poet. Bruce offered to have the poems properly typed, but Ernest replied that they were too personal for anyone else to see. (Gen. C. T. Lanham to author, Sept. 25, 1963, reporting on a conversation with Ambassador David Bruce in Washington, D.C., on September 24.) Ernest was not always so shy about his poems. One afternoon at the Ritz when Mary was not present, he read some of his more serious efforts to Lael and Charles Wertenbaker and Bill Walton. Both his reading and the substance of the verses moved his hearers. Then the "bad boy" phase set in. From the same pocket five minutes later Ernest plucked another poem which he read aloud to the same company. It was a scurrilous attack on his wife Martha. He thought it very funny and watched his listeners narrowly to see if they agreed. They did not. (Lael Tucker Wertenbaker to author, Jan. 7, 1966.)
EH's "Second Poem to Mary": The poem was published along with "To Mary in London" in the *Atlantic*, Vol. 216 (August, 1965), pp. 96–100. Other relevant allusions are in EH to Lanham, Oct. 17, 1944; EH to Lillian Ross, Sept. 18, 1949, and David E. Scherman to author, March 18, 1966.
EH hopes to write novel of Land, Sea, and Air: EH to Perkins, Oct. 15, 1944. This is the earliest allusion I have found to the big book to which he referred so often in 1951–54. *Across the River and into the Trees* (composed 1949) and a few short stories largely siphoned off his experience with the infantry. *The Sea Chase* (composed 1951) covered his sub-hunting adventures. He wrote no fiction about his flights with the RAF, though many letters allude to it, often misleadingly.
EH reaches Hürtgenwald: Col. Thomas A. Kenan to author, June 25, 1962.
Reunion with Colonel Lanham: Lanham's *Memoir*, p. 22.
Capture of EH's son John: John H. Hemingway to author, Aug. 2, 1964.
Martha asks for a divorce: on Nov. 3, 1944, Martha Hemingway wrote Ernest, suggesting that they be divorced.
EH's premonition of the death of the major: Gen. Lanham, *Memoir*, pp. 23–24. **Hürtgen campaign:** Boice, *History of the 22nd Infantry Regiment;* pp. 57–60; General Lanham's *Memoir*, pp. 24–25; Gen. John F. Ruggles to author, June 22, 1966.
EH's conduct among the officers: Col. E. W. Edwards to author, Feb. 5, 1962.
EH on religion and psychiatry: General Lanham's *Memoir*, p. 44. On this or another occasion, Dr. Maskin was discoursing about the nature of battle fatigue when Hemingway interrupted witheringly: "Dr. Maskin, you know everything about fuckoffs and nothing about brave men." (General Lanham's *Memoir*, p. 48.) William Walton, who was also present, traced some at least of Hemingway's scornful treatment of Maskin to anti-Semitism. The evening's debate, as he recalled it, was gross and cruel, both towards the doctor him-

self and the whole psychiatric brotherhood. It ended when the well-drubbed doctor shook a finger at Hemingway and predicted, "You'll be coming to me yet." (William Walton to author, Apr. 2, 1964.) The prediction was fulfilled at the Mayo Brothers Clinic in Rochester, Minnesota in 1960–61. In this way, unhappily, Hemingway fulfilled a prediction of his own, often voiced to friends in these days; whatever we say we will never do we are sure to do sooner or later. (EH to Lanham, Oct. 17, 1944.)
EH as senior counselor: Col. Thomas A. Kenan to author, June 25, 1962.
EH and Swede Henley: C. M. Henley to author, March 9, 1962. In fact, said General Lanham, EH went back to Divisional headquarters every night. EH told Malcolm Cowley a curious story about the gray Kraut sheeplined vest which he wore for warmth. One night in Hürtgen he took a fountain pen and drew pictures of all his decorations at the proper place over the heart. Then, on the right side, he listed the battles in which he had participated up to that time. Finally, he inked out all his handiwork, telling others that he was camouflaging the vest. (EH to Malcolm Cowley, Feb. 10, 1949.)
EH in Lanham's trailer: General Lanham, *Memoir*, p. 41.
German attack repulsed by EH and others: General Lanham's *Memoir*, pp. 26–27; Gen. John F. Ruggles to author, June 22, 1966; Cyrus Sulzberger, *The Resistentialists*, NY, 1962, pp. 26–27. A rumor had recently been circulating in London that EH had been taken prisoner about Nov. 10th. This may have resulted from confusion of names with his son Bumby, who had been captured October 28th. On Nov. 24, SHAEF issued a statement that EH was still hard at work as correspondent with the First Army. *New York Times*, Nov. 25, 1944, p. 7.
American artillery bombards American forward positions: General Lanham's *Memoir*, pp. 28–29; Gen. John F. Ruggles to author, June 22, 1966; Col. James S. Luckett to author, Nov. 8, 1962. Colonel Luckett believed that the entire Hürtgen operation was stupidly conceived, "since it would have been relatively simple to bypass this dank, dark, muddy mass of mines, prepared positions, and prepared fireplans for mortars and artillery."
Situation at Grosshau: General Lanham's *Memoir*, p. 37. EH used the flattened GI and the roasted German in *Across the River and into the Trees*, NY, 1950, p. 257. In one of Colonel Cantwell's recollections, a soldier says, "Sir, there is a dead GI in the middle of the road up ahead, and I'm afraid it is making a bad impression on the troops." And again: "We had put an awful lot of white phosphorus on the town [Grosshau] before we got it for good. . . . That was the first time I ever saw a German dog eating a roasted German Kraut. Later on I saw a cat working on him too. It was a hungry cat, quite nice looking, basically. You wouldn't think a good German cat would eat a good German soldier. . . . Or a good German dog eat a good German soldier's ass which had been roasted by white phosphorus." The first passage is characteristic of Hemingway's early habit of understatement. The second overdoes the event and commentary, and may

even reflect a kind of show-off delight in the elaboration of horror.
EH in Grosshau: General Lanham, *Memoir*, pp. 37–38. William Walton to author, Apr. 2, 1964.
Early morning German counterattack on Lanham's decimated regiment: General Lanham, *Memoir*, pp. 34–35.
Casualties, 22nd Infantry Regiment, Hürtgenwald: *History of the 22nd Infantry Regiment* p. 107. EH later estimated that American casualties in this campaign approximated those of the Union Army at Gettysburg. (EH to Malcolm Cowley, Aug. 25, 1948.)
EH and Walton strafed by Luftwaffe: William Walton to author, Apr. 2, 1964.

Sec. 62. Paris Command Post

SOURCES

Letters of EH: to Mary Welsh, ca. late Jan., 1945; to Gen. Charles T. Lanham, Feb. 14, ca. late Feb., and March 2, 1945; to Mary Welsh, March 5; to Gen. R. O. Barton, Sept. 3, 1945. To Barton, June 9, 1948. To Charles Scribner, Nov. 1, 1950. To Harvey Breit, Apr. 16, 1952. To R. M. Brown, Aug. 8, 1956.
Other documents: Mary Welsh's Diaries, entries of Dec., 1944.
EH's work: Published: "Second Poem to Mary," *Atlantic*, Vol. 216 (Apr., 1965).
Books: Leicester Hemingway, *My Brother, Ernest Hemingway*, 1962; General Lanham, *Memoir*, 1962–63 (unpublished); Malcolm Cowley, *The Faulkner-Cowley File*, 1966.
Author's interviews and correspondence: with William Walton, Apr., 1962; with John H. Hemingway, August, 1964. From Gen. H. W. Blakely, Nov. 30, 1961; from Gen. R. O. Barton, March 30, 1962; from Col. James S. Luckett, Nov. 8, 1962; from Gen. Charles T. Lanham, Aug. 20, 1963, and Apr. 5, 1964; from Mary Hemingway, Oct. 1, 1964; from Air Marshal Sir Peter Wykeham, Aug. 30, 1965; from William Saroyan, Dec. 30, 1965; from Air Marshal Sir Peter Wykeham, Jan. 6, 1966; from Gen. John F. Ruggles, June 22, 1966; from Gen. Charles T. Lanham, March 14–22, 1968; from Mary Hemingway, July, 1968.

NOTES

EH plans return to U.S.A. in Dec., 1944: General Lanham to author, Aug. 20, 1963.
Visit from Sartre: Leicester Hemingway, *My Brother, Ernest Hemingway*, Cleveland, 1962, pp. 261–262.
EH tells Sartre that Faulkner is the better writer: Malcolm Cowley, *The Faulkner-Cowley File*, NY, 1966, p. 29.
EH on his illness: EH to Gen. R. O. Barton, Sept. 3, 1945. But he told Cowley (June 28, 1948) that his long period of impotence ended after his return from Hürtgen. His illness is also described in Leicester Hemingway, pp. 259–260.
Battle of the Bulge (Von Rundstedt's winter offensive): Gen. R. O. Barton to author, March 20, 1962. According to General Lanham, "the German effort against the 4th Division was not major. The main effort was to the north of us. There was no fighting to the south of us." Lanham to author, March 14–22, 1968.

EH telephones Barton: Barton to author, March 20, 1962. In a letter to Charles Scribner (Nov. 1, 1950), EH said that Barton had telephoned him from Luxembourg, asking him to come up with his squad of partisans. This does not square with Barton's testimony.
EH secures jeep and driver from General O'Hare: EH to Barton, Sept. 3, 1945; EH to Scribner, Nov. 1, 1950.
EH reaches Luxembourg: Barton to author, March 20, 1962.
EH put to bed in Lanham's C.P. at Rodenbourg: William Walton to author, Apr. 2, 1964; General Lanham's *Memoir*.
EH and the sacramental wine: EH to Scribner, Nov. 1, 1950; EH to R. M. Brown, Aug. 8, 1956; William Walton to author, April 2, 1964.
EH and Luckett watch attack in Müllerthal: Colonel Luckett to author, Nov. 8, 1962.
EH gathers data for "Life" articles: EH to Barton, June 9, 1948.
Martha reaches Luxembourg: Gen. John F. Ruggles to author, June 22, 1966, and Gen. Lanham's *Memoir*, Addendum.
EH attends Barton's Christmas dinner: Gen. H. W. Blakely to author, Nov. 30, 1961; General Barton to author, March 20, 1962; General Lanham's *Memoir*, Addendum.
Colonel Luckett's outburst: Colonel Luckett to author, Nov. 8, 1962. Apropos of this matter, EH wrote Barton (June 9, 1948) that he himself had only two real gifts. He could fight without worrying and he was loyal. They had all been beat-up after Hürtgen Forest and some of them "behaved different than others." But the way Barton behaved about Jim Luckett on that "awful night" of the Christmas dinner was, said EH, the most exemplary behavior by a commanding officer that he had ever seen. EH was not feeling "too hot" at the dinner because he thought that Buck Lanham should have been invited. Furthermore, he liked Jim Luckett. But Barton had been "damned good" when Luckett sounded off.
Lanham's Christmas morning tour with EH and Martha: Lanham's *Memoir*, Addendum. Another source wishes to remain anonymous.
Walton meets Martha in Luxembourg, with EH's vengeful behavior: William Walton to author, April, 1964.
EH lends pistol to Orwell: EH to Harvey Breit, Apr. 16, 1952. EH added that his favorite books by Orwell were *Burmese Days, Homage to Catalonia, Animal Farm, 1984,* and *Down and Out in Paris and London.*
Saroyan encounters EH: Saroyan to author, Dec. 20, 1965.
The brawl at the Hôtel George V: Air Marshal Sir Peter Wykeham to author, Aug. 30, 1965. Although Saroyan (to author, Dec. 20, 1965) could not recall any such fight, Sir Peter was equally certain that it happened. (Wykeham to author, Jan. 6, 1966.) It is possible that Saroyan had left before the brawl began.
Bumby wounded and captured: John H. Hemingway to author, Aug. 2, 1964.
EH learns of his safety: EH to Lanham, Feb. 14, 1945. In March, Bumby escaped and was again recaptured. He was finally liberated at Muisberg.
EH defines sweating out: "Second Poem to Mary, *"Atlantic,* Vol. 216 (August, 1965.)
EH shoots up Ritz bathroom: EH to Lanham,

March 2, 1945; Lanham to author, Apr. 5, 1964.
Lanham meets Marlene Dietrich: Lanham to author, Apr. 2, 1964.
Walton meets Marlene Dietrich: Walton to author, Apr. 2, 1964.
EH criticizes Walton and Barton: EH to Lanham, late February, 1945. Browning's poem had been composed almost exactly a century before, and was critical of Wordsworth for his alleged political apostasy. The lines Hemingway parodied are the first two: "Just for a handful of silver he left us,/Just for a riband to stick in his coat." Neither the original nor the parody was justified by the facts. General Barton had been relieved of his divisional command on Dec. 26, 1944, owing to persistent illness.
EH's last days in Paris: EH to Lanham, March 2, 1945; EH to Mary, March 5, 1945.
EH pays call on Martha in London: Source wishes to remain anonymous.

Sec. 63. The View from Finca Vigía

SOURCES

Letters of EH: to Perkins, March 16, 1945; to Charles T. Lanham, Apr. 2; to Mary Welsh, April 9, 10, 11, 13, 14, 16, 17, 18, 19, and 20; to Lanham, Apr. 20; to Hadley Mowrer, Apr. 24; to T. J. Welsh, June 19; to Mary Welsh, ca. June 20 and ca. June 21; to Lanham, June 30; to T. O. Bruce, July 18; to Perkins, July 23; to T. O. Bruce, Aug. 2; to Lanham, Aug. 9; to Mary Welsh, Sept. 1, ca. Sept. 3; to Raymond O. Barton, Sept. 3; to Mary Welsh, Sept. 4, 9, 13, 22, 25, 26, 27, 28, and 29; to Perkins, Oct. 31; to Lanham, Dec. 7, 22, and 31, 1945.
Other letters: Mary Welsh to Gen. and Mrs. Charles T. Lanham, ca. June 30, 1945; Mary Welsh to Lanham, Aug. 29, 1945; Gen. R. O. Barton to EH, Sept. 19, 1945.
EH's work: Published: introduction to John Groth, *Studio: Europe,* 1945; foreword to *A Treasury for the Free World,* edited by Ben Raeburn, 1946.
Books and articles: none.
Author's interviews and correspondence: with Gustavo Durán, Feb., 1962; with Gen. Charles T. Lanham, Apr., 1964; with John H. Hemingway, Aug., 1964. From Mrs. Charles T. Lanham, June 1, 1964, and May 10, 1966.

NOTES

EH returns to the Finca Vigía: EH to Perkins, March 16, and EH to Lanham, Apr. 2, 1945. EH recalls the period also in EH to Lanham, Aug. 9, 1945.
EH's April activities: EH to Mary Welsh, Apr. 9, 10, 11, and 17, 1945.
Mary telephones from New York: EH to Mary Welsh, Apr. 13, 1945.
Dr. Herrera examines EH: EH to Mary Welsh, Apr. 14, 1945.
EH prepares for Mary's arrival: EH to Mary Welsh, Apr. 16, 18, 19, and 20, 1945.
EH insults Gustavo Durán: Gustavo Durán to author, Feb. 26, 1962.
EH justifies his return home: EH to Lanham, Apr. 20, 1945. This letter also alludes to Franklin D. Roosevelt's death. EH's curious remark that he might have ended as "a bum" if he had not returned home when he did

sounds like an echo of the advice given him by Agnes von Kurowsky in 1918, when she urged him to go back to Oak Park instead of staying on in Italy with Jim Gamble.

Mary's arrival: EH to Lanham, June 30, 1945. Mary Welsh to General and Mrs. Lanham, ca. June 30, 1945.

Bumby arrives to recuperate: EH to Lanham, June 30, 1945. Bumby is also mentioned in the Log of the *Pilar* (June 2–9, 1945). He had argued the German surgeons out of amputating his right arm and they had repaired the wound by removing a muscle from the back of one shoulder. He said that this helped to loosen his tennis service and increased his skill in flycasting.

EH and Mary hurt in car accident: two notes from EH to Mary, ca. June 20–21, 1945, while she was in the private clinic: EH to Lanham, June 30; EH to T. O. Bruce, July 18; EH to Perkins, July 23; EH to T. O. Bruce, Aug. 2, 1945.

EH outlines his changing religious views: EH to Thomas J. Welsh, June 19, 1945.

EH's substitute for orthodox religion: EH to Mary Welsh, ca. Sept. 3 and Sept. 4, 1945.

EH writes introduction for John Groth: Groth, *Studio: Europe*, NY, 1945, pp. 7–9. The introduction was dated from San Francisco de Paula, Aug. 25, 1945. On receiving the finished book early in December, Ernest privately complained that it was full of horrible crap and lavish praising lies about his exploits in the Schnee Eifel. He held (quite falsely) that Groth had inserted the praise in galley proof after he himself had passed on it, out of gratitude for his kindness in agreeing to write the introduction. Reading it, said he, had made him "sick for a week." EH to Lanham, Dec. 7, 1945. But this was sophistry. In succeeding years he would make similar pronouncements about other books and articles whose authors he had assisted. This happened with Malcolm Cowley's article in *Life* and Lillian Ross's profile in *The New Yorker*.

Mary flies to Chicago: EH to Mary Welsh, Sept. 1, 1945. In this letter, EH included a flood of early recollections for Mary's information: boyhood trips to Chicago theaters with his grandfather Anson, high-school football games and swimming meets; visits to the Chicago Art Institute; his stay at Y. K. Smith's apartment on the Near North Side; crap games with Jack Pentecost; visits to Hinky Dink's, a German beer cellar, and to Wurz 'n' Zepp's; and some account of his ancestry. This was continued in EH to Mary, Sept. 13, 1945. Much of what he said was true, but much was also invented.

EH's exchange with General Barton: EH to Barton, Sept. 3 and Barton to EH, Sept. 19, 1945.

Visit to the Finca by General and Mrs. Lanham: EH to Mary Welsh, Sept. 13, 22, 25, 26, 27, 28, and 29, 1945; General Lanham to author, Apr., 1964; Mrs. Lanham to author, June 1, 1964, and May 10, 1966.

EH on the state of his health and spirits: EH to Mary Welsh, Sept. 9 and Sept. 27, 1945.

EH writes foreword for another anthology: *A Treasury for the Free World*, edited by Ben Raeburn, NY, 1946, pp. xiii–xv, datelined from San Francisco de Paula, Sept., 1945.

EH sells short stories to films: EH to Lanham, Dec. 7, 1945. He thought of this as a harvest. In EH to Perkins, Oct. 31, 1945, he had mentioned the productivity of sixty trees he had set out, and of the alligator pears, sugar apples, soursops, sapadillos, lichees, tamarinds, figs, almonds, mameys, coconuts, and bananas that the Finca provided him.

EH helps Jean Décan: EH to Lanham, Dec. 22 and Dec. 31, 1945.

Sec. 64. *The Nettle and the Flower*

SOURCES

Letters of EH: to Lambert Davis, May 7, 1940. To Harford Powel, Jan. 12, 1946; to Charles T. Lanham, Jan. 20; to Patrick Hemingway, Jan. 21; to Mary Welsh, Jan. 24; to Charles Scribner, Jan. 28; to Patrick and Gregory Hemingway, Feb. 14; to Lanham, Feb. 21 and March 12; to Patrick and Gregory, March 28; to Perkins, Apr. 28; to Patrick and Gregory, May 16; to Konstantin Simonov, June 20; to Lanham, June 30, July 14, and July 20; to Milton Wolff, July 26; to Lanham, Aug. 25, Aug. 28, and Sept. 7; to T. O. Bruce, Sept. 26; to Perkins, Oct. 4; to Lanham, Oct. 10; to Perkins, Oct. 23; to Lanham, Nov. 2; to Perkins, Nov. 7; to T. O. Bruce, Nov. 9; to Perkins, Nov. 18 and Nov. 22; to Lanham, Nov. 28, Dec. 23–24, 1946, and Jan. 19, 1947.

Other letters: Konstantin Simonov to EH, June 26, 1946; J. D. Salinger to EH, July 27; Col. Charles Sweeny to Max Perkins, Nov. 18, 1946.

EH's work: Unpublished: *The Garden of Eden*, a novel.

Articles: Mary Hemingway, "The Man I Married: Ernest Hemingway," *Today's Woman*, Vol. 27 (Feb., 1963); Helen Markel, "A Look Back, A Look Ahead," *Good Housekeeping*, Vol. 156 (Feb., 1963); Charlotte Curtis, "Gardiners Island, A Family Refuge," *New York Times*, Sept. 8, 1964.

Author's interviews and correspondence: with Gen. Charles T. Lanham, Sept., 1964; with Waldo Peirce, June, 1966. From Michael Blankfort, June 8, 1963; from Ellis O. Briggs, Feb. 27, 1964; from Milton Wolff, Oct. 5, 1964; from Mary Hemingway, May 20 and May 27, 1966.

NOTES

EH praises Lanham—and himself: The statement on Lanham was meant for publication and was made in a letter, EH to Harford Powel, Jan. 12, 1946. It was to be used in connection with some articles by Lanham in a nationally circulated magazine.

Activities at the Finca: EH to Patrick Hemingway, Jan. 21, 1946; EH to Mary Welsh, Jan. 24; EH to Scribner, Jan. 28; EH to Patrick and Gregory Hemingway, Feb. 14; EH to Lanham, Feb. 21 and March 12; EH to Patrick and Gregory, March 28; EH to Perkins, Apr. 28, 1946.

Marriage of EH and Mary: Mary Hemingway to author, May 27, 1966. EH's old friend Waldo Peirce was also married for the fourth time on the same day in New York. Like Mary Welsh, Ellen Peirce had been born in Minnesota. Waldo Peirce to author, June 2, 1966. Winston Guest and the Richard Coopers gave Mary a set of table silver. She had it engraved with a specially devised hiero, made up of an arrangement of mountains, arrows, and military insignia. The mountains represented the three mountains of Paris. The arrows represented the Indians whom Mary and Ernest had known in Minnesota and Michigan. A double bar below saluted Bumby's attainment of the rank of captain, as well as the assimilated rank of Mary and Ernest as war correspondents.

EH begins "The Garden of Eden": Mary Hemingway generously supplied the author with a carbon typescript prepared from EH's lengthy manuscript. EH's fascination with hair was a special psychic quirk. According to Mary, his interest in the sexual connotations of hair was all the greater because he thought it the one part of a woman's anatomy that could be changed for fun and without permanent damage. (Mary Hemingway to author, May 20, 1966.) He admired Jean Harlow's platinum blond coronal, and she appeared in Robert Jordan's erotic daydreams in *For Whom the Bell Tolls,* Chapter Eleven. Some of his letters to Mary in May, 1947, mentioned below, urged her to change her hair color to ash blond or red as a surprise for him on her return from Chicago.

EH's progress with his new novel: EH to Lanham, Jan. 20, 1946. EH to Patrick and Gregory Hemingway, Feb. 14; EH to Perkins, Apr. 28; EH to Lanham, July 14 and July 20, 1946.

EH advertises his martial exploits: EH to Konstantin Simonov, June 20, 1946, printed in full in *Soviet Literature,* No. 11 (1962), pp. 165–167. Simonov was making a two-month tour of the U.S.A. with Ilya Ehrenburg and Mihail Galaktionov. He sent one of his books to EH, who promptly invited them to the Finca. They were unable to come. Simonov's reply (June 26, 1946) was sent from Boston as he was about to leave for home. Another reminder of the war came in an amusing letter from young J. D. Salinger in Occupied Germany with his CIC Detachment. Salinger facetiously explained his temporary hospitalization in Nürnberg as an attempt to find a nurse who resembled Catherine Barkley. He had managed to accomplish some writing, including part of a play about a boy named Holden Caulfield and his sister Phoebe. The stage, said Salinger, had fascinated him ever since he had played the role of Raleigh in R. C. Sherriff's romantic war drama, *Journey's End.* When the play was done he proposed to act the part of Holden, suitably disguised with crew-cut hair and a Max Factor belly dimple, and to persuade Margaret O'Brien to do the part of Phoebe. Although he had written two more of his "incestuous" short stories, his plans for a book had temporarily collapsed. But he recalled that his talks with Ernest in Europe had given him his only hopeful minutes of the entire war, and named himself national chairman of the Hemingway Fan Clubs. (J. D. Salinger to EH, July 27, 1946.) EH's letter to Milton Wolff of July 26, 1946, appeared in full in *American Dialog,* Vol. 1 (October–November, 1964), pp. 12–13.

Mary's pregnancy: EH to Lanham, July 20, 1946. EH said he hoped for a daughter, who would be named Brigit. Mary hoped the child would inherit EH's eyes, legs, and brains—an ideal legacy for any daughter. Mary Hemingway to Helen Markel, as reported in "A Look Back, A Look Ahead," *Good Housekeeping,* Vol. 156 (Feb., 1963), p. 36.

Plans for Sun Valley: EH to Lanham, July 20, 1946.

Mary's illness in Casper: EH to Lanham, Aug. 25, Aug. 28, and Sept. 7, 1946; EH to T. O. Bruce, Sept. 26, 1946; EH to Perkins, Oct. 4, 1946. Mary Hemingway, "The Man I Married," Ernest Hemingway," *Today's Woman,* Vol. 27 (Feb., 1953), p. 48.

Sun Valley visit: EH to Lanham, Oct. 10 and Nov. 2, 1946; EH to Perkins, Oct. 23, 1946.

EH rewrites Hotspur speech: EH to Lanham, Nov. 2, 1946. Hotspur's metaphor occurs in a soliloquy, *Henry IV, Part I,* Act. II, sc. iii, line 10.

EH's near accident with shotgun: EH to Lanham, Nov. 2; EH to Perkins, Nov. 7; EH to T. O. Bruce, Nov. 9, 1946.

Trip to New York: EH to T. O. Bruce, Nov. 9; EH to Perkins, Nov. 7 and Nov. 18; Col. Charles Sweeny to Perkins, Nov. 18; EH to Perkins, Nov. 22; EH to Lanham, Nov. 28, 1946.

Plans for visit to Gardiners Island: EH to Lanham, Nov. 28, 1946. The island is well described by Charlotte Curtis, *New York Times,* Sept. 8, 1964, pp. 31 and 58. EH to Lanham, Dec. 23, 1946, is a reminiscence of the visit.

Lanham comes to New York: Gen. Charles T. Lanham to author, Sept., 1964.

Visit to Gardiners Island: EH to Lanham, Dec. 23–24, 1946 and Jan. 19, 1947; Lanham to author, Sept., 1964; Ellis O. Briggs to author, Feb. 27, 1964.

EH visits "Daily Worker" offices: from an undated anonymous memorandum, forwarded to author by Milton Wolff, Oct. 5, 1964. It is impossible to vouch for the authenticity of this account, but it is probably what happened.

EH and Michael Blankfort: Blankfort to author, June 8, 1963. EH's letter to Lambert Davis, Blankfort's editor, was dated May 7, 1940.

Sec. 65. Eden Invaded

SOURCES

Letters of EH: to Perkins, ca. Jan. 15, and Feb. 11, 1947; to Lanham, Feb. 19, March 28, and March 30; to Mary Hemingway, Apr. 11, 18, 19, and 28; to Perkins, Apr. 28; to Mary, May 1, 2, 6, 9, 11, 14, and 15; to Lanham, May 24 and June 21; to Mary, June 26; to Charles Scribner, June 28; to Lanham, July 1; to Mary, July 5; to Lanham, July 16 and Sept. 3; to Scribner, Sept. 18 and 20; to Mary, October 2–4; to Scribner, Oct. 29; to Lanham, Nov. 24, Nov. 27, and Dec. 28, 1947. To Scribner, Jan. 3, 1948; to Malcolm Cowley, Feb. 18; to Lanham, Feb. 18; to Lillian Ross, Feb. 21; to Scribner, Apr. 5; to Cowley, Apr. 9 and 13; to Scribner, June 2, 3, and 12; to Lanham, June 12; to Cowley, June 25; to Lanham, June 26; to Cowley, June 28; to Lillian Ross, July 2; to Scribner, July 28; to Lanham, July 28; to Lillian Ross, July 28; to Scribner, Aug. 8, 13, and 25; to Lanham, Aug. 25, 1948. To author, Feb. 24, 1951.

Other letters: Pauline Hemingway to Mary Hemingway, Apr. 18, 1947; Pauline Hemingway to Barklie Henry, ca. May 16, 1947; Mary Hemingway to Gen. C. T. Lanham, May 24–25, 1947; General Lanham to William Faulkner, June 24, 1947; Charles Scribner to EH, June 25, 1947; William Faulkner to General Lanham, June 28, 1947; William Faulkner to EH, June 28, 1947. Mary Hemingway to Clara Spiegel, Jan. 31, 1948.

EH's work: (a) Unpublished: recording of speech for the Veterans of the Abraham Lincoln Brigade, Feb., 1947. **(b) Published:** introduction to illustrated edition of *A Farewell to Arms,* 1948.

Books and articles: Harvey Breit, "A Walk with Faulkner," *New York Times Book Review,* Jan. 30, 1955; Mary Hemingway, "Papa —The Finca Vigía Years," Aug. 26, 1961 (unpublished); Lillian Ross, *Reporting,* 1964; A. E. Hotchner, *Papa Hemingway,* 1966; Malcolm Cowley, *The Faulkner-Cowley File,* 1966. **Author's interviews and correspondence:** with Mrs. E. J. Miller, July, 1964; with Mr. and Mrs. L. S. Weaver, July, 1964; with Lloyd Arnold, July, 1964; with T. O. Bruce, March, 1965; with Dr. Gregory Hemingway, March, 1965; with Patrick Hemingway, Dec., 1965. From Irving Fajans, ca. June 15, 1965; from Lloyd Arnold, Nov. 30, 1965.

NOTES

EH states theme of "The Garden of Eden": EH to Lanham, June 12, 1948.
Patrick stays on at the Finca: EH to Perkins, ca. Jan. 15 and Feb. 11, 1947. EH was agitated only by a buildup of algae in the swimming pool and a visit from his British publisher, Jonathan Cape. Perkins helped him with both problems. EH also went to Havana to record a speech to be played at the reunion of the Lincoln Brigade on Lincoln's Birthday. He addressed the veterans as a "distinguished company of premature anti-Fascists," and said that the United Nations offered the sole hope of world peace. (Recording generously supplied to author by Irving Fajans, ca. June 15, 1965.) EH described his day-to-day life in letters to Lanham on Feb. 19, March 28, and March 30, 1947.
Patrick's concussion: Pauline Hemingway to Barklie Henry, ca. May 16, 1947; EH to Mary Hemingway, April 11, 1947; EH to Perkins, Apr. 28, 1947; Dr. Gregory Hemingway to author, March, 1965; Patrick Hemingway to author, Dec., 1965.
Mary goes to Chicago; EH nurses Patrick; Pauline comes to Finca: Pauline to Mary, Apr. 18, 1947; EH to Mary, April 18, 19, and 28; May 2, 9, and 11, 1947; EH to Perkins, Apr. 28, 1947.
EH urges Mary to dye her hair and experiments with his own: EH to Mary, May 1, 2, 6, 9, 14, and 15, 1947.
Friendship of Mary and Pauline: EH to Lanham, May 24, 1947.
EH's durability: Mary Hemingway to General Lanham, May 24–25, 1947.
Contretemps with William Faulkner: General Lanham to Faulkner, June 24; Faulkner to Lanham, June 28; Faulkner to EH, June 28, 1947. The clearest explanation of his meaning was given by Faulkner to Harvey Breit some years later: "When I talked about Hemingway being a coward, I had in mind this dream of perfection and how the best contemporary

writers failed to match it. I was asked the question . . . who were the best contemporary writers and how did I rate them. And I said Wolfe, Hemingway, Dos Passos, Caldwell, and myself. I rated Wolfe first, myself second. I put Hemingway last. I said we were all failures. All of us had failed to match the dream of perfection and I rated the authors on the basis of their splendid failure to do the impossible. . . . I rated Hemingway last because he stayed with what he knew. He did it fine, but he didn't try for the impossible." (Harvey Breit, "A Walk with Faulkner," *New York Times Book Review,* Jan. 30, 1955, p. 4.)

EH awarded Bronze Star: NY Times, June 14, 1947. EH pretended to be irked because the citation did not mention his exploits around Rambouillet. He also called it a "cooks and bakers medal." He professed not to know who had recommended him for it, though he had helped General Barton to initiate the recommendation in the fall of 1945. He told Lanham that he had always wanted the Nobel Prize. EH to Lanham, June 21 and July 1, 1947; EH to Mary Hemingway, June 26, 1947.
Death of Max Perkins: Scribner to EH, June 25; EH to Scribner, June 28, 1947.
EH sends Mary to Key West: EH to Lanham, June 21; EH to Scribner, June 28, 1947. Mary's illness dated from June 2 and lasted three weeks, leaving her "weak as a kitten." She was "enchanted" by the good care that Pauline gave her.
Hellinger offers to buy four short stories for films: EH to Lanham, July 16 and Sept. 3, 1947. The stories were "Fifty Grand," "My Old Man," "The Snows of Kilimanjaro," and one other to be selected.
EH discovers high blood pressure: EH to Lanham, Sept. 3, 1947.
EH and Bruce drive to Sun Valley: EH to Scribner, Sept. 18; EH to Mary, Oct. 2, 1947. Mrs. E. J. Miller to author, July, 1964; Mr. and Mrs. L. S. Weaver to author, July, 1964; T. O. Bruce to author, March, 1965. The trip occurred Sept. 21–29, 1947. Chub Weaver's wife Laura cooked steaks for the travelers.
Mary designs tower for the Finca Vigía: Mary Hemingway, "Papa—The Finca Vigía Years," (unpublished), Aug. 26, 1961.
EH on his physical condition: EH to Scribner, Oct. 29; EH to Lanham, Nov. 24, Nov. 27, and Dec. 28, 1947.
EH on death of friends: EH to Scribner, Sept. 20, 1947.
Death of Mark Hellinger: EH to Scribner, Jan. 3, 1948.
EH meets Lillian Ross: Lillian Ross, *Reporting,* NY, 1964, pp. 187–188.
Life at MacDonald Cabins: Mary Hemingway to Clara Spiegel, Jan. 31, 1948.
EH and Ingrid Bergman on New Year's Eve: EH, introd. to *A Farewell to Arms,* NY, 1948, p. ix.
Return to the Finca Vigía: Mary Hemingway, "Papa—The Finca Vigía Years," 1961. The article mentions EH's attitude towards the new tower and his affection for Black Dog.
Malcolm Cowley's visit: EH to Cowley, Feb. 18; EH to Lanham, Feb. 18; EH to Lillian Ross, Feb. 21, 1948, and EH to author, Feb. 24, 1951. See also Cowley's *The Faulkner-*

Cowley File, NY, 1966, pp. 100–101. This is an excellent letter, Cowley to Faulkner, July 20, 1948.
EH supplies data to Cowley and Miss Ross: EH to Cowley, Apr. 9 and 13; June 25 and 28; July 15, Aug. 19, and Sept. 5, 1948; EH to Lillian Ross, Feb. 21, July 2, and July 28, 1948.
EH meets Aaron Hotchner: A. E. Hotchner, *Papa Hemingway,* NY, 1966, pp. 3–12.
EH declines membership in American Academy: EH to Scribner, June 2, 3, and 12, 1948.
Cruise to Cay Sal: EH to Lanham, June 26; EH to Lillian Ross, July 2, 1948.
EH finishes introduction to "A Farewell to Arms": although finished and sent on June 29, it is dated June 30, 1948.
EH's views on illustrations: EH to Scribner, Sept. 18, 1947; EH's introduction pursues the topic, pp. viii–ix.
EH's forty-ninth birthday: EH to Lillian Ross, July 28; EH to Lanham, Aug. 25, 1948. The boy Manolito who went on this cruise "appears" in *The Old Man and the Sea,* 1952.
EH's euphoria: reflected in EH to Lanham, July 28 and EH to Scribner, Aug. 13 and 25, 1948.
EH's plans for Europe: EH to Scribner, Apr. 5, 1948; EH to Lanham, June 26, 1948; EH to Lillian Ross, July 28, and EH to Scribner, July 28, 1948.
Maurice Speiser's illness and death: EH to Scribner, July 28, Aug. 8, and Aug. 25; EH to Lanham, Aug. 25, 1948.

Sec. 66. Past and Present

SOURCES

Letters of EH: to Lanham, Oct. 12, 1948; to Scribner, ca. Oct. 21; to Lanham, Nov. 5, 8, and 10; to Cowley, Nov. 16; to Mary Hemingway, Nov. 18 and 20; to Lanham, Nov. 20; to Mary, Nov. 23 and 24; to Lanham, Nov. 24, 25, and 26; to Cowley, Nov. 28 and 30; to Scribner, Dec. 9 and 31, 1948. To Lanham, Jan. 13 and 15, 1949; to Cowley, Jan. 24 and Feb. 10; to Lillian Ross, March 30; to Lanham, March 30; to Lillian Ross, May 10; to James Laughlin, June 2; to Scribner, June 28, July 20, and July 22; to Lanham, July 27; to Scribner, July 28 and Aug. 3; to Lanham, Aug. 7; to Scribner, Aug. 24; to Bernard Berenson (with Mary), Aug. 25; to Scribner, Aug. 26, Aug. 27, and Sept. 1; to Adriana Ivancich, ca. Oct. 1; to Scribner, Oct. 1, 3, 4, and 8; to Lillian Ross, Oct. 6–7; to Cowley, Oct. 11; to Lanham, Oct. 11; to Averell Harriman, Oct. 11; to Scribner, Oct. 12, 28, and 31; to Lillian Ross, Nov. 4; to Scribner, Nov. 8; to Lillian Ross, Nov. 15 (cable); to Scribner, Nov. 28 and Dec. 9; to Lanham, Dec. 10 and 27, 1949. To Lillian Ross, July 3, 1950; to Scribner, Sept. 4, 1950.
Other letters: Mary Hemingway to Malcolm Cowley, Feb. 9, 1949; Mary to Clara Spiegel, Feb. 16, 1949; Mary to Bernard Berenson, Nov. 14, 1949.
EH's work: Published: literary letter, *New York Times Book Review,* July 31, 1949; preface to Elio Vittorini, *In Sicily,* 1949; *Across the River and into the Trees,* 1950.
Books and articles: Malcolm Cowley, "A Portrait of Mr. Papa," *Life,* Vol. 25, (Jan. 10, 1949); A. E. Hotchner, *Papa Hemingway,* 1966.

Author's interviews and correspondence: with Hadley Mowrer, Aug., 1962; with Mary Hemingway, Aug., 1964; with Adriana von Rex, Oct., 1965; with Gianfranco Ivancich, Oct., 1965; with Federico Kechler, Oct. 1965. From Mrs. Walter Houk, March and April, 1964 (via tape recordings).

NOTES

EH rediscovers Italy: EH to Lanham, Oct. 12, and EH to Scribner, ca. Oct. 21, 1948; Mary Hemingway to Clara Spiegel, Feb. 16, 1949.
EH meets Federico Kechler: Count Kechler to author, Oct. 19, 1965.
EH's view of Venice; his boast of having fought at Capo Sile: EH to Lanham, Nov. 5, 1948.
EH revisits Fossalta: this account is based on that of EH to Malcolm Cowley, Nov. 16, 1948, supplemented by the author's personal inspection of Fossalta and environs in 1965. When EH included a comparable episode in *Across the River and into the Trees,* NY, 1950, pp. 17–19, it is amusing to notice that he allowed Colonel Cantwell a successful defecation as well as the ceremonious burial of money. In place of the stick that Ernest had used, Cantwell dug a hole with a "Sollingen clasp knife such as German poachers carry," while the banknote he buried was for 10,000 rather than 1,000 lire. During the author's visit to Fossalta on Oct. 19, 1965, an old local citizen who was serving as guide volunteered the information that the low yellow house behind the dike had been there since 1918. EH's allusion to such a house appeared in "A Way You'll Never Be," *First 49 Stories,* NY, 1938, p. 506. Mary Hemingway's reference to EH's Fossalta visit: Mary Hemingway to Clara Spiegel, Feb. 16, 1949.
EH's month on Torcello: EH to Lanham, Nov. 5, 8, 10, 20, 24, 25, and 26, 1948. EH to Malcolm Cowley, Nov. 16, 28, and 30, 1948; EH to Mary Hemingway, Nov. 18, 20, 23, and 24, 1948.
Mary's meeting with Berenson: Mary Hemingway to author, August, 1964.
EH's shooting with Carlo Kechler and Nanyuki Franchetti: EH to Scribner, Dec. 9, 1949. According to EH to Scribner, Sept. 4, 1950, the Baron Franchetti shared EH's enthusiasm for Africa, and had even given his children such names as Simba, Afdera, and Nanyuki in memory of safaris before the war. Lorian was named for a swamp where her father had killed a world-record buffalo.
EH meets Adriana Ivancich: Contessa Adriana von Rex to author, Oct. 17, 1965.
Christmas at Cortina: EH to Lanham, Dec. 27, 1948; EH to Scribner, Dec. 31, 1948. The letter to Scribner discusses the sale of "My Old Man." The film was released in March, 1950, as *Under My Skin,* starring John Garfield. On July 3 of that year, EH wrote Lillian Ross that he had seen and liked the film: "pretty damned good."
EH accounts for his slow progress with Land-Sea-Air novel: EH to Scribner, Dec. 31, 1948.
EH's views on Irwin Shaw's "The Young Lions": EH to Lanham, Jan. 13 and 15, 1949. EH was angry at this time because the U.S. Treasury Department wanted him to pay an additional $14,000 income tax for 1944, whereas General Eisenhower, by act of Con-

gress, was to be allowed tax-free royalties on his memoirs.
EH writes preface for Vittorini's "In Sicily": NY, New Directions, 1949. Vittorini, born in 1908, was an anti-Fascist who earned his living as a translator in Florence and Milan. The authorities imprisoned him in Milan in 1943. He died Feb. 13, 1966, aged fifty-seven. When James Laughlin of New Directions sent EH a check in payment for the preface, EH promptly sent it to Vittorini "as I had done the Introduction to help him and not to make money" (EH to Laughlin, June 2, 1950). Laughlin's reply on June 25th said that he had seen Vittorini in Milan about Easter time, and that he was "deeply touched" by EH's gesture, but determined to use the money to buy EH a painting. The preface was sent by EH to Vittorini himself, and by him forwarded to Laughlin, April 7, 1949. Laughlin kindly provided author with copies of this correspondence.
Cowley's "A Portrait of Mister Papa": *Life,* Vol. 25 (Jan. 10, 1949). EH's first private reaction to it was in EH to Lanham, Jan. 15, 1949. His letter to Cowley, calling the piece OK, was dated Jan. 24, 1949. His remark about being embalmed and "mounted" was in EH to Lillian Ross, May 10, 1949.
Mary disputes Cowley on EH's athletic prowess: Mary to Cowley, Feb. 9, 1949. **EH's follow-up letter:** EH to Cowley, Feb. 10, 1949. Mary's "short happy wife" witticism: EH to Scribner, Dec. 9, 1948.
EH's erysipelas: EH to Lanham and EH to Lillian Ross, both from Padua, March 30, 1949.
Sinclair Lewis in Venice: EH to Scribner, July 22, 1949.
EH's second meeting with Adriana and his first with Gianfranco: Adriana von Rex to author, Oct. 17, 1965; Gianfranco Ivancich to author, Oct. 18–19, 1965.
Recent history of Ivancich family: Gianfranco Ivancich to author, Oct. 18–21, 1965.
EH's new secretary: Juanita Jensen Houk to author, March, 1964.
EH's June fishing trip: Log of the *Pilar,* June, 1949.
EH's fiftieth birthday: EH to Scribner, June 28, July 20, and July 22, 1949. On July 28th EH asked Scribner for a wire recorder as a belated birthday present and talked of dictating his memoirs, saying that he knew many secrets about the old days in Paris with Pound, Joyce, Ford, and Gertrude Stein. He would also discuss Anderson, Dos Passos, Faulkner, Fitzgerald, and Wolfe, and include chapters on all the bartenders and whores he had known. His proposed title was *The Hard Way.*
Nita Jensen and the cat shark: Nita Jensen Houk to author, Apr., 1964. She dates the incident as Saturday, July 23, 1949.
EH brags of his new novel and speaks of his search for a title: EH to Scribner, Aug. 24, 26, and 27, and Sept. 1, 1949. These letters also mention the woman from *McCall's,* his hatred for his mother, and his alleged murder of the German soldier.
EH begins correspondence with Berenson: EH and Mary to Bernard Berenson, Aug. 25, 1949.
EH shows Hotchner early chapters of novel: A. E. Hotchner, *Papa Hemingway,* NY, 1966, p. 22.
EH decides on title for "Across the River and

into the Trees":** EH to Scribner, Sept. 21 and 29, 1949.
EH sends Mary to Chicago and borrows $10,-000: EH to Scribner, Sept. 21 and 29, 1949.
EH befriends Xenophobia and gossips with Leopoldina: EH to Scribner, Oct. 1 and 4, 1949.
EH gets word count on novel and boasts of its quality: EH to Scribner, Oct. 3, 1949.
Mary's return from Chicago: EH to Lillian Ross, Oct. 6–7, 1949.
EH names his hero Cantwell: According to Nita Jensen, EH's new wire recorder arrived in August. She was at work one day transcribing his recorded dictation when she happened to glance at the bookshelf, where there was a life of Hawthorne by Robert Cantwell. She made a mental note to ask EH if this was where he had found the name of his hero. By the time she remembered it again, the book was missing. She decided that it would not be tactful to ask EH about it.
EH explains his intentions in "Across the River": EH to Lanham, Oct. 11 and Dec. 10, 1949; EH to Scribner, Oct. 31, 1949.
EH's use of autobiographical allusions in "Across the River": the bombed-out Ivancich country house, p. 13; the visit to Fossalta, pp. 17–19; the description of the Gritti Palace, p. 52; the caricature of Sinclair Lewis, p. 87; the attack on Martha Gellhorn, p. 214; introduction of the headwaiter, pp. 55–64; Cipriani, p. 91, and Nanyuki Franchetti, p. 129. There are many others.
EH writes Adriana Ivancich: EH to Adriana, ca. Oct. 1, 1949.
Origin of name Renata: Hadley Mowrer to author, Aug., 1962; Adriana von Rex to author and Gianfranco Ivancich to author, Oct., 1965.
Connections between "The Garden of Eden" and "Across the River": EH told Scribner (Nov. 28, 1949) that he had reduced "another book" from 187,000 to 87,000 words and then "distilled" the remainder down to 17,000 for certain passages in *Across the River.* This may or may not have been true, but it helps to account for the distinct flavor of *The Garden of Eden* in some of the scenes between the Colonel and Renata.
EH on FDR: from a stenographic transcript dated Oct. 11, 1949. EH dictated it to Nita Jensen and gave her permission to copy and keep it. Supplied to author by Nita Jensen Houk, Apr., 1964. The letter to Averell Harriman, promising to help with the Roosevelt concert, bears the date of Oct. 11, 1949.
Preparations for departure: Nita Jensen types finished parts of "Across the River": EH to Scribner, Oct. 28 and Nov. 8, 1949; EH to Lillian Ross, Nov. 4, 1949.
EH plans to get Hotchner a trip to France: EH to Charles Scribner, Sept. 17, 1949.
EH tentatively agrees to let Lillian Ross prepare his profile: EH to L. Ross, Nov. 4, 1949.
Vial of chemicals: Mary Hemingway to Bernard Berenson, Nov. 14, 1949.
EH cables date of arrival at Idlewild: EH to Lillian Ross, Nov. 15, 1949.

Sec. 67. Across the River

SOURCES

Letters of EH: to Scribner, Dec. 10, 1949; to Lanham, Dec. 10; to Scribner, Dec. 13

and 18; to Lillian Ross, Dec. 18; to Nita Jensen, Dec. 22; to L. Ross, Dec. 28; to Scribner, Dec. 29, 1949. To Mr. and Mrs. T. O. Bruce, Jan. 3, 1950; to Scribner, Jan. 6 and Jan. 18; to Nita Jensen, Jan. 24; to Lanham, Jan. 29; to Scribner, Feb. 18 and 20; to Nita Jensen, Feb. 20 and March 4; to Scribner, March 5, ca. March 14, March 22, and March 29; to Adriana Ivancich, Apr. 10 and 11; to L. Ross, Apr. 11; to Lanham, Apr. 15; to Adriana, Apr. 15, 17, and 18; to L. Ross, Apr. 27; to Scribner, May 1; to L. Ross, May 6; to Scribner, May 6 and 7; to Adriana, May 9; to Scribner, May 16; to Dorman-O'Gowan, May 21; to Ross, May 24; to Scribner, May 30 and June 1; to Adriana, June 3; to Ross, June 3; to Scribner, June 11; to Ross, June 16; to Adriana, June 16; to Scribner, June 18 and 19; to Lanham, June 20; to Ross, June 23; to Harvey Breit, June 24; to Ross, June 25; to Fraser Drew, June 25; to Adriana, June 27 and 28; to Breit, June 30; to Ross, July 3; to Adriana, July 3; to Milton Wolff, July 5; to Lanham, July 5; to Scribner, July 7; to Adriana, July 8; to Breit, July 8 and 9; to Scribner, July 8–9; to Dorman-O'Gowan, July 10; to Ross, July 12; to Dorman-O'-Gowan, July 15; to Breit, July 17; to Adriana, July 23; to Dorman-O'Gowan, July 24; to Dorman-O'Gowan, ca. July 27; to Ross, July 27; to Adriana, July 28; to Scribner, July 29; to Ross, July 31; to Adriana, Aug. 1 and 2; to Breit, Aug. 3; to Dorman-O'Gowan, Aug. 8; to Scribner, Aug. 9; to Ross, Aug. 13 and 14; to Breit, Aug. 14; to Kathleen Sproul, Aug. 15; to Scribner, Aug. 16 and 19; to Ross, Aug. 24; to Breit, Sept. 1; to Ross, Sept. 9, 1950. To author, Feb. 24, 1951.
Other letters: Malcolm Cowley to William Faulkner, July 20, 1948; Mary Hemingway to Lillian Ross, Christmas card, ca. Dec. 15, 1949; Miss Olga Rudge to EH, March 13, 1950; Dorman-O'Gowan to EH, Apr. 6; H. W. R. North to EH, Apr. 23, 1950; Evan Shipman to EH, Apr. 23, 1950; Dorman-O'-Gowan to EH, May 13, 1950; Evan Shipman to EH, Oct. 29, 1950.
EH's work: Published: *Across the River and into the Trees,* serial version, *Cosmopolitan,* Vol. 128, Feb.–June, 1950.
Books and articles: Peter Russell, ed., *An Examination of Ezra Pound,* 1950; Lillian Ross, "How Do You Like It Now, Gentlemen?" *The New Yorker,* Vol. 26 (May 13, 1950), collected in *Reporting,* 1964; A. E. Hotchner, *Papa Hemingway,* 1966; Malcolm Cowley, *The Faulkner-Cowley File,* 1966.
Author's interviews and correspondence: with Mary Hemingway, Aug. 2, 1964; with Bertin Azimont and Louis Bréteall, Nov. 2, 1965. From Mary Hemingway, Aug. 14, 1968.

NOTES

EH in New York, Nov 16–19, 1949: Lillian Ross, "How Do You Like It Now, Gentlemen?" *The New Yorker,* Vol. 26 (May 13, 1950), collected in *Reporting,* NY, 1964, pp. 194–222. A. E. Hotchner, *Papa Hemingway,* NY, 1966, pp. 28–35, says wrongly that the visit occurred in October.
Crossing on the Île de France: EH to Lillian Ross, Dec. 18, 1949.
Marlene's gift of roses: Mary Hemingway to Lillian Ross, Christmas card, ca. Dec. 15, 1949.

Hotchner's arrival: *Papa Hemingway,* 1966, pp. 36–37.
EH finishes "Across the River" (ca. Dec. 10, 1949): EH to Scribner, and EH to Lanham, both Dec. 10, 1949; EH to Lillian Ross, Dec. 18, 1949.
EH at the races: Bertin Azimont and Louis Bréteall to author, Nov., 1965; EH to Scribner, Dec. 10, 13, and 18, 1949; EH to Lanham, Dec. 10, 1949; EH to Nita Jensen, Dec. 22, 1949; EH to Mr. and Mrs. T. O. Bruce, Jan. 3, 1950; A. E. Hotchner, *Papa Hemingway,* NY, 1966, pp. 36–63.
EH's praise of Hotchner's character: EH to Scribner, Dec. 13, 1949.
Christmas trip through south of France: EH to Lillian Ross, Dec. 28, 1949; EH to Scribner, Dec. 29, 1949. Hotchner's account (*Papa Hemingway,* pp. 64–65) concludes with the statement that "the Viertels left us in Cannes and we continued on to Venice." EH's contemporaneous letters to Ross and Scribner say that Hotchner returned to Paris with the Viertels.
Visits with the families Franchetti and Carlo Kechler: EH to Scribner, Jan. 6 and Aug. 9, 1950.
EH's social life in Venice: EH to Scribner, Jan. 6 and 18 and Feb. 18, 1950; EH to Lanham, Jan. 29, 1950; EH to Nita Jensen. Jan. 24, 1950.
The case of Princess Aspasia: Mary Hemingway to author, Aug. 2, 1964. Another instance of the same sort occurred in Cortina, where Mary once found EH and a middle-aged contessa in an ardent embrace. The contessa, undeterred, asked EH to come to stay with her in Rome.
Return to Cortina: EH to Lanham, Jan. 29, 1950, and EH to Scribner, Feb. 18, 1950.
EH's new face infection: EH to Scribner, Feb. 18 and EH to Nita Jensen, Feb. 20, 1950. At this time, EH heard from Nita Jensen, who had been left in charge of the Finca, that Gianfranco and his friends were having noisy parties, breaking glassware, and singing. The servant René was so angered when they stuck flowers into the bread that he threatened to stick flowers up their noses. EH replied that he had given Gianfranco full access to the Finca, and would tolerate no further backtalk from the servants. EH to Nita Jensen, Feb. 20, 1950.
Hotchner leaves "Cosmopolitan": EH to Scribner, Feb. 18, 1950.
Mary's ankle broken: EH to Scribner, Feb. 20 and EH to Nita Jensen, March 4, 1950.
Mondadori dinner and Nobel Prize rumor: EH to Scribner, March 5, 1950.
Adriana's dust jacket for "Across the River": EH to Scribner, Feb. 20, 1950.
Leaving Venice for Paris: EH to Scribner, ca. March 14, 1950.
EH and Pound: Miss Olga Rudge to EH, March 13, 1950, received by EH in Paris, March 16. EH's article on Ezra [1925, not 1923] was reprinted in *An Examination of Ezra Pound,* ed. by Peter Russell, NY, New Directions, 1950, pp. 73–76.
EH's feelings on parting from Adriana: EH to Scribner, March 22, 1950.
Homeward voyage on Île de France: EH to Scribner, March 29, 1950.
Social life at the Sherry Netherland: EH to Scribner, March 29, 1950; H. W. R. North to

EH, Apr. 23, 1950. EH met Irwin Shaw one night at Costello's Bar on Third Avenue, but did not "break his jaw" as he had threatened to do on first reading *The Young Lions*. EH to Lillian Ross, Apr. 11, 1950.
EH meets Evan Shipman: recalled in Shipman to EH, Apr. 23 and Oct. 29, 1950.
EH's reunion with Dorman-O'Gowan: EH to Lanham, Apr. 15 and EH to Lillian Ross, Apr. 27, 1950; Dorman-O'Gowan to EH, Apr. 6 and May 13, 1950.
Return to Cuba: EH to Adriana Ivancich, Apr. 10, 11, 15, 17, and 18, 1950; EH to Lillian Ross, Apr. 27, 1950.
Xenophobia at the Yacht Club: EH to Lillian Ross, May 6 and EH to Scribner, May 7 and May 16, 1950. The letter of May 16 describes EH's activities as a solid citizen, including the PTA.
Publication of Miss Ross's profile: for the public reaction and Miss Ross's surprise at adverse views, see her preface to "Portrait of Hemingway," *Reporting*, NY, 1964, pp. 189–191. **EH's predictions on reading the profile in galley proof:** EH to Scribner May 1, 1950. **His remarks to Miss Ross:** EH to Lillian Ross, June 3 and June 16, 1950. EH to author, Feb. 24, 1951, stated that the "thing" was her idea. He was in "full hold" of a novel and did not give a damn. But when he read it, while continuing to defend her right to say whatever she wished, he was "shocked and felt awful."
EH's sentiments about Venice: EH to Scribner, June 11, 18, and 19, and EH to Lillian Ross, June 23, 1950.
EH dedicates "Across the River" to Mary: EH to Scribner, June 11, 1950.
EH writes "The Shot": EH to Scribner, June 11, 1950.
Trip to Megano de Casigua: EH to Lillian Ross, June 16, 1950.
EH's head injury at Rincón: EH to Adriana, July 3, EH to Lillian Ross, July 3; EH to Milton Wolff, July 5; and EH to Scribner, July 7. On the 8th he celebrated the thirty-second anniversary of his wounding at Fossalta by having a drink with Leopoldina and Xenophobia, to whom he showed the film of *The Killers*. He recorded this visit and the remark about the thickness of his skull in EH to Scribner, July 8–9, 1950.
EH's barrage of letters: See above, Sources, *Letters of EH*, for the dates and names of correspondents. EH to Scribner, July 21, 1950, provided an account of his fifty-first birthday party, a virtual duplicate of his fiftieth.
EH's irritability and its causes: EH to Scribner, Aug. 9, 16, and 19 and EH to Lillian Ross, Aug. 24, 1950.
EH's near suicide by drowning: EH to Lillian Ross, Aug. 24, 1950. In a letter to Miss Ross on Apr. 27, 1950, he had deplored the alleged suicide of Thomas Heggen (May 19, 1949), author of *Mr. Roberts*. But on May 1, 1950, he told Scribner that he was tempted to shoot himself. He decided against it since it would make no one happy except the undertakers and the young writers whom he was blocking off from fame by being as famous as he was. Mary Hemingway believes the near-drowning story "entirely fictional." Mary Hemingway to author, Aug. 14, 1968.

Sec. 68. *Slings and Arrows*

SOURCES

Letters of EH: to Scribner, July 19, 1950; to Dorman-O'Gowan, Aug. 8; to Breit, Sept. 1; to Mary, Sept. 8; to Adriana, Sept. 8; to Mary, Sept. 14; to L. Ross, Sept. 19 and 20; to Lanham, Sept. 21; to Scribner, Sept. 26; to Ross, Sept. 29; to Scribner, Sept. 29 and Oct. 2; to Ross, Oct. 5; to Scribner, Oct. 5; to Breit, Oct. 6; to Scribner, Oct. 7, 8, 11, and 15; to Breit, Oct. 16; to Scribner, Oct. 17, 18, and 20; to Ross, Oct. 22; to Breit, Oct. 26; to Scribner, Nov. 1 and 3; to Dorman-O'Gowan, Nov. 10; to Scribner, Nov. 15; to Dorman-O'Gowan, Nov. 28; to Scribner, Nov. 29 and Dec. 4 and 8; to Breit, Dec. 21; to Scribner, Dec. 26, 1950. To Breit, Jan. 1, 1951; to Dorman-O'Gowan, Jan. 4; to L. Ross, Feb. 3; to Breit, Feb. 6; to Carlos Baker, Feb. 17 and 24; to Dorman-O'Gowan, Feb. 27; to Scribner, March 3; to Baker, March 10; to Scribner, March 14; to Adriana, March 18 and 24; to Baker, Apr. 1; to Scribner, Apr. 1; to Baker, Apr. 8; to Scribner, Apr. 11; to Adriana, Apr. 17; to Cowley, Apr. 19; to Baker, Apr. 24 and 29 and May 9; to Cowley, May 13; to Scribner, May 16, 18, 19, and 28; to Ross, May 28; to Cowley, June 1 and 2; to Dorman-O'Gowan, June 13; to Scribner, June 15 and 29; to Baker, June 30; to Scribner, July 4; to Ross, July 5; to Adriana, July 6; to Mary, July 6, 7, and 8; to Scribner, July 8 and 9; to Mary, July 9, 14, ca. July 15, and July 17; to Scribner, July 20; to Cowley, July 24; to Scribner, Aug. 27; to Baker, Aug. 27; to Scribner, Oct. 5, 1951.
Other letters and documents: Mary Hemingway to Scribner, Oct. 12, 1950; Adriana Ivancich to Scribner, ca. Nov. 15, 1950. Malcolm Cowley to EH, Apr. 18, May 9, and May 19, 1951; Cowley to Thomas Bledsoe, May 22; Bledsoe to Cowley, June 8; Cowley to EH, June 8, 1951. Mary Hemingway's Diary for 1951.
EH's works: Published: *Across the River and into the Trees*, publ. Sept. 7, 1950. Preface to Lee Samuels, *A Hemingway Check List*, 1951. Preface to François Sommer, *Pourquoi Ces Bêtes Sont-Elles Sauvages?* March 28, 1951; "The Good Lion" and "The Faithful Bull," *Holiday*, Vol. 9 (March, 1951); "The Shot," *True*, Vol. 28 (Apr., 1951).
Books: Malcolm Cowley, *The Portable Hemingway*, 1944; J. K. M. McCaffery, ed., *Ernest Hemingway, The Man and His Work*, Sept., 1950; Philip Young, *Ernest Hemingway: A Reconsideration*, 1966; A. E. Hotchner, *Papa Hemingway*, 1966.
Author's interviews: with Mary Hemingway, Aug., 1964.

NOTES

Initial American reception of "Across the River": Richard Rovere, *Harper's* Vol. 201 (Sept., 1950), pp. 104–106; Lewis Gannett, *NY Herald Tribune*, Sept. 7, 1950, p. 23; Joseph Henry Jackson, *San Francisco Chronicle* (Sept. 7), p. 18; Maxwell Geismar, *SRL*, Vol. 33 (Sept. 9) pp. 18–19; Morton D. Zabel, *Nation*, Vol. 171 (Sept. 9), p. 230; Alfred Kazin, *The New Yorker*, Vol. 26 (Sept. 9), pp. 101–103; Malcolm Cowley, *NY Herald Tribune Books* (Sept. 10) pp. 1 and 16; *Time*, Vol. 56 (Sept. 11), pp. 110 and 113; Philip

Young, *Tomorrow,* Vol. 10 (Nov., 1950), pp. 55–56. **English reception:** Cyril Connolly, *Sunday Times,* Sept. 3, 1950, p. 3; L. A. G. Strong, *Spectator,* Vol. 184 (Sept. 8), p. 279; London *Observer* profile, Sept. 10, p. 2.
Laudatory American reviews: Elliot Paul, *Providence Sunday Journal,* Sept. 6, 1950, Section VI, p. 8; Charles Poore, *NY Times,* Sept. 7, 1950, p. 29; John O'Hara, *NY Times Book Review,* Sept. 10, 1950, p. 1.
Novel called a memorable swan-song: *Times Literary Supplement,* Oct. 6, 1950, p. 628.
EH categorizes reviewers: EH to Mary, Sept. 14, 1950.
EH sends O'Hara review to Adriana: EH to Adriana, Sept. 8, 1950.
Afdera Franchetti's fantasies: EH to Adriana, Sept. 8, 1950; EH to Harvey Breit, Oct. 6, 1950.
EH's leg pains: EH to Lillian Ross, Sept. 19 and 29, 1950; EH to Lanham, Sept. 21; EH to Scribner, Oct. 7, 15, 17, 18, and 20, 1950; EH to Harvey Breit, Oct. 16, 1950.
Lee Samuels's Hemingway collection: EH to Scribner, Sept. 29, 1950. EH discusses Samuels's generosity in his preface to Lee Samuels, *A Hemingway Check List,* NY, 1951, pp. 5–6.
EH rejects Breit's bid to do his biography: EH to Breit, Sept. 1, 1950.
Domestic problems at the Finca: EH to Lillian Ross, Oct. 5, 1950; EH to Scribner, Oct. 5, 7, 8, and 11, 1950; EH to Harvey Breit, Oct. 6 and Oct. 26, 1950. Mary Hemingway to Scribner, Oct. 12, 1950.
EH tries to account for adverse reviews: EH to Scribner, Oct. 2, 1950.
EH's consolations for poor reception of "Across the River": climbing bestseller listings, EH to L. Ross, Oct. 22, 1950; **affirmative fan mail,** EH to L. Ross, Sept. 29, 1950, EH to Breit, Oct. 26, 1950; **approval of military aspects of book by three generals,** EH to L. Ross, Sept. 20, 1950, and EH to Scribner, Oct. 5, 1950; **prepublication sell-out of first printings,** EH to Mary Hemingway, Sept. 8, 1950; **quarter-million-dollar offer from Hollywood** (alleged), EH to Scribner, Sept. 26, 1950. Another consolation was the naming of the "Escuela Ernest Hemingway," a new elementary school at Guanabacoa. (EH to Scribner, Oct. 20, 1950.)
Arrival of Adriana and Dora Ivancich: Mary Hemingway's Diary for 1951.
EH's happiness: EH to Adriana, ca. March 24, 1951.
His contentment with the Finca: EH to Dorman-O'Gowan, Aug. 8, 1950.
EH avoids scandal: EH to Adriana, March 18, 1951.
EH names White Tower, Incorporated: EH to Adriana, Apr. 17, 1951.
Social activities for the Ivancich family: Adriana to Charles Scribner, ca. Nov. 15, 1950; EH to Scribner, Nov. 1, 3, 15, and 29; Dec. 4 and 8, 1950; EH to L. Ross, Dec. 4, 1950.
Storm at Puerto Escondido: EH to Dorman-O'Gowan, Nov. 28, 1950.
EH's images for Adriana's beauty: EH to Adriana, July 6, 1951.
EH finishes Part 2 of his three-decker on the sea: EH to Scribner, Dec. 26, 1950; EH to Dorman-O'Gowan, Jan. 4, 1951; EH to L. Ross, Feb. 3, 1951. The book was not *finished* in any strict sense.

EH calls Adriana a spur to work: EH to Adriana, ca. March 24, 1951.
Christmas at the Finca: EH to Breit, Dec. 21, 1950 with undated postscript of ca. Dec. 26 or Dec. 27, 1950; EH to Breit, Jan. 1, 1951. Patrick had married Henrietta Broyles of Baltimore in June, 1950.
EH begins Santiago story: EH to Breit, Jan. 17, 1951. His first short version of the story was in "On the Blue Water," *Esquire,* Vol. 5 (Apr., 1936), p. 184, and he had thought of trying to tell it again in 1939 (EH to Perkins, Feb. 7, 1939).
EH's progress with Santiago story, Jan. 18– Feb. 6, 1951: EH to Breit, postscript of Jan. 18 to letter of Jan. 17; EH to Breit, Feb. 6, 1951.
Adriana and her mother leave Cuba: EH to L. Ross, Feb. 3; EH to Dorman O'Gowan, Feb. 27, 1951.
Story reaches 25,000 words: EH to author, Feb. 17, 1951.
Cowley initiates depth study of EH's fiction: *Viking Portable Hemingway,* Sept., 1944, introd., pp. vii–xxiv.
EH's views on McCaffery volume: *Ernest Hemingway: The Man and His Work,* Cleveland and NY, Sept., 1950. EH to Scribner, July 19, 1950 and EH to Breit, Oct. 6, 1950.
EH learns of two other books about him: EH to Charles A. Fenton, Jan. 12, 1951; EH to Carlos Baker, Feb. 17 and 24, 1951.
EH on author's right of privacy: EH to Carlos Baker, Feb. 17, Feb. 24, March 10, Apr. 1, Apr. 8, Apr. 24, and Apr. 29, 1951.
EH hears of a third book about him: Cowley to EH, Apr. 18, May 9, May 19, and June 8, 1951; EH to Cowley, Apr. 19, May 13, June 1, June 2, and June 15, 1951. Cowley to Thomas Bledsoe, May 22, 1951. Bledsoe to Cowley, June 8, 1951. The author of the book, Philip Young, gave an account of his difficulties in "Foreword, Author and Critic," in *Ernest Hemingway: A Reconsideration,* University Park (Pa.) and London, 1966, pp. 1– 28.
EH begins work on a story of sub-hunting during 1942–43: The typescript, labeled in longhand, *The Sea (Main Book Three),* was begun March 5 and finished May 17, 1951. EH often inserted word counts at the bottom of the pages. He wrote "Fait Mars 5/51" to mark the end of Chapter 1. At the bottom of page 29: "1145 fait mars 6, 1951." Midway of page 37 is the date March 16; page 42 says "Fait March 19/51," and so on. By April 9, he had reached page 100. A notation on page 102 beside the phrase "white painted house and the tall old-fashioned light" says, "Correct from West Indies Pilot if wrong." By May 1, he had reached page 161, and by May 7, page 174. From this time onwards the dating ceased, though the laborious page-by-page word count continued. The total from March 5 to May 7 was sixty-four days, which meant an average of two and two-thirds pages a day over a two-month period, with occasional interludes. The concluding forty-four pages took from May 8 to 17. On the 17th, having brought Hudson to the point of death, he wrote "The End" on his typescript, and told Scribner next day that he had now finished Book III of the four books that made up *The Sea.* He computed the length at 45,000 words and said that this part had "written as cleanly"

as the story of Santiago which made up Book IV. (EH to Scribner, May 18, 1951.)
EH's characterization of the action of the book: EH to Dorman-O'Gowan, June 13, 1951.
EH's lesser work completed and published: two fables in *Holiday*, Vol. 9 (March, 1951), pp. 50–51. The decorations were by Adriana Ivancich. The original six-page typescript of "The Good Lion," owned in 1965 by Gianfranco Ivancich, was signed at the end and dated Jan. 17, 1950 at Venice. The typescript of "The Faithful Bull" contained the notation, "By EH, Prince of Greece," and was signed at the end, "For Adriana with love from Mr. Papa. Venezia, 26/1/50." This also was in Gianfranco's possession in 1965. EH received $3,500 for "The Shot," in *True*, Vol. 28 (April, 1951), pp. 25–28, with photographs made on location by Lloyd Arnold. (EH to Scribner, March 14, 1951.) EH's introduction to the Samuels checklist was dated from the Finca Nov. 8, 1950, though not handed to Samuels until Nov. 28th. Sommer's book on animals first appeared in an edition of 500 copies March 28, 1951 in Paris. EH's preface (pp. 9–11) was translated by Paule de Beaumont, and dated from the Finca, February, 1951. But EH to Dorman-O'Gowan, Nov. 10, 1950, seems to indicate that it was written (or begun) at that time.
EH's final word count for Santiago story: EH to Scribner, July 20, 1951.
EH shows story to friends: to Scribner (EH to Scribner, March 3, 1951); to Hotchner (*Papa Hemingway*, 1966, pp. 72–73); to Tedder (EH to Baker, March 10, 1951); to Grieg and Baker (EH to Baker, Apr. 24, 1951).
EH on the story's "mysterious quality": EH to Scribner, June 29, 1951.
The Lear-Santiago comparison: EH to Baker, May 9, 1951.
Completion and celebration of the sea-chase story: EH to Scribner, May 18, 1951 and Oct. 5, 1951. The celebration is described in the letter of May 18.
EH's dietary beliefs and preferences: EH to Scribner, Apr. 1, Apr. 11, May 16, and May 19, 1951.
EH and the annual marlin tournament: EH to Scribner and EH to Ross, both May 28, 1951. The tournament took place May 25–27, with bad weather on the third day. In a field of forty-four boats, the *Pilar* placed second and the *Tin Kid* sixth. Mary was "brave as a badger." Taylor Williams cracked two ribs and banged his head, but caught the biggest fish of the tournament.
EH begins revision of Part 1 of his sea novel: EH to Scribner, June 29, 1951. He computed its length in EH to Scribner, Aug. 27, 1951.
EH rejects "Cosmopolitan" offer on serialization: EH to Scribner, July 8, 1951.
Death of Grace Hall Hemingway, Memphis Hospital, Memphis, Tenn., June 28, 1951: *New York Times*, June 28. She had been staying with her daughter Madelaine (Sunny), Mrs. Kenneth Mainland. Besides Ernest, her other survivors were Marcelline (Mrs. Sterling Sanford of Detroit, Michigan), Ursula (Mrs. J. J. Jepson of Honolulu, Hawaii), Carol (Mrs. John F. Gardner of Garden City, Long Island), and Leicester, whose nominal residence was Key West, Florida.

EH's comments on her death: EH to Scribner June 29, 1951; EH to Baker, June 30, 1951, and EH to Cowley, July 24, 1951. An obituary appeared in *Time*, Vol. 58 (July 9, 1951), p. 70.
Mary leaves for mainland: EH to Mary, July 6, 7, 8, 9, 14, and 17, 1951 and EH to Scribner, July 9, 1951. These letters describe affairs at the Finca, where visitors included Gianfranco Ivancich, Sinsky (Juan Dunabeitia), Dr. Herrera, Lee Samuels, young Mayito Menocal, Nita Jensen, Otto and Betty Bruce, McKinlay Kantor and family, and Jim Cochrane, one of Buck Lanham's officers from the 22nd Infantry Regiment.
EH plans birthday trip to Puerto Escondido: EH to Scribner, July 4 and 8, 1951. In these letters, EH discussed the books he had completed. He spoke of the trip in EH to Mary, July 17, 1951. In an undated note to Mary, ca. July 15, he signed himself, "Mr. Papa, Cazador de Osos Fracasado"—the Failed Hunter of Bears.

Sec. 69. People in Pain

SOURCES

Letters of EH: to Scribner, March 3, March 14, Apr. 11, May 10, and May 18, 1951; to Lillian Ross, July 5; to Scribner, July 8; to Cyrus Sulzberger, ca. July 15; to Scribner, Aug. 7 and 8; to Sulzberger, Aug. 10; to Mary, Aug. 11; to Charles Fenton, Aug. 31; to Sulzberger, ca. Sept. 5; to Scribner, Sept. 9; to Fenton, Sept. 13; to Ross, Sept. 15; to Cowley, Sept. 16; to Fenton, Sept. 23; to Scribner, Sept. 25, 28, 29 and Oct. 2; to Baker, Oct. 7; to Dorman-O'Gowan, Oct. 18; to D. D. Paige, Oct. 22; to Dorothy Pound, Oct. 22; to John Atkins, Oct. 24; to Baker, Nov. 2, 9, and 22; to Ross, Nov. 22; to Scribner, Dec. 1; to Bledsoe, Dec. 9; to Cowley, Dec. 14; to Scribner, Dec. 16; to Jimmy Cannon, Dec. 28; to Cowley, Dec. 31, 1951. To Scribner, Jan. 8, 1952; to Breit, Jan. 15; to Cowley, Jan. 17; to Bledsoe, Jan. 17; to Breit, Jan. 29; to Scribner, Feb. 1; to Vera Scribner, Feb. 18; to Wallace Meyer, Feb. 22; to Ross, Feb. 24; to Breit, Feb. 24; to Charles Scribner, Jr., Feb. 25; to Wallace Meyer, March 4–7; to Philip Young, March 6; to Meyer, March 9, 16, and 20; to Adriana, Apr. 12; to Meyer, Apr. 15; to Breit, Apr. 16; to Meyer, Apr. 21; to Adriana, Apr. 24; to Breit, May 1; to Selden Rodman, May 19, 1952, to Charles Fenton, July 29, 1952.
Other letters and documents: Evan Shipman to EH, ca. June 12, 1951; Mary Hemingway to Charles Scribner, Sept. 3, 1951; D. D. Paige to EH, Oct. 22, 1951; Thomas Bledsoe to EH, Dec. 3, 1951. Mary Hemingway's diary entries, as follows: Oct. 12, 1951; Dec. 12, 1951; March 10–29, 1952; and Apr. 29, 1952.
EH's work: Unpublished: long short story, untitled, about "Michigan long ago," unfinished, begun ca. Apr. 24, 1952.
Books: John Dos Passos, *Chosen Country*, 1951; Cyrus Sulzberger, *The Resistentialists*, 1962; Philip Young, *Ernest Hemingway: A Reconsideration*, 1966.
Author's interviews and correspondence: with William B. Smith, Apr., 1964; with Patrick Hemingway, Dec., 1965; with Dr. John Walker, Nov., 1966. From Nita Jensen Houk,

Apr., 1964; from Professor H. H. Burns, Jan. 23, 1965; from Charles Scribner, Jr., Dec. 8, 1967.

NOTES

Weather conditions, summer and fall, 1951: Summarized in EH to Dorman-O'Gowan, Oct. 18, 1951, and EH to Jimmy Cannon, Dec. 28, 1951. Besides the heat and humidity, there were nine hurricanes in September, though none of them reached the Finca.
Illness of Evan Shipman: Shipman to EH, ca. June 12, 1951.
Case of Jean Décan: EH to Cyrus Sulzberger, ca. July 15, Aug. 10, and ca. Sept. 5, 1951. Décan's story is set forth at length in Sulzberger's *The Resistentialists*, NY, 1962, Chapter 2, where the author calls him Michel Dupont to protect him.
EH attacks James Jones: EH to Scribner, March 3 and 14, Apr. 11, and May 10, 1951. **On Wolfe and Fitzgerald:** EH to Scribner, May 18, 1951. **On Norman Mailer:** EH to Lillian Ross, July 5, 1951. **On Faulkner:** EH to Fenton, Sept. 23 and EH to Scribner, Sept. 28, 1951.
EH on Dos Passos's "Chosen Country": William B. Smith to author, Apr., 1964. Smith supplied from memory EH's note denouncing Dos Passos. The novel portrayed Katy Smith charmingly as Lulie Harrington; her eccentric father as Lulie's father Ezekiel; her aunt, Mrs. Charles, as Aunt Lydia; her brothers, Y. K. and Bill, as Zeke and Ben Harrington; and Dos Passos himself as James K. P. Pignatelli. Dr. Hemingway appeared as Dr. Warner, and EH as George Elbert Warner. Bill Smith called Dos Passos El Paso. He replied to EH's note by saying that he had not cared much for *Chosen Country,* but still liked El Paso. EH to Charles Fenton, July 29, 1952, said that Dos Passos had made him a "loathsome character" in the novel.
EH's death-consciousness: EH to Scribner, Sept. 9, 1951. Other gloomy letters are EH to Scribner, Sept. 28 and 29, 1951.
Death of Pauline Pfeiffer Hemingway: EH to Scribner (2 letters), Oct. 2, 1951. She died of pheochromocytoma, a tumor of the adrenal medulla, which released large quantities of adrenaline and noradrenaline into her bloodstream, producing the symptoms mentioned. Patrick Hemingway to author, Dec. 16, 1965, and Dr. John Walker to author, Nov. 15, 1966, identified and described the disease.
EH rejects Mistral scheme for release of Pound: D. D. Paige to EH, Oct. 15, 1951; EH to Paige and Dorothy Pound (2 letters), Oct. 22, 1951.
EH helps John Atkins with information: EH to Atkins, Oct. 24, 1951. He had done the same for Charles A. Fenton in letters of Aug. 31, Sept. 13, and Sept. 23, 1951. He also evaluated and corrected sample chapters from Baker's book in EH to Baker, Oct. 7, 1951.
EH misconstrues the nature of Young's book: EH to Baker, Oct. 7, 1951.
EH forbids Young to quote from his works: EH to Scribner, Sept. 9, 1951, noted also in EH to Baker, Nov. 2, 1951.
EH objects to lies and myths about his life: EH to Scribner, Dec. 1, 1951.
Death of Dean Christian Gauss: noted in EH

to Baker, Nov. 9, 1951. Dean Gauss had died suddenly in Pennsylvania Station, NY, Nov. 1, 1951.
Illnesses of Sinsky (Juan Dunabeitia) and Don Andrés Untzaín: EH to L. Ross and EH to Baker, both Nov. 22, 1951.
Death of Harold Ross: EH to Cowley, Dec. 14, 1951.
EH's statistics on "The Island the Stream": EH to Scribner, July 8 and Aug. 7, 1951; EH to L. Ross, Sept. 15, EH to Cowley, Sept. 16, and EH to Baker, Oct. 7, 1951.
Visit by Professor Burns: Burns to author, Jan. 23, 1965; Mary Hemingway's diary entry for Oct. 12, 1951. On returning to Seattle, Burns told Theodore Roethke about EH's poems. Roethke urged EH to publish them, but EH apparently did not respond.
EH tells of inception of Jake Barnes's wound: EH to Thomas Bledsoe, Dec. 9, 1951. Bledsoe had written EH about Philip Young's book on Dec. 3.
EH toys with idea of turning critic: EH to Scribner, Dec. 16, 1951. In 1959, EH prepared such a preface, but it was so breezy, slangy, and bellicose in tone that Charles Scribner, Jr., advised him against publishing it, and Mary agreed.
EH's year-end guinea hunt: EH to Cowley, Dec. 31, 1951. He had sketched his dreams of exotic vacations in EH to Scribner, Dec. 1, 1951.
North wind and cold: EH to Scribner, Jan. 8, 1952. A week later EH defended his advertising endorsement of Ballantine Ale in EH to Harvey Breit, Jan. 15, 1952.
Suicide of the servant Clara: EH to Scribner, Feb. 1, 1952.
Austerity vacation begins: EH to Wallace Meyer, Feb. 22 and EH to Harvey Breit, Feb. 24, 1952. The vacation had begun early in February.
Death of Charles Scribner: Charles Scribner, Jr., to author, Dec. 8, 1967. Mr. Scribner died at Harkness Pavilion, Columbia Presbyterian Medical Center, New York. **EH's letters of sympathy:** EH to Vera Scribner, Feb. 18 and EH to Charles Scribner, Jr., Feb. 25, 1952.
Philip Young exchanges letters with EH: Young to EH, Feb. 6, and EH to Young, March 6, 1952. See Philip Young, *Ernest Hemingway: A Reconsideration,* University Park (Pa.) and London, 1966, foreword, pp. 18–19.
Hayward suggests one-shot magazine publication of "The Old Man and the Sea": EH to Wallace Meyer, March 4, 1952, with postscript of March 7.
EH gives his views on the novel: EH to Meyer, March 4–7, 1952.
Second "austerity vacation": EH to Meyer, March 9, 1952; Mary Hemingway's diary entries for March 10–29, 1952. EH describes Paraíso in a letter to Selden Rodman, May 19, 1952.
EH considers various titles: EH to Wallace Meyer, March 16 and 20, 1952.
Batista's coup: Batista seized power on March 10th, the morning the Hemingways left for Paraíso, cancelling the current election campaign and assuming leadership of a "provisional regime."
Approval of novel by Book of the Month and "Life" editors: EH to Meyer, Apr. 15, 1952.

EH prefers large readership to Nobel Prize:
EH to Meyer, Apr. 15, 1952.
Reunion with Herbert Matthews: EH to Breit,
Apr. 16 and EH to Meyer, Apr. 21, 1952.
EH begins story of Michigan: EH to Adriana,
Apr. 24, 1952.
Nita Jensen's wedding: Nita Jensen Houk to
author, Apr., 1964. "Papa came in all dressed
up," wrote Mrs. Houk, "and he just looked
wonderful." The ceremony was followed by
an elegant reception at the Finca, including a
21-gun salute delightedly fired off by Don
Andrés.
EH and Black Dog: EH to Breit, May 1,
1952.
Flora of the Finca: Mary Hemingway's diary
entry, Apr. 29, 1952.

Sec. 70. The Old Man and the Sea

SOURCES

Letters of EH: to Wallace Meyer, May 2 and
May 7, 1952; to Adriana, May 8; to Meyer,
May 12 and May 15; to Breit, May 16; to
Adriana, May 19 (cable); to Selden Rodman,
May 19; to Meyer, May 19 and May 23; to
Philip Young, May 27 (letter and cable); to
Cowley, May 29; to Meyer, May 30 and May
31; to Adriana, May 31; to Baker, June 4; to
Charles A. Fenton, June 12 and June 18; to
Lanham, June 18; to Meyer, June 20; to Breit,
June 21; to Fenton, June 22 (marked unsent
in EH's handwriting); to Philip Young, June
23; to Meyer, June 24; to Breit, June 27, June
29, and July 4; to Daniel Longwell, July 6;
to Fenton, July 13 (4 letters); to Longwell,
July 24; to Fenton, July 29; to Cowley, ca.
Aug. 15; to Lanham, Aug. 19; to Baker, Aug.
26; to Lillian Ross, Aug. 26; to Charles Scribner, Jr., Sept. 3; to Adriana, Sept. 3; to Meyer,
Sept. 13; to Bernard Berenson, Sept. 13; to
Charles Scribner, Jr., Sept. 19; to Meyer,
Sept. 26; to Longwell, Sept. 28; to Breit, Sept.
29; to Bernard Berenson, Oct. 2 and Oct. 14;
to Adriana, Oct. 28; to Lanham, Oct. 28; to
Fanny Butcher, Nov. 1; to Gregory Hemingway, Nov. 6–7; to L. Ross, Nov. 8; to Adri-
ana, Nov. 23; to Patrick Hemingway, Nov.
26; to L. Ross, Dec. 5; to T. O. Bruce, Dec.
15; to Lanham, Dec. 15; to Adriana, Dec. 16;
to Wirt Williams, Dec. 23, 1952.
Other letters and documents: Harvey Breit to
EH, May 5, 1952; Adriana Ivancich to EH,
May 23, 1952 (cable); Philip Young to EH,
May 23 and 28, 1952; Breit to EH, June 25
and July 2, 1952; Daniel Longwell to EH,
Aug. 26 and Sept. 2, 1952; Bernard Berenson
to EH, Sept. 6, 1952; Mary's diary entry for
Sept. 19, 1952; Bernard Berenson to EH, Sept.
21, 1952; Baker to EH, Oct. 23, 1952; Gregory
Hemingway to EH, ca. Nov. 1 and Nov. 19,
1952; Mary to EH, Nov. 27, 1952; Mary's
diary entry for Dec. 26, 1952.
EH's work: (a) Unpublished: "Fragments from
Ernst von Hemingstein's Journals," composed
ca. May 19–June 21, 1952. **(b) Published:** *The
Old Man and the Sea*, published Sept. 1, 1952
in *Life*, and on Sept. 8, 1952, in the regular
trade edition.
Books: Carlos Baker, *Hemingway: the Writer
as Artist*, 1952; David Cecil, *Max, A Biography*, 1965; Malcolm Cowley, *The Faulkner-
Cowley File*, 1966.
Author's interviews and correspondence: with

Hadley Mowrer, Aug., 1962; with Lorine
Thompson, March 1965; with Mrs. Saxe Commins, Aug., 1966. From Mary Hemingway, ca.
Aug. 26, 1952; from Daniel Longwell, Dec.
18, 1961.

NOTES

Life to publish EH's novel: EH to Meyer,
May 6, 1952.
**EH worries about Book of the Month guar-
antee:** EH to Meyer, May 7, 1952.
**Money from "Life" and reassurance from
BOMC:** EH to Meyer, May 12 and May 15,
1952.
EH wants dignified publicity: EH to Meyer,
May 12, 1952.
Adriana's jacket designs: EH to Adriana, May
19 (cable); EH to Meyer, May 19; Adriana
to EH, May 23 (cable); EH to Meyer, May
23, 1952. EH received a photostat of Adriana's
chosen design (EH to Meyer, May 31) and
the same day wrote to congratulate Adriana.
Lee Samuels photographs EH: EH to Meyer,
May 23, 1952. In the same letter EH dis-
claimed personal vanity. The remark that
when he was good-looking he did not know it
was confirmed by Hadley Mowrer to author,
Aug., 1962.
EH decides no disclaimer is required: EH to
Meyer, May 12, 1952. The identification of
the boy Manolito with the fictional Manolo
is the author's surmise, based on EH's account
of Manolito in EH to Lillian Ross, July 28,
1948 and EH to Lanham, Aug. 25, 1948. **EH
requests Baker not to mention the possible
connection between Santiago and Carlos Gutiérrez:** EH to Meyer, May 30, 1952. Lorine
Thompson to author, March 28, 1965, held
that Santiago was probably modeled in part
on Bra Saunders, whose hands were often
afflicted with fisherman's cramp like Santiago's
in the story.
EH's dedication: EH to Meyer, May 31, 1952.
Settlement with Philip Young: Young to EH,
May 23; EH to Young, May 27 (letter and
cable); Young to EH, May 28; EH to Meyer,
May 30, 1952. EH discusses the matter further
in EH to Baker, June 4, 1952.
EH quarrels with Fenton: EH to Fenton, June
12, June 18, June 22 (marked *unsent* in EH's
handwriting), July 13 (4 letters), and July
29, 1952. EH's lighter vein appeared in "Fragments from Ernst von Hemingstein's Journal,"
sent in letters to Selden Rodman and Harvey
Breit on May 19 and June 21, 1952.
Eisenstadt's photography: EH to Meyer, June
20, 1952, which mentions Anselmo Hernández.
This incident had a curious aftermath. In late
Oct., 1965, Hernández (then aged ninety-two)
crossed to Florida with other Cuban refugees.
Hernández told American reporters that he
had served as a model for EH's Santiago. In
a manner of speaking, it was true.
**Breit elicits statement from Faulkner on "The
Old Man and the Sea":** Breit to EH, June 25,
1952. This letter describes Breit's meeting with
Faulkner on June 16, Faulkner's refusal to
write the review, and his sending of the state-
ment. Mrs. Saxe Commins to author, Aug.,
1966, provided a copy of the statement, which
was dated from Oxford, Miss., June 20, 1952.
EH expatiates on Faulkner's statement: EH to
Breit, June 27, June 29, and July 4, 1952.
Faulkner had already made a similar state-

ment in public. In 1950, Evelyn Waugh had attacked the attackers of *Across the River* for "their high supercilious caddishness." He defended EH as a proponent of "Decent Feeling," with "an elementary sense of chivalry—respect for women, pity for the weak, love of honor." (*Tablet*, London, Sept., 1950). *Time* excerpted Waugh's remarks on Oct. 30, 1950, Vol. 56, p. 44. Faulkner's letter in *Time*, Vol. 56, Nov. 13, 1950, p. 6, associated himself with Waugh's position. "Good for Mr. Waugh," wrote Faulkner. "I would like to have said this myself. . . . One reason I did not is, the man who wrote some of the pieces in *Men Without Women* and *The Sun Also Rises* and some of the African stuff (and some—most—of all the rest of it for that matter) does not need defending, because the ones who throw the spitballs didn't write the pieces . . . and . . . don't have anything to stand on while they throw the spitballs. Neither does Mr. Waugh need this from me. But I hope he will accept me on his side." It would appear that upon returning to Oxford in June, 1952, Faulkner resurrected this two-year-old statement and rewrote it for Harvey Breit. EH's remark to Breit that he had built up Faulkner abroad is partly confirmed by a story of Jean Paul Sartre's. He told Malcolm Cowley that EH, while drunk in Paris, had called Faulkner a better writer than himself. (Cowley to Faulkner, Sept. 17, 1945, printed in *The Faulkner-Cowley File*, N.Y. 1966, p. 29.) Cowley also quoted a recent letter of EH's to himself which said that Faulkner had "the most talent of anybody but hard to depend on because he goes on writing after he is tired. . . . I would have been happy just to have managed him." (EH to Cowley, Sept. 3, 1945.) Breit's contrition about sowing friendship and reaping only discord appears in Breit to EH, July 2, 1952. EH's curious spelling of "Anomatopoeio County" will be recognized as a probably intentional pun on onomatopoeia.
Faulkner reviews "The Old Man": *Shenandoah*, Vol. 3 (Autumn, 1952), p. 55.
EH outlines his esthetic position: EH to Lanham, June 18; EH to Young, June 23; EH to Meyer, June 24; EH to Daniel Longwell, July 6 and July 24, 1952. The letter to Meyer discusses "naturalism."
EH rejects doctrine of nature's malignity: EH to Cowley, ca. Aug. 15, 1952.
Advance publicity for EH's novel: Daniel Longwell to EH, Aug. 26, 1952. Longwell was Chairman of the Board of Editors of *Life*; other arrangements were in the hands of Sidney James, Assistant Managing Editor, and Wilson Hicks, Executive Editor. (Daniel Longwell to author, Dec. 18, 1961.)
EH's tax problems: EH to Lanham, Aug. 19 and Oct. 28, 1952. In the midst of all the excitement, EH received an advance copy of Carlos Baker's *Hemingway: The Writer as Artist* in the morning mail of Aug. 25, 1952. He spent the morning reading it down by the pool, and wrote Baker a long letter about it next day, as did Mary. After dinner on the 25th, he told Mary and Gianfranco that the book was "half good," though with many errors of fact. "Nobody really knows or understands," he said, apropos of *The Old Man and the Sea*, "and nobody has ever said the

secret. The secret is that it is poetry written into prose. And it is the hardest of all things to do." (Mary Hemingway's diary entry for Aug. 25, 1952.) Max Beerbohm, on whom he had paid a call in April, 1922, made a similar remark about *The Old Man*. "It's a poem," he said. "I must read more of what I suppose I ought to call old man Hemingway." David Cecil, *Max, A Biography*, Boston, 1965, p. 484.
Sales data on magazine and book publication: Daniel Longwell to EH, Sept. 2, 1952 and EH to Lanham, Oct. 28, 1952. **Tearful reception:** EH to Adriana, Sept. 3, 1952. **Sample American reviews:** Breit, *Nation*, Vol. 175 (Sept. 6, 1952), p. 194; Jackson, *San Francisco Chronicle*, Sept. 7, 1952, p. 20; *Time*, Vol. 60 (Sept. 8, 1952), p. 114. **Abundant fan mail:** Mary Hemingway's diary, Sept. 19, 1952. **Rabbis and ministers preach sermons on "The Old Man and the Sea":** Baker to EH, Oct. 23, 1952.
Unsolicited praise from Berenson: Berenson to EH, Sept. 6, 1952. "I have read [*The Old Man and the Sea*] with boyish zest," wrote BB, "and thank you for the treat." He greatly preferred EH's style to "the inflationary magniloquence of *Moby-Dick*," and liked Santiago "far better than Ahab."
EH asks for blurb from Berenson: EH to Berenson, Sept. 13, 1952.
Berenson's public statement: Berenson to EH, Sept. 21, 1952. **EH relays statement to Scribners:** EH to Meyer, Sept. 26, 1952.
EH on his historical imagination: EH to Berenson, Oct. 2, 1952.
EH on fiction as superlying: EH to Berenson, Oct. 14, 1952. He returned to this theme in roughly the same words in EH to Lanham, Dec. 15, 1952.
EH critical of Batista dictatorship: EH to Lillian Ross, Aug. 26, 1952.
EH accepts Medal of Honor: announced, *NY Times*, Sept. 8, 1952, and awarded Sept. 23, *NY Times*, Sept. 24, 1952, **EH's comment on acceptance:** EH to Meyer, Sept. 26, 1952.
EH declines New York trip: EH to Meyer, Sept. 13, 1952.
Publishing books and making love: EH to Berenson, Oct. 2, 1952.
EH to send Mary to New York: EH to Berenson and EH to Meyer, both Sept. 13, 1952.
EH seeks thirtieth marlin of season: EH to Breit, Sept. 29, 1952.
EH's joy in watching marlin jump: EH to Berenson, Sept. 13, 1952. Janet Flanner made a pertinent observation on EH's style in *The Old Man*. "It is written as if translated out of Spanish," she said, "which gives it an unfair nobility. It has the extremest virile sentimentality both in emotion and in writing style that I ever saw. Only hardy Ernest could have two males fighting to the death and loving each other because that's what they are doing —killing each other or aiming to. The book will achieve mountains of popularity . . . because it is a short story of struggle, the most popular plot ever invented after writing man noticed that living man's pulses beat faster if someone else does the struggle for him that he is in no position to do for himself, on the heroic model." (Janet Flanner to Solita Solano, ca. Sept., 1952; copy kindly furnished to author by Miss Solano.)

EH defines symbolism: EH to Lillian Ross, Nov. 8, 1952.
EH and Gianfranco: EH to Adriana, Oct. 28, 1952.
Exchange with Gigi: Gregory Hemingway to EH, ca. Nov. 1; EH to Gregory, Nov. 6–7; Gregory to EH, Nov. 19; EH to Adriana, Nov. 23, and EH to Patrick Hemingway, Nov. 26, 1952.
Proposal for film of "The Old Man": EH to Adriana, Dec. 16, 1952. Alfred Rice was also on hand for these discussions: EH to T. O. Bruce, Dec. 15, 1952.
Tentative plans for African safari: EH to Berenson, Oct. 14 and EH to Adriana, Oct. 28, 1952. Advance preparations: EH to Patrick Hemingway, Nov. 26. Hunting the Soul of Zanuck: EH to Lillian Ross, Dec. 5, 1952.

Sec. 71. Year of the Hunters

SOURCES

Letters of EH: To Arthur Mizener, Feb. 22, 1950. To Donald Gallup, Sept. 22, 1952; to Bernard Berenson, Oct. 14, 1952; to Patrick Hemingway, Nov. 26, 1952. To Adriana Ivancich, Jan. 6, 1953; to Baker, Jan. 8; to Meyer, Jan. 8 and 13; to Breit, Jan. 15; to Meyer, Jan. 19; to Adriana, Jan. 19; to Meyer, Jan. 21; to Berenson, Jan. 24; to Adriana, Jan. 25; to Meyer, Jan. 27; to Baker, Feb. 1; to Berenson, Feb. 17; to Dorothy Connable, Feb. 17; to Meyer, Feb. 18; to Fenton, Feb. 18; to Gianfranco Ivancich, Feb. 20 and Feb. 22; to Henry W. R. North, Feb. 25; to Berenson, March 6, March 20–21, and March 29; to Breit, Apr. 4; to Berenson, Apr. 13; to Gianfranco, Apr. 15; to Meyer, May 6; to Lillian Ross, May 10; to Charles Scribner, Jr., May 11; to Lanham, May 23; to Adriana, May 24; to Breit, May 30; to Gianfranco, June 5; to Berenson, June 10; to Baker, June 11; to John Hemingway, June 13; to T. O. Bruce, June 30; to Patrick Hemingway, July 11; to Adriana, July 19; to MacLeish, ca. July 19; to Fenton, Aug. 2; to Lanham, Aug. 2; to Gianfranco, Aug. 4 and Aug. 6; to Berenson, Aug. 11; to Lanham, Aug. 13; to Patrick, Aug. 25; to Breit, Sept. 5 or 6; to Berenson, Sept. 15; to Juanito Quintana, ca. Sept. 14–21; to Lanham, Sept. 25; to Meyer, Sept. 30; to T. O. Bruce, ca. Oct. 27; to Gianfranco, Oct. 31; to Adriana, ca. Nov. 2, 1953. To Breit, June 3, 1954.
Other letters and documents: Mary Hemingway's diary entries for Jan. 1 and 17, 1953; Mary to Gianfranco, Feb. 8; Dorothy Connable to EH, ca. Feb. 14; Mary to Gianfranco, March 8; Mary's diary entries for March 24–Apr. 6; Mary to Gianfranco, Apr. 20; Mary's diary entry for May 4; Mary to Gianfranco, May 16; Gianfranco to EH, July 25; Mary's diary entries for Aug. 26–31, Sept. 1–18, and Sept. 24–Oct. 20; Mary to Lillian Ross, Oct. 28; Mary's diary entries for Nov. 2–Dec. 17; Mary to Lillian Ross, Dec. 23; Mary's diary entries for Dec. 24–1953–Jan. 2, 1954. Peter Buckley to EH, Nov. 27, 1956.
EH's work: Published: "The Circus," Ringling Brothers Program and Magazine for 1953; "The Dangerous Summer," Life, Vol. 49 (Sept. 5, 1960).

Articles: Mary Hemingway, "Hemingway's Spain," Saturday Review, Vol. 50 (March 11, 1967).
Author's interviews and correspondence: With Juanito Quintana, Oct., 1965. From Rupert Bellville, Feb. 27, 1962; from Peter Buckley, ca. Nov. 28, 1962; from Richard Percival, Feb. 2, 1964; from Denis Zaphiro, March 7, 1964; from Clive Cookson, Dec. 15, 1962; from Mayito Menocal the younger, Nov. 16, 1964; from Charles Scribner, Jr., ca. Apr. 15, 1968.

NOTES

EH longs for Africa: EH to Berenson, Oct. 14, 1952; EH to Patrick, Nov. 26, 1952; EH to Meyer, Jan. 13, 1953. EH resents postponement: EH to Adriana, Jan. 6, 1953.
EH sharpens shooting eye: Mary's diary entry, Jan. 1, 1953; EH to Breit, Jan. 15, 1953.
EH befriends circus bears: EH to Baker, Jan. 8 and EH to Breit, Jan. 15, 1953. "The Circus," was the lead article in Ringling Brothers' Program and Magazine for 1953, pp. 7 and 62. EH to Henry W. R. North, Feb. 25, 1953, indicates that the program was already in print by that date. EH to Baker, June 11, 1953, said it took him three weeks of hard work to write this article. The statement should be regarded with skepticism.
Burglars at the Finca: EH to Meyer, Jan. 19 and 21, 1953; Mary's diary entry for Jan. 17. This was the third burglary at the Finca in recent months. EH reported to Meyer that the wounded burglar left a blood spoor "very dark like a kidney shot." He had lately been reading Jim Corbett's tiger books, where Corbett identified a kidney shot by black blood. When EH worked this into his letter about the burglar, Charles Scribner, Jr., who had also been reading Corbett, "had that same feeling of mild disillusionment as catching a magician putting the rabbit into the hat" (Scribner to author, ca. Apr. 15, 1968).
The young man from Connecticut: EH to Meyer, Jan. 27, 1953.
EH on books by Atkins and Young: on Atkins, EH to Meyer and EH to Baker, both Jan. 8, 1953; on Young, EH to Baker, Feb. 1 and EH to Meyer, Feb. 18, 1953. The passages in Young to which EH objected were on pp. 41–43; 149, 165, 168, and 207 in the Rinehart edition of 1952. Meantime EH was telling Adriana that Baker's book was "so full of symbolism that it would make you laugh" (EH to Adriana, Jan. 19, 1953) but also assuring Baker that it was "a fine job of criticism" (EH to Baker, Feb. 1, 1953).
EH's exchange with Dorothy Connable: Dorothy Connable to EH, ca. Feb. 14; EH to Dorothy Connable, Feb. 17, 1953. EH told Miss Connable that he might sometime write about 1920 and 1923 in Toronto.
EH mentions possible memoir of Paris days: EH to Meyer, Feb. 18, 1953. This was EH's second allusion to the idea that resulted in A Moveable Feast, 1964. EH had told the Fitzgerald anecdote to Arthur Mizener, Feb. 22, 1950, and the Stein-Toklas story to Donald Gallup, Sept. 22, 1952.
EH denies Fenton the right to quote: EH to Fenton and EH to Meyer, both Feb. 18, 1953.

Death of Sunny's husband, Kenneth Mainland: EH to Adriana, Jan. 25, 1953.
Mary's illness: Mary to Gianfranco Ivancich, Feb. 8, 1953.
Departure of Gianfranco for Italy: EH to Gianfranco, Feb. 20, 1953.
Death of Willie the Cat: EH to Gianfranco, Feb. 22, 1953.
Finca visitors: Mary to Gianfranco, March 8, 1953.
Trips to Paraíso: EH to Gianfranco, Apr. 15, 1953; Mary's diary entries for March 21–Apr. 2, 1953.
Arrival of the Haywards and Spencer Tracy: Mary's diary entries for Apr. 3–6, 1953 and Mary to Gianfranco, Apr. 20, 1953. Bumby and his wife Puck flew in on the Saturday before Easter for a ten-day visit, bringing their three-year-old daughter, nicknamed Miss Muffet, EH's first grandchild, whom everyone admired. See Mary's diary and letter noted above.
EH shows Tracy around Cojimar: EH to Gianfranco, Apr. 15, 1953.
EH objects to transacting business on Easter: EH to Breit, Apr. 4, 1953.
Mary on the tower: Mary's diary entry, Apr. 6, 1953.
EH wins Pulitzer Prize: Mary's diary entry, May 4, 1953; EH to Meyer, May 6; EH to Lillian Ross, May 10; EH to Charles Scribner, Jr. May 11; and EH to Gianfranco, June 5, 1953.
EH endorses prize check to Bumby: EH to Meyer, May 18 and EH to Lanham, May 23, 1953.
Settlement of film arrangements with Hayward: EH to Gianfranco, Apr. 15, 1953.
"Look" editors' offer and Mary's new car: Mary to Gianfranco, May 16, 1953.
Plans for trip to Spain and Africa: Mary to Gianfranco, May 16, 1953. EH, "The Dangerous Summer," *Life* Vol. 49 (Sept. 5, 1960), p. 78.
Leaving the Finca: EH wrote Berenson on June 10, 1953, about his temporary melancholy on leaving Black Dog. He also mentioned rereading *The Sun Also Rises* in preparation for Spain; he thought the book stood up well—only eight words needed to be changed.
First leg of trip: EH to Bumby, June 13 and EH to T. O. Bruce, June 30, 1953. The stopover in New York is described in EH to Breit, Sept. 5 or 6, 1953.
Crossing on the "Flandre": EH to T. O. Bruce, June 30, 1953.
EH reads Fenton dissertation: EH to Fenton, Aug. 2, 1953.
Motor trip from Le Havre to Irún: EH, "The Dangerous Summer," *Life* Vol. 49 (Sept. 5, 1960), p. 85; EH to Adriana, July 19, 1953, in which he mentions feeling like a knight.
Arrival in Spain: Mary Hemingway, "Hemingway's Spain," *Saturday Review*, Vol. 50 (March 11, 1967), p. 49; EH to Adriana, July 19, 1953 and EH to Lanham, Aug. 2, 1953.
Meeting Quintana and Bellville: Bellville to author, Feb. 27, 1962 and Quintana to author, Oct. 2, 1965.
Meeting Buckley: Buckley to author, ca. Nov. 28, 1962. Buckley's early acquaintance with Bumby is noted in Buckley to EH, Nov. 27, 1956.

EH's reception at Pamplona: EH to Lanham, Aug. 2, 1953.
Proposed appendix to Death in the Afternoon: EH to Patrick Hemingway, July 11, 1953. This letter alludes to his admiration for Ordóñez.
EH meets Ordóñez: Ordóñez to Buckley, fall, 1962, relayed by Buckley to author, ca. Nov. 28, 1962.
End of the fiesta: Mary Hemingway; "Hemingway's Spain," *Saturday Review*, Vol. 50 (March 11, 1967), pp. 102–103.
Gianfranco and Bellville to Biarritz: Gianfranco to EH, July 25, 1953.
Mary's cold: EH, "The Dangerous Summer," *Life*, Vol. 49 (Sept. 5, 1960), p. 86.
Trip through mountain terrain: EH to Lanham, Aug. 2, 1953, and Mary's *Saturday Review* article, cited above, p. 103.
Arrival in Madrid: EH to Lanham, Aug. 2, 1953.
Revisiting Prado: EH to Adriana, July 19, 1953; EH, "The Dangerous Summer," *Life*, Vol. 49 (Sept. 5, 1960), p. 87; Mary Hemingway's *Saturday Review* article, cited above, p. 104.
EH awarded Carlos de Céspedes medal: *New York Times*, July 14, 1953.
MacLeish's poem for EH: EH to MacLeish, ca. July 19, 1953.
Valencia-Madrid-Paris-Marseilles: EH to Lanham, Aug. 2, and EH to Gianfranco, Aug. 4 and 6, 1953. They reached Paris July 31, left Aug. 4, and boarded the ship the morning of the 6th.
Passage to Suez: EH to Berenson, Aug. 11 and EH to Lanham, Aug. 13, 1953.
Meeting Clive Cookson: Cookson to author, Dec. 15, 1962.
Mombasa and Machakos: EH to Patrick Hemingway, Aug. 25, 1953; Clive Cookson to author, Dec. 15, 1962.
Staying at Kitanga: Mary's diary entries, Aug. 26–31, 1953.
Zaphiro and the wounded rhino: Mary's diary entry for Aug. 31, 1953. EH made much of the wounded rhino story, telling Lanham that he had shot the beast at ten paces when it charged (EH to Lanham, Sept. 25, 1953), and telling Quintana that he had received it *recibiendo*, as when a matador kills a charging bull with head-on sword-thrust while standing still (EH to Juanito Quintana, dated only *On safari, third week,* i.e., ca. Sept. 14–21, 1953). These were typical exaggerations.
Zaphiro's previous career: Zaphiro to author, March 7, 1964.
Hunting at Salengai: Mary's diary entries, Sept. 1–8, 1953; EH to Breit, Sept. 5 or 6; EH to Berenson, Sept. 15; EH to Lanham, Sept. 25, 1953. The letter to Lanham describes the elephant episode and gives the number as seventy-two.
Roy Home: Mayito Menocal the younger to author, Nov. 16, 1964.
Charo: Mary's diary, *passim,* and EH to Breit, Jan. 3, 1954.
N'Gui: EH to Breit, Jan. 3, 1954 identified N'Gui as son of M'Cola. But he was in fact the son of M'Cola's elder brother, Manai. (Richard Percival to author, Feb. 2, 1964.)
Zaphiro as white hunter to the Hemingways: Zaphiro to author, March 7, 1964.
EH's first lion: Mary's diary entry, Sept. 9, 1953.

EH on lion tenderloin: EH to Berenson, Sept. 15, 1953 said that lion tenderloin, suitably breaded, was as good as wiener schnitzel.

Move to Kajiado District, first sight of Kimana Swamp, Menocal's lion, and EH's shot at buffalo: Mary's diary entries, Sept. 10–11, 1953. The diary loyally omits mention of EH's poor shooting. Percival and Menocal privately agreed that his skill with the rifle was deficient, though he continued to excel as a wingshot.

Hunting in Kajiado region: Mary's diary entries, Sept. 9–18, 1953, and Mayito Menocal the younger to author, Nov. 16, 1964.

N'Bebia's cooking: Mary's diary entries, Sept. 9–18, 1953. Among his achievements were tommy-livers and scrambled eggs, curries of birds with grated coconut, guinea hen sautéed with saffron rice, deep-dish eland pie with carrots and onions, and lion steaks marinated in sherry. He rolled piecrust with a beer bottle, as Dr. Hemingway had done in the Great Smoky Mountains.

Arrival at Figtree Camp: Mary's diary entries, Sept. 24–Oct. 12, 1953; EH to Wallace Meyer, Sept. 30, 1953.

Split-up of safari: Mary's diary entry, Oct. 4, 1953.

Return to Kitanga Farm and EH's flight to Iringa: Mary's diary entry, Oct. 20, 1953; EH to T. O. Bruce, ca. Oct. 27; EH to Gianfranco, Oct. 31; EH to Adriana, ca. Nov. 2, 1953.

Third month on safari: Mary's diary entries, Nov. 2–Dec. 3, 1953.

EH goes native: Mary's diary entries, Dec. 1, 3, and 17, 1953.

EH's leopard hunt: Diary for Dec. 17, 1953. The author queried Denis Zaphiro about EH's subsequent boast that Debba was his fiancée. "I cannot deny the possibility of this altogether," Zaphiro replied, "But I think it is unlikely that he took more than the first tentative steps toward making it true. . . . When I returned to the Kimana Camp just before Christmas there was a native girl hanging around the staff encampment. She came from a nearby village of Wakamba. This was not unusual as the camp was always full of hangers-on. EH was very generous with his change and the word got around that there was a small fortune to be picked up. . . . The girl may well have been there for that purpose. . . . She was a slovenly-looking brat with a primitive greedy face. She was also none too clean. I thought at the time that she was hanging around the African staff. But she may have been there by arrangement." (Denis Zaphiro to author, March 7, 1964.) EH told Harvey Breit that he and N'Gui were in love with two girls in the Wakamba shamba. Both were "heiresses"—like Brenda Frazier, said he—but black and beautiful. He praised Miss Mary for staying the hell out of it and being "understanding and wonderful." (EH to Breit, Jan. 3, 1954.) He had boasted to Lanham and others during the war that in 1933 he had maintained a black harem in a scout car. When asked about the probable truth of such a claim, J. M. Manley remarked, "A quite impossible situation which would not have been tolerated in any safari party at that time." On the same subject, Philip Percival roared with laughter and said, "Bloody optimist!" (Richard Percival to author, Feb. 2, 1964.)

Christmas season, Kimana Camp: Mary's diary entries, Dec. 24, 1953–Jan. 2, 1954.

Sec. 72. Uganda and After

SOURCES

Letters of EH: to Breit, Jan. 3, 1954; to Patrick, Jan. 20; to Adriana, Feb. 1; to Berenson, Feb. 2; to Breit, Feb. 4; to Adriana, Feb. 13; to Meyer, Feb. 21; to Adriana, March 10; to Lanham, March 12; to MacLeish, March 29; to Berenson, March 29; to Meyer, Apr. 1; to Breit, Apr. 9; to Berenson, Apr. 9, Apr. 29, and May 1; to Adriana, May 1; to Fenton, May 3; to George Plimpton, May 3; to Adriana, May 9, May 19, and June 15; to Bumby, July 8; to Lanham, July 11; to Meyer, July 20; to Bumby, July 26, 1954.

Other documents: Mary's diary entries, Jan. 7–16, 21–28, 1954.

EH's work: Published: "The Christmas Gift," Parts I and II, *Look*, Vol. 18 (Apr. 20 and May 4, 1954).

Books: A. E. Hotchner, *Papa Hemingway*, 1966.

Author's interviews and correspondence: with Count Federico Kechler, Oct., 1965; with Juanito Quintana, Oct., 1965; with Adamo Simon, Oct., 1965. From Mary Hemingway, Apr. 27, 1962; from Denis Zaphiro, March 7, 1964; from Col. James S. Luckett, Feb. 19, 1965.

NOTES

Kimana campsite: Mary's diary entry for Jan. 8, 1954.

Plans for trip to the Congo: Mary's diary entry for Jan. 7, 1954.

EH as Honorary Game Warden: Denis Zaphiro to author, March 7, 1964; EH to Harvey Breit, Jan. 3, 1954; EH to Patrick Hemingway, Jan. 20, 1954.

EH's popularity with villagers: EH to Breit, Jan. 3, 1954; Mary's diary entry for Jan. 14, 1954.

The two plane crashes: account based mainly on Mary's diary entries for Jan. 21–28, 1954, supplemented by EH, "The Christmas Gift," Parts I and II, *Look*, Vol. 18 (Apr. 20, 1954, pp. 29–37 and May 4, 1954, pp. 79–89).

Extent of EH's injuries: Mary Hemingway to author, Apr. 27, 1962.

EH's determination to "ride it out": EH to Berensen, Feb. 2, 1954.

Concussion turns EH maudlin: EH to Berenson, Feb. 2; EH to Adriana, Feb. 1, 2, and 13; EH to Breit, Feb. 4, 1954.

Fishing plans for Indian Ocean: Mary Hemingway to author, Apr. 27, 1962.

EH dictates "Look" article: EH to Meyer, Feb. 21 and EH to Lanham, March 12, 1954.

EH in Shimoni: Mary Hemingway to author, Apr. 27, 1962; EH to Adriana, March 10, 1954; EH to MacLeish, March 29; EH to Berenson, March 29; and EH to Meyer, Apr. 1, 1954.

Mombasa to Venice and arrival at Gritti Palace: EH to Berenson, March 29 and EH to Meyer, Apr. 1, 1954.

Medical examinations in Venice: EH to Berenson and EH to Breit, both Apr. 9, 1954; EH to Berenson, Apr. 29 and May 1, 1954.

EH satirizes Henry James: EH to Adriana, May 9, 1954.

EH visits Torcello and Codroipo: EH to Berenson, Apr. 9, 1954; Count Federico Kechler to author, Oct. 19, 1965.
EH receives Colonel and Mrs. Luckett: Colonel Luckett to author, Feb. 19, 1954.
EH lunches with Ambassador and Mrs. David Bruce: EH to Adriana, May 1, 1954.
EH sees Adriana: EH to Adriana, May 1 and May 9, 1954.
EH accepts Award of Merit from American Academy in absentia: *NY Times,* March 24, 1954; EH to Meyer, Apr. 1, 1954.
Arrival of Adamo and Hotchner: EH to Fenton, May 3, 1954; A. E. Hotchner, *Papa Hemingway,* NY, 1966, pp. 81–96.
EH driven to Spain: EH to Adriana, May 9, 1954; Adamo to author, Oct. 20, 1965; Juanito Quintana to author, Oct. 3, 1965; A. E. Hotchner, *Papa Hemingway,* NY, 1966, pp. 97–131. When the author met Adamo at San Michele al Tagliamento, Oct. 20, 1965, he ceremoniously presented a snapshot of EH, standing beside a stone bridge outside Burgos, wearing a blue knitted sailor's toque. Adamo understood that this was the bridge of *For Whom the Bell Tolls.*
Arrival in Madrid; bullfights; visit to El Escorial: EH to Adriana, May 19, 1954, and A. E. Hotchner, *Papa Hemingway,* NY, 1966, pp. 131–141.
EH meets Plimpton: EH to George Plimpton, May 3, 1954.
Seeing Dr. Madinaveitia: EH to Bumby, July 8, 1954, and Hotchner, *Papa Hemingway,* NY, 1966, pp. 134–137.
Voyage home on the "Francesco Morosini": EH to Lanham, July 11, 1954.
Surprise letter from Adriana at Madeira: EH to Adriana, June 15, 1954.
State of health on return to Finca: EH to Meyer, July 20, and EH to Bumby, July 26, 1954.

Sec. 73. The Bounty of Sweden

SOURCES

Letters of EH: to MacLeish, March 29, 1954; to Lanham, July 12; to Meyer. July 20; to Lanham, Aug. 5; to Lillian Ross, Aug. 15; to Adriana, Aug. 15; to Lanham, Sept. 5; to Berenson, Sept. 24; to Breit, Sept. 24; to Charles Scribner, Jr., Oct. 30; to Dorman-O'Gowan, Nov. 7; to Lanham, Nov. 10; to Dorman-O'Gowan, Dec. 23 to Scribner, Dec. 28; to Meyer, Dec. 28, 1954. To Scribner, Jan. 14, 1955; to Fred Spiegel, Jan. 27; to Adriana, Jan. 30; to Breit, Feb. 1; to Adriana, Feb. 23; to Breit, Feb. 28 and March 18; to Adriana, March 25; to Baker, Apr. 13; to Dorman-O'Gowan, Apr. 15; to Meyer, Apr. 16; to Baker, May 2; to Breit, May 14; to Meyer, May 31 and June 9; to Lanham, June 19; to Berenson, July 9; to Patrick, July 22 and Aug. 24; to Philip Percival, Sept. 4; to Breit, Sept. 15; to Berenson, Sept. 18; to Adriana, Sept. 20; to Berenson, Oct. 4; to Breit, Oct. 6; to Meyer, Oct. 11; to Breit, Oct. 27, Nov. 3, and Nov. 14; to Bumby, Nov. 28, to Meyer, Dec. 5; to Bumby, Dec. 6, 1955.
Other letters: George M. Abbott to EH, Nov. 8, 1954; Mary Hemingway to Lillian Ross, Apr. 7, 1955.
EH's work: Published: endorsement for Pan American Airways, July 27, 1955; Last Will and Testament, Sept. 17, 1955; Nobel Prize Address, Dec. 10, 1955.
Books and articles: Harvey Breit, interview with EH, *New York Times Book Review,* Nov. 7, 1954; Harvey Breit, "A Walk with Faulkner," *New York Times Book Review,* Jan. 30, 1955; Fraser Drew, interview with EH, Apr. 8, 1955 (unpublished); Robert Manning, "Hemingway in Cuba," *Atlantic,* Vol. 216 (Aug., 1965); A. E. Hotchner, *Papa Hemingway,* 1966.
Author's interviews and correspondence: with General Lanham, June, 1963; with Mary Hemingway, Aug., 1964. From Gelston Hardy, Jan. 14 and Jan. 25, 1962.

NOTES

EH on youth and love: EH to Berenson, Sept. 24, 1954. The same letter discusses fame and adulation.
Rumors of Nobel Prize: EH to Lanham, Aug. 5, 1954.
EH's views on Faulkner's "A Fable": EH to Lanham, Aug. 5; EH to Lillian Ross, Aug. 15; EH to Breit, Sept. 24, 1954.
Mary places parents in nursing-home: EH to Lanham, July 12, and EH to Meyer, July 20, 1954, when she returned.
Gianfranco's activities: EH to Adriana, Aug. 15, 1954. This letter also mentions the peaceful overtures from Gregory.
Ava Gardner and Dominguín: EH to Berenson, Aug. 15, 1954.
African wildlife film: EH to Lanham, Aug. 5 and Sept. 5, 1954. The planners included Bill Lowe and others. EH was also angered by Edward Scott of the *Havana Post,* who got into an argument with Mary over the edibility of lion steaks. EH threatened to beat up Scott for insulting a lady. Scott challenged EH to a duel, which EH rejected, saying that Scott was only seeking publicity for himself. (Mary Hemingway to author, Aug., 1964.) EH to Charles Scribner, Jr., Dec. 28, 1954, darkly hinted that Scott was employed by Sen. Joseph McCarthy, whom EH had attacked in "The Christmas Gift," Part II, *Look,* Vol. 18 (May 4, 1954), p. 80.
EH begins African book: EH to Adriana, Aug. 15, 1954 and Jan. 30, 1955. **On his use of Africans in the book:** EH to Lanham, Nov. 10, 1954.
EH compares Debba and Prudy Boulton: EH to MacLeish, March 29, 1954. The same letter calls Debba a dark version of Marilyn Monroe.
EH telephones Lanham news of Nobel Prize: Lanham to author, June, 1963.
Telephone interview with Harvey Breit: quotations from typed transcript, dated 10 A.M. New York time, Oct. 28, 1954. Discussed in *Times Talk,* Vol. 8 (Nov., 1954), p. 12. See especially Breit's front-page account, *New York Times Book Review,* Nov. 7, 1954.
EH explains mention of Dinesen, Sandburg, and Berenson: EH to Meyer, Dec. 28, 1954.
EH complains of interrupted work: EH to Charles Scribner, Jr., Oct. 30 and EH to Meyer, Dec. 28, 1954.
EH and the Nobel Prize medal: Mary Hemingway, note to the LP recording, "Hemingway Reading," which included the Nobel Prize speech, Caedman Records, 1965. In this note, Mary stated that their first news of the award came "two or three weeks" before

the official announcement when "the Swedish minister to various Latin-American countries including Cuba telephoned from Havana and made an appointment to see Ernest" at the Finca. A "simple private ceremony" was arranged for October 21. There was a short exchange of speeches, with "the Swedish Minister and his wife and a few friends standing around in our library, and afterwards one of those sparkling, singing, gay, four-hour luncheon parties with ten or twelve at the table." The Hemingways ended that day with a half-mile evening swim in the pool. October 28th, she continues, was a bright breezy day with streams of sunlight. The Finca staff served coffee to the crowds, which began arriving about ten A.M. EH made a speech for the Havana TV stations—"the sort of impish, pseudo-tough speech that enchanted the Cubans, who knew him widely as a soft touch and an outsize tipper."

EH arranges to receive prize in absentia: George M. Abbott, Chargé d'Affaires, American Embassy, Stockholm, to EH, Nov. 8, 1954.

EH's Nobel Prize address: from a typescript sent by EH to Dorman-O'Gowan, Dec. 23, 1954.

EH interviewed by Manning: EH to Robert Manning, Nov. 17, 1954, from Manning's typescript, "Notes on a conversation with Hemingway," used in part in *Time* cover story, Vol. 64 (Dec. 13, 1954), pp. 70–77, and later adapted by Manning for "Hemingway in Cuba," *Atlantic*, Vol. 216 (Aug., 1965), pp. 101–108.

EH's secret resentment towards Nobel Prize committee: EH to Dorman-O'Gowan, Nov. 7, 1954.

Trip aboard "Pilar" and turtle-meat handshake: EH to Dorman-O'Gowan, Dec. 23, 1954.

EH's January illness: EH to Scribner, Jan. 14, 1955.

Writing as relief from pain: EH to Adriana, Jan. 30, 1955.

Death of Thomas Welsh: EH to Adriana, Feb. 23, 1955.

Pressure from people: EH to Breit, Feb. 1, 1955. In another letter to Breit, March 18, 1955, EH called Santiago a composite portrait of many fishermen, including old Marcos Puig, now dead, who had gone eighty-six days without catching a fish.

EH visited by undergraduates from Princeton and Rutgers: Mary Hemingway to Lillian Ross, Apr. 7, 1955; EH to Carlos Baker, April 13, 1955. The Princeton undergraduates carried a letter of introduction from Baker, who had unwisely written it without supposing that the boys would actually use it. EH's letter to Baker gave an account of the visit, mildly upbraiding Baker for having sired the interruption, but concluding, "I didn't mind seeing those kids at all. They were very cheerful and pleasant. I just wish it had been possible to have told them a convenient time to have seen them." In EH to Baker, May 2, 1955, he sent the boys his best wishes. Their account of the visit appeared in the *Daily Princetonian* for April 14, 1955.

Talk with Fraser Drew: from Professor Drew's transcript, which he generously allowed the author to excerpt.

Trip on "Pilar" (Apr. 17–May 4): EH to Dor-

man-O'Gowan, Apr. 15; EH to Meyer, Apr. 16; EH to Baker, May 2, 1955. On EH's return, Alfred Rice arrived for several days of business conferences: EH to Breit, May 14, 1955.

State of EH's health: EH to Meyer, May 31, 1955.

Arrival of Hayward and Viertel: EH to Meyer, May 31, 1955, with a postscript of June 9; and EH to Lanham, June 19, 1955.

Death of Don Andrés: EH to Adriana, Sept. 20, 1955.

Visit to Key West: EH to Berenson, July 9, 1955.

Business visit by Hotchner: *Papa Hemingway*, NY, 1966, pp. 155–166.

EH at age fifty-six: EH to Berenson, July 9, 1955. His comment on passing years is in EH to Patrick, July, 22, 1955. The author is indebted to Gelston Hardy for an account of his visit to EH at the Finca on July 27th to secure EH's signature on a ghost-written statement about the pleasures of foreign travel for the J. Walter Thompson Co., agents for Pan American World Airways. EH rejected the statement, typed out one of his own, gave Hardy a swim in the pool, and asked him to lunch. Gelston Hardy to author, Jan. 14 and 25, 1962.

EH assists film-makers: EH to Patrick, Aug. 24, 1955; EH to Philip Percival, Sept. 4, and EH to Breit, Sept. 15, 1955.

Arrival of George Brown: EH to Breit, Oct. 6, 1955.

EH's will: Admitted to probate, Aug., 1961, and published in facsimile in *New York Times*, Aug. 25, 1961, p. 27. The other two witnesses were René Villeréal and Lola Richards, servants at the Finca. According to Mary Hemingway, EH never wrote or spoke the "instructions."

EH on his sons: EH to Berenson, Sept. 18 and Oct. 4, and EH to Meyer, Oct. 11, 1955.

EH shoots buzzards: EH to Meyer, Oct. 11, 1955.

EH condemns literary people: on DeVoto, EH to Breit, Nov. 3; on Faulkner, EH to Breit, Nov. 14, 1955, and also EH to Breit, Feb. 1 and Feb. 28, 1955. Another of EH's nicknames for Faulkner was "Corncob."

Domínguin and Ordóñez: EH to Breit, Nov. 3 and Nov. 14, 1955.

EH's year-end illness: EH to Bumby, Nov. 28; EH to Meyer, Dec. 5; EH to Bumby, Dec. 6, 1955. It is also referred to in retrospect in EH to Meyer, Feb. 10, 1956.

EH's bedside reading: This included Sloan Wilson's *The Man in the Gray Flannel Suit* and Norman Mailer's *The Deer Park*, which EH disliked, and Anthony West's *Heritage* and P. H. Newby's *The Picnic at Sakkara*, which he greatly enjoyed. EH also named J. A. Pitts-Rive's *The People of the Sierra* (a gift from Rupert Bellville), and Volume 2 of Fuller's *Military History*.

Sec. 74. Looking Backward

SOURCES

Letters of EH: To Breit, Jan. 28, 1956; to Meyer, Feb. 10, March 13, and March 31; to Philip Percival, Gianfranco Ivancich, and R. M. Brown, all May 25; to Breit, May 28; to Lanham, June 10; to Breit, June 18 and July 3; to Meyer, July 5; to William Attwood,

July 10; to Ezra Pound, July 19; to Breit, July 2; to a Mr. Rider, July 29; to Berenson, Aug. 2; to Charles Scribner, Jr., Aug. 14; to Breit, Sept. 16; to Patrick, Sept. 28; to Berenson, Oct. 4; to Patrick, Oct. 26; to T. O. Bruce, Oct. 30; to Breit, Nov. 5; to Scribner, Nov. 5; to Patrick, Nov. 14 and Dec. 15; to Meyer, Dec. 28, 1956. To George Plimpton, March 4, 1957; to Lanham, Apr. 8; to Plimpton, Apr. 26; to Berenson, Apr. 30; to Meyer, May 18 and May 24; to MacLeish, ca. June 6; to Breit, June 16; to Patrick, June 18; to Robert Frost, June 28; to T. O. Bruce, Aug. 17; to Patrick, Sept. 4; to Breit, Sept. 8 and Oct. 12; to Lanham, Dec. 16, 1957. To Lanham, Jan. 9, 1958; to Gianfranco, Jan. 31; to Juanito Quintana, June 26; to L. H. Brague, July 31; to Lanham, Sept. 18, 1958. **Other letters:** Margaret Marshall to EH, Sept. 7, 1956; MacLeish to EH, Dec. 15, 1956; Mary to Patrick, Dec. 27, 1956. MacLeish to EH, Jan. 8 and Jan. 14, 1957; Mary to Berenson, Apr. 8, 1957; MacLeish to EH, June 3, June 19, and July 21, 1957; Ezra Pound to EH, Apr. 16, 1957. Pound to EH, July 17, 1958; Mary to Gianfranco, Sept. 19, 1958; MacLeish to EH, Sept. 27, 1958. **EH's work: Published:** "A Situation Report," *Look,* Vol. 20 (Sept. 4, 1956). "Two Tales of Darkness:" "A Man of the World," and "Get Yourself a Seeing-Eyed Dog," *Atlantic,* Vol. 200 (Nov., 1957). **Books and articles:** Ronald Duncan, "Pull Down Thy Vanity," *London Sunday Times,* Feb. 11, 1962. Unsigned article, "The Humble Wanderer" [Pio Baroja], *M.D., Medical News Magazine,* Vol. 6 (Dec., 1962); Mary Hemingway, "The Making of the Book: A Chronicle and a Memoir," *New York Times Book Review,* May 10, 1964. A. E. Hotchner, *Papa Hemingway,* 1966. **Author's interviews and correspondence:** with Mario Casamassima, Oct., 1965. From Mary Hemingway, March 24, 1963; from William Attwood, Apr. 13, 1963; from Denis Zaphiro, March 7, 1964; from Dr. Louis Schwartz, Oct. 1, 1964; from Irving Stone, June 27, 1966; from General Charles T. Lanham, Feb. 18, 1968.

NOTES

Anemia of Mary and EH: EH to Breit, Jan. 28, 1956, and EH to Meyer, Feb. 10, 1956.
Plans for Peru: EH to Meyer, March 31, 1956.
EH seals up his African book: EH to Meyer, March 13, 1956.
EH swears off movie involvements: EH to Meyer, March 13, 1956. His views on the squabbling are in EH to Meyer, March 31, and on the casting in EH to Meyer, July 5, 1956.
Fishing off Peru: EH to Percival, Gianfranco, and R. M. Brown, all written May 25, 1956. EH to Breit, May 28 and EH to Lanham, June 10, 1956. See also, EH, "A Situation Report," *Look,* Vol. 20 (Sept. 4, 1956), pp. 23–31.
Benefits to the Hemingways' health: EH to Percival, May 25 and EH to Breit, May 28, 1956. On his return EH learned that Philip Percival had successfully survived his cancer operation and that the Finca cat, Boise, had died of old age.

EH writes piece for "Look": William Attwood to author, Apr. 12, 1963. EH took up a few editorial changes in EH to Attwood, July 10, 1956. The piece was published September 4th.
EH sends Pound $1,000: EH to Pound, July 19, 1956. Pound later alluded to the check in an interview. "Somehow I didn't like to cash it—didn't know how hard up he might be, too. So I turned it into a paper-weight." Donald Duncan, "Pull Down Thy Vanity," *London Sunday Times,* Feb. 11, 1962, p. 33. Pound wrote to thank EH for the check from Merano, Italy: Pound to EH, July 17, 1958.
EH's uncharitable remarks on Faulkner: EH to a Mr. Rider, July 29, 1956. This letter was reproduced in facsimile in Charles Hamilton's Auction Catalogue No. 5, Oct. 8, 1964, and is undoubtedly genuine. Also genuine was EH's admiration for his sister Ursula, who was on hand for his fifty-seventh birthday. He praised her courage in having overcome the effects of three cancer operations in 1955: EH to Breit, July 23, 1956.
EH's new short stories: EH to Berenson, Aug. 2, 1956. The stories are listed by title in EH to Charles Scribner, Jr., Aug. 14, 1956.
Mary's continuing poor health: EH to Scribner, Aug. 14, 1956.
Breit offers New York house to EH: EH to Breit, June 18 (EH's request) and EH to Breit, July 3 (EH accepts), 1956.
EH's reunion with Lanham: General Lanham to author, Feb. 18, 1968. EH also spoke on the telephone to Sylvia Beach, who had done her memoirs and wanted him to read the chapter pertaining to himself. Margaret Marshall of Harcourt, Brace sent him the chapter to Paris on Sept. 7, 1956. Though it was filled with factual errors, there is no indication that he corrected them.
Irving Stone on the Île de France: Stone to author, June 27, 1966.
Casamassima as EH's driver: Casamassima to author, Oct. 20, 1965.
Paris to Madrid: EH to Breit, Sept. 16, 1956. They met Peter Viertel and Rupert Bellville at St.-Jean-de-Luz. EH described the *corrida* at Logroño in EH to Patrick Hemingway, Sept. 28, 1956.
Settling into Hotel Felipe II: EH to Patrick, Sept. 28, 1956.
EH on the good fall weather: EH to Berenson, Oct. 4, 1956.
Feria at Zaragoza: EH to Patrick, Sept. 28, 1956 anticipates this trip. See also Hotchner, *Papa Hemingway,* NY, 1966, pp. 169–174. On EH's excessive drinking, Irving Stone to author, June 27, 1966, and Hotchner, pp. 182–188.
EH calls on Baroja: see "The Humble Wanderer," in *M.D., Medical News Magazine,* Vol. 6 (December, 1962), pp. 140–143, copy kindly supplied to author by Samuel Putnam. The article included a picture of EH and Baroja, both looking old and ill. EH's account of attending Baroja's funeral is in EH to Breit, Nov. 5, 1956.
EH and Mary visit Dr. Madinaveitia: EH to T. O. Bruce, Oct. 30; EH to Breit, Nov. 5; EH to Scribner, Nov. 5; EH to Patrick, Oct. 26, 1956; and EH to Lanham, Apr. 8, 1957. Mary Hemingway to author, March 24, 1963.
EH plans for safari: EH to Patrick, Oct. 26, 1956.

EH defies doctor's advice: EH to Breit, Nov. 5, 1956.

Suez blockage and cancellation of bookings: EH to Patrick. Nov. 14 and Dec. 15, 1956.

EH's trunks in storage: Mary Hemingway, "The Making of the Book: A Chronicle and a Memoir," *New York Times Book Review*, May 10, 1964, pp. 26–27.

Dr. Schwartz attends EH: Schwartz to author, Oct. 1, 1964. He saw EH first on Nov. 30th, 1956 and last on Jan. 3, 1957.

The Hemingways' life in Paris: Mary Hemingway to author, March 24, 1963. According to Mary, the friends they saw included Gianfranco, Peter Viertel, John Huston, Dan Teeters, Philip Hardwick, Capt. Alastair Mackintosh, Charles Ritz, Princess Aspasia of Greece, and others.

Visit from Leonard Lyons: Lyons Den Column, *NY Post*, Jan. 24, 1957.

EH's boredom with diet: EH to Patrick, Dec. 15; Mary to Patrick, Dec. 27; and EH to Meyer, Dec. 28, 1956.

Death of Black Dog: EH to Patrick, Dec. 15, 1956.

MacLeish plan to secure Pound's release: MacLeish to EH, December 15, 1956 and January 8 and 14, 1957. William P. Rogers had just succeeded Herbert Brownell as Attorney General, and it was to Rogers that the letter was sent. It stated that the signers were interested both in Pound as a writer and in the reputation of their country. Medical evidence indicated that Pound would continue to be unfit for trial. They regretted the failure of the Department of Justice to nol pros the indictment and turn the case over to the medical authorities. MacLeish to EH, January 8, 1957, asked him to write Christian Herter in Pound's behalf. I have been unable to discover if EH complied with this request. MacLeish's document was sent to Attorney General Rogers on Jan. 14, 1957.

EH's remark to Lyons: Lyons Den Column, *NY Post*, Jan. 24, 1957.

Return to New York and Cuba: Mary Hemingway to author, March 24, 1963, based in part on her diary entry for Feb. 3, 1957, where she summed up the trip.

EH's depressed state: EH to Meyer, May 18, 1957. Mary's progress report is in Mary to Berenson, Apr. 8, 1957. During this spring he answered by hand a series of questions for George Plimpton to use in his Hemingway interview (*Paris Review* 18, Spring 1958, pp. 61–89). EH to Plimpton, March 4 and April 26, 1957.

EH writes memoir of Fitzgerald for Atlantic centenary but does not submit it: EH to Breit, June 16, 1957. This memoir was EH's first formal step towards the collection posthumously published as *A Moveable Feast*. "A Man of the World," composed between mid-May and mid-June, 1957 (EH to Breit, June 16, 1957), together with "Get Yourself a Seeing-Eyed Dog," composed in the summer of 1956, appeared together as "Two Tales of Darkness," *Atlantic*, Vol. 200 (November, 1957) pp. 64–68.

MacLeish moves to free Pound: MacLeish to EH, June 3, 1957. EH says he cannot go to Washington, but takes his duties seriously: EH to MacLeish, ca. June 6, 1957. MacLeish rehearses history of the case from December,

1955, to present and asks EH to write Frost: MacLeish to EH, June 19, 1957. EH writes Frost as requested: EH to Frost, June 28, 1957. MacLeish reports on his visit to Washington with Frost: MacLeish to EH, July 21, 1957. Throughout this period, Pound continued writing EH in what EH laughingly referred to as the "Unknown Tongue." On April 16th, Ezra said, "Dear Archie [is] still pickin lillies in the valley of asphodel . . . but yr letters lighten captivity." On June 13 he referred to "Carl Sandbag's" life of Lincoln, and on July 15 wanted to know "wotever THE hell evur beKom of Marse Henry Stretter"—meaning Henry Strater, the artist. The reference to Archie MacLeish was illtimed, since MacLeish was actively engaged in Pound's behalf, and had been for some months.

EH predicts bad year for 1957: EH to Meyer, Dec. 28, 1956.

Instances of bad luck: poor weather (EH to Patrick, June 18, 1957); illness of Bumby and Gregory (EH to T. O. Bruce, Aug. 17; EH to Patrick, Sept. 4; EH to Lanham, Dec. 16, 1957).

Zaphiro visit: Denis Zaphiro to author, March 7, 1964; EH to Patrick, Sept. 4, 1957.

EH's complaint of changes in Cuba: EH to Berenson, Apr. 30, 1957.

Cuban patrol shoots dog Machakos: *NY Times*, Aug. 22, 1957.

New York trip with Zaphiro: EH to Breit, Sept. 8 and Oct. 12, 1957; Mary Hemingway, *New York Times Book Review*, May 10, 1964.

EH's tax-bill: EH to Lanham, Dec. 16, 1957.

EH's feeling of strangeness: EH to Gianfranco, Jan. 31, 1958.

Inception and development of the Paris sketchbook: Mary Hemingway, "The Making of the Book: A Chronicle and a Memoir," *New York Times Book Review*, May 10, 1964, pp. 26–27. The "book" of her title was *A Moveable Feast*, the name assigned to the collection before its posthumous publication in 1964.

EH calls the book done except for two incomplete sketches: EH to L. H. Brague, July 31, 1958.

EH revises "The Garden of Eden": EH to Juanito Quintana, June 26, 1958; EH to L. H. Brague (who had succeeded Wallace Meyer as his editor at Scribners) July 31, 1958; and EH to Lanham, September 18, 1958. Mary to Gianfranco, September 19, 1958, said that EH had finished the Paris book and three quarters of another. Mary's article on *A Moveable Feast* in the *New York Times Book Review*, May 10, 1964, states that "soon after we returned from New York" (in October, 1957), Ernest "gave me a manuscript on which he had been working, a novel set in southern France in the twenties, to put into one of our safe deposit boxes in Havana." If this is true, it was taken out again around Christmas, 1957, and worked over through the winter, spring, and summer. He had it in Ketchum in the fall of 1958, since Chapters 25–27 are all labeled "Rewrote, 19/11/58" in Ernest's hand.

Pound's release from St. Elizabeth's: *NY Times*, Apr. 18, 1958. MacLeish provided EH with a summary of the final moves: MacLeish to EH, Sept. 27, 1958.

Mary's report on EH's health: Mary to Gianfranco, Sept. 19, 1958.

Sec. 75. A Man of Sixty

SOURCES

Letters of EH: to Lanham, Sept. 18, 1958; to Breit, Sept. 21; to Bronislaw Zielinski, Nov. 4 (wire) and Nov. 5; to L. H. Brague, Nov. 10; to Zielinski, Nov. 11; to Patrick, Nov. 24; to Zielinski, Nov. 24; to T. O. Bruce, Nov. 27; to Brague, Dec. 22, 1958. To Gianfranco, Jan. 7, 1959; to Brague, Jan. 24; to Gianfranco, Feb. 4; to Brague, Feb. 22; to Nathan (Bill) Davis, Feb. 22; to Bumby, March 30; to William Seward, March 31; to Charles Scribner, Jr., March 31 and Apr. 12; to Zielinski, Apr. 12; to Nathan Davis, Apr. 12; to Brague, May 24; to Scribner, June 3; to Juanito Quintana, June 6; to T. O. Bruce, June 7; to Lanham, ca. June 10; to Scribner, June 13 and June 20; to Zielinski, June 24; to Patrick, Aug. 5; to Brague, Aug. 6 and Aug. 26; to Scribner, Aug. 27; to Brague, Sept. 11; to Lanham, Sept. 16; to T. O. Bruce, Sept. 17; to Scribner, Oct. 11; to T. O. Bruce, Oct. 11; to Dr. George Saviers, Oct. 15, 1959.
Other letters: Lloyd Arnold to EH, Aug. 25, 1958; Mary to Patrick, Sept. 20, 1958; Mary to Mr. and Mrs. T. O. Bruce, November 3, 1958; Mary to Clara Spiegel, Nov. 3, 1958. Mary to Patrick, Jan. 13, 1959; Mary to Clara Spiegel, April 19, 1959; Mary to Clara Spiegel, Aug. 18, 1959; Annie (Mrs. Nathan) Davis to Dr. and Mrs. George Saviers, Aug. 26, 1959; Mary to General Lanham, Aug. 26, 1959; Mary to Patrick, Aug. 30, 1959; Ezra Pound to EH, Oct. 1, 1959; Eaton Adams to Douglas F. Smith, Dec. 18, 1962.
EH's work: Unpublished: "The Art of the Short Story," completed ca. June 13, 1959.
Books and articles: A. E. Hotchner, *This Week* magazine, Oct. 18, 1959; Kenneth Tynan, "Papa and the Playwright," *Playboy*, Vol. 11 (May, 1964); Valerie Danby-Smith, "Reminiscence of Hemingway," *Saturday Review*, Vol. 47 (May 9, 1964); John Crosby, "No Time for Heroes," *New York Herald Tribune*, March 11, 1965; A. E. Hotchner, *Papa Hemingway*, 1966.
Author's interviews and correspondence: with Gen. C. T. Lanham, July, 1963; with Don Anderson, Lloyd Arnold, Chuck Atkinson, and Dr. George Saviers, July, 1964; with Nathan (Bill) Davis, Oct. 1965; with Waldo Peirce, June, 1966. From John Crosby, Apr. 6, 1965; from Lloyd Arnold, Nov. 30, 1965 and April 4, 1966.

NOTES

EH's year of all work and no play: EH to Lanham, Sept. 18, 1958.
EH on time and writing: EH to Breit, Sept. 21, 1958.
Cuban weather: Mary to Patrick, Sept. 20 and EH to Breit, Sept. 21, 1958.
Plans for Ketchum: Mary to Patrick, Sept. 20, 1958, with an insert by EH.
Driving to Idaho: EH to Patrick, Nov. 24, 1958; Mr. and Mrs. T. O. Bruce to author, March 22, 1965.
Arrival in Ketchum (Oct. 7, 1958): Don Anderson, Lloyd Arnold, Chuck Atkinson, and Dr. George Saviers to author, July, 1964.
EH's rented house: Occupied until just before Christmas, this house belonged to Clark and

Marge Heiss. Lloyd Arnold had found it for them at $175 a month (Arnold to EH, Aug. 25, 1958).
EH's euphoria: EH to T. O. Bruce, Nov. 27, 1958.
Shooting with Anderson and MacMullen: Don Anderson to author, Aug. 3, 1964; EH to T. O. Bruce, Nov. 27, 1958. On Oct. 25, the first day of the pheasant season, they drove to Hagerman Valley, hunting along the Snake River in late-summer weather. On Nov. 2, a chilly Sunday with leaden skies, they went down to Bud Purdy's ranch near Picabo with Taylor Williams, MacMullen, and the Arnolds, putting up many coveys of chukar partridge and jumping dozens of ducks in the irrigation ditches. (Mary to the Bruces, Nov. 3, and Mary to Clara Spiegel, Nov. 3, 1958.)
Arrival of Zielinski: EH to Zielinski, Nov. 4 (wire) and Nov. 5, 1958; EH to Brague, Nov. 10; group postcard to Mrs. Zielinski from EH, Mary, the Arnolds, and Zielinski, Nov. 11, 1958.
EH offers Polish prize: EH to Zielinski, Nov. 24, 1958. Announced in *NY Times*, Dec. 3, 1958.
Arrival of Hotchner: Lloyd Arnold to author, Apr. 4, 1966; A. E. Hotchner, *Papa Hemingway*, NY, 1966, pp. 190-196.
EH talks to Hailey schoolchildren: published by Hotchner in *This Week* (Oct. 18, 1959) pp. 10-11 and 24-26, and quoted in *Papa Hemingway*, pp. 197-201.
Arrival of Gary Cooper: EH to Gianfranco, Feb. 4, 1959; and Hotchner, *Papa Hemingway*, pp. 201-202.
EH works on Paris sketchbook: EH to Brague, Dec. 22, 1958.
EH revises parts of "The Garden of Eden": In EH's hand, the MS. bears annotations beside Chapters 25-27, "Rewrote, 19/11/58." The notation beside Ch. 25 reads "very good," a considerable overstatement. On Nov. 10 he wrote Brague that he hoped he would not be dead before his next books appeared.
EH on Cuban situation: EH to Patrick, Nov. 24 and EH to Brague, Dec. 22, 1958.
Flight of Batista: EH to Gianfranco, Jan. 7, 1959. EH's farewell words for Batista were "Sic transit hijo de puta."
News of the Finca: EH to Gianfranco, Jan. 7; Mary to Patrick, Jan. 13, 1959.
EH wishes Castro well: EH to Brague, Jan. 24, 1959.
Move to Whicher house: Mary to Patrick, Jan. 13, 1959.
EH looks at Topping house: Lloyd Arnold to author, Nov., 1964; Chuck Atkinson to author, Aug., 1964. Mary did not like the place: Mary to Clara Spiegel, Apr. 19, 1959.
Death and burial of Taylor Williams: Don Anderson to author, Aug., 1964; Lloyd Arnold to author, Nov., 1964; EH to Brague, Feb. 22, 1959.
EH plans Spanish summer: EH to Nathan Davis, Feb. 22, 1959. Davis had known EH slightly since 1940. He had met Pauline in the 1930s, visited Sun Valley in 1940, entertained EH and Martha in Mexico City in 1941, and seen EH briefly in 1947. Davis to author, Oct. 9, 1965. Ordóñez was fighting the South American circuit, and EH telephoned him Feb. 21 at Bogotá, Colombia.
Drive home from Ketchum: EH to Bumby, March 30; EH to William Seward, March 31;

EH to Nathan Davis, Apr. 12, 1959; Hotchner, *Papa Hemingway*, pp. 202–205.
Purchase of Topping house: Chuck Atkinson to author, Aug., 1964. According to EH, the house was built in 1955 at a cost of $150,000. "Fun will be had in that house," he said. EH to T. O. Bruce, June 7, 1959.
Reunion with Peirce: Waldo Peirce to author, June 1, 1966. Ellen Peirce was subject to sinus infection and the dry air of Tucson was beneficial.
EH on Castro revolution: EH to Bumby, March 30; EH to Scribner, March 31 and Apr. 12; EH to Bronislaw Zielinski, Apr. 12, 1959.
EH meets Tennessee Williams: Kenneth Tynan, "Papa and the Playwright," *Playboy*, Vol. 11 (May, 1964), pp. 97 and 138–141.
EH at Davis estate: Davis to author, Oct., 1965; EH to Brague, May 24, 1959. The place lies about one kilometer north of the main road between Málaga and Torremolinos.
EH at Hotel Suecia: EH to Brague, May 24, 1959.
EH praises Segura bullfight in Madrid: Eaton Adams to Douglas F. Smith, Dec. 18, 1962, an unpublished eyewitness account.
EH's end-of-May bullfight trips: EH to Scribner, June 3 and EH to T. O. Bruce, June 7, 1959.
Mary's nose-and-throat infection: EH to Scribner, June 3, and Mary to Clara Spiegel, Aug. 18, 1959.
EH at Aranjuez with John Crosby: Crosby, "No Time for Heroes," *New York Herald Tribune*, March 11, 1965.
Ordóñez gored at Aranjuez: EH to Scribner, June 3; EH to Juanito Quintana, June 7, 1959, and EH, "The Dangerous Summer," *Life*, Vol. 49 (Sept. 5, 1960), pp. 100–109.
Ordóñez recuperates at Málaga: "The Dangerous Summer," *Life*, Sept. 12, 1960, pp. 64–66.
EH completes short-story preface: EH to Scribner, June 13 and June 20, 1959. The preface, called "The Art of the Short Story," was disliked by Mary and rejected by Scribner in July.
EH's admiration for Ordóñez: EH to Lanham, ca. June 10, 1959.
EH visits Ordóñez's bull ranch: EH to Patrick, Aug. 5, 1959. The same letter speaks of his wish to buy land at Conil.
EH follows Ordóñez's late-June schedule: EH to Lanham, ca. June 10; EH to Zielinski, June 24, 1959; Hotchner, *Papa Hemingway*, pp. 207–211.
EH at Pamplona and Aoiz: "The Dangerous Summer," *Life*, Vol. 49, Sept. 12, 1960, pp. 64–66.
Valerie Danby-Smith as secretary: Miss Danby-Smith, "Reminiscence of Hemingway," *Saturday Review*, Vol. 47 (May, 1964), pp. 30–31 and 37. She stated there that she joined EH's *cuadrilla* in July after the "maddest" of all Spanish fiestas, Pamplona.
EH's sixtieth birthday party: Mary to Patrick, Aug. 30, 1959; EH, "The Dangerous Summer," *Life*, Vol. 49 (Sept. 12, 1960), p. 75.
Dr. Saviers treats EH's kidney infection: Dr. Saviers to author, Aug. 6, 1964.
EH's singular behavior: Gen. C. T. Lanham to author, July, 1963, with supplementary comments, Feb. 18, 1968.
EH in Valencia: Mary to Patrick, Aug. 30, 1959; Lanham to author, July, 1963; EH, "The

Dangerous Summer," *Life*, Vol. 49 (Sept. 12, 1960), pp. 76–82.
Final duels between Antonio and Luis Miguel: "The Dangerous Summer," *Life*, Vol. 49 (Sept. 19, 1960), pp. 74–96.
EH's contract with "Life": EH to Brague, Aug. 6, 1959.
Antonio trampled at Dax: EH to Brague, Aug. 26, 1959.
Lancia accident: Annie [Mrs. Nathan] Davis to Dr. and Mrs. Saviers, Aug. 26; EH to Brague, Aug. 26 and Sept. 11; EH to Lanham, Sept. 16, 1959.
EH surfeited with spectator sports: EH to Scribner, Aug. 27, 1959.
Mary's views on Papa Sportif and Papa Penseroso: Mary to Lanham, Aug. 26, 1959.
Antonio's late-season debarment: EH to Lanham Sept. 16, 1959. Shortly before this time, Mary had a long heart-to-heart talk with Valerie: Mary to Patrick, Aug. 30, 1959.
Hotchner's television deal: EH to T. O. Bruce, Sept. 17, 1959.
EH begins "Life" article: EH to Scribner, Oct. 11; EH to T. O. Bruce, Oct. 11; and EH to Dr. George Saviers, Oct. 15, 1959.
Pound complains of fatigue: Ezra Pound to EH, Oct. 1, 1959.
EH anticipates shooting in Ketchum: EH to Dr. Saviers, Oct. 15, 1959.

Sec. 76. Journey Down

SOURCES

Letters of EH: to Nathan and Annie Davis, Oct. 28, 1959 (one letter to each), and Oct. 31, 1959 (one letter to each); to Charles Scribner, Jr., Nov. 3; to Nathan [Bill] Davis, Nov. 8 and 28; to Baker, Dec. 8; to T. O. Bruce, Dec. 14, 1959. To Davis, Jan. 7, 1960; to Lanham, Jan. 12; to Davis, Jan. 13; to Scribner, Jan. 16; to Davis, Feb. 8; to Patrick, Feb. 10; to Davis, Apr. 1 and May 9; to Gianfranco, May 30; to Juanito Quintana, June 1; to Scribner, July 6; to Bumby, July 31; to Mary, Aug. 5, 8, 15, 19, and 26; to Mary, Sept. 3, 7, 9, 18, and 23, 1960. To Brague, Jan. 8, 1961; to President-elect John F. Kennedy, Jan. 13 (wire); to Lanham, Jan. 16; to Patrick, Jan. 16; to Baker, Jan. 16; to Ellis O. Briggs, Jan. 17; to Thomas Shevlin, Jan. 17; to Hyatt Waggoner, Jan. 18; to Milton Wolff, Jan. 18; to Col. James Luckett, Jan. 18; to Brague, Jan. 19; to Leonard Lyons, Jan. 20; to Peter Barrett, Jan. 20; to Baker, Jan. 20; to Brague, Jan. 20; to Patrick, Jan. 25 (cable); to Brague, Feb. 6; to Patrick, ca. Feb. 15 and March 22; to Scribner, June 10; to Fritz Saviers, June 15, 1961.
Other letters: Mary to Dr. George Saviers, Nov. 10, 1959. Mary to Clara Spiegel, Feb. 29, 1960. Mary to Gen. C. T. Lanham, March 16, 1960. Mary to T. O. Bruce, July 30, 1960. Mary to William D. Horne, Aug. 7, 1960. Mary to Patrick, ca. Dec. 5, 1960. Mary to T. O. Bruce, ca. Dec. 5, 1960. President-elect John F. Kennedy to EH, Jan. 12, 1961 (wire). Dr. Hugh R. Butt to EH, Jan. 19, 1961. Mary to Peter Briggs, Feb. 19, 1961. Mary to T. O. Bruce, Apr. 7, 1961. John Dos Passos to EH, Apr. 28, 1961. Gary Cooper to EH, Apr. 29, 1961 (wire). Mary to Clara Spiegel, May 8, 1961; Mary to T. O. Bruce, May 17, 1961; Dr. George Saviers to EH, June 13, 1961.

EH's work: Published: "The Dangerous Summer," *Life,* Vol. 49, Sept. 5, 12, and 19, 1960.
Books and articles: Seymour Betsky, "A Last Visit," *Saturday Review,* Vol. 44 (July 29, 1961); Arthur Schlesinger, *A Thousand Days: John F. Kennedy in the White House,* 1965; A. E. Hotchner, *Papa Hemingway,* 1966; Andrew Turnbull, "Perkins's Three Generals," *New York Times Book Review,* July 16, 1967.
Author's interviews and correspondence: with Mary Hemingway, Dr. George Saviers, Dr. Scott Earle, Don Anderson, and Chuck Atkinson, Aug., 1964; with Bill Davis, Oct., 1965; with Joseph North, Apr., 1966. From Hadley Mowrer, Apr., 1962; from Mary Hemingway, Apr. 16, 1962; from Luis Kutner, May 8, 1962; from Dr. X, Oct. 16, 1964; from Don Anderson, Nov. 10, 1964; from Dr. David Butsch, Sept. 9, 1965; from General C. T. Lanham, Feb. 18, 1968; from Dr. Howard P. Rome, Feb. 19, 1968; from Dr. Hugh R. Butt, March 6 and Apr. 11, 1968.

NOTES

EH crossing on "Liberté": EH to Bill and Annie Davis, Oct. 28 and Oct. 31, 1959 (2 letters to each). These and other letters from EH to the Davises were sold at auction by Charles Hamilton, Catalogue No. 19, May 24, 1967. This auction catalogue published liberal excerpts from them all, a few of which have been quoted below.
Meeting Andrew Turnbull: Turnbull, "Perkins's Three Generals," *New York Times Book Review,* July 16, 1967, p. 26.
EH in New York: EH to Annie Davis, Oct. 31, 1959. This letter sums up Mary's alleged views of his character, and may be read in the Hamilton auction catalogue noted above, p. 83.
EH inspects new apartment in New York: EH to Bill Davis, Nov. 8, 1959. Charles Scribner, Jr., to author, ca. Apr. 15, 1968. See also Hotchner, *Papa Hemingway,* NY, 1966, pp. 229–232.
EH lends Paris sketchbook to Scribner: EH to Scribner, Nov. 3, 1959.
EH to Havana: EH to Bill Davis, Nov. 8, 1959.
Flag episode: Joseph North to author, Apr., 1966.
Mary prepares Ketchum house for guests: Mary to Dr. George Saviers, Nov. 10, 1959.
EH goes west with Antonio and Carmen: EH to Bill Davis, Nov. 28 and EH to T. O. Bruce, Dec. 14, 1959. These letters allude to Antonio's hasty departure for Mexico.
Mary shatters elbow: EH to Davis, Nov. 28 and EH to Baker, Dec. 8, 1959.
EH's hypertension and insomnia: EH to Lanham, Jan. 12, 1960.
EH on view from window: EH to Davis, Jan. 13, 1960. Quoted from published excerpt in Charles Hamilton catalogue noted above, p. 86. In EH to Davis, Jan. 7, 1960, he records that Hotchner, paying his third visit to Ketchum, shot well on targets but "disasterously" in the field.
EH on Harold Loeb's autobiography: EH to Baker, Dec. 8, 1959.
EH on dying young vs. growing old: EH to his father, Oct. 18, 1918, published in *Oak Parker,* Nov. 16, 1918, pp. 6–7.

Return to Cuba: Mary to Clara Spiegel, Feb. 29, 1960; EH to Scribner, Jan. 16, 1960, says their train is leaving that night.
EH resumes bullfight article: EH to Davis, Feb. 8, and EH to Patrick, Feb. 10, 1960.
Arrival of Valerie and visit from Mikoyan: Mary to Clara Spiegel, Feb. 29, 1960.
Arrival of Herbert Matthews: Mary to Lanham, March 16, 1960.
EH tires of bullfight article: EH to Davis, Apr. 1, 1960.
EH's eye trouble: EH to Davis, May 9, 1960.
EH completes book-length bullfight article: EH to Gianfranco, May 30, 1960.
EH hints at imminent failure of reason: EH to Juanito Quintana, June 1, 1960.
EH summons Hotchner: EH to Scribner, July 6, 1960. See also *Papa Hemingway,* pp. 240–247, where Hotchner notes completion of sale to *Life* magazine.
EH calls self necessary to Ordóñez: EH to Baker, Dec. 8, 1959.
EH's concern about Valerie's legal status: Mary Hemingway to author, Aug., 1964.
EH, Mary, and Valerie to New York: Mary to T. O. Bruce, July 30, 1960. On Aug. 7, Mary wrote W. D. Horne that they came to New York ten days ago (i.e., ca. July 29). Hotchner (*Papa Hemingway,* p. 247) says they all arrived on Friday, July 13, though July 13 was a Wednesday.
EH in New York: EH to Bumby, July 31, 1960; Charles Scribner to author, ca. Apr. 15, 1968; Hotchner, *Papa Hemingway,* pp. 247–251.
EH flies to Madrid: EH to Mary, Aug. 5 (cable on arrival) and EH to Mary, Aug. 8, 1960. Luis Kutner to author, May 8, 1962.
EH's crack-up: Nathan Davis to author, Oct. 9, 1965. EH to Mary, Aug. 15, 19, and 26; Sept. 3, 7, 9, 18, and 23, 1960. The letter of Aug. 19 refers to his complete physical and nervous "crack-up," ironically echoing Fitzgerald's phrase of 1936. The letter of Sept. 3 says the trouble has been coming on for a month; that of Sept. 23 says he wishes Mary were there to keep him from "cracking up."
EH's insane behavior in Madrid: Hotchner, *Papa Hemingway,* pp. 251–263.
Train trip west: Mary Hemingway to author, Apr. 16, 1962.
Fears and delusions in Ketchum: Mary Hemingway to author, Aug. 3, 1964. Hotchner's account of his arrival there is in *Papa Hemingway,* pp. 264–268.
Visit from professors: Seymour Betsky, "A Last Visit," *Saturday Review,* Vol. 44 (July 29, 1961), p. 22. EH to Brague, Jan. 19, 1961, ordered two of Fiedler's books from Scribners and told Harry Brague about the visitation. At the time he had been unable to recall what Fiedler had written about him, except for Malcolm Cowley's opinion that it was "all rot." When Fiedler asked what he thought of them, EH (so he said) answered that he probably disagreed with them, but would defend to the death his right to his opinions. This, said EH, shook Fiedler slightly, and he managed to get his visitors out of the house and get back to work.
Decision to hospitalize EH: Mary Hemingway to author, Aug. 3, 1964; Dr. George Saviers to author, Aug. 6, 1964; Dr. Scott Earle to author, Aug. 7, 1964.

Diagnosis by New York psychiatrist: Dr. X to author, Oct. 6, 1964.
Flight to Rochester: EH to Lanham, Jan. 16 and EH to Brague, Jan. 19, 1961; Dr. Saviers to author, Aug. 6, 1964. Dr. Howard P. Rome to author, Feb. 19, 1968, says that EH occupied Room 1–126 in St. Mary's Hospital.
EH's medical examinations: Mary to Patrick and Mary to T. O. Bruce, both ca. Dec. 5, 1960.
EH's organic ailments: Dr. Hugh Butt to EH, Jan. 19, 1961, a report written at EH's request, and therefore made available to his biographer. In giving his medical history, EH noted his severe hepatitis of late 1918; jaundice, dark urine, enlarged liver, and edema of ankles from 1956; and, beginning in June, 1960, difficulty in working in afternoons after wine with lunch, continued weight loss despite good food intake, and increased insomnia. This history was of course ridiculously incomplete. On admission to Mayo Clinic, he weighed 175.5, with blood pressure of 160/98, and pulse of 80. Laboratory studies showed normal urine with trace of albumin and specific gravity of 1.025. Hemoglobin was 14.7 grams per cent; blood urea 46 milligrams per cent; fasting true blood sugar 115 milligrams per cent; Bromsulphalein dye retention test for liver function was 0; prothrombin time was 23 seconds. Serum bilirubin direct was negative; total proteins 6.05 grams with 3.44 grams albumin and a normal electrophoretic pattern. Cephalin cholesterol was negative; plasma cholesterol was 182 milligrams. Leukocyte count was 5300; differential count was normal. Blood cells were normochromic and normocytic; routine flocculation test for syphilis was negative. X rays of head and chest were negative. Electrocardiographic tracing showed a rate of 60 sinus rhythm with an inverted T in lead III. An electroencephalographic tracing was within normal limits. For several weeks prior to Jan. 19, 1961, blood pressure remained within normal range of 140/80.
EH presents books to doctors and nurses: EH to Brague, Jan. 8, 1961.
EH visits Dr. Butt's home: Dr. David Butsch to author, Sept. 9, 1965. Dr. Butt to author, Mar. 7, and Apr. 11, 1968.
EH shows signs of recovery: EH to Patrick, Jan. 16; EH to Lanham, Jan. 16; EH to Baker, Jan. 16; EH to Ellis O. Briggs, Jan. 17; EH to Tom Shevlin, Jan. 17; EH to Col. James Luckett, Jan. 18; EH to Hyatt Waggoner, Jan. 18; EH to Milton Wolff, Jan. 18; EH to Peter Briggs, Jan. 19; EH to Brague, Jan. 19; EH to Lanham, Jan. 19; EH to Leonard Lyons, Jan. 20; EH to Peter Barrett, Jan. 20; EH to Brague, Jan. 20; EH to Baker, Jan. 20, 1961. These letters are probably only a fraction of those he dictated in this five-day period. He said that after ten hours' work and no exercise, his blood pressure rose to 173/93 on January 20: EH to Brague, Jan. 20, 1961. "Anyway," said EH, "it's mobile."
President-elect Kennedy's invitation to inaugural: Kennedy to EH, Jan. 12, 1961, telegram.
EH sends regrets: EH to Kennedy, Jan. 13, 1961, telegram.
He watches inauguration on television and sends second message: message quoted by Arthur Schlesinger, *A Thousand Days,* Boston, Massachusetts, 1965, p. 732. On

two small bits of paper torn from a pocket notebook occurs the following in EH's handwriting. It was evidently a follow-up to an unauthorized release by the public relations department of Mayo Clinic: "Mr. Hemingway was not queried by a spokesman for the Mayo Clinic yesterday and did not issue a flat no comment on whether he would attend the inauguration ceremonies as reported. He replied to the valued invitation of the President Elect and Mrs. Kennedy and his reply is a matter of record which may be confirmed in Washington." It is not clear whether this statement was released to the press. Aaron Hotchner was summoned to see EH at this time and flew out on January 13th. He was distressed to find EH still in the grip of his delusions, particularly the fear of arrest and prosecution for having "brought" Valerie Danby-Smith to the United States while she was still legally a minor. Hotchner reported that feelings of guilt in connection with Valerie showed themselves in EH's ambivalent treatment of Mary, to whom he was alternately deferential and fiercely abusive. Hotchner added that he was present when EH composed his first reply to the Kennedy invitation: "We spent some time composing a proper reply of declination." A. E. Hotchner, *Papa Hemingway,* NY, 1966, pp. 277–281.
EH's flight home: EH to Baker, Jan. 20, 1961.
EH asserts he is working hard: EH to Patrick, Jan. 25, 1961 (cable).
EH's daily habits, walks, etc.: EH to Brague, Feb. 6, 1961.
Walks on Route 93: Mary Hemingway to author, Aug. 3, 1964. EH told Patrick ca. Feb. 15, 1961, that things had been rough but that he was cheered by the sight of ten cow elk browsing on a mountain ridge.
EH becomes recluse: Don Anderson to author, Aug. 3, 1964.
EH ignores view outside window: Mary Hemingway to Peter Briggs, Feb. 19, 1961.
EH labors over Kennedy message: Mary Hemingway to author, Aug. 3, 1964. Mrs. Hemingway assigns Feb. 20 as the approximate date.
EH weeps over inability to write: Dr. Saviers to author, Aug. 6, 1964.
EH fears onset of cancer: Chuck Atkinson to author, Aug. 2, 1964.
EH fears lawsuits against Paris sketchbook: Mary Hemingway to author, Aug. 3, 1964.
EH telephones Hadley: Hadley Mowrer to author, Apr. 9, 1962.
EH declines to attend Baldy Mountain races: Don Anderson to author, Aug. 3, 1964.
EH complains of not feeling well: EH to Patrick, March 22, 1961.
Mary's fall downstairs: Mary to T. O. Bruce, Apr. 7, 1961.
EH's first suicide threat: Mary Hemingway to author, Aug. 3, 1964.
EH's second suicide attempt: Don Anderson to author, Aug. 3, 1964, with supplementary details forwarded to author, Nov. 10, 1964.
EH flown back to Rochester: Don Anderson to author, Aug. 3, 1964; Dr. George Saviers to author, Aug. 6, 1964. Mr. Anderson stated that he did not touch EH when he walked towards the whirling propellers.
Messages from Dos Passos and Gary Cooper: Dos Passos to EH, Apr. 28, 1961 and Cooper to EH, Apr. 29, 1961 (wire).

EH on honor not to try suicide: Mary Hemingway to author, Aug. 3, 1964.
Mary in Ketchum: Mary to Clara Spiegel, May 8, 1961; Mary to T. O. Bruce, May 17, 1961.
Mary in New York and Rochester: Mary Hemingway to author, Aug. 3, 1964.
EH likes book on Yellowstone: EH to Scribner, June 10, 1961.
EH writes Fritz Saviers: Dr. Saviers to EH, June 13 and EH to Fritz Saviers, June 15, 1961. The letter was published in facsimile in *Life*, Vol. 51 (Aug. 25, 1961), p. 7.
Drive from Rochester to Ketchum: Mary Hemingway to author, Aug. 3, 1964.
Sunday morning: Mary Hemingway to author, Aug. 3, 1964; Chuck Atkinson to author, Aug. 2, 1964; Dr. George Saviers to author, Aug. 6, 1964; Don Anderson to author, Aug. 4, 1964; Dr. Scott Earle to author, Aug. 7, 1964.

Post mortem: Dr. Scott Earle was summoned at 7:40 A.M. to certify the death. He found EH's body slumped crosswise in the entryway. The entire cranial vault had been blown away. When Don Anderson reached the house, the suicide weapon was still there. He opened it and found that both shells had been fired.

Blaine County Coroner Ray McGoldrick filed a certificate stating that EH had died of a "self-inflicted gunshot wound in the head." The sheriff, Frank Hewitt, impounded the gun, which was held for about two weeks. Mary Hemingway and Chuck Atkinson were anxious that it should not fall into the hands of souvenir hunters. Chuck cut the gun to pieces with a blowtorch and buried them in a secret place. He and Don had gone together to the Ketchum cemetery to buy a plot of six 10 by 6 lots near the graves of Taylor Williams and Gene Van Guilder. The body was prepared for burial in Hailey. The services began at 10:30 A.M. July 5th. Father Robert J. Waldmann of Our Lady of the Snows Church (Catholic) in Ketchum read the burial service. Don Anderson, Lloyd Arnold, Chuck Atkinson, George Brown, Forrest MacMullen, Leonard (Bud) Purdy, and Dr. George Saviers served as pallbearers. EH's three sons, his brother, and three of his four sisters were at the funeral. Old friends in attendance included Mr. and Mrs. William D. Horne, Charles Thompson, Mrs. Clara Spiegel, and Gianfranco Ivancich. A large flat gravestone was subsequently installed over the place of burial, with EH's name and his dates of birth and death. He had died nineteen days short of his sixty-second birthday.

DEBTS AND CREDITS

My debts are nearly innumerable. The mere listing below cannot begin to represent or redeem the many hours that generous people gave over, not only to the making of this book but also to increasing its accuracy and enriching the text at all points. My obligations embrace institutions and libraries as well as hundreds of men and women. Were it not for the free time provided by leaves and grants from Princeton University, this book would not now have attained its present form. I owe a special debt to Dr. Gordon N. Ray, President of the John Simon Guggenheim Memorial Foundation, and to Mrs. Elizabeth Ames, Director of Yaddo, for initiating proceedings which led to substantial sequences of uncluttered working hours.

For assistance and encouragement far beyond the call of any conceivable duty, for reading part or all of the manuscript at various stages, and for invaluable suggestions for its improvement, I offer special thanks to Dorothy S. Baker, Professor Cecil Eby, Mrs. Ernest Hemingway, Morton D. Hull, Major General Charles T. Lanham (USA, Ret.), Professor A. W. Litz, Herbert L. Matthews, Mrs. E. J. Miller, Mr. and Mrs. Paul Scott Mowrer, Charles Scribner, Jr., J. H. Taylor, and Dale Wilson.

For interviews, sometimes repeated and often supplemented by extensive correspondence, my heartfelt thanks go to Floyd Allington, Paolo Altamura, Don Anderson, Mr. and Mrs. Lloyd Arnold, Mr. and Mrs. Charles Atkinson, Bertin Azimont, Lawrence T. Barnett, Professor Charles W. Bernardin, Pio Bertoli, William Bird, Ambassador Spruille Braden, Louis Bréteall, Mr. and Mrs. T. O. Bruce, J. C. Buck, Peter Buckley, Mrs. Margaret H. Bundy, Professor Harry H. Burns, Nathaniel Burt, Morley Callaghan, Mario Casamassima, Duncan D. Chaplin, Jr., Lewis Clarahan, Gregory Clark, Mrs. Louis H. Cohn, Charles Collingwood, Mrs. Saxe Commins, Dorothy Connable, Sister Conceptor, James A. Cowan, Mr. and Mrs. Robert Cox, Nathan Davis, Mr. and Mrs. Robert Davis, Mr. and Mrs. George H. Dennis, Mrs. F. W. Dilworth, Mr. and Mrs. John Dos Passos, Ambassador Angier Biddle Duke, Albert Dungan, Mr. and Mrs. Gustavo Duran, Dr. Scott Earle, Professor Louis Fischer, Jerome Flaherty, Janet Flanner, Donald Friede, Robert Frost, Lewis Galantiere, Donald Gallup, John Gardner, Dean Christian Gauss, Martha Gellhorn, Mrs. F. R. B. Godolphin, Mrs. Irene Gordon, C. Roy Greenaway, Winston F. C. Guest, Professor Ramon Guthrie, Gelston Hardy, Mrs. Ernest Hemingway, Dr. Gregory Hemingway, John H. Hemingway, Patrick Hemingway, Mr. and Mrs. Barklie Henry, Andree F. Hickok, Mrs. Guy Hickok, Mr. and Mrs. William D. Horne, Allin K. Ingalls, Gianfranco Ivancich, Howell G. Jenkins, G. M. Johnson, Walter Johnson, Waring Jones, Mr. and Mrs. Robert P. Joyce, Count and Countess Federico Kechler, Fred Keller, Jr., Mrs. Susan L. Kesler, Mrs. Eric Knight, General and Mrs. Charles T. Lanham, Ramon Lavalle, Harold Loeb, Colonel James S. Luckett, Mr. and Mrs. Archibald MacLeish, Sara Mayfield, William L. McGeary, Mrs. Ernest J. Miller, W. M. Mills, Mrs. Theodore Morrison, Mr. and Mrs. Paul Scott Mowrer, Mrs. Auguste Nels, Josef Nels, Mrs. Olive Nordquist, Katherine T. Norris, Joseph North, E. G. Pailthorp, Frances Pailthorp, Earle Pashley, Air Commander G. J. C. Paul, Laud Payne, Waldo Peirce, Archie Pelkey, Bernard Peyton, Karl Pfeiffer, Hazel Potter, Ezra Pound, Juanito Quintana, Adriana von

Rex, Charles Ritz, Mr. and Mrs. John Rogers, Paul Romaine, Mrs. W. W. E. Ross, Major General John F. Ruggles, Mr. and Mrs. Sterling S. Sanford, Dr. George Saviers, Charles Scribner, Thomas Shevlin, Adamo Simon, Ernest Smith, Mr. and Mrs. William B. Smith, Mr. and Mrs. Y. K. Smith, Mrs. Clara Spiegel, Frederick Spiegel, Mrs. William Stanfield, Jr., Mrs. R. W. Steele, Wing Commander K. Stevens, Henry Strater, J. B. Sullivan, Janet H. Taylor, Mr. and Mrs. Charles Thompson, Virgil Thomson, Edith Treleaven, Dr. John Walker, Ivan Wallace, William Walton, Dale Warren, Mr. and Mrs. L. S. Weaver, Mrs. Lael Tucker Wertenbaker, John N. Wheeler, Owen S. White, Professor William White, Dale Wilson, Edmund Wilson, Rosalind Wilson, Ira Wolfert, Dr. W. H. York, and Bronislaw Zielinski.

The following were good enough to supply me with copies of letters by Hemingway. In many instances these included long and valuable sequences covering many years: J. Donald Adams, Jay Allen, Milton Altman, Milford Baker, Major General Raymond O. Barton, Roland Baughman, Michael Blankfort, Harvey Breit, Gene M. Brown, J. Edward Brown, Robert M. Brown, Mr. and Mrs. T. O. Bruce, Peter Buckley, Professor Harry Burns, Morley Callaghan, Richard J. Callahan, Ned Calmer, Cyril Clemens, Mrs. Raiberto Comini, Dorothy Connable, Malcolm Cowley, Kenneth C. Cramer, Lambert Davis, Lieutenant General E. E. Dorman-O'Gowan, John Dos Passos, Professor Fraser Drew, Gustavo Durán, Irving Fajans, Charles E. Feinberg, Mrs. Charles A. Fenton, Charles D. Field, Robert Frost, Donald Gallup, Mr. and Mrs. Antonio Gattorno, Arnold Gingrich, Dr. Fiorella Superbi Gioffredi, Mrs. F. R. B. Godolphin, John D. Gordan, Mrs. Irene Gordon, Mark Gormley, Dr. Howard Gotlieb, George P. Hammond, Mrs. Ernest Hemingway, Patrick Hemingway, Mr. and Mrs. Barklie Henry, Mrs. Guy Hickok, Hans Hinrichs, Mary M. Hirth, William D. Horne, Mrs. Walter Houk, Miss Bert Hunt, Henry Hunter, Gianfranco Ivancich, Howell G. Jenkins, Waring Jones, Professor Alfred Kazin, Mrs. Eric Knight, Dr. Lawrence Kubie, Major General Charles T. Lanham (USA, Ret.), Mrs. Ellen Lasley, James Laughlin, Ramon Lavalle, Harold Loeb, Mrs. J. C. Long, Daniel Longwell, Mrs. Janet Lowrey, Archibald MacLeish, Charles W. Mann, Jr., Elisabetta Mariano, Herbert L. Matthews, David C. Mearns, Mrs. Cynthia D. Meyer, Professor Arthur Mizener, Mrs. Laura V. Monti, Mrs. Theodore Morrison, Mrs. Paul Scott Mowrer, Michael E. Murphy, Josef Nels, Henry W. R. North, Mrs. Amy Nyholm, Professor Ronald Paulson, Professor Norman Holmes Pearson, Waldo Peirce, Karl Pfeiffer, George Plimpton, Captain John C. Pratt (USAF), Juanito Quintana, Adriana von Rex, James C. Rikhoff, Charles Ritz, Selden Rodman, Paul Romaine, Lillian Ross, Dr. George Saviers, Charles Scribner, Charles Scribner, Jr., Dean Gilbert Seldes, Professor William W. Seward, Jr., Thomas Shevlin, William B. Smith, Jr., Solita Solano, Mrs. Clara Spiegel, Henry Strater, Charles B. Strauss, Mrs. J. S. Thomas, Mr. and Mrs. Charles Thompson, Lawrence Towner, Diana Trilling, Hyatt Waggoner, Dale Warren, James Wells, Wirt Williams, Dale Wilson, Milton Wolff, John Cook Wyllie, Bronislaw Zielinski, Lester Ziffren.

For valuable information about Hemingway, chiefly by correspondence, I owe special thanks to Eaton Adams, Richard W. Adams, Mrs. Dorothy Allen, Jay Allen, Don Anderson, Margaret Anderson, Mr. and Mrs. Lloyd Arnold, Nathan Asch, Jerome Bahr, Mrs. Arturo Barea, Major General Raymond O. Barton, Clyde Beatty, Wing Commander R. P. Beaumont, Samuel Bell, A. A. Bernabei, Alvah Bessie, William Bird, Major General H. W. Blakely, Michael Blankfort, W. L. Bond, Vance Bourjaily, Professor Charles R. Bouslog, Ambassador Ellis O. Briggs, John Brooks, Ambassador David K. E. Bruce, Commander Hugo V. B. Burgerhout, Michael Burke, Professor H. H. Burns, Dr. Hugh Butt, Mrs. Elsa Spear Byron, James M. Cain, Richard J. Callahan, Ned Calmer, Whitney Campbell, Kathleen Cannell, Jimmy Cannon, Sally Carrighar, Duncan D. Chaplin, Jr., Professor Thomas Caldecott Chubb, Lewis Clarahan, Morrill Cody, Mrs. L. H. Cohn, Charles Collingwood, Dr. Guy C. Conkle, Dorothy Connable, Clive Cookson, James A. Cowan, Mrs. Virginia Crawley, John Crosby, Russel Crouse, Roald

Dahl, J. E. Davis, Sefton Delmer, Mrs. Russell Doherty, Lieutenant General E. E. Dorman-O'Gowan, John Dos Passos, Professor Fraser Drew, Air Marshal C. R. Dunlap, Professor Cecil D. Eby, George C. Edberg, Colonel Earl W. Edwards, Air Marshal Sir Charles Elworthy, Air Marshal Sir Basil Embry, Professor Ben Euwema, Irving Fajans, James T. Farrell, S. Kip Farrington, Janet Flanner, Professor John Gassner, Mr. and Mrs. Antonio Gattorno, Dean Christian Gauss, Ruth Bradfield Gay, John Gehlmann, Raymond E. George, Arnold Gingrich, Mrs. Irene Gordon, Mrs. John Grace, Winston F. C. Guest, Gelston Hardy, Professor Hornell Hart, Carl Hayden, Richard Haywood, Mrs. Edith Heal, Mrs. Dorothy Heckendorn, Lillian Hellman, Mrs. Ernest Hemingway, Dr. Gregory Hemingway, John Hemingway, Mrs. Mary Williams Hemingway, Patrick Hemingway, C. M. Henley, Josephine Herbst, John Hersey, Mary Hickok, Frank B. Hines, Margarette Hines, Hans Hinrichs, Richard Hokin, Mrs. Lansing C. Holden, Jr., George Houghton, Mrs. Walter Houk, Mrs. Carl Howe, Jr., A. R. Ingalls, Douglas M. Jacobs, Keith Jennison, Mrs. Jasper Jepson, Robert Joyce, Colonel Thomas A. Kenan, Mrs. Susan Lowry Kesler, Clinton King, Steven Kokes, Luis Kutner, Major General Charles T. Lanham (USA, Ret.), Raymond Larsson, Ramon Lavalle, William J. Lederer, Michael Lerner, Read Lewis, Howard Lindsay, Joseph W. Lippincott, Harold Loeb, Maurice E. Lovén, Jacob H. Lowrey, Colonel James Luckett, Alan Lynn, Mr. and Mrs. Archibald MacLeish, Forest H. MacMullen, Tom Mahoney, Brigadier General S. L. A. Marshall, G. Grant Mason, Sara Mayfield, William L. McGeary, Mario Menocal, Jr., Charles Meyers, Mrs. Robbins Milbank, Lewis Milestone, Nancy W. Milford, Colin Miller, J. Miller, Marianne Moore, Professor Samuel French Morse, Arthur Moss, Mr. and Mrs. Paul Scott Mowrer, Gerald Murphy, Michael Murphy, Professor John Murra, Mrs. Olive Nordquist, H. W. R. North, John North, Joseph North, John O'Hara, Earl Pashley, George W. Pay, Laud Payne, Philip Percival, Richard Percival, Prudencio de Pereda, Mr. and Mrs. Edmund I. Phillips, Fred A. Picard, George A. Plimpton, Katherine Anne Porter, Dawn Powell, J. B. Priestley, John Pudney, Ken W. Purdy, Alfred Putnam, Mrs. Ben Ray Redman, Adriana von Rex, Mrs. Albert Roos, Major General John F. Ruggles, Harold Sampson, Mr. and Mrs. Sterling S. Sanford, William Saroyan, Dr. George Saviers, David E. Scherman, Dr. Louis Schwartz, George Seldes, Dean Gilbert Seldes, Professor William W. Seward, Jr., Louis Sheaffer, Vincent Sheean, Gordon Shepherd, Gordon D. Shorney, Dr. Charles A. Siler, Francis G. Smith, Jr., William B. Smith, Jr., Solita Solano, Ambassador A. E. Southard, Mrs. William Stanfield, Jr., Professor Marshall W. Stearns, John Steinbeck, Mrs. Edith M. Stern, Mrs. Holly Stevens, Marcus O. Stevenson, Donald Ogden Stewart, Irving Stone, Colton Storm, F. Sturgis Stout, Henry Strater, Charles B. Strauss, Dr. Carl Stroven, Allen Tate, Janet Taylor, Josephine G. Taylor, Mrs. Ellen Teague, Sir William Teeling, Mrs. J. S. Thomas, Mr. and Mrs. Charles Thompson, Mrs. James Thurber, Calvin Tompkins, Bob Trout, R. G. Tugwell, Andrew Turnbull, Mrs. Anthony J. Ulchar, Commander H. J. E. van der Kop, Henry S. Villard, Nat Wartels, L. S. Weaver, Colonel George S. Wertenbaker, Mrs. Lael Tucker Wertenbaker, Professor John G. Westover, John N. Wheeler, Professor Ray Lewis White, Mrs. William Carlos Williams, Colonel Roger Willock, Dale Wilson, Mrs. Ella Winter, Milton Wolff, Air Marshal Sir Peter Wykeham, Philip Wylie, Professor Philip Young, Denis Zaphiro, and Lester Ziffren.

For various help of other kinds, I wish to thank the following: Robert Allen, Mrs. Sherwood Anderson, Dr. William C. Archie, Veronica Arlunas, Frederick L. Arnold, Mr. and Mrs. A. E. Baker, Brian A. Baker, Brian C. Baker, Professor Sheridan Baker, John Bareto-Leite, Mrs. Rodney M. Barker, Peter Barrett, Peter H. Beard, Rupert Bellville, Professor G. E. Bentley, Paul Benton, John Bernstein, Mary Bertagni, Gordon Birch, Jane M. Birch, L. G. Birch, G. Bogart Blakely, Professor R. P. Blackmur, Professor Joseph Blotner, Reverend W. S. Boice, Kay Boyle, Thomas J. Brandon, Richard Brantley, Dan Bronson, Andreas Brown, R. M. Brown, Jackson Bryer, Martin Bucco, John A. Buche, Dr. Roger A. Burgos, Dr. David W. Butsch, Dr. John L. Butsch, Judith

B. Campbell, Dr. and Mrs. Frank Campo, Stanley A. Carlin, Mr. and Mrs. Paul D. Carter, Marthe Cella, Douglas Chambers, Professor Kenneth K. S. Ch'en, Alexander P. Clark, Richard T. Clarke, H. B. Collamore, Michael Collins, Major E. R. Conway, Professor R. L. Cook, Seymour A. Copstein, Malcolm Cowley, Bert Daga, Mrs. Claude Dauphin, Professor Donald Davidson, John D. Davies, H. A. Decker, Anthony Del Balso, Perine Di Verita, Dr. William S. Dix, Professor A. S. Downer, Cecile Driggs, Helen Duncombe, Sister Dutton, Mary Elizabeth Duykinck, Professor and Mrs. Richard Eberhart, Peter Ehlers, Mrs. H. W. Elliot, Garrett Evans, Mrs. Dwight Follett, Professor Russell Fraser, Anne Freudenberg, Robert Frey, Herbert Furlow, Mrs. John Gardner, E. B. Garnett, George Garrett, Maxwell Geismar, Jonathan Goodwin, E. M. Halliday, Audre Hanneman, C. A. Harper, Mr. and Mrs. Clinton Harriman, Raymond C. Harwood, Edward Hattam, Justin Herman, Granville Hicks, Helen Ann Hillebrand, Dr. Helmut Hirsch, H. W. Hoisington, Mr. and Mrs. William Homer, Professor John M. Howell, Professor John B. Hughes, Ralph Ingersoll, Sturgis Ingersoll, Melvin Jacobson, Mrs. Jean Wilton Jaffe, Douglas C. James, Lucien Jansen, David Jeffrey, Professor A. E. Jensen, Professor E. D. H. Johnson, Richard Colles Johnson, Waring Jones, Dr. E. S. Judd, Hans-Joachim Kann, Leona Keene, Professor Maurice Kelley, Dr. and Mrs. Charles W. Kennedy, C. D. Kerr, Arthur F. Kinney, Günter R. Klatovsky, Savage Klein, Victor Knight, Elsie Koeltl, Professor Jerzy R. Krzyzanowski, Professor and Mrs. Louis A. Landa, Roberta Latham, Jon Leon, Professor Robert W. Lewis, Jr., Mrs. Samuel J. Lanahan, Landon Laird, Erling Larsen, Meyer Levin, Professor Peter Lisca, Professor A. W. Litz, Adrian B. Lopez, Edmund Ludwig, Professor Richard M. Ludwig, Sergeant Leonard Lumbert, Radu Lupan, Patricia Lutz, Leonard Lyons, W. H. Lyons, Nathaniel Mackey, Mr. and Mrs. Edward B. Marks, Patricia Marshall, J. C. Douglas Marshall, Professor R. B. Martin, Anthony Maruca, Robert G. Mayer, Joseph McBride, Allan McCune, Alexander A. Mackenzie, Harry M. Meacham, Professor James Meriwether, Charles L. Michod, Jr., Professor H. K. Miller, Mrs. Janet Miller, Burroughs Mitchell, Judge Worrall F. Mountain, William F. Nolan, Russell O'Brien, Dorothy O'Donnell, George V. Packard, William A. B. Paul, Jordon Pecile, Alice Perkins, Ted Pittenger, Mariquita Platov, George Preucil, Helen E. Price, Alan F. Randolph, Arthur Raybold, Mrs. Gustav Regler, Donald H. Reiman, Charlotte W. Reinheimer, William H. Reinheimer, Alfred Rice, Howard C. Rice, Jr., Robert Richardson, Alice Rickards, Professor W. R. Robinson, Mrs. Leicester Rogers, Dr. Howard P. Rome, Melville J. Ruggles, Professor Charles Ryskamp, Lee Samuels, Mr. and Mrs. Norvell Brockman Samuels, Alan Sandy, H. H. Sargeant, Frederick G. Schmidt, Professor Mark Schorer, Adamo Simon, William Sloane, Red Smith, Lawrence E. Spellman, Professor Peter J. Stanlis, Cuyler Stevens, Janet H. Taylor, G. B. Tennyson, Halsey Thomas, Professor Lawrance R. Thompson, Professor Willard Thorp, Timothy L. Towell, Gene Tunney, Dorothy L. Tyler, Mrs. Roland Usher, Mrs. B. van Benschoten, Professor Edmond L. Volpe, Helmut von Erffa, E. W. Wade, Professor I. O. Wade, Mr. and Mrs. Lansing Wagner, Alexander Wainwright, Marilyn Walden, Mrs. Eleanor Waldman, Robert Wallace, Bruce Wallis, V. I. Wexner, Kenneth S. White, James S. Whiton, Professor Raymond S. Willis, David Williamson, Thomas W. Wilson, L. L. Winship, Sue Wood, Mrs. Jeanne H. Wright, Dr. W. H. York, and Louis Zara. Omissions are inadvertent; it is probably too much to hope that they are nonexistent. Other debts and credits are acknowledged in the Notes section. To all, named and unnamed, go the author's most humble and hearty thanks.

Carlos Baker

FURTHER ACKNOWLEDGMENT

I owe a special note of thanks to Henry Strater for his kindness in allowing the use of prints of his three portraits of Hemingway, one for the jacket of the book, the others in the picture section. I wish also to thank Dr. Richard Brantley and Dr. Lee Johnson for their expert help with the index.

INDEX

NOTE: The following index applies mainly to the people, places, and ideas in the text of the book. Notes are glossed only (or chiefly) when they contain information or proper names not mentioned in the text. Sources, including the bibliographical, are not included in the index because they have been systematically set forth along with the notes to each section. Names of major cities, as well as of streets and hotels, are often omitted.

Under the heading of "Hemingway, Ernest" will be found a list of his books, short stories, and poems. Titles of his books are usually abbreviated:

Across the River and into the Trees: *ARIT*
Death in the Afternoon: *DIA*
A Farewell to Arms: *FTA*
For Whom the Bell Tolls: *FWBT*
Green Hills of Africa: *GHOA*
in our time and *In Our Time*: *iot* and *IOT*
Men Without Women: *MWW*
A Moveable Feast: *AMF*
The Old Man and the Sea: *OMATS*
The Sun Also Rises: *SAR*
To Have and Have Not: *THAHN*
Winner Take Nothing: *WTN*

Titles of EH's articles are not indexed, since they will be found seriatim among the Sources. A selection of EH's opinions on various subjects (e.g., suicide, war, death) has been indexed.

C.B.

Chronology: Ancestry, 1–2, 565. Born and baptized, 3. Infancy, 3–6; boyhood, 7–17; adolescence, 17–29. Kansas City cub reporter, 29–37. Ambulance driver, Italy, 38–44. Wound and recuperation, 44–56. Love affair with Agnes von Kurowsky, 49–59. Return home, 56–60. First postwar summer in Michigan, 61–64. Writing in Petoskey, 65–66. Winter in Toronto, 67–69. Work on *Toronto Star,* 68–70. Second postwar summer in Michigan, 70–74. Work in Chicago and courtship of Hadley Richardson, 75–80. Marriage to Hadley, 80–82.

Voyage to Europe, 83–84. Residence in Paris,